W9-CUF-577

FINANCIAL ACCOUNTING

INFORMATION FOR DECISIONS

Robert W. Ingram
Ph.D. and C.P.A.
Ross-Culverhouse Chair in Accounting
University of Alabama
Tuscaloosa, Alabama

COLLEGE DIVISION South-Western Publishing Co.
Cincinnati Ohio

To my wife, Chris, my best friend and critic, without whose help this book would not have been written.

AO77AA

ISBN: 0-538-82702-5

2 3 4 5 6 7 Ki 9 8 7 6 5 4

Printed in the United States of America

Publisher: Mark R. Hubble
Developmental Editor: Sara E. Bates
Production Editor II: Nancy Ahr
Production Editor I: Robin Schuster
Cover Design and Illustration,
Internal Design: Joseph M. Devine
Internal Illustrations: Rick Moore
Marketing Manager: Martin W. Lewis

Library of Congress Cataloging-in-Publication Data

Ingram, Robert W.
Financial accounting : information for decisions / Robert W. Ingram. -- 1st ed.
p. cm.
Includes bibliographical references and index.
ISBN 0-538-82702-5
1. Accounting--Decision making. 2. Managerial accounting.
I. Title.
HF5635.I484 1994
657--dc20 93-15809
CIP

I(T)P
International Thomson Publishing
South-Western is an ITP Company. The ITP trademark is used under license.

PREFACE

How to Make an A in this Course (For Students Only)

I am going to let you in on some trade secrets instructors seldom tell students. That's why this section is labeled, "For Students Only." If instructors find out I have revealed these secrets, I'll probably get a lot of mail.

Getting good grades is not a matter of luck. That's not the secret. Also, it is no secret that doing assignments (on time), going to class (regularly), getting enough sleep and exercise, eating properly, and studying throughout the semester (instead of just at exam time) will improve your grades. But, this is hard work. So, what you want is a way to get good grades and not work so hard, right? Well, pay attention—the secret is to work smarter! That's not the same as being smarter, which is a matter of luck. Here's how you work smarter.

Step 1: Determine why this course is important for you. First, figure out why you're taking this class. What are your goals for the class? Do you care about this course? Do you have a strong motivation to learn about accounting? Perhaps being an accountant comes on your list of career options just below sweeping up at McDonalds. Maybe your goal is to make lots of money. Or, maybe you're just in college to have a good time until you inherit the family fortune. In any case, this course is designed for you. One of the surest ways to have a million dollars is to start with ten million and not know anything about accounting and business management. If you don't inherit wealth, you're not likely to get it without speaking the language of business. Accounting is the language! Maybe you just want to get a good job, but you're pretty sure you don't want to be an accountant. Fine! This course isn't going to make an accountant out of you. It will help you understand some of the "mystical rituals" of accounting that non-accountants often find confusing. Whatever type of management position you have in any organization, you can be pretty sure you're going to have to have to work with accountants and with accounting information. You should know they can have a major effect on your life. Many organizations use accounting information to evaluate their employees for salary and promotion decisions. You should understand how to interpret this information. You may even learn accounting isn't what you think. Whether you grow to love or hate accounting, decide what you can get out of this course that will be useful to you.

Step 2: Find out what your instructor expects of you in the course. Next, check out your instructor. If you're lucky, your instructor is sensitive, warm, caring, has a good sense of humor, is witty, loves teaching, and wants you to do well in the course. If instead, your instructor is more normal (and less perfect), remember, I'm OK, you're OK, and the instructor is still the instructor. And, as the instructor she/he has power over your life. So, find out what she/he expects from you. What are her/his goals for the course? What does she/he want you to know or be able to do once you complete the course? Perhaps, she/he will tell you (good sign), but if not, ask. You should say: "Professor Whatever-Your-Name-Is (it would be wise to use the right name) what's the lowdown on the layout for this course?" This is education jargon for "what are your goals for this course?" This may catch her/him off guard, so give her/him a minute or two to think. You may even have to wait until the next class meeting to get your answer. Make sure you and your instructor understand each other's goals. Some accounting instructors expect all their students to become accountants. If you have one of these, make it clear. Tell your instructor: "I don't plan to be no account*ant*!" (Make sure you add the *ant*, or you may get fast agreement.) Find out what's in this course for you.

Step 3: Find out how you will be graded. Now, find out how you will be graded. How does the instructor test? Is she/he one of the picky types: "What is the third word on the fifth line on page 211?" Or, does she/he go in for the broader, thought questions: "Explain how accounting was instrumental in negotiating the third treaty of Versailles in 1623." Does she/he go in for multiple guess, or are short answers her/his cup of tea? I expect my students to be able to interpret financial statements. My exams require students to interpret actual corporate statements. If students come to the exam expecting picky questions from the text, they're likely to be very disappointed. Whatever the method, you need to know what is expected of you and how these expectations translate into grades. Occasionally, you'll find an instructor whose stated expectations don't agree with how she/he tests and grades. That's why you need to find out about both expectations and grades. If they don't seem to be consistent, you'll have to determine what the instructor really expects.

Step 4: Emphasize learning what's important. Figure out what you need to do to accomplish your goals and meet the instructor's (real) expectations. A major lesson you should learn, if you haven't already, is "what you take from a course (and almost anything else) depends on what you bring to it." Your attitude is important. If you decide something is worth learning, you'll probably find a way to learn it. Not because you're supposed to learn it, but because you want to. "Wanting to" is the biggest part of working smarter. Wanting to learn will go a long way toward helping you get a good grade. Unfortunately, it may not be enough unless what you want to learn is also what your instructor wants you to learn. Therefore, you need to make sure you and your instructor are on the same wave length. If you're not, talk it over. Find out why the instructor has a different outlook. You may change your opinion about what's important. Determine how to focus your efforts. Not everything in this book or course is equally important. Focus on what's most important to you and to your instructor.

Step 5: Communicate with your instructor. Try to remember your instructor is a person. Even the author of this book is a person. I belong to a wife, two teenagers, and a dog. The dog and I are pretty normal; everybody else is a little neurotic. They claim its because they have to live with the dog and me. Of course, for teenagers, neurosis goes with the territory. There are a few instructors around who get their jollies from treating students like peasants. Luckily, most of us really want to see you do well, but we need your help. Instructors don't know everything. In particular, we can't read your mind. You need to let your instructor know if you're having problems understanding the material you're expected to learn, figuring out what the instructor expects of you, or figuring out how to prepare for tests and other assignments. Talk with your instructor about problems you're having with the class. Remember, your instructor really is human.

This is your class. You paid for it. OK, maybe it was your parents, or somebody else who put out hard, cold cash for you to take this course. Don't let anybody keep you from getting your money's worth. Working smarter means determining what's important and focusing your attention and efforts on these things. Then, don't be distracted from your goals. If you run into problems, deal with them. If you don't understand something in class or in the book, ask questions. If you're afraid of asking dumb questions in class, remember: looking dumb in class is better than looking dumb on an exam. If you think you may be missing key points, talk with your instructor. If you want to learn, you can.

That's it. Give it a try. I think you'll find the course more enjoyable and the experience more rewarding. Of course, you might also try doing assignments, going to class, getting enough sleep and exercise, eating properly, and studying throughout the semester. They usually help, even though they are hard work. Finally, there's no guarantee you'll make an A in this course. But remember, what you take from class depends on what you bring to it.

Best wishes to you, not only in this course, but throughout life.

Rob Ingram

A side note:

To aid you in the learning process, basic concepts are indicated by margin icons. The concepts and their respective icons are shown below.

Transformation Process

Control of Accounting Systems

Reporting Rules, Standards

Cash, Cash Flow

Decisions, Decision Making, Analysis, Understanding

Time, Accrual Accounting

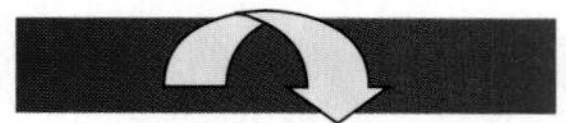

Organizations, Management, Professionals

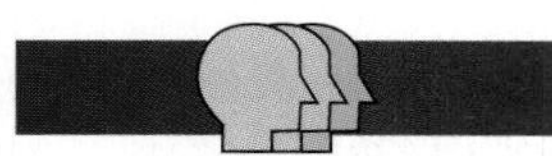

International

Financial Reports

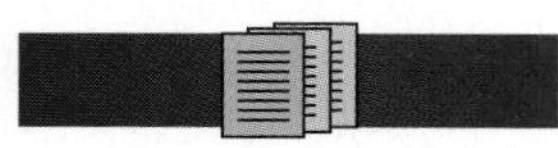

Stockholders

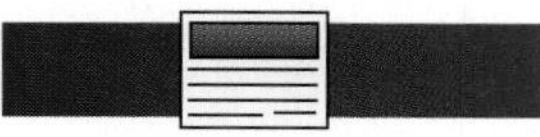

Accounting Information Systems

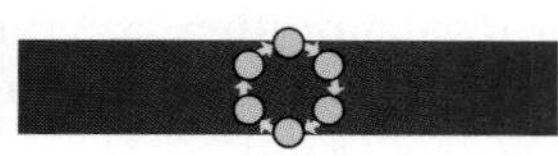

Obligations, Valuation, Contracts

Accounting, Processing Accounting Information

Effect of Business Activities (Risk and Return, Efficiency and Effectiveness, Business Results)

Computer Processing/ Applications

PREFACE

To the Instructor

This book is an introduction to financial accounting. It introduces the reader to concepts of accounting and financial reporting. These concepts are essential to understanding how decision makers use accounting information. Since the purpose of the book is to help students learn how to use accounting information, emphasis is on analyzing and interpreting the information rather than on information preparation. Very little attention is given to such preparation.

Two primary concepts explain accounting information in the book. The first of these is the transformation process in which organizations create goods and services. Accounting measures, records, and reports economic activities in the transformation process. A major philosophy of the book is students cannot understand accounting unless they first understand how organizations operate. The second concept is the need to measure performance in distinct time periods. Accounting measurement and reporting rules focus on timing differences between when events occur that create or use resources and when cash is received or paid. A second major philosophy of the book is students must understand the relationship between accrual and cash flow measures in order to interpret accounting information.

The book emphasizes three pedagogical devices to assist in the learning process. The first device is redundancy. Concepts are introduced and reinforced through repetition and use. Foreshadowing and flashbacks link material in each chapter to previous and future discussion of relevant issues. The second device is the use of real-world examples and illustrations. The real world is more complex than text books sometimes lead students to believe. A goal of this book is for students to be able to understand and use actual financial reports. Excerpts from these reports are used to illustrate concepts and as a basis for interpreting accounting information. Though early chapters use hypothetical examples to illustrate basic concepts, students are introduced to real-world problems and examples. Real-world problems and examples provide the content for most of the later chapters of the book. The third device is an emphasis on active learning. Exercises, problems, cases, and projects at the end of each chapter offer a variety of opportunities for students to become involved in the learning process. Many of these require students to interpret accounting information, to solve problems, and to communicate their solutions in essays, memos, and short reports. Additional suggestions for using cooperative learning techniques in your class setting are provided in the instructor's resource guide.

Accounting for U.S corporations is the primary subject of this book. Students are expected to develop an ability to analyze and interpret corporate annual reports. Accounting for proprietorships and partnerships is considered in examples and in discussion of owners' equity. U.S. and foreign corporate accounting and reporting are compared throughout the book to introduce students to similarities and differences. Taxation, auditing, internal control, and ethical issues that affect interpretation and use of accounting information also are considered throughout the book. An overview of the accounting profession is provided in Chapter 7. Major accounting and reporting differences between public and private sector organizations are examined in Chapter 15.

The author gratefully acknowledges faculty suggestions and comments, and would like to thank those whose suggestions have become part of this text.

K.R. Balachandran
New York University

Bruce Baldwin
Arizona State University
West Campus

Lawrence Bergin
Winona State University

Kathy Bindon
University of Alabama

Chee Chow
San Diego State University

Masako Darrough
Columbia University

Susan Downs
Babson College

Michael Dugan
University of Alabama

Paul Frishkoff
University of Oregon

Vince Guide
Clemson University

Ray Johnson
Portland State University

Charles Konkol
University of Wisconsin,
Milwaukee

Wayne Label
University of Nevada,
Las Vegas

Ronald Mannino
University of Massachusetts
at Amherst

Patrick McKenzie
Arizona State University

Melanie Mogg
College of St. Scholastica

Joe Mori
San Jose State University

Lynn Mazzola Paluska
Nassau Community College

Donald F. Putnam
California State Polytechnic
University, Pomona

William Read
Bentley College

William Samson
University of Alabama

George Sanders
University of Miami

Mike Shields
San Diego State University

Kevin Stocks
Brigham Young University

Mary Stone
University of Alabama

Torben Thomsen
California State University, Fresno

Donna Ulmer
Southern Illinois University, Edwardsville

Neal Ushman
Santa Clara University

Glenn Van Wyhe
Pacific Lutheran University

Sheila Viel
University of Wisconsin, Milwaukee

John Wanlass
DeAnza College

Dan Ward
University of Southwestern Louisiana

Dick Wasson
Southwestern College

The author also gratefully acknowledges the professional assistance of those at South-Western Publishing Co. who took his ideas and rough drafts and created a text book: Sara Bates, Robin Schuster, Mark Hubble, Joe Devine, Rick Moore, Holly Knoechel, and Jennifer Mayhall.

ABOUT THE AUTHOR

Robert W. Ingram is the Ross-Culverhouse Chair in the Culverhouse School of Accountancy at the University of Alabama. He teaches courses in financial accounting and has been actively involved in course and curriculum development. He has served as Director of Education for the American Accounting Association, as a member of the Accounting Education Change Commission, and as editor of *Issues in Accounting Education,* a journal dedicated to accounting education research.

Professor Ingram is a Certified Public Accountant and holds a Ph.D. from Texas Tech University. Prior to joining the faculty at the University of Alabama, he held positions at the University of South Carolina and the University of Iowa, and a visiting appointment at the University of Chicago. His research, which examines financial reporting and accounting education, has been published widely in accounting and business journals. He is recipient of the National Alumni Association Outstanding Commitment to Teaching Award and the Burlington Northern Foundation Faculty Achievement in Research Award at the University of Alabama. He has also received the Notable Contribution to Literature Award of the Government and Nonprofit Section of the American Accounting Association, and the Award for Excellence and Professional Contributions of the Alabama Association for Higher Education in Business.

Professor Ingram is married and has two children. He and his family enjoy sports, travel, reading, music and art. They live contentedly in Tuscaloosa, Alabama.

BRIEF CONTENTS

SECTION I
The Accounting Information System

1	Accounting and Organizations	1
2	Information in Organizations	45
3	Accounting Measurement	89
4	Processing Accounting Information	133
5	Reporting Accounting Information	181
6	Reporting Accruals and Cash Flows	233
7	The Accounting Profession	287

SECTION II
Analysis and Interpretation of Financial Accounting Information

8	Financing Activities: Equity	329
9	Financing Activities: Debt	377
10	Analysis of Financing Activities	421
11	Investing Activities	467
12	Analysis of Investing Activities	517
13	Operating Activities	563
14	Analysis of Operating Activities	611
15	Nonbusiness Organizations	661

APPENDICES

A	Sources of Information About Companies and Industries	A-1
B	General Mills, Inc. Financial Report	B-1
C	General Mills, Inc. 10-K Report	C-1
D	General Mills, Inc. Proxy Statement	D-1
E	Compaq Computer Corp. Statement of Cash Flows	E-1
	Glossary	G-1
	Index	I-1

CONTENTS

SECTION I
THE ACCOUNTING INFORMATION SYSTEM

1 Accounting and Organizations 1

The Accounting Process 2
Accounting Records 2 Summary Reports 3 Steps in the Accounting Process 4 Uses of Accounting Information 5

The Purpose of Organizations 6
Transformation of Resources 7 Creation of Value 8 An Illustration of Creating Value 10 Investment by Owners 11 The Market for Investors 12 Nonbusiness Organizations 13

Decisions in Organizations 14
Financing Activities 14 Investing Activities 21 Operating Activities 22

Summary of the Transformation Process 27

Definition of Accounting 28

2 Information in Organizations 45

Information for Decision Makers 47
Risk and Return 48 Evaluating Exchanges 49 Financial Accounting 54 Managerial Accounting 55 Accounting and Information Needs 57

Information Systems 58
Management Information Systems 59 The Accounting Information System 60

Processing Accounting Information 63
Assets, Liabilities, and Owners' Equity 63 Revenues and Expenses 65 An Illustration of an Accounting System 67

Contracts and Accounting Information 69

3 Accounting Measurement 89

Accounting for the Transformation Process 91

Accounting for Incomplete Transformations 95

Time and Accounting Measurement 96

Cash Flows 96 Cash Flows from Operating Activities 97 The Accrual Basis of Accounting Measurement 98

Reconciling Accrual and Cash Measurements 103

Measuring the Transformation Process 105

The Purpose of Accrual Basis Accounts 108

Assets, Liabilities, and Owners' Equity 108 Revenues and Expenses 109 Accounts and Time 109

4 Processing Accounting Information 133

Processing Transactions 135

Accounting Systems 135

Manual Accounting Systems 135 An Illustration of a Manual Accounting System 136 The Accounting Cycle 148

Computerized Accounting Systems 149

Microcomputer Systems 149 Large Computer Systems 152

Control of Accounting Systems 161

Control of Manual Systems 161 Control of Computer Systems 162

The Accounting System and Management Decisions 163

5 Reporting Accounting Information 181

The Purpose of Financial Statements 183

Income Statement 184 Statement of Stockholders' Equity 184 Balance Sheet 184 Statement of Cash Flows 184

Financial Statement Content and Presentation 186

The Income Statement 186 The Statement of Stockholders' Equity 191 The Balance Sheet 193 The Statement of Cash Flows 197

Use of Financial Statements 202

Interrelationships Among Financial Statements 202 Consolidated Financial Statements 203 Limitations of Financial Statements 204 Usefulness of Financial Statements 207

Financial Statements and the Transformation Process 207

Transformation and Time 208

6 Reporting Accruals and Cash Flows 233

Internal Transactions 235

Depreciation 238 Insurance 239 Supplies 239 Interest 240 Wages 241 Notes Payable 241 Summary of Adjustments 242

Accruals and Deferrals 245

Accrued Revenues 245 Accrued Expenses 247 Deferred Revenues 249 Deferred Expenses 250 Summary of Accruals and Deferrals 251

Reconciliation of Net Income and Cash Flows 252

Accounts Receivable 256 Inventory 256 Accounts Payable 257 Interest Payable 258 Depreciation 259 Other Adjustments for the Indirect Method 259

Interpretation of Cash Flows 260

Financial Statements and the Transformation Process 262

7 The Accounting Profession 287

Accounting as a Profession 289
Management Accounting 289 Public Accounting 292 Governmental and Nonprofit Organizations 301 Education 302 Preparation for an Accounting Career 303

The Historical Development of Accounting 304
Historical Developments to the Early 1900s 304 Federal Regulation in the 1900s 306

The Development of Accounting Standards 308
The AICPA Committee on Accounting Procedure 308 The Accounting Principles Board 308 The Financial Accounting Standards Board 309 Governmental Accounting Standards 309 International Accounting Standards 309

The Purpose of Accounting Standards 310
Providing a Basis for Contracting 310 Assuring Reliability of Information 310 Controlling the Cost of Reporting and Maintaining Equity 311 Determining Fair Business Practices and Economic Analysis 311 Providing a Basis for Litigation 312

Setting Accounting Standards 312
The Standard-Setting Process 313 The Conceptual Framework for Accounting Standards 313

SECTION II ANALYSIS AND INTERPRETATION OF FINANCIAL ACCOUNTING INFORMATION

8 Financing Activities: Equity 329

Stockholder Investment and Retained Earnings 333
Contributed Capital 334 Shares of Stock and Treasury Stock 335 Retained Earnings 337 Summary of Measuring and Reporting Stockholders' Equity 337

Changes in Stockholders' Equity 338
Net Income 339 Cash Dividends 339 Issuance of Stock 340 Acquisition of Other Companies 343 Conversion of Bonds 343 Stock Dividends 344 Other Adjustments to Stockholders' Equity 345

Classes of Stock 350

Complexity and Limitations of Stockholders' Equity 352

International Reporting of Equity 354

Summary of Financial Statement Reporting of Equity 356

9 Financing Activities: Debt 377

Types of Obligations 379

Present and Future Value 380
Compound Interest 381 Annuities 382

Obligations to Lenders 384
Bonds Payable 385 Notes Payable 391 Cash and Accrual Measures of Interest and Principal 393
Obligations to Suppliers and Customers 395
Obligations to Employees 397
Pension Plans 397 Other Post-Employment Benefits 400
Obligations to Governments 402
Other Obligations 404
Liabilities Reported by Foreign Corporations 406
Control of Liabilities 406

10 Analysis of Financing Activities **421**

Risk and Return 423
Security Prices 424 Other Financing Instruments 430
The Effect of Financing Activities on Risk and Return 431
Attributes Affecting Financial Leverage 436
The Importance of Accounting Information 439
Dividend Payments 439 Short-Term and Long-Term Debt 440 Employee Benefits and Other Commitments 444
An Illustration of Financial Decision Analysis 445

11 Investing Activities **467**

Types of Assets 469
Investments in Cash and Securities 470
Investments in Equity Securities 472
Short-Term Equity Investments 473 Long-Term Equity Investments 474 Mergers and Acquisitions 479
Investments in Debt Securities 482
Notes and Other Debt Securities 482 Long-Term Investments in Bonds 483
Plant Assets 485
Depreciation 485 Disposal of Plant Assets 489 Depletion of Natural Resources 490 Leased Assets 492 Construction and Capital Improvement Costs 494
Intangible Assets, Deferred Charges, and Other Assets 495
Cash and Accrual Measurement 497
Control of Assets 498

12 Analysis of Investing Activities **517**

Asset Value 518
Required Rate of Return 520 Evaluating Investment Decisions 523
The Effect of Investing Activities on Risk and Return 526
Segment Reporting 528 Merger and Acquisition Decisions 529 Fair Market Values 533 Financial Assets and Liabilities 534
Comparing Investment Decisions 537
Comparing Companies Over Time 539
Operating Leverage 542
Cash Analysis and Management 545

13 Operating Activities 563

Reporting Operating Results 565

Gross Profit 565
Revenue Recognition 566 Accounts Receivable 569

Cost of Goods Sold and Inventories 572
Reporting Cost of Goods Sold and Inventory 513 Manufacturing Companies 574 Inventory Measurement 576 Weighted Average Method 580 Comparing Inventory Costs Among Companies 518

Other Items Affecting Net Income 582
Operating Income 528 Other Revenues and Expenses 583 Income Taxes 584 Special Items 587 Minority Interest in Income 589 Net Income Available for Common Stockholders 590

Earnings Per Share 591

Cash Flow From Operating Activities 592

Subsequent Events 594

International Reporting of Operating Activities 594

14 Analysis of Operating Activities 611

Analysis of Revenues and Expenses 613
Components of Income 614 Percentage of Analysis of Income 616 Operating Revenues 617 Product Demand 617 Profit Margins 621

Comparing Operating Results Among Companies 624
Return on Assets 624 Return on Equity 631

Problems with Interpreting Earnings 633
Choice of Accounting Methods 633 Earnings Management 634 Restructuring 635 Historical Costs 636

Cash Flow Analysis 636

Business Failure 639

Forecasting Operating Results 640

15 Nonbusiness Organizations 661

Purpose of Nonbusiness Organizations 663
Types of Nonbusiness Organizations 663 Governments 663 The Transformation Process 665

Efficiency and Effectiveness 665
Budgets 666 Fund Accounting 667 Expenditures and Encumbrances 669

Accounting Measurement 670
Measurement Focus 670 The Financial Reporting Entity 672

Accounting Reports 672
Governmental Reporting 673 Governmental Funds and Account Groups 674 Statement of Revenues and Expenditures 676 Comparison of Actual and Budgeted Amounts 678 Proprietary and Fiduciary Funds 679 Financial Statements of Other Nonprofit Organizations 680

Accounting Standards 682

Analysis of Accounting Information 683
Economic Environment 683 Effectiveness and Efficiency 684 Operating and Financial Leverage 686 Compliance 689

APPENDICES

A Sources of Information About Companies and Industries A-1
B General Mills, Inc. Financial Report B-1
C General Mills, Inc. 10-K Report C-1
D General Mills, Inc. Proxy Statement D-1
E Compaq Computer Corp. Consolidated Statement of Cash Flows E-1
Glossary G-1
Index I-1

SECTION I

THE ACCOUNTING INFORMATION SYSTEM

CHAPTER 1

ACCOUNTING AND ORGANIZATIONS

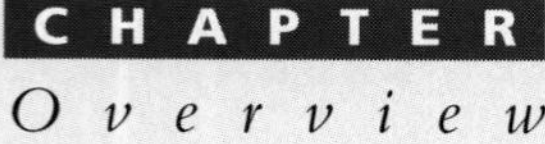

This book introduces basic concepts of accounting. It will help you understand why accounting information is important, how accounting information is produced, and how you can use this information in making decisions about organizations. Accounting describes economic events that occur in organizations. Therefore, to understand accounting you need to understand organizations. This chapter will introduce the purposes of organizations, how they achieve their purposes, the types of decisions made in organizations, and the role of accounting information in making these decisions. **Once you have completed this chapter you should understand that accounting is a system that produces information for making decisions about organizations.**

Major topics covered in this chapter include:

- An illustration of the accounting process.
- The purposes and functions of organizations.
- Decisions made in organizations.
- The role of accounting in making decisions about organizations.

CHAPTER
Objectives

Once you have completed this chapter you should be able to:

1. Identify the purpose of accounting.
2. Explain why accounting is an information system.
3. Compare major types of organizations.
4. Explain how organizations contribute to society.
5. Explain why markets are important.
6. Explain why owners invest in businesses.
7. Explain why accounting information is useful to investors.
8. Identify reasons some goods and services are not sold in markets.
9. Identify financing activities and the types of decisions they require.
10. Compare forms of business ownership.
11. Identify investing activities and the types of decisions they require.
12. Identify operating activities and the types of decisions they require.
13. List steps in an organization's transformation process.
14. Define accounting.

THE ACCOUNTING PROCESS

Objective 1
Identify the purpose of accounting.

The purpose of accounting is to help people make decisions about economic activities. Economic activities involve the allocation of scarce resources. People allocate scarce resources any time they exchange money or other resources for goods and services. These activities are so common that almost every adult in our society uses the accounting process to assist in decision making.

Accounting Records

To illustrate accounting, let's look at a common activity. You probably have a checking account at a financial institution, such as a bank or a credit union. A checking account provides a way to protect and keep track of your money. It simplifies paying bills. When you receive cash or checks written to you, you deposit them in your checking account. Then, when you need money, you write checks or withdraw money from an automatic teller machine. The activities that affect your checking account are making deposits, writing checks, withdrawing money, and paying the bank for service charges.

Learning Note

The terms "money" and "cash" often are used interchangeably. In everyday speech, money refers specifically to paper bills and coins. Cash is a broader term that includes checks, bank accounts, and other resources that are easily converted to money. A general term for money and items easily converted to money is "financial resources."

With your checks and deposit slips, you have a check register similar to the example in Exhibit 1-1. The register helps you manage and control your money by keeping track of amounts you deposit or withdraw, the source of the deposits, the recipients of the checks, the date of these events, and the amount available in your account.

Exhibit 1-1 Check Register

Date	Check Number	Check Issued To/ Deposit Received From	Amount of Deposit	Amount of Check	Balance
July 31					360.00
Aug. 5		Wages	375.00		735.00
8	324	Campus Apartments		200.00	535.00
11	325	West Side Grocery		180.00	355.00
16	326	Campus Bookstore		240.00	115.00
17		Wages	375.00		490.00
20	327	Cash (for entertainment)		50.00	440.00
21		Transfer from savings	500.00		940.00
21	328	My University		500.00	440.00
25	329	Any City Utility Dept.		75.00	365.00

Summary Reports

If you wanted to know how much you spent last month and for what purposes, you could summarize the information from the register to help you understand these activities. For example, you might prepare a summary similar to Exhibit 1-2.

The bank provides you with a statement that reports your checking account activities for the month. The statement lists deposits you made with the bank and checks you wrote that the bank paid during the month. The bank provides this report so you can verify the accuracy of the information you have recorded in your check register and the accuracy of the bank's information about your account. You verify the accuracy by comparing your check register with the bank statement.

Exhibit 1-2

Your Checking Account Summary of Deposits and Payments for August			
Beginning cash balance			$360
Cash deposits:			
Wages received	$750		
Transfer from savings	500		
Total cash deposited		$1,250	
Cash payments:			
Rent	$200		
Food	180		
Tuition	500		
Utilities	75		
Books and supplies	240		
Entertainment	50		
Total cash paid		1,245	
Excess of deposits over payments			5
Ending cash balance			$365

Steps in the Accounting Process

Some of the most important steps in the accounting process occur in this example of a checking account. In a checking account, you are accounting for money held by a bank for your use. The basic information unit in an accounting system is an account. **An *account* is a record of increases and decreases in the dollar amount associated with a specific resource or activity.** All information you record in your check register involves one account, your cash account with the bank. The register helps you keep track of the increases, decreases, and balance in your checking account.

The information in your check register summarizes the activities of your checking account. You record information in the register when an event occurs that increases or decreases the money in your account. **A *transaction* is an event that increases or decreases an account balance.** Transactions identify changes in resources and activities that affect resources. For example, when you write a check to pay for textbooks, you exchange money from your checking account for the books. This event is a transaction you record in your check register by noting the amount of the check and the reduction in your cash balance.

The bank maintains an account for each of its customers. Each time a customer deposits money or writes a check, the bank records the transaction in the customer's account. The account balance is the amount available for use by the customer. The monthly bank statement summarizes the transactions recorded by the bank for the customer's account.

The activities associated with a checking account provide an example of a typical accounting process. This process includes four basic steps that are shown at the top of the next page.

Objective 2
Explain why accounting is an information system.

A *system* is a set of interrelated activities or processes that work together to achieve a goal. Because accounting involves recording, summarizing, and reporting economic information used in making decisions, it is an information system.

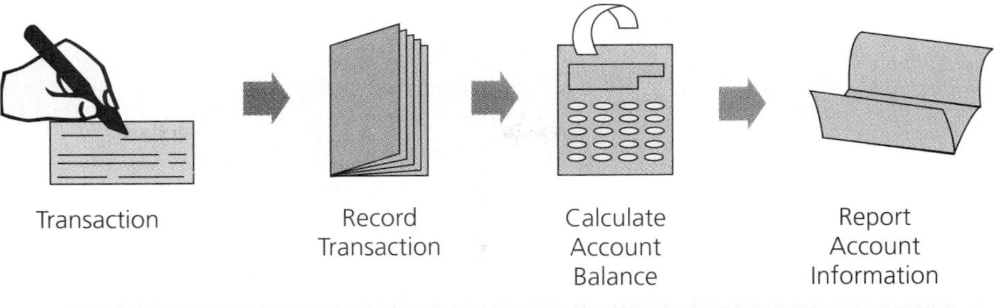

Step	Example
1. A transaction occurs. 2. Record the transaction in the proper accounts. 3. Calculate account balance. 4. Summarize and report transactions periodically to serve a specific need.	1. Purchase textbooks. 2. Record payment in check register. 3. Subtract amount of check from balance. 4. Prepare summary of checking account activities for the month.

Uses of Accounting Information

The decisions made by users of an accounting information system determine the type of information reported by the system. A check register and a bank statement are examples of accounting information. They exist to help the depositor. Information about your checking account can help you understand how you have used your money. How much did you spend for food last month? It can help you plan for future expenditures. Can you afford to go to a movie this weekend? It can provide assurance that you have the amount of money you think you have. Accounting information helps people make decisions.

Most individuals use accounting information regularly. Besides accounting for checking or savings accounts, people use accounting information when they borrow money and repay loans for houses, automobiles, and other personal possessions such as furniture or appliances. Workers file income tax returns to account for their taxable income.

This book explains accounting for organizations. **An *organization* is a group of people who work together to develop, produce and/or distribute goods or services.** Business organizations sell these goods and services to customers. Some organizations, for example social or religious organizations, provide services to their members or other recipients. Accounting provides information for managers, owners, members, and other stakeholders who make decisions about organizations. Stakeholders include those with an economic interest in an organization and those who are affected by its activities.

The next section of this chapter discusses the purpose of organizations and the role of accounting in organizations. Before proceeding, test your understanding of what you have read by solving the following self-study problem.

SELF-STUDY PROBLEM 1-1

The following list contains transactions for Horatio Garcia's checking account at the Central National Bank for April 1995:

April 1 Paid rent of $300 to Northside Apartments.
5 Deposited payroll check of $400.
7 Withdrew $70 for miscellaneous uses from an automatic teller machine.
12 Purchased food for $125 from Miller's Grocery.
14 Deposited payroll check of $400.
17 Withdrew $50 for miscellaneous uses from an automatic teller machine.
20 Paid car payment of $200 to Citizen's Loan Co.
21 Deposited payroll check of $400.
25 Paid utility bill of $60 to City Light and Water.
27 Purchased food for $140 from Wang's Grocery.
28 Purchased clothes for $80 from Street Clothiers.
28 Deposited payroll check of $400.
30 Transferred $500 (by check) to savings account at First Savings and Loan.

The beginning balance in Horatio's checking account was $450. Check numbers should be recorded sequentially beginning with 346.

Required

1. Record each transaction as it would appear in Horatio's check register. Use the format provided below.

Date	Check Number	Check Issued To/ Deposit Received From	Amount of Deposit	Amount of Check	Balance

2. Prepare a summary report for Horatio of his cash deposits and payments for April.
3. List the steps in the accounting process associated with Horatio's checking account.

The solution to Self-Study Problem 1-1 appears at the end of the chapter.

THE PURPOSE OF ORGANIZATIONS

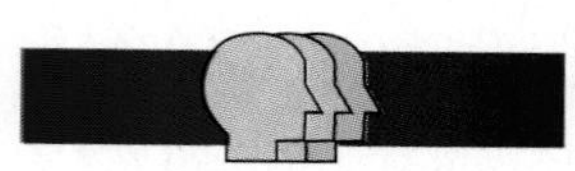

Objective 3
Compare major types of organizations.

Many types of organizations exist to serve society. Why do these organizations exist? Most exist because people need to work together to accomplish their goals. The goals are too large, too complex, or too expensive to be achieved without cooperation. All organizations provide goods and/or services. By working together, people can produce more and better goods and services.

Organizations differ as to the types of goods or services they offer. *Merchandising* **(or** *retail***)** *companies* **sell to consumers goods that are produced by other companies.** Grocery, department, and hardware stores are examples. *Manufacturing companies* **produce goods that they sell to consumers, to merchandising companies, or to other manufacturing companies.** Examples include automobile manufacturers, petroleum refineries, furniture manufacturers, computer companies, and paper companies. *Service companies* **sell services rather than goods.** These companies include banks, insurance companies, hospitals, colleges, law firms, and accounting firms. Some companies may be a combination of types. For example, gas stations are retail and service companies. Restaurants are both manufacturing and service companies.

Types of Organizations

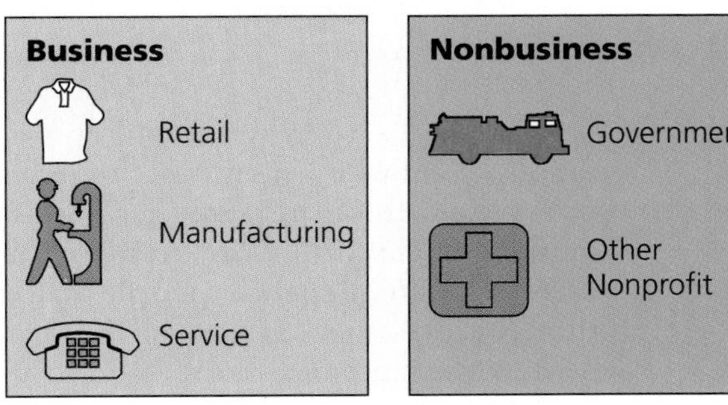

Another way to classify organizations is by whether they attempt to earn a profit. Profits result from selling goods and services to customers at prices greater than the cost of the items sold. **Organizations that sell their goods and services to make a profit are for-profit or business organizations.** *Governmental and nonprofit organizations,* **sometimes referred to as nonbusiness organizations, provide goods or, more typically, services without the intent of making a profit.** *Nonbusiness organizations* include civic, social, and religious organizations. Some types of services are provided by both business and nonbusiness organizations. Examples include education and health care services. Though the products are similar, the goals of the organizations providing these services are different. Nevertheless, all organizations need accounting information for decision making.

Transformation of Resources

A common purpose of organizations is to transform resources from one form to a different, more valuable, form to meet the needs of people. Resources include: natural resources such as minerals and timber, physical resources such as buildings and equipment, management skills, labor, financial resources, legal rights such as patents and trademarks, and information and the systems that provide information. The transformation process combines these resources to create goods and services. Transformation may involve making goods or services easier or less expensive for customers to obtain, as in most merchandising and service companies. Or, it may involve physically converting resources by processing or combining them, as in manufacturing companies.

Objective 4
Explain how organizations contribute to society.

Organizations are created because many transformations are too difficult or too expensive for individuals to accomplish without working together. By combining their managerial skills, labor, and money, individuals create organi-

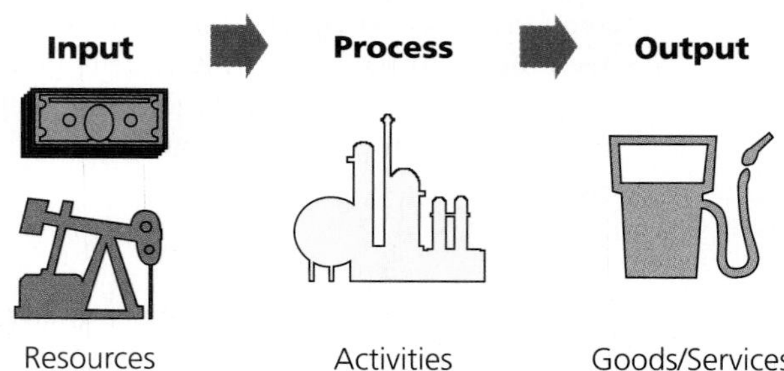

zations to provide benefits that otherwise would be unavailable. These benefits occur when an organization transforms resources from a less desirable form to a more desirable form. **The transformation, if it meets a need of society, creates value because people are better off after the transformation than before.** For example, a company that manufactures shirts creates value because the shirts are more useful to those who purchase them than would be the material from which the shirts are made or the cotton or synthetic fibers used to make the material.

To increase its welfare, a society must encourage organizations to increase the value they create. Because resources are in scarce supply, a society should attempt to use its resources wisely. **A major purpose of accounting information is to help decide how to get the most value from scarce resources.**

Creation of Value

How can a society determine how to use its resources? Decisions about using scarce resources wisely are not easy. Because society is made up of many individuals, disagreement often exists as to how resources should be used. In our society and many others, markets are the means used to promote the wise use of many resources.

Objective 5
Explain why markets are important.

Markets exist to allocate scarce resources used and produced by organizations. **A *market* is any location or process that permits resources to be bought and sold.** Competition in a market determines the amount and value of resources available for exchange. The more valuable a resource is in meeting your needs, the more you are willing to pay for it as a buyer, or the more you want for it as a seller.

The price paid for a resource in a competitive market is an indication of the value assigned to it at the particular time the buyer and seller negotiate an exchange. For example, when you buy a car, you exchange money for the car. The amount of money is a measure of the value you place on the car. Thus, the price of goods and services in a market is a basis for measuring value. **Accounting measures the increase in value created by a transformation as the difference between the total price of goods and services sold and the total cost of resources consumed in developing, producing, and selling the goods and services.**

Learning Note

Distinguish between prices charged by a business to its customers and prices paid by a business for resources it consumes. A price charged by a business is a **sales price**. A price paid by a business to purchase resources that will be consumed in providing goods and services is a **cost** to the business.

What value results when you purchase a car? The amount you pay for the car is an indication of the value you expect to receive from owning it. But, resources were consumed in producing the car and making it available to you.

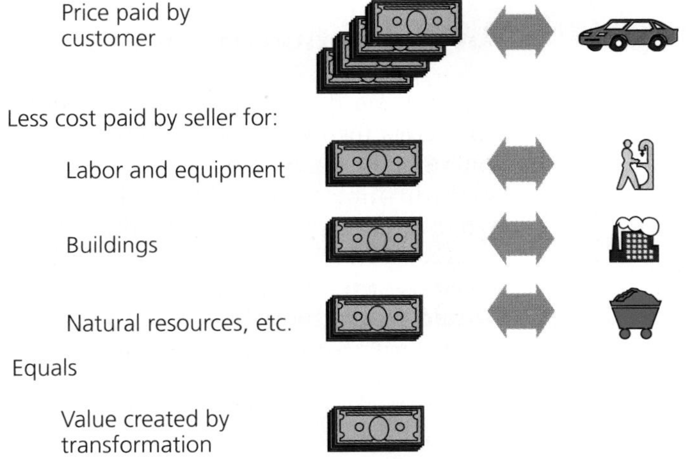

The total cost of these resources, such as metals, plastics, rubber, fabric, machinery and labor used in the manufacturing process, the cost of money to acquire other resources, and the cost of transportation to the dealer, is the cost of resources consumed in making the car available to you. The increase in value from the transformation that produced the car is the difference between the price you pay and the total cost of the resources consumed.

For example, if you pay $12,000 for a car and the total cost of producing the car and making it available to you is $10,000, the value added by the transformation is $2,000. The difference between the price you pay and the total cost of the car to the seller is profit for the automobile manufacturer and the dealership, or more precisely, for the owners of those firms. ***Profit*** **is the difference between the price a seller receives for goods or services and the total cost to the seller of all resources consumed in developing, producing and selling these goods or services during a particular period.** Thus, profits are the net resources generated by the sales events (resources received from the sales minus resources used in making the sale).

Learning Note

A "period" is an important concept in accounting. A period may be any length of time used to measure the effects of transactions. Common periods include months, quarters, and years. An accounting period often is called a fiscal period, because it may not coincide with a calendar period. For example, a company's fiscal year might begin on July 1.

Several markets are important in our economy. Markets exist for resources used by organizations. Organizations compete in **financial markets** for financial resources. Investors choose where to put their money to work by selecting among competing organizations. Organizations compete in **supplier markets** for other resources needed to produce goods and services. Competition in these markets determines the costs of materials, labor, equipment, and other resources available to organizations. Organizations compete in **product markets** (markets for goods and services). These markets determine the prices of goods and services available to customers. From the perspective of organizations, financial and supplier markets are input markets; markets for goods and services are output markets. All of these markets allocate scarce resources.

An Illustration of Creating Value

Suppose you decide to open a clothing store, New Styles, in a shopping mall. Your costs for December include rent on the shop, $2,000; the cost of clothes sold, $7,500; utilities, $300; maintenance, $250; advertising, $400; and wages for a part-time assistant, $500. The selling price of goods sold in December was $15,000. How much profit did the business earn during December?

Exhibit 1-3 reports profit earned by New Styles in December. **An *income statement* measures profit by subtracting the cost of resources consumed from the prices of goods or services sold for a period of time.** Other terms for profit are net income and net earnings. Net income of $4,050 represents the difference between the price of the goods sold to customers and the total cost of resources consumed in providing those goods.

Exhibit 1-3

New Styles Clothing Store
Income Statement
For December 1995

Revenues from clothing sold		$15,000
Expenses:		
Clothes	$7,500	
Rent	2,000	
Utilities	300	
Maintenance	250	
Advertising	400	
Wages	500	
Total cost		10,950
Net income		$ 4,050

The sales prices of goods sold are known as **revenues.** The costs of resources consumed in producing the goods sold and in making them available to customers are known as **expenses.** ***Net income* (or *net earnings*) is the difference between revenues and expenses for a period:** Net Income = Revenues − Expenses. Of course, a business venture may not produce net income. It may result in a net loss. **A *net loss* occurs when expenses are greater**

than revenues for a period. In other words, a net loss results when the cost of resources used to make sales exceeds the value of resources generated by the sales.

Investment by Owners

Objective 6
Explain why owners invest in businesses.

Businesses earn profits (net income) by providing goods and services demanded by society. **Owners invest in a business to receive a return on their investments from profits earned by that business.** By investing their money in a business, owners are foregoing its use for other purposes. In exchange, they expect to share in a business's earnings. ***Return on investment* is the amount of profits earned by a business that could be paid to owners.**

Profits represent net resources that have been earned through sales transactions. These resources belong to owners; a business may distribute profits to its owners. Alternatively, owners (or managers acting on their behalf) may decide to reinvest profits in a business to acquire additional resources. The business uses the additional resources to earn more profits by expanding its size or by expanding into new locations or product lines. Either way, the owners are better off. They receive cash from their investments if profits are withdrawn, or they own a business that is more valuable if profits are reinvested.

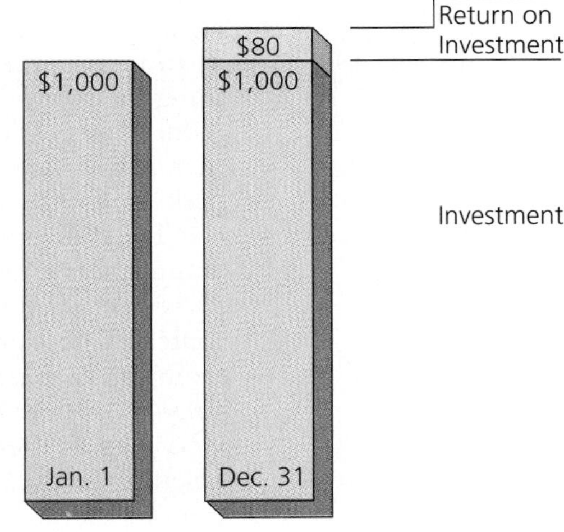

Investing in a business is similar in some ways to investing in a savings account. If you put $1,000 in a savings account, you expect to receive interest on your savings. Interest is the return you earn on your investment. For example, if you earn $80 of interest on your savings in a year, you have received an $80 (or 8%) return on your investment. You may choose to withdraw some of the interest, or you may choose to leave the interest in the account. You either have $80 to spend or you have an investment worth $80 more than your initial investment.

Learning Note

If you withdraw more than $80 from your account, the additional amount withdrawn is a return ***of*** investment, not a return ***on*** investment. It is a return of a portion of the amount you originally invested. For a company to maintain its capital (the amount invested by its owners), it must pay a return to owners from profits the company has earned. Otherwise, the company is reducing its capital by returning a portion of owners' investments to them.

Investing in a business differs in some ways from investing in a savings account. The amount you receive from your savings account is determined by the current interest rate the financial institution agrees to pay. The amount of return you receive from a company depends on the success the company has in earning a profit. If you are the primary owner of a business, success depends primarily on your ability and effort. If you invest in a large company, success depends largely on the abilities and efforts of those who manage the business. When you invest in a business, you have no guarantee it will be successful. You are taking a risk that you may not receive a return on your investment, that the return may be smaller than you expected, or even that you might lose your investment. Greater risk means greater uncertainty about the return that will be received.

Why invest in a business if the investment is risky? If a business is successful, its owners can expect to earn a higher rate of return on their investments relative to a safer alternative such as a savings account. One such example is the Microsoft Corporation, which earned a return of almost 40% per year for its investors between 1987 and 1991. The return on a savings account during this period would have been about 6% per year.

To earn profits and pay returns to owners, businesses must operate effectively and efficiently. **An *effective business* is one that is successful in providing goods and services demanded by customers.** Another measure of success is how socially responsible a business is. That is, not only should a business meet the demands of customers, but it should do so in a way that has a positive effect on society. Drug dealers may be effective in meeting customer demands, but they are not beneficial to society. Effective management involves identifying the right products and putting them in the right locations at the right times. **An *efficient business* is one that provides goods and services at low costs relative to their selling prices.** Managers must control costs by using the proper mix, qualities, and quantities of resources to avoid waste and to reduce costs. The risk of owning a business is lower if it is effective and efficient than if it is ineffective or inefficient. Efficient and effective businesses are competitive in financial, supplier, and product markets.

The difference between effectiveness and efficiency can be viewed from examining companies' revenues and net incomes. For example, assume two companies are identical with respect to products, selling prices, financing, and resources. Company A has revenues of $10 million and net income of $2 million. Company B has revenues of $9 million and net income of $2.2 million. Company A has been more effective in selling its products than Company B because it has higher sales volume and greater revenues. Company B has been more efficient than Company A, however, because it has produced greater net income from its sales by controlling its costs better.

The Market for Investors

Businesses must compete, not only for resources and customers, but also for investors. Business owners expect to receive a return on their investments. Investors choose among alternate investments by evaluating the amount, timing, and uncertainty of the returns they expect to receive. Businesses that earn high profits and are capable of paying returns have less difficulty in obtaining investors than other businesses. A business that cannot earn sufficient profits will be forced to become more effective and efficient or to go out of business.

Objective 7
Explain why accounting information is useful to investors.

The accounting information system is a major source of information investors use in deciding about their investments. **Accounting information helps investors assess the effectiveness and efficiency of businesses.** It helps them estimate the returns that can be expected from investing in a business and the amount of risk associated with their investments. Financial, supplier, and product markets create incentives for businesses to provide products society demands. These market forces help ensure that scarce resources are used to improve society's welfare. Markets help allocate scarce resources to those organizations that can best transform them to create value. Market-based economies have proven to be better means of resource allocation than planned economies.

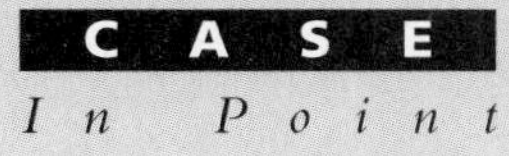

In 1990, a remarkable restructuring began in Eastern Europe as country after country threw off many years of communist domination and began converting to a market system. Since the end of World War II in 1945, countries such as Poland, Hungary, East Germany, and Romania had suffered under planned economies. Central planners decided what to produce, how much to produce, and the prices at which goods were sold.

After more than 40 years of watching their Western European neighbors advance economically, the people and governments of Eastern Europe decided their planned economies were disasters. Shortages of goods were common and available goods often were of low quality. For example, at one time pencils were unavailable at any price in Poland. By the time the pencil shortage was relieved, however, writing paper had disappeared from stores.

Nonbusiness Organizations

Objective 8
Identify reasons some goods and services are not sold in markets.

Not all resources are provided through competitive markets. Governmental and nonprofit organizations provide public services such as police and fire protection, public education, highways and streets, and national defense. These organizations exist primarily to provide goods and services that are difficult to sell in markets or that society has determined should be available to those who cannot purchase them in competitive markets.

Some goods and services are difficult to sell in markets. Public protection and national defense are examples. If the government provides for your protection and defense, it also is providing for the protection and defense of others in your community. People normally will not purchase these services in a market because the benefits they receive cannot be determined from a competitive market price. If you were asked to make a voluntary payment for police and fire protection, how much would you pay? You might have difficulty in determining a fair price because you do not know how much others are paying. A government would have difficulty raising sufficient money to pay for these services if it made requests for voluntary payments. Instead, public services are provided by governmental organizations that pay for them by taxing their citizens. Taxpayers share in the cost of government services to ensure their availability to the entire society.

Other goods and services are not provided in markets because society desires they be available to everyone regardless of ability to pay. As an example, education can be provided by business organizations. Privately owned institutions sometimes sell these services to earn a profit. Still, our society has decided these services should be available to all members of society. Therefore, public schools provide free education to all eligible members of society. Governmental organizations levy taxes to pay for these services.

Political competition substitutes for market competition in governmental organizations. Citizens elect representatives who determine public policies and manage governments. If citizens believe elected representatives are not providing services efficiently and effectively, they can support competing candidates.

Most of this book focuses on accounting for business organizations. We will consider nonbusiness organizations in a separate chapter. Many of the accounting concepts that apply to business organizations also apply to nonbusiness organizations. Nevertheless, important differences exist because nonbusiness organizations do not sell all of their goods and services in competitive markets. Accounting procedures differ among organizations because of the economic and social purposes organizations serve. These differences may affect the way accounting information is used or interpreted.

SELF-STUDY PROBLEM 1-2

John Bach owns a music store in which he sells and repairs musical instruments, and sells sheet music. The following transactions occurred for Bach's Music Store during December 1995:

1. Sold $8,000 of musical instruments that cost the company $4,300.
2. Sold $1,400 of sheet music that cost the company $870.
3. The price of repair services provided during the month was $2,200.
4. Rent on the store for the month was $650.
5. The cost of supplies used during the month was $250.
6. The cost of advertising for the month was $300.
7. The cost of utilities for the month was $200.
8. Other miscellaneous costs for December were $180.

Required

1. Determine the profit (net income) earned by Bach's Music Store for December by preparing an income statement.
2. Explain how the income statement measures value created by Bach's Music Store.

The solution to Self-Study Problem 1-2 appears at the end of the chapter.

DECISIONS IN ORGANIZATIONS

Many types of decisions are made in organizations. Accounting provides important information to make these decisions. In this section, we will consider three organizational activities that use accounting information for decision making: financing, investing, and operating activities.

Financing Activities

Objective 9
Identify financing activities and the types of decisions they require.

Organizations require financial resources to obtain other resources used to produce goods and services. They compete for these resources in financial markets. *Financing activities* **are the methods an organization uses to obtain financial resources from financial markets and how it manages these resources.** Primary sources of financing for most businesses are owners and creditors. The following sections consider these sources.

Objective 10
Compare forms of business ownership.

Business Ownership. Businesses may be classified in two categories: those that are distinct legal entities apart from their owners and those that are not distinct legal entities. **A *corporation* is a legal entity with the right to enter into contracts, the right to own, buy, and sell property, and the right to sell stock.** Resources are owned by the corporation, not by the owners directly.

Corporations may be very large or fairly small organizations. Small corporations often are managed by their owners. The owners of most large corporations do not manage their companies. Instead, they hire professional managers. These owners have the right to vote on certain major decisions, but they do not control the operations of their corporation on a day-to-day basis. One reason most large businesses are organized as corporations is that they typically have greater access to financial markets than other types of organizations.

Corporations often are owned by many investors who purchase shares of stock (certificates of ownership) issued by corporations. **Each share of *stock* represents an equal share in the ownership of a corporation.** An investor who owns 10% of the shares of a corporation owns 10% of the company and has a right to 10% of the return available to stockholders. ***Stockholders*, or shareholders, are the owners of a corporation.**

Shares of stock often are traded in stock markets, such as the New York, London, and Tokyo Stock Exchanges, that are established specifically for this purpose. These markets facilitate the exchange of stock between buyers and sellers. Therefore, unlike other businesses, ownership in many corporations can change easily, simply by buying or selling shares of stock. Major corporations, such as General Motors, Exxon, or IBM, have received billions of dollars from stockholders.

***Proprietorships* and *partnerships* are business organizations that do not have legal identities distinct from their owners. Proprietorships have only one owner; partnerships have more than one owner.** For most proprietorships and partnerships, owners also manage their businesses. In fact, in a legal sense, the owners are the businesses. Owners have a major stake in the business because often much of their personal wealth is invested in it. The amount of a proprietor's personal wealth and his ability to borrow limits the size of a proprietorship. If a proprietorship is profitable, profits earned by the proprietor can be reinvested and the business can become fairly large.

Percentage of Companies and Volume of Sales by Type of Organization

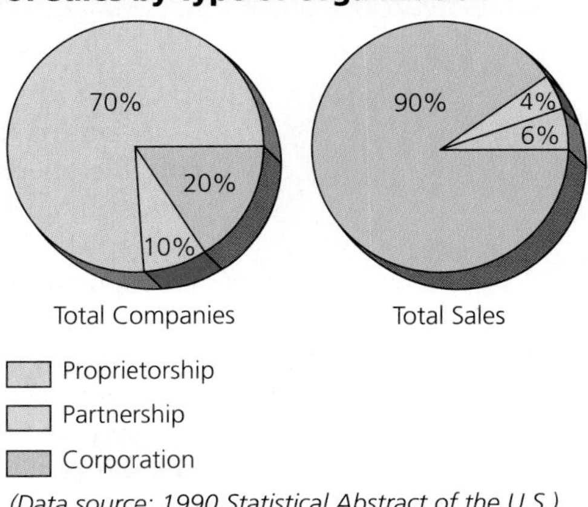

(Data source: 1990 Statistical Abstract of the U.S.)

Partnerships can include several partners; therefore, the money available to finance a partnership depends on the money available from all the partners. New partners can be added, making new money available to the business. While most partnerships are small, large businesses (with as many as a thousand or more owners) sometimes are organized as partnerships.

Management of Corporations. Exhibit 1-4 provides an organizational chart for a typical corporation that describes the formal organization structure among its managers.

Exhibit 1-4 Corporate management functions.

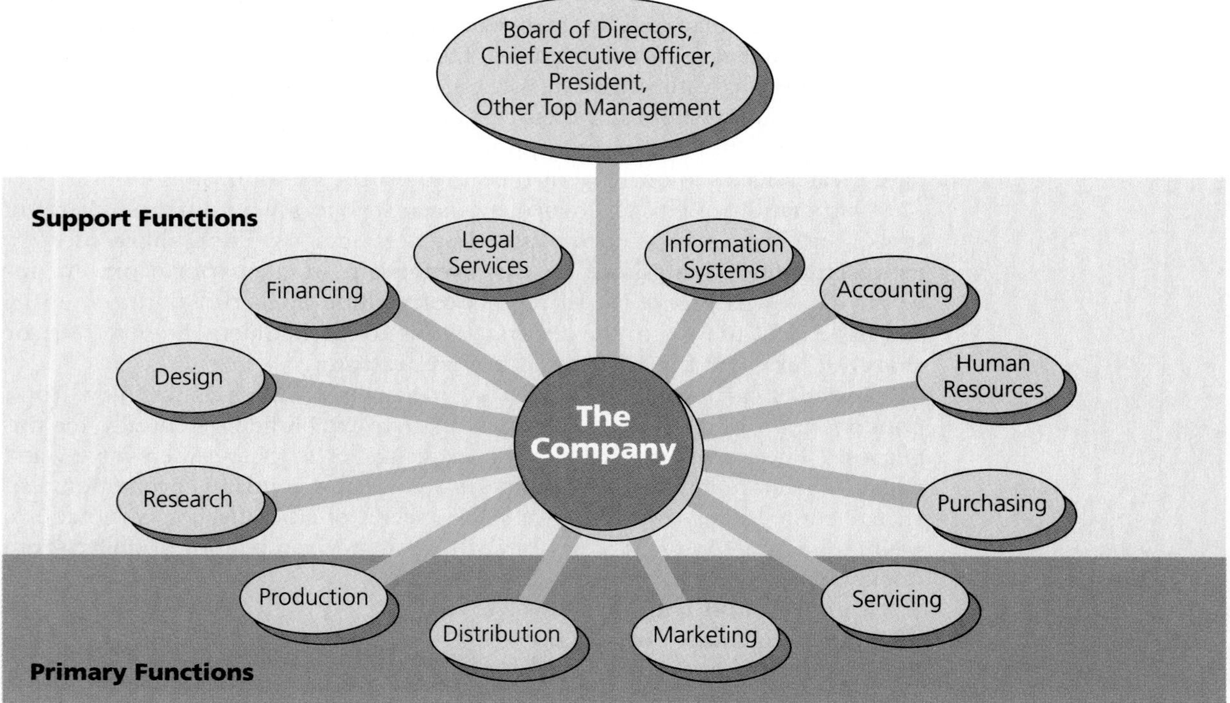

A **board of directors** oversees the decisions of management, and is responsible for protecting the interests of stockholders. Normally, the board is appointed by management with the approval of stockholders. Top managers often serve on the board along with outside directors who are not part of the corporation's management. The **chairman of the board** often holds the position of **chief executive officer** (CEO) with the ultimate responsibility for the success of the business. The **president,** as **chief operating officer,** is responsible for the day-to-day management of a corporation. In some cases, the president also may be the CEO. The company may appoint any number of **vice-presidents** who are responsible for various functions in the organization. The titles and roles of these managers will vary from corporation to corporation. Along with the CEO and president, the vice-presidents constitute the top management of a corporation. Together, they make planning decisions and develop company goals and policies.

Functions performed within a corporation may be separated into support and primary services. Support services assist the primary functions and top management by providing information and other resources necessary to produce and sell goods and services. Primary functions are those actually involved in producing and selling goods and services. These functions include distribution of goods and services to customers and servicing the goods and services to meet customer needs.

Among the support services are research and development, product and production design, finance, legal services, accounting, purchasing, and human resources. The **chief financial officer** (CFO), who also may be the **treasurer,** is responsible for obtaining financial resources and managing a corporation's cash flows. If these positions are separate, the treasurer is responsible primarily for managing and protecting a corporation's cash. The **controller,** as the chief accounting officer, is responsible for accounting and financial reporting, development and maintenance of the accounting information system, and reporting to tax and regulatory authorities.

Primary functions involve the operation of production, distribution, and sales facilities. *Plant managers* oversee production for specific product lines or geographical locations. These managers often have their own staffs at the divisional or plant level. For example, divisional or plant level controllers exist in many corporations. Research, design, and development staffs also exist at the divisional or plant level in some organizations.

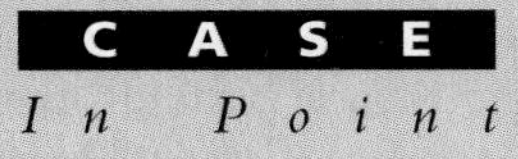

Humana Corporation owns and manages hospitals throughout the U.S. Each hospital provides services to a particular community, and has its own administrator and management team, doctors, nurses, and other staff.

Corporations may be organized by functions such as those described in Exhibit 1-4. Other corporations are organized primarily by region or product line. For example, multinational companies may be organized into North American, European, or Pacific divisions. Functional areas, such as development and production, are subordinate to regional or product managers. Many corporations are finding advantages in changing from a traditional organizational structure to, for example, teams of managers working together on specific projects. Thus, the idea for a new product may be the responsibility of a team of employees from a company's functional areas. Together, the team decides how best to design the product and production process to increase efficiency and product quality.

An important function of top management is creating an organization's structure. Structure determines the functional areas, divisions, and other components of an organization; also, it establishes relationships among managers and employees of these components. Thus, it affects how information flows through an organization, lines of authority and responsibility, and how components of an organization will work together to accomplish its goals.

The distinction between managers and employees is not always clear; therefore, the term "manager" is used broadly in this book to include those in an organization who make decisions affecting the organization's transformation process. Many levels and types of managers exist in many large organizations. Some of these managers are supervisors of departments and divisions of the organization. Others play key roles in developing, designing, producing, distributing, and marketing an organization's products. Others provide and analyze information to assist other managers. The term "employees" will refer primarily to those who perform duties in an organization but do not have major decision-making responsibility.

Advantages of Corporations. Several advantages exist for a corporate form of organization over proprietorships or partnerships. Corporations have **continuous lives** apart from those of their owners. If a proprietor or partner sells her share of a business or dies, the business ceases to exist as a legal entity. The new owner of the business must reestablish the business as a new legal entity. Most corporations, however, continue unchanged if current owners sell their stock, donate it to charity, give it to relatives, or otherwise dispose of their shares.

Shareholders normally are not liable personally for the debts of a corporation. This is a characteristic known as **limited liability**. If a corporation defaults on debt or enters bankruptcy, its owners may lose a portion or all of their investments in the company. But, they are not obligated to repay creditors from their personal wealth for losses incurred by the creditors. Proprietors and partners are personally liable for the debts of their companies and could be required to use their personal wealth to repay their creditors. A proprietorship or partnership is not a separate legal entity apart from its owners.

Shareholders of most corporations do not manage the company. They elect members of the board of directors who then hire **professional managers** to run the corporation. Investors can own part of a corporation or parts of many corporations without having to participate in the day-to-day decisions of running the companies. Many Americans own stock in corporations through personal investments and retirement plans and, thus, are not required to commit large amounts of their personal time to corporate concerns.

Shareholders do not have the right of mutual agency. ***Mutual agency*** **permits a partner to enter into contracts and agreements that are binding on all members of a partnership.** Shareholders cannot enter into contracts or agreements that are binding on a corporation unless they are managers or directors. Therefore, investors in a corporation do not have to be concerned about the abilities of other stockholders to make good business decisions. In contrast, bad decisions by one partner can result in the personal bankruptcy of all partners in a partnership.

By selling shares to many investors, a corporation can obtain a large amount of financial resources. The ability to **raise large amounts of capital** permits corporations to become very large organizations. Thus, corporations can invest in plant facilities and undertake production activities that would be difficult for proprietorships or partnerships.

Disadvantages of Corporations. Several disadvantages exist for the corporate form of ownership. Most **corporations must pay taxes on their incomes.** Corporate taxes are separate from the taxes paid by shareholders on dividends received from the company. Some corporations, especially smaller ones, are not taxed separately. Another disadvantage is **corporations are regulated** by various state and federal government agencies. These regulations require corporations to comply with many state and federal rules concerning business practices and reporting of financial information. Corporations must file many reports with government agencies and make public disclosure of their operating activities. **Compliance with these regulations is costly.** Also, some of the **required disclosures may be helpful to competitors.** Partnerships and proprietorships are regulated also, but the degree of regulation is much less than for corporations.

Owners of corporations normally do not have access to information about the day-to-day activities of their companies. They depend on managers to make decisions that will increase the value of their investments. On the other hand, managers' personal interests sometimes conflict with the interests of stockholders. This problem produces a condition known as moral hazard. Moral hazard arises when one group, known as agents (such as managers), is responsible for serving the needs of another group, known as principals (such as investors). ***Moral hazard* is the condition that exists when agents have superior information to principals and are able to make decisions that favor their own interests over those of the principals.**

Without disclosure of reliable information, corporations would have difficulty in selling stock, and investors would be unable to determine whether managers were making decisions that increased stockholder value or were making decisions that took advantage of the stockholders. Accounting reports are major sources of information to stockholders to help them assess the performance of managers. For example, an income statement helps owners evaluate how well managers have used owners' investments to earn returns for the owners. **Moral hazard imposes costs on corporations because managers must report to stockholders and, generally, these reports are audited.** An audit verifies the reliability of reported information.

The size of many corporations makes them difficult to manage. An individual manager cannot be involved directly with all the decisions made in operating a large organization. Top level managers depend on lower level managers to make decisions and to keep them informed about a corporation's operations. This process is costly because coordination among managers may be difficult to achieve. Moral hazard exists among managers and employees, not just between managers and investors. Corporate goals and policies provide guidance for manager decisions; but, communicating goals and policies and providing incentives for managers to implement them often is difficult and expensive. Employees and lower level managers may not report reliable information about their activities to higher level managers if the information is not in their best interests. Multinational corporations, in particular, are complex and difficult to manage. Distant locations for facilities and differences in languages and local customs can cause special problems.

Creditors. In addition to money provided by owners, businesses (and other organizations) may borrow money. Money may be obtained from banks and other financial institutions, or it may be borrowed from individual lenders. **A lender or *creditor* is someone who loans financial resources to an organization.**

Most organizations depend on banks and similar institutions to lend them money. Corporations often borrow money from individuals or other companies. Exhibit 1-5 describes the amount of money several large corporations have received from owners and creditors.

Creditors loan money to organizations to earn a return on their investments, just as do owners. Creditors, however, usually loan money for a specific period and are promised a specific rate of return on their investments. Usually, this is a fixed rate (say 10%). In contrast, owners invest for a nonspecific period (until they decide to sell their ownership rights) and receive a return that depends on the profits earned by the business.

Exhibit 1-5 Financing Arrangements of Selected Corporations

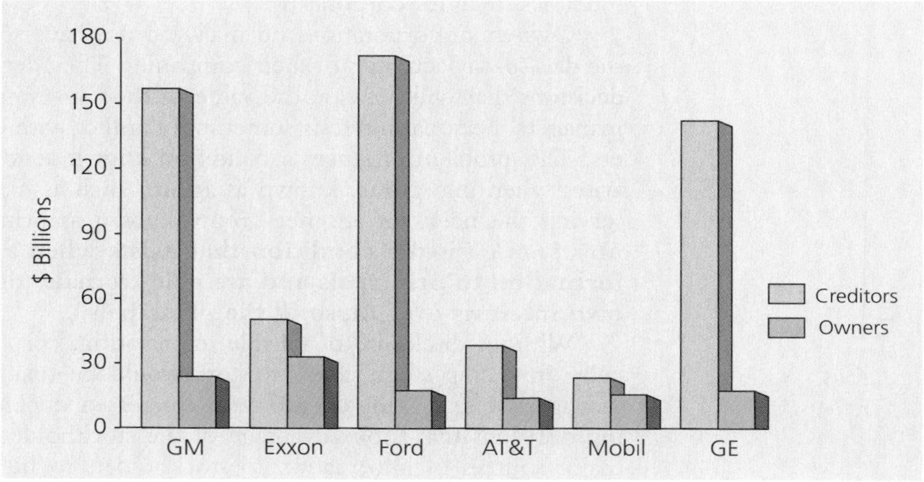

Data source: Fortune, April 22, 1991.

The success of a business determines whether or not creditors will receive the amount promised by the borrower. When a business fails to generate sufficient cash from its revenues to pay its expenses and to pay its creditors, they may not receive the amount promised. Therefore, creditors evaluate the probability an organization will be able to repay debt and interest. Risk is a concern of both creditors and owners. Exhibit 1-6 illustrates financing activities.

Financing Decisions. Financing decisions involve choices about when and where to obtain financial resources and about the amount needed. A corporation must decide how much stock and debt to issue, when they should be is-

Exhibit 1-6 Components of Financing Activities

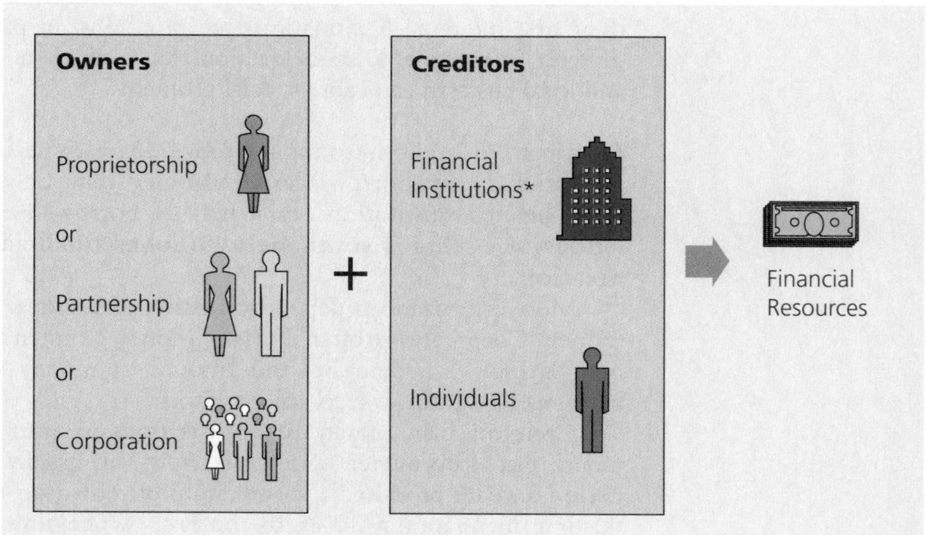

***The term "financial institutions" refers to banks, savings and loans, etc.*

sued, and to whom they should be issued to obtain favorable prices. These decisions depend on the business's need for money and on its ability to repay owners and creditors for their investments.

Financing decisions are made by owners, creditors, and managers. Owners and creditors need to know how managers are using their money and how much risk they are taking. Managers decide how much money a business needs, how much return they will pay to investors, how they will invest capital, and the probable effect of financing arrangements on the profitability and survival of an organization. Questions answered by financing decisions include:

How much financing does an organization need?
Where should an organization obtain its financing?
When should an organization obtain financing?
How will capital be used?
What effect will financing have on profitability and survival?

Investing Activities

Managers use capital from financing activities to acquire other resources used in the transformation process. Having the right mix of resources is essential to efficient and effective operations. The wrong set of resources or having resources in the wrong place or at the wrong time can lead to disastrous results.

Objective 11
Identify investing activities and the types of decisions they require

Investing activities **involve the selection and management of resources that will be used to develop, produce, and sell goods and services.** Resources include supplies, insurance, land and natural resources, buildings, equipment, information systems, people, legal rights such as patents and trademarks, and other resources necessary for an organization to produce goods and services. Organizations compete in supplier markets for these resources. Exhibit 1-7 illustrates investing activities.

Exhibit 1-7 Components of Investing Activities

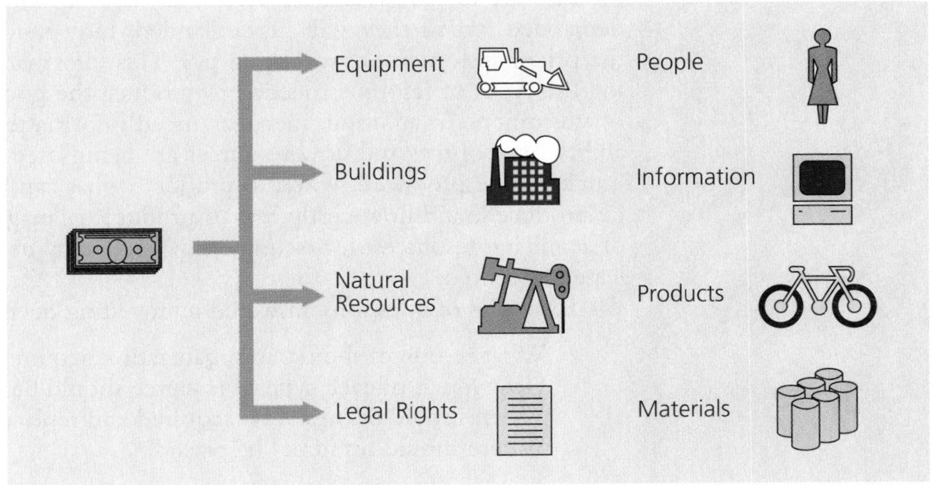

Many manufacturing companies require large investments in buildings and equipment to develop, produce, transport, and market their products. Exhibit 1-8 identifies the amount some large corporations have invested in resources.

Exhibit 1-8 Amounts Invested in Resources by Selected Corporations

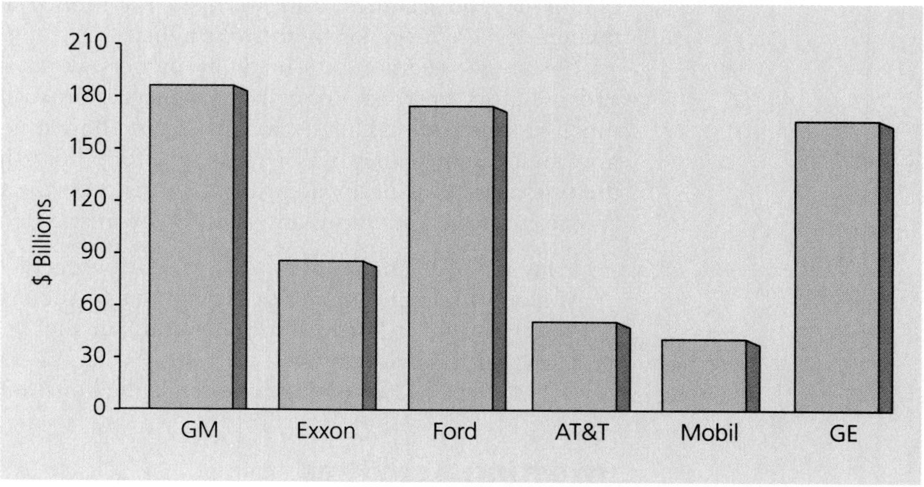

Data source: Fortune, April 22, 1991.

Learning Note

Don't confuse investments made by owners and creditors (financing activities) with investments made by managers (investing activities).

Investing Decisions. Managers decide how much to invest in resources and the types of resources to acquire. Often these decisions involve large amounts of money and have a major effect on the future of an organization. These decisions affect future profitability, future supply of goods and services, and future return to owners and creditors.

In making investing decisions, managers need information for predicting the demand for goods and services. They need to know which products will be demanded, when they will be demanded, how much will be demanded, and the prices customers are willing to pay. This information is useful for determining the types of resources needed to produce the goods and services demanded by customers. In addition, managers need information about the current availability of resources and how resources are being used. They need to know how much can be produced, when to produce, what can be produced, where it can be produced, and how costly it is to produce. Managers evaluate alternate ways of acquiring resources; for example, resources may be purchased or they may be leased or rented.

Examples of questions answered by investing decisions include:

What resources should an organization acquire?
How much of each type of resource should be acquired?
When should resources be acquired and replaced?
Where should resources be placed?

Operating Activities

Objective 12
Identify operating activities and the types of decisions they require.

Operating activities **involve the use of resources to design, produce, distribute, and market goods and services.** Operating activities include research and development, design and engineering, purchasing, personnel, production, distribution, marketing and selling, and servicing. Organizations compete in supplier and labor markets for resources used in these activities. Also, they compete in product markets to sell the goods and services created by operating activities. Exhibit 1-9 features components of operating activities.

Exhibit 1-9 Components of operating activities

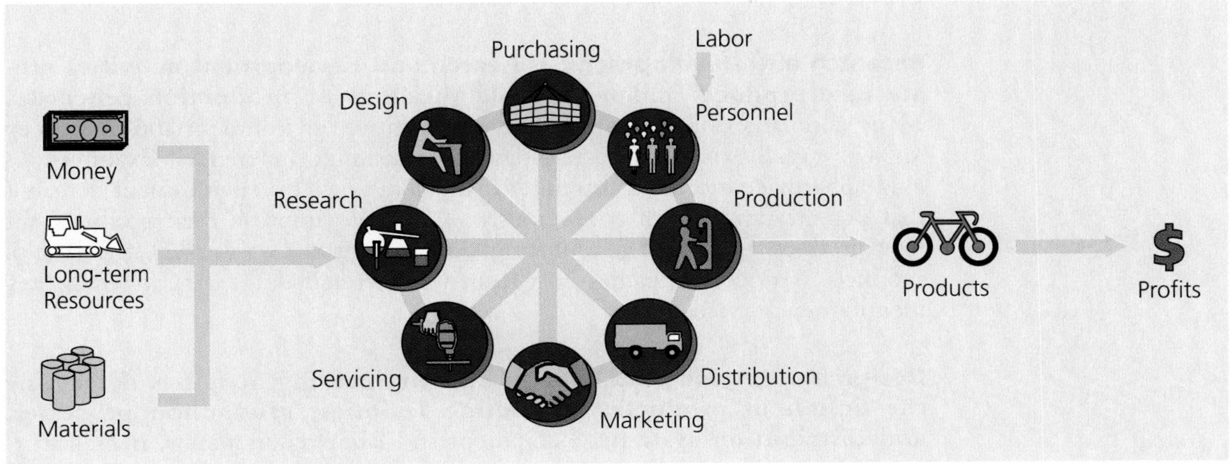

These activities often exist as individual departments or divisions of an organization. Each division may have its own manager who is responsible for decisions in that division. Not every organization needs each of these activities. For example, merchandising and service organizations generally do not require engineering and production. Often, some activities are combined in a division. For example, distribution, marketing, and servicing may be combined in a single division with one chief manager.

Exhibit 1-10 describes the interrelationship of financing, investing, and operating activities. The exhibit illustrates the value to an organization resulting from the transformation of resources into goods and services.

Exhibit 1-10 Value from Transforming Resources into Goods and Services

Support Activities
Top Management
Accounting and Finance
Research and Development
Design and Engineering
Purchasing
Personnel

Primary Activities
Production
Distribution
Marketing and Selling
Servicing

Value Produced
Revenues
− Expenses
= Net Income

Data source: Michael E. Porter, Competitive Advantage, New York, Free Press, 1989, p. 37.

Support activities are those activities not directly involved in making goods and services available to customers; they include general management, financing, and investing activities. Personnel, research and development, and purchasing activities are included as well. These activities support a company's primary activities, which produce goods and services and make them available to customers. The value created by all of these activities is a company's net income. The following sections consider each component of a company's operating activities.

Research and Development. Research and development activities create new products and update old products or production processes. Many companies operate in a highly competitive environment and must keep up with rapidly changing technology and consumer preferences. Examples include pharmaceutical and computer manufacturers. This environment demands that organizations search continuously for ways to improve their products, for new products that meet consumer needs, and for ways to reduce the cost of products. Service companies engage in research and development when they identify new services.

Design and Engineering. Design and engineering activities determine the design of products, production facilities, production processes, and distribution systems. Equipment and labor requirements, manufacturing and assembly processes, and other features of the way goods are produced and distributed have a major effect on product costs and marketability.

Purchasing. Purchasing activities involve acquiring and managing the materials and supplies needed for production or sale. Materials used in manufacturing must be purchased in the appropriate amounts and at the right times to ensure availability. Materials are expensive to acquire and store, but, production cannot occur unless the proper materials are available in the quantities needed. Purchasing decisions involve obtaining the proper types, qualities, and quantities of materials to minimize purchase, storage, and production costs. This function also is important in merchandising companies. Purchasing controls the selection and acquisition of goods that are available for resale and also is important in service organizations such as hospitals.

Personnel. In addition to materials, labor is a primary factor in producing and selling goods and services. **Personnel or human resource activities involve obtaining the needed amount of human resources with the appropriate skills.** Primary functions involve hiring, firing, and training employees, as well as coordination of payroll and employee benefits such as retirement and health care. Salary negotiations and maintaining employee satisfaction also may be important responsibilities of the personnel function.

Production. Production activities involve the manufacture and assembly of goods for sale. Decisions must be made to schedule the production process so labor, materials, and equipment are available when needed. The appropriate mix of these factors is necessary to ensure the required quantity and quality of goods can be produced. Production decisions affect the cost and quality of products. Most companies monitor the production process closely to ensure quality and cost control.

Production activities exist in a simplified form in many service organizations. The production of services involves primarily human labor. Skills are applied in providing for specific consumer needs, such as information, repair, or maintenance. Facilities may be important in providing the services, but materials are not placed into production to create physical goods for sale.

Distribution. Distribution is a key activity in many merchandising companies whose primary transformation function is putting goods in an appropriate location for the convenience of customers. It is also important to many manufacturing and service companies. **Distribution activities involve getting the right goods to the right location at the right time.** Because transportation is costly, decisions must be made about how goods will be shipped, when they will be shipped, and how much will be shipped. Distribution activities are especially important for companies that operate in global markets. Goods often must be shipped from countries where they are produced to other countries where they are sold.

Marketing and Selling. Marketing and selling activities involve making potential buyers aware of products and selling them to customers. Providing information for potential buyers through promotion, advertising, and personal contact is essential for most businesses. Managers decide how to reach buyers effectively and how to present the company's products to create sales. Decisions involve the amount and type of advertising and sales force to use, the types and amounts of credit and discounting to give to different buyers, and the determination of consumer needs and demands. Therefore, selling involves more than the actual sale of goods and services. It involves careful monitoring of consumer needs and tastes. This information, in turn, is important in guiding the research and manufacturing efforts of the company to produce the amount and types of goods and services demanded by customers.

Servicing. The sale of goods and services is not the final step in the transformation process for many organizations. **Servicing products often continues after the sale.** Servicing activities involve the assistance provided to buyers after goods have been sold. Companies provide warranties on many products that require the company to repair and replace defective merchandise. Additionally, manufacturers or sellers often provide service for merchandise after the warranty period. Some organizations provide installation and training for products they sell. For example, computer companies often contract to install computer systems and to train employees to use them. Computers, automobiles, and other high-technology products require periodic maintenance after the sale.

Creation of Profits. In summary, this section has described the operating activities observed in most organizations, though not all activities will exist in every organization. The profitability of a company depends on its success in selling its products and controlling its costs. Profits are a measure of a company's ability to manage its capital and resources. How a company operates depends on the particular strategies management chooses for the organization. These strategies may involve providing goods and services at lower costs than competitors or providing goods and services that differ from those of competitors. Differences may be observed in product performance, quality, or features. Exhibit 1-11 describes profits or losses earned by several large corporations.

Exhibit 1-11 Operating Results of Selected Corporations

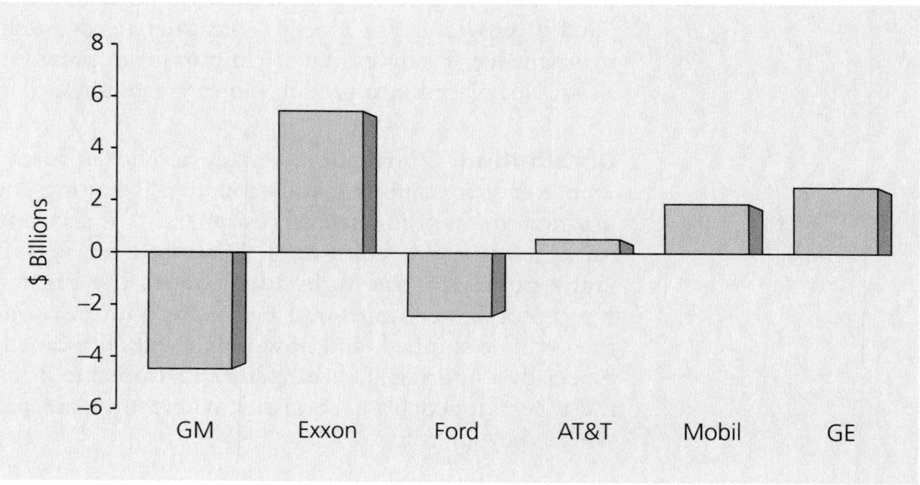

Data source: Fortune, April 22, 1991.

Operating Decisions. Producing and distributing the right set of products efficiently is critical to the success of a business organization. Having the wrong products or producing the right products inefficiently often leads to serious financial problems.

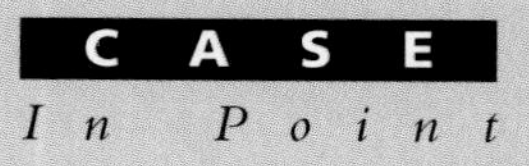

One of the most serious difficulties faced by the U.S. auto industry arose in the mid 1970s. Fuel shortages and high gas prices stimulated a demand for small, fuel-efficient cars. U.S. automakers had little experience in designing, manufacturing, or selling small cars. Foreign automakers, who had a lot of experience with small cars, imported their cars to the U.S. to meet the demand. The U.S. industry lost much of its competitive advantage and has yet to regain it. The loss resulted from an inability to react quickly to a changing economic environment.

Questions answered by operating decisions include:

Research and Development: How can new products be made or existing ones be improved?

Engineering: How should products be designed and produced?

Purchasing: What quantity and types of resources should an organization acquire that will be used to produce goods and services?

Personnel: How many and what types of employees are needed? What kind of training do employees need? How should they be compensated?

Production: How should production activities be scheduled? Should production occur in domestic or foreign locations?

Distribution: How should goods be shipped and stored so they are available to customers when needed?

Marketing and Selling: What activities are necessary to promote and sell goods and services?

Servicing: What types of installation, repair, and maintenance services should be provided to customers for the goods they purchase?

SUMMARY OF THE TRANSFORMATION PROCESS

Objective 13
List steps in the transformation process.

Decisions made in financing, investing, and operating activities require information. The accounting information system is designed to meet certain information needs, particularly those involving the financial effects of the transformation process. **The** ***transformation process*** is a cycle that begins with the **acquisition of capital from owners and creditors**. This capital is **invested in facilities, equipment, people, and other resources** needed to create goods and services. Organizations use these resources in **developing, producing, distributing, and selling goods and services**. Selling goods and services results in the **inflow of additional financial resources** so the cycle can continue.

While the flow of resources typically is from financing to investing and operating decisions, information often follows the reverse path. For example, decisions about how much and what kind of products are demanded by customers are necessary before products can be designed. These decisions are necessary to plan production and distribution. The number of units produced affects the need for materials, labor, and equipment used in the production process. The need for materials, labor, and equipment determines the need for financing to provide money for these resources. Thus, planning often begins with expectations about the sale of goods and services and works backward to determine the resources and activities needed to produce the goods and services. Make sure you have a good understanding of how organizations transform resources into goods and services as illustrated in Exhibit 1-12.

Exhibit 1-12 A Summary of the Transformation Process

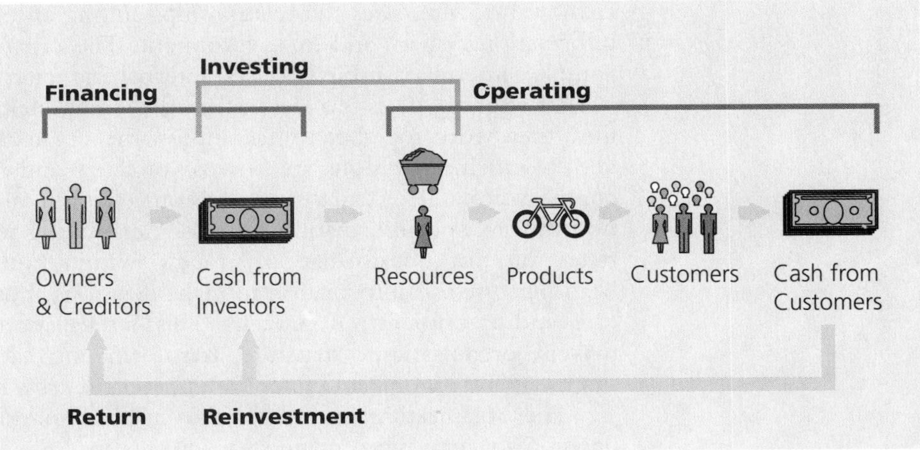

DEFINITION OF ACCOUNTING

Objective 14
Define accounting.

What role does accounting play in an organization's transformation process? *Accounting* **is an information system for the measurement and reporting of the transformation of resources into goods and services and the sale or transfer of these goods and services to consumers.** Accounting uses the prices and costs of resources to measure value created by the transformation process and to trace the flow of resources through the transformation process. By tracing the flow of resources, managers and other decision makers can determine how efficiently and effectively resources are being used.

This chapter began by illustrating the accounting process as one of identifying, measuring, recording, summarizing, and reporting transactions. The accounting system in organizations also contains these steps. Transactions occur any time an organization acquires financial or other resources, uses the resources, or sells goods and services. The effects of these transactions are measured by their prices (or costs) and are recorded in individual accounts for each type of resource or activity. The account balances are summarized periodically and are reported to owners, creditors, managers, and others who make decisions about an organization. Accounting for organizations is much more complex than keeping a checking account because the number of events and accounts is much larger. Also, decisions about when to record events in a checking account are fairly simple. You should record a check when you write it. Decisions about when to record events in an organization's accounts are not so simple, as we will see in a later chapter.

Businesses account for financing, investing, and operating activities that are components of their transformation processes. They record:

1. capital invested by owners,
2. loans from creditors,
3. investments in land, buildings, equipment, and other resources,
4. the use of resources to develop, produce, and sell goods and services, and
5. financial resources from the sale of goods and services.

Accounting exists to serve the needs of those who make decisions about organizations. To understand accounting, you should first understand the purposes and functions of organizations. Also, you should understand the sociopolitical and economic environment in which organizations exist. This environment shapes organizations and affects the information needs of decision makers. Exhibit 1-13 illustrates the relationships among an organization, its accounting information system, and its environment. The organizational environment is a complex interrelationship between internal and external decision makers.

Structuring decisions determine the components of an organization and how they work together to accomplish the organization's goals. For example, key structuring decisions are how to organize and motivate employees to accomplish activities. Structuring decisions establish an organization's transformation process and information systems. Accounting information measures attributes of the transformation process within the organization's structure. Managers use this information to make decisions about the organization's structure and transformation process. This interrelationship of internal decision makers, organizational structure, transformation activities, and internal measurement and reporting defines the organization as a unique entity.

The organization operates within a larger external environment. External decision makers, who include participants in competitive markets and regula-

Exhibit 1-13 Accounting and the Organizational Environment

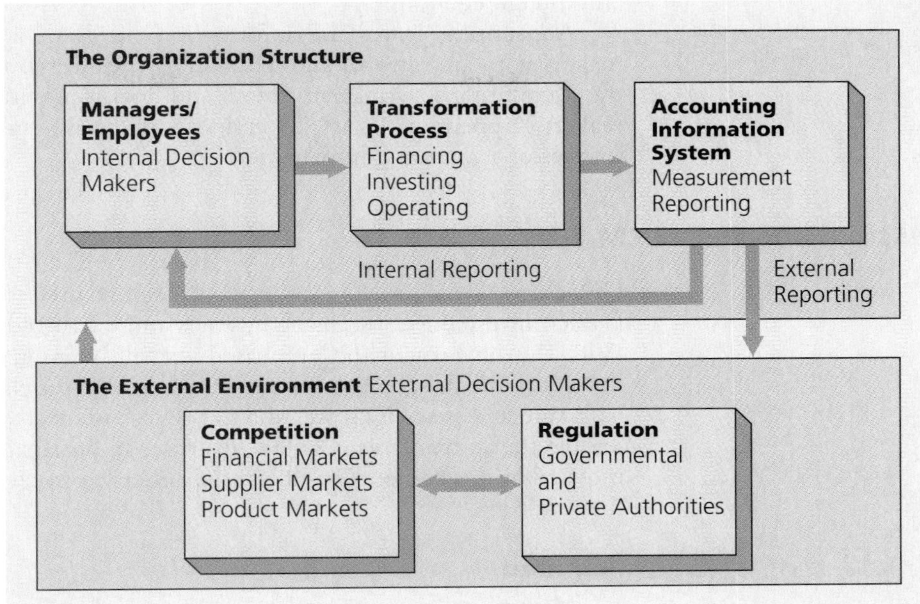

tors, also use accounting information to make decisions that affect the organization. Organizations compete for financial resources provided by investors. They compete for other resources: materials, technology, human skills, equipment, etc. Also, they compete with other organizations to sell their goods and services. Regulators supervise organizational activities to protect the interests of investors, employees, suppliers, competitors for products, and society in general. Governmental agencies, such as the Federal Trade Commission, regulate business practices. Private organizations establish accounting and reporting requirements that are enforced by government agencies. Chapter 7 discusses organizations that regulate accounting.

This book emphasizes accounting and financial reporting for corporations. Moral hazard from the separation of owners and managers has created a strong regulatory environment for corporations. This environment oversees the development of accounting and reporting requirements for corporations. This book will examine this environment and the resulting requirements in detail. While accounting is important in other forms of organizations, owners normally manage these organizations; therefore, the formal regulation of reporting by managers to owners is unnecessary. Accounting information reported by managers to owners and other external decision makers is the subject of financial accounting. This information also is used by managers. Though managers have access to information that extends beyond that reported to external decision makers, internal and external decisions are related. Therefore, this book will consider internal and external decisions that rely on financial accounting information.

The modern multinational corporation is a complex entity. Many familiar corporations, Coca Cola, IBM, and McDonald's to name a few, maintain headquarters in the U.S. They rely on U.S. markets for a major portion of their financing, but their production, marketing, and distribution facilities are spread throughout the world. These companies compete in a global market. Information is a critical resource for internal and external decision makers in both U.S. and foreign economies.

Accounting serves the information needs of a wide variety of decision makers who are internal and external to organizations. Chapter 2 will examine the accounting information system and how it provides information to decision makers. Appendix A, at the end of this book, summarizes some important sources of accounting information.

SELF-STUDY PROBLEM 1-3

G. Galileo owns Galileo Glassware, a manufacturer of small optical instruments. Galileo invested $7,500 in the business and borrowed $2,500 from a local bank. With this investment, he purchased a small building and some equipment. He develops and designs the instruments he sells, purchasing materials from local hardware and specialty stores and has two assistants to help him fabricate and assemble the instruments. Galileo advertises in professional journals. He produces most of his instruments to fill special orders from customers to whom he ships the products.

Required

1. Identify each stage of the transformation process that occurs for Galileo Glassware.
2. What prices and costs are likely to be associated with each stage of the transformation?

The solution to Self-Study Problem 1-3 appears at the end of the chapter.

REVIEW *Summary of Important Concepts*

1. The accounting process:
   A. Accounting is an information system for recording, summarizing, and reporting the financial effects of economic events to help in making decisions.
   B. The account is the basic unit of accounting information. The effect of transactions are recorded in accounts.
   C. The typical accounting process includes: (1) the occurrence of an event to be accounted for, (2) the recording of the effects of the events in accounts, (3) the calculation of account balances, and (4) the summary of the recorded events of a period and the reporting of those summaries.
2. Organizations:
   A. Organizations exist to benefit society by transforming resources from one form to another form that is more valuable in meeting the needs of people.
   B. Because most resources are in scarce supply, society attempts to use its resources to create the greatest benefit for its members.
   C. Markets provide a way for people to express their perceptions of the value of goods and services by the products they purchase and the prices they pay. The increase in value created by a transformation process can be measured by the total price of the goods and services sold less the total cost of resources consumed to produce them.

   D. Owners invest in a business to receive a return on their investments from business profits. Businesses that operate effectively and efficiently normally will earn greater profits.
   E. Businesses that are not profitable will have difficulty attracting investors and will be forced to change their behavior or to go out of business. Therefore, markets make financial and other scarce resources available to organizations that can best transform them to maximize their value for society.
   F. Some goods and services are not sold in competitive markets. Governmental and nonprofit organizations provide these goods and services. Accounting procedures differ among various types of organizations, but the fundamental purposes of accounting for these types of organizations are similar.
3. Organizational decisions:
   A. Managers, owners, and creditors require information for assessing the effectiveness and efficiency of an organization, to ensure the protection of their interests, and to evaluate investment risk and return on investment.
   B. The transformation process involves the conversion of financial and other resources into goods and services. This process can be divided into financing, investing, and operating activities.
   C. Financing decisions are decisions an organization makes about how it will obtain financial resources. Businesses obtain capital from owners (proprietors, partners, or stockholders) and from creditors.
   D. Investing decisions involve choices managers make about resources an organization uses to produce goods and services for its customers.
   E. Operating decisions involve choices managers make about how resources will be transformed into goods and services. Decisions are made about the development and design of products, the purchase of materials, the selection and training of employees, the production process, and the distribution, marketing and selling, and servicing of products.
4. Accounting's role in decision making:
   A. Accounting is an information system for measuring and reporting the transformation of resources into goods and services. Accounting information is used by internal and external decision makers who have a stake in an organization's activities.

DEFINE *Terms and Concepts Defined in this Chapter*

account
accounting
corporation
creditor
effective business
efficient business
financing activities
governmental and nonprofit organizations
income statement
investing activities
manufacturing companies
market
merchandising companies
moral hazard
mutual agency
net earnings
net income
net loss
nonbusiness organizations
operating activities
organization
partnerships
profit
proprietorships
retail companies
return on investment
service companies
stock
stockholders
system
transaction
transformation process

SOLUTIONS

SELF-STUDY PROBLEM 1-1

1. Check Register

Date	Check Number	Check Issued to/ Deposit Received from	Amount of Deposit	Amount of Check	Balance
April 1		Balance			450
1	346	Northside Apartments		300	150
5		Payroll check	400		550
7		Cash withdrawn		70	480
12	347	Miller's Grocery		125	355
14		Payroll check	400		755
17		Cash withdrawn		50	705
20	348	Citizen's Loan Co.		200	505
21		Payroll check	400		905
25	349	City Light and Water		60	845
27	350	Wang's Grocery		140	705
28	351	Street Clothiers		80	625
28		Payroll check	400		1,025
30	352	First Savings and Loan		500	525

2.

Horatio Garcia
Summary of Cash Deposits and Payments
For April 1995

Beginning cash balance			$450
Deposits:			
Payroll		$1,600	
Cash payments:			
Rent	$300		
Food	265		
Car payment	200		
Clothes	80		
Utilities	60		
Miscellaneous	120		
Transfer to savings	500		
Total cash paid		1,525	
Increase in cash for April			75
Ending cash balance			$525

3. The steps in the accounting process include: (1) Horatio receives money or checks and deposits them in his account. He writes checks to exchange money for goods and services. (2) Each transaction is recorded in Horatio's check register. (3) His cash balance is calculated by adding or subtracting the effect of each transaction. (4) The transactions are summarized and a report is prepared to tell Horatio how he spent his money during April and how much money he has at the end of the month.

SELF-STUDY PROBLEM 1-2

1.

Bach's Music Store
Income Statement
For December 1995

Revenue from goods and services sold:		
Musical instruments	$8,000	
Sheet music	1,400	
Repair of instruments	2,200	
Total revenue		$11,600
Expenses from resources consumed:		
Cost of instruments sold	$4,300	
Cost of sheet music sold	870	
Rent	650	
Supplies used	250	
Advertising	300	
Utilities	200	
Miscellaneous	180	
Total expenses		6,750
Net income		$ 4,850

2. The value created by a transformation of resources is the difference between the total price of the goods and services sold and the total cost of the resources consumed in producing these goods and services. This difference is net income, or profit, for the seller.

SELF-STUDY PROBLEM 1-3

1. The stages of the transformation process are:
   a. Galileo financed his business by investing his own money and by borrowing from a bank.
   b. Financial resources were invested in a building and equipment and used to acquire other resources for the business to operate.
   c. Galileo operates the business. Operations involve:
      (1) Development of instruments.
      (2) Design of the instruments.
      (3) Purchase of materials and supplies for manufacturing the instruments.
      (4) Hiring employees to help with production.
      (5) Manufacture of instruments.
      (6) Marketing and sale of instruments.
      (7) Distribution of instruments to customers.

2. The prices and costs associated with the transformation include:
   a. A cost is incurred in borrowing money for use in the business.
   b. A cost is incurred in the purchase of buildings and equipment.
   c. Operating costs include: materials and wear on building and equipment used in development, engineering, and production activities; wages of assistants; advertising; and distribution of products.
   d. The price of the instruments sold provides income for Galileo.

EXERCISES

1-1. In your own words write a short, yet complete, definition for each of the terms listed in the *Terms and Concepts Defined in this Chapter* section.

1-2. At the beginning of February, A. Schwartzen had $400 in his checking account. The following events occurred during February:
a. wrote a check for payment on auto loan, $180.
b. deposited payroll check from employer, $650.
c. wrote a check for groceries, $100.
d. wrote a check for rent, $375.
e. wrote a check for clothing, $60.

Complete the following table for each event and then prepare a short report describing the changes in Schwartzen's cash account for February.

Transaction	Amount of Check	Amount of Deposit	Balance
Balance on February 1			400

1-3. Assume that you have a friend, Alice Wonderland, who has no knowledge of accounting. She asks you to explain the purpose of accounting and to provide a brief description that will help her understand the accounting process. Draft a short, yet complete, memo to Alice that will help her understand the purpose of accounting and the accounting process. Use the format provided below.
DATE: (today's date)
TO: Alice Wonderland
FROM: (your name)
SUBJECT: Inquiry about accounting
(your response)

1-4. Identify primary attributes of each of the following types of organizations and list an example of each:
a. Merchandising
b. Manufacturing
c. Service
d. Government
e. Nonprofit

1-5. The processes involved in making a particular pair of cotton slacks include:
a. Cotton is planted, grown, harvested, and shipped to a textile manufacturer. The cost of the cotton associated with the slacks is $2.00. This amount of cotton is sold to the manufacturer for $2.25.

b. Raw cotton is processed into cotton fabric. The cost of producing the fabric for the slacks, including the cost of the raw cotton, is $6.00. This fabric is sold to a garment manufacturer for $8.00.
c. Cotton fabric is cut and sewn to produce a pair of slacks. The cost of making the slacks, including the cost of the fabric, is $12. The slacks are sold to a retailer for $15.
d. The cost of making the slacks available for sale, including the cost of the slacks, is $17 for the retailer. The retailer sells the slacks for $28.

How much profit is earned at each step in the production and selling process? How much total profit is earned by those involved in making and selling the slacks? Why are customers willing to pay the costs and profits earned by those involved in this process?

1-6. A. Doubleday makes baseball gloves by hand. He buys leather for $50 a yard; padding costs $4 a pound; thread and other materials cost $6 for a month's supply. He pays $200 a month rent for a small shop, where utility costs average $100 a month. Shipping costs are about $3 per glove. In an average month, Doubleday produces and sells 6 gloves. Each glove requires a half yard of leather and a half pound of padding. What is the average cost of a glove made by Doubleday? How much profit does Doubleday earn on each glove if he sells them for $300 each? How much profit does Doubleday earn each month, on average?

1-7. Franco's is a restaurant specializing in Italian food. During October, Franco's recorded the following revenues and expenses:

Sales to customers	$7,800
Cost of food products	2,300
Cost of building and equipment	1,750
Cost of employee labor	1,500
Maintenance and utilities	800

Prepare an income statement for Franco's Restaurant for October.

1-8. The Stop 'n Chew is a fast food restaurant. During January, Stop 'n Chew recorded the following revenues and expenses:

Sales to customers	$4,400
Cost of food products	2,100
Cost of building and equipment	1,250
Cost of employee labor	1,000
Maintenance and utilities	600

Prepare an income statement for Stop 'n Chew for January.

1-9. Pat Hurst is a high school student who delivers papers to earn spending money. During May, she received $300 from customers in payment of subscriptions for the month. She paid $200 for the papers she delivered. In addition, she paid $30 to her parents for use of their car to deliver the papers, and she paid $20 for gas. Prepare a statement to compute the amount of net income Pat earned from her paper route in May.

1-10. On January 1, 1995, S. Clemens invested $2,000 in a savings account. At the end of January, the account balance had increased to $2,010.00. The balance at the end of February was $2,020.05. The balance at the end of March was $2,030.15. The increases occurred because of interest earned on the account. What was Clemens's return on investment in January, February, and March? What was the total return for the three months?

1-11. M. Twain invested $10,000 in Sawyer Rafting Co. in 1996. At the end of the year, Twain's investment was worth $11,500 because of earnings during the year. Sawyer paid Twain $2,000 at the end of the year. What was Twain's return *on* investment for 1996? What was his return *of* investment for the year? Did Sawyer Rafting Co. maintain its capital as a result of these events? Explain.

1-12. Armond and Hammer are two companies that are identical with respect to the products they sell. They are owned by different individuals and are located in different parts of the same city. During September, Armond sold $12,000 of goods, while Hammer sold $9,000. Armond produced $4,000 of profit, and Hammer produced $2,000. What general reasons can you give for the different results for the two companies?

1-13. Spitz and Hives are two companies that compete in the same market with the same product, a brand of steak sauce. The companies are the same size and sell to the same grocery retailers. Both products are sold by the retailers at the same price. During 1997, Spitz sold 800,000 bottles of its sauce at a profit of 20¢ per bottle. Hives sold 650,000 bottles at a profit of 30¢ a bottle. Which company was more effective? Which was more efficient? Which company was more profitable?

1-14. You have a choice of investing in either of two companies, Lewis or Clark. Both companies make the same products and compete in the same markets. Over the last five years, the operating results for the two companies have been:

	Lewis	**Clark**
Sales revenue	$6,000,000	$7,500,000
Net income	$550,000	$900,000

Which company is more efficient? Which is more effective? In which company would you invest? State the reasons for your answers.

1-15. A. Ladin Lamps produces and sells specialty lamps to retail stores. During the latest year, the company sold 30,000 lamps at an average price of $80 per lamp. The production and distribution costs per lamp were $30, on average; other expenses for management salaries and facilities were $1,200,000 for the year. Total investment in the company is $3,000,000. How much profit did A. Ladin Lamps earn for the year? Describe the steps you went through to get your answer. Suggest some changes A. Ladin could make to improve its profitability.

1-16. Refer to Exercise 1-15. If A. Ladin increased its average price by $1 per lamp, how much would its profit increase? If it increased its sales volume by 2,000 lamps, how much would its profit increase? If it reduced its average production and distribution cost by $1 per lamp, how much would its profit increase?

1-17. Willard Filmore does not understand why some goods and services are provided by businesses and others are provided by governments. Write a short, yet complete, memo to Filmore explaining the reasons. Use the following format for your memo:

DATE: (today's date)
TO: Willard Filmore
FROM: (your name)
SUBJECT:
(your response)

1-18. Identify each of the following as to whether it is describing corporations, proprietorships, and/or partnerships:

a. Distinct legal entity separate from its owners.
b. More than one owner.
c. Ownership by stockholders.
d. Controlled by a board of directors.
e. Company changes legal identity when it is sold.
f. Limited liability.
g. Mutual agency.
h. Access to large amounts of capital.
i. Direct taxation of profits.
j. Moral hazard usually is not a major problem.

1-19. Ann Moore is considering opening a small retail store to sell knives and other kitchen utensils. She has a small amount of money to invest and wants to maintain as much control over the business as she can. She has asked you to help her decide how to finance her business. Describe the primary issues you would suggest Ann consider.

1-20. Amen Hotep has started a small business making sundials. He has asked you to help him design a system to record cash received and paid by his business. Cash receipts are deposited daily in a bank account and payments are made by checks written against the account. Develop an information system you would recommend to Amen. Demonstrate how the system functions using the following transactions:

April 1	Cash balance	$1,200
3	Cash received from customers	250
4	Cash paid for rent	400
5	Cash paid for supplies	750
7	Cash received from customers	800
8	Cash paid for taxes	240

1-21. B. Ruth owns a small business selling baseball cards. She maintains a checking account with a local bank and keeps a record of her deposits and checks in a check register. Each month Ms. Ruth receives a bank statement describing the transactions in her account. B. looks at the statements and then throws them away each month. She thinks it is a waste of the bank's money to prepare and mail the statements each month since she already has a record of her checking account transactions in her register. She asks you why the bank goes to the trouble of sending her the statements. How would you respond?

1-22. Adolph's Pork is a major corporation in the pigskin industry. The company has decided it needs an additional $1,000,000 in financing to build a new pickling plant. What are the major sources of financing available to Adolph's? What issues should company management consider in deciding on the type of financing to use?

1-23. Harvey Ferrari has obtained $5,000 from savings and a bank loan to start an automobile garage. Identify the types of resources Harvey will need for his business. How might Harvey choose to pay for these resources?

1-24. Prepare a table to describe the major operating activities you would expect in each of the following organizations: (a) Chrysler Corporation, (b) Wal-Mart, (c) Humana Hospital, a for-profit, community hospital. The table should be organized so it is easy to understand.

1-25. Sandy Dune overheard some friends from your accounting class discussing the "transformation process." She is curious about what this term means and how it applies to organizations and accounting. Explain to Sandy your understanding of the transformation process and why it is an important concept in accounting.

PROBLEMS

PROBLEM 1-1 Summary Information About a Checking Account

Oscar Wright had the following checking account activity during February: Oscar made deposits of $2,000 from salary and $600 from royalties on inventions. He wrote checks of $500 for house payment, $300 for food, $125 for clothing, $100 for entertainment, $90 for utilities, $75 for flying lessons, $200 for insurance, $250 for car payment, and transferred $500 to savings. The beginning balance in his checking account was $580.

Required Prepare a report in good form, following the example of Exhibit 1-2, to describe Oscar's financial activities for February. What is the source of the information described in this report? Why might this information be useful for Oscar? Describe some decisions Oscar might make using this information.

PROBLEM 1-2 Information from a Bank Statement

At the end of February, Oscar Wright received the statement on the next page from his bank.

Oscar Wright
Bank Statement
for February

Beginning balance			$ 700
Deposits received:			
Feb. 17	$2,000		
24	600		
Total deposits		$2,600	
Checks paid:			
Feb. 2	$ 120		
5	500		
8	300		
9	125		
13	100		
16	90		
19	75		
22	200		
25	250		
Total checks		1,760	
Excess of deposits over checks			840
Ending balance			$1,540

Required What information is contained in the bank statement that is not available to Oscar from his summary in Problem 1? Why are some of the numbers in the bank statement different from those in his summary in Problem 1? Why is this information useful to Oscar?

PROBLEM 1-3 A Basic Accounting System

The Go-for-Broke Company is a financial institution that lends money to individuals to purchase personal items such as furniture, appliances, and vacations. Once a loan application is processed, a check is written to approved applicants. The loan recipient then makes a payment to the company each month to repay the loan and to pay interest.

Required Describe an accounting system that Go-for-Broke might use in its financial activities with its customers. Include in your description a discussion of the accounts, events, and reports that would be part of the process. What would be the primary purpose served by accounting reports prepared by the company? Illustrate your accounting system with example transactions for a customer. Prepare example reports for the customer.

PROBLEM 1-4 Developing a Cash Plan

Mary Antoinette is planning to start a new business as a hair stylist. She has saved $2,000 to invest in the business, expecting to receive $800 each month, on average, from sales to customers. She expects that she will need cash to pay the following items each month, on average: rent, $200; supplies, $100; utilities, $75; other, $50. She will need to purchase $3,000 of equipment to start the business; in addition, she thinks she will need $500 to cover initial operating costs. A local bank has agreed to consider a loan to help Mary start her business and has asked her to develop a plan that describes her expected cash receipts and payments for the first year. The plan should show how much cash she will need for the business, how much she will need to borrow, and how she expects to pay back the loan. Monthly payments will be required to pay off the loan and interest. The bank will charge $10 per year in interest for each $100 borrowed until the loan is repaid at the end of the year. Mary has asked you to prepare a plan for her to submit to the bank.

Required Prepare a plan for Mary. Describe any assumptions you make.

PROBLEM 1-5 Determining Net Income and Return on Investment

Harry Ford owns a small car dealership. He rents the property he uses, buys cars from a manufacturer, and resells them to customers. During July, Harry sold 8 cars that cost him a total of $64,000. The total amount he received from the sale of these cars was $80,000. Other costs incurred for the month included rent, $1,500; utilities, $600; insurance, $350; maintenance of property and cars, $200; advertising, $180; and property taxes and business license, $120.

Required Provide an income statement that describes the amount of net value created by Harry during July. How much profit did he earn for July? What can he do with the profit he earned? Assuming Harry invested $500,000 in the dealership, what was the return on his investment for July expressed as a percentage of his investment?

PROBLEM 1-6 Determining Prices and Return on Investment

The Thomasville Electric Company produces electricity. It is investor owned, the only electric utility in the geographical area that it serves, and is regulated by a public service commission. The commission has determined that the rate the company should charge its customers should be sufficient for investors to earn a 10% return on investment. At the end of 1995, the total investment in the company was $1,000,000. The commission considers rate requests from the company each January based on prior year costs and anticipated levels of production. Thomasville's cost for 1995 per kilowatt hour (kwh) of electricity produced was $.09. The company anticipates producing 20,000,000 kwhs of electricity during 1996.

Required (a) What rate per kwh should the commission permit the company to charge to earn a 10% return on investment? (b) Thomasville maintains that it needs to increase the amount of investment by $250,000 to increase its production capacity for the future. If the commission permits the company to earn a 10% return on an investment of $1,250,000, what would the effect be on the rate charged per kwh?

PROBLEM 1-7 Making Financing Decisions and Maintaining a Check Register

Part A. Patty Ross wants to start a business making flags. She has calculated she will need $50,000 to start the business. The money will be used to rent a building, purchase equipment, hire workers, and begin production and sales. Patty has $10,000 in savings she can invest in the business.

Required What alternatives does Patty have for obtaining the additional $40,000 she needs for her business? What information will be important in determining the amount and kind of financing that will be available to her? What decisions will she have to make in deciding on which sources of financing to use?

Part B. Patty Ross started the Ross Flag Company on September 1 with an investment of $10,000 from savings and $40,000 borrowed from Independence Bank. The money was deposited in a checking account in the name of the company. During September, Patty wrote checks for the following purchases for the company:

Date	Check	Amount	Payee
9/3	101	$ 500	Gina Washington (for rent)
9/5	102	12,000	SingSong Sewing Machine Co.
9/12	103	23,000	Fulton Fabric Co.
9/18	104	400	City (for business license)
9/22	105	200	City (deposit on utilities)
9/25	106	3,600	Franklin Construction Co.
9/30	107	2,000	Tyler Jefferson (for wages)
9/30	108	500	Independence Bank (for interest)

Required Complete the check register for Ross Flag Company for September, using the following format. Remember to record the deposits.

Check Register, ROSS FLAG CO.

Date	Check Number	Check Issued to/ Deposit Received From	Amount of Deposit	Amount of Check	Balance

PROBLEM 1-8 Accounting for Cash

Ross Flag Co. received cash for goods sold of $13,000 during October. The beginning cash balance for October was $7,900. The company made cash payments during the month, as follows:

Employee salaries	$2,000
Fabric	3,000
Utilities	1,200
Shipping	800
Interest	500

Required Prepare a schedule that calculates the company's net change in cash for the month of October. Explain why this information might be useful to managers and creditors.

PROBLEM 1-9 Identifying Financing, Investing, and Operating Activities and Reporting Cash

The following events occurred as part of the activities of the Town of Teapot Dome during June:

Borrowed $50,000 from local bank
Received $81,800 in property taxes from taxpayers
Received $32,400 in sales taxes from businesses
Received $12,000 for fees and licenses
Paid $43,000 to employees for salaries
Paid $21,000 for new equipment
Paid $8,200 for maintenance and repair
Paid $4,600 for utilities
Paid $2,500 for supplies
Paid $4,200 for interest

Required (a) Identify the financing, investing, and operating decisions associated with these events. (b) Prepare a schedule reporting Teapot Dome's cash received and paid in June. Assume that the town's cash balance at the beginning of the month was $12,700.

PROBLEM 1-10 Activities in the Transformation Process

Businesses can be divided into three general categories based on the types of products they provide: merchandising, manufacturing, and service.

Required For each category of business, describe how the transformation process makes use of the following activities: (a) financing, (b) investing, (c) research and development, (d) design and engineering, (e) purchasing, (f) personnel, (g) production, (h) distribution, (i) marketing and selling, (j) servicing. If any category of activity is not used, explain why not.

PROBLEM 1-11 Cash Flow in the Transformation Process

Required Prepare a chart containing the major components of the transformation process. Use arrows to show the flow of cash through the process and the exchange of cash with external parties at each stage of the process. Make the chart complete yet simple and easy to understand.

PROBLEM 1-12 Ethics and Moral Hazard

As manager of a retail electronics store, you purchased 100 Whizbang portable radios from a wholesaler in a going out of business sale. These units cost $40 each, about half of the normal cost of other brands you sell for $130. You expected to sell these units at the regular price and earn an above normal profit. After your purchase, you discovered the units were poorly constructed and would probably last about a third as long as other major brands.

Customers often ask you for a recommendation when considering the purchase of a radio. If you tell them the truth about the Whizbang model, you may have difficulty selling these units, even if you offer a steep discount.

Required What should you tell a customer who asks about these radios? What are the short-run and long-run implications for your company's profits if (a) you conceal the quality of the units and sell them at their regular price or (b) reveal the quality problem? If you were to choose alternative b, what options might you consider in an effort to minimize the effect of these units on your profits?

PROBLEM 1-13 Ethics and Moral Hazard

You manage an auto service store. One of your major services is brake replacement. You purchase replacement parts at an average cost of $20 per set. Each set contains parts for four wheels and will repair one car. You charge an average of $60 per car for replacing worn brakes, including an average labor cost of $8. Your current volume for brake replacements is about 1,000 jobs per month. A new vendor has contacted you with an offer to sell you replacement parts at an average cost of $15 per set. After checking on the quality of these parts, you find that their average life is about 60% of that of the parts you are currently using.

Required What are the short-run profit implications of using the $15 brakes instead of the $20 brakes? What are the long-run profit implications? What ethical issues should be considered in choosing which brakes to use?

PROBLEM 1-14 Multiple Choice Overview of the Chapter

1. The basic purpose of accounting is to:
   a. minimize the amount of taxes a company has to pay.
   b. permit an organization to keep track of its financial activities.

c. report the largest amount of net income to stockholders.
d. reduce the amount of risk experienced by investors.

2. The four primary steps in the accounting process are listed in random order. In what chronological order do these steps really occur?
   A. A summary is prepared of the events of the period.
   B. A transaction occurs.
   C. An account balance is increased or decreased.
   D. The effect of an event is recorded.
   a. C, B, D, A
   b. A, B, C, D
   c. D, C, B, A
   d. B, D, C, A
3. A primary purpose of all organizations in our society is to:
   a. make a profit.
   b. minimize the payment of taxes.
   c. provide employment for the largest number of workers possible.
   d. transform resources from one form to another.
4. Mustafa Company is a manufacturer of pharmaceuticals. Which of the following events ordinarily would be expected to create value for the company?

	The firm sells shares of its own stock	**Raw materials are converted to finished products and sold**
a.	Yes	Yes
b.	Yes	No
c.	No	Yes
d.	No	No

5. Which pair of terms describes the same thing?
   a. net income, profit
   b. financing activities, operating activities
   c. partnership, proprietorship
   d. political market, economic market
6. Tammy Faye invested $4,000 in a partnership. One year later, the partnership was sold and cash from the sale was distributed to the partners. On that date, Tammy received a check for her share of the company in the amount of $4,500. What was Tammy's return on investment?
   a. $-0-
   b. $500
   c. $4,000
   d. $4,500
7. P. Sternberg Enterprises developed a new type of roller skate that is very popular because of its high quality and reasonable price. Sternberg is losing money on the product, however, because several key production personnel recently resigned and replacements are not as skilled. Which of the following terms properly describes the firm?

	Effective	**Efficient**
a.	Yes	Yes
b.	Yes	No
c.	No	Yes
d.	No	No

8. Which of the following is an investing activity?
   a. A manufacturer borrows from creditors.
   b. A service firm pays a return to its stockholders.
   c. A retailer sells goods to a nonprofit agency at cost.
   d. A government agency purchases a new mainframe computer system.
9. The primary difference between business and nonbusiness organizations is:
   a. the kinds of goods and services they provide.
   b. their relative sizes.

c. whether efficiency and effectiveness can be controlled.
d. whether they attempt to earn profits.

10. The term "transformation process" refers to:
    a. a repetitive cycle of financing, investing, and operating activities.
    b. the conversion of materials into goods for sale.
    c. procedures designed to reduce a company's risk.
    d. training methods by which unskilled workers become efficient and effective.

CASES

CASE 1-1 Understanding the Transformation Process

The A. Lincoln Company is a designer and builder of log homes. Financing is provided by owners and creditors, primarily banks. The company owns buildings and equipment it uses in the management, design, transportation, and construction process, but purchases logs and other building materials from other companies. These materials are shipped by the sellers. Homes are specially designed for customers, so logs are cut to the dimensions called for in a design and shipped to the customer's building site with other materials for assembly. Lincoln employs design engineers, construction and assembly workers, maintenance personnel, and marketing and service personnel, in addition to its management and office staff. The company is in charge of the construction process until the home is completed and ready for occupancy. Lincoln Company warranties the completed home for one year after completion to be free of defects from materials or construction.

Required Discuss the stages of the transformation process for A. Lincoln Company and provide a chart describing the flow of resources through the transformation process. Note the events in the transformation process that will result in money flowing into or out of the company in exchange for other resources.

CASE 1-2 Financing, Investing, and Operating Activities as Part of the Transformation Process

Refer to the information provided in Case 1.

Required List decisions Lincoln's managers would make at each stage of the transformation process involving the acquisition, use, or disposal of resources.

PROJECTS

PROJECT 1-1 Accounting for Cash

Maintain a record of all of your cash receipts and payments for one week. Prepare a report showing your sources and uses of cash for the week. Group uses into categories such as educational supplies, food, and recreation. Determine the net change in your cash balance for the week.

PROJECT 1-2 Organizations and Their Purposes

Different types of organizations exist in our society, including: service organizations, retail organizations, manufacturing organizations, and government and nonprofit organizations. Identify the names of three organizations that fit into each type. Prepare a table listing (a) the type of organization, (b) the name of the organization, (c) the primary purpose for which the organization exists, (d) major resources the organization consumes in carrying out its purpose, and (e) the goods and services the organization produces in carrying out its purpose.

PROJECT 1-3 Organizations and Their Purposes

Visit your library and locate where corporate annual reports are kept. Most university libraries receive annual reports either in their published form or on microfiche or in computer readable format. Select a corporation whose name begins with the same first letter as your first name. Consult the most recent annual report you can find for this company. Read through the annual report and identify the following information: (a) the year covered by the annual report, (b) the major products or services sold by the organization, (c) the primary resources consumed by this organization in producing goods and services, and (d) the amount of net income earned by this company during the year covered by the report as described on its income statement. (Be sure to determine if that number is expressed in thousands, millions, or billions of dollars).

PROJECT 1-4 Financing, Investing, and Operating Activities

Assume you are trying to explain to a friend what is meant by the following terms: financing activities, investing activities, and operating activities. Write a short explanation of each term so it can be understood by someone who has not studied accounting. Provide examples of each type of activity to illustrate the decisions managers make about the activities in an organization with which your friend is likely to be familiar. Show your description to a friend who has not had accounting and ask her/him to write a brief note indicating any problems with understanding your description.

PROJECT 1-5 Financing, Investing, and Operating Activities

Review Appendix A of this book, then:

a. In the current periodical room of your college or university library locate the following newspapers and magazines: *The Wall Street Journal*, *Barrons*, *Business Week*, *Forbes*, and *Fortune*.
b. Find an example of a financing, investing, or operating decision discussed in an article in a recent issue of one of these periodicals.
c. Write a brief summary of your reading that includes the name of the periodical, the date of the issue, the name of the article, its page number, and the type of decision discussed.
d. Briefly describe the decision you identified in the article.

PROJECT 1-6 Identifying Revenues and Profits

Several publications available in most college libraries list financial information about major corporations. Review Appendix A of this book. Then, examine one of the listed publications, such as *Fortune*, *Value Line*, or *Moody's Industrial Manual*. Select 10 U. S. corporations and prepare a table listing each corporation, its revenues (net sales) and net income for the most recent year available. Compute the ratio of net income to revenues. Rank the firms from most to least efficient using this ratio.

CHAPTER 2

INFORMATION IN ORGANIZATIONS

CHAPTER *Overview*

Chapter 1 described an organization as a transformation process. This process converts resources into goods and services that are sold to customers or distributed to recipients. Chapter 1 examined decisions owners, creditors, and managers make about organizations. Chapter 2 considers the information used by decision makers in greater detail. The need for information occurs from the interaction among those who provide resources and services to an organization. Also, this chapter describes major components of information systems. Several information systems may exist in an organization, each serving a different purpose. Accounting is a particular type of system that provides information about economic consequences of the transformation process. This chapter considers features of the accounting system. After reading this chapter you should understand accounting is an information system for measuring, summarizing, and reporting the economic consequences of an organization's transformation process. This information is used by decision makers to form and evaluate contracts that identify the rights and responsibilities of the decision makers.

Major topics covered in this chapter include:

- Information needs of external and internal decision makers.
- Primary functions of information systems.
- Components of an accounting information system.
- Processing information in an accounting system.

CHAPTER *Objectives*

Once you have completed this chapter, you should be able to:

1. Explain why contracts affect the need for information about organizations.
2. Explain why risk and return are important for investors.
3. Explain how debt and equity financing affect risk and return.
4. Discuss the effect of compensation on managers' decisions.
5. Identify uses of accounting information by managers, employees, suppliers, customers, and government agencies.
6. Identify the purpose of Generally Accepted Accounting Principles and audits.
7. Define financial accounting.
8. Define managerial accounting.
9. Identify the primary activities in an information system.
10. Explain the purpose of a management information system.
11. Explain the purpose of an accounting information system.
12. Identify activities in an accounting information system.
13. List the types of accounts included in an accounting information system.
14. Define assets, liabilities, and owners' equity.
15. Define revenues and expenses.
16. Explain the relationships among contracts, transactions, and accounting information.

INFORMATION FOR DECISION MAKERS

As discussed in Chapter 1, the purpose of accounting is to provide information for decision makers about an organization's transformation process. The value of accounting information is determined by how well it meets the needs of those who use it. Accounting information describes economic consequences of the transformation process. It is concerned with measuring financial resources used to acquire other resources, the conversion of resources into goods and services, and the prices of goods and services sold to customers. Information needs arise within the organizational environment as depicted in Exhibit 2-1.

Exhibit 2-1 Accounting and the Organizational Environment

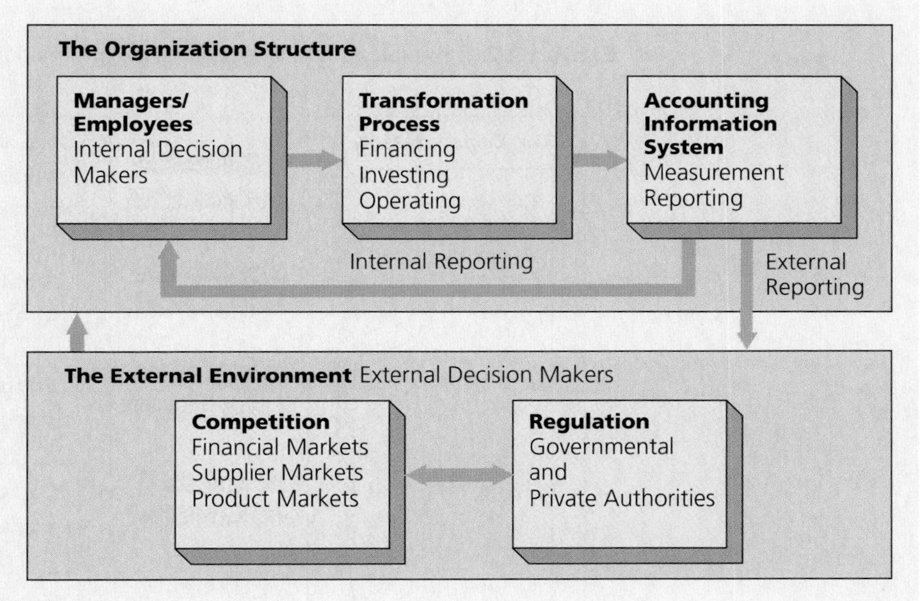

Objective 1
Explain why contracts affect the need for information about organizations.

Information needs of decision makers arise from the many relationships that occur among an organization's stakeholders: managers, investors, suppliers, employees, customers, and government authorities. Many of these decision makers are participants in the transformation. They compete in markets for resources, or they regulate these markets. They exchange resources or services with an organization as part of its transformation process.

Contracts **are legal agreements for the exchange of resources and services.** They provide legal protection for the parties to an agreement if terms of the agreement are not honored. Contract terms establish the rights and responsibilities of the contracting parties. Contracts are "give and get" relationships. Each party to the contract expects to receive something in exchange for something given. For example, a contract by an employee to provide labor to a company involves the giving of labor services by the employee in exchange for wages and benefits. Contracts with proprietorships and partnerships are between the owners/managers, and other contracting parties. In contrast, because corporations are legal entities, contracts can be formed with the corporation as one of the contracting parties. Managers make contracts on behalf of corporations and their owners.

Contracts are enforceable only to the extent contracting parties can determine whether the terms of the contract are being met. Assume you and I sign a contract that calls for you to invest $1,000 in my company, and I agree to pay you 10% of the amount my company earns each year. Unless you have reliable information about my company's earnings, you cannot determine whether I am paying you the agreed amount. Therefore, you probably would not agree to the contract. Contracts require information contracting parties accept as reliable and sufficient for determining if terms of the contract have been met. **Accounting information is important for forming and evaluating contracts.**

Exhibit 2-2 identifies examples of exchanges among stakeholders for which contracts and information about organizations are important. The following sections discuss these exchanges.

Exhibit 2-2 Examples of Exchanges Requiring Information

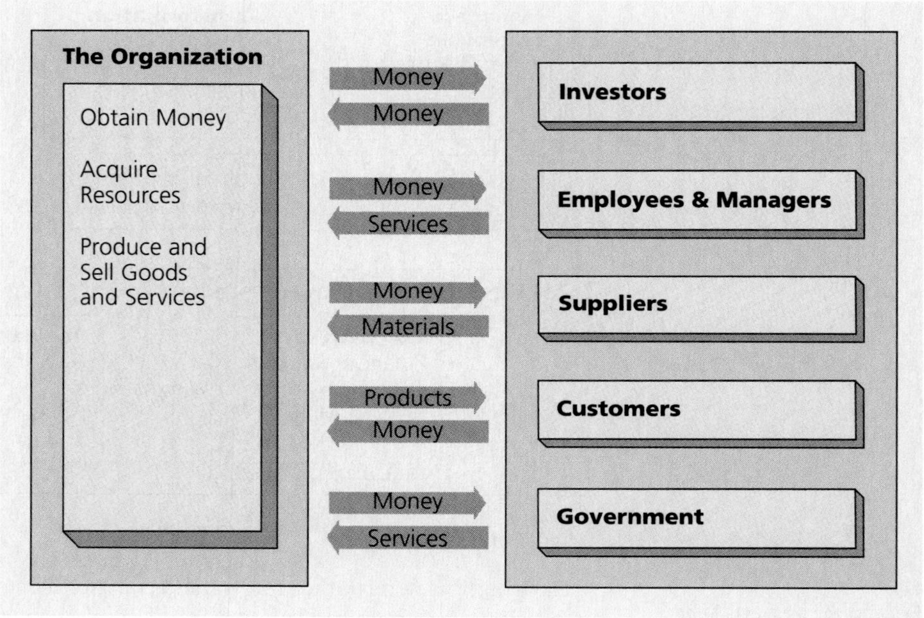

Risk and Return

Contracts are formed to identify rights and responsibilities. These rights and responsibilities establish how risk and return will be shared among contracting parties. Information about risk and return is needed to determine contract terms. Chapter 1 defined return on investment as the amount of profits earned by a business that could be distributed to owners. Risk results from uncertainty about the amount and timing of return. Exhibit 2-3 contains the returns of two investments (A and B) over several time periods. Which investment is riskier? Returns for investment A are relatively stable and predictable; they are growing at a steady rate. Returns for investment B are less predictable. Investment B is riskier than A, though it may produce higher returns over time than A.

Management decisions about financing, investing, and operating activities affect risk and return for an organization's stakeholders. An organization's exter-

Exhibit 2-3 An Illustration of Risk and Return

	Returns	
Time Period	**Investment A**	**Investment B**
1	$6	$10
2	6	12
3	7	7
4	7	3
5	8	8
6	8	11

nal environment also affects risk and return. Competition and regulation affect the cost and availability of resources used in the transformation process, as well as the demand for a company's goods and services and their prices. Competition and regulation vary across companies and time because of different market conditions, types of products and production processes, and changing political and social concerns. For example, concern about product safety can change a relatively stable market into a very uncertain market.

Objective 2
Explain why risk and return are important to investors.

Those who invest in a company expect to earn returns from their investments. At the same time, they must evaluate the risk inherent in investing in the company. What should they earn if the company does well? What might happen if the company does poorly? Risk and return are related in most situations; investors expect to earn higher returns from riskier investments. The higher returns compensate them for accepting higher risk, but actual returns may differ from expected returns. Therefore, riskier investments may actually result in higher or lower returns than less risky investments. On average, however, higher return should be associated with greater risk; otherwise, investors will not participate in risky investments. Accounting information helps investors predict risk and return associated with investments. The following sections consider the risk and return evaluations made by those who contract with an organization.

Evaluating Exchanges

Investors. Owners and creditors are *investors* in an organization. They contract with managers to provide financial resources in exchange for future returns. They need information to decide whether to invest in a company and how much to invest. **Accounting information helps investors evaluate the risk and return they can expect from their investments. Also, it helps them determine whether managers are meeting the terms of their contracts.**

Objective 3
Explain how debt and equity financing affect risk and return.

Financing decisions are a major source of risk in a company. ***Debt financing* results when a company obtains financial resources from creditors. *Equity financing* results when a company obtains financial resources from owners.** Decisions to use debt or equity financing affect a corporation's risk and return. Obtaining resources from creditors often increases the risk of a company. A company has a legal obligation to pay creditors interest on their loans and to repay the amount borrowed. ***Interest* is a return earned by a creditor. The amount borrowed is the *principal* of a loan.** Interest is an amount paid to a creditor in addition to repayment of the principal. If a company does not earn sufficient profits, it may be unable to make these payments, and creditors can force a company into bankruptcy. Bankruptcy is a legal status in which a company is largely controlled by and for its creditors. Creditors also may require a company to liquidate its resources to repay its debts.

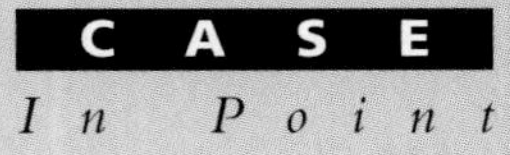

R. H. Macy & Co. declared bankruptcy in 1992. The company operated 251 stores throughout the U.S. Less than six years earlier, the company's management had purchased the company by issuing large amounts of debt. They used the proceeds of the debt to buy out the owners in a "leveraged buy-out," or LBO. The recession of the early 1990's resulted in declining profits for the company, which was unable to generate sufficient cash from its sales to pay interest and maturing principal on its debt. In late 1991 and early 1992, Macy's earnings, before interest and taxes were deducted, dropped to about half of the amount for the preceding year. After considering the effect of interest expense, the company incurred a large loss with little hope of recovery in the near future.

Adapted from The Wall Street Journal, January 28, 1992.

If a company is forced to liquidate (sell all of its noncash assets), creditors are paid amounts owed them before stockholders receive any payments. On the other hand, if a company is profitable, stockholders normally earn higher returns than creditors because stockholders have a right to share in a company's profits. Creditors receive only the amount of interest agreed to when debt is issued. Consequently, investors and managers choose between risk and return.

Assume a company has $300,000 of debt and $500,000 of stock outstanding. Creditors agreed to lend the company money at 10% interest per year. Consider the three scenarios presented below:

	Scenario 1	**Scenario 2**	**Scenario 3**
Income before interest	$100,000	$50,000	$ 0
Interest	(30,000)	(30,000)	(30,000)
Net income	$ 70,000	$20,000	$(30,000)

In scenario 1, the company earns $100,000. After paying interest (and disregarding taxes), the company earns net income of $70,000. Thus, while creditors earn a 10% return, stockholders earn a 14% return ($70,000/$500,000). In scenario 2, stockholder return is only 4% ($20,000/$500,000), and in scenario 3, it is −6% (−$30,000/$500,000). Creditor return is less risky than stockholder return, but the potential for higher (and lower) returns exists for stockholders, relative to creditors. Also, the risk to the company and its stockholders increases as its debt increases. If the company were to incur losses, as in scenario 3, for several periods, it might be unable to pay amounts owed to creditors. The more debt a company has outstanding, the more cash it must generate to make these payments. If a company is unprofitable, it may have difficulty generating the cash it needs.

Managers select the relative amounts of debt and equity financing to use. These decisions depend on a company's need for financial resources. What opportunities exist for the company to invest the additional resources? How profitable are these investments likely to be? Will they generate sufficient profits to enable the company to pay higher returns to owners? These decisions are interrelated with investor decisions. Investors determine the return required for investing in a company from evaluating its risk relative to the risk and return of alternate investments. For example, an investor willing to take higher levels of risk might prefer investment B in Exhibit 2-3. An investor wanting a relatively safe investment might prefer investment A.

Objective 4
Discuss the effect of compensation on managers' decisions.

Managers. Owners generally do not manage large corporations. Instead, they hire managers who operate the businesses for them. Managers contract with owners to provide services in exchange for salaries and other compensation. Because compensation is tied to performance, managers' investments of time and effort in a company are risky. Owners, or directors who represent them, need information to determine how well managers are performing and to reward managers when they do well. To provide incentives for managers to perform well, owners may offer managers bonuses when a company is profitable. **Accounting information provides a means for owners and managers to determine the amount of compensation managers will receive.**

CASE *In Point*

A popular form of bonus compensation is the stock option. A corporation grants a manager the option (right) to buy shares of its stock at a certain price during a particular period. If the market price of the company's stock is higher than the option price, the manager can buy shares at the option price and resell them at the market price or hold them for future price increases and dividends.

A recent survey of major U.S. corporations revealed that stock options provided more than half of the total annual compensation earned by many top corporate managers. The following illustration indicates the average salary and stock compensation for the 100 largest companies in each group. With such large amounts involved, managers have strong incentives to take actions they believe will increase the value of their companies' stocks.

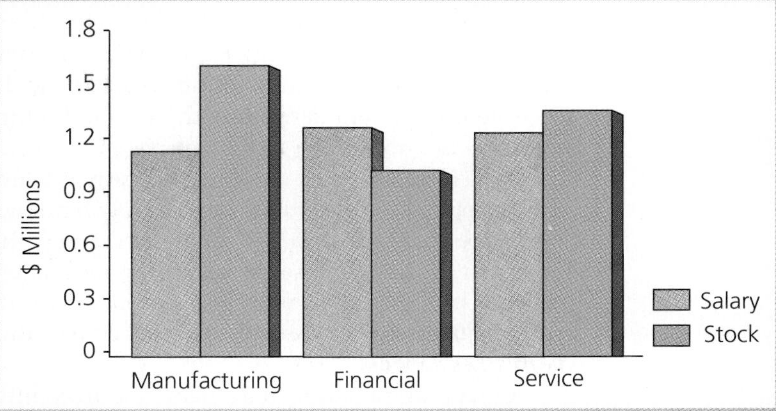

Data source: "Executive Stock Options Seen Gaining: Poll," Accounting Today, September 24, 1990.

Compensation arrangements also encourage managers to present their companies' performances in the best light. Often, compensation is linked to profits and other accounting information, giving managers incentives to report numbers that will maximize their compensation. The combination of management control over information and manager incentives to make their companies look good provides an ethical dilemma for managers. Sometimes, they must choose between the best interests of the company and their own best interests.

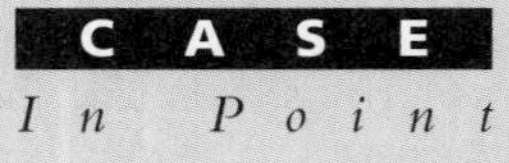

Suppose you are the manager of a company. You are paid a salary of $80,000 a year. In addition, you will receive a 50% bonus ($40,000) if the company's profits exceed $500,000 for the year. You have worked hard during the year and the company has done well. However, your calculations suggest the company's profits will be only $450,000. The company owns some stock in another company that was purchased for $100,000. The market value of the stock is now about $200,000. By selling the stock, you will generate an additional after-tax profit of $65,000. The company will pay $30,000 of additional taxes and about $5,000 in fees associated with the sale. If you sell the stock, you will probably repurchase it (or similar stock) again because it has been valuable to the company. What is the best decision for you as manager? What is the best decision for the company? What would you do?

Objective 5
Identify uses of accounting information by managers, employees, suppliers, customers, and government agencies.

Managers' investing and operating decisions have a direct effect on the risk and return of those who contract with a company. Managers decide which resources to acquire, when to acquire them, and how much to pay for them. The value of a resource to a business depends on the contribution the resource is expected to make in earning future profits. For example, Machine X may be able to produce 50 units an hour, while machine Y may be able to produce 75 units an hour; but machine X may cost less than machine Y. Machine Y may be more reliable and require less maintenance; it may produce units of higher quality; it may last longer, and therefore, it may be a better investment. The expected benefits from a resource should be compared with its expected costs. The difference between the benefits and costs affects the return expected from the resource.

Each investment in a resource involves decisions about risk and return associated with the investment. An organization is a portfolio (collection) of individual resources. In combination, the risks and returns on the investments in these resources help determine the risk and return on investment of the organization as a whole. One task of management is to select a portfolio of resources that will yield a desired amount of return at a level of risk managers and owners find acceptable. Investments in proven technology and established products generally are less risky than investments in new technology or products. Investments in resources in some countries are riskier than those in other countries because of their political and economic environments. **Accounting information is useful for identifying the types and locations of an organization's resources.**

Operating activities transform resources into goods and services. A major purpose of accounting is to measure costs associated with the flow of resources through the transformation process. Accounting also measures resources obtained from selling goods and services. The profits earned by a corporation from its operating activities are a major determinant of risk and return. **Infor-**

mation about the results of operating activities is used to estimate, compare, and manage companies' risks and returns.

Employees. Employees have a major effect on a company's risk and return. Wages and quality of work directly affect product quality, sales, costs, and profits. Companies attempt to locate new facilities in areas where they will have access to ample numbers of qualified workers. Since the cost of labor is an important consideration in these decisions, companies often locate in areas where labor is relatively inexpensive and may move from high cost to low cost areas. In recent years, many U.S. companies have moved facilities to foreign countries to take advantage of lower wages.

Companies evaluate the cost and productivity of their employees. They compare employee performance with management expectations, examine changes over time, and compare different divisions with each other. **Accounting information helps managers assess employee performance.**

Employees negotiate for wages, benefits, and job security. Compensation is affected by a company's performance and financial condition. Labor unions and other employee groups use accounting information to evaluate a company's ability to compensate its employees. Like other contracting parties, employees evaluate risk and return in an employment relationship. If a company does well, employees expect to be rewarded. If it does poorly, they may face lay-offs, wage and benefit cuts, and loss of jobs. **Accounting information helps employees assess the risk and return of their employment contracts.**

Suppliers. An organization purchases materials, merchandise, and other resources from suppliers. Many businesses limit amounts of materials they purchase to those needed for current production to reduce the costs of storing and handling these materials. They depend on suppliers to deliver materials just-in-time for use. Careful negotiation of prices, credit, and delivery schedules between management and suppliers is required. Costs and efficiencies associated with these negotiations affect a company's risk and return. If it cannot obtain quality materials when they are needed, a company may incur major losses from idle production, waste, lost sales, and dissatisfied customers. If a supplier goes out of business or cannot fulfill its commitments, a company may have difficulty obtaining needed resources. **Accounting information helps companies evaluate the abilities of their suppliers to meet their resource needs.**

Suppliers often sell resources to companies on credit. These suppliers are creditors who are financing the sale of resources to a company in anticipation of future payments. Usually, these loans are for short periods of 30-60 days, though longer financing sometimes is arranged. When a company, like Macy's, declares bankruptcy, it often owes large amounts to suppliers. Suppliers may have difficulty collecting these amounts or may be unable to collect them. Therefore, suppliers evaluate the risk they are taking in selling on credit to other companies. Terms of these sales, including prices and payment schedules, are affected by a seller's perception of risk associated with these sales. **Suppliers often use accounting information about their customers to evaluate the risk of a buyer not being able to pay for goods and services acquired.**

Customers. A company is a supplier to its customers. Thus, it evaluates customers in the same way it is evaluated by suppliers. Managers decide the terms of sales by evaluating the risk and return associated with the sales. Riskier customers normally receive less favorable terms. For example, a customer with good credit can purchase a house, car, appliances, and other goods on more favorable terms than can a customer with bad credit.

Customer decisions to buy products often are affected by their perception of quality and dependability, as well as price. These decisions also may depend on the financial reputation of the seller. Will the company be in business in the future when maintenance, repair, or replacement is needed? Will it be able to honor warranties? Are its profits sufficient to invest in new technology and maintain quality products. **Accounting information is used to assess the risks of buying from specific companies and selling to specific customers.**

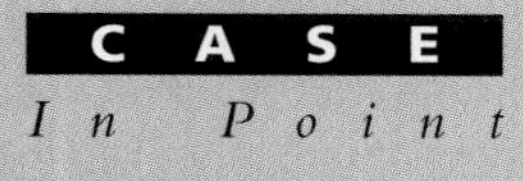

In 1991, several major airlines, including Eastern and Pan Am, abruptly ceased operations after periods of financial distress. Aircraft were grounded and most employees were discharged. Many thousands of customers held reservations and prepaid tickets and were inconvenienced by the events. Many other potential customers had been wary of the airlines because of their ongoing financial problems over the prior months. The refusal of these potential customers to purchase tickets from these airlines was one problem leading to the demise of these companies.

Government Agencies. Organizations are required to provide information to government agencies. Governments require businesses to purchase licenses for selling goods and services and to pay fees for various government services. Often these amounts are determined by the amount of sales or profitability of an organization. Governments collect information about organizations as a basis for economic forecasts and planning at the local, state, and national levels. Businesses are required to report information to state and federal authorities that regulate business activities to ensure fair trade, fair treatment of employees, and fair disclosure to investors.

Businesses report information to taxing authorities at various levels of government. Reports are required for filing sales, property, payroll, excise, and income taxes. The amount of these taxes is determined by how much a company sells, the costs it incurs, and amounts paid to employees. **Government agencies use accounting information to make taxation and regulatory decisions.**

Financial Accounting

Objective 6
Identify the purpose of Generally Accepted Accounting Principles and audits.

Because of concerns about information reliability and moral hazard, managers of major corporations prepare accounting information for investors and other external users according to specific rules called Generally Accepted Accounting Principles (GAAP). ***GAAP*** **are standards developed by professional accounting organizations to identify appropriate accounting and reporting procedures.** GAAP establish minimum disclosure requirements and increase comparability of information from one period to the next and among different companies.

Learning Note GAAP apply only to information prepared for use by external decision makers. Because managers control information available inside an organization, accounting standards such as GAAP are not necessary for this information.

Accounting information reported to investors by most corporations must be audited. **An *audit* is a detailed examination of an organization's financial reports.** It includes an examination of the information system used to prepare the reports, and involves an examination of control procedures organizations use to help ensure the accuracy of accounting information. The purpose of an audit is to evaluate whether information reported to external decision makers is a fair presentation of an organization's economic activities. Standards (GAAP) for the preparation and reporting of information help ensure the reliability of accounting information. The auditors, who are independent certified public accountants (CPAs), examine this information to confirm it is prepared according to GAAP. To be a CPA, a person must pass a qualifying exam and meet education and experience requirements. CPAs are independent of the companies they audit because they are not company employees; rather they are hired by corporate investors. Also, they should have no vested interests in the companies that might bias their audits.

Objective 7
Define financial accounting.

Accounting information prepared for use by external decision makers is financial accounting information. ***Financial accounting* is the process of preparing, reporting, and interpreting accounting information that is provided to external decision makers.** As a primary source of information for investors, this information is important for the financing activities of organizations. It also may affect the decisions of suppliers, customers, and employees.

Learning Note Managers, as internal decision makers, use financial accounting information in addition to managerial accounting information. They are also concerned about the effect of financial accounting information on the decisions of other stakeholders.

Many corporations must report audited financial accounting information to governmental agencies. Corporations whose stock is traded publicly in the U.S. report to the Securities and Exchange Commission (SEC). This agency examines corporate financial reports to verify their conformance with GAAP and SEC requirements. A corporation whose stock may be listed on stock exchanges in more than one country must report to local authorities in each of those countries. Because countries do not use the same GAAP, reporting may involve preparation of separate reports for the investors in the different countries. In the U.S., banks and other financial institutions, defense contractors, hospitals, and many other organizations also report accounting information to governmental agencies.

Managerial Accounting

Objective 8
Define managerial accounting.

Managers need information to evaluate the efficiency and effectiveness of their companies in addition to that provided to external decision makers. ***Managerial* (or *management*) *accounting* is the process of preparing, reporting, and**

interpreting accounting information for use by an organization's internal decision makers. Managers develop accounting systems for internal use to meet their own decision needs. These systems often are separate from the systems used to report financial accounting information. Managerial accounting is used by managers to make planning and control decisions.

Planning **decisions require managers to identify goals and to develop strategies and policies to achieve these goals.** Planning decisions involve choices about which goods and services a company will provide, where a company will locate its facilities, what technology it will acquire, and how it will expand into new markets. These decisions determine the structure of an organization. Managers estimate the profitability of alternate strategies and the risks associated with these alternatives.

Control **decisions require managers to evaluate the accomplishments of their organization and to make changes if the organization is not meeting its goals.** These decisions focus on how well the company is implementing the strategies and policies developed in the planning process. In addition, they require evaluation of employees who have responsibilities for accomplishing an organization's goals. Evaluations motivate employees to make decisions consistent with an organization's goals.

Planning decisions are future oriented: What do managers want to happen in the future? Control decisions are past and present oriented: What has the company accomplished and what changes should be made to improve performance? Planning decisions often are long-run decisions: What objectives exist for the next five years? Control decisions are more immediate: Are objectives being met now? If not, what can be done to improve the situation?

Planning and control decisions are made about financing, investing, and operating activities. Managers plan for a company's financial resource needs and decide how these resources will be invested. They evaluate how financial resources were used and the success of the investments they have made. They plan for new products, product design, and the acquisition of materials and labor to produce products. They plan for the production, distribution, marketing, and servicing of goods and services. Control decisions evaluate these activities. Control of costs is a major management task affecting a company's efficiency.

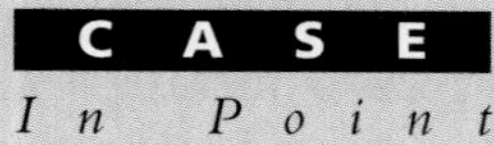

Assume that you own a business that processes film for customers. Your current store is located in a mall. You have invested in state-of-the-art equipment that has the capacity to process 1,000 rolls of film a day. Currently, you are processing an average of 500 rolls a day.

In your planning decisions you want to identify a strategy to increase your processing volume to take advantage of your unused capacity. One strategy would be to open small stores in different locations around town where customers could drop off their film. Twice daily, the film would be picked up from the outlets and delivered to the processing location in the mall. Once processed, the film would be returned to the outlets on the next trip.

This strategy should increase the number of customers because they would not have to take their film to the mall. Also, it would increase the visibility of your business in different parts of town. Whether this is a good strategy depends on how much additional business you can create and on how much additional cost will be necessary to open the outlets and transport the film.

Thus, the planning process depends on weighing the relative benefits and costs that you anticipate if you adopt this strategy. The control process becomes important once you decide on a strategy. Success will depend on how well each outlet performs its mission. You must evaluate each outlet you open. Is it creating sufficient business? Is the film being delivered on time? How expensive is the outlet to operate? How well are employees serving customers? By answering these questions, you may decide some outlets should be closed or moved, or some personnel should be replaced. You may decide the entire strategy is unsuccessful and you should look for an alternative, or you may decide the strategy is successful and you need to enlarge your operations. Planning and control work together. Through planning, you decide what to do. Through control, you decide how well you have done and what to do differently to improve performance.

Accounting and Information Needs

The accounting information system should be adaptable to provide the information demanded of an organization. Specialized accounting systems often are necessary to provide information for different needs of managers, for reporting to investors, for tax planning and reporting, and for reporting to other governmental authorities. These systems work together to meet the needs of those who make decisions about an organization. Decisions managers make in an organization are not independent of decisions made by investors, customers, suppliers, and others. Information reported to external parties affects internal decisions. Financial accounting provides a window for those external to a company to view the consequences of decisions made by managers. Thus, management decisions are the primary concern of both financial and managerial accounting.

Accounting information can be divided into financial and managerial components:

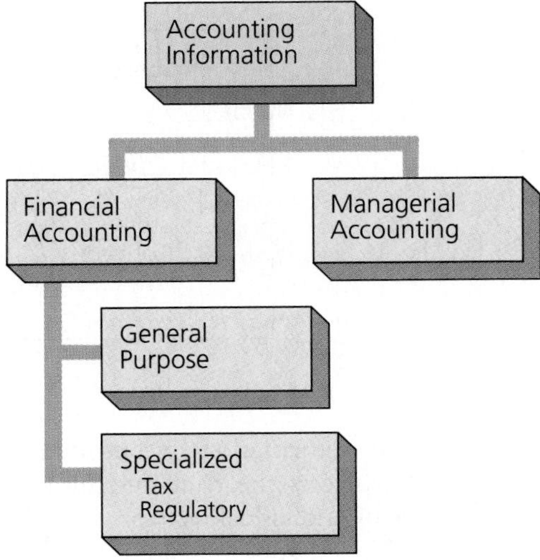

Financial accounting includes general purpose and specialized reporting to external decision makers. General purpose reports are provided to investors, customers, suppliers, employees, and others with a need for information about a company's overall performance. Specialized reports are prepared for tax and regulatory authorities who have a need for specific information, and often are prepared using different accounting rules from those for general purpose reports. Managerial accounting serves numerous needs of internal decision makers. This information is reported in a wide variety of formats and can be designed for specific needs that arise within an organization.

SELF-STUDY PROBLEM 2-1

R. Floorshine is a manufacturer of shoes. The company operates as a corporation and has issued shares of stock to its owners and debt to creditors. It has purchased and leased buildings and equipment. It purchases materials on short-term credit and converts the materials into shoes. The shoes are sold to retail stores, also on a short-term credit arrangement.

Required

Identify the primary exchanges and contracts between the company and those who interact with R. Floorshine. Describe the primary information needs associated with these exchanges and contracts.

The solution to Self-Study Problem 2-1 appears at the end of the chapter.

INFORMATION SYSTEMS

To meet the many information needs of internal and external users, organizations develop systems to collect, process, and report information. Exhibit 2-4 illustrates the primary activities in an information system.

Exhibit 2-4 Primary Activities in an Information System

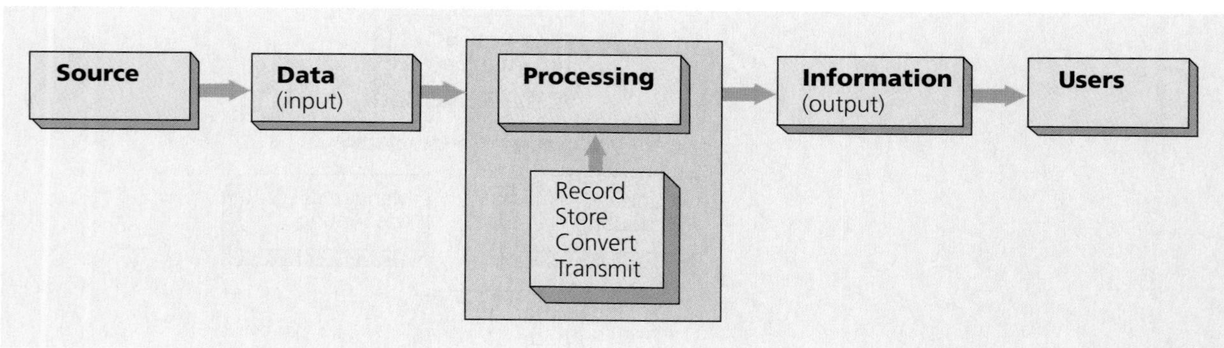

Objective 9
Identify the primary activities in an information system.

An information system identifies and collects data from appropriate sources and converts the data into information that can be used in making decisions. Data are individual facts or symbols that can be converted into useful information.

The purpose of an information system may be to change data to make them more useful before they are received by users or to make information more accessible to users. For example, sound or visual images may be converted by microphone and camera to signals stored on compact disks or tapes. When the disks or tapes are played on appropriate equipment, the signals are converted back to sounds and images. The storage devices make the information more useful by preserving it until it is needed.

Computers are a familiar type of information system. Data are entered through a keyboard into a processing unit. The processing unit converts the data into signals that can be displayed on a monitor or printer or that can be stored until needed. An important aspect of this type of system is that data are transformed into information by the computer. Software is used to rearrange the data, to summarize it, or to tabulate it, so the output is useful information.

The ability to store and manipulate data before they are output is an important attribute of many information systems. One part of an information system that plays an important role in permitting the storage and manipulation of information is a data base. **A *data base* is a physical or electronic arrangement of data that allows the data to be retrieved and manipulated systematically.** Telephone directories and dictionaries are common types of data bases. If you need to find someone's phone number or the meaning of a word, you can look it up in the data base because information is stored in an alphabetical format. An accounting data base might be a computer file containing information about amounts owed to individual creditors.

Management Information Systems

Objective 10
Explain the purpose of a management information system.

Information systems designed to meet the needs of managers are a source of information to be reported to investors, creditors, government authorities and others with whom managers interact. A management information system provides information managers need to operate an organization. In theory, a management information system might be designed so it receives input from all parts of an organization. The system stores the input in a data base, which then provides information for many decisions of internal and external users. In reality, such comprehensive management information systems are not found currently in most organizations. New technology probably will make them more common in the near future.

Exhibit 2-5 presents a model of a comprehensive management information system. In this system, each part of an organization provides input into the data base. For example, marketing provides data about the number of units and dollar amount of sales of each type of product for each geographical location. Personnel provides information about the number of employees in different divisions and the amount of wages and benefits earned and paid. From this comprehensive data base, data are converted into information in the form of schedules and reports that are provided to internal and external users. Computers provide a means for organizations to link managers so information can flow among divisions. To illustrate, a computerized system could allow production to obtain information about the number of units to produce to meet sales orders, purchasing could determine the quantity of materials to order to meet manufacturing requirements, and so forth.

Instead of one comprehensive management information system, organizations normally maintain several information systems (or subsystems) that serve different purposes. Each subsystem is part of the total management information system. Thus, separate information subsystems may exist for marketing, production, and personnel. Each subsystem collects input from activities occurring in that part of the transformation process. The subsystem stores these data and converts them to information as needed to meet the requirements of the partic-

Exhibit 2-5 A Comprehensive Management Information System

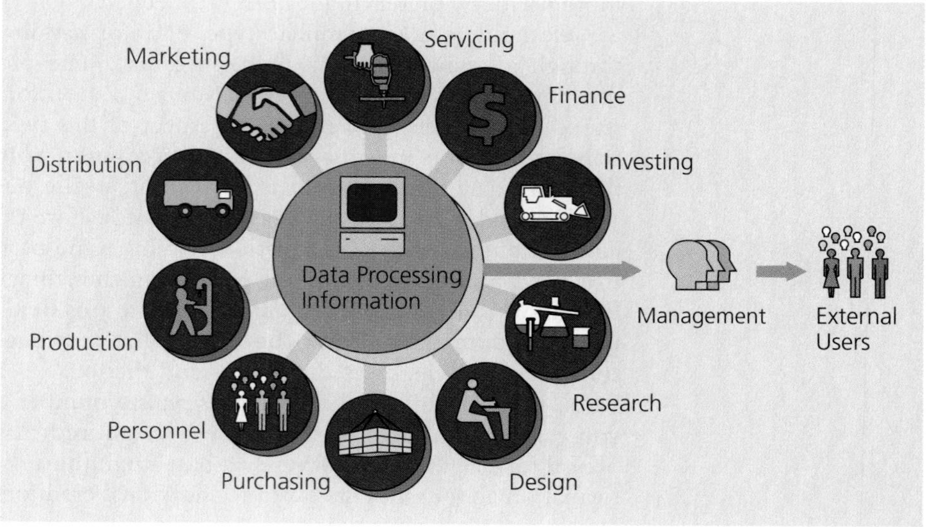

ular managers of that division. Periodically, data from each division are converted into reports and provided to other parts of an organization or to top management.

Objective 11
Explain the purpose of an accounting information system.

Whether comprehensive or not, the management information system provides information about the types, quantities, locations, and uses of resources from the time they are acquired until they are consumed, sold, or discarded as part of the transformation process. **The *accounting information system,* a specific subsystem of the management information system, is responsible for: (1) identifying the resources of an organization, (2) tracking the transformation of resources into goods and services sold to customers or provided to recipients, (3) determining the costs of resources used by an organization, and (4) reporting information about these activities to internal and external users.**

The Accounting Information System

Objective 12
Identify activities in an accounting information system.

Like other information systems, the accounting system is a process in which data are input, recorded and stored in a data base, converted into summaries and tabulations, and transmitted as schedules, reports, and other types of information to users. Primary inputs to the accounting system are (1) costs of resources acquired and used by an organization, (2) prices of goods and services sold by an organization, and (3) management policies affecting these activities. Exhibit 2-6 illustrates the activities that occur in an accounting information system.

The source of data for the accounting information system is an organization's transformation process. The financing, investing, and operating activities of an organization are sources of data about resources that are acquired, transformed, and consumed.

Measurement rules are criteria that determine which attributes of the transformation process enter the accounting system. They identify

Exhibit 2-6 The Accounting Information System

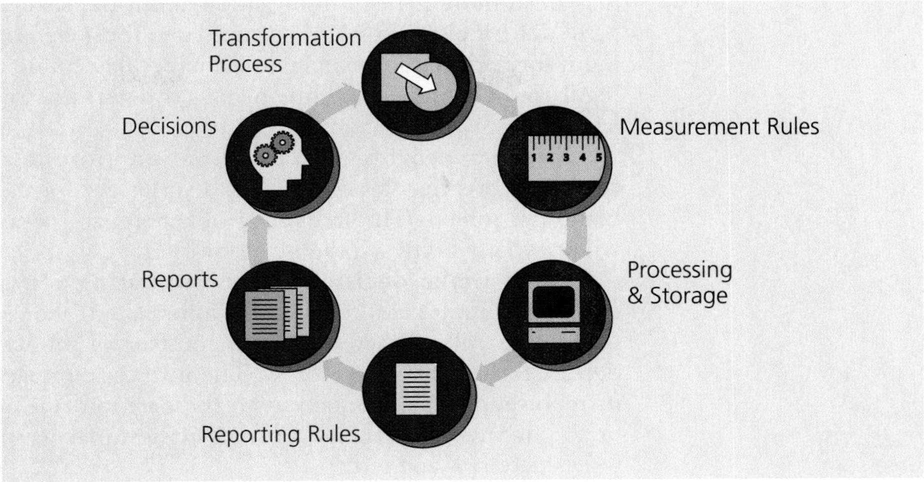

data collected by the system. For example, the system records the cost paid for equipment when it is purchased, but it usually does not record the price the equipment could be sold for unless it is actually sold. The cost of equipment is recorded in the accounting system but not its size, or weight, or color. Measurement rules are designed to select those attributes of the transformation process important to users of the system. GAAP are a primary source of measurement rules for general purpose financial accounting information. Government authorities determine rules for tax and regulatory requirements, while managers develop their own measurement rules for management accounting information.

The transformation process attributes, measured by the accounting system, are recorded in one or more accounting data bases where they may be stored and processed. **Accounting data bases often are books or computer files containing accounts in which an organization's transactions are recorded, summarized, and stored.**

Each transaction is recorded by identifying the accounts affected by an event along with the amount of the transaction. Assume a company purchased equipment for $500. An account for the equipment would be increased by $500, and an account for cash would be decreased by $500. Each transaction is separated into two parts. Often these parts identify an exchange between a company and customers, suppliers, investors, and others. Thus, a company receives equipment and gives up cash.

Recording a transaction is similar to recording a check in a check register. The date, purpose, and amount of a transaction are recorded. Data bases permit account data to be summarized in a variety of ways. An organization can determine how much money it spent in a particular period, the purposes for which money was used, as well as the other resources it acquired, when they were acquired, and how they were used. Users can obtain different types of information from the data base depending on their needs.

Reporting rules are criteria that determine the information that will be reported by an information system. Reporting rules determine which data from the data base will be presented for specific uses and the format of the presentation. Some users may need information about which products were sold and how much was sold in different locations or periods. Other users may need more general information about the total amount of sales for a company. GAAP also provide reporting rules for general purpose financial accounting information. Government authorities determine reporting rules for tax and regulatory information, while managers determine rules for reporting managerial accounting information.

Reports provide the information output by the accounting system. Reports may be available in a variety of forms, such as on paper or on a computer screen. The frequency of reports and amount of detail they contain will vary depending on the needs of users.

Users make decisions after evaluating reported information. Users employ decision rules to interpret information. For example, an investor might decide she will sell her stock in a company if profits reported by the company decline for three years in a row. The investor compares information about profits reported by the company with the decision rule and decides whether to sell or to continue to own the stock. Decision makers use accounting information to evaluate risk and return.

An important step in the system described in Exhibit 2-6 is the link between decisions and the transformation process. User decisions affect the organization. If investors decide not to buy stock in a company or if creditors decide not to lend it money, it may have difficulty obtaining the financial resources it needs to operate or to stay in business. If customers are concerned about the continued existence of a company, they may decide not to buy its products.

SELF-STUDY PROBLEM 2-2

Nap Bonapart is purchasing manager for a company that sells suits. On April 12, Nap received the following weekly report for the suits purchased from one of the company's suppliers:

Merchandise Report
April 12, 1995

Fabric Type	Usual Order Quantity	Unit Cost	Last Order Date	Actual Number on Hand	Desired Number on Hand
Wool	12	$120	Feb. 15	5	10
Cotton	20	80	Mar. 2	8	15
Synthetic	25	75	Mar. 10	20	15

Nap immediately ordered another 12 wool suits and another 20 cotton suits from the manufacturer.

Required

1. What information did Nap consider in making his decision?
2. How does the Merchandise Report assist Nap with the decision? Does this report appear to meet his information needs for the decision he made?
3. What effect does the information in the report and Nap's decision have on the future of the company?

The solution to Self-Study Problem 2-2 appears at the end of the chapter.

PROCESSING ACCOUNTING INFORMATION

This section describes the accounting data base in more detail. To understand the accounting system, you must understand how the system categorizes and stores data. As discussed in Chapter 1, an account is the basic unit for recording data in the accounting system. It contains a record of when an event occurred, the dollar amount of the increase or decrease in the account, and the balance of the account. Accounts are categories for storing data. The number of accounts will vary depending on the complexity and information needs of an organization.

Objective 13
List the types of accounts included in an accounting information system.

The accounting information system in a business organization contains five types of accounts to record the transformation process:

1. Assets
2. Liabilities
3. Owners' Equity
4. Revenues
5. Expenses

These types of accounts capture all the transactions occurring in a company's transformation process. Accounts are like a filing system. A separate file exists for each account. The accounts are arranged by type to make them easy to locate and to make reports easier to prepare, as illustrated below:

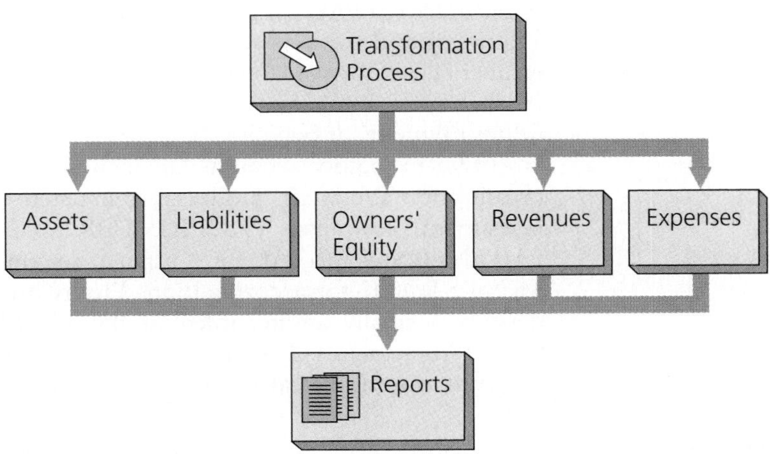

Assets, Liabilities, and Owners' Equity

Objective 14
Define assets, liabilities, and owners' equity.

Assets **are resources purchased by an organization or otherwise under its legal control and available for its use in the future.** Included under the asset category are accounts for financial resources such as CASH and ACCOUNTS RECEIVABLE. *Accounts receivable* **are amounts of cash to be received in the future from credit sales to customers.** Assets also include accounts for physical resources such as INVENTORY (merchandise for sale), MATERIALS, SUPPLIES, EQUIPMENT, BUILDINGS, LAND, and NATURAL RESOURCES, and accounts for other resources that provide legal rights of value to an organization, such as PATENTS and TRADEMARKS. Asset accounts are increased when assets are acquired and are decreased when they are consumed or sold.

Learning Note Account titles are shown in capital letters in the first few chapters to make them easier to identify.

Liabilities **are obligations owed by an organization to its creditors.** ***Owners' equity*** **is the amount of investment made by owners in a business.** Both direct investments and reinvested profits are part of owners' investment. **Owners' equity for corporations usually is called *stockholders'* (or *shareholders'*) *equity*.**

Some liability and owners' equity accounts result from financing activities. The balances of these accounts indicate the amount invested by creditors and owners in an organization. A separate account is used for each major source of financing. A liability account is increased when creditors provide money to an organization, and decreased when an organization repays amounts to creditors. Liability accounts include NOTES PAYABLE for amounts borrowed from banks and other lending institutions and BONDS PAYABLE for amounts borrowed by selling bonds. ***Notes payable*** **are contracts with creditors that affirm the borrower will repay the amount borrowed plus interest at specific dates. A *bond* is a certificate of debt issued by an organization.** Most bonds can be traded in securities markets. The balances of these accounts increase when a company borrows money and decrease when it repays money to its creditors.

Other liabilities are associated with operating activities. Examples include ACCOUNTS PAYABLE, amounts owed to suppliers; WAGES PAYABLE, amounts owed to employees; and TAXES PAYABLE, amounts owed to governmental authorities. Suppliers, employees, governments, and others become creditors of a company when they provide goods and services in exchange for future payments or benefits.

Owners' equity accounts are increased when owners invest money in an organization and when profits are reinvested. Various titles are used for owner investment accounts: PROPRIETOR'S CAPITAL for a proprietorship, PARTNERS' CAPITAL for a partnership, and CAPITAL STOCK or COMMON STOCK for a corporation. Profits earned by a proprietorship or partnership normally are recorded in the PROPRIETOR'S OR PARTNERS' CAPITAL accounts. **Profits earned by a corporation are recorded in an account normally called *RETAINED EARNINGS.***

Learning Note Capital refers to the investment in a company (liabilities and owners' equity), which equals the resources acquired from these investments (assets). Thus, a company's total capital is its total assets or its total liabilities and owners' equity.

An important relationship exists between assets and liabilities plus owners' equity. Liabilities and owners' equity provide financial resources to a business. Assets are resources acquired with the financial resources provided by creditors and owners. Therefore, a relationship exists between the amount of assets available to an organization and the amount of its liabilities and owners' equity.

The accounts included in the following illustration are examples of accounts for each category. Many other accounts could be listed. The right hand side of this equation represents the claims of owners and creditors who provide resources to an organization. The left hand side represents how managers have used investors' capital to acquire resources for the organization. **One of the primary accounting reports describes the relationship among assets,**

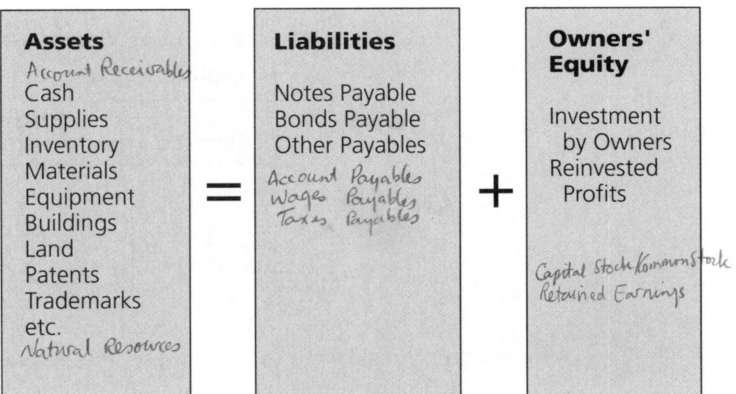

liabilities, and owners' equity. This report is called a *balance sheet* because of the balancing relationship (assets = liabilities + owners' equity). Other names for the balance sheet are statement of financial position and statement of financial condition.

Amounts associated with asset, liability, and owners' equity accounts are for a *particular date*. A company may have assets of $500,000, liabilities of $200,000, and owners' equity of $300,000 on January 1, 1995. If an event occurs on January 2, 1995 that affects these accounts (for example, owners invest an additional $50,000), the account balances will differ between the two days. Accordingly, a report of assets, liabilities, and owners' equity for a company should identify the specific date of the report.

Revenues and Expenses

Objective 15
Define revenues and expenses.

As explained in Chapter 1, revenues result when a business creates resources by selling goods and services to customers. More technically, ***revenues* are increases in assets or decreases in liabilities from selling goods or services that constitute the primary operating activities of an organization.** To illustrate, the sale of merchandise for $1,200 results in the recognition of revenue of $1,200. The resource created is either cash or accounts receivable. Expenses result when an organization consumes resources in producing, selling, and delivering goods and services. More technically, ***expenses* are decreases in assets or increases in liabilities from producing and delivering goods or providing services that constitute the primary operating activities of an organization.** If the cost of merchandise sold is $800, the sale results in an expense of $800. The resource consumed is the merchandise from inventory delivered to a customer. Together, revenues and expenses measure the results of the operating activities of a business *for a period*.

Recall from Chapter 1 that an organization creates value when the total prices of goods and services it provides to its customers are greater than the total costs of the resources the organization consumed in producing and making available these goods and services. This created value is called profit, or net income. In the accounting system, profit is the difference between the amount of revenues and the amount of expenses a business records during a period. Thus, the profit earned by a business for a period can be expressed as shown on the next page.

As discussed in Chapter 1, profit earned by a company for a period is reported on the income statement as net income. Revenues, expenses, and net

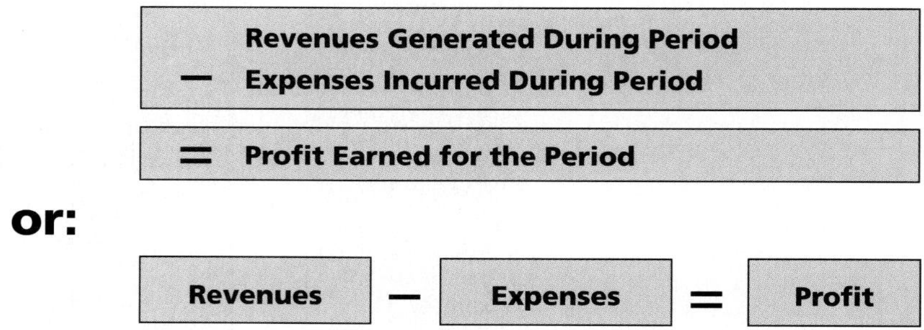

income result from the operating activities of an organization for a fiscal period. A fiscal period can be any length of time: for example, the month of June, the first quarter of 1996, or the year ended September 30, 1995. When reporting revenues, expenses, and net income, it is important to know the fiscal period covered by the report. Reporting net income is something like reporting the score in a baseball game. You need to know the inning or if the game is over. Once a game is over, the score is reset to zero to start a new game. Net income is zero at the beginning of each new fiscal period. The amount at the end of the period is the score for the period.

Owners may receive cash payments from a business. This cash normally is a portion of the amount generated by a company's profitable operations. For corporations, these payments are called ***dividends***. For proprietorships and partnerships, they are called ***withdrawals***. The balances of PARTNERS' or PROPRIETOR'S CAPITAL and CASH are reduced when withdrawals are recorded. RETAINED EARNINGS and CASH are reduced when dividends are recorded.

Exhibit 2-7 describes relationships among types of accounts in the accounting system.

Exhibit 2-7 Relationships Among Types of Accounts

Resources Available for Use (Assets)
Cash
Inventory
Equipment
Buildings
etc.

Operations
Revenues from Sale of Goods and Services
Less
Expenses from Consumption of Resources
Equals
Net Income

Finances
Liabilities
Owners' Equity
Direct Investment
Reinvested Profits

Net income measures the results of operating activities. The amount of net income not paid to owners increases the amount of reinvested profits and is a source of financing used to acquire additional resources. These resources, in turn, are used in the operations of the organization to produce revenues. Thus, the five account categories used in the accounting data base record the results of the transformation process of an organization. A numerical example is useful to illustrate how the transformation process is reported by the accounting system.

An Illustration of an Accounting System

Assume you start a small merchandising business in a local shopping mall, selling electronic equipment. You invest $10,000 in the business from savings and borrow $40,000 by issuing a note payable to a local bank. These transactions occur on January 1. Because of these transactions, the following data would appear in the accounting data base after the events of January 1:

Assets		Liabilities + Owners' Equity		Revenues − Expenses	
Cash	$50,000	Notes payable	$40,000	Sales	$0
		Investment by owner	10,000	Expenses	0
Total	$50,000	Total	$50,000	Total	$0

On January 1, the only asset available to the business is cash. This resource resulted from the financing activities of the business. No investing or operating activities have occurred.

On January 2, you purchase (a) merchandise to sell and pay $20,000 in cash. This merchandise becomes an inventory of goods available for sale to customers. In addition, you purchase (b) equipment for $12,000 and (c) supplies for $4,000. You pay cash for these items which leaves you with $14,000 of cash. Each of these three transactions exchanges one type of asset for another. The accounting data base would now contain the following data:

Assets		Liabilities + Owners' Equity		Revenues − Expenses	
Cash	$50,000	Notes payable	$40,000	Sales	$0
	(20,000) (a)	Investment by owner	10,000	Expenses	0
	(12,000) (b)				
	(4,000) (c)				
	14,000				
Inventory	20,000 (a)				
Equipment	12,000 (b)				
Supplies	4,000 (c)				
Total	$50,000	Total	$50,000	Total	$0

Note: Parentheses indicate decreases in column totals.

During January, you sell (d) at a price of $8,000 in cash, one-fourth of the inventory. The inventory sold had cost you (e) $5,000. After recording these transactions, the data base would contain the following data:

Assets		Liabilities + Owners' Equity		Revenues − Expenses	
Cash	$50,000	Notes payable	$40,000	Sales	$8,000 (d)
	(20,000)	Investment by		Cost of	
	(12,000)	owner	10,000	goods	
	(4,000)	Reinvested		sold	(5,000) (e)
	8,000 (d)	profit	3,000		
	22,000				
Inventory	20,000				
	(5,000) (e)				
	15,000				
Equipment	12,000				
Supplies	4,000				
Total	$53,000	Total	$53,000	Total	$3,000

Because of the sales transaction, cash has increased by $8,000, and inventory has been reduced by $5,000. Therefore, the total amount of assets has increased by $3,000 to $53,000. Sales revenue of $8,000 has been recorded, representing the amount of the sale. Resources (inventory) amounting to $5,000 were consumed in the sale, resulting in an expense of $5,000. ***Cost of goods sold* is an expense representing the cost of inventory sold to customers.** The result of operating activities for January was net income of $3,000. Assuming you do not withdraw money from the business, the net income is reinvested (as reinvested profit) and becomes part of owners' equity. Both resources and finances have increased by $3,000 (assets = liabilities + owners' equity).

Exhibit 2-8 illustrates how the accounting data base reports the flow of resources through the transformation process.

Exhibit 2-8 Accounting Information and the Transformation Process

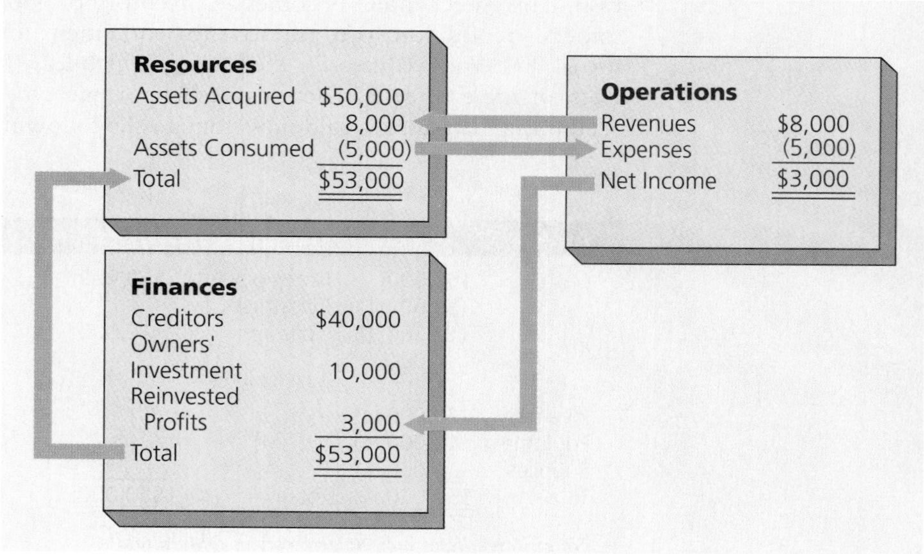

Note from the illustration that the three parts of the transformation process are interrelated. Investments by owners and creditors are used to acquire resources, and some of these resources are consumed in the operating activities of

the business. Additional resources are generated from the sale of goods and services. The excess of resources generated from sales over resources consumed provides additional financing for the company. By identifying exchanges among contracting parties, amounts recorded in accounts are useful for determining whether the rights and responsibilities of those who contract with a company have been met. Also, these recorded amounts are a basis for formulating contracts that will affect the future allocation of scarce resources.

CONTRACTS AND ACCOUNTING INFORMATION

Objective 16
Explain the relationships among contracts, transactions, and accounting information.

Accounting provides information to help those who make decisions about organizations. These decisions result from contractual relationships among investors, managers, employees, suppliers, customers, and government agencies. Contracts specify services and resources each party to a contract is to provide and what each party can expect to receive in return. Contracts identify what is to be given and what is to be received. In other words, they identify how scarce resources will be allocated. Participants in these contracts need information to determine whether terms of the contracts are being met and to evaluate the risk and return they expect from contractual relationships. This information helps determine the terms of contracts and helps decision makers determine whether to participate in contractual relationships.

Information systems are an important mechanism for providing information needed by decision makers. They collect data, process them, and report resulting information. The accounting information system collects data about resources, their sources, and their uses. Data are stored in accounts classified as assets, liabilities, owners' equity, revenues, and expenses. The source of these data are transactions in an organization's transformation process. Transactions identify what is given and what is received in exchanges involving an organization. The system summarizes these data and reports them to decision makers. The reported information is the basis for many of the decisions contracting parties make in evaluating risk and return.

Exhibit 2-9 summarizes the relationship between contracts, transactions, and accounting information.

Exhibit 2-9 Contracts, Transactions, and Accounting Information

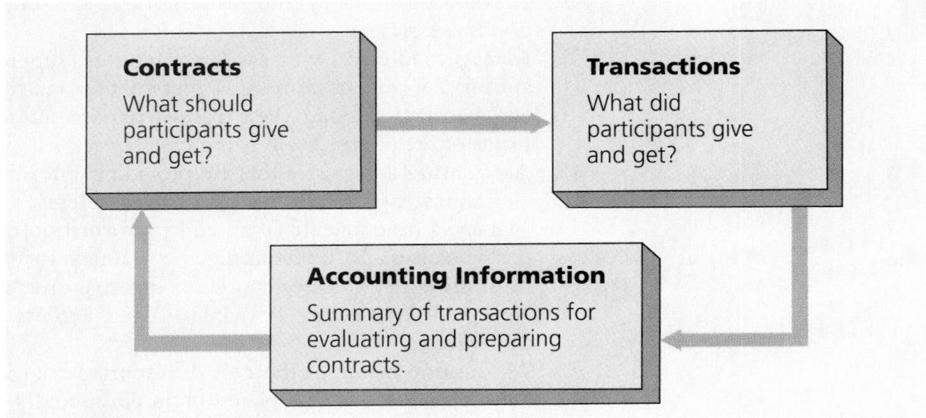

Contracts identify the rights and responsibilities of the contracting parties. Transactions identify actual exchanges among contracting parties and events resulting from their activities. Accounting summarizes the transactions and provides the parties information for evaluating whether contract terms have been met and for preparing future contracts.

The next chapter will examine how accounting measures exchanges and other events occurring in transactions. Accounting measurement rules provide a basis for forming and evaluating contracts.

SELF-STUDY PROBLEM 2-3

Harvey Benedict owns a restaurant called Eggs. He opened the restaurant in November by investing $20,000 from savings and borrowing $20,000 from a local bank. The following additional events occurred for Eggs during November:

1. Purchased equipment for $12,000.
2. Purchased food supplies for $9,000.
3. Sold $14,000 in meals for cash. The food used for the meals cost Eggs $6,000.
4. Paid the following expenses: employee wages of $3,000, rent of $1,000, utilities of $800, other expenses of $500.

Required

1. Use the format of Exhibit 2-8 to describe the data that would be contained in the accounting data base after recording transactions for November. Draw arrows to show the relationships among the accounts in the data base.
2. Identify the resources that are available to Eggs at the end of November. List each asset and the amount available.

The solution to Self-Study Problem 2-3 appears at the end of the chapter.

REVIEW *Summary of Important Concepts*

1. Information needs of external and internal decision makers:
   - A. Accounting provides information about the transformation of resources into goods and services.
   - B. Managers interact with owners, creditors, suppliers, employees, government authorities, and customers as part of the transformation process. Exchanges and contracts among these parties require information to determine if the terms of the contracts are being met.
   - C. Accounting assists investors by providing information for evaluating the risk and return expected from alternate investments.
   - D. Managers have incentives to report information that reflects favorably on their performances. To limit management ability to manipulate reported information, managers prepare reports for external users that conform with Generally Accepted Accounting Principles. These reports are audited by independent accountants.
   - E. Accounting measures the cost of resources used in the transformation process and compares the cost of resources consumed with the amount of resources created from the sale of goods and services.

F. Managers make planning decisions in selecting strategies and policies for achieving organizational goals.
G. Managers make control decisions when they evaluate an organization's operations to determine whether goals are being met and whether changes are needed to improve operations.

2. Primary functions of information systems:
   A. Management information systems help managers make decisions about an organization's operations. Also, it provides information managers report to other decision makers.
   B. The accounting information system is the specific part of a management information system responsible for (1) identifying the resources of an organization, (2) tracking the transformation of resources into goods and services sold to customers, (3) determining the cost of resources used by the organization, and (4) reporting information about these activities to managers and external users.
3. The primary components of an information system are a data source; data; a process for collecting, storing, transmitting, and converting the data; information produced by the system; and decision makers who use the information.
4. Processing information in an accounting system:
   A. The source of data for the accounting information system is an organization's transactions. Measurement rules determine the types of data the system collects. Data are recorded in accounting data bases. These data are summarized and reported according to reporting rules that determine the content and format of reports. Users apply decision rules to determine how to interpret the information and make decisions. These decisions affect the organization.
   B. Transactions are recorded in the accounting data base in five account types: assets, liabilities, owners' equity, revenues, and expenses.
   C. Data recorded in accounts represent an organization's transformation process. These data identify exchanges and other activities useful for evaluating and forming contracts.

DEFINE *Terms and Concepts Defined in this Chapter*

accounting information system
accounts receivable
assets
audit
balance sheet
bond
contracts
control
cost of goods sold
data base
debt financing
dividends
equity financing
expenses
financial accounting
generally accepted accounting principles (GAAP)
interest
investors
liabilities
managerial accounting (management accounting)
notes payable
owners' equity
planning
principal
retained earnings
revenues
stockholders' equity (shareholders' equity)
withdrawals

SOLUTIONS

SELF-STUDY PROBLEM 2-1

1. **Exchanges and contracts between managers, owners, and creditors:** Owners and creditors exchange money with Floorshine for the right to receive

cash in the future from the company. Contracts exist among managers, owners, and creditors. Managers contract with owners and creditors for money to acquire resources that will generate profits for the company and to employ the resources effectively and efficiently. Managers expect to be rewarded for their effectiveness and efficiency and owners and creditors expect a fair return on their investments. These contracting parties need information to assess how well managers have performed and to determine how much cash from the company's operations should be distributed to each party. Managers, owners, and creditors decide whether the terms of contracts are being met. Companies hire independent auditors (CPAs) to examine the financial information provided by managers to owners and creditors to ensure its reliability.

2. **Exchanges and contracts between suppliers and managers:** Suppliers exchange goods and services with the company for the right to receive cash. Contracts between suppliers and managers require information to determine that the company receives the correct types and quantities of goods and services at the appropriate times. Also, information is needed to demonstrate the company has made timely payments for these goods and services.
3. **Exchanges and contracts between employees and managers:** Employees exchange labor services with the company for wages and benefits. Contracts between employees and managers describe the payments, benefits, and rights employees have negotiated with managers. Information is needed to demonstrate that labor services have been provided and employees have been treated fairly. The demands of employees for future wages and benefits depend, in part, on the profitability of the company. Employees and managers need information about the performance of the company to negotiate future contracts.
4. **Exchanges and contracts between customers and managers:** Customers exchange cash for goods and services provided by the company. Customers, such as retail stores, may receive the goods and pay for them later, say within 30 or 60 days. Managers expect to receive the payments when due. Contracts between customers and managers call for the delivery of goods to customers and payment to the company. Customers decide whether to continue to purchase the company's goods. The quality and costs of the goods and future prospects for obtaining the goods when needed are relevant information. Managers must decide whether to continue to extend credit to customers.
5. **Exchanges and contracts between government authorities and managers:** Government authorities monitor companies to determine if they are engaged in fair trade and labor practices. Managers provide information to demonstrate the company is conforming to government regulations. Governments provide services to companies in the form of police and fire protection, utilities, sanitation, and streets and roads. Companies pay taxes and fees for these services. Information is required to verify appropriate amounts of taxes and fees are being paid.

SELF-STUDY PROBLEM 2-2

1. Nap compared the actual number of suits of each type on hand with the minimum number of suits the company desires to have in stock.
2. The Merchandise Report provides information about the number of suits of each type on hand and the minimum number desired. This information is sufficient for Nap's decision and is available in a form that is easy to understand.
3. The decisions Nap makes determine when additional units will be ordered and how many units will be purchased to provide for future sales. This information system provides a means for the company to maintain an adequate amount of merchandise.

SELF-STUDY PROBLEM 2-3

1.

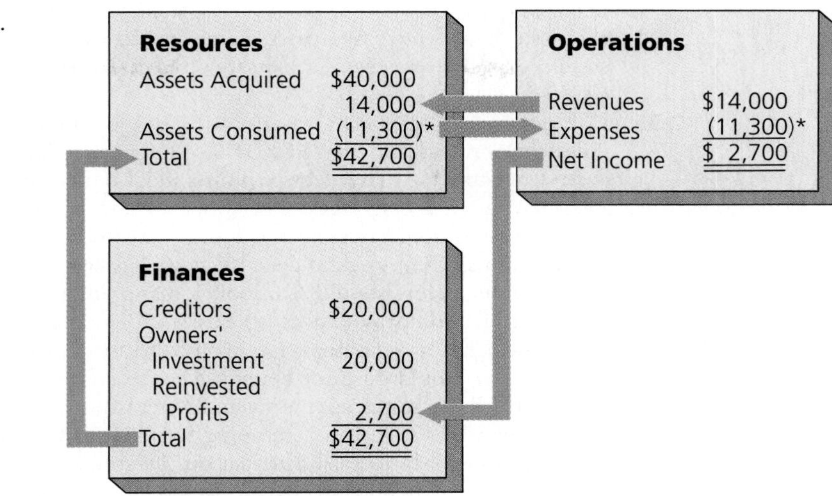

$11,300 = $6,000 supplies consumed + $3,000 wages + $1,000 rent + $800 utilities + $500 other expenses

2.

Cash from financing		$40,000
Cash from sales		14,000
Cash available in November		54,000
Cash used:		
for equipment	$12,000	
for supplies	9,000	
for wages	3,000	
for rent	1,000	
for utilities	800	
for other expenses	500	
Total cash used		(26,300)
Cash at end of November		27,700
Equipment acquired		12,000
Supplies acquired	9,000	
Supplies consumed	(6,000)	
Supplies at end of November		3,000
Total resources available at end of November		$42,700

EXERCISES

2-1. Write a short definition for each of the terms listed in the *Terms and Concepts Defined in this Chapter* section.

2-2. Marjorie Morning has saved $10,000 that she would like to invest. She has been offered two investment alternatives. One alternative is to purchase a five-year certificate of deposit (CD) with a local bank. The CD will pay 7% interest annually. Another alternative is to purchase shares of a mutual stock fund. The earnings from the fund fluctuate with stock prices and interest rates. The fund's rate of return for the last five years has been: 8%, 3.5%, 9%, 6%, and 10%. Assuming the fund's return is expected to be about the same in the next five years, compute the average annual rate of return Marjorie should expect to receive. Explain the concept of risk. Which investment alternative is riskier?

2-3. Gazzooks Co. is preparing to raise $100,000 of additional capital for plant expansion. The company currently has $100,000 of long-term debt and $200,000 of stock (40,000 shares) outstanding. The debt pays an annual return of 9% to creditors. The stock has been paying an average return of about 14% to stockholders. The company has been advised that it could borrow the funds it needs at a 10% interest rate. To obtain the needed money from stockholders, the company would need to sell 20,000 shares of new stock. What factors should Gazzooks's management consider in making its decision? Assuming the company expects to earn a 20% return on investment for the foreseeable future, which form of financing would be most beneficial to current stockholders? Which form would be most beneficial if the company fears a downturn in the economy and believes it may earn only an 8% return on investment over the next few years?

2-4. Read Exercise 2-3. If you were going to invest in Gazzooks Co. and you believed the company was likely to earn a return on investment of 20% per year, would you rather be a creditor or stockholder? Why? Would your answer differ if you expected the company to earn a return on investment of 8%? Why?

2-5. To encourage its managers to earn a profit for its stockholders, Plumtree Corporation pays a bonus to top managers if the company earns at least a 12% return on investment each year. The return is computed as the ratio of net income to total assets. To determine whether a bonus will be paid, the Board of Directors requires management to submit an income statement and balance sheet at the end of each fiscal year. Should the Board and stockholders be concerned about the reliability of the financial reports? What can they do to make sure the reports faithfully represent the company's economic activities?

2-6. Financing activities occur when organizations obtain financial resources to invest in other resources and to engage in providing goods and services. Who makes financing decisions? List some factors that are important in making these decisions.

2-7. Jean Roget does not understand the concept that an organization is a portfolio of individual resources. Explain to Jean why the selection of a portfolio is important to the success of a business. Use Wal-Mart as an example to explain the concept to Jean.

2-8. Wendy Hu is considering two new products for her office products manufacturing business. One is a laser printer. Wendy has had numerous calls for the product, which will compete with other major brands. The other is a new computer projection system that permits a presenter to display color computer images without the need for a regular computer or projection system. The product would have little competition. Wendy believes the market will be receptive to this product. What are some of the risks inherent in the decision of whether or not to produce the two products?

2-9. Identify each of the following as planning or control decisions:

a. Decision to buy a new production facility.
b. Decision to change the mix in a chemical compound used to produce a synthetic fiber to reduce the cost of the product.
c. Decision to replace a machine that is no longer serviceable.
d. Decision to retrain workers to enhance long-run productivity.
e. Decision to open retail stores in a foreign country.
f. Decision to count goods for sale to verify inventory records.
g. Decision to sell a production plant that is no longer profitable.
h. Decision to survey customers to determine their satisfaction with a company's products.

2-10. USX is a major manufacturer of steel. Identify a planning and a control decision USX managers are likely to make concerning each of the following: (a) financing, (b) investing, and (c) operating activities.

2-11. Vladimire Polyester owns a small men's clothing store and employs a small sales force. He buys from manufacturers and sells to customers. His financing comes from operations and a loan from a local bank. He pays sales, payroll, and income taxes. He also pays for electricity, water, and telephone utility services. List each of the parties involved in an exchange with Vladimire's store. For each, identify the resources or services that are exchanged. Also, briefly identify the type of information required to complete each exchange.

2-12. A telephone book is an example of an information system. How is the system designed to meet the needs of users? What limitations does the way a telephone book is organized place on its use?

2-13. Listed below are types of information available in a company's management information system. Identify those types that are likely to be provided by the accounting information system by writing Yes next to the item. Write No next to those that are not provided by the accounting system.

a. The cost of merchandise sold to customers.
b. The number of units of product 101A sold to customers on 12/24/95.
c. The number of customers who made purchases during April.
d. The dollar amount of sales for April.
e. The product styles available for sale.
f. The ages of employees.
g. The number of machines used to produce product 12C.
h. The cost of the machines used to produce product 12C allocated to production in January.
i. The quality of goods produced in division B.
j. The cost of goods produced in division B.

2-14. The Ink Co. is a small printing company owned and managed by B. Franklin. Franklin takes orders from customers and writes the pertinent information on an order form. One copy of the order form is given to the customer. Another copy is sent to the print shop where the job is completed. The shop operator writes a bill that lists the charges for materials and labor for the job. Then the bill is attached to the order and sent back to Franklin. Customers return for their orders and pay the amounts listed on the bills. The bills then are marked PAID. One copy is given to the customer and a second copy is sent to the bookkeeper, who records the sale in the company's accounting records. Franklin deposits the cash or checks received from customers at a local bank. The bank deposit slip is sent to the bookkeeper for confirmation and to record available cash. Develop a simple diagram to chart the flow of documents and information through the system Ink Co. uses to process orders and record sales transactions.

2-15. K. Khan is owner of an import business, Khan's Imports. He wants to develop a management information system for his business. He is unclear about the particular role of an accounting system in a management information system. Explain to Khan the purpose of an accounting system and how it differs from other parts of a management information system.

2-16. Able Transportation Co. is a trucking company that delivers freight throughout the U. S. and Canada. One of the primary costs of the company's operations is gas used to fuel the trucks. The truck operators purchase gas from commercial suppliers. These purchases are accumulated and recorded to expense each month for each region based on the number of miles travelled in the region. The expenses are included in the regional income statements prepared each month that top managers use to evaluate the performance of regional managers. Identify the components of the accounting information system represented by these events.

2-17. Louise McEnroe is a stockholder of National Concrete Co., a major supplier of building materials. Today, Louise received information that National Concrete sustained a major loss from operations during the most recent quarter and is expecting even bigger losses during the coming quarter. How can this information, available to Louise and other decision makers, affect the transformation process of National Concrete during the coming fiscal period?

2-18. Yashiko Takawa is a loan officer at a major bank. Hendrick Swindler recently applied for a small business loan for his dry cleaning company, Take 'Em to the Cleaners. As part of the application, Swindler was asked to provide an income statement and balance sheet for his company. These statements revealed impressive performance information. What concerns might Yashiko have about the information provided by Swindler? What actions might she take to relieve these concerns?

2-19. Dr. Ben Gazara is a general practitioner. Among his financial records is a list of patient charges and payments. An example record follows:

Patient: Ben Cartwright, One Ponderosa, Beverly Hills, CA, 90201

Date	Charges	Payments	Balance Due
6/18/95	$120.00		$120.00
7/4/95		$120.00	0
9/23/95	$350.00		$350.00

How is this information system useful to Dr. Gazara's practice? For what kinds of decisions could the system be used?

2-20. Listed below are some of the accounts that appear in the accounting system of Hides, Inc., a manufacturer of leather goods. Indicate the type of account by writing asset, liability, owners' equity, revenue, or expense next to each account title.

a. Accounts Receivable
b. Accounts Payable
c. Sales
d. Cash
e. Leather Products
f. Display Equipment
g. Leather (materials)
h. Common Stock
i. Cost of Goods Sold
j. Interest Expense
k. Notes Payable
l. Retained Earnings
m. Supplies Expense
n. Utilities Expense
o. Wages Expense
p. Wages Payable

2-21. Balance sheet accounts for Fern's Florist are listed below. Prepare a schedule to demonstrate that assets = liabilities + owner's equity for the company.

Accounts Payable	$13,700
Accounts Receivable	8,300
Buildings	159,000
Cash	2,400
Equipment	25,500
Flowers and Plants	37,000
Notes Payable	122,000
Proprietor's Capital	94,900
Wages Payable	1,600

2-22. The following events occurred during December for the Christmas Cookie Co.:

a. Consumed $80,000 of flour, sugar, and other ingredients for cookies sold.
b. Paid $130,000 for December wages.
c. Paid $32,000 for utilities consumed in December.
d. Sold $312,000 of cookies, receiving $250,000 of cash. The remainder was an increase in Accounts Receivable.
e. Consumed $20,000 of supplies and other items.

Prepare an income statement and a schedule showing resources acquired and consumed for December for the company.

2-23. Amora Mudala opened a music store in a local mall, selling CDs and tapes. She invested $40,000 in the business and borrowed $60,000 from a local bank. The following additional events occurred during April, the first month of operations:

a. Paid cash for equipment costing $25,000.
b. Purchased an inventory of CDs and tapes for $60,000 in cash.
c. Sold one-third of the CDs and tapes for a cash sales price of $40,000.
d. Paid expenses:

employee wages	$5,000
rent	8,000
utilities	2,000
interest	600

e. Recorded an expense for use of equipment for month of $500.

Use the following format to describe the data that would be contained in the accounting data base after recording these transactions for April.

RESOURCES:
Assets Acquired:
Assets Consumed:
Total Assets

OPERATIONS:
Revenues:
Expenses:
Net Income

FINANCES:
Creditors:
Owner's Investment:
Reinvested Profits:
Total Finances

2-24. Listed below are transactions for Perez Manufacturing Co. For each transaction, describe the accounts that are involved and how each account is affected by the transaction. Show expenses as negative amounts. The first transaction is described as an example.

a. Juanita Perez invested $20,000 in the company.

Assets		Liabilities and Owners' Equity		Revenues and Expenses	
a. Cash	+$20,000	Owner's investment	+$20,000		

b. Sale of goods for $60,000 on credit (increase in Accounts Receivable).
c. Purchase of raw materials for $90,000. Cash is paid.
d. Payment of wages for services provided, $15,000.
e. Paid back part of loan to a bank (Notes Payable), $3,000.
f. Purchase of equipment for $8,000 on credit (increase in Accounts Payable).
g. Paid utilities company for services consumed, $1,200.

2-25. The Har-Mone Co. is a producer of perfumes and cosmetics. The following changes were recorded in the company's accounting records during October. For each item, describe the transaction that would have resulted in the recording. The first item is described as an example.

a. Cash increased $20,000; Owners' Investment increased $20,000. *The owners invested $20,000 in the company.*
b. Accounts Receivable increased $30,000; Sales Revenue increased $30,000.
c. Equipment increased $15,000; Cash decreased $15,000.
d. Materials increased $18,000; Accounts Payable increased $18,000.
e. Supplies expense increased $3,000; Supplies decreased $3,000.
f. Cash increased $10,000; Notes Payable increased $10,000.
g. Inventory decreased $9,000; Cost of Goods Sold increased $9,000.

2-26. Edgar Feinstein is considering an investment of $10,000 in either of two companies. Summary financial statement information is provided for each company below. From an analysis of the information presented, what advice would you give Edgar about which company to invest in? Why?

	Arsino Chemical Co.	Basalt, Inc.
Balance Sheet:		
Assets	$1,500,000	$20,000,000
Liabilities	1,000,000	12,000,000
Equity	500,000	8,000,000
Income Statement:		
Revenues	$400,000	$2,400,000
Expenses	220,000	1,400,000
Net Income	180,000	1,000,000

PROBLEMS

PROBLEM 2-1 Risk and Return

Carlotta Icon is considering a major investment in the common stock of one of the companies listed below. She has asked your assistance in determining the comparative risk and return of these investments. Your extensive financial knowledge leads you to suggest that past earnings performance could be evaluated as a potential indicator of future performance. Comparative historical information is presented below for both firms.

(amounts in millions of dollars)

	1986	1987	1988	1989	1990
USX					
net income	$ 8	$ 9	$10	$11	$13
total assets	61	59	68	73	70
TWA					
net income	$42	$(5)	$13	$31	$(23)
total assets	62	63	64	65	66

Required Compute (a) the return on assets (net income ÷ total assets) for each year for each company and (b) the average ratio of net income to total assets over the five years for each company. (c) Compare the returns for the two companies. Write a brief memo to Carlotta Icon describing your findings as to comparative risk and return of these two firms. (d) Which firm would you recommend to Carlotta? Why?

PROBLEM 2-2 Identifying Information Desired from the Accounting System

Tree-Top Airlines began as a small commuter line 10 years ago but has grown into the seventh largest airline in America with a strong regional route system. In addition, it has many routes to America's commercial centers and a few selected international routes. Tree-Top has a fleet of 300 planes and approximately 9,000 employees who (by company policy) must all be stockholders. After airline deregulation, the company grew rapidly by using a clever combination of long-term financing from banks and leasing companies. It is now the largest employer in its home state. Its stock is widely traded on the American Stock Exchange. In light of the company's rapid growth, the controller is performing a detailed and complete reevaluation of the firm's accounting information system. While the system has been updated and improved constantly through the years, the controller is concerned whether it is providing useful information to the appropriate parties.

Required (a) Identify the parties that have an economic interest in Tree-Top Airlines. (b) For each party, identify the type of information that should be provided by Tree-Top's accounting information system.

PROBLEM 2-3 Compensation Arrangements for Managers

You are a member of the Executive Compensation Committee of the Board of Directors for the Fresh Catch Food Company. Your committee has been directed to investigate the feasibility of adopting an incentive compensation plan for the company's top-level management. Included in this group is the CEO, the president, the controller, and the vice presidents of finance, marketing, and manufacturing. The Board of Directors has requested that you consider the following options and prepare a recommendation for the full Board of Directors.

1. Year-end cash bonuses based on exceeding sales targets for the year
2. Year-end cash bonuses based on exceeding profit targets for the year
3. Free shares of company stock if the stock price goes up by a target amount over a three year period

Related to your full-time executive position in another firm, you recently attended a seminar where it was claimed that executive compensation plans can sometimes affect the content of financial reports provided to owners. The chair of the Executive Compensation Committee has asked you to write a brief memo to the rest of the committee describing the potential effects and problems you see in a compensation plan.

Required Prepare that memo (in good form). Be sure to include examples to support your main points.

PROBLEM 2-4 Planning and Control Decisions

Connie Thompson is manager of the Long-Term Care Division of the Cooper County Health Department. With its $150 million budget, the division is responsible for provision of long-term care services (often in nursing homes) to the elderly and physically disabled. The division contracts with providers for nursing home care, adult day care, in-home visiting nurses, and a variety of other long-term care services. In her position of manager, Connie makes a variety of planning and control decisions on a daily basis. On a recent Tuesday morning, Connie sat at her desk with the following issues and decisions needing attention:

1. Two months ago, the child of a nursing home patient filed a complaint alleging mistreatment of his parent. An investigation revealed substance to the complaint and several remedial actions have been developed. Connie must decide which actions to require of the nursing home.
2. For nearly a year, a task force in Connie's department has been developing an experimental alternative to nursing home care. It will require a waiver of the federal Medicaid rules but has the potential to provide better quality care at a lower cost to

taxpayers. Connie must decide whether to proceed with this initiative via a formal request to Washington, D.C.

3. Budget problems caused the state legislature to reduce funding for a certain program. A citizens' committee has recommended priorities to Connie for trimming the program. Connie must make and announce the final decision today.
4. Connie is contemplating engagement of a consultant to conduct an evaluation of her division. Such an evaluation would judge whether the goals and objectives of her unit are being carried out in an effective and efficient manner.
5. Connie's immediate superior has proposed moving a service unit currently located in another division to the Long-Term Care Division. The unit is not operating effectively because of a variety of problems within the unit. Connie must provide a written recommendation to her supervisor by tomorrow about how this new unit could be integrated into the work of her Division.

Required (a) Discuss the differences between a planning decision and a control decision. (b) Specify whether each issue described above is a planning decision or a control decision. Briefly justify your answer.

PROBLEM 2-5 The Components of an Information System

The West Side Church is a local congregation of about 500 members and regular attenders. At each church service an offering is taken; nearly all contributions are by check. At the end of each service, the head ushers, Fred Westlund and Dale Chapetta, turn over the proceeds to the church treasurer, Margaret Gorsey. Margaret makes a confidential record of each identifiable contribution (for year-end tax statements to contributors), totals the amount received, and deposits it. The deposit slip is given to the church bookkeeper, Zenia Flowers. Zenia enters the deposit in the church's ledger each week. At the end of the month, Zenia summarizes all accounts and prepares a Statement of Contributions, Expenditures, and Cash on Hand. This document is distributed to members of the congregation.

Required Prepare a diagram like the one in Exhibit 2-4 that shows the components of an information system. For each component of the system, identify the persons, documents, or events from the narrative above that correspond to the component.

PROBLEM 2-6 Entering Data Into an Accounting Information System

Melocky Beach Company sells a variety of trinkets and do-dads to tourists on the beach. Each day teenagers are paid 20% of the sales they make by hawking the wares up and down the beach. The company was formed only recently and given approval by the local city council to operate this business. The following events are the first in the company's short history:

a. The company was formed when José Melocky contributed $2,300 to the firm.
b. The Ocean Bank loaned the firm $7,000 in exchange for the firm's one-year note payable.
c. Merchandise costing $6,000 was purchased on 30-day credit from Cabo Company.
d. Goods costing $1,500 were sold to tourists at prices totalling $4,500 in cash, and the teenagers were paid their commissions.
e. A payment of $2,000 was made to Cabo Company.
f. Goods costing $1,900 were sold for cash totalling $5,500, and the teenagers were paid their commissions.
g. A payment of $2,800 is made to the Ocean Bank. (Ignore interest.)
h. José Melocky withdrew $2,000 from Reinvested Profits for personal uses.

Assume the company uses the following set of accounts:

Cash	Reinvested Profits
Inventory	Sales
Payable to Cabo	Cost of Sales
Notes Payable	Commissions Expense
Investment by Owner	

Required (a) For each event above, identify whether it is a financing activity, an investing activity, or an operating activity. (b) Determine how each event affects the accounting data base. Show the account balances that should appear in the accounting data base after each of the events above has been recorded. Assume profits are immediately reinvested in the company. Event (a) is done for you as an example.

	Assets		Liabilities and Owners' Equity				Revenues and Expenses		
	Cash	Inventory	Payable to Cabo	Notes Payable	Investment by Owner	Reinvested Profits	Sales	Cost of Sales	Commissions Expense
a. Financing	+2,300				+2,300				
	$2,300				$2,300				

PROBLEM 2-7 Entering Data Into an Accounting Information System

Randy had a hard time finding a summer job when he went home from college this summer so he decided to go into the lawn mowing business for himself. He had the following business activities during the month of June.

a. Used $200 of his own money and borrowed $700 from his father to start the business.
b. Spent $200 to purchase a used lawnmower; an additional $75 for a lawn edger; $50 for a wheelbarrow; and $25 for hand clippers and shears.
c. Bought a (very) used pickup truck for $800 from Bettis Motors. He made a $250 down payment and signed a note payable for the balance.
d. During the first two weeks, Randy performed $300 of lawnmowing services. Customers paid $200 of this in cash and promised the remaining payment the next week (use Accounts Receivable). He paid $40 for gas, oil, and other supplies.
e. Collected the remaining amount of cash from prior lawnmowing.
f. During the last half of the month, Randy performed $510 of lawnmowing services. All but $50 was collected in full at the completion of each respective job. He paid out $75 for gas, oil, and other supplies.
g. Paid back one-half of the amount he had borrowed from his father.
h. Randy withdrew $100 from Reinvested Profits for his personal use.

Randy knew from taking an accounting class at college that the following accounts would be needed to keep track of his business activities.

Cash	Investment by Owner
Accounts Receivable	Reinvested Profits
Equipment	Sales Revenue
Note Payable—Dad	Expense
Note Payable—Bettis Motors	

Required (a) Show what the various account balances will be after each transaction is entered into the accounting data base. Assume that any profits are immediately reinvested in the business. Transaction (a) is done for you as an example. (b) Prepare a financial report (as of the end of June) that lists the firm's resources and finances. List the resources on the left side and the finances on the right. Total each list to show that they are equal in amount. (c) Prepare a financial report that summarizes operations for the month of June. List revenues first and then expenses.

	Assets			Liabilities and Owners' Equity				Revenues and Expenses	
	Cash	Accounts Receivable	Equipment	Note Payable—Dad	Note Payable—Bettis	Investment by Owner	Reinvested Profits	Sales Revenue	Expenses
a.	+900 $900			+700 $700		+200 $200			

PROBLEM 2-8 Reconstructing Events from Information in the Accounting Data Base

Horace and Hortense have just established a home-cleaning service. They charge $15 per hour per person and usually are paid by check upon completion of a job. For certain customers, they send a bill immediately and are paid promptly by return mail. Their out-of-pocket expenses are rather low, usually only cleaning supplies and transportation. They use a simple accounting system in which they update their account balances after each transaction. Revenues and expenses are recorded immediately in Reinvested Profits. Listed below are their updated account balances after each of the ten transactions that occurred during their first week in business.

	Cash	Accounts Receivable	Supplies	Notes Payable	Investment by Owner	Reinvested Profits	Sales Revenue	Expenses
a.	$ 100				$100			
b.	250			$ 250				
c.	– 75		$ 75					
d.	300	$ 60				$ 360	$360	
e.			–40			– 40		$40
f.	– 50		50					
g.	–160			–160				
h.	60	–60						
i.	400	50				450	450	
j.			–60			– 60		60
k.	–500					–500		
l.	50	–50						

Required Describe each of the firm's first twelve transactions, specifying the amounts involved.

PROBLEM 2-9 Ethics and Accounting Systems

Charlie Clancy owns an appliance store that sells major appliances such as washers and refrigerators. Charlie obtained financing for his business from a local bank. In January of each year, the bank requires Charlie to prepare and submit an income statement and balance sheet for the past year. Charlie also prepares his personal income tax return at this time and includes the profits earned from his appliance business.

Charlie purchases appliances from a major manufacturer throughout the year. Because of inflation, the costs of the appliances to Charlie typically increase during the year. Often the units purchased at the end of the year cost 10% to 15% more than those purchased at the beginning of the year.

In preparing his financial statements for the bank, Charlie uses the costs of the earliest units from his stock in computing Cost of Goods Sold for the year. These costs are subtracted from revenues to compute net income on the income statement. The last units purchased are reported as part of Inventory on the balance sheet. In preparing his tax return, Charlie subtracts from revenues the costs of the *most recent* units purchased to compute taxable income.

Required (a) What are the financial implications of the measurement rules Charlie uses for his financial statements and income tax return? (b) Are there ethical problems with Charlie's decisions about measurement rules?

PROBLEM 2-10 Ethics and Accounting Systems

(a) Henry Bradshaw owns a furniture store. In January 1996, Henry applied for a loan from a local bank because of a cash shortfall he has been facing. As part of the loan application, the bank required Henry to submit an income statement for the most recent year, ended in December 1995. Henry owes a sizeable sum to a furniture manufacturer for merchandise he purchased and received in 1995. Much of the merchandise was sold in 1995. Henry delayed payment for the merchandise until January 1996. Also, he did not record an expense for the cost of the merchandise sold until January, though he recorded the sales as revenue in 1995.

Required What are the financial and ethical implications of Henry's actions?

(b) Alley Smith is Budget Director for a midwestern state that is facing a financial crisis. It is required by law to spend no more than the total revenues it collects during its fiscal year, which ends on September 30. State employees are paid on the last day of each month, and the wages are recorded in the accounting system as an expenditure when paid. Because of the current financial crisis, the state is in danger of spending more than the revenues it expects to collect during the current year. To help solve the problem, Alley changed the state's accounting system in September of the current year so employee wages are not recorded until the first of the month. Therefore, September wages will be recognized in October of the next fiscal year.

Required What are the financial and ethical implications of Alley's actions?

PROBLEM 2-11 Design and Use of an Information System

C. Miranda is owner of a company that manufactures wax fruit, Miranda Fruit Co. The fruit, which is sold to hat makers, florists, and novelty shops, is packaged in lots of 100 and is manufactured in three sizes: small, medium, and large. Orders are received from customers by mail or phone. Customers indicate the size and quantity of product they desire, and orders are filled and shipped within three days. Bills are shipped with the orders, which customers are expected to pay in full within 30 days of the billing date. Delinquent accounts are noted for a second billing. Those that are over 60 days old are marked so no additional orders are accepted until the accounts have been paid. The following account balances were outstanding at the end of March, 1995:

Company	Amount	Due Date
Tropical Hats	$9,000	March 10
Penway Florists	4,000	April 4
Hurley Hats	12,000	April 12
Oscar's Novelties	7,000	April 20

Lots are priced at $100 for large, $85 for medium, and $75 for small. The following transactions occurred during April:

April 3 Received payment of $4,000 from Penway Florists.
7 Received order from Hurley Hats for 20 lots of large, 30 lots of medium, and 10 lots of small.
9 Shipped Hurley order with bill.
10 Billed Tropical Hats for overdue account.
12 Received payment from Hurley Hats for $12,000.
18 Received order from Penway Florists for 10 lots of large, 25 lots of medium, and 40 lots of small.
19 Received payment of $7,000 from Oscar's Novelties.
21 Shipped order to Penway with bill.
24 Received payment of $5,000 from Tropical Hats.
28 Received payment from Penway for total amount owed.

Required Design a form as part of an information system Miranda Fruit Co. can use to keep track of its customers' orders and payments. Using the form, record data for each of the April transactions.

PROBLEM 2-12 Multiple Choice Overview of the Chapter

1. The value of accounting information is greatest when it:
   a. has been obtained at low cost.
   b. meets the needs of users.
   c. supports expansion of the business into new products or markets.
   d. reports favorable results allowing dividends and bonuses to be paid.
2. An investor is evaluating the potential investments described below. Past financial results of these two companies are judged to be indicative of future returns and risk.

Year	Ball Bearing Profits	Beach Ball Profits
A	$ 8	$ 3
B	9	22
C	10	7

Which investment appears to have the highest return and highest risk from the information provided?

	Highest return	Highest risk
a.	Ball Bearing	Ball Bearing
b.	Ball Bearing	Beach Ball
c.	Beach Ball	Ball Bearing
d.	Beach Ball	Beach Ball

3. Which combination below correctly matches the type and audience of accounting information?

	Information prepared primarily for decision makers inside the firm	Information prepared primarily for decision makers outside the firm
a.	managerial accounting	managerial accounting
b.	financial accounting	managerial accounting
c.	managerial accounting	financial accounting
d.	financial accounting	financial accounting

4. The primary difference between a planning decision and a control decision is that:
   a. investors make planning decisions while management makes control decisions.
   b. planning decisions involve dollars while control decisions involve qualitative factors.
   c. planning decisions involve revenues while control decisions involve expenses.
   d. planning decisions are developmental while control decisions are corrective.
5. Accounting information is developed by an organization to assist its managers in dealing with which of the following?

	Suppliers	Government officials
a.	Yes	Yes
b.	Yes	No
c.	No	Yes
d.	No	No

6. Which of the following is a true statement concerning an information system?
   a. It must be computerized to function efficiently.
   b. It increases risk but decreases expected return.
   c. It eliminates the need for an audit.
   d. It creates information from data.
7. Management information systems supply information:

	Needed by managers for internal decision making	Managers must provide to persons outside the firm
a.	Yes	Yes
b.	Yes	No
c.	No	Yes
d.	No	No

8. The accounting information system used by Ombozzi Medical Supply keeps track of the cost of each inventory item, its purchase date, and its supplier. No record is kept of the transportation company that delivered the goods. These facts deal most closely with which component of the accounting information system?
   a. reporting rules
   b. transformation process
   c. measurement rules
   d. decision processes
9. Liability and owners' equity accounts usually arise from which type of activities?
   a. investing
   b. financing
   c. operating
   d. manufacturing
10. Expresso Delivery Service purchased a new delivery truck for $21,000 by making a $4,000 cash payment and giving a $17,000 note payable to the seller. The net effect of the transaction on the company's total assets and total liabilities was:

	Assets	Liabilities
a.	increased	increased
b.	no change	increased
c.	increased	decreased
d.	decreased	increased

CASES

CASE 2-1 Designing an Accounting Information System

For about a year, Frank Poppa has been operating a hot dog stand in the parking lot of a major discount retailer in a suburban area. The stand appears to be a pushcart but is actually a small trailer that is towed from home each day. Frank cleverly designed the stand to include storage compartments, a propane gas cooker, insulated coolers for canned sodas, and plenty of space for condiments, napkins, etc. What started out as a "weekend gig" to pick up a few extra bucks has turned into a full-time vocation. Frank soon found that on a hot summer day, he could easily take in more than $1,000 from sales of a full line of fancy hot dogs and cold sodas.

About four months ago, he decided to expand to more locations. He found that large discount retailers were quite happy to provide him adequate space near the front door because customers enjoyed the convenience and the stand helped build traffic for the retailer. Frank formed Poppa's Dogs Co. and negotiated contracts with several retailers to provide pushcart operations outside their stores. The contracts generally call for Poppa's Dogs to pay a location fee to the retailer plus 3% of the pushcart's sales.

Frank plans to be very careful when hiring the people necessary to operate the five new pushcart locations. He is confident he can assess good moral character and avoid hiring anyone who would take advantage of him. Frank will have to spend about $3,000 for each new pushcart and related equipment. In addition, he will have to invest in an inventory of hot dogs, condiments, and sodas for each location. A local bank has agreed to provide financing.

Up to now, Frank has maintained an informal accounting system consisting of an envelope full of receipts and his personal checking account. The system has served him well so far, but he is finding that more often he is getting his personal financial activities confused with those of his business. Frank is positive the business is profitable because he seems to have more money left at the end of the month than he did when he was working full-time as an auto mechanic. He has decided he needs a better accounting system and has decided to consult with a CPA he knows to see what she might recommend.

Required What information does Frank obtain from his current accounting system? What information should Frank be able to obtain from a new accounting system? Make recommendations to Frank regarding how he can improve his accounting system and identify a chart (list) of accounts that you would expect to find in Frank's new accounting system. For each account, identify whether it is an asset, liability, owners' equity, revenue, or expense.

CASE 2-2 Determining Measurement Rules for an Accounting System

(Read Case 2-1 before reading the additional information below.) In general, Frank expects the daily operations of Poppa's Dogs to go as follows: All carts will be parked at his home each evening. Each morning, each operator will pick up a trailer and a supply of hot dogs, condiments, sodas, and a change fund. At the end of each day the trailers, remaining inventory, supplies, and the day's receipts will be returned to Frank. Operators will be paid each Friday.

Required (a) Describe what a measurement rule is in relation to an accounting information system. (b) For each event that follows, recommend and defend a measurement rule. Also, specify what information this measurement rule would exclude from the accounting data base. (c) Identify two additional events that are likely for the company and construct a measurement rule to fit those situations.

1. On Wednesday, June 5, 1995, five gallons of relish ($5.50) and five gallons of mustard ($3.86) were ordered on credit from Wallace Food Supply. The goods were picked up that same day at 4 p.m.
2. On Thursday, June 6, 1995, a hot dog (Cajun style—$1.75) and can of soda (7-Up—$0.50) were sold for cash to Julie Wyndross at 11:15 a.m.
3. On Friday, June 7, 1995, a new employee (Pat Carlucci) was hired to operate pushcart #6 at Home Center Discount Club.

CASE 2-3 Designing an Information System for Large Quantities of Data

Your client Gary Gearshift has unexpectedly obtained national publicity and is suddenly hot property in the entertainment world with his music played on the Oilpan Flute. As his agent, you are arranging for a 3-cassette package of his "best loved favorites" to be marketed on late night cable TV. After consulting with experts, you reasonably expect that you will receive up to 1,000 telephone orders per day for approximately 30 days. After that, you expect orders to fade away to near zero.

Given the tremendous outpouring of national enthusiasm for this fad, you will charge a premium price of $45 and offer three easy monthly payments of $15 each. There will be a separate charge for shipping and handling ($6 due with the first installment) and 6% sales tax on each order (also due with the first installment). A deal has been made with a music production company to provide 3-cassette packages to you for $5 each. They can be ordered in batches of 500 and will be delivered in 7 days. You decide to build an accounting system to keep track of this venture.

Required (a) List the information you would like the accounting system to provide you (for example, total sales for each day). Briefly explain why the information is important. (b) Design an information system that will produce the information you need. Identify the components of the system (what are the primary inputs, processes, and outputs of the system?).

PROJECTS

PROJECT 2-1 Interviewing a Decision Maker

Select an organization in your community that interests you. This might be a business firm, a government agency, or some other nonprofit organization. Make an appointment with the owner, general manager, or a department manager to interview them about how they use accounting information to make decisions in their jobs. Every organization and manager is different but, in general, you want to understand the types of decisions the manager has to make and whether he or she relies on financial information to guide any of those decisions. Further, you want to learn how the information affects the decision that needs to be made. Ask the manager to give you some specific examples of decisions that were affected by accounting information. Another way of addressing the issue is to ask which management decisions would be tougher (or riskier) to make if there were no financial information available to the decision maker. Write a short report from the information and examples you obtained in your interview.

PROJECT 2-2 Comparing Risk and Return

Go to the library and find the latest edition of *Moody's Industrial Manual*. From the alphabetical index, select three companies, including at least one that operates in the state where you are attending college. Estimate risk and return for each company for the most recent ten years. Estimate return by computing the ratio of net income to total assets (net income ÷ total assets) for each year. Prepare a graph of the returns for ten years for the three companies. (You will need to use several different years of *Moody's* manual to obtain the data you need.) Assume you are advising your instructor about potential investments. Write a memo evaluating the companies you have chosen. Include your graph and provide an assessment of the relative returns and risks of the companies. Recommend one for investment.

PROJECT 2-3 Compensation Contracts with Managers

Select three companies whose annual reports are in your library. Try to find one company whose name starts with the same letter as your first name, a second company using the first letter of your middle name, and a third company using the first letter of your last name. Find the most recent annual report for each of your three companies. In the back half of each annual report you should find the financial statements which will be followed by several Notes to the Financial Statements. These notes generally include important information explaining specific items on the financial statements. Carefully read through these notes to find any information about executive compensation. Common forms of executive compensation that are disclosed in the notes include bonus plans, profit-sharing plans, and stock option plans. Make a photocopy of this information and label it with the company's name. Your choices must have information on executive compensation. If any of your choices do not, substitute another firm having the same first letter in its name. Write a memorandum to your instructor that compares and contrasts the practices of the three different firms, and list any questions these disclosures bring to mind. Attach the photocopies to your memo.

PROJECT 2-4 Corporate Balance Sheets

Select three companies whose annual reports are in your library. Try to find one company that is a manufacturer, one that is a retailer, and one that is a utility. Find the most recent annual report for each of your three companies. In the back half of each annual report you should find the financial statements. Find the statement titled Balance Sheet (often Consolidated Balance Sheet or Statement of Financial Position). List the major resources reported for each company for the most recent year. Which resources appear to be most important for each company? Also, list the major liabilities and the total amount of stockholders' equity. Compute the ratio of total assets to total liabilities for each company (total assets ÷ total liabilities). Compare the ratios for the three companies. What reasons can you provide for why different companies rely on different types of resources and financing?

PROJECT 2-5 Personal Balance Sheet

Prepare a list of the major types of resources that belong to you: clothing, stereo equipment, car, etc. Estimate the value of each type of resource from what you paid for it or what you think it would cost to replace it. Also, list your personal debts: bank loans, student loans, car loans, etc. Prepare a balance sheet that organizes your resources and finances, and report the difference between your assets and liabilities as Personal Capital. Along with your balance sheet, prepare notes that explain how you computed the value of each type of asset and liability.

PROJECT 2-6 Planning and Control Decisions

In recent issues of business publications, such as *The Wall Street Journal*, *Business Week*, and *Fortune*, find three articles or news items that describe management planning decisions. Also, find three that describe management control decisions. Briefly summarize the decisions described in the articles. Note the publication, date, and page number for each article.

CHAPTER 3

ACCOUNTING MEASUREMENT

CHAPTER
Overview

Chapter 1 described organizations as a transformation process, which is the primary source of data for the accounting system. Chapter 2 examined information needs of decision makers that affect the development of information systems, and introduced the accounting information system as illustrated below. This chapter examines some fundamental concepts of accounting measurement. These concepts guide the development of measurement rules in the accounting information system. The concepts determine which events in the transformation process are recorded by the accounting system and when they are recorded.

Major topics covered in this chapter include:

- Accounting measurement of the transformation process.
- The importance of time in accounting measurement.
- The relationship between accrual and cash measurements.
- The purpose of accrual basis accounts.

CHAPTER
Objectives

Once you have completed this chapter, you should be able to:

1. Demonstrate the use of an accounting system to record financing, investing, and operating activities.
2. Summarize the information an accounting system provides about a transformation process.
3. Explain the implications of the going concern principle for the transformation process.
4. Explain the implications of periodic measurement for accounting information.
5. Explain why change in cash is not a valid measure of an organization's performance for a period.
6. Explain why cash flow from operating activities is not a complete measure of an organization's performance for a period.
7. Distinguish the accrual basis from the cash basis and explain why the accrual basis is used.
8. Reconcile cash and accrual measures of operating activities.
9. Identify information reported by an accrual basis accounting system.
10. Explain the purposes of different account types in an accrual accounting system.

ACCOUNTING FOR THE TRANSFORMATION PROCESS

Objective 1
Demonstrate the use of an accounting system to record financing, investing, and operating activities.

The accounting information system provides a means of recording, summarizing, and reporting an organization's transformation process. This process consists of (1) **financing activities:** the acquisition and management of financial resources, (2) **investing activities:** the investment of financial resources in other resources, and (3) **operating activities:** the use of resources to produce, sell, and distribute goods and services.

The complexity of an organization's accounting system depends on the complexity of the organization's transformation process. Factors such as the size of the organization, the number of geographical locations in which it operates, the number of different products it manufactures and sells, and the types of financing it uses affect the size and complexity of the accounting system. Thus, a small business, like a hair styling salon, requires a relatively simple accounting system, while a chain of Wal-Mart stores requires a relatively complex system. A multinational company like Ford Motor Company is extremely complex. Accounting systems may need to accommodate language, currency, and regulatory differences among countries. The information needs of decision makers increase with the size and complexity of an organization. An organization's accounting system becomes more complex as the information needs of decision makers increase.

Though some accounting systems are more complex than others, most accounting systems have similar objectives and use similar procedures. As a basis for discussion, consider the transformation cycle of a small business, Produce Transit Co., owned by Y. Lemon. The company contracts with a chain of grocery stores in Michigan to provide them with fresh produce from Florida. Lemon invests $2,000 from savings and borrows $1,000 from a friend to finance the business venture, agreeing to pay interest of $25 a week, beginning June 1, until the loan is repaid. With $3,000 available, Lemon rents a truck for one week for $500 and leaves for Florida on June 1.

On June 1, the account balances shown in Exhibit 3-1 represent the financial situation for Produce Transit Co. immediately after renting the truck but before leaving for Florida.

Exhibit 3-1

Produce Transit Company
Account Summary
June 1, 1996

Assets =		Liabilities + Owner's Equity		Revenues − Expenses	
Cash	$2,500	Loan	$1,000	Revenues	$0
Prepaid rent—truck	500	Investment by owner	2,000	Expenses	0
Total	$3,000	Total	$3,000	Total	$0

Analysis of cash:

Cash received:	Investment by owner	$2,000
	Loan	1,000
Cash paid:	Truck rental	(500)
	Total	$2,500

The company obtained $3,000 of financing but spent $500 for rent on the truck. In exchange for the cash, the company has a resource available for use (a truck) that was not available previously. The truck is represented in the accounts by PREPAID RENT because the company did not purchase the truck but rented it for one week. ***Prepaid rent* is an asset representing the cost of a rented resource to be consumed in the near future.** For example, if you pay your apartment rent at the beginning of a month, you have an asset, prepaid rent. Note that in Exhibit 3-1 the amount of assets equals the amount of liabilities plus owners' equity.

Lemon returned to Michigan on June 6. The following costs were incurred as part of the trip:

Purchase of produce	$2,000
Food and lodging	220
Gas	280

On June 6, immediately before selling the produce, the company has an additional resource, $2,000 of produce. But, all of its cash has been consumed:

Cash received:	Investment by owner	$2,000
	Loan	1,000
Cash paid:	Truck rental	(500)
	Food/lodging	(220)
	Gas	(280)
	Produce	(2,000)
	Total cash	$ 0

On June 7, Lemon sells the produce to the grocery chain for $3,500 and pays back the loan of $1,000 and interest of $25. After selling the produce on June 7 and repaying the loan plus interest, the company's financial condition would appear as illustrated in Exhibit 3-2.

Exhibit 3-2

Produce Transit Company
Account Summary
For Week Ended June 7, 1996

Assets =		Liabilities + Owner's Equity		+ Revenues − Expenses		
Cash	$2,475	Loan	$ 0	Revenues		$3,500
Prepaid rent	0	Investment by owner	2,000	Expenses:		
Produce	0			Cost of goods sold	(2,000)	
				Truck rental	(500)	
				Food and lodging	(220)	
				Gas	(280)	
				Interest	(25)	(3,025)
Total	$2,475	Total	$2,000	Total		$ 475

Analysis of cash:

Cash received:	Investment by owner	$2,000
	Loan	1,000
	Sales	3,500
Cash paid:	Truck rental	(500)
	Food	(220)
	Gas	(280)
	Produce	(2,000)
	Loan repayment	(1,000)
	Interest	(25)
	Total	$2,475

During a fiscal period, the accounting equation ASSETS = LIABILITIES + OWNERS' EQUITY must be extended to include revenues and expenses:

ASSETS = LIABILITIES + OWNERS' EQUITY + REVENUES − EXPENSES

In Exhibit 3-2 this equation contains the following amounts: $2,475 (assets) = $0 (liabilities) + $2,000 (owners' equity) + $3,500 (revenues) − $3,025 (expenses). If the revenue and expense account balances ($475 = $3,500 − $3,025) were transferred to owners' equity on June 7, the first two columns in the exhibit would be equal: $2,475 (assets) = $0 (liabilities) + $2,475 (owners' equity). This relationship can be illustrated as follows:

Assets =		Liabilities + Owner's Equity		+ Revenues − Expenses	
Cash	$2,475	Investment by owner	2,000	Revenues	$0
		Reinvested profit	475	Expenses	0

The linkage between revenues and expenses and owners' equity is provided through reinvested profit (retained earnings account for corporations and partnership or proprietor's capital accounts for other businesses). Reinvested profit is increased by revenues and decreased by expenses for a period. Therefore, when examining account balances, it is important to know whether the revenue and expense account balances have been transferred to reinvested profit. **If revenue and expense account balances have been transferred to reinvested profit: ASSETS = LIABILITIES + OWNERS' EQUITY. If revenue and expense account balances have not yet been transferred to reinvested profit: ASSETS = LIABILITIES + OWNERS' EQUITY + REVENUES − EXPENSES.** Organizations often do not transfer revenue and expense account balances until the end of a fiscal year. Thus, during a fiscal period, these balances normally are part of the accounting equation.

As of June 7, the company has earned $475 in net income after its sale of $3,500. The price of the goods sold is $475 greater than the total cost of all the resources consumed in making the goods available for sale. Lemon now has $2,475 in cash and is $475 better off than before the venture. Because of the transactions associated with this transformation, Lemon's wealth has increased by $475. This fact is verified by the amount of cash available once all activities of the venture have been completed. The amount also is verified by the amount of net income earned from the venture. The net income figure is important because it clearly distinguishes the return *on* investment from the venture ($475) from the return *of* investment from the venture ($2,000). As explained in Chapter 1, return *of* investment is recovery by an owner of an amount invested in a business.

Objective 2
Summarize the information an accounting system provides about a transformation process.

The accounting system in this example described the economic consequences of the transformation from start to finish. It described the resources that were available during the transformation, and how the company obtained financial resources to acquire other resources. It measured the price of goods sold. It measured the costs associated with the transformation process, $3,025. It measured how well the business performed: Lemon received a return on investment of $475. These measures provide a basis for estimating future performance if Lemon chooses to continue the business.

In addition, the accounting system can be used to summarize the economic consequences of contracts the company formed with other parties.

Contracting Party	Given in Exchange	Received in Exchange	Contract Completed
Owner	Investment of $2,000	Return on investment of $475	Yes
Lender	Loan of $1,000	Repayment of loan plus interest of $25	Yes
Suppliers of:			
Truck	Use of truck	Rent of $500	Yes
Food and lodging	Food and lodging	Payment of $220	Yes
Gas	Gas	Payment of $280	Yes
Produce	Produce	Payment of $2,000	Yes
Customers	Payment of $3,500	Produce	Yes

This information is important for identifying the various participants in the transformation process and what they gave and received. Also, it is helpful to know all contracts have been completed. Anyone interested in contracting with the company in the future can use this information to evaluate the risk and return associated with the contract.

SELF-STUDY PROBLEM 3-1

On December 1, 1996, S. Claus signed a one-month contract with a toy manufacturer, Elves, Inc. Under the terms of the contract, Claus will deliver merchandise from Elves' Far North plant to locations throughout the U.S. On December 1, Claus signed a one-month lease on a sleigh and a team of reindeer for which he paid $1,500 from his savings. As an additional investment, he withdrew $3,500 from savings to cover his operating costs for the month. From these resources, he paid the following expenses in December:

Lodging	$ 750
Meals	600
Hay and oats	1,800

At the end of December, Claus was paid $5,000 by Elves, Inc., for providing delivery services.

Required

Complete the following account summary for S. Claus for December. Show the amounts of revenue and expense for Claus before the balances of these accounts are transferred to reinvested profit for December.

S. Claus
Account Summary
For Month Ended December 31, 1996

Assets =		Liabilities + Owner's Equity		+ Revenues − Expenses	
Cash		Investment by owner		Revenues	
				Expenses	____
Total	____	Total	____	Total	____

The solution to Self-Study Problem 3-1 appears at the end of the chapter.

ACCOUNTING FOR INCOMPLETE TRANSFORMATIONS

Objective 3
Explain the implications of the going concern principle for the transformation process.

The Produce Transit Co. illustration, in two respects, is not typical of the activities of most organizations. First, the transactions were simpler and fewer than those observed in most organizations. Second, and more important for the current discussion, the illustration considered a transformation that began and ended during a short period. The transformation began with the investment on June 1 and ended a week later with the sale of the produce and repayment of the loan. The transformation began with cash and ended when all resources were converted back to cash. Most organizations are going concerns: their transformation processes are continuous, extending beyond the current fiscal period. **A *going concern* is an organization with an indefinite life that is sufficiently long so that, over time, all currently incomplete transformations will be completed.**

Consider a trucking company that owns many trucks and that continuously hauls produce to different parts of the country. Cash is invested in trucks and produce and is paid to employees. The company does not stop operations periodically to sell all its trucks and produce to determine how well it is performing. The company must evaluate its performance while its transformation process is still unfinished.

Managers, owners, creditors, and other decision makers need frequent information about how well a company is doing. Important questions need to be answered before a company knows the final results of all its current activities: How much money is available to pay bills and purchase resources? How much profit has the company earned? How much money can the company distribute to owners? Therefore, organizations report the results of their financing, investing, and operating activities periodically, even though they do not know all the results of these activities. Because the results are not fully known, managers must estimate the results they expect from the operations of a particular fiscal period. These estimates may not always be precise or accurate. Often, they are better, however, than having no information until all results are known. For some companies, all the results cannot be determined for years after the period in which activities occur.

Objective 4
Explain the implications of periodic measurement for accounting information.

The accounting systems of most organizations report periodically the estimated results of financing, investing, and operating activities. ***Periodic measurement*** **occurs when the accounting system measures and reports the performance of an organization for particular fiscal periods so decisions can be made using timely information.** Managers often receive reports monthly, though more frequent reporting is common for purposes such as ordering materials, controlling production, and shipping goods.

The going concern and periodic measurement principles are important for the development of Generally Accepted Accounting Principles (GAAP). Accounting rules used to prepare reports for external users assume an organization is a going concern. If evidence exists that an organization is not a viable going concern, different accounting rules are used to measure and report its economic activities. Many corporations report summary information to their stockholders and other external users quarterly and prepare a detailed annual report. The choice of how often to report represents a tradeoff between the cost of providing the reports and the benefits users derive from timely information. Reporting frequency also results from a tradeoff between the timeliness and accuracy of information. For example, quarterly reports are more timely than annual reports, but they typically contain more estimates because some events cannot be measured until fiscal year end.

TIME AND ACCOUNTING MEASUREMENT

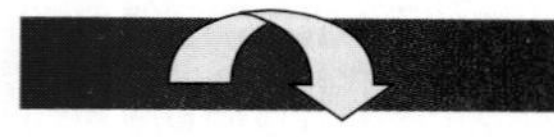

Major decisions in estimating the results of a transformation process are when to recognize the sale of goods and services and when to recognize the consumption of resources. Recognition occurs in accounting when transactions are recorded in the accounting system. The following sections describe alternate approaches for identifying when transactions should be recorded.

Cash Flows

Objective 5
Explain why change in cash is not a valid measure of an organization's performance for a period.

One alternative for measuring the economic consequences of an organization's activities is by the amount of cash resulting from the transformation process during a fiscal period. ***Cash flow*** **is the amount of cash received (cash inflow) or paid (cash outflow) during a period.** For example, assume you manage a business, A. Einstein Electronics. On May 1, 1995, owners invested $200,000 in the business, and the business borrowed an additional $100,000 from creditors. You used this financing to purchase equipment for $25,000, a building for $125,000, and land for $30,000. In addition, you purchased $75,000 of merchandise for sale, which left you $45,000 of cash. These transactions occurred during May. On May 31, the company's account balances would appear as illustrated in Exhibit 3-3.

Exhibit 3-4 reports cash received and paid for A. Einstein Electronics for May. Cash increased $45,000 for the company in May. This amount does not represent the results of operating activities, however, because no operating activities occurred in May. No goods were produced or sold. The $45,000 does not represent a return on investment to owners. It is simply the cash that remains from the owners' investments after other resources have been acquired. Therefore, the change in cash for a period is not a valid measure of how much better off the owners of a company are from the company's activities for a period.

Exhibit 3-3

A. Einstein Electronics
Account Summary
For Month Ended May 31, 1995

Assets =		Liabilities + Owners' Equity		+ Revenues − Expenses	
Cash	$ 45,000	Loans	$100,000	Revenues	$0
Merchandise	75,000	Owners' investment	200,000	Expenses	0
Equipment	25,000				
Building	125,000				
Land	30,000				
Total	$300,000	Total	$300,000	Total	$0

Exhibit 3-4

A. Einstein Electronics
Cash Received and Paid
For Month Ended May 31, 1995

Cash received:		
Loans from creditors	$100,000	
Investment by owners	200,000	$300,000
Cash paid:		
Purchase of merchandise	75,000	
Purchase of equipment	25,000	
Purchase of building	125,000	
Purchase of land	30,000	255,000
Increase in cash		$ 45,000

Cash Flows from Operating Activities

Objective 6
Explain why cash flow from operating activities is not a complete measure of an organization's performance for a period.

Another possible measure of performance is the amount of cash flow from operating activities, rather than the total cash flow for a period. Assume that during June, the first month of operations, you sell for $67,500 half of the merchandise you purchased. Of these sales, $50,000 was for cash and the remainder was on credit, with the cash to be received within 30 days. The company paid wages of $10,000 to employees and owed $3,000 of additional wages at the end of the month. The company paid other operating costs (e.g., utilities, licenses, insurance, and maintenance) amounting to $1,200. Exhibit 3-5 reports the cash flow from operating activities for A. Einstein Electronics for June.

Cash has increased to $83,800 ($45,000 from May + $50,000 of cash sales in June − $11,200 of cash payments in June). This summary reports net cash flow of $38,800 based on the difference between the cash received from operating activities ($50,000) and the cash paid for these activities ($11,200) during June.

Does $38,800 represent a complete measure of performance for June? Consider the following problems related to Exhibit 3-5:

1. Sales of $17,500 made on credit have not been recognized. Customers owe this amount to the company, though cash was not received in June.

Exhibit 3-5

A. Einstein Electronics
Account Summary
For Month Ended June 30, 1995

Assets =		Liabilities + Owners' Equity		+ Net Cash Flow from Operating Activities		
Cash	$ 83,800	Loans	$100,000	Cash received		$50,000
Merchandise	75,000	Owners' investment	200,000	Cash paid:		
Equipment	25,000			Wages	(10,000)	
Building	125,000			Other	(1,200)	
Land	30,000					(11,200)
Total	$338,000	Total	$300,000	Total		$38,800

2. The amount of merchandise reported at the end of June is incorrect. Half the merchandise has been sold; therefore, the cost of merchandise available for sale at the end of June is $37,500, instead of $75,000. No cash outflow occurred for merchandise in June, though some merchandise was consumed. The cash outflow occurred in May when the merchandise was purchased.
3. The $3,000 owed to employees has not been recorded. The cash outflow will not occur until July, but an obligation for the payment exists in June, when employee services were received. The cost is related to services received in June, not July.

These problems suggest reporting operating activities, as well as financing and investing activities, on a cash flow basis is not adequate. The issue is one of timing. Cash flows do not always occur at the same time goods are sold or resources are consumed as part of the transformation process. This limitation does not mean information about cash flows is unimportant to managers, owners, and others who provide and use cash. The amount of cash flow resulting from an organization's operating activities should approximate the results of its operating activities over a long period. But, over short periods, such as a month, a quarter, or even a year, cash flow usually will not be a complete indicator of a company's performance.

Individuals often use cash as a basis for measuring their financial conditions. When you and I make decisions about going to a movie, buying a car, or going on a vacation, we look at how much cash we have available. Cash is important to businesses and other organizations, as well. But, cash is not the primary measure most organizations use to evaluate their operating activities. The next section examines the accrual basis of measurement.

The Accrual Basis of Accounting Measurement

Objective 7
Distinguish the accrual basis of accounting from the cash basis and explain why the accrual basis is used.

Instead of cash measurement, businesses typically use the accrual basis of measurement. Accrual measurement focuses on events that create or consume resources, in addition to cash flows. **The *accrual basis* of accounting measurement recognizes revenues when resources are created as part of an organization's operating activities. It recognizes expenses when re-**

sources are consumed as part of operating activities. The following sections describe accrual measurement and compare it with cash measurement.

Sales and Receivables. In most situations, revenue is recognized when goods and services are sold. A sale is a contract between a company and a customer. A customer takes possession of goods or receives services. In exchange, the customer pays cash or agrees to pay cash in the future for these goods or services.

To illustrate the relationship between accrual and cash measures, consider A. Einstein Electronics again. The accrual measurement of the June sales transactions can be represented as:

Assets =	Liabilities + Owners' Equity	+ Revenues − Expenses
Cash $50,000 Accounts receivable 17,500	$0	Sales revenue $67,500

The accrual basis reports $67,500 of revenue for June because this is the price of the goods sold to customers during June. It is the amount of the contract between the company and its customers. The contract calls for customers to exchange $67,500 of financial resources for goods. Of this amount, $50,000 is a CASH asset. The remaining $17,500 is a receivable asset (indicating the right to receive cash in the future). ACCOUNTS RECEIVABLE represents the amount owed to an organization by its customers. The revenue account indicates how much current and future cash ($67,500) was generated and where it came from (sale of merchandise to customers). The assets indicate which resources were generated by the sale and their amounts, cash ($50,000) and future cash ($17,500).

Recognizing revenue and receiving cash may occur at the same time, as when goods are sold for cash. The critical event for purposes of accounting revenue recognition, however, is the sale, not the receipt of cash. An exception is made for contracts that extend over several years. For example, a portion of revenues often are recognized on long-term construction contracts before the contracts are completed. The revenues are allocated to different fiscal periods in proportion to the percentage of the contract completed during each period. We will examine this and other exceptions in later chapters.

Cost of Goods Sold. The accrual basis recognizes $37,500 of expense for merchandise consumed from sales made in June. COST OF GOODS SOLD is an expense for the cost of merchandise sold to customers. This transaction can be illustrated as:

Assets =	Liabilities + Owners' Equity	+ Revenues − Expenses
Merchandise $(37,500)		Cost of goods sold $(37,500)

The expense for merchandise is recognized in the period in which revenue from the sale is recorded. The accrual basis matches the expense with the revenue produced from the resources consumed.

Wages. The accrual basis recognizes wages for June, as illustrated at the top of the next page.

Assets =	Liabilities + Owners' Equity	+ Revenues − Expenses
Cash $(10,000)	Wages payable $3,000	Wages expense $(13,000)

The accrual basis recognizes $13,000 of WAGES EXPENSE because this is the cost of employee services consumed during June. Of this amount, $10,000 is cash paid to employees, a reduction in the balance of the cash account. The remaining $3,000 is a liability, WAGES PAYABLE. WAGES PAYABLE is an amount owed by a company to its employees for services they have already provided. This liability represents a contractual obligation of the company to pay cash in the future. Part of this amount is paid during the current period (CASH) and part will be paid in the future (WAGES PAYABLE).

Interest. A. Einstein Electronics pays interest on a loan at periodic intervals. The accrual basis records an expense for the interest each fiscal period. For example, if the loan requires interest payments of $3,000 every three months, the company records one-third of the interest as an expense of each of the three months. Therefore, A. Einstein would record $1,000 of INTEREST EXPENSE for June. ***Interest expense* is the cost associated with borrowing money during a fiscal period.** This $1,000 is owed to creditors because the company has used the creditors' money during June. ***Interest payable* is an amount owed to creditors for the use of the creditors' money during a fiscal period.** Like WAGES PAYABLE, INTEREST PAYABLE is a contractual obligation to pay cash in the future for a resource (use of borrowed money) that has been consumed. The transaction can be illustrated as:

Assets =	Liabilities + Owners' Equity	+ Revenues − Expenses
$0	Interest payable $1,000	Interest expense $(1,000)

In this transaction, assets are not affected during the current period because cash will not be paid out for two more months.

Depreciation. Two other accounts need to be considered, BUILDING and EQUIPMENT. These accounts are examples of fixed assets. ***Fixed assets* or *plant assets* are long-term, physical resources.** The company purchased the building for $125,000 and the equipment for $25,000. Because the business is a going concern, we assume the building will be used until it wears out or outlives its usefulness and has to be replaced. The same is true of equipment. Both assets are expected to last for several years. It is misleading to report the entire cost of the building or equipment as expense in the period in which they are purchased or in the period in which they are replaced. Instead, the accrual basis allocates a portion of the cost of these assets to expense during each fiscal period that benefits from their use.

For example, assume the building has a useful life of 25 years. The company might allocate $5,000 ($125,000/25 years) of the building's cost to expense each year or approximately $417 ($125,000/300 months) each month of this 25 year period. In the same manner, if the equipment has a useful life of 10 years, the company might allocate $2,500 ($25,000/10 years) of cost to expense each year or approximately $208 ($25,000/120 months) each month. **The process of allocating the costs of fixed assets to expense over the use-**

ful lives of the assets is known as *depreciation*. Total depreciation for A. Einstein Electronics would be $625 for June. This transaction can be illustrated as:

Assets =	Liabilities + Owners' Equity	+ Revenues − Expenses
Accumulated depreciation $(625)		Depreciation expense $(625)

***Depreciation expense* is the cost of fixed assets recognized as being consumed during a fiscal period.** Instead of reducing the building and equipment accounts directly, accounting normally uses an accumulated depreciation account. ***Accumulated depreciation* is the portion of fixed asset costs allocated to depreciation since the assets were acquired.** Accumulated depreciation is a contra-asset account. It offsets the asset account to which it relates. **A *contra account* is any account that offsets or reduces the amount of another account.** Thus, on its balance sheet, A. Einstein Electronics will report the cost of its fixed assets less the accumulated depreciation recognized for these assets. Some fixed assets, notably land, are not depreciated because it is assumed they will not wear out.

The measurement of depreciation is an estimation procedure. The amount of depreciation recorded depends on assumptions about the lives of assets. The company assumed the building would last 25 years. Also, it chose to allocate an equal amount of depreciation expense to each month of the asset's life. A different assumption as to the building's life or a different allocation method would change the amount of depreciation expense and accumulated depreciation recorded each month.

Numbers such as $417 and $208 for depreciation expense appear to be very precise. Nevertheless, this precision is misleading because the numbers are the result of allocation decisions. Different allocation methods would produce different numbers. Because the amounts are estimates, it makes little sense to report numbers that make the amounts appear to be more precise than they are. Thus, reports to decision makers usually round amounts to hundreds, thousands, or even millions of dollars, depending on an organization's size.

Other Expenses. The final transaction for A. Einstein Electronics is the payment of other expenses of $1,200. The payment can be illustrated as:

Assets =	Liabilities + Owners' Equity	+ Revenues − Expenses
Cash (1,200)		Other expenses (1,200)

The cash payment for expenses reduces the amount of cash available to A. Einstein Electronics. In this transaction, like many others in most organizations, a cash payment occurs at the time an expense is recorded.

Product and Period Costs. Accrual accounting attempts to match expenses with revenues. Most revenues are recognized when goods are sold. Therefore, expenses directly associated with specific goods also are recognized when the goods are sold. For example, cost of goods sold for specific items of merchandise is recorded when this merchandise is sold. The expense is matched with the revenue from the sale. **Costs directly associated with specific goods are *product costs.* Product costs are expensed in the fiscal period the goods with which they are associated are sold.** Product costs are inventoried until the related goods are sold. Merchandise acquired by A. Einstein Electronics for $500 in May is an asset, merchandise inventory, until this merchandise is sold. At the time it is sold, the inventory account is decreased and COST OF GOODS SOLD is recognized. Manufacturing companies inventory the costs of goods produced until the goods are sold. These costs include the costs of labor, materials, and other resources that are part of the production process. For example, assume a company pays $100 for labor and $150 for materials that are used to produce a washing machine in September. The washing machine is sent to a warehouse and later sold to a retailer in December. The total manufacturing cost of $250 is recorded as an asset, inventory, in September. COST OF GOODS SOLD and a reduction in INVENTORY by $250, are recorded when the machine is sold in December.

Some costs cannot be associated directly with specific goods. Examples include management salaries, depreciation and insurance on office facilities, and advertising costs. ***Period costs* are costs not directly associated with specific goods. Period costs are reported as expenses in external accounting reports in the period in which they occur (in other words, the period benefitting from the cost).** Cash may be paid for these resources in a period other than when they are consumed. For example, interest expense for A. Einstein Electronics is a period cost. It is recognized in June, the period benefitting from the cost, though cash is not paid until August.

Managers may allocate certain costs differently for internal reporting and decision purposes than for external reporting purposes. GAAP require some costs, for example, those associated with research and development, to be expensed when they are incurred. Managers may treat these costs as product costs for planning or control purposes. Accounting procedures used in external reporting may differ from those used in internal reporting.

Summary of Accrual Accounting. Exhibit 3-6 illustrates the result of recording all of A. Einstein Electronics' June transactions using the accrual basis.

Exhibit 3-6

A. Einstein Electronics
Accrual Basis Account Summary
For Month Ended June 30, 1995

Assets =		Liabilities + Owners' Equity		+ Revenues − Expenses	
Cash	$83,800	Loans	$100,000	Sales revenue	$67,500
Accounts receivable	17,500	Wages payable	3,000	Cost of goods sold	(37,500)
Merchandise	37,500	Interest payable	1,000	Wages expense	(13,000)
Equipment	25,000	Owners' investment	200,000	Depreciation expense	(625)
Building	125,000			Interest expense	(1,000)
Accumulated depreciation	(625)			Other expense	(1,200)
Land	30,000				
Total	$318,175	Total	$304,000		$14,175

Analysis of cash:		
Cash received:	Sale of merchandise	$50,000
Cash paid:	Payment of salaries	(10,000)
	Payment of other expenses	(1,200)
Net increase in cash		38,800
Beginning cash balance		45,000
Ending cash balance		$83,800

The accrual basis reports $14,175 of net income for A. Einstein Electronics in June. Though an estimate, this amount is a measure of performance based on the economic consequences of the company's operating activities in June. It is a measure of how much better off the owners are as a result of the company's operating activities during June. Observe that the accounting process can become complex very quickly. Even a few transactions result in a complex set of data that must be organized carefully if it is to make sense to users.

Like the analysis for Produce Transit Company, the accounts for A. Einstein Electronics provide information about the status of contracts involving the company:

Contracting Party	Given in Exchange	Received in Exchange	Contract Completed
Owner	Investment of $200,000	Return on investment of $14,175	No, business is a going concern
Lender	Loan of $100,000	Interest earned of $1,000	No, interest and principal not yet paid
Suppliers:	Merchandise Equipment Buildings Land Other items	Payment of $75,000 Payment of $25,000 Payment of $125,000 Payment of $30,000 Payment of $1,200	Yes Yes Yes Yes Yes
Employees	Labor	Payment of $10,000 and right to $3,000 more	No, a portion of wages not yet paid
Customers	Payment of $50,000 and promise to pay of $17,500	Merchandise	No, a portion of price not yet received

The information identifies the contracting parties, the exchanges that occurred or will occur, and whether the contracts have been completed.

RECONCILING ACCRUAL AND CASH MEASUREMENTS

Objective 8
Reconcile cash and accrual measures of operating activities.

The relationship between accrual and cash measurements is critical to understanding accounting information. Exhibit 3-6 provides an analysis of changes in cash during June for A. Einstein Electronics. Changes in the cash account result from transactions that produce cash inflows and outflows. Several items recorded using the accrual basis sales for credit and noncash expenses, such as cost of goods sold, depreciation, and interest did not affect cash flows in June.

Accrual and cash numbers provide different measures of operating activities for the month. These two measures can be reconciled, as in Exhibit 3-7.

Exhibit 3-7

A. Einstein Electronics
Reconciliation of Net Cash Flow from Operating Activities and Net Income
For Month Ended June 30, 1995

	Cash Flow from Operating Activities for June			**Net Income from Operating Activities for June**		
	Past	**June**	**Future**	**Revenues**	**Expenses**	**Total**
Cash received for June sales		$50,000		$50,000		
Cash to be received for June sales			$17,500	17,500		
Total June sales						$67,500
Cash paid in June for resources consumed in June:						
Wages		(10,000)			$(10,000)	
Other		(1,200)			(1,200)	
Cash to be paid for resources consumed in June:						
Wages			(3,000)		(3,000)	
Interest			(1,000)		(1,000)	
Cash paid in past for resources consumed in June:						
Inventory	$(37,500)				(37,500)	
Depreciation	(625)				(625)	
Total resources consumed in June						(53,325)
Net cash increase in June		$38,800				
Net income for June						$14,175
Net cash increase	$(38,125)+	$38,800 +	$13,500	→	→	$14,175

This illustration indicates the timing of cash flows associated with revenues and expenses recorded in June. Net cash flows from operating activities for June were $38,800, corresponding to Exhibit 3-5, but some cash inflows associated with revenues recorded in June will be received in the future. Some cash outflows associated with expenses recorded in June were paid in May, and some will be paid in the future. Thus, while net cash flow from operating activities was $38,800 in June, the net result of all cash flows (past, present, and future) from revenues and expenses recorded in June is only $14,175. This amount is the company's net income for June. **The accrual basis attempts to measure the economic consequences of operating activities during the period in which they occur.** This accrual measure should approximate the cash flow that will result from these operating activities, once *all* of these cash flows occur.

Therefore, it should provide a more accurate measure of the economic consequences of operating activities during a period than cash flows provide for the period.

MEASURING THE TRANSFORMATION PROCESS

Objective 9
Identify information reported by an accrual basis accounting system.

The major purpose of an accounting system is to provide information about an organization's transformation process. With this information, users can measure the financing, investing, and operating results of the process. Exhibit 3-8 illustrates the scope of information available from the accounting system. The information in the exhibit includes all transactions related to the transformation process of A. Einstein Electronics for both May and June.

Exhibit 3-8

Summary of Transformation Process
A. Einstein Electronics

Income Statement
For Two Months Ended June 30, 1995

Sales revenue		$67,500
Expenses:		
Cost of goods sold	$37,500	
Wages	13,000	
Interest	1,000	
Depreciation	625	
Other	1,200	
Total expenses		53,325
Net income		$14,175

Statement of Cash Flows
For Two Months Ended June 30, 1995

Cash flow from operating activities:		
Sale of merchandise	$ 50,000	
Less: cash paid for expenses	(11,200)	
cash paid for merchandise	(75,000)	$ (36,200)
Cash flow for investing activities:		
Purchase of equipment	(25,000)	
Purchase of building	(125,000)	
Purchase of land	(30,000)	(180,000)
Cash flow from financing activities:		
Loans from creditors	100,000	
Investment by owners	200,000	300,000
Net increase in cash		83,800
Cash balance, May 1		0
Cash balance, June 30		$ 83,800

Balance Sheet
June 30, 1995

Assets:		
Cash		$ 83,800
Accounts receivable		17,500
Merchandise inventory		37,500
Equipment	$ 25,000	
Building	125,000	
	150,000	
Less: Accumulated depreciation	(625)	149,375
Land		30,000
Total assets		$318,175
Liabilities:		
Wages payable	$ 3,000	
Interest payable	1,000	
Loans payable	100,000	
Total liabilities		$104,000
Owners' equity:		
Investment by owners	200,000	
Reinvested profits	14,175	
Total owners' equity		214,175
Total liabilities and owners' equity		$318,175

The information provided in this exhibit is typical of the financial statements reported by an accounting system. The economic consequences of transactions occurring in an organization's transformation process are summarized in accounts. Accounts are created as needed to capture information from transactions. As a group, the accounts form a data base in which information is stored until needed by users. Periodically, the account information is summarized and reported in a form that enables users to understand the transactions that occurred in the transformation process.

The income statement reports the costs of resources consumed in producing, selling, and distributing goods and services and the prices of goods and services sold during a period. The statement of cash flows reports the cash consequences of financing, investing, and operating activities during a period. The balance sheet reports the resources available for use in the transformation process and claims to those resources at a point in time. Observe that reinvested profits are reported on the balance sheet after revenues and expenses for the current fiscal period have been transferred to this account.

Reports by large corporations to external users often summarize accounts by general categories. For example, "operating expenses" may be reported instead of individual expenses such as wages and depreciation. Corporations report additional information along with their financial statements to help readers understand and interpret the statements. Later chapters will examine this additional information.

Learning Note

Assets are the resources reported by a company. All other accounts provide information about where resources came from and how they were used. Students often have trouble interpreting some of these accounts. For example, revenues are not cash. Cash is an asset on the balance sheet. Revenues describe where some resources (including some cash) were obtained during a period: from customers. Net income and reinvested profits (or retained earnings) also are not cash. These accounts provide information about the amount of resources generated from operating activities, but they are not resources themselves. An organization must have cash to acquire other resources and to pay its bills. It cannot pay for anything with revenues, net income, or retained earnings.

Both accrual and cash measures of the transformation process are useful. The accrual basis estimates the economic consequences of the transformation process during a period. The cash basis measures the net amount of cash provided by the transformation process during the period. Accrual basis measurements provide information about whether an organization's operations are sufficiently effective and efficient for long-run success. Cash basis measurements provide information about whether an organization is generating sufficient cash to meet its current obligations and survive in the short-run. Either measure can be misleading when considered in isolation.

For example, a company may report a large amount of net income for a period. That income may result from a large amount of revenue that does not generate current cash inflow. Thus, the company may not have sufficient cash to meet its operating needs and pay its creditors. A profitable company can be forced into bankruptcy because of inadequate cash flow. On the other hand, a company may report a large amount of cash flow for a period because of collections on sales to customers from a prior period. Though cash flow may look good, net income may demonstrate the company is having difficulty selling its products. Both accrual and cash flow measures are important in evaluating a company's performance. A successful company normally will demonstrate good accrual and cash basis performance.

SELF-STUDY PROBLEM 3-2

N. Bates is owner and manager of Bates' Motel. He purchased the motel at the end of 1993. On January 1, 1995, the asset, liability, and owners' equity account balances for Bates' Motel were as follows:

Bates' Motel
Account Summary
January 1, 1995

Assets		**Liabilities & Owners' Equity**	
Cash	$ 4,200	Notes payable	$ 80,000
Supplies	7,300	Investment by owners	45,000
Furniture and equipment	19,500	Reinvested profits	9,600
Buildings	93,600		
Accumulated depreciation	(5,000)		
Land	15,000		
Total	$134,600	Total	$134,600

During 1995, the motel earned $88,000 from room rentals. Of this amount, $82,000 was received in cash by year end; $6,000 was accounts receivable from corporate clients. Expenses incurred during the year included: wages, $30,000; utilities, $8,400; supplies consumed, $5,300; depreciation on furniture and equipment, $2,000; depreciation on buildings, $3,000; interest on note, $7,000; and miscellaneous, $2,400. Other than depreciation and supplies consumed, all expenses were paid in cash when incurred, except that $1,500 of wages (of the $30,000) were owed to employees at year end. Other cash payments included $2,200 for purchase of supplies and $10,000 paid on the principal of the notes payable. Bates withdrew $20,000 from the business during the year for living expenses.

Required

Prepare a summary of the transformation process for Bates' Motel for 1995 using the format of Exhibit 3-8.

The solution to Self-Study Problem 3-2 appears at the end of the chapter.

THE PURPOSE OF ACCRUAL BASIS ACCOUNTS

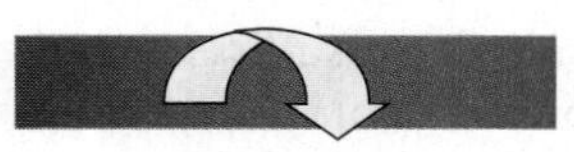

Objective 10
Explain the purposes of different account types in an accrual accounting system.

Each of the types of accounts in an accounting system plays an important role in accrual measurement. Each type of account provides information about economic consequences of an organization's transformation process and contractual relationships in the process. Also, these accounts link events together that occur in different fiscal periods. The following sections examine how accounts provide this link.

Assets, Liabilities, and Owners' Equity

The balance sheet reports accounts that represent resources and claims to those resources by creditors and owners. These resources and claims resulted from events occurring prior to the balance sheet date. Also, they provide information about future events that will occur.

Assets are resources available for future use by an organization to which it has a legal right. They may be resources purchased in the past that will be consumed in the future, such as merchandise, equipment, and buildings. Other assets, such as accounts receivable, represent legal rights to receive cash in the future. A company may invest cash in securities, such as stocks or bonds issued by other companies, with the expectation of receiving returns in the future. Cash is a financial resource that represents the legal right to purchase other resources. Therefore, assets consist of: (1) past cash outflows for resources to be used in the future, such as INVENTORY, BUILDINGS, EQUIPMENT, and PATENTS, (2) future cash inflows resulting from sales made by an organization, such as ACCOUNTS RECEIVABLE, (3) future cash inflows from INVESTMENTS held by a company, and (4) financial resources, such as CASH, currently available for use.

Liabilities represent legal obligations of an organization to provide cash or goods and services to external parties in the future. Some liabilities arise from financing activities. These liabilities, such as NOTES PAYABLE and BONDS

PAYABLE, will be repaid in the future. Thus, these liabilities result from past cash inflows to an organization that will result in future cash outflows. Other liabilities include obligations to pay cash for resources acquired or consumed in the past, such as ACCOUNTS PAYABLE, WAGES PAYABLE, and INTEREST PAYABLE. Accounts payable are amounts owed to suppliers for merchandise, materials, and other resources purchased on credit. Liabilities also include **UNEARNED REVENUES, which are obligations to provide goods and services in the future.** These liabilities arise when an organization receives financial resources from customers in exchange for goods and services to be provided in the future. An example is a publisher that sells magazine subscriptions. The publisher receives cash from customers in advance of publishing the magazine. The amount received is recorded as UNEARNED REVENUE. Revenue is not recognized for these goods or services until they are distributed to customers. At that time, UNEARNED REVENUE is decreased and REVENUE is increased. Thus, liabilities include (1) cash inflows in the past that will require cash outflows in the future, (2) resources acquired or consumed in the past that will require cash outflows in the future, and (3) cash received in the past for goods and services that will be provided in the future.

Owners' equity includes investments in an organization by owners and reinvested profits. Owners of proprietorships and partnerships recover their investments when they sell their businesses. A corporation, however, is under no obligation to repay amounts invested by stockholders as long as it is a going concern. A corporation may choose, however, to repurchase shares of stock that it has issued. Thus, it may pay cash to owners for their stock. In addition, owners expect to receive returns on their investments. These returns may be in the form of cash payments from the organization or in the form of higher values for their investments, such as increases in stock prices. If returns are paid to owners as dividends (corporations) or withdrawals (proprietorships and partnerships), the owners receive cash directly from the company. Therefore, owners' equity involves past cash inflows for which future cash outflows are expected. Information about assets, liabilities, and owners' equity is reported on a company's balance sheet.

Revenues and Expenses

Revenues and expenses provide information about resources generated and consumed during a fiscal period. They report the economic consequences of transactions that help explain why resources changed from the beginning to the end of a fiscal period. Revenues result during the current period from the sale of goods and services to customers. Cash inflows associated with the sales may be received in past, current, or future periods. Similarly, expenses result from the consumption of resources during a period, irrespective of whether cash is paid for these resources in past, present, or future periods. Information about revenues and expenses is reported on a company's income statement; information about cash flows is reported on a statement of cash flows.

Accounts and Time

As a whole, an accrual accounting system provides information about revenues and expenses during a fiscal period for an organization that is a going concern.

Also, it provides information about cash flows that occurred during the fiscal period. Asset, liability, and owners' equity accounts provide information about future cash flows, revenues, and expenses that will result from transactions that occurred in prior fiscal periods.

This information is necessary because the economic consequences of an organization's transformation process must be separated into distinct periods of time:

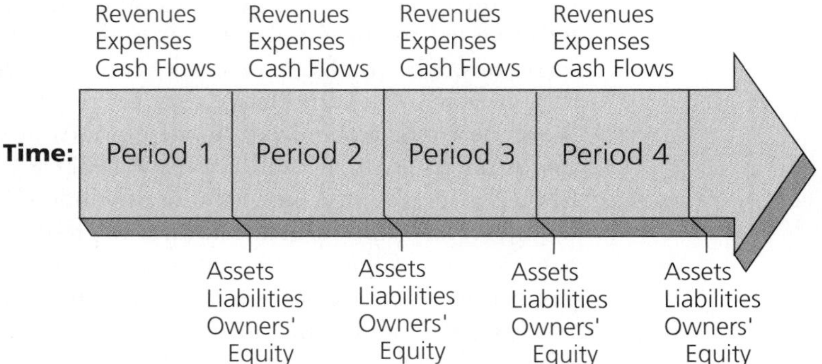

Separation into periods is necessary to report activities on a timely basis. Assets, liabilities, and owners' equity identify resources and claims to those resources at distinct intervals, the beginning and end of fiscal periods. Revenues, expenses, and cash flows identify events that change an organization's resources and claims to the resources during a period. Together, these accounts provide a dynamic picture of the economic consequences of the transformation process. They provide information about past events that created and consumed resources, affected claims to the resources, and created and consumed cash flows. They provide information about current resources and claims to the resources. And they provide information about expected future changes in resources, claims, and cash flows resulting from events that have already occurred.

How the accounting system functions to create and report this information is the subject of Chapter 4.

SELF-STUDY PROBLEM 3-3

The following are independent transactions:

1. An organization purchased supplies in February for $6,000 cash. $1,000 of the supplies was consumed in February; $2,000 was consumed in March.
2. An organization sells $10,000 of merchandise in March; $8,000 for cash and $2,000 on credit.
3. An organization buys $5,000 of merchandise in March and sells it during the month. It paid $1,000 for the merchandise in March. The remainder will be paid in April.
4. An organization consumes $3,000 of merchandise in March that was purchased in February. $1,200 was paid for the merchandise in February, and the remainder is paid for in March.
5. An organization borrows $20,000 from a bank in March. The loan will be repaid over a 10 year period beginning in April. Consider only the loan and repayment of principal.

6. An organization buys equipment priced at $7,000 in March and pays cash. $500 of the equipment value is consumed in March; the remainder will be consumed in the future.

Required

For each transaction, indicate the amount of revenue, expense, and cash flow that would result. Use the format provided below and place the appropriate amount in each box to indicate when the revenue, expense, or cash flow would be recorded. Transaction 1 is worked for you:

1.	Past	March	Future	Total
Revenues				
Expenses	$1,000	$2,000	$3,000	$6,000
Cash Received				
Cash Paid	$6,000			$6,000

The solution to Self-Study Problem 3-3 appears at the end of the chapter.

REVIEW

Summary of Important Concepts

1. Transformation process:
   A. The accounting information system provides a means of recording, summarizing, and reporting an organization's transformation process.
   B. Together, assets, liabilities, owners' equity, revenues, expenses, and cash flows measure the outcome of an organization's transformation process.
2. Time and accounting measurement:
   A. Most organizations are going concerns: their transformation processes are continuous.
   B. Going concerns report results of their financing, investing, and operating activities periodically, even though all results of these activities are not fully known and must be estimated.
   C. Major decisions in estimating the results of a going concern are when to recognize the sale of goods and services and when to recognize the cost of resources consumed in providing goods and services.
3. Accrual and cash measurement:
   A. The accrual basis of accounting measures revenues when resources are created from sales and expenses when resources are consumed in operating activities, irrespective of when cash is received or paid.
   B. Revenues and expenses measure the results of an organization's operating activities on an accrual basis. Cash flows measure the cash provided by and used in an organization's operating activities, as well as by its financing and investing activities.
4. Accrual basis accounts:
   A. Assets measure the amount of resources available to an organization to be consumed in the future and the amount of cash expected in the future from revenues earned and other transactions in the current or prior periods.

B. Liabilities measure the amount of obligations owed by an organization that will be paid in the future for resources acquired or consumed in the current or prior periods.
C. Owners' equity measures the amount invested by owners in an organization either as direct investments or as reinvested profits.

DEFINE *Terms and Concepts Defined in this Chapter*

accrual basis	depreciation	interest expense	plant assets
accumulated depreciation	depreciation expense	interest payable	prepaid rent
cash flow	fixed assets	period costs	product costs
contra account	going concern	periodic measurement	unearned revenue

SOLUTIONS

SELF-STUDY PROBLEM 3-1

S. Claus
Account Summary
For Month Ended December 31, 1996

Assets =		Liabilities + Owners' Equity		+ Revenues − Expenses	
Cash	$5,350	Investment by owner	$5,000	Revenues	$5,000
				Expenses:	
				Lease	(1,500)
				Lodging	(750)
				Meals	(600)
				Hay and oats	(1,800)
Total	$5,350	Total	$5,000	Total	$ 350

SELF-STUDY PROBLEM 3-2

Summary of Transformation Process
Bates' Motel

Income Statement
For Year Ended December 31, 1995

Rent revenue		$88,000
Expenses:		
Supplies	$ 5,300	
Wages	30,000	
Utilities	8,400	
Interest	7,000	
Depreciation	5,000	
Other	2,400	
Total expenses		58,100
Net income		$29,900

Statement of Cash Flows
For Year Ended December 31, 1995

Cash provided by operating activities:		
From room rental	$82,000	
Less: cash paid for expenses (Note 1)	(46,300)	
cash paid for supplies	(2,200)	$33,500
Cash used for financing activities:		
Payment of loan	(10,000)	
Withdrawal by owner	(20,000)	(30,000)
Cash used for investing activities:		0
Net increase in cash		3,500
Cash balance, January 1, 1995		4,200
Cash balance, December 31, 1995		$ 7,700

Note 1: Cash paid for expenses:

Wages	$28,500
Utilities	8,400
Interest	7,000
Miscellaneous	2,400
Total cash paid	$46,300

Balance Sheet
December 31, 1995

Assets:		
Cash		$ 7,700
Accounts receivable		6,000
Supplies (Note 2)		4,200
Furniture and equipment	$ 19,500	
Buildings	93,600	
	113,100	
Less: Accumulated depreciation	(10,000)	103,100
Land		15,000
Total assets		$136,000
Liabilities:		
Wages payable	1,500	
Notes payable	70,000	
Total liabilities		71,500
Owner's equity:		
Investment by owner	45,000	
Reinvested profits (Note 3)	19,500	
Total owners' equity		64,500
Total liabilities and owners' equity		$136,000

Note 2:

Supplies on hand, beginning	$7,300
Supplies purchased	2,200
Supplies consumed	(5,300)
Supplies on hand, ending	$4,200

Note 3:

Reinvested profits, beginning	$ 9,600
Net income, 1995	29,900
Owner withdrawal, 1995	(20,000)
Reinvested profits, ending	$19,500

SELF-STUDY PROBLEM 3-3

2.	Past	March	Future	Total
Revenues		$10,000		$10,000
Expenses				
Cash Received		$8,000	$2,000	$10,000
Cash Paid				
3.				
Revenues				
Expenses		$5,000		$5,000
Cash Received				
Cash Paid		$1,000	$4,000	$5,000
4.				
Revenues				
Expenses		$3,000		$3,000
Cash Received				
Cash Paid	$1,200	$1,800		$3,000
5.				
Revenues				
Expenses				
Cash Received		$20,000		$20,000
Cash Paid			$20,000	$20,000
6.				
Revenues				
Expenses		$500	$6,500	$7,000
Cash Received				
Cash Paid		$7,000		$7,000

EXERCISES

3-1. Write a short definition for each of the terms listed in the *Terms and Concepts Defined in this Chapter* section.

3-2. Compare and contrast the accounting systems of (1) a large retail company such as Sears and (2) a small local retail store such as Marvin's Men's Store. Consider the following attributes in your comparison: (a) number of accounts in the system, (b) relative number of decision makers and their information needs, (c) effect of locations and departments on the complexity of the system, and (d) the primary types of accounts included in the system.

3-3. Jerry Reed drives for a large moving company. The company contacts Jerry when it has a job for him and furnishes a truck for his use. Jerry picks up the truck, drives to the mover's home, loads, transports, and delivers the mover's belongings. He returns the truck to the company and receives his pay. Jerry is paid $2 per mile for the job. He is responsible for paying for his own gas, food, and lodging. Also, he must hire any helpers he needs to load and unload the truck. Jerry travelled 1,200 miles on a recent job. He paid $250 for gas, $58 for food, $102 for lodging, and $40 for helpers. How much did Jerry earn for the job? How much net cash did he receive? Was the amount he earned more or less than the net cash he received? Why?

3-4. Alice Ekberg makes wooden mailboxes in her garage. She makes a supply of boxes during the week. On the weekend, she rents a booth at a flea market where she sells her products. She paints the purchaser's name and address on a mailbox when it is sold. During a recent week, Alice paid $200 for wood and supplies she used to construct 10 mailboxes. On Saturday, she sold 5 of the boxes for $50 each. On Sunday, she sold 4 of the remaining boxes, also for $50 each. She had to pay $10 each day for rent for the booth. How much net cash did Alice receive on Saturday? How much on Sunday? How much did each box cost Alice (excluding rent)? How much did Alice earn on Saturday, on Sunday, and for the week? What was her net cash flow for the week? Was the amount earned more or less than the net cash received? Why?

3-5. Refer to Exercise 3-4. How much additional cash will Alice have available to spend during the week following her sales from making and selling mailboxes? If she expects to sell the same number of mailboxes next weekend, how much should she expect to earn then? How many mailboxes should she make during the coming week? What will her net cash flow be for the coming week if she purchases materials to make the additional boxes she plans to sell at the same costs as last week and sells these for $50 each? She again will pay $10 rent for Saturday and for Sunday. Is the amount earned for the week more or less than the net cash received? Why?

3-6. Acorn Products Co. is a manufacturer of oak furniture. It began operations in 1994. During its first year of operations, Acorn paid $4,300,000 for wood and other raw materials for its products. From these materials, it produced 17,200 pieces of furniture. The average cost of raw materials for each piece was $250 ($4,300,000/17,200). During 1994, Acorn sold 14,000 pieces of the furniture it manufactured at an average price of $600 per piece. All sales were for cash. Assuming the total of other expenses incurred by Acorn during 1994 was $3,000,000, how much net income did Acorn earn in 1994? If other expenses were paid in cash, how much was Acorn's net cash flow from operations? Was the net income more or less than the net cash flow? Why? Which measure is a better predictor of next year's operating results? Why?

3-7. Refer to Exercise 3-6. During its second year of operations, Acorn began with inventory of $800,000, representing 3,200 pieces of furniture. During 1995, Acorn paid $3,000,000 for materials, sufficient to produce 12,000 pieces of furniture at an average cost of $250 per piece. During the year, the company sold 14,000 pieces of furniture at an average price of $600 per piece. All sales were for cash. Other expenses amounted to $3,000,000, all paid in cash. How much net income did Acorn earn in 1995? How much net cash flow did it receive from operations? Was the net income more or less than the net cash flow? Why?

3-8. Meteor Transport Co. is a trucking company. It owns a large fleet of trucks that transports freight throughout the country. Some of these trucks cost hundreds of thousands of dollars and are operated for 15 years or more before being replaced. The company issues long-term debt to pay for most of its equipment. The company's fiscal year ends on June 30. The company prepares financial reports for each fiscal year that include estimates of its results of operations for the year. How do the operations of Meteor illustrate the periodic measurement and going concern principles of accounting?

3-9. South Plains Grain Co. began operations in January of 1995. It is investor-owned and provides storage facilities for farmers who grow wheat in the South Plains area. During 1995, the company issued $3,000,000 of stock and $2,000,000 of long-term debt. $4,800,000 of the capital was used to purchase land, construct grain silos, and purchase equipment for their operations. $1,400,000 of storage fees was paid by farmers. An additional $300,000 of fees was owed to the company at year end. $1,000,000 was paid by the company for wages, utilities, interest, insurance, and taxes during the year. An additional $200,000 was owed by the company at year end for resources consumed during the year. How much was South Plains' net cash flow for 1995? What was its net cash flow from financing, investing, and operating activities? Why is this information useful? Does this information provide an adequate measurement of the performance of the company for the current fiscal year? Does it provide a good indicator of cash flows that should be anticipated during 1996? Why?

3-10. Oscar Wheatfield is a farmer. He owns farm equipment and buildings that cost him $750,000 when he purchased them several years ago. He owes a local bank $500,000 for loans used to purchase these assets. In 1995, Oscar sold $800,000 of wheat he raised during the year. He incurred operating costs of $740,000 to produce the wheat, including $45,000 of interest on the bank loans and $70,000 of depreciation on the plant assets. In addition, Oscar repaid $50,000 of the amount he owed on the loans. The sales and all operating costs but depreciation were for cash. How much net income did Oscar earn? What was his net cash flow for the year? Explain the difference.

3-11. Bernstein Piano Co. sold $89,000 of goods during September. It collected $30,000 from these sales plus $66,000 from sales of prior months. Complete the following table:

	Cash Flow in September	**Cash Flow in Future**	**Sales Revenue for September**
Cash from prior sales	?		
Cash from September sales	?	?	?
Total cash received in Sept.	?		

3-12. Mercy Hospital paid $200,000 in wages during May. Of these, $24,000 was for wages earned in April. An additional $16,000 of wages was owed to employees for services provided in May. These wages will be paid in June. Complete the following table:

	Cash Flow in May	**Cash Flow in June**	**Wages Expense for May**
Cash paid for prior wages	?		
Cash paid for May wages	?	?	?
Total cash paid in May for wages	?		

3-13. Chin Construction Co. purchased $460,000 of materials during February. It owed $150,000 for material purchased during January. It paid the amount for January plus $240,000 of the amount purchased during February. $75,000 of the materials purchased in January was used in February along with $400,000 of the materials purchased in February. What was Chin's cash flow for materials in February? What was its expense for materials used in February?

3-14. Luna Pottery Works paid $110,000 for materials purchased in October. $75,000 of these materials plus $25,000 of materials purchased in September were sold during October. All materials available at the beginning of October were consumed during October. What was Luna's cost of goods sold for October? What amount of materials was left in inventory at the end of October?

3-15. George Carver borrowed $300,000 on January 1 to open a peanut processing plant. Interest on the loan is $3,000 each month and is paid quarterly. The first interest payment will be made on March 31. Complete the following table:

	January	February	March	Total for Quarter
Cash paid for interest	?	?	?	?
Interest expense	?	?	?	?

3-16. Pasteur Pharmaceutical Co. manufactures prescription drugs. The company recently purchased $600,000 of equipment. Cash was paid for the equipment on January 1, 1995. The company will depreciate the equipment over a three year period at $200,000 each year. Complete the following table:

	1995	1996	1997	Total for 3 Years
Cash paid for equipment	?	?	?	?
Depreciation expense	?	?	?	?

Explain the difference between cash flows each year and the amount of depreciation expense recorded.

3-17. The Ali Baba Rug Co. manufactures oriental rugs. It pays utility bills at the end of the month that services are received. The company received the following bills for June, July, and August: $700, $850, $650. Complete the following table:

	June	July	August	Total for 3 Months
Cash paid for utilities	?	?	?	?
Utilities expense	?	?	?	?

When are cash and accrual basis measures different? When are they the same?

3-18. Complete the following table:

	Past Cash Flow	April Cash Flow	Future Cash Flow	April Revenues/ Expenses
Cash received for April sales		$90,000	$25,000	?
Cash paid for resources consumed in April:				
Merchandise	$15,000	$30,000	$5,000	?
Wages		$10,000	$3,000	?
Equipment	$20,000	$0	$0	?
Net cash increase in April		?		
Net income for April				?

Why was cash flow from operations in April different from net income in April?

3-19. Listed below are definitions for four types of assets:

a. Financial resources available for use
b. Financial resources paid in past for resources that will be consumed in future
c. Goods and services sold in past that will result in future cash receipts
d. Financial resources paid in past for resources that will yield future cash receipts

Place the letter (or letters) of the appropriate definition beside each of the assets below:

_______ Buildings
_______ Investments
_______ Supplies
_______ Cash
_______ Equipment
_______ Accounts Receivable
_______ Patents
_______ Inventory

3-20. Listed below are definitions for three types of liabilities:

a. Financial resources received in past that will be repaid in future
b. Merchandise and other resources and services acquired in past that will result in future cash payments
c. Financial resources received in past for goods and services that will be provided to customers in future

Place the letter of the appropriate definition beside each of the liabilities below:

_______ Notes Payable
_______ Wages Payable
_______ Unearned Revenues
_______ Interest Payable
_______ Accounts Payable
_______ Bonds Payable
_______ Rent Payable
_______ Insurance Payable

3-21. For each of the transactions listed below, indicate the amount of revenue, expense, and cash flow that would result. Use the format provided and place the appropriate amount in each box.

a. $10,000 of supplies was purchased in August, of which $3,000 was consumed that month and $5,000 was consumed in September.
b. $30,000 of merchandise was sold in September. $12,000 of the sales were on credit.
c. Merchandise that cost the seller $15,000 was sold in September. The seller paid $10,000 for the merchandise in August, the rest was paid for in September.
d. $100,000 was borrowed in August. $5,000 will be repaid each month for 20 months beginning in September.
e. $50,000 of equipment was purchased and paid for in August. $1,000 of the equipment value was consumed in September, the remainder will be consumed in the future.

	Past	**September**	**Future**	**Total**
Revenues				
Expenses				
Cash received				
Cash paid				

3-22. For each of the following transactions, indicate the amount of cash, other assets, liabilities, and/or owners' equity that would result. Record your responses in the table provided below. Show revenues and expenses as additions or deductions to owners' equity. Place decreases in parentheses.

a. $10,000 of supplies were purchased in June.
b. $3,000 of the supplies was consumed in June.
c. $30,000 of merchandise was sold in June. $12,000 of the sales was on credit. The merchandise cost the seller $14,000.
d. $100,000 was borrowed in June.
e. Interest of $1,000 was incurred and paid in June.
f. $50,000 of equipment was purchased in June.
g. $2,000 of equipment value was consumed in June.

Transaction	Cash	Other Assets	Liability	Owners' Equity
a				
b				
c				
d				
e				
f				
g				

3-23. Sit and Sleep is a retail furniture store. At the end of the 1995 fiscal year, the company had a balance in accounts receivable of $130,000. During 1996, it received $790,000 in payments from customers, including the receivables from 1995. The balance in accounts receivable at the end of 1996 was $100,000. During 1997, it received $840,000 in payments from customers, including the receivables from 1996. The balance in accounts receivable was $120,000 at the end of 1997. How much revenue did Sit and Sleep earn from sales to customers in 1996? How much did it earn in 1997?

3-24. Complete the following table. Each column represents an independent situation. All receivables are collected in the year following the sale.

	(a)	(b)	(c)
Cash received from customers for 1996	$200,000	$350,000	?
Sales revenue for 1996	$215,000	$320,000	$180,000
Accounts receivable at beginning of 1996	$45,000	?	$30,000
Accounts receivable at end of 1996	?	$70,000	$38,000

PROBLEMS

PROBLEM 3-1 The Effect of Transactions on Accounts

The Z. Taylor Mortuary had the following account summary at April 1:

Z. Taylor Mortuary
Account Summary
April 1, 1995

Assets =		Liabilities + Owners' Equity		+ Revenues − Expenses	
Cash	$ 5,600	Wages payable	$ 3,500	Revenues	$0
Equipment	34,900	Loan from bank	40,000	Expenses	0
Building	100,000	Owners' investment	55,000		
Land	24,000	Reinvested profits	66,000		
Total	$164,500	Total	$164,500	Total	$0

The following transactions occurred during April:

a. All amounts owed to employees at the beginning of the month were paid in full.
b. Services were sold to customers for cash at prices totaling $6,590.
c. The owners withdrew $5,500 from the business for personal use.
d. Depreciation expense was recorded as follows: Equipment, $500; Building, $900.
e. One month's interest (at a 12% annual rate) was paid to the bank.

Required (a) Prepare a new account summary that incorporates April's transactions. (b) Prepare a separate explanation of changes in the cash account. (c) Discuss the return on investment that occurred during April.

PROBLEM 3-2 Determining Transactions from Changes in an Account Summary

The A. Capone Correctional Facility is a private enterprise prison which contracts services to a midwestern state. At the end of September the organization had the following account summary.

A. Capone Correctional Facility
Account Summary
September 30, 1996

Assets =		Liabilities + Owners' Equity		+ Revenues − Expenses	
Cash	$ 29,150	Accounts payable	$ 18,900	Revenues	$0
Supplies	43,800	Bonds payable	300,000	Expenses	0
Equipment	200,000	Owners' investment	700,000		
Buildings	900,000	Reinvested profits	589,050		
Land	435,000				
Total	$1,607,950	Total	$1,607,950	Total	$0

During the month of October, a number of economic events occurred and were entered into the accounting data base. At the end of October the company had the following correct account summary:

A. Capone Correctional Facility
Account Summary
For Month Ended October 31, 1996

Assets =		Liab. + Owners' Equity		+ Revenues − Expenses	
Cash	$ 39,150	Accounts payable	$ 18,900	Revenues	$540,000
Supplies	18,800	Bonds payable	0	Expenses:	
Equipment	200,000	Owners' investment	700,000	Supplies	(25,000)
Buildings	900,000	Reinvested profits	589,050	Depreciation	(5,750)
Accumulated depreciation	(5,750)			Wages	(230,000)
Land	435,000				
Total	$1,587,200	Total	$1,307,950	Total	$279,250

Required Identify the transactions that occurred during October. Also, prepare a separate analysis of the cash account detailing all changes.

PROBLEM 3-3 Preparing an Account Summary for a Fiscal Period

On March 1, Carl Caldwell started the Caldwell Furniture Repair Company. He invested $4,000 of his own money, borrowed $8,000 from his father-in-law at 9% annual interest, and obtained an additional $1,500, 12% loan from Maxibank. He purchased $7,500 of tools and equipment (some new, some used), and bought $2,600 of supplies such as paints, resins, and glue. Caldwell rented a shop at a local business park, paying in advance for the months of March, April and May, $1,800. During March he performed repairs totalling $3,800 and used up $1,200 of supplies. Of the repair services performed, 75% were paid for in cash by the end of the month and the balance was expected to be collected in April. Carl estimated that wear and tear on the equipment and tools during March was $125. On March 31, he owed $166 to the electric company and $39 to the water company for services consumed. Also on that date, he paid interest totalling $75 on the two loans.

Required (a) Prepare an account summary for the Caldwell Furniture Repair Company for the month of March. (b) Prepare a separate presentation that details the changes in the cash account during March. (c) Is the transformation cycle complete or incomplete at the end of March? Explain your answer.

PROBLEM 3-4 Explaining the Difference Between Cash and Accrual Accounting

The accounting department at Klinger Realty sent the financial reports found at the top of the next page to Robin Garrison, general manager. Attached was a note indicating that both sets of data are based on the same set of events that occurred during the quarter just completed. Robin was only recently promoted to this position and is unfamiliar with accounting information and procedures.

After reviewing this report, Robin is somewhat disturbed because she always thought accounting was an exact process. How, she wonders, can there be two different results from the same set of facts? Furthermore, how could they be so different? Which one is the "true" or "correct" report?

Required Assume you are called in to advise Ms. Garrison. Write a memo to her explaining why there can be two measures of operating results and why they differ.

Klinger Enterprises
Results of Operating Activities
Third Quarter, 1995

	Cash Basis		Accrual Basis	
Cash receipts/revenues:				
Sales commissions	$300,000		$400,000	
Property management	310,000		165,000	
Total		$610,000		$565,000
Cash payments/expenses:				
Office employee wages	53,000		48,000	
Advertising	10,000		90,000	
Office supplies	0		3,400	
Depreciation—office equipment	0		1,800	
Rent	6,000		6,000	
Sales staff commissions	150,000		200,000	
Property managers' salaries	116,000		90,000	
Total		335,000		439,200
Net cash flow		$275,000		
Net income				$125,800

PROBLEM 3-5 Preparing a Report of Net Cash Flow from Operations

Weintraub Water Products is a retailer of water sports products for backyard swimming pools. During August, the firm had the following operating activities:

Aug. 1 Bought $5,000 of goods for resale from Pinetree Wholesalers on credit.
5 Paid $450 to the local newspaper for advertising during July.
6 Paid $1,000 rent for the month of August.
9 Sold goods on credit for $7,300. These goods cost the firm $3,600.
10 Paid $3,000 to Pinetree Wholesalers for goods purchased August 1.
11 Collected $5,200 from goods sold on August 9.
13 Paid cash for $9,200 of goods for resale from Stanley Company.
16 Paid employee wages to date, $1,150.
19 Sold goods on credit for $6,350. These goods cost the firm $2,190.
25 Collected $3,700 from the sales made on August 19.
29 Paid $1,000 rent for the month of September.
31 Employees earned $1,200 of wages but will not be paid until September 1.

Required Prepare a report of net cash flow from operating activities.

PROBLEM 3-6 Preparing an Accrual Basis Income Statement

The Computer Den is a retailer of computer hardware and software. It had the following operating activities during the month of April:

April 1 Purchased $8,000 of inventory on credit from Big Byte Wholesalers.
3 Paid $1,800 rent for the months of March and April.
8 Sold goods to customers for $14,200; 40% of that was for cash. These goods cost the firm $8,600.
11 Paid $6,000 to Big Byte Wholesalers for goods purchased April 1.
14 Collected $7,700 from goods sold on April 8.
17 Paid cash for $23,200 of goods for resale to Tech-O Company.

April 18 Paid employee wages to date, $1,150.
21 Sold goods to customers on credit for $12,350. These goods cost the firm $8,190.
22 Contributed $100 to the local United Way campaign.
24 Collected $9,000 from the sales made on April 21.
27 Paid $1,500 to the local newspaper for an ad campaign during April.
30 Paid May rent, $900.
30 Employees earned $1,200 of wages but will not be paid until September 1.

Required Prepare an accrual basis income statement.

PROBLEM 3-7 Converting Net Income to Net Cash Flow

The following accrual basis information is available about Syria Corporation for 1996.

Total revenue from sales to customers	$30,000
Total expenses	23,000
Net income	$ 7,000

In addition, the following account information is known:

	Accounts Receivable	Accounts Payable
Beginning of year balance	$3,000	$5,000
End of year balance	7,000	3,000

Required Determine (a) the amount of cash collected from customers during the year, (b) the amount of cash paid out for expenses during the year, and (c) the net cash flow for the year.

PROBLEM 3-8 Converting Net Cash Flow to Net Income

Mizzi Retail Company reported the following cash flow information at the end of its first year in business.

Cash received from customers		$94,000
Cash paid out to suppliers of inventory	$22,000	
Cash paid out to employees	31,000	
Cash paid out for advertising	5,000	
Cash paid out for taxes	12,000	70,000
Net cash flow for the year		$24,000

Also known at year end was the following:

Amounts not yet collected from customers	$34,000
Amounts owed to suppliers	6,000
Wages owed to employees	9,000
Additional taxes still owed	4,000

Required Prepare an accrual basis income statement for Mizzi Company's first year in business.

PROBLEM 3-9 Preparing Cash Basis and Accrual Basis Reports

Madison Remodelers has the following information available at the end of November concerning operating activities during the last three months:

	September	October	November
Cash collections from customers:			
For services provided during September	$ 90,000	$ 60,000	$ 32,000
For services provided during October	5,000	80,000	55,000
For services provided during November		7,000	65,000
Cash paid out:			
For goods & services used in September	100,000	30,000	20,000
For goods & services used in October	10,000	80,000	30,000
For goods & services used in November		8,000	75,000

Required (a) Prepare a report of October's net cash flow from operating activities. (b) Prepare an accrual basis income statement for October, assuming all of October's revenues and expenses resulted in cash flows in September through November.

PROBLEM 3-10 Revenue Recognition in Accrual Accounting

Daisy Political Consultants has been in existence for many years. During the month of November the following events occurred.

a. The owners contributed an additional $13,000 to the business to finance an expansion of operations.
b. Consulting services totalling $22,000 were performed on credit during November and billed to customers.
c. A loan in the amount of $50,000 was obtained from a wealthy campaign contributor.
d. Expenses in the amount of $12,000 were incurred during the month. One-third had been paid for by month-end.
e. Cash of $37,000 was collected from customers for whom services had been performed during September and October.
f. Services totaling $9,000 were performed for customers who had previously paid for the services during October.

Required Daisy uses accrual basis accounting. For which of the events above should revenue be recorded in November? In each case, how much revenue should be recorded? If an event does not involve revenue, specify why not.

PROBLEM 3-11 Expense Recognition in Accrual Accounting

The local chapter of Special People, a social service organization, had the following economic events occur during the month of May.

a. A luncheon honoring volunteers was held at a cost of $700. By month end the bill hadn't been received or paid.
b. Bought new letterhead and envelopes that were printed at a cost of $400. The new items will not be used, however, until the old supply is exhausted sometime in June.
c. The executive director was paid her usual monthly salary of $3,000.
d. Paid cash for prizes, ribbons and awards for events upcoming in July, $7,500.
e. Paid the electric bill for April totalling $124.

f. Radio, TV, and newspaper advertising related to a special fundraising campaign during May. The $6,500 cost had been paid in April.

Required Special People uses accrual basis accounting. For which of the events above should an expense be recorded in May? In each case, how much expense should be recorded? If an event does not involve an expense, specify why not.

PROBLEM 3-12 Distinguishing Among Types of Accounts

Bishop Auto Glass uses the following accounts when preparing its financial reports. Place a mark in the appropriate column to indicate the type of account.

	Asset	Liability	Equity	Revenue	Expense
a. Wages payable					
b. Accounts receivable					
c. Reinvested profits					
d. Buildings					
e. Supplies expense					
f. Inventory					
g. Sales					
h. Marketable securities					
i. Loan from bank					
j. Land					
k. Owners' investment					
l. Supplies					
m. Cost of Goods Sold					
n. Bonds payable					
o. Prepaid advertising					
p. Wages expense					
q. Utilities expense					

PROBLEM 3-13 Ethics and Accounting Measurement

Hardy Rock is proprietor of a jewelry store. In January, he applied for a bank loan and was asked to submit an income statement for the past year, ended in December. Near the end of the prior year, Hardy had purchased merchandise for resale that cost him $120,000. He still owed $90,000 for this merchandise at year end. Half of the merchandise was sold during the Christmas holidays for $150,000. Customers owed Hardy

$100,000 for these purchases at year end. Hardy included these transactions as part of his financial statements as follows:

Added to revenues	$150,000
Added to expenses	15,000
Added to net income	$135,000

Hardy reasoned that, because he sold half the merchandise in December, he should report it as revenue, though he had not received all of the cash from customers. Also, he reasoned that, because he had paid $30,000 for the merchandise by year end and had sold half of the merchandise, he should report $15,000 of this amount as cost of goods sold.

Required What problems do you see with Hardy's reasoning? Is there an ethical problem with Hardy's treatment of these transactions? What should the effect of these transactions have been on net income?

PROBLEM 3-14 Ethics and Accounting Measurement

Nick Nash, Fred Ford, and Dick Dodge are partners in an automobile dealership, Chic Chevrolet. Nick keeps the accounting records for the partnership because the other partners do not have much knowledge of accounting and depend on Nick for his expertise. The partners have agreed they will share equally in the company's profits at the end of each year. For fiscal 1996, the first year of operations, the company sold $3,300,000 of merchandise. Of this amount, $800,000 was still owed the company by customers at year end. The company purchased and paid cash for merchandise costing $1,700,000 during 1996. $500,000 of this merchandise remained in inventory at year end. The company purchased and paid for $600,000 of equipment, which should have a useful life of six years. Other expenses amounted to $290,000, all paid for in cash. Nick prepared the following income statement and distribution of profits for 1996:

Income Statement

Revenues		$2,500,000
Expenses:		
Merchandise	$1,700,000	
Equipment	600,000	
Other	290,000	
Total expenses		2,590,000
Net loss		$ 90,000
Distribution of net loss:		
Reduction in owner's capital:		
Dick Dodge		30,000
Fred Ford		30,000
Nick Nash		30,000
Total distribution of net loss		$ 90,000

Dick and Fred were mystified by these results because they believed the company had been performing above their expectations. Nick assured his partners his numbers were correct.

Required What problems do you see with Nick's financial report? How might Nick have used the information in his report to take advantage of his partners? Prepare a proper income statement and distribution of profits schedule for Chic Chevrolet.

PROBLEM 3-15 Multiple-Choice Overview of the Chapter

1. Which of the following are part of an organization's transformation process?

	Investing activities	Operating activities
a.	Yes	Yes
b.	Yes	No
c.	No	Yes
d.	No	No

2. A going concern:
   a. need not prepare financial reports.
   b. should be expected to go out of business in the near future.
   c. need not concern itself with cash flow but should concentrate instead on generating net income.
   d. is assumed to have an expected life sufficiently long to complete any transformation cycles currently in process.
3. Tempel Manufacturing uses accrual accounting. Each of the following events occurred during the month of February. Which one of them should be recorded as a revenue or expense for the month of February?
   a. Sales of $30,000 were made on credit. They will be collected during March.
   b. Collections of $10,000 were made from sales that occurred during January.
   c. Materials costing $18,000 were purchased and paid for. It is expected that they will be used during March.
   d. A bill in the amount of $8,600 was received from a supplier for goods purchased during January. It was paid immediately.
4. Zinsli Company uses the accrual basis of accounting. Each of the following events occurred during July. Which one of them should be reported as an expense of July?
   a. Office supplies costing $800 were used up. They had been purchased and paid for during April.
   b. A new delivery truck was purchased on the last day of July. It was not put into use until August.
   c. On the third day of the month, $8,000 was paid to employees for hours worked during the month of June.
   d. Near the end of the month, August rent of $1,500 was paid in advance.
5. Montvise, Incorporated started operations during 1995. By year end, cash collections from customers totalled $153,000. In addition, the firm had accounts receivable from customers of $20,000. What amount of revenue should Montvise report on its 1995 income statement if it uses accrual accounting?
   a. $0
   b. $133,000
   c. $153,000
   d. $173,000
6. Periodic measurement requires that:
   a. the transformation process of an organization be measured and reported regularly.
   b. financial events be measured using a periodic chart of accounts.
   c. the life of a company should be long enough so that all incomplete transformation cycles can be completed.
   d. financial statements be prepared for owners at least every month.
7. The following information is available for two companies for the year 1996:

	Handle-Bar Mustache Company	Pencil-Thin Mustache Company
	Cash Operating Statement For the Year 1996	*Accrual Income Statement For the Year 1996*
Receipts/Revenues	$50,000	$55,000
Payments/Expenses	38,000	31,000
Net Cash/Net Income	$12,000	$24,000

Which of the following statements can be determined from the information provided?

a. Pencil-Thin collected more cash from customers during 1996 than did Handle-Bar.
b. Pencil-Thin was profitable during 1996, while Handle-Bar may have been profitable.
c. Pencil-Thin is twice as profitable as Handle-Bar.
d. Handle-Bar consumed more total resources during 1996 than did Pencil-Thin.

8. Which of the following accounts is a liability?

	Depreciation Expense	Accounts Receivable
a.	Yes	Yes
b.	Yes	No
c.	No	Yes
d.	No	No

9. On January 1, 1995, a company bought machinery for $15,000. The machinery was expected to last for 5 years and to be of no value after that point. The firm will depreciate the machinery $3,000 per year. At the end of the second year, the machinery is appraised to be worth $11,000 on the open market. How much depreciation did the company record on the asset for the first two years?
   a. $4,000
   b. $11,000
   c. $6,000
   d. $9,000
10. Using accrual-based measurement, expenses should be recognized when:
    a. a business owner recognizes that the firm is incurring too many expenses.
    b. resources are used rather than when they are paid for.
    c. cash is paid for resources.
    d. sufficient revenue is earned to offset the expenses.

CASES

CASE 3-1 Evaluating the Transformation Process

The Provolone Pizza Company has just completed its first month in business. The owners, Charla and Pauline, had previously worked for a major pizza chain but were convinced they could offer a better product in a better atmosphere. They knew the importance of accurate financial records and hired a bookkeeper. Yesterday, the bookkeeper hand-delivered an account summary to the owners and promptly fell over dead. You have been retained by Charla and Pauline to interpret the following financial report and explain its significance.

Provolone Pizza Company
Account Summary
For First Month of Business

Assets =		Liabilities + Owners' Equity		+ Revenues − Expenses	
Cash	$ 2,240	Wages payable	$ 180	Revenues	$4,000
Food products	980	Advertising payable	400	Expenses:	
Supplies	1,000	Loan from bank	6,800	Store rent	(800)
Prepaid rent	2,400	Owners' capital	5,500	Food products	(1,475)
Equipment	5,100			Wages	(990)
				Advertising	(1,430)
				Interest	(40)
				Supplies	(375)
				Depreciation	(50)
Total	$11,720	Total	$12,880	Total	$(1,160)

Required (a) Discuss whether the information provided by the summary could be helpful to the owners and, if so, describe how. If not, describe why not. (b) Identify at least ten events that occurred as part of the transformation process during the firm's first month in business, identifying the amounts of cash involved. (c) Prepare an analysis of cash that explains how the cash balance changed during the period covered by the report. (d) Did Charla and Pauline make a good judgment when they decided to get into this business? Would you recommend they continue with the pizza business or discontinue it? What additional information would be helpful to you in making such a recommendation?

CASE 3-2 Evaluating the Results of an Organization's Transformation Process

Spivey Software Corporation has been in business for several years and is publicly traded on a major U.S. stock exchange. It is a wholesaler of a variety of commercial software applications including word processing, spreadsheet, and database applications. On January 1, 1996, the company's balance sheet appeared as follows (all amounts are in thousands of dollars):

Spivey Software Corporation
Balance Sheet
January 1, 1996

Assets		Liabilities & Stockholders' Equity	
Cash	$ 4,240	Wages payable	$ 640
Accounts receivable	7,800	Capital stock	32,000
Inventory	15,200	Retained earnings	13,600
Buildings and equipment	12,000		
Land (for plant expansion)	7,000	Total liabilities and	
Total assets	$46,240	stockholders' equity	$46,240

During the first quarter of 1996 (January, February, March), the following events occurred.

a. New office furniture costing $500 was purchased with cash on the last day of March. This was to be used in a new sales office that was scheduled to open April 1.
b. Wages and salaries totalling $3,200 were paid. 20% of this amount was to liquidate wages payable that arose in the 4th quarter of the previous year. The company has a policy of not making wage or salary advances to employees.
c. All accounts receivable outstanding at January 1 were collected.
d. The company's advertising agency billed the firm $1,000 for a campaign running during the current quarter. The company is planning to pay the bill during April.
e. Sales were made to customers totalling $18,000. Of these sales, 60% was collected during the first quarter and the balance is expected to be collected during the next quarter. The goods that were sold cost the company $13,000 when they were purchased.
f. Dividends were declared and paid to stockholders in the amount of $1,500.
g. Inventory (software programs) costing $10,500 was purchased. 10% was paid for by the end of the quarter.
h. A three-year, $4,000, 12% loan was obtained from a local bank on the last day of the quarter.
i. New shares of stock were sold by the company for $2,000 in cash.
j. A new three-year lease agreement was signed and executed. The lease required that a $900 monthly rental be paid in advance for the first two quarters of the current year.
k. The accountants calculated that depreciation totalling $300 should be recorded for the quarter regarding the firm's buildings and equipment that had originally cost $16,870.
l. Sold the land that had been held for plant expansion for $7,000.

Required Did the company have a satisfactory first quarter? Prepare any summary documents you believe might help management (or interested external parties) better understand the effectiveness or efficiency of the firm's first quarter transformation process.

PROJECTS

PROJECT 3-1 Bibliographic Indexes for Business

Bibliographic indexes list magazine, journal, or newspaper articles by topic. Using an index, you are to identify a published article, find it, copy it, and write a summary of it that will be discussed in class or turned in to your instructor. To begin, go to the reference area of your library and locate one or more of the following: *The Business Periodicals Index*, *The Accounting and Taxation Index*, *ABI/INFORM* (a computerized system). In one of the indexes, look up categories such as cash flow, cash basis accounting, cash management, and accrual basis accounting. Select two articles that appear to address examples of how cash flow (or cash basis) accounting information is used. Alternatively, you might look for articles that compare the usefulness of accrual and cash basis information. Read the articles and write a one-page summary.

PROJECT 3-2 Comparing Cash Versus Accrual Financial Reports

Under GAAP, a company must report the results of its operating activities on both the accrual basis and the cash basis. Users then can compare the amount of cash generated by operating activities to the amount of net income generated by operating activities. The purpose of this exercise is to locate and compare cash and accrual information in annual reports. The results of operating activities are reported in two separate places. Accrual basis information is reported on the income statement, while cash basis information is reported on the statement of cash flows. In this assignment you are to choose three companies. Choose one merchandising company, one manufacturing company, and one service company (e.g. utility, bank, or insurance). From your library's collection of annual reports, obtain the four most recent annual reports of each company you selected. Because each report contains two years' information, you will have at least five years of data. In each annual report, find the income statement and statement of cash flows. Prepare a schedule of information in the format below.

	Results of Operating Activities	
	From the Cash Flow Statement	**From the Income Statement**
	Cash Flow From Operating Activities	*Net Income (or Operating Income)*
Company #1:		
19__	$________	$________
19__	$________	$________
19__	$________	$________
19__	$________	$________
19__	$________	$________
Total for 5 years	$________	$________
Average per year	$________	$________

Use the amount labeled operating income if you can find it. If not, use net income as an approximation. Start with the most recent year first and work backwards. Continue similarly for the second and third companies. For each company, write a short description of how its cash flow pattern compares to its net income. Are they similar? Opposite? Do any trends emerge? If the cash flow is different from the net income (and it will be), explain how this can occur.

PROJECT 3-3 Identifying Cash Flows

Identify recent annual reports for five companies in five different industries. Find the statement of cash flows in each company's report. Make a list of the cash flows from operating, financing, and investing activities for each company. List the primary financing and investing activities identified in each company's report. Write a short report to accompany your lists that discusses how these activities appear to differ in importance across industries.

PROJECT 3-4 Cash and Accrual Measures

Assume you are trying to explain to a friend the differences between cash and accrual accounting. Write a short comparison of the two types of measurement. Provide examples of each to show how they differ when used to measure a common type of transaction. Show your comparison to someone who does not have much understanding of accounting and ask this person to write a brief note indicating any problems with understanding your explanation.

PROJECT 3-5 Unethical Behavior

Use an index of business periodicals (e.g., *The Business Periodicals Index* or *The Accounting and Taxation Index*) in the reference room of your library to identify articles about recent cases in which businesses or their managers have been accused or convicted of fraud. Find one that discusses how the fraud occurred and write a brief summary that includes a citation for the article. Explain the general effect the fraud had on the company's financial condition and on its financial statements. How were investors and others who had contractual relationships with the company affected by the fraud? What legal remedies (if any) were being sought for the fraud?

CHAPTER 4

PROCESSING ACCOUNTING INFORMATION

CHAPTER *Overview*

This chapter examines the processing phase of the accounting information system. The chapter considers procedures accountants use to record, store, and summarize accounting data in a form that provides useful information for decision makers. The processing phase is the third stage of the accounting information system described in Chapter 2:

Also covered in this chapter are manual and computerized accounting systems. Both types of systems serve the same basic function: to convert data about economic events into information useful for decision makers. Therefore, all accounting systems require the analysis of events to determine transactions that should be recorded in the system. How transactions are recorded and how the system processes transactions differ, however, among systems. We will consider how transactions are identified and recorded and how accounting systems process data to create useful information. Also, we will consider controls used with accounting systems to increase their reliability and the accuracy of accounting information.

Major topics covered in this chapter include:

- The effects of transactions on accounting records and reports.
- Components and functions of manual and computerized accounting systems.
- Control procedures to improve the reliability of accounting systems.

CHAPTER *Objectives*

Once you have completed this chapter, you should be able to:

1. Summarize the purpose of the processing phase of an accounting information system.
2. Explain what is meant by the term "double-entry bookkeeping."
3. Explain the purpose of the journal and the ledger.
4. Explain the purpose of debits and credits.
5. Explair. the purpose of a subsidiary ledger.
6. Analyze transactions and determine their effects on account balances.
7. Explain the purpose of closing the books.
8. Summarize the steps in the accounting cycle.
9. Describe the components of a microcomputer accounting system.

10. Identify the modules of a large accounting system.
11. Distinguish between master and transaction files.
12. Trace the flow of data through a large accounting system.
13. Explain the purpose of accounting controls for manual and computerized accounting systems.
14. Identify the types of management decisions an accounting system facilitates.

PROCESSING TRANSACTIONS

The processing phase of the accounting information system begins with identifying and recording transactions, which are events that occur within the transformation process. The financial effects of transactions are recorded in the accounting system as increases or decreases in the balances of individual accounts. Account balances are stored in a data base. Reports for internal and external decision makers summarize information from the data base.

Objective 1
Summarize the purpose of the processing phase of an accounting system.

Transactions occur when an organization obtains financial resources, when it invests its financial resources in other resources, when it consumes these resources to produce goods and services, and when it sells goods and services. An organization's resources include financial resources (such as cash and securities), physical resources (such as buildings and equipment), services (such as human labor), or legal rights (such as patents). An organization obtains financial resources when it borrows from creditors and receives investments from owners; it invests in other resources when it purchases, borrows, or rents them. An organization consumes resources when it uses them in the transformation process to produce goods and services. When the goods and services are sold to customers, an organization earns the right to receive additional financial resources. **The purpose of the processing phase of the accounting information system is to record resource acquisition and consumption activities in a systematic form that can be summarized and reported.**

ACCOUNTING SYSTEMS

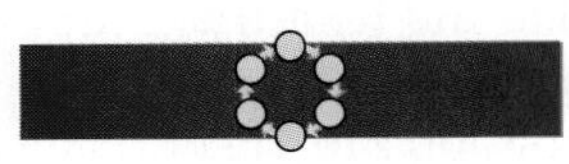

Systems for processing accounting information come in a variety of forms. These systems fulfill the purpose discussed in the previous section and lead to similar results. How they work may be quite different, however. Major differences depend on whether the system is manual or computerized.

Manual Accounting Systems

Objective 2
Explain what is meant by the term "double-entry bookkeeping."

The traditional approach used to process transactions is known as *double-entry bookkeeping*, a systematic method for recording transactions. Double-entry bookkeeping involves a series of interrelated steps. The organization creates a set of accounting "books" to record and store the effects of transactions on accounts. For many centuries, these transactions were recorded manually in bound books or loose-leaf documents. The term "double-entry" comes from the requirement that each transaction be recorded in two or more accounts. A transaction identifies an exchange of resources or other event in which a "give and take" has occurred. The "give and take" process affects at least two elements of the accounting equation.

Recall that the balance sheet equation is a fundamental expression of the relationship among accounting elements:

ASSETS = LIABILITIES + OWNERS' EQUITY

During a fiscal period, an organization accumulates revenues and expenses that are transferred to owners' equity at the end of the period. At the end of a fiscal period, owners' equity is adjusted to include the effects of revenues and expenses for the period:

Owners' equity at beginning of period
\+ Revenues for the period
− Expenses for the period
= Owners' equity at end of period

This adjustment transfers the amount of net income earned during a period to the balance sheet. During a fiscal period, before the adjustment is made, the accounting equation must be expanded to include the effects of revenues and expenses:

ASSETS = LIABILITIES + OWNERS' EQUITY + REVENUES − EXPENSES

This equation is critical to understanding how transactions are recorded in an accounting system. **A balance must be maintained at all times among the elements of the equation.** Therefore, if one element changes in the equation, some other element also must change to maintain the balance. Thus, the title "double-entry." The following section provides an example of transactions associated with a manual accounting system. We will use the transactions to illustrate double-entry bookkeeping.

An Illustration of a Manual Accounting System

Round-O Tires is a small retail business selling automobile and light truck tires. The business also provides related services, such as balancing, repairing flats, and aligning front-ends. Round-O is owned and managed by Johnny Treads. The business employs three other people, including a part-time bookkeeper, Nora Specks. Most of the company's sales are for cash, though it sells on credit to a few major business customers.

Objective 3
Explain the purpose of the journal and the ledger.

Round-O, like many small businesses, records transactions using a journal and a ledger. **A *journal* is a book for recording transactions in the order in which they occur. A *ledger* is a book for summarizing account balances.** The journal and ledger are the data base for a manual accounting system. Manual accounting systems almost always use at least one primary journal and one primary ledger, called the **general journal** and **general ledger**. Special journals and ledgers may be used for specific purposes. Transactions are recorded in the journal after being analyzed to determine which accounts are affected, the amount of the effect, and whether the transaction increases or decreases these accounts. Source documents provide a basis for determining the effect of transactions on accounts. ***Source documents*** **are records of specific transactions such as sales invoices, receiving notices, bills, and cash register receipts.**

Processing data in the accounting system involves the analysis of transactions, often from source documents, to determine their effect on the balances of individual accounts. ***Transaction analysis*** **is the determination of which accounts a transaction affects, the amount of the effect, and whether the transaction increases or decreases affected account balances.**

Sales and Inventory Transactions. Most of Round-O's transactions involve the sale of goods and services, collecting cash from customers, obtaining inventory, and paying suppliers. Exhibit 4-1 provides an illustration of the flow of data through the accounting system to record these transactions.

Exhibit 4-1 Recording Sales and Inventory Transactions

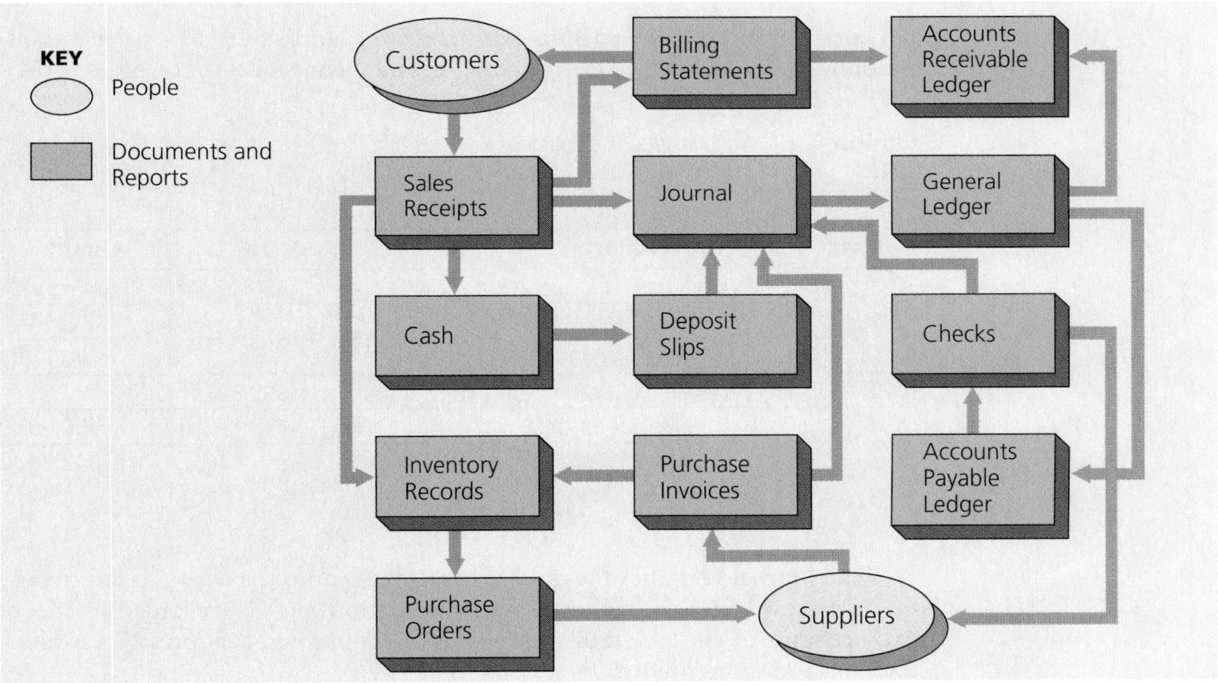

When a customer makes a purchase, Johnny writes a **sales receipt**, which describes the items or services sold, and lists the quantity and prices of the sales, and the date and customer's name. Cash sales are marked "Paid" on the sales receipt. For credit sales the customer's signature is required on the sales receipt.

At the end of each day, Johnny counts the cash, including checks and credit card slips. Cash of $200 for change is kept in the cash drawer; the remaining cash, representing the day's cash sales, is deposited at a local bank. A copy of the deposit slip is placed with the sales receipts.

Cash Sales. Each morning, Nora collects the sales receipts and deposit slips from the prior day's sales. She records the total sales in the journal. Exhibit 4-2

Example of a Sales Receipt

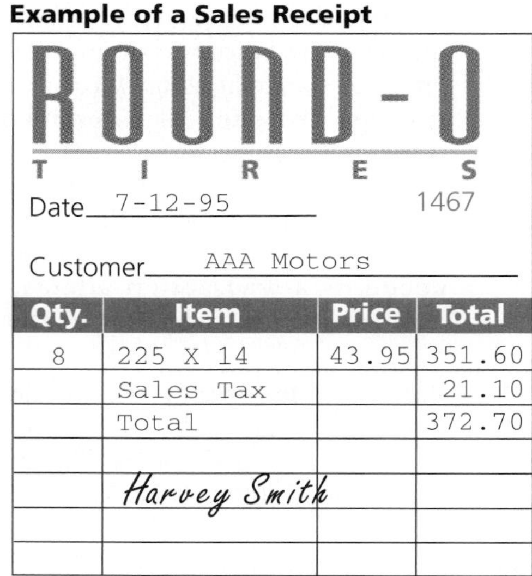

ROUND-O TIRES

Date 7-12-95 1467

Customer AAA Motors

Qty.	Item	Price	Total
8	225 X 14	43.95	351.60
	Sales Tax		21.10
	Total		372.70
	Harvey Smith		

provides an example of a portion of a page from Nora's journal. The first transaction records sales of tires for cash; the second records sales on credit.

Exhibit 4-2 An Example of a Journal

Page 23

Date	Transaction		Debit	Credit
Oct. 3	Cash	✔	1,300.39	
	Sales Tax Payable	✔		73.61
	Sales Revenue	✔		1,226.78
Oct. 3	Accounts Receivable		893.86	
	Sales Tax Payable			50.60
	Sales Revenue			843.26

The journal identifies the date of each transaction, the accounts affected by the transaction, and the amounts. Each transaction must be recorded in at least two accounts to preserve the balance of the accounting equation. We can illustrate this process as follows:

Assets =	Liabilities + Owners' Equity	+ Revenues − Expenses
Cash 1,300.39	Sales Tax Payable 73.61	Sales Revenue 1,226.78

An increase in the asset CASH of $1,300.39 is balanced by an increase in SALES TAX PAYABLE of $73.61 and an increase in SALES REVENUE of $1,226.78. Note that Round-O collects 6% sales tax for local governments. These collections result in obligations to remit the taxes to government authorities, and thus, are recorded as liabilities.

The elements of the accounting equation can be thought of in the following way:

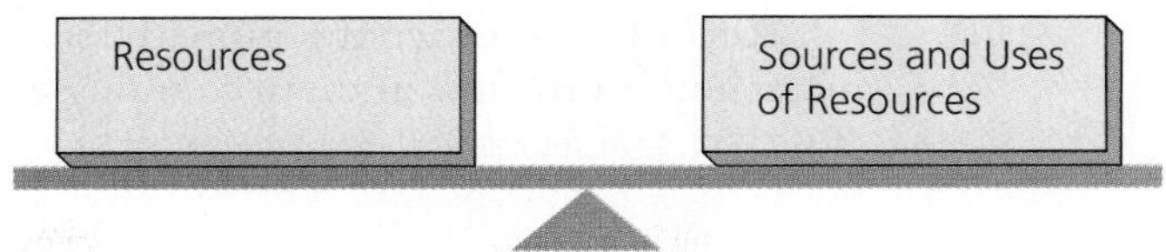

Assets are resources. Resources originate from those who invest in an organization (liabilities, owners' equity) and those who purchase its goods and services (revenues). Resources are consumed in payments to investors and in materials and services that are used to provide goods and services for customers (expenses). Thus, the balance between resources and the sources and uses of resources must always be maintained.

Objective 4
Explain the purpose of debits and credits.

Traditionally, accountants have recorded transactions using debits and credits. **Debits and credits refer to increases and decreases in account balances. *Debits* are increases in asset and expense account balances and decreases in liability, owners' equity, and revenue account balances. *Credits* are decreases in asset and expense account balances and increases in liability, owners' equity, and revenue account balances.** In Exhibit 4-2, CASH was increased by a debit, while SALES TAX PAYABLE and SALES REVENUE were increased by credits. By convention, the left-hand side of the accounting equation (assets) is increased by debits, while the right-hand side (liabilities and owners' equity) is increased by credits. Revenues increase owners' equity and, therefore, are increased by credits. Expenses are an offset to revenues and reduce owners' equity. Therefore, they are increased by debits:

Assets =	Liabilities + Owners' Equity	+ Revenues	− Expenses
Debit +	Debit −	Debit −	Debit +
Credit −	Credit +	Credit +	Credit −

These rules preserve the mathematical relationship in the accounting equation. At the same time, they provide a check on the accuracy of recorded transactions. The total of debits recorded in the journal for any period should be equal to the total of credits. If debits do not equal credits, an error has occurred in recording one or more transactions for the period.

The mathematical relationship of debits and credits with the accounting equation is readily observable if the equation is transformed by moving expenses from the right-hand to the left-hand side:

ASSETS + EXPENSES = LIABILITIES + OWNERS' EQUITY + REVENUES

The left-hand side of the equation is increased by debit entries and the right-hand side is increased by credit entries:

Recording transactions properly so debits are equal to credits results in maintaining a balance in the accounting equation.

Learning Note

The format shown above for debits and credits is referred to as the T-account format. It is a commonly used approach for demonstrating the effect of transactions on accounts. For example, the sales transaction of October 3 in Exhibit 4-2 could be represented as:

CASH		=	SALES TAX PAYABLE		+	SALES REVENUE	
Debit	Credit		Debit	Credit		Debit	Credit
1,300.39				73.61			1,226.78

T-accounts are not part of an accounting system. They are simply a device often used to explain transactions.

As illustrated in Exhibit 4-2, by convention, debit entries in a journal are recorded first and are followed by credit entries for each transaction. Credit entries are indented from the left-hand margin to make them easier to identify. An explanation might follow below the journal entry describing the event that produced the transaction.

A ledger provides a summary of transactions affecting individual accounts. The check marks in Exhibit 4-2 indicate that the transactions recorded in the journal have been **posted** to (recorded in) the ledger. Exhibit 4-3 illustrates a portion of Round-O's general ledger for the cash account:

Exhibit 4-3 An Example of a General Ledger

Account: CASH — Account Number: 101

Date	Ref.	Debit	Credit	Balance
Sept. 26	GJ 22	879.25		17,892.34
	GJ 22		578.91	17,313.43
27	GJ 22		490.18	16,823.25
	GJ 22	133.82		16,957.07
Oct. 3	GJ 23	1,300.39		18,257.46

A ledger page is maintained for each account. Accounts are numbered for ease of reference. **A *chart of accounts* is a list of account titles and numbers for an organization.** Often, assets are numbered from 100-199, liabilities from 200-299, etc. Account numbers may have subcodes to identify divisions, departments, or individual customers. For example, account 301-16 may identify an ACCOUNTS PAYABLE account (301) for Never-Wear Tire Company (16). Account 425-06-112 may identify utility expenses (425), at the North Dakota plant (06), in the maintenance department (112).

The October 3 entry in the reference column indicates the source of the entry was the General Journal (GJ), page 23. Increases in asset and expense accounts are posted to the debit column of the ledger account. These debit entries increase the balances of the asset and expense accounts. Increases in liability, owners' equity, and revenue accounts are posted to the credit column, as shown below for the sales revenue account. This entry posts the transaction recorded on October 3 in the journal, Exhibit 4-2.

Account: SALES REVENUE — Account Number: 401

Date	Ref.	Debit	Credit	Balance
Sept. 28				43,249.75
Oct. 3	GJ 23		1,226.78	44,476.53

An advantage of using two columns, one for additions and one for subtractions, is the ease of computing totals. Remember that, for most of history, bookkeepers did not have adding machines, calculators, or computers. Mathematical calculation was a mental activity. It is easier to add a column of debits and another column of credits and then compute the difference than it is to mix pluses and minuses in the same column. Adding columns to verify totals has been a routine part of bookkeeping. The debit and credit system is designed to help the bookkeeper maintain accurate records. Much of this advantage is lost in an age of computers. Debits and credits are still part of the language of accounting, but their importance for accounting systems is much diminished. Computers identify pluses and minuses, rather than debits and credits, and do not care about the order in which they occur.

The goal of this book is not to make you proficient in using debits and credits. Instead, a goal is to help you understand the effect of transactions on accounting reports. It is important that you be able to analyze transactions to determine their effect on financial statements. **A set of financial statements is a summary of transactions.** Therefore, to understand financial statements you should understand the underlying transactions. Our concern is that you understand which elements of the accounting equation are affected, how they are affected, and how the effects are observed in the financial statements. However, debits and credits are part of the language of accounting and business you should include in your vocabulary.

Credit Sales and Accounts Receivable. Credit sales are recorded to the accounts receivable and sales revenue accounts:

Assets =		Liabilities + Owners' Equity		+ Revenues − Expenses	
Accounts Receivable	893.86	Sales Tax Payable	50.60	Sales Revenue	843.26

Nora separates the sales receipts for credit sales and places them in a file for future reference.

At the end of each week, Nora prepares a billing statement for each credit customer, listing sales to the customer for the week and the balance owed by the customer. She mails the billing statement to the customer and files a copy. When a payment is received from a credit customer, Nora compares the amount on the customer's check with the appropriate billing statement (see

Exhibit 4-1). She records the amount received in the journal to the cash and accounts receivable accounts:

Assets =	Liabilities + Owners' Equity	+ Revenues − Expenses
Cash 657.00 Accounts Receivable (657.00)		

Parentheses indicate decreases in column totals.

Observe that exchanging one asset for another preserves the balance in the accounting equation.

In addition to posting this transaction to ACCOUNTS RECEIVABLE in the general ledger, Nora also must post it to specific customer accounts in the **accounts receivable ledger**. This ledger lists each customer who buys from Round-O on credit. When customers purchase goods, Nora debits their accounts; when they pay for goods they have purchased, she credits their accounts:

Accounts Receivable Subsidiary Ledger

Account: DEPENDABLE AUTO Account Number: 103-08

Date	Ref.	Debit	Credit	Balance
Sept. 18	GJ 21	456.33		1,556.90
Sept. 29	GJ 22		690.12	866.78
Oct. 3	GJ 23	893.86		1,760.64

Objective 5
Explain the purpose of a subsidiary ledger.

The accounts receivable ledger is a subsidiary ledger. **A *subsidiary ledger* contains accounts that are subcategories of a general ledger account.** By using subsidiary ledgers, a company can maintain detailed information separate from the summary record found in the general ledger. The totals of all customer accounts in the subsidiary accounts receivable ledger should be equal to the balance of the accounts receivable account in the general ledger. The general ledger account is a **control account**. The accounts in the accounts receivable ledger are **subsidiary accounts** that support the balance of the control account:

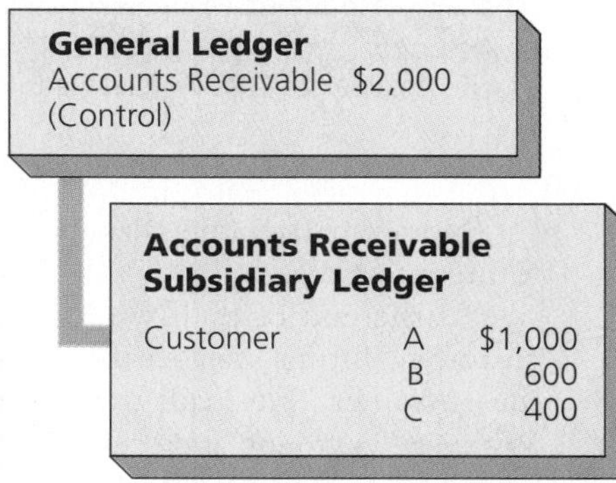

Cost of Goods Sold and Inventory. After recording sales, Nora records the cost of inventory sold to the cost of goods sold and inventory accounts for items listed on the sales receipts. This transaction reduces inventory and increases expense, thereby reducing net income:

Assets =	Liabilities + Owners' Equity	+ Revenues − Expenses
Inventory (1,076.12)		Cost of Goods Sold (1,076.12)

Nora uses the sales receipts to update inventory records. The records are maintained on index cards, though they could be maintained in an inventory subsidiary ledger. A separate card is kept for each inventory item. Thus, each brand and size of tire is listed on a separate card, along with its cost. The card lists the number of units in inventory. Nora subtracts the number of units sold during the prior day to update the record each morning.

Purchases and Accounts Payable. When the number of units in inventory drops below a predetermined number, Nora prepares a purchase order for additional tires (see Exhibit 4-1). Johnny signs the purchase order and mails it to the tire manufacturer's regional warehouse. Nora files a copy of the purchase order.

When an order is received, Nora compares the packing slip (a list of items shipped) accompanying the shipment with the purchase order. Then, she updates the inventory records for the new tires or informs Johnny of any discrepancy in the order. A purchase invoice is mailed by the warehouse to Round-O. The purchase invoice identifies the costs of items and the amount owed the supplier. When the invoice is received, Nora records the purchase in the journal to the inventory and accounts payable accounts:

Assets =	Liabilities + Owners' Equity	+ Revenues − Expenses
Inventory 8,460.93	Accounts Payable 8,460.93	

Nora also records the purchase in an **accounts payable ledger**. This subsidiary ledger lists accounts for each supplier and the amount Round-O owes each supplier. (The terms "supplier" and "vendor" are used interchangeably in practice.) The accounts payable ledger functions for suppliers in the same manner as the accounts receivable ledger does for customers.

At the end of each month, Nora writes checks for purchase invoices received during the month. She records the payments in the journal to the accounts payable and cash accounts:

Assets =	Liabilities + Owners' Equity	+ Revenues − Expenses
Cash (5,794.68)	Accounts Payable (5,794.68)	

Learning Note

Observe that a transaction is not recorded when merchandise is ordered. A transaction is recorded once ownership of the merchandise is transferred to the purchaser. This transfer generally takes place at time of delivery. Also, orders received for goods and services are not recorded until ownership of the goods is transferred or the services are provided to the customer.

Other Transactions. Bills received for utilities, advertising, and other expenses are placed in a file when received. At the end of each week, Nora writes checks for these bills. In the journal she records the payments to the expense and cash accounts. Also at the end of each week, Nora writes a payroll check for each employee. Nora maintains a payroll record for each employee, listing the amount paid and the amount withheld for taxes and social security. In the journal she records the payments to the wages expense and cash accounts. Also, she records PAYROLL TAX EXPENSE and PAYROLL TAXES PAYABLE for the amount that has to be distributed to the government. Johnny signs the checks and distributes them to employees or mails them to other service providers.

Nora records purchases of equipment and other fixed assets in the journal to the appropriate asset account and to CASH or ACCOUNTS PAYABLE. A record for each fixed asset is maintained on an index card (though a subsidiary ledger could be used). The card describes the asset and lists the date of purchase and the purchase price. The company's accountant reviews the cards each year and computes depreciation rates for the fixed assets.

The following illustration summarizes the transactions identified in this section:

Assets =		Liabilities + Owners' Equity		+ Revenues − Expenses	
Cash	1,300.39	Sales Tax Payable	73.61	Sales Revenue	1,226.78
Accounts Receivable	893.86	Sales Tax Payable	50.60	Sales Revenue	843.26
Cash Accounts Receivable	657.00 (657.00)				
Inventory	(1,076.12)			Cost of Goods Sold	(1,076.12)
Inventory	8,460.93	Accounts Payable	8,460.93		
Cash	(5,794.68)	Accounts Payable	(5,794.68)		
Cash	(465.89)			Utilities Expense	(465.89)
Cash	(7,234.97)			Wages Expense	(7,234.97)
		Payroll Tax Payable	1,320.12	Payroll Tax Expense	(1,320.12)
Equipment Cash	2,047.39 (2,047.39)				
Total	**(3,916.48)**	**Total**	**4,110.58**	**Total**	**(8,027.06)**

Objective 6
Analyze transactions and determine their effects on account balances.

Note the **accounting equation is in balance after each transaction is recorded.** At any time, the column totals for transactions recorded for a period will demonstrate that the equation is balanced. Also, be careful to observe that transactions change account balances. **The amounts recorded are not the balances of the accounts but changes in the balances.** Therefore, after all the transactions described above have been recorded, the assets column reports a decrease in total assets of $3,916.48. This amount is the change in assets resulting from the transactions. It is *not* the amount of assets available after the transactions have been recorded.

Exhibit 4-4 illustrates the effect of Round-O's transactions on its account balances:

Exhibit 4-4 The Effect of Transactions on Account Balances

	Balances Before Transactions	+ or − Transaction Effects	= Balances After Transactions
Assets:			
Cash	$16,957.07	+1,300.39 +657.00 −5,794.68 −465.89 −7,234.97 −2,047.39 −13,585.54	$3,371.53
Accounts receivable	24,305.91	+893.86 −657.00 +236.86	24,542.77
Inventory	89,570.12	−1,076.12 +8,460.93 +7,384.81	96,954.93
Property, plant, and equipment	186,452.55	+2,047.39	188,499.94
Total assets	**317,285.65**	**−3,916.48**	**313,369.17**
Liabilities:			
Accounts payable	20,410.33	+8,460.93 −5,794.68 +2,666.25	23,076.58
Sales tax payable	8,100.47	+73.61 +50.60 +124.21	8,224.68
Payroll tax payable	5,326.84	+1,320.12	6,646.96
Notes payable	187,500.00		187,500.00
Total liabilities	**221,337.64**	**+4,110.58**	**225,448.22**
Owner's equity	**87,532.14**		**87,532.14**
Sales revenue	**43,249.75**	+1,226.78 +843.26 +2,070.04	**45,319.79**
Expenses:			
Cost of goods sold	(17,687.08)	−1,076.12	(18,763.20)
Utilities expense	(2,590.10)	−465.89	(3,055.99)
Wages expense	(12,399.26)	−7,234.97	(19,634.23)
Payroll tax expense	(2,157.44)	−1,320.12	(3,477.56)
Total expenses	**(34,833.88)**	**−10,097.10**	**(44,903.98)**
Total liabilities, owner's equity, revenues and expenses	**$317,285.65**	**−3,916.48**	**$313,369.17**

The transactions change the balances of Round-O's accounts. The equality, ASSETS = LIABILITIES + OWNERS' EQUITY + REVENUES − EXPENSES, is maintained before ($317,285.65) and after ($313,369.17) the transactions are recorded.

Exhibit 4-5 Common Types of Transactions

Transaction	Source Documents	Accounts Affected		
		Assets	Liabilities and Owners' Equity	Revenues and Expenses
Sales for cash	Sales slips and invoices	Cash (Inventory)		Sales Revenue (Cost of Goods Sold)
Sales on credit	Sales slips and invoices	Accounts Receivable (Inventory)		Sales Revenue (Cost of Goods Sold)
Collections from customers	Checks and billing statements	Cash (Accounts Receivable)		
Purchase merchandise or materials for cash	Purchase orders and invoices	(Cash) Inventory		
Purchase merchandise or materials on credit	Purchase orders and invoices	Inventory	Accounts Payable	
Payment to vendors	Bills and checks	(Cash)	(Accounts Payable)	
Other purchases for cash	Purchase orders and invoices	(Cash) Equipment or other assets		
Other purchases on credit	Purchase orders and invoices	Equipment or other assets	Accounts or Notes Payable	
Payment of operating expenses	Bills and checks	(Cash)		(Expenses—Wages, Utilities etc.)
Borrow from creditors	Loan agreements	Cash	Notes or Bonds Payable	
Repay creditors	Checks	(Cash)	(Notes or Bonds Payable)	
Pay interest to creditors	Checks	(Cash)		(Interest Expense)
Investment by owners	Owner or stockholder agreements	Cash	Owners' Capital or Stockholders' Equity	
Payment of return to owners	Checks	(Cash)	(Owners' Capital or Dividends)	

Transactions that decrease column totals are shown in ( ).

Summary of Transactions. Though many types of transactions occur in an organization, a few types of transactions account for most activity recorded in an accounting system. Exhibit 4-5 summarizes primary transactions between an organization and external parties. Other than adjustments (considered in Chapter 6), these are the types of transactions you will observe most often in a business.

Completing the Accounting Process. After posting journal entries to the general ledger at the end of each month, Nora prepares a trial balance from the ledger accounts. **A *trial balance* is a listing of each account in the general ledger and its balance at a particular date.** It is used to verify the accuracy of the ledger account balances. Exhibit 4-6 provides an example of a trial balance. Amounts correspond with those in Exhibit 4-4. Column totals demonstrate that total debits equal total credits. They have no other meaning.

Exhibit 4-6

Round-O Tires
Trial Balance
October 31, 1996

Account	Debit	Credit
Cash	$ 3,371.53	
Accounts receivable	24,542.77	
Merchandise inventory	96,954.93	
Property, plant, and equipment	188,499.94	
Accounts payable		$ 23,076.58
Sales tax payable		8,224.68
Payroll tax payable		6,646.96
Notes payable		187,500.00
Owner's capital		87,532.14
Sales revenue		45,319.79
Cost of goods sold	18,763.20	
Utilities expense	3,055.99	
Wages expense	19,634.23	
Payroll tax expense	3,477.56	
Total	**$358,300.15**	**$358,300.15**

At the end of each month, Nora also adjusts the accounts for events that affect account balances but have not been recorded. These adjustments arise because of differences between (1) when revenues and expenses are recognized using the accrual basis of accounting and (2) when cash is received or paid. For example, fixed assets are purchased and then depreciated as they are used. Chapter 6 examines adjusting entries.

After recording any necessary adjustments, Nora prepares an **adjusted trial balance**. The adjusted trial balance shows account balances after the effects of adjustments have been recorded. Then, she prepares **financial statements** for the month. At the end of the year, she prepares annual financial statements. These statements are reviewed by a public accountant, who also prepares a tax return for Johnny, including the company's taxable earnings.

Objective 7
Explain the purpose of closing the books.

A final step in processing accounting information involves transferring revenue and expense account balances to owners' equity. Accountants refer to this process as closing the accounts or **closing the books.** A closing transaction adjusts each revenue and expense account so it has a zero balance at the end of a fiscal period, usually a fiscal year. For example, assume the sales revenue account for Round-O has a balance of $289,000 at the end of the 1996 fiscal year. This balance represents the company's total sales since the beginning of the fiscal year. The balance is eliminated by deducting $289,000 from the revenue account (debiting the account for $289,000). This balance is added (credited) to an owners' equity account. For proprietorships and partnerships, this account usually is the OWNER'S CAPITAL account. For a corporation, it is the RETAINED EARNINGS account.

The balances of expense accounts are eliminated by deducting (crediting) the balance from each account and subtracting (debiting) it from OWNER'S CAPITAL or RETAINED EARNINGS.

Once these adjustments have been made, (1) the balances of all revenue and expense accounts are zero and (2) the balances of these accounts have been transferred to owners' equity. Therefore, once the books are closed, the accounting equation ASSETS = LIABILITIES + OWNERS' EQUITY is balanced because revenue and expense accounts are all equal to zero. When a company begins a new fiscal year, it accumulates new revenues and expenses for the new period.

The Accounting Cycle

Objective 8
Summarize the steps in the accounting cycle.

The *accounting cycle* is the process of analyzing transactions, recording transactions in the journal, posting the journal entries to the ledger accounts, and preparing financial reports from the ledger account balances. Following is a summary of the accounting cycle.

1. Collect and prepare source documents.
2. Analyze and record transactions in journal.
3. Post transactions to ledger.
4. Prepare trial balance.
5. Record adjustments.*
6. Prepare adjusted trial balance.*
7. Prepare financial statements.*
8. Record closing transactions.
   Return to step 1.

Covered in Chapter 6.

Learning Note

The steps described above for the accounting cycle are a general indication of what you will find in practice. Each organization develops its accounting procedures to meet its specific information needs. The timing and order of the steps may differ. The procedures themselves will vary somewhat in practice as well. You should be aware that variations exist.

SELF-STUDY PROBLEM 4-1

Leonardo's is a retail store that specializes in artists' supplies. The following transactions occurred during May. Identify the effect of each transaction on Leonardo's accounts by completing the table provided. Use ( ) to identify decreases in column totals. Demonstrate that the accounting equation is balanced after all transactions have been recorded.

1. Sold $300 of merchandise for cash.
2. The merchandise sold in (1) cost Leonardo's $135.
3. Sold $800 of merchandise on credit.
4. The merchandise sold in (3) cost Leonardo's $320.
5. Purchased on credit $3,400 of merchandise from suppliers.
6. Paid $2,000 to suppliers for credit purchases.
7. Paid $230 for utilities expense.
8. Paid $690 to employees for wages.

Assets =	Liabilities + Owners' Equity	+ Revenues − Expenses
Total	Total	Total

The solution to Self-Study Problem 4-1 appears at the end of the chapter.

COMPUTERIZED ACCOUNTING SYSTEMS

Many organizations, even small ones, maintain their accounting records on computers in the U.S. and other developed countries. Though taken for granted in the U.S., computers and computer systems are rare in some countries, where manual systems still prevail. An advantage of a computerized accounting system is the journal and ledger functions are performed by the computer. Accounts are updated automatically. The computer can print transaction and account records. Also, it can prepare financial statements from the accounting records. Therefore, the amount of manual work is limited primarily to entering transactions on the computer. Fewer opportunities for error exist than with a manual system. A computer system normally is faster and less expensive than a manual system for all but very small organizations.

Microcomputer Systems

Objective 9
Describe the components of a microcomputer accounting system.

Within computerized systems, there are small systems that operate on a microcomputer as well as large systems that require mainframe computers or computer networks. Smaller companies often use accounting programs designed for personal computers. These programs provide accounting records similar to those provided by a manual bookkeeping system. For example, the program provides a **sales invoice** template. The template is an invoice with blanks for customer name, address, items purchased, and amounts. A computer operator completes an invoice template on the computer with the name of the customer and a description of items purchased. The operator enters the quantity of each item purchased and the computer fills in the price from **product pricing records** stored on the computer. Appropriate taxes are determined by the computer program. The program automatically records the transaction to the appropriate sales and inventory accounts and updates inventory records and customers' accounts for credit sales. The operator can print a copy of the sales invoice for the customer. Exhibit 4-7 illustrates a sales invoice, which documents the items sold to the customer.

Exhibit 4-7 Example of a Sales Invoice

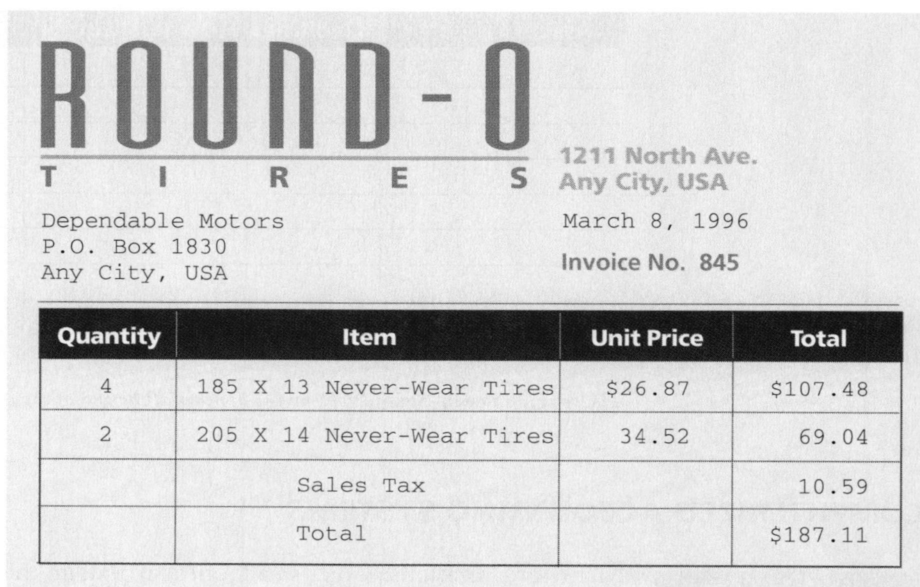

ROUND-O TIRES
1211 North Ave.
Any City, USA

Dependable Motors
P.O. Box 1830
Any City, USA

March 8, 1996

Invoice No. 845

Quantity	Item	Unit Price	Total
4	185 X 13 Never-Wear Tires	$26.87	$107.48
2	205 X 14 Never-Wear Tires	34.52	69.04
	Sales Tax		10.59
	Total		$187.11

The sales invoice template is part of an **accounts receivable module** in the system. Other major modules usually include **accounts payable**, **payroll**, and **general ledger and financial statements**. These are the primary accounting activities, in volume of transactions, for most small companies.

The accounts receivable module maintains customer records. It can be used to print reports of customer activity for a period, current amounts owed, and overdue accounts. Also, it is used to print periodic **billing statements** to customers. These statements are used to prompt payment from customers. Exhibit 4-8 provides an example of a billing statement.

A purchase order template in the **accounts payable module** permits the operator to prepare a purchase order on the computer with the name of the supplier and a description of the items ordered. The operator prints a copy of the purchase order for mailing to the supplier. When a shipment and purchase invoice are received from the supplier, a template is completed for the items and amount of the purchase. The computer updates inventory and accounts payable accounts and records. The module permits an operator to prepare checks for operating expenses and other purchases, and can be used to print reports of current accounts payable balances.

Exhibit 4-8 Example of a Billing Statement

ROUND-O
TIRES
1211 North Ave.
Any City, USA

TO: Dependable Motors
P.O. Box 1830
Any City, USA

DATE: 3/31/96
ACCT NO: 103-12
AMOUNT DUE: $187.11
DELINQUENT AFTER: 4/10/96

Please detach and return top portion with check

Date	Transaction	Invoice No.	Cash Received	Amount
1/12/96	Invoice	769		$395.20
2/6/96	Payment		$395.20	-395.20
3/8/96	Invoice	845		187.11

A **payroll module** permits an operator to update employee records for hours worked during a pay period. The computer prepares payroll forms and prints checks for employees. The system also prepares payroll tax reports for government authorities.

The **general ledger and financial statements module** permits other transactions to be recorded for nonroutine transactions such as bank loans and owner investments. The general ledger is updated by transactions recorded in other modules. It prepares financial statements for various periods, such as the current month, the year-to-date, or the current fiscal year.

A computerized system may be fairly simple. One operator may enter all transactions and maintain the system. For larger organizations, several operators may be involved. Different operators may be responsible for different types of transactions: accounts receivable, accounts payable, payroll, etc. Their computers may be part of a network so data entered at different work stations are maintained as part of one data base.

The accounting cycle for a microcomputer accounting system is similar to that for a manual system. The primary difference is the computer performs some of the functions the bookkeeper must perform in a manual system:

Step	Performed By
1. Collect and prepare source documents.	Bookkeeper/Operator
2. Analyze and record transactions in computer.	Bookkeeper/Operator
3. Post transactions to ledger.	Computer
4. Prepare trial balance.	Computer
5. Record adjustments.*	Bookkeeper/Operator
6. Prepare adjusted trial balance.*	Computer
7. Prepare financial statements.*	Computer
8. Record closing transactions.	Computer

** Covered in Chapter 6.*

Large Computer Systems

In large companies, computerized accounting systems can become quite complex. Many employees may be involved in entering data in the computer. Separate departments often are used for accounts receivable, accounts payable, payroll, etc. Computer operators are linked to a large mainframe computer, a (medium-sized) minicomputer, or a network of microcomputers. Operators may be in different geographical locations.

One of the advantages of a computerized accounting system is the ability it affords managers to access information about current activities. For example, a manager in a company's headquarters in the Northeast can query the system for sales information for a division across town or on the West Coast. Other advantages are a reduction in duplication of data and the ability to produce a wide variety of reports. Computer systems can share data bases; therefore, data entered in a system for one purpose can be accessed for other purposes. Computer data files can be manipulated to produce reports for different products, regions, customers, and time periods. Multinational companies use computer systems to link facilities throughout the world. These systems compile data from various locations and translate data measured in foreign currencies into dollars. Thus, these systems are major assets for large companies.

Objective 10
Identify the modules of a large computer accounting system.

Exhibit 4-9 depicts the accounting system for Never-Wear, Inc., a manufacturer of tires for cars and trucks.[1] The company sells to new car and truck manufacturers and to retail chains throughout the nation. A large accounting system, such as Never-Wear's, consists of several computer modules that interact with each other. Each module accesses one or more data bases. These data bases store information about customers, products, vendors, and other aspects of the business's activities. Each module also includes programs that manipulate and summarize information in the data bases. Numbers in Exhibit 4-9 identify relationships among modules. The following sections examine each of these modules and the relationships.

Objective 11
Distinguish between master and transaction files.

Master and Transaction Files. Large computerized accounting systems use master files and transaction files. These files are the data bases for the modules depicted in Exhibit 4-9. **A *master file* maintains relatively permanent information that occurs once for each entity or item** (e.g., a customer, vendor, or inventory item). For example, a customer's name, identification number, and address would be maintained in an accounts receivable master file. **A *transaction file* contains transactions during a specific period for the entities contained in the master file.** For example, a new sales order transaction file would contain the date and amount of a customer's purchase. The entity's (e.g., customer's) identification code is used to link the transaction to the master file.

A transaction is processed in the modules (Exhibit 4-9) by entering transaction data on a terminal. Data also can be entered through optical scanners. Scanners read data directly from bar codes or other tagging devices. Exhibit 4-10 illustrates the processing of a transaction. The transaction file contains a series of records. A record contains data for a specific customer, including an

[1] Much of this section is adapted from a description of an accounting system marketed by IBM presented in J. Page and P. Hooper, *Accounting and Information Systems,* 4th ed., Prentice-Hall, 1992.

Exhibit 4-9 Modules in a Computerized Accounting System

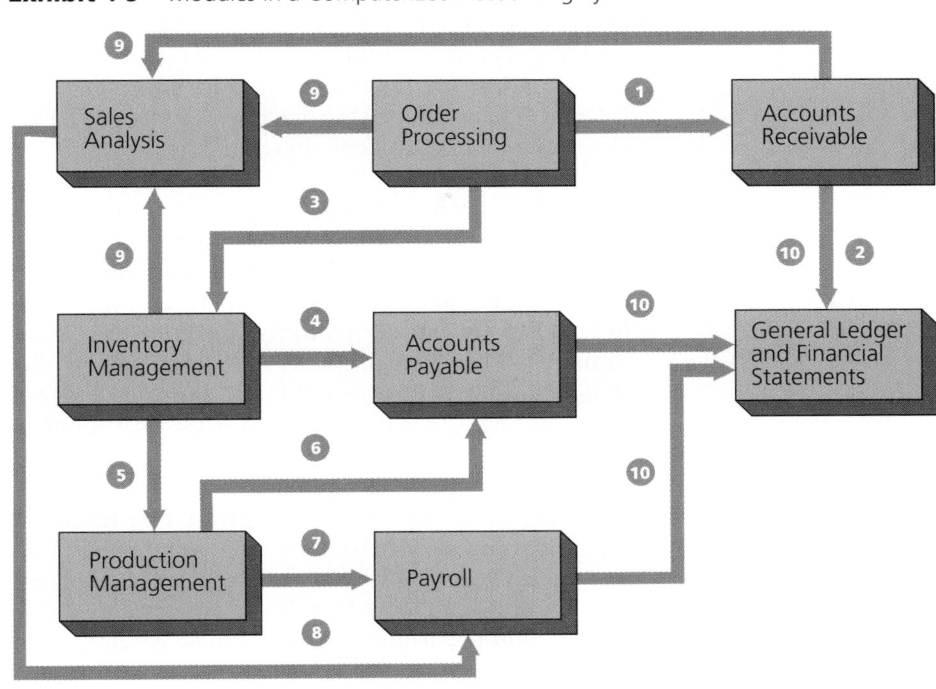

identification number, the date of a transaction, and the amount of the transaction. In this example, a payment of $312.85 has been received from Round-O Tires. A computer program opens the master file and matches the transaction against the customer's record in the master file using the identification number.

Exhibit 4-10 Updating Files in a Computer Module

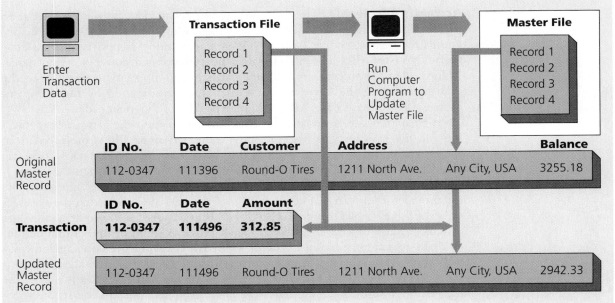

Enter Transaction Data

Transaction File

Record 1
Record 2
Record 3
Record 4

Run Computer Program to Update Master File

Master File

Record 1
Record 2
Record 3
Record 4

	ID No.	**Date**	**Customer**	**Address**		**Balance**
Original Master Record	112-0347	111396	Round-O Tires	1211 North Ave.	Any City, USA	3255.18

	ID No.	**Date**	**Amount**
Transaction	**112-0347**	**111496**	**312.85**

Updated Master Record	112-0347	111496	Round-O Tires	1211 North Ave.	Any City, USA	2942.33

In this example, the customer's record in the master file contains the ID number, the date, the name and address of the customer, and the amount of the customer's accounts receivable balance. The program updates the customer's record in the master file for the transaction information by adjusting the accounting balance. Then, the next transaction is processed. This procedure continues until all transactions have been entered.

Order Processing. Never-Wear's sales force submits customer orders to the company's order department (see Exhibit 4-9). Here they are entered on a terminal in a **new sales order transaction file**. This file identifies the customer and information about the products ordered by the customer. Information from this file is transferred to the accounts receivable module (relationship 1, in Exhibit 4-9) and to the inventory management module (relationship 3). The transaction file is used to produce a list of orders by item and a list of orders by customer. Also, it is used to prepare a list for shipping goods to customers. This list is used by warehouse employees to prepare the customer's order, and may then serve as a packing slip to accompany the order.

Optical scanners and **computer terminals** throughout a business or factory often are important parts of a computerized accounting system. Scanners read codes from tags on materials or merchandise and enter identification codes directly into computer files. Such devices are common in retail stores, such as grocery and department stores. Similar systems assist in manufacturing and distribution processes. These files can be used to identify prices, costs, and inventory data, and may become part of transaction files. Even without scanners, codes can be keyed into the computer as a basis for updating accounting records. These devices reduce the amount of labor required to input data into the accounting system and reduce the opportunity for error in data entry.

A comprehensive summary of source data, files, and reports for each module is included in Exhibit 4-16, later in the chapter. You may wish to reference this exhibit for an overview of the flow of data through each module.

Accounts Receivable. The order processing department transfers information to the accounts receivable department (relationship 1 in Exhibit 4-9). The accounts receivable module of Never-Wear's accounting system includes a **customer master file**. The file contains the customer's account number, name, address, credit limit, current account balance, and amounts received from the customer during the current year. Other information used by the company, such as a customer credit rating, also may be part of the master file.

The master file is updated by two transaction files: the new sales invoices file and the cash receipts file. The **new sales invoices file** is produced from the new sales order transaction file (from order processing). It contains information about sales activity for a period. Transactions in this file increase the ACCOUNTS RECEIVABLE balances for customers in the master file. Also, the file provides a summary of sales activity for the period for updating the balances of SALES REVENUE and ACCOUNTS RECEIVABLE in the general ledger module (relationship 2 in Exhibit 4-9). It provides some of the same functions as a sales journal in a manual system. The **cash receipts file** contains information about cash received from customers during a period. Transactions in this file decrease the ACCOUNTS RECEIVABLE balances for customers in the master file. Exhibit 4-11 illustrates the effect of transactions in the accounts receivable module.

Exhibit 4-11 The Accounts Receivable Module

Step 1	Step 2	Step 3		
Customer makes purchase for $500 on credit	Transaction is recorded in new sales invoice file	Update Accounts Receivable for customer	Balance Sale Balance	$1,300 + 500 $1,800
Customer makes payment of $800	Transaction is recorded in cash receipts file	Update Accounts Receivable for customer	Balance Receipt Balance	$1,800 – 800 $1,000

The computerized accounting system uses the accounts receivable module to prepare several reports. These include a report of sales activity by customer and a report of cash collections by customer. The computer also prepares billing statements and delinquency notices. These are mailed to customers to initiate payment. Exhibit 4-12 summarizes the relationships between the order processing and accounts receivable modules.

Exhibit 4-12 Relationships Between Order Processing and Accounts Receivable Modules

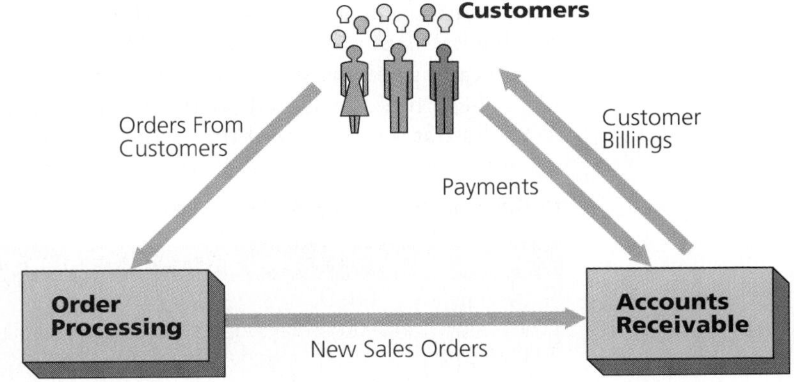

Inventory Management. The order processing department also transfers information to the inventory management department (see relationship 3 in Exhibit 4-9). The inventory management module of Never-Wear's accounting system includes an **inventory item master file**. This file includes information about each item of inventory, item identification numbers, costs per unit, unit selling prices, quantity available, quantity on order, number received and number sold during current fiscal year, and vendor identification.

The inventory master file is updated for current period sales by the new sales order transaction file (from order processing). It provides information about the current availability of inventory items needed for processing customer orders. When insufficient inventory is available or the quantity of inventory drops below a set number, new purchase orders are prepared and submitted to vendors.

A **new purchase orders transaction file** is created from orders placed with vendors during the current period. The inventory master file is updated for new purchase orders from this transaction file. This information also is transferred to the accounts payable module.

The inventory module produces inventory reports listing inventory items ordered from vendors, received from vendors, and shipped to customers during a period. It reports the quantities of each inventory item available at the end of a period. This report also includes unit and total costs for each item, and provides management with information about sales volume and profitability for each inventory item. Also, it provides information for determining when and what amount of inventory items to order.

Accounts Payable. Purchase order information is transferred from the inventory management department to the accounts payable department (see relationship 4 in Exhibit 4-9). The master file for accounts payable is a **vendor file** that contains information for each vendor. Information contained in the file includes vendor name, identification number, address, current amount owed to the vendor, and payments made during the current fiscal period.

Transaction files in the accounts payable module include an **open purchase invoices file**, a **new purchase invoice file**, and a **cash payments file**. The open purchase invoices file contains information for each unpaid invoice and about specific items purchased from each vendor. The new purchase invoice file is prepared from the new purchase orders transaction file (from inventory management) and contains information about purchase transactions made during the current fiscal period. This file is used to increase accounts payable balances in the master file. The cash payments file contains information about cash payment transactions that decrease payable balances in the master file. These files are linked to the master file by the vendor number. Exhibit 4-13 illustrates the effect of transactions in the accounts payable module.

Exhibit 4-13 The Accounts Payable Module

Step 1	Step 2	Step 3		
Company acquires inventory for $700 on credit	Transaction is recorded in new purchase invoices file	Update accounts payable for vendor	Balance Purchase Balance	$ 400 + 700 $1,100
Company makes payment of $400	Transaction is recorded in cash payments file	Update accounts payable for vendor	Balance Purchase Balance	$1,100 − 400 $ 700

The accounts payable module produces reports listing cash payments made during a fiscal period, purchases made during a period, and amounts owed to individual vendors. The module also produces checks to pay vendor accounts. Exhibit 4-14 illustrates the relationships among the order processing, inventory management, and accounts payable modules.

Production Management. The inventory management department provides information about product demand and orders for goods to the production department (see relationship 5 in Exhibit 4-9). The **product structure master file** identifies the type and quantity of materials, components, and subassemblies associated with each finished product. The **routing master file** identifies each activity necessary to manufacture each product and where these products are manufactured in the factory. Changes in product design and manufacturing

Exhibit 4-14 Relationships Among Order Processing, Inventory Management, and Accounts Payable Modules

Order Processing
Inventory Availability
New Sales
Inventory Management
Goods
Vendors
Payments
New Orders
Accounts Payable
Purchase Orders

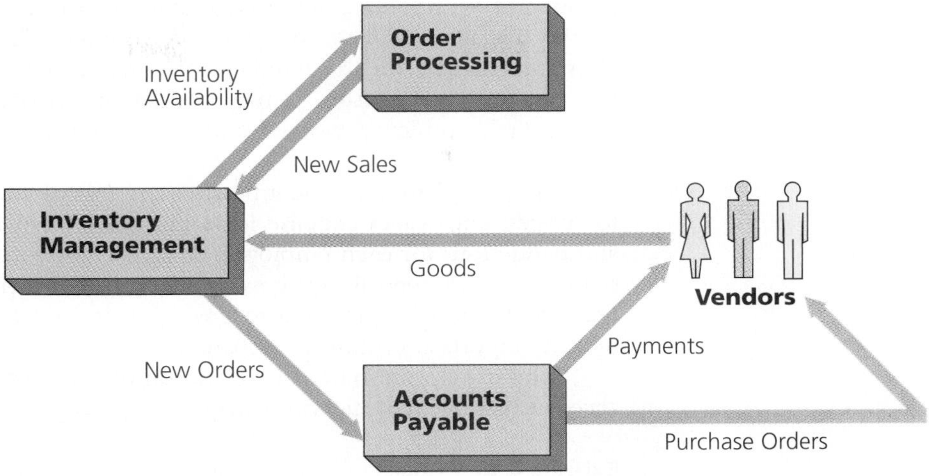

processes are recorded in a **manufacturing changes transaction file**. This file updates the master files. A **manufacturing order summary file** collects information necessary to process each order. It contains information on schedule dates for manufacturing specific orders, routing information, costs accumulated in the manufacturing process, and customer identification.

From the files in the production management module, several reports are created. A bill of materials lists each component of a product and its cost. A routing report identifies the path through the manufacturing process for each product. Product cost reports identify the cost of manufacturing each product. Purchase requisitions identify needed materials or components for some portion of a manufacturing process. Requisitions are used to prepare purchase orders which are linked with the accounts payable module (relationship 6 in Exhibit 4-9). Purchase orders are used to acquire additional materials for the production process. Work-in-process cost reports identify the costs associated with the manufacturing process during a period. These costs include materials, labor, scrap, utilities, and other items necessary for the manufacture of goods. Order status reports identify the location of each order in the manufacturing process, its cost, and its expected completion date.

The production module is unnecessary for merchandising and service organizations. Inventory management and accounts payable modules process the inventory transactions for these organizations.

Payroll. The payroll department receives information from the production department (relationship 7 in Exhibit 4-9) and from sales analysis (relationship 8), which is described in the next section. The production department provides information about employee wages. Sales analysis provides information about salaries and commissions for the sales force. The master file for the payroll module is the **employee master file**. This file contains information for each employee, including name, identification number, address, social security number, pay rate, tax exemption and status data, total hours worked and total earnings for the current fiscal year, and withholding information. Withholding information reflects federal and state taxes, social security taxes, and any other amounts withheld from payroll.

Transaction files include a **tax and deduction file** and a **current employee activity file**. The tax file provides information to determine the amount of withholding for each employee. In conjunction with the current activity file, it is used to compute net earnings. The current activity file contains information on the number of hours worked by each employee during the current period. Also, it may contain information on the department in which each employee worked and special adjustments for overtime or other activities.

The payroll module identifies the amount of wages payable, amounts paid for wages, and wages expense for a period. It prepares reports listing earnings and deductions for each employee. Also, it is used to prepare payroll checks for employees and reports for government tax authorities. W-2 Wage and Tax Statements must be provided to governments and employees each year. Social security reports also must be prepared.

Exhibit 4-15 illustrates the relationships among the inventory management, accounts payable, production management, and payroll modules.

Exhibit 4-15 Relationships Among Inventory Management, Accounts Payable, Production Management, and Payroll Modules

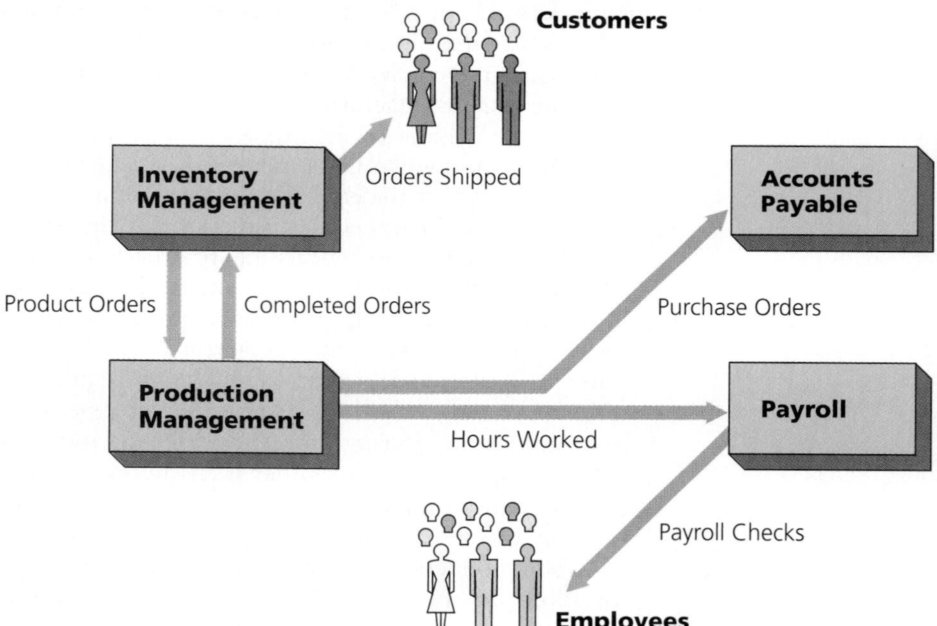

Sales Analysis. The sales analysis module utilizes information from the files maintained in the accounts receivable, order processing, and inventory modules to prepare reports and provide information for payroll (see relationship 9 in Exhibit 4-9). This information is used to report sales and profitability by salesperson. This report identifies sales of products by person and territory. It provides a basis for forecasting future sales activity. The module prepares a report of sales and profits by inventory item. This report also is useful for forecasting sales and for determining inventory requirements and advertising expenditures. A sales and profits by customer report describes customer activity for a period. It helps management identify primary customers and changes in their demands for goods.

Exhibit 4-16 Flow of Data Through Modules in an Accounting System

Module	Source Data	Transaction Files	Master Files	Output	Accounts
Order Processing	1. Customer orders	1. New sales order		1. Orders by item and customer 2. Shipping list and packing slip	
Accounts Receivable	1. Sales invoices 2. Cash receipts	1. New sales invoices 2. Cash receipts	1. Customer master file	1. Sales by customer 2. Cash received 3. Billing statements 4. Delinquency notices	1. Sales Revenue 2. Accounts Receivable 3. Cash
Inventory Management	1. Sales invoices 2. Purchase invoices	1. New purchase orders	1. Inventory item master file	1. Inventory reports	1. Inventory 2. Cost of Goods Sold
Accounts Payable	1. Purchase invoices 2. Cash payments	1. Open purchase invoices 2. New purchase invoices 3. Cash payments	1. Vendor master file	1. Purchases by vendor 2. Amounts owed 3. Cash paid 4. Checks to vendors	1. Inventory 2. Equipment 3. Supplies 4. Accounts Payable 5. Cash
Production Management	1. Sales invoices	1. Manufacturing changes 2. Manufacturing order summary	1. Product structure master file 2. Routing master file	1. Routing 2. Bill of materials 3. Purchase requisition 4. Purchase orders 5. Work-in-process cost 6. Order status	1. Production Costs—Materials Labor, etc. 2. Inventory
Payroll	1. Hours worked 2. Wage rate 3. Tax data	1. Current employee activity 2. Tax and deduction	1. Employee master file	1. Payroll list 2. Employee earnings 3. Payroll checks 4. Tax statements	1. Wages Payable 2. Cash 3. Wages Expense 4. Payroll Tax Payable 5. Payroll Tax Expense
Sales Analysis	1. Sales orders			1. Sales and profitability by salesperson item, customer	
General Ledger and Financial Statements	1. Files from other modules 2. Other transaction data	1. Current period transaction 2. Cumulative transaction	1. General ledger master	1. Transactions by date and account 2. Financial statements	1. Those not provided by other modules

General Ledger and Financial Statements. Other modules in the accounting system transfer information to the general ledger module (relationship 10 in Exhibit 4-9). The general ledger module contains a **general ledger master file**. This file contains each account title, its number, its classification (e.g., asset), its current balance, and additions and subtractions for the current fiscal year.

The master file is updated by a **current period transaction file**. This file identifies each transaction for the current period. This transaction file receives input from other modules of the accounting system, such as accounts receivable, accounts payable, and payroll. Non-routine transactions, such as issuing stock, are entered directly in the transaction file.

The current period transaction file also is used to update a **cumulative transaction file**. This file provides a permanent record of transactions. It is used in preparing tax and other reports and as a basis for auditing the company's accounting records.

The general ledger module is used for preparing a variety of financial reports. It may be used to prepare a listing of transactions in chronological order like a general journal in a manual system. It can prepare a summary of transactions by account like a general ledger. It is used to prepare financial statements for the company and for different regions and divisions. These statements can be prepared for any fiscal period needed (e.g., month, quarter, or year).

Objective 12
Trace the flow of data through a large computer accounting system.

Exhibit 4-16 provides a summary of inputs, processing activities, and outputs of the modules in Never-Wear's accounting system.

SELF-STUDY PROBLEM 4-2

The accounting system for the Stop-U Brake Co. includes the following modules:

a. order processing
b. accounts receivable
c. inventory management
d. accounts payable
e. production management
f. payroll
g. sales analysis
h. general ledger

The master and transaction files used in the system include:

_______ cash payments transaction file
_______ cash receipts transaction file
_______ cumulative transaction file
_______ current employee activity file
_______ current period transaction file
_______ customer master file
_______ employee master file
_______ general ledger master file
_______ inventory item master file
_______ manufacturing changes transaction file
_______ manufacturing order summary file
_______ new purchase invoice transaction file
_______ new purchase orders transaction file
_______ new sales invoices transaction file
_______ new sales order transaction file
_______ open purchase invoice transaction file
_______ product structure master file
_______ routing master file
_______ tax and deduction file
_______ vendor master file

Required

Place the letter of the module associated with each file in the blank to the left of the file.

The solution to Self-Study Problem 4-2 appears at the end of the chapter.

CONTROL OF ACCOUNTING SYSTEMS

Objective 13
Explain the purpose of accounting controls for manual and computerized accounting systems.

A primary concern about any accounting system is its reliability. For accounting information to be useful, it must accurately measure economic events that affect an organization. A variety of difficulties can arise that result in unreliable information. For example, data may be recorded incorrectly in the accounting system. Errors may be made in source documents or as data are entered into the system. Deliberate errors may be made by managers or employees to cover mismanagement, fraud, or theft. Events may go unrecorded because of oversight or because of theft or misuse of resources. Programming errors in the system may result in improper processing of data, leading to erroneous reports. Events may not be recorded for the period in which they occur. Whatever the cause, unreliability is a serious problem in an accounting system.

To reduce the likelihood of error, omission, or misstatement, controls are built into accounting systems. These controls are part of an organization's system of internal accounting controls. **Internal control** consists of procedures designed to protect an organization's resources and to ensure the reliability of its accounting records. This section considers internal control procedures designed to ensure the reliability of accounting records. We will consider both manual and computerized systems. Other internal control procedures will be considered in Chapter 7.

Control of Manual Systems

Some of the most important internal control features of an accounting system are integral to the system itself. Many features of double-entry bookkeeping were developed to increase the reliability of the system. Debits and credits simplify the recording of transactions, and provide a means for identifying errors if debits are not equal to credits. Comparing subsidiary ledger balances with general ledger account balances can detect errors in recording data. Trial balances also are useful for this purpose. Therefore, one of the most important control features of a manual system is use of a double-entry system by a trained bookkeeper.

Manual systems most often are used by small, owner-managed companies. These systems are operated by one or a few employees. Therefore, control of these systems depends on the integrity and ability of these employees. The following internal control procedures can be helpful in maintaining a reliable accounting system:

1. Hire qualified employees. Bookkeepers and other office staff should have the necessary training and experience to meet job requirements. Employees must be honest and dependable.
2. Establish clear policies to define the authority and responsibilities of employees. Employees should understand their duties and the limits of their authority. Record-keeping responsibilities should be separated from physical control over cash, inventory, and other resources whenever possible.

3. Establish procedures for proper processing of transactions. Transactions should be authorized by the owner or appropriate manager who should sign checks, invoices, or other documents.
4. Use proper forms and prenumbered documents. Preprinted and prenumbered forms permit validation of all transactions. Proper forms reduce the opportunity for error through omission of data or failure to document transactions. Prenumbered forms permit the owner to determine that all transactions have been recorded.
5. Maintain control over documents and resources. Documents should be filed for future reference and later verification. They should be maintained in safe locations for protection from unauthorized access or destruction. Cash should be deposited daily. Inventory should be stored in a safe location.
6. Accounting records should be independently verified. The cash account should be reconciled with bank statements. Inventory account records should be verified by periodic physical counts. An audit by an independent accountant is useful for verifying accounting records.

Control of Computer Systems

A computerized accounting system creates many internal control problems. Much of the documentation of a manual system is replaced by computer records. These records are subject to manipulation after they are created; therefore, they may not provide independent verification of transactions. Computers can make mistakes with the speed of light and are not capable of judging the reasonableness of their actions. Whether a check is written for $100 or $100,000 does not matter to a computer. Computerized data can be destroyed. Computer systems can fail, resulting in the loss of programs and data. Employees can change programs and erase data. Numerous examples exist of disgruntled employees who deliberately sabotaged computer systems, costing companies millions of dollars.

In addition to the types of internal control procedures described in the prior section, the following procedures often are used with computerized systems:

1. Control access to the system. An important safeguard is physical access to the computer. Control over the computer itself is important. Terminals and microcomputers should be protected from unauthorized use. They should not be accessible by unauthorized personnel. Passwords should be used to prevent access to the system and to specific data files and programs.
2. Identify responsibility for specific functions. Employee identification codes can be used to determine who processed certain transactions. Employees should have access only to those files and programs they need to perform their duties.
3. Substantial error checking should be built into the computer system. Programs should be designed to determine the reasonableness of data entered in the system and to check for mathematical accuracy and completeness. Data entered in one part of the system should be verified against data from other parts; for example, purchase invoices should agree with purchase orders. Limits should be placed on what the computer can do without special authorization; for example, a limit might be placed on the amount that can be printed on a check.

4. Computer programs should be checked carefully when they are installed. They should be rechecked periodically to determine that they are functioning properly. To illustrate, test transactions can be run through the system and outputs can be compared with expected results to verify the system's accuracy.
5. Data files should be backed up regularly, and copies should be secured. Extra copies of programs and documentation should be maintained, as well. Even access to backup computer systems may be necessary for some organizations.
6. Segregate duties among data processing employees. Design and operation of computer systems should be separate functions. If employees who enter data and process records do not understand how the programs are designed, they will have little opportunity to modify the programs for personal gain.
7. Document the system, programs, and operating procedures. Documentation of how the system works and the proper procedures to be used by employees is important. Documentation is needed when the system is modified to determine the appropriateness of changes. Documentation is useful when employees are trained for new duties. Finally, it is important when the system is audited to make sure the system is functioning properly. Reliable accounting information depends on reliable processing. Internal controls are important for ensuring the accounting system is processing data accurately.

THE ACCOUNTING SYSTEM AND MANAGEMENT DECISIONS

Objective 14
Identify the types of management decisions an accounting system facilitates.

An accounting system serves a variety of needs, providing information for internal and external decision makers. External decision makers receive reports prepared by the system. We will examine these in Chapters 5 and 6. The system serves various needs of managers. The design of an accounting system is important to facilitate effective and efficient operations within an organization. This section discusses some of the needs served by the modules of the accounting system we considered in the prior section.

Order processing is designed to facilitate the timely and accurate processing of customer orders. Prompt and reliable servicing of customer orders is necessary in competitive markets. Customers want fast service and delivery. Fast order processing increases customer satisfaction because of quicker response to customer demands. Customers need to know when they will receive their orders, so order processing must interact with inventory management to identify available items or with production management to schedule customer orders for manufacturing. Customers require up-to-date prices and product descriptions. Order processing must be linked with inventory management to provide this information.

Sales analysis provides information for identifying high demand and profitable products. It helps managers make pricing decisions. It helps managers decide which products to emphasize, which product lines to expand, and which products to eliminate. Also, it helps managers identify profitable territories and customers. Thus, managers can decide where to invest in additional marketing efforts. Managers need to predict future sales activity to determine how much to invest in production capacity and inventory. By anticipating fluctuations in demand, managers can control resources and cash flows to meet changing financial and market conditions.

The processing of accounts receivable and cash from sales provides information to help a company manage its cash flow. Management needs information to help it control cash and reduce the delay in collecting receivables. Also, managers need information to minimize losses from uncollectible receivables. The accounts receivable module of an accounting system assists in providing information about who owes a company money, how long receivables have been outstanding, and past experiences with a customer. Management uses this information to decide whether to extend credit, what type of credit terms to provide, and whether or not special actions are necessary to collect accounts.

Inventory management provides information to control inventory and costs associated with inventory. Managers determine the amount of inventory to maintain, and should protect it from theft and obsolescence. Too much or too little inventory is costly because sales are lost or cash is tied up in nonproductive resources.

Information about accounts payable helps managers control cash outflows. Managers want to delay outflows as long as they do not incur substantial costs from the delay. They do not want to pay high financing charges or late fees; they want to take advantage of discounts for early payment. Also, they want to maintain favorable relations with vendors. Managers use information from accounts payable to determine when to make payments and to monitor future cash requirements. Planning for cash inflows and outflows is an important management function. A company does not wish to maintain too much cash that could be invested in productive assets. On the other hand, it does not wish to be short of cash for meeting obligations and current operating needs.

Production is a primary activity in many organizations. The production process can be extremely complex. The accounting system can assist managers in controlling this process. Information on production costs and resource constraints can make a major difference in a company's profitability. Managers schedule production activities to make efficient use of available materials, labor, and equipment. Accounting systems can help managers plan for the efficient use of resources.

Payroll is a major expense in most organizations. Control over this expense and cash flows is an important activity. Accounting information helps managers monitor labor costs. It also provides for information needs of employees, labor unions, and tax and regulatory authorities.

The effective design of an accounting system involves trade-offs between costs and benefits. Computerized systems reduce the cost of information processing and reporting and increase the flexibility of the system to meet management needs. They can be very expensive, however. Hardware and software needed by the system may require a significant investment. Therefore, an organization must assess its information needs and determine the type of system which is best suited to meet those needs at a reasonable cost.

SELF-STUDY PROBLEM 4-3

Deborah Stinger works in the systems development department of a major company. She helped develop the company's computerized accounting system. Occasionally, she fills in for one of the operators in the accounts payable department. This operator is responsible for processing checks to vendors for purchases made by the company. While filling in, Deborah created an account for a fictitious company, just to see if the system could be tricked into writing checks for nonexistent purchases. She added data to the company's master vendor file and entered some phony purchase invoice numbers and data in the purchase orders transaction file. The computer wrote the checks, and they were mailed to a post office box Deborah opened. Over the last few years, Deborah has written over $80,000 in checks to her fictitious company.

Required

Identify some internal control deficiencies in the accounting system that have allowed Deborah to embezzle money from her company.

The solution to Self-Study Problem 4-3 appears at the end of the chapter.

REVIEW

Summary of Important Concepts

1. The effects of transactions on accounting records and reports:
   A. Financial effects of transactions are recorded in the accounting system as increases or decreases in account balances.
   B. Debits and credits refer to increases and decreases in account balances.
   C. Double-entry bookkeeping requires each transaction be recorded in two or more accounts to maintain the balance in the accounting equation.
   D. Transactions are recorded in chronological order in a journal. A ledger provides a summary of account balances.
   E. Subsidiary ledgers provide details about transactions affecting a control account such as accounts receivable and accounts payable.
   F. Closing transactions transfer revenue and expense account balances to owners' equity.
2. Components and functions of manual and computerized accounting systems:
   A. Major differences in accounting systems depend on whether the systems are manual or computerized.
   B. A computer provides the journal and ledger functions in a computerized accounting system.
   C. A large computerized accounting system consists of modules that work together to process transactions. Modules include order processing, accounts receivable, inventory management, accounts payable, production management, payroll, sales analysis, and general ledger.
   D. In a large computer system, transactions are recorded in transaction files that are used to update master files in each module.
3. Control procedures to improve the reliability of accounting systems:
   A. Accounting systems include controls to reduce the likelihood of error, omission, or misstatement of accounting records.
   B. By following good internal control procedures, such as hiring qualified employees, establishing clear policies and procedures, using proper forms and prenumbered documents, controlling access to documents and resources, and having accounting records verified, a reliable accounting system can be maintained.
   C. Internal control procedures helpful when the accounting system is computerized include thorough check of the system at installation, control of access to the system, identification codes indicating function responsibilities and segregation of duties, built-in error checking, regular backup of data files, secure storage of backup copies, and documentation of the system, programs, and operating procedures.
   D. Accounting systems facilitate effective and efficient operations within an organization by providing information for management decisions.

DEFINE *Terms and Concepts Defined in this Chapter*

accounting cycle	ledger	subsidiary ledger
chart of accounts	journal	transaction analysis
credits	master file	transaction file
debits	source documents	trial balance
double-entry bookkeeping		

SOLUTIONS

SELF-STUDY PROBLEM 4-1

Assets =		Liabilities + Owners' Equity		+ Revenues − Expenses	
1. Cash	300			Sales Revenue	300
2. Inventory	(135)			Cost of Goods Sold	(135)
3. Accounts Receivable	800			Sales Revenue	800
4. Inventory	(320)			Cost of Goods Sold	(320)
5. Inventory	3,400	Accounts Payable	3,400		
6. Cash	(2,000)	Accounts Payable	(2,000)		
7. Cash	(230)			Utilities Expense	(230)
8. Cash	(690)			Wages Expense	(690)
Total	1,125	Total	1,400	Total	(275)

SELF-STUDY PROBLEM 4-2

Answer	File
d	cash payments transaction file
b	cash receipts transaction file
h	cumulative transaction file
f	current employee activity file
h	current period transaction file
b	customer master file
f	employee master file
h	general ledger master file
c	inventory item master file
e	manufacturing changes transaction file
e	manufacturing order summary file
d	new purchase invoice transaction file
c	new purchase orders transaction file
b	new sales invoices transaction file
a	new sales order transaction file
d	open purchase invoice transaction file
e	product structure master file
e	routing master file
f	tax and deduction file
d	vendor master file

SELF-STUDY PROBLEM 4-3

Internal control deficiencies include lack of sufficient barriers to the accounting system that would prevent access by an unauthorized employee. Limitations on physical access, passwords, and employee identification numbers should have prevented Deborah from accessing the system. Deborah should not have authority to use the system. Another deficiency was the failure to separate systems development from computer operations personnel. Deborah was able to embezzle funds because she understood the computer programs that created master and transaction files. Computer operators normally do not have sufficient knowledge of the system to manipulate it in this manner. A third deficiency was the failure of the system to verify transactions or compare amounts from one part of the system to another. Use of sequentially numbered purchase orders should make it difficult for an employee to create fictitious data without the system identifying a problem.

EXERCISES

4-1. Write a short definition for each of the terms listed in the "Terms and Concepts Defined in this Chapter" section.

4-2. For each of the types of transactions listed below, indicate whether it is a financing, investing, or operating activity; and indicate the effect of the transaction on net income and cash flows. The first item is provided as an example.

Transaction	Type of Activity	Effect on Net Income	Effect on Cash Flows
a. Purchase merchandise	Operating	None	Outflow
b. Repay creditors			
c. Sale of goods & services			
d. Borrow from creditors			
e. Sale of long-term assets			
f. Investment by owners			
g. Consume resources to produce goods			
h. Pay return to owners			

4-3. The following transaction occurred for Pittman Co. on March 23, 1995: The company sold merchandise for cash, $5,000. Diagram the flow of information resulting from this transaction through a manual accounting system. Include the following items in your diagram, in the proper order: ledger, sales invoice, financial statements (balance sheet, income statement, statement of cash flows), journal.

4-4. For each of the situations below, indicate whether a debit or a credit entry is required by placing an X in the appropriate box.

Transaction Type	Debit	Credit
Increase a liability account		
Decrease an equity account		
Increase a revenue account		
Decrease a contra account to an asset		

Transaction Type	Debit	Credit
Increase an expense account		
Decrease an asset account		
Decrease a liability account		
Increase an equity account		
Increase a contra account to an asset		
Increase an asset account		
Close a revenue account		
Close an expense account		

4-5. Complete the chart below by indicating whether the type of transaction would require a debit or credit entry in an organization's journal. Place an X in the appropriate box to indicate your response.

Transaction Type	Debit	Credit
Increase in cash		
Decrease in accounts payable		
Increase in sales revenue		
Decrease in equipment		
Increase in cost of goods sold		
Decrease in accounts receivable		
Increase in notes payable		
Decrease in owners' investment		
Increase in inventory		
Decrease in cash		
Increase in wages expense		
Decrease in inventory		

4-6. For each of the accounts listed below, indicate whether you would expect the account to have a debit or a credit balance. Place an X in the appropriate column to indicate your answer.

Account	Debit	Credit
Cash		
Accounts payable		
Sales revenues		
Owners' capital		
Inventory		
Equipment		
Cost of goods sold		

Account	Debit	Credit
Notes payable		
Wages expense		
Wages payable		
Buildings		
Accounts receivable		

4-7. Excerpts from the ledger of Merrylynn's Craft Store are provided below. For each excerpt, describe the type of transaction that would have produced the effects reported in the ledger at each date.

	Date	Debit	Credit	Balance
a. INVENTORY				
	Jan. 1			12,000
	Jan. 15		4,000	8,000
	Jan. 23	2,000		10,000
b. ACCOUNTS PAYABLE				
	Jan. 1			7,000
	Jan. 10	3,000		4,000
	Jan. 25		1,000	5,000
c. SALES REVENUES				
	Jan. 1			0
	Jan. 8		6,000	6,000
	Jan. 19		3,000	9,000

4-8. Sweitzer's is a medical supply company. For each of the following events indicate in the box provided whether the balance of the listed account would increase or decrease as a result of the transaction:

Event	Account	Increase or Decrease
Cash is paid	Cash	
Land is sold	Cash	
Merchandise is acquired	Merchandise Inventory	
Merchandise is sold for cash	Merchandise Inventory	
Merchandise is sold on credit	Sales Revenue	
Wages are paid for month	Wages Expense	
Wages are paid for month	Cash	
Cash is received from a loan	Notes Payable	
Merchandise is sold on credit	Merchandise Inventory	
Merchandise is purchased on credit	Accounts Payable	

4-9. Record each of the following transactions for Park's Tree Service. Use the format provided at the end of this exercise.

a. On July 1, Chung Park invested $8,000 in the business.
b. On July 5, Chung borrowed $4,000 from a local bank for the business by signing a note.
c. On July 8, Chung purchased equipment for $10,000 cash.
d. On July 8, Chung purchased insurance for $600 for a one-year period.
e. On July 10, Chung completed his first job and received payment of $500.
f. On July 14, Chung signed a contract to provide services for a local community. The contract provides for specific services to be provided each month and for payment of $100 at the end of each month.
g. On July 18, Chung completed the services required by the contract for July and sent a bill to the community.

Assets =	Liabilities + Owners' Equity	+ Revenues − Expenses

4-10. Record the following transactions for Rose's Flower Shop. Use the format provided below.
a. Purchased merchandise for sale on October 1 for $800 to be paid by October 30.
b. Sold merchandise for $200 cash on October 3. The merchandise cost Rose's $60.
c. Sold merchandise for $400 on credit on October 6. The merchandise cost Rose's $130.
d. Ordered $500 of merchandise on October 7 from a supplier.
e. $100 of the merchandise purchased on October 1 spoiled on October 9 and had to be trashed resulting in spoilage expense.
f. Paid $600 on October 9 to suppliers for merchandise purchased on October 1.
g. Received $300 on October 10 from customers for sales of October 6.

Assets =	Liabilities + Owners' Equity	+ Revenues − Expenses

4-11. A trial balance for Marta's Vineyard is shown below. The trial balance includes all transactions for the fiscal year except closing the books. Using the information provided in the trial balance at the top of the next page, indicate the accounts that would require closing at the end of December. What is the purpose of this closing process?

4-12. The following events occur as part of an accounting cycle. List the events in the order in which they should occur in the cycle.
a. Record adjustments.
b. Post transactions to ledger.
c. Prepare adjusted trial balance.
d. Collect and prepare source documents.
e. Record closing transactions.
f. Prepare trial balance.
g. Prepare financial statements
h. Analyze and record transactions in journal.

4-13. Woody's Building Supplies uses a computerized accounting system on a personal computer. The system includes accounts receivable, accounts payable, payroll, and general ledger modules. What is the purpose of each of these modules? Give examples of transactions that would be recorded in each.

Marta's Vineyard
Preclosing Adjusted Trial Balance
December 31, 1996

Account	Debit	Credit
Cash	$ 1,300	
Inventory	5,600	
Supplies	2,000	
Prepaid Insurance	900	
Equipment	7,100	
Accumulated Depreciation		$ 3,400
Interest Payable		300
Notes Payable		4,000
Investment by Owner		8,350
Sales Revenue		4,400
Cost of Goods Sold	1,800	
Wages Expense	700	
Utilities Expense	300	
Depreciation Expense	100	
Insurance Expense	200	
Supplies Expense	150	
Interest Expense	300	
Total	$20,450	$20,450

4-14. Differentiate between master and transaction files in a computerized accounting system. Give examples of each type of file.

4-15. Explain the purpose of the order processing module of a large computerized accounting system. What relationship does this module have with other modules in the system?

4-16. Primary source documents for an accounting system include customer orders, sales invoices, purchase invoices, cash receipts, and checks. State which of these documents is important to the following modules in an accounting system and explain why each document is important: order processing, accounts receivable, inventory management, accounts payable, and production management.

4-17. Computerized accounting systems create special control problems for an organization. Common control procedures used by organizations include:

a. Use of passwords to access terminals and program.
b. Limits placed on amounts that the computer will accept for various transactions.
c. Use of test transactions.
d. Regular backup of data and programs.
e. Separation of design from operation of systems.

Explain the purpose of each control procedure.

4-18. The following are subsidiary accounts for Uptown Auto Parts:

Accounts Receivable	**Accounts Payable**
AAA Auto	Ford Motor Co.
Highway 20 Honda	General Motors Corp.
Fred's Garage	Honda Corp.
Macedonia Buick	Ted's Rebuilt Parts

Identify the purpose of these accounts. Explain how the subsidiary accounts are related to the accounts appearing on Uptown Auto Parts' financial statements.

4-19. Describe the events that would produce each of the following transactions:

Assets =		Liabilities + Owners' Equity		+ Revenues − Expenses	
a. Cash	400			Sales Revenue	400
Inventory	(150)			Cost of Goods Sold	(150)
b. Inventory	700	Accounts Payable	700		
c. Equipment	1,000				
Cash	(1,000)				
d. Cash	2,500	Notes Payable	2,500		
e. Cash	(500)	Accounts Payable	(500)		
f. Cash	(100)			Interest Expense	(100)

4-20. The Flushing Pipe Co. closes its books on December 31 each year. Explain what is meant by "closing the books" and why this procedure is part of Flushing's accounting process.

4-21. Harvey Hammer owns a hardware store, Harvey Hammer's Hardware. Harvey receives information from his bookkeeper each month that includes a chart of accounts, a list of journal transactions, ledger account balances, an adjusted trial balance, and financial statements. Harvey is bewildered by all of the information. The following list includes the kinds of information Harvey needs from the system. For each item, indicate which component of the system Harvey would use to obtain the information.

a. Profits earned for the month.
b. Transactions that occurred on June 22.
c. The amount of cash available on June 10.
d. A list of asset accounts included in the system.
e. Total liabilities at the end of the month.
f. Verification that the accounts are in balance.
g. The amount of cash paid to creditors during the month.
h. Expenses for the month.

PROBLEMS

PROBLEM 4-1 Processing Accounting Information

Your college roommates are microbiology majors and have had little exposure to accounting. They've heard references to debits and credits and are vaguely aware that something called journals and ledgers are involved. In their view, accounting is recordkeeping and doesn't seem very important. They don't understand why anyone needs to know how accounting information is processed, unless you want to be a bookkeeper.

Required Prepare an explanation for your roommates of why the processing function is an important and critical part of an accounting information system.

PROBLEM 4-2 Debits and Credits

For each of the accounts in the table at the top of the next page, identify the type of account (asset, liability, owners' equity, revenue, or expense), and the type of entry (debit or credit) that increases the account.

PROBLEM 4-3 Recording Transactions

On March 1, 1995, Anita and Louise started the Appliance Rescue Company. They offer a complete line of appliance parts and repair services. Below are the transactions that occurred during the first month of business.

a. The business was started by each partner contributing $5,000.
b. Each partner also contributed personal tools with a value of $4,000.

	Account Type	Increase With
a. Prepaid Insurance		
b. Retained Earnings		
c. Accumulated Depreciation		
d. Wages Expense		
e. Commissions Revenue		
f. Interest Payable		
g. Supplies		
h. Insurance Expense		
i. Unearned Rent		
j. Prepaid Advertising		
k. Notes Payable		
l. Cost of Goods Sold		
m. Machinery		
n. Owners' Capital		
o. Accounts Receivable		
p. Bonds Payable		
q. Supplies Expense		

c. The annual business license and permits totalled $250 and were paid in cash.
d. A used service truck was purchased by paying $3,000 down and signing a 3-year, 12% note payable for the $6,600 balance.
e. An inventory of repair parts was purchased on credit for $10,000.
f. A shop was rented for $800 monthly and the first month's rent was paid.
g. Newspaper advertising cost $600. The bill had not yet come by the end of the month, so it had not been paid.
h. Services totaling $2,200 were performed during the month for cash
i. Services totaling $3,500 were performed during the month on credit.
j. Parts costing a total of $2,000 were sold to customers for $3,100 cash.
k. Gas, oil, and maintenance on the service truck costing $385 was charged to the company's credit card.
l. At the end of the month, Anita and Louise each withdrew $1,000 from the business for personal expenses.

Required Below is a list of the company's accounts. Use them to record each transaction. Use the format illustrated.

Accounts Payable	Owners' Capital—Anita
Advertising Expense	Owners' Capital—Louise
Accounts Receivable	Repair Parts Inventory
Cost of Goods Sold	Rent Expense
Cash	Tools
Gas, Oil, & Maintenance Expense	Sales Revenue
Note Payable	Truck
License and Permit Expense	Service Revenue

Assets =	Liabilities + Owners' Equity	+ Revenues − Expenses

PROBLEM 4-4 Identifying and Recording Transactions

Bill Collector has worked for many years in the credit evaluation business and recently decided to open his own collection agency on August 1. Following are the events that occurred during the first month of business.

Aug.	1	Bill started the firm by investing $9,500.
	3	An office suite was rented at $1,000 per month and the first month's rent was paid.
	5	Furnishings for the office were purchased on credit at a cost of $5,400.
	6	A $6,000 loan was obtained from a relative at 10% annual interest.
	7	Three employees were hired. They will start training next Wednesday.
	12	Bill arranged for promotional literature to be printed for distribution to potential clients. It was printed and distributed at a cost of $2,100 cash.
	23	Services provided to clients totalled $4,500. 40% was collected in cash, with the balance on accounts receivable.
	31	Utilities used during the month totalling $480 have not been paid.
	31	Employee wages for the month were $3,200, of which 30% was still owed at month end.
	31	Three more clients contracted for service that would begin during the following month. Bill estimated that these clients would generate $6,000 of billings per month. No cash has yet been received.

Required (a) For each event, identify the accounts affected, the amount, and whether the effect was to increase or decrease the account. If no accounts were affected, write No Effect. Use the format shown below. (b) Provide a total for each account at the end of the month and demonstrate that assets = liabilities + owners' equity + revenues − expenses.

Assets =	Liabilities + Owners' Equity	+ Revenues − Expenses

PROBLEM 4-5 Describing an Accounting System

Weiser Fruit Co. uses an accounting system that includes a journal, a ledger, a trial balance, and financial statements. Prunella Weiser, daughter of the owner, recently completed college and is new to the company. Prunella majored in music and doesn't have much understanding of accounting. You have been asked to help her become familiar with the accounting system.

Required Write a memo to Prunella describing briefly the purpose of each part of the system and how the parts work together to provide information for management and other users. Also, indicate your willingness to meet with her to discuss the system in detail and provide further information.

PROBLEM 4-6 Describing an Accounting System

On March 12, Barney Pfife ordered a uniform from the Ace Detective Uniform Company. On April 18, Barney received the uniform and a bill for $87.59. On April 26, Ace received a check from Barney.

Required Trace the flow of information through the accounting system of Ace Detective Uniform Company associated with these events. Identify source documents and transactions associated with the events in each of the following departments: sales, accounts receivable, inventory, shipping, and accounts payable.

PROBLEM 4-7 Evaluating an Accounting System

Angelo Sarcozzi is a vegetable grower. He buys seeds, plants, fertilizers, insecticides, and other products from local vendors. Most purchases are on credit. Angelo receives bills monthly and writes checks to pay his accounts. He owns his land and has borrowed money to purchase a tractor and other equipment. Angelo sells his crops to local merchants at grocery stores and restaurants; most of the sales are for cash; some are for credit. He records cash payments and receipts in his personal checkbook. He records noncash sales in a notebook, listing the customer, date, and amount of the sale. When he receives checks from these customers, he marks off the amount in the notebook.

Required Evaluate Angelo's accounting system. What problems do you see with the system? What changes would you recommend to improve it?

PROBLEM 4-8 Master and Transaction Files

Listed below are transaction files used in a large company's computerized accounting system:

Cash payments file	New purchase invoices file
Cash receipts file	New purchase orders file
Cumulative transactions file	New sales invoice file
Current employee activity file	New sales order file
Current period transactions file	Open purchase invoices file
Manufacturing changes file	Tax and deductions file
Manufacturing order summary file	

Required For each file, identify the module of the accounting system in which the file is used, the master file with which it is associated, and the primary purpose of the transaction file.

PROBLEM 4-9 Ethical Issues in an Accounting System

Ethel Spikes works for the Hard Rock Candy Company. She enters customer orders in the company's accounting system. The orders are written on prepared forms by the company's sales representatives (reps). The company employs 10 sales reps who work different territories. The reps are paid on a commission basis for sales made during the preceding month. Sales reports prepared by the accounting department supervisor are used to determine the commissions. Sales reps drop off the forms to the accounting supervisor each week. The supervisor then delivers the forms to Ethel. She enters the orders in a computer and prints out a sales report and sales invoices for each customer. These are picked up by the supervisor who delivers them to payroll and to shipping. The result of entering the orders in the accounting system is to increase accounts receivable and to increase sales revenue.

Ethel has discovered an interesting regularity in some of the orders. One of the sales reps always reports abnormally high orders from a particular customer. A few days after the end of each month, the rep submits a cancellation form for the customer to eliminate a large portion of the customer's order. The supervisor directs Ethel to record the cancellation by reducing accounts receivable for the customer and recording an increase in an operating expense account. Ethel doesn't know much about accounting. When she asked her supervisor about this procedure, she was told it was standard for this customer and not to worry about it.

Ethel smells a rat, however, and has considered discussing the matter with the vice-president of finance. But, she is concerned she may simply be making waves that will alienate her supervisor.

Required Ethel has sought your advise as a friend about this matter. What would you recommend to Ethel? What problems do you see in Hard Rock's accounting system? How might these problems be solved?

PROBLEM 4-10 Economics of Accounting Systems

Oscar Grinch is president of the Sesame Garbage Can Company. Grinch is a notorious miser, who spends as little as possible on new technology, especially in support services. You were recently hired by the company to manage its accounting department. You were aware the company's system was antiquated before taking the job, but, soon after beginning work, you realized it is hopelessly outdated. The system relies on manual procedures that have been in place since the company was a small operation first founded by Grinch.

You have contacted some vendors and have a good idea about the type of system that would meet the company's needs. A new computerized system would cost about $50,000 for hardware and software.

Required Write a memorandum to Grinch explaining the benefits of a new system. Justify the cost of the system by identifying how it can improve the company economically.

PROBLEM 4-11 Multiple-Choice Overview of the Chapter

1. The processing phase of the accounting information system includes which of the following events?

	Deciding how to raise needed capital	Recording transactions
a.	Yes	Yes
b.	Yes	No
c.	No	Yes
d.	No	No

2. A important characteristic of a double-entry bookkeeping system is that:
   a. errors cannot occur.
   b. the total of debit entries must always equal the total of credit entries.
   c. a computer is never needed.
   d. source documents are not needed if the double-entry system is used.
3. Office supplies were purchased on credit for $900. Which of the following changes in account balances is the correct result of the transaction?

	Office Supplies	Accounts Payable
a.	Increased	Increased
b.	Increased	Decreased
c.	Decreased	Decreased
d.	Decreased	Increased

4. Which of the following is a true statement regarding the journal and ledger?
   a. Transactions are recorded in the ledger before being posted to the journal.
   b. Normal entries are recorded initially in the journal while closing entries are recorded initially in the ledger.
   c. Transactions are arranged chronologically in the journal but are recorded in separate accounts in the ledger.
   d. Account balances are easily determinable from the journal but more difficult to determine from the ledger.
5. The balance of the merchandise inventory account increased by $3,000 during February. Which of the following statements can be made as a result of this information?
   a. Credit sales for the month were $3,000 greater than cash received from customers.
   b. Purchases of inventory for the month were $3,000 less than the cost of merchandise sold for the month.
   c. Purchases of inventory for the month were $3,000 greater than the cost of merchandise sold for the month.
   d. Merchandise purchased for the month totalled $3,000.

6. All of the following are advantages of a computerized accounting system except:
   a. Journal and ledger functions are performed by the computer.
   b. It is easier to control than a manual system.
   c. It is faster than a manual system.
   d. Fewer opportunities for error exist than in a manual system.
7. Cash received by a company from customers would be recorded initially in a microcomputer accounting system in the:
   a. accounts receivable module.
   b. accounts payable module.
   c. payroll module.
   d. general ledger module.
8. An inventory report from an accounting system probably would provide all of the following information except:
   a. the amount of inventory purchased during a period.
   b. the amount of inventory sold during a period.
   c. the cost of each inventory item.
   d. the amount owed to the company by those who purchased inventory.
9. To protect its assets and accounting information, a company should:
   a. hire employees with college degrees.
   b. update accounts daily.
   c. permit access to accounting records by top managers only.
   d. independently verify accounting records.
10. An effective accounting system should:
    a. increase customer satisfaction.
    b. eliminate the need to borrow money.
    c. improve a company's products.
    d. reduce the speed of cash inflows.

CASES

CASE 4-1 Developing an Accounting System

Peggy Sue is a close friend who has recently purchased a specialty store in a local mall. Peggy has little understanding of accounting. She has asked for your assistance in developing an accounting system. She needs information about her business to determine how well the business is performing. In a recent visit, she showed you the following documents that she uses to keep track of her business activities: (a) Sales receipts are written for each sales transaction. The sales receipt notes the items sold and the sales price. A copy is given to the customer, and another copy is placed in a box. (b) Cash or checks received from customers are placed in a cash register. Deposit slips are made out each day and the receipts are deposited in a local bank. (c) Peggy keeps a checkbook for the company. When bills are received from suppliers, or for rent, utilities, etc., Peggy writes a check and fills out a check register that is maintained in the checkbook. Wages, interest on a bank note, and other expenses are paid by check, as well. (d) Index cards are maintained for each inventory item. As merchandise is received, the quantity obtained is noted on the appropriate card along with the unit cost. The index cards are updated weekly for merchandise sold by referencing the sales receipts for the week. (e) Receipts for equipment and other asset purchases are maintained in a file folder.

Required Recommend an accounting system for Peggy that would make use of the documents she is using. Describe the components of the system and how they can provide information for Peggy. Use some example transactions to demonstrate for Peggy how the system would work.

CASE 4-2 Correcting Errors

Hansel and Gretel Cook own a bakery, famous for its gingerbread. Neither is a trained accountant. They have devised a system for recording transactions that they believe is sufficient. Listed below are a series of transactions for a recent month. The transactions were recorded as shown in the table.

a. Received orders for goods. Payment of $500 to be made when delivered.
b. Placed an order for supplies of $300.
c. Shipped goods to customers and received $500 cash.
d. Received supplies and paid $300 cash.
e. Paid interest to bank of $200 cash.
f. Purchased equipment on credit for $3,000.

Assets =		Liabilities + Owners' Equity		+ Revenues − Expenses	
Orders Received	500			Sales	500
Supplies Ordered	300			Supplies Expense	(300)
Cash Orders Shipped	500 (500)				
Cash Supplies Received	(300) 300				
Cash Paid	200			Interest Paid	(200)
		Accounts Payable	3,000	Equipment Expense	(3,000)

Required Explain to the Cooks the misunderstanding they have about recording transactions. Correct the recording errors they have made.

PROJECTS

PROJECT 4-1 Preparing a Trial Balance from Financial Statements

Select a recent corporate annual report from your library. Use the balance sheet and income statement from the annual report to prepare a trial balance for the company. The trial balance should list the accounts reported in the financial statements. Debit and credit columns should be provided for the account balances. Demonstrate that total debits equal total credits.

PROJECT 4-2 Developing and Analyzing Transactions

Develop a set of hypothetical transactions for a fictional company following the pattern of Problem 4-4. Create a minimum of 10 transactions and identify the accounting effects of each.

PROJECT 4-3 Developing a Personal Accounting System

Develop an accounting system you could use to provide information about your economic activities. Write a short report describing your system. The report should include:

a. a list of decisions the system should help you make.
b. a list of source documents that would provide data for your system.
c. examples of the system, demonstrating how it operates, including transactions for at least a week.
d. example reports that help you with the decisions identified in part a.

PROJECT 4-4 Identifying Components of an Accounting System

Visit a nearby business or talk with a business manager you know. Ask for a list of source documents that provide data for the accounting system. Ask for copies of any documents the manager can share with you. Also, ask the manager to describe how the business maintains its accounting records and for a chart of accounts for the business. Write a short report that summarizes your findings and includes the examples you obtained.

PROJECT 4-5 Evaluating Accounting Systems

Assume you are an employee of a small business. The business has been using a manual accounting system, but your boss has decided to consider a microcomputer system. You have been assigned the responsibility of identifying the features of the system that need to be evaluated. Also, your boss wants you to identify at least three brands of computer systems and compare their costs and features. Research some commonly used types of accounting software, and write a short report for your boss. Include references to the sources of information you used in preparing your report. (Hint: Use a periodical index to identify some articles that evaluate accounting computer packages for use on personal computers.)

CHAPTER 5

REPORTING ACCOUNTING INFORMATION

CHAPTER *Overview*

This chapter introduces the reporting phase of the accounting information system. The output of the accounting system consists of reports and schedules. For these outputs to be useful to decision makers, the reports must accurately summarize the transactions in the transformation process. Therefore, the system must measure the effects of transactions accurately. It must process transactions to produce reliable information. And, it must summarize the information in a form understandable to users.

This chapter discusses stages 4 and 5 of the accounting information system, reporting rules and reports:

Reporting rules define how data are combined and summarized in preparing reports and schedules. Reports present information in a form consistent with reporting rules.

The form and content of reports from the accounting system depend on the needs of users. This chapter introduces some of the most common accounting reports, financial statements. The purpose of this chapter is to explain how financial statements report transactions that occur in an organization's transformation process. **Once you have completed this chapter you should understand the purpose of financial statements.**

Major topics covered in this chapter include:

- The purpose and content of financial statements.
- Special attributes and limitations of financial statements.

CHAPTER *Objectives*

Once you have completed this chapter you should be able to:

1. Identify the primary financial statements issued by businesses.
2. Summarize the information reported on a company's income statement.
3. Explain reporting rules that determine the format of an income statement.
4. Summarize the information reported on a company's statement of stockholders' equity.
5. Summarize the information reported on a company's balance sheet.
6. Explain reporting rules that determine the format of a balance sheet.
7. Summarize the information reported on a company's statement of cash flows.

8. Explain reporting rules that determine the direct format of a statement of cash flows.
9. Discuss how financial statements work together to present a picture of a company for a fiscal period.
10. Explain why many corporations publish consolidated financial statements.
11. Identify some of the primary limitations of financial statements.
12. Discuss how financial statements relate to the transformation process and the time periods in which companies operate.

THE PURPOSE OF FINANCIAL STATEMENTS

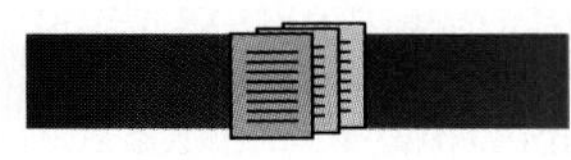

Objective 1
Identify the primary financial statements issued by businesses.

Accounting information may serve general and specific purposes. Financial statements are the primary format organizations use to report general purpose accounting information to external decision makers. Most business organizations prepare three financial statements:

1. **an income statement,**
2. **a balance sheet,** and
3. **a statement of cash flows.**

Many corporations prepare a fourth statement, **a statement of stockholders' equity,** because of the variety and complexity of their ownership transactions. The following sections examine the purpose and content of these four financial statements. Information contained in financial statements and information accompanying the statements provide the subject for much of the remainder of this book. Specific-purpose accounting reports and other information used by internal decision makers is the subject of managerial accounting.

The form and content of financial statements have evolved throughout the twentieth century and continues to change to meet user needs. Financial statements are used by internal and external decision makers. The format and content of the statements used by managers to make financing, investing, and operating decisions often follow those of statements prepared for external users. Statements for internal use may be prepared in any form and with any content desired by management.

For many years the balance sheet was the primary financial statement reported to external users. It was designed to meet the needs of creditors who wanted information about resources available to pay debts and claims to these resources. Banks and other creditors still provide the primary sources of financing for corporations in some countries and for many companies, including some corporations, in the U.S. The income statement developed to meet the needs of corporate investors who wanted information about earnings. Earnings information is useful for evaluating management decisions that affect dividends and stock values. The statement of stockholders' equity describes transactions affecting stock and the amount and use of retained earnings. A recent addition to external reports, the statement of cash flows provides information for investors and other users to assess the ability of a company to meet its cash requirements.

Financial statements for general-purpose external reporting normally are prepared according to generally accepted accounting principles (GAAP). GAAP specify the format and content of the statements, though they permit managers to choose among alternate procedures in reporting some transactions. Chapter 7 provides a more extensive discussion of GAAP.

Income Statement

An income statement (sometimes called an earnings statement or a profit and loss (P & L) statement) reports an organization's revenues and expenses for a fiscal period. The income statement presents operating results on an accrual basis. It measures the amount of goods and services provided to customers and resources consumed in providing these goods and services.

Revenues and expenses result from the sale and consumption of resources for a fiscal period. Therefore, the income statement reports the results of these operating activities for a particular period such as a month, quarter, or fiscal year. For example, the income statement might report operating results for the month of July, the first quarter ending September 30, or the fiscal year ending June 30.

Statement of Stockholders' Equity

A *statement of stockholders' equity* **reports changes in a corporation's stockholders' equity for a fiscal period.** These changes result from profits earned during a period, from dividends paid to owners, and from the sale or repurchase of stock by a corporation. This statement links the income statement to the balance sheet because it describes how much net income was reinvested as part of stockholders' equity.

Balance Sheet

A balance sheet reports the balances of the asset, liability, and owners' equity accounts at a particular date. Other names for the balance sheet are **statement of financial position** and **statement of financial condition,** sometimes used by financial institutions. These names are good descriptions of the statement because it reports the cost of resources available to an organization at a particular date and the sources of financing used to acquire those resources. In combination, the resources and financing are the financial position, or condition, of the organization at the report date.

Statement of Cash Flows

A *statement of cash flows* **reports events that resulted in cash inflows and outflows for a fiscal period.** The statement of cash flows and the income statement both report operating activities for a fiscal period, but these statements differ in two important ways. First, the cash flow statement reports financing and investing activities in addition to operating activities, while the income statement reports operating activities. Second, the cash flow statement reports operating activities on a cash basis while the income statement reports them on an accrual basis. The income statement provides an *estimate* of the cash flows that will result once all cash inflows and outflows associated with current period operating activities have been received or paid. The statement of cash flows reports *actual* cash flows received or paid during the current fiscal period.

The income statement and statement of cash flows reflect a trade-off in the value of information that can be reported from an accounting system. An income statement provides an estimate of how well an organization has performed when all events are completed that had, or will have, an economic effect on the period's operating activities. Because the information reported is an estimate, it is not always precise. In contrast, the statement of cash flows is precise because it reports events that have been completed. But, this information normally is not as good a measure of current period operating results as that contained on the income statement. The statement of cash flows reports cash flows of the current financial period irrespective of when the operating activities occurred that caused the cash flows.

To illustrate, assume during October a company sells $30,000 of goods and services and collects $26,000 from customers. The $26,000 of cash inflow is a precise measure of cash received from sales during October. It is not, however, a complete measure of the amount of goods sold by the company to customers during October. Some portion of the $26,000 may represent sales made in prior months that were collected in October. Some portion of the cash from sales made in October may not be collected from customers until later months.

Information about cash flows is useful for decisions about an organization's ability to pay current obligations. Profitability, as measured by the income statement, is only one aspect of performance. An organization may be profitable but may not have sufficient cash to pay its debts. This situation may arise, for example, when a business is unable to collect on a large amount of sales made on credit. The sales are reported as revenue on the income statement when goods are sold. Yet, the cash is not available for use by the business until it collects the accounts receivable resulting from the sales.

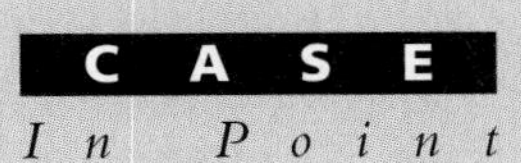

Having a popular product line and a large backlog of orders does not guarantee a company will have cash available to pay its bills on time. In one of the most famous cash-flow shortages in American business history, Douglas Aircraft of California was forced into a 1967 merger with McDonnell Company of St. Louis. The merger formed the McDonnell Douglas Corporation.

At the time, Douglas Corporation's DC-8 and DC-9 aircraft had found an enthusiastic market with airlines and had accumulated a $3.2 billion backlog of orders. Douglas literally could not make its airliners fast enough. A severe shortage of skilled employees and jet engines disrupted production and raised costs sharply. Rather suddenly, Douglas needed additional cash of $350–$400 million to continue production. As word of the company's plight spread, its stock price plummeted from a 1966 high of $112 per share to $45 at the time of the merger.

Unable to raise the money from banks, Douglas was forced to merge with its old rival, McDonnell, which previously had attempted a takeover of Douglas. As part of the merger agreement, McDonnell provided $68.7 million of cash to Douglas. Douglas was then able to borrow another $300 million to restart its production lines.

FINANCIAL STATEMENT CONTENT AND PRESENTATION

Financial statements summarize account balances. This section illustrates financial statements that report typical business transactions. Assume you manage a company, Rockyfellow, Inc., that operates a small chain of gas stations. Exhibit 5-1 lists account balances for Rockyfellow, Inc., at December 31, 1996, the end of the fiscal year. The following sections illustrate how these data are reported in the company's financial statements.

Exhibit 5-1

Rockyfellow, Inc.
Account Balances
December 31, 1996

Account	Balance
Cash	$ 15,600
Accounts Receivable	22,430
Merchandise Inventory	43,500
Supplies	12,670
Prepaid Insurance	8,290
Equipment	93,070
Allowance for Depreciation—Equipment	22,350
Buildings	275,000
Allowance for Depreciation—Buildings	83,510
Land	36,810
Patents	32,000
Accounts Payable	24,790
Wages Payable	4,100
Interest Payable	11,250
Income Taxes Payable	2,400
Notes Payable, Current Portion	14,400
Notes Payable, Long-Term	177,600
Owners' Investment (Contributed Capital)*	125,000
Reinvested Profits (Retained Earnings), 1/1/96	62,700
Dividends	5,000
Sales Revenue	186,230
Cost of Goods Sold	73,350
Wages Expense	42,700
Utilities Expense	6,430
Depreciation Expense	9,650
Insurance Expense	3,420
Supplies Expense	8,390
Interest Expense	10,300
Advertising Expense	7,120
Patent Expense	3,000
Income Tax Expense	5,600

**Explained later in this chapter.*

The Income Statement

The income statement reports the revenue and expense account balances and the net income for the period. Exhibit 5-2 illustrates a multiple-step income statement, which is a commonly used format.

Exhibit 5-2

Objective 2
Summarize the information reported on a company's income statement.

Rockyfellow, Inc.
Income Statement
For the Year Ended December 31, 1996
(Multiple-Step Format)

Sales revenue		$186,230
Cost of goods sold		73,350
Gross profit		112,880
Operating expenses:		
Wages	$42,700	
Utilities	6,430	
Depreciation	9,650	
Insurance	3,420	
Supplies	8,390	
Advertising	7,120	
Patent*	3,000	
Total operating expenses		80,710
Income from operations		32,170
Other revenues and expenses:		
Interest expense		10,300
Pre-tax income		21,870
Income tax expense		5,600
Net income		$ 16,270
Earnings per share of common stock* (12,500 shares outstanding)		$1.30

Explained later in this chapter.

Learning Note

Amount columns are used on financial statements to facilitate addition and subtraction. The number and format of columns is a matter of convenience. The objective is clarity of presentation.

In interpreting the income statement, it is important to remember revenues and expenses are measured on an *accrual basis*. Revenues indicate the sales price of goods and services sold during a period. They do *not* indicate how much cash was received from the sales during a current fiscal period. Expenses identify the cost of resources consumed in producing and selling goods and services sold during a period. They do *not* identify how much cash was paid for resources during a period. **Net income is not cash flow.**

As shown in the income statement for Rockyfellow, Inc., a **multiple-step income statement** is divided into several sections or steps. The usual sections are shown in the exhibit at the top of the next page.

Gross Profit. The income statement reports *gross profit,* **which is the difference between the selling price of goods or services sold to customers during a period and the cost of the goods or services sold.** For a merchandising company, the cost of goods sold is the cost of the merchandise inventory sold during a period. For a manufacturing company, cost of goods sold includes the dollar amounts of materials, labor, and other resources that are

Objective 3
Explain reporting rules that determine the format of an income statement.

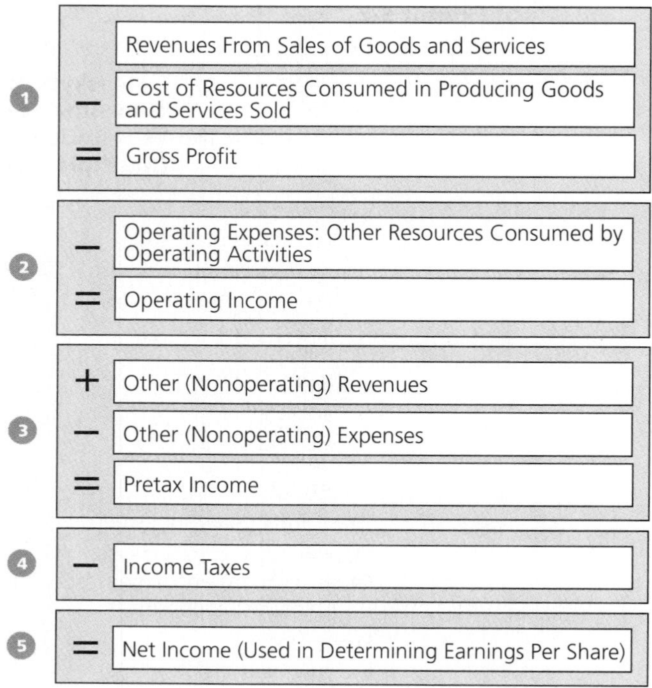

consumed directly in producing the goods sold during a period. As explained in Chapter 3, these costs are product costs. Product costs are recorded as an asset (INVENTORY) until goods are sold. Then the costs are matched against the revenues generated from the sale by recording an expense (COST OF GOODS SOLD) during the same fiscal period as the sale.

Cost of services rather than cost of goods are important for service companies. **The *cost of services sold* is the cost of material, labor, and other resources consumed directly in producing services sold during a period.** For example, the cost of nursing and other patient care costs in a hospital are costs of services. These costs cannot be inventoried and therefore are expensed in the period in which the services are provided.

Other Operating Expenses and Operating Income. The second section of a multiple-step income statement lists operating expenses other than cost of goods sold or cost of services sold. ***Operating expenses* identify costs of resources consumed as part of operating activities during a fiscal period in addition to those directly associated with specific goods or services. Most operating expenses are period costs because they are recognized in the fiscal period in which they occur.** Operating expenses include administrative and selling expenses incurred during a period. Salaries for managers and their support staffs who are not involved directly in producing goods and the cost of resources used by managers are operating expenses. These expenses include depreciation, taxes, insurance on office buildings and equipment, and the costs of supplies and utilities consumed in operating these facilities. GAAP require most marketing and selling costs and research and development costs incurred during a fiscal period to be reported as operating expenses of the period in which they occur. Because identifying how much of these costs is associated with benefits of future periods is difficult to determine,

Expenses and Net Income as a Percentage of Total Revenues
for Several Large U.S. Corporations

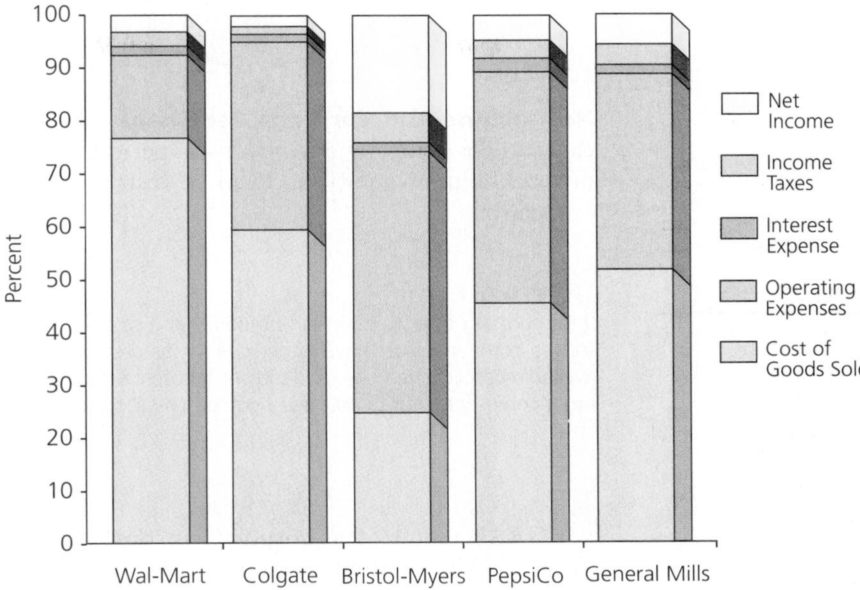

Data source: 1991 Annual Reports.

GAAP are conservative in requiring these amounts to be expensed to avoid an overstatement of profits during the current fiscal period.

The excess of gross profit over operating expenses is *income from operations,* **or** *operating income.* If operating expenses are greater than gross profit, a loss from operations results.

Other Revenues and Expenses. Revenues and expenses may occur that are not directly related to a company's primary operating activities. These are reported separately as *other revenues and expenses.* This category sometimes is labelled *financial revenues and expenses* because most items reported in this section result from financing activities. The largest item listed in this category often is interest expense on debt issued by an organization. This expense results from a financing activity rather than from an operating activity. **Borrowing money frequently is necessary for an organization's operations; however, except for financial institutions, it is not part of its operating activities.** Accordingly, other expenses and revenues are reported on the income statement after income from operations. This separate listing distinguishes them from revenues and expenses that result from operating activities.

Income Taxes. Most corporations pay income taxes on their earnings. **The amount of income tax expense is determined by applying tax rates required by current tax laws and regulations to the income earned by a company during a fiscal period.** Exhibit 5-2 reports Rockyfellow, Inc., incurred income taxes of $5,600 on pretax income of $21,870 in 1996.

Proprietorships and partnerships do not pay income taxes on their profits directly. Instead, those profits are treated as personal income of the owners. The owners pay income tax on a proprietorship's profits or on their share of the profits of a partnership.

Learning Note

Not all U.S. corporations pay income taxes on profits. Certain small corporations, known as Subchapter S corporations in the tax laws, are treated like partnerships for tax purposes.

Net Income and Earnings Per Share. Net income is the amount of profit earned by a company during a fiscal period. It represents an increase in owners' or stockholders' equity, and can be distributed to owners or reinvested in the company.

Learning Note

It is important to note that cash dividends and cash withdrawals are paid out of cash. Therefore, a company must have either current or past undistributed profits and sufficient cash available before it can pay dividends or before owners can withdraw money. Remember that net income does not guarantee a company will have favorable cash flows during a period.

GAAP require that corporate income statements prepared for distribution to shareholders and other external users present earnings per share as part of the statement. ***Earnings per share* is a measure of the earnings performance of each share of stock during a fiscal period. In general, it is computed by dividing net income by the average number of shares of common stock outstanding during a fiscal period.**[1]

Single-Step Format. The income statement presented in Exhibit 5-2 is typical of the type of information reported by companies in their income statements. Nevertheless, the format and content of income statements vary in practice. An alternative format to that described in Exhibit 5-2 is a **single-step statement.** In this type of statement, all revenues, such as sales, service, and interest are grouped together in the first section of the statement and are added together to compute total revenues. All expenses, including cost of goods sold, operating expenses, and other expenses are grouped together as total expenses. Total expenses are subtracted from total revenues to compute net income. Exhibit 5-3 illustrates a single-step income statement for Rockyfellow, Inc.

Internally used income statements may be prepared in a variety of formats and may use different reporting rules from those described in Exhibits 5-2 and 5-3. The statements may be prepared for different divisions of a company, for different product lines, or for different regions. The type and amount of information included in a statement will depend on the needs of managers who use them. The format and content of these statements are not governed by GAAP.

Externally used income statements, especially those of large corporations, may be more complex than the ones presented in Exhibits 5-2 and 5-3. In addition, most corporations report income statements for the most recent three fiscal years in their annual reports. Some income statement information often is reported for the latest five or ten year period in schedules accompanying the financial statements. Later chapters examine additional information that may appear on or accompany income statements.

[1] Common stock is explained in Chapter 8. The computation of earnings per share can be quite complex. Chapter 13 will examine this computation in more detail.

Exhibit 5-3

Rockyfellow, Inc.
Income Statement
For the Year Ended December 31, 1996
(Single-Step Format)

Sales revenue		$186,230
Expenses:		
Cost of goods sold	$73,350	
Wages	42,700	
Utilities	6,430	
Depreciation	9,650	
Insurance	3,420	
Supplies	8,390	
Advertising	7,120	
Patent	3,000	
Interest	10,300	
Income tax	5,600	
Total expenses		169,960
Net income		$ 16,270
Earnings per share of common stock (12,500 shares outstanding)		$1.30

SELF-STUDY PROBLEM 5-1

An income statement for IBM Corporation for a recent fiscal year is provided at the top of the next page. Use this statement to answer the following questions:

1. How much revenue did IBM earn from selling computers?
2. How much revenue did it earn from other operating activities?
3. How much revenue did it earn from nonoperating activities?
4. How much gross profit did IBM earn from the sale of computers?
5. How much gross profit did it earn from the sale of software?
6. How much expense did it incur for nonoperating activities?
7. Approximately how many shares of stock did IBM have outstanding during the year?
8. What were IBM's product costs for equipment and software sold for the period?
9. How much profit did IBM earn during the fiscal year?
10. How much cash did IBM receive from its operating activities during the year?

The Statement of Stockholders' Equity

Recall that the statement of stockholders' equity provides information about changes in owners' equity accounts for a corporation during a fiscal period. Exhibit 5-4 provides an example of this statement for Rockyfellow, Inc.

Objective 4
Summarize the information reported on a company's statement of stockholders' equity.

Stockholders' equity consists of two major divisions: contributed capital and retained earnings. ***Contributed capital*** **is the amount of direct investment by owners in a corporation.** It is the amount paid in to the corporation by stockholders for the ownership shares at the time the stock was sold by

INTERNATIONAL BUSINESS MACHINES CORPORATION
CONSOLIDATED STATEMENT OF EARNINGS
For the Year Ended December 31, 1990

(Dollars in millions except per share amounts)		
Revenue:		
Sales of equipment	$43,959	
Software	9,952	
Support services	11,322	
Rentals and financing	3,785	
		$69,018
Cost of goods and services sold:		
Sales of equipment	19,401	
Software	3,126	
Support services	6,617	
Rentals and financing	1,579	
		30,723
Gross profit		38,295
Operating expenses:		
Selling, general and administrative	20,709	
Research, development and engineering	6,554	
		27,263
Operating income		11,032
Other income, principally interest		495
Interest expense		(1,324)
Earnings before income taxes		10,203
Provision for income taxes		4,183
Net earnings		$6,020
Per share amounts:		
Net earnings		$10.51

Data source: IBM, 1990 Annual Report. Slight modifications in format have been made to the original.

The solution to Self-Study Problem 5-1 appears at the end of the chapter.

the corporation. The balance of contributed capital changes during a fiscal period when a corporation sells additional shares of stock. The balance also changes when the company buys its own shares back from stockholders and retires those shares so they cannot be resold.

Retained earnings is the cumulative amount of net income earned that has been reinvested in the corporation. It is the amount of profit that has not been paid out as dividends to stockholders. Retained earnings increases during a fiscal period by the amount of net income. It decreases by the amount of any net loss and by the amount of dividends paid or promised during a period.

Dividends are not reported on the income statement because they are not expenses. They are a distribution of net income to owners. **DIVIDENDS is a contra-owners' equity account.** It is a direct reduction in retained earnings and is reported on the statement of stockholders' equity.

The statement of stockholders' equity provides a link between the income statement and the balance sheet. The ending balances from the statement of

Exhibit 5-4

Rockyfellow, Inc.
Statement of Stockholders' Equity
For the Year Ended December 31, 1996

	Contributed Capital	Retained Earnings	Total
Balance at January 1, 1996	$100,000	$62,700	$162,700
Common stock issued	25,000		25,000
Net income		16,270	16,270
Dividends paid		(5,000)	(5,000)
Balance at December 31, 1996	$125,000	$73,970	$198,970

stockholders' equity are the amounts reported as stockholders' equity on the balance sheet. Corporations typically provide a statement of stockholders' equity for the most recent three fiscal years in their annual reports.

Learning Note

Corporations sometimes report an abbreviated version of the statement of stockholders' equity that contains only the retained earnings section of Exhibit 5-4. Accountants refer to this abbreviated version as a **statement of retained earnings**. Some corporations combine **the statement of retained earnings with the income statement.**

The Balance Sheet

Objective 5
Summarize the information reported on a company's balance sheet.

Objective 6
Explain reporting rules that determine the format of a balance sheet.

A balance sheet reports the asset, liability, and owners' equity account balances for a company at the end of a fiscal period. Exhibit 5-5 provides a balance sheet for Rockyfellow, Inc.

Recall that the total amount of assets reported on the balance sheet at the end of a fiscal period must be equal to the total amount of liabilities and owners' equity (after the balances of revenue and expense accounts have been transferred to owners' equity). This relationship of assets = liabilities + owners' equity is the fundamental balance sheet equation.

Exhibit 5-5 provides a **classified balance sheet** in which assets and liabilities are separated by type. Also, the exhibit illustrates a **comparative balance sheet** because it provides information for more than one fiscal period. A balance sheet provides information for a particular date; thus, information for the beginning and ending dates of a fiscal period is useful for determining changes in balance sheet accounts during that period. GAAP require classified and comparative balance sheets in reports to external users. Supplemental schedules may disclose some balance sheet information for the most recent five or ten years.

A balance sheet can be classified into seven primary sections, as shown in the illustration at the top of page 195.

Current Assets. ***Current assets* are cash or other resources management expects to convert to cash or consume during the next fiscal year.** Most current assets are liquid assets. ***Liquid assets* are resources that can be**

Exhibit 5-5

Rockyfellow, Inc.
Balance Sheet
December 31, 1996

	1996	1995
Assets		
Current assets:		
Cash	$ 15,600	$ 11,700
Accounts receivable	22,430	13,850
Merchandise inventory	43,500	44,450
Supplies	12,670	9,920
Prepaid insurance	8,290	5,950
Total current assets	102,490	85,870
Property, plant, and equipment:		
Equipment	93,070	79,570
Buildings	275,000	235,000
	368,070	314,570
Less: Accumulated depreciation	105,860	96,210
	262,210	218,360
Land	36,810	45,000
Total property, plant, and equipment	299,020	263,360
Other assets:		
Patents	32,000	35,000
Total assets*	$433,510	$384,230
Liabilities		
Current liabilities:		
Accounts payable	24,790	22,630
Wages payable	4,100	5,510
Interest payable	11,250	9,920
Income taxes payable	2,400	3,000
Notes payable, current portion	14,400	9,320
Total current liabilities	56,940	50,380
Long-term liabilities:		
Notes payable, long-term	177,600	171,150
Total liabilities	234,540	221,530
Stockholders' Equity		
Contributed capital	125,000**	100,000
Retained earnings	73,970**	62,700
Total stockholders' equity	198,970**	162,700
Total liabilities and stockholders' equity	$433,510	$384,230

***Total assets = Total current assets + Total property, plant, and equipment + Other assets**

****From Exhibit 5-4**

converted to cash in a relatively short period. In addition to cash, current assets include: (1) accounts receivable for which a company expects to receive cash during the next fiscal year, (2) inventory a company expects to sell during the next fiscal year, and (3) resources it expects to consume during the next fiscal year, such as supplies and prepaid insurance.

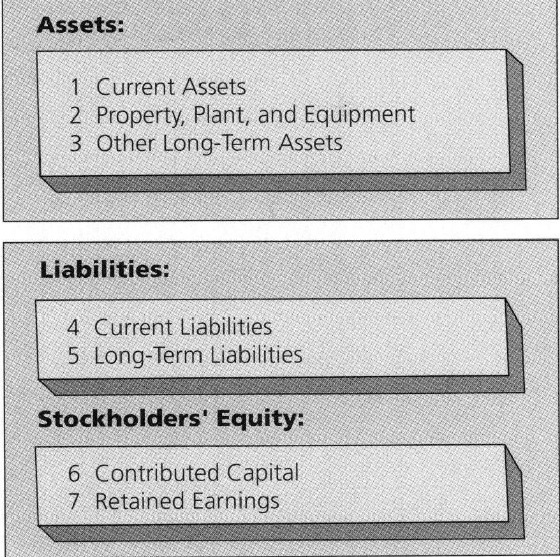

Assets:
1 Current Assets
2 Property, Plant, and Equipment
3 Other Long-Term Assets
Liabilities:
4 Current Liabilities
5 Long-Term Liabilities
Stockholders' Equity:
6 Contributed Capital
7 Retained Earnings

Learning Note

An organization's operating cycle is the period from the time cash is used to acquire or produce goods until these goods are sold and cash is received. The operating cycles of most organizations are less than 12 months. A fiscal year is the primary reporting period for these companies. Occasionally, a company's operating cycle is longer than 12 months. In such cases, which are rare, current assets are defined as those a company expects to convert to cash or consume during the next operating cycle.

Property, Plant, and Equipment. *Property, plant, and equipment,* **often called fixed or plant assets, are long-term, tangible assets that are used in a company's operations.** Unlike inventory, these assets are not intended for resale. U.S. GAAP require fixed assets, other than land, to be depreciated over their estimated useful lives. Depreciation allocates the cost of these assets to the fiscal periods that benefit from their use as a means of matching expenses with revenues. GAAP in some countries permit the immediate expensing of plant assets.

Other Long-Term Assets. *Other assets* **include long-term investments in other companies, noncurrent receivables, fixed assets held for sale, prepaids not expected to be consumed in the next fiscal year, and long-term legal rights such as patents, trademarks, and copyrights.** These types of assets may be listed on the balance sheet under separate headings, such as Long-Term Investments, if they constitute a significant portion of a company's assets. *Long-term investments* **occur when one company purchases the stock or bonds of another company.** Companies often invest in other companies to share in their earnings or to obtain access to resources, management skills, technology, and markets available to other companies.

Accounts and notes receivable a company does not expect to collect during the next fiscal year (or longer operating cycle) are not included among current assets. These items are reported in the Other Assets category. This category includes supplies, prepaid insurance, and similar assets that will not be consumed during the next fiscal period. Property, plant, and equipment items a company is not using currently but is holding for future use, disposal, or sale also are in-

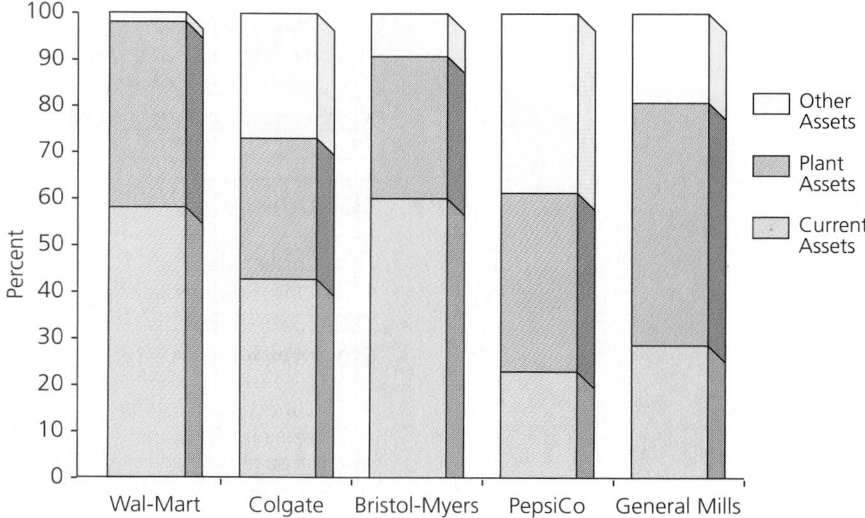

Data source: 1991 Annual Report.

cluded in this category. For example, land held for a future factory site would be listed here.

Long-term legal rights resulting from the ownership of patents, copyrights, trademarks, and similar items are known as *intangible assets*, in contrast to tangible assets such as property, plant, and equipment. The cost of these assets is allocated over their estimated useful lives in a similar manner to the allocation of fixed asset costs. *Amortization* **is the process of systematically allocating a cost to expense over a period of time**. Intangible assets usually are amortized on a straight-line basis. That is, the cost of the assets is allocated to expense equally over the fiscal periods management expects will benefit from their use. This allocation attempts to match expense with revenue. PATENT EXPENSE, reported on the income statement in Exhibit 5-2, is the amortization expense for patents. Unlike fixed assets, an accumulation account, such as ACCUMULATED DEPRECIATION, normally is not used to record the cumulative amortization of intangibles. The amortization expense for a period is subtracted directly from the appropriate intangible asset account when the expense is recorded.

To illustrate, assume that on January 1, 1995, a company purchased a patent, giving that company the exclusive right to produce a product. The cost of the patent was $10,000, and it was expected to have a useful life for the company of 10 years. The amount of amortization expense for the patent would be $1,000 per year for the 10 year period. The balance of the patent account reported on the company's December 31, 1995, balance sheet would be $9,000. The balance on December 31, 1996, would be $8,000, and so forth.

Liabilities. A balance sheet separates liabilities into current and long-term categories. *Current liabilities* **are those management expects to pay during the next fiscal year (or longer operating cycle).** *Long-term liabilities* **are those not classified as current liabilities.**

When long-term debt is paid in installments, the amount that will be paid during the next year is a current liability (such as NOTES PAYABLE, CURRENT PORTION in Exhibit 5-5). For example, assume a company issues $20,000 in long-term notes payable on January 1, 1992. The principal is to be paid in four equal annual installments. Therefore, $5,000 of the notes would be reported as a current liability on any balance sheets prepared prior to January 1, 1996. The remaining unpaid balance would be reported as a long-term liability ($15,000 in 1992, $10,000 in 1993, and $5,000 in 1994). There would be no long-term liability during 1995 because the final installment is paid at the end of 1995 and is classified as a current liability in 1995.

Liabilities and Stockholders' Equity as a Percentage of Total Assets for Some Large U.S. Corporations

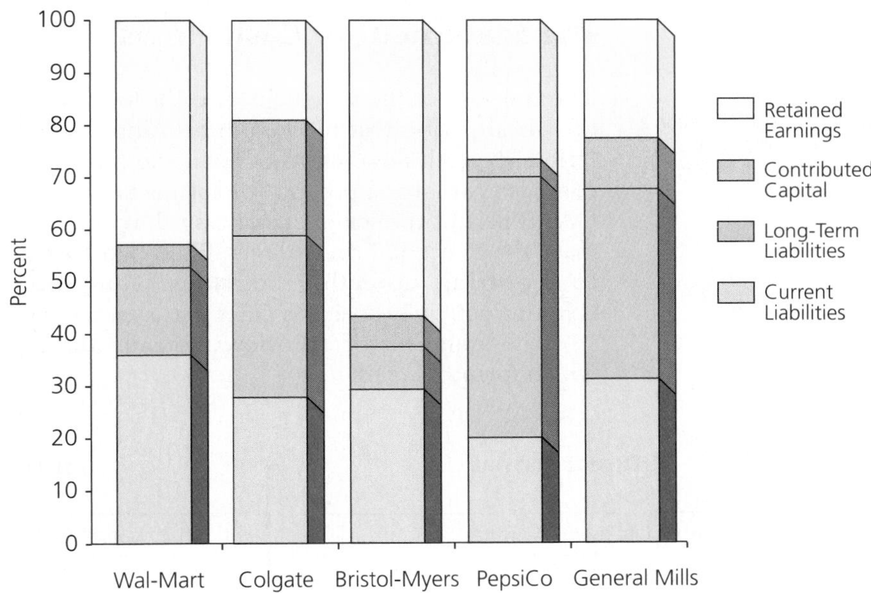

Data source: 1991 Annual Reports.

Working Capital. Financial statement users often are interested in the relationship between an organization's current assets and current liabilities. *Working capital* **is the amount of current assets minus the amount of current liabilities**. Rockyfellow, Inc.'s working capital for 1996 is $45,550 ($102,490 of current assets − $56,940 of current liabilities). Working capital often is expressed as a ratio. **The** *working capital ratio,* **or** *current ratio,* **is the amount of current assets divided by the amount of current liabilities**. Rockyfellow's working capital ratio for 1996 is 1.8 ($102,490/$56,940). Working capital is a commonly used measure of a company's *liquidity* **(having sufficient liquid assets to pay current obligations)**. A large amount of working capital, or a high working capital ratio, often implies a company has satisfactory liquidity and will be able to pay its current obligations on a timely basis. Measures of liquidity and their use will be examined in later chapters.

Stockholders' Equity.[2] The balances of stockholders' equity accounts on the balance sheet are the ending balances reported for these accounts on the state-

2 More extensive coverage of stockholders' equity appears in Chapter 8.

ment of stockholders' equity (see Exhibit 5-4). These balances normally include the cumulative amount of contributed capital and retained earnings obtained by a corporation since its beginning.

Other Balance Sheet Formats. Like the income statement, the balance sheet may appear in a variety of formats in practice. Companies may use different reporting rules from those previously described. Some types of companies, for example, many utilities, report fixed assets prior to current assets and report stockholders' equity prior to liabilities. Foreign companies often use formats that differ from those used in the U.S. Examples of various formats will be illustrated throughout this book.

The Statement of Cash Flows

Objective 7
Summarize the information reported on a company's statement of cash flows.

The purpose of the statement of cash flows is to identify the primary activities of a fiscal period that resulted in cash inflows and outflows. The statement describes the cash flow results of financing, investing, and operating activities for a company for a fiscal period. It explains the change in a company's cash balance. GAAP permit the statement of cash flows to be presented in either of two formats: the direct and the indirect. **The two formats differ only with respect to reporting operating activities**. Thus, the presentation of financing and investing activities does not differ between the two formats.

The statement of cash flows contains three primary sections regardless of which format is used:

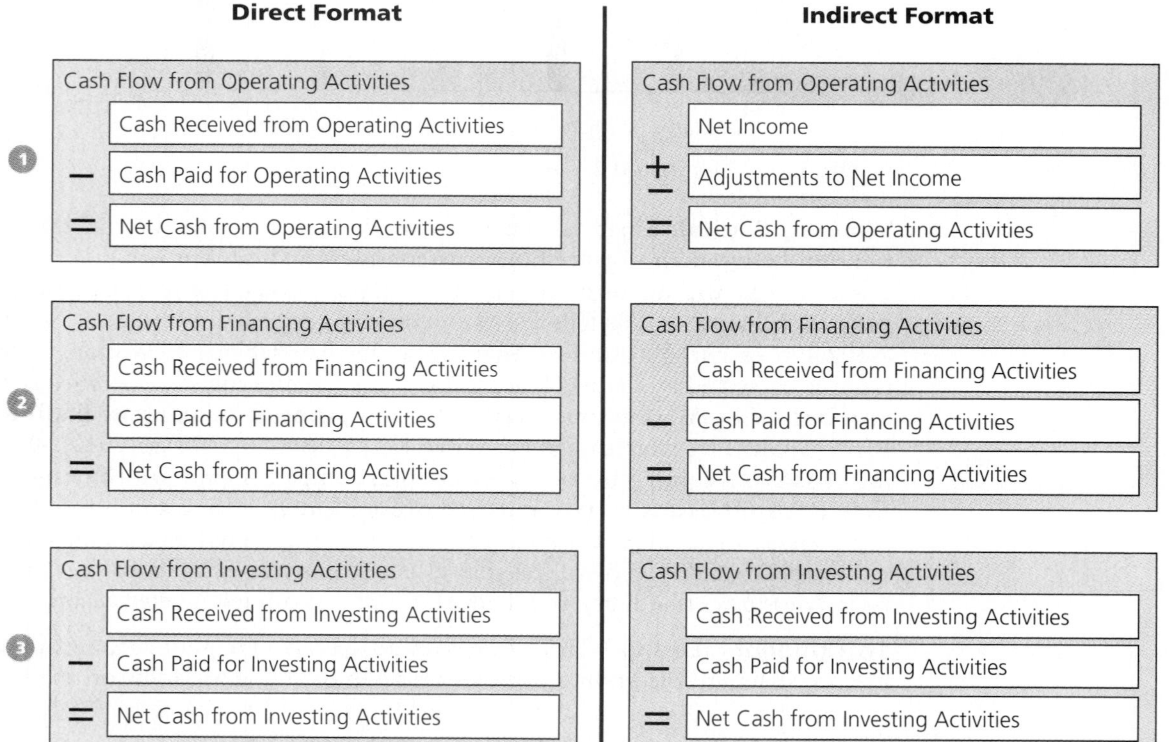

This chapter considers the primary content of the direct format. The indirect format will be examined in Chapter 6.

Exhibit 5-6 provides an example of the cash flow statement for Rockyfellow, Inc., using the direct format.

Exhibit 5-6

Rockyfellow, Inc.
Statement of Cash Flows
For the Year Ended December 31, 1996
(Direct Format)

Cash flow from operating activities		
Receipts:		
Collections from customers		$177,650
Payments:		
To suppliers of inventory	$(70,240)	
To employees	(44,110)	
For utilities	(6,430)	
For insurance	(5,760)	
For supplies	(11,140)	
For interest	(8,970)	
For advertising	(7,120)	
For income taxes	(6,200)	
Total cash payments		(159,970)
Net cash flow from operating activities		17,680
Cash flow from financing activities		
Proceeds from issuing common stock	25,000	
Proceeds from issuing long-term debt	32,000	
Payment of long-term debt	(20,470)	
Payment of dividends	(5,000)	
Net cash flow from financing activities		31,530
Cash flow from investing activities		
Purchase of plant assets	(53,500)	
Sale of plant assets	8,190	
Net cash flow from investing activities		(45,310)
Net increase in cash		3,900
Cash balance, December 31, 1995*		11,700
Cash balance, December 31, 1996*		$15,600

***From Exhibit 5-5**

Note: Cash outflows are indicated on the statement by parentheses. Often cash flow from investing activities is listed before cash flow from financing activities.

Objective 8
Explain reporting rules that determine the direct format of a statement of cash flows.

The direct format of reporting the statement of cash flows presents each major source and use of cash. Amounts of cash received from customers and amounts paid to suppliers for inventory, to employees for wages, etc., are listed on the statement. The cash balances reported in Exhibit 5-6 correspond with those of the comparative balance sheet in Exhibit 5-5. The statement of cash flows is divided into three sections corresponding to the three phases of the transformation process: financing, investing, and operating.

Operating Activities. Operating activities are transactions involving the purchase, production, or sale of goods and services. Cash flow from operating activities identifies cash received from the sale of goods and services. Also it identifies cash paid for resources used to provide goods and services. An important relationship exists between the income statement and the operating activities section of the statement of cash flows. Both are based on the same set of activities. On the income statement, operating activities are measured on an accrual basis. On the cash flow statement, these activities are measured on a cash basis. These amounts can be compared to determine timing differences between accrual basis recognition of revenues and expenses and cash flows for the period.

Current asset and current liability transactions normally result from the operating activities of a company, for example, from buying and selling merchandise. Therefore, cash flows associated with working capital items, such as the purchase of inventory, supplies, or prepaid insurance, and payment of wages, are part of the operating activities section of the statement of cash flows.

Learning Note

Interest is included as an operating activity on the cash flow statement because it appears on the income statement. Interest is the result of a company's financing activities rather than its operating activities, however.

Financing Activities. Financing activities are transactions between a company and its owners or between a company and its long-term creditors. The financing activities section reports only the cash flow effects of transactions associated with long-term debt and investments by owners. Cash flows result when debt is issued or repaid and when stock is issued or repurchased. Payments of dividends also is a financing activity.

Investing Activities. Investing activities are acquisitions or disposals of long-term assets during a fiscal period. Depreciation and amortization expenses are not cash flow items. These expenses are not listed either in the operating or investing sections of the statement of cash flows when the direct format is used. Cash flow occurs when fixed or intangible assets are purchased or sold, not when the costs of these assets are amortized.

Some transactions affect investing and financing activities without affecting cash directly. Assume a company borrows $300,000 from a bank to purchase a building; the transaction increases BUILDINGS and NOTES PAYABLE but does not have a direct effect on cash. GAAP require such transactions to be disclosed in notes to the financial statements. Some companies list these items on the statement of cash flows below the cash flow items.

Other special items also may appear on the statement of cash flows that do not fit into one of the three primary divisions of the statement. The effect of exchange rate changes (considered in Chapter 8) is an example of this type of item. Appendix E of this book contains the statement of cash flows for Compaq Computer Corporation, prepared using the direct format.

GAAP also require a schedule to reconcile cash flows from operating activities with net income when the direct format is used. This schedule is similar to the presentation of the statement of cash flows using the indirect format examined in Chapter 6.

SELF-STUDY PROBLEM 5-2

Listed below are account balances, cash receipts and payments, and other data for Lewy Pasture, Inc., a company that distributes pharmaceutical supplies, for the fiscal year ended October 31, 1996:

Accounts payable	$ 22,000
Accounts receivable	11,000
Accumulated depreciation	164,000
Buildings	412,000
Cash	16,000
Cash collections from customers	360,000
Cash from disposal of equipment	8,000
Cash from issuance of notes payable	60,000
Cash paid for acquisition of buildings	32,000
Cash paid for acquisition of land	5,000
Cash paid for acquisition of long-term investments	8,000
Cash paid to repurchase stock	35,000
Cash payments for income tax	11,000
Cash payments for insurance	9,000
Cash payments for interest	23,000
Cash payments for notes payable	30,000
Cash payments for supplies	10,000
Cash payments to employees	100,000
Cash payments to suppliers	154,000
Contributed capital	300,000
Cost of goods sold	146,000
Dividends (declared and paid)	17,000
Equipment	245,000
General and administrative expenses	96,000
Income tax expense	14,000
Income tax payable	6,000
Interest expense	25,000
Interest payable	14,000
Land	35,000
Long-term investments	35,000
Merchandise inventory	62,000
Notes payable, current portion	10,000
Notes payable, long-term	278,000
Prepaid insurance	7,000
Retained earnings, October 31, 1995	25,000
Sales revenue	357,000
Selling expenses	47,000
Supplies	13,000
Trademarks	13,000
Wages payable	18,000
Shares of common stock: 10,000	

Required

From the data presented above, determine the amount of each of the following items for Pasture's financial statements:

1. Gross profit
2. Income from operations
3. Net income
4. Earnings per share
5. Current assets
6. Property, plant, and equipment
7. Other assets
8. Total assets
9. Current liabilities
10. Working capital and working capital ratio
11. Total liabilities

12. Retained earnings, October 31, 1996
13. Total stockholders' equity
14. Total liabilities and stockholders' equity
15. Net cash flow from (for) operating activities
16. Net cash flow from (for) investing activities
17. Net cash flow from (for) financing activities
18. Net increase or decrease in cash

The solution to Self-Study Problem 5-2 appears at the end of the chapter.

USE OF FINANCIAL STATEMENTS

Financial statements are a primary source of accounting information for external decision makers. External users analyze statements to evaluate the ability of an organization to use its resources effectively and efficiently. By comparing changes in assets, liabilities, earnings, and cash flows over time, users form expectations about return and risk. Comparisons across companies help determine which companies are being managed effectively and provide the best investment opportunities.

Section 2 of this book describes methods of analyzing and interpreting financial statements in detail. The remainder of this chapter considers attributes of financial statements decision makers should understand when interpreting them.

Interrelationships Among Financial Statements

Objective 9
Discuss how financial statements work together to present a picture of a company for a fiscal period.

Taken as a whole, the financial statements describe the economic events that changed the financial condition of a company from the beginning to the end of a fiscal period. Information on the income statement and statement of cash flows explains changes in balance sheet accounts during a period.

For example, Rockyfellow, Inc., reported a beginning balance for accounts receivable of $13,850 and an ending balance of $22,430 (Exhibit 5-5). This increase of $8,580 can be explained by two other financial statement numbers. Sales revenue on the income statement was $186,230 for the period (Exhibit 5-3). The statement of cash flows reports cash of $177,650 collected from customers for the period (Exhibit 5-6). The increase in accounts receivable is the difference between sales for the period and the amount of cash collected from customers: $8,580 = $186,230 − $177,650.

The summary information presented in financial statements does not always provide sufficient detail to explain the change in every balance sheet account. Access to the ledger accounts would be necessary to provide a complete explanation. Nevertheless, the relationships among the financial statements are important. Balance sheets for the beginning and ending of a fiscal period reveal changes in the resources and finances of a company. The company's income statement and statement of cash flows reveal major events that caused these changes. **The relationship among financial statements in which the numbers on one statement explain numbers on other statements is called *articulation*.** You should remember a company's financial statements are not independent of each other. They work together to explain the events that changed the company's financial condition:

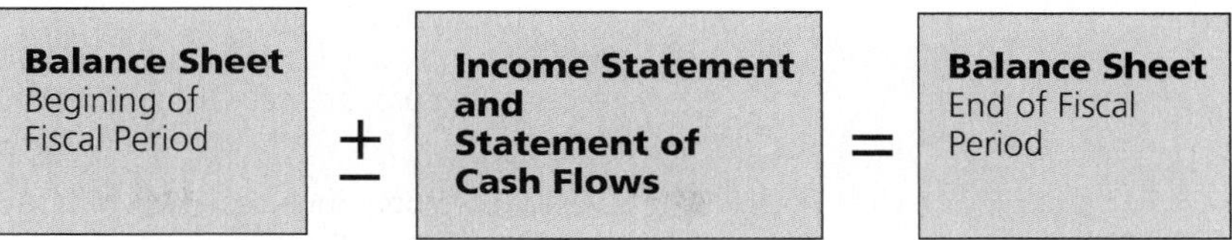

Consolidated Financial Statements

Objective 10
Explain why many corporations publish consolidated financial statements.

Most large corporations publish consolidated financial statements. ***Consolidated financial statements*** **report the combined economic activities of two or more corporations owned by the same stockholders.** Most major corporations own a controlling interest in other corporations. If one corporation owns a sufficient number of shares of another corporation (generally more than 50%), it is able to control the management of the corporation it owns. **A corporation that controls another corporation is known as a *parent corporation*. Corporations controlled by another corporation are *subsidiaries*.** A subsidiary may be wholly owned (100% owned by a parent), or partially owned (less than 100%). Consolidated financial statements report the activities of a parent and its subsidiaries as though they were one company. A parent and its subsidiaries are sometimes referred to as a group. This term is particularly common in financial reports of European corporations. These reports refer to "group accounts" or "group financial statements" when referring to consolidated statements.

Consolidated statements combine the accounts of a parent and its subsidiaries for reporting purposes. Assume Push Automotive Co. owns Slick Tire Co. and Sticky Brakes Co. At the end of fiscal 1995, the cash account for the three companies appears as follows:

Push Automotive	$180,000
Slick Tire	60,000
Sticky Brakes	40,000
Total cash	$280,000

The consolidated balance sheet for Push Automotive for 1995 would report a cash balance of $280,000.

All accounts cannot be combined in the same way as cash, however. For example, assume sales revenue for the three companies was as follows:

Push Automotive	$1,400,000
Slick Tire	500,000
Sticky Brakes	300,000
Total revenue	$2,200,000

The combined total represents the consolidated revenues of Push Automotive and its subsidiaries only if no sales were made *among* the three companies. Assume Slick Tire sold goods to Push that amounted to $300,000 of its sales. Sticky Brakes sold goods to Push that amounted to $180,000 of its sales. Consolidated revenues would be:

Push Automotive		$1,400,000
Slick Tire	$500,000	
Less intercompany sales	300,000	200,000
Sticky Brakes	300,000	
Less intercompany sales	180,000	120,000
Total consolidated revenue		$1,720,000

Intercompany sales must be eliminated from total revenues because these sales are not transactions with customers outside the consolidated business. Cost of goods sold would have to be adjusted as well for the costs associated with intercompany sales. Other accounts that require adjustments include intercompany payables and receivables. In addition, subsidiary stockholders' equity is eliminated because it is owned by the parent.

The consolidated statements represent the economic activities of a parent and its subsidiaries as though they were one business organization. Owners of a parent firm are also owners of the subsidiaries controlled by the parent. Therefore, consolidated statements provide information about the activities of a group of companies owned by particular stockholders. The stockholders should be concerned about the activities of both parent and subsidiaries. The value of the stockholders' investments is determined by the value of the parent and its subsidiaries.

Some countries do not require consolidation of parent and subsidiary financial statements. Each company reports its own statements. When statements are not consolidated, investors have more difficulty in assessing the performance of a parent company.

Limitations of Financial Statements

Objective 11
Identify some of the primary limitations of financial statements.

In spite of the abundant information financial statements provide, their usefulness is limited by certain constraints of the reporting process. Some of these limitations include:

1. use of estimates and allocations,
2. use of historical costs,
3. omission of transactions,
4. omission of resources and costs, and
5. delay in providing information.

These constraints result primarily from costs associated with the reporting process. Information is a resource. It is costly to provide. Its value is determined by benefits derived by those who use the information. For information to be valuable, its cost must be less than the benefits it provides to users. Therefore, the amount and type of reported information is constrained by costs and benefits.

The following sections consider these limitations. Users should keep these limitations in mind when interpreting financial statement information.

Use of Estimates and Allocations. Many of the numbers reported in financial statements result from estimates and allocations. For example, depreciation and amortization represent allocations of asset costs to expenses over the estimated lives of the assets. These estimates often are imprecise because the amount of the asset consumed in a particular fiscal period is difficult to determine. Decisions about when to recognize revenues and expenses frequently require management judgment. Sometimes it is not clear when a revenue has been earned or when an expense has been incurred. For example, revenues earned on long-term contracts, such as those in the construction industry, are known with certainty only after the contract has been completed. But, if the contract takes several years to complete, determination of the revenue that should be recognized each year during the contract period requires management judgment. Different managers and companies may use different methods for recognizing certain revenues and expenses. Managers estimate the amount of credit sales that will be uncollectible, and determine when to recognize a loss from obsolete inventory or from plant assets that have experienced an unexpected decline in value. These subjective decisions and estimates mean accounting numbers are not as precise as they might initially appear. Precision is limited by the cost of obtaining precise information in a timely manner.

Use of Historical Costs. Financial statements report primarily the historical cost of assets and liabilities. ***Historical cost*** **is the purchase or exchange price of an asset or liability at the time it is acquired or incurred.** The recorded values of many assets are reduced over time by depreciation and amortization. They are not adjusted for changes in the purchasing power of money or for changes in the current value of the assets or liabilities. The purchasing power of money changes over time because of inflation; for example, a dollar in 1994 buys less than a dollar would purchase in 1980. The current value of an asset is the amount at which that asset, in its current condition, could be bought or sold at the present time. A building purchased in 1980 for $500,000 may be reported in the financial statements at a book value (cost minus accumulated depreciation) of $200,000 in 1994. This amount has not been adjusted for inflation. Suppose inflation has been 100% since the building was purchased; the current cost of that building in its 1994 condition would be about $400,000. However, disclosure of current cost and the impact of purchasing power changes are not required by GAAP. Rather, financial statements report most assets and liabilities at their historical costs, adjusted for accumulated depreciation or amortization when appropriate.

Some countries such as the United Kingdom and the Netherlands permit financial statements to be reported using current values. Assets and liabilities are restated to approximate their market values at the end of a fiscal period.

Net income should provide financial statement users a reasonable estimate of the amount a company can distribute to its owners and maintain the company's capital. If economic conditions are stable, a company that maintains its capital should be able to earn profits indefinitely at approximately the same level as in the past. Unfortunately, economic conditions are seldom stable across fiscal periods. Companies must contend with changing economic conditions such as variations in interest rates and inflation, changing markets and competition, variations in the price and availability of materials, plant assets, labor, and changing technology. **Therefore, the amount of net income reported by a company may overstate or understate the amount a company can distribute to its owners and still maintain its capital.** Numerous factors must be examined by users in interpreting a company's earnings and in forecasting its prospects for the future.

Omission of Transactions. Financial statements include the primary transactions that occur as part of a company's transformation process. Nevertheless, **a guarantee does not exist that all important transactions are fully reported in a company's financial statements.** Some transactions do not result from specific exchanges. They result when revenues or expenses are allocated to fiscal periods. Accountants and managers sometimes disagree about when certain activities should be recognized. Also, they may disagree about the amount that should be reported in the financial statements for these activities. The accounting profession has debated extensively such issues as how to recognize the costs of employee retirement benefits. Today, companies report certain liabilities, assets, and expenses associated with these items that were not reported 10 years ago. Undoubtedly, other issues will arise that will alter information reported in the financial statements.

The importance of information changes over time. Companies develop new financing and compensation arrangements. Reporting rules for these arrangements may not be covered by existing GAAP. If the arrangements become common such that new reporting rules would increase the benefits of information for users, GAAP may be created for transactions involving these new arrangements. GAAP are dynamic. They change as the needs of users and economic activities of organizations change. Chapter 7 examines the process used to establish GAAP.

Omission of Resources and Costs. Certain types of resources and costs are not reported in the financial statements. The value of employees is not an asset listed on most balance sheets. Nevertheless, a well-trained and stable work force and skilled managers may be the resource that adds most to the value of many companies. Without skilled labor and management, the remaining resources of a company often would have little value. Financial statements do not report these human resources. They are not owned by a company, and their values are difficult and costly to determine. A major portion of the value of many companies derives from their research and development activities that create new and improved products. The costs of these efforts are expensed when they are incurred each fiscal period even though they may have a major effect on the future earnings of a company. Such costs are expensed because of the difficulty and cost of identifying the timing and amount of future benefits a company will receive from these efforts. Nevertheless, the economic value of a company differs from the amount reported on its financial statements because of these measurement limitations.

Delay in Providing Information. Financial statement information is not always timely. Annual financial statements may lag actual events by a year or more; even monthly statements may lag events by several weeks. While such delays may not be a major problem for certain types of decisions, they may be critical for others. Users often need more timely sources. Managers, in particular, may need information on an ongoing basis to make effective decisions. Traditional financial statements are only one type of accounting information. Because financial statements are costly to produce and distribute, external reporting is limited to distinct fiscal periods. As information technology reduces the cost of reporting, more frequent reporting to external users may become feasible.

Usefulness of Financial Statements

A variety of problems impair the usefulness of financial statements. Do these problems negate the usefulness and purpose of the statements? Clearly, the answer is no. Financial statements continue to be a primary source of information for managers and external users about a company's activities. But, these problems mean considerable care is needed to understand accounting information and to use it correctly in making decisions. Careful analysis of the information is necessary. Different types of decisions sometimes require different subsets of information. The way accounting information is used by a company's production managers will be different than the way it is used by a company's president or by investors and creditors. Much of the remainder of this text will consider problems associated with understanding and using accounting information and methods for solving these problems.

FINANCIAL STATEMENTS AND THE TRANSFORMATION PROCESS

Objective 12
Discuss how financial statements relate to the transformation process and the time periods in which companies operate.

The first five chapters of this book have examined the purpose and function of business organizations and the role of the accounting information system. Organizations transform resources into goods and services. The accounting information system identifies events associated with the transformation process. It includes these events in financial information that can be summarized and reported to decision makers.

Exhibit 5-9 illustrates the accounting information system as it represents the transformation process.

Exhibit 5-9 Accounting Information and the Transformation Process

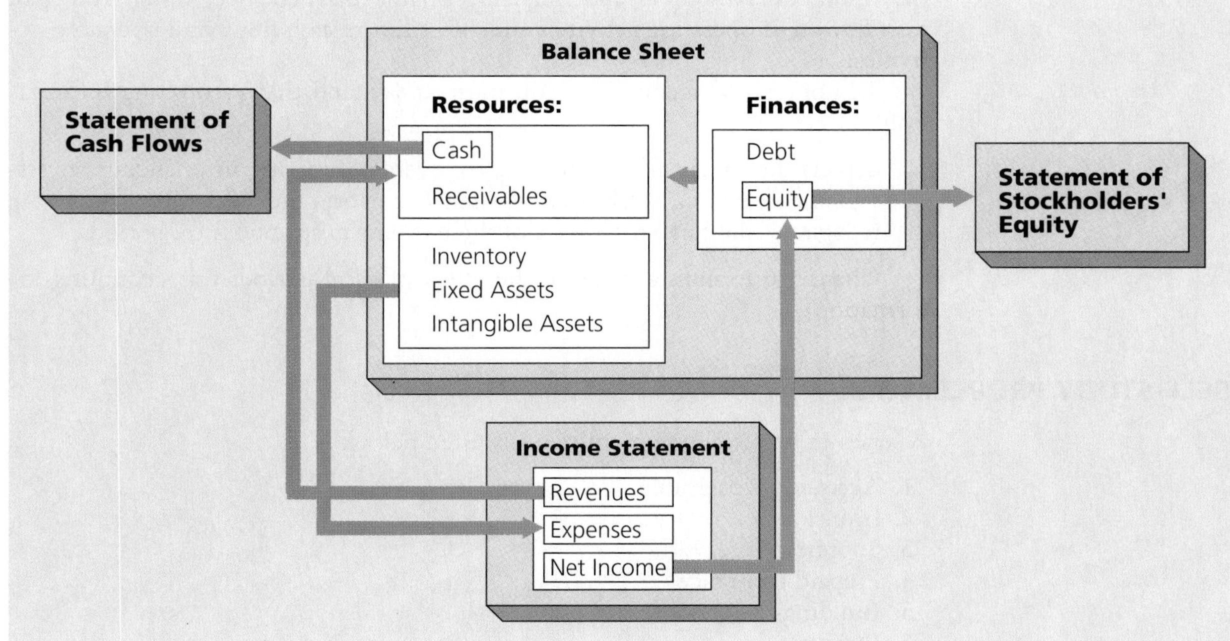

Financial statements and individual accounts originate within the transformation process. The balance sheet identifies sources of financing for a company and how the financing was invested in resources available to the company. The income statement identifies operating activities that provide additional financial resources and equity. These operating activities also require the consumption of resources. Their consumption is measured by expenses. Events from financing, investing, and operating activities affect a company's cash flows. The statement of cash flows identifies these events. Both investments by owners and reinvestment of profits affect stockholders' equity. These events are identified in the statement of stockholders' equity.

Transformation and Time

Two essential concepts must be mastered to understand accounting information. One of the concepts is the transformation process. Transactions associated with the transformation process are the basis for accounting information. Accounting information is meaningful only when it is a reasonable representation of an organization's transformation process. To interpret accounting information, you must understand the transformation process.

The second concept is the importance of time in measuring financial performance. A company's activities are separated into periods of time, fiscal periods. The events that occur in a company's transformation process should be associated with the periods in which they occur. But, many events extend to more than one fiscal period. Contracts often begin in one period and end in a subsequent period. Cash flows may occur in one period, while revenues or expenses may occur in another. Cash flows are reported on the statement of cash flows. Revenues and expenses are reported on the income statement. The balance sheet identifies resources and sources of financing for the resources. Resources and financing on the balance sheet result from past cash flows and operating activities and affect future cash flows and operating activities.

To understand accounting, you must understand that accounting information:

1. depicts the financial consequences of events occurring in financing, investing, and operating activities in the transformation process, and
2. recognizes the financial effects of these events in specific fiscal periods.

Chapter 6 examines in detail the effect of fiscal periods on accounting information.

SELF-STUDY PROBLEM 5-3

A series of financial statement items is listed below:

1. Accounts Receivable
2. Inventory
3. Supplies
4. Prepaid Insurance
5. Buildings
6. Patents
7. Accounts Payable

8. Wages Payable
9. Interest Payable
10. Notes Payable
11. Contributed Capital
12. Retained Earnings
13. Dividends
14. Sales Revenue
15. Cost of Goods Sold
16. Depreciation Expense
17. Wages Expense
18. Interest Expense
19. Cash Collected from Customers
20. Cash Paid to Suppliers
21. Cash Received from Issuing Debt
22. Cash Paid for Equipment

Required

For each account, indicate the financial statement on which the account would appear. Then, identify the information provided by the account and the meaning of the account for an organization's transformation process. Use the format provided below. The first item is provided as an example:

Item	Financial Statement	Activity Reported
1. Accounts Receivable	Balance Sheet	Cash to be received in the future from prior sales

The solution to Self-Study Problem 5-3 appears at the end of the chapter.

REVIEW *Summary of Important Concepts*

1. Purpose and content of financial statements:
   A. Financial statements include the balance sheet, the income statement, the statement of cash flows, and the statement of stockholders' equity.
   B. The income statement reports the results of operations of a company for a fiscal period on the accrual basis. It reports information about the creation and consumption of resources in producing and selling goods and services, not about actual cash flows.
   C. Income statement formats vary, but typical statements are prepared using a multiple-step or single-step format.
   D. Corporations often report a statement of stockholders' equity. It describes the results of transactions that have changed the amount of contributed capital and retained earnings of a company during a fiscal period.
   E. A balance sheet identifies asset, liability, and owners' equity account balances at the end of a fiscal period. Balance sheets often classify accounts into current and long-term asset and liability categories. Comparative balance sheets report account balances for more than one fiscal period.
   F. The statement of cash flows reports the cash inflows and outflows associated with operating, investing, and financing activities of a company for a fiscal period. The statement may be presented in a direct or indirect format.

G. Two essential concepts describe the information reported by financial statements: (1) financial statements represent the transformation process of an organization for a fiscal period and (2) financial statements report the effects of transactions for specific periods.

2. Special attributes and limitations of financial statements:
   A. The interrelated financial statements, as a set, describe the financial impact of economic events of a company from the beginning to the end of a fiscal period.
   B. Consolidated financial statements report the economic activities of a parent and its subsidiaries as though they were one business entity.
   C. Limitations exist in financial statements that affect the usefulness of the information they report. Limitations include the need for estimates of financial results, the use of historical costs for representing asset values, and incomplete measures for some resources or transactions that might affect a company's value.

DEFINE *Terms and Concepts Defined in this Chapter*

amortization
articulation
consolidated financial statements
contributed capital
cost of services sold
current assets
current liabilities
current ratio
earnings per share
financial revenues and expenses
gross profit
historical cost
income from operations
intangible assets
liquid assets
liquidity
long-term investments
long-term liabilities
operating expenses
other assets
other revenues and expenses
parent corporation
property, plant, and equipment
statement of cash flows
statement of stockholders' equity
subsidiary
working capital
working capital ratio

SOLUTIONS

SELF-STUDY PROBLEM 5-1

1. Revenue from sale of equipment	$43,959,000,000
2. Other operating revenue:	
Software	9,952,000,000
Support services	$11,322,000,000
Rentals and financing	3,785,000,000
Total	$25,059,000,000
3. Other income	$495,000,000
4. Gross profit from sale of equipment:	
Sales revenue	$43,959,000,000
Cost of goods sold	19,401,000,000
Gross profit	$24,558,000,000
5. Gross profit from sale of software:	
Sales revenue	$9,952,000,000
Cost of goods sold	3,126,000,000
Gross profit	$6,826,000,000

6. Interest expense $1,324,000,000

7. Number of shares outstanding ($6,020,000,000/$10.51) = 572,787,821 shares.

8. Cost of goods sold:

For equipment	$19,401,000,000
For software	3,126,000,000
Total	$22,527,000,000

9. Net earnings $6,020,000,000

10. Net cash from operations cannot be determined from the income statement.

SELF-STUDY PROBLEM 5-2

1. Gross profit:

Sales revenue		$357,000
Cost of goods sold		146,000
Gross profit		$211,000

2. Income from operations:

Gross profit		$211,000
General and administrative expenses	$96,000	
Selling expenses	47,000	
Total operating expenses		143,000
Income from operations		$ 68,000

3. Net income:

Income from operations		$ 68,000
Interest expense	$25,000	
Income tax expense	14,000	39,000
Net income		$ 29,000

4. Earnings per share:
Net income ÷ shares of common stock ($29,000/10,000) = $2.90

5. Current assets:

Cash	$ 16,000
Accounts receivable	11,000
Merchandise inventory	62,000
Supplies	13,000
Prepaid insurance	7,000
Current assets	$109,000

6. Property, plant, and equipment:

Land	$ 35,000
Buildings	412,000
Equipment	245,000
Accumulated depreciation	(164,000)
Property, plant, and equipment	$528,000

7. Other assets:

Long-term investments	$ 35,000
Trademarks	13,000
Other assets	$ 48,000

8. Total assets:

Current assets	$109,000
Property, plant, and equipment	528,000
Other assets	48,000
Total assets	$685,000*

9. Current liabilities:

Accounts payable	$ 22,000
Wages payable	18,000
Interest payable	14,000
Income tax payable	6,000
Notes payable, current portion	10,000
Current liabilities	$ 70,000

10. Working capital and working capital ratio:

Current assets	$109,000
Current liabilities	70,000
Working capital	$ 39,000

Working capital ratio ($109,000/$70,000) = 1.557

11. Total liabilities:

Current liabilities	$ 70,000
Notes payable, long-term	278,000
Total liabilities	$348,000

12. Retained earnings, October 31, 1996:

Retained earnings, October 31, 1995	$ 25,000
Net income	29,000
Dividends	(17,000)
Retained earnings, October 31, 1996	$ 37,000

13. Total stockholders' equity:

Contributed capital	$300,000
Retained earnings	37,000
Stockholders' equity	$337,000

14. Total liabilities and stockholders' equity:

Total liabilities	$348,000
Stockholders' equity	337,000
Total liabilities and stockholders' equity	$685,000*

15. Net cash flow from operating activities:

Collections from customers	$360,000
Payments for income tax	(11,000)
Payments for insurance	(9,000)
Payments for interest	(23,000)
Payments for supplies	(10,000)
Payments to employees	(100,000)
Payments to suppliers	(154,000)
Cash flow from operating activities	$ 53,000

16. Net cash flow from (for) investing activities:

Disposal of equipment	$ 8,000
Acquisition of buildings	(32,000)
Acquisition of land	(5,000)
Acquisition of long-term investments	(8,000)
Cash flow from (for) investing activities	$ (37,000)

17. Net cash flow from (for) financing activities:

Issuance of notes payable	$ 60,000
Repurchase of stock	(35,000)
Payments for notes payable	(30,000)
Payment of dividends	(17,000)
Cash flow from (for) financing activities	$ (22,000)

18. Net increase or decrease in cash:

Cash flow from operating activities	$ 53,000
Cash flow from (for) investing activities	(37,000)

Cash flow from (for) financing activities	(22,000)
Net decrease in cash	$ (6,000)

****Note: Total assets = total liabilities + stockholders' equity.***

SELF-STUDY PROBLEM 5-3

Item	Financial Statement	Activity Reported
1. Accounts Receivable	Balance Sheet	Cash to be received in future from prior sales
2. Inventory	Balance Sheet	Cost of resources acquired in past to be used in future operations
3. Supplies	Balance Sheet	Cost of resources acquired in past to be used in future operations
4. Prepaid Insurance	Balance Sheet	Cost of resources acquired in past to be used in future operations
5. Buildings	Balance Sheet	Cost of resources acquired in past to be used in future operations
6. Patents	Balance Sheet	Cost of resources acquired in past to be used in future operations
7. Accounts Payable	Balance Sheet	Cash to be paid in future for resources acquired in past
8. Wages Payable	Balance Sheet	Cash to be paid in future for services used in past operations
9. Interest Payable	Balance Sheet	Cash to be paid in future for use of money borrowed in past
10. Notes Payable	Balance Sheet	Cash borrowed in past to acquire resources, to be repaid in future
11. Contributed Capital	Balance Sheet and Stockholders' Equity	Cash received in past from owners used to acquire resources
12. Retained Earnings	Balance Sheet and Stockholders' Equity	Profits earned from operations used to acquire additional resources
13. Dividends	Stockholders' Equity	Cash paid or promised to owners from results of operations
14. Sales Revenue	Income Statement	Cash received or to be received from past operations
15. Cost of Goods Sold	Income Statement	Cost of resources consumed in past operations
16. Depreciation Expense	Income Statement	Cost of resources consumed in past operations
17. Wages Expense	Income Statement	Cost of services consumed in past operations
18. Interest Expense	Income Statement	Cost of services consumed in past operations
19. Cash from Customers	Cash Flows	Cash received from sales
20. Cash to Suppliers	Cash Flows	Cash paid for resources acquired
21. Cash from Debt	Cash Flows	Cash received from creditors
22. Cash for Equipment	Cash Flows	Cash paid for resources acquired

EXERCISES

5-1. Write a short definition for each of the terms listed in the *Terms and Concepts Defined in this Chapter* section.

5-2. Listed below are typical accounts that appear on financial statements. For each account, identify the financial statement(s) on which it appears:

a. Wages expense
b. Wages payable
c. Cash received from customers
d. Common stock
e. Dividends paid
f. Accounts receivable
g. Sales revenue
h. Common stock issued during year
i. Cash used to purchase equipment
j. Inventory
k. Net income
l. Retained earnings
m. Contributed capital

5-3. A list of information contained in financial statements is provided below. For each item, indicate which financial statement provides the information.

a. Changes in a corporation's stockholders' equity for a fiscal period
b. The dollar amount of resources available at a particular date
c. Cash used for investing activities
d. Accrual based operating results for a fiscal period
e. The cost of resources consumed in producing revenues for a period
f. The sources of finances used to acquire resources
g. The effect of issuing stock on the amount of contributed capital during a period
h. Cash received from operating activities during a period
i. Revenues generated during a fiscal period

5-4. Both a company's income statement and its statement of cash flows provide information about operating activities during a fiscal period. Why are both statements included in the company's financial report? How can information in each statement be used by decision makers?

5-5. The Johansen Co. sells, rents, and services ski equipment. Information about the company's financial performance for a recent fiscal period is provided below:

Average shares outstanding, 10,000
Cost of sales and services, $34,000
Debt outstanding, $65,000
General and administrative expenses, $12,000
Income tax expense, $20,000
Interest expense, $8,000
Payments to owners, $30,000
Rental revenue, $45,000
Sales revenue, $79,000
Selling expense, $27,000
Service revenue, $23,000

From the information provided, compute the following amounts for the period:

a. Gross profit
b. Operating expenses
c. Income from operations
d. Pretax income
e. Net income
f. Earnings per share

5-6. An income statement provides information about product and period costs. Distinguish between these types of costs. Classify each of the following as a product or period cost:

a. advertising expenses
b. wages for factory workers
c. wages for management
d. commissions for sales staff
e. depreciation on factory equipment
f. depreciation on office equipment
g. materials used in production
h. merchandise purchased for resale
i. utilities used by management facilities
j. utilities used by a factory

5-7. Adorondike, Inc., manages resort property. Use the following information to prepare a statement of stockholders' equity for the year ended September 30, 1995:

a. The company paid $20,000 of dividends during the fiscal year.
b. The company issued $200,000 of common stock during the year.
c. The company paid off $160,000 of long-term debt during the year.
d. Net income for the year was $60,000.
e. Contributed capital on October 1, 1994, was $350,000. Retained earnings was $70,000.

5-8. Differentiate between contributed capital and retained earnings. Identify events that affect the amount of contributed capital or retained earnings for a corporation.

5-9. Listed below are selected account balances for the Navaho Rug Co. for June 30, 1994:

Accounts payable, $67,000
Accounts receivable, $56,000
Accumulated depreciation, $212,000
Buildings, $500,000
Cash, $23,000
Contributed capital, $600,000
Cost of goods sold, $560,000
Equipment, $300,000
Interest payable, $29,000
Land, $200,000
Merchandise inventory, $460,000
Notes payable, current portion, $40,000
Notes payable, long-term, $480,000
Prepaid insurance, $32,000
Retained earnings, $186,000
Supplies, $38,000
Trademarks, $30,000
Wages expense, $250,000
Wages payable, $25,000

Use this information to compute the following amounts:

a. Current assets
b. Current liabilities
c. Property, plant, and equipment
d. Total assets
e. Long-term liabilities
f. Total liabilities
g. Stockholders' equity
i. Total liabilities and stockholders' equity
j. Working capital

5-10. The following information reflects cash flow and other activities of the MaGoo Eyeglass Co. for three months ended March 31, 1995:

Paid for advertising, $300
Paid for equipment, $42,000
Paid for income taxes, $3,000
Paid for insurance, $200
Paid for interest, $450
Paid for utilities, $790
Paid to employees, $18,000
Paid to owners, $12,000
Paid to suppliers, $42,000
Depreciation expense, $13,000
Received from customers, $87,000
Received from issuing long-term debt, $20,000
Received from sale of land, $33,000

Use this information to answer the following questions:

a. What was net cash flow from operating activities for the period?
b. What was net cash flow from financing activities?
c. What was net cash flow from investing activities?
d. What was the net change in cash for the period?

5-11. For each of items listed below, identify whether it would appear on the statement of cash flows as part of the computation of cash flow from operating activities, cash flow from financing activities, cash flow from investing activities, or if it would not appear at all. Also, indicate whether the item is added or subtracted in computing cash flow using the direct method of preparing the statement of cash flows:

a. Purchase of plant assets
b. Cash paid to suppliers
c. Cash collected from customers
d. Payment of long-term debt
e. Net income
f. Depreciation expense
g. Payment of dividends
h. Issuing stock
i. Cash paid to employees
j. Cash paid for income taxes
k. Disposal of plant assets

5-12. The following information is available for Hourglass Watch Co. for the first six months of 1995:

Cash collected from customers	$130,000
Cash paid to suppliers	45,000
Cash paid for utilities	8,000
Cash paid for insurance	12,000
Cash paid for equipment	35,000
Cash paid to employees	23,000
Cash paid for interest	3,000
Cash paid for dividends	2,000
Cash received from disposal of equipment	9,000

Determine the cash flow from operating activities for the six month period.

5-13. Listed below are account balances. For each item, indicate the future implications for cash flows and/or operating activities. Item (a) is provided as an example.

Account Balance	Implication
a. Accounts receivable, $10,000	$10,000 of cash should be received from customers during the next fiscal year.
b. Accounts payable, $7,500	
c. Inventory, $50,000	
d. Notes payable, long-term, $100,000	
e. Equipment, $80,000	
f. Prepaid insurance, $22,000	
g. Wages payable, $8,000	
h. Unearned revenue, $13,000	
i. Notes payable, current, $5,000	

5-14. An income statement for Delta Airlines for a recent fiscal year follows:

CONSOLIDATED STATEMENT OF OPERATIONS
For the year ended June 30, 1992

(In Thousands, Except Per Share Amounts)	**1992**
Operating Revenues:	
Passenger	**$10,115,185**
Cargo	**587,633**
Other, net	**133,967**
Total operating revenues	**10,836,785**
Operating Expenses:	
Salaries and related costs	**4,436,402**
Aircraft fuel	**1,482,372**
Aircraft maintenance materials and repairs	**445,947**
Aircraft rent	**641,914**
Facilities and other rent	**355,412**
Landing fees	**224,351**
Passenger service	**524,223**
Passenger commissions	**1,153,184**
Depreciation and amortization	**634,528**
Other	**1,613,358**
Total operating expenses	**11,511,691**
Operating Income (Loss)	**(674,906)**
Other Income (Expense):	
Interest expense	**(151,430)**
Gain on disposition of flight equipment	**34,563**
Write-off of Pan Am reorganization costs	**(43,000)**
Miscellaneous income, net	**48,400**
	(111,467)
Loss Before Income Taxes	**(786,373)**
Income Tax Savings	**(280,055)**
Net Income (Loss)	**(506,318)**
Preferred Stock Dividends, Net of Tax Benefits	**(18,567)**
Net Income (Loss) Attributable to Common Stockholders	**$(524,885)**
Net Income (Loss) Per Share	**$(10.60)**

Note: Slight modifications have been made to the format of the statement for purposes of simplifying the presentation.

Use this income statement to answer the following questions:

a. What were Delta's main sources of revenues?
b. What were its largest expenses?
c. How much revenue did Delta earn from transporting passengers?
d. How much revenue did it earn from other operating activities?
e. How much revenue did it earn from nonoperating activities?
f. How much operating income did Delta earn?
g. How much expense did it incur for nonoperating activities?
h. Approximately how many shares of stock did Delta have outstanding during the year?
i. How much profit did Delta earn during the fiscal year?

5-15. Procter and Gamble reported the following income statement in a recent year:

CONSOLIDATED STATEMENT OF EARNINGS
Year Ended June 30 (Millions of Dollars Except Per Share Amounts)

	1992
Income	
Net sales	$29,362
Interest and other income	528
	29,890
Costs and Expenses	
Cost of products sold	17,324
Marketing, administrative, and other expenses	9,171
Interest expense	510
	27,005
Earnings Before Income Taxes	2,885
Income Taxes	1,013
Net Earnings	$ 1,872
Net Earnings Per Share	$2.62

Note: Slight modifications have been made to the format of the statement for purposes of simplifying the presentation.

a. What was Procter and Gamble's gross profit for the year?
b. What was the amount of the company's product costs expensed during the year?
c. What was its total operating expense?
d. What was its operating income?
e. What was its nonoperating income or expense?

5-16. International Paper Company reported the following information in a recent year (dollars in millions):

Accounts and notes receivable	$1,841
Accounts payable	1,110
Accrued income taxes	102
Accrued payroll and benefits	216
Cash and temporary investments	238
Contributed capital	1,147
Deferred charges and other assets (long-term)	1,020
Deferred income taxes	1,044
Intangibles	816
Inventories	1,780
Investments (long-term)	383
Long-term debt	3,351
Notes payable and current maturities of long-term debt	1,699
Other accrued liabilities	600
Other current assets	272
Other long-term liabilities	1,080
Plants, properties, and equipment, net of depreciation	7,848
Retained earnings	4,592
Timberlands	743

Note: Slight modifications have been made to the data for purposes of simplifying the presentation.

Accrued liabilities are current liabilities. Deferred income taxes are long-term liabilities.

Use the information provided to prepare a balance sheet for International Paper Co. in good form. The fiscal year end is December 31, 1991.

5-17. Selected information reported by Xerox Corporation in a recent year included (in millions):

Contributed capital at December 31, 1989	$1,251
Retained earnings at December 31, 1989	4,283
Retirement of stock	787
Net income	704
Dividends	349

Use this information to prepare a basic statement of stockholders' equity for Xerox for the year ended December 31, 1990.

5-18. The following information (with slight modification) was reported by IBM in a recent year (in millions of dollars):

Acquisition of property, plant, and equipment	$6,497
Sale of investments in other companies	5,028
Issuance of long-term debt	5,776
Repurchase of IBM stock	196
Other receipts from financing activities	67
Disposal of property, plant and equipment	645
Net increase in short-term borrowings	2,676
Purchase of stock in other companies	4,848
Cash dividends paid	2,771
Investment in software	2,014
Reduction of long-term debt	4,184

Using the information listed, calculate the net cash flow from financing activities and the net cash flow from investing activities for IBM.

5-19. The following chart provides cash flow information for three corporations for a recent fiscal year.

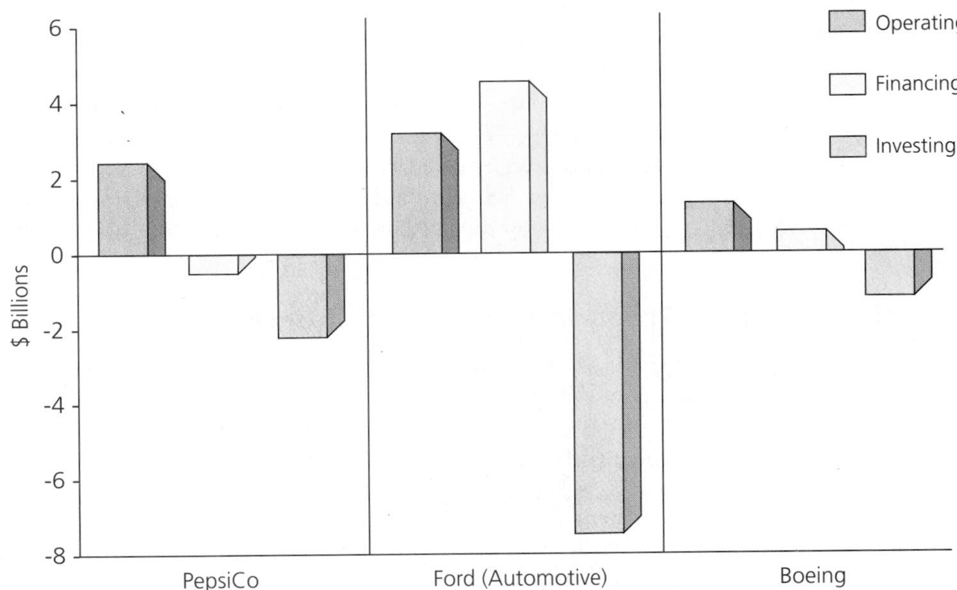

Use the chart to answer each of the following questions:

a. Which company had the largest amount of cash flow from operating activities? Which had the smallest?
b. For fiscal year 1989, Boeing reported cash flow from operating activities of −$514 million. What might have caused Boeing's cash flow from operating activities to be negative?
c. Would you expect cash flow associated with investing activities to be negative? Why?
d. Why might Ford's cash flow associated with financing activities differ from that of PepsiCo and Boeing?
e. Which company appears to have had the most favorable cash flow situation? Explain your answer.

5-20. Though U.S. companies report their plant assets at historical cost, some foreign companies report current values for their plant assets. For example, a recent annual report for Nestlé, a Swiss company disclosed:

> Tangible fixed assets are shown in the balance sheet at their net replacement values arrived at as follows:
> - Land: market value prudently estimated.
> - Other tangible fixed assets: replacement new value (the amount which theoretically would have to be invested in order to replace an asset by a similar new asset duly installed and rendering the same service) less the accumulated depreciation calculated on this value.
>
>   These amounts are recalculated each year.

Using this method, the company reported plant assets of 14,867 million Swiss francs. The book value of these assets using historical cost would have been 10,616 million Swiss francs. What are some of the advantages and disadvantages of the asset valuation method used by Nestlé relative to that used by U.S. companies? What implications does the use of current value have for Nestlé's return on assets and return on stockholders' equity?

PROBLEMS

PROBLEM 5-1 Identifying the Purpose of Financial Statements

Assume you are a financial manager with a U.S. corporation. A. Suliman is a recently employed manager in the Middle Eastern division of your corporation and a visitor to the U.S. He has little familiarity with U.S. financial reporting practices. Your boss has given you the responsibility of explaining financial reports to Mr. Suliman.

Required Write a short report describing each of the four basic corporate financial statements for Suliman. Make sure you are clear about the purpose of each statement, its contents, and its relationships to the other financial statements.

PROBLEM 5-2 Preparing Financial Statements

Argyle Co. manufactures socks. A list of account balances for December 31, 1995, the end of the company's fiscal year is provided at the top of the next page. Argyle had 10,000 shares of stock outstanding during the year.

Required From this list, prepare an income statement and balance sheet for the fiscal year. Use the multiple-step format for the income statement. Include titles for each statement.

Argyle Co.
Account Balances
December 31, 1995

Account	Balance
Cash	$ 9,300
Accounts Receivable	32,700
Inventory	61,000
Supplies	15,400
Prepaid Insurance	7,100
Equipment	85,000
Allowance for Depreciation—Equipment	35,000
Buildings	340,000
Allowance for Depreciation—Buildings	210,000
Land	20,000
Patents	6,000
Accounts Payable	36,500
Wages Payable	6,900
Interest Payable	3,400
Income Taxes Payable	8,100
Notes Payable, Current Portion	5,000
Notes Payable, Long-Term	75,000
Owners' Investment	50,000
Reinvested Profits, December 31, 1995	120,300
Dividends	30,000
Sales Revenue	260,000
Cost of Goods Sold	125,000
Wages Expense	32,000
Utilities Expense	4,000
Depreciation Expense	2,100
Insurance Expense	3,000
Supplies Expense	4,600
Interest Expense	7,300
Advertising Expense	2,900
Patent Expense	800
Income Tax Expense	22,000

PROBLEM 5-3 Interpreting an Income Statement

Recent income statements for Microsoft Corporation are provided at the top of the next page.

Required Ratios often are used to assess changes in financial statement information over time. Use the income statements to answer the following questions:

a. What was the ratio of net income to net revenues each year?
b. What was the ratio of cost of revenues (cost of goods sold) to net revenues each year?
c. What was the ratio of operating expenses to net revenues each year?
d. What was the percentage change in net income between 1990 and 1991, and between 1991 and 1992? (Hint: divide the increase in net income from 1990 to 1991 by the net income for 1990.)
e. Did Microsoft's operating results improve between 1990 and 1991? Between 1991 and 1992? Explain your answers.

INCOME STATEMENT

(In thousands, except net income per share)	Years Ended June 30		
	1992	**1991**	**1990**
Net revenues	$2,758,725	$1,843,432	$1,183,446
Cost of revenues	466,424	362,589	252,668
Gross profit	2,292,301	1,480,843	930,778
Operating expenses:			
Research and development	352,153	235,386	180,615
Sales and marketing	854,537	533,619	317,593
General and administrative	89,632	61,996	39,332
Total operating expenses	1,296,322	831,001	537,540
Operating income	995,979	649,842	393,238
Interest income—net	55,894	37,265	30,837
Nonoperating expense	(10,608)	(16,463)	(13,511)
Income before income taxes	1,041,265	670,644	410,564
Provision for income taxes	333,205	207,901	131,378
Net income	$ 708,060	$ 462,743	$ 279,186
Net income per share	$2.41	$1.64	$1.04

Note: Slight modifications have been made to the format of the statement for purposes of simplifying the presentation.

PROBLEM 5-4 Limitations of Financial Statements

Markus O'Realius is considering the purchase of a business, the Caesar Co. The potential seller has provided Markus with a copy of the business's financial statements for the last three years. The financial statements reveal total assets of $350,000 and total liabilities of $150,000. The seller is asking $300,000 for the business. Markus believes the business is worth only about $200,000, the amount of owners' equity reported on the balance sheet. He has asked your assistance in determining a price to offer for the business.

Required Write a memo to Markus explaining why he should not interpret the balance sheet as an accurate measure of the value of the business. Describe limitations of financial statements that might result in the market value of the business being higher (or lower) than the financial statement amounts.

PROBLEM 5-5 Accounting Concepts

Latin Specialties is an import company, financed primarily by stockholders and bank loans. It imports handmade goods from Central and South America to the U.S. where they are sold to retail stores. The company's buyers contract with small companies for goods that the buyers ship to a central location in the U.S. The goods are inventoried and then redistributed as orders are received from retailers. Latin Specialties receives a bill from the manufacturers along with the goods it receives and makes payments each month. The company sends bills to retailers along with orders. Most retailers pay their bills each month, as well. Several months can pass from the time goods are shipped to the U.S. until cash is received from retailers.

Required Explain how Latin Specialties' financial statements represent the company's transformation process. Consider the events and transactions in the transformation process and how they are described in the financial statements. In particular, consider the relationships the company has with investors, suppliers, and customers. How does the timing of the events in the transformation process affect the financial statements? Why is it important that time be considered in reporting accounting information?

PROBLEM 5-6 Interpreting a Balance Sheet

A recent balance sheet for The Walt Disney Company is provided below:

CONSOLIDATED BALANCE SHEET
(in millions)

September 30	**1991**	**1990**
Assets		
Cash	$ 886.1	$ 819.8
Marketable securities	782.4	588.1
Receivables	1,128.2	851.5
Merchandise inventories	311.6	269.2
Film and television costs (a)	596.9	641.1
Theme parks, resorts and other property, at cost		
Attractions, buildings and equipment	5,628.1	4,654.6
Accumulated depreciation	(1,667.8)	(1,405.1)
	3,960.3	3,249.5
Projects in progress	540.9	594.0
Land	70.4	67.0
Other assets	1,151.7	942.1
	$9,428.5	$8,022.3
Liabilities and Stockholders' Equity		
Accounts payable and other accrued liabilities	$1,433.8	$1,158.1
Income taxes payable	296.2	200.3
Borrowings (a)	2,213.8	1,584.6
Unearned royalties and other advances (a)	859.5	841.9
Deferred income taxes (a)	753.9	748.8
Stockholders' equity		
Common stock	549.7	502.8
Retained earnings	3,950.5	3,401.1
Adjustments	(628.9)	(415.3)
	$9,428.5	$8,022.3

(a) Noncurrent

Note: Slight modifications have been made to the format of the statement for purposes of simplifying the presentation.

Required From the information provided, answer the following questions:

a. What was the total amount of current assets for the company in 1990 and 1991?
b. What was the total amount of current liabilities for both years?
c. What was the amount of working capital, and what was the working capital ratio for 1990 and 1991?
d. What were the amounts of noncurrent assets and noncurrent liabilities for both years?
e. What was the amount of contributed capital for 1990 and 1991?
f. What were the amounts of total assets, total liabilities, and stockholders' equity for 1990 and 1991?

g. How much net cash flow should the company expect during the following fiscal period from the assets and liabilities that existed on September 30, 1991? How does this amount compare with 1990?
h. What were the percentage changes in total assets and total liabilities between 1990 and 1991? (Hint: Divide the change in the account balance from 1990 to 1991 by the amount for 1990.) What were the ratios of total liabilities to total assets in both years?
i. Did the company's financial position improve between 1990 and 1991?

PROBLEM 5-7 Ethical Issues in Financial Reporting

Morgan Beetlejuice is a regional sales manager for Green-Grow, Inc., a producer of garden supplies. The company's fiscal year ends on April 30. In mid-April, Morgan is contacted by the president of Green-Grow, B. Elzebulb, explaining that the company is facing a financial problem. Two years ago, the company borrowed heavily from several banks to buy a competitor company and to increase production of its primary products, insecticides and fertilizers. As a part of the loan agreement, Green-Grow must maintain a working capital ratio of 1.2 and earn a net income of at least $2 per share. If the company fails to meet these requirements, as reflected in its annual financial statements, the banks can restrict future credit for the company or require early payment of their loans, potentially forcing the company into bankruptcy.

The president explains that this fiscal year has been a difficult one for Green-Grow. Sales have slipped because of increased competition, and the rising prices of chemicals have increased the company's production costs. The company is in danger of not meeting the loan requirements and could be forced to make drastic cuts or to liquidate its assets. B. Elzebulb informs Morgan her job could be in danger. The president asks Morgan to help with the problem by dating all sales invoices that clear her office during the first half of May as though the sales were made in April. May is a month of heavy sales volume for the company as retail stores stock up for the coming season. The president believes the added sales would be sufficient to get the company past the loan problem. He explains this procedure will be used only this one time; by next year, the company will be in better shape because of new products it is developing. Also, he reminds Morgan her bonus for the year will be higher because of the additional sales that will be recorded in April. He points out the company is fundamentally in sound financial shape and he would hate to see its future jeopardized by a minor bookkeeping problem. He is asking for the cooperation of all of the regional sales managers. He argues the stockholders, employees, and managers will all be better off if the sales are pre-dated. He wants Morgan's assurance she will cooperate.

Required What effect will pre-dating the sales have on Green-Grow's balance sheet, income statement, and statement of cash flows? Be specific about which accounts will be affected and why. How will this practice solve the company's problem with the banks? What would be the appropriate behavior for B. Elzebulb under the circumstances the company is facing? What would be the appropriate behavior for Morgan?

PROBLEM 5-8 Evaluating Financing Arrangements

Selected financial statement information is presented below for two companies, the Debt Co. and the Equity Co. The companies are in the same industry, and both have fiscal years ending September 30. All amounts are in millions.

	Debt Co.	Equity Co.
Current assets	$2.00	$2.00
Total assets	5.00	5.00

Total liabilities	4.00	1.00
Interest expense	.60	.10
Operating expenses	.80	.80

Cost of goods sold is 40% of sales revenue for both companies. Income taxes are 30% of pretax income for both companies. Debt Co. has 250,000 shares of stock outstanding. Equity Co. has 1,000,000 shares outstanding.

Required Prepare an income statement for each company assuming sales revenues are:

a. $3 million
b. $2.5 million
c. $2 million

Explain the changes in net income and earnings per share for the companies for the different amounts of sales revenues. If you had $100,000 to invest in either of these companies and this amount would purchase the same number of shares in either, in which would you buy stock?

PROBLEM 5-9 Estimating Future Activities

Van Gogh is considering a business opportunity selling artificial flowers, especially irises and lilies. He needs $50,000 in financing to begin operations. He has $30,000 in savings he can invest and has spoken with a local bank about borrowing the additional $20,000 he needs. The bank has indicated it will consider the loan but has asked for a set of financial statements that describes what Van believes the company's financial condition will look like at the end of the first three months of operations. Van has asked for your assistance in preparing the financial statements. He has provided you with the following expectations:

a. Plant assets costing $45,000 will be needed at the beginning of the three month period.
b. Inventory of $10,000 will be purchased for the first month. The inventory will be paid for in the month following purchase. The amount of inventory purchased each subsequent month will equal the amount sold in the prior month.
c. Average monthly sales should be about $15,000. Two-thirds of the sales will be for cash each month, and one-third will be for credit. Credit sales will be collected in the month following sale.
d. The cost of the inventory sold will be $8,000 each month.
e. The interest on the loan will require a payment of $250 at the end of each month. An additional $200 will be paid to the bank each month to repay the loan.
f. Operating expenses, other than depreciation, each month should be $2,000. These will be paid in cash. Depreciation should be $400 each month.
g. Van expects to withdraw $2,000 from the business each month for living expenses.

In addition, he has provided the worksheet at the top of the next page, completed for the first month of operations.

Required Complete the worksheet for the second and third months.

PROBLEM 5-10 Multiple-Choice Overview of the Chapter

1. Which of the following is not a statement you would expect to find in a corporate annual report?
   a. Statement of financial position
   b. Statement of earnings
   c. Statement of cash flows
   -d. Statement of accounts receivable

	First Month	Second Month	Third Month
Sales revenues	$15,000		
Cost of goods sold	(8,000)		
Gross profit	7,000		
Depreciation	(400)		
Other operating expenses	(2,000)		
Income from operations	4,600		
Interest expense	(250)		
Net income	$4,350		
Cash	$10,550		
Accounts receivable	5,000		
Inventory	2,000		
Plant assets, net of depreciation	44,600		
Total assets	$62,150		
Accounts payable	$10,000		
Notes payable	19,800		
Investment by owner	30,000		
Reinvested profits	2,350		
Total liabilities & owners' equity	$62,150		
Cash collected from customers	$10,000		
Cash paid to suppliers	0		
Cash paid for operating expenses	(2,000)		
Cash paid for interest	(250)		
Cash paid for plant assets	(45,000)		
Cash received from bank	20,000		
Cash received from owner	30,000		
Cash paid to repay loan	(200)		
Cash paid to owner	(2,000)		
Change in cash	$10,550		

2. The following assets appear on the balance sheet for Astroid Co.:

Accounts receivable	$ 25,000
Accumulated depreciation	80,000
Cash	10,000
Intangible assets	30,000
Inventory	50,000
Plant assets	200,000

The amount of current assets reported by Astroid is:

a. $85,000
b. $75,000
c. $115,000
d. $235,000

3. The following information was reported on the income statement of Wagon Wheel Co.:

Sales revenues	$900,000
Cost of goods sold	400,000
Selling, general and administrative expenses	300,000
Interest expense	60,000

Wagon Wheel's gross profit and operating income would be:

	Gross Profit	Operating Income
a.	$600,000	$140,000
b.	$500,000	$140,000
c.	$500,000	$200,000
d.	$200,000	$140,000

4. Which of the following is a *false* statement regarding the statement of stockholders' equity?
   a. It lists changes in contributed capital and retained earnings for a fiscal period.
   b. It contains information about net income and dividends for a fiscal period.
   c. It reports the net change in stockholders' equity for a fiscal period.
   d. It reports increases or decreases in stocks and bonds for a fiscal period.
5. A balance sheet that provides information for more than one fiscal period is:
   a. a classified balance sheet
   b. a comparative balance sheet
   c. a consolidated balance sheet
   d. a combined balance sheet
6. Working capital is the amount of:
   a. cash and cash equivalents available to a company at the end of a fiscal period.
   b. long-term investments available at the end of a fiscal period less long-term debt at the end of the period.
   c. current assets available at the end of a fiscal period less current liabilities at the end of the period.
   d. total assets available at the end of a period that can be converted to cash.
7. The statement of cash flows for the Fieldspar Exploration Co. reported:

Cash paid for equipment	150,000
Cash paid to employees	200,000
Cash paid to owners	75,000
Cash paid to suppliers	280,000
Cash received from loans	100,000
Cash received from customers	600,000

What were Fieldspar's net cash flows from operating, financing, and investing activities?

	Operating	Financing	Investing
a.	$120,000	$ 25,000	$(150,000)
b.	$250,000	$100,000	$(430,000)
c.	$320,000	$100,000	$(430,000)
d.	$120,000	$100,000	$(430,000)

8. A statement of cash flows, prepared using the direct method, would report cash collected from customers as:
   a. an addition to cash flow from financing activities.
   b. a subtraction from cash flow from financing activities.
   c. an addition to cash flow from operating activities.
   d. an addition to cash flow from investing activities.
9. The Flag Ship Co. reported depreciation and amortization expense of $300,000 for the latest fiscal year. The depreciation and amortization expense would:
   a. increase cash flow for the year $300,000.
   b. decrease cash flow for the year $300,000.
   c. have no effect on cash flow for the year.
   d. have an effect on cash flow if assets were purchased during the year.
10. The Grape Bowl Co. reported plant assets for the latest fiscal year of $5 million, net of accumulated depreciation. From this information, which of the following is an accurate statement about the company?
    a. The amount the company would receive, if it sold its plant assets at the end of the fiscal year, would be $5 million.
    b. The company would have to pay $5 million dollars to replace its assets if they were replaced at the end of the fiscal year.
    c. The historical cost of the company's plant assets at the end of the fiscal year, adjusted for depreciation, was $5 million.
    d. The amount the company paid for the plant assets it controlled at the end of the fiscal year was $5 million.

CASES

CASE 5-1 Analysis of Corporate Financial Statements

Financial statements for McDonald's Corporation are provided on the next page from a recent annual report. Examine these statements and answer the questions that follow.

Required Use the financial statements to answer each of the following questions:

a. What were the accrual basis operating results for McDonald's for 1991? What was its primary nonoperating expense? What were the major sources of income and major operating expenses for the company?
b. What was the company's ratio of net income to total assets and ratio of net income to stockholders' equity for 1991? If you owned 10,000 of the company's shares of stock, what was your claim on the company's earnings for 1991? How much cash would you have received from the company?
c. What have been McDonald's major sources of financing? What changes occurred in the company's finances during 1991?
d. What were McDonald's most important assets? What changes occurred in its assets during 1991? What assets may be important to the company that are not reported on its balance sheet?

Consolidated Statement of Income

In millions of dollars, except per common share data	**Year Ended December 31, 1991**
Revenues	
Sales by Company-operated restaurants	$4,908.5
Revenues from franchised restaurants	1,786.5
Total revenues	6,695.0
Operating costs and expenses	
Company-operated restaurants	
Food and packaging	1,627.5
Payroll and other employee benefits	1,259.2
Occupancy and other operating expenses	1,142.4
	4,029.1
Franchised restaurants—occupancy expenses	306.5
General, administrative and selling expenses	794.7
Other operating income—net	(113.8)
Total operating costs and expenses	5,016.5
Operating income	1,678.5
Interest expense	(391.4)
Other nonoperating income—net	12.3
Income before provision for income taxes	1,299.4
Provision for income taxes	439.8
Net income	$ 859.6
Net income per common share	$2.35
Dividends per common share	$.36

Consolidated Balance Sheet

(In millions of dollars)	**December 31, 1991**	**1990**
Assets		
Current assets		
Cash and equivalents	$ 220.2	$ 142.8
Accounts receivable	238.4	222.1
Notes receivable	36.0	32.9
Inventories	42.6	42.9
Prepaid expenses and other current assets	108.8	108.3
Total current assets	646.0	549.0
Other assets		
Notes receivable due after one year	123.1	102.2
Investments in and advances to affiliates	374.2	335.2
Miscellaneous	278.2	250.0
Total other assets	775.5	687.4
Property and equipment		
Property and equipment, at cost	12,368.0	11,535.5
Accumulated depreciation and amortization	(2,809.5)	(2,488.4)
Net property and equipment	9,558.5	9,047.1
Intangible assets, net of amortization	369.1	384.0
Total assets	$11,349.1	$10,667.5

Liabilities and shareholders' equity		
Current liabilities		
Notes payable	$ 278.3	$ 299.0
Accounts payable	313.9	355.7
Income taxes	157.2	82.6
Other taxes	82.3	68.6
Interest payable	185.7	133.2
Other liabilities	201.4	194.9
Current maturities of long-term debt	69.1	64.7
Total current liabilities	1,287.9	1,198.7
Long-term debt	4,267.4	4,428.7
Security deposits by francises and other long-term liabilities	224.5	162.7
Deferred income taxes	734.2	695.1
Shareholders' equity		
Capital stock	546.3	419.6
Retained earnings	5,925.2	5,214.5
Other adjustments	(1,636.4)	(1,451.8)
Total shareholders' equity	4,835.1	4,182.3
Total liabilities and shareholders' equity	$11,349.1	$10,667.5

Note: Slight modifications have been made to the format of the statements for purposes of simplifying the presentation.

CASE 5-2 Comparing Financial Statement Information

Selected financial statement information for a recent fiscal year are provided below for Ford Motor Company and Honda Motor Company. The data are expressed in $millions for Ford and ¥(yen)billions for Honda.

	Ford*	**Honda**
Sales revenue	$72,050.9	$4,391.9
Cost of goods sold	71,826.6	3,199.4
Operating expenses	3,993.4	1,039.1
Net income (loss)	(2,258.0)	64.9
Net cash inflows (outflows) from operating activities	3,340.5	233.9
Net cash inflows (outflows) from investing activities	(7,515.2)	(398.6)
Net cash inflows (outflows) from financing activities	4,146.7	153.7
Current assets	21,851.9	1,808.9
Plant assets, net	22,522.3	1,096.9
Total assets	52,397.4	3,156.2
Current liabilities	21,816.8	1,398.9
Long-term debt	6,538.7	603.2
Stockholders' equity	22,690.3	1,102.7

****All amounts except net income and stockholders' equity are for the automotive operations only. Net income and stockholders' equity are for the entire corporation.***

Required Compare the financing, investing, and operating activities of the two companies from the information provided. Comparisons can be made by converting income statement numbers to percentages by dividing by sales revenues. Divide balance sheet numbers by total assets. Divide cash flow numbers by cash from operating activities. Also, you may wish to compare income and cash flow numbers to balance sheet numbers (e.g., sales to total assets).

CASE 5-3 INTERPRETING CASH FLOWS

Appendix E of this book contains the statement of cash flows for Compaq Computer Corporation. This statement is prepared using the direct format.

Required Use the appendix to answer the following questions:

1. What were Compaq's primary sources of cash in 1991? What were its primary uses of cash in 1991?
2. What was the primary cause of the decrease in cash flow from operating activities from 1990 to 1991?
3. Was Compaq growing from 1989 to 1991? Explain.
4. Evaluate Compaq's cash flows. Did the company appear to be obtaining sufficient cash to meet its needs?
5. What primary explanations are provided for the difference between Compaq's cash flow from operating activities and net income?

PROJECTS

PROJECT 5-1 Comparing Financial Statements

Select three recent corporate annual reports from your library. Select firms from the same industry (e.g., automobile manufacturing, paper, chemicals, airlines, etc.). Prepare a comparative analysis for these companies using the following table as a guide:

	Company 1	Company 2	Company 3
Current assets/Total assets			
Plant assets, net of depreciation/Total assets			
Total liabilities/Total assets			
Current assets/Current liabilities			
Cost of goods sold/Sales revenues			
Operating expenses/Sales revenues			
Income from operations/Total assets			
Income from operations/Stockholders' equity			
Net cash from operating activities/Net income			
Net cash from investing activities/Total assets			
Net cash from financing activities/Total assets			

Write a short report comparing the three companies. The report should address the questions: Which of the companies appears to be in the best financial condition? Which appears to be in the worst?

PROJECT 5-2 Comparing Financial Statements

Follow the format of Project 5-1, but select three companies from different industries. Try to find a utility, a retail company, and a manufacturing company. Use the table in Project 5-1 as a format to compare the companies. Write a report describing similarities and differences in the financial information among the three companies.

PROJECT 5-3 Comparing Financial Statements

Locate recent annual reports for 10 different companies in your library. Prepare a table or list that identifies the following financial statement information. List the different titles you find for the balance sheet, income statement, statement of stockholders' equity, and statement of cash flows and indicate how many times each was used. List each of the major headings in each of the financial statements and indicate how many times each was used. List how many fiscal years were included in each of the financial statements. How many of the statements of cash flows were prepared using the direct method? How many using the indirect method? What conclusions can you draw about the formats and captions used by companies in their financial statements?

PROJECT 5-4 Answering Financial Reporting Questions

Find a recent issue of *Accounting Trends and Techniques* (published by the American Institute of Certified Public Accountants) in your library. Look for information in this publication to answer the following questions:

a. In what month do most corporations end their fiscal years? What are the second and third most popular months?
b. What are the most popular titles used for the balance sheet?
c. What titles are used by corporations to refer to the stockholders' equity section of the balance sheet?
d. What titles are used for the income statement?
e. What proportion of companies uses the multiple-step form of the income statement?
f. What titles are used for cost of goods sold on the income statement?
g. What proportion of companies uses the indirect method of presenting the statement of cash flows?

PROJECT 5-5 Researching Financial Problems

Suppose you were interested in investing in the airlines industry. Develop an approach you might use to find out which airline companies have demonstrated strong financial health in the last 10 years and which have demonstrated poor financial health. What information would you want to examine to assist in your decision? How would you obtain this information? List the periodicals and other publications that would be relevant for your analysis.

PROJECT 5-6 Using Business Journals

Use a periodicals index, such as the *Accounting and Taxation* or the *Business Periodicals Index*, to identify recent articles that discuss problems or limitations of financial statements. Use key words such as financial statements and financial reporting. Select an article from a journal available in your library. Read the article and write a summary of the problem or limitation discussed in the article.

CHAPTER 6

REPORTING ACCRUALS AND CASH FLOWS

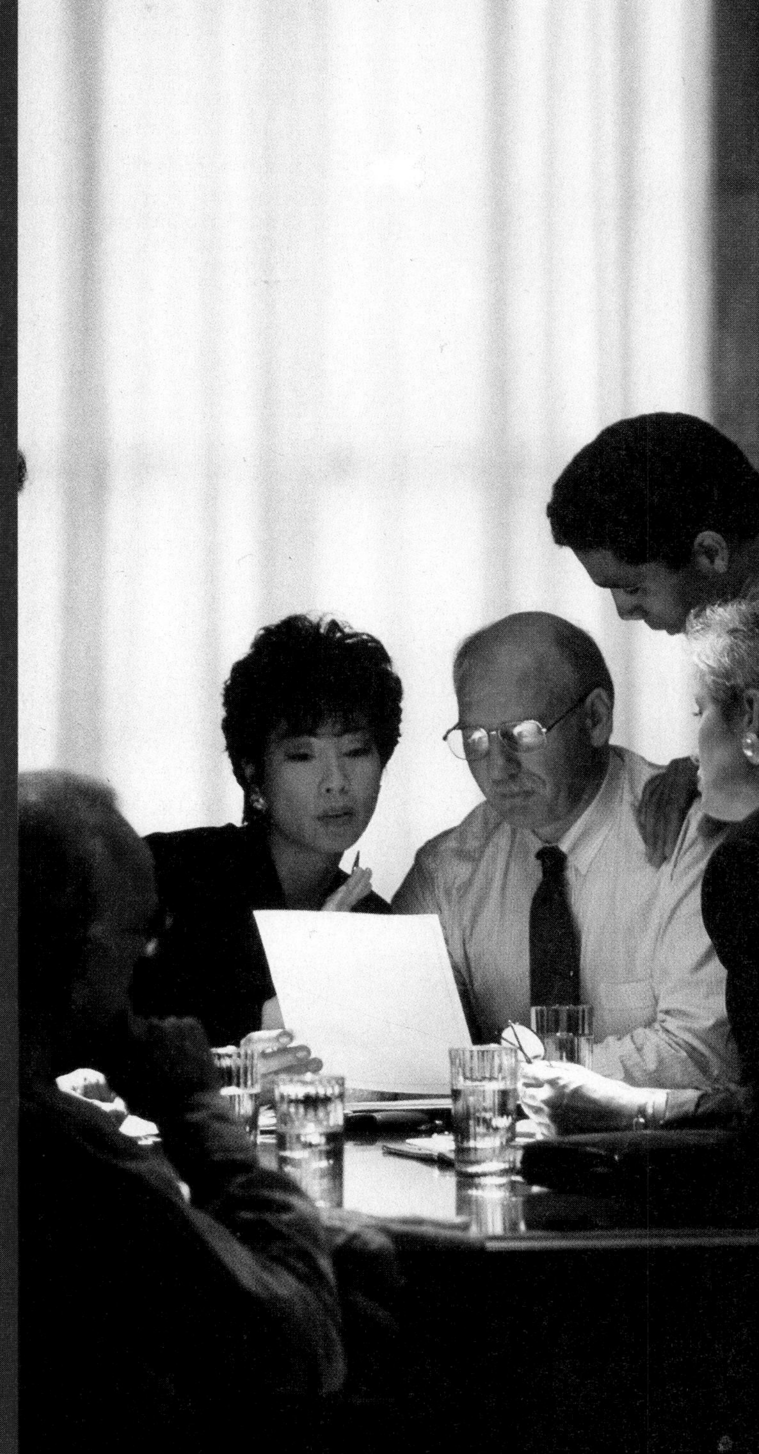

CHAPTER *Overview*

This chapter considers relationships between accrual and cash measures of operating activities. These relationships have a major effect on information reported in financial statements. Understanding the relationships is essential to understanding accounting information. The chapter examines timing differences between when revenues and expenses occur and when cash is received or paid. These transactions affect the income statement through the recognition of revenues and expenses. They affect the balance sheet primarily through current asset and liability accounts. These accounts capture differences in timing between (1) recognition of revenues and expenses and (2) cash flows. These events also affect the statement of cash flows when the statement reconciles accrual and cash basis measures of operating activities.

This chapter examines relationships between measurement rules and accounting reports.

Major topics covered in this chapter include:

- Internal transaction adjustments for timing differences between accrual and cash measures.
- The effects of accrual and deferral adjustments on balance sheet and income statement accounts.
- The effects of timing differences on the reporting of cash flows.
- The importance of cash flow information for interpreting performance.

CHAPTER *Objectives*

Once you have completed this chapter you should be able to:

1. Differentiate external from internal transactions and explain the purpose of both.
2. Identify examples of internal transactions.
3. Define accrual and deferral accounts and transactions.
4. Identify accrued revenues.
5. Identify accrued expenses.
6. Identify deferred revenues.
7. Identify deferred expenses.
8. Compare the direct and indirect formats of the statement of cash flows.
9. Explain the relationship between the indirect format of the statement of cash flows and accruals and deferrals.

10. Interpret cash flow information as a basis for analyzing corporate financial performance.
11. Identify relationships between financial statements and components of the transformation process.

INTERNAL TRANSACTIONS

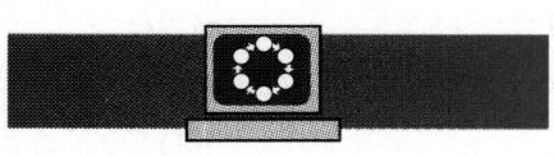

Objective 1
Differentiate external from internal transactions and explain the purpose of both.

In addition to **external transactions**, such as the exchange of goods for cash, organizations also account for **internal transactions**. External transactions occur when resources are exchanged between an organization and those with whom it contracts. Internal transactions identify economic consequences of these exchanges in the appropriate fiscal periods. For example, an organization pays $6,000 for an insurance policy on December 1, 1993. The policy provides insurance coverage for 1994 and 1995. An external transaction occurs when the policy is purchased in 1993. Internal transactions are recorded in 1994 and 1995 to recognize the consumption of the resource in the periods that benefit from its use. These transactions are necessary if the financial statements are to report the proper amount of assets and expenses for each of these years. **Recording internal transactions is necessary because of timing differences between (1) activities that produce and sell goods and services and (2) cash flows.** Recognition of internal transactions occurs through a process of adjusting account balances, normally at the end of a fiscal period. Adjustments result in the recognition of revenues or expenses in one fiscal period, though cash flows have occurred or will occur in a different period.

Adjustments occur when contracts extend beyond the current fiscal period. For instance, a contract may be initiated when goods are transferred from seller to buyer. The contract may be completed when cash is transferred from buyer to seller. If these events occur in one fiscal period, accounting for the transactions is relatively simple. If these events occur in different periods, however, the accounting becomes more complex. Decisions must be made about when to recognize revenues or expenses and how much to recognize. Internal transactions are the results of these decisions.

To illustrate adjustments, consider the following example. Exhibit 6-1 provides the balance sheet for The Party Animal, Inc., a retailer of party goods, at the end of its 1994 fiscal year.

The following (12) summary transactions occurred during 1995:

1. Sold goods that cost $123,000 for $357,000. All sales were on credit.
2. Collected $370,000 in cash from customers.
3. Purchased $140,000 of merchandise on credit.
4. Paid $132,000 to suppliers for merchandise.
5. Paid $93,000 of wages to employees.
6. Paid $5,000 for utilities expenses.
7. Purchased $12,500 of supplies for cash.
8. Paid $14,000 for advertising.
9. Paid $18,000 in interest.
10. Paid $26,000 for principal on notes payable.

11. Paid $24,000 in income taxes.
12. Paid $20,000 in dividends.

Exhibit 6-1

The Party Animal, Inc.
Balance Sheet
December 31, 1994

Assets	
Current assets:	
Cash	$ 20,600
Accounts receivable	50,400
Merchandise inventory	88,000
Supplies	13,500
Prepaid insurance	12,000
Total current assets	184,500
Property, plant, and equipment:	
Equipment	92,100
Buildings	180,000
	272,100
Less: accumulated depreciation	110,700
	161,400
Land	60,000
Total property, plant, and equipment	221,400
Total assets	$405,900
Liabilities	
Current liabilities:	
Accounts payable	$ 46,800
Wages payable	17,900
Interest payable	18,000
Income taxes payable	5,000
Notes payable, current portion	26,000
Total current liabilities	113,700
Long-term liabilities:	
Notes payable, long-term	120,000
Total liabilities	233,700
Stockholders' Equity	
Common stock, no par, 100,000 shares authorized and issued	100,000
Retained earnings	72,200
Total stockholders' equity	172,200
Total liabilities and stockholders' equity	$405,900

These are external transactions. They represent exchanges with customers, suppliers, creditors, and owners. They do not include all of the transactions that need to be reported on Party Animal's financial statements, however. For example, there is no transaction to recognize depreciation expense or insurance expense. The transactions missing from this list are internal transactions.

Once the effects of the external transactions are recorded, the balance sheet account balances would appear as follows (transaction numbers are in parentheses):

December 31,	1994	External Transaction Effects	1995
Assets			
Current assets:			
Cash	$ 20,600	+370,000 (2) −132,000 (4) −93,000 (5) −5,000 (6) −12,500 (7) −14,000 (8) −18,000 (9) −26,000 (10) −24,000 (11) −20,000 (12) 25,500	$ 46,100
Accounts receivable	50,400	+357,000 (1) −370,000 (2) −13,000	37,400
Merchandise inventory	88,000	+140,000 (3) −123,000 (1) 17,000	105,000
Supplies	13,500	+12,500 (7)	26,000
Prepaid insurance	12,000		12,000
Total current assets	**184,500**		
Property, plant, and equipment:			
Equipment	92,100		92,100
Buildings	180,000		180,000
	272,100		
Less: accumulated depreciation	110,700		110,700
	161,400		
Land	60,000		60,000
Total property, plant, and equipment	**221,400**		
Total assets	**$405,900**		
Liabilities			
Current liabilities:			
Accounts payable	46,800	+140,000 (3) −132,000 (4) 8,000	54,800
Wages payable	17,900	−93,000 (5)	−75,100
Interest payable	18,000	−18,000 (9)	
Income taxes payable	5,000	−24,000 (11)	−19,000
Notes payable, current portion	26,000	−26,000 (10)	0
Total current liabilities	**113,700**		
Long-term liabilities:			
Notes payable, long-term	**120,000**		120,000
Total liabilities	**233,700**		

December 31,	1994	External Transaction Effects	1995
Stockholders' Equity			
Common stock	100,000		100,000
Retained earnings		64,190 (a) 20,000 (12) 44,190	
	72,200		116,390
Total stockholders' equity	**172,200**		
Total liabilities and stockholders' equity	**$405,900**		

(a) Adjustments for revenues and expenses. These accounts will be examined in detail later.

The following sections consider internal transactions.

Depreciation

Objective 2
Identify examples of internal transactions.

Assume management expected the equipment, costing $92,100, to have a useful life of 10 years when it was purchased. The equipment was purchased prior to 1995, but a portion of the cost of the equipment has been consumed during 1995, because the equipment wears out as it is used. To recognize the portion consumed, management might allocate one-tenth of the cost of the equipment to each year of its useful life. Then, the company would record $9,210 ($92,100/10 years) of depreciation expense for the equipment in 1995.

Cost of Asset = $92,100/10 years of Useful Life

Year 1	Year 2	Year 3	Years 4–9	Year 10
$9,210	$9,210	$9,210	@$9,210	$9,210

Assume management expected the buildings, costing $180,000, to have a useful life of 30 years when they were purchased. Management might allocate one-thirtieth of the cost of the buildings to each year. The depreciation expense for 1995 would be $6,000 ($180,000/30 years). Therefore, total depreciation for buildings and equipment would be $15,210 for the year. This internal transaction would be recorded as an increase in ACCUMULATED DEPRECIATION and as an increase in DEPRECIATION EXPENSE. Therefore, assets and income are reduced:

Assets =	Liabilities + Owners' Equity	+ Revenues − Expenses
Accumulated Depreciation (15,210)		Depreciation Expense (15,210)

Parentheses denote decreases in column totals.

The 1995 balance for accumulated depreciation is the prior year balance plus the amount of depreciation recorded in 1995 ($125,910 = $110,700 + $15,210). Note that recognition of depreciation expense does not involve cash. The cash payment for the assets occurred when they were acquired. Also, note that no external exchanges occurred in recognizing depreciation.

Insurance

Assume prepaid insurance was purchased in 1994 and provides coverage for a three-year period, beginning in 1995. Since one-third of the cost of the insurance was consumed during 1995, the company should record INSURANCE EXPENSE of $4,000 ($12,000/3 years) for 1995:

Cost of Insurance = $12,000/3 Years

Year 1	Year 2	Year 3
$4,000	$4,000	$4,000

This internal transaction would be recorded as a decrease in PREPAID INSURANCE and as an increase in INSURANCE EXPENSE. Therefore, assets and income are reduced:

Assets =		Liabilities + Owners' Equity + Revenues − Expenses	
Prepaid Insurance	(4,000)	Insurance Expense	(4,000)

As in the depreciation example, recognition of insurance expense does not involve cash. Cash was paid when the asset was purchased in 1994. No external exchanges occurred for insurance during 1995.

Supplies

Another asset that has been consumed without any explicit recognition is supplies. Office and maintenance supplies are consumed throughout the year as part of the company's operations. To determine how much of the asset has been consumed, the company must count or estimate the amount of asset left at the end of the fiscal period. For example, if $16,000 of supplies remain at the end of 1995, management can assume the company has consumed $10,000 of supplies:

Supplies available at beginning of year	$13,500
Supplies purchased during 1995	12,500
Total supplies available during year	26,000
Less: supplies remaining at end of year	16,000
Supplies consumed	$10,000

This internal transaction would be recorded as a decrease in SUPPLIES and as an increase in SUPPLIES EXPENSE. Therefore, assets and net income are reduced:

Assets =	Liabilities + Owners' Equity	+ Revenues − Expenses
Supplies (10,000)		Supplies Expense (10,000)

As in the prior examples, recognition of supplies expense does not involve cash. Cash was paid when the supplies were purchased.

Interest

An additional adjustment is needed for interest expense incurred during the year on the debt owed to the bank. Interest accumulates on debt throughout a fiscal period. Management recognizes these expenses during the period in which they occur, rather than waiting until cash is paid.

Assume Party Animal pays interest and principal to the bank at the beginning of each fiscal year. The $18,000 of interest paid in transaction 9 was paid at the beginning of 1995 for interest incurred during 1994. Assume the company incurred 10% interest on notes payable during 1995. The balance of notes payable is $120,000 after the payment of $26,000 at the beginning of 1995. Thus, the company incurred $12,000 ($120,000 × .10) of interest expense for 1995. The company will pay this interest to the bank when it is due in January 1996.

Interest expense recognized in 1995 would be recorded as an increase in INTEREST PAYABLE and as an increase in INTEREST EXPENSE. Therefore, liabilities are increased and income is reduced:

Assets =	Liabilities + Owners' Equity	+ Revenues − Expenses
-0-*	Interest Payable 12,000	Interest Expense (12,000)

Remember that the equation Assets = Liabilities + Owners' Equity + Revenues − Expenses must balance. Therefore, when no asset account is affected by a transaction, a zero is shown to complete the equation.

As in the prior examples, recognition of interest expense does not involve cash. Cash is paid when interest becomes due to creditors. For example, assume Party Animal pays the amount owed for interest incurred in 1995 at the beginning of 1996. The transaction would be recorded in 1996 by decreasing CASH and decreasing INTEREST PAYABLE:

Assets =	Liabilities + Owners' Equity	+ Revenues − Expenses
Cash (12,000)	Interest Payable (12,000)	

Note the cash payment for interest occurs in 1996. The expense associated with interest was recognized in 1995 when it was incurred.

Wages

A company incurs wages expense when employees earn the wages by providing services. Employees may not be paid at the time wages are earned. Therefore, the amount of wages expense may not equal the amount paid to employees during a fiscal period. Party Animal had $17,900 of wages payable at the end of 1994. This amount would have been paid to employees early in 1995 for services they provided in 1994. Assume employees earned $85,000 of wages during 1995. The company paid $93,000 in wages during the year (transaction 5). Therefore, the company owes $9,900 of wages at the end of 1995:

Wages payable at beginning of 1995	$ 17,900
Wages expense for 1995	85,000
Total wages to be paid	102,900
Less: wages paid during 1995	93,000
Wages payable at end of 1995	$ 9,900

This liability would be recognized as an increase in WAGES PAYABLE and an increase in WAGES EXPENSE for wages incurred during 1995:

Assets =	Liabilities + Owners' Equity		+ Revenues − Expenses	
-0-	Wages Payable	9,900	Wages Expense	(9,900)

The liability would be reduced during 1996 when the wages owed are paid to employees.

Income Taxes

Corporations pay taxes on income earned during a fiscal year. A portion of taxes incurred in one period may be paid in another period. Therefore, like wages, the amount of income tax expense and the amount paid for income taxes often differ for a fiscal period. (The use of different rules for computing taxable and financial income also complicate the recognition of income taxes. We will consider these differences in a later chapter.) Assume Party Animal incurred $22,000 of income tax expense on income earned during 1995. It would recognize the tax by increasing INCOME TAXES PAYABLE and increasing INCOME TAX EXPENSE, which reduces net income:

Assets =	Liabilities + Owners' Equity		+ Revenues − Expenses	
-0-	Income Taxes Payable	22,000	Income Tax Expense	(22,000)

Notes Payable

A final internal transaction occurs when Party Animal recognizes the amount of notes payable that will become due in 1995. This amount is transferred from

NOTES PAYABLE, LONG-TERM, to NOTES PAYABLE, CURRENT PORTION. The amount of the transfer depends on the repayment schedule that is part of the loan agreement with the bank. Assume Party Animal is obligated to pay $20,000 of the note principal during 1996. The transaction reduces the long-term liability and increases the current liability at the end of 1995:

Assets =	Liabilities + Owners' Equity		+ Revenues − Expenses
-0-	Notes Payable, Current Portion	20,000	
	Notes Payable, Long-Term	(20,000)	

Summary of Adjustments

Once the effects of the adjustments for internal transactions are added to the external transaction effects, Party Animal can prepare its income statement and balance sheet for 1995 as shown in Exhibits 6-2 and 6-3.

Exhibit 6-2

The Party Animal, Inc.
Income Statement
For the Year Ended December 31, 1995

Sales revenue		$357,000
Cost of goods sold		123,000
Gross profit		234,000
Operating expenses:		
Wages expense	$85,000	
Utilities expense	5,000	
Depreciation expense	15,210	
Insurance expense	4,000	
Supplies expense	10,000	
Advertising expense	14,000	
Total operating expenses		133,210
Income from operations		100,790
Other revenues and expenses:		
Interest expense		12,000
Pre-tax income		88,790
Income tax expense		22,000
Net income		$ 66,790
Earnings per share of common stock (100,000 shares outstanding)		$ 0.67

Recording and reporting adjustments for internal transactions are essential parts of the accounting process. Most of these adjustments result from timing differences between the recognition of revenues and expenses and the payment or receipt of cash. External transactions also may be associated with timing differences. The next section classifies by category internal and external transactions associated with timing differences.

Exhibit 6-3

The Party Animal, Inc.
Balance Sheet

December 31,	1994	All Transaction Effects	1995
Assets			
Current assets:			
Cash		+370,000 (2) −132,000 (4) −93,000 (5) −5,000 (6) −12,500 (7) −14,000 (8) −18,000 (9) −26,000 (10) −24,000 (11) −20,000 (12)	
	$ 20,600	25,500	$ 46,100
Accounts receivable		+357,000 (1) −370,000 (2)	
	50,400	−13,000	37,400
Merchandise inventory		+140,000 (3) −123,000 (1)	
	88,000	17,000	105,000
Supplies		+12,500 (7) −10,000 (i)	
	13,500	2,500	16,000
Prepaid insurance	12,000	−4,000 (i)	8,000
Total current assets	**184,500**		**212,500**
Property, plant, and equipment:			
Equipment	92,100		92,100
Buildings	180,000		180,000
	272,100		272,100
Less: accumulated depreciation	110,700	+ 15,210 (i)	125,910
	161,400		146,190
Land	60,000		60,000
Total property, plant, and equipment	**221,400**		**206,190**
Total assets	**$405,900**		**$418,690**
Liabilities			
Current liabilities:			
Accounts payable		+140,000 (3) −132,000 (4)	
	46,800	8,000	54,800
Wages payable		−93,000 (5) 85,000 (i)	
	17,900	−8,000	9,900
Interest payable		−18,000 (9) +12,000 (i)	
	18,000	−6,000	12,000

December 31,	1994	All Transaction Effects	1995
Income taxes payable	5,000	−24,000 (11) +22,000 (i) −2,000	3,000
Notes payable, current portion	26,000	−26,000 (10) +20,000 (i) −6,000	20,000
Total current liabilities	**113,700**		**99,700**
Long-term liabilities:			
Notes payable, long-term	120,000	−20,000 (i)	100,000
Total liabilities	**233,700**		**199,700**
Stockholders' Equity			
Common stock	100,000		100,000
Retained earnings	72,200	+66,790 (a) −20,000 (12) 46,790	118,990
Total stockholders' equity	**172,200**		**218,990**
Total liabilities and stockholders' equity	**$405,900**		**$418,690**

(a) Adjustments for revenues and expenses. (i) Internal transactions.

SELF-STUDY PROBLEM 6-1

Consider each of the following independent transactions.

Required

Identify the effect of each transaction by writing the account titles and amounts in the table provided on the next page. Use ( ) to indicate a reduction in the column totals.

a. A company recognizes $2,000 of unpaid wages earned by employees.
b. A company identifies $1,200 of supplies remaining at the end of the month. It had $1,800 of supplies on hand at the beginning of the month and purchased $5,000 of supplies during the month.
c. A company recognizes $2,400 of interest on notes payable incurred during the month. The interest will be paid next month.
d. A company recognizes $3,700 of income taxes owed on current period income. The taxes will be paid during the coming fiscal period.
e. A company recognizes $8,000 of depreciation for the current fiscal period.
f. A company transfers $10,000 of notes payable, long-term, to notes payable, current portion.
g. A company recognizes the consumption of one-third of a prepaid insurance policy for which it paid $6,000 last period.

Assets =		Liabilities + Owners' Equity		+ Revenues − Expenses	
Account	**Amount**	**Account**	**Amount**	**Account**	**Amount**
a.					
b.					
c.					
d.					
e.					
f.					
g.					

The solution to Self-Study Problem 6-1 appears at the end of the chapter.

ACCRUALS AND DEFERRALS

Objective 3
Define accrual and deferral accounts and transactions.

Differences in timing between when (1) goods or services are produced or sold and (2) cash is received or paid often result in transactions in which revenues or expenses are recognized in one period and cash flows are recognized in another. This section classifies these types of transactions which are common for most companies. The adjustments considered earlier in the chapter are examples of accruals and deferrals.

Accrued revenues **and** *accrued expenses* **occur when revenues and expenses are recognized before cash is received or paid.**

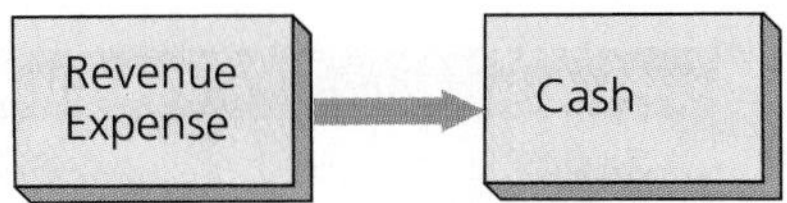

Deferred revenues **and** *deferred expenses* **occur when revenues and expenses are recognized after cash is received or paid.**

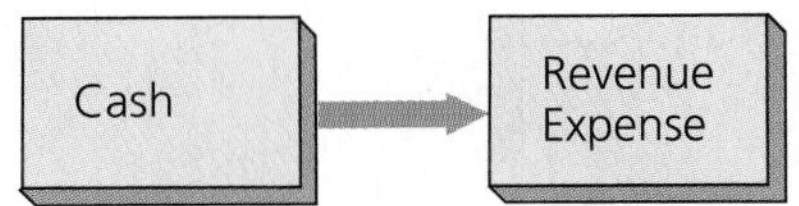

Internal transactions are examples of accruals and deferrals, but accruals and deferrals also may result from external transactions.

Accrued Revenues

Objective 4
Identify accrued revenues.

Assume that, beginning March 1, a company agrees to sell $1,200 of merchandise on the first of each month for three months to a customer. The customer agrees to pay $3,600 for the merchandise at the end of the three-month period.

The company has provided goods to the customer on March 1, April 1, and May 1, but cash is not received until May 31. Visualize the relationship between the revenues and cash flows as:

	March	April	May
Revenue	1,200	1,200	1,200
Cash Inflow	0	0	3,600

The company should recognize revenue of $1,200 on March 1, April 1, and May 1 when goods are provided to the customer. On each of these dates, it recognizes accounts receivable of $1,200 as well:

Assets =			Liab. + Owners' Equity	+ Revenues − Expenses		
Accounts Receivable	March	1,200		Sales Revenues	March	1,200
	April	1,200			April	1,200
	May	1,200			May	1,200

The asset, ACCOUNTS RECEIVABLE, represents the cash that will be received in the future. Once the cash is received in May, the balance of ACCOUNTS RECEIVABLE decreases and the balance of CASH increases:

Assets =		Liabilities + Owners' Equity	+ Revenues − Expenses
Cash	3,600		
Accounts Receivable	(3,600)		-0-

ACCOUNTS RECEIVABLE provides a record of the expected future cash flow until it is received. This account adjusts for the difference between the time revenue is recognized and cash is received. It is important to recognize the relationship among SALES REVENUE, ACCOUNTS RECEIVABLE, and CASH:

Event	Revenue Recognition	Timing Adjustment	Cash Flow
1	Sales Revenue 3,600	Accounts Receivable 3,600	
2		Accounts Receivable (3,600)	Cash 3,600

The first transaction records revenue earned and a receivable for cash expected from the sale. The second transaction eliminates the receivable and records cash received. The net effect of these transactions is to increase cash and sales revenue by $3,600. Accounts receivable provides a means of adjusting for timing differences.

Accrued Expenses

Objective 5
Identify accrued expenses.

Timing differences can occur between expenses and cash flows. For example, assume a company borrows $10,000 from a bank on July 1 and pays $300 in interest each quarter. If the first interest payment is due September 30, the company would recognize $100 of interest expense at the end of July, August, and September, but it would not record a cash outflow until September 30. Visualize the relationship between the expense and the cash flow as:

	July	August	September
Expense	(100)	(100)	(100)
Cash Outflow	0	0	(300)

Just as ACCOUNTS RECEIVABLE represents an expected future cash inflow (until it is received) in the previous example, INTEREST PAYABLE represents an expected future cash outflow (until it is paid):

Assets =	Liabilities + Owners' Equity			+ Revenues − Expenses		
	Interest Payable	July	100	Interest Expense	July	(100)
		August	100		August	(100)
-0-		Sept.	100		Sept.	(100)

The amount to be paid to the bank accumulates as INTEREST PAYABLE until it is paid. Once the cash is paid, the balance of INTEREST PAYABLE is reduced:

Assets =		Liabilities + Owners' Equity		+ Revenues − Expenses
Cash	(300)	Interest Payable	(300)	

The net effect of these transactions is to decrease net income by $300 and to decrease cash by $300:

Event	Expense Recognition	Timing Adjustment	Cash Flow
1	Interest Expense (300)	Interest Payable 300	
2		Interest Payable (300)	Cash (300)

A similar relationship exists between other expenses, payables, and cash outflows. For some transactions, other assets also may be involved. For example, assume a company purchases $800 of inventory during February. The purchase is made on credit. $800 is paid to the supplier for the merchandise in March. $300 of the merchandise is sold in February and the remaining $500 is sold during March. The company should recognize the purchase as an asset when the purchase occurs in February. Cash is paid in March:

	February	March
Asset	800	0
Cash Outflow	0	(800)

A portion of the asset is consumed in February and the remainder in March. Therefore an expense is recognized in both months:

	February	March
Expense	(300)	(500)

When the inventory is purchased, INVENTORY increases along with ACCOUNTS PAYABLE:

Assets =		Liabilities + Owners' Equity		+ Revenues − Expenses
Inventory	800	Accounts Payable	800	

As the asset is consumed, an expense, COST OF GOODS SOLD is recognized:

Assets =			Liab. + Owners' Equity	+ Revenues − Expenses		
Inventory	Feb.	(300)		Cost of	Feb.	(300)
	March	(500)		Goods Sold	Mar.	(500)

Finally, when the supplier is paid, CASH and ACCOUNTS PAYABLE are reduced:

Assets =		Liabilities + Owners' Equity		+ Revenues − Expenses
Cash	(800)	Accounts Payable	(800)	

Note the net effect of these transactions: the company has paid $800 in cash and has incurred a decrease in net income of $800 during the two months of February and March.

Event	Asset	Expense Recognition	Timing Adjustment	Cash Flow
1	Inventory 800		Accounts Payable 800	
2	Inventory (800)	Cost of Sales (800)		
3			Accounts Payable (800)	Cash (800)

The accounting process is complicated by the need to identify economic events with the fiscal period that benefited from the events. The same adjustment process would be necessary if these transactions occurred in different fiscal years instead of different months. The timing of the expense and cash flow are different. Therefore, the accounting system provides a means for identifying the period in which transactions should be recognized. Payables provide an accounting record for adjusting between the time when expenses (and sometimes assets) are recognized and when cash is paid.

Deferred Revenues

Objective 6
Identify deferred revenues.

Deferred revenue occurs when cash is received before revenue is earned. Assume that on October 1, a company rents equipment to a customer for three months for $250 per month. The customer pays the $750 rental fee in advance on October 1. While the company receives the cash on that day, the rent will not be earned until a portion of the rental period has passed. The customer receives services in October, November, and December. The cash flow occurs in October. As a result, the company defers the revenue on October 1 until it is earned in October, November, and December. Visualize the relationship between the revenue and the cash flow as:

	October	November	December
Revenue	250	250	250
Cash Inflow	750	0	0

When cash is received before revenue is earned, it is recorded in a liability account such as UNEARNED RENT. **Deferred revenues are liabilities.** They represent an obligation to provide goods and services to customers in the future. The obligation arises because customers have paid for goods and services they have not received yet:

Assets =		Liabilities + Owners' Equity		+ Revenues − Expenses
Cash	750	Unearned Rent	750	

As the rent is earned during the three months, revenue is recognized and the liability is reduced:

Assets =	Liabilities + Owners' Equity			+ Revenues − Expenses		
-0-	Unearned Rent	Oct.	(250)	Rent Revenue	Oct.	250
		Nov.	(250)		Nov.	250
		Dec.	(250)		Dec.	250

Thus, unearned revenue accounts, such as UNEARNED RENT, provide a means of adjusting for timing differences between when cash is received and when revenue is earned:

Event	Cash Flow	Timing Adjustment	Revenue Recognition
1	Cash 750	Unearned Rent 750	
2		Unearned Rent (750)	Rent Revenue 750

The net effect of the transactions is to increase cash and rent revenue by $750.

Deferred Expenses

Objective 7
Identify deferred expenses.

A deferred expense results when cash is paid out before an expense has been incurred. For example, assume a company purchases a three-month property insurance policy for $2,400 on January 1 and pays cash at that time. While the cash outflow occurs on January 1, the benefits associated with the policy are consumed over the months of January, February, and March. The company should recognize an expense for the insurance each month as the policy is consumed. Visualize the relationship between the expense and the cash flow as:

	January	February	March
Expense	(800)	(800)	(800)
Cash Outflow	(2,400)	0	0

An asset account, such as PREPAID INSURANCE, represents the amount of a short-term resource available until it is consumed. **A deferred or prepaid expense account is an asset**, a resource expected to be consumed in the future for which cash has been paid:

Assets =		Liabilities + Owners' Equity	+ Revenues − Expenses
Cash	(2,400)		
Prepaid Insurance	2,400	-0-	-0-

As the asset is consumed, PREPAID INSURANCE is reduced and INSURANCE EXPENSE is recognized:

Assets =			Liabilities + Owners' Equity	+ Revenues − Expenses		
Prepaid Insurance	Jan.	(800)		Insurance Expense	Jan.	(800)
	Feb.	(800)			Feb.	(800)
	Mar.	(800)			Mar.	(800)

The net effect of these transactions is to reduce cash and income by $2,400:

Event	Cash Flow		Timing Adjustment		Expense Recognition	
1	Cash	(2,400)	Prepaid Insurance	2,400		
2			Prepaid Insurance	(2,400)	Insurance Expense	(2,400)

Summary of Accruals and Deferrals

Many of the transactions organizations record in their accounting systems result from timing differences. Asset and liability accounts, such as ACCOUNTS RECEIVABLE, INTEREST PAYABLE, UNEARNED RENT, and PREPAID INSURANCE, result from accrual and deferral transactions. Note that **accruals and deferrals result in transactions that must be recorded on more than one date**. At least one entry is required to record revenues or expenses and at least one additional entry is required to record cash received or paid.

A close relationship exists between (1) current asset and liability accounts and (2) revenue and expense accounts. Current asset and liability accounts provide a link between the time revenues and expenses are recognized and the time cash is received or paid:

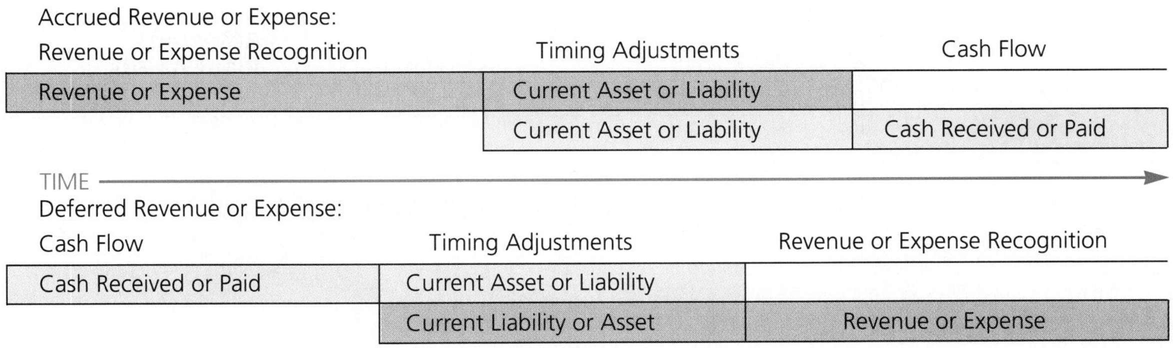

Accrued Revenue or Expense:

Revenue or Expense Recognition	Timing Adjustments	Cash Flow
Revenue or Expense	Current Asset or Liability	
	Current Asset or Liability	Cash Received or Paid

TIME →

Deferred Revenue or Expense:

Cash Flow	Timing Adjustments	Revenue or Expense Recognition
Cash Received or Paid	Current Asset or Liability	
	Current Liability or Asset	Revenue or Expense

SELF-STUDY PROBLEM 6-2

For each of the following independent situations, identify the effect on the balance sheet account. Use + and − to indicate an increase or decrease in the account. Complete each set of transactions using the format provided. The first one is done for you.

a. **Transaction**	**Effect on Accounts Receivable**
Sold $12,000 of goods on credit	+ $12,000
Collected $10,000 from customers	− 10,000
Net change	+ 2,000
b.	**Effect on Inventory**
Sold goods costing $8,000	
Purchased $9,500 of inventory on credit	
Net change	
c.	**Effect on Accounts Payable**
Purchased $9,500 of inventory on credit	
Paid $11,500 in cash to suppliers	
Net change	
d.	**Effect on Wages Payable**
Accrued $7,000 of unpaid wages	
Paid $6,300 in wages to employees	
Net change	
e.	**Effect on Prepaid Insurance**
Consumed 1 month of a 6-month insurance policy costing $6,000	
Paid $6,000 for a 6-month insurance policy	
Net change	
f.	**Effect on Unearned Rent**
Earned 1 month's rent from a 1-year lease of property for $12,000 per year	
Received $12,000 cash in advance for a 1-year lease	
Net change	
g.	**Effect on Plant Assets**
Recognized $4,000 of depreciation expense	
Net change	

The solution to Self-Study Problem 6-2 appears at the end of the chapter.

RECONCILIATION OF NET INCOME AND CASH FLOWS

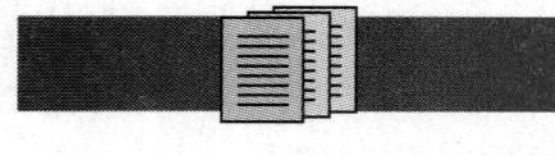

The statement of cash flows reports the cash flow effects of transactions during a fiscal period. For example, the cash flow statement for The Party Animal, Inc., for 1995 would appear as in Exhibit 6-4. This statement is prepared using the direct format described in Chapter 5.

Exhibit 6-4

The Party Animal, Inc.
Statement of Cash Flows
For the Year Ended December 31, 1995
(Direct Format)

Cash flow from operating activities:		
Receipts:		
Collections from customers		$370,000
Payments:		
To suppliers of inventory	$(132,000)	
To employees	(93,000)	
For utilities	(5,000)	
For supplies	(12,500)	
For advertising	(14,000)	
For interest	(18,000)	
For income taxes	(24,000)	
Total cash payments		298,500
Net cash flow from operating activities		71,500
Cash flow from financing activities:		
Payment of notes payable	(26,000)	
Payment of dividends	(20,000)	
Net cash flow from financing activities		(46,000)
Net increase in cash		25,500
Cash balance, December 31, 1994		20,600
Cash balance, December 31, 1995		$ 46,100

This statement provides a description of the events that resulted in the receipt or payment of cash during the fiscal year. Exhibit 6-3 showed these events as transactions affecting the cash balance during 1995. External decision makers do not have access to information about individual transactions. Therefore, the financial statements provide information summarizing the effects of the transactions.

Objective 8
Compare the direct and indirect formats of the statement of cash flows.

The direct format does not explain the relationship between cash flows for the year and the results of operations reported on the income statement. Net income for Party Animal was $64,190, while net cash inflow from operating activities was $71,500. An explanation of this difference is provided by a separate schedule accompanying the statement of cash flows. This schedule is similar to information presented on the statement of cash flows when it is prepared following the indirect format. This section describes the reconciliation by examining the indirect format, which is used by most corporations.

The indirect format of the statement of cash flows does not report cash flow effects of operating activities directly. Instead, this method converts net income on an accrual basis to cash flow from operating activities on a cash basis. Therefore, **the indirect format adjusts accrual basis information to a cash basis rather than reporting cash flow information directly**. Both the direct and indirect methods yield the same amount of cash flow from operating activities. Exhibit 6-5 presents the indirect format of the statement for The Party Animal, Inc., which is explained in following paragraphs.

Exhibit 6-5 does not present the sources and uses of cash associated with operating activities directly. Instead, it presents them as the indirect result of

Exhibit 6-5

The Party Animal, Inc.
Statement of Cash Flows
For the Year Ended December 31, 1995
(Indirect Format)

Cash flow from operating activities:		
Net income		$ 66,790
Noncash adjustments to income:		
Depreciation expense	$15,210	
Decrease in accounts receivable	13,000	
Increase in inventory	(17,000)	
Increase in supplies	(2,500)	
Decrease in prepaid insurance	4,000	
Increase in accounts payable	8,000	
Decrease in wages payable	(8,000)	
Decrease in interest payable	(6,000)	
Decrease in income tax payable	(2,000)	
Net adjustments to income		4,710
Net cash flow from operating activities		71,500
Cash flow from financing activities:		
Payment of notes payable	(26,000)	
Payment of dividends	(20,000)	
Net cash flow from financing activities		(46,000)
Net increase in cash		25,500
Cash balance, December 31, 1994		20,600
Cash balance, December 31, 1995		$ 46,100

changes in working capital accounts and other adjustments. This presentation is more complex than the direct method. Nevertheless, it is commonly used in practice. **The cash flow from the operating activities section in the indirect format is designed to reconcile accrual and cash basis performance measures.**

The cash flow from investing and financing sections are identical between the direct and indirect formats. Therefore, the following discussion will focus only on the operating section.

Percentage of Major Corporations Reporting Cash Flows Using the Direct and Indirect Formats

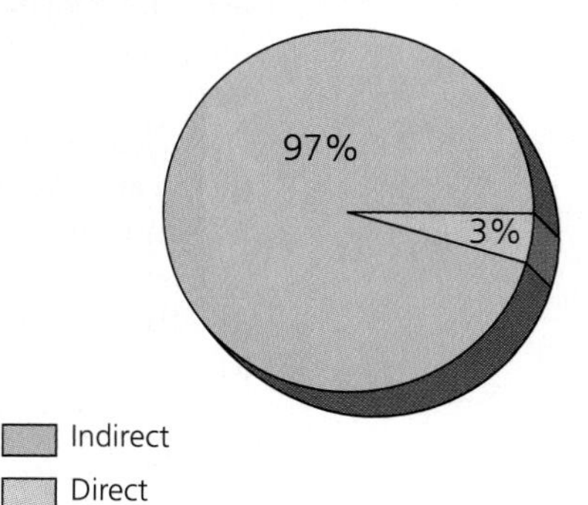

(Data source: Accounting Trends and Techniques, 1991

Objective 9
Explain the relationship between the indirect format of the statement of cash flows and accruals and deferrals.

To understand the indirect format, you must understand accruals and deferrals. The difference between net income and cash flow from operating activities results from accruals and deferrals for a fiscal period. Recall that accruals and deferrals occur because of timing differences between cash flows and revenues or expenses. These timing differences affect the balances of current asset and current liability accounts:

Accrued Revenue or Expense:

Revenue or Expense Recognition	Timing Adjustment	Cash Flow
Revenue or Expense	Current Asset or Liability	
	Current Asset or Liability	Cash Received or Paid

TIME →

Deferred Revenue or Expense:

Cash Flow	Timing Adjustment	Revenue or Expense Recognition
Cash Received or Paid	Current Liability or Asset	
	Current Liability or Asset	Revenue or Expense

The difference between cash and accrual measures is equal to the change in the relevant current asset or liability account. Consider the prepaid insurance example we examined earlier. A company purchases a three-month property insurance policy for $2,400 on January 1 and pays cash at that time. While the cash outflow occurs on January 1, the value associated with the policy is consumed over the months of January, February, and March. The company recognizes an expense for the insurance each month as the policy is consumed:

	January	**February**	**March**
Expense	(800)	(800)	(800)
Cash Outflow	(2,400)	0	0

The amount of expense recognized in January is $800. The amount of cash paid is $2,400. The link between insurance expense and cash paid for insurance is prepaid insurance.

Cash (2,400)	Prepaid Insurance 2,400	
	Prepaid Insurance (800)	Insurance Expense (800)
	Change 1,600	

The effect of the expense is to reduce net income in January by $800. The transactions reduced cash in January by $2,400. The difference is the increase in prepaid insurance in January of $1,600:

Effect on net income	$(800)
Less increase in prepaid insurance	(1,600)
Effect on cash flow from operating activities	$(2,400)

The adjustments to net income on the statement of cash flows result from accruals and deferrals. The amount of the accruals and deferrals can be determined, in most cases, by the change in the appropriate current asset or current liability account. The following sections examine these changes.

Accounts Receivable

Consider the relationships among sales revenue, accounts receivable, and cash flow. Sales revenue results in an increase in net income, but it results in an increase in cash only when cash has been collected. Exhibit 6-3 indicates that Party Animal experienced a decrease in accounts receivable of $13,000 during 1995:

	1994	Transactions	1995
Sales on credit		+357,000 (1)	
Cash collected from customers		−370,000 (2)	
Accounts receivable	50,400	−13,000	37,400

Accounts receivable decreases when cash collected during a period ($370,000) is greater than sales made on credit ($357,000). The difference between the amount reported as an increase in income for the year ($357,000) was $13,000 less than the amount of cash flow from customers for 1995 ($370,000). Therefore, to determine the amount of cash flow from operating activities for the year, the $13,000 decrease in accounts receivable should be added to net income.

Net Income	Adjusted for Timing Differences	= Cash Flow from Operating Activities
Sales Revenue	+ Decrease in Accounts Receivable	= Cash Collected from Customers
$357,000	+ $13,000	= $370,000

Thus, the direct format (Exhibit 6-4) reports cash flow from sales directly by reporting cash collected from customers. The indirect format reports the same result but does so indirectly by adding the decrease in accounts receivable to net income (Exhibit 6-5). An increase in accounts receivable for a period would be subtracted from net income in calculating cash flow.

Inventory

The change in inventory during a period results from inventory sales and purchases. In Exhibit 6-3, Party Animal's inventory balance increased $17,000 in 1995:

	1994	Transactions	1995
Purchase of inventory		+140,000 (3)	
Cost of goods sold		123,000 (1)	
Merchandise inventory	88,000	17,000	105,000

Therefore, $17,000 more of inventory was purchased during 1995 than was sold. The inventory sold was part of cost of goods sold for 1995 and reduced net income. But, inventory purchased was $17,000 more than the amount of expense recorded:

Net Income	Adjusted for Timing Differences	= Amount Purchased
Cost of Goods Sold	− Increase in Merchandise Inventory	= Purchase of Inventory
$(123,000)	− $17,000	= $(140,000)

Because expense was less than the purchase by $17,000, this amount is subtracted from net income in calculating cash flow from operating activities. If merchandise inventory had decreased during the period, the company would add the decrease to net income in computing cash flow from operating activities.

Cash flow associated with inventory also involves accounts payable. Remember that payment for inventory is a two-step process. Party Animal acquired inventory on credit in step 1. Then, it paid cash to the creditors in step 2. Step 2 involves an adjustment to the balance of accounts payable, considered next.

Accounts Payable

Exhibit 6-3 reveals accounts payable increased during 1995:

	1994	Transactions	1995
Purchase of inventory		+140,000 (3)	
Payment to suppliers		−132,000 (4)	
Accounts payable	$46,800	8,000	54,800

The increase in accounts payable indicates Party Animal purchased more inventory during 1995 than it paid for during the year. That is, the amount of inventory acquired was $8,000 more than the amount of cash paid for inventory:

Amount Purchased	Adjusted for Timing Differences	= Cash Flow from Operating Activities
Purchase of Inventory	+ Increase in Accounts Payable	= Cash Paid to Suppliers
$(140,000)	+ $8,000	= $(132,000)

Because the cash outflow was less than the amount purchased, the increase in accounts payable should be added back to net income in computing cash flow from operating activities (Exhibit 6-5). If accounts payable had decreased during the period, the company would subtract the decrease from net income.

The amount of cash paid to suppliers during 1995 can be determined by looking at the change in MERCHANDISE INVENTORY (step 1) and the change in ACCOUNTS PAYABLE (step 2) together. Changes in both of these accounts explain the difference between the cost of goods sold (inventory consumed during the period) and the cash paid to suppliers during 1995.

Net Income	**Adjusted for Timing Differences**	**= Cash Flow from Operating Activities**
Cost of Goods Sold	− Increase in Merchandise Inventory + Increase in Accounts Payable	= Cash Paid to Suppliers
$(123,000)	− $17,000 + $8,000	= $(132,000)

This amount agrees with the amount of cash paid to suppliers for inventory reported on the direct format of the statement of cash flows (Exhibit 6-4).

The statement of cash flows reports the two-step adjustment in two parts, the change in inventory and the change in accounts payable. Understanding the relationship between these accounts is important for interpreting the statement.

Interest Payable

Exhibit 6-3 indicates interest payable decreased $6,000 during 1995:

	1994	**Transactions**	**1995**
Payment of interest		−18,000 (9)	
Interest expense		+12,000	
Interest payable	18,000	−6,000	12,000

The decrease resulted from a payment of $18,000 for interest and recognition of interest expense of $12,600. Therefore, the effect on net income was $6,000 less than the cash outflow:

Net Income	**Adjusted for Timing Differences**	**= Cash Flow from Operating Activities**
Interest Expense	− Decrease in Interest Payable	= Cash Paid for Interest
$(12,000)	− $6,000	= $(18,000)

More cash was paid out than was recognized as expense in computing net income. Therefore, the decrease in interest payable is subtracted from net income in computing cash flow from operating activities (Exhibit 6-5).

Depreciation

Party Animal recognized $15,210 of depreciation expense in computing current period income (Exhibit 6-2). This expense also is represented on the balance sheet by the increase in accumulated depreciation. No cash flow was associated with the expense during the current period. The cash outflow occurred previously when fixed assets were purchased, not during the current period when they were used. The cash outflow appeared on the statement of cash flows as an investing activity in the period in which the assets were purchased. Therefore, no additional cash outflow is associated with depreciation expense during the current fiscal period. Because depreciation expense was subtracted from revenues on the income statement in calculating net income, it must be added back to net income in computing cash flow from operating activities:

Net Income	Adjusted for Timing Differences	= Cash Flow from Operating Activities
Depreciation Expense	+ Increase in Depreciation	= Cash Paid for Depreciation
$(15,210)	+ $15,210	= $0

Depreciation does not affect current assets or liabilities. Accumulated depreciation plays much the same kind of role. The change in accumulated depreciation results from a timing difference between when depreciation expense is recognized and when cash is paid. Perhaps it is simpler to remember, however, that noncash expenses, like depreciation, are added to net income in computing cash flow from operating activities.

Other noncash expenses include amortization expense for patents and other intangible assets. These expenses also should be added back to net income in computing cash flow from operating activities. Cash outflow occurs when intangible assets are purchased or when costs are incurred in creating them, not when they are amortized. Like depreciation, amortization is an expense that reduces net income. But, it does not reduce cash. Therefore, expenses that do not affect cash, such as depreciation and amortization, must be added back to net income in computing cash flow from operating activities.

Other Adjustments for the Indirect Method

The reasoning behind other adjustments to net income using the indirect format is the same as that for accounts receivable, merchandise inventory, accounts payable, and interest payable. This reasoning leads to the observations that:

1. Increases in current asset balances are subtracted from net income in computing cash flow from operating activities. Decreases in current asset balances are added to net income.
2. Increases in current liability balances are added to net income in computing cash flow from operating activities. Decreases in current liability balances are subtracted from net income. (Note that this is the opposite of the current asset treatment.)

3. Noncash expenses, such as depreciation and amortization, are added to net income in computing cash flow from operating activities. Occasionally, a company will report a noncash revenue that is subtracted from net income.

Net Income
+ Depreciation and Amortization Expense
− Increases in Current Asset Accounts
+ Decreases in Current Asset Accounts
+ Increases in Current Liability Accounts
− Decreases in Current Liability Accounts
= Cash Flow from Operating Activities

You should verify from Exhibit 6-5 that these relationships are followed consistently on the statement of cash flows using the indirect format.

Note that net income is not adjusted for the change in notes payable, current portion, though it is a current liability. This change is associated with the payment of long-term debt and is reported as a financing activity. Notes payable are not part of the operating activities of the company because they have no effect on net income or cash flow from operating activities. Interest associated with the notes does affect net income and cash flow, and is included as part of the adjustments.

The indirect format reconciles net income and cash flow. The reconciliation is made by examining changes in accounts that adjust for differences in timing between (1) revenues and expenses and (2) cash flows. Most of these timing differences are captured in working capital accounts. These accounts identify accruals and deferrals necessary to adjust for timing differences between the accrual basis and the cash basis. **You will find it difficult to understand accounting information without understanding these relationships.** They are central to accounting measurement and to reporting the transformation process.

INTERPRETATION OF CASH FLOWS

Objective 10
Interpret cash flow information as a basis for analyzing corporate financial performance.

Changes in current asset and current liability accounts can reveal strengths and weaknesses in a company's operating activities. For example, a significant increase in accounts receivable during a period may indicate a company is having difficulty collecting on its sales. Thus, while net income may appear favorable, cash flows may be unfavorable. Similarly, a significant increase in accounts payable may indicate a company is having difficulty meeting its current obligations. Profitability is not sufficient to ensure success in a business organization. Profits must be accompanied by favorable cash flows that signal the ability of a company to convert its revenues into cash on a timely basis.

For example, Exhibit 6-6 illustrates a major increase in cash flow for Johnson & Johnson in 1990, compared with 1989. This increase was accompanied by a modest increase in net income. The increase in cash flow can be explained by an increase of $360 million in accounts payable during 1990. Accounts payable had decreased in 1989 by $42 million. Increases in accounts payable in 1991 were accompanied by increases in accounts receivable. Receivables increased by $244 million in 1991, compared with $127 million in 1990. These changes help explain the pattern of cash flows reported by the company.

Exhibit 6-6 A Comparison of Net Cash Inflow from Operating Activities and Net Income for Johnson & Johnson

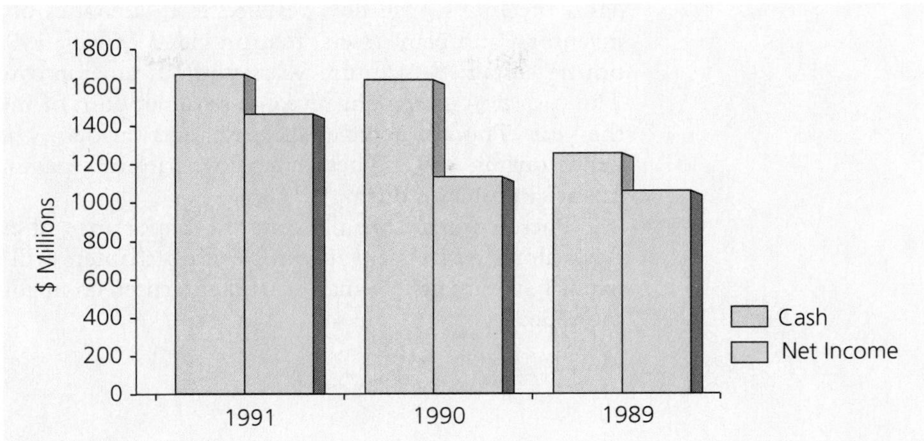

Exhibit 6-7 compares cash flows and net income for Johnson & Johnson with Unisys for 1991. The exhibit illustrates important differences in the financial activities of the two firms. Johnson & Johnson reported net income and operating cash flows that were positive and of similar amounts. The company also reported major cash outflows for investing and financing activities which are consistent with a healthy financial condition. The statement of cash flows reveals that Johnson & Johnson's investment in new plant assets was approximately twice the amount of depreciation recorded for the period. Plant expansion indicates growth and expected future profitability. The company also paid dividends to stockholders at amounts above prior years. It retired debt and repurchased common stock. These activities indicate the company was using its cash to strengthen its financial position.

Exhibit 6-7 Comparison of Income and Cash Flows for Johnson & Johnson and Unisys

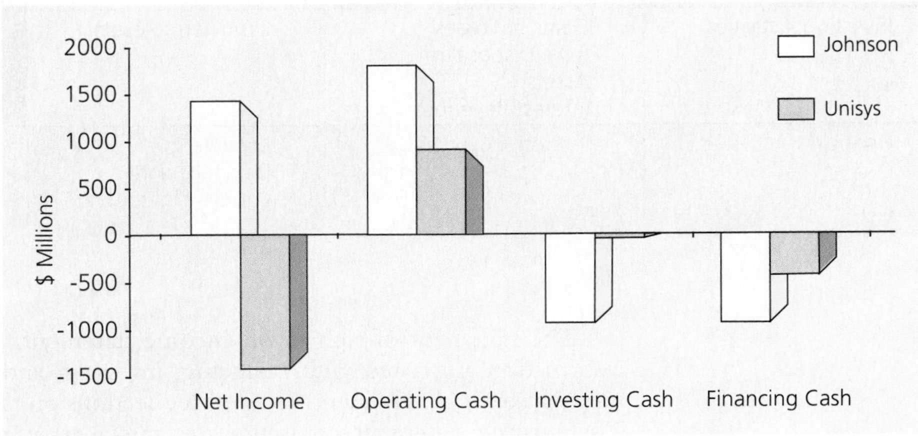

Unisys, on the other hand, provides a very different picture. Large losses were accompanied by a positive cash flow from operating activities. In addition

to noncash expenses (depreciation and amortization), decreases in receivables and inventories explain most of the difference between income and cash flow. Most of Unisys' cash flow resulted from activities of prior periods (receivables, inventory, and plant assets) that provided cash in 1991. These cash flows could not be sustained in future years without an improvement in operating results. The cash flow statement reveals a small amount of investment in plant assets for the year. Though it did make payments on debt, the company curtailed dividends during 1991. These cash flow patterns suggest Unisys was facing major financial problems during 1991.

These comparisons illustrate the importance of evaluating a company's cash flows along with its net income. Future chapters will examine the use of the financial statements to analyze and interpret companies' economic activities in more depth.

FINANCIAL STATEMENTS AND THE TRANSFORMATION PROCESS

Objective 11
Identify relationships between financial statements and components of the transformation process.

A summary of the relationships between financial statements and the transformation process concludes this chapter. Exhibit 6-8 depicts these relationships. Components of the transformation process include financing, investing, and operating activities. The financial statements provide information about each of these activities and interrelationships among them. Later chapters of this book will examine this information and its use in decision making.

Exhibit 6-8 Financial Statement Reporting of Major Components of the Transformation Process

Statement of Cash Flows	Income Statement	Balance Sheet	Statement of Stockholders' Equity
Operating Activities	Income from Operations	Current Assets and Current Liabilities	
Investing Activities	Gains or Losses from Disposal of Assets, Interest Revenues	Long-Term Assets	
Financing Activities	Interest Expenses	Long-Term Liabilities and Equity	Changes in Stockholders' Equity

The statement of cash flows, income statement, and balance sheet provide information associated with financing, investing, and operating activities. This information is clearly identified in three sections on the statement of cash flows. The income statement communicates information primarily about operating activities. Gains and losses associated with selling assets other than inventory represent results of investing activities. Interest revenue often results from investing activities, as well. Interest expense results from financing activities. Financing activities result in long-term liabilities and equity on the balance sheet. Long-term assets are the result of investing activities. Most current assets and liabilities result from operating activities, timing differences between revenues and cash inflows or expenses and cash outflows. The statement of changes in stockholders' equity provides detailed information about results of equity financing activities.

SELF-STUDY PROBLEM 6-3

Consider each of the following independent situations. Identify the adjustment that would be made to net income in computing cash flow from operating activities. Parentheses indicate a negative effect on net income. Use ( ) to indicate a cash outflow. Use the format provided:

a.	**Amount**
Sales revenues	$12,000
Increase in accounts receivable	2,000
Cash collected from customers	
b.	
Cost of goods sold	$(8,000)
Increase in inventory	1,500
Decrease in accounts payable	2,000
Cash paid to suppliers	
c.	
Wages expense	$(7,000)
Increase in wages payable	700
Cash paid to employees	
d.	
Insurance expense	$(1,000)
Increase in prepaid insurance	5,000
Cash paid for insurance	
e.	
Rent revenue	$1,000
Increase in unearned rent	11,000
Cash received in advance from customer	
f.	
Depreciation expense	$(4,000)
Decrease in plant assets	4,000
Cash paid for depreciation	

Once you have completed the problem, compare it with Self-Study Problem 6-2.

The solution to Self-Study Problem 6-3 appears at the end of the chapter.

REVIEW *Summary of Important Concepts*

1. Internal transactions:
   A. Internal transactions are important for complete recognition of revenues and expenses during a fiscal period.
   B. Internal transactions adjust account balances for revenues and expenses that should be recognized though external transactions have not occurred.
   C. Internal transactions often involve current asset or liability accounts in addition to revenues and expenses.
2. Adjustments and the balance sheet and income statement:
   A. Accruals and deferrals adjust for timing differences between when revenues or expenses are recognized and when cash is received or paid.
   B. Accrued revenues occur when revenues are recognized before cash is received.
   C. Accrued expenses occur when expenses are recognized before cash is paid.
   D. Deferred revenues occur when revenues are recognized after cash is received.
   E. Deferred expenses occur when expenses are recognized after cash is paid.
3. Timing differences and cash flow reporting:
   A. The indirect format of the statement of cash flows reconciles net income with cash flow from operating activities.
   B. The indirect format adjusts net income for changes in current asset and current liability account balances and for noncash expenses or revenues in computing cash flow from operating activities.
   C. Changes in working capital account balances identify differences between the amounts of revenues and expenses recognized during a fiscal period and the amounts of cash received or paid.
4. Cash flow information:
   A. Information about the sources and uses of cash provides a picture of a company's ability to meet its payment obligations now and in the future.
   B. Cash flow information, along with that on the income statement and balance sheet, provides insight into a company's operating, investing, and financing activities.

DEFINE *Terms and Concepts Defined in this Chapter*

accrued expenses
accrued revenues
deferred expenses
deferred revenues

SOLUTIONS

SELF-STUDY PROBLEM 6-1

Assets =		Liabilities + Owners' Equity		+ Revenues − Expenses	
Account	**Amount**	**Account**	**Amount**	**Account**	**Amount**
a.	-0-	Wages Payable	2,000	Wages Expense	(2,000)
b. Supplies	(5,600)*			Supplies Expense	(5,600)
c.	-0-	Interest Payable	2,400	Interest Expense	(2,400)
d.	-0-	Income Taxes Payable	3,700	Income Tax Expense	(3,700)
e. Accumulated Deprec.	(8,000)			Depreciation Expense	(8,000)
f.	-0-	Notes Payable, Current Portion Notes Payable, Long-Term	10,000 (10,000)		
g. Prepaid Insurance	(2,000)			Insurance Expense	(2,000)

****$1,800 beginning supplies + $5,000 purchased − $1,200 remaining = $5,600 used during the month.***

SELF-STUDY PROBLEM 6-2

a. **Transaction**	**Effect on Accounts Receivable**
Sold $12,000 of goods on credit	+$12,000
Collected $10,000 from customers	−10,000
Net change	+$2,000
b.	**Effect on Inventory**
Sold goods costing $8,000	−$8,000
Purchased $9,500 of inventory on credit	+9,500
Net change	+$1,500
c.	**Effect on Accounts Payable**
Purchased $9,500 of inventory on credit	+$9,500
Paid $11,000 in cash to suppliers	−11,500
Net change	−$2,000
d.	**Effect on Wages Payable**
Accrued $7,000 of unpaid wages	+$7,000
Paid $6,300 in wages to employees	−6,300
Net change	+$700
e.	**Effect on Prepaid Insurance**
Consumed 1 month of a 6-month insurance policy costing $6,000	−$1,000
Paid $6,000 for a 6-month insurance policy	+6,000
Net change	+$5,000

f. **Transaction**	**Effect on Unearned Rent**
Earned 1 month's rent from a 1-year lease of property for $12,000 per year	−$1,000
Received $12,000 cash in advance for a 1-year lease	+12,000
Net change	+$11,000
g.	**Effect on Plant Assets**
Recognized $4,000 of depreciation expense	−$4,000
Net change	−$4,000

SELF-STUDY PROBLEM 6-3

a.	**Amount**
Sales revenues	$12,000
Increase in accounts receivable	−2,000
Cash collected from customers	**$10,000**
b.	
Cost of goods sold	$(8,000)
Increase in inventory	−1,500
Decrease in accounts payable	−2,000
Cash paid to suppliers	**$(11,500)**
c.	
Wages expense	$(7,000)
Increase in wages payable	+700
Cash paid to employees	**$(6,300)**
d.	
Insurance expense	$(1,000)
Increase in prepaid insurance	−5,000
Cash paid for insurance	**$(6,000)**
e.	
Rent revenue	$1,000
Increase in unearned rent	+11,000
Cash received in advance from customer	**$12,000**
f.	
Depreciation expense	$(4,000)
Decrease in plant assets	+4,000
Cash paid for depreciation	**$0**

EXERCISES

6-1. Write a short definition for each of the terms listed in the *Terms and Concepts Defined in this Chapter* section.

6-2. Distinguish between external and internal transactions. Why are internal transactions necessary?

6-3. Identify each of the following as external or internal transactions. Also, identify the accounts that would be affected by each transaction:

a. Sold merchandise to customers for $3,000 on credit (ignore effect on inventory).
b. Collected $2,500 in cash from customers for prior sales.
c. Rented building space to a customer for $48,000. The rent covers one year and the customer paid in advance.
d. Earned rent for the first month from transaction c.
e. Purchased property insurance for one year and paid $24,000.
f. Incurred expense for first month from transaction e.

6-4. The Zung Tea Co. purchased property insurance on January 1, 1995, for $600. The insurance covers a three-month period. Insurance expense is recorded each month. Complete the following tables for transactions in January, February, and March 1995. What was the net effect of the transactions for the three months on the company's financial statements?

	January	**February**	**March**	**Total**
Expense				
Cash Outflow				

Effect for three months:

Cash		
		Insurance Expense

6-5. The Pierre Tire Co. borrowed $10,000 from a bank on April 1, 1996. $300 of interest is paid on the loan each quarter, beginning June 30. Interest is accrued each month. Complete the following tables for July, August, and September 1996. What was the net effect of the transactions for the three months on the company's financial statements?

	July	**August**	**September**	**Total**
Expense				
Cash Outflow				

Effect for three months:

Interest Expense		
		Cash

6-6. The Big Bang Chemical Co. signed a contract with Holes 'R Us Construction, Inc., on April 1, 1995. Big Bang agreed to provide Holes 'R Us with goods priced at $10,000 each month for three months, beginning April 1. Holes 'R Us agreed to pay $30,000 for the goods on June 30. Complete the following tables for Big Bang for April, May, and June. What was the net effect of the transactions for the three months on the company's financial statements?

	April	May	June	Total
Revenue				
Cash Inflow				

Effect for three months:

Sales Revenue		
		Cash

6-7. Wowee Press, Inc., publishes a weekly magazine. Subscriptions for 3 months are $36. Customers submit payment in December for issues beginning in January. By December 31, 1995, Wowee Press had received $720,000 in subscriptions. Revenues are recorded each month as earned. Complete the following tables for transactions in December 1995 and for January, February, and March 1996. What was the net effect of the transactions for the four months on the company's financial statements?

	December	January	February	March	Total
Revenue					
Cash Inflow					

Effect for four months:

Cash		
		Sales Revenue

6-8. Consider each of the following independent transactions. Identify the effect of each transaction by writing the account titles and amounts in the table provided below. Use ( ) to indicate amounts that reduce the column balance.

a. A company recognizes $3,000 of unpaid wages earned by employees.
b. A company identifies $2,000 of supplies remaining at the end of the month. It had $1,300 of supplies on hand at the beginning of the month and purchased $7,000 of supplies during the month.
c. A company recognizes $1,800 of interest on notes payable incurred during the month. The interest will be paid next month.
d. A company recognizes $6,000 of income taxes owed on current period income. The taxes will be paid during the coming fiscal period.
e. A company recognizes $5,000 of depreciation for the current fiscal period.
f. A company transfers $20,000 of notes payable, long-term, to notes payable, current portion.
g. A company recognizes the consumption of one-third of a prepaid insurance policy for which it paid $9,000.

Assets =		Liabilities + Owners' Equity		+ Revenues − Expenses	
Account	**Amount**	**Account**	**Amount**	**Account**	**Amount**
a.					
b.					
c.					
d.					
e.					
f.					
g.					
Total		Total		Total	

6-9. Determine whether each of the following sentences indicates an accrued revenue, accrued expense, deferred revenue, or deferred expense.

1. Cash is paid in June and a related expense is recognized in July.
2. A revenue is recognized in June for which cash is received in July.
3. Expense is recognized in June for which cash is paid in July.
4. Cash is received in June and a related revenue is recognized in July.

6-10. For each of items listed below, identify whether it would appear on the statement of cash flows as part of the computation of cash flow from operating activities, cash flow from financing activities, or cash flow from investing activities. Also, indicate whether the item is added or subtracted in computing cash flow using the indirect method of preparing the statement of cash flows:

a. Purchase of plant assets
b. Increase in accounts payable
c. Decrease in accounts receivable
d. Payment of long-term debt
e. Net income
f. Depreciation expense
g. Payment of dividends
h. Issuing stock
i. Increase in inventory
j. Decrease in taxes payable
k. Disposal of plant assets

6-11. The following information is available for Hourglass Watch Co. for the first six months of 1995:

Revenues	$130,000
Expenses	75,000
Increase in accounts receivable	8,000
Decrease in inventory	12,000
Decrease in supplies	5,000
Increase in accounts payable	13,000
Decrease in wages payable	3,000
Depreciation expense	9,000
Patent expense	2,000

Determine the cash flow from operating activities for the six-month period.

6-12. Use the information provided in each of the following independent situations to answer the questions. Briefly explain your answer to each question.

a. Cash collected from customers for a fiscal period was $30,000. Accounts receivable increased during the period by $6,000. What was sales revenue for the period?
b. Cash paid to suppliers for merchandise during a period was $55,000. Accounts payable decreased during the period by $4,000. Inventory increased during the period by $7,000. What was cost of goods sold for the period?
c. Interest paid during a period was $6,000. Interest payable decreased during the period by $1,500. What was interest expense for the period?
d. Cash flow from operations for a period was $40,000. Current assets decreased during the period by $8,000. Current liabilities decreased by $5,000. What was net income for the period?

6-13. Use the information provided in each of the following independent situations to answer the questions. Briefly explain your answers.

a. Net cash flow from operations for a period was $26,000. Noncash revenues were $14,000. Noncash expenses were $17,000. What was net income for the period?
b. Wages expense for a period was $47,000. Wages payable increased during the period by $7,000. How much cash was paid to employees during the period?
c. Cash collected from customers for a fiscal period was $83,000. Sales revenue for the period was $94,000. Accounts receivable at the beginning of the period was $22,000. What was the balance in accounts receivable at the end of the period?

d. Net income for a period was $33,000. Current assets increased during the period by $5,000. Current liabilities increased by $8,000. How much was cash flow from operations for the period?

6-14. Listed below are account balances. For each item, indicate the future implications for cash flows and/or operating activities. Item (a) is provided as an example.

Account Balance	**Implication**
a. Accounts receivable, $10,000	Approximately $10,000 of cash should be received from customers during the coming fiscal year.
b. Accounts payable, $7,500	
c. Inventory, $50,000	
d. Notes payable, long-term, $100,000	
e. Equipment, $80,000	
f. Prepaid insurance, $22,000	
g. Wages payable, $8,000	
h. Unearned revenue, $13,000	
i. Notes payable, current, $5,000	

6-15. The following information was reported by Boeing Company in a recent year (in millions):

Decrease in inventories	1,585
Decrease in unearned revenues	362
Depreciation and amortization	678
Increase in accounts payable	554
Increase in accounts receivable	233
Increase in income taxes payable	227
Increase in other receivables	301
Net earnings	1,385
Noncash revenues	197

What was Boeing's cash flow from operating activities for the fiscal year?

6-16. Following is a statement of cash flows reported by Time-Warner for a recent fiscal year.

Consolidated Statement of Cash Flows

Year Ended December 31, (millions)	*1991*
Operations:	
Net loss	$ (99)
Adjustments for noncash and nonoperating items:	
Depreciation and amortization	1,109
Noncash losses	70
Changes in related balance sheet accounts:	
Receivables	(138)
Inventories	18
Accounts payable and other liabilities	71
Other balance sheet changes	66
Cash provided by operations	1,097

Year Ended December 31, (millions)	*1991*
Investing activities:	
Acquisitions and investments	(478)
Capital expenditures	(527)
Proceeds from dispositions	186
Cash used by investing activities	(819)
Financing activities:	
Decrease in debt	(2,454)
Proceeds from Stock Rights Offering	2,558
Dividends paid	(363)
Other	8
Cash used by financing activities	(251)
Increase in cash and equivalents	**$ 27**

Note: Slight modifications have been made to the format of the statement for purposes of simplifying the presentation.

Use the statement to answer the following questions:

a. What was the primary source of cash flow for the company?
b. Why did the company receive a net cash inflow from operations when it incurred a net loss for the period?
c. What were the primary uses of cash during the period?
d. Did receivables, inventories, and accounts payable increase or decrease during the year?
e. If revenues were $12,021 million for 1991, how much cash was collected from customers for the year?

6-17. Consider the following pattern in selected year-end data for the Profit Company:

Year	**1**	**2**	**3**	**4**	**5**	**6**
Cash flow from operating activities	$20,000	$25,000	$18,000	$12,000	$ 6,000	$ 2,000
Receivables	35,000	37,000	42,000	45,000	50,000	53,000
Inventory	70,000	76,000	80,000	84,000	86,000	90,000
Payables	24,000	28,000	32,000	46,000	57,000	66,000
Net income	50,000	53,000	55,000	59,000	63,000	55,000

Provide an explanation for the changes over the six-year period. What difficulties do you believe the company is facing?

6-18. Capital Company has experienced the following results over the past three years:

(in thousands)

Year	**1**	**2**	**3**
Net income (loss)	$ 2,000	$(10,000)	$ (8,000)
Depreciation and amortization	(9,000)	(11,000)	(14,000)
Net cash flow from operating activities	13,000	15,000	18,000
Net expenditures for plant assets	9,000	6,000	5,000

The price of Capital Company's common stock has declined steadily over the three-year period. At the end of year 3, it is trading at $10 per share. Early in year 4, Boone Icahn, who specializes in taking over poorly performing businesses, has offered shareholders of Capital $18 per share for their stock. Why would Icahn be willing to pay such an amount? What does he see in the company that suggests value?

6-19. Martha Rosenbloom holds stock in several major corporations. Each year she receives a copy of the companies' annual reports. She looks at the pictures, reads the discussion by management, and examines some of the primary financial statement numbers. She has a pretty good understanding of some of the financial statement information. She tells her friends she doesn't know how to make heads or tails of the statement of cash flows, however. She doesn't understand how depreciation and changes in current assets and liabilities have anything to do with cash. A mutual friend, Arthur Doyle, has found out that you are taking accounting and asks you to help Martha. Write Martha a letter explaining the cash flow from operating activities section of the statement of cash flows found in most annual reports. Martha's address is 945 Oak Lane, Anytown, USA.

6-20. Explain how a company can have a net loss for a fiscal period but have a net increase in cash from operating activities.

6-21. The Dollar Sign Corporation sold $30,000 of merchandise on credit during April. The merchandise cost the company $18,000. It purchased $25,000 of inventory on credit during April. Also, it collected $22,000 from customers and paid $16,000 to suppliers. What effect did these transactions have on cash, accounts receivable, inventory, accounts payable, revenues, and expenses?

6-22. Complete the following table describing the relationship between financial statements and components of the transformation process:

Statement of Cash Flows	Income Statement	Balance Sheet	Statement of Stockholders' Equity
Operating Activities			
Investing Activities			
Financing Activities			

PROBLEMS

PROBLEM 6-1 Adjustments

The Gorby Chef Restaurant reported the following balance sheet and income statement:

The Gorby Chef Restaurant
Balance Sheet
For Month Ended March 31, 1996

Assets	
Current assets:	
Cash	$ 12,200
Supplies	13,900
Prepaid rent	9,000
Total current assets	35,100
Plant assets:	
Building	100,000
Accumulated depreciation	(20,000)
Total plant assets	80,000
Total assets	$115,100

Liabilities and Stockholders' Equity	
Current liabilities:	
Unearned revenue from gift certificates	10,700
Total current liabilities	10,700
Notes payable	30,000
Total liabilities	40,700
Stockholders' equity:	
Common stock	40,000
Retained earnings	34,400
Total stockholders' equity	74,400
Total liabilities and stockholders' equity	$115,100

The Gorby Chef Restaurant
Income Statement
For the Three Months Ended March 31, 1996

Sales revenue	$96,000
Cost of dinners sold	(33,000)
Wages expense	(29,400)
Rent expense	(6,000)
Total expenses	(68,400)
Net income	$27,600

The company failed to record the following adjustments at the end of March:

a. The prepaid rent account represents three months rent paid at the beginning of March. Rent expense has not been recorded for March.
b. Wages owed but unpaid at the end of March total $4,100.
c. In addition to the sales revenue shown, gift certificates totalling $9,200 were redeemed during the period.
d. The building is being depreciated over a 25-year estimated useful life. No depreciation has been recorded for the current quarter.
e. The amount of supplies available at the end of March was $3,000.
f. Interest accumulates on the note payable at 12% per year. No interest has been recorded for the quarter.

Required Make adjustments in the following tables to prepare a corrected balance sheet and income statement for Gorby Chef.

The Gorby Chef Restaurant
Balance Sheet
March 31, 1996

	Uncorrected	Adjustments	Corrected
Assets			
Current assets:			
Cash	$ 12,200		
Supplies	13,900		
Prepaid rent	9,000		
Total current assets	35,100		

	Uncorrected	Adjustments	Corrected
Plant assets:			
Building	100,000		
Accumulated depreciation	(20,000)		
Total plant assets	80,000		
Total assets	$115,100		
Liabilities and Stockholders' Equity			
Current liabilities:			
Unearned revenue from gift certificates	10,700		
Total current liabilities	10,700		
Notes payable	30,000		
Total liabilities	40,700		
Stockholders' equity			
Common stock	40,000		
Retained earnings*	34,400		
Total stockholders' equity	74,400		
Total liabilities and stockholders' equity	$115,100		

Retained earnings must be adjusted for the change in net income resulting from the corrections.

The Gorby Chef Restaurant
Income Statement
For the Three Months Ended March 31, 1996

	Uncorrected	Adjustments	Corrected
Sales revenue	$ 96,000		
Cost of dinners sold	(33,000)		
Wages expense	(29,400)		
Rent expense	(6,000)		
Total expenses	(68,400)		
Net income	$ 27,600		

PROBLEM 6-2 Accruals and Deferrals

The Nifty Threads Clothing Store had the following information available at December 31, 1996.

a. A 12%, $8,000 note payable had been outstanding since August 1, 1996. Under the terms of the note, the amount of the note plus interest is to be paid on February 1, 1997. No interest has been recorded on the note.
b. In December 1996, a local high school band made a $6,000 deposit toward new uniforms. At December 31, 1996, one-third of the order had been delivered to the customer. Unearned revenue had been recorded when cash was received.
c. Part of the store space is rented to Van Johnson, who operates an alteration shop. At year end, Van had not yet paid the $500 rent for December 1996 and no revenue had been recorded
d. On August 1, 1996, Nifty Threads had purchased and paid for a one-year fire insurance policy costing $2,400. This amount had been recorded as prepaid insurance.

Required Complete the following table for the transactions described above:

Assets =	Liabilities + Owners' Equity	+ Revenues − Expenses

Parentheses denote decreases in column balances.

PROBLEM 6-3 Effects of Transactions on Current Assets and Liabilities

For each of the following independent situations, identify the effect on the balance sheet account. Use + and − to indicate an increase or decrease in the account. Complete each set of transactions using the format provided.

a. **Transaction**	**Effect on Accounts Receivable**	**Effect on Net Income**	**Effect on Cash Flow**
Sold $8,000 of goods on credit			
Collected $11,000 from customers			
Net change			
b.	**Effect on Inventory**	**Effect on Net Income**	**Effect on Cash Flow**
Sold goods costing $3,000			
Purchased $2,400 of inventory for cash			
Net change			
c.	**Effect on Wages Payable**	**Effect on Net Income**	**Effect on Cash Flow**
Accrued $2,000 of unpaid wages			
Paid $1,700 in wages to employees			
Net change			
d.	**Effect on Prepaid Insurance**	**Effect on Net Income**	**Effect on Cash Flow**
Consumed 1 month of a 3-month insurance policy costing $9,000			
Paid $9,000 for a 3-month insurance policy			
Net change			
e.	**Effect on Unearned Rent**	**Effect on Net Income**	**Effect on Cash Flow**
Earned 1 month's rent from a 6-month lease of property for $18,000 per 6 months			
Received $18,000 cash in advance for a 6-month lease			
Net change			

f. **Transaction**	**Effect on Plant Assets**	**Effect on Net Income**	**Effect on Cash Flow**
Recognized $14,000 of depreciation expense			
Net change			

PROBLEM 6-4 Ethical Issues in Accounting

Hides, Inc., manufactures leather goods: belts, purses, and specialty items. These goods are sold to retailers throughout the country. The company's fiscal year ends December 31. In December, 1995, the company received orders for $12,000 of goods. Checks were received with the orders. The goods will be manufactured and shipped in January. Hides recorded the orders in December as:

Assets =		**Liabilities + Owners' Equity**	**+ Revenues − Expenses**	
Cash	12,000		Sales Revenue	12,000

The company reported the following summary information in its financial statements for 1995:

Assets	$250,000
Liabilities	240,000
Owners' Equity	10,000
Revenues	90,000
Expenses	83,000

Required Discuss any concerns you would have with the way in which Hides recorded the December orders. How should the transaction have been reported? What effect would the entry have on the company's summary financial information? What ethical problems are posed by this situation?

PROBLEM 6-5 Adjustments

The Flash-In-The-Pan Co. manufactures cooking products. On August 1, 1996, the company borrowed $100,000 from creditors. Semiannual interest payments of $6,000 are to be made to creditors beginning January 31, 1997. On July 1, 1996, the company purchased a one-year insurance policy for $8,000 and recorded it as prepaid insurance. On January 1, 1996, the company purchased equipment with an expected life of 4 years for $40,000. On October 1, 1996, the company rented some of its unused warehouse space to another company who agreed to pay $12,000 for the space every six months, beginning April 1, 1997.

Summary information reported by Flash for the fiscal year ended December 31, 1996, included:

Assets	$500,000
Liabilities	200,000
Owners' Equity	300,000
Revenues	120,000
Expenses	90,000

Flash failed to record any adjustments at the end of 1996 for interest, prepaid insurance, depreciation, and rent.

Required Complete the following table for the adjustments that Flash should make and describe the effect the transactions would have on the summary financial information:

Assets =	Liabilities + Owners' Equity	+ Revenues − Expenses

PROBLEM 6-6 Adjustments

The following account balances existed for Sounds, Inc., a recording studio, for three months ended August 31, 1995, prior to adjustments:

	Unadjusted	Adjustments	Adjusted
Cash	$ 35,000		
Accounts Receivable	23,500		
Supplies	12,800		
Prepaid Insurance	2,700		
Equipment	312,000		
Accumulated Depreciation—Equipment	(86,000)		
Buildings	433,000		
Accumulated Depreciation—Buildings	(57,000)		
Land	39,000		
Total Assets	**715,000**		
Unearned Revenues	$ 24,000		
Accounts Payable	18,600		
Interest Payable	4,000		
Wages Payable	0		
Note Payable	280,000		
Common Stock	200,000		
Retained Earnings*	149,400		
Total Liabilities & Stockholders' Equity	**676,000**		
Rent Revenues	$ 67,000		
Wages Expense	(24,000)		
Supplies Expense	0		
Insurance Expense			
Interest Expense	(4,000)		
Depreciation Expense			
Net Income	**$ 39,000**		

Net income has not been added for the current year.

The following additional information is available for transactions that have not been recorded for August:

a. Unearned revenues represent contracts for use of studio facilities. $8,000 of this amount had been earned by August 31.

b. $6,700 of supplies remained on hand on August 31.
c. Interest accumulates on the note in the amount of $2,000 per month. Interest has not been recorded for August.
d. $2,900 of wages earned in August are unpaid.
e. The insurance provides coverage for one year. The cost was $3,600 for the year.
f. Depreciation on equipment is $1,000 per month. Depreciation on buildings is $400 per month. No depreciation has been recorded for the quarter.

Required Record necessary adjustments in the table.

PROBLEM 6-7 Interpreting a Cash Flow Statement

A statement of cash flows is provided for Procter & Gamble Company for a recent fiscal year:

CONSOLIDATED STATEMENT OF CASH FLOWS
For Year Ended June 30 (Millions of Dollars)

	1992
Cash and Cash Equivalents, beginning of year	$ 1,384
Operating Activities	
Net earnings	1,872
Depreciation, depletion and amortization	1,051
Deferred income taxes	125
Decrease in accounts receivable	23
Decrease in inventories	160
Increase in payables and accrued liabilities	45
Other	(206)
	3,070
Investing Activities	
Capital expenditures	(1,911)
Proceeds from asset sales and retirements	291
Acquisitions	(1,240)
	(2,860)
Financing Activities	
Dividends to shareholders	(788)
Change in short-term debt	(156)
Additions to long-term debt	1,608
Reduction of long-term debt	(433)
Repurchase of shares	(49)
	182
Increase in Cash and Cash Equivalents	$ 392
Cash and Cash Equivalents, end of year	$ 1,776

Note: Slight modifications have been made to the format of the statement for purposes of simplifying the presentation.

Required Use the information from the statement of cash flows to answer the following questions:

a. What was the amount of change in Procter & Gamble's cash account for 1992?
b. What were the primary sources of cash for the company?

c. What were the primary uses of cash?
d. Why were depreciation and amortization added to net income in computing cash flow from operating activities?
e. Why were the decrease in receivables and inventory added and the increase in accounts payable added to net income in computing cash flow from operating activities?
f. Why were capital expenditures, asset sales and retirements, and acquisitions listed as investing activities?
g. Did short-term debt increase or decrease during the year?
h. How much new long-term debt was issued during the year? How much old long-term debt was paid off?
i. Does the company appear to be facing a cash flow problem? Explain your answer.

PROBLEM 6-8 Evaluating Income and Cash Flows

Selected financial statement information is reported below for the High Rise Co., a real estate developer. All amounts are in thousands.

For the year ended December 31, 1996		
Sales revenue	$5,600	
Cost of goods sold	3,200	
Operating expenses	1,400	
Net income	1,000	
Dividends paid	500	
For December 31	**1996**	**1995**
Cash	$ 670	$ 970
Accounts receivable	2,300	1,100
Inventories	4,700	2,500
Accounts payable	1,900	1,300
Notes payable	5,000	3,000

Required Prepare a statement of cash flows for High Rise, assuming that all important cash flow activities are reflected in the information provided above. What financial problems do you see in examining the financial information presented for High Rise? What are some potential causes of these problems?

PROBLEM 6-9 Interpreting the Cash Flow Statement

Portions of the consolidated statement of cash flows and income statement for Carnival Cruise Lines, Inc., are provided below:

YEAR ENDED NOVEMBER 30,	(in thousands) **1991**
Net income	$ 84,988
Adjustments:	
Depreciation and amortization	85,166
Non-cash interest	15,089
Loss from discontinued segment	168,836
Other	1,129

	(in thousands) 1991
Changes in operating assets and liabilities:	
Increase in receivables	(1,171)
Increase in inventory	(3,643)
Increase in prepaid and other	(5,305)
Decrease in accounts payable	(356)
Increase in accrued liabilities	1,559
Increase in customer deposits	3,539
Increase in deferred taxes	1,909
Net effect of discontinued operation	(7,322)
Net cash from operations	$344,418

YEAR ENDED NOVEMBER 30,	**1991**
Revenues	$1,404,704
Costs and Expenses	1,088,799
Operating Income	315,905
Other Income (Expense):	
Interest income	10,596
Interest expense	(65,428)
Other income	1,746
Income tax expense	(8,995)
	(62,081)
Income from Continuing Operations	253,824
Discontinued Operations:	
Loss from operations of Hotel and Casino segment	(33,373)
Estimated loss on disposal of Hotel and Casino segment	(135,463)
Net Income	$ 84,988

Required Use the information from the financial statements to answer each of the following questions:

a. How much cash did Carnival collect from customers in fiscal 1991? Consider all working capital adjustments related to customer receipts.
b. How much cash did Carnival pay for operating costs for 1991? Consider all working capital adjustments related to operating expenses.
c. How much cash did Carnival pay for interest in 1991?
d. What was Carnival's net cash flow from discontinued operations? (Adjust income statement items for cash flow items related to discontinued operations.)
e. What was Carnival's net cash flow from continuing operations? (Net cash from continuing operations = net cash from operating activities − net cash from discontinued operations.)

PROBLEM 6-10 Comparing Cash Flows

Following are portions of the statements of cash flows for two corporations for the fiscal year ended in 1991:

(In millions)	Toys "R" Us Inc.	Texas Instruments
Net income	$326	$(409)
Adjustments:		
Depreciation	79	590
(Increase) decrease in accounts receivable	(20)	11
(Increase) decrease in inventories	(45)	55
(Increase) decrease in other assets	(10)	1
Increase (decrease) in payables	(54)	63
Other adjustments	17	106
Net cash provided by operating activities	293	417
Net cash used in investing activities	(500)	(533)
Net cash provided by financing activities	201	165
Net change in cash	$(6)	$49

Required Write a short report comparing the financial performances of the two companies.

PROBLEM 6-11 Interpreting Cash Flows

A portion of the statement of cash flows is provided below from the 1991 Annual Report of Eastman Kodak Co.:

(In millions)	1991	1990	1989
Cash flows from operating activities:			
Net earnings	$ 17	$ 703	$ 529
Adjustments to reconcile net earnings to net cash provided by operating activities			
Depreciation and amortization	1,477	1,309	1,326
Provision (benefit) for deferred taxes	(147)	(165)	—
Retirement of properties	330	320	322
Increase in receivables	(15)	(88)	(174)
Decrease in inventories	114	82	518
Increases in liabilities excluding borrowings	755	414	334
Other items, net (mostly prepaid assets)	26	(65)	(236)
Total adjustments	2,540	1,807	2,090
Net cash provided by operating activities	$2,557	$2,510	$2,619

Required Prepare a short report comparing the operating activities of Kodak for the three years.

PROBLEM 6-12 Multiple-Choice Overview of the Chapter

1. Which of the following is an internal transaction:
   a. purchase of inventory on credit
   b. recognition of depreciation on plant assets

c. payment of amount owed to creditors
d. receipt of cash for rent to be earned in the future

2. The April Shower Company recognized $500 of interest on notes payable during September. The interest will be paid in December. Which of the following is the correct effect of the transaction in September?

	Interest Payable	Income from Operations
a.	+$500	−$500
b.	+$500	$0
c.	−$500	$0
d.	−$500	−$500

3. The Finkle Stein Company recognized $800 of rent earned during November. The rent was received in October. Which of the following is the correct effect of this transaction in November:

	Cash	Income from Operations
a.	+$800	+$800
b.	+$800	−$800
c.	$0	−$800
d.	$0	+$800

4. The primary purpose of adjustments is to:
   a. increase net income.
   b. minimize income taxes payable.
   c. correct errors that have been made during a period.
   d. obtain the proper account balances at the end of a period.
5. At December 31, Dinosaur Pest Control had not yet paid December's rent of $3,000. As of the same date, Dinosaur had collected $2,500 from customers for services that had not yet been performed. Which combination of the following items does the firm have at December 31?
   a. accrued revenue, accrued expense
   b. accrued revenue, deferred expense
   c. deferred revenue, accrued expense
   d. deferred revenue, deferred expense
6. A statement of cash flows, prepared using the indirect method, would report an increase in accounts receivable as:
   a. an addition to cash flow from financing activities.
   b. a subtraction from cash flow from financing activities.
   c. an addition to net income in computing cash flow from operating activities.
   d. a subtraction from net income in computing cash flow from operating activities.
7. The Horace Co. reported depreciation and amortization expense of $500,000 for the latest fiscal year. The depreciation and amortization expense would:
   a. increase cash flow for the year $500,000.
   b. decrease cash flow for the year $500,000.
   c. have no effect on cash flow for the year.
   d. have an effect on cash flow if assets were purchased during the year.
8. Rust Iron Co. purchased a three-month insurance policy on March 1, 1995. The company paid $3,000 for the policy. The amount of interest expense and cash outflow the company should report for March would be:

	Interest Expense	Cash Outflow
a.	$3,000	$3,000
b.	3,000	1,000
c.	1,000	3,000
d.	1,000	1,000

9. The Micro Fish Company recognized $20,000 of interest expense in 1996. The balance of the company's interest payable account decreased $4,000. The amount of cash paid by the company for interest in 1996 was:

a. $20,000
b. $24,000
c. $4,000
d. $16,000

10. Operating activities are reflected on a company's balance sheet primarily in:
    a. plant assets
    b. current assets and liabilities
    c. income from operations
    d. cash flow from operating activities

CASES

CASE 6-1 Analysis of Corporate Financial Statements

Financial statements from a recent annual report for Hewlett-Packard, a manufacturer of electronic equipment, are provided below and on the next two pages. Examine these statements and answer the questions that follow the statements.

Consolidated Statement of Earnings
For the year ended October 31
In millions except per share amounts

	1992
Net revenue:	
Equipment	$12,354
Services	4,056
	16,410
Costs and expenses:	
Cost of equipment sold	6,625
Cost of services	2,533
Research and development	1,620
Selling, general and administrative	4,228
	15,006
Earnings from operations	1,404
Interest income and other income	17
Interest expense	96
Earnings before taxes and effect of accounting change	1,325
Provision for taxes	444
Earnings before effect of accounting change	881
Transition effect of accounting change, net of taxes	332
Net earnings	$549
Net earnings per share	$2.18

Consolidated Balance Sheet
For the year ended October 31
In millions

	1992	1991
Assets		
Current assets:		
Cash and cash equivalents	$641	$625
Short-term investments	394	495
Accounts and notes receivable	3,497	2,976
Inventory	2,605	2,273
Other current assets	524	347
Total current assets	7,679	6,716
Property, plant and equipment	6,592	5,961
Accumulated depreciation	(2,943)	(2,616)
	3,649	3,345
Long-term receivables and other assets	2,372	1,912
	$13,700	$11,973
Liabilities and shareholders' equity		
Current liabilities:		
Notes payable and short-term borrowings	$1,384	$1,201
Accounts payable	925	686
Employee compensation and benefits	913	837
Taxes on earnings	490	381
Deferred revenues	449	375
Other accrued liabilities	933	583
Total current liabilities	5,094	4,063
Long-term debt	425	188
Other liabilities	633	210
Deferred taxes on earnings	49	243
Shareholders' equity:		
Common stock	874	1,010
Retained earnings	6,625	6,259
Total shareholders' equity	7,499	7,269
	$13,700	$11,973

Consolidated Statement of Cash Flows
For the year ended October 31
In millions

	1992
Cash flows from operating activities:	
Net earnings	$549
Adjustments to reconcile net earnings to cash provided by operating activities:	
Transition effect of accounting change	332
Depreciation and amortization	673
U.S. federal deferred taxes on earnings	(35)
Changes in assets and liabilities:	
Accounts and notes receivable	(480)
Inventories	(267)
Accounts payable	226
Taxes on earnings	31
Other current assets and liabilities	328
Other, net	(69)
	1,288

	1992
Cash flows from investing activities:	
Investment in property, plant and equipment	(1,032)
Disposition of property, plant and equipment	183
Purchase of short-term investments	(782)
Maturities of short-term investments	883
Purchase of long-term investments	(53)
Maturities of long-term investments	4
Acquisitions, net of cash required	(411)
Other, net	(58)
	(1,266)
Cash flows from financing activities:	
Increase in notes payable and short-term borrowings	186
Issuance of long-term debt	309
Repayment of current maturities of long-term debt	(79)
Issuance of common stock under employee stock plans	293
Repurchase of common stock	(530)
Dividends	(183)
Other, net	(2)
	(6)
Increase in cash and cash equivalents	16
Cash and cash equivalents at beginning of year	625
Cash and cash equivalents at end of year	$641

Note: Slight modifications have been made to the format of the statement for purposes of simplifying the presentation.

Required Use the financial statements to answer each of the following questions:

a. What were Hewlett-Packard's major operating activities during 1992? What were the major differences between the accrual and cash flow effects of these activities?
b. What were the ratios of net income to total assets and net income to stockholders' equity for 1992? If you owned 10,000 of the company's 250,824,000 shares of stock, what was your claim on the company's earnings for 1992? How much cash would you have received from the company?
c. What were the company's major sources of cash for 1992? What have been its major sources of financing? What major financing activities occurred in 1992?
d. What major investing activities occurred in 1992? What were the company's most important assets? What assets may be important to the company that are not reported on its balance sheet?

CASE 6-2 Interpreting Cash Flows

Review the financial report of General Mills, Inc., in Appendix B.

Required Prepare a short report analyzing each of the following issues:

a. What were the accrual and cash basis results of operating activities for 1992? Explain any major differences between the two results.
b. Identify which current assets and liabilities increased and decreased during 1992.
c. What has been the relationship between net income and cash flow from operating activities over the 1990–1992 period? What accounts for changes in the relationship over the three years?
d. How would you assess the company's financial performance for 1992?

PROJECTS

PROJECT 6-1 Comparing Financial Statements

Locate recent annual reports for three different companies in your library. Prepare a table comparing the cash flow from operating activities of the companies. List each company, major adjustments to net income, and net cash flow from operating activities. Describe the major differences you observe among the companies.

PROJECT 6-2 Researching Cash Flow

Write a comparative analysis of three companies in a particular industry. Focus your analysis on cash flow from operating activities. Explain major differences among the companies and draw conclusions about the relative strengths of each company. Explain differences between the amount of net income and amount of cash flow from operating activities for each company.

PROJECT 6-3 Using Business Journals

Use a periodicals index, such as the *Accounting and Tax Index* or the *Business Periodicals Index*, to identify recent articles that discuss cash flow problems faced by specific companies. Select an article from a journal available in your library. Read the article and write a summary of the problem discussed in the article.

PROJECT 6-4 Accruals and Deferrals

Assume you are trying to explain to someone who has little knowledge of accounting the reason for accruals and deferrals. Write an explanation that defines these terms, describes why they are necessary, and gives examples. Show your explanation to a friend and ask whether the person understands your explanation. If necessary, revise your explanation to respond to your friend's understanding of these concepts.

PROJECT 6-5 Examining Changes in Cash Flow

Examine a recent corporate annual report. Write a memo to your instructor in which you compare the cash flow statements for the three most recent years. What major changes occurred during the period that affected cash flows from operating, financing, and investing activities? What conclusions can you draw about the financial performance of the company from these changes?

CHAPTER 7

THE ACCOUNTING PROFESSION

CHAPTER *Overview*

The first six chapters of this book introduced the accounting information system. This chapter looks at the accounting profession. Accountants develop accounting systems, establish measurement and reporting rules, manage the processing of accounting information, and interpret accounting reports. The profession includes accountants in every segment of society and in every type of organization. Also, it includes rule-making, enforcement, and professional organizations that promote quality and integrity in the work performed by accountants.

This chapter examines the different types of work performed by accountants. It discusses the educational background and skills necessary for entry into the accounting profession. It provides a historical overview of the development of the profession and of the contemporary practice of accounting. And, it describes the process by which accounting measurement and reporting rules are developed in the U.S.

Major topics covered in this chapter include:

- The functions of the accounting profession.
- The historical development of accounting.
- The development of accounting standards.

CHAPTER *Objectives*

Once you have completed this chapter, you should be able to:

1. Explain the term "accounting profession."
2. Identify responsibilities of accountants in business organizations.
3. Identify responsibilities of public accountants.
4. Identify the purpose of an audit report.
5. Identify responsibilities of accountants in governmental and nonprofit organizations.
6. Explain the role of accountants in education.
7. Discuss educational requirements for entry into the accounting profession.
8. List important events in the development of accounting and understand their effects on contemporary accounting.
9. Identify organizations responsible for setting accounting standards in the U.S.
10. Explain why accounting standards are important to our economy.
11. List steps in the process of establishing accounting standards.
12. Identify the primary components of the conceptual framework used in establishing accounting standards for businesses in the U.S.

ACCOUNTING AS A PROFESSION

Objective 1
Explain the term "accounting profession."

A profession is a group of individuals who share specific skills and training. This group is accepted by society as being qualified to engage in certain services or activities that serve the public need. Most professions require their members to meet licensing requirements and often are regulated by government authorities. The accounting profession includes those who have attained a high level of knowledge of accounting through education and experience. These individuals use their skills to develop accounting systems, to prepare and evaluate accounting information, and to assist decision makers with the analysis and interpretation of this information. Some of these responsibilities require accountants to be licensed to perform certain services. To acquire a license, an accountant generally must complete a college degree with a specified number of business and accounting courses, pass a qualifying examination administered by the profession, and obtain experience in accounting practice.

Percentage of 1.2 Million U.S. Accountants in Various Organizations

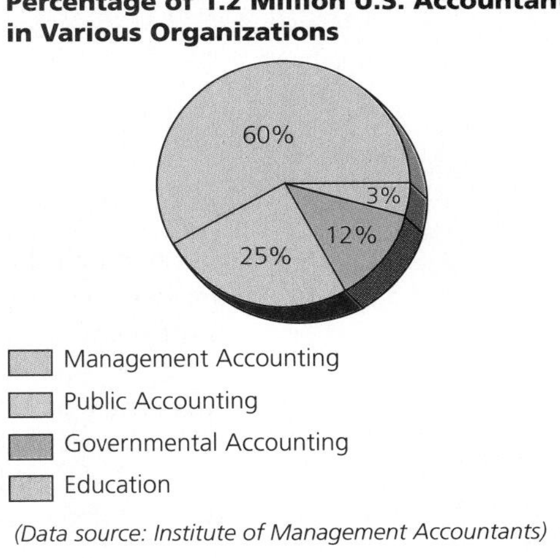

(Data source: Institute of Management Accountants)

The accounting profession encompasses accountants who work in businesses, public accounting firms, government and nonprofit organizations, and educational institutions. One of the distinguishing features of a profession is self-regulation. The accounting profession includes several professional organizations that oversee the activities of accountants. These organizations establish standards that are designed to promote competency and ethical behavior on the part of accounting practitioners for entry and continuation in the accounting profession.

The following sections examine the qualifications and responsibilities of accountants in more depth.

Management Accounting

Accountants play several roles in supporting the management of business organizations, as illustrated at the top of the next page.

Management accounting includes all accounting functions within business organizations. Many accountants who work in business organizations belong to the Institute of Management Accountants (IMA). The IMA is a national professional organization of management accountants and the sponsor of the Certified Management Accountant (CMA) program for individuals who meet education requirements and pass the CMA Examination, which is offered twice each year. The CMA designation is intended to indicate the attainment of professional competency in managerial accounting. Becoming a CMA normally is not required for employment in accounting, though it may enhance professional career opportunities. The IMA promotes ethical standards, continuing education,

Objective 2
Identify responsibilities of accountants in business organizations.

and research that assists in the practice of management accounting. Accountants are expected to update their knowledge and skills on an ongoing basis. CMAs must meet continuing education requirements each year.

Information Systems Development. All organizations require information systems to collect, summarize, and report information needed by internal and external decision makers. Larger organizations often maintain an information systems department. This department is responsible for designing and implementing information systems for a variety of functions, such as accounting, production, purchasing, and customer orders. Typically, these systems are computerized. Therefore, employees of these departments include programmers and computer systems analysts who understand how computers process data. Accountants assist in the development of these systems, particularly those needed to process accounting information. These accountants normally have been educated in both accounting and computer information systems.

Financial Accounting Management. Accountants oversee the processing of accounting information. While entering transactions in the accounting system is primarily a clerical activity, accountants are responsible for managing this activity to ensure efficiency and accuracy. Accountants are responsible for adjusting and closing entries and other nonroutine bookkeeping activities for which a detailed understanding of accounting is required. Also, accountants are responsible for providing information from the accounting system to meet the needs of other managers. They work with the information systems department in designing reports and procedures to get the needed information to the appropriate users promptly and accurately.

Financial Reporting. Accountants prepare financial statements and other reports for distribution to owners, creditors, employees, and regulatory authorities. Most large corporations prepare these reports quarterly. Most of these reports must be prepared in accordance with generally accepted accounting principles (GAAP) if they are distributed to owners, creditors, and other external users. Reports filed with regulatory authorities, such as the Securities and Exchange Commission, also must conform with GAAP. Some organizations must report to other regulatory authorities. For example, businesses that contract with government agencies must report to a contracting authority such as the Department of Defense. Most financial institutions must report to federal and state banking authorities. These authorities establish reporting requirements for the organizations that report to them.

Various government authorities require reports to determine conformity with fair trade and labor regulations. Other reports collect data for government economic planning. These reports provide indicators of how well the economy is performing, such as the amount of sales and the number of employees during a period.

Most businesses are required to file a variety of reports with taxing authorities at the federal, state, and local levels. These reports are used to determine compliance with income, sales, payroll, and other tax regulations.

Financial Planning and Analysis. Accountants play a direct role in the management of organizations making decisions that require an understanding of accounting information. Accountants analyze and interpret financial statements and other accounting reports to determine how well a company is performing. This information is used by managers in planning future operations and in making strategic decisions about obtaining and using resources.

Accountants assist in decisions about obtaining new capital from owners and creditors, the purchase of new assets, mergers with and acquisitions of other companies, sale of divisions, development of new product lines, expansion into new locations, replacement of assets, and strategies for improving performance and profitability.

Cost Accounting and Management. *Cost accounting* **includes those functions necessary to accumulate and report a company's costs.** *Cost management* **includes strategies and methods to reduce costs and increase competitiveness.** Accountants monitor a company's operations to determine whether actual costs for developing, purchasing, producing, marketing, and servicing products are consistent with expectations. They develop and analyze information to determine that a company is operating efficiently and effectively. If costs are out of line with expectations, they notify managers and employees and work with them to identify corrective actions. Accountants may work with managers and engineers in production and development to find ways to improve efficiency by reducing production costs.

Internal Auditing. Internal auditing is the process of evaluating a company's activities to assess whether appropriate procedures are being used and whether management policies are being implemented. Internal auditors identify ways for departments to improve their operations. Also, they consider whether departments and divisions are operating in the best interest of the company as a whole. Thus, they are concerned with how decisions are made and with how decisions made in one department affect other departments. Internal auditors also are concerned with the procedures a company uses to safeguard its resources to prevent theft, fraud, and mismanagement.

Internal control **is an organization's plan and the procedures it uses to safeguard its assets, ensure reliable information, promote efficiency, and encourage adherence to policies.** Federal law requires corporations that report to the SEC to have a system of internal controls. Internal control procedures include various techniques for promoting the control objectives. Procedures should be developed to identify, train, and retain competent employees. Employee responsibilities should be clearly defined so employees understand what is expected of them and how they will be evaluated. Company policies should establish how decisions are to be made and who has the authority to make them. Appropriate authorization for the use of resources is an important internal control procedure. Employee responsibilities should be divided so no single employee has control over acquisition, use, and record-keeping associated with resources. Separation of duties reduces the likelihood an employee can steal or misuse resources without being discovered by someone else in the organization. The following illustration summarizes some major internal control procedures:

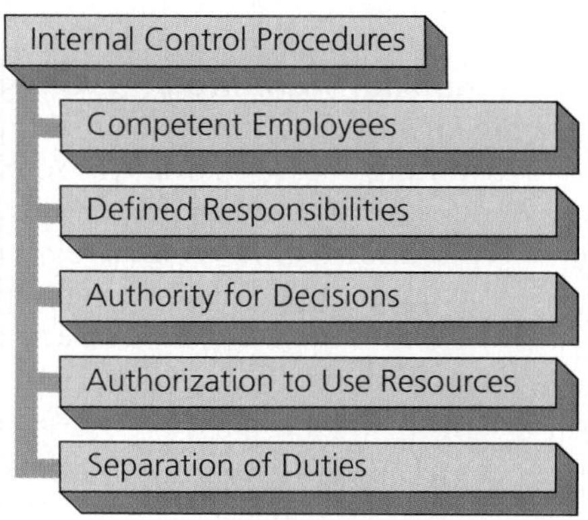

Internal auditors help in developing and evaluating a company's system of internal controls to ensure the system is operating effectively. They monitor the activities of employees to determine procedures are being followed. They investigate areas in which internal controls may be deficient or may not be operating properly. From the investigation, they determine whether inefficiency or misuse of resources is a problem. Internal auditors normally report to top management or to a company's board of directors any problems that warrant attention.

Many internal auditors belong to the Institute of Internal Auditors (IIA). The IIA, a national professional organization, sponsors the Certified Internal Auditor (CIA) Examination, which is offered nationally each year. The CIA designation is intended to indicate the attainment of professional competency in internal auditing. Being a CIA is not a normal requirement for employment in accounting, though, like the CMA, it may enhance professional career opportunities. Also, like the IMA, the IIA develops standards of professional and ethical conduct for internal auditors. CIAs are expected to complete continuing education requirements each year. An individual may be both a CMA and a CIA.

Public Accounting

Accountants provide services to the public as auditors, compilers and reviewers of financial statements, tax advisers, and consultants, as illustrated on the next page.

Independent auditing services are provided in the U.S. by certified public accountants (CPAs). A CPA is an individual who has met education, examination, and experience requirements imposed by a state government. A State Board of Public Accountancy is responsible for establishing and overseeing certification requirements.

Objective 3
Identify responsibilities of public accountants.

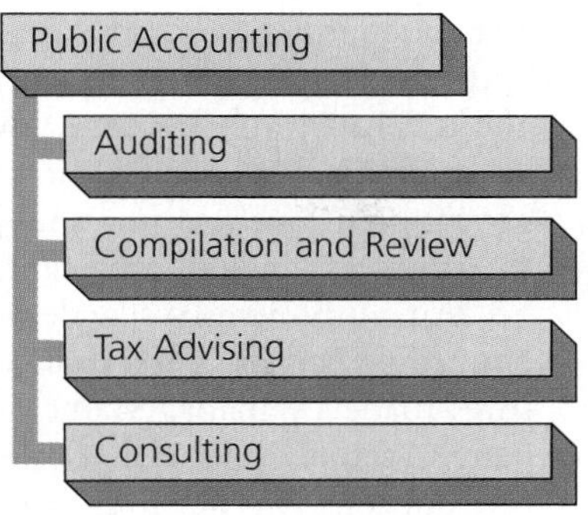

To become a CPA, an individual must pass the Uniform CPA Examination. This national examination, which is offered twice a year (May and November) in all states and territories, includes three sections (Practice and Theory, Business Law, and Auditing). Most states require applicants for the examination to have a college degree that includes a minimum number of hours in accounting and business administration courses. The number of hours varies from state to state. Many states have passed legislation requiring applicants to have completed a minimum of 150 semester (or equivalent quarter) hours of course work, including a bachelor's degree. This legislation generally requires at least 30 hours of accounting courses. Some states require experience in accounting, usually by working for a CPA, before licensing a person who has passed the CPA Examination to practice as an independent accountant.

Many CPAs belong to the American Institute of Certified Public Accountants (AICPA) and to a State Society of CPAs in the state where they practice. The AICPA is a national professional organization that, along with the State Societies, oversees the practice of public accounting in the U.S. Members are required to complete an average of 40 hours of continuing professional education each year and to abide by a strict code of ethics and professional conduct. These requirements are intended to ensure that CPAs remain current in their knowledge and provide quality professional service to the public.

CPA firms may be large, with thousands of professionals, or may be small, perhaps with only one professional. The largest international accounting firms have offices throughout the world. The six largest firms, known as the "Big Six," are: Arthur Andersen, Coopers and Lybrand, Deloitte and Touche, Ernst and Young, KPMG Peat Marwick, and Price Waterhouse.

Learning Note

All CPAs are not in public practice. A CPA may work in business, in governmental and nonprofit organizations, and in education. Anyone who passes certification requirements can be a CPA. A CPA also may be a CMA and a CIA.

Certification of accountants in public practice is common in most countries. The European equivalent of the CPA is the Chartered Accountant (CA). To become a Chartered Accountant, candidates must pass several exams and serve an apprenticeship with a Chartered Accounting firm.

Auditing. The public practice of auditing differs from internal auditing. Internal auditors are employees of the organizations they audit; therefore, they are not independent of those organizations. To provide auditing services, external auditors must be independent, in fact and appearance, of the organizations they audit. Therefore, they are referred to as independent auditors or independent accountants. An external financial audit provides assurance to owners, creditors, government authorities, and others who rely on a company's financial reports that they are faithful representations of the company's economic activities.

An audit involves a detailed, systematic investigation of a company's accounting records. The auditor attempts to verify that the numbers and disclosures made by management in its financial reports are consistent with the company's actual financial position and operating results. Records, operating procedures, contracts, resources, and management policies and decisions are examined to provide evidence of the fairness of financial report information. Auditors determine internal control procedures exist and are being used. They compare the information in financial reports with information from prior years and other sources to confirm their fairness.

Objective 4
Identify the purpose of an audit report.

A primary purpose of public accounting is attestation. ***Attestation* occurs when an auditor affirms the fairness of financial statements by signing an audit report.** Auditors issue an audit report upon completion of their audit work. **The *audit report,* or *audit opinion,* provides public notice of the auditor's belief about the fairness of the accompanying financial information.** Only a licensed CPA may give a formal opinion about audited financial information. Exhibit 7-1 provides an example of an auditor's report.

Exhibit 7-1 Example Auditor's Report

Report of Independent Accountants

To the Shareholders and
Board of Directors
of Pennzoil Company

We have audited the accompanying consolidated balance sheets of Pennzoil Company (a Delaware corporation) and subsidiaries as of December 31, 1991 and 1990, and the related consolidated statements of income, shareholders' equity, and cash flows for each of the three years in the period ended December 31, 1991. These financial statements are the responsibility of the Company's management. Our responsibility is to express an opinion on these financial statements based on our audits.

We conducted our audits in accordance with generally accepted auditing standards. Those standards require that we plan and perform the audit to obtain reasonable assurance about whether the financial statements are free of material misstatement. An audit includes examining, on a test basis, evidence supporting the amounts and disclosures in the financial statements. An audit also includes assessing the accounting principles used and significant estimates made by management, as well as evaluating the overall financial statement presentation. We believe that our audits provide a reasonable basis for our opinion.

In our opinion, the financial statements referred to above present fairly, in all material respects, the financial position of Pennzoil Company and subsidiaries as of December 31, 1991 and 1990, and the results of their operations and their cash flows for each of the three years in the period ended December 31, 1991 in conformity with generally accepted accounting principles.

As discussed in Note 5 to the Consolidated Financial Statements, as of January 1, 1991, the Company changed its method of accounting for post-retirement costs other than pensions.

ARTHUR ANDERSEN & CO.

Houston, Texas
February 20, 1992

The audit report contains several important sections as described in Exhibit 7-2.

Exhibit 7-2 Sections of an Audit Report

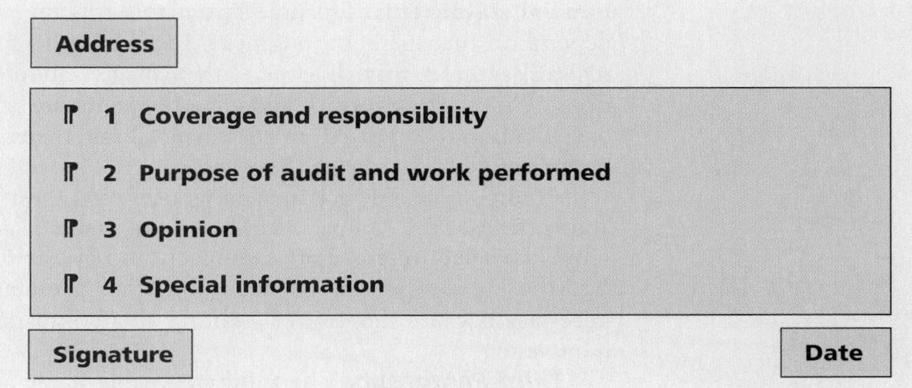

An audit report often is addressed to the shareholders of the company. Normally, an audit is performed on behalf of the shareholders and other external parties. Audits may be requested for special purposes, for example, to secure a bank loan or as part of merger negotiations. The audit report may be addressed to specific users who will receive the report, such as bank loan officers. Auditors are responsible for protecting the interests of those who will use audited financial statements.

Many corporations have formed audit committees. **An *audit committee* is composed of members of a corporation's board of directors who discuss the audit and its findings with the independent auditors.** The audit committee is informed by auditors of any important problems discovered during the audit. The committee keeps other members of the board informed of audit activities.

First Paragraph. The first paragraph of the audit report identifies the statements and fiscal periods covered by the audit. A typical audit will cover all the primary financial statements: income statement, balance sheet, and statement of cash flows. The most recent three years of operations normally are covered by the audit. For most large corporations, the audited financial statements are the consolidated statements of the parent and its subsidiaries.

The first paragraph also describes the responsibilities of auditors and management. Management is responsible for preparing the statements. By publishing the statements for external users, management asserts the statements are a fair and accurate description of a company's economic activities. Auditors are responsible for competently using the technology available to them to confirm (or disconfirm) the assertions of management. This technology includes procedures to obtain evidence to support the auditors' beliefs. For example, auditors inspect certain resources, such as inventory and fixed assets, to confirm their existence.

Second Paragraph. The second paragraph of the audit report summarizes the audit process. *Generally Accepted Auditing Standards (GAAS)* **include procedures used in conducting an audit to help auditors form an opinion about the fairness of the audited statements.** GAAS are developed in the U.S. by the Auditing Standards Board (ASB). The ASB is a division of the AICPA. Auditing standards are published and updated periodically by the AICPA. Failure to conform with GAAS in an independent audit is a major violation of a CPA's responsibilities.

From evidence collected from using GAAS, auditors assert the financial statements are free of material misstatement. *Materiality* **is a criterion for establishing the importance of a potential misstatement in audited financial statements.** Financial statements contain estimates and allocations that depend on management judgment. In addition to finding errors in accounting records, auditors may disagree with managers about their estimates and allocations. Unless these errors and disagreements are material (important) to the overall amounts reported on the financial statements, however, auditors are not required to take action on these issues.

Auditors examine accounting records on a "test basis." Auditors do not examine 100% of a company's transactions. Instead, auditors use sampling techniques to select representative transactions. By verifying these transactions, auditors form an opinion about the financial statements as a whole. Sampling is necessary because the cost of auditing all a company's records generally is prohibitive.

Third Paragraph. The third paragraph of the audit report states the auditor's opinion. An opinion may be one of several types:

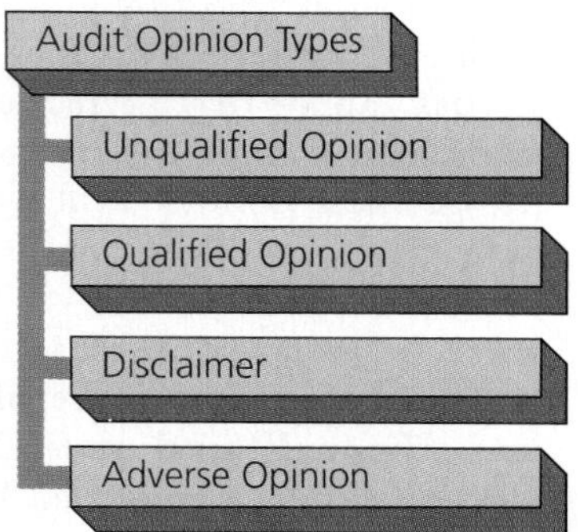

Most audit reports provide an **unqualified opinion**. This opinion states that the auditor believes the financial statements fairly present the company's actual economic events for the period covered by the audited statements. Fair presentation means the financial statements are prepared in conformity with GAAP and are free from material omissions and misstatements.

A **qualified opinion** is issued when the auditor believes the statements are fairly presented except for the presentation of specific items. The exceptions are for accounting procedures the auditor does not believe conform with GAAP.

A **disclaimer** is issued when the auditor does not believe sufficient evidence is available or the auditor cannot perform sufficient audit work to form an opinion about the fairness of the financial statements. This problem may arise because of limitations placed on the audit by management or because of missing or incomplete records.

An **adverse opinion** is issued when the auditor believes the financial statements do not fairly represent a company's economic activities. Such an opinion is issued if the auditor believes the statements are potentially misleading. A company whose statements contain major departures from GAAP would receive an adverse opinion.

Almost all audit reports for major corporations contain unqualified opinions or opinions with minor qualifications. The SEC requires these corporations to file reports that do not contain major qualifications, disclaimers, or adverse opinions. Therefore, these corporations are required to conform with GAAP and to provide the information necessary to satisfy their auditors that their statements are fairly presented. When a major disagreement exists between an auditor and a client company, the auditor may withdraw from the audit without issuing an opinion or the company may seek a different auditor. SEC regulated corporations must report major disagreements and auditor changes to the SEC.

Qualified opinions, disclaimers, and even adverse opinions are more common for businesses that are not regulated by the SEC and for governmental and nonprofit organizations. These organizations may not be required to conform with GAAP, and their audit reports may include departures from GAAP.

Fourth Paragraph. The first three paragraphs are standard for most corporate audit reports. A fourth paragraph is included only if the auditor believes additional information should be noted in the opinion that is not contained in the earlier paragraphs. In Exhibit 7-1, the auditor notes the company has changed accounting methods for a particular item. Companies are expected to be consistent in their application of accounting methods from year to year. When a company changes methods that may have an effect on the amounts reported in the financial statements, the auditor is required to note the change in the audit report to alert readers.

Signature and Date. Audit reports must be signed by the public accounting firm that performed the audit, thus indicating its responsibility. The date of the audit report is the date all audit work was completed for the periods covered by the report. The auditor is responsible for disclosing any material information that might affect a decision maker's interpretation of the financial statements through the date of the audit report.

Other Audit Report Formats. The standard audit report described above is the most common report included in annual reports of U.S. corporations. Variations exist, however. Some public accounting firms prefer a modified format of the standard report. For example, the following audit report was included in the 1991 annual report of Hewlett-Packard Company:

> In our opinion, the accompanying consolidated balance sheet and the related consolidated statements of earnings, of cash flows and of shareholders' equity present fairly, in all material respects, the financial position of Hewlett-Packard Company and its subsidiaries at October 31, 1991 and 1990, and the results of their operations and their cash flows for each of the three years in the period ended October 31, 1991, in conformity with generally accepted accounting principles. These financial statements are the responsibility of the company's management; our responsibility is to express an opinion on these financial statements based on our audits. We conducted our audits of these statements in accordance with generally accepted auditing standards which require that we plan and perform the audit to obtain reasonable assurance about whether the financial statements are free of material misstatement. An audit includes examining, on a test basis, evidence supporting the amounts and disclosures in the financial statements, assessing the accounting principles

> used and significant estimates made by management, and evaluating the overall financial statement presentation. We believe that our audits provide a reasonable basis for the opinion expressed above.
>
> Price Waterhouse (Signature)
> San Francisco, California
> November 31, 1991

Careful reading of the paragraph reveals that it contains the same information as the standard three-paragraph report issued by most auditors. The audit report normally will convey the same information for most major corporations, regardless of variations in format.

Audit reports for foreign corporations differ from those of U.S. corporations. Different countries establish their own auditing and accounting standards. The format of the audit report depends on the auditing standards of the country in which a company has its principal operations. For example, the following report appeared in the 1991 annual report of the British Petroleum Company:

> We have audited the accounts set out on pages 34 to 52 in accordance with Auditing Standards.
>
> In our opinion the accounts give a true and fair view of the state of affairs of the company and of the group at 31 December 1991 and of the profit and source and application of funds of the group for the year then ended and have been properly prepared in accordance with the Companies Act of 1985.
>
> Ernst & Young
> Chartered Accountants
> London
> 13 February 1992

Though shorter than U.S. audit reports, the British report includes similar information. Several terminology differences are apparent: "true and fair view" substitutes for present fairly. "State of affairs" refers to financial position; "profit" refers to operating results, and "source and application of funds" to changes in cash and other working capital items. The term "group" is common in European reporting and refers to a parent and its consolidated subsidiaries. The Companies Act is legislation regulating accounting and financial reporting in the United Kingdom.

Management Responsibilities for Financial Statements. The audit report for U.S. corporations notes that financial statements are the responsibility of management. Most corporate annual reports include a statement by management identifying their responsibilities. For example, the following was included in the 1991 annual report of Johnson & Johnson:

> Report of Management
>
> The management of Johnson & Johnson is responsible for the integrity and objectivity of the accompanying financial statements and related information. The statements have been prepared in conformity with generally accepted accounting principles, and include amounts that are based on our best judgments with due consideration given to materiality. The financial statements are consistent in all material respects with guidelines issued to date by the International Accounting Standards Committee.
>
> Management maintains a system of internal accounting controls monitored by a corporate staff of professionally trained internal auditors who travel worldwide. This system is designed to provide reasonable assurance, at reasonable cost, that assets are safeguarded and that transactions and events are

recorded properly. While the Company is organized on the principles of decentralized management, appropriate control measures are also evidenced by well-defined organizational responsibilities, management selection, development and evaluation processes, communicative techniques, financial planning and reporting systems and formalized procedures.

It has always been the policy and practice of the Company to conduct its affairs ethically and in a socially responsible manner. This responsibility is characterized and reflected in the Company's Credo and Policy on Business Conduct which are distributed throughout the Company. Management maintains a systematic program to ensure compliance with these policies.

Coopers & Lybrand, independent auditors, is engaged to audit our financial statements. Coopers & Lybrand obtains and maintains an understanding of our internal control structure and conducts such tests and other auditing procedures considered necessary in the circumstances to express the opinion in the report that follows.

The Audit Committee of the Board of Directors, composed solely of outside directors, meets periodically with the independent auditors, management and internal auditors to review their work and confirm that they are properly discharging their responsibilities. In addition, the independent auditors, the General Counsel and the Vice President, Internal Audit, are free to meet with the Audit Committee without the presence of management to discuss results of their work and observations on the adequacy of internal financial controls, the quality of financial reporting and other relevant matters.

Signed by Ralph S. Larsen, Chairman, Board of Directors and Chief Executive Officer, and by Clark H. Johnson, Vice President, Finance and Chief Financial Officer.

Through this report, management acknowledges its responsibility for the financial statements, for implementing a system of internal controls to ensure reliability of the statements, to maintain ethical business practices in the company, and to work with its external auditors. The report also describes the role of the corporation's audit committee. Most large U.S. corporations are required by law to maintain a system of internal controls and to provide a statement of management responsibility with their annual financial reports.

Limitations of the Audit. Auditors are responsible for being competent in audit technology and for using this technology to the best of their abilities. They are expected to use reasonable judgment and due diligence in performing the audit, and should demonstrate the highest integrity and remain unbiased in their judgments. But, no audit, however well-performed, can provide complete assurance that a company's financial statements are totally accurate. While auditors should be alert to the possibility of management fraud, elaborate schemes have been perpetrated by some managers to prevent the auditor from detecting the fraud and its effect on the financial statements. Most cases in which auditors have failed to discover material misstatements have involved fraud on the part of a company's managers and/or employees.

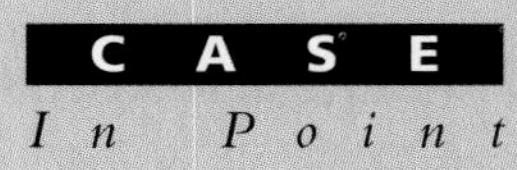

One of the most elaborate of recent management frauds was the ZZZZ Best case. The company was started by a young entrepreneur on a small budget to provide cleaning services for businesses and other clients. The business grew rapidly and became a major corporation. The top managers of the company colluded to defraud their investors by reporting exaggerated revenues. They reported cleaning contracts that did not exist. These nonexistent contracts and revenues were used to raise additional capital. Instead of investing the money in the company, managers used it for their own purposes.

The managers engaged in major deception to prevent the company's auditors from discovering their fraud. The auditors were shown several locations throughout the country where the company supposedly was working on contracts. In reality, these locations had been rented or borrowed temporarily and were made to look like work sites. Records and contracts were forged to make the auditors believe the work was legitimate.

Compilation and Review. In addition to audits, public accountants provide compilation and review services, especially for smaller businesses. ***Compilation*** **occurs when an independent accountant prepares financial statements for a client from the client's accounting records.** ***Review*** **occurs when an independent accountant examines a client's financial statements to provide assurance they appear to be in good order.** Compilation is a service requested by organizations that may not have the expertise to prepare their own financial statements. Review is a service requested by organizations that do not require an audit. Instead, they need an independent examination of their financial statements to provide some assurance the statements report the organization's economic activities. For example, as part of a loan arrangement, a bank may request a company provide financial statements that have been reviewed by an independent accountant. Financial statements that have been compiled or reviewed by a public accountant are unaudited. Therefore, they should not be relied on as being a faithful representation of a company's economic activities to the extent of audited statements.

Tax Advising. Another service performed by public accountants is tax advising. Public accountants work with individuals and businesses to prepare tax returns and to help with tax planning. Tax laws and regulations often are complex. Most people do not have the time or expertise to comply with reporting requirements and to avoid overpayment of taxes. Businesses may employ their own tax professionals to assist with reporting and planning requirements. Most companies, however, rely on public accountants for part or most of this work.

Tax regulations change frequently; therefore, tax professionals continuously update their knowledge to remain current. They use this expertise to advise clients on business and personal financial strategies that will minimize their tax obligations. Much of this advice focuses on income taxes, especially at the federal level. State, local, and international tax issues are important, as well, for many corporations. Estate and gift taxes are an important concern for many individuals.

Since many corporations pay taxes on their income, effective tax planning can save these companies large amounts of money. Taxes can have a major effect on the accounting methods used by businesses. Accounting methods determine how much revenue or expense will be reported during a fiscal period. By selecting methods that reduce revenues and increase expenses for a period, a company can reduce its required tax payments. Accounting and tax measurement rules limit the choices available to companies. Thus, considerable skill may be required to identify methods that will reduce taxes and not violate accounting or tax rules. The effect of taxes on accounting methods will be considered in future chapters.

Consulting. Another major service provided by public accountants is consulting. Consulting encompasses a wide variety of activities:

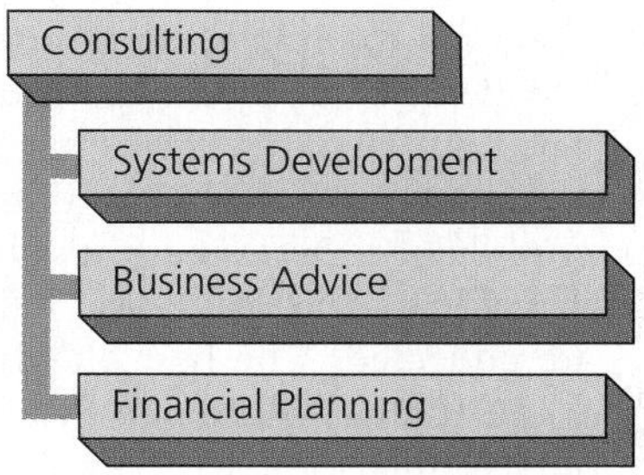

Accountants assist businesses in designing and implementing information systems. This assistance may involve selecting hardware and software, tailoring the system to the needs of the business, and training employees to use the system and understand the information it provides. Public accounting firms also may provide bookkeeping services for their clients, especially for those too small to have their own accounting departments. Accounting firms often use computers to maintain accounting records and prepare financial statements for clients.

Accountants assist managers in understanding financial information about their businesses. They may examine a company to identify ways it could operate more effectively or efficiently. They may examine other companies that are merger or acquisition prospects to estimate the value of these companies. They may help companies identify personnel for positions in a company, especially where specific managerial or financial skills are required for the positions.

Accountants also work with individuals and small business owners. They help them understand their finances and plan their personal or business financial activities. They advise them on investments, resource acquisitions, insurance needs, retirement plans, and many other issues. Accountants are multipurpose financial advisers.

Governmental and Nonprofit Organizations

Objective 5
Identify responsibilities of accountants in governmental and nonprofit organizations.

Accounting activities in federal, state, and local governments and in nonprofit organizations, such as nonprofit hospitals and universities, are similar to those of businesses. These nonbusiness organizations require accounting systems, prepare financial reports, analyze financial information for decision purposes, and develop internal control systems. Often they are audited by independent accountants. In these respects, the earlier discussion of business organization accounting applies to nonbusiness organizations as well. Management accountants work in governmental and nonprofit organizations as they do in businesses. Public accountants provide auditing and other services to governmental and nonprofit organizations.

Nonbusiness organizations are different from businesses in several respects. The production of goods is not a major activity for most nonbusiness organizations. Therefore, some of the cost accounting issues that are critical for many businesses are not as important for these organizations. Most nonbusiness organizations are tax-exempt. Therefore, the tax issues that apply to businesses are not of concern. Tax-exempt organizations are required to file tax reports, however, and to establish that they have met requirements for tax-exempt status.

A major accounting issue for governments involves the receipt, rather than payment, of taxes. Taxes are a major source of revenues for governments. Accountants who work in government are concerned with tax assessment and compliance. Assessment involves determination of the amount of taxes owed by individuals and businesses. Compliance involves ensuring that amounts owed are collected. The best known of the organizations concerned with these issues is the Internal Revenue Service (IRS), which is a major employer of accountants. Similar organizations exist at the state government level.

Governments also are involved in audit activities. State governments have an audit division responsible for auditing the various departments and divisions of state government. In some states, these auditors have responsibility for local governments, as well. The General Accounting Office (GAO) is responsible for auditing the federal government. The GAO audits federal government departments and activities and reports its findings to Congress. Other government agencies are involved in audits of organizations that receive government funds and contracts. Government agencies also audit businesses regulated by federal agencies, such as certain banks, savings and loans, and other financial institutions.

Accountants also are employed by government organizations such as the Federal Bureau of Investigation (FBI). Criminal behavior often involves theft and fraud. Accountants investigate suspected cases of financial mismanagement to identify the existence, type, and amount of criminal behavior.

Education

Objective 6
Explain the role of accountants in education.

Accounting is taught in high schools, community colleges, four-year colleges and universities, and graduate schools. The number of accounting faculty has risen sharply in the past two decades as the demand for accounting courses and graduates has increased. Accounting faculty are educated as accountants, as educators, and as researchers. Many have been employed in the practice of accounting.

Accounting faculty typically have completed a masters degree in accounting or business administration. Many have completed a doctorate with a specialization in accounting. The doctorate is particularly important for those who want faculty positions in universities with research expectations. The task of these faculty is both to disseminate knowledge through teaching and to expand knowledge in the accounting discipline through research. Faculty in larger universities often specialize in a particular area of accounting, such as managerial, auditing, accounting systems, or taxation.

Preparation for an Accounting Career

Objective 7
Discuss educational requirements for entry into the accounting profession.

The previous section described employment opportunities available in accounting. The flexibility an accounting degree offers for employment in a wide variety of organizations has made accounting a popular college major. To take advantage of these opportunities, students must obtain both a high level of technical knowledge and a broad level of professional skills.

Accounting is a technical profession. Students typically take courses in the preparation and analysis of financial accounting information, in management and cost accounting, in governmental and nonprofit accounting, in accounting information systems, in taxation of individuals and corporations, and in auditing. Along with courses in business administration, these courses help develop the technical and business skills needed by accountants.

In addition to technical knowledge, skills in communication, group behavior, problem solving, and logical reasoning are required of accountants. Knowledge of accounting is not sufficient. An accountant must be able to communicate technical information to those who use accounting information. Clear and effective presentation and writing skills are essential. Accountants often work in teams with managers, engineers, and other accountants; they must be able to work effectively in these settings to achieve team objectives. They must be able to provide leadership and guidance in achieving group goals when the need arises.

Accountants are required to use judgment in solving problems. Often, problems do not have obvious answers. Choices have to be made among alternatives. An ability to grasp the relevant facts, identify alternatives, and propose workable solutions is critical to success. Accountants should enjoy working with people. Public accountants, in particular, must market their services to clients. A willingness to accept responsibility, without close supervision, is an important attribute.

Perhaps the most important requirement for success in accounting is integrity. Accountants must make difficult choices. They are under constant pressure to make choices that will affect the welfare of managers, stockholders, colleagues, and other individuals. These choices require accountants to be fair and unbiased in their decisions. The reputation of the accounting profession for fairness and ethical behavior is essential for the role it plays in society.

Students interested in accounting careers should take every opportunity to develop the skills required by the profession. For example, courses in writing, public speaking, and group behavior are highly desirable. Courses in business ethics and leadership can be valuable. Humanities and liberal arts courses that require exercising independent thought and judgment can be useful. Mathematics can help in developing reasoning skills.

Another skill increasingly useful for accountants is the ability to speak a foreign language. The globalization of business has led to increasing interrelationships between accountants and managers of multinational corporations. The ability to converse with foreign managers, along with an understanding of their cultures, can be extremely valuable. An understanding of international business and accounting is important in addition to developing these skills.

Accounting provides an excellent background for a variety of career opportunities. Corporate managers often find an accounting education prepares them for their decision-making responsibilities. Financial analysts and bank officers frequently have accounting backgrounds. An accounting education also is good preparation for those who plan to attend law school, especially if they are interested in corporate or tax law.

SELF-STUDY PROBLEM 7-1

Listed below are responsibilities of the accounting profession. For each item, identify whether the responsibility is provided by management accountants, public accountants, governmental and nonprofit accountants, or accounting educators. Some responsibilities may be provided by more than one type of accountant.

1. Development of accounting systems.
2. Evaluation of whether company policies are being implemented.
3. Preparation of tax returns.
4. Determination that taxpayers have complied with tax regulations.
5. Development of new accounting knowledge.
6. Independent evaluation of an organization's financial statements.
7. Advising managers about the interpretation of financial information.
8. Determination of the cost of producing goods and services.
9. Preparation of those who wish to enter the accounting profession.
10. Providing financial planning advice to individuals and business managers.

The solution to Self-Study Problem 7-1 appears at the end of the chapter.

THE HISTORICAL DEVELOPMENT OF ACCOUNTING

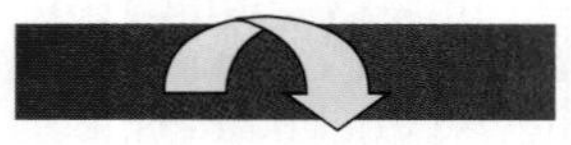

Accounting has evolved over a long period of time. It has changed in response to economic, social, and political events that have affected the need for accounting information. Exhibit 7-3 lists some of the important events in the development of accounting.

Historical Developments to the Early 1900s

Accounting is as old as recorded history; in fact, writing and math sprang from the need for record keeping. Ancient Babylonian cuneiform tablets recorded information about the quantity and types of agricultural goods produced. Modern forms of record keeping can be traced to the Middle Ages. Trade became important in Europe with the development of ships and navigation tools. Bookkeeping developed to document resources exchanged in commerce and debtor and creditor relationships. It was a common practice for an accountant

Objective 8
List important events in the development of accounting and understand their effects on contemporary accounting.

Exhibit 7-3 Important Events in Accounting History

Date	Event
2000 B.C.	Development of Record Keeping
1200–1400 A.D.	Development of Modern Bookkeeping
1494	Pacioli's Method of Venice
1750–1850	Industrial Revolution and Rise of the Corporation
1792	New York Stock Exchange Formed
1887	American Institute of Accountants Formed
1896	First CPA Examination
1913	Income Taxation Approved in the U.S.
1929	Collapse of Stock Market
1933	Securities Act of 1933
1934	Securities and Exchange Act of 1934 and Formation of Securities and Exchange Commission
1936	Committee on Accounting Procedure Formed
1959	Accounting Principles Board Formed
1973	Financial Accounting Standards Board and International Accounting Standards Committee Formed
1984	Governmental Accounting Standards Board Formed
1991	Federal Accounting Standards Advisory Board Formed

to accompany commercial voyages. The accountant was responsible for keeping track of goods to be traded, recording amounts of exchanges, and reporting to investors on the outcomes of their ventures.

One of the first known descriptions of double-entry bookkeeping was published in 1494 by Luca Pacioli, an Italian monk. Italy was the center of commerce in the Western world at the beginning of the Renaissance. It lay on the major trade routes between Europe and Asia. Therefore, it is no surprise that accounting was practiced in Italy during this period. Pacioli referred to his method of bookkeeping as the Method of Venice. This method provided the foundation for modern accounting.

The Industrial Revolution. Accounting advanced during the Industrial Revolution (approximately 1750-1850). This was a period of rapid development of manufacturing technology. New products and production processes required greater investments of capital and better management skills than before. The corporation became an important form of business organization because of its ability to raise large amounts of capital. Corporate managers required more sophisticated accounting systems than their predecessors to provide information necessary for operating complex organizations. Managerial accounting techniques developed to assist managers in tracking manufacturing costs and in evaluating the performances of their companies.

The corporate form of organization has had an important effect on the use of accounting information by managers. A single manager cannot oversee the activities of a large, complex organization. Therefore, an organized hierarchy of managers performing specific tasks is needed in these corporations. Lower levels of managers report to higher levels. Managers in different divisions or locations must communicate with managers in other divisions or locations. Accounting information provides a means for managers to communicate with each other about many aspects of corporate activities. Many accounting procedures and reporting formats have been developed to meet these needs. This information is not regulated, as is information provided to stockholders, since managers are the providers and users of the information. Thus, each corporation develops its own internal reporting procedures to help managers make planning and control decisions.

Market and Professional Developments. The New York Stock Exchange (NYSE) was formed in 1792. The exchange was important for facilitating the growing trade in corporate stocks. Also, it was important because it required financial reporting by member corporations by the early 1900s. The NYSE's efforts were one of the first attempts in the U.S. to regulate reporting to stockholders.

Increasing operating complexity and demand for capital created a need for accounting information and for greater accounting skills. The earliest major professional accounting organization in the U.S. was created in 1887. The American Institute of Accountants later became the American Institute of Certified Public Accountants (AICPA). Since its formation, the AICPA has played a major role in determining the qualifications of public accountants and in regulating their activities.

Income Taxation. Adoption of the 16th amendment to the U.S. Constitution in 1913 permitted federal taxation of individual and corporate income. Taxation of income is not possible without rules and reporting requirements that determine how income will be computed. Therefore, taxation has had an important effect on accounting practice and the accounting profession. The Internal Revenue Service (IRS) was created as a government agency to oversee tax reporting and collection. The Internal Revenue Code legislates tax accounting and reporting rules. These tax rules were developed primarily from the accounting and financial reporting rules used by businesses.

Income taxes are important to business accounting for two reasons. First, they create an incentive for the federal government to monitor accounting practices. The government is concerned with full and fair reporting of income to ensure the proper payment of taxes. Second, most individuals and many small businesses rely on accounting rules used in computing their taxes when they report on their financial conditions. For example, if an individual wishes to obtain a mortgage to purchase a home, the lending financial institution may ask for a copy of the person's most recent federal tax return. Also, many proprietorships, partnerships, and some small corporations maintain their accounting records using accounting rules acceptable for tax reporting. When they wish to borrow money, they often provide financial reports developed from these accounting records to lending institutions.

Federal Regulation in the 1900s

The early 1900s was a period of intense corporate activity. Many corporations were created and many individuals invested in stock. The collapse of the stock market in 1929 resulted in the loss of much personal wealth and a demand for increased regulation of corporate financial reporting. Many people believed a cause of the collapse was a lack of sufficient information about corporate activities and a lack of government oversight of the stock markets.

In response to these concerns, the U.S. Congress passed the **Securities Act of 1933**. This legislation required most corporations to file registration statements before selling stock to investors. As a part of these statements, corporations were required to provide financial reports containing balance sheets and income statements. Additional legislation, the **Securities and Exchange Act of 1934,** required corporations to provide annual financial reports to stockholders. The legislation also required that these reports be audited by independent accountants. The 1934 act also created the Securities and Exchange Commission (SEC) as a federal agency reporting to Congress. The SEC was given responsibility for overseeing external financial reporting by publicly-traded corporations.

Learning Note

Corporate stocks and bonds are referred to as securities. Stocks are equity securities. Bonds are debt securities. Publicly-traded corporations are those whose securities are traded through security exchanges and brokers.

Currently, the SEC requires publicly-traded corporations to publish annual and quarterly financial reports. These reports contain information about the corporations' business activities and their financial statements. Annual financial statements must be audited by independent CPAs.

In addition, annual and quarterly registration statements must be filed by corporations with the SEC. **Annual registration statements filed by corporations with the SEC are known as *Form 10-K reports*.** They are required by Section 10-K of the 1934 act. A 10-K describes a corporation's business and its management and financial activities. Much of the information referred to in a 10-K is provided in the annual report. Appendix C of this book contains an example 10-K report. Quarterly statements are known as 10-Q's. Other statements are required periodically if specific events occur. For example, if a corporation issues new shares of stock, it must file a registration statement. If it changes auditors, it must file a Form 8-K report.

Another document that corporations are required to provide to stockholders is a proxy statement. **A *proxy statement* provides information about matters that will be considered at a corporation's annual stockholders' meeting**. These matters frequently include election of members of the board of directors, adoption of management compensation plans, and selection of an independent auditor. The proxy statement provides information about the members of the board of directors and their compensation, major stockholders, stock owned by managers, compensation of managers, and management and employee compensation and retirement plans. Appendix D of this book contains a proxy statement.

A *proxy* is a document that authorizes management to cast votes for its stockholders at a stockholders' meeting. If stockholders cannot attend the meeting and wish for management to vote for them, they can sign and return the proxy to the managers.

During the 1900's financial accounting has become a highly regulated and formalized process. Publicly-traded corporations must provide audited financial reports to their stockholders. These statements should provide full disclosure of accounting information in accordance with GAAP. The managers and auditors of companies who fail to provide this information or who do so fraudulently are subject to civil and criminal prosecution.

SELF-STUDY PROBLEM 7-2

Several major events have been important for the development of modern accounting practice in the U.S. Explain the importance of each of the following events:

a. The Industrial Revolution
b. The income tax
c. The securities legislation of 1933 and 1934

The solution to Self-Study Problem 7-2 appears at the end of the chapter.

THE DEVELOPMENT OF ACCOUNTING STANDARDS

Objective 9
Identify organizations responsible for setting accounting standards in the U.S.

The SEC is responsible for enforcement of reporting and auditing requirements. Occasionally, the SEC also establishes accounting standards for corporations to use in providing financial reports to their investors. For the most part, accounting standards (GAAP) have been established in the U.S. by private, rather than governmental, organizations. Private standard setting is not common outside the U.S. Most other nations rely on laws enacted by government to establish accounting standards. These standards frequently serve the needs of the government for information about corporate activities.

The AICPA Committee on Accounting Procedure

In 1939, the AICPA Committee on Accounting Procedure (CAP) began to issue accounting and financial reporting standards. This organization and its replacements have been recognized by the SEC as the source of GAAP for U.S. corporations. GAAP consist of the pronouncements of the authoritative organizations that have been established to set accounting standards. Members of the CAP participated in the organization on a part-time basis. Most were practicing accountants who maintained their own firms.

The CAP was replaced in 1959. Nevertheless, the AICPA continues to play a role in setting accounting standards. Its committees are instrumental in identifying accounting issues and in recommending appropriate accounting procedures. In addition, the AICPA, through its Auditing Standards Board, remains the primary organization for establishing procedures used by independent auditors. The AICPA regulates the auditing profession by requiring auditors to comply with auditing standards and to meet continuing education requirements. Accounting firms that are AICPA members must be reviewed periodically by other accounting firms to assess the quality of their audit work.

The Accounting Principles Board

The CAP was criticized as being controlled by the AICPA and audit firms. In 1959, the Accounting Principles Board (APB) replaced the CAP. The APB was not controlled by the AICPA. Most members of the APB participated on a part-time basis and included representatives who were not practicing accountants. The APB was more independent of the accounting profession than was the CAP. Nevertheless, the APB also was criticized as being too much under the control of the accounting profession.

The Financial Accounting Standards Board

Perceived inadequacies in the operations of the APB, led to its being replaced in 1973 by the Financial Accounting Standards Board (FASB). The FASB continues as the primary organization for setting GAAP for businesses in the U.S. The FASB has seven full-time members appointed by a supporting organization, the Financial Accounting Foundation (FAF). The FASB is privately funded through the efforts of the FAF. The FAF includes representatives from the accounting profession, industry, government, financial institutions, the securities industry, and the investing public. Thus, it is intended to be broadly representative of those who have an interest in accounting and financial reporting. The FASB issues standards that establish GAAP for corporations and other businesses.

The FASB also sets accounting and financial reporting standards for nonprofit organizations other than governmental units. These organizations are not subject to SEC regulation, however, and compliance with GAAP is largely voluntary. Many organizations that receive federal funding are required by the federal government to be audited for compliance with GAAP.

Governmental Accounting Standards

The Governmental Accounting Standards Board (GASB) was created in 1984 to establish GAAP for state and local governmental units. Like the FASB, the GASB reports to the FAF, which appoints its members and oversees its activities.

The federal government is not subject to FASB or GASB standards but establishes its own accounting rules. The federal government does not have a coherent set of GAAP for all of its agencies and departments. The Federal Accounting Standards Advisory Board (FASAB) was created in 1991 to assist with the establishment of accounting standards for agencies and departments of the federal government. The FASAB attempts to identify the needs of users of federal financial information and to develop financial reports to meet those needs.

Chapter 15 describes governmental and nonprofit accounting standards in more detail.

International Accounting Standards

The regulation of financial accounting and reporting is an international activity. Considerable diversity exists in accounting standards among nations. The International Accounting Standards Committee (IASC) was created in 1973 as an international effort to study accounting issues and to reduce the diversity of standards. The IASC has issued accounting standards that identify preferred accounting methods for activities such as inventory estimation and consolidation but has no enforcement power. Nevertheless, it influences accounting practices in most developed and developing nations because of the growing globalization of trade and security markets. Some countries, especially developing ones, have adopted IASC standards as their GAAP.

THE PURPOSE OF ACCOUNTING STANDARDS

Objective 10
Explain why accounting standards are important to our economy.

Accounting standards prescribe financial accounting and reporting practices for most major corporations. The rules used by corporations to measure and report their transformation activities should conform to GAAP. An elaborate regulatory procedure exists for establishing accounting standards, and also serves to monitor compliance with the standards. This process serves several important functions in our society.

Providing a Basis for Contracting

Managers contract with stockholders to manage the operations of corporations for the stockholders' welfare. Stockholders contract with managers to compensate the managers for their services; this compensation depends on company performance. Without accounting information, these contracts would be unenforceable since stockholders could not judge company performance. Accounting information provides an important means of assessing manager performance and determining compensation.

Specific performance measures are needed in contracts to define the rules of the game. Accounting standards provide a basis for determining performance measures that can be verified by both managers and stockholders. For example, compensation contracts may provide for a bonus to be paid to certain managers if a corporation's earnings increase by 10% over the prior year. Standards are needed to determine how earnings will be measured so managers and stockholders can agree earnings increased by 10 percent.

Contracts also are important for creditors, employees, and other groups. For example, creditors are concerned about how much of a corporation's resources are transferred to stockholders as dividends. Limitations often are placed on these payments that depend on the amount of earnings or working capital. Accounting rules define how earnings and other amounts will be measured. Employees contract for compensation and benefits, including retirement and health care. Accounting information can assist them in determining whether benefits are being funded and whether an organization is likely to be able to continue to provide jobs, compensation, and benefits.

Assuring Reliability of Information

Managers need to assure investors that the information they report about the performance of their businesses is accurate and reliable. GAAP and audits by independent CPAs help meet this need. GAAP limit managers' abilities to select the methods they use to calculate accounting numbers. Since measurement rules are established by someone other than management, investors have some assurance accounting information is not being manipulated to serve the interests of managers.

Accounting standards provide a basis against which a corporation's accounting information can be audited. An auditor examines whether the procedures used by managers to develop and report accounting information to external users are in compliance with GAAP. If the procedures are not in compliance with GAAP, auditors should note the discrepancy in their audit reports. GAAP provide a standard of measurement for auditors, as well as for managers who report accounting information.

Controlling the Cost of Reporting and Maintaining Equity

Reporting to external users is expensive. Corporations must maintain information systems for financial reporting. Standards control the amount and type of information corporations are expected to provide. Individual users cannot force a corporation to provide information not mandated by regulation. All corporations in a particular industry are subject to the same reporting requirements. Therefore, no corporation or user has an unfair advantage over others.

The public reporting of information is important so all users have equal access to important information. Standards require the reporting of information useful to those who make investment decisions. Federal laws prohibit the use of information for personal gain by those with unfair access to information. In particular, managers, directors, and others who have access to inside information are prohibited from using this information to earn profits by trading in corporate securities.

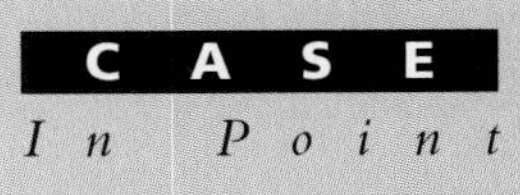

In March 1992, Sheldon M. Stone, a former Boston real estate developer, pleaded guilty to securities fraud. Stone assisted a law firm employee in securing a mortgage for a condominium she was buying by financing her down payment. In return, the employee provided Stone with confidential information regarding a pending takeover of Parisian, Inc. The law firm was assisting with the takeover. Stone, and a partner, purchased 22,000 shares of Parisian and later sold the stock for a profit of $273,375.

Determining Fair Business Practices and Economic Analysis

The federal and state governments use accounting information in regulating business practices and in setting economic policies. The government monitors corporate profits and trade activities. Policies are enacted to control business activities that lead to unreasonable profits or noncompetitive trade.

The government insures depositors in many financial institutions against loss of their deposits. Federal and state agencies are responsible for overseeing the activities of these institutions to protect the interests of depositors. The accounting practices of these institutions are important so their financial conditions can be monitored reliably.

Other organizations, such as public utilities, are under the direct supervision of regulatory agencies. These agencies set the rates these organizations can charge to earn a fair return for their investors. Accounting standards are important to ensure rates are determined fairly and similar organizations receive equitable treatment from regulators.

Also, the government sets policies to promote economic activity and to control inflation and unemployment. It uses accounting information from companies in setting these policies. Accounting standards ensure the availability of reliable information for these purposes.

Providing a Basis for Litigation

Investors and other users of accounting information can sue managers and auditors for issuing false or misleading information. Litigation protects users from unscrupulous managers and from gross negligence on the part of auditors. It is the responsibility of managers to provide accurate and timely accounting information. Auditors certify that financial statement information fairly presents a company's economic activities, while GAAP provide a benchmark against which reported information can be compared. Failure to comply with accounting and auditing standards is a basis for litigation.

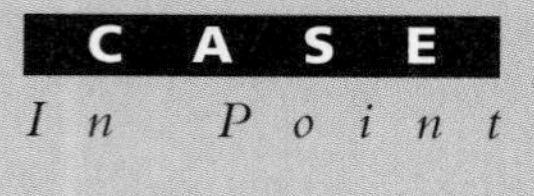

In May 1992, a jury awarded $338 million to a British corporation for negligence by Price Waterhouse in its audits of an Arizona bank. The bank was purchased in 1987 by the British company. Price Waterhouse audited the bank in 1985 and 1986. After the purchase, the bank was forced to write down the reported value of some of its major assets.

Several other major CPA firms settled lawsuits in the early 1990's for audits of savings and loan and other companies. For example, Ernst & Young paid $63 million for investor claims from the collapse of Lincoln Savings & Loan Association. Coopers & Lybrand paid approximately $50 million to settle a suit over failure to discover financial statement misstatements in its audits of MiniScribe Corporation.

SETTING ACCOUNTING STANDARDS

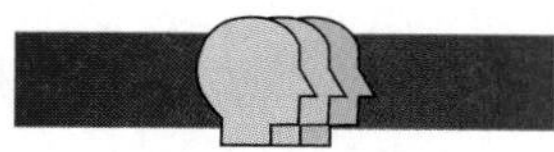

Accounting standards are important to protect the interests of investors, managers, and the general public. Therefore, the standards must be perceived as being reasonable and responsive to the needs of different constituents. Arbitrary and unnecessary standards do not serve the needs of society. For these reasons, accounting standards are established through a political process. This process provides an opportunity for interested parties to express their opinions and to provide information that may have a bearing on prospective standards. The fact that accounting standards are referred to as *Generally Accepted* Accounting Principles is not accidental. To serve the needs of society, accounting standards must be accepted by those who are affected by them. Therefore, the process of establishing standards includes an opportunity for all interested parties to inform standard setters of their needs and concerns. This process increases the likelihood that standards will be accepted by those affected and that the benefits derived from the standards will exceed the costs of standard setting and reporting.

The Standard-Setting Process

Objective 11
List steps in the process of establishing accounting standards.

The process used by the FASB is typical of that used by other organizations, such as the GASB and the IASC. The process consists of the following steps:

1. Accounting issues are identified and evaluated for consideration.
2. A discussion memorandum is issued and responses are solicited.
3. Public hearings are held.
4. An exposure draft is issued and responses are solicited.
5. Additional public hearings are held as needed.
6. A standard is issued.
7. Existing standards are reviewed and modified as needed.

Accounting issues may be identified by the accounting profession, managers, investors, or by the FASB staff. The staff evaluates the issues, and the Board determines those issues that appear to be important for it to address.

A *discussion memorandum* is a document that identifies accounting issues and alternative approaches to resolving the issues. All interested parties are encouraged to respond to a discussion memorandum. The FASB staff summarizes responses to a discussion memorandum for the Board. Public hearings may be held to obtain additional information.

The Board develops a proposed standard after reviewing responses. Alternatively, the Board can decide to drop an issue or postpone further consideration. If a proposal is issued, it represents the views of the Board, not necessarily the views of a majority of respondents. Nevertheless, the Board must justify its views and demonstrate that its decisions are not arbitrary.

The Board issues its proposal in the form of an exposure draft. **An *exposure draft* is a document that describes a proposed accounting standard.** It identifies requirements that may be contained in an actual standard. Responses again are solicited and public hearings sometimes are held.

Once the Board reviews responses to an exposure draft, it may modify and reissue the exposure draft or issue a standard. **An *accounting standard* is an official pronouncement establishing acceptable accounting procedures or financial report content.** FASB standards are known as *Statements of Financial Accounting Standards.* To be issued, a standard must be agreed to by at least five of the seven members of the Board. The views of Board members who vote against a standard are issued as part of the standard.

Once a standard has been issued, it becomes part of GAAP. An effective date is part of each standard; as a result, financial reports issued after this date must comply with it. Standards can be reviewed at any time to determine if they are serving their intended purposes and can be modified or replaced if found to be ineffective.

The Conceptual Framework for Accounting Standards

The conceptual framework was developed by the FASB in the late 1970's and early 1980's to provide guidance in the development of accounting standards.

The *conceptual framework* is a set of objectives, principles, and definitions to guide the development of new accounting standards.

Objective 12
Identify the primary components of the conceptual framework used in establishing accounting standards for businesses in the U.S.

The FASB conceptual framework includes four major components: (1) objectives of financial reporting, (2) qualitative characteristics of accounting information, (3) elements of financial statements, and (4) recognition and measurement in financial statements.

The objectives of financial reporting provide an overall purpose for financial reports. The purpose of financial reports is to provide information useful to current and potential investors, creditors, and other users in making decisions. Financial reports should help these decision makers assess the amounts, timing, and uncertainty of prospective cash flows to the decision makers and to business organizations. Financial reports should also provide information about resources, claims to resources, and changes in resources for business organizations.

Qualitative characteristics are attributes that make accounting information useful. The characteristics of information are described as a hierarchy, with understandability and usefulness for decision making being the most important, as depicted in Exhibit 7-4:

Exhibit 7-4 Qualitative Characteristics of Accounting Information

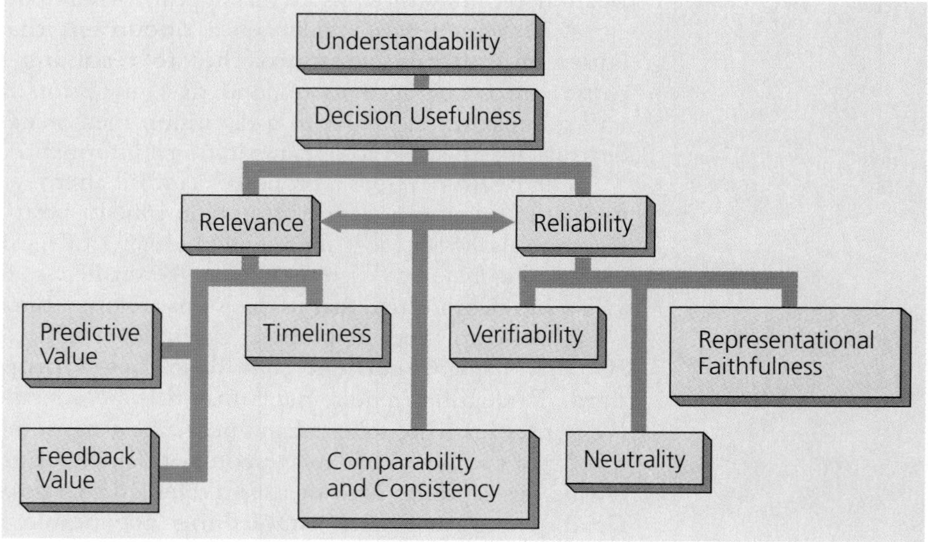

Adapted from Statement of Financial Accounting Concepts No. 2: Qualitative Characteristics of Accounting Information, FASB, May 1980.

Relevance and reliability are considered to be the two primary qualities that result in accounting information being useful. Relevant information should be timely and have predictive or feedback value. Reliable information should faithfully represent economic events and should be verifiable and neutral. Information about an organization is more valuable when it can be compared with information from other organizations and when it is prepared using consistent methods over time.

Elements of financial statements provide definitions of the primary classes of items contained in financial statements. Elements include assets, liabilities, equity, investments by owners, distributions to owners, revenues, expenses, gains, and losses.

Recognition and measurement criteria identify information that should be contained in financial statements. The primary financial statements are described in the conceptual framework, along with the items that should be contained in each statement. To be included in the financial statements, an item should meet the definition of an element of a financial statement. Also, it should be relevant to decision makers and measurable with sufficient reliability to be useful. Revenues should be recognized when earned—that is, when an organization has substantially accomplished what it must do to be entitled to the benefits from the revenues. Expenses are recognized when an organization's resources are consumed in revenue-generating activities.

When the FASB is deciding on new accounting standards, it refers to the conceptual framework for guidance. The guidance helps the FASB resolve new and emerging accounting problems. If standards are consistent with the framework, they are likely to be consistent among themselves. Therefore, preparers and users of financial accounting information should find a logical pattern to the information. The framework should help them better understand the content and limitations of financial reports.

SELF-STUDY PROBLEM 7-3

Descriptions are provided below for organizations that have had an effect on the accounting profession. Identify the name of each organization.

1. Creates auditing standards in the U.S.
2. Creates accounting standards in the U.S. for businesses and certain other organizations.
3. Enforces compliance with accounting standards for most corporations.
4. Enhances professional behavior for internal auditors.
5. Enhances professional behavior for public accountants.
6. Creates local and state governmental accounting standards.
7. Advises the federal government on the creation of accounting standards for federal agencies.
8. Attempts to develop uniformity in accounting standards among different nations.
9. Enhances professional behavior for management accountants.

The solution to Self-Study Problem 7-3 appears at the end of the chapter.

REVIEW *Summary of Important Concepts*

1. The accounting profession:
   A. The accounting profession includes those who have developed a high level of knowledge of accounting through education and experience. The profession includes management accountants, public accountants, governmental and nonprofit accountants, and accounting educators.
   B. Management accountants provide services as employees of businesses and other organizations, including information systems development, financial accounting management, financial reporting, financial planning and analysis, cost management and control, and internal auditing.

C. Public accountants provide services to businesses, governmental and nonprofit organizations, and individuals. These services include auditing, compilation and review of financial statements, tax advice, and consulting.
D. An audit report summarizes the audit process and expresses the auditor's opinion about an organization's financial statements.
E. Governmental and nonprofit accountants provide management accounting services to these organizations. In addition, they are concerned with tax assessment and compliance.
F. Accounting educators create and disseminate accounting knowledge.

2. The historical development of accounting:
   A. Contemporary accounting has developed from the needs of individuals and organizations to maintain systematic records of their resources and transactions. Accounting is as old as written history.
   B. Contemporary accounting can be traced to the accounting methods developed in Europe at the beginning of the Renaissance.
   C. The Industrial Revolution increased the need for accountants to help manage corporations.
   D. The growing trade in corporate stocks led to increased professionalism and regulation of corporate accounting and reporting in the early 1900's.
   E. Income taxation led to increased federal involvement with accounting procedures, which were the basis for calculation of taxable income.
   F. The collapse of the stock market in 1929 led to legislation that created the SEC and led to federal regulation of corporate financial accounting.
3. The development of accounting standards:
   A. Accounting standards are set in the U.S. primarily by private organizations. Corporate and nonprofit organization (except for government) standards are established by the Financial Accounting Standards Board. State and local governmental standards are established by the Governmental Accounting Standards Board.
   B. Accounting standards are important in our society as a basis for contracting, for assuring reliability of financial information, for controlling the cost of reporting and maintaining equity among investors, for determining fair business practices and economic analysis, and as a basis for litigation.
   C. Accounting standards are established through a lengthy due process that provides opportunity for all concerned parties to express their opinions about an accounting issue. The process involves issuing a discussion memorandum, written responses and public hearings, issuing an exposure draft, further responses and hearings, and issuing a standard. Standards may be reviewed, revised, or replaced at any time.
   D. A conceptual framework provides guidance for the FASB in establishing accounting standards.

DEFINE *Terms and Concepts Defined in this Chapter*

accounting standard
attestation
audit committee
audit opinion
audit report
compilation
conceptual framework
cost accounting
cost management
discussion memorandum
exposure draft
Form 10-K reports
Generally Accepted Auditing Standards (GAAS)
internal control
materiality
proxy
proxy statement
review

SOLUTIONS

SELF-STUDY PROBLEM 7-1

1. Accounting systems may be developed by management accountants or by public accountants. Larger corporations generally employ their own staffs for this purpose. Public accountants may assist these staffs or may provide services for organizations that do not have their own staffs.
2. Internal auditors, who are management accountants, evaluate company policies to ensure they are being implemented.
3. Public accountants prepare tax returns, though one does not have to be a CPA to provide this service. Some companies employ their own tax staffs.
4. Governmental accountants are responsible for tax compliance.
5. Accounting educators are primarily responsible for the development of new accounting knowledge.
6. Public accountants provide independent audit services.
7. Management accountants and public accountants help managers interpret financial information.
8. Management accountants are primarily responsible for cost accounting. Public accountants may consult with managers about cost management.
9. Educators prepare students for entry into the accounting profession.
10. Public accountants provide financial planning advice.

SELF-STUDY PROBLEM 7-2

Three major events include:

1. **The Industrial Revolution** produced large organizations that required access to large amounts of capital. As a means of obtaining this capital, corporations were formed. Because corporations generally result in a separation of owners from managers, a need for reliable reporting of financial activities by managers to owners and other external parties was created. This information is necessary for enforcing contracts among the parties. In addition, the size and complexity of corporations create a need for accounting systems to assist managers in planning and control decisions.
2. **Income taxation** of corporations increased government involvement with corporate accounting practices. These practices became the basis for determining taxable income. Standard practices were needed to determine reliably the amount of taxable income and to maintain equity among corporations so each organization was taxed fairly.
3. The collapse of the stock market in 1929 created a demand for **government regulation of corporate securities markets**. Regulation of accounting practices was a major part of the resulting legislation of 1933 and 1934. The federal government formed the SEC to oversee corporate accounting and financial reporting procedures and to enforce compliance with accounting standards. The SEC relied on the accounting profession to form organizations for the establishment of accounting standards. The SEC also required corporations to issue audited annual financial reports. The securities laws made corporate managers and their auditors subject to litigation for providing false or misleading accounting information. Increased growth and complexity of the security markets and corporations have resulted in greater regulation of accounting information reported to external parties. Accounting standard setting organizations, such as the FASB, have created GAAP to control the reporting of accounting information and to help maintain user confidence in this information.

SELF-STUDY PROBLEM 7-3

1. Auditing Standards Board (ASB)
2. Financial Accounting Standards Board (FASB)
3. Securities and Exchange Commission (SEC)
4. Institute of Internal Auditors (IIA)
5. American Institute of Certified Public Accountants (AICPA)
6. Governmental Accounting Standards Board (GASB)
7. Federal Accounting Standards Advisory Board (FASAB)
8. International Accounting Standards Committee (IASC)
9. Institute of Management Accountants (IMA)

EXERCISES

7-1. Write a short definition for each of the terms listed in the *Terms and Concepts Defined in this Chapter* section.

7-2. Self-regulation is an important attribute of a profession like accounting. What is the purpose of self-regulation? Describe some of the self-regulation procedures of the accounting profession.

7-3. Management accountants are responsible for those activities in an organization necessary for ensuring that accounting information is available to information users when it is needed. What are some activities of management accountants necessary for completing these responsibilities?

7-4. Sigfreid Fromm is a recent graduate in accounting. She has taken a position with the Hand Writer Co. The company has three divisions that manufacture three products: pencils, pens, and colored markers. Financial information for the most recent fiscal period for each division includes:

Division	Pencils	Pens	Markers
Divisional Revenues	$200,000	$ 300,000	$100,000
Divisional Expenses	140,000	260,000	60,000
Divisional Assets	600,000	1,000,000	200,000

One of Sigfreid's regular duties is to prepare an analysis of the performance of each division. Prepare an analysis of divisional performance from the information provided that Sigfreid might provide to her supervisor. Which of the divisions appears to be most profitable? How is this responsibility typical of the tasks often performed by management accountants?

7-5. What is the purpose of internal auditing? Why is it important to an organization? Why is internal auditing an accounting responsibility?

7-6. List and briefly describe the primary internal control procedures discussed in the chapter.

7-7. Identify each of the following and explain how it relates to the professional practice of accounting in the U.S.:

a. CPA
b. CMA
c. CIA
d. AICPA
e. IMA
f. IIA
g. State Board of Public Accountancy

7-8. How does the public practice of auditing differ from internal auditing? What services are provided by external auditors?

7-9. Identify each of the sections of an audit report and explain its purpose.

7-10. Meese, Neese, and Reese is a CPA firm. The following situations arose in the firm's audits of several clients:

a. The Bagdad Co. was determined to have used an accounting procedure for recording inventory that was inconsistent with generally accepted accounting principles. The CPA firm determined the procedure did not result in a material misstatement but believed the procedure should be revealed to financial statement users.
b. The Stockholm Co. prepared its financial statements using accounting procedures that were inconsistent with generally accepted accounting principles. The CPA firm determined the procedures resulted in a material misstatement of financial position and operating results.
c. The Bejing Co. prepared financial statements in conformity with generally accepted accounting principles. These statements revealed a loss during the fiscal year.
d. The Nairobe Co. prepared financial statements but did not have sufficient accounting records to verify the accuracy of the statements.

What type of audit opinion would the CPA firm issue for each of these situations? How should users interpret the financial statements in response to the opinions?

7-11. Occasionally, financial reports are issued that contain misstatements. Managers sometimes engage in fraudulent behavior that is not uncovered by the company's auditors. As a result, the auditors issue an unqualified opinion on the misstated financials. Auditors often are blamed in these circumstances for failing to discover the fraud and report it to stockholders. What are the responsibilities of auditors for disclosing misstatements and revealing fraud?

7-12. Bill Flamingo owns a small pet store. He has applied for a loan from a local bank to expand his business. The bank has asked Bill to provide financial statements for the business that have been reviewed by a CPA. Bill relies on a local CPA firm to maintain his accounting records and to prepare his financial statements. He is unsure about what the bank is requesting for the business. He asks his CPA for guidance. Does the bank want audited financial statements? He is concerned that an audit would be too expensive for the size of his business and for the amount he wants to borrow. Assume you are Bill's CPA. Write a short memo to Bill explaining the difference between an audit and a compilation and review.

7-13. Many of the responsibilities of accountants in businesses are similar to those in governmental and nonprofit organizations. What are some of major responsibilities of accountants in governments that do not exist for accountants in businesses?

7-14. A close friend knows you are taking an accounting class. The friend tells you he has thought about majoring in accounting but doesn't know what kind of preparation he needs for an accounting career. He asks you to describe the preparation he will need. What can you tell him?

7-15. Why can it be said that accounting is as old as recorded history? Why is it not surprising that modern accounting developed during the early Renaissance in Italy?

7-16. Three major developments in the history of accounting involved the Industrial Revolution, the 16th amendment to the U.S. Constitution, and the events subsequent to the stock market crash of 1929. Explain briefly the significance of each of these events for contemporary accounting.

7-17. Identify the major reporting requirements associated with each of the following:

a. Securities Act of 1933
b. Securities and Exchange Act of 1934
c. 10-K report
d. 10-Q report
e. Proxy statement

7-18. Identify each of the following:

a. The private sector organization currently responsible for setting financial accounting standards in the U.S.
b. The private sector organization currently responsible for setting state and local governmental accounting standards in the U.S.

c. The organization currently responsible for setting auditing standards in the U.S.
d. The organization that exists to influence the development of international accounting standards.
e. The private sector organization responsible for setting financial accounting standards in the U.S. from 1959 to 1973.
f. The organization responsible for helping with the establishment of accounting standards for federal government agencies.
g. The organization responsible for the enforcement of financial accounting standards in the U.S.

7-19. How would you react to the following statement? "Accounting standards impose costs on corporations and their managers to protect the interests of investors."

7-20. What is meant by the term "generally accepted accounting principles"? What is the significance of the phrase "generally accepted"?

7-21. What is the purpose of the qualitative characteristics of financial reports? What are the primary qualitative characteristics as defined by the FASB?

7-22. What is the primary objective of financial reporting according to the FASB?

PROBLEMS

PROBLEM 7-1 Describing the Accounting Profession

The high school from which you graduated is sponsoring a career day to inform students about career opportunities in various disciplines. You have been asked to participate in a panel discussion on professional careers that will be part of the career day. Your task is to present a 10-minute overview of the accounting profession and career opportunities in accounting.

Required Prepare a detailed topic outline for your presentation that includes the issues you believe would be most important for your discussion. Consider how you might make the topic interesting and informative for a high school audience.

PROBLEM 7-2 Evaluating Internal Control

The Spring Valley Church is a small congregation with about 50 members. The church is financed by member donations. Most of these donations are collected during the Sunday morning service. Many of the donations are in cash. Other donations are by checks made payable to the church. Harvey Plump has served as treasurer for the church since becoming a member a few years ago. The church accepted Harvey's offer to serve as treasurer as an indication of his interest in being active in the church. Harvey listed several previous experiences with financial matters on his resumé as qualifying him for the position.

Once donations are collected each week, Harvey takes the money to the church office, where he counts it. He makes out a deposit slip and deposits the money in the church's account at a local bank. He records the deposit in the church's check register. He writes checks to pay the church's expenses. In some cases, he writes small checks to himself as reimbursement for incidental expenses he pays for the church. He opens bank statements received by the church each month and reconciles them with the church's check register. Harvey prepares a monthly statement of cash received and disbursed that is distributed to members of the congregation.

The church always seems to be lacking sufficient financial resources. A recent meeting was held to discuss expansion of the church's building, but current finances seem to make expansion impossible. Some members don't understand why the church's financial condition appears to be so bleak, since they believe they are making large donations.

The church has asked you, as a local accountant, to help them evaluate their financial situation.

Required Evaluate the internal control problems of the Spring Valley Church. What explanation can be provided for the church's financial problems? How might you confirm your explanation?

PROBLEM 7-3 Evaluating Internal Control Procedures

Consider each of the following situations:

(a) Sales clerks in a retail store are assigned to a specific cash register. They are given a cash drawer containing $100 in change at the beginning of their shifts. They are required to enter the amount of each purchase on the cash register. The cash register records an identification and price for each item purchased. Cash payments are collected from customers and placed in the cash register. A copy of the cash register sales slip is given to the customer. At the end of each shift, the employee takes the cash drawer and cash register tape to a supervisor who counts the cash, verifies the sales, and signs an approval form. The sales clerk also signs the form that identifies the amount of cash and amount of sales for the day.

(b) A ticket seller at a movie theater is issued a cash drawer with $100 in change and a roll of prenumbered tickets when the theater opens each day. The seller collects cash from customers and issues the tickets. Each customer hands a ticket to a ticket taker who tears the ticket in half and gives half back to the customer. At the end of the day, the ticket seller returns the cash drawer and tickets to a supervisor.

Required For each situation, discuss why the procedures are used and how they provide effective internal control.

PROBLEM 7-4 Understanding the Audit Report

A standard audit report contains reference to each of the following:

a. Responsibility
b. Generally accepted auditing standards
c. Material misstatement and material respects
d. A test basis
e. Present fairly . . . in conformity with generally accepted accounting principles

Required Explain why each of these terms is important for understanding the audit report and audit process.

PROBLEM 7-5 Public Accounting Services

Mirna McKenzie owns and manages several apartment complexes near a local college. She has maintained her own accounting records, but her business has grown past the point she feels competent to do her own accounting. Your CPA firm is near her apartments. You received a letter the other day from Mirna asking for a description of the kinds of services you could provide her business.

Required Write a letter to Mirna describing the services of your firm. Assume you provide a full range of public accounting services. Her address is: Mirna McKenzie, McKenzie Apartments, 2200 Placid Place, Your Town.

PROBLEM 7-6 Ethical Issues in Public Accounting

A series of independent situations involving accountants in public practice is described below:

a. Martin Hooper, CPA, accepted an engagement to provide a financial audit of the Bremer Co. Hooper owns 15% of the stock Bremer has issued.
b. Andrea Doria, CPA, accepted an engagement to provide an audit for the First State Bank. She has never audited a bank and has no specific training in bank audits.
c. Zeeman Kline, CPA, audited the Klasp Co. and issued an unqualified opinion on its financial statements. During the audit, he discovered a major discrepancy between certain assets reported on the financial statements and those owned by the company. He discussed the matter with the company president and was assured the accounts would be corrected next year.
d. Florence Nightingale, CPA, audited Community Hospital. She did not have time to complete all of the audit work prior to the time an audit report was needed by the hospital's board of directors. She decided to issue an unqualified report to meet the board's deadline and then complete the audit work. She felt sure she would not find any audit problems.

Required For each situation, explain why the CPA's actions violated ethical standards for external audits.

PROBLEM 7-7 The Importance of Financial Accounting Standards

Accounting and financial reporting to external decision makers is highly regulated in the U.S. Standards specify the types of information to be reported and how accounting numbers are to be calculated. Listed below are groups who benefit from these standards:

a. managers
b. stockholders
c. creditors
d. government authorities
e. auditors
f. employees

Required Explain why financial accounting standards are important to each of these groups.

PROBLEM 7-8 Setting Accounting Standards

Accounting standards are set in the U.S. in the private sector. Public hearings and written comments provide feedback during development of the standards. Opportunity is provided to those affected by standards to provide information to standard-setting organizations such as the FASB.

Required Draw a diagram describing the major steps in the standard-setting process. Explain the purpose of each of the primary documents that results from the process.

PROBLEM 7-9 Ethical Issues in Auditing

Larry Clint is the president of Hometown Bank. The bank has several thousand depositors and makes loans to many local businesses and homeowners. Blanche Granite is a partner with a CPA firm hired to audit Hometown Bank. The financial statements the bank proposes to issue for the 1996 fiscal year include the following information:

Loans receivable	$4,000,000
Total assets	5,000,000
Net income	1,000,000

During the audit, Blanche discovers that many of the loans were made for real estate development. Because of economic problems in the region, much of this real estate remains unsold or vacant. The current market value of the property is considerably less than its cost. Several of the developers are experiencing financial problems, and it appears unlikely that the bank will recover its loans if they default. Blanche described this problem to Larry and proposed a write-down of the receivables to $2,800,000. The $1,200,000 write-down would be written off against earnings for 1996.

Larry is extremely upset by the proposal. He notes the write-off would result in a reported loss for the bank for 1996. Also, the bank would be in jeopardy of falling below the equity requirements imposed by the bank regulatory board to which the bank is accountable. He fears the board would impose major constraints on the bank's operations. Also, he fears depositors would lose confidence in the bank and withdraw their money, further compounding the bank's financial problems. He cites several economic forecasts indicating an impending improvement in the region's economy. Further, he notes the bank's demise would be a major economic blow to the local economy and could precipitate the bankruptcy of some of the bank's major customers.

Blanche acknowledges that Larry is correct in his perceptions of the possible outcomes of the write-off. Larry proposes an alternative to Blanche. The bank will write down the receivables by $300,000 for 1996. The remaining losses will be recognized over the next three years, assuming property values have not improved. Larry also tells Blanche that if she is unwilling to accept his proposal, he will fire her firm and hire new auditors. The bank has been a long-time client for Blanche's firm and is one of its major revenue producers. Blanche also recognizes Larry's proposal is not consistent with accounting principles.

Required What are the ethical problems faced by Blanche? What action would you recommend she take?

PROBLEM 7-10 The Purpose of the Conceptual Framework

The Financial Accounting Standards Board developed a conceptual framework to provide guidance in the development of financial accounting standards.

Required Discuss the primary components of the conceptual framework for business organizations and explain the purpose of each component.

PROBLEM 7-11 Evaluating the Quality of Financial Reports

The following statements describe the annual report issued by Short Sheet company for the fiscal year ended December 31, 1995:

a. The report was issued on October 1, 1996.
b. Income included management's estimates of the increased value of certain fixed assets during 1995.
c. Procedures used to calculate revenues and expenses were different for 1995 than for 1994 and earlier years.
d. Procedures used by Short to calculate its net income differ from those used by the rest of its industry.
e. Short's financial statements were audited by an accounting firm owned by the president's brother.
f. Some of the company's major liabilities were not included in the annual report.

Required For each statement, identify the qualitative characteristic that has been compromised and explain the effect on report users.

PROBLEM 7-12 Multiple-Choice Overview of the Chapter

1. Which of the following is not a characteristic of a profession?
   a. a high level of knowledge and skills
   b. self-regulation
   c. government regulation of fees
   d. acceptance by society of qualifications to provide services
2. Management accountants may provide all of the following services except:
   a. financial reporting
   b. financial planning and analysis
   c. financial accounting management
   d. financial auditing
3. An organization's plan and the procedures it uses to safeguard its assets, ensure accurate information, promote efficiency, and encourage adherence to policies is its:
   a. internal control system.
   b. cost accounting system.
   c. financial accounting system.
   d. management information system.
4. An audit report of an independent accountant:
   a. is addressed to a company's managers.
   b. must contain only three paragraphs.
   c. is dated at the balance sheet date of the audited financial statements.
   d. identifies the responsibilities of the auditor.
5. Members of a corporation's board of directors responsible for working with the independent auditor are:
   a. the internal control committee.
   b. the audit committee.
   c. the management compensation committee.
   d. the management supervision committee.
6. Procedures used by an auditor in conducting an audit that form a basis for the auditor's opinion are:
   a. generally accepted auditing standards.
   b. generally accepted auditing principles.
   c. generally accepted accounting principles.
   d. generally accepted accounting standards.
7. A major development in the history of accounting was:
   a. the Method of Venice.
   b. the 13th amendment to the Constitution.
   c. the management revolution.
   d. the Securities Act of 1932.
8. A 10-K report is:
   a. a quarterly financial report for the SEC.
   b. a registration for a new stock issue with the SEC.
   c. an annual financial report for the SEC.
   d. a report of change in auditors for the SEC.
9. Financial accounting standards for businesses currently are established in the U.S. primarily by the:
   a. Federal Accounting Standards Board.
   b. Financial Accounting Standards Board.
   c. Securities and Exchange Commission.
   d. Accounting Principles Board.
10. All of the following are qualitative characteristics of financial reporting except:
    a. relevance
    b. reliability

c. representational faithfulness
d. conservatism

CASES

CASE 7-1 Examining a 10-K Report

Appendix C of this book contains a 10-K report for General Mills. This report provides a comprehensive overview of the corporation that must be filed with the SEC within 90 days after fiscal year end. Appendix D contains a proxy statement for General Mills.

Required Review the 10-K and proxy and write a short report in which you identify each of the following:

a. Description of the business, including:
   1. the principal products and services provided, including the major lines of business.
   2. the location of the company's principal plants and other properties.
   3. any pending legal proceedings.
   4. the date of shareholders' meetings and major issues voted on.
b. Description of securities and accounting matters, including:
   1. the market where the company's common stock is traded.
   2. reasons for references to the corporation's annual report to stockholders.
   3. any disagreements with accountants about financial accounting and disclosure issues.
c. Description of directors and officers, including:
   1. the names and offices of principal executive officers.
   2. compensation of officers for 1992.
   3. stock owned by officers.
   4. specific factors considered in evaluation of officers.

CASE 7-2 Examining a Statement of Financial Accounting Standards

Locate a copy of the FASB's Statement of Financial Accounting Standards No. 107 in your library.

Required Review the statement and write a short report in which you identify each of the following:

a. the topic covered by and the purpose of the statement
b. the date the statement was issued
c. the effect of statement requirements on financial statements
d. the effect of statement requirements on financial disclosures
e. the effective date of the statement
f. the vote of the FASB members
g. topics covered by appendices to the statement

CASE 7-3 Examining an Audit Report

Examine the auditor's report and the report of the audit committee provided as part of the annual report of General Mills, Inc., in Appendix B of this book and answer the following questions:

a. Who was General Mills' external auditor? What date did the auditor complete its audit work?
b. What was the auditor's responsibility with respect to the company's financial statements? What was the responsibility of management?
c. What are generally accepted auditing standards? Why are they important in an audit?
d. What kind of opinion did General Mills' auditors issue? Why is this opinion important to the company?
e. What is an audit committee? How does the company's audit committee benefit its stockholder?

PROJECTS

PROJECT 7-1 Audits and Audit Reports

Obtain the most recent annual report available for each of three corporations from your library. Find the auditor's report in each annual report, usually just before or just after the financial statements; make a photocopy of each one; and label it with the company's name. Read and compare the three audit reports. What similarities do you find? What differences? Write a memorandum to your instructor reporting your findings. Attach the photocopies of the audit reports to your memo.

PROJECT 7-2 Interviewing an Accountant

Make an appointment with an accountant at a CPA firm, a business organization, or a governmental or nonprofit organization. Ask the accountant to describe his or her primary responsibilities and what kinds of activities occur during a regular business day. Ask the accountant to identify the primary skills and training needed for his or her position. Write a memorandum to your instructor reporting the results of your interview. Identify the person interviewed and the date of the interview.

PROJECT 7-3 Requirements of an Accounting Major

Review the requirements for a major in accounting at your college or university or at a university where you may be planning to complete your undergraduate degree. Identify the prerequisites and admission requirements for the accounting program, the course requirements for the major (including accounting, business, and nonbusiness courses), and other degree requirements. Determine if the program offers a fifth year or graduate degree program and the requirements of the program. Write a short report in which you describe the degree requirements.

PROJECT 7-4 The Development of an Accounting Standard

Locate a copy of the FASB's *Statements of Financial Accounting Standards* in your library. Select one of these standards and review the appendix on "Background Information." Make a copy of this section. Draw a diagram that illustrates the steps that occurred prior to the issuance of the statement. For each step, identify the event and the date it occurred. Attach the copy of the statement section to the diagram.

PROJECT 7-5 Examining an Audit Failure

Use an index, such as the *Business Periodicals Index* or *Accounting and Tax Index,* to identify a recent article that describes an example of an actual or suspected audit failure. Make a copy of the article. Write a memo to your instructor identifying the event and the reasons cited in the article for the audit failure. Attach the copy of the article to the memo.

SECTION II

ANALYSIS AND INTERPRETATION OF FINANCIAL ACCOUNTING INFORMATION

CHAPTER 8

FINANCING ACTIVITIES: EQUITY

CHAPTER
Overview

Every business organization has owners who have invested in that business to receive a return on their investments. This chapter examines information corporations report about stockholders' equity—information that is useful for understanding part of a company's financing activities.

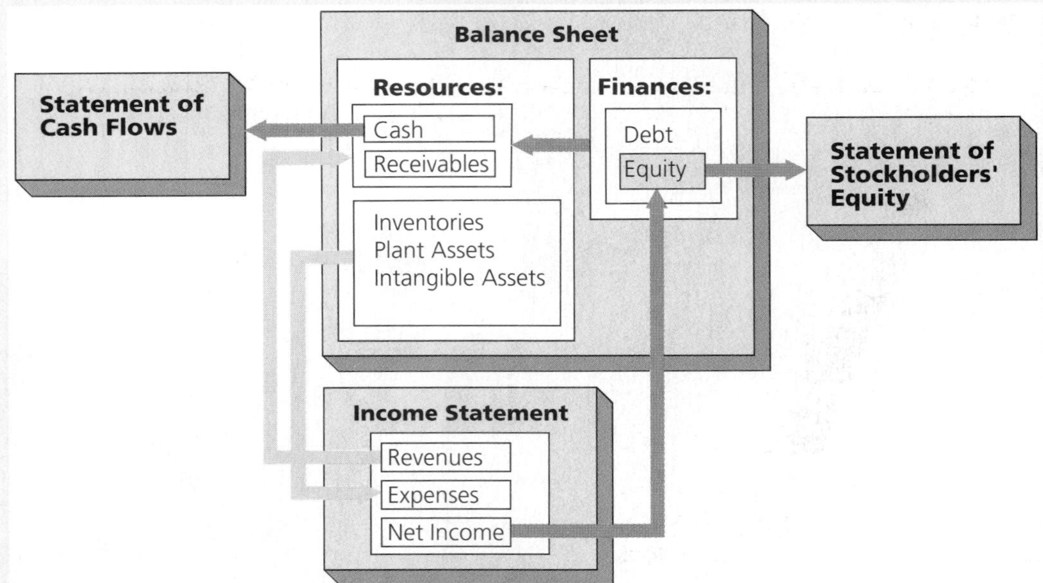

Reporting of equity transactions occurs primarily on the balance sheet and statement of stockholders' equity. The statement of cash flows reports cash flows associated with financing activities. Equity financing activities occur when owners provide financial resources to a business by investing in it and when a business distributes a return to its owners. This chapter discusses accounting and reporting requirements followed by publicly-traded corporations when reporting to external decision makers.

Major topics covered in this chapter include:

- Stockholder investment and retained earnings.
- Transactions affecting stockholders' equity.
- Classes of stock.
- Limitations of stockholders' equity reporting.
- International reporting of equity.

CHAPTER
Objectives

Once you have completed this chapter, you should be able to:

1. Identify the primary information reported in the stockholders' equity section.
2. List the primary components of contributed capital and explain how the components are measured.
3. Summarize balance sheet information about stock shares authorized, issued, and outstanding.
4. Explain what retained earnings reveals about a corporation.
5. Identify the types of events that change stockholders' equity during a fiscal period.

6. Distinguish stock dividends from cash dividends and explain the effect of dividends on equity.
7. Explain how dividends affect the value of a corporation and the wealth of stockholders.
8. Discuss the effect foreign operations may have on stockholders' equity.
9. Distinguish preferred stock from common stock and discuss why more than one type of stock may be issued.
10. Explain how accounting rules affect the complexity of stockholders' equity.
11. Compare and contrast the reporting of stockholders' equity for U.S. and foreign corporations.
12. Summarize the effects stockholders' equity transactions have on net income and cash flow.

STOCKHOLDER INVESTMENT AND RETAINED EARNINGS

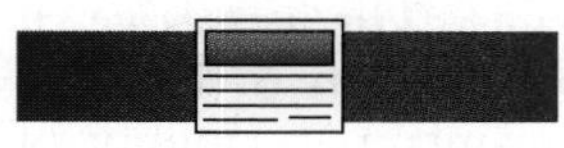

Objective 1
Identify the primary information reported in the stockholders' equity section.

Exhibit 8-1 reproduces the owners' equity section of a recent balance sheet for First Financial Management Corporation, a provider of data processing services.

Exhibit 8-1

First Financial Management Corporation
Shareholders' Equity
(Excerpt from the Annual Report Consolidated Balance Sheet)

(Dollars in Thousands) December 31,	1991	1990
Shareholders' equity:		
Common stock; $.10 par value; authorized 150,000,000 shares; issued 55,753,365 shares (1991) and 41,639,741 shares (1990)	$ 5,575	$ 4,164
Paid-in capital	740,157	430,988
Retained earnings	254,094	168,279
Treasury stock at cost, 425,715 shares (1991) and 207,294 shares (1990)	(6,866)	(2,760)
Total shareholders' equity	$992,960	$600,671

Minor modifications have been made to the format.

This exhibit illustrates the basic information corporations report in their balance sheets about their owners' equity. Corporate owners' equity is referred to as **stockholders'** or **shareholders' equity,** because owners hold shares of stock as an indication of their ownership.

Two categories of information about stockholders' equity are presented in Exhibit 8-1. The first category is contributed capital. ***Contributed capital*** **is the direct investment made by stockholders in a corporation.** Contributed capital for First Financial consists of **common stock** and **paid-in capital.** The second category is retained earnings, profits reinvested in a corporation. (Treasury stock, a contra-equity account, is explained later in this chapter.)

Contributed Capital

Objective 2
List the primary components of contributed capital and explain how the components are measured.

Corporations issue shares of stock to their owners in exchange for cash (and occasionally other resources such as property). ***Common stock*** **represents the ownership rights of investors in a corporation.** The term *capital stock* sometimes is used instead of common stock. Each share of common stock represents an equal share in the ownership of a corporation. Owners of these shares have a right to vote on the activities of a corporation and to share in its earnings. An owner of 10,000 shares of common stock of a corporation that has 100,000 shares of stock outstanding has a right to 10% of the dividends paid to owners. Also, this owner controls 10% of the votes that can be cast on issues voted on by the stockholders.

Par Value. U.S. corporations must be chartered by a specific state. **A *charter* is the legal right granted by a state that permits a corporation to exist.** The charter establishes a corporation as a legal entity and sets limits on its activities to protect its owners and others who contract with it. Among other things, a corporation's charter specifies the maximum number of shares the corporation is authorized to issue.

Some states require corporate stock to have a par value. **The *par value* of stock is the value assigned to each share by a corporation in its corporate charter.** A state may require a corporation to maintain an amount of equity equal to or greater than the par value of its stock. This amount cannot be transferred back to the owners unless the corporation liquidates its assets and goes out of business. Originally, par value was intended to protect a corporation's creditors by requiring owners to maintain a certain level of investment in a corporation. Such protection was important in the late 1800's and early 1900's because, at that time, corporations were not required to provide financial reports to their creditors or investors. Managers argued that public reporting of financial information could jeopardize a company's competitive position by allowing competitors to learn about the company's operations.

With the increased requirements for financial reporting that have developed during the 1900's, par value has lost much of its significance. For corporations chartered in states that do not require a par value, stock is issued without a par value and is known as no-par stock. When a par value exists, it often is set at a low amount, as in Exhibit 8-1 (10¢ per share).

Paid-In Capital in Excess of Par. Normally, stock is sold by a corporation at a price greater than its par value. For example, if 10,000 shares of $1 par value stock are sold by a corporation for $5 per share, stockholders' equity would include:

Common stock, par value	$10,000
Paid-in capital in excess of par	40,000
Total contributed capital	$50,000

Paid-in capital in excess of par value **is the amount received by a corporation from sale of its stock in addition to the stock's par value.** Corporate financial reports refer to paid-in capital in excess of par as paid-in capital, contributed capital in excess of par, proceeds in excess of par value, additional paid-in capital, surplus, premium on capital stock, and a variety of other names.

The total contributed capital from par value stock is the sum of capital stock (at par value) and paid-in capital in excess of par value. Total contributed capital for First Financial at the end of 1991 was $745,732,000 as shown in Exhibit 8-1.

Occasionally, a corporation will establish its own **nominal,** or **stated, value** for its no-par stock. That value will appear on the balance sheet in place of par value. In such cases, contributed capital will equal the sum of the stated value of the capital stock and the paid-in capital in excess of stated value.

Percentage of Major Corporations with Par, No Par, and Stated Value Stock

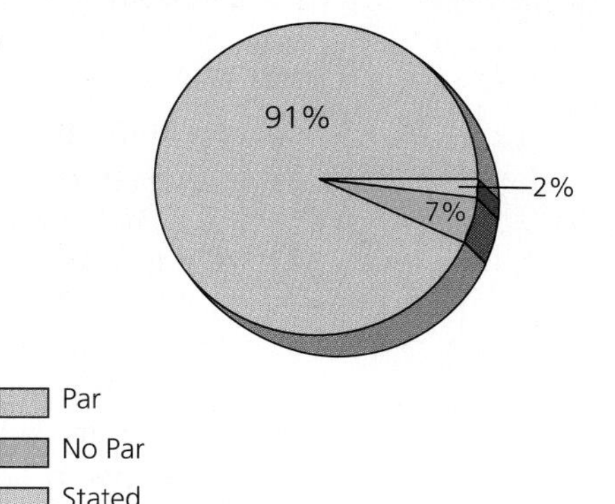

(Data source: Accounting Trends & Techniques, 1991)

If a corporation issues no-par stock and does not establish a stated value, total contributed capital for that stock is reported as a single amount in the equity section of the balance sheet. For example, a recent balance sheet for Ford Motor Company of Canada reported:

December 31 (in millions of dollars)	**1991**	**1990**
Capital stock		
Authorized-Unlimited number of common shares without nominal or par value. Issued 8,291,132 shares.	13.4	13.4

The total capital stock of $13.4 million is the total contributed capital for the corporation.

While the various terms associated with capital stock can be confusing, take care to understand the basic concept. **Contributed capital is the amount paid in to a corporation directly by its stockholders.** The amount of contributed capital may be reported in various formats, such as:

1. Contributed capital = common stock (par value) + paid-in capital in excess of par,
2. Contributed capital = common stock (stated value) + paid-in capital in excess of stated value, or
3. Contributed capital = common stock (or capital stock) when no par or stated value exists.

Shares of Stock and Treasury Stock

Objective 3
Summarize balance sheet information about stock shares authorized, issued and outstanding.

A corporation discloses in its annual report the number of shares of stock authorized by its charter. First Financial reported 150,000,000 shares authorized (see Exhibit 8-1). ***Authorized shares*** **are the maximum number of shares a corporation can issue without receiving approval from stockholders and the state to amend its charter.** Also, a corporation reports the number of shares of stock that have been issued (sold) to investors and the number of shares currently held by investors. ***Issued shares*** **are the number of shares that have been sold by a corporation to investors.** ***Outstanding shares*** **are the number of shares currently held by investors.** The difference (if any) between the number of shares issued and the number of shares outstanding represents the number of shares a corporation has repurchased from its investors.

Learning Note

Ford Motor Company of Canada reported that it could issue an unlimited number of shares. Securities regulations in Canada differ from those in the U.S. In the U.S., authorized shares are limited to a maximum number specified in a corporation's charter.

First Financial reported 425,715 shares of treasury stock at the end of 1991 (see Exhibit 8-1).

At the end of 1991, the number of shares outstanding was 425,715 less than the number issued. Therefore, 55,327,650 shares were outstanding at the end of 1991 (55,753,365 − 425,715). ***Treasury stock*** **is stock a corporation sold to its investors and then repurchased from them.** Because it is held by the corporation, it is not outstanding. TREASURY STOCK is a contra-stockholders' equity account. The cost of treasury stock is subtracted from other equity accounts to compute total stockholders' equity. The cost of treasury stock is the amount a corporation paid to investors to repurchase the stock.

First Financial notes (Exhibit 8-1) that the cost of treasury stock held at the end of 1991 was $6,866,000. The average price it paid for this stock was about $16.13 per share ($6,866,000/425,715). It may have repurchased the stock at several different times at different prices.

Once a corporation repurchases shares of its stock, it may choose to retire those shares rather than hold them in treasury. Shares that have been retired are not included in the number of shares issued. The amount a corporation paid to repurchase shares is deducted from the balance of contributed capital and retained earnings in the year of the retirement. For example, in 1991 IBM purchased and retired 2,127,400 shares at a total cost of $196 million. IBM reduced contributed capital on its balance sheet by the amount of the original par value and paid-in capital in excess of par recorded for this stock ($24 million). Retained earnings was reduced by the amount IBM paid for the stock in 1991 in excess of the amount for which it was sold originally ($172 million).

Percentage of Major Corporations Reporting Treasury Stock

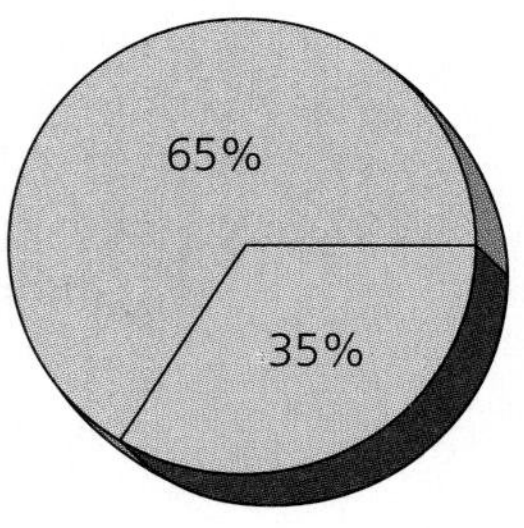

(Data source: Accounting Trends & Techniques, 1991)

Learning Note

Amounts shown on the balance sheet are totals accumulated over the life of a company. They are not the result of current year activities only. Therefore, the 6,866,000 of treasury stock First Financial reported for 1991 was the total stock it held in treasury at the end of 1991. The net increase in treasury stock held by the company in 1991 was $4,106,000 ($6,866,000 − $2,760,000).

Retained Earnings

Objective 4
Explain what retained earnings reveals about a corporation.

Recall from Chapter 2 that **retained earnings is profit reinvested in a corporation.** Other titles appearing in annual reports for retained earnings include reinvested earnings; net income, earnings, or profit retained in the business; or net income, earnings, or profit reinvested in the business. The amount of retained earnings indicates the accumulated net income invested in corporate resources. For example, assume that Harbor Co. began business on January 1, 1991. Its net income and dividends for 1991 through 1995 were:

Year	Net Income	Dividends	Increase in Retained Earnings	Balance of Retained Earnings
1991	$250,000	$100,000	$150,000	$ 150,000
1992	340,000	100,000	240,000	390,000
1993	416,000	200,000	216,000	606,000
1994	434,000	200,000	234,000	840,000
1995	500,000	300,000	200,000	1,040,000

Retained earnings is the accumulation of net income earned by a corporation over its life less the amount of dividends it has paid to investors.[1]

First Financial had accumulated $254,094,000 of retained earnings by December 31, 1991 (Exhibit 8-1). Thus, in addition to over $745 million of financing provided directly by owners as contributed capital, First Financial generated $254 million of financing from profitable operations.

Summary of Measuring and Reporting Stockholders' Equity

In addition to reporting the amount of par value and paid-in capital in excess of par, corporations are required by GAAP to report the number of shares of stock authorized, issued, and outstanding. This information may be reported either on the balance sheet or as a part of accompanying notes. The cost of stock a corporation has repurchased from its stockholders is deducted on the balance sheet as treasury stock in reporting total stockholders' equity (see Exhibit 8-1).

Percentage of Total Stockholder's Equity Composed of Stock and Retained Earnings for Some Major U.S. Corporations

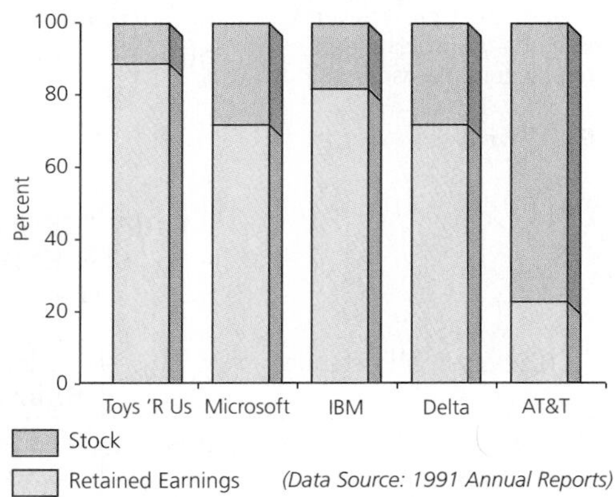

(Data Source: 1991 Annual Reports)

Learning Note

Corporations occasionally issue stock in exchange for noncash resources, such as the stock of another corporation or plant assets such as land and buildings. In these cases, the amount of contributed capital is measured by the stock's fair market value at the time of the exchange or by the fair market value of the resource received in the exchange, if it is easier

[1] Other transfers can be made from retained earnings for special purposes. Some of these transfers are examined later.

The primary events in the transformation process that affect stockholders' equity are the issuance of stock (contributed capital) and the reinvestment of net income (retained earnings). The accounting system measures these events by the amount of cash received from the sale of stock by a corporation and by the amount of net income reinvested in the corporation.

SELF-STUDY PROBLEM 8-1

The Bovine Co. began operations in January 1993. At that time, it issued 100,000 shares of $1 par value common stock. The stock sold for $5 per share. The company's charter permits it to issue 250,000 shares of stock. In 1995, the company repurchased 8,000 shares of stock at a cost of $7 per share. Bovine's net income and cash dividend payments have been:

Year	Net Income	Dividends
1993	$ (60,000)	$ 0
1994	140,000	50,000
1995	220,000	100,000

Required

Draft the stockholders' equity section of Bovine's balance sheet for the years ended December 31, 1995 and 1994.

The solution to Self-Study Problem 8-1 appears at the end of the chapter.

CHANGES IN STOCKHOLDERS' EQUITY

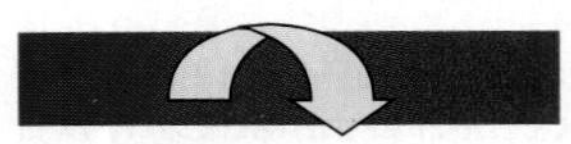

Objective 5
Identify the types of events that change stockholders' equity during a fiscal period.

The statement of stockholders' (or shareholders') equity describes events that have changed the amount of stockholders' equity during the fiscal periods covered by the statement. Exhibit 8-2 provides the statement of stockholders' equity for First Financial Management Corporation for 1991. The following sections describe each of the items listed in the exhibit.

Exhibit 8-2

FIRST FINANCIAL MANAGEMENT CORPORATION
STATEMENT OF SHAREHOLDERS' EQUITY
(Excerpt from 1991 Annual Report)

(Dollars in Thousands)	Common Stock		Paid-In	Retained	Treasury Stock	
	Shares	Amount	Capital	Earnings	Shares	Cost
Balance, December 31, 1990	41,639,741	$4,164	$430,988	$168,279	(207,294)	$(2,760)
1 Stock issued	6,503,400	650	144,150			
2 Stock issued in acquisitions			183		18,579	300
3 Debentures converted	7,297,908	730	161,493			
4 Stock options exercised	188,909	19	1,644			
5 Shares issued for employee stock purchase plan	42,575	4	488			
6 Cash dividends ($.07 per share)				(3,224)		
7 Net income				89,039		
8 Other adjustments	80,832	8	1,211		(237,000)	(4,406)
Balance, December 31, 1991	55,753,365	$5,575	$740,157	$254,094	(425,715)	$(6,866)

Note: Items have been numbered for ease of reference. Minor adjustments have been made to the format.

The format of the statement of stockholders' equity varies from corporation to corporation. Nevertheless, the statement lists the events that have resulted in changes in stockholders' equity during the past fiscal year. Though Exhibit 8-2 provides information for only one year, the complete statement includes information for two prior years as well.

Net Income

Exhibit 8-2 identifies transactions typical of those considered in prior chapters. For example, current year net income of $89,039,000 was added to retained earnings (from Exhibit 8-2):

(Dollars in thousands)	Common Stock		Paid-In Capital	Retained Earnings
	Shares	Amount		
7 Net income				89,039

The transfer was made by closing the revenue and expense accounts (see Chapter 4):

Assets =		Liabilities + Equity		+ Revenues − Expenses	
	-0-	Retained Earnings	89,039	Revenues	(1,507,103)
				Expenses	1,418,064

Parentheses denote decreases in column totals. Numbers are in thousands of dollars.

In total, revenues were $1,507,103,000 and expenses were $1,418,064,000 (from First Financial's income statement). The balances of these accounts are transferred to retained earnings, increasing it by the amount of net income. This transaction preserves the relationship: assets = liabilities + owners' equity + revenues − expenses.

Cash Dividends

During 1990, First Financial paid cash dividends totalling $3,224,000 to stockholders (from Exhibit 8-2):

(Dollars in thousands)	Common Stock		Paid-In Capital	Retained Earnings
	Shares	Amount		
6 Cash dividends ($.07 per share)				(3,224)

This transaction resulted in the payment of cash to stockholders, reducing the amount of cash held by the company and reducing its retained earnings:

Assets =		Liabilities + Equity		+ Revenues − Expenses
Cash	(3,224)	Retained Earnings	(3,224)	-0-

Cash dividends are paid only on shares outstanding. They are not paid on shares held in treasury, because a company would be paying dividends to itself.

Several dates are important for dividend transactions. **The *date of declaration* for dividends is the date a corporation's board of directors announces that a dividend will be paid. The *date of record* for a dividend is the date used to determine the recipients of the dividend.** All registered owners on the date of record receive the dividend. Anyone purchasing shares too late to be registered by the date of record will not receive dividends. **The *date of payment* for a dividend is the date the dividends are mailed to recipients.**

Dividends **declared** during a fiscal period are reported on a corporation's statement of stockholders' equity as a reduction in retained earnings. Dividends paid during a fiscal period are reported on the corporation's statement of cash flows. These amounts will not always be the same. For example, a company may declare a dividend near the end of its fiscal year but not pay the dividend until the following fiscal year. Dividends that have been declared but that have not been paid are reported as a current liability, DIVIDENDS PAYABLE.

Issuance of Stock

First Financial issued 6.5 million shares of new stock to stockholders (from Exhibit 8-2):

(Dollars in thousands)	**Common Stock**		**Paid-In**	**Retained**
	Shares	**Amount**	**Capital**	**Earnings**
1 Stock issued	6,503,400	650	144,150	

The sale of these shares resulted in a cash inflow of $144,800,000, an increase in common stock of $650,000 (par value at $.10 per share), and an increase of $144,150,000 in paid-in capital:

Assets =		**Liabilities + Equity**		**+ Revenues − Expenses**
Cash	144,800	Common Stock	650	
		Paid-In Capital	144,150	-0-

A corporation's annual report includes explanatory information about its financial statements. Notes accompanying financial statements are useful for understanding events described in the statements. GAAP require organizations to provide sufficient explanatory information so external users can understand data presented in financial statements. A note describing the stock offering by First Financial is included in its annual report, as shown in Exhibit 8-3.

Exhibit 8-3

NOTE DESCRIBING STOCK OFFERING FOR
FIRST FINANCIAL MANAGEMENT CORPORATION
(Excerpt from 1991 Annual Report)

In July 1991, the Company completed an equity offering of 6.5 million shares of its common stock, resulting in net proceeds to the Company of $144.8 million.

This note describes the sale of stock. The number of shares issued and the net proceeds (cash received by First Financial) correspond with the information in the statement of shareholders' equity (Exhibit 8-2). The proceeds of $144.8 million included $650,000 of common stock at par value plus $144,150,000 of paid-in capital in excess of par value.

When a company issues new shares of stock, each current stockholder normally has a right to purchase a portion of these shares equal to the percentage of shares owned prior to the sale. **The right to maintain the same percentage of ownership when new shares are issued is known as the *preemptive right* of stockholders.** This right prevents management from diluting the control (and wealth) of current owners by selling new shares to someone other than the current owners. When a company is preparing to issue new shares, it normally issues stock rights to existing owners. These certificates authorize the recipient to purchase new shares. The number of rights a stockholder receives depends on the number of shares owned. Stock rights may be sold to others interested in purchasing the company's stock if the original recipient does not wish to purchase the new shares.

Stock Options. First Financial issued 188,909 shares of stock as part of a stock option plan (from Exhibit 8-2):

(Dollars in thousands)	Common Stock		Paid-In	Retained
	Shares	**Amount**	**Capital**	**Earnings**
4 Stock options exercised	188,909	19	1,644	

Stock options are rights to purchase shares of stock at a specified price. Options frequently are granted to employees and managers of a company as part of incentive compensation arrangements. A note to First Financial's statements describes the option arrangement, as shown in Exhibit 8-4.

Exhibit 8-4

Note Describing Stock Options and Awards for First Financial Management Corporation

The Company has various plans that provide for the granting of stock options and restricted shares to certain officers, employees and non-employee members of the Company's Board of Directors. A total of 5.8 million shares of FFMC common stock has been authorized for issuance under these plans. The Company has reserved the appropriate number of shares of common stock to accommodate these plans and other outstanding options.

Options to purchase shares of the Company's common stock are generally granted at not less than the common stock's fair market value at the date of grant, have ten-year terms, and become exercisable in five equal annual increments beginning six months after the grant.

This note describes options issued to managers and employees as part of their compensation arrangements. ***Stock options* permit those to whom the options have been granted to purchase a specified number of shares of a company's stock at a predetermined price.** For example, assume that employees receive options to purchase 10,000 shares of First Financial's stock on January 2, 1995. The options permit the employees to purchase the shares at

$48 per share on January 2, 1996. The stock is selling at $45 per share when the options are granted. If the company does well in 1995, so that the stock price increases above $48 per share by the end of the year, the employees will profit from exercising their options. The options provide an incentive for employees to be productive and help their company's stock price to increase.

The transaction for First Financial recording the exercise of the options resulted in cash inflow to the company for the amount employees paid for the stock. The transaction also increased First Financial's contributed capital as shown in Exhibit 8-2. Under certain circumstances, options result in recognition of compensation expense by the issuing company. For example, if the exercise price is less than the market price of a company's stock at the time options are granted, compensation expense normally is recognized over the period from the grant to the exercise date. Most options, however, do not result in compensation expense. Exercise of these options simply increases contributed capital and increases cash inflow for the amount received for the stock.

First Financial options were issued at "not less than the common stock's fair market value" (Exhibit 8-4). Therefore, the company did not recognize compensation expense.

When a corporation sponsors an employee stock option plan (ESOP), it sometimes repurchases shares for later distribution to employees. It must acquire these shares from owners who are willing to sell them at their current market price. This is one of the reasons a corporation might wish to acquire treasury stock. As services are provided by employees each fiscal period, they will receive the shares.

The amount of compensation expense associated with a stock option plan often is determined at the time options are granted. Shares of stock are issued by a company to an ESOP for later distribution to employees. Compensation expense is not incurred by a company, however, until services are received from employees over the life of the plan. Therefore, compensation is deferred at the time options are granted and then recognized as expense as employees provide service to a company. The amount of deferred compensation reduces stockholders' equity by the amount of stock issued to the ESOP but not yet earned by employees. For example, Exhibit 8-5 contains an excerpt from the stockholders' equity portion of a recent balance sheet issued by Chevron Corporation.

Exhibit 8-5

Chevron Corporation
Stockholders' Equity
(Excerpt from Annual Report)

At December 31 Millions of dollars	**1991**	**1990**
Common stock (authorized 500,000,000 shares, $3.00 par value, 356,243,534 shares issued)	1,069	1,069
Capital in excess of par value	1,839	1,835
Deferred compensation—employee stock ownership Plan (ESOP)	(964)	(979)
. . .		
Retained Earnings	13,349	13,195

Minor modifications have been made to the format of the statement for presentation purposes.

Deferred compensation is the amount employees will earn over the life of the stock option plan. As shares of stock are issued to employees over the life of the plan, the amount reported as deferred (future) compensation is reduced and compensation expense is recognized.

Accounting for stock option plans can be complex. Many types of plans exist and accounting recognition varies according to plan type and terms. Stock option plans often result in tax benefits to corporations. Therefore, tax regulations often determine the terms of stock option plans so corporations can benefit from tax deductions associated with their options.

Acquisition of Other Companies

First Financial issued 18,579 shares of stock to acquire another company (from Exhibit 8-2):

(Dollars in Thousands)	Paid-In Capital	Retained Earnings	Treasury Stock	
			Shares	Cost
2 Stock issued in acquisitions	183		18,579	300

The stock was issued to the previous owners of other companies in exchange for their stock holdings in those companies. Treasury stock worth $483,000 was issued in the exchange. The cost of the stock when it was repurchased by First Financial was $300,000. The excess of the value of the treasury stock when reissued ($483,000) over its cost ($300,000) is recorded as paid-in capital. The transaction also increased First Financial's total assets by the same amount:

Assets =		Liabilities + Equity		+ Revenues − Expenses
Long-term Investment In Other Companies	483,000	Paid-In Capital	183,000	
		Treasury Stock	300,000	

The acquisition by First Financial of other companies is an example of a corporation (First Financial) issuing stock in exchange for assets other than cash.

Conversion of Bonds

First Financial issued 7,297,908 shares of common stock in exchange for the conversion of debenture bonds (from Exhibit 8-2):

(Dollars in Thousands)	Common Stock		Paid-In Capital	Retained Earnings
	Shares	Amount		
3 Debentures converted	7,297,908	730	161,493	

Debentures **are bonds that are unsecured by specific assets.** Thus, if a corporation defaults on payment of the bonds, the bondholders have a claim against the company as a whole. But, they do not have a claim on specific assets that must be sold to repay the debt. *Convertible bonds* **are bonds that can be converted into shares of stock.** When bonds are converted, they are exchanged by bondholders for shares of common stock. The contract that permits this exchange was established when the bonds were first sold. (Chapter 9 will examine bonds in more detail.) For First Financial, the transaction reduced the amount of debt the company had outstanding and increased its contributed capital by $162,223,000 ($730,000 of par value and $161,493,000 of paid-in capital):

Assets =	Liabilities + Equity		+ Revenues − Expenses
	Bonds Payable	(162,223)	
	Common Stock	730	
-0-	Paid-In Capital	161,493	-0-

Convertible bonds attract investors who want protection in case a company is not successful in its operations but who also want an opportunity to share in a company's earnings if it is successful. Bondholders are promised an annual interest payment and are provided more protection than stockholders if a company liquidates. But, if a company is successful, convertible bondholders can convert their bonds into stock to take advantage of higher returns. Because of the conversion feature, convertible bonds often pay a smaller interest rate than comparable non-convertible bonds.

Stock Dividends

Corporations sometimes issue stock dividends. *Stock dividends* **are shares of stock distributed by a company to its current stockholders without charge to the stockholders.** For example, the notes to First Financial's 1989 statements report: "All share and per share data in the accompanying financial statements have been restated to reflect a 5% stock dividend paid on July 1, 1989 to shareholders of record as of June 1, 1989."

Objective 6
Distinguish stock dividends from cash dividends and explain the effect of dividends on equity.

The effect of a stock dividend is to increase the number of shares of stock a company has outstanding and the number held by each stockholder. The increase in shares for each stockholder is proportional to the number owned before the distribution. For example, assume you owned 1,000 shares of First Financial's stock on June 1, 1989. You would have received 50 additional shares of stock on July 1 (1,000 shares × 5%). The total number of shares of common stock outstanding increased by 5% as a result of this distribution.

Unlike cash dividends, stock dividends do not decrease a corporation's cash since no cash is paid out. Stock dividends are subtracted from retained earnings and do not change the total amount of stockholders' equity. They simply transfer an amount from retained earnings to contributed capital. The amount of the transfer is determined by the market price of the stock at the time the dividend is declared.

Occasionally, corporations issue large stock dividends known as stock splits. **When a corporation declares a *stock split*, it issues a multiple of the**

number of shares of stock outstanding prior to the split. First Financial split its stock in 1992. A note to the financial statements reported:

> On January 29, 1992, the Company's Board of Directors authorized a stock split of each two $.10 par value shares into three $.10 par value shares of the Company's common stock and increased the number of authorized shares from 100 million to 150 million.

This event did not change First Financial's total stockholders' equity. In some cases, a company will reduce the par value of its common stock in proportion to the magnitude of a stock split. Thus, if the par value is $10 per share prior to a 2-for-1 split, the par value will be $5 per share after the split. By changing the par value, the company maintains the same amount of contributed capital on its books after the split as before, and no account balances are altered. If a company does not reduce its par value, as in the example of First Financial, an amount is transferred from retained earnings to contributed capital equal to the par value of the additional stock issued.

The Value of Dividend Payments

The payment of dividends, whether cash or stock, does not increase the wealth of shareholders. If you receive a cash dividend, you have more cash than you did before the dividend was paid to you. But, the value of the shares of stock you own has decreased by the amount of the cash you received.

For example, assume you purchased a share of stock on January 1, 1995, for $40. Because of the profitable operations of the issuer, the market value of the share has increased to $50 on June 30, 1995. On July 1, 1995, the issuer pays you a $1 cash dividend. Therefore, on July 1, you have $1 that you did not have on June 30. However, assuming no other economic changes between June 30 and July 1, your stock will be worth only $49 on July 1. The corporation's cash (and thus its assets) was reduced by the amount paid out as dividends to stockholders. Therefore, the corporation's value has decreased by the amount of the dividend. However, your wealth has increased by $10 from January 1 to July 1, whether or not the company pays a dividend.

Objective 7
Explain how dividends affect the value of a corporation and wealth of stockholders.

Observe that the increase in wealth is before the effect of income taxes. Stockholders pay taxes on cash dividends they receive. Therefore, a $1 dividend results in a net cash flow to the stockholder of only $.70, if the stockholder's tax rate is 30%.

A stock dividend or split increases the number of shares of stock you own but does not increase the value of the corporation in which you own stock. Assume you own a share of stock in a company with a market value of $50. The company splits the stock 2-for-1, so you own two shares after the split. If no economic changes occur at the time of the split, each share will be worth only $25.[2] Shareholder wealth is increased by the profits earned by a corporation through its operating activities, not by the payment of dividends.

Then, why do corporations pay cash dividends or issue stock dividends? Investors in many corporations expect to receive dividends. They purchase stock with the expectation of receiving cash they can use for personal expenses. Most

[2] Economic changes may accompany a stock split. For instance, a split may signal management's expectations about a company's future financial performance, or it may increase the marketability of a company's stock. Stock prices reflect expectations about future events, not just the results of past events.

corporations pay regular cash dividends because they know their stockholders expect them.

Some corporations do not pay cash dividends. These companies usually have high growth potential and can invest their cash flows in high return projects that will increase investor wealth. Stockholders of these corporations recognize their growth potential and prefer the companies reinvest their cash rather than pay it out as dividends. (Dividend policies will be considered in a later chapter.)

The *dividend payout ratio* is the percentage of a corporation's net income paid out as dividends. It is calculated by dividing the total cash dividend for a fiscal period by net income for the period and may vary from 0 to 100%. Payout ratios for most corporations are less than 50%. **The *dividend yield*, a measure of the cash return to the stockholder during a period, is the ratio of the dividend paid on each share of stock to the price of the stock.**

While having little economic value, a stock dividend may be psychologically rewarding to stockholders. Therefore, if a company cannot pay a cash dividend because it does not have sufficient cash or does not want to pay additional cash dividends, it might issue a stock dividend.

A stock split permits a company to reduce its stock price. For example, assume a corporation's stock is selling at $100 per share at the time it issues a 4 for 1 stock split. The price per share after the split should be approximately $25 per share. This reduced price increases the marketability of the company's stock because more people can afford to buy the stock at $25 per share than at $100 per share. Brokerage fees are lower when shares are purchased in round lots (100 shares or multiples of 100 shares) than in odd lots (fewer than 100 shares). Therefore, investors could purchase a round lot for $2,500 after such a split but would have to pay $10,000 before the split.

Other Adjustments to Stockholders' Equity

Item 8 in First Financial's statement of shareholders' equity (from Exhibit 8-2) refers to other adjustments:

(Dollars in thousands)	Common Stock		Paid-In Capital	Retained Earnings	Treasury Stock	
	Shares	Amount			Shares	Cost
8 Other adjustments	80,832	8	1,211		(237,000)	(4,406)

These adjustments were not considered to be material and reasons for the adjustments were not disclosed by First Financial.

You will discover a variety of activities listed in corporations' statements of shareholders' equity. These will vary from company to company. Those discussed for First Financial indicate common types of activities that explain changes in stockholders' equity. Other adjustments are considered below.

Foreign Currency Adjustments. A common adjustment for multinational corporations is a foreign currency adjustment. ***Multinational corporations* are companies that operate in foreign and domestic markets.** Therefore, a portion of their operations is conducted in foreign currency, such as British pounds or Japanese yen. When preparing financial statements, multinationals chartered in the U.S. translate their foreign operations into U.S. dollars. ***Foreign currency translation*** **is the process of converting the financial results of operations that occur in a foreign currency into U.S. dollars for financial reporting purposes.**

Objective 8
Discuss the effect foreign operations may have on stockholders' equity.

For example, assume Multinational Co., a U.S. corporation, purchased assets in Britain for £5 million. The dollar equivalent at the time of the purchase was $10 million. But, assume the dollar equivalent at the end of Multinational Co.'s fiscal year is $9.9 million. A change in the exchange rate between pounds and dollars has reduced the dollar equivalent value of the assets. This change in value is reported on the balance sheet as an adjustment to stockholders' equity.

Exhibit 8-6 provides a recent balance sheet presentation of stockholders' equity for IBM.

Exhibit 8-6

International Business Machines Corporation
Stockholders' Equity
(Excerpt from Annual Report)

(Dollars in millions)	**1991**	**1990**
Capital stock, par value $1.25 per share	6,531	6,357
Shares authorized: 750,000,000		
Issued: 1991—571,349,324; 1990—571,618,795		
Retained earnings	27,339	33,234
Translation adjustments	3,167	3,266
Less: Treasury stock, at cost	(31)	(25)
Shares: 1991—331,665; 1990—227,604		
Total Stockholders' Equity	37,006	42,832

Learning Note

Note that while IBM reports a par value for its stock ($1.25 per share), it does not separate the amount of contributed capital between common stock and paid-in capital. It reports the entire amount as capital stock. This is another example of the many variations you will encounter in financial reporting practices among corporations.

A *translation adjustment* represents the effect of translating the operations of a company's foreign subsidiaries into U.S. dollars for purposes of reporting consolidated financial statements. These adjustments may result in gains or losses depending on whether the dollar has gained or lost value relative to other currencies during a period. Translation adjustments may be reported either as a separate item in the stockholders' equity section of the balance sheet or on the income statement. How these adjustments are reported depends on the type of foreign activities in which a company is involved.

If a subsidiary's foreign activities are sufficient that a foreign currency is the primary medium of exchange for its activities, the foreign currency is the subsidiary's functional currency. ***Functional currency*** **is the currency a company or division uses in conducting its operating activities.** For example, assume that a company owns a subsidiary that operates largely independent of the parent in a foreign country. The functional currency for the foreign operations would be the local currency of the foreign country. Because the foreign subsidiary would be included on the parent company's consolidated financial statements, asset and liability accounts are translated from their foreign currency amounts to dollars at the exchange rate that exists at the balance sheet date. Revenue and expense accounts are translated at the average rate of exchange for the fiscal period. Gains and losses associated with changes in exchange rates are reported as part of stockholders' equity on the consolidated balance sheet as in Exhibit 8-6.

On the other hand, assume the subsidiary is simply an extension of the parent company. It exists primarily as a means for the parent to sell goods produced in the U.S. in a foreign market. Or, it might exist so the U.S. company has access to raw materials produced in a foreign country. The subsidiary's functional currency would be the dollar. The subsidiary's account balances would be translated into dollars on the parent's consolidated statements using a complex procedure that distinguishes between monetary and nonmonetary assets and liabilities. Monetary items are those that have a fixed monetary value, such as cash, receivables, and marketable securities, while nonmonetary items include inventory and fixed assets. This method also is used for translating accounts of subsidiaries that operate in highly inflationary environments, such as many Latin American countries. When this method is used, gains and losses resulting from exchange rate changes are included on the income statement.

Exhibit 8-7 summarizes some of the primary differences between the methods used to report foreign currency translation gains and losses.

Exhibit 8-7

Foreign Currency Translation Methods

Level of Foreign Activity	Functional Currency	Effect on Balance Sheet	Effect on Income Statement
High	Foreign	Balance sheet accounts translated at balance sheet date; Gains or losses reported as part of stockholders' equity	Income statement accounts translated at average exchange rate for the fiscal period
Low	US$	Monetary accounts translated at balance sheet date; Nonmonetary accounts translated at rate when they were acquired	Income statement accounts translated at rate when transactions occurred; Gains or losses reported on income statement

Thus, when you observe translation adjustments on the balance sheet, you should recognize these adjustments result from foreign currency gains and losses of foreign subsidiaries. The functional currency for these operations is the foreign currency. **Gains or losses from translating the accounts of these subsidiaries to U.S. dollars have not been included as part of net income.** The cumulative amount of the gains and losses is reported as an addition to (for a cumulative gain) or a subtraction from (for a cumulative loss) stockholders' equity.

The gain or loss recognized during a specific fiscal year is added to or subtracted from the cumulative translation adjustment balance. For example, assume that Far East Company has a cumulative translation adjustment balance of

$10 million at the end of 1994, representing a net translation gain. Translation of account balances for its foreign subsidiaries results in a loss of $2 million for fiscal 1995. The balance added to stockholders' equity on the consolidated balance sheet for the 1995 fiscal year would be $8 million. As long as a company maintains its foreign operations and does not convert its foreign investment into dollars, these gains and losses do not reflect economic changes in the company's operations because foreign currency has not actually been exchanged for dollars. The adjustment reported on the balance sheet identifies the approximate amount of gain or loss that would result if the foreign investment were converted into dollars at the balance sheet date.

Minority Interest. ***Minority interest*** **is the portion of a subsidiary's stockholders' equity owned by shareholders other than the parent corporation.** For example, assume that Parent Co. owns 80% of Subsidiary Co.'s stock. Subsidiary reports total stockholders' equity of $2,000,000 for fiscal 1995. The minority interest associated with the 20% of the stock that Parent does not own would be $400,000. Parent would report this amount as minority interest on its balance sheet.

Corporations differ in their reporting of minority interest. Some report it as part of stockholders' equity—a portion of the consolidated company's total equity held by outside interests. Some corporations report minority interest as a liability—a claim by outside interests against a portion of the consolidated company's resources. Other companies include minority interest as a separate category between liabilities and equity.

Appropriation of Retained Earnings. **An** ***appropriation of retained earnings*** **transfers part of the retained earnings balance to a restricted retained earnings account.** It is used to signal management's intent to conserve cash for a specific purpose by restricting it from being distributed as dividends. The new account title might be RETAINED EARNINGS—APPROPRIATION FOR PLANT EXPANSION or something similar. Appropriations are rare among U.S. companies but sometimes are found in financial statements of foreign companies.

SELF-STUDY PROBLEM 8-2

Excerpts from financial statements for Vulcan Materials Co. are provided on the next page. From this information, answer the following questions:

1. What was Vulcan's total contributed capital for 1990?
2. How many shares of common stock were outstanding at the end of 1990?
3. Did Vulcan report a gain or loss from foreign currency translation adjustments during 1990 as reported on the balance sheet?
4. Was the functional currency U.S. dollars or foreign currency for the operations associated with the translation adjustments on the balance sheet?
5. What dollar amount of treasury stock did Vulcan hold at the end of 1990?
6. What was the net change in the number of treasury shares held by Vulcan during 1990?
7. What was the amount of dividend per share paid by Vulcan during 1990, assuming that 38,680,000 shares were outstanding when dividends were paid?

8. What was the dividend payout ratio for 1990 for Vulcan?
9. How much net cash flow was generated from financing activities associated with stockholders' equity during the current year? What were the sources of this cash flow?
10. How much net income was generated from financing activities associated with stockholders' equity during the current year?

Vulcan Materials Company
(Excerpt from the Consolidated Balance Sheet)

(Amounts in thousands)	1990	1989
Shareholders' equity		
Common stock, $1 par value	$ 46,573	$ 46,573
Capital in excess of par value	2,758	1,477
Retained earnings	912,173	838,311
Accumulated foreign currency translation adjustment	—	(445)
Total	961,504	885,916
Less cost of stock in treasury	281,312	222,371
Total stockholders' equity	$680,192	$663,545

Statement of Shareholders' Equity
for 1990

(Amounts and shares in thousands)	Shares	Amount
Common stock, $1 par value		
Authorized: 160,000 shares		
Issued at beginning of year	46,573	$ 46,573
Issued at end of year	46,573	46,573
Capital in excess of par value		
Balance at beginning of year		1,477
Distributions under Performance Share Plan		1,281
Balance at end of year		2,758
Retained earnings		
Balance at beginning of year		838,311
Net earnings		120,278
Cash dividends on common stock		(46,416)
Balance at end of year		912,173
Accumulated foreign currency translation adjustment		
Balance at beginning of year		(445)
Translation adjustments		445
Balance at end of year		—
Common stock held in treasury		
Balance at beginning of year	(7,078)	(222,371)
Purchase of common shares	(1,423)	(59,242)
Distributions under Performance Share Plan	34	301
Balance at end of year	(8,467)	(281,312)
Total		$680,192

The solution to Self-Study Problem 8-2 appears at the end of the chapter.

CLASSES OF STOCK

Objective 9
Distinguish preferred stock from common stock and discuss why more than one type of stock may be issued.

Some corporations issue more than one type or class of stock. The classes may differ with respect to voting and dividend rights. A corporation's annual report will describe the different classes of stock issued by a company. One type of stock issued by many companies, in addition to common stock, is preferred stock.

Preferred stock **is stock that has a higher claim on dividends and assets than common stock.** Cash dividends must be paid to preferred stockholders before they can be paid to common stockholders. Preferred stockholders also often have a liquidation preference over common stockholders. If a corporation becomes unable to meet its obligations and must liquidate its assets, preferred stockholders will be paid before common stockholders. Therefore, preferred stock is a less risky investment. Preferred stockholders normally do not have voting rights in a corporation. Thus, preferred stockholders participate in the profits of a corporation but not in decisions about its operations. Like bonds, some preferred stock is convertible. Convertible preferred stock can be exchanged for shares of common stock under the provisions of the preferred stock agreement. In rare cases, preferred stock may be exchanged for bonds rather than common stock.

Percentage of Major Corporations Issuing Preferred Stock

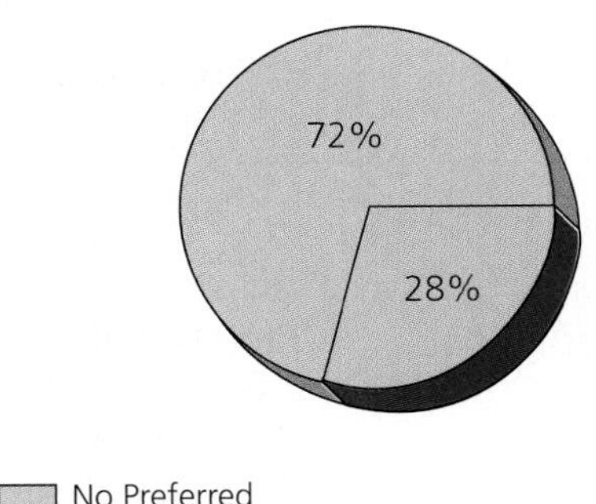

(Data source: Accounting Trends & Techniques, 1991)

Corporations issue preferred stock to attract investors who do not want to take as much risk as common stockholders. If a company does well, preferred stockholders will receive a reasonable return on their investments and may be able to convert their shares to common stock. If a company does poorly, preferred stockholders are likely to receive higher returns than common stockholders and are more protected against loss in case of liquidation.

Exhibit 8-8 provides an example of the stockholders' equity presentation from a recent annual report of Sears, Roebuck and Co. Preferred stock is presented on the balance sheet before common stock. The numbers of shares authorized, issued, and outstanding also are reported on the statement or in the notes. Thus, the reporting of preferred stock is similar to that of common stock. The issuance of preferred stock results in cash inflow to a corporation, just as does the issuance of common stock.

A note to the Sears statement discloses:

> In November 1991, Sears, Roebuck and Co. issued 3.25 million 8.88% Preferred Shares. . . . All shares were outstanding as of Dec. 31, 1991. Dividends of $3.9 million were accrued during 1991. The 8.88% Preferred Shares have cumulative dividends and a liquidation preference of $100 per share . . . plus accrued and unpaid dividends. On or after Nov. 9, 1996, Sears may, at its option, redeem the 8.88% Preferred Shares, in whole or in part, at any time at a redemption price of $100 per share, plus accrued and unpaid dividends to the redemption date.

Exhibit 8-8

SEARS, ROEBUCK AND CO.
SHAREHOLDERS' EQUITY
(Excerpt from Annual Report)

December 31 (millions)	**1991**	**1990**
Preferred shares, ($1 par value, 3.25 shares outstanding in 1991)	$ 325.0	$ —
Common shares ($.75 par value, 344.1 and 343.1 shares outstanding)	289.5	289.1
Capital in excess of par value	2,153.4	2,137.9
Retained earnings	13,514.3	12,927.1
Treasury stock (at cost)	(1,746.4)	(1,765.8)
Other adjustments	(347.6)	(764.5)
Total stockholders' equity	$14,188.2	$12,823.8

Minor modifications have been made to the format of the statement for presentation purposes.

The 8.88% rate associated with the Sears preferred stock is the dividend rate. This percentage times the liquidation value (8.88% × $100) equals the amount of annual dividend ($8.88) promised to preferred stockholders on each share of stock. Preferred stockholders are not guaranteed this amount. But, they will receive this amount before any cash dividend can be paid to common stockholders.

The Sears preferred stock is **cumulative.** When stock is cumulative, **any dividends that were not paid in prior years must be paid in the current year before a dividend can be paid to common stockholders.** For example, if Sears failed to pay a cash dividend in 1994, it would have to pay a dividend of $17.76 (2 × $8.88) in 1995 for each share of preferred stock outstanding before it could pay a dividend to common stockholders.

The **liquidation value** is the amount preferred stockholders will receive per share before any payments can be made to common stockholders, if the company were to liquidate. Other major features of the stock, such as **conversion** and **exchange rights,** also are disclosed in the note to the financial statements. An issuer of **redeemable preferred stock** reserves the right to repurchase the stock at specific times and prices. If the stock is redeemed, the issuer repurchases it at the redemption price, and may establish a sinking fund to provide for the redemption. **A *sinking fund* is a long-term investment to which a company makes payments for a period of time to accumulate financial resources to repurchase stock or pay debt.**

Payments of cash dividends are made to preferred stockholders in the same manner as to common stockholders. The amount of dividend payment, however, often differs between the two types of stock. Usually, preferred stockholders receive the stated dividend rate. Dividends to common stockholders usually depend on the profitability of a company. When a company is highly profitable, it normally pays larger dividends to common stockholders than when it is less profitable. If it is unprofitable, it may skip dividends for the current year. As noted earlier, if preferred stock is cumulative, these dividends must be paid in a future year. Most often, cash dividends are paid quarterly on both common and preferred stock, resulting in a cash outflow and reduction of retained earnings.

Participating preferred stock permits stockholders to participate in the earnings of the issuer in an amount greater than the stated rate. For example, assume the stated rate on preferred stock is 5%, but a cash dividend is paid to common stockholders that is 10% of par. If the preferred stock is participating, the preferred stockholders may receive a dividend of up to 10%.

Accountants disagree about whether preferred stock and similar securities are properly classified as equity. These securities have some of the characteristics of equity and some of debt. The fact that preferred stock pays a fixed rate and does not provide voting rights makes it similar to debt. The fact that a legal obligation to pay dividends does not exist unless sufficient profits are earned to make the payment makes it similar to equity. The classification of some securities as debt or equity is arbitrary because the securities have some attributes of each.

Redeemable preferred stock, in particular, is controversial because a company has the right to pay off the stockholders just as it would if it were repaying creditors. Therefore, redeemable preferred stock often is reported as a separate item on the balance sheet between liabilities and equity.

Care should be used in examining a corporation's financial statements to distinguish common stock from other types of stock. Though not an expense, preferred dividends reduce the amount of net income available for distribution to common stockholders. Normally, these dividends must be paid before dividends can be paid to common stockholders.

COMPLEXITY AND LIMITATIONS OF STOCKHOLDERS' EQUITY

Objective 10
Explain how accounting rules affect the complexity of stockholders' equity.

Stockholders' equity can be complex for some corporations because of the many types of transactions that can occur as part of a company's financing activities. Transactions such as the issuance or repurchase of stock for cash, the issuance of stock to acquire other businesses, the issuance of stock to employees, the conversion of bonds and preferred stock to common stock, and the payment of cash dividends and stock dividends are typical.

Some of the complexity of stockholders' equity arises because of the way GAAP permit or require the reporting of certain transactions. For example, gains or losses from foreign currency adjustments may be reported on the income statement or on the balance sheet. If they are reported on the income statement, they are transferred to retained earnings (on the balance sheet) as part of reinvested profits. If they are reported on the balance sheet, they appear as a reduction in stockholders' equity.

This complexity results from the political process in which accounting standards are established. Managers do not like to report items on the income statement that affect the volatility of net income or over which they have little control. Foreign currency adjustments result from changes in exchange rates. These changes occur frequently and cannot be controlled by a company's managers; therefore, managers have argued that these adjustments should not be reported on the income statement. As a result, GAAP permit them to be reported as part of stockholders' equity under certain conditions.

Some transactions do not fit well into traditional financial statement classifications (assets, liabilities, owners' equity, revenues, and expenses). The accounting rules developed to report these transactions sometimes are complex.

An important limitation of financial reporting that can add complexity to financial statements is the requirement that most items be reported at historical cost. This constraint results in a reported book value for equity that may differ significantly from its market value. Exhibit 8-9 provides part of the stockholders' equity section of a recent balance sheet for Holiday Corporation, parent company of Holiday Inns.[3]

Exhibit 8-9

HOLIDAY CORPORATION
STOCKHOLDERS' EQUITY
(Excerpt from Annual Report Balance Sheet)

(In thousands, except share amounts)	**1990**	**1989**
Common stock, $1.50 par value, authorized 120,000,000 shares, outstanding 26,225,980 and 23,592,569 shares (excluding 14,613,417 and 17,246,828 shares held in treasury)	39,339	35,389
Capital surplus	12,625	205,717
Retained earnings (deficit)	(791,021)	404,655

The deficit in retained earnings for 1990 resulted from the payment of a $65 per share dividend by the company to prevent a takeover.[4] A **takeover** attempt occurs when investors try to purchase large numbers of shares of a corporation's stock to take control of the company from its current managers and directors. Holiday Corporation financed the dividend by issuing debt that greatly exceeded the book value of its assets, resulting in a deficit in retained earnings (total liabilities were greater than total assets).

Holiday was able to borrow a large amount of money to pay the dividends because the market value of its assets, particularly real estate, was much greater than their book (accounting) value. The assets were used as collateral for the debt. Thus, this transaction permitted Holiday to obtain a large amount of cash, because the market value of its assets was greater than its liabilities, even after issuing the debt. The financial statements present the book value of Holiday's assets, which are far less than the amount of its liabilities. The takeover was avoided because the large cash dividend and increased borrowings made the company less attractive by reducing its value. The value was distributed to current stockholders as dividends.

It is important to recognize in this example that Holiday Corporation's deficit resulted from GAAP that restrict the measurement of most assets to their historic costs. Otherwise, it would appear as though the company had become unprofitable and was in danger of bankruptcy. Readers of the company's financial statements would be unaware of the reasons for the deficit if they did not read management's explanations. Also, they should interpret the statements in light of the measurement rules used in preparing them.

[3] In an event unrelated to this discussion, Holiday Corporation was acquired by Bass PLC, a British company.

[4] Data source: M. Roberts, W. Samson, and M. Dugan, "The Stockholders' Equity Section: Form Without Substance?" *Accounting Horizons,* Volume 4, No. 4, December, 1990, pp. 35-46.

INTERNATIONAL REPORTING OF EQUITY

Objective 11
Compare and contrast the reporting of stockholders' equity for U.S. and foreign corporations.

The reporting of stockholders' equity by foreign corporations is similar to that by U.S. corporations. Most industrialized nations use similar reporting rules, though some major differences exist. It is not safe to assume that amounts reported in the financial statements of foreign corporations are measured using the same rules as those reported by U.S. corporations. Each nation sets its own accounting and reporting rules.

Learning Note

Foreign corporations whose stock is listed on U.S. stock exchanges issue annual financial reports that conform with U.S. GAAP. These companies may issue a different annual report to stockholders in their own countries, using different accounting rules.

Exhibit 8-10 provides the stockholders' equity section from a recent annual report of Sony Corporation, a Japanese company.

Exhibit 8-10

SONY CORPORATION
STOCKHOLDERS' EQUITY
(Excerpt from Annual Report)

(Millions of Yen) March 31	**1991**	**1992**
Common stock, ¥50 par value—		
Authorized—1,350,000,000 shares		
Issued: 1991—338,592,899 shares	296,483	
1992—373,077,895 shares		297,949
Additional paid-in capital	437,921	439,430
Legal reserve	16,295	19,118
Retained earnings appropriated for special allowances	26,151	30,683
Retained earnings	766,390	861,227
Cumulative translation adjustment	(66,826)	(111,612)
Total stockholders' equity	1,476,414	1,536,795

Minor modifications have been made to the format of the statement for presentation purposes.

Sony reports its stockholders' equity in a manner similar to U.S. companies. It reports the amount of common stock at par (in yen, ¥), along with paid-in capital in excess of par. Also, it reports the number of shares authorized and issued. It reports retained earnings, appropriated and unappropriated, and a translation adjustment. All of these items are like those reported by U.S. corporations. As noted earlier, appropriations of retained earnings are rare for U.S. corporations.

Learning Note

Sony reported data for the latest year in the right-hand column. Most U.S. companies report the latest year in the left-hand column. Be careful when you read statements to note which year is the most recent.

An item that differs from U.S. reports is the legal reserve. Many countries, including Japan, require corporations to restrict a portion of their equity so it cannot be paid out to investors. A note to Sony's statement discloses:

> The Japanese Commercial Code provides that an amount equal to at least 10% of cash dividends and other distributions from retained earnings paid by the company and its Japanese subsidiaries be appropriated as a legal reserve. No further appropriation is required when the legal reserve equals 25% of stated capital.

Legal reserves are established to protect creditors and others with claims on corporate resources from excessive distributions to owners. Such distributions could erode corporate capital to the point creditors and other claimants would have little protection. Legal reserves serve a similar function to par value: protection of creditors.

Notes to Sony's statements provide a description of changes in stockholders' equity like that provided by a statement of stockholders' equity. These changes are of the type reported by U.S. corporations: issuing new stock, converting debt, and exercise of warrants. Thus, Sony's report about equity is very similar to that of U.S. companies.

Exhibit 8-11 illustrates the stockholders' equity section of Nestlé S.A., a Swiss company. The contents differ in several respects from those of U.S. corporations and from those of Sony.

Exhibit 8-11

NESTLÉ S. A.
STOCKHOLDERS' EQUITY
(Excerpt from Annual Report)

In francs	**1991**	**1990**
Share capital and reserves:		
Share capital	364 000 000	346 500 000
Participation capital	24 000 000	24 000 000
General reserve	4 912 658 820	4 336 247 400
Special reserve	4 885 270 362	4 360 000 000
Total share capital and reserves	**10 185 929 182**	**9 066 747 400**
Earned surplus:		
Balance brought forward after appropriations	2 448 484	4 308 908
Net profit for the year	1 002 430 321	933 491 576
Total earned surplus	**1 004 878 805**	**937 800 484**

The format has been modified slightly.

Nestlé's balance sheet does not report information about the number of shares authorized, issued, or outstanding. This information is reported in a note that describes the number of shares outstanding. Also, Nestlé does not report treasury stock as a deduction from stockholders' equity. Instead, it discloses that any treasury shares are included as current assets on the balance sheet. This procedure is forbidden in the U.S.

Nestlé identifies two classes of capital, share capital and participation capital. **Share capital** corresponds to the par value of common stock and **participation capital** is similar to the par value of preferred stock. Participation capital entitles the owner to participate in corporate profits and has value in case of liquidation. It does not have voting rights.

General reserve and special reserve are similar to paid-in capital in excess of par. Like Sony, Nestlé is required to maintain a legal reserve for the protection of creditors. Thus, a portion of contributed capital is maintained. Other reserves may be established for specific purposes similar to an appropriation of retained earnings.

Note that Nestlé calls its retained earnings **earned surplus.** On the balance sheet, it presents its beginning balance after appropriations for dividends and reserves along with its net income for the year.

Differences in terminology provide a major barrier to understanding foreign corporate reports, especially for stockholders' equity accounts. For example, the stockholders' equity sections of British corporate reports refer to **called-up share capital.** This title refers to the amount of par value of common and/or preferred stock the corporation has collected from stockholders at the balance sheet date. European stockholders often purchase stock in installments. A portion of the total price of the stock is paid periodically as demanded by the issuer. Thus, the amount of cash collected from stockholders may be less than the par value of stock at a particular time.

Instead of paid-in capital in excess of par, British reports refer to **share premium** or a similar title. Instead of retained earnings, they use a title such as **profit and loss. Reserve accounts** are used for various purposes by British corporations. For example, foreign currency translation adjustments may be reported as part of a reserve account. British companies are permitted to recognize increases in the market values of assets, if the increases are expected to be permanent. The increases in assets are accompanied by increases in equity, recognized in a **revaluation reserve** account.

Care should be used in comparing the accounting numbers reported by foreign companies with those of U.S. companies. The notes to the financial statements may reveal important differences in the way the numbers are prepared and in the meaning of terms used to report stockholders' equity.

SUMMARY OF FINANCIAL STATEMENT REPORTING OF EQUITY

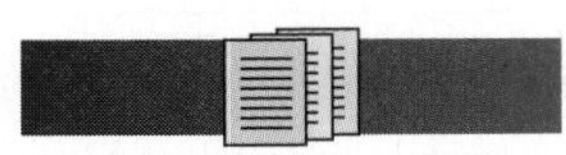

Objective 12
Summarize the effects stockholders' equity transactions have on net income and cash flow.

The effects of most stock-related transactions are observed on the balance sheet and on the statement of stockholders' equity—these transactions are financing activities. Because they do not involve the operating activities of a business, revenues and expenses are not affected. Therefore, the income statement is not affected by stock-related transactions. In fact, **a corporation cannot create income through transactions involving its own stock.**

When a corporation issues stock, it receives cash, but it does not earn revenue since it has not provided goods or services to customers. Even if a corporation repurchases some of its stock (as treasury stock) and resells the stock at a higher price, it does not earn revenue, though it creates additional cash inflow. The link between stockholders' equity and the income statement is in the transfer of net income to retained earnings. The results of a company's operating activities (net income) increase (or decrease in the case of a loss) stockholders' equity. But, stock-related transactions do not increase (or decrease) net income.

Learning Note

When a corporation issues stock options, an expense may result. This expense occurs because of the difference between the cash the company will receive when the options are exercised and the market value of stock issued. This expense is the result of an operating activity, not a financing activity. Options are issued to compensate employees for their services, not to provide a source of cash.

Two stock-related cash flow items are prominent on the statement of cash flows. Both appear in the financing activities section. One is the payment of cash dividends to stockholders, a cash outflow; the other is the issuance or repurchase of stock. Generally when stock is issued, a corporation receives cash, and when stock is repurchased, cash is paid out. For example, a recent statement of cash flows for Mobil Corporation reported:

($ in millions)	
Cash Flow from Financing Activities:	
Cash dividends paid	(1,045)
Proceeds from issuance of preferred stock	800
Proceeds from issuance of common stock	62
Purchase of common stock for treasury	(222)

Parentheses denote cash outflows.

Exhibit 8-12 summarizes the stockholders' equity transactions considered in this chapter.

Exhibit 8-12

Summary of Financial Statement Effects of Stockholders' Equity Transactions

Transaction	Cash	Other Assets	Liabilities	Contributed Capital	Retained Earnings	Net Income
Issue stock	I			I		
Repurchase stock	D			D(a)		
Transfer net income					I	D(b)
Acquire companies		I		I		
Conversion of bonds			D	I		
Exercise options	I			I		D(c)
Pay cash dividends	D				D	
Issue stock dividends				I	D	
Translation adjustments		I/D(d)		I/D(d)		

I=Increase, D=Decrease

(a) Reported as Treasury Stock that is deducted as part of stockholders' equity.
(b) Net effect of transferring net income to retained earnings.
(c) Options sometimes result in a compensation expense accrued over the life of the options.
(d) Translation adjustments may either increase or decrease the reported amount of assets, liabilities, and stockholders' equity depending on whether the dollar increases or decreases in value relative to other currencies. The adjustment is to stockholders' equity as a whole, rather than to contributed capital or retained earnings.

SELF-STUDY PROBLEM 8-3

IBM reported the following equity transactions in recent years (in $millions):

1. Net loss transferred to retained earnings: $2,827
2. Cash dividends: $2,771
3. Capital stock repurchased: $196 (includes $172 deducted from retained earnings)
4. Translation adjustments: $(99)
5. Capital stock issued: $172

Required

(a) Complete the following table by placing the appropriate amounts in each column, indicating the effect of each transaction:

Transaction	Cash	Other Assets	Liabilities	Contributed Capital	Retained Earnings	Net Income
1. Transfer net loss						
2. Cash dividends						
3. Repurchase stock						
4. Translation adjustments						
5. Capital stock issued						

(b) What were the total cash flow effects of these transactions?
(c) How much net income was generated by these transactions?

The solution to Self-Study Problem 8-3 appears at the end of the chapter.

REVIEW *Summary of Important Concepts*

1. Stockholder investment and retained earnings:
   A. The balance sheet reports the amount of a corporation's contributed capital and retained earnings.
   B. Contributed capital includes the par or stated value of stock and paid-in capital in excess of par or stated value. If stock has no par or stated value, the entire amount of contributed capital is reported as common or capital stock.
   C. Stock repurchased by a corporation from its stockholders is reported on the balance sheet as treasury stock.
2. Transactions affecting stockholders' equity:
   A. The statement of shareholders' equity reports events that affected the amount of stockholders' equity during a fiscal period. Common events include net income, cash dividends, issuing stock, repurchasing stock, stock dividends, exercise of stock options or warrants, and conversion of preferred stock or bonds.
   B. Foreign currency adjustments for which a foreign currency was the functional currency are reported on the balance sheet as additions or subtractions in computing stockholders' equity.

C. A company cannot create income through transactions involving its own stock.
D. The primary stockholders' equity transactions that affect cash flow are the issuance or repurchase of stock and the payment of cash dividends.

3. Classes of stock:
   A. Corporations may issue preferred stock in addition to common stock. Preferred stock has a higher claim to dividends and assets than common stock.
4. Limitations of stockholders' equity reporting:
   A. The reporting of stockholders' equity often is complex because of the variety of transactions that affect equity and because of GAAP that permit some items, such as translation adjustments, to be reported in more than one way.
5. International reporting of equity:
   A. Amounts reported in the financial statements of foreign corporations often are measured using rules that differ from those in the U.S.

DEFINE *Terms and Concepts Defined in this Chapter*

appropriation of retained earnings
authorized shares
charter
common stock
contributed capital
convertible bonds
date of declaration
date of payment
date of record
debentures
dividend payout ratio
dividend yield
foreign currency translation
functional currency
issued shares
minority interest
multinational corporation
outstanding shares
paid-in capital in excess of par
par value
preemptive right
preferred stock
sinking fund
stock dividends
stock options
stock split
translation adjustment
treasury stock

SOLUTIONS

SELF-STUDY PROBLEM 8-1

Bovine Co.
Stockholders' Equity

December 31,	**1995**	**1994**
Contributed capital:		
Common stock: $1 par, 250,000 shares authorized, 100,000 shares issued	100,000	100,000
Paid-in capital in excess of par	400,000	400,000
Retained earnings	150,000	30,000
Less treasury stock, 8,000 shares at cost	(56,000)	
Total stockholders' equity	594,000	530,000

SELF-STUDY PROBLEM 8-2

1. Total contributed capital: $46,573,000 + 2,758,000 = $49,331,000.
2. Common shares outstanding: 46,573,000 issued − 8,467,000 in treasury = 38,106,000.
3. Vulcan reported a foreign currency translation gain of $445,000.
4. Amounts reported on the balance sheet are for translation adjustments in which the functional currency is the foreign currency.
5. Treasury stock: $281,312,000.
6. Net change in treasury stock: 1,423,000 shares purchased − 34,000 shares reissued = 1,389,000 net increase in shares held in treasury.
7. Dividend per share: $46,416,000 paid/38,680,000 shares outstanding = $1.20.
8. Dividend payout ratio: $46,416,000 dividends/$120,278,000 net earnings = 38.6%.
9. Net cash outflow: $46,416,000 dividends + $59,242,000 purchase of stock = $105,658,000.
10. Net income is not generated by financing activities.

SELF-STUDY PROBLEM 8-3

(a) **Transaction**	**Cash**	**Other Assets**	**Liabilities**	**Contributed Capital**	**Retained Earnings**	**Net Income**
1. Transfer net loss					(2,827)	2,827
2. Cash dividends	(2,771)				(2,771)	
3. Repurchase stock	(196)			(24)	(172)	
4. Translation adjustments		(99)		(99)		
5. Capital stock issued	172			172		

(b) The net cash effect was a cash outflow of $2,795,000,000 (sum of cash column).
(c) No net income was generated from these transactions.

EXERCISES

8-1. Write a short definition for each of the terms listed in the *Terms and Concepts Defined in this Chapter* section.

8-2. The stockholders' equity section of the balance sheet of Caterpillar, Inc. is presented below:

December 31 (Dollars in millions)	**Consolidated 1991**
STOCKHOLDERS' EQUITY	
Common stock of $1.00 par value:	
Authorized shares: 200,000,000	
Outstanding shares: 100,911,799 at paid-in amount	$ 798
Profit employed in the business	3,138
Foreign currency translation adjustment	108
TOTAL STOCKHOLDERS' EQUITY	$4,044

How much contributed capital did Caterpillar report for 1991? What was the total par value of Caterpillar's stock? What was the amount of paid-in capital in excess of par? How much retained earnings did Caterpillar report?

8-3. Stockholders' equity often includes contributed capital, common stock, paid-in capital in excess of par, and retained earnings. Draw a diagram to illustrate the relationship among the divisions of stockholders' equity and describe each division.

8-4. The Diamond Jim Corporation issued 200,000 shares of common stock in March 1993. It was authorized to issue up to 1,000,000 shares. The stock had a par value of $1 per share and sold at $10 per share. In December 1993, the company reported net income for 1993 of $150,000. It paid dividends of $50,000 during 1993. In May 1994, the company repurchased 20,000 shares of its stock at $20 per share. It reported net income of $200,000 in 1994, and paid dividends of $75,000 during the year. Prepare the stockholders' equity section of the company's balance sheet for 1993 and 1994.

8-5. For December 31, 1991, Coca-Cola Enterprises, Inc., reported 500 million shares of common stock authorized; 140,718,062 shares issued; and 12,217,898 shares of treasury stock. Explain the meaning of each of these amounts.

8-6. Kimberly-Clark Corporation reported the following information for the fiscal year ended December 31, 1991:

	Treasury Stock	
(Millions of dollars except share amounts)	**Shares**	**Amount**
Balance at December 31, 1990	2,072,866	$66.8
Exercise of stock options	(260,626)	(8.2)
Purchased for treasury	17,084	.8
Balance at December 31, 1991	1,829,324	$59.4

Explain why the exercise of stock options reduced the amount of treasury stock during the year. Why is the preemptive right of stockholders a factor in this situation? What was the approximate cost per share of the new shares of treasury stock purchased during the year?

8-7. What is the purpose of the statement of stockholders' equity? What does this statement report that is not reported on the balance sheet?

8-8. Rubbermaid, Inc. reported the following information for the fiscal year ended December 31, 1991:

Net earnings: $162,650,000; cash dividends: $49,643,000; stock issued for employee stock plans: par value $102,000; paid-in capital in excess of par $3,771,000; foreign currency translation adjustment: $756,000; Two-for-one stock split: par value $80,094,000; paid-in capital in excess of par ($41,569,000); retained earnings ($38,525,000); other adjustments to retained earnings ($100,000). Complete the following statement of stockholders' equity for Rubbermaid.

(Dollars in thousands)	Par Value of Common Shares	Paid-In Capital in Excess of Par	Retained Earnings	Foreign Currency Translation Adjustment	Total Shareholders' Equity
Balance at December 31, 1990	$79,993	$37,857	$638,551	$11,803	$768,204
Net earnings					
Cash dividends					
Employee stock plans					
Foreign currency adjustment					
Two-for-one stock split					
Other					
Balance at December 31, 1991					

8-9. Archer Daniels Midland Company reported the following information about changes in its no-par common stock in the statement of stockholders' equity for the fiscal year ended June 30, 1992 (numbers are in thousands):

	Shares	Amount
Acquisitions	2,636	$72,764
Purchase treasury shares	(3,329)	(85,889)
5% stock dividend	15,547	389,996

If the stock issued for acquisitions represented the total compensation the company paid to acquire other companies, what was the assumed fair market value of the acquired companies? What was the approximate market value per share of the company's stock at the time of the acquisitions? At the time of purchase of treasury shares? At the time of the stock dividend? What was the effect of each of these transactions on the company's cash flows for the year? What was the effect of the purchase of treasury shares and the stock dividend on the company's net income for the year?

8-10. During its 1995 fiscal year, the Colridge Co. had the following transactions:

a. Issued 100,000 shares of stock with a market value of $3.4 million to acquire the Tennyson Co.
b. Sold 200,000 shares to investors for $6.6 million.
c. Repurchased 30,000 shares of its stock at a cost of $980,000.
d. Transferred $4.7 million of net income to retained earnings.
e. Paid cash dividends of $2 million.
f. Issued a stock dividend, totalling 250,000 shares. The market value of stock issued was $860,000.
g. Issued stock worth $500,000 in exchange for convertible bonds with the same value.

Complete the following table by indicating the effect each transaction would have on each account or account type:

	Cash	Other Assets	Liabilities	Contributed Capital	Retained Earnings	Net Income
a.						
b.						
c.						
d.						
e.						
f.						
g.						

8-11. The Micro Nesia Company issued 600,000 shares of common stock in 1996. The stock sold for $10 per share. What amount would the company report for common stock, paid-in capital in excess of par, and total contributed capital for this transaction? Complete the table on the next page based on these assumptions:

a. the stock had a par value of $1 per share
b. the stock was no-par
c. the stock had a stated value of $2 per share

	Common Stock	Paid-In Capital in Excess of Par	Total Contributed Capital
a.			
b.			
c.			

8-12. The Creole Pepper Co. had 100,000 shares of no-par common stock and 20,000 shares of 7%, $10 par preferred stock outstanding at the end of its 1995 fiscal year. The company paid a 50¢ a share dividend to common stockholders and the required dividend to preferred stockholders. Net income for the year was $300,000. How much total dividend did Creole pay? What was the amount of net income available for common stock in 1995?

8-13. The Cardboard Box Company issued 100,000 shares of $1 par value stock during 1996 at a price of $18 per share. The company earned net income of $500,000 for the year and paid dividends of $200,000. It had a translation gain of $60,000 on foreign subsidiaries for which the functional currency was the foreign currency. It sold 10,000 shares of treasury stock for $17 per share, but the market price was $12 per share when the treasury stock was purchased. The company reported the following information at the end of its 1995 fiscal year:

Common stock	$ 400,000
Paid-in capital	3,000,000
Retained earnings	5,200,000
Translation adjustments	(460,000)
Treasury stock	(350,000)
Total stockholders' equity	$7,790,000

Determine the amounts that would be reported for stockholders' equity at the end of the 1996 fiscal year. (Hint: the difference between the sales and purchase price of treasury stock should be included in paid-in capital.)

8-14. The Mack-a-Roni Company issued 200,000 shares of $1 par value stock during 1996 at a price of $8 per share. The company earned net income of $340,000 for the year and paid dividends of $250,000. Cash flow from operating activities was $355,000. It had a translation loss of $50,000 on foreign subsidiaries for which the functional currency was the foreign currency. It sold 20,000 shares of treasury stock for $8 per share, but the market price was $6 per share when the treasury stock was purchased. Calculate the effect of these transactions on the company's net income and cash flows for the year. (Hint: the difference between the sales and purchase price of treasury stock is included in paid-in capital).

8-15. What is minority interest? What alternatives does a company have for reporting minority interest?

8-16. Explain why treasury stock is deducted on the balance sheet in the computation of total stockholders' equity.

8-17. U.S. corporations use two methods of reporting translation adjustments for foreign operations and foreign subsidiaries. Explain the primary accounting and reporting requirements of each method. What factors are important in determining which method is used for a particular operation?

8-18. Nippon Oil Company, a Japanese corporation, provided the following information in its 1992 annual report:

	Millions of Yen
Stockholders' equity:	
Common stock;	
Authorized—2,000,000,000 shares	
Issued—1,225,662,793 shares	¥123,841
Capital surplus	105,045
Legal reserve	13,038
Retained earnings	337,521
	579,447*
Less treasury common stock, at cost;	
391,529 shares	(971)
Total stockholders' equity	¥578,476

Column does not total due to rounding.

Compare and contrast the stockholders' equity reported by Nippon Oil with the report of stockholders' equity you would expect of a U.S. corporation. What is the significance of the legal reserve?

8-19. The Better-Than-Average Company granted options for 100,000 shares of its $1 par common stock to employees early in 1994. The exercise price of the shares was equal to its market value at the date the options were granted, $20 per share. The options were exercised late in 1994 when the market value of the stock was $25 per share. What effect would these transactions have on the company's 1994 financial statements?

8-20. The Armor Plate Company began business in 1980. It issued most of its 500,000 shares of outstanding stock at that time at a market price of $15 per share. At the end of 1995, the company reported retained earnings of $5.3 million; also the company's stock was selling for $50 per share. What was the total market value of the company's stock at the end of 1995? What was the amount of stockholders' equity reported on the company's balance sheet? Explain why the market value is likely to differ from the reported amount for most companies.

PROBLEMS

PROBLEM 8-1 Interpreting Stockholders' Equity on the Balance Sheet

The following information was reported by Borden, Inc., on its 1991 balance sheet:

(In millions) December 31,	**1991**
Shareholders' Equity	
Common stock—$.0625 par value	
Authorized 480,000,000 shares	
Issued 201,983,374 shares	$ 126.2
Paid-in capital	314.9
Accumulated translation adjustment and other	(52.7)
Retained earnings	2,127.3
	2,515.7
Less common stock in treasury	
(at cost)—54,499,760 shares	(541.2)
	$1,974.5

Required Answer the following questions:

a. What is the purpose of each of the stockholders' equity items on the balance sheet?
b. What is the difference between authorized and issued shares? How many shares of stock did Borden have outstanding at the end of 1991?
c. What was the functional currency used by Borden for the translation adjustment items reported on the balance sheet? What was the effect of this adjustment on net income? on cash flow?
d. What average price did Borden pay for the shares held in treasury?

PROBLEM 8-2 Determining Stockholders' Equity

The Ricardo Ball Co. began operations in October 1992. It issued 300,000 shares of $1 par value common stock and 10,000 shares of 8%, $100 par value preferred stock. The preferred stock is cumulative, non-voting, and non-participating. The common stock sold for $10 per share and the preferred sold at par. The company is authorized to issue 1 million shares of common and 50,000 shares of preferred stock. In June 1994, the company repurchased 20,000 shares of common stock at a cost of $20 per share. The company's net income and cash dividend payments to common stockholders have been:

Year	Net Income	Common Dividends
1993	$100,000	$ 0
1994	$400,000	$100,000
1995	$600,000	$200,000

The required cash dividends were paid to preferred stockholders each year.

Required Draft the stockholders' equity section of Ricardo Ball Co.'s balance sheet for the 1994 and 1995 fiscal years.

PROBLEM 8-3 Interpreting a Statement of Stockholders' Equity

A statement of stockholders' equity for Georgia-Pacific Corporation is provided below:

STATEMENT OF SHAREHOLDERS' EQUITY (MILLIONS EXCEPT SHARES) — **GEORGIA-PACIFIC CORPORATION AND SUBSIDIARIES**

COMMON STOCK SHARES		TOTAL	COMMON STOCK	ADDITIONAL PAID-IN CAPITAL	RETAINED EARNINGS	LONG-TERM INCENTIVE PLAN DEFERRED COMPENSATION	OTHER
86,704,000	BALANCE AT DECEMBER 31, 1990	$2,975	$69	$ 995	$1,939	$(30)	$ 2
	NET LOSS	(142)	—	—	(142)	—	—
	CASH DIVIDENDS DECLARED	(140)	—	—	(140)	—	—
	COMMON STOCK ISSUED:						
145,000	STOCK OPTION PLAN	8	—	8	—	—	—
580,000	EMPLOYEE STOCK PURCHASE PLANS	20	1	19	—	—	—
(8,000)	LONG-TERM INCENTIVE PLAN	25	—	23	—	2	—
	OTHER	(10)	—	—	—	—	(10)
87,421,000	BALANCE AT DECEMBER 31, 1991	$2,736	$70	$1,045	$1,657	$(28)	$(8)

Notes to the statement indicate that 8,000 shares of previously awarded shares for the long-term incentive plan were cancelled during the year.

Required Answer each of the following questions:

a. What primary events affected owners' equity for the company during 1991?
b. How many shares of common stock were issued during 1991? For what purposes were they issued? Who received these shares?
c. What was the par value of the company's stock? What was the average per-share issue price of the company's stock?
d. How much treasury stock did the company have outstanding at the end of 1991?
e. Did the company maintain its capital during 1991? Explain your answer.

PROBLEM 8-4 Interpreting Stockholders' Equity Transactions

Portions of the statement of stockholders' equity and statement of cash flows for Genuine Parts Company are provided below:

Consolidated Statement of Shareholders' Equity
Genuine Parts Company and Subsidiaries

(dollars in thousands)	Common Stock	Additional Paid-In Capital	Retained Earnings	Treasury Stock	Total Shareholders' Equity
Balance at December 31, 1990	$80,405	$9,449	$1,057,083	$(113,837)	$1,033,100
Net income	-0-	-0-	207,677	-0-	207,677
Cash dividends declared	-0-	-0-	(110,558)	-0-	(110,558)
Purchase and retirement of stock	(120)	-0-	(4,296)	-0-	(4,416)
Stock options exercised	-0-	(278)	-0-	1,193	915
Balance at December 31, 1991	**$80,285**	**$9,171**	**$1,149,906**	**$(112,644)**	**$1,126,718**

Consolidated Statement of Cash Flows
Genuine Parts Company and Subsidiaries

(dollars in thousands)	Year Ended December 31, 1991
—	—
Net Cash Provided by Operating Activities	$ 218,082
—	—
Net Cash Used in Investing Activities	(42,674)
Financing Activities	
—	—
Stock options exercised	915
Dividends paid	(109,281)
Purchase of stock	(4,416)
—	—
Net Cash Used in Financing Activities	(139,423)
Net Increase in Cash and Cash Equivalents	$ 35,985

— *indicates items omitted*

Required Explain the relationship between items reported on the statement of stockholders' equity and the statement of cash flows. Also, explain the relationship between items reported on the statement of cash flows and the income statement for Genuine Parts.

PROBLEM 8-5 Stock Option Plans

In its 1991 Annual Report, ConAgra, Inc., reported the following information about its stock option plans:

> Stock option plans approved by the stockholders provide for the granting of options to employees for the purchase of common stock at prices equal to the fair market value at the time of the grant, and for the issuance of restricted or bonus stock without direct cost or at reduced cost to the employee. During fiscal 1991 and 1990, 76,000 and 390,000 shares of restricted stock were issued. The value of the restricted and bonus stock, equal to fair market value at the time of the grant, is being amortized as compensation expense. . . . The compensation expense for fiscal 1991 and 1990 was $1.2 million and $1.0 million. For the most part, options granted are exercisable in five equal annual installments and expire ten years after date of grant. For participants under the long-term senior management incentive plan, options are not exercisable for three to five years from the date of grant. . . .

ConAgra goes on to report that 1.5 million shares were granted as options in fiscal 1991. 1.1 million shares were exercised, and .2 million shares were cancelled.

Required Answer the following questions:

a. What is the purpose of stock options such as those issued by ConAgra? What benefits do employees derive from the options?
b. What is the purpose of the exercise restrictions described by ConAgra?
c. What is meant by "granted," "exercised," and "cancelled," as these terms apply to stock options?
d. Why is the value of the stock options amortized as compensation expense? What effect do stock option transactions have on the financial statements?

PROBLEM 8-6 Interpreting Stock Transactions

Peggy Sue owned 1,000 shares of Holly Co.'s 1 million shares of common stock at the beginning of 1994. She paid $10,000 for her shares of stock in 1990. On January 1, 1994, the company's stock had a total par value of $1 million and a total paid-in capital value of $9 million. The stock had a total market value of $50 million. The company sold 200,000 shares of stock during the year at a price of $60 per share. Peggy Sue purchased 200 shares of the new issue. After the sale of stock, the company issued a 4 for 1 stock split, reducing the par value of the stock to $.25 per share. During 1994, the company earned net income of $4 million and paid a cash dividend of $1.5 million.

Required Answer each of the following questions:

a. What percentage of the company's stock did Peggy Sue own at the beginning of 1994? At the end of 1994?
b. Explain how each of the following affected the market value of the stock owned by Peggy Sue: net income earned by the company, payment of the cash dividend, the stock split.
c. What was the total par value and total contributed capital for Holly Co. stock at the end of 1994?
d. What amount of dividend did Peggy Sue receive in 1994? What was the dividend payout ratio for the company? What was the cash dividend yield for Peggy Sue?

PROBLEM 8-7 Ethical Issues in Stock Transactions

Consider each of the following independent situations:

George W. Bush, son of then President Bush, reportedly sold $848,560 of Harken Energy Co. stock one week before Harken reported poor earnings, followed by a severe decline in stock price. At the time, Bush was a director of the company and a member of a committee investigating the company's financial problems.

Securities analyst Bert Boksen sold $107,500 of Cascade International stock he owned in 1991. At the time, Boksen was recommending to clients they buy Cascade's stock. Five weeks later, Boksen notified clients he was changing his buy recommendation. A few months later, Cascade filed for bankruptcy. Its stock was selling at $2.50 per share, down from approximately $10 per share, at which Boksen sold his stock.

During February 1992, over 1,000 company executives, directors, and major shareholders sold more than 10% of their holdings in their companies' stocks. The insiders appeared to be taking advantage of a strong surge in security prices.

Required What ethical problems do you see in each of these events? Explain why you think, or do not think, a problem exists.

PROBLEM 8-8 Ethical Issues in Stock Transactions

Perka Wits is an operations manager for the Tall Timber Co. Through the company's stock option plan and other purchases, Perka has obtained 20,000 shares of the company's stock, less than one percent of the total shares of the company. The stock is currently trading at about $25 per share. The price has risen steadily over the last couple of years as the company has taken advantage of favorable industry conditions. Perka has advised a number of friends and relatives to buy the company's stock because she believes the company will continue to do well.

Perka is in charge of most of the company's timber holdings. One of Perka's field supervisors has informed her that employees have discovered a new disease in a portion of the company's trees. The trees are dying at an alarming rate, and the disease is spreading rapidly. Though the supervisor believes a treatment can be developed and hopes to minimize the effects, he believes the disease will create a major financial problem for the company in the near future. Perka realizes she will have to inform the company president of the problem and is preparing the necessary information. She wonders if she should sell her stock in the company before the information becomes public. Also, she is considering informing her friends and relatives that they should sell the stock, though she would not tell them the reason for her advice.

Required What should Perka do?

PROBLEM 8-9 Understanding Preferred Stock

Sprint Corporation reported it had 232,000 shares of redeemable preferred stock outstanding at December 31, 1991. The stock had a stated value of $100 per share for a total stated value of $23.2 million. The stock was non-participating, non-voting, cumulative, with a 7¾% annual dividend rate. The company reported the stock is "redeemed through a sinking fund at the rate of 12,000 shares, or $1.2 million per year, until 2008, at which time all remaining shares are to be redeemed. . . . In the event of default, the holders of the company's redeemable preferred stock are entitled to elect a certain number of directors until all arrears in dividend and sinking fund payments have been paid." (From Sprint Corporation Annual Report, 1991).

Required Answer each of the following questions:

a. What is preferred stock? What preferences do preferred stockholders normally obtain? What preferences did Sprint's preferred stockholders obtain?
b. What do the terms "non-participating," "non-voting," and "cumulative" mean in terms of the rights of the stockholders?

c. How much total dividend was the company expected to pay each year on the preferred stock? What effect did these payments have on common stockholders?

d. What is redeemable stock? Why would Sprint issue redeemable stock? What is the purpose of a sinking fund? How much stock will the company need to redeem in 2008 if it follows its stated redemption policy?

PROBLEM 8-10 Interpreting Financial Statements

Excerpts from financial statements for Dresser Industries, Inc., are provided below.

Dresser Industries, Inc.
Excerpt from Balance Sheet

In Millions—October 31,	1991	1990
Shareholders' Investment		
Common shares, $0.25 par value	$ 41.6	$ 41.6
Capital in excess of par value	419.4	423.3
Retained earnings	1,760.5	1,694.3
Cumulative translation adjustments	(27.3)	11.4
Other adjustments	(3.0)	(1.7)
	2,191.2	2,168.9
Less treasury shares, at cost	430.0	405.2
Total shareholders' investment	$1,761.2	$1,763.7

Statement of Shareholders' Investment

In Millions—Year Ended October 31,	1991
Common Shares, Par Value	
Beginning of year	$ 41.6
End of year	$ 41.6
Capital in Excess of Par Value	
Beginning of year	$ 423.3
Shares issued under employee benefit and dividend plans	(3.9)
End of year	$ 419.4
Retained Earnings	
Beginning of year	$1,694.3
Net earnings	146.8
Dividends on common shares	(80.6)
End of year	$1,760.5
Cumulative Translation Adjustments	
Beginning of year	$ 11.4
Adjustments due to translation rate changes	(38.7)
End of year	$ (27.3)
Other Adjustments, End of Year	$ (3.0)
Treasury Shares, at Cost	
Beginning of year	$ (405.2)
Shares acquired	(36.0)
Shares issued under employee and director benefit plans	11.2
End of year	$ (430.0)
Total Shareholders' Investment, End of Year	$1,761.2

Required Answer the following questions:

1. What was Dresser's total contributed capital for 1991?
2. Did Dresser report a gain or loss from foreign currency translation adjustments during 1991 as reported on the balance sheet?
3. Was the functional currency for the operations associated with the translation adjustments on the balance sheet dollars or foreign currency?
4. What dollar amount of treasury stock did Dresser hold at the end of 1991?
5. What was the amount of dividend per share paid by Dresser during 1991, assuming that 134,333,333 shares were outstanding when dividends were paid?
6. What was the dividend payout ratio for 1991 for Dresser?
7. How much net cash flow was generated from financing activities associated with stockholders' equity during the current year? What were the sources of this cash flow?
8. How much net income was generated from financing activities associated with stockholders' equity during the current year?

PROBLEM 8-11 Interpreting Foreign Financial Reports

A portion of a recent balance sheet of Imperial Chemical Industries, a British corporation, appears below:

At December 31, 1990	**£m**
Capital and reserves attributable to parent company	
Called-up share capital	708
Reserves	—
Share premium account	446
Revaluation reserve	50
Other reserves	381
Profit and loss account	3,014
Associated undertaking's reserves	72
Total reserves	3,963
Total capital and reserves attributable to parent company	4,671

Required Compare and contrast the reported information with what would be reported for a U.S. corporation.

PROBLEM 8-12 Multiple-Choice Overview of the Chapter

1. Which of the following is not a caption that might appear as part of a corporation's contributed capital?
   a. common stock
   b. retained earnings
   c. paid-in capital in excess of par
   d. additional paid-in capital
2. A stockholder who owns 5% of the common stock of a corporation has a right to each of the following except:
   a. to 5% of any dividends paid to common stockholders
   b. to cast votes on matters brought to stockholders for a vote
   c. to receive a dividend of 5% of net income for the current period
   d. to purchase 5% of any additional common stock issued by the company

3. If a company sells 100,000 shares of $1 par value stock for $8 per share, the amount of paid-in capital in excess of par from the sale would be:
   a. $700,000
   b. $800,000
   c. $100,000
   d. $900,000
4. If a company is authorized to issue 1 million shares of common stock, has issued 300,000 shares, and holds 50,000 shares in treasury, the number of shares outstanding would be:
   a. 250,000
   b. 300,000
   c. 350,000
   d. 650,000
5. A corporation had retained earnings of $400,000 at December 31, 1993. Net income for 1994 was $175,000, and the company paid a cash dividend of $75,000. Also, the company repurchased shares of its stock during the year at a total cost of $50,000. The balance of retained earnings at December 31, 1994, would be:
   a. $450,000
   b. $550,000
   c. $575,000
   d. $500,000
6. A corporation paid a cash dividend of $100,000 during its 1994 fiscal year. Which of the following correctly identifies the effect of this transaction on the financial statements?

	Assets	Equity	Net Income
a.	increase	decrease	no effect
b.	decrease	decrease	no effect
c.	decrease	decrease	decrease
d.	increase	decrease	decrease

7. When a company grants stock options to employees, it may recognize compensation expense:
   a. at the time the options are granted
   b. at the time the options are exercised
   c. over the period the options are outstanding
   d. when the exercise price is less than the market price
8. A corporation issued a 10% stock dividend during its 1994 fiscal year. The market value of the stock was $20 per share at the time the dividend was issued. One million shares of stock were outstanding. The par value of the stock was $1 per share. Which of the following correctly identifies the effect on the financial statements of this transaction?

	Assets	Equity	Net Income
a.	increase	decrease	no effect
b.	no effect	decrease	no effect
c.	no effect	no effect	no effect
d.	no effect	decrease	decrease

9. Translation adjustments are recognized in the stockholders' equity section of a corporation's balance sheet when a foreign subsidiary:
   a. is largely independent of the parent in conducting business in the foreign country
   b. is primarily an extension of the parent to sell goods in a foreign market
   c. is operating in a highly inflationary foreign economy
   d. is using the U.S. dollar as its functional currency
10. All of the following are typically true of preferred stock except:
    a. it has a fixed dividend rate
    b. it has a higher claim to dividends than common stock
    c. it has a higher liquidation claim than common stock
    d. it has greater voting rights than common stock

CASES

CASE 8-1 Interpreting Stockholders' Equity

A portion of the consolidated balance sheet of Unisys Corporation follows:

December 31 (Millions)	1991	1990
Total assets	**$8,432.0**	$10,288.6
Total liabilities	**6,417.6**	6,803.2
Stockholders' equity		
Preferred stock	**1,578.0**	1,578.4
Common stock, shares issued: 1991–162.2; 1990–162.1	**1.6**	810.4
Retained earnings (accumulated deficit)	**(497.0)**	900.8
Other capital	**931.8**	195.8
Stockholders' equity	**2,014.4**	3,485.4
Total liabilities and stockholders' equity	**$8,432.0**	$10,288.6

A note to the statement reveals:

> The Company has 360,000,000 authorized shares of common stock. In April of 1991, the Certificate of Incorporation of the Company was amended to change the par value of the common stock from $5 per share to $.01 per share . . .
>
> In February 1991, the Board of Directors of the Company suspended the quarterly dividend on the Company's cumulative convertible preferred stock. At December 31, 1991, preferred dividends of $94.3 million were in arrears, . . .

At the beginning of 1990, Unisys's common stock was priced at about $15 per share. At the end of 1991, it was priced at about $4 per share.

Required Prepare a report that explains the following:

a. Of what economic significance is the par value of a company's stock? What is the significance of the decision by Unisys to restate the par value of its stock? What advantage exists for the company?
b. What are the primary attributes of preferred stock? In what ways is preferred stock equity? In what ways is it debt? Why do companies issue preferred stock?
c. What effect does the suspension of dividends on the preferred stock have on Unisys's financial statements? What economic effect does it have on the company? If the preferred stock and dividends in arrears were reported by Unisys as liabilities, what would the effect be on its balance sheet?
d. Assess the financial condition of Unisys's common stockholders at the end of 1991.

CASE 8-2 Analyzing Stockholders' Equity

Review the financial statements of General Mills, Inc. provided in Appendix B of this book.

Required Write a report that answers the following questions.

a. Explain the meaning and importance of each of the major items reported as part of the company's stockholders' equity.

b. If alternative accounting methods exist for items reported as part of stockholders' equity, describe the alternatives and identify the method used by the company.
c. Describe each of the major stockholders' equity transactions that occurred during the 1992 fiscal year. Identify the cash flow and income statement effect of each transaction.

PROJECTS

PROJECT 8-1 Analysis of Stockholders' Equity

Locate recent annual reports for corporations in three different industries, identifying the primary similarities and differences in the companies' stockholders' equities. Write a short report comparing the captions, primary transactions, and relative amounts of different items in the stockholders' equity section of the balance sheets and in the statements of stockholders' equity.

PROJECT 8-2 Comparison of U.S. and Foreign Reporting

Locate copies of three recent annual reports of U.S. corporations and three annual reports of foreign corporations from three different countries. Write a short report comparing the captions, primary transactions, and relative amounts of different items in the stockholders' equity section of the balance sheets and in the statements of stockholders' equity. The report should focus on primary differences between the U.S. and foreign corporation reports. You may need to consult a book on international accounting or financial reporting for assistance in defining terms in the foreign reports. Provide definitions in your report of any terms that are not explained in this chapter.

PROJECT 8-3 Identifying Stock Transactions

Use a journal index (for example, the *Business Periodicals Index* or the *Accounting and Tax Index*) or *The Wall Street Journal Index* to locate recent articles that discuss preferred stock transactions of major corporations. Summarize two articles that discuss reasons for the transactions. Make sure you include complete references to the articles.

PROJECT 8-4 Unethical Behavior

Use a journal index (for example, the *Business Periodicals Index* or the *Accounting and Tax Index*) or *The Wall Street Journal Index* to locate a recent article that discusses a case involving insider trading or fraudulent trading activities of corporate stock. Summarize the article by explaining key activities associated with the insider trading or fraud. If the case resulted in penalties, identify them. Make sure you include a complete reference to the article.

PROJECT 8-5 Comparing Financial Statement Numbers

Locate recent annual reports of five corporations. Alternatively, use *Moody's Industrial Manual* or another source of financial statement information. Select companies from different industries. Include at least one utility, one financial institution, and one retail company. Complete the following table by identifying the ratio of the amount of each component of stockholders' equity to the company's total assets. For example, if a company has $1 million in preferred stock and $5 million in total assets, the amount of preferred stock would be .20. Preferred stock and common stock should include both par and paid-in capital in excess of par amounts for each class of stock.

Name of Company	Industry	Preferred Stock	Common Stock	Retained Earnings	Total Stockholders' Equity

Write a short report to accompany the table comparing the components of stockholders' equity for the corporations. Indicate the source of your data.

CHAPTER 9

FINANCING ACTIVITIES: DEBT

CHAPTER *Overview*

Chapter 8 considered stockholders' equity as a source of financing for business organizations. This chapter examines debt as a source of financing. An organization incurs debt when it borrows from other organizations or individuals. Debt consists of short-term and long-term obligations. These obligations are contractual relationships in which an organization receives cash, other resources, or services. In exchange, an organization agrees to repay creditors or provide future services or benefits. Debt is a major source of financing for many organizations because financial resources obtained from it are used to acquire other resources. Organizations report information about their debt transactions on their balance sheets and statements of cash flows:

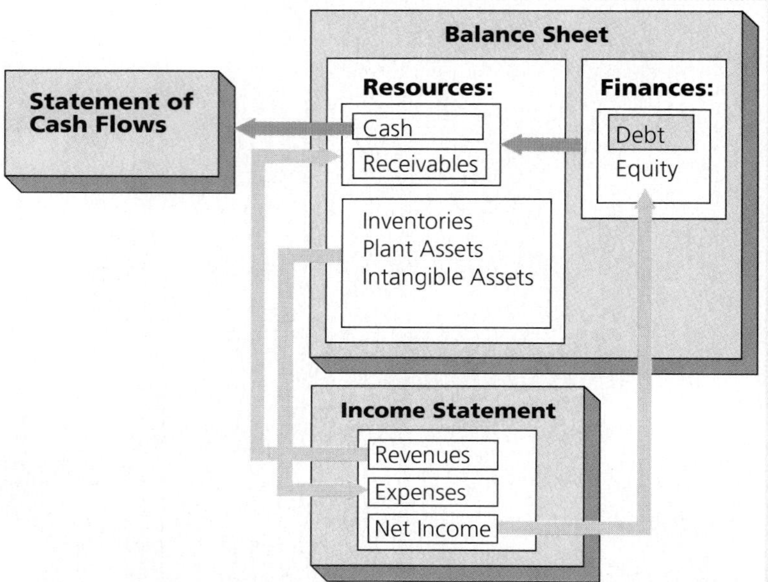

Other information accompanying these statements describes terms of debt contracts and constraints imposed on an organization because of its obligations. This chapter describes this information and accounting rules (GAAP) organizations use to measure and report their obligations.

Major topics covered in this chapter include:

- Characteristics and measurement of obligations.
- Obligations to lenders.
- Obligations to suppliers and customers.
- Obligations to employees.
- Taxes and other obligations.

CHAPTER *Objectives*

Once you have completed this chapter you should be able to:

1. Identify primary types of debt transactions.
2. Determine the present and future values of liabilities.
3. Identify information companies report about obligations to lenders.
4. Determine the price and interest expense for bonds payable.
5. Explain why accrual and cash flow measures of interest may differ.

6. Identify obligations to suppliers and creditors.
7. Explain major accounting issues associated with employee obligations.
8. Distinguish between current and deferred income tax liabilities.
9. Identify other types of obligations reported by corporations.
10. Identify problems in comparing liabilities of foreign and U.S. corporations.
11. Explain how accounting information is useful in controlling liabilities.

TYPES OF OBLIGATIONS

Objective 1
Identify primary types of debt transactions.

Organizations engage in a variety of debt transactions that obligate organizations to make future payments of cash or provide goods or services. Most of these obligations are reported by organizations as liabilities on their balance sheets. Liabilities represent contractual relationships with creditors, suppliers, customers, employees, and others.

An organization incurs debt when it borrows from creditors. A debt transaction occurs when a company borrows from a financial institution, such as a bank, another company, or an individual. The company signs a note (a contract) in which a lender agrees to provide financial resources to a borrower in exchange for a legally enforceable promise by the borrower to repay the amount borrowed (the principal) plus interest. Companies borrow from financial institutions, such as banks, from other companies, and from individuals.

In addition to contracts with creditors, organizations contract with suppliers, employees, and other providers of goods and services. For example, a department store acquires merchandise on credit from a manufacturer and agrees to pay for the goods in the near future. Companies contract with employees for their services in exchange for compensation, of which a portion (such as retirement benefits) may be deferred to the future. Thus, obligations to creditors, suppliers, and employees are part of an organization's liabilities.

The term "liability" encompasses an organization's obligations to provide future payments, goods, or services. **Three attributes define a liability: (1) a present responsibility exists for an organization to transfer resources to some other entity at some future time, (2) the organization cannot choose to avoid the transfer, and (3) the event causing the responsibility has already occurred.**[1] A liability links a past event (receiving something of value) and a future event (giving something of value in exchange for what was received).

Exhibit 9-1 provides an excerpt showing company liabilities reported on a recent IBM balance sheet. IBM's liabilities are similar to those of many large corporations. They represent obligations to governments (taxes and deferred income taxes), lenders (short-term and long-term debt), suppliers (accounts payable), employees (compensation and benefits), and customers (deferred income). Future sections of this chapter examine each of these types of obligations. The next section, however, describes the concepts of present and future value. These concepts are important for understanding the measurement and reporting of liabilities.

[1] "Elements of Financial Statements," *FASB Statement of Financial Accounting Concepts No. 6* (Stamford, Conn.: FASB, 1985), par. 36.

Exhibit 9-1

INTERNATIONAL BUSINESS MACHINES CORPORATION (Excerpt from Consolidated Statement of Financial Position)		
(Dollars in millions) At December 31:	**1991**	**1990**
Liabilities		
Current Liabilities:		
Taxes	$ 2,449	$ 3,159
Short-term debt	13,716	7,602
Accounts payable	3,507	3,367
Compensation and benefits	3,241	3,014
Deferred income	2,879	2,506
Other accrued expenses and liabilities	7,832	5,628
	33,624	25,276
Long-Term Debt	13,231	11,943
Other Liabilities	6,685	3,656
Deferred Income Taxes	1,927	3,861
Total Liabilities	$55,467	$44,736

PRESENT AND FUTURE VALUE

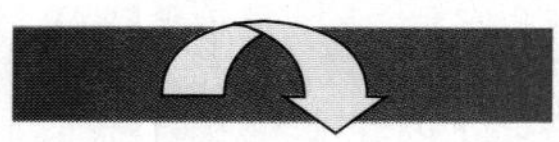

Objective 2
Determine the present and future values of liabilities.

The *present value* of a liability or investment is the amount it is worth at the beginning of a time period. The *future value* is the amount a liability or investment is worth at some time in the future. Liabilities and investments are two sides of the same coin. If a company issues debt in exchange for financial resources, the lender has invested in the issuer. This chapter examines present and future value concepts primarily as they relate to liabilities, that is, from the perspective of the issuer of debt. The same concepts apply to investments. The investor's perspective will be examined in more detail in later chapters.

To illustrate the concepts of present and future value, assume Central Transit Company borrows $1,000 from a local bank on March 1, 1993. The present value of the company's obligation at March 1 is $1,000. If the bank requires interest on the loan at an annual rate of 8%, Central Transit will incur interest expense of $80 for the year ended March 1, 1994. If no payments are made during the year, the company's total liability to the bank at the end of the first year will be $1,080. This amount is the future value of the liability at March 1, 1994. The future value (FV) is equal to the present value (PV) plus interest:

$$FV = PV + \text{Interest},$$
$$FV = PV + (PV \times R^t), \text{ or}$$
$$FV = PV\,(1 + R)^t$$

R is the rate of interest earned and t is the number of periods in the investment. In the present example:

$$\$1{,}080 = \$1{,}000 + (\$1{,}000 \times 0.08^1),$$
$$\$1{,}080 = \$1{,}000\,(1 + 0.08)^1, \text{ or}$$
$$\$1{,}080 = \$1{,}000\,(1.08)^1$$

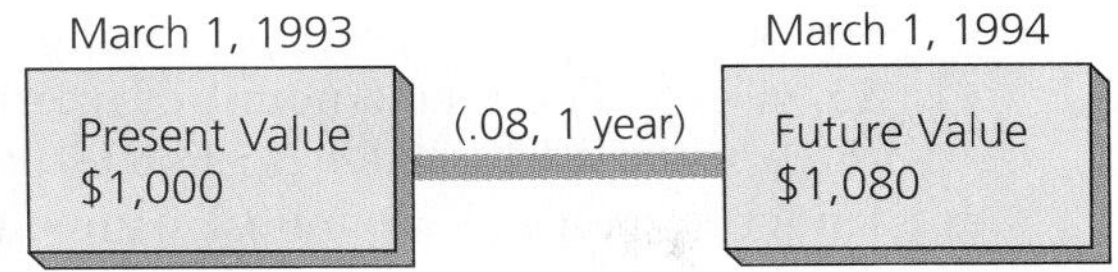

During the second year, assuming no payment to the bank or change in interest rate, Central Transit will incur additional interest expense of \$86.40 (\$1,080 × 0.08). The company will incur interest expense on its original loan of \$1,000 and on the interest expense incurred in year 1, \$80. The future value of the obligation at the end of two years will be:

$$\$1,166.40 = \$1,000\,(1.08)^2$$

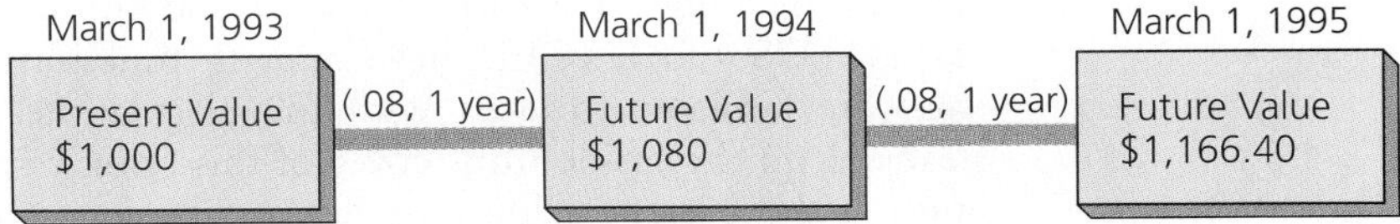

Compound Interest

As long as Central Transit continues to borrow at 8% and does not pay any of the principal or interest on its debt, its obligation will continue to grow at a compound rate of 8% per year. (In reality, creditors require frequent periodic payments of principal and interest as considered later in this chapter.) Compounding results from interest expense incurred on interest accumulated in prior periods. **Compound interest** is a useful concept because it describes the amount of interest expense a company would incur on an obligation over a particular period at a specific interest rate. Thus, 8% interest compounded over two years on a \$1,000 principal amount borrowed at the beginning of those two years equals \$166.40.

Compounding of interest can be viewed in reverse, also. For example, assume Central Transit could obtain a loan that will require it to pay a total of \$5,000 at the end of three years. This \$5,000 is the loan's future value, which also is known as the **maturity value** of the loan. The maturity value of an obligation is the amount the borrower will pay when the obligation matures. If the amount Central Transit will be required to pay on June 1, 1997, has a known future value of \$5,000, how much cash will Central Transit receive from the lender at the beginning of the three-year period (June 1, 1994) if the lender requires an annual compound interest return of 8%? By rearranging the terms of the future value equation, the present value is computed as:

$$PV = FV / (1 + R)^t \text{ or,}$$
$$\$3,969.16 = \$5,000 / (1.08)^3$$

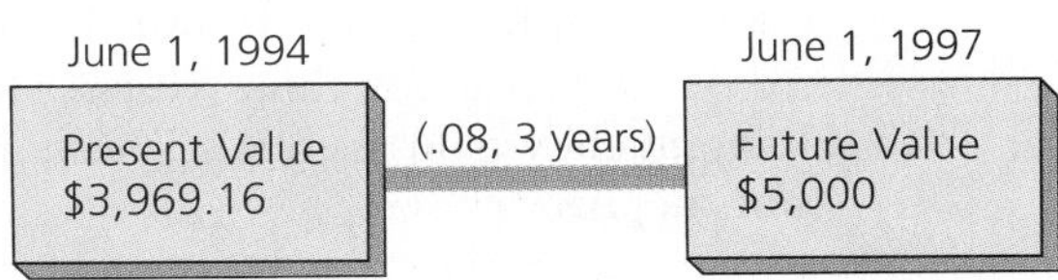

Therefore, the principal amount of the loan made on June 1, 1994, is \$3,969.16. The total amount of interest expense incurred on the loan over the three years is \$1,030.84 (\$5,000.00 − \$3,969.16). We can determine that the lender has earned an annual compound rate of 8% as follows (minor adjustments have been made for rounding):

Interest incurred in Year 1: \$3,969.16 × .08 = \$317.53.
Interest incurred in Year 2: \$3,969.16 + \$317.53 = \$4,286.69 × .08 = \$342.94
Interest incurred in Year 3: \$3,969.16 + \$317.53 + \$342.94 = \$4,629.63 × .08 = \$370.37
Total paid at end of three years: \$3,969.16 + \$317.53 + \$342.94 + \$370.37 = \$5,000.00

Computers or programmable calculators are useful for computing present and future values. Certain calculators and computer spreadsheet programs, such as LOTUS and EXCEL, have built-in functions for these calculations. Tables also are available to assist with the calculations if a computer is unavailable. Table 1 on the inside front cover of this book provides interest factors for computing the present value of a future amount. The table reports values for the expression $[1 / (1 + R)^t]$ for interest rates (R) in the columns and for periods (t) in the rows. To use the table, select an interest factor for the appropriate number of periods and interest rate. The future value (FV) is multiplied by the interest factor (IF) to compute the present value (PV): PV = FV × IF. For example, the interest factor for 3 periods at 8% is 0.79383 (see Table 1). Therefore, \$3,969.16 = \$5,000 × 0.79383. The interest factor 0.79383 from Table 1 equals $1 / (1.08)^3$. Remember to *multiply* the future value by the interest factor to compute the present value.

Obligations may incur interest at a rate compounded more frequently than annually. For example, an obligation may incur interest compounded semi-annually or monthly. If the \$5,000 loan described above were priced to pay 8% interest compounded semi-annually, the correct calculation for the amount received by Central Transit would be:

$PV = \$5,000 / (1.04)^6$, or
PV = \$5,000 × 0.79031 (from Table 1) = \$3,951.55

In this calculation, t is six semi-annual periods, and R is 4% earned each six months. If interest were compounded monthly, t would be 36 (3 years × 12 months per year) and R would be .0067 (.08 / 12 months).

Annuities

Instead of single payments, such as \$5,000 at the end of 3 years, borrowers normally pay periodic amounts over the life of a loan. For example, assume a bank makes a loan to Central Transit that requires the company to pay \$1,000 at the end of each year for three years. The bank requires 8% interest on the loan. How much would Central Transit receive at the beginning of the first year from the loan?

The obligation may be depicted as follows:

Present Value of the Loan at Beginning of Year One	Future Value of the Loan at End of Year One	Future Value of the Loan at End of Year Two	Future Value of the Loan at End of Year Three
?	$1,000		
?	←	$1,000	
?	←	←	$1,000

The present value of the obligation is the sum of the present values of each of three payments:

$$PV = \frac{\$1,000}{(1.08)^1} + \frac{\$1,000}{(1.08)^2} + \frac{\$1,000}{(1.08)^3}$$

This equation can be written as:

$$PV = \sum_{t=1}^{3} \frac{\$1,000}{(1.08)^t}$$

(The symbol Σ is a summation sign. It means to calculate the sum of the expression following the summation sign. The t=1 below the summation sign and the 3 above it means the summation is for the values of time periods 1 through 3.) Using Table 1, the present value can be calculated as:

$$PV = (\$1,000 \times .92593) + (\$1,000 \times .85734) + (\$1,000 \times .79383) = \$2,577 \text{ (rounded)}$$

Thus, the amount Central Transit would borrow at the beginning of the 3 years is $2,577. Since it would pay a total of $3,000 (3 × $1,000) to the bank over the 3-year period, Central Transit would incur a total interest expense of $423 ($3,000 − $2,577).

This kind of obligation is known as an annuity. **An *annuity* is a series of equal payments over a specified number of equal time periods.** Spreadsheet and other computer programs calculate present values of annuities. Alternatively, Table 2 on the inside back cover of this book can be used for this purpose. The table provides interest factors for annuities. To use the table, find the interest factor for the appropriate interest rate and number of periods. Multiply the annuity payment (P) by the interest factor for an annuity (IFA) to compute the present value of the annuity (PVA): PVA = P × IFA. The interest factor for this example would be identified in the 8% column and the row for 3 periods. The factor is 2.57710. The present value of an annuity payment of $1,000 per period for three periods at 8% interest per period would be $2,577.10 = $1,000 × 2.57710.

Liabilities often involve cash flows paid in future periods. Therefore, measuring the amount of a liability frequently involves computing the present value of future cash flows. The following sections will consider these measurement issues.

OBLIGATIONS TO LENDERS

An organization's short-term and long-term borrowings are obligations to lenders. Typically, these obligations are a major portion of an organization's liabilities. They usually are reported on the balance sheet as short-term and long-term debt (see Exhibit 9-1). An organization has an obligation to repay short-term debt during the coming fiscal period. Short-term debt includes obligations that mature in the coming fiscal year, including installments of long-term debt that will become due in the coming year. For example, notes issued in 1993 that will become due in 1994 are classified as short-term debt on the December 31, 1993, balance sheet. In addition, any portion of long-term debt that will become due in 1994 is classified as short-term on the December 31, 1993, balance sheet.

Objective 3
Identify information companies report about obligations to lenders.

Additional information about IBM's long-term debt is provided in notes accompanying its financial statements, as described in Exhibit 9-2:

Exhibit 9-2

IBM CORPORATION
(Excerpt from Notes to Consolidated Financial Statements)

(Dollars in millions) At December 31:	Maturities	**1991**	**1990**
Long-Term Debt			
U.S. Dollars:			
Debentures—			
7⅞% convertible, subordinated*	2004	$ 1,254	$ 1,254
8⅜%	2019	750	750
9⅜%		—	238
Notes—			
5¾% to 7⅝%	1992–1994	987	354
7¾% to 8⅞%	1992–1995	1,820	2,370
. . .		. . .	. . .
		8,810	8,664
Other Currencies (average interest rate at December 31, 1991, in parentheses):			
Japanese yen (6.7%)	1992–2026	3,367	532
Swiss francs (6.9%)	1992–1996	1,204	1,125
. . .		. . .	. . .
		17,611	13,662
Less: Net unamortized discount		17	15
		17,594	13,647
Less: Current maturities		4,363	1,704
Total		$13,231	$11,943

Annual maturity and sinking fund requirements in millions of dollars on long-term debt outstanding at December 31, 1991, are as follows: 1992, $4,363; 1993, $3,377; 1994, $3,115; 1995, $2,024; 1996, $1,386; 1997 and beyond, $3,346.

****The 7⅞% convertible, subordinated debentures are unsecured subordinated obligations of IBM, which are convertible into IBM capital stock at a conversion price of $153.6563 per share. They are redeemable, at the option of the company, as of November 1991 at a price of 102.363% of the principal amount, and at decreasing prices thereafter. Sinking fund payments starting in 1994 are intended to retire 75% of the debentures prior to maturity. During 1991, conversions of debentures resulted in the issuance of 25 shares of IBM capital stock.***

. . . Denotes data have been omitted from the original note.

Two primary types of debt are reported in this exhibit, debenture bonds and notes. The following sections examine accounting and reporting issues for each of these types of debt.

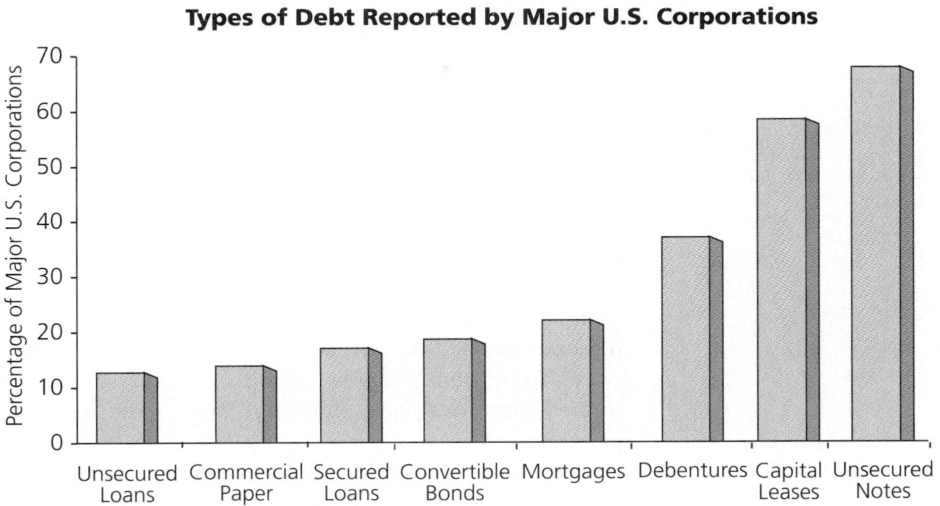

Data source: AICPA, Accounting Trends & Techniques, 1991.

Bonds Payable

A bond is a contract between a borrower and a creditor. It certifies that the borrower will repay the amount borrowed at a specified maturity date and pay interest for specific periods up to the maturity date. Some companies issue bonds that are secured by specific assets, such as real estate. ***Debentures*, which are unsecured bonds,** frequently are issued by major corporations. If a company is forced to liquidate to repay its creditors, secured debt is repaid from the sale of the assets provided as collateral for the debt. Unsecured debt is paid from the sale of other assets. Secured debt typically is less risky than unsecured debt.

Bonds can be issued with any maturity date. Most are issued for 10, 20, or 30 years. Exhibit 9-2 reveals the amount of principal IBM is obligated to repay in future years when its debt matures. For example, it is obligated to repay $1,254 million of bonds in 2004. Note that $238 million of 9⅜% bonds matured in 1991. These bonds were reported as part of the current liability at the end of 1990. Most bonds have a maturity value of $1,000 per bond, which is the amount the issuer promises to pay the bondholder at maturity. Thus, $238 million of bonds represents 238,000 bonds, each with a maturity value of $1,000.

A note near the bottom of Exhibit 9-2 describes the amount of debt IBM is obligated to pay in specific future years. These are obligations existing at the end of 1991. **Sinking funds** are investments that can be used to repay debt. IBM has made such investments over the life of its debt so it will have the resources needed for repayment. Those sinking funds are reported on IBM's balance sheet as a part of its investment assets.

A note also explains the conversion features of convertible, subordinated debentures. **Subordinated debt** is debt that will be repaid after other debt has been repaid, in case of bankruptcy or liquidation. The conversion price ($153.6563) determines the number of shares of stock a bondholder will receive for each bond converted to stock. Thus, each $1,000 bond could be converted into approximately 6.5 shares of stock ($1,000 / $153.6563). The stock was selling at approximately $105 per share at the end of 1991. Therefore, it is not surprising that very few shares were converted during 1991.

Objective 4
Determine the price and interest expense for bonds payable.

Nominal and Market Rates of Interest. The interest rate associated with a bond indicates the amount the issuer promises to pay the bondholder each year, as a percent of maturity value. Thus, if you owned one of IBM's $1,000, 8⅜% bonds, you would receive $83.75 in interest each year until the bond matures. At the maturity date, you would receive $1,000 as payment of principal, in addition to interest. Since most bonds pay interest twice a year, you probably would receive $41.88 every six months, assuming you hold the bond until its maturity date. **The interest rate paid on a bond is its *nominal* or *coupon rate*.** (Some bonds are issued with coupons. A bondholder clips a coupon each interest payment date and submits it to the issuer in exchange for an interest payment.)

Because bonds often are sold at prices other than their maturity values, the actual return on a bond may not be equal to the nominal rate. Bonds are sold in markets to the highest bidders. The amount a bond sells for depends on economic conditions at the time it is sold and on investors' assessments of the bond's risk. For example, assume a company wants to issue $10 million of 20-year, 8% bonds in 1994. The company promises to pay $80 interest on each bond for 20 years and to pay $1,000 to each bondholder when the bonds mature in 2014. Potential buyers would consider expected interest and inflation rates over the 1994–2014 period. They would consider the risk that the issuer might default on interest or principal payments over the life of the bonds.

From this information, they decide how much to bid for the bonds. They might bid more or less than $10 million for the bonds. If the bonds were sold for less than $10 million, the actual return to investors would be greater than 8%. If the bonds were sold for more than $10 million, the actual return would be less than 8%. **The actual market return on bonds is their *effective rate of return* or *yield to maturity*.**

To illustrate, assume the bonds sold at 95% of their maturity value. Investors would pay $950 for each bond. They would receive $80 interest each year for 20 years. At the end of 20 years, they would receive $1,000 of principal. The yield to maturity of the bond would be greater than 8% because, in addition to the $80 interest each year, investors earned $50 as the difference between the amount they paid for the bonds in 1994 and the amount received at maturity in 2014. If investors paid more than $1,000 per bond, they would earn less than 8%. For example, if they paid 105% of maturity value, they would pay $1,050 for each bond. Because they pay $1,050 but receive only $1,000 at maturity, bondholders earn less than the nominal rate on the bonds. To summarize:

- If bonds sell for *less* than maturity value, the effective rate or yield to maturity is *greater* than the nominal rate.
- If bonds sell for their maturity value, the effective rate or yield to maturity is *equal to* the nominal rate.
- If bonds sell for *more* than maturity value, the effective rate or yield to maturity is *less* than the nominal rate.

Determining Bond Prices. The price of a bond is the present value of the future cash flows bondholders expect to receive. Assume the Smart Money Corporation sells bonds that mature in 5 years and that pay a 5% annual coupon rate. Interest is paid every six months ($25 per $1,000 bond). The bonds sell at a price that will yield an effective rate of 6% (3% semi-annually) for investors. The cash flows from a bond consist of periodic interest payments (an annuity) and principal (a single amount) paid at maturity. Therefore, the price of a bond is the present value of *future interest payments plus principal.*

Present Value of 5 Year, 5% Bond With Semi-Annual Payments Discounted At 6%

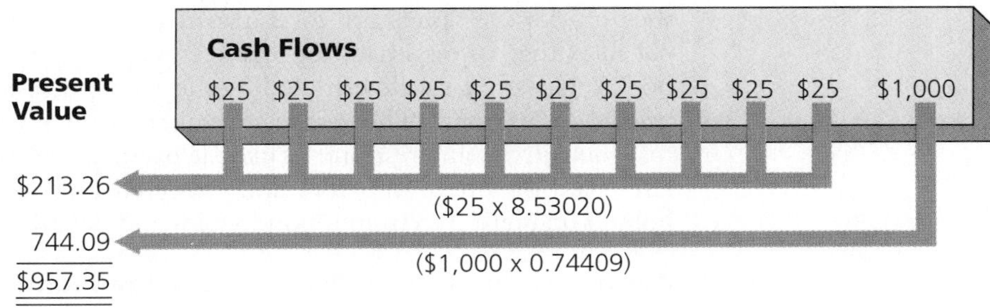

The present value of the interest payments in this example can be computed as:

$$\text{PV (of interest)} = \sum_{t=1}^{10} \frac{\$25}{(1.03)^t}$$

Table 2 provides the interest factor for an annuity of 10 periods at 3% per period as 8.53020. Therefore, the present value of the interest payments is $213.26 ($25 × 8.53020).

The present value of the principal payment can be computed as:

$$\text{PV (of principal)} = \frac{\$1{,}000}{(1.03)^{10}}$$

Table 1 provides the interest factor for a single amount at the end of 10 periods at 3% as 0.74409. Therefore, the present value of the principal is $744.09 ($1,000 × .74409).

The price of a bond is the present value of interest *plus* the present value of principal:

$$\text{PV (of bond)} = \$957.35 = \$213.26 + \$744.09$$

If Smart Money sold $10 million of bonds, it would receive $9,573,500.

This example illustrates the relationship between nominal (or coupon) and market (or effective) rates of interest. **The nominal rate indicates the rate of interest paid annually. The market rate indicates the annual return bond investors expect to earn and the rate of interest the issuer expects to incur.** The market rate may be higher, lower, or the same as the coupon rate. If the market and coupon rates are the same, bonds will sell at maturity value (sometimes called **par** or **face value**). If the market rate is higher than the coupon rate, bonds will sell at a **discount**, an amount less than maturity value. By bidding less than maturity value, investors increase their effective returns. If the market rate is less than the coupon rate, bonds will sell at a **premium,** an amount greater than maturity value. By bidding more than maturity value, investors decrease their effective returns. Remember bonds are sold in a competitive market. Investors will pay an amount equal to the what they believe bonds are worth.

A bond's nominal rate is determined by the issuer. It can be any amount the issuer decides is appropriate. For example, zero-coupon bonds have a nominal rate of 0%. The return earned by investors is the difference between what they pay for the bonds and their maturity value. Most bonds are issued at nominal rates that approximate the market rate at the time the bonds are issued. A bond's market rate is determined by the return investors require before they will purchase the bond. The market rate increases with the risk that a bond issuer may default on interest and principal payments. Also, it is affected by interest rates paid on other securities and expected inflation rates over the life of the bond. Chapter 10 examines bond yields and default risk.

Amortization of Bond Discount and Premium. Interest expense for the issuer of bonds is determined by the market rate on the bonds at the time they are issued, not by their nominal rate. For example, assume Smart Money issues five-year, 5% bonds with a maturity value of $10,000,000. The bonds pay interest semi-annually. They sell at 95.735 percent of par to yield an effective rate of 6%. Exhibit 9-3 describes the computation of interest expense on the bonds over their lives. This schedule is known as an **amortization schedule**.

Exhibit 9-3

Amortization Schedule for Bonds Issued at a Discount

a	b	c	d	e	f	g
Period	**Present Value at Beginning of Period**	**Unamortized Discount ($10 million − b)**	**Interest Expense (b × 3%)**	**Interest Payment (nominal rate × maturity value)**	**Amortization (d − e)**	**Present Value at End of Period (b + f)**
1	$9,573,500	$426,500	$287,205	$250,000	$37,205	$ 9,610,705
2	9,610,705	389,295	288,321	250,000	38,321	9,649,026
3	9,649,026	350,974	289,471	250,000	39,471	9,688,497
4	9,688,497	311,503	290,655	250,000	40,655	9,729,152
5	9,729,152	270,848	291,875	250,000	41,875	9,771,026
6	9,771,026	228,974	293,131	250,000	43,131	9,814,157
7	9,814,157	185,843	294,425	250,000	44,425	9,858,582
8	9,858,582	141,418	295,757	250,000	45,757	9,904,339
9	9,904,339	95,661	297,130	250,000	47,130	9,951,470
10	9,951,470	48,530	298,530	250,000	48,530	10,000,000

Some adjustments were made due to rounding.

Smart Money received $9,573,500 for the bonds when they were sold at the beginning of period 1. This transaction would be recorded in the company's accounts as follows:

Assets =		Liabilities + Equity		+ Revenues − Expenses	
Cash	9,573,500	Bonds Payable	10,000,000		
		Discount on Bonds Payable	(426,500)		-0-

DISCOUNT ON BONDS PAYABLE **is a contra-liability account resulting from the sale of bonds at a price less than their maturity value.** It offsets BONDS PAYABLE. The company's balance sheet would report a net liability of $9,573,500 at the time the bonds were issued.

The amortization schedule reports the present value of the bonds in column b, which is the amount Smart Money received at the beginning of period 1. The unamortized discount in column c is the difference between the maturity value of the bonds ($10 million) and their present value. Interest expense each period in column d is the effective interest rate for the period times the present value (column b) at the *beginning* of the period. Interest payments in column e are determined by the nominal rate of interest. Amortization of the bond discount is the difference between the interest expense (column d) and interest payments (column e). It is the amount of additional interest recognized each period because of the difference between the amount received for the bonds and their maturity value.

At the end of the first six months, the company would pay $250,000 interest on the bonds. Also, it would amortize a portion of the discount on the bonds, as follows:

Assets =		Liabilities + Equity		+ Revenues − Expenses	
Cash	(250,000)	Discount on Bonds Payable	37,205	Interest Expense	(287,205)

The amount amortized is determined from Exhibit 9-3. DISCOUNT ON BONDS PAYABLE is reduced by the amount of the discount amortized ($37,205), increasing the net liability (present value) by this amount. The company's balance sheet would report a net liability for the bonds of $9,610,705 at the beginning of period 2 (see Exhibit 9-3).

The amortization process transfers the discount to interest expense over the life of the bonds. At the end of period 10, all of the discount has been amortized (see Exhibit 9-3). The net liability for the bonds is equal to their maturity value ($10 million), which is the amount repaid at the end of period 10, in addition to the final interest payment. The final interest payment would affect the company's accounts as follows:

Assets =		Liabilities + Equity		+ Revenues − Expenses	
Cash	(250,000)	Discount on Bonds Payable	48,530	Interest Expense	(298,530)

Repayment of the principal of the bonds then would affect the accounts as:

Assets =		Liabilities + Equity		+ Revenues − Expenses
Cash	(10,000,000)	Bonds Payable	(10,000,000)	

The difference between the accrual and cash flow measurement of the transactions can be viewed as follows:

Period	Cash Flow	Expense
at issue date	$ 9,573,500	$ 0
1	(250,000)	(287,205)
2	(250,000)	(288,321)
3	(250,000)	(289,471)
4	(250,000)	(290,655)
5	(250,000)	(291,875)
6	(250,000)	(293,131)
7	(250,000)	(294,425)
8	(250,000)	(295,757)
9	(250,000)	(297,130)
10	(10,250,000)	(298,530)
Total	$(2,926,500)	$(2,926,500)

Some adjustments were made due to rounding.

The net cash flow is equal to the interest expense recognized for the bonds over the 10-year period. The discount affects cash flow because of the difference between the amount received for the bonds and the amount repaid at the end of period 10. The amortization of a discount allocates the cost of selling bonds at a discount to the fiscal periods during which the bonds are outstanding.

IBM disclosed that its net unamortized discount was $17 million at the end of 1991 (Exhibit 9-2). This amount was subtracted to compute IBM's net liability. This disclosure indicates some of IBM's bonds were sold at less than their maturity value. The discount is being amortized over the life of the bonds. Therefore, the amount of interest *expense* recorded each year on these bonds was greater than the interest *paid* to bondholders.

When bonds are issued at a premium, the amount of interest expense recognized each period is less than the amount of interest paid. **A *premium on bonds payable* increases the liability recognized by a bond issuer because bonds are sold at more than their maturity value.** The premium is reduced over the life of the bonds as it is amortized. The following self-study problem considers bonds issued at a premium.

SELF-STUDY PROBLEM 9-1

The Real-Smooth Glass Co. issued $1 million of 5-year bonds on January 1, 1992. The bonds paid interest at 10% with semiannual payments on July 1 and January 1. The bonds sold to yield an effective rate of 8%.

Required

a. At what price did the bonds sell?
b. Prepare an amortization schedule using the following format:

a	b	c	d	e	f	g
Period	Present Value at Beginning of Period	Unamor-tized Premium	Interest Expense (b × 4%)	Interest Payment	Amortiza-tion (d − e)	Present Value at End of Period (b + f)

c. Use the following format to indicate the transaction Real-Smooth would record on January 1, 1992.

Assets =	Liabilities + Equity	+ Revenues − Expenses

d. How much interest did the company pay on July 1, 1992? On January 1, 1993? On January 1, 1997?
e. How much interest expense did Real-Smooth record on July 1, 1992? On January 1, 1993? On January 1, 1997?
f. Why did the interest payments differ from interest expense?

The solution to Self-Study Problem 9-1 appears at the end of this chapter.

Notes Payable

Notes are similar to bonds in many respects. Notes are contracts with lenders (generally financial institutions), who provide cash in exchange for future interest and repayment of principal. The interest rate reported for a note determines the amount of interest payments on the note. Often, a portion of the principal of a note is repaid along with interest. For example, assume the Car Toon Company finances the purchase of equipment costing $10,000. The company signs a note with a bank at an effective annual rate of 10% to be repaid over 4 years. (This example will assume four annual payments to simplify the calculations, although monthly or quarterly payments are a more common practice.)

Car Toon will make four equal, annual payments on the note. The four payments are an annuity with a present value of $10,000. Therefore, determine the amount of the annuity payments by solving the equation:

PVA = Annuity Payments × Interest Factor (from Table 2)
$10,000 = Annuity Payments × 3.16987 (10%, 4 periods)
Annuity Payments = $10,000 / 3.16987 = $3,155

An amortization schedule for the note would indicate:

a	b	c	d	e	f
Period	**Present Value at Beginning of Period**	**Total Payment**	**Interest Expense (b × 10%)**	**Amount of Principal Paid (c − d)**	**Present Value at End of Period (b − e)**
1	$10,000	$3,155	$1,000	$2,155	$7,845
2	7,845	3,155	785	2,370	5,475
3	5,475	3,155	548	2,607	2,868
4	2,868	3,155	287	2,868	0

The four payments of $3,155 result in a 10% effective return in addition to repayment of $10,000 principal. Differences between this amortization schedule and the one in Exhibit 9-3 are (1) no discount or premium exists for this note and (2) a portion of the note principal is repaid each period along with interest.

The transactions associated with the note would affect Car Toon's accounts as follows:

	Assets =		Liabilities + Equity		+ Revenues − Expenses	
At issue date	Cash	10,000	Notes Payable	10,000		
End of year 1	Cash	(3,155)	Notes Payable	(2,155)	Interest Expense	(1,000)
End of year 2	Cash	(3,155)	Notes Payable	(2,370)	Interest Expense	(785)
End of year 3	Cash	(3,155)	Notes Payable	(2,607)	Interest Expense	(548)
End of year 4	Cash	(3,155)	Notes Payable	(2,868)	Interest Expense	(287)

The total cash outflow for the note ($2,620) is equal to the interest expense recorded over the life of the note. Cash outflows are allocated equally to the four years.

This example is typical of procedures used for auto and home loans. Loan payments are annuity payments calculated in the manner described above. Observe from the amortization schedule that a large portion of the payment made in the first year is for interest. The amount paid on principal is much smaller in the first year than in the last year. Very little of the payment made on a 30-year mortgage is applied to principal in the early years of the loan. After paying for 5 years on a 30-year mortgage, a borrower still owes almost as much on the principal of the note as the amount originally borrowed.

A wide variety of attributes can be found among notes. They vary with respect to how cash flows are arranged; some may require interest and principal payments over the life of the note; some may require principal repayments at the end of the note's life; others may require interest *and* principal payments at the end. A note may be issued at a discount, and, although uncommon, a premium is possible.

Bond attributes also vary. Some bond issues are repaid at the end of a fixed period, such as 10 years. Others are issued so a portion of the bonds are repaid each year over the life of the bonds. For example, an organization might issue $10 million of 10-year bonds. Each year, one-tenth of the bonds are repaid. Such bonds are known as serial bonds and are commonly issued by governments.

Cash and Accrual Measures of Interest and Principal

Objective 5
Explain why accrual and cash flow measures of interest may differ.

Interest payments and interest expense for a fiscal period are seldom the same. IBM reported interest expense for 1991 of $1,423 million. It reported interest payments for 1991 of $2,617 million. Prior sections of this chapter have illustrated how the amortization of discounts or premiums can result in differences between interest expense and interest payments. In addition, some interest may be capitalized (recorded to asset accounts) rather than being expensed. Chapter 11 will examine interest capitalization.

Cash flow associated with debt principal also may not equal the change in debt reported by a company for a fiscal year. Consider the changes in IBM's debt for 1991. The balance sheet (Exhibit 9-1) reported:

(in millions)	**1991**	**1990**
Short-term debt	$13,716	$ 7,602
Long-term debt	13,231	11,943

The company's statement of cash flows indicated proceeds from new debt of $5,776 million and payments to settle debt of $4,184 million. In addition, it reported short-term borrowings of $2,676 million. The note to the financial statements in Exhibit 9-2 described current maturities of long-term debt at the end of 1991 of $4,363 million. Most of the change in IBM's debt can be explained from these amounts:

Short-term debt at end of 1990	$ 7,602
New maturities of long-term debt	4,363
Short-term borrowings	2,676
Less: Payments to settle debt in 1991	(4,184)
Short-term debt at end of 1991	$10,457
Long-term debt at end of 1990	$11,943
New debt issued in 1991	5,776
Less: Maturities of long-term debt	(4,363)
Long-term debt at end of 1991	$13,356

IBM reported short-term debt of $13,716 million and long-term debt of $13,231 million at the end of 1991. Differences between the amounts computed above and the amounts reported by IBM can be explained by two events. A company may repurchase (redeem) debt for an amount different from the amount at which the debt is shown on its balance sheet. For example, assume a company has bonds outstanding that are reported on its balance sheet at $12 million. It decides to repurchase these bonds and retire them. The bonds can be repurchased for $10 million at current market prices. The company has reduced the debt on its balance sheet by $12 million but has paid only $10 million. The difference is a gain of $2 million:

Assets =		Liabilities + Equity		+ Revenues − Expenses	
Cash	(10,000,000)	Bonds Payable	(12,000,000)	Gain from Redemption of Bonds	2,000,000

Unlike transactions involving the repurchase of a company's own stock, transactions involving the repurchase of debt can result in revenues or expenses.

Learning Note

Gains increase net income and losses decrease net income. These terms sometimes are used in place of revenues and expenses for items that are not a primary part of a company's operating activities.

Another explanation of the change in IBM's debt is found in a note discussing acquisitions of other companies. IBM acquired a subsidiary during 1991. The subsidiary was included in the 1991 consolidated financial statements. Therefore, the subsidiary's debt was added to IBM's other debt for 1991. To illustrate this type of event, assume Parent Company pays $10 million to purchase Sub Company's assets for $15 million and liabilities for $5 million. The transaction would affect Parent's accounts as follows:

Assets =		Liabilities + Equity		+ Revenues − Expenses
Cash	(10,000,000)	Liabilities (from Sub)	5,000,000	
Assets (from Sub)	15,000,000			

The actual transaction would record individual assets such as inventory, equipment, and buildings rather than a total of $15 million for ASSETS. Also, it would record individual liabilities, such as accounts, notes, and bonds payable, rather than $5 million for LIABILITIES. Chapter 11 examines acquisitions in more detail.

In summary, a corporation's reported debt changes in response to several types of events:

- Issuance of new short-term or long-term debt
- Repayment or redemption of existing debt
- Transfer of current maturities from long-term to short-term debt
- Purchase (or sale) of subsidiaries

A corporation's financial statements and accompanying notes provide information to help users determine the amount of debt the company has outstanding, changes in the amount during a fiscal period, interest rates on its debt, interest expense recorded during a period, and current and future cash flows associated with existing debt and interest payments.

OBLIGATIONS TO SUPPLIERS AND CUSTOMERS

Objective 6
Identify obligations to suppliers and creditors.

Most corporations purchase goods or services from suppliers on credit. These transactions produce accounts payable, sometimes referred to as trade payables. IBM reported accounts payable of $3,507 million in 1991 (Exhibit 9-1). These liabilities result from the purchase of merchandise, materials, and supplies from suppliers. Typically, they are short-term obligations that will be repaid within 60 days. Though accounts payable are a source of short-term financing, they result from operating activities. They facilitate the acquisition of resources used frequently in operating activities. Once credit has been established, a company can order merchandise or materials from suppliers without having to arrange prepayment.

Suppliers frequently offer discounts to purchasers if they pay their accounts within a specified period. The discounts are offered to speed the payment of accounts and, therefore, to speed cash inflow for the supplier. For example, assume the Ball Bearing Company orders a supply of steel ingots from the Steel Ingot Company. The cost of the order is $300,000. The company placed the order on June 1, 1994, and received the order on June 20 with a billing statement. The bill is for $300,000 payable within 30 days after June 20. In addition, Steel Ingot offers a 2% discount if the payment is received within 10 days (by June 30). Credit terms of this type often are reported in a form such as 2/10, n/30 (2% discount if paid in 10 days, net amount due in 30 days). Thus, if Ball Bearing takes advantage of the discount, it will save $6,000 (2% × $300,000) on its purchase. The 2% discount results from paying the account 20 days earlier than it otherwise would be due. On an annualized basis, this discount amounts to about a 36% interest rate.[2] Therefore, companies should take advantage of these savings. The purchase should be recorded at the amount the company expects to pay for the order, which should be $294,000. The following transactions are likely:

June 1, 1994: No transaction is recorded because no exchange or contractual relationship has occurred.

June 20, 1994: The order is received.

Assets =		Liabilities + Equity		+ Revenues − Expenses
Materials Inventory	294,000	Accounts Payable	294,000	

June 28, 1994: Payment is made.

Assets =		Liabilities + Equity		+ Revenues − Expenses
Cash	(294,000)	Accounts Payable	(294,000)	

If the account is not paid within the discount period, the additional $6,000 of payment should be recorded as an expense. A separate account, such as DIS-

[2] To determine the annualized rate, divide 365 days by 20 days to determine the number of 20-day periods in a year: 365/20 = 18.25. Then, multiply the number of 20-day periods by the discount rate permitted for payment within 20 days: 18.25 × .02 = .365 or 36.5%.

COUNTS LOST, is useful for drawing attention to management's failure to take advantage of discounts:

Assets =		Liabilities + Equity		+ Revenues − Expenses	
Cash	(300,000)	Accounts Payable	(294,000)	Discounts Lost	(6,000)

Managing credit is an important function in most organizations. Accounting information can help managers understand the importance of these decisions.

Corporations also may incur obligations to customers. IBM reported deferred income in 1991 of $2,879 million. **Deferred income is another title for unearned revenues.** These liabilities result when customers pay for goods and services they will receive in a future fiscal period. Thus, IBM had received a total of $2,879 million by the end of 1991 for goods and services it would provide in 1992. We can assume the goods and services were provided in 1992 because the deferred income was reported as a current liability at the end of 1991.

Information was not provided by IBM to determine the specific types of contracts represented by deferred income. Given the nature of IBM's business activities, it is safe to assume these are contracts for computer systems, and installation and service arrangements. Customers have paid in advance for these goods and services, or they have made partial payments (such as deposits) for them.

Warranties are another important customer obligation for many companies. **A *warranty* is a promise by a seller to repair or replace defective products or to service products over a period of time.** Typically, products are warrantied for a limited period, such as 90 days or one year. Estimated warranty costs should be recognized at the time goods and services are sold. For example, if Ford Motor Company sells $5 billion of automobiles in September, it would recognize a liability and expense for the estimated warranty costs associated with the automobiles sold. If this amount were $100 million, it would record:

Assets =	Liabilities + Equity		+ Revenues − Expenses	
	Obligation for Warranties	100,000,000	Warranty Expense	(100,000,000)

Warranty expenses are accrued to match them with revenue earned from the sale of warrantied products. When warranty costs are incurred on products that have been sold, warranty obligations are reduced. For example, assume Ford incurred a cost of $3 million during December to replace defective parts. The costs would affect the company's accounts as follows:

Assets =		Liabilities + Equity		+ Revenues − Expenses
Parts Inventory	(3,000,000)	Obligation for Warranties	(3,000,000)	

Most corporations do not report separately the amount of accrued or actual warranty costs in their financial statements. These amounts are included with other liability and expense items. For competitive reasons, some companies are not anxious to disclose their warranty costs.

OBLIGATIONS TO EMPLOYEES

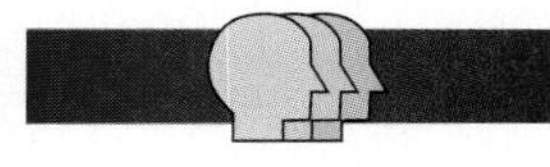

Many companies provide both current and deferred compensation for their employees. Current compensation consists of wages, medical benefits, vacation and sick leave, and disability income. Deferred compensation includes retirement benefits, such as retirement income and medical benefits. Companies recognize current compensation as expense when it is incurred. Wages expense is recognized at the time employees earn the wages. The same is true of other current benefits. Unpaid wages and benefits are accrued as expense at the end of a fiscal year and are reported as current liabilities. IBM reported a current liability for compensation and benefits of $3,241 million in 1991 (Exhibit 9-1).

Deferred compensation poses more complex accounting issues. Until recently, many companies did not record liabilities for deferred compensation. Retirement benefits were expensed in the period in which benefits were paid or at the time employees retired. At the same time, sufficient resources were not being invested by some companies to provide for retirement benefits. These unfunded obligations were not reported, and, in some cases, the amounts were not even known by management. The FASB now requires corporations to report information about deferred compensation in their annual reports.

Objective 7
Explain major accounting issues associated with employee obligations.

Reporting of deferred compensation can be very complex. The discussion which follows identifies the information major corporations report about these obligations. Also, it describes how these items are measured. **The primary accounting issues for employee obligations are (1) determining the amount of benefits earned by employees and owed by a company, and (2) determining the amount invested by a company to meet these obligations and the amount earned on these investments.** When a company owes more than it has invested to meet the obligation, it has an unfunded liability. When employees earn more benefits during a period than a company earns on its investments, the company incurs an expense.

Pension Plans

A pension plan is a contract between a company and its employees. The company agrees to provide future retirement benefits in exchange for current services provided by employees. Two types of pension plans are common. A **defined contribution plan** invests contributions by an employer and/or its employees during the period of employment. These investments and their earnings are then used to provide retirement benefits. The amount employees receive is determined by the value of their investments. A **defined benefit plan** promises employees retirement income that is a percentage of their pre-retirement earnings. Typically, a formula is used to determine the amount of income a retired employee receives each month. The formula generally includes the number of years the employee worked and the wages the employee earned prior to retirement.

Pension plans may be contributory or non-contributory. A **contributory plan** requires employees to invest a portion of their wages in the plan. A **non-contributory plan** is fully funded by the employer.

Pension plans provide a trade-off between current and future compensation for employees. They are beneficial to employees because they provide for retirement with "before-tax dollars." That is, employees normally do not pay income taxes on amounts contributed to pension plans until retirement benefits are received. Thus, they can accumulate much higher investments to provide retirement incomes than if contributions were taxed.

Employers benefit from pension plans because the plans encourage workers to be productive. Employees have a stake in the future welfare of the company because they are relying on it to pay retirement benefits. Often, employers also receive tax benefits for contributions made to employee pension plans. Further, pension plans may permit a company to reduce its current cash outflow by deferring employee compensation to future periods.

Deferred contribution plans transfer the risk associated with plan earnings to employees. Employee retirement benefits are determined by plan earnings and accumulations. The employer does not guarantee the level of benefits employees will receive. Defined benefit plan risk remains primarily with the employer, and plan terms stipulate the level of benefits employees will receive when they retire. The employer is obligated to provide these benefits whether or not plan assets have accumulated a sufficient amount to pay the costs.

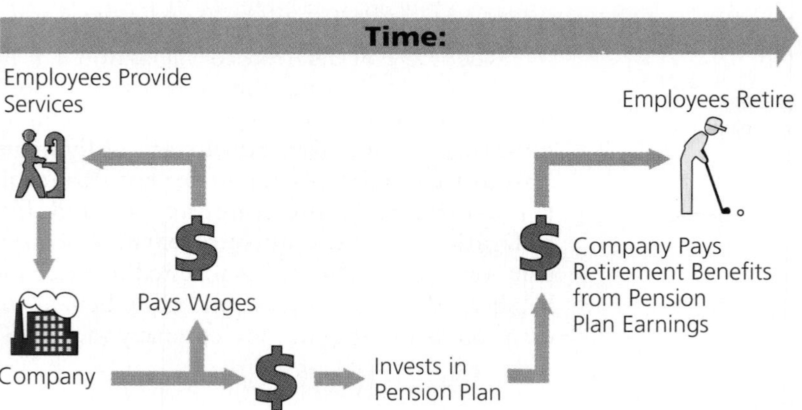

Defined Contribution Plans. Accounting for a defined contribution plan is relatively simple. Periodic contributions are made to an investment fund. The fund manager invests the contributions in stocks, bonds, real estate, and other investments. An account is maintained for each employee until the employee retires. Then, the employee is paid retirement benefits from his or her account. Unpaid benefits may become part of the employee's estate, upon death. Contributions made by a company to a defined contribution plan are recorded as an expense when contributions are made to the plan investment account. For example, Humana Incorporated reported the following information in its 1991 annual report:

> The Company maintains a noncontributory defined contribution retirement plan covering substantially all employees. Benefits are determined as a percentage of a participant's earned income and are vested annually. Retirement

plan expense was $39 million for 1991, $33 million for 1990 and $25 million for 1989. Amounts equal to retirement plan expense are funded annually.

Defined Benefit Plans. Accounting for defined benefit plans is much more complex. A company is obligated to pay retired employees a promised amount, regardless of whether it has invested amounts sufficient to make the payments. The measurement of benefits, expenses, and obligations is quite complex. A company, or its pension plan administrators, must estimate (1) how long individual employees will work for the company, (2) how much their wages will increase until they retire, (3) how long employees will live after they retire, and (4) how much plan assets will earn to provide for retirement benefits. From this information, an estimate is made of the present value of expected future benefits earned by employees and the present value of expected earnings from pension plan assets each fiscal period. The following paragraphs describe the primary disclosures companies provide for their defined benefit plans.

IBM included the schedule in Exhibit 9-4 in its 1991 annual report.

Exhibit 9-4

RETIREMENT PLAN DISCLOSURE
(Excerpt from IBM Annual Report)

The funded status at December 31 was as follows:	U.S. Plan	
(Dollars in millions)	**1991**	**1990**
Actuarial present value of benefit obligations:		
1 Vested benefit obligation	$(16,194)	$(13,112)
2 Accumulated benefit obligation	$(16,229)	$(13,146)
3 Projected benefit obligation	$(19,700)	$(17,091)
4 Plan assets at fair value	25,196	22,225
5 Projected benefit obligation less than plan assets	5,496	5,134
6 Unrecognized net gain	(3,732)	(2,665)
7 Unrecognized prior service cost	1,890	1,323
8 Unrecognized net asset established at January 1, 1986	(2,543)	(2,747)
9 Prepaid pension cost recognized in the statement of financial position	$ 1,111	$ 1,045
Net periodic pension cost for the years ended December 31:	**1991**	**1990**
10 Service cost—benefits earned during the period	$ 691	$ 573
11 Interest cost on the projected benefit obligation	1,488	1,309
Return on plan assets—		
12 Actual	(4,044)	(160)
13 Deferred	1,961	(1,859)
14 Net amortizations	(162)	(253)
15 Net periodic pension cost	$ (66)	$ (390)

Minor modifications have been made in the format. Items have been numbered for ease of reference. Non-U.S. plan data have been omitted.

The disclosures provided in Exhibit 9-4 are required by GAAP. They consist of two major sections. Items 1–9 provide information about the asset or liability reported at the end of the fiscal year. IBM reported an asset of $1,111 million at the end of 1991 (item 9). This asset resulted from the excess value of pension plan assets over the present value of benefit obligations to employees. The second section (items 10–15) calculates the amount of current period gain or loss associated with the pension plan. IBM reported a gain of $66 million in 1991, item 15. Parentheses were used by IBM for item 15 to denote a negative cost (a gain). This gain resulted from 1991 earnings on plan assets exceeding the benefits earned currently by employees during 1991.

The schedule includes several items useful for understanding a company's pension plan status. Vested benefits (item 1) are those that cannot be taken from employees who leave the company prior to retirement. Accumulated benefit obligation (item 2) is the present value of estimated pension benefits based on current wage rates. Projected benefit obligation (item 3) is the present value of estimated benefits assuming wages will increase at an expected rate. These amounts are estimates of future retirement benefits earned currently by employees. Plan assets at fair value (item 4) is the market value of assets available for meeting pension obligations at the end of the current year. Items 6, 7, and 8 are adjustments for differences between actual and expected earnings on plan assets and adjustments associated with the establishment or modification of the plan in prior years.

Service cost (item 10) is the amount of estimated pension benefits earned by employees during the current year. Interest cost (item 11) is an estimate of the cost associated with the passage of time until the benefits are received by employees. Employees are one year closer to retirement in 1991 than in 1990. Therefore, the present value of their projected benefits is larger than in the prior year. This increase in present value is reported as interest cost. The total of service and interest costs (items 10 and 11) is compared with the estimated return on plan assets, including adjustments, (items 12, 13 and 14) to compute the pension cost for the current year (item 15).

The funding of pension plans is an important consideration when examining a company's financial position. Substantial unfunded obligations will require future cash payments just as though the company had borrowed from creditors. Failure to provide for these obligations can increase the risk to investors that a company will not be able to generate cash flows to pay interest or dividends.

Though accounting for pension obligations for defined benefit plans is very complex, two amounts are of primary importance. The net asset or liability (item 9) indicates whether a company is investing sufficiently in its pension plans to meet expected future obligations. The net periodic pension cost (item 15) indicates whether a company's pension plan assets are earning a sufficient amount to cover benefits earned by employees during the current period.

Other Post-Employment Benefits

Many companies provide retired employees with health care, life insurance, and other benefits. Accounting for these benefits is similar to accounting for pensions. The FASB adopted a new standard in 1990 requiring publicly-traded corporations to report information about their obligations for these post-employment benefits. IBM was one of the first companies to adopt the new standard. Most major corporations were required to adopt the standard prior to issuing financial statements for their 1994 fiscal years.

IBM disclosed in its 1991 annual report that it provided medical, dental, and life insurance for retirees and eligible dependents. Exhibit 9-5 provides information about IBM's post-employment benefits, other than pensions.

Exhibit 9-5

OTHER POST-EMPLOYMENT BENEFIT DISCLOSURE
(Excerpt from IBM Annual Report)

(Dollars in millions)
The funded status at December 31, 1991 was as follows:

Accumulated postretirement benefit obligation:	
Retirees	$(3,277)
Fully eligible active plan participants	(303)
Other active plan participants	(1,869)
Total	(5,449)
Plan assets at fair value	1,632
Accumulated postretirement benefit obligation in excess of plan assets	(3,817)
Unrecognized net loss	117
Accrued postretirement benefit cost recognized in the statement of financial position	$(3,700)

Net periodic postretirement benefit cost for 1991 included the following:

Service cost—benefits attributed to service during the period	$132
Interest cost on the accumulated postretirement benefit obligation	389
Return on plan assets—	
Actual	(325)
Deferred	198
Net periodic postretirement benefit cost	$394

Minor modifications have been made to the format.

This information is similar to the information IBM reported about its pension plans. The first section of the exhibit calculates the amount of asset or liability included on the balance sheet. IBM reported a liability of $3,700 million at the end of 1991. This amount was the excess of its benefit obligations over the value of its plan assets. The liability is reported as part of Other Liabilities on IBM's balance sheet (Exhibit 9-1).

The second section of Exhibit 9-5 reports the current-year cost of other post-employment benefits. This cost was $394 million. It was the excess of benefits earned by employees in 1991 over 1991 earnings on plan assets to provide these benefits. This cost was reported as part of expenses on IBM's 1991 income statement.

Like pension benefits, other post-employment benefits can result in obligations that affect a company's future cash flows and profitability. Many U.S. corporations have underfunded their obligations for employee benefits. Recognition of these obligations will have a major effect on the balance sheets and income statements of some of these organizations.

SELF-STUDY PROBLEM 9-2

The following information is excerpted from the 1991 annual report of PepsiCo, Inc.

(in millions)		1991
1	Service cost of benefits earned	$ 46.8
2	Interest cost on projected benefit obligations	69.2
	Return on plan assets:	
3	Actual	(224.1)
4	Deferred gain	134.2
		(89.9)
5	Amortization of net transition gain	(19.0)
6	Pension expense	$ 7.1
7	Accumulated benefit obligation	$(813.9)
8	Effect of projected compensation increases	(133.0)
9	Projected benefit obligation	(946.9)
10	Plan assets at fair value	1,199.3
11	Plan assets in excess of projected benefit obligation	252.4
12	Unrecognized prior service cost	48.7
13	Unrecognized net gain	(103.4)
14	Unrecognized net transition gain	(129.1)
15	Prepaid pension liability	$ 68.6

Minor modifications have been made to the format. Items have been numbered for ease of reference.

Required

Answer each of the following questions:

a. What amount of pension benefit was earned by PepsiCo's employees in 1991? How much revenue or expense did the company report that year as a result of these benefits? Why was the amount of revenue or expense different from the amount of benefit earned by employees?

b. What was the market value of PepsiCo's pension plan assets at the end of 1991? Was this amount greater or less than the company's obligations to its employees for pension benefits at the end of the year? Did PepsiCo report an asset or a liability for its pension plan at the end of 1991?

The solution to Self-Study Problem 9-2 appears at the end of the chapter.

OBLIGATIONS TO GOVERNMENTS

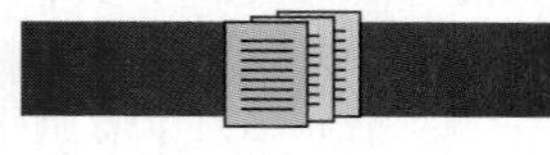

Most companies pay taxes, including local, state, federal, and foreign income taxes, property taxes, sales taxes, and social security taxes. Many of these are recognized in the period in which the obligation for the taxes arises. For example, assume a company receives a statement for property taxes of $500,000. The taxes are for July 1, 1992, to June 30, 1993. The amount of the tax is an expense for this period. If the company's fiscal year ends December 31, half of the tax is an expense for 1992 and half for 1993.

Objective 8
Distinguish between current and deferred income tax liabilities.

Income taxes pose a special accounting problem for many corporations. Most large corporations are required to pay income taxes on their earnings. These companies report an income tax expense (sometimes labeled "provision for income taxes") on their income statements. For example, IBM reported a provision for income taxes of $685 million in 1991, which is based on the income reported for the current year. The U.S. federal income tax rate on corporations in 1991 was 34%. Therefore, a corporation's income tax expense in 1991 should have been approximately 34% of pretax earnings. Adjustments would be made for tax rates on foreign earnings and state and local tax rates, which differ from the federal tax rate. IBM reported that, after these adjustments, its effective tax rate was 40%.

The amount of income tax obligation a company incurs for a fiscal period generally is not the same as the amount reported on its income statement. Income tax expense is the amount a company is obligated to pay on the income recognized on its income statement. The amount of income recognized for tax purposes (on a company's tax return) often differs from the income statement amount. Tax rules permit some revenues to be deferred. The amount of expenses a company recognizes for tax purposes also may differ from the amount reported on its income statement. Thus, taxes owed for a fiscal year often differ from income tax expense. ***Deferred income tax*** **is the accumulated difference between the amount of income tax expense and income tax liability over the life of a company.** For example, assume a company reports income before taxes of $9 million in 1994. It reports its income for tax purposes to be $7.5 million because of differences between tax and accounting recognition of revenues and expenses. The company reports income tax expense on $9 million of income as $3 million. The amount owed on $7.5 million is determined to be $2.5 million. The transaction recognizing these amounts would affect the company's accounts as follows:

Assets =	Liabilities + Equity		+ Revenues − Expenses	
	Income Taxes Payable	2,500,000	Income Tax Expense	(3,000,000)
	Deferred Income Taxes	500,000		

INCOME TAXES PAYABLE is a current liability that will be paid when current period taxes are due. DEFERRED INCOME TAXES typically are reported as part of long-term liabilities. They represent future taxes that may be owed to the government when income that was deferred for tax purposes is recognized in a future period. This method assumes the $500,000 of deferred tax will be paid when the $1.5 million of income deferred for tax purposes in 1994 becomes taxable in some future period.

Under current GAAP, only deferred taxes that represent expected future tax obligations should be recognized. IBM reported $1,927 million of deferred taxes in 1991. In the past, some corporations recognized large amounts of deferred taxes that had little relationship with expected future tax payments. No attempt is made (under current or former GAAP) to discount these expected future tax obligations to their present value. These measurement issues pose a problem in trying to estimate a company's tax liabilities. Future chapters will examine tax issues in greater detail.

OTHER OBLIGATIONS

Objective 9
Identify other types of obligations reported by corporations.

A variety of other obligations may be reported by organizations. Some of these appear on the balance sheet, while others are reported only in notes. Examples include lines of credit, foreign exchange contracts, lease commitments, and other commitments and contingencies.

IBM reported in notes to its financial statements unused **lines of credit** at the end of 1991 of approximately $6,900 million. These lines of credit permitted the company to borrow on a short-term basis from various banks. Lines of credit are important as a source of short-term financing should a company need additional cash. Unused lines of credit are not a liability and, therefore, are not reported on the balance sheet. Amounts that have been borrowed using lines of credit are reported as liabilities, usually as short-term debt.

IBM also reported in notes to its financial statements that it was a party to **foreign exchange contracts**. These contracts permit a company to hedge against changes in foreign exchange rates. Such changes can have an adverse effect on a company's profits.

For example, assume IBM sold £5 million of computer equipment to a British company on credit on January 1. At the time of the sale, the exchange rate was $2/£. Therefore, IBM recognized revenue from the sale of $10 million. When the British company settled its account on April 1, the exchange rate had declined to $1.90/£. IBM would receive a payment of £5 million, but the payment would be exchangeable for only $9,500,000 (£5 million × $1.90/£), resulting in an exchange loss of $500,000. To protect itself against exchange rate losses, over which it has no control, IBM could enter into a hedging contract on January 1. It would borrow £5 million and agree to repay the loan on April 1. It then could exchange the pounds for $10 million dollars on January 1. Then, on April 1, it could use the £5 million received from the sale of equipment to repay the loan. The hedging contract would permit IBM to avoid the exchange loss. The company would incur interest expense on the loan. The company would have to decide whether the potential exchange loss was sufficient to warrant the interest expense incurred on the loan.

Hedging obligations are reported as part of a company's liabilities. Exhibit 9-2 reports several notes that are repayable in foreign currencies. A portion of these notes hedges IBM's foreign operations.

GAAP require companies to report contingencies and commitments that may result in future obligations. **A *contingency* is an existing condition that may result in an economic effect if a future event occurs.** For example, IBM reported in its 1991 annual report:

> IBM has guaranteed certain loans and commitments of various ventures to which it is a party. Additionally, the company is contingently liable for certain receivables . . . . These commitments, which in the aggregate are approximately $1 billion, are not expected to result in a material adverse effect on the company's financial results.

A current obligation does not exist for these contingencies. If some future event occurs, however, an obligation might result. For example, if another entity defaults on a loan guaranteed by IBM, the company could become liable for repayment of the loan.

Another common type of contingency involves litigation. Corporations often are involved in lawsuits. Disclosures are provided in their annual reports,

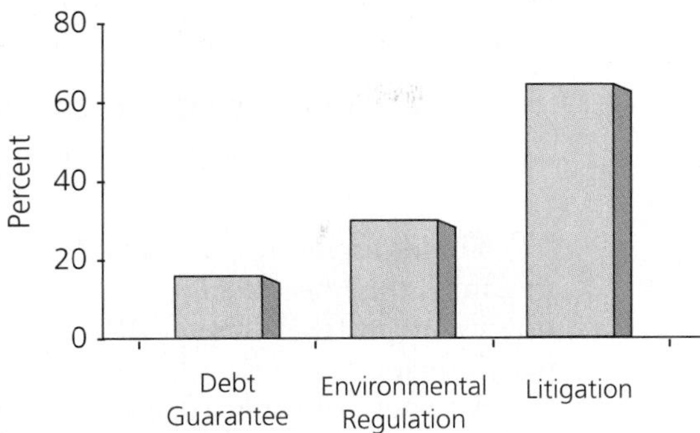

Data source: AICPA, Accounting Trends & Techniques, 1991.

summarizing existing litigation. For example, Chrysler Corporation reported in its 1991 annual report:

> Chrysler is a party to various legal proceedings, including some purporting to be class actions against the Company and some which assert claims for damages in large amounts. Chrysler believes each proceeding constitutes routine litigation incident to the business conducted by Chrysler. Although the amount of its exposure at December 31, 1991 with regard to these matters cannot be determined, Chrysler believes that the ultimate disposition of these matters will not have a material adverse effect on its consolidated financial position.

If a probable loss will result from a contingency and the amount of the loss can be estimated reasonably, it should be included as a liability on a company's balance sheet. Also, the amount of expected loss is recognized as a deduction in computing net income. Such occurrences are rare. Texaco, Inc. reported claims by the Internal Revenue Service in 1991 for taxes from prior years. While arguing the claims were not valid, Texaco noted that it had recorded obligations for these amounts.

A *commitment* **is a promise to engage in some future activity that will have an economic effect.** Commitments often involve future sales or purchases. For example, Delta Airlines reported in 1991 that it had committed to purchase 199 aircraft expected to cost $5.15 billion. This amount was not a liability on Delta's balance sheet. A liability does not result until the company purchases the aircraft, usually after they have been manufactured.

A common form of commitment is for leased assets. Certain leases, known as **capital leases,** are treated as purchase arrangements. The present value of future lease payments are treated as liabilities and are reported on the balance sheet. For example, Delta Airlines reported a liability for capital leases of $120.5 million in 1991. Capital leases will be examined in Chapter 11. In addition to capital leases, companies use **operating leases** to acquire access to resources. The cost of operating leases is recorded as an expense in the period in which the leased assets are used. Liabilities are not recorded for these activities. Some of these leases are non-cancellable, however, resulting in a commitment for future payments. The minimum amount of these future payments is reported in notes to the financial statements. For example, Ford Motor Company disclosed the following operating lease commitments in its 1991 annual report (in millions):

1992	1993	1994	1995	1996	After 1996	Total
$305	$303	$237	$194	$167	$501	$1,707

These disclosures are intended to assist investors and other decision makers in evaluating the effect existing conditions are likely to have on future cash flows and profits. Chapter 10 examines the use of information about a company's financial activities by decision makers.

A variety of other obligations may be reported by corporations. For example, dividends declared but unpaid at the end of a fiscal year are reported as a current liability, DIVIDENDS PAYABLE. The types of liabilities reported by companies vary for different industries. Customer deposits are common for utility companies. Air traffic liability for unused tickets is reported by airlines. Terminology varies considerably among corporations. Careful reading of explanations provided in notes to the financial statements often will clarify the items listed on the balance sheet.

LIABILITIES REPORTED BY FOREIGN CORPORATIONS

Objective 10
Identify problems in comparing liabilities of foreign and U.S. corporations.

Foreign corporations report most of the same types of liabilities as U.S. corporations. The liability section of the balance sheets of foreign corporations often appear very similar to those of U.S. corporations. Accounting rules for measuring these liabilities may differ, however. Many countries do not require corporations to accrue employee pension benefits during the periods in which they are earned. Post-employment health care benefits are not a responsibility of many foreign corporations. These benefits are provided by the government rather than by corporations. Practices concerning deferred income taxes also vary considerably among countries. Many Japanese corporations do not recognize deferred taxes. Measurement of lease obligations also varies across nations. Considerable care must be used in comparing liabilities of foreign and U.S. corporations.

CONTROL OF LIABILITIES

Objective 11
Explain how accounting information is useful in controlling liabilities.

Ensuring proper accrual of liabilities and related expenses is an important internal control procedure for many organizations. Careful monitoring of records, especially near the end of a fiscal year, is needed to make sure liabilities and expenses are recognized properly. For example, accounts payable should be recorded in the period in which materials and merchandise are acquired. Acquisition occurs when legal title to goods is transferred to the purchaser, typically at the time the goods are received. Shipping terms determine the owner of goods in transit between seller and buyer. Warranty obligations and expenses should be recognized in the period when revenues are recognized from sales of warrantied products.

Interest obligations and expenses should be recognized in the period in which they are incurred. For example, assume a company has $100 million of bonds payable outstanding. The bonds pay interest on March 1 and September 1 at a 10% annual rate. If the company's fiscal year ends on December 31, it should accrue interest on the bonds from September through December. The amount accrued would be $3,333,333 ($100 million × .10 × 4/12). Material amounts of discount or premium also should be accrued. Proper measurement of obligations and related expenses is an important accounting function.

SELF-STUDY PROBLEM 9-3

The following information is excerpted from the liabilities section of the 1991 balance sheet of Philip Morris Companies, Inc. (in millions):

Short-term borrowings	$ 514
Current portion of long-term debt	1,355
Accounts payable	2,820
Accrued liabilities:	
Marketing	1,396
Taxes, except income taxes	781
Employment costs	895
Income taxes	1,603
Dividends payable	486
Long-term debt	13,420
Deferred income taxes	731
Accrued postretirement health care costs	1,854

Required

From this list, identify the amount of obligations Philip Morris had to suppliers of goods and services, customers, lenders, governments, employees, and stockholders at the end of 1991.

The solution to Self-Study Problem 9-3 appears at the end of the chapter.

REVIEW *Summary of Important Concepts*

1. The characteristics and measurement of obligations:
   A. Liabilities result from contractual relationships with lenders, suppliers, customers, employees, governments, and other parties.
   B. Three attributes of a liability are (1) a present responsibility exists for an organization to transfer resources to some other entity at some future time, (2) the organization cannot choose to avoid the transfer, and (3) the event causing the responsibility has already occurred.
   C. Proper measurement of obligations and related expenses is an important accounting control function.
   D. The present value of a liability or investment is the amount of expected future cash flows paid or received, discounted at a required rate of return.

2. Obligations to lenders:
   A. The price of a bond is the present value of expected future cash flows from interest and principal.
   B. The effective rate of return on a bond may differ from its nominal rate. If the effective rate is higher than the nominal rate, a bond has been sold at a discount. If the effective rate is lower than the nominal rate, a bond has been sold at a premium.
   C. Discounts and premiums on bonds payable are amortized to interest expense over the life of the bonds. Amortization of a discount increases interest expense, and amortization of a premium decreases interest expense each period.
   D. An amortization schedule can be used to determine the interest expense on bonds, notes, and similar financial instruments.
3. Obligations to suppliers and customers:
   A. Accounts payable, deferred income (unearned revenues), and warranties are examples of obligations to suppliers and customers.
4. Obligations to employees:
   A. Obligations to employees result from deferred compensation for pensions and other post-employment benefits.
   B. The primary accounting issues for employee obligations are (1) determining the amount of benefits earned by employees and owed by a company, and (2) determining the amount invested by a company to meet these obligations and the amount earned on these investments.
5. Taxes and other obligations:
   A. Deferred income taxes result from differences between income tax expense and the amount of current tax obligation for income taxes as reported on a company's tax return.
   B. Contingencies and commitments are potential future liabilities. The existence and amount of the liabilities depends on future events. If a probable loss will result from a contingency and the amount of the loss can be estimated reasonably, it should be included as a liability on a company's balance sheet.
   C. Though foreign corporations report many of the liabilities reported by U.S. corporations, comparing reported liabilities sometimes is difficult because different accounting measurement rules are used.

DEFINE *Terms and Concepts Defined in this Chapter*

annuity
commitment
contingency
coupon rate of return
debentures
deferred income tax
discount on bonds payable
effective rate of return
future value
nominal rate of return
premium on bonds payable
present value
warranty
yield to maturity

SOLUTIONS

SELF-STUDY PROBLEM 9-1

a. The price would be the present value of a single payment of $1,000,000 at the end of 10 periods, discounted at 4%, plus the present value of 10 payments of $50,000 ($1,000,000 × .10/2), discounted at 4%:

PV of single amount factor from Table 1 = .67556 × $1,000,000 =	$ 675,560
PV of annuity factor from Table 2 = 8.1109 × $50,000 =	405,545
Total price =	$1,081,105

b.

a	b	c	d	e	f	g
Period*	**Present Value at Beginning of Period**	**Unamortized Premium**	**Effective Interest (b × 4%)**	**Interest Payment**	**Amortization (d – e)**	**Present Value at End of Period (b + f)**
1	1,081,105	81,105	43,244	50,000	−6,756	1,074,349
2	1,074,349	74,349	42,974	50,000	−7,026	1,067,323
3	1,067,323	67,323	42,693	50,000	−7,307	1,060,016
4	1,060,016	60,016	42,401	50,000	−7,599	1,052,417
5	1,052,417	52,417	42,097	50,000	−7,903	1,044,514
6	1,044,513	44,513	41,781	50,000	−8,219	1,036,295
7	1,036,294	36,294	41,452	50,000	−8,548	1,027,747
8	1,027,746	27,746	41,110	50,000	−8,890	1,018,857
9	1,018,856	18,856	40,754	50,000	−9,246	1,009,611
10	1,009,610	9,611	40,389	50,000	−9,611	1,000,000

In this problem, each period is 6 months long.

Some adjustments were made due to rounding.

c.

Assets =		Liabilities + Equity		+ Revenues – Expenses
Cash	1,081,105	Bonds Payable	1,000,000	
		Premium on Bonds Payable	81,105	

d. Interest paid:

July 1, 1992	$50,000
January 1, 1993	$50,000
January 1, 1997	$50,000

e. Interest expense:

July 1, 1992	$43,244
January 1, 1993	$42,974
January 1, 1997	$40,389

f. Interest expense includes the effect of premium amortization over the life of the bonds. The premium is amortized to match the lower cost of selling the bonds at a premium with the periods in which the bonds are outstanding. For the 10 periods as a whole, the net cash flow is equal to the total expense recognized:

Total expense (from amortization schedule) = $418,895 (adjusted for rounding error)

Net cash outflow = $1,081,105 cash inflow – [(10 × $50,000) + $1,000,000 cash outflow] = $418,895

SELF-STUDY PROBLEM 9-2

a. PepsiCo's employees earned pension benefits of $46.8 million for current services (item 1). In addition, the company incurred interest cost associated with these benefits of $69.2 million (item 2). PepsiCo reported an expense of $7.1 million for

1991 (item 6). The expense was less than the benefits earned by employees because of earnings of the company's pension plan assets.

b. The market value of PepsiCo's pension plan assets was $1,199.3 million at the end of 1991 (item 10). This amount was greater than the projected benefit obligation (item 9) and greater than the obligation after adjustments were made (items 12–14). PepsiCo reported an asset of $68.6 million (item 15).

SELF-STUDY PROBLEM 9-3

Obligations in millions	
Suppliers:	
Accounts payable	$ 2,820
Accrued liabilities: marketing	1,396
Total	$ 4,216
Customers	none reported
Lenders:	
Short-term borrowings	$ 514
Current portion of long-term debt	1,355
Long-term debt	13,420
Total	$15,289
Governments:	
Accrued liabilities: Taxes, except income taxes	$ 781
Income taxes	1,603
Deferred income taxes	731
Total	$ 3,115
Employees:	
Accrued liabilities: Employment costs	$ 895
Accrued postretirement health care costs	1,854
Total	$ 2,749
Stockholders:	
Dividends payable	$ 486

EXERCISES

9-1. Write a short definition for each of the terms listed in the *Terms and Concepts Defined in this Chapter* section.

9-2. List major types of liabilities businesses report on their balance sheets. How are these liabilities classified on the balance sheet?

9-3. On May 12, 1994, the High Tech Company contracted with Zermatt Labs to construct robotic equipment according to specifications provided by Zermatt. In exchange, Zermatt agreed to pay $300,000 to High Tech on June 1, 1994, and an additional $300,000 to High Tech when construction is completed and the equipment is installed. High Tech has agreed to complete the construction and installation by August 1, 1995. Should Zermatt report a liability on its financial statements for the fiscal year ended June 30, 1994, as a result of this contract? Should High Tech report a liability on its financial statements for the same period? Explain.

9-4. On November 22, 1993, Dairy Farms, Inc., signed an agreement with the First Farmer's Bank. The agreement permits Dairy Farms to obtain up to $500,000 of cash from the bank anytime during the coming year. Any amount obtained is to be repaid in monthly installments of 5% of the amount borrowed plus interest at an annual rate of

10% of the amount borrowed. At the end of its fiscal year, on December 31, 1993, Dairy Farms had not obtained any money from the bank. Should Dairy Farms report a liability on its 1993 financial statements? Explain.

9-5. Assume you borrow $10,000 on April 1, 1994, at an annual rate of 7%. What will be the future value of your loan on March 31, 1995? If you do not pay interest and the loan continues to accrue interest at 7%, what will be the future value of your loan on March 31, 1996? If you pay the interest incurred for the first year on March 31, 1995, what will be the future value of your loan on March 31, 1996?

9-6. Assume you received a loan on July 1, 1990. The lender charges annual interest at 5%. On June 30, 1995, you owe the lender $510.52. Assuming you made no payments for principal or interest on the loan during the five years, how much did you borrow?

9-7. Edgar Poe owns the Raven Co. On January 1, 1992, the beginning of the company's fiscal year, Poe borrowed $600,000 at 10% annual interest to purchase equipment. The loan is to be repaid over 5 years in equal annual installments. How much will Poe pay each year? What will be the amount of interest expense reported by Raven Co. for the loan in 1992? In 1993?

9-8. The Waldo Company issued $1 million of 5-year, 8% bonds on January 1, 1994. The bonds pay interest semiannually. How much did the bonds sell for under each of the following situations?

a. The bonds sold to yield 8%.
b. The bonds sold to yield 6%.
c. The bonds sold to yield 10%.

9-9. For each of the following independent situations determine (a) whether the bonds sold at face value, at a premium, or at a discount, and (b) whether interest expense recognized each year for the bonds was less than, equal to, or greater than the amount of interest paid on the bonds:

a. Bonds with a coupon rate of 8% were sold to yield a market rate of 10%.
b. Bonds with a coupon rate of 10% were sold to yield a market rate of 8%.
c. Bonds with a coupon rate of 8% were sold to yield a market rate of 8%.

9-10. The Gen Sing Company issued 10-year bonds with a face value of $10 million on October 1, 1994. The bonds pay interest at 7% annually. The bonds sold at 93.29% of face value to yield an effective rate of 8%. How much interest expense should Gen Sing recognize on the bonds for the fiscal year ended September 30, 1995? What amount of net liability would the company report for the bonds on its 1995 balance sheet? How much total expense would the company recognize for the bonds over the 10 years they are outstanding?

9-11. The Turn Buckle Company financed new equipment costing $50,000 with a five-year loan from a local bank. The bank charged 11% interest on the note. What would Turn Buckle's annual payments be to the bank each year, assuming the note and interest are paid in equal annual installments? How much interest expense would the company record for the first year of the note? For the second year?

9-12. The Long Fellow Company ordered $100,000 of materials from the Wads Worth Company on March 23, 1994. Long Fellow received the materials on April 5, with terms 3/10, n/30. On April 12, Long Fellow paid for the materials. What transactions should Long Fellow record on March 23, April 5, and April 12? Use the following format:

Assets =	Liabilities + Equity	+ Revenues − Expenses

If Long Fellow made the payment on April 22, instead of April 12, what transaction would it record?

9-13. The Natty Bumpo Company sold $3 million of merchandise to customers in fiscal 1994. The merchandise was sold with a one-year warranty. Bumpo agreed to repair or replace defective merchandise that was returned to the company within one year of the purchase date. At the end of the 1994 fiscal year, Bumpo estimated that outstanding warranties would cost the company $200,000 during 1995. Actual warranty costs during fiscal 1995 amounted to parts—$80,000, labor—$118,000, shipping—$9,000. What transactions should Bumpo record in 1994 and 1995 for the warranties? Use the following format:

Assets =	Liabilities + Equity	+ Revenues − Expenses

9-14. H.J. Heinz Company reported net pension costs of $6,764,000 for its 1992 fiscal year. The company also reported prepaid pension costs of $156,303,000 at the end of the year. What effect did these amounts have on the company's 1992 balance sheet and income statement. What information do these disclosures provide about the funding status of the company's pension plan?

9-15. While auditing the 1995 financial statements of Monte Zuma Company, you discover that no provision has been made for post-employment benefit obligations associated with the company's provision of health care benefits to retired employees. When asked about the matter, Mr. Zuma, the president of the company, responded that the company paid for health care costs of retired employees each year as the costs were incurred. Therefore, no obligation existed. Write a short memo to the president explaining why post-employment benefits result in an obligation for the company that should be reported on its balance sheet.

9-16. Archer Daniels Midland Company reported income taxes of $255,812,000 in 1992. Of this amount, $6,643,000 was deferred and $249,169,000 was for the current period. What transaction would the company have recorded for its taxes in 1992? Use the following format:

Assets =	Liabilities + Equity	+ Revenues − Expenses

Explain why corporations recognize deferred taxes. What effect do these have on the income statement?

9-17. The Pork Barrel Corporation reported the following information at the end of its 1994 fiscal year:

Accounts payable to suppliers	$ 800,000
Notes payable	3,500,000
Unfunded pension obligations	4,200,000
Loan guarantees for subsidiaries	2,000,000
Pending lawsuit against the company	5,000,000
Commitment to purchase materials in 1995	1,500,000
Capital leases (present value of future payments)	4,000,000
Noncancellable operating leases for 1995	1,800,000

All required principal and interest payments on the loans guaranteed by the company were paid by subsidiaries during the current year. The company's legal counsel believed the company would not have to pay any claims from the lawsuit. How much total liability did the company report for these items on its 1995 balance sheet? Explain your answer.

9-18. The Quaker Oats Company disclosed the following in its 1992 annual report:

Foreign Currency Forward Contracts. At June 30, 1992, the Company had forward contracts for the purchase and sale of European, Canadian and other currencies, purchases totalling $14.6 million and sales totalling $116 million.

What is the purpose of foreign currency contracts? What information does the existence of these contracts provide about Quaker's foreign operations?

9-19. Organizations often lease resources rather than purchasing them. What two types of leases are commonly used to acquire access to resources? How do they differ? How does the type of lease affect a company's reported liabilities?

9-20. The Jewels Vern Company ordered $200,000 of merchandise for resale during December 1994. Title to the goods is transferred to the company at the time the merchandise is received. By the end of December, the company had received billing invoices for $100,000 of the merchandise, it had received $125,000 of the merchandise, it had paid $50,000 of the bills for merchandise received, and it had sold merchandise received during December that cost it $30,000. How would these events affect the company's assets, liabilities, and expenses for the year ended December 31, 1994? Explain your answer.

PROBLEMS

PROBLEM 9-1 Identifying Liabilities

A business may contract with banks, individuals, and other companies to borrow money. Also, it may contract with suppliers, employees, and customers.

Required Identify the types of obligations that a business may incur in these contractual relationships. How are these obligations reported by a business on its balance sheet? What are the purposes of the obligations?

PROBLEM 9-2 Interpreting Long-Term Debt

BellSouth reported the following information in its 1990 annual report:

Long-term debt consists primarily of debentures issued by the telephone subsidiaries. Interest rates and maturities of the amounts outstanding are summarized as follows at December 31:

Description	Interest Rates	Maturities	1990	1989
Debentures	3¼%–6⅞%	1993–2004	**$ 675.0**	$ 675.0
	7⅜%–8¼%	1999–2017	**2,785.0**	2,785.0
	8½%–10¾%	2001–2029	**2,925.0**	2,925.0
			6,385.0	6,385.0
Other long-term debt			**. . .**	. . .
Unamortized discount, net			**(53.1)**	(54.3)
Total			**$7,781.0**	$7,054.6

Maturities of long-term debt outstanding at December 31, 1990, are summarized below:

	1991	1992	1993	1994	1995	Thereafter	Total
Maturities	$210.6	$183.1	$335.7	$87.2	$86.6	$7,141.5	$8,044.7

Required Answer each of the following questions:

a. What are debentures? How do they differ from other forms of long-term debt?

b. What is unamortized discount? Why is it subtracted in calculating total long-term debt?

c. What is the purpose of the schedule reported by BellSouth? What information does it provide for external decision makers?

PROBLEM 9-3 Amortization of Bond Premium

The Icabod Crane Company sold $10 million of 4-year, 9% debentures on July 1, 1993. The bonds sold to yield 8%. Interest is paid annually on June 30.

Required

a. Determine the price of the bonds.

b. Prepare an amortization schedule to amortize the premium.

c. Use the following format to identify the transaction that Icabod Crane would use to record interest on the bonds on June 30, 1994:

Assets =	Liabilities + Equity	+ Revenues − Expenses

PROBLEM 9-4 Interpreting Pension Costs

Westinghouse reported the following information in its 1991 annual report:

Net Periodic Pension Costs *(in millions)*	1991	1990	1989
Service cost	$ 65	$ 65	$ 69
Interest cost on projected benefit obligations	439	438	432
Amortization of unrecognized net obligation	48	44	46
Amortization of unrecognized prior service cost	8	11	12
	560	558	559
Return on plan assets:			
Actual return on plan assets	(699)	53	(662)
Unrecognized return on plan assets	216	(525)	212
Recognized return on plan assets	(483)	(472)	(450)
Net periodic pension cost	$ 77	$ 86	$ 109

Funding Status *(in millions)* *At December 31*	1991	1990
Actuarial present value of benefit obligations		
Vested	$(4,365)	$(4,323)
Nonvested	(409)	(347)
Accumulated benefit obligation	(4,774)	(4,670)
Effect of projected future compensation levels	(324)	(436)
Projected benefit obligation for service to date	(5,098)	(5,106)
Plan assets at fair value	4,856	4,098
Projected benefit obligations in excess of plan assets	(242)	(1,008)
Unrecognized net loss	643	862
Prior service costs not yet recognized	13	98
Unrecognized transition obligation at January 1, net of amortization	450	494
Prepaid pension contribution	$ 864	$ 446

Minor modifications have been made to the format.

Required Answer each of the following questions:

a. How much pension expense or revenue did Westinghouse recognize during 1991?
b. What was the return on plan assets in 1991? How did the return affect the amount of pension expense or revenue reported by Westinghouse?
c. What amount of retirement benefits was earned by employees in 1991? Why did the company incur interest cost on pension obligations in 1991?
d. What amount of asset or liability did Westinghouse recognize for its pension obligations in 1991?
e. What amount of obligation is owed to employees for services performed to date based on current wage rates? Based on projected increases in wage rates?

PROBLEM 9-5 Ethical Issues Related to Debt

Hiram Snerdly is an investment broker. Recently he contacted potential investors and offered to sell them bonds that were paying a 10% annual rate of interest. He noted that the bonds were paying a return much higher than other investments and that similar bonds were selling at a market rate of 6% interest. The bonds had a ten-year maturity and paid interest semiannually. Several investors purchased the bonds because of the high rate of interest but later were concerned to learn that the maturity value of $1,000 per bond was considerably less than the purchase price of $1,350.

Required Compare the price of the bonds sold by Snerdly to bonds yielding a market rate of 6%? What was the approximate real rate of return earned by the investors? Did they have a right to be concerned about their investments? Do you see any ethical problems with Snerdly's sales pitch?

PROBLEM 9-6 Defining Liabilities

Reichman Company reported income taxes payable and compensation and benefits payable among its current liabilities on its 1993 balance sheet. Also, the company reported deferred income taxes and deferred benefits and compensation among its long-term liabilities.

Required What criteria should be met for an item to be reported as a liability? Differentiate between current and long-term liabilities. What arguments can you provide for reporting these items as liabilities? What arguments can you provide for not reporting these items as liabilities?

PROBLEM 9-7 Bond Interest and Cash Flows

Tazaki Company is planning to issue $10 million of 4-year bonds that will pay interest annually. The company needs $10 million to finance the acquisition of new facilities. The market rate of interest for the company's bonds is 8%. As an employee of the company's finance department, you have been asked to evaluate different coupon rates the company might use for the bonds.

Required Answer each of the following questions:

a. What determines the market rate of interest for a company's bonds?
b. What amount of interest expense and interest payment would the company incur each year over the life of the bonds if they were issued at a coupon rate of 6, 8, or 10%?
c. What total amount of expense and cash outflow would be incurred over the 4-year period for each of the alternatives in b? What recommendation would you make to the company's top management about which coupon rate to use?

PROBLEM 9-8 Calculation of Notes Payable

You have decided to purchase a car. You have found a clean used car that will cost you $7,500. You can finance your purchase with a note at a local credit union at an annual rate of 12% for 24 months. The credit union will require a down payment of $500.

Required How much will your monthly payments be to the credit union? How much will you pay the credit union over the life of the note? How much of this amount will be interest? If you decide to pay off the note at the end of the first year, how much will you owe the credit union?

PROBLEM 9-9 Explaining Changes in Debt

Warner-Lambert Company reported the following information on its 1991 balance sheet:

(in millions)	1991	1990
Current liabilities:		
Notes payable—banks and other	$113.7	$222.6
Current portion of long-term debt	14.7	7.7
Long-term debt	447.9	306.8

The following information was reported on the company's cash flow statement:

(in millions)	1991
Financing Activities:	
Proceeds from borrowings	$281.5
Principal payments on borrowings	(230.6)

Of the proceeds, $150 million was from long-term debt. The payments were for notes payable and current portion of long-term debt.

Required Explain the change in short-term (notes payable and current portion of long-term debt) and long-term debt balances to the extent possible from the information provided above.

PROBLEM 9-10 Analysis of Other Post-Employment Benefits

Energen Corporation reported the following information in its 1992 annual report:

As of Year Ended (in thousands)	1992	1991
Accumulated net post-employment benefit obligation	$(16,891)	$(15,077)
Unamortized net transition obligation	11,836	10,095
Accrued post-employment benefit obligation	$ (5,055)	$ (4,982)

For the year ended September 30 (in thousands)	**1992**	**1991**
Service cost	$ 321	$ 290
Interest cost on accumulated post-employment benefit obligation	1,276	1,279
Amortization of transition obligation	842	842
Net periodic post-employment benefit expense	$ 2,439	$ 2,411

The company adopted the accounting standard requiring disclosure of post-employment benefit obligations in its 1992 statements. The unamortized net transition obligation arose from initial adoption of the standard, which permitted a portion of the initial obligation from adopting the standard to be deferred and to be amortized over several years. The amount amortized is reported as a part of the net expense ($842,000) recognized in 1992.

Required Why do accounting standards require companies to report post-employment benefit obligations? What effect did the obligation have on Energen's balance sheet and income statement in 1992? What steps can a company take to reduce its liability and expense for post-employment benefits?

PROBLEM 9-11 Reporting Income Taxes

SYSCO Corporation reported income taxes on its 1992 income statement of $109,427,000. It reported deferred taxes on its balance sheet of $86,545,000 for 1991 and $100,488,000 for 1992. Its statement of cash flows indicated the company paid income taxes of $89,478,000 in 1992.

Required Use the following format to identify the transactions SYSCO recorded during 1992 to account for these events:

Assets =	Liabilities + Equity	+ Revenues − Expenses

What information do deferred taxes provide external users about a company's future cash flows? Is the amount of deferred taxes reported by a company a reliable estimate of the company's current obligation for future tax payments? Explain your answer.

PROBLEM 9-12 Multiple-Choice Overview of the Chapter

1. A company borrowed $100,000 from a bank on July 1, 1994, making monthly payments of $5,235 on the note at the end of each month from July through December. Total interest expense on the note for this six-month period was $4,410. The total amount the company would report on its December 31, 1994, balance sheet for notes payable for this note would be:
   a. $100,000
   b. $95,590
   c. $73,000
   d. $68,590
2. Kibuki Company issued $5 million of bonds at a market rate of 7%. The bonds have a coupon rate of 8%. Which of the following is correct:

	The bonds sold at a	The annual rate of interest paid on the bonds is
a.	Discount	7%
b.	Discount	8%
c.	Premium	7%
d.	Premium	8%

3. Rubble Company sold 10-year bonds at a discount. Net cash flow on the bonds includes the effects of issue price, interest payments, and principal payment. Over the total life of the bonds, the amount of interest expense on the bonds:
   a. would be greater than net cash flow
   b. would be equal to net cash flow
   c. would be less than net cash flow
   d. would not be determinable from available information
4. On May 1, Ishida Company purchased $10,000 of merchandise on credit with terms 2/10, n/30. The amount the company would pay for the merchandise on each of the following dates would be:

	May 8	May 12	June 2
a.	$ 9,800	$10,000	$10,000
b.	9,800	9,800	10,000
c.	9,800	9,800	9,800
d.	10,000	10,000	10,000

5. A company's pension plan assets are estimated to have a market value of $8 million at the end of the 1994 fiscal year. The company's estimated obligation to employees for pension benefits at the end of 1994 is $14 million. As a result of these events, the company would probably report which of the following on its 1994 balance sheet:
   a. an asset
   b. a liability
   c. an asset and a liability
   d. neither an asset nor a liability
6. Which of the following indicates the amount of post-employment benefits earned by a company's employees for a fiscal year:
   a. accumulated post-employment benefit obligation
   b. net periodic post-employment benefit obligation
   c. accrued post-employment benefit cost
   d. service cost
7. Axel Corporation reported income taxes on its 1995 income statement of $300,000. It reported taxes payable for 1995 of $250,000, based on its taxable income. As a result of these events, the company's deferred income taxes account:
   a. increased by $50,000
   b. decreased by $50,000
   c. decreased income tax expense by $50,000
   d. Increased income tax expense by $50,000
8. Weimar Company reported an unused line of credit of $2 million and a contingency for loan guarantees of $1.3 million at the end of 1994. The amount of liability the company would report on its 1994 balance sheet associated with these items would be:
   a. $0
   b. $1.3 million
   c. $2 million
   d. $3.3 million
9. Echo Company reported the following operating lease commitments in its 1995 annual report (in millions): 1996—$12, 1997—$10, 1998—$9, 1999—$5, 2000—$3, after 2000—$8. The amount of liability the company would report on its 1995 annual report for these leases would be:
   a. $47 million
   b. the present value of $47 million

c. $12 million
d. $0

10. Oshima Company issued $10 million of 6% bonds on November 1, 1994. The bonds pay interest semiannually on May 1 and November 1 each year. The amount of interest payable the company should report on its December 31, 1994, balance sheet would be:
a. $0
b. $100,000
c. $300,000
d. $600,000

CASES

CASE 9-1 Making Credit Decisions

As an employee of the loan department of Metropolitan Bank, one of your primary tasks is analyzing information provided by organizations applying for commercial loans. Most applicants are small businesses seeking additional capital to acquire long-term assets. Other applicants are seeking financing to acquire existing businesses. A typical applicant is Cleopatra Jones, who owns Cleopatra's, a women's clothing store. Ms. Jones has applied for a loan of $30,000 to finance an expansion of her business.

Required Identify the types of information you would need from Ms. Jones to help you make a loan decision. Explain why each type of information would be useful.

CASE 9-2 Analyzing Liabilities

Review the financial statements and accompanying notes of General Mills, Inc. provided in Appendix B of this book.

Required Write a report that answers the following questions:

a. What were the company's most important liabilities in 1992? How did the relative importance of the liabilities change from the prior year?
b. How did changes in the company's liabilities affect cash flows associated with financing activities for 1992? How did the company's liabilities affect its net income in 1992?
c. Describe major changes in the company's long-term debt during 1992.
d. What effect did the company's retirement plans have on its balance sheet and income statement in 1992?

PROJECTS

PROJECT 9-1 Analysis of Liabilities

Locate recent annual reports for corporations in three different industries. Identify the primary similarities and differences in the companies' liabilities. Write a short report comparing the captions and relative amounts of different items in the liabilities section of the balance sheets.

PROJECT 9-2 Comparison of U.S. and Foreign Reporting

Locate copies of three recent annual reports of U.S. corporations and three annual reports of foreign corporations from three different countries. Write a short report comparing the titles and relative amounts of different items in the liabilities section of the balance sheets. The report should focus on primary differences between the U.S. and foreign corporation reports. You may need to consult a book on international accounting or financial reporting for assistance in defining terms in the foreign reports. Provide definitions in your report of any terms used in the reports that are not explained in this chapter.

PROJECT 9-3 Identifying Debt Transactions

Use a journal index (for example, the *Business Periodicals Index* or the *Accounting and Tax Index*) or *The Wall Street Journal Index* to locate recent articles that discuss debt transactions of major corporations, such as the issuance of new debt. Summarize two articles that discuss reasons for the transactions. Include complete references to the articles.

PROJECT 9-4 Default and Bankruptcy

Use a journal index (for example, the *Business Periodicals Index* or the *Accounting and Tax Index*) or *The Wall Street Journal Index* to locate a recent article that discusses a recent case in which a company defaulted on its debt or declared bankruptcy because it could not make its debt payments. Summarize major effects of the default or bankruptcy on the company. Include a complete reference to the article.

PROJECT 9-5 Comparing Financial Statement Numbers

Locate recent annual reports of five corporations. Alternatively, use *Moody's Industrial Manual* or another source of financial statement information. Select companies from different industries, including at least one utility, one financial institution, and one retail company. Complete the following table by identifying the ratio of the amount of debt to the company's total assets. For example, if a company has $1 million long-term debt and $5 million in total assets, the ratio for long-term debt would be .20. Short-term debt should include notes payable, current portions of long-term debt, and other similar items.

Name of Company	Industry	Short-Term Debt	Current Liabilities	Long-Term Debt	Total Liabilities

Write a short report to accompany the table comparing the relative amount of liabilities for the corporations. Indicate the source of your data.

CHAPTER 10

ANALYSIS OF FINANCING ACTIVITIES

CHAPTER *Overview*

Chapters 8 and 9 described accounting for equity and debt. These chapters identified various financial instruments and obligations corporations use to finance their assets and operating activities. Among these were common and preferred stock, bonds, notes, and accounts payable, deferred employee benefit obligations, and leases. This chapter examines the use of accounting information by those who analyze financing activities. This analysis affects contractual relationships among managers, providers of capital, and providers of goods and services. Managers have a responsibility to make decisions that are in the interest of a company's owners. At the same time, they should operate within the constraints imposed by contracts with creditors, employees, and other resource providers, which are designed to protect the interests of these contracting parties. Thus, managers should make decisions that increase the value of a corporation to its stockholders and meet the company's obligations to creditors and other parties.

Managers use accounting information to make financing decisions. Investors use accounting information to evaluate whether management decisions are consistent with maximizing stockholder value. Creditors and other contracting parties use accounting information to evaluate whether management decisions are consistent with their interests.

The first part of this chapter examines the relationship between risk and return attributes of financial instruments. Risk and return associated with securities, such as stocks and bonds, affect their prices. Financing activities, in turn, affect security risk and return, as examined in the second part of the chapter. The latter part of the chapter considers how financing activities can be analyzed to assess their effect on risk and return.

Major topics covered in this chapter include:

- Risk, return, and pricing of financial instruments.
- The effect of financing decisions on risk and return.
- Using accounting information to evaluate financing activities.

CHAPTER *Objectives*

After completing this chapter, you should be able to:

1. Explain the concept of capital structure.
2. Define the price of a security.
3. Distinguish between primary and secondary markets.
4. Explain the effect of default and interest rate risk on bond prices.
5. Explain the effect of financial and interest rate risk on preferred stock prices.
6. Explain the effect of financial and interest rate risk on common stock prices.
7. Determine the effect of financial leverage on a company's earnings.
8. Identify economic and company attributes that affect financial leverage.
9. Explain how accounting information is useful for evaluating financing activities.
10. Analyze a company's financing decisions.

RISK AND RETURN

Financing activities involve choices about how a company obtains cash to acquire other resources and to pay for services. Managers have several types of financial instruments from which to choose, including common stock, preferred stock, short-term debt, long-term debt, and leases. The risk and return attributes of these instruments vary. Managers have some discretion over these attributes, such as coupon rates, repayment schedules, conversion rights, call and redemption provisions, voting rights, and dividend payments. Exhibit 10-1 depicts financing arrangements of several major corporations. The exhibit illustrates the proportion of each company's finances composed of different types of liabilities and equities.

Exhibit 10-1 Financing Arrangements for Some Major Corporations

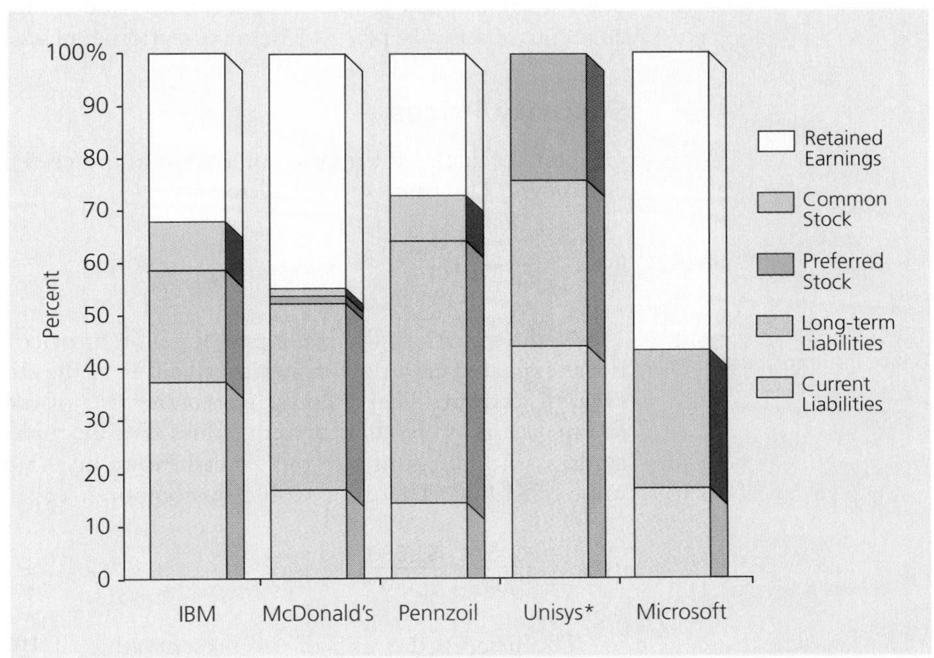

Unisys had an accumulated deficit and other negative adjustments to the stockholders' equity section at the end of 1991. The impact of this is reflected in a reduction of the preferred stock proportion from 34% to 24%. Note that while Unisys has some common stock, its proportion is negligible.

Data source: 1991 Annual Reports

Objective 1
Explain the concept of capital structure.

Financing arrangements vary depending on a company's operating activities and performance. **The way in which a company chooses to finance its assets and operating activities is its *capital structure*.** For example, Pennzoil's capital structure includes a large proportion of long-term debt. Pennzoil is in an industry that requires a large amount of investment in plant assets. Long-term debt is used to finance these assets. In contrast, Microsoft does not require a large investment in plant assets. Its capital structure contains no long-term debt.

Companies in the same industry may have different capital structures. For example, compare IBM with Unisys. Unisys's financial condition was much worse than IBM's in 1991. This condition is indicated by large proportions of current and long-term liabilities in Unisys's capital structure. Unisys exhibits almost no common stock or retained earnings, which have been eroded by poor operating performance. IBM exhibited large proportions of common stock along with a significant amount of retained earnings. Note that McDonald's and Microsoft have been successful in financing their assets from profits generated by operating activities, as exhibited by high proportions of retained earnings. Thus, capital structures vary across companies as a result of industry attributes and operating performance. Capital structures also vary for companies in different countries. High proportions of debt financing are common in some countries, Japan for example, because of economic and political conditions in those countries.

Accounting information about a company's capital structure is used by decision makers in assessing the risk and return they expect from contractual relationships with the company. To understand how accounting information is important for evaluating financing activities, one should understand fundamental concepts of security prices. The next section explains these concepts.

Security Prices

Chapter 9 calculated the price of a bond as the present value of expected future cash flows. The price was calculated as:

$$PV = \sum_{t=1}^{M} \frac{C_t}{(1 + R)^t}$$

Objective 2
Define the price of a security.

In this equation, PV is the present value or price, M is the maturity date, C is the expected cash flow in period t, and R is the **discount rate,** or **required rate of return.** The discount rate is the rate of return necessary to discount future cash flows to their present values. For example, assume a bond of 10 periods, with a discount rate of 4%, cash flows of $45 per period, and a maturity value of $1,000. The price would be computed as:

$$PV = \sum_{t=1}^{10} \frac{\$45}{(1.04)^t} + \frac{\$1{,}000}{(1.04)^{10}}$$

The price is the sum of the present value of 10 interest payments of $45, plus one payment of principal, in period 10, of $1,000.

More generally, the price of a security can be defined by the ratio:

$$\text{Price} = \frac{\text{Expected Future Cash Flows}}{\text{Discount Rate}}$$

The price of a security increases as the expected future cash flows from owning the security increase or as the discount rate decreases. At a more conceptual level, price can be expressed as the relationship between return and risk associated with a security:

$$\text{Price} = \frac{\text{Return}}{\text{Risk}}$$

Exhibit 10-2 illustrates changes in the price of a security that pays $100 per period, as the number of periods and discount rate change. The price increases more rapidly and to a higher amount for lower discount rates; it also increases as the number of periods increases and as the discount rate decreases. Future

Exhibit 10-2 Effect of Number of Periods and Discount Rate on the Price of a Security Paying $100 per Period

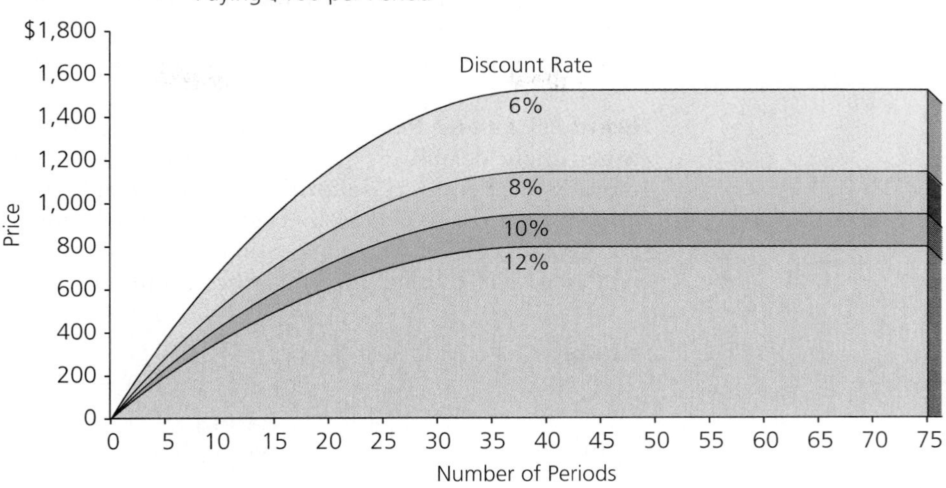

cash flows increase as the number of periods increases. Observe that prices increase rapidly in the early periods for each alternative. Cash flows received in the near future affect the price of a financial instrument much more than those received in later periods. Also, observe that prices reach a maximum at the number of periods at which a line becomes horizontal. For example, the price of an investment discounted at 12%, reaches a maximum after about 50 periods. Each of the other lines also reaches a maximum, but in later periods.

The maximum price for any security with a constant expected cash flow each period is:

$$\text{Price} = \frac{\text{Cash Flow per Period (C)}}{\text{Discount Rate (R)}}$$

The price of a security that pays $100 per period for an indefinite number of future periods with a discount rate of 10% is $1,000 ($100 / 0.10). This amount is the price in Exhibit 10-2, at which the line for a 10% discount rate becomes horizontal. This price equation is important because it describes the price of equity securities, such as common and preferred stocks, that have an indefinite life. If a stock is expected to yield a constant cash flow per period (C) over an indefinite number of periods with a required return (R), the price (P) can be defined as $P = C / R$. This equation is a useful conceptual explanation of stock prices, though expected cash flows are not constant for common stocks. This issue will be addressed later.

First, let's examine the discount rate or required rate of return (R). The value of R depends on general economic conditions and conditions specific to the company issuing a financial instrument. The discount rate increases with the rise of both the level of interest rates in the economy and the uncertainty of future cash flows from owning an instrument. The level of interest rates is affected by expected inflation and government policies. **Uncertainty about interest rates is *interest rate risk*.** The discount rate for a security also depends on ***business risk*, uncertainty associated with a company's financing, investing, and operating activities that affect its ability to generate cash**

flows. Business risk affects *financial risk,* the risk that a company may be unable to make payments to investors as promised. Thus, risk for security owners includes two components, interest rate and financial risk. The next section illustrates the effect of these risks on bond prices.

Bond Prices and Risk. A primary concern of bond investors is the risk that an issuer might default on the payment of interest or principal. This financial risk often is referred to as **default risk.** The default risks of bonds are signaled by bond ratings. Rating agencies, such as Moody's and Standard and Poor's, evaluate default risk and assign a rating to many bonds, especially those that are widely traded. Exhibit 10-3 describes commonly used ratings:

Exhibit 10-3 Bond Ratings

Grade	Rating Moody/S&P	Explanation
Investment Grade	Aaa/AAA	Best quality, lowest risk
	Aa/AA	High quality
	A/A	Upper medium quality
	Baa/BBB	Medium quality
Speculative Grade	Ba/BB	Speculative quality
	B/B	Low quality
	Below B	Very low quality

Bonds rated Baa/BBB and above are **investment grade bonds.** Banks, insurance companies, and certain other organizations are permitted to invest only in investment grade bonds. Bonds rated Ba/BB and below are **speculative grade bonds,** also known as **junk bonds.** Deregulation of savings and loan institutions in the 1980's permitted these organizations to invest in junk bonds. Defaults on these bonds were associated with failures of many savings and loans.

In addition to letters to denote quality ratings, bonds are separated into groups within each rating class. For example, Moody's designates bonds in the highest group in each class with a 1, those in the middle group with a 2, and those in the lowest group with a 3. Bond ratings for some major corporations are listed below:

Corporation	Moody's Bond Rating
International Business Machines	Aa2
General Mills	Aa3
Wal-Mart	Aa3
PepsiCo	A1
General Motors	A2
Delta Airlines	Baa1
Chrysler	B2
Unisys	B2
Continental Airlines	Ca

Data source: Moody's Investors Service, Moody's Bond Record, May 1992.

Chrysler's and Unisys' bonds were speculative grade. Continental Airlines' rating (Ca) reflected the bankruptcy status of the company.

Bonds with high ratings typically pay lower market returns (or yields) than those with low ratings. For example, Exhibit 10-4 describes average market returns for bonds of different ratings:

Exhibit 10-4 Yield and Risk for Corporate Bonds

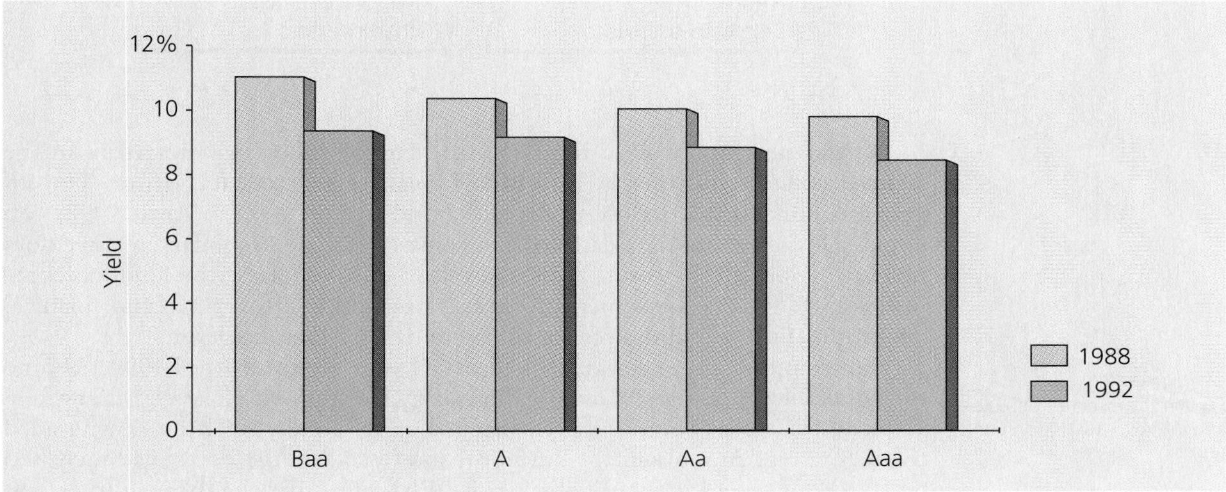

Data source: Moody's Investors Service, Moody's Bond Record, May 1992. Data are for April of each year.

Yields were lower for higher rated bonds for both 1988 and 1992. Yields were higher, however, for all ratings in 1988 than in 1992. The higher yields resulted from higher interest rates throughout the economy in 1988. For example, the interest paid on short-term government securities was over 6% in 1988. By 1992, this interest rate was approximately 4%. Short-term government securities are default free. Therefore, they provide a measure of the general level of interest rates in the economy.

To illustrate the effect of changes in risk on bond prices, assume Capital Company issued $10 million of 10-year bonds in April of 1992 at a nominal rate of 8%. The bonds were rated Aa, were sold to yield an 8% market rate, and paid interest semiannually. The price of each bond at the time it was issued would have been:

$$PV = \sum_{t=1}^{20} \frac{\$40}{(1.04)^t} + \frac{\$1{,}000}{(1.04)^{20}}$$

From Table 2, the interest factor for an annuity of 20 periods at 4% is 13.59033. From Table 1, the interest factor for a single payment at the end of 20 periods at 4% is .45639. Therefore, the price of each bond was $1,000 = [($40 × 13.59033) + ($1,000 × .45639)]. The bonds sold at maturity value because the nominal and market rates were equal.

Objective 3
Distinguish between primary and secondary markets.

The *primary market* is the market in which new (or original) issues of stocks and bonds are sold. This market determines the amount of cash a company will receive for its securities. Ignoring sales fees, Capital Company would have received $10 million for its bonds issued in April 1992.

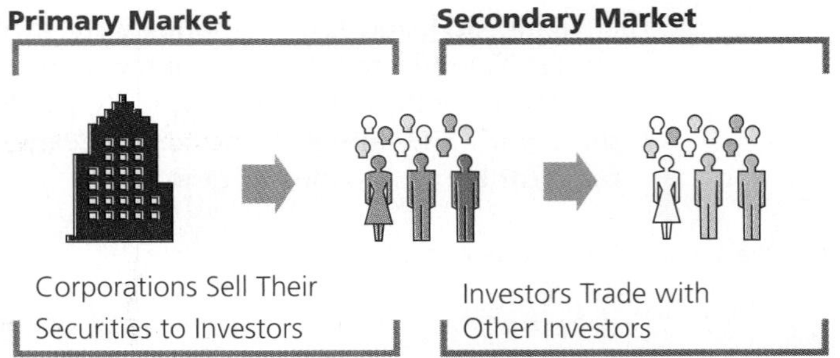

Once these bonds have been sold to investors, they may be resold in the ***secondary market,*** **a market in which investors sell to each other.** Thus, if you had purchased $10,000 of Capital's bonds for $10,000 in April 1992, you could sell them at a later date to other investors. The secondary market does not have a direct effect on the amount received by Capital or on amounts it reports on its financial statements. Capital's operating performance and financial condition affect its bond prices in the secondary market, however.

Objective 4
Explain the effect of default and interest rate risk on bond prices.

For example, suppose you wished to sell your bonds in April 1994. Assume the general level of interest rates had not changed from April 1992. But, assume Capital's financial condition had worsened so its bonds had been downgraded to an A rating. As a result, the current market yield on the bonds had increased to 10% because of increased default risk. What effect did the increase in default risk have on the price of the bonds? The price of the bonds would be computed using an effective yield of 5% per semi-annual period for a remaining life of 16 periods. Using values from Tables 1 and 2, the price per bond would be $891.62 = [($40 × 10.83777) + ($1,000 × .45811)]. Your investment of $10,000 has decreased in value to $8,916.20. If Capital's financial condition had improved, the value of your investment would have increased.

Changes in the rate used to discount the cash flows received from a bond affect the price of the bond. In addition to changes in the default risk of a bond, changes in the level of interest rates also affect a bond's price. Thus, if the level of interest rates in the economy had increased between April 1992 and April 1994, the price you would receive for your bonds in 1994 would be lower than the amount you paid, even if their default risk remained unchanged. Most bonds pay a cash flow that is fixed at the time they are issued. For example, Capital Company promised to pay $40 each six months plus $1,000 at maturity. This amount does not change even if market conditions, interest rates, or company attributes change, unless the company defaults. Therefore, the expected cash flows from a bond remain constant each period. Default risk does change, however, and accounting information is useful for bondholders and other creditors in assessing that default risk.

Stock Prices and Risk. Risk affects the prices of both preferred and common stock. The amount of risk associated with each type of stock depends on certain attributes of the stock, as discussed in the following sections.

Preferred Stock. Preferred stock is an alternative financial instrument to either long-term debt or common stock. Preferred stock is less risky than common stock. Therefore, a company expects to pay a lower return on preferred than on common stock. In contrast to common stock, preferred stock may provide a source of cash without diluting control of a company, because preferred stock normally does not have voting rights.

Because dividends usually are a fixed amount, preferred stock often provides financial leverage, similar to debt. For example, assume a company's preferred stock is paying a 10% return and the company can earn a 15% return on its investments. Then, earnings per share on common stock will be higher than if all financing were provided by common stock. Unlike interest payments, dividend payments can be skipped without a threat of bankruptcy. Preferred stockholders, like common stockholders, face the risk that a company will not pay dividends.

Objective 5
Explain the effect of financial and interest rate risk on preferred stock prices.

Because preferred stocks generally do not have maturity dates, they have an indefinite life. Therefore, the price (P) of a share of preferred stock can be calculated from the expected cash flow to owners (C) and the required rate of return (R): P = C / R. For example, assume Capital Company issued preferred stock with a par value of $100 and an annual dividend rate of $5. If the stock sold at a market return of 5%, the price of the stock should be $100 = ($5 / .05). A change in the rate of return after the sale would affect the price of the stock in the secondary market. If the rate decreased to 4.5% because of improvements in Capital's financial condition or a decrease in interest rates, the price should increase to approximately $111 = ($5 / .045).

Dividends paid on preferred stock, like interest, reduce the amount of profit and cash flow available for common stockholders. Though interest is deducted in computing net income and cash flow from operating activities, preferred dividends are not deducted in these computations. They are reported on the statement of stockholders' equity and are included in the computation of earnings per share. Care should be used in evaluating net income and cash flow to consider the effect of preferred dividends. For example, Procter & Gamble reported net income of $1,773 million in 1991. It paid $78 million in dividends to preferred stockholders. Therefore, earnings available for common stockholders were $1,695 million ($1,773 − $78). Also, the company's cash flow from operating activities of $2,069 million should be adjusted by the preferred dividends to calculate the cash flow available for common stockholders: $1,991 million ($2,069 − $78).

A disadvantage of stock financing is that, unlike interest, dividends cannot be deducted from taxes. Thus, if a company pays $1 million in dividends, its actual cost and cash outflow is $1 million. If it pays $1 million in interest and its tax rate is 34%, it saves $340,000 in taxes by deducting the interest expense from its income. Its net cash outflow is only $660,000.

Common Stock. Common stock differs from both bonds and preferred stock because cash flows are not fixed. Cash flow available to common stockholders depends on a company's operating results. This cash flow is the difference between the amount of cash received from customers and the amount paid for resources consumed, interest, dividends to preferred stockholders, and taxes. This cash flow is more volatile than the cash flow for other types of securities. Accordingly, the financial risk associated with common stock is higher than for bonds or preferred stock and the required rate of return also is higher.

Objective 6
Explain the effect of financial and interest rate risk on common stock prices.

As an illustration, assume Capital Company issued common stock in 1992. At the time of sale, the expected cash flow available to stockholders for the foreseeable future was $10 per share. The stock sold at an effective rate of 12%. The expected price of the stock would have been $83.33 = ($10 / .12). This calculation assumes a constant cash flow. If investors expected the cash flow to grow at a constant rate, the price equation should include the expected growth. The equation would be:

$$\text{Price} = \frac{\text{Expected Cash Flow}}{\text{Discount Rate} - \text{Expected Growth Rate}}$$

Thus, if investors expected an annual growth rate in cash flows of 4%, the expected price of Capital's stock would be $125 = [$10 / (.12 − .04)]. **Therefore, stock prices are affected by the level of interest rates and by factors that affect the expected cash flows available to stockholders.** These factors may affect both the numerator and denominator of the price equation.

The price equation described above is the basis for measures of stock risk and performance used by professional stock analysts. Net income (actual or forecasted) often is substituted for expected cash flow in the analysis. Net income is assumed to be a signal of expected cash flows. If price is expressed on a per share basis, then earnings per share can be used as an estimate of expected cash flow. Thus, the price equation becomes:

$$\text{Price per Share} = \frac{\text{Earnings per Share}}{\text{Discount Rate} - \text{Expected Growth Rate}}$$

The equation can be rewritten as:

$$\frac{\text{Price per Share}}{\text{Earnings per Share}} = \frac{1}{\text{Discount Rate} - \text{Expected Growth Rate}}$$

The ratio of price per share to earnings per share is known as the *price-earnings,* or *PE, ratio.* This ratio is a measure of the risk associated with a company's stock. The higher the PE ratio, the lower the risk. As an example, McDonald's PE ratio was 19, General Mills' was 22, and Microsoft's was 33 at the end of 1992.[1] PE ratios normally are not computed for companies, such as IBM and General Motors in 1992, that reported net losses in the preceding fiscal period.

The use of earnings in the ratio assumes earnings are a reliable measure of cash flow available for common stockholders. This assumption is not always valid. Later chapters will examine measurement issues affecting the relationship between cash flows and reported earnings. In general, however, earnings are expected, over the long run, to approximate cash flows from operating activities. Later sections of this chapter consider this issue in more depth.[2]

Other Financing Instruments

In addition to stocks and bonds, corporations issue promissory notes, generally with a maturity of one to seven years, and short-term notes, often referred to as **commercial paper.** These notes normally are issued to financial institutions and to other corporations. They generally are marketable, and their prices are affected by changes in risk much the way bond prices are affected. Most other

1 Data source: *The Wall Street Journal,* December 31, 1992.
2 Actual stock price behavior is largely consistent with the price equation. For example, approximately 93% of the variation in aggregate stock prices from 1981 to 1991 could be explained by interest rates and corporate earnings.

obligations, such as accounts payable and deferred compensation, are not marketable. A company's business risk affects the uncertainty of cash flows to these creditors, suppliers, and employees, however. They may assess risk in much the same way as bond and stockholders, though their investments are not priced in a securities market.

This section has examined the relationships between the prices of a company's financial instruments and their expected cash flows and risks. Financing activities affect expected cash flows and risks. The following sections examine capital structure decisions that affect security prices, cash flows, and risks.

SELF-STUDY PROBLEM 10-1

The El Roncho Salsa Company issued $10 million of 8%, 10-year bonds on April 1, 1992. The bonds sold at their maturity value of $1,000 per bond. They pay interest semiannually on April 1 and September 1. Because of changes in the level of interest rates and changes in El Roncho's default risk, the market rate on the bonds increased to 10% by September 1, 1995.

El Roncho's net income for 1994 was $14 million. The company's 10 million shares of common stock were selling at $8 per share. In August 1995, the company projected that its net income for that year would decrease to $10 million.

Required

(a) Compute the price you would expect to pay for El Roncho's bonds in September 1995. (b) Explain the effect you would expect the information reported in August 1995 to have on the price of El Roncho's stock.

The solution to Self-Study Problem 10-1 appears at the end of the chapter.

THE EFFECT OF FINANCING ACTIVITIES ON RISK AND RETURN

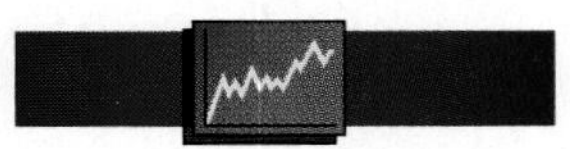

The following example illustrates the effects a company's financing activities can have on its financial instruments. At the end of 1994, the Heavy Metal Company had assets of $339.6 million, totally financed by equity:

	1994	1993
Total assets	$339,600,000	$300,000,000
Total liabilities	0	0
Total stockholders' equity	$339,600,000	$300,000,000

The company had 10 million shares of stock outstanding. It reported net income for 1994 as follows:

Operating income	$60,000,000
Interest expense	0
Income taxes (at 34%)	20,400,000
Net income	$39,600,000
Earnings per share (10,000,000 shares)	$3.96

A commonly used measure of a company's performance for a fiscal period is the relationship between the company's earnings and its equity or between its earnings and its assets. **The ratio of earnings to equity is known as *return on equity.* The ratio of earnings to assets is known as *return on assets,* or return on investment.** Return on equity (sometimes called return on common equity) is a measure of return on investment by common stockholders. Return on assets is a measure of return on total (debt and equity) investment.

These return measures are calculated as:

$$\text{Return on Assets} = \frac{\text{Net Income} + \text{Interest Expense } (1 - \text{Tax Rate})}{\text{Average Total Assets}}$$

$$\text{Return on Equity} = \frac{\text{Net Income} - \text{Dividends on Preferred Stock}}{\text{Average Common Stockholders' Equity}}$$

The numerator in the return on assets calculation is net income adjusted for the cost of debt financing. Interest expense is added back to net income to measure earnings from operating activities without consideration of how the operating activities were financed. Interest expense normally is measured on an after-tax basis: interest expense × (1 − tax rate). If the interest had not been incurred, it would not have been deducted from income taxes. Therefore, the net effect of interest on net income is its after-tax effect.

The numerator in the return on equity calculation is income to common stockholders, after considering the effect of returns to creditors (subtracted in computing net income) and preferred stockholders. The par value plus paid-in capital in excess of par on preferred stock should be deducted from total stockholders' equity to calculate common stockholders' equity.

Average investment normally is used as the denominator in these calculations, measured by adding beginning and ending investment (total assets or common stockholders' equity) for the year and dividing by 2. In 1994, average assets for Heavy Metal were $319.8 million = [($339.6 + $300.0)/2].

Learning Note

Variations exist in practice in the calculation of ratios. For example, return on assets sometimes is calculated simply as net income divided by total assets. If you are using ratios to analyze company activities, be sure you know how the ratios were computed and be sure the ratios were computed consistently for all companies in your analysis.

Heavy Metal earned a return of 12.4% on assets in 1994 (net income ÷ average total assets = $39,600,000 / $319,800,000). Its return on equity also was 12.4%, because assets were financed completely by equity.

During 1995, management is considering the acquisition of additional assets that will cost the company $100 million. Management believes these assets will permit the company to expand into new product lines that will yield a return of 22% ($22 million) before taxes. It is considering whether to finance the additional assets with debt or with equity. The company's stock currently is selling at $40 per share. Management believes 2.5 million new shares could be issued at this price if the acquisition is financed with equity ($100 million / $40 per share). The company can issue the debt it needs to finance its acquisitions at a market rate of 8%. It has no preferred stock.

The alternatives may be evaluated by examining accounting information describing expected results from each financing alternative:

	Equity Financing	Debt Financing
Total assets	$439,600,000	$439,600,000
Total liabilities	$ 0	$100,000,000
Total stockholders' equity	$439,600,000	$339,600,000
Operating income ($60,000,000 + $22,000,000)	$ 82,000,000	$ 82,000,000
Interest expense	0	(8,000,000)
Pretax income	82,000,000	74,000,000
Income tax expense (34%)	(27,880,000)	(25,160,000)
Net income	$ 54,120,000	$ 48,840,000
Earnings per share (12,500,000 shares)	$4.33	
Earnings per share (10,000,000 shares)		$4.88
Average total assets ($339,600,000 + $439,600,000)/2	$389,600,000	$389,600,000
Net income adjusted for interest:		
($54,120,000 + $0)	$ 54,120,000	
($48,840,000 + [$8,000,000 × (1−34%)]		$ 54,120,000
Return on assets ($54,120,000 / $389,600,000)	13.9%	13.9%
Average total equity:		
($339,600,000 + $439,600,000)/2	$389,600,000	
($339,600,000 + $339,600,000)/2		$339,600,000
Return on equity:		
($54,120,000 / $389,600,000)	13.9%	
($48,840,000 / $339,600,000)		14.4%

These calculations project the expected results for 1995 if the additional assets had been acquired and expected results had been achieved. This type of analysis of expected results is known as "what-if" analysis. Accounting information prepared using this analysis is known as "pro-forma" information. Pro-forma financial statements report the expected results for a period from a set of hypothetical assumptions. What-if analysis commonly is used by managers and analysts to evaluate the likely results of a decision.

Debt financing produces a higher return on equity because less equity is outstanding if debt financing is used, even though net income is lower. If equity financing were used, current stockholders would be required to invest an additional $100 million in the company. Otherwise, their ownership would be diluted by the sale of stock to new owners. If the company's price-earnings (PE) ratio (about 10 to 1) remained unchanged after the decision, the price of the stock should be about $43 per share (10 × $4.33) if equity financing is used and about $49 (10 × $4.88) if debt financing is used. From this return information, debt financing appears to be the better alternative.

The effect of the decision on risk also needs to be considered, however. In particular, debt financing increases the risk of the company. The use of debt financing increases the possibility of lower earnings, reduced dividends, and even bankruptcy, which could result if the company did not generate sufficient cash to pay the interest and principal on its debt. For example, assume the debt is to be repaid in 10 annual installments of $10 million. In 1995, Heavy Metal would need $18 million ($8 million for interest and $10 million for principal) to pay principal and interest on the debt. If the company continues to perform as it did in 1994, these payments should not be a problem. Suppose, however, economic conditions are worse than anticipated and the company earns only $40 million of operating income in 1995. Heavy Metal's net income would be:

Operating income	$40,000,000
Interest expense	(8,000,000)
Income taxes (at 34%)	(10,880,000)
Net income	$21,120,000
Earnings per share (10,000,000 shares)	$2.11

Cash flow from operating activities probably would be much lower than in 1994. The company could have difficulty paying $10 million of debt principal and meeting its other cash needs.

Exhibit 10-5 illustrates the effect of the financing decision on earnings per share. The graph illustrates the relationship between operating income and taxes and earnings per share for Heavy Metal.

Exhibit 10-5 The Effect of Capital Structure on Earnings per Share

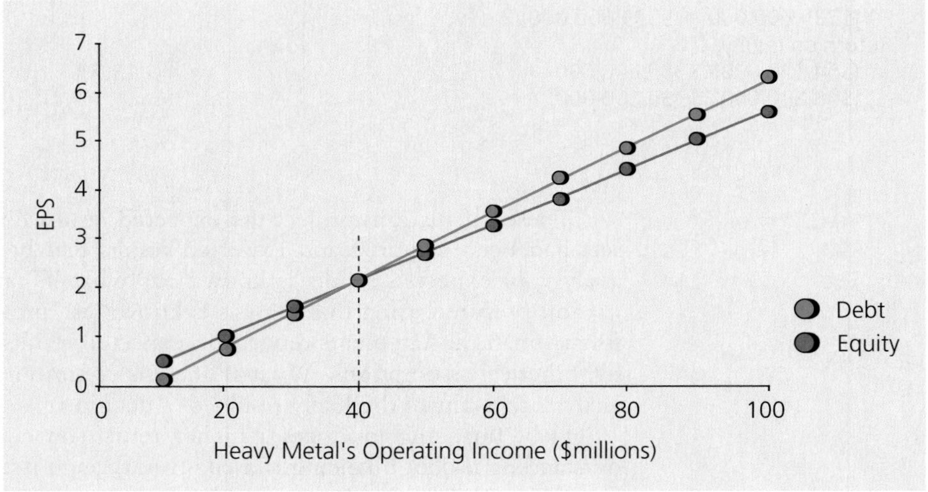

Objective 7
Determine the effect of financial leverage on a company's earnings.

For amounts of operating income above $40 million, earnings per share is higher if debt is used to finance the additional assets. For amounts below $40 million, earnings per share is higher if equity is used. The company's earnings per share is more sensitive to changes in income when debt financing is used, as indicated by the steeper slope of debt line in Exhibit 10-5. The increase in risk caused by debt financing is likely to affect the company's PE ratio. Investors may discount Heavy Metal's earnings at a higher rate because of the added risk. The effect of debt financing on the PE ratio depends on investors' expectations about the company's future earnings and its ability to meet its debt payments.

The use of debt in a company's capital structure is referred to as *financial leverage*. The higher the proportion of debt, the more highly levered the company. Financial leverage increases a company's earnings per share as sales increase. Leverage decreases earnings per share, however, as sales decrease. A major financing decision for managers is selection of an appropriate amount of financial leverage. Note that return on equity is larger than return on assets when the effect of leverage is beneficial to stockholders.

What mix of debt and equity is optimal for Heavy Metal? Assume instead of deciding how to finance additional assets, management is deciding whether to issue debt to repurchase a portion of Heavy Metal's equity. Would current stockholders be better off if a portion of the company's equity were repurchased? If so, how much should be acquired?

This decision can be evaluated if assumptions are made about the company's future earnings and the amount of interest it will have to pay for various amounts of debt. For example, assume the company will continue to earn operating income of $60 million per year in the foreseeable future as it did in 1994. Assume the company can repurchase as many shares of its stock as it wishes at the current market price of $40 per share. Also, assume the following schedule of interest rates would apply to debt issued by the company:

Proportion of Debt	Interest Rate
10%	7%
20%	7.50%
30%	8.55%
40%	9.70%
50%	12%
60%	14%

As the proportion of debt in the capital structure (ratio of debt to equity) increases, the risk of default on interest and principal increases. Therefore, the interest rate required by creditors increases. Also, stockholders will expect a higher return on their investments to compensate them for the higher risk of bankruptcy and uncertainty about cash flows.

Exhibit 10-6 provides information about the effect of additional amounts of debt on Heavy Metal's earnings per share (assuming a 34% tax rate).

Exhibit 10-6 The Effect of Debt on Earnings per Share

(In Millions Except Percentages and EPS)

Percent Debt	Interest Rate	Total Assets	Total Debt	Total Equity	Operating Income	Interest	Pretax Income	Net Income	Shares	EPS
0%	0%	$300.00	$0.00	$300.00	$60.00	$0.00	$60.00	$39.60	10.00	$3.96
10%	7%	300.00	30.00	270.00	60.00	2.10	57.90	38.21	9.25	4.13
20%	7.50%	300.00	60.00	240.00	60.00	4.50	55.50	36.63	8.50	4.31
30%	8.55%	300.00	90.00	210.00	60.00	7.70	52.30	34.52	7.75	4.45
40%	9.70%	300.00	120.00	180.00	60.00	11.64	48.36	31.92	7.00	4.56
50%	12%	300.00	150.00	150.00	60.00	18.00	42.00	27.72	6.25	4.44
60%	14%	300.00	180.00	120.00	60.00	25.20	34.80	22.97	5.50	4.18

As the proportion of debt in the capital structure increases, earnings per share increases because debt is used to reduce the number of shares of stock outstanding. Eventually, however, the increasing interest rate on the debt becomes so large that it offsets the effect of fewer shares. For Heavy Metal, earnings per share, under the above assumptions, will be maximized when the proportion of debt in the capital structure is 40%.

Exhibit 10-6 does not consider the effect of increased risk on the company's stock price, however. As the proportion of debt increases, the PE ratio is likely to decrease. The discount rate in the price equation (price = expected cash flow ÷ discount rate) should increase as the amount of debt in the capital structure increases. Therefore, the effect of the increase in earnings per share on the company's stock price will be offset by a higher required return. Thus, while return (expected cash flow) increases, risk also increases. Consequently, the effect of increased leverage on price depends on both the increase in expected cash flow and the increase in risk. The optimal capital structure will be less than 40% debt. How much less depends on the effect of increased amounts of debt on the required rate of return for the company's stock.

Capital structure can be measured by the **ratio of debt (total liabilities) to equity** (sometimes called **debt to net worth).** Net worth is total assets minus total liabilities. Another common measure is the **ratio of debt to total capitalization** (liabilities plus stockholders' equity), also called the **debt to total assets ratio** or the **debt ratio.**

Learning Note

Analysts sometimes include only long-term debt in these ratios. They may exclude unfunded pension obligations and deferred taxes from the debt category and may include the present value of future operating lease payments. They may include preferred stock as part of debt rather than equity. These adjustments are logical when the purpose of the analysis is to measure the relationship between long-term financing provided by creditors and that provided by owners.

Greater financial leverage is associated with higher risk, on average. The amount of financial leverage used by companies in some industries is larger than in other industries. For example, petroleum refining companies are more highly levered, on average, than are pharmaceutical companies. The next section examines some economic and company attributes that affect financing activities.

Attributes Affecting Financial Leverage

The amount of financial leverage a company uses depends on economic conditions, such as the level of interest rates. Also, it depends on attributes of a company, such as the type of assets it uses and the stability of its earnings.

Objective 8
Identify economic and company attributes that affect financial leverage.

The level of interest rates in the economy is affected by federal government policies. Rates increase and decrease as the Federal Reserve Board increases and decreases the rate banks pay for funds. During the recession of the early 1990's, the Federal Reserve decreased rates sharply to stimulate the economy. Lower interest rates increase the amount of money companies and individuals borrow. More money means more buying, and more buying means more production, more profits, more jobs, and more taxes. As interest rates decline, the prices of existing stocks and bonds increase. As the Discount Rate in the equation Price = Expected Cash Flow ÷ Discount Rate decreases, Price increases if Expected Cash Flow remains constant.

The level of interest rates has several effects on capital structure. Companies may choose to borrow more, thereby increasing their financial leverage. Lower interest rates also may stimulate companies to refinance existing debt. For example, assume a company's liabilities in 1990 included $30 million of long-term debt, paying 10% interest. If interest rates decreased in 1990 so the company could issue the same debt at 8%, the company could save $600,000 ($30 million × 2%) a year, before taxes, by refinancing its outstanding debt. The company might issue new debt at the lower rate and use the proceeds to repay its existing debt.

If the debt consisted of bonds, the price of the bonds in the secondary market would increase as interest rates decreased. Therefore, the current market price of the company's 10% bonds would be high relative to the price it would receive from issuing 8% bonds. Many bonds contain call provisions so a company can repurchase its bonds if interest rates decrease. The call price for most bonds is slightly higher than their face value. By selling $30 million of 8% bonds, the company could call its 10% bonds and repay them at only slightly more than $30 million, making call provisions useful for that company. Similarly, preferred stock may have a redemption provision that serves the same purpose.

Another way companies take advantage of lower interest rates is to reduce their financial leverage by issuing additional stock. At the beginning of the 1990s, many companies were highly levered. The amount of leverage was a cause of the recession, as many companies struggled to repay principal and interest on their debt. Bankruptcies were frequent. As stock prices increased, many companies took the opportunity to issue new shares of stock at higher market prices, and proceeds from these shares were used to repay debt.

Company attributes also affect capital structure decisions. Some companies rely on a large amount of plant assets. Large amounts of equipment and other facilities are needed to produce goods such as petroleum products, automobiles, or airplanes. Companies in these industries often use long-term debt to finance the acquisition of these assets. These companies generally are more highly levered than companies that do not need large amounts of plant assets; for example, service companies usually have small amounts of long-term debt.

Some companies' earnings are more volatile than others. Demand for some products remains relatively unchanged if the economy hits a downturn; examples include pharmaceutical and food products. Demand for other products decreases in an economic slump: automobiles, major appliances, and housing. Demand for some products actually increases in a downturn: fast foods and discount merchandise. A company with a stable demand, and therefore relatively stable earnings, can afford to be more highly levered than other companies. Companies with stable earnings face less likelihood that their earnings will decrease to a level at which they are unable to repay principal and interest on their debt.

Exhibit 10-7 illustrates the stability of earnings for two companies for 1981–1991.

Johnson & Johnson's earnings were more stable than Chevron's. Johnson's debt to equity ratio was .89 in 1991 compared with a debt to equity ratio of .67 for Chevron. Though Johnson was more highly levered, its PE ratio was 25, compared with a PE ratio of 12 for Chevron. Chevron's higher risk can be explained, in part, by the instability of its earnings relative to those of Johnson & Johnson.

Exhibit 10-7 Stability of Earnings

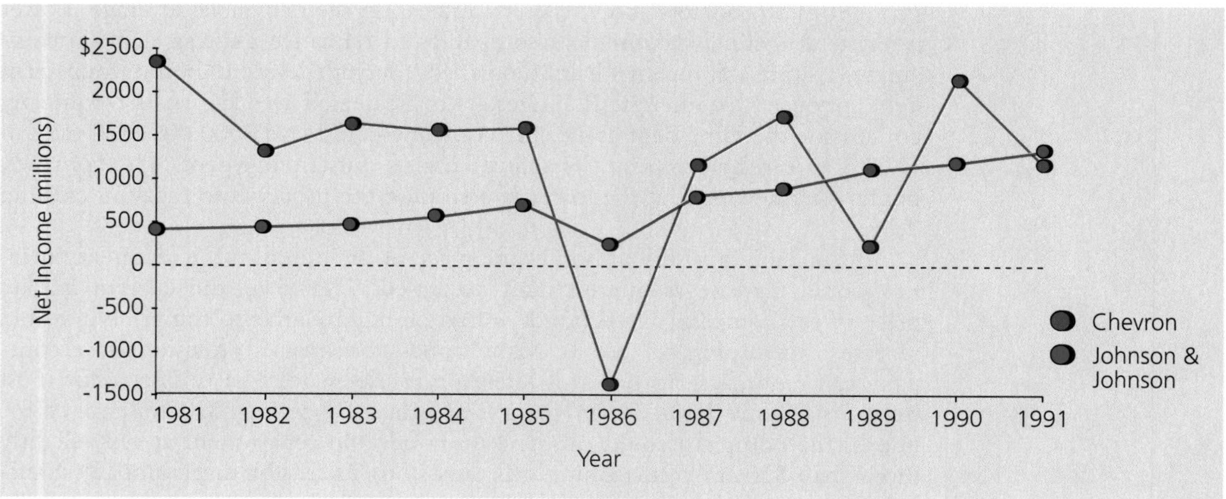

This section has explained how financing activities can affect the risk and return of a company's financial securities. The next section examines specific uses of accounting information in analyzing financing activities.

SELF-STUDY PROBLEM 10-2

Andromeda Corporation began operations in October 1995. Common stock was issued at that time for a total of $80 million (10 million shares). During the fiscal year ended September 30, 1996, Andromeda's net income was $16 million after taxes of $8 million and its stock increased in value to $10 per share, its current price.

The company has an opportunity to expand its operations into a new product line, but the expansion will require new investment of $30 million. Management is considering how it might raise the new capital for this investment. Three alternatives are being considered. Option A provides for issuing new shares of common stock to raise the amount. Management believes the stock will sell at its current price. Option B provides for issuing 300,000 shares of $100 par value preferred stock with a $10 dividend rate. Management believes the shares would sell at their par value. Option C provides for issuing $30 million of 20-year, 8% bonds. Management believes the bonds would sell at face (maturity) value.

Assume the new investment will provide additional annual operating income to Andromeda of $9 million for the foreseeable future. Without the investment, Andromeda expects an annual net income of $16 million for the foreseeable future.

Required

What would be the effect of each option on Andromeda's common stockholders? What recommendations would you make to Andromeda's managers concerning this investment?

The solution to Self-Study Problem 10-2 appears at the end of the chapter.

THE IMPORTANCE OF ACCOUNTING INFORMATION

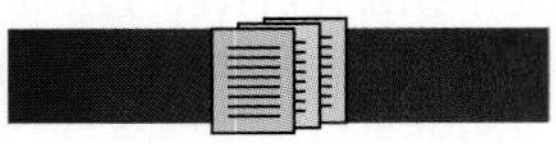

Objective 9
Explain how accounting information is useful for evaluating financing activities.

A primary use of accounting information is to help managers make capital structure decisions. This information also helps investors and other external users evaluate these decisions, which affect their own decisions to invest and extend credit. Financial statements and related disclosures provide information to evaluate financing activities. In addition to the amount of liabilities, preferred stock, and common stock, these reports provide information about dividend payments, the use of short-term and long-term debt, obligations to employees, and other commitments.

Dividend Payments

Net income is a source of financing, increasing a company's equity. Cash flows from operating activities can be used to finance acquisition of additional assets. How much of a company's cash flow is available to finance assets depends on how much cash dividend it pays. Decisions about dividend payments during a fiscal period depend on a company's financial performance and on its dividend policy. The amount of dividends companies pay varies considerably. Some companies pay out most of their net income as dividends while other companies pay no dividends. Commonly used measures of dividend decisions are **dividends per share** and the ***dividend payout ratio,*** **the ratio of dividends per share to earnings per share.** Exhibit 10-8 describes 1991 dividend payout ratios for several major corporations.

Exhibit 10-8 Dividend Payout Ratios

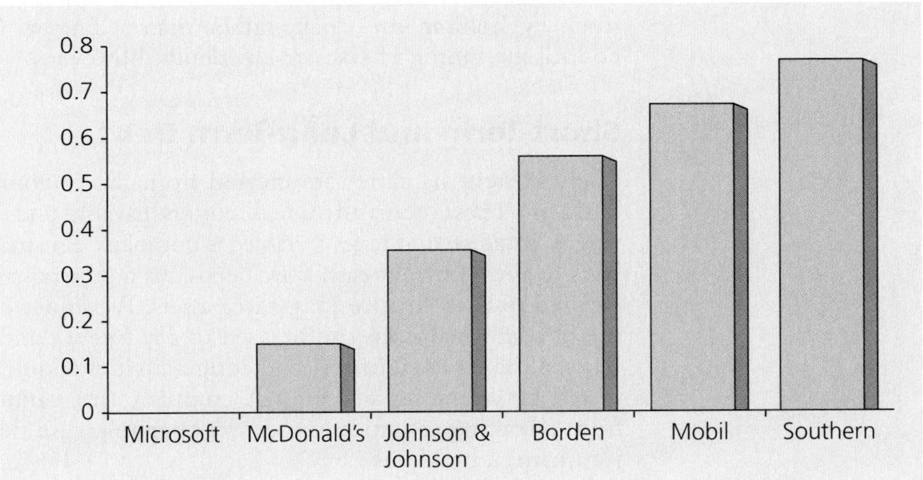

The dividend payout ratios for the companies in the exhibit vary from 0 (for Microsoft) to 77% (for Southern Co., a utility company). Companies with high growth potential, such as Microsoft and McDonald's, reinvest most of their profits. Companies in mature, stable industries, such as utilities, pay out most of their income to stockholders.

Investors often select stocks because of a particular investment strategy. Some investors want to own stocks that pay a stable dividend so they can use the cash receipts. Other investors want to own stocks that will grow in value because the issuing companies reinvest profits in new technology, products, and product markets. Therefore, different dividend policies appeal to different investors.

Corporations that pay dividends often attempt to maintain a stable dividend policy so investors can anticipate the amount of cash they will receive. These companies increase dividend payments only when they believe they will be able to sustain higher payments. They are reluctant to reduce dividend payments unless they expect a long-term decline in earnings. Therefore, a change in the amount of dividend per share paid by a company often is an important signal about a company's expected financial performance.

Remember that dividends paid out of earnings are a return on investment. Dividends paid in excess of earnings are a return of investment. A company that consistently pays dividends in excess of its earnings usually is not maintaining its capital. It is jeopardizing its ability to sustain its current level of earnings or to take advantage of growth opportunities.

The amount of dividends a company pays depends largely on the alternatives it has for investing its cash. If sufficient investment alternatives exist for a company to use cash from operating activities to create higher profits and cash flows, it should take advantage of these alternatives. For example, assume a company can reinvest its profits at a return of 15%, after taxes, while individual stockholders can earn only 10% on investments of similar risk, after taxes. Stockholders should prefer that the company retain the cash rather than pay dividends. Therefore, a company's dividend payments reveal information about its growth potential and dividend policies.

Taxation of dividends is another reason stockholders might want a company to reinvest profits rather than pay dividends. Dividends received are taxable income to the stockholders. Reinvested profits are not taxed to stockholders until stock is sold. Profits earned when investors sell their stock are taxed at a somewhat more favorable rate than dividends. Stockholders can defer the taxes on stock by holding the stock, rather than selling it. Most stockholders cannot control the timing of taxes on dividends, however.

Short-Term and Long-Term Debt

Many current liabilities are created from the ongoing operating activities of a business. These items include accounts payable and accrued liabilities, such as wages, interest, and taxes payable. A company also may borrow on a short-term basis to meet current cash flow needs. As a general rule, long-term debt should be used only to finance long-term assets. Revenues earned by a company from use of additional assets can be used to pay interest and principal on debt used to finance the assets. Current operating activities should be financed by cash generated by operating activities. A company that cannot generate sufficient cash from operating activities to meet its operating cash needs typically is facing major financial problems.

The analysis of short-term cash flows and obligations is important for managers and external decision makers. Creditors should have a particular interest in whether a company is generating sufficient cash flows to meet its current obligations. Exhibit 10-9 provides accounting information to illustrate this point.

This information reveals that, at the end of 1991, Unisys had obligations of $3,663 million that were to be paid in 1992. Almost all of these current liabilities required cash payments by the company. Current assets amounted to $4,295.9 million for a **current ratio** (current assets/current liabilities) of 1.17 ($4,295.9/$3,663). All of the company's current assets were not likely to produce cash flows in 1992, however. Other current assets, in particular, consisted largely of prepaid expenses. These resources were consumed in 1992 but did

Exhibit 10-9

UNISYS CORPORATION
SELECTED FINANCIAL STATEMENT INFORMATION

December 31 (Millions)	1991
Current assets	
Cash and cash equivalents	$ 813.6
Accounts and notes receivable	1,777.2
Inventories	1,024.8
Other current assets	680.3
Total	4,295.9
Current liabilities	
Notes payable	277.4
Current maturities of long-term debt	313.4
Accounts payable	1,058.4
Other accrued liabilities	1,634.2
Estimated income taxes	379.6
Total	3,663.0
Net cash provided by operating activities	919.5

not produce additional cash. Inventories produce cash if the goods in inventory can be sold and receivables can be collected. Assuming inventories and receivables were converted to cash, the company could be expected to generate $3,615.6 ($813.6 + $1,777.2 + $1,024.8) million in cash in 1992 from current assets available at the beginning of the year. This amount was less than the amount needed to pay the company's current liabilities of $3,663 million.

Current assets and liabilities provide partial information about a company's cash generating potential and cash needs at the beginning of a fiscal period. In addition, **the statement of cash flows provides important information about the ability of a company to meet its cash needs.** Unisys expected to generate cash from operating activities in 1992 to pay its current liabilities and to meet its operating needs. The amount of cash generated from operating activities was $919.5 million in 1991 (see Exhibit 10-9). This cash flow was available to repay principal on debt that matured in 1992 and for asset replacements. Current maturities of long-term debt to be repaid in 1992 (see Exhibit 10-9) were reported to be $313.4 million. Additional notes payable were $277.4 million. Therefore, $590.8 million ($313.4 + $277.4) of Unisys' cash flow from operating activities was used to pay these obligations in 1992. If the company's cash flows from operating activities fell short of the 1991 amount, the company could have difficulty in paying these obligations. This problem was likely to become worse in 1993. Notes to the financial statements reveal that Unisys' maturing long-term debt in 1993 was $1,398.7 million. Thus, the company would need to increase its cash flows above the 1991 level to be able to make these payments.

Unisys' management discussed some effects of its financial problems in its 1991 annual report:

> In September 1990 and February 1991, the Board of Directors of the Company suspended the quarterly dividend on the Company's common and preferred stock, respectively. At December 31, 1991, cumulative preferred dividends in arrears amounted to $94.3 million.

> Since 1989, the credit ratings for the Company's public debt have been lowered. The credit ratings on the Company's senior long-term debt were lowered from . . . Ba3 to B2 by Moody's Investors Service in April 1991 . . . .
>
> Effective June 30, 1991, the Company entered into an amendment to its revolving credit agreement.[3] The amended agreement lowered the net worth requirement, as defined therein from $3.5 billion to $2.05 billion. The amendment also provides that the aggregate principal amount outstanding under the revolving credit agreement will not exceed $1.05 billion unless and until the loans under the agreement are secured to an extent and by collateral satisfactory to the lenders. Additional amendment terms include a restriction on the payment of dividends and prepayment of debt, limitations on capital expenditures and the setting of minimum levels of income before interest and income taxes. The amendment also increased the interest rates and commitment fees payable by the Company.

In 1991 Unisys was a company struggling to survive. It had suspended dividends because of the shortage of cash. Its debt rating had been revised to a highly speculative grade, indicating an increase in default risk. Its creditors had amended loan agreements and had increased interest rates on the company's debt. *Loan agreements* **and** *debt covenants* **are restrictions placed on a company's economic activities by its creditors.** These contract terms protect creditors from management decisions that might reduce the value of their loans. These terms often restrict the amount of debt a company can issue, restrict dividends when profits are low, and require a company to maintain a certain level of working capital, equity, or profits. Accounting information is used by creditors to determine whether contract terms are being met. If the terms are not met, creditors can require early payment of their loans, require renegotiation of credit terms, take control of a company, or force a company into bankruptcy.

Loan agreements and debt covenants often are expressed in terms of accounting ratios. Ratios such as debt to equity, current, dividend payout, cash flow to current maturities of long-term debt, times interest earned, and quick (or acid-test) are common in loan agreements.[4] For example, an agreement might specify that a company should not exceed a debt to equity ratio of 1.2 to 1.

These ratios, other than those defined earlier, are calculated as follows:

Cash Flow to Current Maturities of Long-Term Debt Ratio = Net Cash Flow from Operating Activities ÷ Current Maturities of Long-Term Debt. This ratio measures the sufficiency of cash to meet current debt payments.

Times Interest Earned Ratio = Income Before Interest and Taxes ÷ Interest Expense. This ratio measures the sufficiency of current income to cover interest requirements.

Quick (or Acid-Test) Ratio = (Cash + Marketable Securities + Receivables) ÷ Current Liabilities. This ratio measures the sufficiency of current cash generating assets to meet current obligations. It is a more conservative form of the current ratio.

[3] A revolving credit agreement provides for borrowing up to an agreed amount. Periodic payments are made to cover interest and principal charges. A common form of revolving credit agreement used by individuals is a credit card.

[4] Charles H. Gibson, *Financial Statement Analysis*, South-Western Publishing Co., 1992, p. 551.

Exhibit 10-10 illustrates the ratios with accounting information from the 1991 annual reports of four companies.

Exhibit 10-10

Accounting Ratios for Selected Companies

	Unisys	IBM	McDonald's	Microsoft
1991 Financial Statement Information (in millions)				
Total Debt	$6,417.6	$55,467.0	$6,514.0	$ 293.4
Preferred Stock	1,578.0	0.0	298.2	0.0
Total Equity	2,014.4	37,006.0	4,835.1	1,350.8
Current Assets	4,295.9	40,969.0	646.0	1,028.5
Current Liabilities	3,663.0	33,624.0	1,287.9	293.4
Cash Flow from Operating Activities	919.5	6,725.0	1,423.2	557.9
Current Maturities of Long-Term Debt	313.4	4,363.0	69.1	0.0
Operating Income	−578.9	942.0	1,678.5	649.8
Interest Expense	407.6	1,423.0	391.4	4.5
Cash, Securities, Receivables	2,590.8	29,468.0	494.6	929.6
Ratios				
Debt to Equity	3.19	1.50	1.35	0.22
Debt + Preferred Stock/Common Equity	18.32	1.50	1.50	0.22
Current	1.17	1.22	0.50	3.51
Cash Flow to Current Maturities of Long-Term Debt	2.93	1.54	20.60	
Times Interest Earned	−1.42	.66	4.29	144.40
Quick	0.71	0.88	0.38	3.17

Unisys' problems can be observed from the debt to equity, cash flow to current maturities of long-term debt, and times interest earned ratios. The debt to equity ratio is especially high if preferred stock is added to the numerator and subtracted from the denominator (as shown for debt + preferred stock/common equity in Exhibit 10-10). Like debt, preferred stock requires fixed payments each year before dividends can be paid on common stock. Therefore, preferred stock sometimes is treated by analysts as though it were debt rather than equity. Times interest earned is negative because the company reported an operating loss in 1991. In contrast, Microsoft's debt consisted of current liabilities. Therefore, it had no current maturities of long-term debt in 1991. From this analysis, it is apparent that Unisys was facing a problem because of the high proportion of debt and preferred stock in its capital structure. The company was having difficulty meeting its interest, principal, and preferred dividend payments.

Information about cash flows, current assets, and current liabilities is especially important for evaluating a company's ability to meet its current obligations. This analysis often is referred to as an analysis of liquidity. Current, cash flow, and quick ratios are called **liquidity ratios.** Information about profits and long-term or total assets, liabilities, and stockholders' equity is important for evaluating a company's ability to meet its long-term obligations. Ratios involving long-term obligations, such as the debt to equity ratio, sometimes are referred to as **debt** or **leverage ratios.** Profits generally are a good measure of long-run cash flow generating ability. In the short-run, however, they may not provide an accurate description of cash flow. Cash flow from operating activities often is a better measure of the ability of a company to meet its current cash requirements.

Ratios are useful for revealing relationships and patterns in accounting information. Many types of ratios can be computed. Memorizing ratios is much less important than understanding concepts that make ratios useful, however.

Learning Note

Considerable care must be used in comparing ratios for companies from different countries. Numbers used in ratios are affected by GAAP used in creating the numbers. Because GAAP vary among countries, accounting numbers, and therefore ratios, are not always comparable for companies from various countries.

Employee Benefits and Other Commitments

Long-term obligations such as deferred benefits, deferred taxes, leases and other commitments, contingencies, and minority interest require special consideration in assessing a company's capital structure. With the exception of leases and certain other commitments, the measurement of these items often is imprecise. Contingencies often are not included on the balance sheet at all. The amount of a contingency, such as the outcome of a lawsuit, is difficult to determine. Also, the probability of the contingency becoming an actual liability, frequently is difficult to determine.

The amounts of deferred pension and other post-employment benefits also are "soft" numbers. They depend on management assumptions that vary considerably across companies. Assumptions about the rate at which wages and health care costs will increase are educated guesses. Managers have considerable latitude over the accrual of certain expenses associated with these plans. Though these amounts may provide some idea of future commitments for employee benefits, they should be viewed as only rough approximations. Trends in cash flows associated with these benefits may provide a better measure of the effect of the plans on a company's financial condition.

Financial decisions affect the risk associated with pension and other benefit plans. Employees contract with a company to provide services in exchange for current and future compensation. As a company's financial condition deteriorates, the potential for default on employee compensation increases. Companies that become bankrupt may default on their benefit plans. Certain plans, especially pension plans, often are insured by the federal government. Other types of benefit plans are not insured. Also, if a company's financial condition deteriorates, it may modify plan terms to reduce costs and cash outflows. For example, Unisys reported in 1991:

> In 1990, The Company took action to reduce costs, including the suspension of Company matching contributions to certain U.S. employee savings plans and the amendment of the U.S. . . . pension plan to change the benefit formula . . .

Accounting information can be used by employees in negotiating for current and deferred compensation and benefits.

Deferred taxes do not represent actual obligations because they are not legally owed to the government. An examination of trends in cash payments for income taxes may be a better measure of future requirements. Recent changes in accounting standards may improve the accuracy of amounts reported for this obligation. A new standard, effective for financial statements issued after December 15, 1992, requires the amount of deferred tax to be adjusted for amounts that are not likely to result in actual tax payments. Prior to 1992, such adjustments were not made and deferred tax amounts sometimes had little relationship with actual obligations for future tax payments. The fact that these liabilities are not discounted to their present value (under the new or old standards) also means that they are likely to be overstated.

Minority interest results when a parent company owns less than 100% of a consolidated subsidiary. The equity represented by other owners (minority owners) is reported on the balance sheet, generally between liabilities and stockholders' equity. This item does not represent an existing obligation to make payments or to transfer other resources. Therefore, some analysts ignore this amount in evaluating a company's obligations and capital structure. It is not clear that minority interest, deferred taxes, and deferred benefit obligations increase the risk of a company in the same way as other liabilities. Comparing these liabilities among companies is difficult because of the variation in assumptions used in computing the amounts. Comparison is especially difficult for foreign corporations because they frequently do not report deferred benefits, taxes, and other commitments.

Lease commitments are contractual obligations to make future payments. Capitalized lease obligations are reported as a part of liabilities. Minimum future rental or lease payments for operating leases are disclosed in notes to financial statements. These commitments will affect a company's future cash requirements; therefore, they should be considered in evaluating its ability to meet maturing obligations. For example, Unisys disclosed in 1991 that it had minimum net rental commitments of $238.9 million in 1992. These should be considered in evaluating the company's ability to meet its current obligations in 1992. Some analysts include these amounts, or their discounted values, as part of liabilities when calculating liquidity and debt ratios.

Preferred stock is part of a company's equity. As noted earlier, preferred dividends usually are fixed payments that reduce cash flow available to common stockholders. They should be deducted from net income or cash flow in calculating accounting ratios such as return on equity. Some analysts consider material amounts of preferred stock as part of a company's obligations rather than as part of its equity. They include preferred stock in the numerator rather than the denominator of the debt to equity ratio.

This section has described how accounting information is helpful in evaluating financial decisions. The final section of this chapter examines financing decisions of Vulcan Materials Company using information from the company's financial statements and related disclosures.

AN ILLUSTRATION OF FINANCIAL DECISION ANALYSIS

Exhibit 10-11 provides information reported by Vulcan Materials Company in its 1991 annual report.

The type of analysis performed on accounting information depends on the purpose of the analysis. Different decision makers may have somewhat different reasons for analyzing this information. For example, the concerns of short-term creditors are different from those of long-term creditors. The concerns of cred-

Exhibit 10-11

Vulcan Materials Company
Selected Annual Report Information

(in thousands except per share amounts)

December 31	**1991**	**1990**	**1989**
Income Statement:			
1. Operating income	$ 84,652	$ 186,987	$ 207,480
2. Interest expense	(11,205)	(7,758)	(6,117)
3. Provision for income taxes	(20,867)	(58,951)	(67,943)
4. Net income	$ 52,580	$ 120,278	$ 133,420*
5. Earnings per share	$1.38	$3.10	$3.30*
6. Dividends per share	$1.20	$1.20	$1.12
7. Average common shares outstanding	38,216	38,830	40,395
Cash Flow Statement:			
8. Net cash from continuing operating activities	$ 184,858	$ 205,899	$ 255,751
9. Payment of debt principal	(16,942)	(17,675)	(10,096)
10. Purchase of plant assets	(63,645)	(119,886)	(102,974)
11. Cash dividends paid	(45,664)	(46,416)	(45,042)
12. Cash available for other purposes	$ 58,607	$21,922	$ 97,639
Balance Sheet:			
13. Current assets	$ 285,147	$ 295,312	$ 333,252
14. Plant assets, net of depreciation	675,440	720,691	602,483
15. Other assets	112,524	101,994	66,804
16. Total assets	$1,073,111	$1,117,997	$1,002,539
17. Current liabilities	$ 135,388	$ 233,839	$ 140,916
18. Long-term debt and capitalized leases	111,106	44,674	55,154
19. Other noncurrent liabilities	35,666	37,554	32,576
20. Deferred compensation and benefits	38,397	36,566	36,663
21. Deferred income taxes	69,626	85,172	73,685
22. Total liabilities	$ 390,183	$ 437,805	$ 338,994
23. Contributed capital	$ 50,036	$ 49,331	$ 48,050
24. Retained earnings	919,089	912,173	837,866
25. Treasury stock	(286,197)	(281,312)	(222,371)
26. Total stockholders' equity	682,928	680,192	663,545
27. Total liabilities and stockholders' equity	$1,073,111	$1,117,997	$1,002,539
28. Market value of stock	$1,368,000	$1,295,400	$1,757,750
29. Price per share	$36	$34	$44.50
30. Shares outstanding	38,000	38,100	39,500
31. Price-earnings ratio	26.1	11.0	13.5
32. Debt to equity ratio	57.1	64.4	51.1

****In 1989, reported net income was further reduced by a net $2,561 million from the disposal of a segment and from a change in an accounting principle. For purposes of our analysis, the net income before these adjustments and the related earnings per share are used.***

itors are different from those of owners. The general analysis that follows focuses on the issues that can be useful to a variety of users. Modifications would need to be made to meet the needs of specific decision makers.

Objective 10
Analyze a company's financing decisions.

As a first step in the analysis, observe the company's overall financial condition and changes in the condition for the years reported. Net income (item 4) and earnings per share (item 5) have decreased each year, declining sharply in

1991. This trend was typical of many companies during the recession of the early 1990's.

The company's dividends per share (item 6) increased in 1990 and remained at the same level in 1991, suggesting the company was not facing a major financial problem. Also, the company's cash flow from operating activities remained strong. Though cash flow from operating activities declined during the recessionary period (item 8), they remained high relative to cash requirements. Cash flow from operating activities includes the effect of cash payments for interest and taxes. This cash flow was considerably higher than the amount needed by Vulcan to pay principal on debt (item 9). Thus, the company did not face a major risk of default or bankruptcy, even in 1991.

Vulcan used a substantial portion of its cash flow from operating activities to acquire additional plant assets (item 10), especially in 1989 and 1990. After using its cash flow from operating activities to purchase new assets, the company had a surplus of cash after payment of dividends (item 12). The company was not facing a cash flow problem.

As a second step in the analysis, observe the financing activities made by the company's management. At the end of 1989, Vulcan's capital structure consisted of approximately 34% debt and 66% equity. By the end of 1990, it consisted of approximately 40% debt and 60% equity. Two primary events accounted for the change in capital structure, an increase in debt and a repurchase of stock. Vulcan borrowed approximately $100 million in short-term debt during 1990 (as part of item 17), which financed the acquisition of additional plant assets in 1990 (item 14). Other assets (item 15) also increased. Notes to the financial statements reveal this increase was due primarily to acquisitions of other companies, also financed by the new debt. The short-term debt was converted to long-term debt in 1991 (see changes in items 17 and 18), and a portion of the debt was repaid in 1991. Total liabilities decreased by almost $50 million (item 22). The company repurchased approximately $60 million of its own stock in 1990 and an additional $5 million in 1991 (item 25). Other financial statement amounts remained relatively unchanged from 1989 to 1991.

As a third step, analyze the effects of the financing activities on the risk and return of creditors and stockholders. Assume that when the decision to issue debt was made in 1990, Vulcan's management expected the company's operating income to remain at the 1989 level of approximately $200 million per year. Information in the annual report indicates the company's average return on assets for the 1981 to 1990 period was approximately 18% before taxes. Therefore, it can be assumed management expected the new investments to produce a return of at least 18%. Notes to the financial statements indicate the company issued approximately $100 million of new debt at an average market rate of 8.5%. The company's effective tax rate was 34%. The *expected* effect of these decisions on earnings per share can be demonstrated as shown in Exhibit 10-12.

The expected (pro-forma) effect of the debt financing and new investment was to increase expected earnings per share to $3.40 from $3.24. Once the effect of the repurchase of common shares is included in the analysis, expected earnings per share increased to $3.52.

Actual results for 1991 were much worse than those anticipated above. The increased interest pushed the company's earnings per share lower in 1991. Earnings on the new investments were undoubtedly lower than expected, as well. Were these bad decisions? This question should not be answered by reference to results for one year, especially when the year was one in which many companies experienced major declines in net income. Instead, the answer depends on

Exhibit 10-12 Expected Effect of Financing Decision

	Before New Financing	**After New Financing**
Operating income	$200,000,000	$200,000,000
Earnings on new investment (at 18%)		18,000,000
Interest expense (from 1989, item 2)	(6,000,000)	(14,500,000)
Pretax income	194,000,000	203,500,000
Income tax expense (at 34%)	(66,000,000)	(69,200,000)
Net income	128,000,000*	134,300,000
Earnings per share (39,500 shares, item 30)	$3.24*	$3.40
Earnings per share (38,100 shares, item 30)		$3.52

These numbers do not exactly agree with those of 1989 since approximations are being used for illustrative purposes.

the effect the decisions will have on the long-run profitability of the company and cash flows available to its owners. How did investors react to these decisions? Observe that Vulcan's stock price increased in 1991, though it dropped in 1990 (item 29 in Exhibit 10-11).

Vulcan's price-earnings ratio in 1991 was about double the 1989 level (item 31). This increase can be explained, in part, by a decrease in the level of interest rates from 1989 to 1991. Also, the PE ratio can be affected by a temporary decline in earnings. Stock prices reflect long-run expectations about a company's cash flows. A temporary decline in earnings is not likely to have a major effect on a stock's price as long as investors expect a fairly quick turnaround. If a company's stock price remains relatively stable while its earnings decrease, its PE ratio will be higher than normal. Therefore, **the PE ratio often is computed using average earnings over a period of several years or expected earnings for future periods.** In some cases, analysts' forecasts of future earnings are used to calculate the ratio. Regardless of these influences on the PE ratio, Vulcan's stock price remained relatively stable during a period of declining earnings. By June of 1992, the price had increased to over $42 per share; thus, investors appeared to be pleased with the company's performance.

Vulcan's financial statements reveal a strong company with excess cash flows. These cash flows were used to acquire long-term assets, to repurchase stock, and to repay debt. The company easily handled the increased leverage from financing decisions made in 1990, even when earnings for the following year decreased dramatically from prior levels. There is no indication of a company struggling to meet current obligations or of one overburdened by principal and interest payments. The company's debt to equity ratio (item 32) remained relatively stable during this period. Its stockholders' equity (item 26) increased and its liabilities (item 22) decreased from 1990 to 1991.

Financing decisions provide financial resources for the acquisition and replacement of assets. Chapter 11 examines investing activities as part of the transformation process.

SELF-STUDY PROBLEM 10-3

The following information is excerpted from the 1992 annual report of Wal-Mart Stores, Inc.:

(Amounts in millions except per share data)	**1992**	**1991**
Operating income	$ 2,819	$ 2,212
Interest expense	266	169
Pretax income	2,553	2,043
Income taxes	945	752
Net income	1,608	1,291
Earnings per share	1.40	1.14
Total current assets	8,575	6,415
Inventories and prepaid expenses	7,445	5,857
Plant assets, net of depreciation	5,079	3,724
Total assets	15,443	11,389
Current liabilities:		
Commercial paper	454	395
Accounts payable	3,454	2,651
Other accrued liabilities	1,056	914
Long-term debt due within one year	5	6
Capital lease obligations due within one year	35	24
Total current liabilities	5,004	3,990
Long-term debt	1,722	740
Long-term capital lease obligations	1,556	1,159
Deferred taxes	172	134
Total liabilities	8,454	6,023
Retained earnings	6,249	4,836
Total shareholders' equity	6,990	5,366
Net cash provided by operating activities	1,357	1,296
Net cash used in investing activities	(2,150)	(1,526)
Net cash provided by financing activities	811	230

Wal-Mart had no preferred stock.

Required

Answer each of the following questions:

a. What was the amount of each of the following ratios for Wal-Mart:
   1. current ratio for 1992 and 1991
   2. quick ratio for 1992 and 1991
   3. debt to equity ratio for 1992 and 1991
   4. return on assets for 1992
   5. return on equity for 1992

b. What were the primary financing decisions made by Wal-Mart's management in 1992?

c. Evaluate Wal-Mart's financing decisions based on its financial position, profitability, and cash flows.

REVIEW *Summary of Important Concepts*

1. Capital structure:
   A. A company's capital structure is determined by the way it finances its assets and operating activities.

   B. Higher proportions of debt increase the return to common stockholders when a company performs well but reduce returns when it performs poorly. Therefore, risk increases as the proportion of debt in capital structure increases.
2. Security prices:
   A. The price of a security is defined by the discounted future cash flows investors expect to receive. The price increases as the expected cash flows from owning the security increase or as the discount rate decreases.
   B. A security's discount rate (or required rate of return) is affected by interest rate and financial risk.
   C. Expected cash flows for bonds and preferred stock usually are fixed. Expected cash flows for common stock are variable and depend on a company's operating results.
3. Primary and secondary markets:
   A. Securities are sold in primary (original issue) and secondary (resale) markets.
   B. Prices in secondary markets change as expected cash flows, interest rate, and financial risk change.
4. Security prices and risk:
   A. Risk and return attributes of financial instruments differ.
   B. The price-earnings ratio is a commonly used measure of risk for common stocks.
5. Financial leverage and company earnings:
   A. The proportion of debt to equity in a company's capital structure is financial leverage. Financial leverage affects the risk and return of its debt and equity securities. It affects earnings per share and return on equity.
   B. Financial leverage increases earnings per share when sales are high but decreases earnings per share when sales are low.
6. Economic and company attributes and financial leverage:
   A. Analysis of financial decisions involves consideration of whether cash flows are sufficient to pay for current obligations and are likely to be sufficient in the future to pay for long-term obligations.
   B. The proportion of debt in a company's capital structure often is higher for companies whose earnings are relatively stable over time. If earnings remain stable though the economy worsens, the company is able to pay higher amounts of principal and interest.
7. Evaluation of financing activities:
   A. Loan agreements and debt covenants protect the rights of creditors. If a company violates these agreements, creditors may require immediate repayment of debt or force a company into bankruptcy. These agreements often are expressed in terms of accounting ratios. Therefore, an analysis of accounting information is useful for determining whether agreements and covenants have been violated.
   B. The analysis of accounting information may require special consideration of deferred compensation, deferred taxes, minority interest, operating lease commitments, and preferred stock.

Ratios discussed in this chapter:

$$\text{Price-Earnings or PE Ratio} = \frac{\text{Price per Share of Common Stock}}{\text{Earnings per Share of Common Stock}}$$

The PE ratio is a measure of the risk associated with a company's stock. The higher the PE ratio, the lower the risk.

$$\text{Return on Assets} = \frac{\text{Net Income} + \text{Interest Expense } (1 - \text{Tax Rate})}{\text{Average Total Assets}}$$

Return on assets is a measure of return on total (debt and equity) investment that ignores whether a company used debt or equity financing.

$$\text{Return on Equity} = \frac{\text{Net Income} - \text{Dividends on Preferred Stock}}{\text{Average Common Stockholders' Equity}}$$

Return on equity (sometimes called return on common equity) is a measure of return on investment by common stockholders.

$$\text{Debt to Equity Ratio} = \frac{\text{Total Debt}}{\text{Total Stockholders' Equity}}$$

The debt to equity ratio is a measure of capital structure and is sometimes called debt to net worth. Net worth is total assets minus total liabilities.

$$\text{Debt to Total Assets Ratio} = \frac{\text{Total Debt}}{\text{Total Assets}}$$

The debt to total assets ratio is another common measure of capital structure. It also is known as debt to total capitalization (liabilities plus stockholders' equity) and as simply the debt ratio. Analysts sometimes include only long-term debt in these ratios. They may exclude unfunded pension obligations and deferred taxes from the debt category and may include the present value of future operating lease payments. They may include preferred stock as part of debt rather than equity.

$$\text{Dividends per Share} = \frac{\text{Dividends on Common Stock}}{\text{Average Number of Shares of Common Stock Outstanding}}$$

Dividends per share is a commonly used measure of dividend payment decisions.

$$\text{Dividend Payout Ratio} = \frac{\text{Dividends per Share}}{\text{Earnings per Share}}$$

The dividend payout ratio is another common measure of the relative amount of dividends paid by a corporation during a fiscal period.

$$\text{Cash Flow to Current Maturities of Long-Term Debt Ratio} = \frac{\text{Net Cash Flow from Operating Activities}}{\text{Current Maturities of Long-Term Debt}}$$

This ratio measures the sufficiency of cash to meet current debt payments.

$$\text{Times Interest Earned Ratio} = \frac{\text{Income Before Interest and Taxes}}{\text{Interest Expense}}$$

This ratio measures the sufficiency of current income to cover interest requirements.

$$\text{Current Ratio} = \frac{\text{Total Current Assets}}{\text{Total Current Liabilities}}$$

The current ratio is a measure of the ability of a company to meet its current obligations.

$$\text{Quick (or Acid-Test) Ratio} = \frac{\text{Cash} + \text{Marketable Securities} + \text{Receivables}}{\text{Total Current Liabilities}}$$

The quick ratio measures the sufficiency of current cash-generating assets to meet current obligations. This ratio is a more conservative form of the current ratio.

DEFINE *Terms and Concepts Defined in this Chapter*

business risk
capital structure
debt covenants
dividend payout ratio
financial leverage
financial risk
interest rate risk
loan agreements
price-earnings (PE) ratio
primary market
return on assets
return on equity
secondary market

SOLUTIONS

SELF-STUDY PROBLEM 10-1

a. The price of El Roncho's bonds would be computed as follows:

Present value of interest payments of $40 per period for 14 remaining periods, discounted at 5%:

PV = $40 × 9.89864 = $395.95

Present value of a single payment of $1,000 at the end of 14 periods, discounted at 5%.

PV = $1,000 × .50507 = $505.07

The price of each bond would be $901.02 ($395.95 + $505.07).

b. El Roncho's common stock had been selling for $8 per share and its earnings per share was $1.40 ($14 million / 10 million shares). Therefore, its PE ratio was 5.7 ($8 / $1.40). Its earnings per share would drop to $1 ($10 million / 10 million shares), based on the projection. If the PE ratio remained constant, the price would drop to about $5.70 per share; however, it is unlikely the PE ratio would remain constant. Much would depend on investors' expectations about the long-run profitability of the company. If they viewed the decline in profits as a permanent decrease, the price of the company's stock should decrease below $5.70.

SELF-STUDY PROBLEM 10-2

	Current	Option A	Option B	Option C
Operating income	$24,000,000	$33,000,000	$33,000,000	$33,000,000
Interest expense	0	0	0	2,400,000
Pretax income	24,000,000	33,000,000	33,000,000	30,600,000
Income tax (33⅓%)	8,000,000	11,000,000	11,000,000	10,200,000
Net income	16,000,000	22,000,000	22,000,000	20,400,000
Preferred dividends	0	0	3,000,000	0
Net income available for common stockholders	16,000,000	22,000,000	19,000,000	20,400,000
Common shares	10,000,000	13,000,000	10,000,000	10,000,000
Earnings per share	$1.60	$1.69	$1.90	$2.04

The new project would increase income before interest and taxes by $9 million. If Option A is adopted, 3 million new shares of common stock must be issued at the current price to raise $30 million, and earnings per share would be $1.69. If Option B is adopted, dividends will be paid on preferred stock. After this payment, earnings per share would be $1.90 per share. If Option C is adopted, interest will be paid on the bonds. Earnings per share would be $2.04. Therefore, Option C provides the highest earnings per share from the assumptions provided.

Management should consider other factors in making a decision. Potential dilution of ownership will result if additional common stock is issued. If the company does not do as well as expected, preferred stock or bonds may have a negative effect on income available for common shareholders. Bonds increase the risk of bankruptcy and loss of control by stockholders.

SELF-STUDY PROBLEM 10-3

a.	**1992**	**1991**
1. current ratio = current assets ÷ current liabilities	8,575/5,004 = 1.71	6,415/3,990 = 1.61
2. quick ratio = current assets − inventories and prepaid expenses ÷ current liabilities	8,575 − 7,445 = 1,130 1,130/5,004 = .23	6,415 − 5,857 = 558 558/3,990 = .14
3. debt to equity ratio	8,454/6,990 = 1.21	6,023/5,366 = 1.12
4. return on assets: average assets tax rate = income tax ÷ pretax income net income + interest (1 − tax rate) return on assets	 (11,389 + 15,443)/2 = 13,416 945/2,553 = .37 1,608 + [266(1 − .37)] = 1,776 1,776/13,416 = .13	
5. return on equity: average equity net income − preferred dividends return on equity	 (5,366 + 6,990)/2 = 6,178 1,608 1,608/6,178 = .26	

b. The primary financing decision was to increase liabilities. Accounts payable, long-term debt, and long-term capital lease obligations increased. An increase in accounts payable can indicate increased operating activity or difficulty in meeting current obligations. Long-term debt and lease obligations have the greatest impact in future years as they become current liabilities.

c. Wal-Mart's financing decisions appear to be justified by its financial position, profitability, and cash flows. The amount of current liabilities is consistent with the amount of current assets. Accounts payable and short-term debt appear to be used primarily to finance inventories, which are a large portion of the assets of a retail company. Long-term debt is small relative to plant and long-term assets. These assets are financed primarily by operating activities. Observe that long-term liabilities are small relative to stockholders' equity, especially retained earnings, and that a significant portion of the cash flow used for investing activities comes from cash flow from operating activities. The company's profits and cash flows both appear to be quite strong, net income and net cash from operating activities increasing in 1992 relative to 1991. The company's PE ratio increased from 29.4 ($33.50/$1.14) to 46.2 ($64.625/$1.40), indicating a favorable assessment of risk by investors. Wal-Mart appears to be a strong company with no apparent financial problems.

EXERCISES

10-1. Write a short definition for each of the terms listed in the *Terms and Concepts Defined in this Chapter* section.

10-2. What is capital structure? Why do the capital structures of companies vary?

10-3. On June 1, 1990, the share price of General Mills stock was approximately $35. One year later, the price was approximately $60. What factors could account for the increase in price? How can accounting information be useful in evaluating a company's stock price?

10-4. A security is expected to pay a return of $100 per year. The discount rate for the security is 6%. What will the price of the security be if it has a life of 5 years? 10 years? 20 years? The life is infinite?

10-5. A security has a life of 10 years with a discount rate of 6%. What will the price of the security be if it is expected to pay a return of $10 per year? $100 per year? What will be the price of the security if it has an infinite life and is expected to pay a return of $10 per year? $100 per year?

10-6. Alicia Smith is considering an investment in securities. She has heard that stocks have provided higher returns than bonds or certificates of deposit (CDs) in recent years. Why should Alicia expect stocks to perform better on average than other investments? What types of risks should Alicia consider when evaluating alternate investments? How are investments in stocks, bonds, and CDs affected by these types of risk?

10-7. On August 1, 1990, the Feinman Company issued $4 million of 8%, 20-year bonds. The bonds were rated Aa and sold to yield a return of 8%. Sue Lin Tang purchased $20,000 of the bonds when they were issued. At the end of 1995, Tang decided to sell the bonds. The bond rating had been lowered to A early in 1995. What price did Sue pay for the bonds when she purchased them? Would the price of the bonds in the secondary market at the end of 1995 be lower or higher than the price Sue paid for the bonds? What factors, other than those associated with the bond rating, would affect the price? What factors might account for the lower rating?

10-8. Deidrich Knickerbocker is considering an investment in common stocks. He has read summary information about stocks in the financial press and noted that analysts often discuss PE ratios when evaluating stocks. Deidrich does not understand the meaning of PE ratios and asks you for an explanation. What assistance can you provide?

10-9. The Hester Prinn Company had total assets of $24 million and stockholders' equity of $18 million at the end of 1994. At the end of 1993, total assets were $22 million and stockholders' equity was $16.3 million. Stockholders' equity in 1994 consisted of 1 million shares of common stock with a book value of $15 million and 30,000 shares of preferred stock with a book value of $3 million. No changes were made in the amount of preferred stock during 1994. During 1994, the company reported net income of $4 million, while interest expense was $500,000 for the year. The company's income tax rate was 30%. The company paid preferred dividends of $10 per share and common dividends of $2 per share in 1994. Compute Hester Prinn's return on assets and return on equity for 1994. What would these amounts have been if the company had issued $5 million of bonds at the beginning of 1994 and had used the proceeds to repurchase 250,000 shares of its common stock at $20 per share, reducing common stockholders' equity at the end of 1994 to $11,450,000? Assume interest expense increased to $800,000, net income decreased to $3.79 million, and dividends per share remained at $2 per share for common stock.

10-10. Why are return on assets and return on equity commonly used to evaluate a company's performance in addition to its net income? Why are return on assets and return on equity both used in evaluating performance? Assume a company issued long-term bonds during a fiscal period, increasing its interest expense. The bonds were used to finance new plant assets. What effect would the financing and asset acquisition have on the company's financial leverage? What effect should the additional financing have on the company's risk and return?

10-11. The Words Worth Company expects net income of $5 million from the pretax earnings of $7 million for 1995. The company's average total assets during 1995 were $25 million. It had no long-term debt or preferred stock. It had 1 million shares of common stock outstanding. Words Worth is considering issuing $10 million of debentures to repurchase 300,000 shares of its common stock. If the debt had been outstanding in 1995, the company would have paid $900,000 in interest expense. Calculate the company's earnings per share, return on assets, and return on equity for 1995 as reported and as it would have been if the debt had been issued. Assume average stockholders' equity of $15 million for computing pro-forma amounts.

10-12. The Kip Ling Company had stockholders' equity of $100 million in 1994 and long-term debt of $10 million. It had 10 million shares of common stock outstanding. The company's interest expense was $800,000, and its income tax rate was 30%. It believes its annual income before interest and taxes will vary between $5 million and $15 million for the foreseeable future, the average expected to be about $8 million. The company is considering issuing $25 million of additional debt to replace 3 million shares of its common stock. The additional debt would cost the company $3 million a year in interest. If you were asked by the company for advice on whether to issue the debt, what advice would you provide?

10-13. What is meant by optimal capital structure? What effect does capital structure have on a company's interest costs? What effect does it have on its PE ratio? Why is optimal capital structure difficult to determine in practice?

10-14. The Carlyle Company has assets of $200 million and long-term debt of $110 million. The debt consists primarily of callable debentures with interest rates of 10 to 12%. Over the last couple of years, the general level of interest rates has decreased by about 2.5%. Carlyle could issue its debt at current rates of approximately 8%. Also, over the two-year period, Carlyle's stock price has increased approximately 30%. What effect might these changes have on Carlyle's financing decisions?

10-15. Selected information is provided below for Georgia-Pacific Corporation from its 1991 annual report:

(in millions)	**1991**	**1990**	**1989**	**1988**	**1987**
Interest expense	$ 656	$ 606	$ 260	$ 197	$ 124
Income tax expense	266	354	426	311	340
Net income (loss)	(142)	365	661	467	458
Cash from operations	630	1,223	1,358	865	781
Total assets	10,622	12,060	7,056	7,115	5,870
Shareholders' equity	2,736	2,975	2,717	2,635	2,680

Evaluate the effect of the company's capital structure on its profitability, cash flow from operations, and risk for the five years presented.

10-16. Information for two companies is provided below from their 1991 annual reports:

(in millions)	**1992**	**1991**	**1990**	**1989**	**1988**
General Mills					
Net income	$ 495.6	$ 472.7	$ 381.4	$414.3	$283.1
Dividends	245	211	181	154	139
Wal-Mart					
Net income	$1,608.5	$1,291.0	$1,076.9	$837.2	$627.6
Dividends	195	159	125	90	69

What do the dividend policies indicate about future prospects for the two companies?

10-17. Selected information from the 1991 annual report of Allied Products Corporation is provided below:

Net loss	$ (34,043,000)
Interest expense	16,761,000
Income tax expense	0
Net cash from operating activities	34,521,000
Cash flow from financing activities:	
Proceeds from issuance of long-term debt	13,057,000
Payments of long-term debt	(80,323,000)
Preferred dividends paid	0
Current assets:	
Cash and marketable securities	7,558,000
Notes and accounts receivable, net	127,972,000
Inventories	93,245,000
Prepaid expenses	4,106,000
Total current assets	232,881,000
Current liabilities:	
Current portion of long-term debt	130,291,000
Accounts payable	35,965,000
Other accrued liabilities	39,908,000
Total current liabilities	206,164,000

If you were a creditor, what concerns would you have about Allied Products' ability to pay its current obligations in 1992?

10-18. The following information was reported in the 1991 annual report of Westinghouse Electric Corporation:

> In December 1991, the Corporation entered into a three-year $6 billion revolving credit facility agreement with a syndicate of 49 domestic and international banks. . . . The facility is available for use by the Corporation . . . subject to the maintenance of certain ratios and compliance with other covenants. Among other things, these covenants place restrictions on the incurrence of liens, the amount of debt on a consolidated basis and at the subsidiary level, and the amount of contingent liabilities. The covenants also require the maintenance of a leverage ratio, a minimum coverage ratio, and minimum consolidated net worth among other things.

The revolving credit agreement permitted Westinghouse to borrow up to $6 billion over a three-year period, as needed. What are debt or loan covenants? Why are they required in conjunction with many loan agreements? What restraints are placed on Westinghouse by the loan agreements discussed above? What are contingent liabilities, leverage ratios, coverage ratios, and net worth? What incentives do these covenants provide for Westinghouse's management that might affect the company's reported accounting information?

10-19. Westinghouse Electric Corporation reported the following information in its 1991 annual report:

(in millions)	**1991**	**1990**
Long-Term Liabilities:*		
Long-term debt	$ 1,264	$ 931
Other noncurrent liabilities:		
Deferred income taxes	625	182

(in millions)	1991	1990
Long-Term Liabilities:*		
Minimum pension liability	0	1,018
Other	313	387
Total long-term liabilities	2,202	2,518
Contingent liabilities and commitments	—	—
Minority interest	173	171
Stockholders' Equity:		
Common stock	393	370
Capital in excess of par value	1,039	659
Common stock held in treasury	(1,264)	(1,887)
Other	(4)	(346)
Retained earnings	3,582	5,101
Total stockholders' equity	$ 3,746	$ 3,897

****These liability amounts do not include the financing services segment of the corporation.***

Minor modifications have been made to the original format.

Contingent liabilities included litigation, for which no costs were anticipated; purchase agreements and loan guarantees, considered by management to be immaterial; and lease commitments. Minimum rental payments were listed as 1992—$172, 1993—$149, 1994—$117, 1995—$88, 1996—$73, subsequent years—$784, total—$1,383. Compute the long-term debt to equity ratio for Westinghouse for 1990 and 1991. Explain which amounts you would include in your computation and why.

10-20. The Ali Baba Company's capital structure includes $8 million of long-term debt that pays 10% annual interest. It also includes $2 million of preferred stock and $7 million of common stock and retained earnings. The preferred stock is cumulative and pays a 6% annual dividend. What effect does the preferred stock have on the risk and return of the long-term debt and common stock? Should the preferred stock be considered debt or equity?

PROBLEMS

PROBLEM 10-1 Identifying Capital Structure Choices

You are a financial manager with a medium-sized company, Kangaroo Express. The company is owned and managed by the Marsupial family. Currently, 60% of the company's total liabilities and stockholders' equity is composed of long-term notes. Current liabilities account for 20%, and the remainder consists of stock held by members of the Marsupial family. You have been asked to meet with the company's top management to discuss the company's capital structure and plans to raise capital for expansion.

Required Write a short report describing alternative types of financing Kangaroo Express might consider. Explain the risk and return implications of each alternative for the Marsupials.

PROBLEM 10-2 Computing Bond and Stock Prices

A security's price is a function of expected cash flows from owning the security and the rate used to discount the expected cash flows. Listed below are attributes of several securities:

a. A bond with a maturity value of $1,000, a 10-year maturity, paying 8% interest, with semiannual payments.
b. A share of preferred stock with a par value of $100, paying an 8% annual dividend.
c. A share of common stock with a par value of $10, expected cash flows for the current year are $2 per share and are expected to grow at a rate of 5% per year.

Required Calculate the price of each security, assuming a discount rate of (1) 6%, (2) 8%, and (3) 10%. What conclusions can you draw about the effects of discount rates on the prices of bonds and stocks?

PROBLEM 10-3 Evaluating the Effect of Earnings on Stock Prices

Information is provided below for Chrysler Corporation:

Year	1982	1983	1984	1985	1986	1987	1988	1989	1990	1991
Earnings per Share	.82	2.57	8.37	6.16	6.25	5.90	4.66	1.55	.30	−3.28
Stock Price	4.95	11.00	12.15	17.10	24.85	33.80	24.15	23.85	14.75	12.85

Required Evaluate the relationship between Chrysler's stock price and earnings per share. Does earnings per share appear to be a good signal of the expected cash flows to stockholders? Compute Chrysler's PE ratio for the periods shown. Why does the PE ratio vary over time? What factors other than expected cash flows affect stock price? How do these factors affect the PE ratio?

PROBLEM 10-4 Analyzing Credit Paying Ability

Digital Equipment Corporation disclosed the following information in its 1991 annual report:

(in millions)	1991	1990
Net income (loss)	$ (617.4)	$ 74.4
Net cash flow from operating activities	1,040.9	1,434.1
Net cash flow from financing activities	(99.2)	22.8
Interest payments	42.6	33.4
Bank loans and current portion of long-term debt	23.3	12.5
Total current liabilities	4,091.0	3,289.8
Total liabilities	4,250.9	3,472.9
Total current assets	7,654.0	7,621.6
Total assets	11,874.7	11,654.8

You are a financial analyst with a large investment company. Several clients are creditors and stockholders of Digital. One client in particular, Magnolia Smythe, has expressed concern about the company's recent net loss. She is concerned about the company's ability to meet its principal and interest payments and the effect of this ability on the company's stockholders.

Required Write a memo to Magnolia explaining whether you think she should be concerned about the company's ability to meet its obligations and whether stockholders should be concerned about the company's performance. Use relevant information from the data presented to support your explanations.

PROBLEM 10-5 Evaluating Stock Repurchase Transactions

Corporations frequently repurchase shares of their own stock. For example, in September 1987, Hospital Corporation of America repurchased approximately 12 million shares of its own stock at $47 per share. By the end of the year, the stock price had dropped to approximately $31 per share.

Required Answer each of the following questions:

a. Why do companies repurchase shares of their own stock?
b. How did the purchase of the stock and its subsequent decline in price affect Hospital Corporation of America's financial statements?
c. Do financial statements adequately report the effects of a decline in price? Explain your answer.

PROBLEM 10-6 Comparing Capital Structures

Financial statement information is provided below from the 1991 annual reports of two companies. Intel Corporation is a manufacturer of computer microprocessors. Pacific Gas and Electric is a stockholder owned utility.

(in millions)		(in millions)	
Intel Corporation	**1991**	**Pacific Gas & Electric**	**1991**
Current assets	$3,604	Plant assets	$16,959
Plant assets, net	2,163	Other noncurrent assets	2,316
Other noncurrent assets	525	Current assets	2,913
Total assets	6,292	Total assets	22,901
Current liabilities	1,228	Common stock equity	7,681
Long-term debt	363	Preferred stock	987
Other noncurrent liabilities	284	Long-term debt	8,249
Preferred stock	0	Other noncurrent liabilities	2,888
Stockholders' equity	4,418	Current liabilities	3,096

Required Compare the capital structures of the two companies. Explain why differences are likely to exist between the companies, considering their risk and return attributes.

PROBLEM 10-7 Assessing Default Risk

Information is provided below for Sears, Roebuck and Co. from its 1991 annual report:

(in millions)	1991	1990	1989	1988	1987
Net income	$ 1,279	$ 902	$ 1,509	$ 1,454	$ 1,633
Interest expense	3,252	3,370	3,224	2,937	2,721
Total assets	106,435	96,253	86,972	77,952	75,014
Short-term debt	9,788	15,314	12,714	8,978	7,055
Long-term debt	19,170	12,636	10,036	9,736	9,562
Shareholders' equity	14,188	12,824	13,622	14,055	13,541

The company's income tax rate was approximately 20%. In September 1990, Moody's Investors Service lowered its rating on Sears' debt.

Required Why do you think Moody's lowered its rating? Prepare an analysis of the accounting information provided above to justify your answer. Specific references should be made to ratios that substantiate your conclusions.

PROBLEM 10-8 Analyzing Capital Structure Decisions

Late in 1988, RJR Nabisco was acquired by a group of investors in a leveraged buyout (LBO). Accounting information from the company's 1990 and 1987 annual reports, before and after the buyout, is presented below.

(in millions)	1990	1989	1987
Net income (loss)	$ (429)	$ (1,149)	$1,209
Operating income	2,818	2,053	2,304
Interest expense	(3,000)	(2,937)	(489)
Interest paid	(1,424)	(1,909)	not reported
Free cash flow*	2,702	647	not reported
Current maturities of long-term debt	1,425	2,632	162
Total current liabilities	5,205	6,568	4,123
Long-term debt	16,955	21,948	3,884
Other noncurrent liabilities	2,653	2,873	1,797
Deferred income taxes	3,813	3,786	846
Redeemable preferred stock	1,795	0	173
Common stockholders' equity	2,494	1,237	6,038

Free cash flow is cash flow from operating activities less capital expenditures.

Required Answer each of the following questions:

a. From the information before and after the LBO, how would you define an LBO?
b. What explanation can you provide for why interest expense in 1990 and 1989 was considerably higher than interest paid?
c. At the time of the LBO, RJR Nabisco's debt was rated below investment grade (to junk bond status). In late 1991, the debt was upgraded to investment grade by both Moody's and Standard and Poor's. What reasons can you provide for why these events might have occurred?
d. If you were analyzing the company's performance after the LBO, what information would you consider to be most important? Why?

PROBLEM 10-9 Ethical Issues in Financing Decisions

Until late 1991, when he died, Robert Maxwell was chief executive officer and a major stockholder of Maxwell Communications Corporation. The company's performance declined in 1990 and 1991. To prevent a major decrease in the value of the company's stock, Maxwell secretly diverted £200 million from other companies he owned to purchase shares of Maxwell Communications' stock. The purchased shares were used by other companies owned by Maxwell as collateral for bank loans. Cash from the loans was used to finance interest payments and losses on operations. After Maxwell's death and discovery of the stock transactions, the stock lost most of its value.

Required Were these transactions unethical? Why?

PROBLEM 10-10 Analysis of Capital Structure

Information is provided below for Citicorp from its 1991 annual report:

In millions	**1991**	**1990**
Interest revenue	$ 24,354	$ 30,983
Interest expense	17,089	23,798
Net interest revenue	7,265	7,185
Provision for credit losses	3,890	2,662
Net interest revenue after provision for credit losses	3,375	4,523
Other revenue	7,485	7,402
Other expense	11,097	11,099
Income before taxes	(237)	826
Net cash provided by (used in) operating activities	(3,929)	4,240
Net cash provided by (used in) investing activities	(1,755)	9,556
Net cash provided by (used in) financing activities	4,306	(12,610)
Total loans (receivable), net of allowance for credit losses	147,636	151,857
Total assets (including loans)	216,922	216,986
Total deposits	146,475	142,452
Total liabilities (including deposits)	207,433	207,256
Preferred stock	2,140	1,540
Total stockholders' equity (including preferred stock)	9,489	9,730

Citicorp is one of the nation's largest banks. U.S. banking regulations require banks to maintain an equity to total assets ratio of 4%. In March 1992, Citicorp sold $150 million of additional preferred stock with a dividend rate of 9.05%. The bank's common stock was not paying a dividend. The sale prompted Standard and Poor's to lower Citicorp's credit rating to BBB−, the lowest investment grade.

Required Answer each of the following questions:

a. What are Citicorp's primary revenues, expenses, assets, and liabilities?
b. What was Citicorp's equity to asset ratio at the end of 1991?
c. What effect did issuing additional preferred stock have on the bank's equity to asset ratio?
d. What other activities could the bank use to increase this ratio? What are the advantages and disadvantages of using preferred stock?
e. Why did Standard and Poor's lower Citicorp's credit rating as a result of its issuing additional preferred stock?

PROBLEM 10-11 Evaluating Financial Leverage

Information is provided below for Baker Hughes Incorporated:

In thousands, except per share amounts	1991
Interest expense	$ 83,561
Income taxes	38,893
Net income	173,458
Earnings per share	1.26
Total assets	2,905,602
Short-term borrowing	25,657
Current portion of long-term debt	75,962
Total current liabilities	705,272
Long-term debt	545,242
Deferred income taxes	61,039
Other long-term liabilities	44,980
Minority interest	3,708
Total stockholders' equity	1,545,361

Assume that during 1991, Baker Hughes had the opportunity to acquire additional assets at a price of $500 million. At the time, the company's stock was selling at $30 per share. The additional assets were expected to increase the company's income before interest and taxes by $80 million annually for the foreseeable future.

Required Prepare a pro-forma income statement, beginning with operating income, to explain whether Baker Hughes should finance the acquisition with debt or stock. Assume stock could be sold at $30 per share and debt could be issued at the average interest associated with the company's existing short-term and long-term debt.

PROBLEM 10-12 Multiple-Choice Overview of the Chapter

1. The way a company finances its assets and operating activities is its:
   a. capital structure
   b. financial leverage
   c. return on equity
   d. present value
2. The price of a security can be calculated as:
   a. expected cash flows to investors times its discount rate
   b. expected cash flows divided by its discount rate
   c. its discount rate divided by expected cash flows
   d. the sum of expected future cash flows
3. The price of a share of common stock with expected annual cash flow of $4 per share, a required rate of return of 10%, and an expected growth rate of 4% would be:
   a. $40
   b. $41.60
   c. $100
   d. $66.67
4. Junk bonds are another name for:
   a. debentures
   b. speculative grade bonds
   c. investment grade bonds
   d. bonds in default

5. The market in which investors sell securities to each other is the:
   a. primary market
   b. commodities market
   c. secondary market
   d. over-the-counter market
6. Audabon Company had net income of $3 million in 1993. Its interest expense was $1 million for the year. It had no preferred stock. Its average total assets were $15 million, and its average total equity was $5 million. Audabon's return on assets was:
   a. much higher than its return on equity
   b. slightly higher than its return on equity
   c. about the same as its return on equity
   d. much lower than its return on equity
7. Baker Company expects net income of $10 million in 1994 after taxes of $5 million. The company has 1 million shares of common stock outstanding. To raise $20 million of additional capital, Baker can either issue debt with an interest rate of 10% or issue 600,000 shares of additional common stock. Investment of the additional capital is expected to increase income, before the effect of additional interest and taxes, by $8 million. To maximize earnings per share, Baker should:
   a. increase its financial leverage
   b. reduce its financial leverage
   c. not alter its financial leverage
   d. issue only common stock
8. High amounts of financial leverage are most common for companies with:
   a. small proportions of plant assets and stable earnings
   b. large proportions of plant assets and stable earnings
   c. small proportions of plant assets and unstable earnings
   d. large proportions of plant assets and unstable earnings
9. Low dividend payout ratios are common for companies
   a. with low growth potential
   b. in stable industries
   c. with high growth potential
   d. with stable earnings
10. If a company is having difficulty paying interest and principal on its debt, creditors should be particularly concerned with:
    a. its return on assets
    b. its return on equity
    c. its debt to equity ratio
    d. its cash flows

CASES

CASE 10-1 Evaluating Capital Structure

Selected information from Motorola, Incorporated's 1991 annual report is provided below:

(in millions except per share amounts)	1991	1990
Earnings before interest and taxes	$742	$799
Interest expense	129	133

(in millions except per share amounts)	1991	1990
Earnings before income taxes	613	666
Income taxes	159	167
Net earnings	454	499
Net earnings per share	$3.44	$3.80
Average shares outstanding	131.9	131.3
Total current assets	4,487	4,452
Total assets	9,375	8,742
Total current liabilities	3,063	3,048
Long-term debt	954	792
Deferred income taxes	196	203
Other liabilities	532	442
Total stockholders' equity	4,630	4,257
Net cash provided by operations	1,358	1,307
Net cash used for investing activities	(1,232)	(1,443)
Net cash provided by financing activities:		
Increase (decrease) in notes payable and current portion of long-term debt	(143)	208
Increase in long-term debt	135	7
Issuance of common stock	19	55
Payment of dividends	(100)	(100)
Net cash provided by (used for) financing activities	(89)	170

Required Write a short report describing Motorola's capital structure. Consider changes in Motorola's capital structure in 1991, and identify the causes of these changes. Identify Motorola's primary source of financing in 1991 and evaluate the company's financial condition at the end of that same year.

CASE 10-2 Evaluating Capital Structure Decisions

The Water Bed Company's capital structure at the end of 1994 included $10 million of 9% bonds, $2 million of 7%, $100 par preferred stock, and $20 million of common stock. The company's 10 million shares of common stock are selling at $5 per share. During 1994, the company earned $4 million of net income after tax expense of $1.5 million. It paid preferred dividends of $140,000 and dividends to common stockholders of $1 million.

Required For each of the following independent events, explain the effect the event would have on the company's earnings per share, return on assets, and return on equity. What effect would you expect the event to have on the price of each type of security?

a. The company issued $15 million of new bonds to finance the purchase of additional plant assets. The bonds were issued at a market rate of 12%. The new assets are expected to produce additional pretax profits of $2 million.
b. The company issued $10 million of new common stock to repurchase its bonds. The stock sold at $5 per share.
c. The company issued $4 million of new 7% preferred stock to repurchase shares of the company's common stock. The preferred stock sold at its par value of $100. The common stock was repurchased at $6 per share.
d. Because of new competition, the company's profits are expected to decline to $3 million for the foreseeable future.

CASE 10-3 Evaluating Financing Decisions

Appendix B of this book contains a copy of the 1992 annual report of General Mills, Inc.

Required Review the annual report and write a short report in which you:

a. Evaluate the company's financial condition in 1992 and changes in the condition from 1991 to 1992.
b. Identify the company's primary financing activities in 1992.
c. Analyze the effects of the 1992 financing activities on the risk and return of the company's long-term debt and common stock.

PROJECTS

PROJECT 10-1 Comparing Capital Structures

Obtain the most recent annual report available for each of three corporations from your library. Look for companies in different industries. Identify the primary components of the capital structure of each company. In particular, determine the relative proportion of short-term debt, other current liabilities, long-term debt, other long-term liabilities, preferred stock, and common stock in each company's capital structure. Provide a graph or diagram to illustrate the comparisons and write a brief analysis of differences in the capital structures. What explanations can you provide for why the capital structures are different or are similar?

PROJECT 10-2 Comparing Stock Price Behavior

Obtain stock price information for five companies for the last 10 years. Use closing prices at the end of the companies' fiscal years. Prepare a chart illustrating the relationship between each company's stock price and its earnings per share over the 10-year period. What conclusions can you draw about the relationship between earnings and stock price for each company?

PROJECT 10-3 Comparing Bond Ratings

Use Standard and Poor's or Moody's bond surveys to identify corporate bond ratings for five companies, making sure all the companies you identify do not have the same ratings. Examine the companies' accounting information to evaluate their debt and liquidity ratios. Write a short report explaining why you believe the companies have different ratings.

PROJECT 10-4 Evaluating Capital Structure

Identify a recent article in the *The Wall Street Journal* or in a business periodical describing a company that has made a significant change in its capital structure—by issuing stock or debt, for example. Make a copy of the article. Write a memo to your instructor identifying the event and the reasons cited in the article for the change in capital structure. Attach the copy of the article to the memo.

PROJECT 10-5 Evaluating Credit Risk

Identify a recent article in the *The Wall Street Journal* or in a business periodical describing a company that has had its bond rating changed. Make a copy of the article. Write a memo to your instructor identifying the event and the reasons cited in the article for the change in rating. Attach the copy of the article to the memo.

CHAPTER 11

INVESTING ACTIVITIES

CHAPTER
Overview

The primary purpose of financing activities is to obtain financial resources for organizations, as we have seen in Chapters 8, 9, and 10. Investing activities determine how financial resources will be used. In particular, they involve choices about which assets an organization will obtain for use in its operating activities. Organizations invest their financial resources in assets, such as merchandise, materials, buildings, and equipment, that are required for use in their operating activities. Some of these assets, such as merchandise and materials, are associated directly with operating activities and will be considered when those activities are discussed in Chapters 13 and 14. Investing activities considered in this chapter include investments in such assets as cash, securities, other companies, buildings, equipment, and patents. Accounting for these investments includes accounting for their acquisition and disposal, accounting for expenses associated with use of the assets, identification of amounts reported for these assets on the balance sheet, and disclosure of information about the investing activities in notes to the financial statements. Protection and control of assets also is an important issue affecting accounting information. The measurement and reporting of investing activities affect the income statement and statement of cash flows in addition to the balance sheet, as illustrated below:

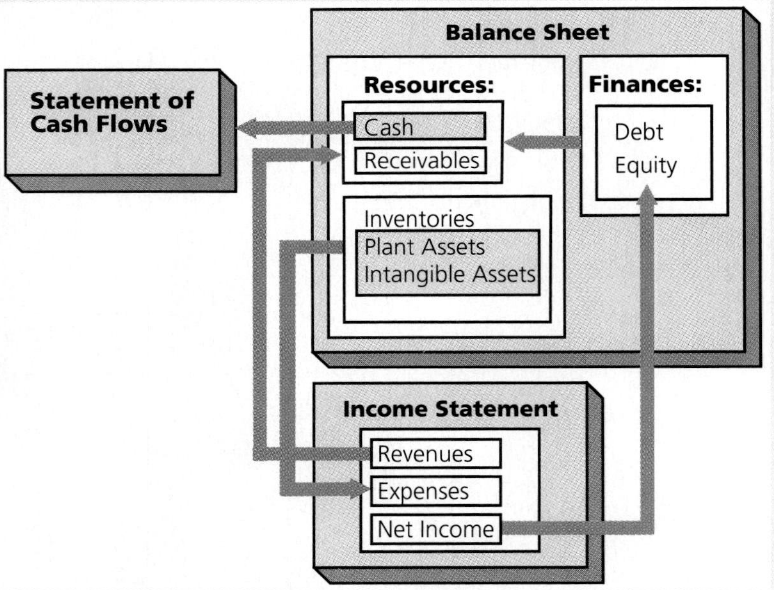

Major topics covered in this chapter include:

- Investments in cash and securities.
- Investments in plant and other long-term assets.
- Cash flow and accrual measures of investing activities.
- Control of assets.

CHAPTER
Objectives

Once you have completed this chapter, you should be able to:

1. Identify the purpose of investing activities.
2. Identify types of securities and explain why companies invest in them.
3. Explain accounting rules for investments in equity securities.

4. Identify methods used to account for acquisitions and mergers.
5. Explain accounting rules for investments in debt securities.
6. Distinguish between straight-line and accelerated depreciation methods.
7. Determine the accounting effects of disposing of plant assets.
8. Explain accounting rules for investments in natural resources.
9. Distinguish between operating and capital leases.
10. Explain accounting issues associated with construction and capital improvements.
11. Explain accounting issues associated with intangible assets, deferred charges, and other assets.
12. Compare cash and accrual measurement of investing activities.
13. Identify asset control procedures.

TYPES OF ASSETS

Objective 1
Identify the purpose of investing activities.

Investing activities provide the resources an organization needs to operate. These resources are reported primarily as assets. Not all resources are included among assets, however. A company's balance sheet reports those assets for which identifiable costs can be reasonably determined. Exhibit 11-1 contains the asset section of the balance sheet reported by International Paper Co. in its 1991 annual report. This exhibit will be used as a basis for discussing the types of assets reported by most corporations.

Exhibit 11-1

INTERNATIONAL PAPER COMPANY
EXCERPT FROM CONSOLIDATED BALANCE SHEET

In millions at December 31	1991	1990
Assets		
Current Assets		
Cash and temporary investments, at cost, which approximates market	$ 238	$ 256
Accounts and notes receivable, less allowances of $74 in 1991 and $57 in 1990	1,841	1,798
Inventories	1,780	1,638
Other current assets	272	247
Total Current Assets	4,131	3,939
Plants, Properties and Equipment, Net	7,848	7,287
Timberlands	743	751
Investments	383	103
Goodwill	816	687
Deferred Charges and Other Assets	1,020	902
Total Assets	$14,941	$13,669

Data source: 1991 Annual Report

Minor modifications have been made to the format of this statement for presentation purposes.

Most companies divide their assets into two primary categories: current and long-term. **Current assets are those management expects to convert to cash or consume during the coming fiscal year.**[1] Some current assets are associated closely with a company's operating activities, which involve the use of those assets in producing and selling goods and services. Those assets (accounts receivable, inventories, and prepaid expenses) are examined in Chapter 13. Other current assets result from investment decisions concerning the amount of cash and short-term securities an organization needs to support its operating activities. Long-term assets include investments in securities, plant assets, and intangible assets.

INVESTMENTS IN CASH AND SECURITIES

Cash is central to an organization's financing, investing, and operating activities. These activities affect the amount of cash available to a company. Few measurement or reporting problems arise with cash. An organization increases its cash account when cash is received. It decreases the account when cash is paid. The primary accounting issues related to cash are cash management and control. Control is considered later in this chapter. Chapter 12 examines cash management.

The amount of cash reported on a company's balance sheet normally includes cash and cash equivalents. **Cash and equivalents** encompass bank accounts, currency, checks, certain short-term investments, and other instruments that represent ready sources of money. The definition of cash equivalents varies across organizations. A note to International Paper's financial statements provides a typical definition: "Temporary investments with a maturity of three months or less are treated as cash equivalents and are stated at cost." These investments are easily and quickly converted into cash. Therefore, they can be used to meet a company's cash needs. A company's statement of cash flows explains changes in cash and equivalents during a fiscal year.

Securities that are part of an organization's assets include financial instruments such as stocks, bonds, certificates of deposit, and notes in which it has invested. These securities do not include a company's issuance or repurchase of its own financial instruments, such as bonds or stock. A company's own bonds and stocks are reported as part of the company's debt and equity, the repurchase of which is shown as a reduction of the liability or equity sections. A company's investments in another company's debt or equity securities are reported as assets, however. (Debt securities include bonds, notes, and other debt instruments. Equity securities include preferred and common stock.) For certain accounting rules (GAAP), only common stock is included in the equity category. This chapter examines some of these rules.

Companies report investments in securities in a variety of ways. Typically, these investments are classified as current or noncurrent. Short-term **marketable securities** are reported as current assets since the company expects to convert them to cash during the coming fiscal year.[2] Other investments in securities are classified as long-term or noncurrent. It is the intent of management

[1] In rare cases, a company's cycle of conversion, or operating cycle, is longer than a year. An operating cycle is the period from the time cash is paid for inventory until the inventory is sold and converted back to cash. In such cases, the longer operating cycle, rather than the fiscal year, is used as a basis for determining current assets.

[2] Securities are marketable if they are readily exchangeable for cash. Examples include stocks, bonds, and commercial paper of major corporations, and government securities.

to convert securities to cash, not the type of securities, that determines their classification as current or long-term. Thus, an investment by General Motors in 10,000 shares of IBM stock may be either a current or noncurrent investment, depending on whether GM management expects to sell the stock in the coming year. Investments in securities that are not readily marketable should not be classified as current assets, even if management plans to sell them during the coming year. If a market does not exist for the securities, management may have difficulty selling them.

Objective 2
Identify types of securities and explain why companies invest in them.

For most companies, short-term marketable securities result from a temporary excess of cash. The cash is invested to earn a return until the cash is needed. Long-term investments represent several different investment needs. For example, companies often create investments to fund the repurchase or repayment of their own debt. Investment funds are created to pay for retirement and other employee benefits. Investments are made in other companies to gain access to markets, resources, and technology. Thus, investments in securities serve a variety of purposes.

How a company accounts for its investments in securities depends on three attributes of the securities: type, length of investment, and amount of control. The type of investment is determined by whether a security is an equity, particularly common stock, or a debt security. Length of investment is determined by whether management expects to sell an investment during the coming year. Amount of control applies only to long-term investments in equity securities. Control is determined by the extent of ownership a company has in other companies in which it invests. Exhibit 11-2 categorizes investments by type, length of investment, and control. Accounting measurement and reporting rules are associated with these categories.

Exhibit 11-2 Accounting for Investments in Securities

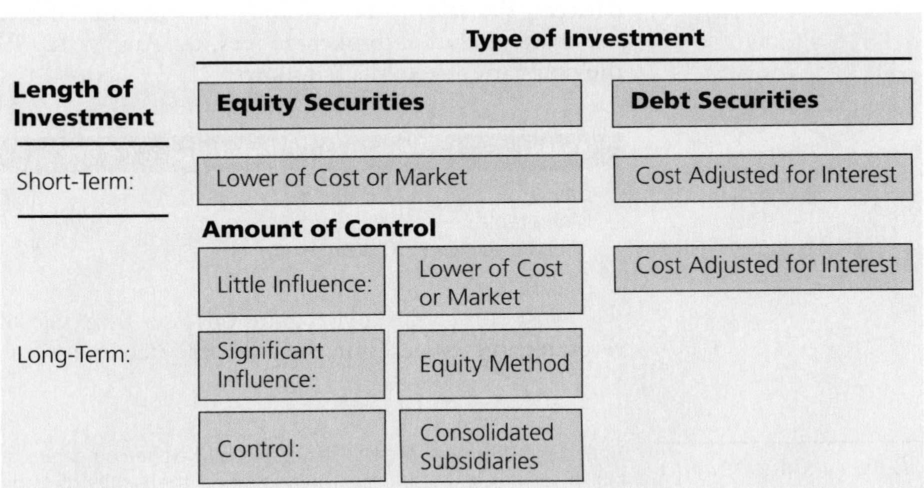

Type of Investment
Length of Investment
Equity Securities
Debt Securities
Short-Term:
Lower of Cost or Market
Cost Adjusted for Interest
Amount of Control
Little Influence:
Lower of Cost or Market
Cost Adjusted for Interest
Long-Term:
Significant Influence:
Equity Method
Control:
Consolidated Subsidiaries

As a general rule, GAAP require investments in securities to be reported on a company's balance sheet at their cost. Cost is the amount paid for an investment. Specific rules for different types of securities require adjustments to cost. The following sections describe adjustments required by GAAP for each category of investment.

In addition to cost-based reporting on the balance sheet, GAAP require fair value reporting of most securities. Fair values of investments in financial instruments should be disclosed on financial statements or in accompanying notes. The methods or assumptions used to estimate fair values also must be disclosed. Market prices should be used when they are available. If an organization cannot reasonably estimate the fair value of some instruments, the reasons for not disclosing the estimates should be explained.

INVESTMENTS IN EQUITY SECURITIES

Objective 3
Explain accounting rules for investments in equity securities.

Several types of investment transactions are common for equity securities. These include purchase and sale of securities, recording dividends or other investment income, and valuation of securities at the end of a fiscal period. The effect of these transactions on a company's financial statements depends on the length of the investment and, for long-term investments, the extent of control the investor has over the issuer of stock.

Equity investments are recorded at cost, including brokerage fees, when they are purchased. For example, if Silicon Company purchased 10,000 shares of Alfonso Company stock at a cost of $100,000 on November 1, 1994, the transaction would affect Silicon's accounts as follows:

Assets =		Liabilities + Equity	+ Revenues − Expenses
Cash	(100,000)		
Marketable Securities	100,000	-0-	-0-

When investments are sold, a gain or loss is recognized for the difference between the sales price and the cost. Assume Silicon sold all the shares at $12 per share, including brokerage fees, on August 12, 1995. The sale would affect the company's accounts as follows:

Assets =		Liabilities + Equity	+ Revenues − Expenses	
Cash	120,000		Gain on Sale of Investments	20,000
Marketable Securities	(100,000)			

Most companies report gains or losses from sale of securities as part of other revenues and expenses on their income statements.

Learning Note

Financial institutions, such as banks and brokerage companies, are in the business of investing in securities. These organizations report the results of trading activities as part of their operating revenues and expenses.

Dividends from these investments should be recognized at the time they are earned. For example, assume Alfonso paid a dividend of $.10 a share on December 15, 1994. Silicon should record the transaction as:

Assets =		Liabilities + Equity	+ Revenues − Expenses	
Cash	1,000		Investment Revenue	1,000

These rules apply to most investments in equity securities. Certain measurement and reporting rules vary, however, for investments, depending on the extent of control, as described below.

Short-Term Equity Investments

Short-term equity investments are accounted for using the lower of cost or market method. **The *lower of cost or market method* for securities requires investments be reported at their aggregate cost or market value, whichever is lower.** To illustrate, assume Silicon owned short-term marketable securities costing $300,000 on December 31, 1995, its fiscal year end. The market price of these securities was $270,000 on this date. Silicon would report the securities on its balance sheet at $270,000. The $30,000 decline in value would be recognized as part of other expenses on the income statement.

The lower of cost or market measurement rule recognizes losses on marketable securities in the period in which a decline in market value occurs. The rule is applied to the aggregate (whole) amount of marketable securities, not to individual securities. For example, assume Silicon owned the following short-term equity securities on December 31:

	Cost	Market
Alfonso Stock	$200,000	$160,000
Beatlejuice Stock	100,000	110,000
Total	$300,000	$270,000

The effect of recording the decline in value on Silicon's accounts would be:

Assets =		Liabilities + Equity	+ Revenues − Expenses	
Allowance for Decline in Value of Marketable Securities	($30,000)		Loss on Decline in Value of Marketable Securities	($30,000)

ALLOWANCE FOR DECLINE IN VALUE OF MARKETABLE SECURITIES is a contra-asset account, which offsets MARKETABLE SECURITIES. Silicon would report the net amount of marketable securities on its balance sheet as $270,000.

The comparison to determine lower of cost or market is made using the total cost and market value of all short-term marketable securities. If the aggregate market value is higher than cost, a gain is not recognized until the securities are sold. The lower of cost or market method is one of several examples of conservative accounting measurement. Losses or expenses are recognized before an actual sale occurs, but gains or revenues are not recognized until a sale occurs. For tax purposes, gains and losses on investments are not recognized until securities are sold.

GAAP require the application of lower of cost or market only to investments in equity securities. Some companies apply the method to all short-term marketable securities, including debt securities. Other companies report short-term investments in debt securities at cost, without adjusting for any decline in market value. The FASB has considered requiring many debt securities, particularly those currently held for resale, to be reported at an amount equal to the present value of expected future cash flows. Therefore, if expected future cash flows change, for instance because of a default by the issuer, the securities would be reported at an amount less than their cost.

Long-Term Equity Investments

Accounting methods for long-term investments in equity securities depend on the amount of control a company has over another company in which it has invested. Control is determined by the percentage of an issuer's common stock owned by an investor. The greater the ownership, the greater the control. Three types of accounting rules (GAAP) are used:

Extent of Control	Accounting Rule
Little influence	Lower of cost or market
Significant influence	Equity method
Control	Consolidation

The following sections describe accounting procedures for each of these rules.

Lower of Cost or Market. The **lower of cost or market method** applies to long-term equity investments in which the buyer has little influence over the company whose stock it has purchased. GAAP assume that an acquisition of less than 20% of a company's common stock results in little influence. Preferred stocks normally do not provide voting rights. Because owners of these securities cannot influence the issuer, most preferred stocks are accounted for using the lower of cost or market method.

The total cost of all long-term investments that meet the 20% rule is compared with their total market value at the end of the fiscal year. If the market value is below cost, the investments are written down to their market value. As an example, assume Silicon owns long-term marketable equity securities at the end of 1995. The company paid $100,000 for these securities, whose market value at the end of 1995 was $80,000. The company would report the securities on its 1995 balance sheet at $80,000. Unlike short-term equity investments, the $20,000 decline in the long-term equity securities is not reported on the income statement. It is deducted from stockholders' equity in a manner similar to the deduction of treasury stock.

The effect of the decline in value on Silicon's accounts would be:

Assets =		Liabilities + Equity		+ Revenues − Expenses
Allowance for Decline in Value of Long-Term Investments	($20,000)	Loss from Decline in Value of Long-Term Investments	($20,000)	

Remember, LOSS FROM DECLINE IN VALUE OF LONG-TERM INVESTMENTS is not an income statement account. It is a contra-stockholders' equity account.

Justification for this reporting rule is based on the long-term nature of the investments. Because the investments are long-term, the market value of the securities may change substantially before they are sold. Therefore, a loss is not recognized on the income statement until a sale is made. Short-term investments, on the other hand, are likely to be sold at a price approximating their market value. Therefore, losses on those investments are reported on the income statement. An increase in market value above cost, for short-term or long-term investments, is not recognized on the balance sheet or income statement until an investment is sold, a procedure justified by conservatism.

Learning Note

Some accountants argue that conservatism is not an appropriate accounting practice. Conservatism results in biased earnings numbers because expenses and losses are recognized in the fiscal period in which a decline in value occurs but revenues and gains are deferred until actual sales occur.

The lower of cost or market method applies to long-term investments in equity securities only when the investor cannot exert significant influence or control over the company in which it has invested. GAAP assume significant influence exists when a company owns at least 20%, but no more than 50%, of another company's common stock. Control is assumed when more than 50% is owned. The following sections consider accounting for these situations.

Equity Method. If an investor has significant influence over another company, the lower of cost or market method may not present an accurate description of transactions between the companies. For example, assume Big Company owns 30% of the common stock of Little Company. It purchased the stock for $30 million on January 1, 1995. The purchase affected Big Company's accounts as follows:

Assets =		Liabilities + Equity	+ Revenues − Expenses
Cash	(30,000,000)		
Long-Term Investments	30,000,000	-0-	-0-

During 1995, Little Company earned net income of $6 million. Big Company had a poor year and generated a smaller than expected net income of $10 million. To bolster its profits, it used its influence over Little Company to have its management pay a $4 million dividend in December 1995. Because Big Company owned 30% of Little's stock, it received $1.2 million of the dividend. If the lower of cost or market measurement rule were used, the dividend would increase Big Company's revenues for 1995.

Because of the influence problem, GAAP require companies with significant influence to use the equity method of accounting for these investments. **The *equity method* requires an investor company to recognize revenue from an investee company's net income in proportion to the investor's ownership.** For example, if Little Company reported net income of $6 million in 1995, Big Company would record 30% of the net income as an increase in its investment and as revenue:

Assets =		Liabilities + Equity	+ Revenues − Expenses	
Long-Term Investments	1,800,000		Investment Revenue	1,800,000

This investment revenue sometimes is reported on the income statement as **equity in earnings of affiliated companies.**

Dividends received from Little Company reduce Big Company's investment because they are considered to be a return of part of the $1,800,000 investment recognized by Big Company. For example, if Little Company paid $4 million in dividends, Big Company would record its 30% share as:

Assets =		Liabilities + Equity	+ Revenues − Expenses
Cash	1,200,000		
Long-Term Investments	(1,200,000)	-0-	-0-

Thus, while Little Company's retained earnings increased by $2 million in 1995 ($6 million of net income − $4 million of dividends), Big Company's investment increased proportionately by $600,000 ($2 million × .30):

Little Co.			**Big Co.**	
Net Income	$6,000,000		Revenue	$1,800,000
Less: Dividends	$4,000,000	**x 30%**	Less: Cash Received	$1,200,000
Equals: Increases in Retained Earnings	$2,000,000		Equals: Increase in Long-Term Investment	$600,000

The book value of Big Company's investment in Little Company would be $30.6 million after these transactions have been recorded ($30,000,000 + $1,800,000 − $1,200,000).

If, during 1996, Big Company decided to sell its investment in Little Company at a price of $30.3 million, the sale would affect its accounts as follows:

Assets =		Liabilities + Equity	+ Revenues – Expenses	
Cash	30,300,000		Loss on Sale of Investments	(300,000)
Long-Term Investments	(30,600,000)			

The balance of LONG-TERM INVESTMENTS is reduced by the book value of Big Company's investment in Little Company. The difference between the cash received and the book value of the investment is a gain or loss on sale.

If the amount is material, the total amount of investments using the equity method often is reported as a separate asset. For example, DuPont reported investments in affiliates of $1,580 million on its 1991 balance sheet.

Consolidation of Subsidiaries. If a company owns over 50% of another company's voting stock, it controls the other company. The controlled company is a **subsidiary** of the controlling, or **parent,** company. The subsidiary's financial statements normally are consolidated as part of the parent corporation's consolidated financial statements. The consolidated statements report the parent and its subsidiaries as though they were one company.

For example, assume Parent Corporation owns 90% of Sub Corporation's common stock at the end of 1995. Parent paid $45 million for Sub's stock at the beginning of the year. The acquisition affected Parent's accounts as follows:

Assets =		Liabilities + Equity	+ Revenues – Expenses
Cash	(45,000,000)		
Long-Term Investment	45,000,000	-0-	-0-

A part of Parent's assets and Sub's liabilities is a loan from Parent to Sub for $12 million. In addition, Sub sold goods priced at $5 million to Parent during the current fiscal year. Sub's cost for these goods was $3 million. Exhibit 11-3 describes the consolidation of the companies' financial statements at the end of 1995.

The consolidated balance sheet includes the assets and liabilities of both companies as shown in the right-hand column of Exhibit 11-3. For example, the consolidated assets of $235 million equal Parent's assets of $212 million plus Sub's assets of $80 million minus the adjustments for intercompany notes receivable (item a) and the long-term investment in Sub (item b). The intercompany receivable (item a) and payable (item c) are eliminated. In addition, the long-term investment account on the books of Parent (item b) and 90% (the parent's share) of Sub's stockholders' equity (item d) are eliminated. The remaining 10% ($5 million) of Sub's stockholders' equity is reported as minority interest. ***Minority interest*** **is the percentage of a subsidiary not owned by the parent.**

The consolidated income statement includes revenues and expenses as shown in the right-hand column. The intercompany revenue (item e) and cost of goods sold (item f) are eliminated. 10% of Sub's net income (item g) is reported as **minority interest in earnings** on the consolidated income statement.

Exhibit 11-3 Preparation of Consolidated Financial Statements

(in millions)	Parent Corporation Balances	Sub Corporation Balances	Adjustments Necessary for Consolidation		Parent Corp. Consolidated Statements
Total Assets	$212	$80	**a** Note Receivable	(12)	
			b Long-Term Investment	(45)	$235
Total Liabilities	$ 96	$30	**c** Note Payable	(12)	$114
Stockholders' Equity—Sub		50	**d**	(45)	Minority Interest 5
Stockholders' Equity—Parent	116				116
Liabilities and Stockholders' Equity	$212	$80		(57)	$235
Revenues	$160	$70	**e**	(5)	$225
Expenses	(140)	(60)	**f**	3	(197)
Minority Interest			**g**	(1)	(1)
Net income	$20	$10		(3)	$ 27

Consolidation procedures apply only to Parent Company's consolidated financial statements. The consolidation and elimination adjustments described in Exhibit 11-3 are not recorded in Parent Company's accounting records. Instead, Parent Company accounts for its investment in Sub in its accounting records using the same type of procedures as described previously for the equity method. If it were to sell its investment, Parent would record a gain or loss as the difference between the book value of the investment in its accounting records and the amount received from the sale.

Corporations report their consolidation procedures in describing their accounting policies. International Paper reported in 1991:

> The consolidated financial statements include the accounts of International Paper Company and it subsidiaries (the Company). Minority interest represents minority shareholders' proportionate share of the equity in several of the Company's consolidated subsidiaries, ... All significant intercompany balances and transactions are eliminated. Investments in affiliated companies owned 20% or more, and the Company's investment in Carter Holt Harvey Limited where the Company has the ability to exercise significant influence, are accounted for by the equity method. The Company's share of affiliates' earnings is included in the Consolidated Statement of Earnings.

Learning Note

Not all countries require corporations to issue consolidated financial statements. Parent corporations may issue statements that do not include their subsidiaries. Also, rules about which companies must be included as part of consolidated reports vary among countries. Therefore, caution should be used in examining reports to determine which subsidiary companies have been included and which have been excluded.

Mergers and Acquisitions

Business combinations involve the merger of two companies or the acquisition of one company by another. **An *acquisition* occurs when one company acquires a controlling interest in another company, which continues to exist as a separate legal entity.** In the previous example, Parent Company acquired a majority of Sub Company's common stock. Parent could accomplish this transaction in two primary ways. It could purchase Sub's shares. Sub's former stockholders would receive cash but would no longer be owners in Sub or Parent. Alternatively, Parent could have issued shares of its own stock in exchange for the stock of Sub. Sub's former stockholders would now be stockholders of Parent and its subsidiary. Under either of these arrangements, if Sub continued as a separate legal entity, Parent would issue consolidated financial statements.

On the other hand, if Parent owned all of Sub's common stock, it could retire Sub's stock and eliminate Sub as a separate legal entity. Sub's assets and liabilities would be combined with Parent's as part of a merger. **A *merger* occurs when companies combine their resources and operations so only one legal entity continues to exist.**

Objective 4
Identify methods used to account for acquisitions and mergers.

Two methods are used to account for mergers and acquisitions: the purchase method and the pooling of interests method. The **pooling of interests method** is used only when an acquisition or merger is accomplished primarily through the issuance of common stock. At least 90% of the common stock of one company in an acquisition or merger must be acquired through an exchange of the other company's common stock.[3] The **purchase method** is used when stock is acquired primarily through the exchange of cash, debt, or arrangements other than issuance of common stock. Most mergers and acquisitions are accounted for as purchases.

Purchase Method. In a purchase, the assets and liabilities of an acquired company are reported in consolidated financial statements at their **fair market value** at the date of acquisition. If a merger occurs, the assets and liabilities of the acquired company are combined in the new entity's accounting records at their fair market value. Therefore, the transaction is treated similarly to the company's purchase of new equipment or other assets. The purchase price determines the amount reported for the new assets and liabilities.

As an example, assume Parent Company purchased all of Sub Company's common stock, paying $65 million in cash. At the time of the purchase, Sub's balance sheet reported assets with a book value of $80 million, liabilities of $30 million, and stockholders' equity of $50 million. Therefore, Parent paid $65 million for Sub's net assets (assets − liabilities) with a book value of $50 million. Parent paid the additional $15 million because it considered the value of Sub as a going concern to be higher than its book value. Book value does not consider the fair market value of assets and liabilities or the value of trained employees and established markets.

Sub's assets and liabilities would be valued by Parent at their fair market value, to the extent determinable. Assume Sub is merged with Parent. An appraisal of the value of Sub's identifiable assets and liabilities reveals assets with a

[3] Other conditions also must be met for the pooling of interests method to be used. These conditions restrict the use of the method to situations in which stock for stock exchanges occur.

market value of $93 million and liabilities with a market value of $34 million. Therefore, Parent has paid $65 million for net assets with an identifiable market value of $59 million ($93 − $34). Parent records the remaining $6 million it paid for Sub as goodwill. ***Goodwill* is the excess of cost over the market value of identifiable net assets resulting from the purchase of one company by another.** Goodwill represents the value of trained employees, established markets, and other resources that are not identified on Sub's balance sheet. It is an intangible asset.

The purchase of Sub would affect Parent's accounts as follows:

Assets =		Liabilities + Equity		+ Revenues − Expenses
Cash	(65,000,000)	Liabilities of Sub (identifiable)	34,000,000	
Assets of Sub (identifiable)	93,000,000			
Goodwill	6,000,000			

Parent would record Sub's individual assets and liabilities at their estimated market values. GAAP require goodwill to be amortized over a period not to exceed 40 years. If Parent amortized its goodwill over 10 years, it would recognize $600,000 of amortization expense each year.

If the transaction had been an acquisition rather than a merger, Parent would have recorded LONG-TERM INVESTMENTS of $65 million. The individual asset, liability, and goodwill amounts would have been reported on Parent's consolidated balance sheet but not as part of Parent's own accounting records because Sub would continue to be a separate legal entity.

Learning Note

Some countries, such as Great Britain, permit corporations to write off goodwill against stockholders' equity in the period in which goodwill is acquired. By writing off the goodwill, the corporation eliminates the amortization expense that would reduce its net income in future periods. Therefore, a company's reported net income will be higher than if goodwill had been amortized. Thus, a British company might report higher net income than an identical U.S. company because of the difference between U.S. and British GAAP concerning the amortization of goodwill.

Pooling of Interests. If the merger were a pooling of interests, Parent would have exchanged shares of its stock for Sub's shares. The new shares would be recorded at an amount equal to the *book value* of Sub's stockholders' equity. The assets and liabilities of Sub would be recorded by Parent at their book values as determined by Sub's accounting records:

Assets =		Liabilities + Equity		+ Revenues − Expenses
Assets of Sub	80,000,000	Liabilities of Sub	30,000,000	
		Common Stock	50,000,000	

Parent would have recorded Sub's individual assets and liabilities. Assets and liabilities have been pooled rather than purchased. Goodwill does not result from a pooling of interests.

Companies describe merger and acquisition activities in notes to the financial statements. As an example, International Paper disclosed in its 1991 annual report:

> During the first quarter of 1991, the Company purchased certain packaging and sheeting facilities located in France . . . . [A description of various mergers and acquisitions follows.]
>
> All of the 1991 and 1990 acquisitions, except the merger with Leslie Paper Company, were accounted for using the purchase method. The operating results of all 1991 and 1990 mergers and acquisitions have been included in the Consolidated Statement of Earnings from the dates of acquisition.

For tax purposes, corporations normally report mergers and acquisitions using the pooling of interests method. Assets and liabilities are reported at the same amount after the merger or acquisition as before. Therefore, the amount of depreciation that can be taken for tax purposes is determined by the book value of the assets acquired, not by their market value, even if the purchase method were used for financial reporting purposes.

SELF-STUDY PROBLEM 11-1

Consider each of the following independent long-term investment transactions that occurred on July 1, 1994:

a. Adam Company acquired 35% of Smith Company's common stock for $20 million cash.
b. Adam acquired 100% of Smith Company's common stock in exchange for shares of Adam Company's own common stock. Smith was merged with Adam and no longer continued as a separate legal entity.
c. Adam purchased 10% of Smith Company's common stock for $8 million cash ($8 per share).
d. Adam acquired 95% of Smith Company's common stock in exchange for $84 million cash. Smith continued as a separate legal entity.

For each transaction in which Smith continued as a separate legal entity, assume Smith's net income for the fiscal year ended June 30, 1995, was $5 million. Also, assume Smith paid $2 million in dividends for the year ended June 30, 1995. No other intercompany transactions occurred during the year. The price of Smith's stock was $7 per share on June 30, 1995. Adam Company owned no other long-term equity securities on this date.

Required

For each transaction, explain the accounting measurement and reporting rules Adam would use to account for the investment. Also, explain how, if at all, Smith's net income and dividends would affect Adam's accounts for the fiscal year ended June 30, 1995.

The solution to Self-Study Problem 11-1 appears at the end of the chapter.

INVESTMENTS IN DEBT SECURITIES

Objective 5
Explain accounting rules for investments in debt securities.

When a company invests in debt securities, it is making loans to the issuer of the securities. These investments may be in the form of bonds, notes, or commercial paper issued by other organizations. Banks issue debt instruments in the form of certificates of deposit. The issuer of debt securities has an obligation to repay the principal borrowed from investors and to pay interest.

Notes and Other Debt Securities

Accounting for investments in debt securities involves transactions associated with their purchase, interest earned, interest received, and their sale. For example, assume Silicon purchased $60,000 of short-term government notes on September 1, 1995. The notes pay interest at an annual rate of 5%. On September 1, the transaction to purchase the securities would affect Silicon's accounts as follows:

Assets =		Liabilities + Equity	+ Revenues − Expenses	
Cash	(60,000)			
Marketable Securities	60,000			

At the end of its fiscal year, on December 31, Silicon would recognize $1,000 interest earned on the note for four months ($60,000 × .05 × 4⁄12):

Assets =		Liabilities + Equity	+ Revenues − Expenses	
Interest Receivable	1,000		Interest Revenue	1,000

At the end of 1995, Silicon would include the investment and interest receivable in its current assets.

If the notes mature on February 28, 1996, Silicon would record cash for the principal ($60,000) and interest received ($1,500 = $60,000 × .05 × 6⁄12). The company records the additional interest earned for two months during 1996 ($500 = $60,000 × .05 × 2⁄12) as interest revenue. These transactions would affect the company's accounts as follows:

Assets =		Liabilities + Equity	+ Revenues − Expenses	
Cash	61,500		Interest Revenue	500
Marketable Securities	(60,000)			
Interest Receivable	(1,000)			

Amortization schedules may be used for notes receivable to identify the amount of revenue recognized during a fiscal period. These schedules are common for long-term investments that pay principal and interest in installments over several fiscal periods. They serve the same purpose as those for notes payable, as discussed in Chapter 9.

Long-term receivables are common for financial services companies and for financial divisions of other companies. For example, automobile companies include divisions that finance the sale of automobiles to customers. Ford's financial services division reported receivables of $89,701 million in 1991. Also, short- and long-term notes and other loans are major assets for financial institutions such as banks.

Long-Term Investments in Bonds

Accounting rules for long-term investments in bonds mirror those used to account for bonds payable. A company records the investment at cost, including brokerage fees. For example, assume Silicon purchased 100 Alfonso Company bonds on July 1, 1995. The bonds pay interest semiannually on June 30 and December 31 at an annual coupon rate of 8%. The bonds sold at an effective yield of 10%. The effect of brokerage fees are included in computing the effective yield. The bonds mature on December 31, 1997, at a value of $1,000 per bond.

The price Silicon paid for each bond would be the present value of $40 each six months for 5 semiannual periods (July 1995 through December 1997), plus the present value of $1,000 at the end of 5 periods. The discount factor is 5% for each six-month period.

The interest factor for an annuity of 5 periods at 5% is 4.32948 (Table 2). The interest factor for a single payment at the end of 5 periods at 5% is .78353 (Table 1). Therefore, the price of each bond would be:

$$\$956.71 = (\$40 \times 4.32948) + (\$1{,}000 \times .78353)$$

The effect of the purchase transaction on Silicon's accounts would be:

Assets =		Liabilities + Equity	+ Revenues − Expenses
Cash	(95,671)		
Long-Term Investments	95,671	-0-	-0-

At each interest payment date, Silicon would record interest revenue and amortize the bond discount. Exhibit 11-4 provides an amortization schedule for the bonds.

Exhibit 11-4 Amortization Schedule for Bond Investment

a	b	c	d	e	f	g
Period	**Present Value at Beginning of Period**	**Unamortized Discount**	**Interest Revenue (b × .05)**	**Interest Received**	**Amortization (d − e)**	**Present Value at End of Period (b + f)**
1	$95,671	$4,329	$4,784	$4,000	$784	$ 96,455
2	96,455	3,545	4,823	4,000	823	97,278
3	97,278	2,722	4,864	4,000	864	98,142
4	98,142	1,858	4,907	4,000	907	99,049
5	99,049	951	4,951	4,000	951	100,000

Therefore, on December 31, 1995, Silicon would record interest on the bonds:

Assets =		Liabilities + Equity	+ Revenues − Expenses	
Cash	4,000		Interest Revenue	4,784
Long-Term Investments	784			

Silicon would report the bonds as long-term investments on its balance sheet at the end of 1995 at their book value of $96,455. The book value is the cost of the bonds, adjusted for amortization of the discount.

On June 30, 1996, Silicon would record:

Assets =		Liabilities + Equity	+ Revenues − Expenses	
Cash	4,000		Interest Revenue	4,823
Long-Term Investments	823			

Amortization of the discount increases LONG-TERM INVESTMENT and INTEREST REVENUE. The company would continue to record interest until the bonds mature. On December 31, 1997, it would record the final interest payment:

Assets =		Liabilities + Equity	+ Revenues − Expenses	
Cash	4,000		Interest Revenue	4,951
Long-Term Investments	951			

Also, it would record receipt of principal:

Assets =		Liabilities + Equity	+ Revenues − Expenses
Cash	100,000		
Long-Term Investments	(100,000)	-0-	-0-

Amortization of the discount has increased the long-term investment account to $100,000 on December 31, 1997. This is the amount of principal repaid on this date.

If Silicon decided to sell the bonds prior to their maturity, it would receive an amount determined by the market value of the bonds at the date of sale. For example, assume Silicon sold the bonds on June 30, 1996, at a price of $98,000. The book value of Silicon's investment on this date, after recording interest, was $97,278. Therefore, the sale of the bonds would result in a gain of $722:

Assets =		Liabilities + Equity	+ Revenues − Expenses	
Cash	98,000		Gain on Sale of Investments	722
Long-Term Investments	(97,278)			

The gain (or loss) is the difference between the amount received from the sale and the amortized cost (book value) of the investment.

When bonds are bought or sold between interest payment dates, interest must be accrued on the bonds. For example, assume the sale in the previous example occurred on February 28, 1997, instead of on December 31, 1996. Silicon would have earned $1,333 ($100,000 × .08 × 2/12) of interest on the bonds for two months. Therefore, assuming the bonds are sold for $98,000 plus accrued interest, Silicon would record the sale as:

Assets =		Liabilities + Equity	+ Revenues − Expenses	
Cash	99,333		Interest Revenue	1,333
Long-Term Investments	(97,278)		Gain on Sale of Investments	722

In essence, two transactions have been recorded. Silicon received the interest it had earned since the last payment of interest ($1,333), in addition to the price of the bonds ($98,000). Silicon must collect the interest it has earned from the buyer because the buyer will receive the next interest payment for a full six months.

PLANT ASSETS

Plant assets include land, buildings, and equipment used in a company's operating activities. International Paper reported plant assets of $7,848 million in 1991 (Exhibit 11-1). This amount was net (after subtraction) of accumulated depreciation.

Transactions associated with plant assets include their purchase and disposal and their valuation on the balance sheet at the end of a fiscal period. Plant assets are recorded at cost, which includes the amount paid for them plus the cost of transportation, site preparation, installation, and construction necessary to make the assets usable. Plant assets are reported on the balance sheet at cost less accumulated depreciation.

Land is not subject to depreciation because it is not consumed. The cost of land associated with natural resources, such as oil or timber, that are consumed is allocated to expense through depletion (explained later in this chapter). Land generally is acquired as a site for office, manufacturing, and other facilities. The cost of land includes site preparation necessary for construction. Land improvements, such as paving and lighting, are treated as separate assets that are depreciated.

Often land is acquired along with other assets. The purchase price includes land, buildings, and improvements. In this situation, the cost must be allocated between the land and other assets. Allocation methods generally consider the appraised value of the land and other assets as a basis for allocation.

The next section considers depreciation for plant assets other than land.

Depreciation

Objective 6
Distinguish between straight-line and accelerated depreciation methods.

Plant assets that are consumed, such as buildings and equipment, are depreciated over their estimated useful lives. **Depreciation is the process of allocating the cost of plant assets to expense over the fiscal periods that benefit from their use.** Companies use a variety of depreciation methods.

These methods fall into two general types: straight-line and accelerated. A third type, units-of-production, is used for certain assets described later. ***Straight-line depreciation*** **allocates an equal amount of the cost of a plant asset to expense during each fiscal period of the asset's expected useful life.** ***Accelerated depreciation*** **allocates a larger portion of plant asset cost to expense early in the asset's life.**

To illustrate, assume Silicon Company purchased equipment on January 1, 1993, at a cost of $100,000. Management expects the equipment to have a useful life of 5 years. At the end of 5 years, management expects to sell the equipment as scrap metal with negligible value. Therefore, the depreciable cost of the asset is $100,000.

Depreciation Methods Used by Major U.S. Corporations for Financial Reporting

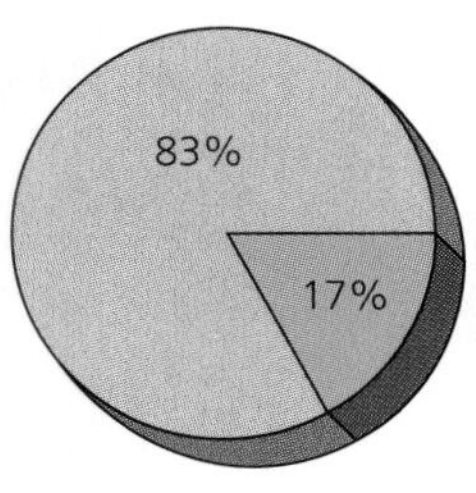

Straight Line
Accelerated

(Data source: AICPA, Accounting Trends and Techniques, 1991.)

Straight-Line Depreciation.
Straight-line depreciation would allocate $20,000 ($100,000/5) of cost to depreciation expense each year over the life of the asset:

Depreciation Expense = Depreciable Cost ÷ Expected Life of Asset

Therefore, in 1993, depreciation would affect the company's accounts as follows:

Assets =		Liabilities + Equity	+ Revenues − Expenses	
Accumulated Depreciation	(20,0000)		Depreciation Expense	(20,000)

ACCUMULATED DEPRECIATION is a contra-asset account offsetting EQUIPMENT. The net, or book value, of plant assets is the cost of assets minus accumulated depreciation. The book value of the equipment purchased on January 1 would be $80,000 at the end of 1993, $60,000 at the end of 1994, and so forth.

If the asset were expected to have a material sales or trade-in value at the end of its useful life, this value should be deducted from the cost in calculating depreciation. For example, if the equipment was expected to have a sales value of $5,000 at the end of its useful life, annual depreciation expense would be $19,000 = [($100,000 − $5,000)/5 years]. The amount an organization expects to receive for a plant asset at the end of its useful life is the asset's **residual,** or **salvage, value.** The residual value for many assets is negligible and often is omitted in calculating depreciation expense.

Accelerated Depreciation. Two methods of accelerated depreciation are common: the declining balance method and the sum-of-the-years'-digits method. *Declining balance depreciation* **allocates a multiple of the straight-line rate times the book value of an asset to depreciation expense.** A common multiple is two, known as double-declining balance. An asset with a five-year life would be depreciated at a straight-line rate of 20% ($\frac{1}{5}$) if the straight-line method were used. Thus, double the straight-line rate would be 40% ($\frac{1}{5} \times 2$). If Silicon used the double-declining balance method for its asset, depreciation for 1993 would be calculated as:

Depreciation Expense = Book Value × (2 ÷ Expected Useful Life)
\$40,000 = \$100,000 × $\frac{2}{5}$

The company would record accumulated depreciation and depreciation expense of \$40,000 in 1993. Depreciation expense for 1994 would be calculated as:

\$24,000 = \$60,000 × $\frac{2}{5}$

The book value at the beginning of 1994 (\$60,000) was multiplied times twice the straight-line rate.

Sum-of-the-years'-digits depreciation **allocates depreciation according to a fraction, n/N, in which n is remaining life of the asset at the beginning of the period and N is the sum of the years of the expected useful life of the asset.** For an asset with a five-year useful life, the sum would be 15 (1 + 2 + 3 + 4 + 5). Depreciation expense in the first year of the asset's life would be computed as:

Depreciation Expense = Cost × $\frac{5}{15}$
\$33,333 = \$100,000 × $\frac{5}{15}$

The remaining life of the asset at the beginning of the second year is four years. Therefore, depreciation expense in the second year would be:

\$26,667 = \$100,000 × $\frac{4}{15}$

Observe that cost, not book value, is used in the calculation. If the asset had a residual value of \$5,000, the depreciation expense would be computed as (\$100,000 − \$5,000) × $\frac{5}{15}$ in year one and as (\$100,000 − \$5,000) × $\frac{4}{15}$ in year two.

Units-of-Production Depreciation. In addition to the straight-line and accelerated methods, the units-of-production method is used by some companies for production equipment and facilities. **The** ***units-of-production depreciation*** **method produces a level amount of depreciation expense per unit of output, rather than per fiscal period.** For example, assume Silicon purchased for \$30,000 a machine used to cut metal parts. Management expects the machine to produce 3 million components over its useful life. Depreciation could be computed based on the number of units produced during a fiscal period. The depreciation rate on the equipment would be \$.01 per unit (\$30,000/3,000,000). If 600,000 units were produced in 1995, \$6,000 (600,000 × \$.01) of depreciation expense would be recorded on the asset. If approximately the same number of units are produced each period, results of this method will be similar to those of straight-line depreciation.

Comparison of Depreciation Methods. A depreciation schedule reports the depreciation expense and book value of an asset over its useful life. Exhibit 11-5 provides a depreciation schedule for Silicon's asset for each of the methods previously considered.

Exhibit 11-5 Depreciation Schedule

	Straight-Line		Declining Balance		Sum-of-the-Years'-Digits	
Year	**Book Value**	**Depreciation**	**Book Value**	**Depreciation**	**Book Value**	**Depreciation**
0	$100,000		$100,000		$100,000	
1	80,000	$ 20,000	60,000	$ 40,000	66,667	$ 33,333
2	60,000	20,000	36,000	24,000	40,000	26,667
3	40,000	20,000	21,600	14,400	20,000	20,000
4	20,000	20,000	12,960	8,640	6,667	13,333
5	0	20,000	0	12,960	0	6,667
Total		$100,000		$100,000		$100,000

Year 0 is the purchase date at the beginning of the five-year period. As depreciation expense is recorded each year, accumulated depreciation increases and the book value of the asset decreases. Observe that the amount of depreciation recorded in years one and two is higher using the accelerated methods than using the straight-line method. Each method allocates the cost of the asset to depreciation over the asset's life. Observe that the declining balance method requires the remaining book value of an asset to be expensed in the last year of its life, regardless of the amount. The $12,960 of depreciation expense computed using this method in Exhibit 11-5 was the amount necessary to write off the cost of the machine. It was not 40% of the book value at the beginning of the year.

Depreciation expense is prorated for plant assets acquired during a fiscal period. If a company acquired assets in April 1996, and its fiscal year end was December 31, it would record 9/12 of the full-year depreciation expense for these assets in 1996.

When a company continuously purchases and replaces plant assets, accelerated depreciation will result in lower net income than will straight-line depreciation. Most companies use straight-line depreciation for the majority of their assets, thereby reporting higher net incomes. Companies may use different depreciation methods for financial reporting and tax purposes. Accelerated depreciation is permitted for tax purposes for most plant assets. Accelerated depreciation reduces the amount of taxable income and the cash outflow for taxes. Tax rules specify the type of depreciation method and useful life that can be used for computing depreciation for tax purposes. For example, most office furniture and factory equipment can be depreciated for tax purposes over 7 years using the double-declining balance method.

As an example of accounting and tax reporting differences, assume Silicon purchased equipment at a cost of $100,000. The equipment has no residual value and an expected useful life of 10 years. Silicon depreciates the equipment for financial reporting purposes using the straight-line method and a ten-year life. Depreciation expense would be $10,000 for the first year. For tax purposes, it uses the double-declining balance method and a seven-year life. Depreciation expense would be $28,571 ($100,000 × 2/7) for the first year for tax purposes. The higher amount of expense for tax purposes would result in lower income for tax purposes than for financial reporting purposes. The difference would result in deferred income taxes as discussed in Chapter 9.

GAAP require corporations to report the depreciation methods they use. A note to International Paper's financial statements disclosed:

> Plants, properties and equipment are stated at cost, less accumulated depreciation. For financial reporting purposes, the Company uses the units-of-production method for depreciating its major U.S. pulp and paper mills and certain wood products facilities, and the straight-line method for other plants and equipment. . . . For tax purposes, depreciation is computed utilizing accelerated methods.

In addition, International Paper reported a schedule of its major classes of plant assets:

In millions at December 31	1991	1990
Pulp, paper and packaging facilities		
Mills	$ 9,194	$ 8,459
Packaging plants	922	791
Wood products facilities	975	913
Other plants, properties and equipment	1,642	1,493
Gross cost	12,733	11,656
Less: Accumulated depreciation	4,885	4,369
Plants, properties and equipment, net	$ 7,848	$ 7,287

Thus, at the end of 1991, the company had paid $12.7 billion for assets with a book value of $7.8 billion. Approximately, one-third of the cost of plant assets had been depreciated by the end of 1991.

Foreign corporations may use accounting methods for depreciation that differ from those used in the U.S. For example, Swiss companies may expense plant assets in the year in which they are acquired. These assets are reported on the companies' balance sheets at a book value of one Swiss franc. This practice results in lower reported net income and lower asset values for these companies relative to those of most nations. This extremely conservative practice helps protect creditors, such as banks, that provide most of the financing for Swiss companies.

Disposal of Plant Assets

Objective 7
Determine the accounting effects of disposing of plant assets.

Disposal of plant assets occurs when the assets are retired, sold, or traded for new assets. Each of these transactions involves elimination of an asset's cost and accumulated depreciation from the accounting records. For example, assume Silicon retired the equipment described in Exhibit 11-5 at the end of year 4 because it had become obsolete and had no sales value. If Silicon had used straight-line depreciation, it would record the retirement by eliminating the asset and related accumulated depreciation from its accounts:

Assets =		Liabilities + Equity	+ Revenues − Expenses	
Equipment	(100,000)		Loss on Disposal of Plant Assets	(20,000)
Accumulated Depreciation	80,000			

Through the end of year 4, $80,000 of accumulated depreciation had been recorded on the asset. The book value of the asset is recorded as a loss if the asset is retired before being fully depreciated.

If the asset were sold at the end of year 4 for $12,000, Silicon would follow a similar procedure:

Assets =		Liabilities + Equity	+ Revenues − Expenses	
Cash	12,000		Loss on Disposal of Plant Assets	(8,000)
Equipment	(100,000)			
Accumulated Depreciation	80,000			

The difference between the amount received for the asset and the asset's book value is a gain or loss. If Silicon had received more than $20,000 for the asset, it would have recorded a gain.

If the asset were traded in on a newer model, the cost of the asset would be recorded, in addition to accounting for the disposal of the old asset. Assume Silicon's asset was traded in at the end of year 4 for a new model, priced at $135,000. The seller allowed Silicon $15,000 for the old asset, resulting in a cash payment of $120,000 ($135,000 − $15,000). The transaction would affect Silicon's accounts as follows:

Assets =		Liabilities + Equity	+ Revenues − Expenses	
Cash	(120,000)		Loss on Disposal of Plant Assets	(5,000)
Equipment (new)	135,000			
Equipment (old)	(100,000)			
Accumulated Depreciation	80,000			

The old asset and related accumulated depreciation are eliminated as in the prior transactions. The new asset is recorded. The difference between the amount allowed for trade-in value and the book value of the old asset is a gain or loss on disposal.

Depletion of Natural Resources

Objective 8
Explain accounting rules for investments in natural resources.

Paper, petroleum, mining, and other companies invest in natural resources. They purchase or lease land that contains timber, oil, or minerals. The cost of the land is primarily for the natural resources it contains. For example, International Paper reported timberlands of $743 million in 1991.

The amount reported for natural resources on a company's balance sheet is the cost of the asset less depletion. ***Depletion*** **is the systematic allocation of the cost of natural resources to the periods that benefit from their**

use. Assume Silicon purchased land containing minerals on April 1, 1995, for $8 million. The transaction affected the company's accounts as follows:

Assets =		Liabilities + Equity	+ Revenues − Expenses
Cash	(8,000,000)		
Mineral Deposits	8,000,000	-0-	-0-

The company estimated the land contained 80,000 tons of minerals when it was purchased. Thus, the estimated cost per ton was $100 ($8 million/80,000 tons). During 1995, Silicon mined the land and removed 16,000 tons of the minerals. The cost of the asset consumed during 1995 would affect the company's accounts as follows ($100 × 16,000 tons):

Assets =		Liabilities + Equity	+ Revenues − Expenses
Inventory	1,600,000		
Mineral Deposits	(1,600,000)	-0-	-0-

The minerals are inventoried until they are consumed or sold. Cost of goods sold should be increased when the inventory is sold. This example assumes the land has negligible value apart from the value of the mineral deposits. If the land is valuable apart from the deposits, the estimated cost of the land should be recorded as a separate asset. Only the estimated value of the deposits should be depleted.

GAAP require corporations to describe accounting procedures for natural resources. A note to International Paper's financial statements disclosed:

> The Company . . . controlled approximately 6.3 million acres of timberlands in the United States at December 31, 1991. Timberlands are stated at cost, less accumulated depletion representing the cost of timber harvested.

GAAP require that natural resources be reported by companies at their amortized costs. The market values of these resources is not reported on the financial statements, though some companies disclose information about the current value of these assets in notes to the financial statements. For some companies, the market values may be much higher than book values. Companies owning oil and timber reserves, for example, may have experienced dramatic increases in the market values of these resources in recent years because of increasing demand. The market value of a company's stock may reflect the unrecorded value of these assets.

SELF-STUDY PROBLEM 11-2

The Banana Boat Company purchased equipment on January 1, 1996, at a cost of $400,000. The equipment has an expected life of 8 years, at which time it is anticipated to have negligible value. The company's management is considering whether to depreciate the equipment on a straight-line, double declining balance, or sum-of-the-years'-digits basis. The company's tax rate is 30%. For tax purposes, the equipment will be depreciated over 7 years using the double-declining balance method, regardless of which method is used for financial reporting purposes.

Required

What effect would each of the three methods have on Banana Boat's net income in 1996? What effect would each method have on the company's cash flows for the year?

The solution to Self-Study Problem 11-2 appears at the end of the chapter.

Leased Assets

Objective 9
Distinguish between operating and capital leases.

In addition to purchasing plant assets, some companies lease assets from other companies. Leasing is common in certain industries, such as airlines. Leases are of two major types: operating and capital. **An *operating lease* is a contract that permits one organization to use property owned by another organization for a limited period of time. The costs of operating leases are expensed in the period in which leased assets are used.** For example, assume Silicon paid $60,000 for equipment it leased in 1995. If the leases were accounted for as operating leases, Silicon would record $60,000 of lease expense in 1995. Minimum future payments associated with operating lease contracts must be disclosed by corporations as discussed in Chapter 9.

A *capital lease* is a contract that permits one organization to use property owned by another organization as though the property had been purchased. Capital leases transfer most of the risks and rights of ownership to the company leasing the assets. These lease contracts are for most of the useful life of an asset and may provide an option for the lessor to purchase the asset. For accounting purposes, capital leases are treated as purchase contracts. Leased assets are reported on the balance sheet, along with other plant assets. For example, American Airlines reported the following information on its 1991 balance sheet (in millions):

	1991	**1990**
Equipment and Property Under Capital Leases		
Flight equipment	$1,826	$1,641
Other equipment and property	286	288
	2,112	1,929
Less accumulated amortization	546	634
	$1,566	$1,295

About 15% of American's plant assets were leased in 1991.

In addition, American reported current obligations under capital leases of $75 million and long-term capital lease obligations of $1,928 million in 1991 as part of its liabilities. These obligations represent the financing arrangements implicit in the lease contracts.

The amount recorded for leased assets is the present value of future lease payments. Capital leases are a form of financing in which a company acquires the right to use a resource in exchange for payments over a specified period.

The payments compensate the owner of the asset for the asset cost and for interest for financing the lease. In substance, the arrangement is the same as a company borrowing money to purchase an asset. An asset is acquired, and a loan is created that must be repaid with interest.

For example, assume Silicon leased equipment on January 1, 1993. The lease contract called for 5 annual payments of $3,000. Silicon could have borrowed cash at 9% to purchase the equipment. On January 1, 1993, the leased asset would be recognized by Silicon as the present value of the lease payments. The present value of an annuity of 5 periods at 9% is 3.88965 (Table 2). The present value of the lease payments would be $11,669 ($3,000 × 3.88965). The lease would affect Silicon's accounts as follows:

Assets =		Liabilities + Equity		+ Revenues − Expenses	
Equipment Under Capital Lease	11,669	Capital Lease Obligation	11,669		

The transaction is treated as though Silicon purchased the asset and borrowed money to finance the purchase.

Two transactions are necessary at the end of 1993. One of these amortizes the cost of the leased asset as though it were being depreciated. Assuming straight-line depreciation of $2,334 ($11,669/5), the amortization would affect Silicon's accounts as follows:

Assets =		Liabilities + Equity	+ Revenues − Expenses	
Accumulated Amortization	(2,334)		Amortization Expense	(2,334)

The second transaction recognizes the payment of principal and interest on the financing arrangement. Exhibit 11-6 provides a lease payment schedule.

Exhibit 11-6 Lease Payment Schedule

a	b	c	d	e	f
Period	**Lease Obligation at Beginning of Period**	**Interest Expense (b × .09)**	**Lease Payment**	**Principal Payment (d − c)**	**Lease Obligation at End of Period (b − e)**
1	$11,669	$1,050	$3,000	$1,950	$9,719
2	9,719	875	3,000	2,125	7,594
3	7,594	683	3,000	2,317	5,277
4	5,277	475	3,000	2,525	2,752
5	2,752	248	3,000	2,752	0

The lease is treated as an installment loan. A portion of each payment is treated as interest and a portion is treated as a payment of loan principal. At the end of 1993, this transaction would affect Silicon's accounts as follows:

Assets =		Liabilities + Equity		+ Revenues − Expenses	
Cash	(3,000)	Capital Lease Obligation	(1,950)	Interest Expense	(1,050)

Silicon would continue to record transactions at the end of each year. The asset would be amortized at the rate of $2,334 per year. The principal and interest for the financing arrangement would be recorded according to amounts shown in the lease payment schedule.

The net result of these transactions is the inclusion of assets and liabilities on the balance sheet for leased assets. By requiring these amounts to be reported, GAAP attempt to increase the comparability between amounts reported by different corporations. For example, assume Lease Airlines leased its aircraft, and Purchase Airlines purchased its aircraft. If capital leases were not reported on the balance sheets, Lease Airlines would have far fewer assets and liabilities than Purchase Airlines. Attempts to compare the performances of the two companies would be difficult. The return on assets of Lease, for example, would be much higher than that for Purchase if both had the same amount of net income. Reporting leased assets and obligations makes the two companies' financial statements more comparable.

Japanese companies do not include the asset or liability associated with capital leases on their balance sheets. All leases are reported as operating leases. Thus, for industries in which capital leasing is important, the airline and automobile industries for example, a Japanese company would report lower amounts of assets and liabilities than an identical U.S. company.

Construction and Capital Improvement Costs

In addition to purchasing or leasing plant assets, companies may construct their own plant assets. Assets that are under construction are reported on the balance sheet or in accompanying notes. Construction is common for utilities. For example, Commonwealth Edison reported $1,036 million of construction work-in-progress at December 31, 1991.

Objective 10
Explain accounting issues associated with construction and capital improvements.

Construction costs include materials, labor, utilities, equipment used in construction, interest, and other costs associated with the construction. These costs are capitalized (included as part of the cost of the asset that is constructed) rather than expensed. They are then depreciated over the useful life of the asset. For example, assume Silicon constructed a building in 1994. It paid $2 million for materials, $3 million for wages, and $600,000 for other miscellaneous costs associated with construction. In addition, interest associated with financing the construction was determined to be $70,000. These costs are recorded to an asset account, CONSTRUCTION WORK-IN-PROGRESS. Once the building is completed, the amount in CONSTRUCTION WORK-IN-PROGRESS is transferred to BUILDINGS. It is then treated in the same manner as the cost of any other plant asset.

Notes to the financial statements describe the amounts of capitalized interest. International Paper reported:

> Interest costs for the construction of certain long-term assets are capitalized and amortized over the related assets' estimated useful lives. The Company capitalized net interest costs of $36 million in 1991 . . . Interest payments made during 1991 . . . were $385 million . . . .

The amount of interest cost incurred during a fiscal period that is not capitalized is reported as interest expense.

Capital improvements occur when a company adds to or replaces a portion of an existing asset. If the addition or replacement increases the life or serviceability of the asset, it is capitalized. The cost of the improvement is recorded as part of the asset cost and is depreciated over its remaining life. Other repair and maintenance costs are expensed in the period in which they are incurred.

INTANGIBLE ASSETS, DEFERRED CHARGES, AND OTHER ASSETS

Objective 11
Explain accounting issues associated with intangible assets, deferred charges, and other assets.

Intangible assets include the cost of legal rights such as copyrights, patents, brand names, and trademarks owned by a company. The purchase price or legal fees associated with securing the rights are recorded as assets. These costs, then, are amortized over the life of the assets. For example, ConAgra reported intangible assets as follows for 1991, in millions:

Brands, trademarks, and goodwill, at cost less accumulated amortization of $104.8	$2,710.9

Intangible assets are normally amortized on a straight-line basis. ConAgra notes:

> Brands and goodwill arising from the excess of cost of investment over the equity in net assets at date of acquisition and trademarks are being amortized using the straight-line method, principally over a period of 40 years.

Percentage of Major Corporations Reporting Intangible Assets

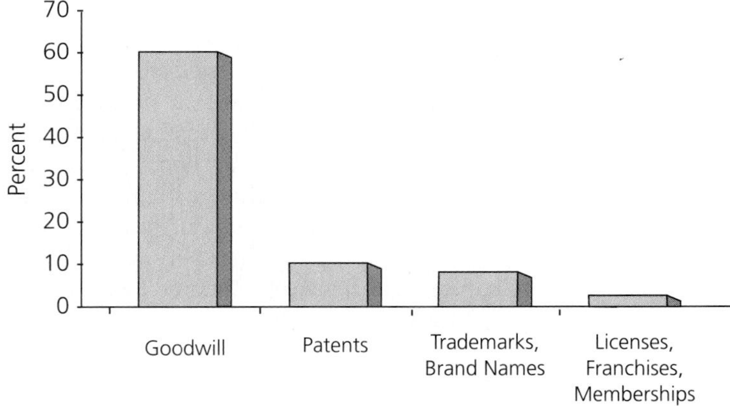

Data source: AICPA, Accounting Trends & Techniques, 1991

GAAP require intangibles to be amortized over a period of 40 years or less. A longer amortization period reduces the amount of expense recognized each year relative to a shorter period. As an example, assume Silicon purchased intangible assets for $1 million. By amortizing the assets over 40 years, it would recognize $25,000 of expense each year (as shown on the next page):

Assets =		Liabilities + Equity	+ Revenues − Expenses	
Intangible Assets	(25,000)		Amortization Expense	(25,000)

A contra-asset, ACCUMULATED AMORTIZATION, could have been used to record the reduction in the book value of intangible assets.

U.S. GAAP do not permit companies to report the estimated market value of their brands, trademarks, and other intangibles as part of their assets. They can report only the cost associated with these items as assets on their balance sheets. Brands and trademarks, however, may be among a corporation's most valuable resources. For example, the Coca-Cola brand name has been estimated to have a value of almost $25 billion.[4] Many companies would report much higher asset and stockholders' equity amounts if the market values of these assets were included. Some countries, such as Great Britain, permit corporations to report the estimated market value of these assets. Therefore, British companies may appear to have higher asset and equity values than their U.S. counterparts.

International Paper reported deferred charges and other assets of $1,020 million for 1991 (Exhibit 11-1). ***Deferred charges*** **are assets resulting when a company prepays expenses that will result in long-term benefits.** These charges typically are amortized over future periods. Start-up costs on new businesses, divisions, or projects often are capitalized and reported as deferred charges. These costs include costs incurred prior to the beginning of operation of a business venture. Typical costs are legal fees, support services, and advertising. These costs are recorded to an asset account such as ORGANIZATIONAL COSTS. International Paper reported:

> Start-up costs on major projects are capitalized and amortized over a five-year period. Unamortized start-up costs were $75 million . . . at December 31, 1991 . . . .

Other assets can include miscellaneous accounts that do not fit under other categories. **Plant assets held for disposal** is an example. If plant assets have been removed from service and a company is attempting to sell them, they are listed as other assets rather than as plant assets. Prepaid and deferred tax charges may be reported as separate items if they are material. Prepaid taxes are current assets. **Deferred tax charges** generally are long-term assets. Both accounts result from differences between financial and tax accounting procedures. These differences can result in liabilities, deferred tax obligations, as described in Chapter 9, or in assets. Chapter 13 examines tax issues in more detail.

Marketing costs sometimes are capitalized if the costs are associated with benefits a company will receive in future periods. For example, PepsiCo reported in 1991:

> Marketing costs deferred consist of media and personal service advertising prepayments, materials in inventory and production costs of future media advertising; these assets are expensed in the year used. Most marketing costs are expensed in the period in which they are incurred.

Research and development activities are important for many companies. These costs are associated with new product design and development. Though

[4] Reported in *USA Today*, August 12, 1992.

these costs are likely to benefit future periods, GAAP require these costs to be expensed in the period in which they are incurred. Uncertainty about the periods that benefit from the costs is the rationale for immediate expensing of the costs.

Prepaid pension costs also may be reported as assets. These prepayments result when the value of pension plan assets is in excess of projected benefit obligations, as described in Chapter 9.

Corporations report other types of assets. Certain assets are important to a specific industry or company. A description of the assets often is provided in notes to the financial statements.

CASH AND ACCRUAL MEASUREMENT

The statement of cash flows reports the amount of cash flow associated with investing activities. International Paper reported the following as part of its statement of cash flows for 1991:

Investment Activities (in millions)	
Invested in capital projects	(1,197)
Mergers and acquisitions	
Plants, properties, equipment and timberlands	(131)
Goodwill	(211)
Other assets and liabilities, net	(115)
Investments in affiliated companies	(258)
Other investment	(31)
Cash Used for Investment Activities	(1,943)

Objective 12
Compare cash and accrual measurement of investing activities.

The company's balance sheet (Exhibit 11-1) reported total long-term assets (total assets − total current assets) of $9,730 million at the end of 1990 and $10,810 million at the end of 1991. Most of the change in long-term assets can be explained by investing activities reported on the statement of cash flows. In addition to acquisitions, the balance of the plant asset accounts is affected by depreciation and amortization. International Papér reported $700 million of depreciation and amortization for 1991. Therefore, the change in the company's long-term assets can be explained as follows:

Beginning balance of long-term assets	$ 9,730
New investment	1,943
Depreciation and amortization	(700)
Ending balance of long-term assets	$10,973

Most of the difference between the ending balance computed ($10,973 million) and the actual amount ($10,810 million) can be explained by the transfer of certain long-term assets, especially deferred charges, to current assets.

The amount of cash received from the sale of long-term assets is reported as cash from investing activities on the statement of cash flows. Gains and losses on these sales are reported on the income statement. Depreciation and amortization expenses are noncash items. In addition, revenue recognized under the equity method, less dividends received, is a noncash item. These revenues and expenses are noncash items on the statement of cash flows. They are adjustments to net income in computing cash flow from operating activities when the indirect format is used.

For example, assume Silicon reported the following transactions for 1995, in millions:

Sale of plant assets with a book value of $22 for $16, reporting a loss of $6.
Sale of securities with a book value of $10 for $14, reporting a gain of $4.
Depreciation and amortization expense for 1995 was $8.
Recognition of investment revenue from equity investments, $5. Dividends received, $2.

If Silicon's net income for 1995 was $40 million, its statement of cash flows would report:

Operating Activities:	
Net income	$40
Adjustments for noncash items:	
Loss on sale of plant assets	6
Gain on sale of securities	(4)
Depreciation and amortization	8
Equity in earnings, less dividends	(3)
Cash flow from operating activities	$47
Investing activities:	
Sale of plant assets	$16
Sale of securities	14
Cash flow from investing activities	$30

The total amount of cash received from the sale of plant assets and securities is reported as part of investing activities. Therefore, the loss from sale of plant assets and gain on sale of securities are noncash items. The loss is added to net income, and the gain is subtracted. Noncash expenses, such as depreciation and amortization, are added to net income. Noncash revenues, such as investment revenue using the equity method, are subtracted from net income. Often these amounts, other than depreciation, are not material and are not reported as separate items on a company's statement of cash flows. Depreciation and amortization often explain the major difference between cash flow from operating activities and net income for many companies.

CONTROL OF ASSETS

Objective 13
Identify asset control procedures.

Control of assets is an important accounting issue. Accounting records should be compared with results of physical inspections of assets on a regular basis. Accounting records identify the amount of cash, securities, inventories, and plant assets a company should have available. The records provide a basis for determining whether assets are missing and for determining who is responsible for the assets. Internal controls in the accounting system are designed to ensure the proper recording of these assets. Chapter 4 described some of these controls.

Physical controls are necessary to protect the assets from theft, misuse, and deterioration. Failure to protect assets can result in misstated account balances because recorded assets do not exist.

Control procedures involve independent verification of assets, security over access to assets, and inspection of assets. Cash and securities are especially vulnerable because they are easily concealed and are readily transferable. Safes, vaults, and banks are used to protect these assets. Many securities are registered in the name of the owner, thereby controlling the transfer of the assets. Surprise audits of cash and securities are used to verify their existence. Retail companies often maintain large amounts of cash. Cash is obtained from the sale of merchandise and is needed to make change for customers. Cash registers are used to protect this cash. Sales receipts or cash register tapes provide independent verification of the amount of cash reported by sales clerks. Surprise cash counts can reveal whether employees are using cash for personal benefit, for example, for unreported short-term loans to themselves.

Accounting records identify the amount of cash and securities deposited in bank accounts or invested with brokerage firms and other financial institutions. These institutions provide monthly or quarterly statements of account balances and transactions for the period. Reconciliation of these statements with the company's accounting records verifies the accuracy of the records.

Physical assets, such as inventories and plant assets, should be secured. Storerooms, warehouses, and other facilities protect these assets. Access is permitted only to authorized personnel. Periodic counts verify the accuracy of accounting records. Proper hiring and training procedures can help with asset security. Retail stores often use magnetic tags to prevent shoplifting. More expensive products are kept in locked cases. Display items may be secured so they cannot be removed.

Tools and equipment are the responsibility of specific employees. These employees may be personally liable for loss of tools or equipment. Cars, trucks, and other vehicles are assigned to individuals who are responsible for their use and protection. Major assets may be insured for fire or theft. Guards and surveillance equipment are used to protect inventories and plant assets.

Control is a major management activity in most organizations. Control involves a combination of accounting and other procedures.

SELF-STUDY PROBLEM 11-3

Wal-Mart Stores, Inc., reported the following information in its 1991 annual report (in millions):

	1991	**1990**
Property, plant and equipment, at cost	$4,698	$3,190
Accumulated depreciation	974	712
Property under capital leases	1,298	1,212
Accumulated amortization	311	260
Net income	1,291	
Depreciation and amortization expense	347	
Loss from sale of assets	3	
Net cash used for plant assets	1,526	

Required

(a) Identify the transactions that explain most of the increase in Wal-Mart's net plant assets (plant assets and capital leases net of accumulated depreciation and amortization) for 1991. (b) How would depreciation and amortization and the loss from sale of plant assets affect Wal-Mart's computation of cash flow from operating activities in 1991? The indirect format of the statement of cash flows was used.

The solution to Self-Study Problem 11-3 appears at the end of the chapter.

REVIEW *Summary of Important Concepts*

1. Investments in cash and securities:
   - A. Investing activities provide resources an organization needs to operate. These resources are reported primarily as assets.
   - B. Cash and equivalants include bank accounts, currency, checks, some short-term investments, and other ready sources of money.
   - C. Marketable securities may be either current or long-term depending on management's intention to sell them during the coming fiscal period.
   - D. Marketable equity securities are reported on the balance sheet at the lower of cost or market. Losses on these investments are recognized in the period in which a decline in market value occurs. These losses are recognized on the income statement for short-term investments and on the balance sheet for long-term investments.
   - E. Corporations report long-term investments in equity securities that represent 20% to 50% of the common stock of another company using the equity method. The owned company's net income is reported as investment revenue by the investor in proportion to the percentage of common stock owned.
   - F. Companies controlled by an investor corporation are reported as consolidated subsidiaries. A parent and its subsidiaries are reported as though they were one entity in the parent's consolidated financial statements.
   - G. Mergers and acquisitions occur when one company obtains a controlling interest in the common stock of another corporation. Mergers and acquisitions are accounted for by the purchase or pooling of interests method.
   - H. Investments in debt securities are recorded at cost. A premium or discount on the securities is amortized over the life of the securities.
2. Investments in plant assets, intangibles, and other assets:
   - A. Plant assets are reported on the balance sheet at cost less accumulated depreciation.
   - B. Several methods of depreciation are used, including: straight-line, declining balance, sum-of-the-years'-digits, and units-of-production. Most corporations use straight-line depreciation for financial statement purposes. Accelerated methods often are used for tax purposes.
   - C. Depletion allocates the cost of natural resources to expense as the assets are consumed.
   - D. Operating leases are expensed during the period leased assets are used. The present values of future payments for capital leases are recorded as assets and liabilities.
   - E. Construction costs, including interest, are capitalized and then depreciated.
3. Cash flow and accrual measures in investing activities:
   - A. The statement of cash flows reports cash flows associated with investing activities. Cash flow and accrual measures of asset transactions often differ.

4. Control concerns:
   A. Control of assets is important to ensure the accuracy of accounting information.

DEFINE *Terms and Concepts Defined in this Chapter*

accelerated depreciation
acquisition
capital lease
declining balance depreciation
deferred charges
depletion
equity method
goodwill
lower of cost or market method
merger
minority interest
operating lease
straight-line depreciation
sum-of-the-years'-digits depreciation
units-of-production depreciation

SOLUTIONS

SELF-STUDY PROBLEM 11-1

a. Adam Company would use the equity method for its investment because it owns 20 to 50% of Smith Company's stock. Adam is assumed to have significant influence over Smith. Adam would recognize 35% ($1.75 million) of Smith's income as investment revenue for 1995. The dividends received from Smith ($700,000) would reduce Adam's investment account. After these transactions have been recorded, the book value of Adam's investment in Smith would be $21.05 million ($20 + $1.75 − $.7).
b. Adam Company would record the merger as a pooling of interests, assuming all conditions for a pooling were met. Smith's account balances would be combined with those of Adam's at their book value. The stock issued by Adam would be recorded at the book value of Smith's stockholders' equity. Consolidated statements would not be necessary because only one legal entity existed after the merger. Smith would have had no net income and would have paid no dividends for 1995 because it ceased to exist as a separate legal entity at the time of the merger.
c. Adam Company would use the lower of cost or market method for its investment since its ownership is less than 20%. The purchase would be recorded at cost. Smith's net income would have no effect on Adam's investment. Dividends received from Adam would be recorded as investment revenue. The investment would be reported by Adam at its market value of $7 million on June 30, 1995, because market value was below cost. The decline in value of $1 million would be subtracted from the stockholders' equity on Adam's balance sheet because the investment was long-term.
d. Adam Company would record the investment at cost since this acquisition is a purchase of greater than 50% interest. Adjustments would be made to Adam's investment account for Smith's net income and dividends in the same manner as under the equity method. 95% of Smith's net income would be added to the investment account, and 95% of Smith's dividends would be subtracted. The investment account would not appear on Adam's consolidated financial statements, however. The statements would report the consolidated results of the two companies as though they were one company. Smith's assets and liabilities would be included on the consolidated balance sheet at their estimated fair market values. Any excess of cost over the fair market value of identifiable net assets would be reported as goodwill.

SELF-STUDY PROBLEM 11-2

Computation of depreciation for 1996 would be:

Straight-line	\$ 50,000 = \$400,000/8 years
Double-declining balance	\$100,000 = \$400,000 × 2/8
Sum-of-the-years'-digits	\$ 88,889 = \$400,000 × 8/36

Depreciation under each method would reduce net income, after taxes, as follows:

Straight-line	\$35,000 = \$50,000 × (1.0 − .3)
Double-declining balance	\$70,000 = \$100,000 × (1.0 − .3)
Sum-of-the-years'-digits	\$62,222 = \$88,889 × (1.0 − .3)

Use of the straight-line method would produce the highest net income. The choice of method for calculating depreciation on the income statement has no effect on Banana Boats' method for tax calculation. Therefore, it does not affect the company's cash flows. Note that, other than reducing taxes, depreciation does not affect cash flows.

SELF-STUDY PROBLEM 11-3

a.

	1991	**1990**
Property, plant and equipment, at cost	\$4,698	\$3,190
Accumulated depreciation	(974)	(712)
Property under capital leases	1,298	1,212
Accumulated amortization	(311)	(260)
Net plant assets	\$4,711	\$3,430
Net increase in plant assets (\$4,711 − \$3,430)	**\$1,281**	
Net cash used for plant assets	\$1,526	
Depreciation and amortization expense	(347)	
Net increase in plant assets explained	**\$1,179**	

Of the net increase in actual plant assets of \$1,281 million, \$1,179 million can be explained by net purchases of plant assets and depreciation and amortization expense.

b. Depreciation and amortization and the loss from sale of assets would be added to net income in computing cash flow from operating activities:

Net income	\$1,291
Depreciation and amortization expense	347
Loss from sale of assets	3
Effect of adjustments to net income on cash flow from operating activities	\$1,641

Depreciation and amortization expense and the loss from sale of assets are noncash items that were deducted in computing net income. Therefore, they should be added to net income to compute cash flow from operating activities.

EXERCISES

11-1. Write a short definition for each of the terms listed in the *Terms and Concepts Defined in this Chapter* section.

11-2. Archer Company produces sporting goods equipment. Identify and describe briefly the types of assets Archer is likely to include in its accounting system.

11-3. At the end of its 1994 fiscal year, Hamlet Company owned the following investments:

a. $100,000 of bonds of major corporations with maturities of 5 years or more.
b. $160,000 of common stock of major corporations.
c. $75,000 of commercial paper issued by major corporations, with maturities of 6 months or less.
d. $50,000 of bonds that are not readily marketable with maturities of 2 years.
e. $40,000 of bonds of major corporations with maturities of 12 months or less.

Determine the amount Hamlet would report as current assets, assuming management plans to sell the bonds and common stock during the next fiscal year. Explain your answer.

11-4. The Ophelia Company owned the following investments at the end of its 1995 fiscal year:

a. 10,000 shares of the common stock of Claudius Company. Claudius had 1 million shares outstanding.
b. 2 million shares of the common stock of Polonius Company. Polonius had 3 million shares outstanding.
c. 300,000 shares of the common stock of Gertrude Company. Gertrude had 1 million shares outstanding.
d. 400,000 shares of the preferred stock of Fortinbras Company. Fortinbras had 500,000 shares of preferred outstanding.

Assume each of these investments is properly accounted for as a long-term investment. How would Ophelia account for each type of investment? Explain the purpose of each accounting rule used by Ophelia to account for its investments.

11-5. Macintyre Company recorded the following transactions during its 1993 fiscal year:

a. Purchased 5% of the outstanding shares of Duncan Company for $300,000, plus brokerage fees of $30,000.
b. Purchased 2% of the outstanding shares of Macduff Company for $400,000, plus brokerage fees of $40,000.
c. Received $50,000 of dividends from Duncan Company.

At the end of 1993, the Duncan shares had a market value of $350,000. The Macduff shares had a market value of $360,000. Macintyre owned no other investments in common stock. The transactions were properly recorded as short-term investments. Use the following format to identify the effect of each event on Macintyre's account balances:

Assets =	Liabilities + Equity	+ Revenues – Expenses

11-6. Isabella Company recorded the following transactions during its 1993 fiscal year:

a. Purchased 5% of the outstanding shares of Othello Company for $300,000, plus brokerage fees of $30,000.

b. Purchased 2% of the outstanding shares of Ferdinand Company for $400,000, plus brokerage fees of $40,000.

c. Received $50,000 of dividends from Othello Company.

At the end of 1993, the Othello shares had a market value of $350,000. The Ferdinand shares had a market value of $360,000. Isabella owned no other investments in common stock. The transactions were properly recorded as long-term investments. Use the following format to identify the effect of each event on Isabella's account balances:

Assets =	Liabilities + Equity	+ Revenues − Expenses

11-7. In 1991, Chandler Company acquired 40% of Pertel Company for $30 million. Pertel's net income and dividend payments since the purchase are shown below:

Year	Net Income	Dividends
1991	$8,000,000	$3,000,000
1992	7,400,000	2,500,000
1993	8,100,000	3,000,000
1994	8,500,000	3,200,000

At the beginning of its 1995 fiscal year, Chandler sold its investment in Pertel for $42 million. Determine the amount Chandler reported on its balance sheet for its investment in Pertel in 1991 through 1994. How much profit (or loss) did Chandler record from its sale of Pertel in 1995?

11-8. Daedulus Company purchased 100% of Icarus Company common stock on June 1, 1994, for $200 million in cash. At the time of the purchase, the fair market value of Icarus's assets was $350 million. The fair market value of its liabilities was $180 million. The transaction was accounted for as a merger using the purchase method. Use the following format to indicate the effect the transaction would have had on Daedulus's accounts:

Assets =	Liabilities + Equity	+ Revenues − Expenses

Explain the meaning of goodwill and how it affects a company's financial reports.

11-9. Castor Company acquired 100% of Pollux Company's common stock during 1994. At the end of the 1994 fiscal year, Pollux's assets had a book value of $80 million and a market value of $93 million. Its liabilities had a book value of $30 million and a market value of $32 million. Castor's assets had a book value of $310 million and a market value of $340 million. Its liabilities had a book value of $130 million and a market value of $140 million. There were no other intercompany transactions during 1994. If Castor exchanged 7 million shares of its common stock for all of Pollux's common stock in a pooling of interests, what amount would it report on its consolidated balance sheet at the end of 1994 for total assets, total liabilities, and total stockholders' equity? Pollux's common stock was selling at $10 per share at the time of the acquisition.

11-10. Pinkerton Company sold merchandise to Aristotle Company on November 1, 1993, at a price of $50,000. The merchandise cost Pinkerton $36,000. Aristotle signed a note to pay Pinkerton the sales price plus interest at an annual rate of 12%. Pinkerton's fiscal year ends December 31. Aristotle paid the note plus interest on April 30, 1994. Use the following format to indicate the effect the transactions related to the sale would have on Pinkerton's accounts.

Assets =	Liabilities + Equity	+ Revenues − Expenses

11-11. Troilus Company purchased $400,000 of Mertle Co. long-term bonds on May 1, 1994, at maturity value plus accrued interest since January 1. Interest at an 8% annual rate was received in semiannual payments on July 1, 1994, and January 1, 1995. Troilus's fiscal year ends December 31. The bonds were sold on March 1, 1995, for $430,000, including accrued interest. Use the following format to indicate the effect the transactions related to the bonds would have on Troilus's accounts:

Assets =	Liabilities + Equity	+ Revenues − Expenses

11-12. Cressida Company purchased delivery equipment on April 1, 1994, at a cost of $200,000. The equipment is expected to have a useful life of 7 years and no salvage value. How much depreciation expense would Cressida record in 1994 using the straight-line, double-declining balance, and sum-of-the-years'-digits methods? The company's fiscal year end is December 31. If the units-of-production method were used, how much depreciation would Cressida record? Assume the equipment is expected to be used for 250,000 miles. During 1994, the equipment was used for 60,000 miles.

11-13. Litten Company purchased a building on March 1, 1980, at a cost of $4 million. For financial reporting purposes, the building was depreciated on a straight-line basis over 372 months at $10,000 per month. The building was sold on October 31, 1994, for $7.2 million. How much gain or loss did Litten record on the sale of the building? Accelerated depreciation was used to record depreciation for tax purposes. As of October 31, 1994, the company had recorded $2.7 million of depreciation on an accelerated basis. How much gain or loss did Litten record on the sale of the building for tax purposes? Why would the company use straight-line depreciation for financial reporting purposes and accelerated depreciation for tax purposes?

11-14. Palamon Company owns rights to coal reserves in several states. The rights cost the company $140 million. The reserves are expected to produce 50 billion tons of coal. During the company's 1995 fiscal year, 5 billion tons of coal were mined from the reserves. Prior to 1995, 30 billion tons of coal had been mined. How much depletion expense would Palamon record in 1995? At what amount would the company report the coal reserves on its balance sheet at the end of 1995? What effect would the depletion expense have on the company's cash flows in 1995?

11-15. Lance Company leased equipment at the beginning of its 1995 fiscal year. The leases call for payments of $100,000 at the end of each year for 5 years. Lance could borrow to purchase the assets at an annual rate of 11%. What amount would the company report as an asset at the end of 1995 for the lease if it were accounted for as a capital lease? Assume straight-line amortization. What amount would the company report as a liability at the end of 1995 if the lease were accounted for as a capital lease? How much expense would Lance report for the lease if it were accounted for as a capital lease? What effect would the lease have on Lance's financial statements and related notes if the lease were accounted for as an operating lease? Why might Lance prefer to report the lease as an operating rather than capital lease?

11-16. Franchesca Company recorded the following transactions during its 1996 fiscal year:

a. Construction costs associated with facilities currently in progress:

Labor	$350,000
Materials	675,000
Utilities	87,000
Tools and special equipment	22,000
Interest on construction loan	94,000

b. The cost of an addition to an existing building was $840,000.

c. The cost of repairs to equipment was $90,000. These repairs are required on a regular basis and do not affect the estimated useful life of the equipment.

How would each of these transactions affect Franchesca's financial statements for 1996? Assume cash had been paid for all costs by the end of the fiscal year.

11-17. The Nestlé Company reported total fixed assets of 17,116 million Swiss francs for the fiscal year ended December 31, 1990. Of this amount, 14,867 million were tangible fixed assets; 1,641 million were investments, and 608 million were other assets, primarily loans to other companies. Notes to the statements disclosed the following:

> Tangible fixed assets are shown in the balance sheet at their net replacement values arrived at as follows:
>
> Land: market value prudently estimated.
>
> Other tangible fixed assets: replacement new value (the amount which theoretically would have to be invested in order to replace an asset by a similar new asset duly installed and rendering the same service) less the accumulated depreciation calculated on this value.
>
> These amounts are recalculated each year.
>
> Depreciation is provided on the straight-line method so as to amortise fully the replacement new values of tangible fixed assets over their estimated useful lives, ...
>
> Goodwill arising on consolidation, which represents the excess of the purchase cost over the fair value of the net tangible assets acquired, is written off against reserves in the year acquired.

The reported book value of tangible fixed assets on a historical cost basis was 10,616 million Swiss francs. Reserves are a portion of stockholders' equity, similar to paid-in capital in excess of par. What major differences exist in the reporting of these long-term assets by Nestlé and the way they would be reported by a U.S. company? What effect do these differences have on the financial statements of Nestlé relative to a U.S. company?

11-18. Companies sometimes sell fixed assets to other companies or to investors and then lease the assets back. For example, General Motors raised about $650 million by selling machines at GM's Saturn plant and other similar assets to investors. GM leased the assets back and paid investors over a period of 18 years for these arrangements at an effective interest rate of about 9%. Investors who purchased the assets were able to depreciate them for tax purposes. During 1991, GM lost over $4.7 billion from its operating activities. Therefore, the depreciation was of no immediate value to GM because it paid no taxes on its operations. What advantages were available to GM from this arrangement? What effect would you expect this arrangement to have on GM's cash flows, income, and balance sheet in 1991? Why?

11-19. At the beginning of its 1993 fiscal year, Madrian Corporation owned 47% of Juvenal Company's common stock. Though it has been profitable, Juvenal has had some financial problems in recent years and is highly levered. During 1993, Madrian acquired Homer Company. Among Homer's investments was an investment in 5% of Juvenal Company's common stock. Before the end of its 1993 fiscal year, Madrian sold a portion of its investment in Juvenal to reduce its total ownership to 50%. What effect did the sale have on Madrian's financial statements for 1993? Why might Madrian prefer one alternative for accounting for its investment in Juvenal to another?

11-20. Why is accounting information useful as a means of controlling assets and ensuring their security?

PROBLEMS

PROBLEM 11-1 Reporting Investments

During its 1994 fiscal year, Portia Company purchased 10% of the common stock of Leonardo Company for $3,470,000, including fees. Also, it purchased 5% of the common stock of Shylock Company for $2,690,000, including fees. During 1994, Portia received $500,000 of dividends from Leonardo. At the end of the fiscal year, the investment in Leonardo had a market value of $3,100,000. The investment in Shylock had a market value of $2,800,000. Portia owned no other stock investments during 1994. During its 1995 fiscal year, Portia sold the Shylock investment for $2,900,000. The company purchased a 3% investment in Balthasar Company for $1,930,000, including fees. During 1995, Portia received $500,000 of dividends from Leonardo. At the end of 1995, the Leonardo investment had a market value of $3,350,000 and the Balthasar investment had a market value of $1,940,000. Portia owned no other stock investments during 1995. All of Portia's investments were properly accounted for as long-term investments.

Required (a) Prepare a schedule calculating the amount Portia would report for long-term investments on its balance sheet at the end of 1994 and 1995. (b) Prepare a schedule calculating the effect of Portia's investment activities on its income for 1994 and 1995.

PROBLEM 11-2 Accounting for Investments

At the end of its 1995 fiscal year, Seuss Company owned the following investments:

a. 2% of Hermia Company stock, purchased at a cost of $375,000.
b. 1% of Lysander Company stock, purchased at a cost of $250,000.
c. 35% of Demetri Company stock, purchased at a cost of $42 million.
d. 10% of Paxton Company stock, purchased at a cost of $5,380,000.

Seuss' management expects to sell its investment in Hermia and Lysander during the 1996 fiscal year. It does not expect to sell its investments in Demetri or Paxton during the 1996 fiscal year. The market value of each investment at the end of the 1995 fiscal year was:

Hermia	$ 390,000
Lysander	240,000
Demetri	44,300,000
Paxton	5,200,000

During 1995, Seuss received $70,000 of dividends from Hermia and $1,800,000 of dividends from Demetri. Demetri Company reported net income of $6 million in 1995. Paxton Company reported net income of $4.8 million. Seuss Company owned no other stock investments during 1995.

Required Prepare a schedule to determine the amount Seuss would report on its balance sheet for investments at the end of 1995.

PROBLEM 11-3 Reporting Consolidations

Penelope Corporation owns 100% of Syrius Corporation's common stock at the end of 1995. Penelope paid $150 million for Syrius' stock at the beginning of the year. A part of Penelope's assets and Syrius' liabilities is a loan from Penelope to Syrius for $20 million. In addition, Syrius sold goods priced at $8 million to Penelope during 1995. Syrius' cost for these goods was $5 million. Syrius earned net income of $30 million in 1995 and paid no dividends.

Required

(a) Use the following format to describe the effect of the investment transaction on Penelope's account balances:

Assets =	Liabilities + Equity	+ Revenues − Expenses

(b) Compute the balance of Penelope's investment in Syrius at the end of 1995 (use the equity method).

(c) Complete the following table to compute the amounts that would be reported on Penelope's consolidated balance sheet and income statement for 1995.

(in millions)	Penelope Corporation	Syrius Corporation	Adjustments	Penelope Corporation Consolidated Statements
Total assets	$570	$230		
Total liabilities	234	50		
Stockholders' Equity—Syrius		180		
Stockholders' Equity—Penelope	336			
Liabilities and Stockholders' Equity	$570	$230		
Revenues	$660	$170		
Expenses	(540)	(140)		
Net income	$120	$30		

PROBLEM 11-4 Accounting for Investments in Bonds

Pirrus Company purchased 100 Achiles Company bonds on April 1, 1995. The bonds pay interest semiannually on March 31 and September 30 at an annual coupon rate of 10%. The bonds sold at an effective yield of 8%. The effect of brokerage fees are included in computing the effective yield. The bonds mature on March 31, 1997, at a value of $1,000 per bond. Pirrus's fiscal year ends on September 31.

Required (a) Compute the price Pirrus paid for Achilles' bonds. (b) Prepare an amortization schedule for Pirrus's investment. (c) Use the following format to indicate the effect transactions associated with the bonds would have on Pirrus's accounts in 1995, 1996, and 1997:

Assets =	Liabilities + Equity	+ Revenues − Expenses

PROBLEM 11-5 Comparing Depreciation Methods

The Chaucer Company purchased equipment with an expected useful life of 4 years. The equipment was purchased on January 1, 1992, for $125,000. It is expected to have a salvage value of $5,000 at the end of 4 years.

Required (a) Prepare a depreciation schedule for the asset showing the book value and depreciation expense on the asset each year using the straight-line, double-declining balance, and sum-of-the-years'-digits methods. (b) Which method would you prefer to use for financial reporting purposes if you were manager of Chaucer Company? Which method would you prefer for tax purposes? Explain. (c) Which method has the greatest effect on cash flow each year? Why?

PROBLEM 11-6 Accounting for Capital Leases

Bath Company signed a lease contract for equipment on January 1, 1993. The contract called for 7 year-end payments of $8,000. Bath could have borrowed to purchase the equipment at 10%.

Required (a) Prepare a lease payment schedule for the asset. (b) Use the following format to identify the effect of the capital lease on Bath's accounts at the time of the contract and at the end of Bath's fiscal year on December 31, 1993. Assume the lease is amortized on a straight-line basis.

Assets =	Liabilities + Equity	+ Revenues − Expenses

(c) How much would Bath report on its balance sheet for 1993 as a capital lease asset and as a capital lease obligation?

PROBLEM 11-7 Analyzing Long-Term Assets

American Home Products reported the following information in its 1991 annual report:

(in thousands)	1991	1990
Balance Sheet:		
Property, plant, and equipment	$2,659,232	$2,532,822
Less accumulated depreciation	1,182,391	1,095,432
Property, plant, and equipment, net	1,476,841	1,437,390
Goodwill	254,551	283,214
Statement of Cash Flows:		
Depreciation and amortization expense	167,166	179,761
Purchase of property, plant, and equipment	(227,911)	(247,693)
Proceeds from sale of assets	30,947	22,005

The company also reported:

> *Property, Plant, and Equipment* is carried at cost. Depreciation is provided over the estimated useful lives of the related assets, principally on the straight-line method.
>
> *Goodwill* is being amortized on the straight-line method over periods not exceeding 40 years. Accumulated amortization was $367,945,000 and $360,314,000 at December 31, 1991 and 1990, respectively.

Required Answer each of the following questions, assuming no other major transactions occurred that affected the company's long-term assets during 1991:

a. Approximately how much amortization expense did American Home Products record in 1991?
b. Approximately how much depreciation expense did the company record in 1991? What is the approximate average useful life of the company's plant assets?
c. What was the net increase in the company's plant assets during 1991? What events account for this increase?
d. Was the net effect of the company's long-term asset transactions on its net income for 1991 greater or less than the effect of these transactions on its cash flows? Explain.

PROBLEM 11-8 Explaining Asset Changes

Intel Corporation reported the following information on its 1991 balance sheet:

(in thousands)	1991	1990
Short-term investments (at cost, which approximates market)	**$ 757,602**	**$ 165,239**
Property, plant and equipment:		
Land and buildings	1,097,526	961,368
Machinery and equipment	2,288,200	1,764,623
Construction in progress	258,430	87,614
	3,644,156	2,813,605
Less accumulated depreciation	1,481,433	1,156,037
Property, plant and equipment, net	**2,162,723**	**1,657,568**
Long-term investments (at cost, which approximates market)	**479,752**	**561,477**

In addition, Intel reported the following information on its statement of cash flows for 1991:

(in thousands)	1991
Cash flows provided by (used for) operating activities:	
Net income	$ 818,629
Adjustments to reconcile net income to net cash provided by Operating activities:	
Depreciation	418,252
Net loss on retirements of plant assets	24,882
(other items omitted)	
Net cash provided by operating activities	**1,349,497**

(in thousands)	**1991**
Cash flows provided by (used for) investing activities:	
Additions to plant assets	(948,289)
Sales and maturities of investments	36,756
Additions to investments	(547,394)
Net cash used for investing activities	**(1,458,927)**
Net cash provided by financing activities	**8,829**

Required Answer each of the following questions:

a. What was the primary source used by Intel to finance its investment activities in 1991?
b. Assume all major transactions affecting plant assets and investments are summarized in the information provided above. Prepare a schedule to explain the change in Intel's plant assets during 1991. Begin with the balance of property, plant and equipment, net of depreciation, at the beginning of 1991.
c. Prepare a schedule to explain the change in Intel's investments during 1991.
d. Did Intel's plant assets increase or decrease during 1991? To what extent does your answer depend on whether the change in plant assets is measured in terms of nominal dollar values, real dollar values, or economic benefits to the company (such as value of goods produced using the plant assets) of plant assets acquired and disposed of during the year.

PROBLEM 11-9 Ethical Issues in Financial Reporting

More Money is a medium-sized bank. The bank's stock is owned primarily by residents in the city where the bank operates. During the 1980's the bank lent money for numerous real estate developments. Much of the loans were used to construct office space by developers who expected to repay the loans from office rent. Aggressive lending and building practices resulted in over-building. A downturn in the local economy drastically reduced demand for office space. As a result, many of the buildings were largely empty in 1992. Rent from the facilities was insufficient to pay interest on several of the bank's larger loans. More Money permitted several borrowers to restructure their loans, providing a longer period of repayment and lower interest rates. The market value of the property has decreased approximately 40% since its construction. The bank's 1992 balance sheet reported loans in the bank's long-term investment portfolio of $43 million. This amount was net of a loan loss reserve of $5 million. The bank also included $18 million of property, resulting from foreclosures the bank had made on several loans, among its assets. The property is valued at the present value of the loan payments, including interest the bank expected from the original borrowers. More Money is collecting rent from tenants and expects to sell the property when real estate values return to higher levels. The bank's total assets were $80 million and total stockholders' equity was $10 million. Its reported profits for 1992 were $6 million. The bank's auditors have questioned its management about its loans and property values. They believe that the current market value of the loan portfolio is about $35 million. They are less sure about the value of the property. The bank's managers have argued that the current market value of the loans is not relevant because they do not expect to sell the loans. Instead, they expect to hold the loans until they mature. Also, they do not plan to sell the property until they can recover the amount More Money invested.

Required At what amount should More Money's loan portfolio be valued? Why? Do you see any ethical problems with the way the bank's managers want to report its assets? What problems may arise for the bank if it reports its loans at their current market value?

PROBLEM 11-10 Exchange of Assets

Garvin Company purchased manufacturing equipment in July 1990 for $1,600,000. The equipment was depreciated over an expected useful life of 5 years using the straight-line method. The equipment was assumed to have a residual value of $100,000. In July 1994, Garvin traded the equipment in on new equipment of the same type. The new equipment sold for $1,850,000. The seller allowed Garvin a discount of $75,000 for the old equipment. Garvin paid cash for the old and new equipment.

Required Answer each of the following questions:

a. Prepare a schedule to determine the gain or loss Garvin should recognize for trading in the old equipment for new equipment.
b. Use the following format to describe the effect of the trade-in on Garvin's accounts:

Assets =	Liabilities + Equity	+ Revenues − Expenses

c. Calculate the net effect all transactions associated with the old equipment had on Garvin's pretax income from 1990 through 1994. Also, calculate the net effect all transactions associated with the equipment had on cash flows for this period. Explain the relationship between the effect on pretax income and the effect on cash flows.

PROBLEM 11-11 Comparing Depreciation Methods

Tax rules permit some assets to be depreciated using an accelerated method during the early years of an asset's life. Once the asset reaches the age that straight-line depreciation produces more favorable tax results, the remaining book value of the asset can be depreciated on a straight-line basis. The Pandora Company purchased equipment on March 1, 1993, at a cost of $1,800,000. The equipment was depreciated for a full year in 1993. It was expected to have a useful life of 6 years. Tax rules permit the use of the double-declining balance method reverting to the straight-line method when it becomes advantageous to the company.

Required Determine the amount of depreciation Pandora should take on the asset each year of its six-year life for tax purposes. Assuming a tax rate of 34%, how much would the company save each year in taxes compared to using the straight-line method over the entire life of the asset?

PROBLEM 11-12 Multiple-Choice Overview of the Chapter

1. Short-term investments in marketable equity securities should be accounted for by a company using the:
   a. equity method
   b. consolidation method
   c. amortized cost method
   d. lower of cost or market method
2. If the market value of a company's portfolio of long-term equity securities is greater than the cost of the portfolio at the end of a fiscal year, the company should report:

a. a loss on its income statement
b. an adjustment to its stockholders' equity
c. its investments at cost
d. its investments at market value

3. Dividends received from investments accounted for using the equity method should be recorded by the investor as:
   a. an increase in investment revenue
   b. an increase in stockholders' equity
   c. a decrease in long-term investments
   d. an increase in long-term investments
4. Long-term investments in the common stock of another company normally should be accounted for as a consolidated subsidiary if the investor owns an interest of:
   a. more than 50%
   b. not less than 90%
   c. not less than 20%
   d. not more than 50%
5. The excess of cost over the market value of identifiable net assets acquired in a purchase of another company should be reported as:
   a. a fixed asset
   b. an intangible asset
   c. an expense of the period in which the acquisition occurs
   d. a revenue of the period in which the acquisition occurs
6. When a company purchases bonds at a premium, amortization of the premium:
   a. increases interest revenue recorded over the life of the bonds
   b. decreases interest revenue recorded over the life of the bonds
   c. increases the book value of the investment over the life of the bonds
   d. is not recorded until the bonds are sold or mature
7. Horner Company recorded $20,000 of depreciation on assets acquired at the beginning of 1994. The assets cost $50,000 and had an estimated useful life of 5 years. The method Horner used for depreciating the assets was the:
   a. straight-line method
   b. cost recovery method
   c. sum-of-the-years'-digits method
   d. double-declining balance method
8. Avery Company traded a truck for a new truck in 1995. At the time of the trade, the old truck had a book value of $10,000. The price of the new truck was $55,000. The dealer allowed Avery $6,000 for the old truck. As a result of this transaction, Avery should record:
   a. a loss of $4,000
   b. a gain of $4,000
   c. a loss of $10,000
   d. a gain of $10,000
9. Costs a business incurs prior to beginning operations normally are accounted for as:
   a. expenses of the period in which they are incurred
   b. expenses of the first year of operations
   c. deferred charges to be amortized over several years after operations begin
   d. reductions in revenues over the first five years of operations
10. The excess of capital expenditures over depreciation expense for a fiscal year:
    a. increases the book value of plant assets during the period
    b. decreases the book value of plant assets during the period
    c. decreases accumulated depreciation during the period
    d. decreases total assets during the period

CASES

CASE 11-1 Comparison of Purchase and Leasing of Plant Assets

The Wakefield Company plans to acquire new equipment costing $2 million on January 1, 1994, the beginning of the company's fiscal year. Wakefield can either borrow $2 million from a bank at 10% interest or lease the equipment. A lease would be accounted for as a capital lease. The equipment is expected to have a useful life of 4 years, which would be the lease period. It would have no residual value at the end of that period. Wakefield normally uses the straight-line method to depreciate its equipment. Lease payments would be $635,000 per year for the 4-year lease. If money is borrowed from a bank, one-fourth of the principal, plus interest, would be repaid each year.

Required As a manager with the company, you have been asked to evaluate the alternatives and to recommend the best choice for acquiring the equipment. Determine the effect of (a) purchasing and (b) leasing the equipment on Wakefield's balance sheet, income statement, and statement of cash flows over the 4-year period. Evaluate the alternatives and make a recommendation.

CASE 11-2 Analysis of Investing Activities

Appendix B of this book contains a copy of the 1992 annual report of General Mills, Inc.

Required Review the annual report and write a short report in which you identify each of the following:

a. Identify the accounting methods used by the company for cash and equivalents, plant assets, intangible assets, and research and development costs.
b. Identify the cost of each of the company's types of plant assets and the total amount of accumulated depreciation on these assets at the end of 1992.
c. Explain the change in the company's plant asset and other long-term asset accounts in 1992 by an analysis of its investment activities and depreciation and amortization reported for 1992.

PROJECTS

PROJECT 11-1 Comparing Types of Assets

Obtain the most recent annual report available for each of three corporations from your library. Look for companies in different industries, identifying the primary types of assets of each company. In particular, determine the relative proportion of current, long-term investment, plant, intangible assets, and other assets for each company. Provide a graph or diagram to illustrate the comparisons. Write a brief analysis of differences in assets. What explanations can you provide for why the assets are different or are similar?

PROJECT 11-2 Comparing Accounting Methods

Examine the annual reports of five companies. Identify the accounting methods used by each to account for investments in securities, plant assets, and intangible assets. Write a short report identifying and comparing the methods. What effects are the methods likely to have on the company's financial statements?

PROJECT 11-3 Evaluating Mergers and Acquisitions

Use *The Wall Street Journal Index* or a business periodical index to identify a recent acquisition or merger involving a major company. Use the company's annual report or financial information from *Moody's* manuals or another source to determine the effects of the merger on the company's financial statements. Compare the company's statements in the year before to the year after the acquisition or merger. Determine which method was used to account for the merger. Write a short report describing the method and the effect it had on major items in the company's financial statements, such as total assets, long-term debt, stockholders' equity, net income, interest expense, and cash flow from operating activities.

PROJECT 11-4 Evaluating Capital Leases

Identify a recent article in *The Wall Street Journal* or in a business periodical describing the use of capital leases by a company. Make a copy of the article. Write a memo to your instructor identifying the event and the reasons cited in the article for the company using the leases. Attach the copy of the article to the memo.

PROJECT 11-5 Evaluating Asset Control

Identify a recent article in *The Wall Street Journal* or in a business periodical describing a company that has reported an asset control problem. These problems usually involve the discovery of employee or management fraud. Make a copy of the article. Write a memo to your instructor identifying the event and the reasons it occurred. Attach the copy of the article to the memo.

CHAPTER 12

ANALYSIS OF INVESTING ACTIVITIES

CHAPTER
Overview

Investment decisions involve choices managers make in acquiring resources. Managers decide which resources to acquire, how to acquire them, and when to replace them. Managers use financial statement information in making their decisions. These decisions also involve information available to managers that is not available to external decision makers. Regardless of the source of information used in their decisions, managers are concerned about the effects of their decisions on their company's performance as revealed in its financial statements. Investors and other external decision makers use financial statement information to evaluate managers' decisions.

This chapter examines investment decisions made by managers. It considers how financial accounting information is used in making these decisions. Also, it considers how financial accounting information can be used to identify and evaluate these decisions.

Major topics covered in this chapter include:

- Investment valuation
- The effect of investment decisions on risk and return
- Comparison of investment decisions
- The effect of operating leverage on earnings
- Analysis of cash management decisions

CHAPTER
Objectives

Once you have completed this chapter, you should be able to:

1. Determine the net present value of an investment.
2. Explain the effect of dividend policy on investment decisions.
3. Evaluate a company's investment decisions.
4. Explain how individual investments affect a company's risk and return.
5. Explain the purpose of segment reporting.
6. Identify the purpose of mergers and acquisitions and the effect they can have on accounting information.
7. Explain why fair market value reporting of assets can be useful.
8. Use accounting information to compare investment decisions among companies and over time.
9. Explain the effect of operating leverage on a company's earnings.
10. Analyze a company's cash management.

ASSET VALUE

Assets are important because they provide future benefits to an organization. An organization employs its resources to generate profits. The value of a resource can be determined from the contribution the resource makes to the future welfare of a company, its owners, and other stakeholders. For example, assume the Ready-Copy Co. provides photocopy services. A new copy machine is capable of producing 5 million photocopies during its life. The company expects to use the machine at a rate of approximately 200,000 copies per month. After considering the cost of paper, toner, electricity, and other related costs, the company expects to earn three cents per copy, or $6,000 per month ($.03 × 200,000). Ready-Copy requires a minimum return of 12% on its investments.

The maximum amount Ready-Copy is willing to pay for the machine is the present value of the future net cash flows it expects to receive. The interest factor for an annuity of 25 periods (5,000,000 copies/200,000 copies per month) at 1% per period (12% per year/12 months) is 22.02316 (Table 2). Therefore, the present value of the future cash flows from the machine is $132,139 ($6,000 × 22.02316). Ready-Copy would be willing to pay an amount less than the present value. Thus, if the cost of the machine were $100,000, Ready-Copy might purchase the machine because it could earn more than 12% on its investment.

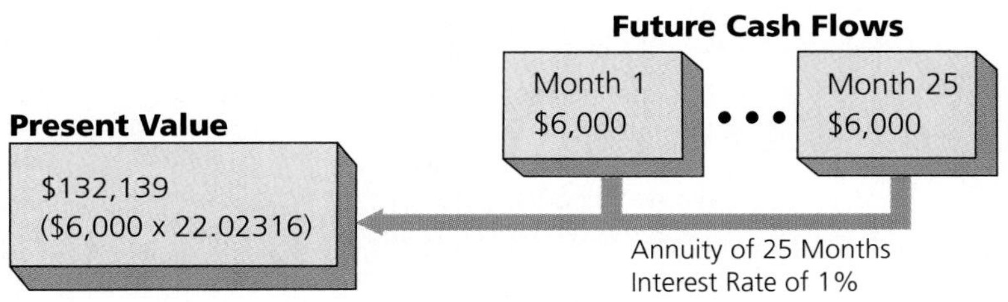

Objective 1
Determine the net present value of an investment.

The *net present value* of an investment is the excess of the present value of future cash inflows expected from the investment over its cost. The net present value of the copy machine would be $32,139 ($132,139 − $100,000). Companies invest in assets with positive net present values. From these investments, companies expect to earn a return greater than a predetermined required rate of return. Actual returns may be greater or less than expected returns, however. For example, assume Ready-Copy buys the machine. An unexpected increase in paper costs reduces its earnings to 2 cents a copy. Competition prevents the company from passing this increased cost on to customers. The present value of future cash flows is reduced to $88,093 ($4,000 × 22.02316). The net present value is a negative $11,907 if the machine costs $100,000 ($88,093 − $100,000), and the company fails to earn 12% on its investment. Therefore, the machine proves to be a bad investment. Managers take risks when they make investment decisions. They evaluate risks and expected returns in making these decisions in an effort to make profitable decisions and limit unprofitable ones. They use accounting information to assist with these evaluations.

Income tax effects should be considered when examining the cost of investments. Government tax policies sometimes are designed to stimulate investment in certain types of assets. A portion of payments for assets, such as equipment, assets used in research activities, or pollution control devices may be deductible in computing taxable income. These tax effects increase net cash flows associated with an investment and increase the investment's net present value. The tax effects are a way in which government shares in the risks of investments that it believes are beneficial to society or to some special interest group.

Required Rate of Return

Companies use different approaches to determine the required rates of return for their investments. At a minimum, the required rate of return should be equal to a company's **average cost of capital,** which is the weighted average cost of its debt and equity (preferred and common). **The weighted average cost of capital is the cost of debt times the percentage of debt in the capital structure plus the cost of equity times the percentage of equity in the capital structure.** To illustrate, McDonald's Corporation reported the following information in its 1991 annual report:

In millions of dollars **Year ended December 31,**	**1991**	**1990**
Interest expense—net of capitalized interest of \$26.2 and \$36.0	391.4	381.2
Income tax expense	439.8	444.0
Net income	859.6	802.3
Preferred stock dividends	19.2	14.0
Long-term debt (including current maturities)	4,336.5	4,493.4
Preferred shareholders' equity	298.2	199.7
Common shareholders' equity (market value)	13,630.6	10,054.8

McDonald's total interest for 1991 was \$417.6 million (\$391.4 + \$26.2). Its income tax rate was approximately 34% [\$439.8/(\$439.8 + 859.6)]. Thus, its after-tax interest cost was \$275.6 million [\$417.6(1 − .34)]. The average long-term debt outstanding during 1991 was \$4,415.0 million [(\$4,336.5 + \$4,493.4)/2]. Therefore, its average after-tax interest rate was approximately 6.2% (\$275.6/\$4,415) in 1991.

McDonald's average preferred stockholders' equity was \$249.0 million [(\$298.2 + \$199.7)/2]. Its return on average preferred stockholders' equity was 7.7% (\$19.2/\$249.0).

Return on common stockholders' equity often is computed using the market value of common equity as the denominator. Market value takes into consideration the return stockholders would earn if they purchased a company's stock at its current market price. Market value can be calculated by multiplying the market price per share of common stock times the number of common shares outstanding at the end of a fiscal period. McDonald's average common stockholders' equity was \$11,842.7 million [(\$13,630.6 + \$10,054.8)/2]. Its earnings available for common stockholders was \$840.4 million (\$859.6 net income − \$19.2 preferred dividends). Therefore, it earned a 7.1% return on average stockholders' equity (\$840.4/\$11,842.7). This return was similar to the return earned in prior years. Therefore, we can assume it approximates the rate owners expect from their investments. McDonald's capital structure consisted of approximately 26.7% long-term debt, 1.5% preferred stock, and 71.8% stockholder's equity:

Long-term debt: 26.7% = $4,415.0/($4,415.0 + $249.0 + $11,842.7)
Preferred stock: 1.5% = $249.0/($4,415.0 + $249.0 + $11,842.7)
Common stock: 71.8% = $11,842.7/($4,415.0 + $249.0 + $11,842.7)

Thus, the company's weighted average cost of capital would be approximately 6.9%:

Cost of debt × percentage of debt in the capital structure: 6.2% × 26.7% = 1.66%
Cost of equity × percentage of equity in the capital structure—
Preferred stock: 7.7% × 1.5% = 0.12
Common stock: 7.1% × 71.8% = 5.10
6.88%

McDonald's should invest in new resources that it expects to yield a return of at least 6.9%. Management might select a higher required return, however. Management realizes that some projects it expects to earn more than 6.9% will earn less. A higher required return provides a margin of protection against investments that turn out to be bad decisions. Also, if management believes its current return on equity is too low, it will set a higher required return.

Some projects are more risky than others. For example, McDonald's might choose between opening a new store in two locations. One location is in an established territory. The territory has demonstrated increasing demands for the company's products. Existing delivery systems could service the location. A second location is in a new territory, perhaps in another country. Demand for the product is uncertain. New delivery systems would need to be created. The potential risks and returns from investing in the second location might be considerably higher than those for the first location. A new McDonald's in Moscow is probably a riskier investment than one in the U.S. Management should consider the higher risk and return in making its choice. A higher required rate of return might be used to discount the expected future cash flows.

A company typically has a variety of new projects in which it can invest. These projects may involve expanding production or sales capacity, developing new product lines, moving into new territories, and renovating or replacing existing facilities. These projects can be ranked according to the rate of return management expects from investing in them. Management will then choose to invest available capital in those projects that it expects to yield the highest return, after considering the expected risk.

For example, assume the New Adventure Company identifies five projects in which it could invest:

Project	Expected Rate of Return	Amount of Investment
A	25%	$150,000
B	22	70,000
C	20	80,000
D	13	100,000
E	10	50,000

The company's required rate of return is 15%. Therefore, it could invest in projects A, B, and C if it has sufficient cash. Whether it will choose to invest in these projects depends on its access to capital.

Objective 2
Explain the effect of dividend policy on investment decisions.

Suppose New Adventure has $290,000 available for investment if no additional financing is provided from new debt or equity. The decision to invest in new projects should consider other cash requirements. For example, assume the company has been paying dividends of $1.40 per share on 100,000 shares for the past few years. Investing decisions are not independent of financing decisions. New Adventure could pay its regular dividend of $140,000 ($1.40 × 100,000 shares), leaving it $150,000 to invest. But, A would be the only project that could be funded. Alternatively, if New Adventure pays a smaller dividend, it could invest in projects A and B or in A, B, and C.

Companies that pay a regular dividend usually are reluctant to reduce the amount because their stockholders expect to receive the dividend. In theory, stockholders are better off, however, if management invests its cash in projects expected to earn higher rates of return than the current cost of capital. These investments should increase future cash flows and the value of the company's stock. For example, assume New Adventure's average stockholders' equity was $1,200,000 during 1995 and its earnings were $180,000. The company's return on equity would have been 15% ($180,000/$1,200,000). Its earnings per share was $1.80. If its PE ratio were 10, its price would have been $18 per share.

If the company chooses to pay its regular dividend, it could invest in project A. Assume New Adventure expects to earn $250,000 in 1996 and for the foreseeable future without any new investment. In addition, if the dividend is paid, the company expects to earn an additional $37,500 after taxes from its investment in project A ($150,000 × .25). If the dividend is not paid, it expects to earn an additional $68,900 after taxes from investments in A, B, and C. Cash flows are expected to be approximately equal to after-tax earnings. The effect of the dividend decision on expected return on equity for 1996 is shown below:

	Dividend	**No Dividend**
Stockholders' equity, end of 1995	$1,200,000	$1,200,000
Dividends	(140,000)	0
Regular earnings	250,000	250,000
Additional earnings from new projects	37,500	68,900
Net income	287,500	318,900
Earnings per share (100,000 shares)	2.875	3.189
Stockholders' equity, end of 1996	1,347,500	1,518,900
Average stockholders' equity	1,273,750	1,359,450
Return on equity	22.6%	23.5%

Stockholders' equity at the end of 1996 is the beginning balance plus net income minus dividends. Return on equity is net income (minus any preferred dividends) divided by average stockholders' equity. This illustration assumes New Adventure had no preferred stock.

If it pays dividends, the company can expect net income of $287,500 and return on equity of 22.6%. If its PE ratio remains at 10, its stock price will be $28.75. If it did not pay the dividend, it would expect net income of $318,900 and return on equity of 23.5%. The expected stock price would be $31.89. Thus, if the dividend is paid, stockholders will receive a dividend of $1.40 per share ($140,000/100,000 shares) and own stock worth $28.75, a total value of $30.15. If the dividend is not paid, stockholders will own stock worth $31.89 per share. Payment of the dividend is expected to cost stockholders $1.74 per share because of the lost earnings from the unfunded projects.

How much a company chooses to reinvest from its operating activities depends on the investment alternatives available. Stockholders are better off if the company invests in projects that earn an amount greater than the company's cost of capital. Examination of a company's financial statements provides evidence of the company's investment alternatives and the results of its investment decisions.

Evaluating Investment Decisions

This section demonstrates how accounting information can be used to identify and evaluate companies' investment decisions. Exhibit 12-1 provides selected information from Microsoft Corporation's 1991 annual report.

Exhibit 12-1

Microsoft Corporation
Selected Accounting Information

In millions	Net Income	Cash—Operating	Cash—Investing	Cash—Financing	Average Total Assets	Long-Term Debt
1989	$171	$222	$(145)	$26	$ 607	$0
1990	279	278	(271)	44	913	0
1991	463	558	(381)	(4)	1,375	0

Cash outflows are in parentheses.

Microsoft invested heavily in new assets over the three years. Its average total assets grew 127% [($1,375 − $607)/$607]. Large amounts of cash were used for investing activities each year. Associated with these investments were rapid increases in net income and cash flows from operating activities. Cash from operating activities was used to finance new investments.

Return on assets is a commonly used measure of a company's investment decisions. Return on assets is computed by dividing net income plus the after-tax cost of interest by average total assets.[1] As a company grows through additional investment, its net income should increase in proportion to its assets. An increase in return on assets over several years suggests management is making good investment decisions. A decrease suggests poor decisions. Care must be used in interpreting the measure, however. Temporary changes in the ratio may indicate short-term changes in the economy that are not related to a company's investment decisions. Another measure for evaluating investment decisions is the ratio of **cash flow from operating activities to average total assets.** This measure provides a cash, rather than accrual, measure of return.

Objective 3
Evaluate a company's investment decisions.

Exhibit 12-2 illustrates return on assets, cash flow from operating activities to average total assets, and stock prices for Microsoft for 1989 to 1991. Return on assets and cash flow to average total assets are shown as percentages. The higher return on assets and cash flows over the three years were associated with

[1] As referenced in other places in this book, a standard definition does not exist for many ratios. Different analysts and companies compute ratios, such as return on assets, using different methods. Be sure ratios you use for comparing companies or periods are calculated using consistent methods.

a sharp increase in stock price. Cash measures typically are more variable over time than accrual measures, as shown in the exhibit.

Exhibit 12-2 Microsoft Corporation Return on Investment and Stock Price

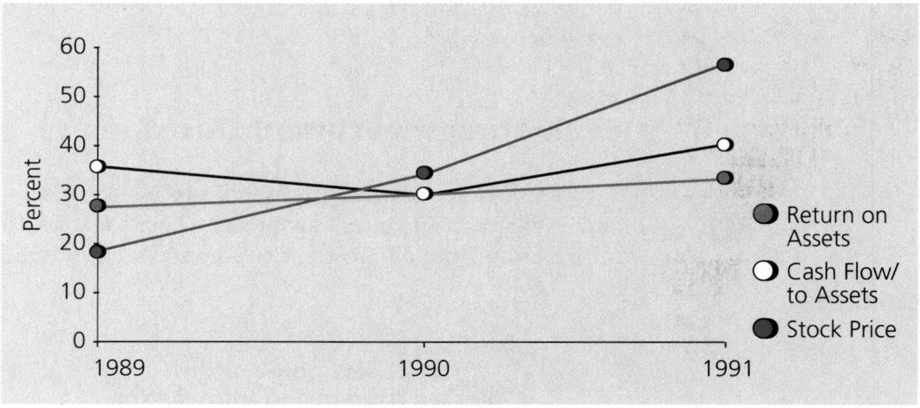

Though other factors, such as general economic conditions, may have contributed to Microsoft's incremental earnings and cash flows, it appears the company was making good investment decisions that increased stockholder value. The company paid no dividends during this period. Stockholders benefited from management investing cash flows in projects that yielded high rates of return.

Another example provides a different assessment of investment decisions. Exhibit 12-3 provides information reported by Allied Products Corporation, which produces agricultural equipment and automotive parts.

Exhibit 12-3

Allied Products Corporation
Selected Accounting Information

In millions	Net Income	Cash—Operating	Cash—Investing	Cash—Financing	Average Total Assets	Long-Term Debt
1986	16.2	(99.8)	(2.6)	97.7	324.3	120.1
1987	(1.7)	(32.1)	(9.9)	41.1	423.1	184.2
1988	5.5	(3.6)	(1.7)	12.3	462.7	171.7
1989	(22.4)	(8.0)	(6.7)	15.0	484.1	232.1
1990	(5.8)	25.7	(6.7)	(14.4)	463.3	53.4
1991	(34.0)	34.5	27.6	(67.3)	383.1	31.0

Net losses and cash outflows are in parentheses.

Allied Products' performance is markedly different from Microsoft's, as revealed by the exhibit. Allied Products' total assets increased steadily from 1986 to 1989. Cash was used for investing activities during this period as shown by the net cash outflows for investing activities in Exhibit 12-3. Total long-term debt increased during this period, as well. A portion of the debt was used to acquire additional assets, but much of the debt provided cash for operating activities. Observe from Exhibit 12-3 the net cash outflow from operating activities.

The company invested in additional plant assets and increased its production capacity, especially in 1986 and 1987, as shown by the increase in total assets. Demand for the company's products declined in the late 1980s and early 1990s, however, as evidenced by the net losses. When major portions of the debt became due in 1990 and 1991, Allied Products was forced to sell much of its assets, especially in 1991. Observe from Exhibit 12-3 the net cash inflow from investing activities in 1991. These sales provided cash flows from investing activities that were used, along with cash flows from operating activities, to repay debt in 1991. Note that cash flows for financing activities were negative in 1990 and 1991, indicating repayment of debt. The liquidation of assets in 1991 accounted for much of the company's net loss because these assets were sold at less than their book values.

Allied Products reported in its 1989 annual report:

> During 1990, capital expenditures will be limited to those which are necessary to maintain current buildings and machinery and equipment or will result in a significant reduction of operating costs. The Company will curtail tractor production in 1990 to . . . reduce tractor inventories and receivables.

The company's investment decisions were influenced by its operating and financing activities. Allied Products' financial situation was so strained that its auditors noted "substantial doubt about the Company's ability to continue as a going concern" in its 1991 annual report.

Exhibit 12-4 illustrates return on assets, cash flow from operating activities to total assets, and common stock price for Allied Products.

Exhibit 12-4 Allied Products Incorporated Return on Investment and Stock Price

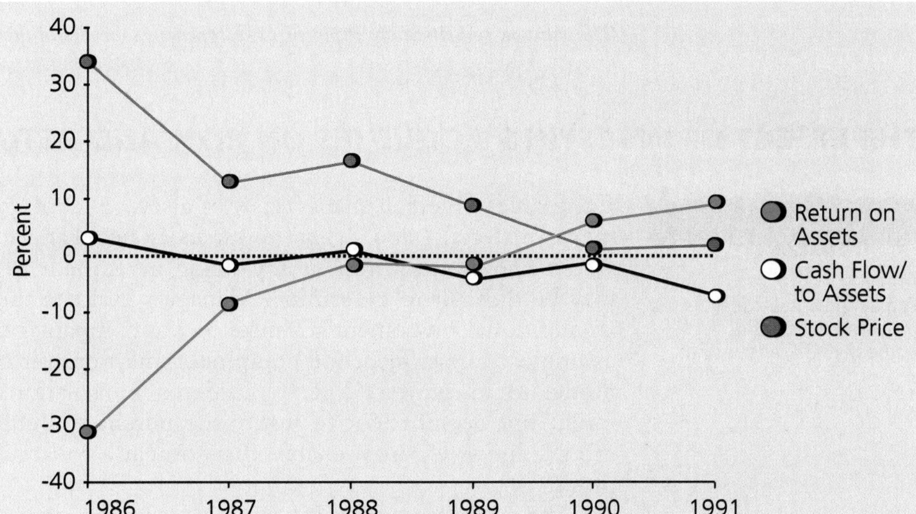

In this illustration, the company's stock price declined from a high of $33 per share at the end of 1986 to $3 per share at the end of 1991. Though cash flows from operating activities exhibit a positive trend, they were negative throughout most of the period. The company's financial statements reveal that the increase in cash flows was obtained by a reduction in operating activities that permitted the company to reduce inventories and to collect outstanding receivables. The decline in return on assets due to losses from operating activities was associated with a decline in stock price.

Microsoft and Allied Products illustrate contrasting results of investment decisions. Microsoft took advantage of a strong market for computer software. Its innovative developments made it a market leader. Allied Products invested in new production capacity at a time when demand for its products was decreasing. Its cash flow and net income problems brought it to the brink of economic disaster.

SELF-STUDY PROBLEM 12-1

Selected accounting information is provided below for Wal-Mart Stores, Inc.

Wal-Mart
Selected Accounting Information

In millions	Net Income	Cash—Operating	Cash—Investing	Cash—Financing	Average Total Assets	Long-Term Debt
1990	1,076	867	(894)	27	7,279	1,388
1991	1,291	1,296	(1,526)	230	9,794	2,033
1992	1,608	1,357	(2,150)	811	13,416	1,722

Required

Identify and evaluate the company's investment decisions for 1990 to 1992. Consider changes in assets and cash flows and the company's return on assets and cash flow to total assets.

The solution to Self-Study Problem 12-1 appears at the end of the chapter.

THE EFFECT OF INVESTING ACTIVITIES ON RISK AND RETURN

Objective 4
Explain how individual investments affect a company's risk and return.

Companies invest in many types of assets. A combination of buildings, equipment, materials, and other resources is necessary to produce goods and services. The contribution of any single investment to a company's performance may be difficult to determine. Managers evaluate the contribution they expect an additional investment to make to the company's overall risk and return. For example, a new piece of equipment may permit a company to add a new model to its product line. Considered in isolation, demand for the product might not be sufficient to justify the purchase. Being able to provide the new model, however, may enable the company to attract customers for its other products.

For example, assume Ink, Inc., purchased a new color printing press in 1993 at a cost of $300,000. The press permitted the company to accept jobs for large-format color posters and other publications it previously could not accept. Though the market for these jobs was not large, relatively few companies were capable of providing the service. Ink's management expected to generate additional net cash flows of $70,000 per year from jobs using the machine for the next 6 years. The company's average cost of capital was 12%. At that rate, the present value of the expected cash flows is $287,800 ($70,000 × 4.11141 from Table 2). From these expected cash flows, management could not justify purchasing the machine. Management believed, however, that the machine would permit the company to compete for work from several companies with which it had not previously done business. The machine enabled the company to meet the full line of printing needs of these companies. Management expected the additional sales from all of these jobs to generate $200,000 of additional net cash flows each year. Accordingly, the expenditure for the machine clearly was justified. The present value of the cash flows is $822,300 ($200,000 × 4.11141). **The overall contribution an investment makes to a company's performance is the critical factor in evaluating the investment.**

Investments in different types of assets also can reduce a company's risk. For example, assume the Ice-Cold Company has invested $30 million in assets it uses to produce air-conditioning equipment. Demand for the company's products varies from year to year depending on the severity of the weather. The company's expected profits for the next eight years are illustrated in Exhibit 12-5. Ice-Cold's management developed the expectations from information about past years. It assumed the pattern of net income from prior years would continue in the future with some additional growth in net income.

Exhibit 12-5 Expected Profits from Different Product Lines (Ice-Cold Company)

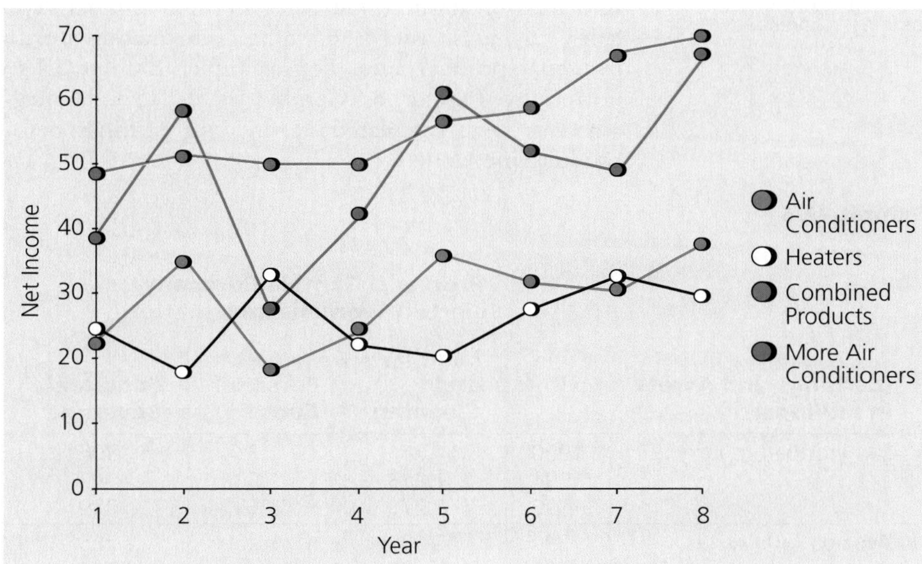

Ice-Cold's expected net income from current production is indicated by Air Conditioners line. The company has decided to invest an additional $20 million to increase its production capacity. If it invests in additional production of air conditioners, net income should increase as shown by the line for More Air Conditioners in Exhibit 12-5. This second line represents the total expected net income from current and additional production of air conditioners. Net income would continue to vary considerably from year to year, because of the variability in demand for air conditioners. As an alternative, the company could invest in the production of a different product, such as heaters. Management expects that variation in demand for heaters would offset the variation in demand for air conditioners, as shown in Exhibit 12-5 by the line for Heaters. When demand for air conditioners is high, demand for heaters is expected to be low and vice versa. By producing and selling both products, the company expects to reduce the variation in its net income (and in its cash flow from operating activities). Total net income from producing two products is shown in Exhibit 12-5 by the line for Combined Products. Net income would be more stable if two products were produced than if only air conditioners were produced. Ice-Cold could reduce the variation in its net income (and cash flows) by investing in a new product line.

Diversification, by investing in the production and sale of various types of products, can lead to more stable income and cash flow patterns. Stability of cash flows reduces the risk that a company will be unable to meet payments to creditors or to provide for its other cash needs. Also, it increases the probability that a company will be able to pay regular dividends to preferred and common stockholders.

Corporations report information about their various product lines in their annual reports. The following section considers these disclosures.

Segment Reporting

Objective 5
Explain the purpose of segment reporting.

Many corporations invest in a variety of product lines. Corporations disclose information about these lines in their annual reports as *segment information*. Sales, earnings, assets, and other information normally are included for each principal product line. For example, Exhibit 12-6 contains information reported by Procter & Gamble in its 1992 annual report. Return on asset amounts were calculated by dividing earnings before taxes by assets for each product line.

Exhibit 12-6

Procter & Gamble Company
Selected Segment Information

(Earnings and Assets in millions)		Laundry and Cleaning	Personal Care	Food and Beverage	Pulp and Chemicals	Total*
Earnings Before Taxes	1990	$ 781	$ 1,314	$ 304	$ 307	$ 2,421
	1991	1,013	1,602	47	222	2,687
	1992	1,278	1,651	229**	74	2,885
Average Total Assets	1990	3,130	8,239	2,285	1,441	17,419
	1991	3,695	9,437	2,556	1,507	19,478
	1992	4,247	11,269	2,529	1,621	22,247
Return on Assets	1990	25%	15.9%	13.3%	21.3%	13.9%
	1991	27.4%	17.0%	1.8%	14.7%	13.8%
	1992	30.1%	14.7%	9.1%	4.6%	13.0%

** The totals also include the effect of corporate assets and earnings, not shown in detail in this exhibit.*

*** The 1992 earnings of this group include a $103 million gain from the nonusual sale of some assets.*

Observe that earnings and return on assets are more stable over the years reported for the company as a whole than for its individual segments. Segment information can be used by external decision makers to identify a company's primary product lines and the relative importance of each line. The overall risk and return of a company is affected by the risk and return of its segments. If the company diversifies its investments into different types of products, the company's risk can be reduced.

Companies also can diversify by investing in different geographic locations. Many large corporations operate internationally. They report information about operating and investing activities in various geographic locations. Investing in certain locations, for example certain foreign countries, is riskier than investing in others. Expected returns also should be higher for higher risk locations.

Diversification can produce its own risk, however. A company that has had success with one type of product or location may have little ability to manage other products or locations. Too much diversification may make it difficult for management to control a company's activities because of increased complexity. As a result, a company's performance could deteriorate. Companies normally invest in related product lines. These lines often rely on similar product designs, raw materials, production processes, and marketing activities. Therefore, the skills necessary for success with one line can be used with other similar lines. When a company is not successful with a particular product line or location, often it will sell the assets associated with the product or location to another company. These sales frequently result in losses when the assets are sold, because the product line has not been successful.

Companies also may sell profitable product lines or locations in an effort to reduce the complexity of their activities or to create cash inflows. Many companies that issued large amounts of debt in the late 1980s sold profitable segments in the early 1990s to raise cash to pay principal and interest. Chapter 13 considers the reporting of information about discontinued product lines or other major segments.

Merger and Acquisition Decisions

Diversification and expansion are primary reasons companies merge with and acquire other companies. These investment decisions often have a major effect on accounting information. The recent merger of Time Incorporated with Warner Communications Incorporated illustrates how accounting numbers can tell a dramatic story. Time acquired 59.3% of Warner's common stock in July 1989. The remaining Warner stock was acquired in January 1990. The companies were merged to form Time Warner Incorporated. The $14 billion acquisition was accounted for using the purchase method. The purchase was financed primarily by $8.3 billion of long-term debt and $5.6 billion of preferred stock. At the beginning of 1989, Warner's common stock was selling at $37 per share. The total market value of the stock was approximately $4,689 million. At the beginning of 1989, Time's common stock was selling at $107 per share and had a total market value of about $6,067 million. Time paid Warner's shareholders $70 per share for their stock, almost twice its market value.

Objective 6
Identify the purpose of mergers and acquisitions and the effect they can have on accounting information.

Why did Time consider Warner to be worth so much more than its apparent market value? Management believed the two corporations would be worth more as a single entity than as two companies, perceiving an opportunity for growth in sales and profitability. The business press noted that Time's direct-mail operations would enhance Warner's record operations. At the same time, Warner's foreign operations were important to Time, which had foreign sales of less than 10%, compared with Warner's 40%. Warner's movie and TV studios could provide programs for HBO and Cinemax cable channels, owned by Time.[2]

Exhibit 12-7 provides information from the firms' annual reports. This information describes certain financial effects of the merger. The exhibit provides information for 1987 and 1988 for Time and Warner as separate corporations. The combined data are the sums of the amounts given for the two companies. Information for 1989, 1990, and 1991 is for the merged entity, Time Warner.

Revenues for Time Warner for 1989–1991 were higher than the total for the separate companies in 1987 and 1988. This increase suggests that the objective of increased growth through the merger had merit. Note, however, that Time Warner incurred losses (see Net Income in Exhibit 12-7) in 1989–1991 in comparison with substantial profits for the separate companies in 1987 and 1988. Earnings per share were markedly lower. The losses can be explained largely by the increase in interest, depreciation, and amortization expenses resulting from the merger.

Exhibit 12-7

Time Warner Incorporated
Selected Accounting Information

In Millions (except per share amounts)		1987	1988	1989	1990	1991
Revenues	Time	$4,193	$4,507			
	Warner	3,404	4,206			
	Combined	**7,597**	**8,713**	**$10,779**	**$11,517**	**$12,021**
Interest Expense	Time	99	111			
	Warner	20	26			
	Combined	**119**	**137**	**1,137**	**1,133**	**966**
Depreciation and Amortization	Time	205	224			
	Warner	142	183			
	Combined	**347**	**407**	**1,082**	**1,138**	**1,109**
Net Income (Loss)	Time	250	289			
	Warner	328	423			
	Combined	**578**	**712**	**(432)**	**(227)**	**(99)**
Earnings (Loss) per Share	Time	4.18	5.01			
	Warner	2.09	2.65			
	Combined			**(17.29)**	**(13.67)**	**(9.60)**
Dividends on Preferred Stock	Time					
	Warner	40	51			
	Combined	**40**	**51**	**555**	**559**	**593**
Cash—Operating	Time	492	535			
	Warner	440	394			
	Combined	**932**	**929**	**693**	**649**	**1,097**
Cash—Investing	Time	(535)	(819)			
	Warner	(218)	(630)			
	Combined	**(753)**	**(1,449)**	**(821)**	**(741)**	**(819)**

[2] *Fortune*, August 14, 1989, p. 59.

In Millions (except per share amounts)		1987	1988	1989	1990	1991
Goodwill	Time	997	986			
	Warner	0	0			
	Combined	**997**	**986**	**9,044**	**9,073**	**8,850**
Total Assets	Time	4,424	4,913			
	Warner	3,872	4,598			
	Combined	**8,296**	**9,511**	**24,791**	**25,337**	**24,889**
Total Liabilities	Time	3,176	3,554			
	Warner	2,394	2,807			
	Combined	**5,570**	**6,361**	**18,035**	**19,023**	**16,391**
Preferred Stock	Time	0	0			
	Warner	758	758			
	Combined	**758**	**758**	**5,584**	**5,954**	**6,256**
Shareholders' Equity	Time	1,248	1,359			
	Warner	1,478	1,791			
	Combined	**2,726**	**3,150**	**6,756**	**6,314**	**8,498**

Time Warner's total liabilities were approximately $12 billion greater in 1989 than the total for the separate companies in 1988. Most of the increase resulted from debt issued to finance the merger. Additional long-term debt resulted in interest expense that was almost $1 billion more in 1989 than in 1988.

Because the acquisition was accounted for as a purchase, Warner's assets and liabilities were recorded in Time Warner's accounting records at their fair market values. Observe that the total assets of the merged company in 1989 were $15 billion larger than the combined assets for the separate corporations in 1988. Goodwill accounted for most of this increase. This goodwill was the excess of the cost paid by Time over the market value of identifiable assets and liabilities of Warner. The higher recorded value of plant assets and goodwill on Time Warner's books resulted in depreciation and amortization expense that was about $600 million higher after the merger than before.

The increase in interest, depreciation, and amortization expenses caused net income to become a net loss. The increase in depreciation and amortization was the result of an accounting adjustment rather than an economic event, however. These expenses did not require cash outflows. Observe that cash flow from operating activities in 1989 and 1990 was positive, though less than in 1987 and 1988. Interest payments accounted for much of the lower cash flow. Cash flow from operating activities was a better measure than net income of the operating results of Time Warner during this period. Net income was adversely affected by the accounting adjustments for depreciation and amortization. These adjustments distorted operating results and performance measures, such as return on assets and return on equity. Thus, these measures should not be compared before and after the merger without considering the effect of the additional depreciation and amortization.

If the additional depreciation and amortization expenses resulting from the merger were eliminated, Time Warner would have reported net income in 1989 and 1990, rather than net losses. Most of these additional expenses were not deductible for tax purposes. Therefore, the company would have reported net income of $504 million in 1990:

Excess of depreciation and amortization in 1990 over 1988:	$731 million ($1,138 − $407)
Net loss in 1990:	(227)
Net income in 1990:	$504

After considering the dividends on preferred stock, earnings per share of common stock would have been negative, but much higher than reported:

Net income in 1990 (adjusted)	$504
Dividends on preferred stock	(559)
Loss attributable to common stockholders	$ (55)
Earnings per share (57 million shares)	$(.96)

Thus, what might appear to be a disastrous event emerges as much less of a catastrophe, if the effects of accounting rules on the reported amounts are considered.

The merger resulted in real economic effects, in addition to the accounting effects. The combined debt (total liabilities) to equity ratio for Time and Warner was 2.02 ($6,361/$3,150) prior to the merger. The debt to equity ratio for Time Warner was 2.67 ($18,035/$6,756) after the merger. The ratio of debt and preferred stock (fixed obligations) to common stockholders' equity was about 95%. Prior to the merger, Time's debt was rated A2 and Warner's was rated A3. After the merger, Time Warner's debt was rated Ba2, barely above speculative grade. The cash flow effect of the capital structure change was dramatic. Payments for interest and dividends on preferred stock were about $1.2 billion per year higher after the merger than before. At the same time, the company was able to generate additional revenues of about $2 billion. Presumably, these revenues would produce higher cash flows. Whether the merger proves to be successful depends on the company's long-run ability to generate cash flows from its operating activities.

Time and Warner's common stock prices during this period provide an interesting description of investors' reactions to the merger. Exhibit 12-8 illustrates common stock price changes during the merger period.

Exhibit 12-8 Common Stock Prices During Period of Time Warner Merger

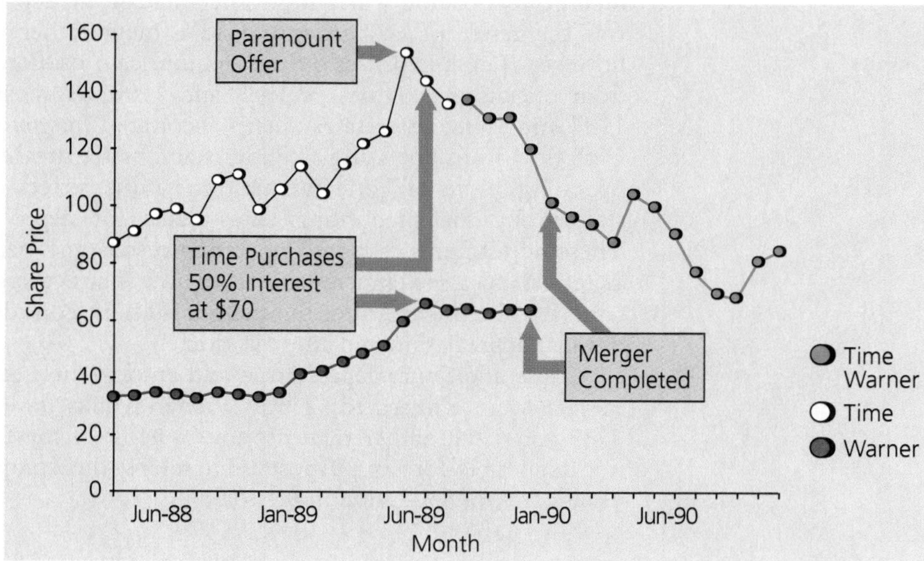

Prior to the merger, Time's stock was trading at about $90 per share and Warner's was trading at about $35 per share. As investors learned of the potential merger, the prices of the companies' stocks increased. By the time the acquisition began, Warner's stock was selling at about $65 per share, near the amount Time paid to acquire the shares. They remained at this level until the merger was completed. Time's shares increased dramatically in mid-1989 as the result of a bid by Paramount Incorporated to purchase Time for $175 per share. Time's board of directors rejected the offer, and the stock price declined. After the merger, Time's (now Time Warner's) stock price declined to a level approximating that of the pre-merger period. By the end of 1991, the stock was still selling at about $87 per share. During this same period, Standard and Poor's stock price index increased about 18%. Therefore, investor response to the merger was not favorable, at least initially.

Considerable care is needed in interpreting accounting information after a major acquisition or merger. The purchase method can result in large increases in assets and increases in depreciation and amortization. The method has been criticized because it mixes book and fair market values and complicates analysis. In the case of Time Warner, Warner's assets and liabilities were added to accounting records at fair market value. Time's assets and liabilities remained in the records at their historical cost values. After the merger, goodwill accounted for about 36% of Time Warner's total assets. This asset has little meaning to many external decision makers. If the merger had involved an exchange of stock and had been accounted for as a pooling of interests, the resulting financial statements in 1989 would have appeared similar to the combined totals for 1988 in Exhibit 12-7. Some would argue that this method would provide a fairer presentation of the results of the merger.

Fair Market Values

Objective 7
Explain why fair market value reporting of assets can be useful.

Some accountants and financial analysts believe that financial statements should report fair market values of assets and liabilities rather than, or in addition to, historical costs. For example, tangible assets, such as inventory and plant assets, might be reported on the balance sheet at their estimated replacement costs at the end of each fiscal year. Such reports would require companies to appraise the value of their assets and liabilities each year. Price indexes for specific types of assets that indicate changes in asset costs during the year might be used for this purpose. Many managers and accountants are concerned, however, that these appraisals are too subjective to provide reliable information. The added cost of providing this information also has been cited as a reason for not reporting current values.

Even if assets were adjusted to their current values, it is not evident that the problem of purchase method accounting would be resolved. Prior to the Time Warner merger, the two companies reported combined total assets of $9.5 billion. After the merger, total assets were reported at $24.8 billion, an increase of $15.3 billion. Of this amount, only $2.1 billion resulted from an adjustment of previously recognized assets to their fair market values. The remaining $13.2 billion resulted from goodwill and other assets that were previously unrecognized. Even if Warner's assets had been recorded at their fair market value prior to the merger, the financial statement amounts of Time Warner would have been dramatically different from those of Time and Warner prior to the merger.

The amounts reported on the balance sheet, whether considered individually or in total, do not represent the fair market value of a corporation. The value of a corporation is determined by its ability to generate cash flows through its operating activities. Investor assessments of this ability, adjusted for risk, determine the market value of a company's stock. Warner Communication's stock had a total market value of $5.2 billion (127 million shares × $41 per share) at the beginning of 1989. The book value of the company's stockholders' equity was $1.8 billion (Exhibit 12-7). Time paid $14 billion for the stock.

A company's balance sheet identifies primarily the historical cost of its assets and the source of financial resources used to acquire them. Changes in the composition of assets, liabilities, and equities over time generally is useful information. In addition, information about changes in the relationship between these amounts and a company's net income or cash flows can be useful. This information helps investors and other external decision makers understand how a company is using its resources. It does not tell them what a company is worth. Investors considered Warner to be worth almost twice its book value at the beginning of 1989. This value was determined by the ability of the company's management to use its resources to generate cash flows from operating activities. The value of a company typically is different from the value of its separate assets. The ability to manage assets, the value of trained employees, and the value of established markets are not reported on the balance sheet.

Two companies may have identical assets but have different market values. For example, a restaurant may go out of business in a specific location because it cannot generate a profit. New owners may buy the building and equipment and create a successful new business. The difference between success and failure often occurs because of how the assets are managed, not because of the assets themselves. A profitable business will be more valuable than an unprofitable business with the same assets.

Time believed Warner was considerably more valuable than its $5.2 billion market value. Time's management believed Warner's assets, employees, products, and markets would be more valuable in combination with those of Time than they were as a separate company. **Value results from the ability to manage resources, including tangible assets, money, and people.**

Nevertheless, many accountants have argued that financial statements should report the current value of assets and liabilities. This information could enhance the ability of decision makers to compare companies and provide for more equitable measurement of performance. Some countries, such as Great Britain and the Netherlands, permit corporations to use current values as the measurement basis for reporting their assets. Therefore, companies in these countries normally would report higher amounts for their assets than identical U.S. companies. Performance measures, such as return on assets, also are affected.

Financial Assets and Liabilities

One area in which fair market accounting has received special attention is in the reporting of financial assets and liabilities, such as debt and equity securities. Many securities are traded on a regular basis, revealing their current market prices. Changes in market values of notes, bonds, and other debt instruments can be determined from changes in market rates of interest and expected cash flows. Financial instruments are primary assets for many financial institutions.

Banks, savings and loans, insurance companies, and other institutions invest heavily in these assets. Cash is provided by depositors or policy owners. Institutions such as banks and savings and loans lend this cash to businesses or individuals. Excess cash is invested in marketable securities until it is needed.

During periods of rapid change in interest rates and other economic conditions, historical costs of financial instruments can be misleading. During the 1980s many savings and loans reported large amounts of financial investments at historical costs. The market values of many of these investments, however, were far below their costs. Therefore, the fair market values of the companies' assets sometimes were less than their liabilities. If fair market amounts had been reported, the companies would have been insolvent (their liabilities would have been greater than their assets).

To illustrate, assume Sly Savings and Loan's assets at the end of 1994 consisted of three financial instruments, each costing $2,000:

1994	**Historical Cost**	**Fair Market Value**
Assets	$2,000	$3,000
	2,000	500
	2,000	300
Total Assets	6,000	3,800
Liabilities	4,000	4,000
Equity	2,000	(200)

During 1995, the company sold the asset with a market value of $3,000, thereby generating income of $1,000, a return on assets of 16.7% and a return on equity of 50%. It invested cash from the sale in another instrument at a cost of $3,000. Therefore, its financial position at the end of 1995 was:

1995	**Historical Cost**	**Fair Market Value**
Assets	$3,000	$3,000
	2,000	500
	2,000	300
Total Assets	7,000	3,800
Liabilities	4,000	4,000
Equity	3,000	(200)

Though the company's financial position appeared to be improving and it appeared to be profitable, the company was insolvent. In 1996, the company's liabilities became due and it sold all of its investments at their fair market values. It incurred a loss of $3,200, and it reported its financial position as:

1996	**Historical Cost**	**Fair Market Value**
Total Assets (Cash)	$3,800	$3,800
Liabilities	4,000	4,000
Equity	(200)	(200)

The company's insolvency now becomes apparent on its historical cost balance sheet. Creditors and owners were misled during 1995 into believing the company was doing well, when, in fact, it was facing a major problem. Many savings and loans and some banks faced this situation in the late 1980s and early 1990s. They were able to hide their financial problems for several years behind historical cost financial statements. These institutions had many loans among their assets that were not paying expected interest. Real estate loans, in particular, often were returning very low yields. In many cases, their market values were far below their historical cost values.

The SEC has argued that financial institutions should value financial instruments at their market values on their balance sheets. Many institutions have been opposed to this accounting requirement because of the added volatility it produces in their net incomes and equities. Regulatory authorities require these institutions to maintain minimum proportions of equity in their capital structures. A sharp drop in market values could result in equities that are below regulatory minimums. The institutions argue they would have to maintain higher levels of equity as protection from market volatility. This requirement would mean they could make fewer loans, which also would affect their profitability.

The accounting methods used by companies affect their financial statements. A company's net income, return on assets, and other profitability and risk measures may look very different if it uses one method rather than another. Management may choose among these methods, for example, straight-line versus accelerated depreciation. In other cases, such as purchase or pooling for mergers and acquisitions, a choice does not exist. Unless a transaction can be structured to meet stringent requirements to be a pooling of interests, purchase accounting is required. Nevertheless, the method used may have a major effect on reported accounting numbers. Decision makers should consider the effect of accounting methods on reported numbers when analyzing accounting information.

SELF-STUDY PROBLEM 12-2

Accounting information as originally reported by ConAgra, Inc., in its 1991 annual report is provided below:

In millions	**1991**	**1990**
Depreciation and amortization expense	$ 250.8	$ 129.7
Income before interest and taxes	789.6	503.4
Interest expense	298.0	170.6
Income before taxes	515.2	356.9
Income taxes	204.0	125.2
Net income	311.2	231.7
Preferred dividends	19.5	1.3
Net income available for common stock	291.7	230.4
Earnings per share	2.13	1.87
Weighted average common shares	136.9	123.2
Total assets	9,420.3	4,804.2
Intangible assets	2,710.9	251.5
Cash flow from operating activities	691.8	316.6

Many of the changes that occurred in ConAgra's financial statements resulted from acquisitions of other companies accounted for using the purchase method. Assume the increase in depreciation and amortization expense, interest expense, preferred dividends, and weighted average common shares resulted from acquisition activity. Also, assume $900 million of plant assets and the increase in intangible assets (primarily goodwill) resulted from recording assets and liabilities of acquired companies at their fair market values instead of at their book values.

Required

(a) Calculate return on assets and cash flow from operating activities to total assets for 1990 and 1991 as reported. Use the total assets reported in each year as the denominator in these calculations. (b) Calculate these amounts for 1991 after adjusting for the effects of the purchase method on net income, cash flows, and total assets. Assume the income tax rate for 1991 was 40%. (c) What would the company's earnings per share have been in 1991 after adjusting net income for the effects of the purchase method?

The solution to Self-Study Problem 12-2 appears at the end of this chapter.

COMPARING INVESTMENT DECISIONS

Objective 8
Use accounting information to compare investment decisions among companies and over time.

Accounting information can provide useful information about investment decisions. It can be used to compare decisions and performances for different companies. It can be used to answer questions such as: How do investment decisions differ among companies? At what rate are companies increasing their assets? How have companies financed their assets? How well are companies using their assets to generate profits and cash flows?

Exhibit 12-9 provides information for ten companies from their 1991 annual reports. Five companies are in the food industry, and five are in the paper and wood products industry. Comparing companies within and between industries provides a basis for analyzing differences among the companies. Panels A and B in the exhibit provide information from the companies' financial statements. This information identifies the relative composition of each company's assets and capital structure. Considerable variation is apparent among the companies.

Ratios often are useful for comparing companies because they provide a common basis of analysis. Ratios are provided in panel C of Exhibit 12-9. For example, the ratio of net plant assets to cost of plant assets indicates the percentage of plant assets that have not been depreciated. If all companies being compared use similar depreciation policies, this ratio measures the relative age of the companies' plant assets. If this ratio is relatively high, a company is newer or has recently acquired a large portion of its plant assets. Depreciation and amortization expenses often are higher for these companies than for companies with older assets.

The ratio of **depreciation and amortization expense to long-term assets** indicates the rate at which long-term assets are being expensed. The ratio of **cash used in investing activities to long-term assets** describes the rate at which new assets are being acquired. Depreciation and amortization include primarily expenses associated with plant, intangible, and other long-term assets. Cash used in investing activities includes primarily cash flows associated with the purchase and sale of long-term assets. A comparison of cash invest-

Exhibit 12-9

Selected Information for Companies in Two Industries

Panel A Dollars in millions	**Current Assets**	**Plant Assets—Cost**	**Plant Assets—Net**	**Intangible Assets**	**Total Assets**	**Current Liabilities**	**Long-Term Debt**
Borden	1,941	3,244	1,904	1,318	5,481	1,434	1,346
Ralston Purina	1,676	3,443	2,184	486	4,632	1,194	2,071
Heinz	2,120	2,764	1,723	749	4,935	1,430	717
ConAgra	4,343	2,740	1,942	2,711	9,420	4,087	2,093
General Mills	1,082	3,337	2,241	79	3,902	1,272	879
Scott Paper	1,481	7,064	4,086	484	6,493	1,510	2,333
Weyerhauser	1,549	9,317	4,987	0	7,550	943	2,592
Georgia-Pacific	1,562	9,775	5,567	1,949	10,622	2,722	3,743
Champion International	1,162	7,462	5,386	0	8,656	794	2,978
International Paper	4,131	12,733	7,848	816	14,941	3,727	3,351

Panel B Dollars in millions	**Total Liabilities**	**Total Equity**	**Depr. & Amort.**	**Cash—Operating**	**Cash—Investing**	**Cash—Financing**	**Net Income**
Borden	3,506	1,975	217	349	(311)	9	295
Ralston Purina	3,848	784	260	711	(391)	(246)	371
Heinz	2,660	2,275	196	733	(487)	(209)	568
ConAgra	7,603	1,817	251	692	(1,057)	960	311
General Mills	2,788	1,114	218	544	(556)	50	473
Scott Paper	4,511	1,982	353	582	(224)	(283)	(70)
Weyerhauser	4,061	3,489	446	729	(509)	(140)	(89)
Georgia-Pacific	7,886	2,736	724	580	746	(1,336)	(79)
Champion International	4,985	3,671	341	370	(498)	182	40
International Paper	9,202	5,739	700	1,152	(1,943)	777	184

Panel C	**Depr. & Amort./Long-Term Assets***	**Cash—Investing/Long-Term Assets***	**Long-Term Assets/Total Assets**	**Plant Assets/Total Assets**	**Intangible Assets/Total Assets**	**Debt/Equity**	**Net Income/Total Assets**	**Cash—Operating/Total Assets**
Borden	6.1%	8.8%	64.6%	34.7%	24.0%	177.5%	5.4%	6.4%
Ralston Purina	8.8%	13.2%	63.8%	47.2%	10.5%	490.8%	8.0%	15.3%
Heinz	7.0%	17.3%	57.0%	34.9%	15.2%	116.9%	11.5%	14.9%
ConAgra	4.9%	20.8%	53.9%	20.6%	28.8%	418.4%	3.3%	7.3%
General Mills	7.7%	19.7%	72.3%	57.4%	2.0%	250.3%	12.9%	13.9%
Average	**6.9%**	**16.0%**	**62.3%**	**39.0%**	**16.1%**	**290.8%**	**8.2%**	**11.6%**
Scott Paper	7.0%	4.5%	77.2%	62.9%	7.5%	227.6%	−1.1%	9.0%
Weyerhauser	7.4%	8.5%	79.5%	66.1%	0.0%	116.4%	−1.2%	9.7%
Georgia-Pacific	8.0%	−8.2%	85.3%	52.4%	18.3%	288.2%	−0.7%	5.5%
Champion International	4.6%	6.6%	86.6%	62.2%	0.0%	135.8%	0.5%	4.3%
International Paper	6.5%	18.0%	72.4%	52.5%	5.5%	160.3%	1.2%	7.7%
Average	**6.7%**	**5.9%**	**80.2%**	**59.2%**	**6.3%**	**185.7%**	**−1.3%**	**7.2%**

*Total assets − Current assets

ment and depreciation ratios provides information about a company's reinvestment and growth policies.

Exhibit 12-9 indicates that companies in the food industry were reinvesting at a much higher rate (average of 16.0%) than those in the paper industry (average of 5.9%). Companies in the food industry were reinvesting at a rate about 10% higher on average than their rate of depreciation and amortization. In contrast, some companies in the paper industry were reinvesting at a lower rate than the rate of depreciation and amortization. Georgia-Pacific sold more long-term assets than it purchased in 1991. International Paper was an exception in this industry, reinvesting at a much higher rate than its rate of depreciation and amortization.

Asset composition ratios, such as **plant, intangible, or total long-term assets to total assets,** indicate the relative importance of various types of assets. Long-term and plant assets were much larger percentages of total assets for companies in the paper industry, on average, than those in the food industry. Intangible assets were a larger percentage of total assets for companies in the food industry, on average. Intangible assets often result from mergers and acquisitions. Mergers also can explain why depreciation and amortization expenses were higher for some companies, such as Georgia-Pacific.

The **debt to equity ratio** describes a company's financial leverage. Companies in the food industry were more highly levered than those in the paper industry, on average. The leverage for Heinz was well below average for food companies, and the leverage for Georgia-Pacific was above average for the paper industry.

Net income to total assets (return on assets) and **cash flow from operating activities to total assets** are performance measures. They indicate the success companies are having in using their assets. Both ratios were higher on average for the food industry. Three of the five companies in the paper industry reported net losses. Observe, however, that two of these companies reported relatively high cash flow from operating activities. Cash flow from operating activities normally will be higher than net income because of the effect of depreciation and amortization. Chapters 13 and 14 will examine this relationship in more detail. The paper industry is more sensitive to changes in the economy than is the food industry. This sensitivity can be observed in the lower return and cash flow amounts for the paper industry. These companies were hurt by the recession of the early 1990s. Demand for their products declined as other companies cut back on production and the demand for shipping containers and other paper goods declined. The food industry was relatively less affected because people, and animals, continue to need food even during a recession.

The type of information provided in Exhibit 12-9 is useful for assessing differences across industries and the relative strengths of companies in an industry. Examining information for only one year can be misleading, however, because the year may not be typical. Examining the performance of companies over time often is helpful in evaluating investment decisions.

COMPARING COMPANIES OVER TIME

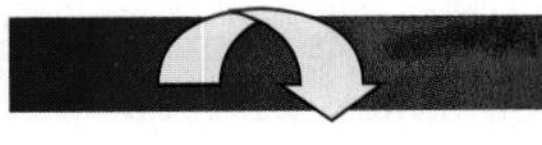

Exhibit 12-10 provides information for Heinz and ConAgra for 1987 to 1991. The exhibit contains accounting information as presented by the companies in supplemental schedules in their annual reports. Most companies report selected accounting information for five- or ten-year periods, in addition to information reported in their financial statements.

Exhibit 12-10 Comparison of Growth Rates

$ in millions	**1987**	**1988**	**1989**	**1990**	**1991**	**Average Growth**
Inflation Index	100	103.9	108.4	112.9	117.0	
Total Assets						
ConAgra	2,483	3,043	4,278	4,804	9,420	12.8%
Heinz	3,364	3,605	4,002	4,487	4,935	2.5%
Depreciation & Amortization						
ConAgra	77	90	102	130	251	11.1%
Heinz	110	133	148	169	196	4.6%
Capital Expenditures						
ConAgra	178	196	241	349	1,160	18.6%
Heinz	185	238	323	355	345	10.7%
Net Income						
ConAgra	149	155	198	232	311	6.3%
Heinz	339	386	440	504	568	3.9%
Long-Term Debt						
ConAgra	429	490	560	635	2,093	15.5%
Heinz	876	780	962	1,257	1,227	2.0%

Data source: 1991 annual reports.

Inflation index is the Gross Domestic Product Implicit Price Deflator from Economic Indicators, U.S. Government Printing Office, March 1992.

This exhibit contains several important financial statement items. The only item not considered in earlier analysis is capital expenditures. *Capital expenditures* **are amounts paid for the purchase, lease, and construction of plant assets.** Thus, they are similar to cash outflows for investing activities as reported on the statement of cash flows. Most companies disclose capital expenditures as part of notes to their financial statements.

The rate of change, or growth, can be a useful measure for comparing information over time. The growth rate is the percentage change in amounts from one period to another. Growth rates may be nominal or real. **Nominal growth rates** are computed from the numbers presented in an annual report without adjustment. **Real growth rates** take inflation into account. Because of inflation, dollar amounts presented for one year are not measured on an equivalent scale with those of other years. For example, assume a company's sales were $100 million in 1987 and $120 million in 1991. Because of inflation, 1987 dollars were worth more than 1991 dollars. A dollar in 1987 would purchase more goods and services than a dollar in 1991. The nominal growth in sales for 1987 to 1991 is calculated as:

$$\text{Nominal Growth} = \frac{\$120 - \$100}{\$100} = 20\%$$

The real growth in sales is computed by first adjusting the sales numbers for inflation. For example, Exhibit 12-10 shows the inflation index in 1987 was 100 and the index in 1991 was 117. Therefore, to restate the 1987 amount in 1991 equivalent dollars, sales would be multiplied by the ratio of the index for 1991 to the index for 1987:

$$\text{Restated 1987 sales} = \$100 \times \frac{117}{100} = \$117$$

Sales of $100 million in 1987 dollars were equivalent to sales of $117 million in 1991 dollars. Thus, the real rate of growth would be:

$$\text{Real Growth} = \frac{\$120 - \$117}{\$117} = 2.56\%$$

What appeared to be a relatively large increase in sales was, in fact, only a small increase when adjusted for inflation.

The growth rates shown in Exhibit 12-10 were calculated by first adjusting the amounts reported for each item each year for inflation. For example, total assets for ConAgra were adjusted for 1987 as: $2,483 × (117/100) = $2,905. For 1988, total assets were: $3,043 × (117/103.9) = $3,427. Then, the percentage changes in the accounting numbers from one year to the next were calculated. The percentage change in total assets for ConAgra from 1987 to 1988 was: ($3,427 − $2,905)/$2,905 = $18.0%. Finally, the average annual growth rate was computed by summing the growth rates for each year and dividing by 5. This amount is reported as the average growth rate in Exhibit 12-10.

A comparison of growth rates for ConAgra and Heinz reveals higher growth for ConAgra for all items reported in Exhibit 12-10. Total assets, depreciation and amortization, capital expenditures, and long-term debt grew at much higher rates for ConAgra than for Heinz. Net income grew at a slightly higher rate. ConAgra invested at a higher rate than Heinz, as shown by capital expenditures. Therefore, ConAgra's assets grew at a faster rate than Heinz's. This growth was financed largely by additional debt. Thus, ConAgra's debt grew at a much faster rate than Heinz's. Though net income also grew faster for ConAgra, it grew at a lower rate than the company's rate of investment. In contrast, net income for Heinz grew at a faster rate than its rate of investment. Heinz invested less than ConAgra but received higher returns from its investments, on average, than did ConAgra from 1987 to 1991, as observed by comparing the growth rate of net income with the growth rate in total assets.

Ratios also can provide useful information for comparing companies' activities over time. Exhibit 12-11 provides ratio information for ConAgra and Heinz. An advantage of ratios is that adjustments for inflation are unnecessary if the numerator and denominator of the ratio are for the same period. Because the numerator and denominator are measured in dollars of the same period, the result is not affected by inflation. Exhibit 12-11 reports ratios as percentages. For example, the depreciation and amortization expense to total assets ratio for ConAgra in 1987 was 3.1% (from Exhibit 12-10: $77/$2,483). (The ratio also might be stated as .031 or as .031 to 1.) These ratios demonstrate that ConAgra invested more heavily through capital expenditures each year than did Heinz. Though ConAgra's depreciation and amortization grew at a faster rate than Heinz's (from Exhibit 12-10: 11.1% compared to 4.6%), it was a smaller percentage of total assets each year (Exhibit 12-11). ConAgra's total assets were growing at a faster rate than its depreciation and amortization. Heinz's total assets were growing also, but at a slower rate than ConAgra's.

Net income was a lower percentage of total assets for ConAgra throughout the five-year period. The ratio decreased over time for ConAgra, while increasing slightly for Heinz. For ConAgra, both capital expenditures and long-term debt increased as a percentage of total assets in 1991. Only in 1991 did ConAgra's financial leverage approach that of Heinz, which was more highly levered throughout the five-year period.

Exhibit 12-11 Comparison of Ratios

	Depreciation and Amortization/ Total Assets		Capital Expenditures/ Total Assets		Net Income/ Total Assets		Long-Term Debt/ Total Assets	
	ConAgra	**Heinz**	**ConAgra**	**Heinz**	**ConAgra**	**Heinz**	**ConAgra**	**Heinz**
1987	3.1%	3.3%	7.2%	5.5%	6.0%	10.1%	17.3%	26.0%
1988	3.0%	3.7%	6.4%	6.6%	5.1%	10.7%	16.1%	21.6%
1989	2.4%	3.7%	5.6%	8.1%	4.6%	11.0%	13.1%	24.0%
1990	2.7%	3.8%	7.3%	7.9%	4.8%	11.2%	13.2%	28.0%
1991	2.7%	4.0%	12.3%	7.0%	3.3%	11.5%	22.2%	24.9%
Average	2.8%	3.7%	7.8%	7.0%	4.8%	10.9%	16.4%	24.9%

Data source: 1991 annual reports.

A more thorough analysis of accounting information than provided above would be needed to determine the relative performances of the two companies. For example, ConAgra's relatively lower net income to total assets ratio can be explained by the higher growth rate in its investment activities. As was discussed earlier for Time Warner, when a company acquires other companies and accounts for the acquisitions using the purchase method, its accounting numbers can be distorted. ConAgra was involved in several acquisitions from 1987 to 1991. A relatively large acquisition was made in 1991. These acquisitions increased its assets, capital expenditures, and long-term debt. The additional interest, depreciation, and amortization expenses reduced its net income. Chapters 13 and 14 examine additional ratios and other accounting measures useful for evaluating management decisions.

OPERATING LEVERAGE

Operating leverage **is the proportion of a company's total expenses that are fixed.** *Fixed costs* **are expenses that do not vary in proportion to sales activity.** *Variable costs* **are expenses that do vary in proportion to sales activity.** Operating leverage is affected by a company's asset composition. Companies with large proportions of long-term assets typically have large fixed costs. As an illustration, assume two companies, Fixed and Variable, are similar except for their asset composition. Exhibit 12-12 provides information for the two companies.

Both companies have the same amount of total assets. Fixed Company has a larger proportion of long-term assets, however. Long-term assets typically are associated with fixed costs, such as depreciation and amortization of plant and intangible assets, repair and maintenance costs, utilities, insurance, and other costs associated with these assets. Current assets include inventory, short-term investments, and prepaid expenses that are more likely to vary with sales activity.

Objective 9
Explain the effect of operating leverage on a company's earnings.

Exhibit 12-12 Comparison of Operating Leverage

	Fixed Company	Variable Company
Current assets	$ 400,000	$ 600,000
Long-term assets	600,000	400,000
Total assets	$1,000,000	$1,000,000
First Scenario		
Sales revenue	$ 500,000	$ 500,000
Variable costs, 20% and 40% of sales	(100,000)	(200,000)
Fixed costs	(200,000)	(50,000)
Income before taxes	200,000	250,000
Income taxes, 30%	60,000	75,000
Net income	$ 140,000	$ 175,000
Earnings per share, 100,000 shares	$1.40	$1.75
Return on assets	14.0%	17.5%
Second Scenario		
Sales revenue	$1,000,000	$1,000,000
Variable costs, 20% and 40% of sales	(200,000)	(400,000)
Fixed costs	(200,000)	(50,000)
Income before taxes	600,000	550,000
Income taxes, 30%	180,000	165,000
Net income	$ 420,000	$ 385,000
Earnings per share, 100,000 shares	$4.20	$3.85
Return on assets	42%	38.5%

As a result, Fixed Company has more fixed costs that are expensed in the First Scenario than does Variable Company. Variable Company has a higher proportion of variable costs that are expensed. Both companies have the same amount of sales. Observe that at a sales level of $500,000, Variable Company earns a higher net income. Thus, its earnings per share and return on assets (net income ÷ total assets) are higher as well.

The second scenario differs from the first because sales are assumed to be $1 million for both companies. Fixed costs remain the same as in the first scenario, but variable costs increase in proportion to sales. Consequently, Fixed Company now earns a higher net income than Variable Company. Operating leverage, like financial leverage, provides a magnifying effect on net income. As sales increase, high leverage improves net income. As sales decrease, however, high leverage has a detrimental effect on net income. The effect of leverage on net income can be observed from Exhibit 12-13. This exhibit illustrates net income relative to sales for Fixed and Variable Companies. Net income is more sensitive to changes in sales revenue for Fixed Company than for Variable Company, as indicated by the steeper slope of the line in Exhibit 12-13. The ratio of operating income to sales often is used in evaluating the effect of operating leverage when interest expense is reported on the income statement. Interest expense results from financial rather than operating leverage. Therefore, the effect of interest expense on income should be excluded in an analysis of operating leverage.

Exhibit 12-14 provides asset composition (as an indicator of operating leverage) and PE ratios for selected companies in the food and paper industries.

Exhibit 12-13 Effect of Operating Leverage on Net Income

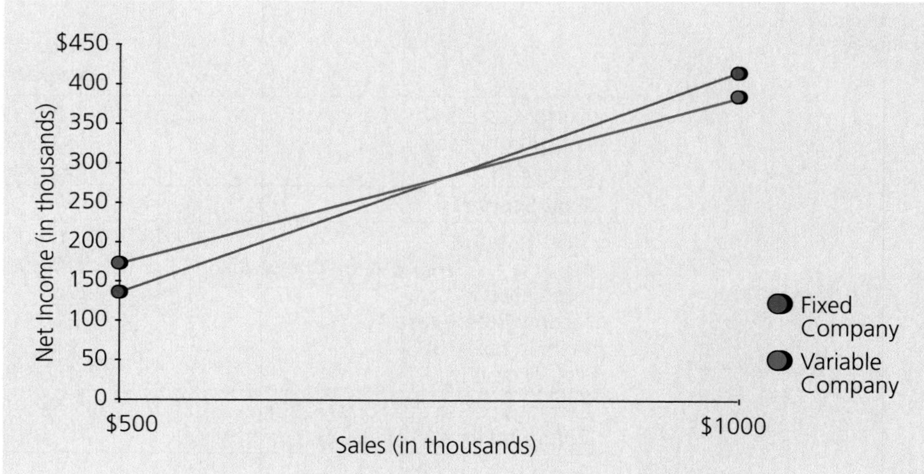

The companies in the paper industry have greater amounts of operating leverage than those in the food industry. Higher operating leverage increases risk because of the greater variability in net income that results from the leverage. Observe that companies in the paper industry have lower PE ratios than those in the food industry, evidence of the increased risk. PE ratios were computed as the average PE ratio for 1987 to 1991 for each company, excluding years in which net income was negative. Because of the higher variability of earnings of the paper companies, investors discount their earnings at a higher rate than those of the food companies.

The relative variability of the earnings for the paper industry can be observed from Exhibit 12-15. This exhibit illustrates the average earnings per share amounts for companies in the food and paper industries for 1987 to 1991.

Exhibit 12-14 Operating Leverage and Risk

	Long-Term Assets/ Total Assets	**Price-Earnings Ratio**
Borden	64.6%	13.9
Ralston Purina	63.8%	13.8
Heinz	57.0%	15.6
ConAgra	53.9%	15.1
General Mills	72.3%	15.5
Average	62.3%	14.8
Scott Paper	77.2%	11.8
Weyerhauser	79.5%	9.3
Georgia-Pacific	85.3%	7.9
Champion International	86.6%	10.4
International Paper	72.4%	8.5
Average	80.2%	9.6

Data source: 1991 annual reports.

Exhibit 12-15 Effect of Operating Leverage on Earnings Volatility

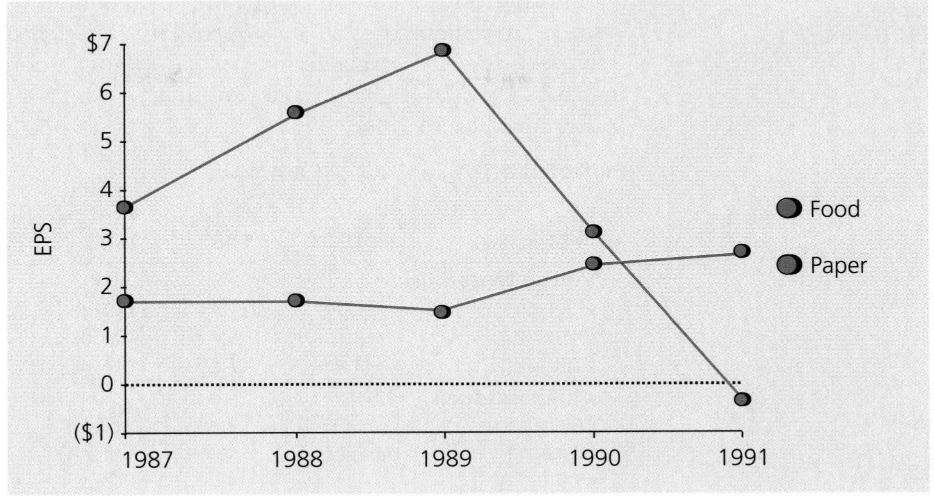

Earnings per share for companies in the food industry were relatively stable over the five-year period. In contrast, earnings per share for those in the paper industry were quite volatile.

Greater amounts of operating leverage are more necessary for some industries than for others. Some industries are capital intensive. They require large amounts of capital assets, particularly plant assets. Manufacturing companies often are capital intensive. Investments in plant assets are necessary to produce manufactured goods. Merchandising companies also may be capital intensive if they require large investments in stores, warehouses, or delivery equipment. Examination of operating leverage and how it is being managed is important in evaluating a company's investment decisions. Chapter 14 examines operating leverage in more detail.

CASH ANALYSIS AND MANAGEMENT

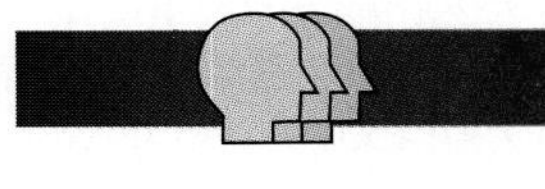

Cash is vital to an organization. Without sufficient cash, an organization cannot survive. Managing cash is a vital function. Too little cash and an organization is incapable of meeting its current obligations, replacing assets, or taking advantage of new opportunities. Too much cash also can be a problem unless a company has good opportunities for investing the cash. Cash does not earn a return until it is invested. Therefore, excess cash should be invested. If excess cash will be needed in the near future for other purposes, investments should be short-term. If excess cash will not be needed for other purposes, a company should look for new investment opportunities, repay existing debt, repurchase stock, or pay cash dividends to its stockholders.

Objective 10
Analyze a company's cash management.

The inability to generate cash is the cause of most business failures. Therefore, careful monitoring of cash flows should be a high priority in every business. Operating cash flows should be used to replace current assets, pay dividends, and pay for operating costs. Financing activities provide cash flows for long-term asset purchases. Many companies maintain lines of credit with financial institutions that permit them to borrow on a short-term basis to meet short-term cash flow needs. Financing for major acquisitions normally requires a company to issue new stock or long-term debt.

The statement of cash flows provides information about a company's cash flow decisions. It is valuable for evaluating how a company is obtaining and using cash. Exhibit 12-16 provides summary cash flow information for two companies for 1986 to 1991.

Exhibit 12-16 Analysis of Cash Flows

In Millions	1986	1987	1988	1989	1990	1991
Vulcan Materials						
Operating	$205.0	$213.4	$175.3	$250.2	$200.1	$183.3
Investing	(120.0)	(99.3)	(102.2)	(120.4)	(249.6)	(98.7)
Financing	(116.7)	(73.7)	(111.2)	(113.6)	(16.2)	(84.2)
Allied Products						
Operating	(99.8)	(32.1)	(3.6)	(8.1)	25.7	34.5
Investing	(2.6)	(9.9)	(1.7)	(6.7)	(6.7)	27.6
Financing	97.7	41.1	12.3	15.0	(14.4)	(67.3)

For most companies, the amount of cash flow from operating activities is approximately equal to the amount of cash flows for financing and investing activities:

Operating Cash In = Cash Used for Investing Cash from (or for) Financing

For example, net cash inflows from operating activities for Vulcan Materials in 1991 were $183.3 million, approximately equal to the total of net cash outflows for investing and financing activities, $182.9 million ($98.7 + $84.2). This relationship is logical because all cash flows result from one of these three types of activities. If a company generated $30 million of cash flow from operating activities and needed $50 million for investing activities, it would need to raise $20 million from financing activities: $30 = ($50) + $20.

The source of cash inflows for Vulcan Materials for the years shown in Exhibit 12-16 was operating activities. These activities provided sufficient cash to meet current operating needs and to provide for the company's investing activities. Excess cash was used to repay debt and to repurchase stock. Therefore, cash was used for financing activities. In contrast, Allied Products relied on financing activities to provide cash inflows from 1987 to 1989, primarily for use by operating activities. It used relatively little of this cash for investing activities. When cash was generated from operating activities in 1990 and 1991, it was used to repay debt. In addition, cash was generated from investing activities by selling long-term assets to repay debt. The company's total new investment for the six years was approximately zero. At the same time, its debt and contributed capital increased by approximately $80 million.

The patterns of cash flows for Vulcan Materials and Allied Products are illustrated in Exhibit 12-17. Vulcan Materials generated cash flows from operating activities that were approximately equal to the cash used for operating and financing activities.

In contrast, Allied Products obtained cash from financing activities sufficient to meet its operating and investing requirements, until 1990. As was discussed earlier in the chapter, the company faced serious problems at the end of 1991 because of its inability to borrow additional cash. A pattern of large and sustained cash outflows from operating activities is a major signal of financial problems. Chapter 14 examines this issue in more detail.

Exhibit 12-17 Cash Flow Patterns

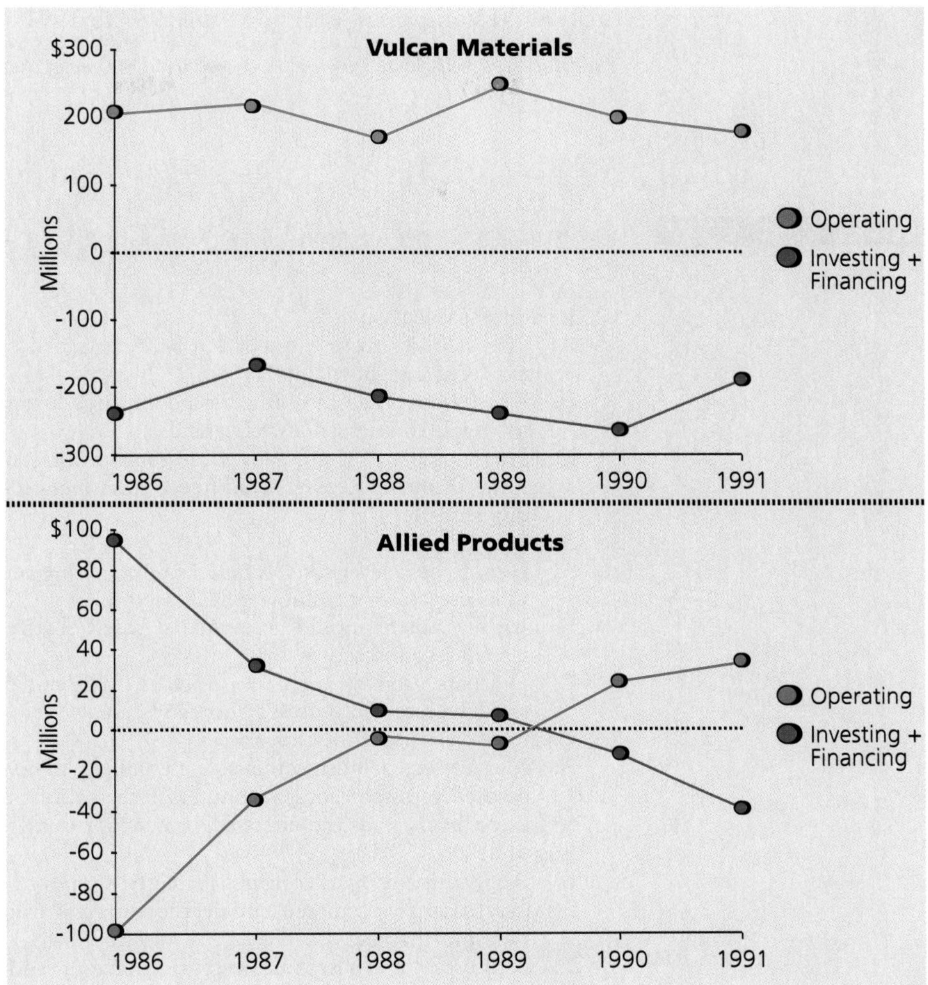

SELF-STUDY PROBLEM 12-3

Cash flow information is provided below for two companies in the computer and electronics industry. Cash outflows are shown in parentheses.

In millions	1991	1990	1989
Tandy Corporation			
Operating activities	$617	$ 58	$353
Investing activities	(141)	(182)	(123)
Financing activities	(426)	200	(360)
Texas Instruments Incorporated			
Operating activities	417	694	799
Investing activities	(533)	(699)	(832)
Financing activities	173	(14)	(83)

Required

Analyze the companies' cash flows for 1989 to 1991.

The solution to Self-Study Problem 12-3 appears at the end of the chapter.

REVIEW *Summary of Important Concepts*

1. Investment valuation:
   A. The value of an investment can be determined by the net present value of its expected cash flows.
   B. The required rate of return for a company's investments should be greater than its weighted average cost of capital.
   C. Stockholders of a company with good investment opportunities are better off if the company reinvests cash flows from operating activities rather than paying dividends.
2. Risk and return:
   A. Return on assets and cash flow from operating activities to total assets are measures used to evaluate investment decisions.
   B. An investment should be evaluated based on the effect it has on a company's overall risk and return.
   C. Diversification through investment in different types of assets, product lines, and locations can reduce a company's risk.
3. Comparison of investment decisions:
   A. Mergers and acquisitions enable a company to diversify and expand. Care must be used in interpreting accounting information after a major merger or acquisition because of the effect the transaction may have on accounting information.
   B. Reporting fair market values for certain types of assets may provide useful information that can prevent decision makers from being misled by historical cost information.
   C. Ratios that measure the composition of assets and the relationship between net income or cash flows and assets are often used to compare investment decisions among companies and industries.
   D. Real and nominal growth rates provide information for evaluating companies' investment decisions over time.
4. Operating leverage:
   A. Operating leverage, the proportion of a company's total expenses that are fixed, affects the amount and volatility of a company's earnings.
5. Cash management decisions:
   A. The statement of cash flows provides information that can be used to analyze a company's cash management decisions. This information can be used to identify cash flow problems.

DEFINE *Terms and Concepts Defined in this Chapter*

capital expenditures
fixed costs
net present value
operating leverage
variable costs

SOLUTIONS

SELF-STUDY PROBLEM 12-1

Wal-Mart's average total assets increased by about 84% over the three years. Cash was invested in new assets throughout the period. Most of this cash was generated from operating activities. Net income to total assets and cash from operating activities to total assets were as follows:

	Net Income/ Average Total Assets	Cash—Operating/ Average Total Assets
1990	14.8%	11.9%
1991	13.2%	13.2%
1992	12.0%	10.7%

These ratios were fairly stable over the three-year period, suggesting Wal-Mart was earning a fairly consistent return on its new investments. Comparisons with other companies or analysis over a longer period would be needed to determine more precisely how well the company's investments were performing. No indication of a financial problem is evident from these data.

SELF-STUDY PROBLEM 12-2

(a)	1991	1990
Return on assets: [net income + interest expense (1 − .40)] ÷ total assets	5.2%	7.0%
Cash flow to total assets	7.3%	6.6%

(b)	1991
Income before taxes	$ 515.2
Excess depreciation and amortization ($250.8 − $129.7)	121.1
Restated income before taxes	636.3
Income taxes, 40%	(254.5)
Net income as restated	$ 381.8
Net income as restated plus interest expense [298.0 × (1 − .40)]	$ 560.6
Total assets	$9,420.3
Intangible assets from acquisition ($2,710.9− $251.5)	(2,459.4)
Write-up of plant assets to fair market	(900.0)
Total assets as restated	$6,060.9
Return on assets ($560.6/$6,060.9)	9.2%
Cash flow to total assets ($691.8/$6,060.19)	11.4%

(c)	1991
Net income as restated	$381.8
Preferred dividends	(19.5)
Net income available for common stock	$362.3
Earnings per share ($362.3/136.9 shares)	$2.65

SELF-STUDY PROBLEM 12-3

Both companies had positive cash flows from operating activities each year. Tandy's operating cash flows were more volatile, but Texas Instruments' operating cash flows evidenced a downward trend over the three years. Texas Instruments used much more cash for investing activities during the period than did Tandy. It invested an amount greater than its operating cash flows each year. Tandy invested a much lower amount of cash. Instead, it used its cash to repay debt and repurchase stock. Thus, its cash management practices differed from those of Texas Instruments. The investing practices might suggest that Texas Instruments had better investment options than did Tandy. Management apparently believed it had good investment opportunities because they invested more cash than generated by operating activities each year. These investments were not generating higher levels of cash flow from operating activities by 1991, however. A longer period might be needed to evaluate these investment decisions.

EXERCISES

12-1. Write a short definition for each of the terms listed in the *Terms and Concepts Defined in this Chapter* section.

12-2. The Yang Company is considering the purchase of equipment. The equipment costs $70,000. The company expects the asset to generate cash inflows of $20,000 per year for 5 years. Yang requires a return of 12% on its investments. What is the net present value of the equipment? Should the company buy the equipment if the net present value is its only criterion?

12-3. The Takeshi Company's weighted average cost of capital is 11%. The company has an opportunity to invest in a project that is expected to generate a cash inflow of $30,000 per year for 8 years. The investment would be made at the beginning of the project's life. What is the maximum price Takeshi should be willing to pay to invest in the project?

12-4. Besserat Company earned net income of $13 million during 1994. The company's common stockholders' equity (market value) was $75 million at the end of 1993 and $80 million at the end of 1994. Interest expense for 1994 was $2 million. Besserat's total short-term and long-term debt at the end of 1993 was $17 million. Its total short-term and long-term debt at the end of 1994 was $16 million. Short-term debt includes current maturities of long-term debt. What was Besserat's weighted average cost of capital for 1994? Of what importance is the weighted average cost of capital for a company's investment decisions?

12-5. Some companies distribute most of their earnings to stockholders in the form of dividends. Other companies distribute a small portion of their earning as dividends or pay no dividends at all. How does a company's dividend policy affect its investment decisions? What does a company's dividend policy signal about its investment opportunities?

12-6. Information is provided below for Motorola Incorporated from its 1991 annual report:

(in millions)	**1991**	**1990**	**1989**	**1988**	**1987**
Interest expense	129	133	130	98	
Net income	454	499	498	445	
Total assets	9,375	8,742	7,686	6,710	5,517

Evaluate Motorola's investing decisions by computing and analyzing its return on assets for 1988 through 1991. Assume an income tax rate of 34%.

12-7. The following information was reported by Monsanto Company in its 1991 annual report:

(in millions)	1991	1990	1989	1988	1987
Interest expense	169	179	182	174	
Net income	296	546	679	591	
Cash flow from operating activities	1,180	1,104	1,037	1,304	
Total assets	9,227	9,236	8,604	8,461	8,455

Evaluate Monsanto's investing decisions by computing return on assets and cash flow from operating activities to total assets for 1988 through 1991. Assume an income tax rate of 34%. Compare the cash flow and accrual measures.

12-8. Companies often invest in assets that will permit them to produce several different product lines. What are the advantages of investing in several product lines as opposed to making larger investments in the production of a single product?

12-9. Segment information is provided below from the 1991 annual report of American Cyanamid Company:

(in millions)	1991	1990	1989
Operating earnings:			
Medical	$ 383.1	$ 297.5	$ 320.3
Agricultural	189.9	133.0	184.9
Chemicals	32.2	142.6	44.7
Total	605.2	287.9	549.9
Assets:			
Medical	1,919.3	1,799.9	1,493.5
Agricultural	1,042.6	1,075.8	1,011.3
Chemicals	745.1	756.1	767.4
Total	3,707.0	3,631.8	3,272.2

Evaluate the performance of each of Cyanamid's segments and the effect they had on the company's overall performance. If you were a manager at Cyanamid, how would this information affect your investment decisions?

12-10. Hockey Company acquired the Puck Company during 1993. The companies merged to form the Hockey Puck Company. The merger was accounted for as a purchase. The fair market value of Puck Company's net assets was $38 million. Hockey Company paid $60 million for the net assets. The merger was financed by the issuance of long-term debt at an interest rate of 12%. Prior to the merger, Hockey Company had total assets of $90 million and total liabilities of $40 million. Its net income for 1993 was expected to be $10 million. Puck expected net income for 1993 of $4 million. How would the merger affect Hockey Puck's financial statements for 1993? What effect would it have on the use of financial statement information by investors and other external parties?

12-11. During 1989 PepsiCo, Incorporated, paid over $3 billion for acquisitions accounted for using the purchase method. Other major acquisitions also occurred in 1990 and 1991 amounting to approximately $1,270 million. Of the company's total assets of $18,775 million at the end of 1991, $5,932 million were goodwill. Total assets were $11,135 million in 1988. Net cash flow from operating activities was $1,895 million in 1988 and $2,430 million in 1991. Net income was $762 million in 1988 and $1,080 million in 1991. Interest expense was $344 million in 1988 and $616 million in 1991. Evaluate the effect of PepsiCo's acquisitions on the company's performance.

12-12. Anthro Poid is a friend who is planning to be a business manager. In a recent discussion about financial matters Anthro made the following statement: "A company's balance sheet measures the value of a company's resources. Investors can use this value for pricing the company's stock and for comparing the values of different companies." How would you respond to Anthro?

12-13. At the end of its 1993 fiscal year, Shangri-La Company owned the following investments in securities:

Investment	Historical Cost	Fair Market Value
A	$650,000	$765,000
B	840,000	730,000

Other assets had a book value of $2.4 million and liabilities had a book value of $2.8 million. Shangri-La's pretax income for 1993 was $400,000 and its tax rate was 30%. If the company sold Investment A at the end of 1993 for cash, what effect would the sale have on its financial statements and return on assets? Assume assets are reported on the financial statements at historical cost. What effect would the sale of Investment B have on the company's financial statements and return on assets? Compare these amounts to those that would be reported if no investments were sold.

12-14. Selected financial information for two companies is reported below from their 1991 annual reports:

(in millions)	Digital Equipment Corporation	Honeywell Incorporated
Plant assets, at cost	$7,429	$2,447
Depreciation expense	492	236
Net cash outflow for investing activities	1,027	197

Compare the depreciation policies and investment rates of the two companies. Both companies use straight-line depreciation, predominantly. Assume cash was invested primarily in plant assets.

12-15. Selected accounting information is provided below for two companies:

	1987	1988	1989	1990	1991
Inflation Index	100	103.9	108.4	112.9	117.0
Total Assets					
Alcoa	9,902	10,538	11,541	11,413	11,178
Warner-Lambert	2,476	2,703	2,860	3,261	3,602
Depreciation & Amortization					
Alcoa	587	623	638	690	698
Warner-Lambert	79	96	105	120	135
Capital Expenditures					
Alcoa	856	866	876	851	850
Warner-Lambert	174	190	218	240	326

What trends in asset investments are apparent from examining the data presented above? Compare the nominal and real growth rates in total assets for the two companies from 1987 to 1991.

12-16. The Ming and Shang Companies both increased sales by 30% between their 1993 and 1994 fiscal years. Ming's net income increased 40% as a result of the increased sales. Shang's net income increased 20%. Explain why differences in operating leverage may have resulted in a higher increase in net income for Ming than for Shang. Provide a diagram to illustrate your explanation.

12-17. The Maglioni Company recorded sales revenues of $5 million in 1994. The company incurred expenses of $4.5 million. Fixed costs accounted for $2 million of these expenses. How much net income would Maglioni have reported if its sales had been $4 million? $6 million? Suppose the company's sales were $5 million in 1994. Its total expenses were $4.5 million and fixed costs accounted for $3 million of these expenses. How much net income would Maglioni have reported if its sales had been $4 million? $6 million? What conclusions can you draw from this analysis about the effect of operating leverage on net income?

12-18. The balance sheet and statement of cash flows provide information about a company's access to and use of cash. What differences would you expect to see in the information related to cash on these statements for a company reporting strong financial performance versus a company reporting weak financial performance?

12-19. Information is provided below from the statement of cash flows of Delta Airlines, Incorporated, for 1992:

(In thousands)	**1992**	**1991**	**1990**
Net cash provided by operating activities	149,514	$ 323,790	$ 803,766
Net cash used in investing activities	(3,039,118)	(2,171,704)	(1,974,069)
Net cash provided by financing activities	2,176,315	2,543,159	709,103

Most of the cash provided by financing activities was from the issuance of long-term debt and from sale and lease-back of fixed assets. Evaluate Delta's cash flows over the three years. What information is communicated about the company's future prospects by its investing and financing activities during this period?

12-20. The Florez Company increased its investment in long-term assets by 20% in the past three years. This investment was financed by rapid increases in cash generated from operating activities. Cash from operating activities also was used to repay about 30% of Florez's long-term debt and to repurchase 10% of its common stock. What effect would you expect these events to have on the company's earnings per share and price-earnings ratio?

PROBLEMS

PROBLEM 12-1 Determining Asset Value

The Sand Castle Company is planning to add a new machine to its production process. The machine will permit the company to produce a better grade of building material. As a result of its new capacity, the company expects to create additional net cash inflows over the life of the machine, as follows: year 1, $300,000; year 2, $300,000; year 3, $400,000; year 4, $500,000; year 5, $500,000. The machine can be purchased for $1,200,000. The company's average cost of capital is 12%.

Required Write a memo to Sandra Alexander, the vice-president of production for the company, explaining why you believe the machine should or should not be purchased.

PROBLEM 12-2 Determining Required Rate of Return

Information is provided below from the 1992 annual report of General Mills:

In millions	**1992**	**1991**
Notes payable	169.3	$ 23.4
Current portion of long-term debt	32.6	129.0
Long-term debt, net of current portion	920.5	879.0
Total stockholders' equity	1,370.9	1,113.5
Interest, including amount capitalized	103.1	103.9
Net income	495.6	472.7

Required Determine General Mills' weighted average cost of capital and explain why the cost of capital is useful for investment decisions. Assume an income tax rate of 34%.

PROBLEM 12-3 Evaluating Investment Decisions

During 1991, Intel Corporation invested $1,459 million of cash in additional assets. Of this amount, $948 million was invested in plant assets. The remainder was invested in securities. The company invested $879 million of cash in additional assets in 1990. Other information reported by the company in its 1991 annual report includes:

(in millions)	**1991**	**1990**	**1989**
Total assets	$6,292	$5,376	$3,994
Interest expense	82	99	96
Net income	819	650	391

Required Compare the results of Intel's investment decisions during 1990 and 1991.

PROBLEM 12-4 Evaluating Investment Decisions

The following information was reported by Intel Corporation in its 1991 annual report:

(in millions, except EPS)	**Total Assets**	**Long-Term Debt**	**Additions to Plant Assets**	**Net Income**	**Earnings per Share**
1991	$6,292	$363	$948	$819	$3.92
1990	5,376	345	680	650	3.20
1989	3,994	412	422	391	2.07
1988	3,550	479	477	453	2.51
1987	2,499	298	302	248	1.38
1986	1,977				

Required Evaluate Intel's investment decisions for the period from 1987 to 1991. Assume an income tax rate of 34%.

PROBLEM 12-5 Evaluating Investment Decisions

The following information was reported by PepsiCo, Incorporated, in its 1991 annual report:

in millions except share price	**1991**	**1990**	**1989**	**1988**	**1987**
Net income	$ 1,080.2	$ 1,076.9	$ 901.4	$ 762.2	$ 594.8
Cash flow—operating	2,430.3	2,110.0	1,885.9	1,894.5	1,334.5
Cash invested in other companies	640.9	630.6	3,296.6	1,415.5	371.5
Cash purchases of plant assets	1,457.8	1,180.1	943.8	725.8	770.5
Cash dividends paid	343.2	293.9	241.9	199.0	172.0
Total assets	18,775.1	17,143.4	15,126.7	11,135.3	9,022.7

Required Identify and evaluate PepsiCo's investment decisions over the five years shown above.

PROBLEM 12-6 Analysis of Segment Information

Segment information is provided below from the 1991 annual report of Cooper Industries:

(in millions)	**1991**	**1990**	**1989**
Electrical Products:			
Earnings	$ 273.4	$ 288.8	$ 280.6
Assets	1,265.8	1,309.7	1,331.2
Automotive Products:			
Earnings	145.2	154.2	95.8
Assets	1,648.9	1,646.6	1,476.9
Petroleum & Industrial Equipment:			
Earnings	310.6	241.2	107.4
Assets	2,423.5	2,417.3	2,304.9
Total Corporate:			
Earnings before taxes	668.6	628.6	474.7
Assets	7,148.6	7,167.5	6,745.0

Cooper also disclosed two smaller segments that are not shown above. Total corporate earnings and assets also include general and administrative expenses and assets that were not allocated to individual segments.

Required What effect have these segments had on Cooper Industries' risk and return for the period shown?

PROBLEM 12-7 Analysis of Acquisitions

The Fast Burn Company is considering the acquisition of Plenty Fuel Company. Fast Burn would acquire all of Plenty Fuel's common stock, which, if purchased for cash, would cost $15 million. The fair market value of Plenty's assets is $18 million, and the fair market value of its liabilities is $6 million. Financial statements for the two companies for their most recent fiscal years reveals:

(in millions)	Fast Burn	Plenty Fuel
Total assets	$30.7	$14.5
Total liabilities	16.9	5.8
Net income	5.6	2.7

To finance the acquisition, Fast Burn would issue additional common stock. The stock could be sold for cash or it could be exchanged directly with Plenty Fuel's current stockholders. Goodwill would be amortized over 10 years. There were no intercompany transactions between the companies.

Required (a) What effect would the acquisition have on Fast Burn's consolidated financial statements and profitability if the acquisition were accounted for as a purchase? (b) What effect would the acquisition have on Fast Burn's consolidated financial statements and profitability if the acquisition were accounted for as a pooling of interests? (c) What effect would the accounting method used (purchase or pooling) have on Fast Burn's cash flows?

PROBLEM 12-8 Comparing Investment Activities

Information is provided below from the 1991 annual reports of The Coca-Cola Company and PepsiCo, Incorporated:

(in millions except per share amounts)	Coca-Cola	PepsiCo
Current assets	$ 4,144	$ 4,566
Investments and other assets	2,885	1,682
Plant assets, at cost	4,445	10,502
Plant assets, net	2,890	6,595
Goodwill and intangibles	304	5,932
Total assets	10,223	18,775
Current liabilities	4,118	3,722
Long-term debt	985	7,806
Other liabilities	694	1,701
Shareholders' equity	4,426	5,546
Net income	1,618	1,080
Interest expense	193	616
Depreciation and amortization	261	1,035
Net cash provided by operating activities	2,084	2,430
Net cash provided by (used in) investing activities	(1,125)	(2,276)
Net cash provided by (used in) financing activities	(1,331)	(131)
Earnings per share	2.04	1.35
Stock price per share	80.25	33.75
Cash from operating activities per share	3.13	3.03

Required Use accounting ratios to compare the investing activities and performances of the two companies for 1991. What important differences exist in the investing and financing activities of the companies? How do these differences affect the risk and return of the companies? How do these differences affect the PE ratios and the price/cash flow from operating activities ratios of the two companies?

PROBLEM 12-9 Comparing Investment Decisions

Information is presented below for Chrysler Corporation and Ford Motor Company from their 1991 annual reports:

(in millions)	Total Assets	Capital Expenditures	Depreciation and Amortization	Dividends	Net Income (Loss)
Chrysler					
1984	$ 9,039	$1,247	$ 555	$ 105	$ 2,373
1985	12,154	1,528	474	116	1,610
1986	14,253	2,054	537	176	1,389
1987	19,745	1,919	868	219	1,290
1988	22,230	1,636	1,121	224	1,050
1989	23,631	1,588	1,248	277	359
1990	24,521	1,697	1,261	269	68
1991	25,544	2,190	1,311	145	(795)
Ford					
1984	51,990	3,554	2,384	370	2,907
1985	75,094	3,803	2,508	443	2,515
1986	93,232	3,464	3,152	592	3,285
1987	115,994	3,758	3,460	807	4,625
1988	143,367	4,782	3,792	1,113	5,300
1989	160,893	6,767	4,228	1,400	3,835
1990	173,663	7,257	4,879	1,388	860
1991	174,429	5,847	5,778	928	(2,258)

Required (a) Compute annual growth rates for the items listed above for each company from 1985 to 1991. (b) Compare the investment decisions of the two companies over these years. Which company appears to have made the best decisions? Why? (c) What assumptions about the companies' accounting methods are important to your analysis?

PROBLEM 12-10 Comparing Operating Leverage

Information is provided below from the 1991 annual reports of The Home Depot, Incorporated, and Pacific Gas and Electric Company. The earnings shown below are operating income (income before interest and taxes).

	The Home Depot		Pacific Gas and Electric	
(in millions)	Sales	Earnings	Sales	Earnings
1987	$1454	$ 96	$7186	$1262
1988	2000	126	7646	1297
1989	2759	182	8588	1623
1990	3815	260	9470	1706
1991	5137	396	9778	1713

Home Depot's plant and other long-term assets constitute about 50% of its total assets. Pacific Gas and Electric's plant and other long-term assets constitute about 80% of its total assets. Almost all of the long-term assets of both companies are plant assets.

Required Prepare a graph to illustrate the relationship between each company's earnings and its sales over the five years. Which company has the highest operating leverage? What effect does operating leverage have on the companies' operating incomes?

PROBLEM 12-11 Comparing Cash Flows

Cash flow information is provided below for two companies in the paper and wood products industry. Cash outflows are shown in parentheses.

In millions	1991	1990	1989	Total
Champion International				
Operating activities	$ 370	$ 532	$ 774	$1,676
Investing activities	(498)	(1,067)	(1,041)	(2,606)
Financing activities	182	538	269	989
Georgia-Pacific				
Operating activities	580	2,073	1,358	4,011
Investing activities	746	(4,229)	(500)	(3,983)
Financing activities	(1,336)	2,191	(897)	(42)

Required Analyze the companies' cash flows for 1989 to 1991 and for the three years in total.

PROBLEM 12-12 Multiple-Choice Overview of the Chapter

1. The net present value of an investment involves a comparison of the cost of the investment with its:
   a. future revenues
   b. future expenses
   c. future cash flows
   d. required rate of return
2. The minimum required rate of return a company should expect to earn on new investments is the company's:
   a. average cost of capital
   b. net present value
   c. current return on assets
   d. current return on equity
3. A company with good investment opportunities normally can increase its stockholders' wealth by:
   a. increasing its cash dividend payout rate
   b. reducing its cash dividend payout rate
   c. reducing the amount invested in new assets
   d. reducing its required rate of return on new assets
4. A company can reduce the volatility of its net income by:
   a. diversifying its product line
   b. increasing its financial leverage

c. increasing its operating leverage
d. investing in projects with high net present values

5. In an acquisition accounted for as a purchase, the assets and liabilities of the acquired company are reported on the consolidated balance sheet of the acquiring company at their:
   a. book value
   b. net present value
   c. estimated fair market value
   d. original cost
6. The amortization of goodwill affects the net income and net cash flow from operating activities of the acquiring company as follows:

	Net Income	Net Cash Flow
a.	Yes	Yes
b.	Yes	No
c.	No	Yes
d.	No	No

7. Company A has a higher proportion of fixed expenses than Company B. The sales revenues of both companies increased by 10%. You would expect:
   a. Company A's expenses to increase more rapidly than Company B's.
   b. Company A's expenses to decrease while Company B's increase.
   c. Company A's net income to decrease while Company B's increase.
   d. Company A's net income to increase more rapidly than Company B's.
8. Company A and Company B are similar in size and in many other respects. The companies reported the following net cash flow from (used for) investing activities in their 1994 annual reports:

($ in millions)	1994	1993	1992
Company A	(460)	(350)	(265)
Company B	200	35	(80)

   From this information you would expect:
   a. Company A to be growing more rapidly than Company B.
   b. Company B to be growing more rapidly than Company A.
   c. Company B to have better investment alternatives than Company A.
   d. Company A to be in greater need of cash than Company B.
9. A company has increased its investment in assets at an average annual rate of 3% over the last decade. The average annual rate of inflation over this period has been 5%. The company's nominal and real growth rates have been:

	Nominal	Real
a.	positive	positive
b.	positive	negative
c.	negative	positive
d.	negative	negative

10. Which of the following net cash flow patterns is typical of a company with high growth potential and strong financial performance:

	Cash Flow from Operating Activities	Cash Flow from Investing Activities
a.	Outflow	Outflow
b.	Outflow	Inflow
c.	Inflow	Inflow
d.	Inflow	Outflow

CASES

CASE 12-1 Analysis of an Acquisition

You are a financial analyst with a major corporation, High Hopes Company. You have been assigned the task of evaluating a potential acquisition candidate, Roll-the-Dice, Incorporated. Selected accounting information for the two companies is presented below. Information for 1993 and 1992 are actual company results. Results for 1994 are projected from information available at the beginning of the year.

(in millions)	1994	1993	1992
High Hopes Company			
Depreciation and amortization expense	$ 13.4	$ 13.1	$ 11.6
Operating income	46.3	42.7	37.5
Interest expense	4.9	5.1	5.5
Provision for income taxes	12.6	11.8	11.0
Net income	28.8	25.8	21.0
Total assets	305.7	292.1	274.8
Total liabilities	125.9	128.0	135.2
Total stockholders' equity	179.8	164.1	139.6
Net cash flow from operating activities	40.4	38.5	32.8
Net cash flow used for investing activities	(14.1)	(12.8)	(9.8)
Net cash flow used for financing activities	(25.3)	(25.7)	(23.0)
Roll-the-Dice, Incorporated			
Depreciation expense	$ 5.4	$ 5.2	$ 4.5
Operating income	22.8	19.3	12.9
Interest expense	3.7	3.5	3.0
Provision for income taxes	6.2	4.7	4.2
Net income	12.9	11.1	5.7
Total assets	114.3	111.0	93.4
Total liabilities	35.8	33.2	31.8
Total stockholders' equity	78.5	77.8	73.5
Depreciation and amortization expense	5.4	5.2	4.5
Net cash flow from operating activities	18.7	16.4	14.6
Net cash flow used for investing activities	(13.7)	(7.9)	(18.3)
Net cash flow from (used for) financing activities	(4.5)	(8.6)	3.8

The acquisition, if it were to occur, would result in High Hopes' purchasing all of the common stock of Roll-the-Dice at a price of $130 million. To finance the acquisition, High Hopes plans to issue $130 million of long-term debt at 10.7% annual interest. The debt would be repaid in equal installments over 10 years. The fair market value of Roll-the-Dice's assets is $127 million. The fair market value of its liabilities are $37 million. The additional assets would increase depreciation on Roll-the-Dice's current assets from $5.4 million to $7.0 million. Goodwill from the acquisition would be amortized over 10 years. There are no intercompany transactions between High Hopes and Roll-the-Dice. Assume High Hopes' income tax rate is 34%.

Required Prepare summary pro-forma income statement and statement of cash flows for High Hopes for 1994, assuming it acquires Roll-the-Dice at the beginning of 1994. What recommendation would you make to High Hopes' management concerning the acquisition?

CASE 12-2 Evaluating Investment Decisions

Appendix B of this book contains a copy of the 1992 annual report of General Mills, Inc.

Required Review the annual report and write a short report in which you identify each of the following:

a. What was the company's weighted average cost of capital for 1992?
b. What major investment decisions did the company make from 1990 to 1992?
c. Compare the ratio of operating income to identifiable assets of the company's major product lines in 1992.

PROJECTS

PROJECT 12-1 Comparing Investment Decisions

Obtain the most recent annual report available for each of three corporations from your library. Calculate the return on assets for each company for each of the most recent three years. Write a brief report comparing the companies' returns. What explanations can you provide for why the returns were different or similar?

PROJECT 12-2 Comparing Investment Decisions

Obtain the most recent annual report available for each of three corporations from your library. Examine the cash flows associated with investing activities for each company for each of the most recent three years. Write a brief report comparing the companies' investing activities. Explain how the companies' investing decisions affected their cash flows. Explain how each company's investing decisions affected its asset growth.

PROJECT 12-3 Comparing Segment Information

Obtain the most recent annual report available for each of three corporations from your library. Find corporations in the same industry. Examine information reported by each company about its industry segments. Compute return on assets for each segment for each company. Write a short report comparing the segments and their performances for each company.

PROJECT 12-4 Evaluating Cash Flows

Use the annual report of a major corporation to determine the company's net cash flows from operating, investing, and financing activities for the last five years. You may need to use reports from earlier years to obtain some of the information. Prepare a graph to illustrate changes in the cash flows over the five-year period. Write a short report describing the changes and explaining their importance for evaluating the company's performance and investing decisions.

PROJECT 12-5 Comparing Operating Leverage

Use annual reports or other sources of accounting information to identify an example of a company with a high amount of operating leverage and a company with a low amount of operating leverage. Examine the relationship between the sales revenues and operating incomes of each company for the last five years. Graph these relationships and write a short report comparing the operating leverages and operating performances of the two companies.

CHAPTER 13

OPERATING ACTIVITIES

CHAPTER
Overview

As discussed in previous chapters, financing and investing activities support operating activities by providing necessary resources. Operating activities create goods and services and market these products to customers. This chapter examines accounting for a company's operating activities. The income statement and statement of cash flows provide information about operating activities. These activities also affect information reported on the balance sheet, as shown in the following illustration:

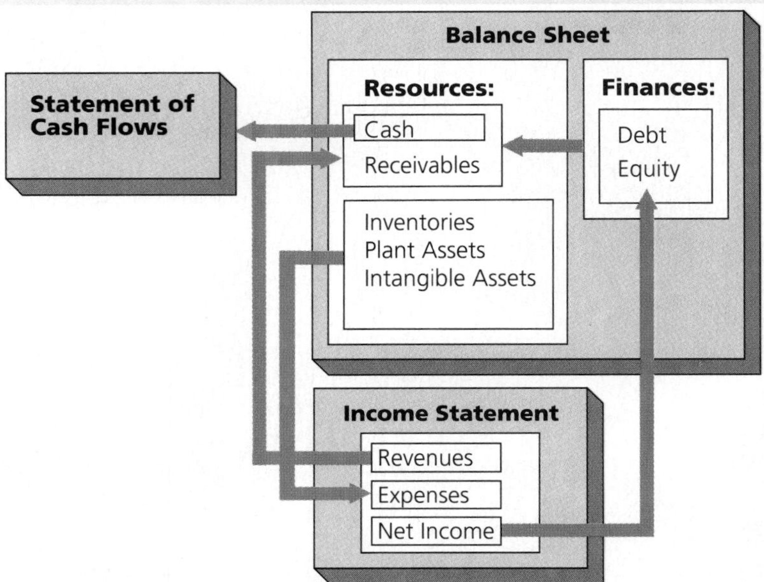

This chapter discusses the contents of the income statement, statement of cash flows, and interrelationships among elements of these statements and those of the balance sheet.

Major topics covered in this chapter include:

- Revenues and accounts receivable
- Cost of goods sold and inventories
- Operating income and expenses, other revenues and expenses, and income taxes
- Special income statement items
- Cash flow from operating activities

CHAPTER
Objectives

Once you have completed this chapter, you should be able to:

1. Identify the purpose and major components of an income statement.
2. Identify transactions that affect gross profit.
3. Determine when a company should recognize revenues.
4. Determine the amount of accounts receivable a company should report.
5. Determine the amount of inventories for merchandising and manufacturing companies.

6. Explain the effect of inventory measurement methods on cost of goods sold and inventory.
7. Explain the reporting and measurement of operating expenses.
8. Explain the reporting and measurement of other revenues and expenses.
9. Explain the reporting and measurement of income taxes.
10. Explain the reporting and measurement of discontinued operations, extraordinary items, and accounting changes.
11. Determine net income available for common shareholders.
12. Distinguish primary and fully diluted earnings per share.
13. Compare accrual and cash operating results.
14. Explain the reporting of subsequent events.

REPORTING OPERATING RESULTS

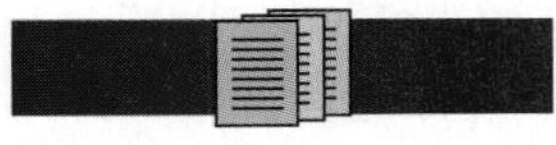

Objective 1
Identify the purpose and major components of an income statement.

The income statement reports the accrual basis results of operating activities for a fiscal period. It includes revenues from sales and services. Expenses associated with production, marketing, distribution, managing, and other functions are subtracted from these revenues to calculate net income. Net income is a primary measure of a company's performance during a fiscal period. It is a measure of the results of operating activities. Therefore, decision makers use net income to evaluate a company's success in providing value for its stockholders and as a basis for forecasting future operating results.

To illustrate the reporting of operating activities, Exhibit 13-1 contains Coca-Cola's income statement from its 1991 annual report. Major items reported on the income statement include operating revenues, gross profit, operating income, income from continuing operations before taxes, income from continuing operations (after taxes), net income, net income available to common stockholders, and earnings per share. These items are typical of those reported by most corporations. The following sections examine reporting and measurement issues associated with each of these items.

GROSS PROFIT

Objective 2
Identify transactions that affect gross profit.

Gross profit **is the excess of operating revenues over cost of goods sold.** It represents the difference between the amount a company expects to receive from its sales and the cost of resources consumed in producing or acquiring goods and services that are sold during a fiscal period. Coca-Cola reported gross profit of $6,923 million in 1991 (item 3 in Exhibit 13-1).

Gross profit results from transactions between a company and its customers and suppliers. Suppliers are providers of resources used in producing goods and services. Customers are purchasers of these goods and services. Merchandising and manufacturing companies acquire resources from suppliers and sell goods to customers. Operating transactions of service companies are simpler than those of other companies. These companies sell services that usually do not require large amounts of inventories or transactions with suppliers. The following sections examine accounting for activities that affect gross profit.

Exhibit 13-1

THE COCA-COLA COMPANY
CONSOLIDATED STATEMENT OF INCOME

Year Ended December 31 (In millions except per share data)	1991	1990	1989
1. **Net Operating Revenues**	$11,571	$10,236	$8,622
2. Cost of goods sold	4,648	4,208	3,548
3. **Gross Profit**	6,923	6,028	5,074
4. Selling, administrative and general expenses	4,604	4,076	3,348
5. **Operating Income**	2,319	1,952	1,726
6. Interest income	175	170	205
7. Interest expense	(192)	(231)	(308)
8. Equity income	40	110	75
9. Other income—net	41	13	66
10. **Income from Continuing Operations before Income Taxes**	2,383	2,014	1,764
11. Income taxes	765	632	571
12. **Income from Continuing Operations**	1,618	1,382	1,193
13. Equity income from discontinued operation	—	—	21
14. Gain on sale of discontinued operation (net of income taxes of $421,021)	—	—	509
15. **Net Income**	1,618	1,382	1,723
16. Preferred stock dividends	1	18	21
17. **Net Income Available to Common Share Owners**	$ 1,617	$ 1,364	$1,702
18. **Income per Common Share**			
19. Continuing operations	$ 2.43	$ 2.04	$ 1.69
20. Discontinued operation	—	—	.77
21. **Net Income per Common Share**	$ 2.43	$ 2.04	$ 2.46
22. **Average Common Shares Outstanding**	666	669	692

Minor modifications have been made to the format for presentation purposes. Items have been numbered for reference.

Revenue Recognition

Objective 3
Determine when a company should recognize revenues.

Operating revenues result from sales of goods and services to customers. For most companies, sales are linked closely with accounts receivable because sales are made on credit. Therefore, the recognition of revenue affects the recognition of accounts receivable.

Coca-Cola reported net operating revenues of $11,571 million in 1991 (item 1 in Exhibit 13-1). For most companies, revenues are recognized at the time title (ownership) to goods or services is transferred to customers. Title to most goods passes to the buyer at the time of delivery or at the time goods are shipped to the buyer. In many retail companies, revenue is recognized at the time of sale, when customers take possession of goods. Service companies normally recognize revenue at the time services are performed. Manufacturing companies and some merchandising companies often ship goods to customers. A company may assume responsibility for the goods until they are received by the customer. Alternatively, a company may assume responsibility for the goods only until they are transferred to a freight company. The freight term associated with these shipments is **free on board (FOB).** When goods are shipped **FOB destination,** title to the goods is transferred to the customer when goods are delivered. When goods are shipped **FOB shipping point,** title passes to the customer when goods are picked up by the shipper.

As a general rule, revenue should be recognized when four criteria have been met:

1. a company has completed most of the activities necessary to produce and sell goods or services,
2. the costs associated with the goods or services have been incurred or can be measured reasonably,
3. the amount of revenue can be measured objectively, and
4. the collection of cash from the purchaser is reasonably assured.

A company usually has earned revenue at the time services are performed or goods are transferred. For example, Georgia-Pacific disclosed its revenue recognition policy in its 1992 annual report as follows:

> The Corporation recognizes revenue when title to the goods sold passes to the buyer, which is generally at the time of shipment.

Hewlett-Packard reported revenue recognition for sales and services in its 1992 annual report as:

> Revenue from equipment sales is generally recognized at the time the equipment is shipped. Services revenue is recognized over the contractual period or as services are performed.

Certain types of revenues result in recognition problems because the activities that produce the revenues occur over more than one fiscal period. The next section considers long-term contracts, which are a common example of this recognition problem.

Revenue Recognition for Long-Term Contracts. Revenue recognition sometimes requires a company to estimate when revenue has been earned. Revenues earned from long-term contracts often are recognized in proportion to the passage of time. For example, if a company contracts to provide maintenance services over a three-year period for $75,000, it might recognize $25,000 per year. This recognition assumes that approximately the same amount of service is provided each year.

Long-term construction contracts can pose special recognition problems, depending on contract terms. For example, Boeing reported the following revenue recognition policies in its 1991 annual report:

> Sales under commercial programs and U.S. Government and foreign military fixed-price type contracts are generally recorded as deliveries are made. For certain fixed-price type contracts that require substantial performance over a long time period before deliveries begin, sales are recorded based upon attainment of scheduled performance milestones. Sales under cost-reimbursement contracts are recorded as costs are incurred and fees are earned.

The *percentage of completion method* for long-term contracts recognizes revenues and expenses for long-term contracts in proportion to the amount of the contract completed each fiscal period. To illustrate, assume Asphalt Company signs a contract on March 1, 1993, with a local government to resurface its streets. The contract calls for payment of $12 million over 3 years, the expected period to complete the project. At the start of the project, Asphalt expects to earn net income of $2 million from the contract. During 1993, the company incurs $2 million in costs and expects to incur an additional $8 million to complete the project. Therefore, the company assumes that 20% ($2 million/$10 million) of the contract has been completed and recognizes 20% of total contract revenue in 1993:

Revenue recognized in 1993 (20% × $12,000,000)	$2,400,000
Expenses recognized in 1993	2,000,000
Net income in 1993	$ 400,000

A variety of methods are used in practice to estimate the proportion of a contract that has been completed.

If Asphalt incurs more costs than expected, it will earn less profit, assuming the contract does not permit the added costs to be transferred to the government. If costs cannot be transferred, the contract is a fixed-cost contract. If costs can be transferred, it is a cost-reimbursement contract. Assume Asphalt incurred $4 million of costs in 1994. The company revises its estimates and now expects to incur an additional $4.5 million after 1994 to complete the fixed-cost contract. Thus, as of the end of 1994, it expects to incur total costs of $10.5 million and earn a profit of $1.5 million. For 1993 and 1994, the company has incurred a total of 57% of the expected costs ($6.0 million/$10.5 million). Therefore, it has earned revenues for the two years of $6,840,000 (57% × $12 million). Of this amount, $2,400,000 was reported as revenue in 1993. Consequently, revenue and net income for 1994 would be:

Revenue recognized in 1994 ($6,840,000 − $2,400,000)	$4,440,000
Expenses recognized in 1994	4,000,000
Net income in 1994	$ 440,000

The percentage of completion method requires a company to estimate revenues earned each period from a long-term contract. It provides a better matching of revenues and expenses, however, than waiting until the project is completed. **The *completed contracts method* recognizes revenue when a long-term contract is completed.** This method should be used only when considerable uncertainty exists about the profits being earned from a project or about the payments being collected.

Long-term contracts provide one example of the need for special revenue recognition methods. A variety of revenue recognition methods are used in different industries because of variations in the earnings process. The following section considers some of these methods.

Other Revenue Recognition Methods. Specific methods of revenue recognition vary across companies, depending on the types of products sold. Following are examples of revenue recognition policies disclosed by companies in various industries in their recent annual reports.

Delta Air Lines:

> Passenger ticket sales are recorded as revenue when the transportation is provided. The value of unused tickets is included in current liabilities as air traffic liability.

Carnival Cruise Lines:

> Customer cruise deposits, which represent unearned revenue, are included in the balance sheet when received and are recognized as cruise revenue upon completion of voyages with durations of 20 days or less and on a pro rata basis for voyages in excess of 20 days. Revenues from tour and related services are recognized at the time the related service is performed.

Walt Disney:

> Revenues from theatrical distribution of motion pictures are recognized in domestic markets when motion pictures are exhibited and in foreign markets when revenues are reported by distributors. Television licensing revenues are generally recorded when the program material is available for telecasting by the licensee and when certain other conditions are met.
>
> Revenues from participants/sponsors at the theme parks are generally recorded over the period of the applicable agreements commencing with the opening of the attraction.

Marvel Entertainment Group:

> Sales of comics are recorded generally two to four weeks after shipment, which approximates the retail sale date. Sales made on a returnable basis are recorded net of a provision for anticipated returns.
>
> Subscription revenues are generally collected in advance for a one year subscription. These revenues are deferred and recognized as income on a pro-rata basis over an annual period.
>
> Income from licensing of characters owned by the Company or third parties and publication rights is recorded at the time collection is assured.

Revenue recognition methods attempt to estimate the revenue earned during a fiscal period. Recognition also requires estimation of discounts and returns that are expected to reduce the revenue earned in a fiscal period. In addition, these recognition issues affect the amount of accounts receivable reported by a company, considered in the next section.

Accounts Receivable

Objective 4
Determine the amount of accounts receivable a company should report.

Accounts receivable are amounts owed an organization by customers. This account links sales revenue with cash received from customers. A company increases the account when it sells goods or services on credit and decreases it when cash is received from the customer. The balance of this account identifies the amount a company expects to collect from its customers.

Sales Discounts and Returns. Revenues are reported on the income statement net of discounts and net of expected returns. Discounts result when a company sells goods at reduced prices. Prices may be discounted for a variety of reasons. Customers who purchase large quantities of goods often receive discounts from the list price. Also, discounts often are provided as an incentive for early payment of accounts receivable by customers (considered in this section). The amount a company expects to receive from a sale is the amount that should be recorded as revenue.

For example, assume Crunchy Foods Company sells goods priced at \$25,000 to a customer with terms 2/10, n30 (2% discount if paid in 10 days, net amount due in 30 days, as discussed in chapter 9). The amount of sales revenue and accounts receivable associated with this transaction should be reported as $24,500, net of the discount of $500 ($25,000 × .02). The amount recognized for revenue is the amount Crunchy Foods expects to receive from its customer. The sale and receipt of cash would affect the company's accounts as follows:

Assets =		Liabilities + Equity	+ Revenues − Expenses	
Accounts Receivable	24,500		Sales Revenue	24,500
Cash	24,500			
Accounts Receivable	(24,500)			

In practice, many companies recognize receivables and sales revenues at their gross amount, $25,000 in this example. Then, if a customer pays within the discount period, they reduce the amount of revenue through a contra-account, such as SALES DISCOUNTS:

Assets =		Liabilities + Equity	+ Revenues − Expenses	
Accounts Receivable	25,000		Sales Revenue	25,000
Cash	24,500		Sales Discounts	(500)
Accounts Receivable	(25,000)			

Sales discounts are subtracted from sales revenues in reporting net operating revenues on the income statement.

Companies also should subtract expected sales returns in computing net operating revenues. Some companies sell merchandise with the expectation that some of the merchandise will be returned from the buyer. For example, publishing companies often allow returns of books and magazines sold to retail stores. If a retailer does not sell all of its supply of a magazine for the current month, it can return them to the publisher for credit against the amount it owes. College bookstores often return unsold textbooks if they have an oversupply.

As an illustration, assume Textbook Publishing Company sold $5 million of books during fiscal 1995. It recorded sales revenue and accounts receivable for the $5 million. From past experience, the company estimates that 15% of sales will result in returns in 1996. Therefore, Textbook Publishing should record an adjustment to its revenues and receivables at the end of the 1995 period. The effect of these transactions on the company's accounts would be:

Assets =		Liabilities + Equity	+ Revenues − Expenses	
Accounts Receivable	5,000,000		Sales Revenue	5,000,000
Allowance for Returns	(750,000)		Sales Returns	(750,000)

Both ALLOWANCE FOR RETURNS and SALES RETURNS are contra-accounts. Textbook Publishing would report net accounts receivable and net sales revenue of $4,250,000 on its 1995 financial statements.

Most companies that sell goods and services on credit expect a portion of their accounts to become uncollectible. Estimated uncollectible accounts also affect the amount of accounts receivable reported for a fiscal period as discussed below.

Uncollectible Accounts. Companies sell goods and services in one fiscal period that prove to be uncollectible in another period. To match the loss associated with the uncollectible accounts with the sales that resulted in the uncollectible accounts, companies should estimate the amount of losses they expect from uncollectible accounts at the end of their fiscal years. For example, assume Crunchy Foods has $2 million of accounts receivable outstanding at the end of 1994. It estimates that approximately 3% of these accounts will not be paid by customers. Though the company will make a reasonable effort to collect from its customers, some accounts will not be collectible. The amount estimated to be uncollectible should be recorded as follows:

Assets =		Liabilities + Equity	+ Revenues − Expenses	
Allowance for Doubtful Accounts	(60,000)		Doubtful Accounts Expense	(60,000)

The *ALLOWANCE FOR DOUBTFUL ACCOUNTS* identifies the amount of accounts receivable a company's management expects is likely to become uncollectible. The allowance account is a contra-asset account that is subtracted from ACCOUNTS RECEIVABLE. Thus, the accounts receivable amount reported on the balance sheet is shown net of the allowance.

Learning Note

Companies refer to the allowance for doubtful accounts by a variety of names, including allowance for uncollectible accounts, allowance for bad debts, or simply allowances.

Once an account is determined to be uncollectible, it is eliminated and the amount is subtracted from a company's accounts receivable balance. For example, assume Crunchy Foods determines on March 12, 1995, that a receivable for the Belly Up Corporation is uncollectible. Belly Up's account balance is $40,000. Crunchy Foods would eliminate the account as follows:

Assets =		Liabilities + Equity	+ Revenues − Expenses
Accounts Receivable	(40,000)		
Allowance for Doubtful Accounts	40,000	-0-	-0-

An additional expense is not recognized on March 12 because it was part of the doubtful accounts expense estimated on December 31, 1994.

Companies estimate the amount of uncollectible accounts from prior experiences. They may examine current overdue accounts, and they may consider current economic conditions in forming their expectations. Uncollectible accounts increase for most companies during recessionary periods.

A company's credit policies affect the amount of uncollectible accounts it expects. A company can increase its sales by accepting customers with higher credit risks. More uncollectible accounts are likely to result from these sales, however. Therefore, doubtful accounts expense is reported as part of selling expenses because it is a cost of selling goods and services to customers who are unable to pay for their purchases.

Companies report accounts receivable on their balance sheets net of the allowance for returns and the allowance for doubtful accounts. For example, Marvel Entertainment Group reported in its 1991 annual report (in thousands):

Accounts receivable	$20,129
Less: Allowance for returns	(7,753)
Allowance for doubtful accounts	(627)
Accounts receivable, net	$11,749

Marvel reported accounts receivable on its balance sheet of $11,749,000.

SELF-STUDY PROBLEM 13-1

The Freddy Stair Company owns and operates dance studios. The company contracts with customers for dance lessons. Customers may pay for their lessons in one of three ways. They may pay $50 at the end of each month. They may pay $550 in advance for the coming year. Or, they may pay $350 at the end of each 6 months.

The following amounts resulted from operating activities for 1995:

Fees collected from customers paying monthly	$120,000
Fees collected from customers paying in advance	55,000
Fees collected from customers paying semi-annually	70,000
Total fees collected	$245,000

Of the fees collected in advance, $20,000 are for lessons to be provided in 1996. Customers paying semi-annually owe $40,000 for lessons received but not yet paid. Approximately 6% of these fees are likely to be uncollectible. The company recognized revenues of $285,000 in 1995 and reported net accounts receivable of $40,000.

Required

Determine the amount of revenues and accounts receivable Freddy Stair should have reported for 1995.

The solution to Self-Study Problem 13-1 appears at the end of the chapter.

COST OF GOODS SOLD AND INVENTORIES

To generate revenues, merchandising and manufacturing companies must acquire or produce inventories. Inventories are assets reported on the balance sheet. Once goods are sold, inventories are reduced and cost of goods sold is recognized on the income statement. Therefore, the amount reported for inventories on the balance sheet affects the amount reported for cost of goods sold on the income statement. Accounting for cost of goods sold and inventories involves measurement and reporting issues. Measurement issues determine how the costs are computed. Reporting rules identify how costs are reported on the income statement and balance sheet. The following sections examine reporting and measurement issues associated with cost of goods sold and inventories.

Reporting Cost of Goods Sold and Inventory

Objective 5
Determine the amount of inventories for merchandising and manufacturing companies.

Inventories are goods a company intends to sell. Cost of goods sold is the cost of goods a company actually has sold during a fiscal period. Coca-Cola reported cost of goods sold of $4,648 million in 1991 (item 2 of Exhibit 13-1). Inventories for merchandising companies consist primarily of merchandise for sale. Inventories for manufacturing companies include goods for sale, goods at intermediate stages of production, and materials and supplies that will be used in the production process. These inventories are referred to as finished goods, work in process, and raw materials. For example, a note to Coca-Cola's 1991 balance sheet provided the following information.

Inventories consist of the following (in thousands):

December 31	**1991**	**1990**
Raw materials and supplies	$615,459	$567,694
Work in process	23,475	18,451
Finished goods	348,830	396,168
	$987,764	$982,313

The totals from this note are the amounts reported as inventories on the company's balance sheet.

The following sections examine reporting of cost of goods sold and inventories for merchandising and manufacturing companies.

Merchandising Companies. Accounting for merchandise inventory transactions is fairly simple. A company increases the balance of MERCHANDISE INVENTORY when inventory is purchased. It decreases the account balance when inventory is sold. For example, assume Crunchy Foods purchased $50,000 of inventory on May 4, 1994, and sold $20,000 on May 6. These transactions would affect the company's accounts as follows:

Assets =		**Liabilities + Equity**	**+ Revenues − Expenses**	
Merchandise Inventory	50,000	Accounts Payable 50,000		
Merchandise Inventory	(20,000)		Cost of Goods Sold	(20,000)

The cost of inventory includes the amount paid for the goods themselves plus shipping costs paid by the buyer. Goods in transit between the seller and buyer should be included as part of the buyer's inventory at year end, if title to the goods and the risk of ownership have been transferred to the buyer at that time.

In addition to recording purchase and sales transactions that affect financial statements, companies maintain detailed records that describe the inventory item and the quantity purchased and sold. These records provide information for determining the number of units on hand, demand for each item, and when to reorder. These records also are used for control purposes. Periodically, physical counts of inventory are verified against inventory records to determine if theft or misplacement has occurred and to check the accuracy of the accounting records.

Manufacturing Companies. Accounting for inventory transactions of a manufacturing company is more complex. The production process can be viewed as involving three stages. Exhibit 13-2 illustrates these stages for Plastic Container Corporation for 1994.

Exhibit 13-2 Inventories for a Manufacturing Company

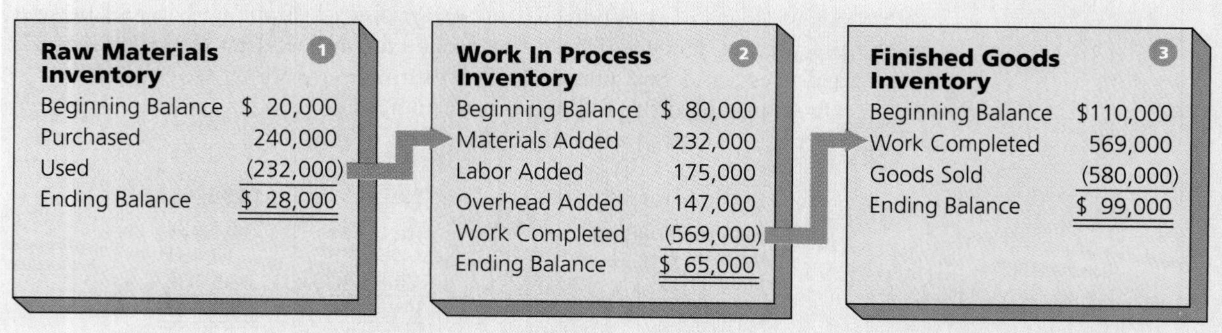

Raw Materials Inventory
1
Beginning Balance $ 20,000
Purchased 240,000
Used (232,000)
Ending Balance $ 28,000
Work In Process Inventory
2
Beginning Balance $ 80,000
Materials Added 232,000
Labor Added 175,000
Overhead Added 147,000
Work Completed (569,000)
Ending Balance $ 65,000
Finished Goods Inventory
3
Beginning Balance $110,000
Work Completed 569,000
Goods Sold (580,000)
Ending Balance $ 99,000

In stage 1, Plastic Container had $20,000 of raw materials available at the beginning of 1994. *Raw materials* **are the physical ingredients of a product, such as chemicals, metals, wood, or components acquired from a supplier.** For example, Plastic Container purchases plastic pellets as raw materials. It heats these pellets and molds them into containers in its production process. Plastic Container purchased $240,000 of raw materials in 1994 and placed $232,000 of the raw materials into production. Therefore, the balance at the end of 1994 was $28,000 as shown in Exhibit 13-2.

These transactions affected the company's accounts as follows:

Assets =	Liabilities + Equity	+ Revenues − Expenses
Raw Materials 240,000	Accounts Payable 240,000	
Raw Materials (232,000) Work in Process 232,000		

RAW MATERIALS and WORK IN PROCESS are inventory accounts. *Work in process* **consists of goods currently in the process of being manufactured.**

In stage 2, the company had $80,000 of goods already in the production process at the beginning of 1994. These goods were partially completed before

1994 but required additional materials and processing during 1994. Raw materials from stage 1 were added to production during 1994, as previously shown. In addition, $175,000 of **wages and benefits of employees who worked directly in the manufacturing process** were added to the cost of production. These costs are ***direct labor*** costs. Also, $147,000 of overhead costs were used in the production process. ***Overhead*** **costs include the costs of supplies ($25,000), utilities ($30,000), depreciation of plant assets ($70,000), and indirect labor ($22,000) used in the production process.** ***Indirect labor*** **includes the cost of wages and benefits paid to maintenance and supervisory employees who are associated with the production process.** All of these costs were added to work in process inventory during the year. The $569,000 cost of goods completed during 1994 was transferred to FINISHED GOODS INVENTORY. ***Finished goods*** **are products awaiting sale.** These transactions would affect Plastic Container's accounts as follows:

Assets =		Liabilities + Equity		+ Revenues − Expenses	
Work in Process	175,000	Wages Payable and Deferred Benefits	175,000		
Work in Process	147,000	Utilities Payable	30,000		
Supplies	(25,000)	Wages Payable and Deferred Benefits	22,000		
Accumulated Depreciation	(70,000)				
Finished Goods	569,000				
Work in Process	(569,000)				

In stage 3, Plastic Container had $110,000 of FINISHED GOODS INVENTORY at the beginning of 1994. Goods completed during 1994 were transferred to finished goods as shown above. The cost of goods sold during 1994 decreased the finished goods inventory account:

Assets =		Liabilities + Equity	+ Revenues − Expenses	
Finished Goods	(580,000)		Cost of Goods Sold	(580,000)

Thus, the final step in the process is recognition of COST OF GOODS SOLD.

Observe that companies do not recognize expenses for materials, labor, and overhead used in the production process until goods are sold. These costs become part of the company's inventories until the finished goods are sold. At the time of sale, these product costs are transferred to expense. This accrual accounting procedure matches expenses with revenues in the period in which revenues are recognized. Product costs of goods that are unsold at year end are reported on the balance sheet as part of a company's inventories.

Exhibit 13-3 illustrates the accounting process associated with inventory for merchandising and manufacturing companies.

Exhibit 13-3 A Summary of Inventory Transactions

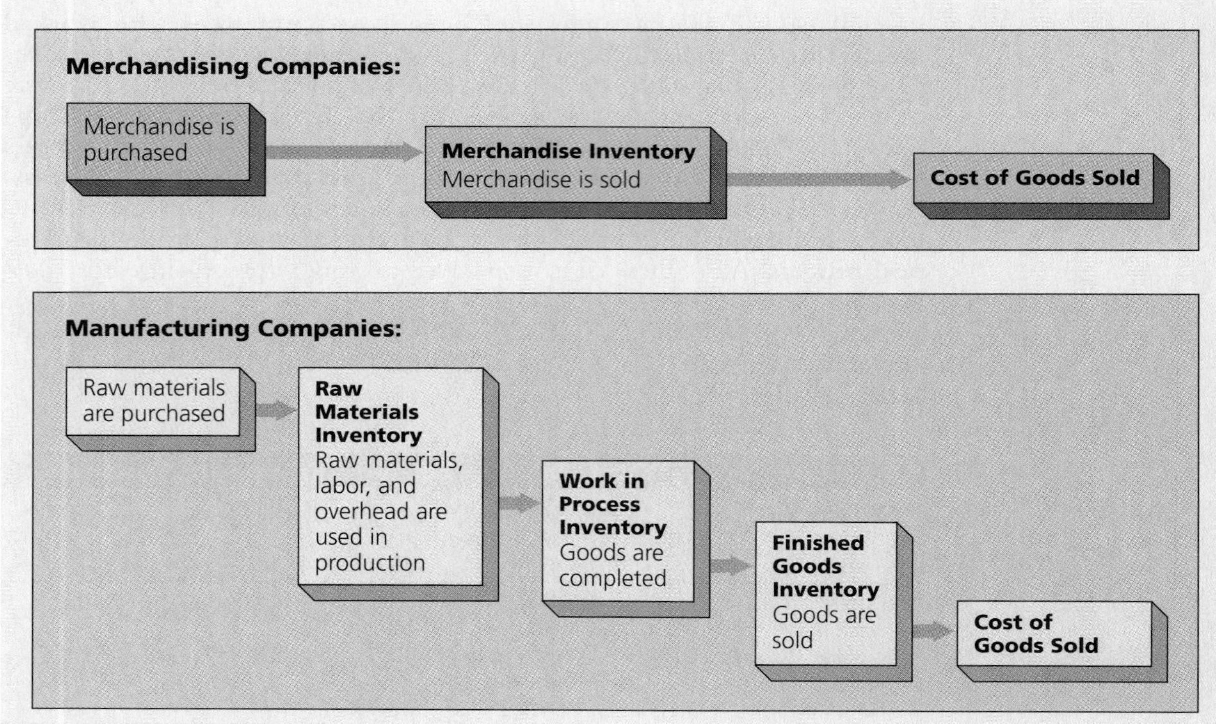

Companies must measure the costs associated with inventory transactions to determine the amount of inventories and cost of goods sold to record for individual transactions and the amount to report on financial statements. The following section examines inventory measurement.

Inventory Measurement

Objective 6
Explain the effect of inventory measurement methods on cost of goods sold and inventory.

In addition to the reporting of inventories discussed in the previous section, measurement of inventories is an important issue for many companies. Estimation issues arise because costs of merchandise, raw materials, labor, utilities, supplies, and other resources change over time. For example, the Fair Deal Automobile Company is a retailer of new cars. In March 1995, Fair Deal purchased six X-14 Flaming Arrows from the manufacturer, all with standard equipment and costing $12,000 each. In May 1995, the company purchased five more X-14 Flaming Arrows with the same equipment. But this time, the cost of the cars to Fair Deal had risen to $12,800 each. In June 1995, Fair Deal sold three of the cars. Should it recognize cost of goods sold of $12,000 or $12,800 for each car?

Fair Deal should have no difficulty in deciding which cost to recognize. Each car was identified in the company's inventory records by the vehicle identification number. Even if all of the cars were the same color, the company must specifically identify which cars were sold and match the cost with sales revenue. Therefore, if it sold two cars that cost $12,000 and one that cost $12,800, it would recognize cost of goods sold and a reduction in inventory of $36,800 in June.

Now consider the example of Fresh Line Markets. The company owns and operates retail grocery stores. It buys canned goods in bulk to take advantage of quantity discounts. In March 1995, the company purchased 100 cases of Caribou Canned Corn for $4.80 a case. Each case contained 24 cans at a cost of $.20 per can. In May 1995, Fresh Line purchased 100 additional cases of corn at $5.28 a case, a cost of $.22 a can. In June 1995, Mrs. Doris Daye purchased two cans of Caribou Canned Corn. Should the company record cost of goods sold for the corn at $.20 or $.22 a can?

The First-In First-Out Method. It is unlikely that Fresh Line can distinguish among cans of corn. Even if it could, the cost of identifying each unit would be prohibitive. Therefore, Fresh Line estimates the cost of goods sold. **It assumes those units of inventory acquired first are sold first, known as the *first-in first-out method,* or *FIFO.*** For example, assume that the company's inventory contained 30 cases of Caribou Canned Corn at the beginning of March. Each case cost $4.32. It purchased 100 cases at $4.80 in March and 100 cases at $5.28 in May. For the three months ended May 31, the company sold 190 cases of the corn. What would cost of goods sold be for the period and how much inventory would be reported at the end of the period?

Exhibit 13-4 illustrates the assumed flow of merchandise and costs for March through May using the FIFO method.

Exhibit 13-4 FIFO Inventory Flow Assumption

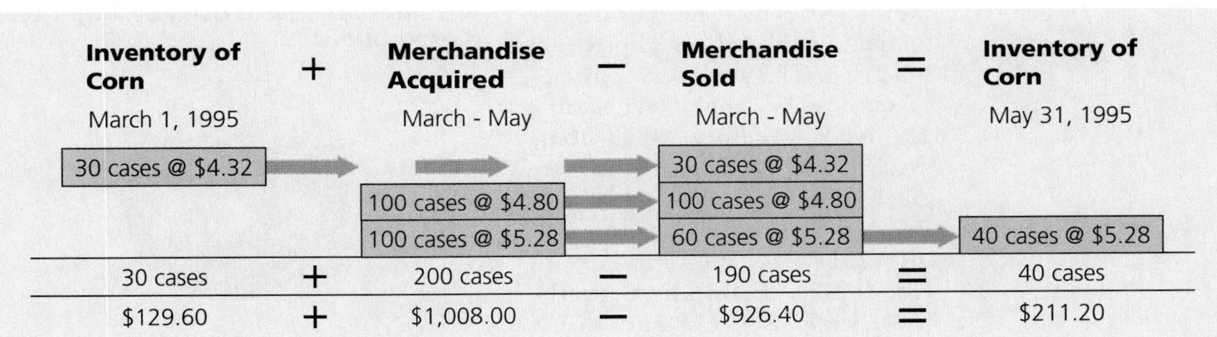

Using the FIFO assumption, Fresh Line would recognize cost of goods sold using the cost of the merchandise acquired first. Therefore, it would recognize 30 cases from beginning inventory plus 100 cases acquired in March and 60 cases acquired in May as being sold. The 40 remaining cases acquired in May would be the company's ending inventory of corn. Cost of goods sold for the three-month period would be $926.40. The inventory balance at the end of May would be $211.20.

Two other inventory estimation methods are common. **One assumes the last units acquired are sold first, the *last-in first-out method,* or *LIFO.* The other assumes an average cost of units available during a period as the cost of units sold, the *weighted average method.***

The Last-In First-Out Method. Exhibit 13-5 illustrates the LIFO method for Fresh Line, using the same data as Exhibit 13-4.

Exhibit 13-5 LIFO Inventory Flow Assumption

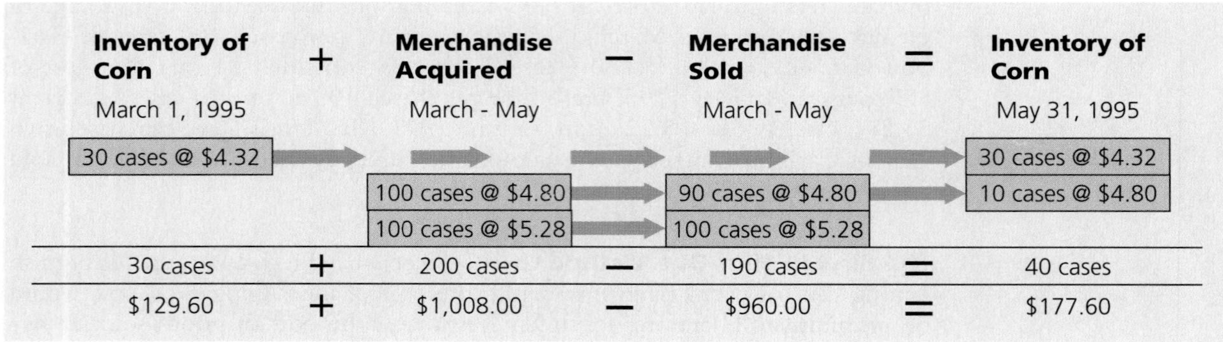

Using the LIFO assumption, Fresh Line would recognize cost of goods sold using the cost of the merchandise acquired last. Therefore, it would recognize 100 cases acquired in May plus 90 cases acquired in March as being sold. The 10 remaining cases acquired in March plus the 30 cases of beginning inventory would be the company's ending inventory of corn. Cost of goods sold for the three-month period would be $960.00. The inventory balance at the end of May would be $177.60.

Fresh Line might use LIFO if it stacks inventory in its warehouse so the most recent cases acquired are placed on display and sold first. This inventory management practice is not likely because the older inventory would eventually spoil. The company is more likely to sell the oldest units first. Nevertheless, the company might use LIFO to measure cost of goods sold. **Estimation methods, such as FIFO and LIFO, are used to measure the amount of inventory reported on a company's balance sheet and the amount of cost of goods sold reported on its income statement. They do not necessarily correspond with the physical flow of goods through a company.** Most companies will sell their oldest goods first to avoid spoilage and obsolescence. They may use LIFO to account for these goods because of tax advantages.

Inventory Methods Used by Major U.S Corporations

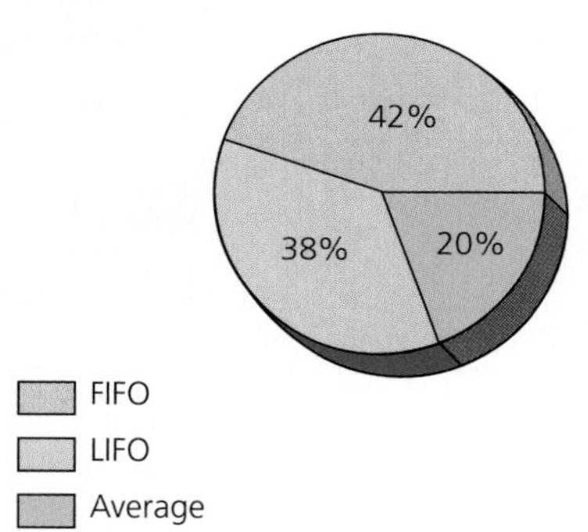

(Data source: AICPA, Accounting Trends and Techniques, 1991)

Because the cost of canned corn rose from March to May, cost of goods sold was higher using LIFO than using FIFO. LIFO matches the most recent cost of goods acquired with sales revenue for a fiscal period. FIFO matches the earliest cost of goods in inventory with sales revenue for a fiscal period. In inflationary periods, LIFO often results in higher cost of goods sold and lower net income than FIFO. At the same time, LIFO normally results in lower inventory balances than FIFO:

	FIFO	LIFO
Inventory costs matched with sales on income statement	Earliest Acquired	Most Recently Acquired
Inventory costs remaining on balance sheet	Most Recently Acquired	Earliest Acquired

When used to measure taxable income, LIFO also reduces the amount of income subject to taxation for many companies. Therefore, for these companies, LIFO reduces cash outflow for income taxes. Federal tax regulations require companies that choose to use LIFO for tax purposes also use that method for financial reporting purposes. Thus, many companies use LIFO in preparing their financial statements so they can use it in preparing their tax returns.

If costs were to decline during a fiscal period, the relationship between FIFO and LIFO would be reversed. LIFO would produce higher net income and lower cash flows because of higher taxes. Therefore, companies whose costs are likely to decline over time normally would not use LIFO. For example, the cost of computer components has declined steadily since the early 1980s. Computer manufacturers seldom use LIFO.

In addition, LIFO can result in higher taxable income if a company sells more inventory than it acquires during a period. For example, assume Plastic Container Corporation uses the LIFO method. At the beginning of 1994, it had an inventory of raw materials consisting of 3,000 tons at a LIFO cost of $400 per ton. During 1994, the company acquired an additional 8,000 tons at a current cost of $700 per ton. Thus, it has 11,000 tons of raw material available for use. If it used 10,000 tons of the raw material to produce goods sold during 1994, the company would be forced to recognize 2,000 tons of materials at a cost of $400 per ton as part of cost of goods sold:

Beginning inventory	3,000 tons	(at $400 per ton)
Inventory purchased	8,000 tons	(at $700 per ton)
Inventory available	11,000 tons	
Inventory sold using LIFO:		
	8,000 tons	(at $700 per ton)
	2,000 tons	(at $400 per ton)
Total inventory sold	10,000 tons	

Profits and taxable income will be higher than if the cost of materials used during the current period were the cost of materials purchased during the period. If the company had been using FIFO, the cost of its beginning inventory would have been much closer to the current price of $700 per ton. LIFO results in inventory costs that often are much lower than current costs. Therefore, the amount reported on the balance sheet for inventory often understates the current cost of inventory when LIFO is used. Companies that cannot control their inventory levels may not find LIFO to be a suitable method if they risk dipping into early inventory layers.

Most countries other than the U.S. do not permit the use of LIFO, and there are no tax advantages for the use of LIFO in these countries. Therefore, multinational firms, including large U.S. corporations, normally use FIFO for inventories held in foreign countries even if they use LIFO for similar inventories held in the U.S. Companies can use LIFO for some inventories and FIFO and/or weighted average for others.

Weighted Average Method. A third commonly used inventory estimation method is the weighted average method. As an illustration, Fresh Line's weighted average inventory cost for March through May would be:

Beginning inventory	30 cases × $4.32 =	$ 129.60
Inventory acquired	100 cases × $4.80 =	480.00
	100 cases × $5.28 =	528.00
Total inventory available	230 cases	1,137.60
Average cost per case	$1,137.60/230 =	$4.9461
Cost of goods sold	190 × $4.9461 =	$939.76
Ending inventory	40 × $4.9461 =	$197.84

The average cost method produces cost of goods sold and ending inventory amounts between those produced by FIFO and LIFO.

Companies use inventory estimation methods to determine the cost associated with inventories and cost of goods sold. In addition, GAAP require companies to compare the costs determined from the estimation methods with the current market cost of inventories. If current market costs are below estimated costs, inventories must be written down to current market. The following section describes this process.

Learning Note

A variety of specialized inventory measurement rules have been devised for companies in different industries. Dollar value LIFO, retail LIFO, and retail dollar value LIFO are examples of specialized methods. Though the mechanics of calculating inventory costs differ, the concepts underlying these methods are similar to those presented above.

Lower of Cost or Market Inventory Valuation. GAAP require inventory to be reported at the **lower of cost or market.** This concept is similar to the lower of cost or market procedure applied to marketable securities. The measurement of inventories is more complex because the market values of inventories are not always readily determinable. GAAP specify a procedure for computing market value that considers current replacement cost and the amount a company expects to receive from selling inventory, less the profit it expects to earn from the inventory. Once market value is determined, the cost of inventory is compared with the market value. If the market value is less than cost, the inventory is written down to market.

For example, assume Plastic Container has inventory costing $100,000 at the end of its 1995 fiscal year. The current market value of the inventory is determined to be $90,000. The inventory would be adjusted as follows:

Assets =		Liabilities + Equity	+ Revenues − Expenses	
Inventory	(10,000)		Loss from Revaluation of Inventory	(10,000)

The loss is recognized in the period in which the inventory declines in value. An excess of market value over cost is not recognized through a valuation adjustment, another example of the application of conservatism to accounting measurement.

Comparing Inventory Costs Among Companies

GAAP require companies to disclose the methods used to measure inventories and cost of goods sold. Also, GAAP require those that use LIFO to disclose the effect of using this method on reported inventory value. For example, Coca-Cola disclosed in its 1991 annual report:

> Inventories are valued at the lower of cost or market. In general, inventories are valued on the basis of average cost or first-in, first-out methods. However, certain soft drink and citrus inventories are valued on the last-in, first-out (LIFO) method. The excess of current costs over LIFO stated values amounted to approximately $27 million and $42 million at December 31, 1991 and 1990, respectively.

The current cost of Coca-Cola's inventory at the end of 1991 would have been approximately equal to its FIFO cost because FIFO results in the most recent inventory costs being reported on the balance sheet. Thus, if Coca-Cola's LIFO inventories had been reported on a FIFO basis, its cost of goods sold would have been $15 million more in 1991 than the amount reported on its income statement. Beginning inventory would have been $42 million larger than reported, while ending inventory would have been $27 million larger. Therefore, on a FIFO basis the company would have reported $15 million more cost of goods sold ($42−$27) than the amount reported using LIFO. Decision makers can use this information in comparing the costs of companies using the LIFO method with those using FIFO. For example, Coca-Cola's income could be analyzed for comparison with companies using FIFO by increasing its cost of goods sold by $15 million and then recomputing other income statement amounts.

FIFO, LIFO, and average estimation methods are used by merchandising and manufacturing companies. Manufacturing companies use these methods for raw materials, work in process, and finished goods inventories. Modern manufacturing methods have eliminated large amounts of inventories for some companies. Materials are obtained from suppliers as they are needed, "just-in-time" for inclusion in the manufacturing process. Work in process flows at a rate sufficient to meet orders without accumulating large amounts of work in process or finished goods inventory. Companies using just-in-time manufacturing procedures will report relatively small amounts of inventory. These companies expense almost all manufacturing costs each period as part of cost of goods sold. Therefore, the choice of inventory estimation methods is less important for these companies than for those with large inventories.

SELF-STUDY PROBLEM 13-2

The Fashion Mart is a clothing retailer. At the end of 1993, the company reported $8 million of inventory on a FIFO basis. During 1994, the company acquired $30 million of inventory. It reported $10 million of inventory at the end of 1994 on a FIFO basis. If the company had used LIFO, it would have reported $6 million of inventory at the end of 1993 and $7 million at the end of 1994. The company's income tax rate is 30%.

Required

(a) What would the difference have been in Fashion Mart's net income and cash flow from operating activities if it had used LIFO instead of FIFO in 1994? (b) What factors should the company consider in deciding which inventory estimation method to use?

The solution to Self-Study Problem 13-2 appears at the end of the chapter.

OTHER ITEMS AFFECTING NET INCOME

Product revenues result from the sale of goods and services. Product costs result from the acquisition and production of goods and services. Gross profit is the excess of product revenues over product costs associated with the goods and services sold during a period. Items reported on the income statement after gross profit include operating expenses, financial revenues and expenses, and special items. When all of these items are included, the income statement would report the following information:

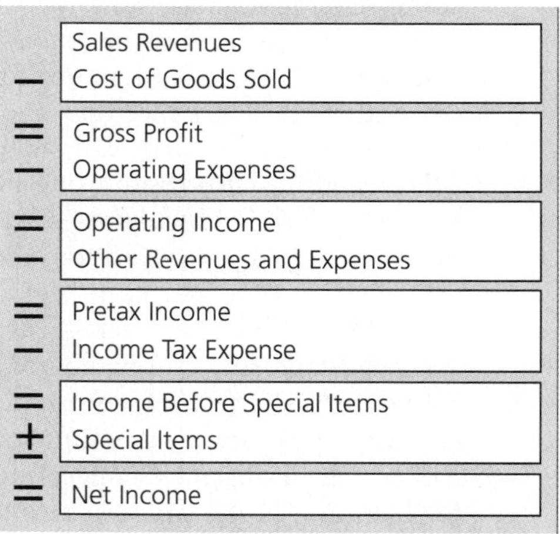

Sales Revenues
− Cost of Goods Sold
= Gross Profit
− Operating Expenses
= Operating Income
− Other Revenues and Expenses
= Pretax Income
− Income Tax Expense
= Income Before Special Items
± Special Items
= Net Income

The following sections consider information reported after gross profit on the income statement.

Operating Income

Objective 7
Explain the reporting and measurement of operating expenses.

Operating income **is gross profit minus other operating expenses. Operating expenses include non-production costs associated with operating activities during a fiscal period.** These costs are expensed in the period in which they occur. For most companies, most of these costs are associated with marketing, research and development, and general administrative activities. Marketing costs include advertising, direct selling, and distribution costs. Depreciation of assets used primarily in selling activities and salaries and commissions of the sales force are included in this category. Administrative costs include depreciation of plant assets used in administrative activities, such as office buildings and equipment, and management office worker salaries. Costs associated with research and development, distribution, marketing, servicing, and general management activities are expensed during the period in which they occur.

Coca-Cola reported selling, administrative, and general expenses of $4,604 million and operating income of $2,319 million in 1991 (items 4 and 5 in Exhibit 13-1):

Year Ended December 31 *(In millions except per share data)*	**1991**	**1990**	**1989**
1. **Net Operating Revenues**	$11,571	$10,236	$8,622
2. Cost of goods sold	4,648	4,208	3,548
3. **Gross Profit**	6,923	6,028	5,074
4. Selling, administrative and general expenses	4,604	4,076	3,348
5. **Operating Income**	2,319	1,952	1,726

Corporations often summarize their operating expenses as one line on the income statement (item 4). Some operating expenses are reported separately on the income statement, however. For example, GAAP require companies to report separately any unusual or infrequent revenues or expenses that are material in amount. Certain other expenses that are important for a company's operating activities, such as research and development expenses and depreciation expenses, also must be disclosed. They may be reported separately on the income statement or disclosed in notes to the financial statements.

Other Revenues and Expenses

Objective 8
Explain the reporting and measurement of other revenues and expenses.

Other revenues include interest and other income from short-term and long-term investments. Other expenses include interest on short-term and long-term debt. These amounts are accrued. Thus, the amount of revenue reported is the amount earned, regardless of whether cash was received. The amount of expense reported is the amount of liability incurred during the current fiscal year, regardless of whether cash has been paid.

As shown in Exhibit 13-1, Coca-Cola reported interest income of $175 million (item 6) and interest expense of $192 million (item 7) in 1991. Also, it reported equity income of $40 million (item 8) and other income of $41 million (item 9):

Year Ended December 31	**1991**	**1990**	**1989**
5. **Operating Income**	2,319	1,952	1,726
6. Interest income	175	170	205
7. Interest expense	(192)	(231)	(308)
8. Equity income	40	110	75
9. Other income—net	41	13	66
10. **Income from Continuing Operations before Income Taxes**	2,383	2,014	1,764

Equity income is revenue from investments accounted for using the equity method, as discussed in Chapter 11. These investments are those in corporations over which Coca-Cola has significant influence. Notes to Coca-Cola's statements reveal other income was primarily from the sale of property and investments in other companies.

Items 6 through 9 represent nonoperating revenues and expenses. They are not part of Coca-Cola's primary operating activities. Therefore, they are reported after operating income. The net effect of these items is included in income before income taxes (item 10). The next section examines income taxes.

Income Taxes

A company's income statement reports the amount of income taxes that a company would incur if its pretax income were all taxable in the current fiscal year. Thus, income taxes reported on the income statement are determined primarily by multiplying pretax income times the corporate tax rate. Coca-Cola reported income taxes of $765 million for 1991 on its income statement (item 11 in Exhibit 13-1):

Year Ended December 31	**1991**	**1990**	**1989**
10. **Income from Continuing Operations before Income Taxes**	2,383	2,014	1,764
11. Income taxes	765	632	571
12. **Income from Continuing Operations**	1,618	1,382	1,193

Objective 9
Explain the reporting and measurement of income taxes.

The effective tax rate used by Coca-Cola was 32.1% ($765/$2,383). The U.S. federal statutory rate for corporate income was 34% in 1991. A note to Coca-Cola's statements disclosed that the actual rate was 32.1% after considering the effect of state and foreign tax rates. For example, the company's earnings associated with operations in Puerto Rico were tax exempt.

The amount of income tax liability a company incurs in a fiscal period often differs from the income tax expense it reports on its income statement. This difference results in deferred taxes. Coca-Cola disclosed that its total income taxes for 1991 included:

Current taxes	$831 million
Deferred taxes	(66 million)
Total taxes	$765 million

Current taxes of $831 million were the company's tax liability for 1991 as computed on its tax return. The difference between the amount reported on the income statement ($765 million) and the amount of liability ($831 million) resulted from differences in the amounts of revenues and expenses reported for financial statement and tax purposes.

Coca-Cola's tax liability was greater than its reported tax expense in 1991:

Assets =	Liabilities + Equity		+ Revenues − Expenses	
-0-	Income Taxes Payable	831,000,000	Income Tax Expense	(765,000,000)
	Deferred Taxes	(66,000,000)		

This transaction reduced the company's deferred tax liability by $66 million in 1991.

Coca-Cola disclosed in its 1991 annual report:

> Deferred taxes are provided principally for depreciation, certain employee compensation-related expenses, and certain capital transactions that are recognized in different years for financial statement and income tax purposes.

These timing differences are typical of those identified as being important for most corporations.

Timing Differences Reported by 600 Major U.S. Corporations

Data source: AICPA, Accounting Trends & Techniques, 1991.

Companies often use accounting methods for financial statements different from those used for tax purposes. The intent of financial statements is to present fairly a company's financial performance in conformity with GAAP. The intent of tax accounting is to report a company's taxable income. Companies will attempt to minimize their tax obligations by minimizing taxable income consistent with tax regulations. However, companies usually want to present the most positive net income allowable under GAAP. Since tax regulations and GAAP do not always coincide, the amount of income for financial reporting purposes often differs from that for tax purposes.

Companies select accounting methods to help them meet their financial and tax reporting objectives. For example, assume Plastic Container Corporation reported the following information for financial reporting and tax purposes in 1994:

	Income Statement	Tax Return
Revenues	$8,000,000	$8,000,000
Depreciation expense	(1,000,000)	(1,600,000)
Other expenses	(5,000,000)	(5,000,000)
Pretax income	2,000,000	1,400,000
Income taxes (34%)	(680,000)	(476,000)
Net income	$1,320,000	$ 924,000

The company used the straight-line method to compute depreciation on its income statement and used the accelerated method permitted by tax regulations on its tax return. The effect of the difference in accounting methods on the company's accounts would be:

Assets =	Liabilities + Equity		+ Revenues − Expenses	
-0-	Income Taxes Payable	476,000	Income Tax Expense	(680,000)
	Deferred Taxes	204,000		

A tax difference may result either in an asset or a liability for deferred taxes. If a company's income tax liabilities (tax return calculations) have been greater than its income tax expenses (financial statement calculations), it will report a deferred tax liability on its balance sheet. The liability represents expected future tax payments. If its income tax liabilities have been greater than its income tax expenses, it will report a deferred tax asset on its balance sheet. The asset represents expected future tax benefits through reduced tax payments.

The transaction for Plastic Container increased its deferred tax liability by $204,000. In future periods, the accelerated depreciation method used for tax purposes will produce less depreciation expense than the straight-line method used for financial reporting purposes. In those years, the amount of taxes computed on the tax return will be greater than the amount reported on the income statement. For example, assume that in 1997 Plastic Container computes income taxes on its income statement as $800,000 and income taxes on its tax return as $920,000. The effect of the computations on the company's accounts will be:

Assets =	Liabilities + Equity		+ Revenues − Expenses	
-0-	Income Taxes Payable	920,000	Income Tax Expense	(800,000)
	Deferred Taxes	(120,000)		

The company's deferred tax liability is reduced by $120,000 in 1997. This is the type of transaction reported by Coca-Cola in 1991 at the top of the preceding page.

For many companies, the amount left after income taxes is deducted from pre-tax income is net income. For other companies, special items that affect net income are reported after income taxes. These items are considered in the following section.

Special Items

In addition to those revenues and expenses that are common to most corporations, special revenue and expense items are reported occasionally. These special items are reported separately from other items and require special disclosure. Separate reporting is required because they affect net income during the current fiscal period but will not affect net income of future periods. Therefore, decision makers should evaluate these items differently from those activities that are expected to affect income in future periods, especially when forecasting future income. Three types of special items may occur: discontinued operations, extraordinary items, and accounting changes.

Discontinued Operations. Coca-Cola reported income from continuing operations of $1,618 million in 1991 (item 12 in Exhibit 13-1):

Year Ended December 31	**1991**	**1990**	**1989**
12. **Income from Continuing Operations**	1,618	1,382	1,193
13. Equity income from discontinued operation	—	—	21
14. Gain on sale of discontinued operation (net of income taxes of $421,021)	—	—	509
15. **Net Income**	1,618	1,382	1,723

This also was the amount of net income (item 15) the company reported for 1991. Continuing operations are those from which a company expects to derive income in future years. In contrast, ***discontinued operations*** **are those from which a company will no longer derive income.** Discontinued operations result when a company sells or closes a major component of its operations.

Objective 10
Explain the reporting and measurement of discontinued operations, extraordinary items, and accounting changes.

In 1989, Coca-Cola reported discontinued operations. Two items were reported, one for equity income, and one for gain on sale of a discontinued operation. The company disclosed:

> In 1989, the Company sold its entire equity interest in Columbia Pictures Entertainment, Inc. (CPE) for approximately $1.6 billion in cash. The equity interest consisted of approximately 49 percent of the outstanding common shares of CPE and 1,000 shares of preferred stock. The sale resulted in a pretax gain of approximately $930 million. On an after-tax basis, the gain was approximately $509 million or $.74 per common share *[plus equity income of $21 million on discontinued operations that resulted in income of $.03 per share].*

A gain or loss on discontinued operations is reported separately from income from continuing operations. Because the operations have been discontinued, the gain or loss from sale is a one-time event. Also, the income (or loss) from the operating activities of the discontinued operation will not reoccur in future years. Therefore, this income (or loss) is reported separately, as well. Thus, in evaluating Coca-Cola's earnings for 1989, decision makers should be aware that net income for the year included a one-time gain of $509 million and operating income of $21 million (equity income from discontinued operations) that will not reoccur in future years. Observe that Coca-Cola's net income declined from 1989 to 1990, largely because of the effect of its discontinued operations.

A gain or loss from sale of a discontinued operation is reported on the income statement net of income taxes. Like the gain or loss, the income tax effect is a one-time event. If Coca-Cola had not had a pretax gain of $930 million ($509 after-tax gain + $421 income tax on gain) on its sale, it would not have incurred taxes of $421 million on the gain.

Extraordinary Items. Gains and losses that are both unusual and infrequent are reported as *extraordinary items*. Unusual and infrequent is determined from the reference point of an individual company. What is unusual and infrequent for one company may not be unusual or infrequent for another. Extraordinary items are reported separately on the income statement (net of taxes) to call attention to their special nature. Like discontinued operations, a specific extraordinary item would not reoccur in future years.

As an example, National Medical Enterprises, Incorporated, reported the following on its 1992 income statement (in millions):

Income before income taxes and extraordinary charges	$ 230
Taxes on income	(97)
Income before extraordinary charges	133
Extraordinary charges	(29)
Net income	$ 104

A note to the statement revealed the extraordinary loss resulted from litigation against the company. The tax effect of the extraordinary item, a reduction in taxes of $13.9 million, also was disclosed in the note. Other causes of extraordinary items are losses from natural disasters such as fires, termination of pension plans, and certain changes in debt agreements.

U.S. GAAP are more restrictive in defining extraordinary items than GAAP in some other countries. Therefore, extraordinary items are more common and include a broader range of transactions in some foreign corporate reports.

Accounting Changes. *Accounting changes* are the effects on income due to changes in the application of accounting principles from one fiscal period to another. Companies report material effects on their income when adopting new accounting standards or changing from one accounting method to another. Georgia-Pacific reported on its 1991 income statement (in millions):

Income before income taxes and accounting changes	$ 187
Provision for income taxes	266
Loss before accounting changes	(79)
Cumulative effect of accounting changes, net of taxes	(63)
Net loss	$(142)

The company disclosed:

> Effective January 1, 1991, the Corporation changed its accounting policy at certain manufacturing facilities to include in inventory certain supplies that were previously expensed. The Corporation believes this method is preferable because it provides a better matching of costs and related revenues and is more consistent with the Corporation's tax reporting method. The cumulative effect of this change for years prior to 1991 was to increase net income by $56 million in 1991 after related income tax expense of $35 million. . . .

> The Corporation adopted Financial Accounting Standard No. 106, "Employers' Accounting for Postretirement Benefits Other than Pensions," as of January 1, 1991. This statement requires the accrual of the cost of providing postretirement benefits, including medical and life insurance coverage, during the active service period of the employee. The Corporation elected to immediately recognize the accumulated liability, measured as of January 1, 1991. This resulted in a one-time, after-tax charge of $119 million (after reduction for income taxes of $73 million) . . . .

These changes account for most of the effect reported on a cumulative basis on the income statement. Reporting on a cumulative basis considers, to the extent determinable, the effect the change would have had on income reported in prior years if the new method had been used in those years.

An accounting change is reported as a separate item on the income statement, net of tax effects. This reporting requirement calls attention to the change. Consistency is an important attribute of accounting methods. A company should not change accounting methods except when justified by changes in the company's economic circumstances or when necessary to adopt a new accounting standard. A paragraph also is added to a company's audit report to bring attention to a change in an accounting method. This paragraph brings to the reader's attention the inconsistency between accounting methods used in prior years and those used in the current year.

A **change in accounting method** is different from a **change in accounting estimate.** Estimates are required by many transactions. For example, when a company records depreciation expense, it must estimate the remaining useful life of its plant assets. These estimates are likely to change from time to time as additional information becomes available to managers or as conditions change. Changes in estimates do not require special reporting or disclosure. Also, they normally do not have a cumulative effect. Rather, they are prospective. That is, the change considers the current and future periods, not the past.

For example, assume Plastic Container Corporation changed its estimate of the remaining useful life of some of its plant assets from 10 years to 8 years. If the book value of the assets was $100,000 per year, it would record $12,500, instead of $10,000, of depreciation expense each year over the remaining life of these assets. No adjustment would be made to depreciation reported in prior years.

A corporation's net income includes income from continuing operations and adjustments for special items. Net income is the amount earned by both preferred and common stockholders for a fiscal period. The next section considers the adjustment necessary to compute net income earned by common stockholders.

Minority Interest in Income

As discussed in Chapter 12, consolidated financial statements include a parent corporation and its subsidiaries. The parent may own less than 100% of some subsidiaries. For example, if a corporation owns 80% (the majority interest) of another corporation, the remaining 20% is minority interest. The consolidated income statement includes revenues and expenses of the parent and its subsidiaries as though they were one company. **The portion of subsidiary net income attributable to minority interest is reported on the income statement as** ***minority interest in income of consolidated subsidiaries.***

As an illustration, Westinghouse Electric Corporation reported the following information on its 1991 income statement:

(In millions) Year Ended December 31	**1991**
Loss before income taxes and minority interest in income of consolidated subsidiaries	$(1,096)
Income taxes	25
Minority interest in income of consolidated subsidiaries	(15)
Net loss	$(1,086)

Westinghouse's income statement contained the same kind of revenue and expense items as Coca-Cola's except for the separate reporting of minority interest in income. Observe that the minority interest is subtracted from pretax income (loss) in computing net income (loss). It is the portion of net income (loss) attributable to owners of subsidiaries rather than to owners of Westinghouse.

Net income (loss) is the remainder after adjustments are made for minority interest in income and special items. It is a measure of the net result of operating activities during a fiscal period. It may not be the amount earned by common stockholders, however, because of dividends paid on preferred stock. The next section considers the computation of net income available for common stockholders.

Net Income Available for Common Stockholders

Dividends on preferred stock are deducted from net income to compute net income available for common stockholders. Preferred dividends represent a claim by preferred stockholders on a company's earnings. This claim almost always takes precedence over the claim of common stockholders. Coca-Cola reported preferred dividends of $1 million in 1991 and net income available for common of $1,617 million (items 16 and 17 in Exhibit 13-1):

Year Ended December 31	**1991**	**1990**	**1989**
15. **Net Income**	1,618	1,382	1,723
16. Preferred stock dividends	1	18	21
17. **Net Income Available to Common Share Owners**	$1,617	$1,364	$1,702

Objective 11
Determine net income available for common shareholders.

Net income available for common is the net result of operating activities for a fiscal period after considering the effects of distributions to suppliers, employees, governments, creditors, and preferred stockholders. It is an accrual measure of the profit earned by common stockholders. It is an estimate of the increase in common stockholder value resulting from a company's performance during a fiscal period. This value also is expressed on a per share basis to provide a means for individual stockholders to estimate the effect of a company's performance on the portion of the company they own.

EARNINGS PER SHARE

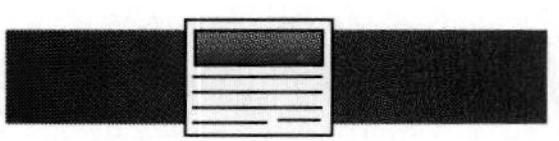

Objective 12
Distinguish primary and fully diluted earnings per share.

GAAP require corporations to report net income on a per share basis. By multiplying earnings per share times the number of shares owned, a stockholder can identify the amount of profit attributable to the stockholders' investment. For many companies, this amount is net income divided by the average common shares outstanding during a fiscal period. A weighted average number of common shares is computed by considering the number of months shares of common stock were outstanding throughout a fiscal period. This average is used in the computation because profits are earned throughout the period. For example, assume Marble Slab Corporation had 2 million shares of common stock outstanding at the beginning of 1994. On October 1, 1994, the company issued an additional 1 million shares. The weighted average number of shares would be 2.25 million [(2 million × 9⁄12) + (3 million × 3⁄12)]. If Marble Slab had reported net income of $5 million for 1994, its earnings per share would have been $2.22 ($5 million/2.25 million).

Coca-Cola reported earnings per share of $2.43 in 1991 on 666 million average shares (items 21 and 22 in Exhibit 13-1):

Year Ended December 31	**1991**	**1990**	**1989**
18. **Income per Common Share**			
19. Continuing operations	$ 2.43	$ 2.04	$ 1.69
20. Discontinued operation	—	—	.77
21. **Net Income per Common Share**	$ 2.43	$ 2.04	$ 2.46
22. **Average Common Shares Outstanding**	666	669	692

Observe that when a company reports special items, such as discontinued operations, it must also report separately earnings per share for these items. Thus, in 1989 Coca-Cola reported earnings per share for continuing operations of $1.69 (item 19) and earnings per share for discontinued operations of $.77 (item 20). Separate reporting also is required for extraordinary items and accounting changes.

Earnings per share is complicated for some companies by the existence of convertible bonds, convertible preferred stock, stock options, or stock warrants. These instruments permit the owner to exchange them for shares of common stock. If an exchange is made, additional shares of common stock will be issued. These companies report two sets of earnings per share numbers, primary and fully diluted earnings per share. ***Primary earnings per share*** **is earnings per share attributable to common stock outstanding and to common stock equivalents.** ***Fully diluted earnings per share*** **is earnings per share attributable to common stock after considering all effects of exercising options and warrants, convertible debt, and convertible preferred stock that would reduce earnings per share.**

Instruments that are substantially the same as common stock are considered **common stock equivalents.** For example, stock options and warrants are common stock equivalents because they permit the owner to acquire common stock. Convertible debt and convertible preferred stock are common stock equivalents if they meet certain criteria. If the effect of exercising options and warrants or converting debt and preferred stock is to dilute (reduce) earnings per share, these instruments are referred to as dilutive securities. Primary earnings per share assumes dilutive common stock equivalents were converted to shares of common stock during a fiscal period. Fully diluted earnings per share assumes all dilutive securities were converted to shares of common stock during a period. It represents the minimum amount of earnings per share a company would report if options, warrants, and convertible securities were exchanged for common stock. Fully diluted earnings per share will always be less than or equal to primary earnings per share.

Corporations report primary and fully diluted earnings per share for various categories of income. For example, National Medical Enterprises reported the following information on its 1992 income statement:

	1992	1991	1990
Earnings (loss) per share:			
Primary:			
Before extraordinary charges	$ 0.77	$ 1.73	$ 1.52
Extraordinary charges	(0.17)	(0.03)	(0.02)
Net	$ 0.60	$ 1.70	$ 1.50
Fully diluted:			
Before extraordinary charges	$ 0.75	$ 1.54	$ 1.33
Extraordinary charges	(0.15)	(0.02)	(0.01)
Net	$ 0.60	$ 1.52	$ 1.32

The income statement presents the results of operating activities on an accrual basis. The statement of cash flows presents the cash flow results of operating activities. Differences between the cash flow and accrual measures were considered in detail in Chapter 6. The following section summarizes information reported about operating activities on the statement of cash flows.

CASH FLOW FROM OPERATING ACTIVITIES

The statement of cash flows presents the results of operating activities for a fiscal period on a cash basis. Exhibit 13-6 contains information Coca-Cola reported in its 1991 annual report. Like most companies, Coca-Cola uses the indirect format for presenting its statement. This format adjusts net income (item A) for noncash revenues and expenses (items B–H).

Depreciation and amortization (item B), foreign currency adjustments (item E), and other noncash items (item G) were expenses recognized in 1991. These expenses did not require cash outflow during 1991. (Other noncash items were miscellaneous items that were not described in detail in Coca-Cola's annual report.)

Objective 13
Compare accrual and cash operating results.

Equity income (item D) and the gain on sale of businesses and investments (item F) were revenues that did not provide cash inflow. Recall from Chapter 11 that a company records equity income when it uses the equity method to recognize a portion of the net income of another company in which it has invested. Dividends received from the equity investment provide cash inflows. Equity income in excess of dividends does not provide cash flow during the period in which the income is recognized. Gains on sale of businesses and investments result when the sales price is greater than the book value of the assets.

Exhibit 13-6

THE COCA-COLA COMPANY
(Excerpt from Consolidated Statement from Cash Flows)

Year Ended December 31, *(in millions)*	**1991**
Operating Activities	
A. Net income	$1,618
B. Depreciation and amortization	261
C. Deferred income taxes	(66)
D. Equity income, net of dividends	(16)
E. Foreign currency adjustments	66
F. Gain on sale of businesses and investments before income taxes	(35)
G. Other noncash items	33
H. Net change in operating assets and liabilities	223
I. Net cash provided by operating activities	2,084
Investing Activities	
Net cash used in investing activities	(1,124)
Financing Activities	
Net cash used in financing activities	(1,331)
Effect of Exchange Rate Changes	458
Cash and Cash Equivalents	
Net decrease in cash during the year	(371)
Balance at beginning of year	1,429
Balance at end of year	$1,058

Minor modifications have been made to the format. Details of investing and financing activities have been omitted. Items have been lettered for reference.

Cash inflows from the sales are reported as cash flow from investing activities. Therefore, the gains do not provide any additional cash flow.

Coca-Cola recorded income tax expense of $765 million on its income statement for 1991 (Exhibit 13-1). Its liability (and required cash payment) for income taxes was $831 million for 1991. Thus, cash payments for income taxes were $66 million greater ($831−$765) than income tax expense. The difference of $66 million was the decrease in deferred taxes for the year. Therefore, on the statement of cash flows, Coca-Cola subtracted the decrease in deferred taxes (item C) to account for the additional cash outflow.

Coca-Cola's net change in operating assets and liabilities (item H) were the changes in current assets and liabilities. A note to the financial statements disclosed details of these changes (in thousands):

Year Ended December 31,	**1991**
Increase in trade accounts receivable	$ (31,826)
Increase in inventories	(3,020)
Increase in prepaid expenses and other assets	(325,595)
Increase in accounts payable and accrued expenses	266,684
Increase in accrued taxes	215,877
Increase in other liabilities	100,717
	$222,837

Changes in these accounts measure the difference between accrual basis recognition of revenues, cost of goods sold, and operating expenses, and cash basis recognition. Recall from Chapter 6 that increases in current assets decrease cash flows and increases in current liabilities increase cash flows.

Coca-Cola's net income of $1,618 million in 1991 (Exhibit 13-1) resulted in net cash flow from operating activities of $2,084 million (item I).

In addition to reporting financial activities for the past fiscal year, corporations report information about events that occurred subsequent to the fiscal year but prior to the time their annual reports are prepared for distribution. The next section considers reporting of subsequent events.

SUBSEQUENT EVENTS

Annual financial statements report the effects of transactions for fiscal years. Thus, if the statements are dated December 31, 1994, they report account balances at this date. The annual report containing the statements usually is published 60 to 90 days after the close of a company's fiscal year. ***Subsequent events*** **are major economic activities occurring after the close of a company's fiscal year but prior to the time its annual report is printed.** GAAP require companies to disclose information about these activities in notes to their financial statements. The disclosure should identify important facts associated with the event, including the amounts of transactions that have occurred. Common types of subsequent events include changes in debt, litigation, business combinations, discontinued operations, and stock dividends or splits.

For example, National Medical Enterprises, Inc., reported in 1992:

Objective 14
Explain the reporting of subsequent events.

> On July 30, 1992, eight insurance companies . . . filed suit against the Company and a subsidiary alleging that psychiatric hospitals owned by lower-tier subsidiaries engaged in certain fraudulent practices. The suit does not allege a specific dollar amount of damages, but seeks the return of alleged over-payments, treble damages and attorney fees. The Company and its subsidiary intend to vigorously defend themselves in this action. At this time, management cannot determine the likelihood or amount of liabilities or losses that may arise from this lawsuit, but based on management's present knowledge, management does not expect the outcome to have a material adverse effect on the Company's consolidated financial position.

These transactions were not included in National's financial statements for its fiscal year ended May 31, 1991. They were included in its financial statements for the fiscal year ended May 31, 1992. This information was reported in the 1991 annual report to inform decision makers of major events that would affect the company's future financial statements. An analysis of National's statements for 1991 should consider the effect on the company's future performance of the subsequent event.

The final section of this chapter explains some of the major differences in reporting the results of operating activities between U.S. and foreign corporations.

INTERNATIONAL REPORTING OF OPERATING ACTIVITIES

Foreign corporations report much of the same income statement information as U.S. corporations. The formats of the statements often are different, however. Exhibit 13-7 contains the income statement of Glaxo Holdings, a British corporation, as reported in its 1992 annual report.

Exhibit 13-7

Glaxo Holdings
Consolidated Profit and Loss Account

For the year ended 30th June	**1992 £m**	**1991 £m**
1. TURNOVER	4,096	3,397
2. Operating costs less other income	2,809	2,293
3. TRADING PROFIT	1,287	1,104
4. Investment income less interest payable	140	179
5. PROFIT ON ORDINARY ACTIVITIES BEFORE TAXATION	1,427	1,283
6. Taxation	386	359
7. PROFIT ON ORDINARY ACTIVITIES AFTER TAXATION	1,041	924
8. Minority Interests	8	12
9. PROFIT BEFORE EXTRAORDINARY ITEMS	1,033	912
10. Extraordinary Items	—	31
11. PROFIT FOR THE FINANCIAL YEAR	1,033	881
12. Dividends	512	420
13. RETAINED PROFIT	521	461
14. EARNINGS PER SHARE	34.3p	30.4p

Items have been numbered for reference.

The title consolidated profit and loss account is used instead of consolidated income statement. Turnover (item 1) is net sales revenue. Operating costs less other income (item 2) include cost of goods sold, operating expenses, and income other than sales. Individual expenses are not reported separately on the income statement. Schedules and notes accompanying the financial statements describe these items in more detail.

Trading profit (item 3) is equivalent to operating income. Investment income less interest payable (item 4), which is other expenses and revenues, is subtracted to compute profit on ordinary activities before taxation (item 5), the equivalent to income before taxes. Taxation (item 6) is income taxes. Minority interests (item 8) and extraordinary items (item 10) have the same meaning as in reports of U.S. companies. Profit for the financial year (item 11) is net income. Dividends (item 12) are subtracted from profit to determine retained profit (item 13), equivalent to retained earnings. Earnings per share (item 14) is computed by dividing net income by the number of shares of stock outstanding at the end of the fiscal year.

The format used by British corporations to report operating results differs from the format used by U.S. corporations. The information reported and reporting rules, however, are similar. Though differences exist in reporting among companies in different countries, the content usually is similar. Care must be used in making comparisons because of differences in reporting and measurement rules.

Considerable diversity exists in reporting cash flows. Some foreign corporations report a statement of cash flows that is similar to that reported by U.S. corporations. Some report a statement of changes in working capital that explains changes in current asset and liability accounts but does not specifically report cash flows. Others report only an income statement without a cash flow or other statement of operating activities.

SELF-STUDY PROBLEM 13-3

The Ben E. King Company reported the following items on its income statement for 1995:

a. Net operating revenues, $845,000
b. Cost of goods sold, $320,000
c. Selling and administrative expenses, $280,000
d. Research and development expenses, $78,000
e. Net interest expense, $4,000
f. Provision for income taxes, $50,000
g. Current year loss from discontinued operations of $30,000, net of tax of $10,000
h. Loss from sale of discontinued operations of $100,000, net of tax of $30,000
i. Cumulative effect (gain) of change in accounting principle of $120,000, net of tax of $40,000
j. Preferred stock dividends, $60,000

The company had 10,000 shares of common stock outstanding throughout the fiscal year.

Required

Compute each of the following:

1. Gross profit
2. Operating income
3. Income (loss) from continuing operations, before taxes
4. Income (loss) before discontinued operations and cumulative effect of accounting change
5. Income (loss) before cumulative effect of accounting change
6. Net income
7. Net income (loss) available for common shareholders

Earnings per share for:

8. Continuing operations
9. Discontinued operations
10. Net income (loss) before cumulative effect of accounting change
11. Cumulative effect of accounting change
12. Net income (loss)

The solution to Self-Study Problem 13-3 appears at the end of the chapter.

REVIEW *Summary of Important Concepts*

1. Revenues and accounts receivable:
   A. Revenues generally are recognized when goods and services are transferred to customers. Revenue recognition methods vary when revenues are earned over long periods (such as long-term contracts), collectibility is not assured, or amounts are not easily estimated.

   B. Accounts receivable are reported net of allowances for doubtful accounts and returns. An expense associated with these amounts is recorded at the end of a fiscal period as an estimate of sales for the period that will not result in cash inflows.
2. Cost of goods sold and inventories:
   A. Merchandising companies report merchandise inventory. Manufacturing companies report raw materials, work in process, and finished goods inventories.
   B. Most companies measure cost of goods sold and ending inventory amounts using FIFO, LIFO, or weighted average estimation methods.
   C. The choice of inventory estimation method affects the amount of net income reported for a period.
   D. Cash flows are affected by the income tax consequences resulting from the choice of inventory estimation method. LIFO generally produces lower income tax obligations.
3. Operating income and expenses, other revenues and expenses, and income taxes:
   A. Gross profit is the excess of net operating revenue over cost of goods sold. Gross profit results from transactions involving customers and suppliers.
   B. Operating income is gross profit minus operating expenses. Operating expenses are period costs not directly related to production or inventory cost.
   C. Financial revenues and expenses are subtracted from operating income to produce income before taxes.
   D. Income tax expense is shown on the income statement as the statutory rate on pretax income for a period. The difference between this amount and the amount of tax obligation computed on a corporation's tax return is deferred tax. Deferred tax results from differences in the recognition of revenues and expenses for financial statement and tax purposes.
4. Special income statement items:
   A. Minority interest in income of consolidated subsidiaries is the portion of subsidiary net income attributable to minority owners of subsidiaries.
   B. Gains and losses associated with discontinued operations, extraordinary items, and accounting changes are reported separately, net of income tax effects.
   C. Dividends on preferred stock are deducted from net income to compute net income available for common stockholders.
   D. Corporations report primary and fully diluted earnings per share for primary categories of net income.
   E. Subsequent events are major economic activities occurring after the end of a fiscal year but before financial statements are printed and made available to decision makers.
5. Cash flow from operating activities:
   A. The income statement reports the accrual basis results of operating activities for a period. The cash flow statement reports the cash basis results of operating activities for a period.

DEFINE *Terms and Concepts Defined in this Chapter*

accounting changes
allowance for doubtful accounts
completed contracts method
direct labor
discontinued operations
extraordinary items
finished goods
first-in first-out (FIFO) method
fully diluted earnings per share
gross profit
indirect labor
last-in first-out (LIFO) method
minority interest in income of consolidated subsidiaries
operating income
overhead
percentage of completion method
primary earnings per share
raw materials
subsequent events
weighted average method
work in process

SOLUTIONS

SELF-STUDY PROBLEM 13-1

	Cash	Revenues	Net Accounts Receivable
Customers paying monthly	$120,000	$120,000	$ 0
Customers paying in advance	55,000	35,000	0
Customers paying semi-annually	70,000	110,000	37,600
Total	$245,000	$265,000	$37,600

Receivables and revenues for customers paying semi-annually include amounts owed of $40,000 less estimated uncollectible accounts of $2,400 ($40,000 × .06).

SELF-STUDY PROBLEM 13-2

(a)

(in millions)	FIFO	LIFO
Beginning inventory	$ 8.0	$ 6.0
Inventory acquired	30.0	30.0
Ending inventory	(10.0)	(7.0)
Cost of goods sold	$ 28.0	$ 29.0
Cost of goods sold, tax benefit (30%)	8.4	8.7
Effect on net income	$ 19.6	$ 20.3

Fashion Mart's cost of goods sold would have been $1 million greater if it had used the LIFO method. It would have saved $300,000 ($8.7−8.4) in taxes if it had used the LIFO method compared with the FIFO method. On an after-tax basis, cost of goods sold would have been $700,000 greater ($20.3−$19.6) if the LIFO method had been used. Therefore, net income would have been $700,000 less under LIFO than under FIFO. Cash outflows would have been $300,000 lower under LIFO, the amount of additional tax savings.

(b) Fashion Mart should consider the effect of the choice of inventory estimation method on its future cash flows. If the company expects its inventory costs to continue to increase and its sales are relatively stable, LIFO will result in lower income tax obligations than will FIFO. If costs or sales are volatile, LIFO might not be an advantage. For example, if the company sells more inventory than it acquires during a fiscal year, LIFO will result in higher net income and tax obligations than will FIFO.

SELF-STUDY PROBLEM 13-3

Net operating revenues	$845,000
Cost of goods sold	(320,000)
1. Gross profit	525,000
Selling and administrative expenses	(280,000)
Research and development expenses	(78,000)
2. Operating income	167,000
Net interest expense	(4,000)
3. Income from continuing operations, before taxes	163,000
Provision for income taxes	(50,000)

4. Income before discontinued operations and cumulative effect of accounting change	113,000
Discontinued operations:	
Current period loss, net of tax of $10,000	(30,000)
Loss from sale of discontinued operations, net of tax of $30,000	(100,000)
5. Loss before cumulative effect of accounting change	(17,000)
Cumulative effect of change in accounting principle, net of tax of $40,000	120,000
6. Net income	103,000
Less: preferred dividends	(60,000)
7. Net income available for common shareholders	$ 43,000
Earnings per share:	
8. Continuing operations ($113,000/10,000 shares)	$11.30
9. Discontinued operations ($130,000/10,000 shares)	(13.00)
10. Net loss before cumulative effect of accounting change ($17,000/10,000 shares)	(1.70)
11. Cumulative effect of accounting change ($120,000/10,000 shares)	12.00
12. Net income ($103,000/10,000 shares)	$10.30

EXERCISES

13-1. Write a short definition for each of the terms listed in the *Terms and Concepts Defined in this Chapter* section.

13-2. Distinguish between the results of operating activities reported on the income statement and the results of operating activities reported on the statement of cash flows. What effect do differences between these statements have on the balance sheet?

13-3. An excerpt of the income statement from the 1992 annual report of General Mills, Incorporated, is provided below:

Amounts in Millions, Except per Share Data	*Fiscal Year Ended* May 31, 1992
Continuing Operations:	
Sales	$7,777.8
Costs and Expenses:	
Cost of sales	4,123.2
Selling, general and administrative	2,504.5
Depreciation and amortization	247.4
Interest, net	58.2
Total Costs and Expenses	6,933.3
Earnings from Continuing Operations before Taxes	844.5
Income Taxes	338.9
Earnings from Continuing Operations	505.6
Discontinued Operations after Taxes	(10.0)
Net Earnings	$ 495.6
Earnings per Share:	
Continuing operations	$3.05
Discontinued operations	(.06)
Net Earnings per Share	$2.99
Average Number of Common Shares	165.7

Write a short explanation of each item presented on the income statement. How much gross profit and operating income did General Mills report for 1992?

13-4. An excerpt of the income statement from the 1991 annual report of Alcoa is provided below:

For the year ended December 31	**1991**
(in millions, except share amounts)	
Revenues	
Sales and operating revenues	$9,884.1
Other income, principally interest	97.1
	9,981.2
Costs and Expenses	
Cost of goods sold	7,444.8
Selling, general administrative and other expenses	579.8
Research and development expenses	251.9
Provision for depreciation, depletion and amortization	697.9
Interest expense	153.2
Taxes other than payroll and severance taxes	122.3
Other operating expenses	330.9
	9,580.8
Earnings	
Income before taxes on income	400.4
Provision for taxes on income	181.7
Income from operations	218.7
Minority interests	(156.0)
Net Income	$ 62.7
Earnings per Common Share	$ .71

Write a short explanation of each item presented on the income statement. How much gross profit and operating income did Alcoa report for 1991?

13-5. Gross profit results from transactions of a company with its customers and suppliers. What types of transactions affect gross profit? How does accounting for timing differences between cash flow and accrual measurements of these transactions affect the financial statements?

13-6. The Aracnoid Company manufactures specialized industrial equipment. The equipment often is sold under credit terms that provide for payment over a two- or three-year period. A substantial prepayment is required before equipment is manufactured. The purchaser accepts title to the equipment at the time it is delivered. Aracnoid also sells service contracts on the equipment it sells. These multi-year contracts stipulate that Aracnoid will provide periodic maintenance on the equipment and will repair the equipment if it breaks down. How should Aracnoid determine its sales and service revenues?

13-7. On June 1, 1994, Milo Construction Company signed a contract to construct a building for MiGrain Agricultural Cooperative. The contract called for MiGrain to pay $4 million to Milo for the building, once construction was completed. Milo expected total construction costs to be $3.2 million. By December 31, 1994, the end of Milo's fiscal year, it had incurred costs of $800,000 on the project. How much revenue and profit should Milo recognize for the project for 1994? Assume the company does not pay income taxes. Also, assume little uncertainty exists about the receipt of payment for the project. How would your answer differ if MiGrain was facing serious financial difficulty at the end of 1994 that could lead to bankruptcy?

13-8. New Cleus Company sold merchandise during its 1995 fiscal year. The total sales price of the merchandise was $30 million. Because of quantity sales discounts, the company billed its customers $28.5 million for the merchandise. New Cleus sells goods to retailers who have a right to return the merchandise if it does not sell within 90 days. New Cleus expects a return rate of 5% of the amount sold. How much revenue should New Cleus recognize for 1995? Justify your answer.

13-9. Karloff Company reported accounts receivable at the end of 1993 of $3,200,000, net of an allowance of $450,000. During its fiscal 1994 year, it recorded sales of $18,600,000, on credit, and collected $18,750,000 from customers. It wrote off $165,000 of bad debts and estimated that it required an allowance for doubtful accounts at the end of 1994 equal to 3% of its 1994 sales. Use the following format to identify how each of these events would affect Karloff's accounts during 1994.

Assets =	Liabilities + Equity	+ Revenues − Expenses

What was the net amount of accounts receivable reported by Karloff on its 1994 balance sheet?

13-10. Rath Bone Company purchased $860,000 of merchandise on credit during its 1995 fiscal year. At the end of 1994, the company reported accounts payable of $90,000 and merchandise inventory of $55,000. It made payments to suppliers of $847,000 and sold merchandise that cost $900,000 during 1995. Use the following format to identify how each of these events would affect Rath Bone's accounts during 1995.

Assets =	Liabilities + Equity	+ Revenues − Expenses

How much merchandise inventory and accounts payable would Rath Bone report on its 1995 balance sheet?

13-11. Sandberg Company purchased $750,000 of materials on credit during its 1994 fiscal year. $775,000 of materials were placed into production. Other production costs included $540,000 of direct labor and $220,000 of overhead. Finished goods costing $1,600,000 were completed during the year, and finished goods costing $1,580,000 were sold. Use the following format to identify how each of these events would affect Sandberg's accounts during 1994. Record overhead to accounts payable.

Assets =	Liabilities + Equity	+ Revenues − Expenses

13-12. Dickinson Company is a wholesaler of garden supplies. At the beginning of its 1993 fiscal year, the company owned 300 bags of X50 lawn fertilizer at a cost of $8 per bag. During April, May, and June of 1993, the following events occurred:

Purchased 800 bags on April 1 at $8.25 each.
Sold 1,000 bags during April.
Purchased 1,500 bags on May 1 at $8.50 each.
Sold 1,350 bags during May.
Purchased 1,200 bags during June at $8.60 each.
Sold 1,275 bags during June.

How much inventory of X50 would Dickinson report on June 30 and how much cost of goods sold would it report for the product for the three months if it used the FIFO estimation method? How much inventory and cost of goods sold would it report if it used the LIFO method? What would its weighted average cost of inventory have been for the month?

13-13. Some corporations use FIFO to estimate their inventory costs. Others use LIFO. What issues are important to this decision? What effect can the choice have on a company's net income and cash flow from operating activities?

13-14. Eli Lilly & Company reported inventories of $673.0 million in 1990 and $599.5 million in 1989. It used LIFO for much of its inventory. If it had used FIFO, it would have reported inventories of $715.7 million in 1990 and $646.5 million in 1989. Assuming an income tax rate of 34%, what effect did the use of LIFO have on the company's reported net income and income taxes?

13-15. GAAP require companies to report inventories on a lower of cost or market basis. What is the purpose of this measurement rule? What effect does it have on a company's financial statements?

13-16. PepsiCo, Incorporated, reported a provision for income taxes of $590.1 million on its 1991 income statement. Deferred income taxes increased from $942.8 million in 1990 to $1,070.1 million in 1991. The company paid $385.9 million of income taxes in 1991. Use the following format to indicate the effect of these transactions on PepsiCo's accounts:

Assets =	Liabilities + Equity	+ Revenues − Expenses

What information is provided by deferred income taxes?

13-17. Paramount Communications Incorporated reported the following information in 1989 (in millions):

Earnings from continuing operations before taxes	$ 19.1
Provision for income taxes	7.6
Earnings from continuing operations	11.5
Earnings from discontinued operations (net of tax of $763.4)	1,453.9
Net earnings	$1,465.4

What are discontinued operations? Why did the company report discontinued operations and the related amount of income taxes separately from continuing operations?

13-18. American Brands, Incorporated, reported net income of $806.1 million in 1991. It reported primary earnings per share of $3.91 and fully diluted earnings per share of $3.74. Distinguish between primary and fully diluted earnings per share. Why were both amounts reported by American Brands?

13-19. Georgia-Pacific Corporation reported a net loss of $142 million in 1991. It reported cash provided by operations of $580 million. Among the adjustments to net income on the statement of cash flows (prepared using the indirect format), the company reported:

depreciation
depletion
amortization of debt discounts and premiums
amortization of goodwill
deferred taxes
gain on sale of assets
and change in receivables, inventories, and payables

Why are these items listed on the statement of cash flows?

13-20. AMR Corporation's fiscal year ends on December 31. In its 1991 annual report, the company reported: "In February 1992, AMR issued 6.5 million shares of common stock, resulting in net proceeds of approximately $454 million." Why is this event reported in the 1991 annual report? What effect did it have on the company's 1991 financial statements?

PROBLEMS

PROBLEM 13-1 Interpreting an Income Statement

Income statement information from the 1991 annual report of Baker Hughes Incorporated is provided below. Baker Hughes provides products and services for the petroleum industry.

Years ended September 30, (In thousands of dollars, except per share amounts)	**1991**	**1990**	**1989**
Revenues:			
Sales	$1,989,336	$1,859,393	$1,763,329
Services and rentals	839,021	754,864	564,666
Total	2,828,357	2,614,257	2,327,995
Costs and Expenses:			
Cost of sales	1,160,915	1,100,762	1,066,835
Cost of services and rentals	402,365	452,209	376,090
Research and engineering	102,558	82,790	70,449
Marketing and field service	617,226	502,720	431,368
General and administrative	221,907	217,827	208,773
Amortization of goodwill and other intangibles	27,926	14,476	5,663
Unusual charges—net	62,946	66,846	—
	2,595,843	2,437,630	2,159,178
Operating income	232,514	176,627	168,817
Gain on sale of subsidiary stock	56,103	65,721	
Interest expense	(83,561)	(77,465)	(60,037)
Interest income	7,295	15,132	8,808
Income before income taxes and extraordinary item	212,351	180,015	117,588
Income taxes	38,893	37,838	34,837
Income before extraordinary item	173,458	142,177	82,751
Extraordinary item:			
Reduction of income taxes arising from carry-forward of prior years' U.S. operating losses	—	—	2,272
Net income	$ 173,458	$ 142,177	$ 85,023
Income per Share of Common Stock:			
Income before extraordinary item	$1.26	$1.06	$.64
Extraordinary item			.02
Net income	$1.26	$1.06	$.66

Minor modifications have been made.

Required Answer each of the following questions:

a. How do sales differ from services and rentals? Why are these amounts shown separately?

b. What was Baker Hughes' gross profit in 1991? What information does this amount provide?

c. Notes to the financial statements indicate unusual charges were for litigation and insurance claims and costs associated with changes in the company's structure. Why are these items reported separately on the income statement?
d. What was the amount of total operating expenses for 1991?
e. Why are gain on sale of subsidiary stock, interest expense, and interest income reported after operating income?
f. Why was the reduction in income taxes reported as an extraordinary item? Why is this item listed separately?
g. Did Baker Hughes have any dilutive securities outstanding during the three years reported on the income statement? How do you know?

PROBLEM 13-2 Revenue Recognition

Paramount Communications, Incorporated, reported the following information in its 1992 annual report:

> Theatrical revenues from domestic and foreign markets are recognized as films are exhibited, revenues from the sale of videocassettes are recognized upon delivery of the merchandise, and revenues from all television sources are recognized upon availability of the film for telecast.

Required What is meant by revenue recognition? Why does Paramount use different revenue recognition principles for different types of revenue? What are the critical events for each of these types of revenue?

PROBLEM 13-3 Operating Transactions

Nabokov Company purchased $4,230,000 of merchandise on credit during its 1995 fiscal year. At the end of 1994, the company reported accounts payable of $870,000 and merchandise inventory of $535,000. It made payments to suppliers of $4,280,000 and sold merchandise that cost $4,060,000 during 1995.

Required Determine the amount of each of the following items reported on Nabokov's 1995 financial statements: merchandise inventory, accounts payable, cost of goods sold, cash paid to suppliers. Explain the difference between the amounts of cost of goods sold and cash paid to suppliers reported for the period.

PROBLEM 13-4 Inventory Transactions of Manufacturing Companies

The O'Neill Company began its fiscal 1994 year with $870,000 of raw materials inventory, $1,390,000 of work in process inventory, and $620,000 of finished goods inventory. During 1994, the company purchased $3,550,000 of raw materials, and used $3,720,000 of raw materials in production. Labor used in production for the year was $2,490,000. Overhead was $1,380,000. Cost of goods sold for the year was $7,500,000. The ending balance of finished goods inventory was $530,000.

Required Use Exhibit 13-2 as a format for developing a diagram to show the effect of these events on O'Neill's inventory accounts for 1994.

PROBLEM 13-5 Preparing an Income Statement

Salinger Company's accounting system listed the following information for the company's 1995 fiscal year (in millions):

Average common shares outstanding	2.4
Cost of goods sold	$170.3
Extraordinary gain	18.2
Gain on sale of securities	8.6
General and administrative expenses	75.5
Income taxes (34% of pretax income)	
Interest expense	12.0
Interest income	5.9
Loss associated with cumulative effect of accounting change	4.0
Loss from discontinued operations	13.1
Sales of merchandise	320.8
Selling expenses	30.2

Required Prepare an income statement for Salinger Company for the year ended December 31, 1995. Assume the tax rate of 34% applies to special items as well as ordinary income.

PROBLEM 13-6 Comparing Inventory Estimation Methods

Information (in millions) about total inventory at year end and cost of goods sold for Axelrod Company is provided below. Axelrod uses the LIFO estimation method. The company's tax rate is 34%.

Year	LIFO Inventory	Inventory Purchased	FIFO Inventory
1990	$24.2	—	$27.5
1991	26.3	502.7	30.0
1992	30.2	510.6	34.4
1993	32.8	522.6	37.4
1994	31.4	535.1	35.8

Required Compute the cost of goods sold that Axelrod would report using the LIFO and FIFO methods. (Cost of goods sold is beginning inventory + purchases − ending inventory). What would be the effect on Axelrod's pretax income and cash flows each year for 1991 through 1994 if the company had used FIFO rather than LIFO? Is the company better off using LIFO or FIFO? Why?

PROBLEM 13-7 Inventory Estimation and Income Control

Kerouac Company uses the LIFO inventory estimation method. At the beginning of its 1994 fiscal year, the company's inventory consisted of the following:

Units	Unit Cost	Total Cost
8,000	$22.00	$176,000
4,000	23.00	92,000
2,000	32.00	64,000
2,000	34.00	68,000

These units were purchased over several years, during which inventory costs increased rapidly. During 1994, Kerouac produced 20,000 additional units of inventory at an average cost of $36 per unit. The average sales price of units sold during the year was $55.

Required Answer the following questions:

a. What would be Kerouac's gross profit and average gross profit per unit if it sold 20,000, 24,000, 28,000, or 36,000 units during 1994?
b. Assume Kerouac sold 36,000 units during 1994. How many units would it need to produce to minimize the tax effect of its gross profit? How many units would it need to produce to maximize its gross profit?
c. If you were a manager of Kerouac and wanted to control the amount of gross profit reported by the company in 1994, what could you do? If you wanted to develop an accounting standard that could prevent this type of management manipulation of income, what kind of standard might you propose?

PROBLEM 13-8 Computing Accounts Receivable

Erdman Corporation reported accounts receivable of $16.5 million at the end of its 1994 fiscal year. This amount was net of an allowance for doubtful accounts of $1,800,000. During 1995, Erdman sold $56.5 million of merchandise on credit. It collected $57.9 million from customers. Accounts valued at $1,980,000 were written off as uncollectible during 1995. Erdman's management estimates that 4% of credit sales made during 1995 will be uncollectible.

Required Answer each of the following questions:

a. What amount will Erdman report for accounts receivable and the allowance for doubtful accounts for 1995?
b. Why do companies record expenses for uncollectible accounts based on estimates from sales during the prior year rather than recording the expenses when accounts are written off in a future period?
c. What perentage of its 1995 credit sales did Erdman expect to become uncollectible? If this percentage were to increase over several years, what information might it provide to decision makers?

PROBLEM 13-9 The Effect of Accounting Choices

The Ginsberg Company is a recently formed, publicly traded company. On December 31, 1994, the company reported the following information.

a. Sales revenues were $13,680,000. 360,000 units were sold. Credit sales were $10,000,000. Uncollectible accounts associated with 1994 credit sales are estimated to be between 3% and 4%.
b. 140,000 units of inventory were available at the beginning of the year at a unit cost of $10 per unit; 250,000 units were purchased during the year at $10.50, and 150,000 units were purchased at $11.50 per unit.
c. Plant assets included equipment with a book value of $3,375,000 and buildings with a book value of $8,260,000. The equipment has an estimated remaining useful life of between 4 and 7 years. The buildings have an estimated remaining useful life of between 25 and 35 years.
d. Intangible assets cost $1,200,000 and have a remaining useful life of no less than 10 years.
e. The company has the option of adopting a new accounting standard for the 1994 fiscal year. If the standard is adopted for 1994, the cumulative effect of the accounting change, before the tax effect, will be a loss of $1,100,000.
f. The company's tax rate is 34%. Other operating expenses were $6,245,000. Interest expense was $460,000. 500,000 shares of common stock were outstanding throughout the year.

Required Provide pro-forma income statements for 1994 showing the minimum and maximum amounts of net income and earnings per share Ginsberg could report under GAAP.

PROBLEM 13-10 Accounting Choice Decisions

Malamud Company reported sales revenue of $10.0 million for its 1995 fiscal year. The company uses FIFO for inventory estimation purposes. Cost of goods sold was $3.8 million. If the company had used LIFO, its cost of goods sold would have been $4.5 million. The company reported depreciation expense of $1.2 million on a straight-line basis. If the company had used accelerated depreciation, it would have reported depreciation expense of $1.7 million. Other expenses, excluding income tax, were $3.0 million. The company's income tax rate was 30%.

Required Compute Malamud's net income as reported and as it would have been reported if LIFO and accelerated depreciation had been used. What effect would the choice of accounting methods have on the company's cash flows from operating activities during 1995, if the same methods were used for both financial reporting and tax purposes?

PROBLEM 13-11 International Reporting of Operating Activities

Dalgety Company reported the following income statement for 1990:

For the year ended 30 June	1990 £m
Turnover	4,634
Group profit on ordinary activities before tax	118.1
Tax	(33.9)
Group profit on ordinary activities after tax	84.2
Minority interests	(2.6)
Profit before extraordinary items	81.6
Extraordinary items	(15.8)
Profit attributable to Dalgety shareholders	65.8
Dividends	(41.1)
Retained earnings	24.7
Earnings per £1 ordinary share	36.5p

The abbreviation for millions is m, and the abbreviation for pence is p. Extraordinary items were net of a tax effect of 2.6m. The average number of common shares outstanding during the year was 223.7m.

Required Reformat Dalgety's income statement as it might appear if it were prepared by a U.S. company.

PROBLEM 13-12 Multiple-Choice Overview of the Chapter

1. The excess of sales revenues over cost of goods sold for a fiscal period is:
   a. net income
   b. income before taxes
   c. operating income
   d. gross profit
2. Timing differences between sales revenues recognized during a fiscal period and cash collected from customers during the period affects the change in the balance of:
   a. accounts receivable
   b. unearned revenue

c. gross profit
d. allowance for doubtful accounts

3. A transaction to estimate the amount of doubtful accounts expense for a fiscal period would affect the:
   a. accounts receivable and doubtful accounts expense accounts.
   b. allowance for doubtful accounts and doubtful accounts expense accounts.
   c. allowance for doubtful accounts and accounts receivable accounts.
   d. allowance for doubtful accounts and sales revenue accounts.
4. The Universal Joint Company publishes a monthly periodical, *Grease Today*. At the beginning of March, the company's unearned revenues included 1,200 annual subscriptions at $36 per subscription. During March, the company received 200 new subscriptions at $36 each. The March issue was shipped to all subscribers on March 25. The amount of subscription revenue the company should recognize in March would be:
   a. $7,200
   b. $4,200
   c. $3,600
   d. $600
5. Two companies are identical except that one used LIFO and the other used FIFO. Both companies produced and sold the same amount of goods during 1995. The company that would report the highest net income:
   a. would be the company that used LIFO.
   b. would be the company that used FIFO.
   c. would depend on the change in inventory costs during the year and whether more goods were produced than sold.
   d. would depend on the price at which the goods were sold and the cost of the goods at the end of the fiscal year.
6. The MacLean Company reported income tax expense on its 1994 income statement of $3.4 million. The amount of income tax the company owed for 1994, determined on its tax return, was $2.8 million. The change in the company's deferred taxes account for 1994 would be:
   a. an increase of $0.6 million.
   b. an increase of $2.8 million.
   c. a decrease of $0.6 million.
   d. a decrease of $2.8 million.
7. The Redford Company reported net income of $40 million for its 1995 fiscal year. The company recorded interest expense of $10 million for the year. Also, it paid preferred dividends of $2 million and common dividends of $5 million. The average number of common shares outstanding for the year was 10 million. The company would report earnings per share of common stock for 1995 of:
   a. $4.00
   b. $3.80
   c. $3.30
   d. $2.30
8. McManus Company reported net income for 1994 of $20 million. The average number of common shares outstanding for the year was 10 million. The company also had convertible bonds outstanding at the end of 1994, though none of the bonds were converted during the 1994 fiscal year. If all the bonds were converted, net income would have increased by $1 million in 1994, and average common shares would have increased by 800,000 shares. McManus would report for 1994:
   a. Primary earnings per share of $2.00 and no amount for fully diluted earnings per share.
   b. Primary earnings per share of $2.00 and fully diluted earnings per share of $2.10.
   c. Primary earnings per share of $2.10 and fully diluted earnings per share of $2.00.

d. Primary earnings per share of $2.00 and fully diluted earnings per share of $1.94.

9. Sontag Company sold plant assets with a book value of $8 million for $10 million during its 1993 fiscal year. The effect of the transaction on the company's pretax income and cash flow from operating activities for 1993 would be:

	Effect on Pretax Income	Effect on Operating Cash Flow
a.	$2 million	$2 million
b.	$2 million	$0
c.	$2 million	$10 million
d.	$8 million	$10 million

10. Vonnegut Company sold a subsidiary in January 1995 for a loss of $10 million. The sale of the subsidiary should be reported in Vonnegut's 1994 annual report as:
    a. an extraordinary item.
    b. a discontinued operation.
    c. a subsequent event.
    d. an infrequent, but not unusual, item.

CASES

CASE 13-1 Examining Operating Activities

Appendix B of this book contains a copy of the 1992 annual report of General Mills, Inc.

Required Review the annual report and answer each of the following questions:

a. What was the primary inventory estimation method used by General Mills? If the company had not used LIFO for valuing any of its inventories, what would the effect have been on the company's cost of goods sold and operating income?
b. What was the amount of the company's allowance for doubtful accounts for 1992? Did the relationship between estimated doubtful accounts and accounts receivable change from 1991 to 1992?
c. How much income tax expense did General Mills recognize for 1992? How much income tax did the company owe for 1992? What were the primary causes of the difference between income tax expense and income tax payable? How much income tax did the company pay in 1992?
d. How much did the company report for interest expense, rent expense, and research and development expense in 1992?

CASE 13-2 Examining Accrual and Cash Flow Measures of Operating Activities

Appendix B of this book contains a copy of the 1992 annual report of General Mills, Inc.

Required Review the annual report and answer each of the following questions:

a. What was the absolute and percentage relationship between cash flow from operating activities and net income for General Mills for 1990 through 1992?
b. What were the primary causes of differences between cash flow from operating activities and net income in 1992?
c. Approximately how much cash did General Mills collect from customers in 1992? Approximately how much cash did the company pay to suppliers?

PROJECTS

PROJECT 13-1 Comparing Revenue and Inventory Methods

Obtain the most recent annual report available for each of three corporations from your library. Use companies from different industries. Examine the revenue recognition and inventory estimation methods used by each company. Write a short report comparing the methods used by each company.

PROJECT 13-2 Comparing Income Statements

Obtain the most recent annual report available for each of three corporations from your library. Compare the amounts reported on the income statements of the companies. Which items were most important relative to the companies' total revenue? What differences and similarities did you find in the format and terminology of the reports? What special items were disclosed? Write a short report summarizing your findings.

PROJECT 13-3 Comparing Income Tax Reporting

Obtain the most recent annual report available for each of three corporations from your library. Find corporations in the same industry. Examine the disclosures provided by each company about its income taxes. How much income tax did each company report on its income statement? How did this amount compare with the amount of income tax the company owed on its taxable income? How much income tax did each company pay during the year? How much deferred tax did it report, and how did the balance of deferred taxes change during the year? What explanations are provided about differences between income taxes reported for financial statements and tax purposes? Summarize your findings in a short report.

PROJECT 13-4 Examining Earnings per Share

Find an example of a company that reported primary and fully diluted earnings per share in a recent year. Examine disclosures in the company's annual report about its earnings per share. What types of dilutive securities were outstanding? How did these securities affect the company's earnings per share? Summarize your findings in a short report.

PROJECT 13-5 Examining Cash Flows

Obtain the most recent annual report available for each of three corporations from your library. Compare the amounts reported on the statements of cash flows of the companies. What explanations were provided for differences between net income and cash flow from operating activities? What differences and similarities did you find in the format and terminology of the reports? Write a short report summarizing your findings.

CHAPTER 14

ANALYSIS OF OPERATING ACTIVITIES

CHAPTER *Overview*

Through its operating activities, an organization develops, produces, distributes, and markets goods and services. These activities are part of an organization's transformation process. The goal of this process is to create value for those who purchase an organization's products. Effective and efficient creation of value results in profits. Operating activities present managers with opportunities, challenges, and uncertainties. Operating decisions are the choices managers make to take advantage of opportunities and to deal with challenges and uncertainties. Accounting information describes the results of operating decisions. It can be used to identify and evaluate management decisions. It can help decision makers understand an organization's current economic circumstances and how these circumstances developed. Also, accounting information can help decision makers forecast an organization's economic future.

Many types of analysis of operating decisions are possible. This chapter examines analytical approaches that are useful for interpreting accounting information. These approaches consider both accrual and cash flow measures of operating activities. They permit evaluation of organizations over time and comparisons among organizations. A primary objective of this analysis is determination and evaluation of a company's risk and return and the effect of risk and return on a company's various stakeholders.

Major topics covered in this chapter include:

- Analysis of revenues and expenses.
- Comparison of operating results among companies.
- Problems associated with interpreting earnings.
- Analysis of cash flows.
- Business failures.
- Forecasting of operating performance.

CHAPTER *Objectives*

Once you have completed this chapter, you should be able to:

1. Identify a company's economic environment and explain why it is important to understanding its performance.
2. Explain how an income statement provides information about effectiveness and efficiency.
3. Analyze the relationships among components of an income statement.
4. Identify factors affecting demand for a company's products.
5. List indicators of economic performance and explain their importance.
6. Explain the importance of profit margins.
7. Identify the components of return on assets and explain their importance.
8. Identify and analyze companies' strategies for success.
9. Identify and analyze components of return on common equity.
10. Identify major problems that affect the interpretation of accounting information.
11. Compare a company's cash flow and net income as a basis for identifying potential financial problems.
12. Identify warning signals of impending business failure.
13. Explain factors that should be considered in forecasting a company's operating results.

ANALYSIS OF REVENUES AND EXPENSES

Objective 1
Identify a company's economic environment and explain why it is important to understanding its performance.

An organization's success or failure results largely from how it responds to its economic environment. Recall from Chapter 1 that an organization's economic environment is composed of internal and external conditions. Exhibit 14-1 summarizes an organization's economic environment.

Exhibit 14-1 Accounting and the Organizational Environment

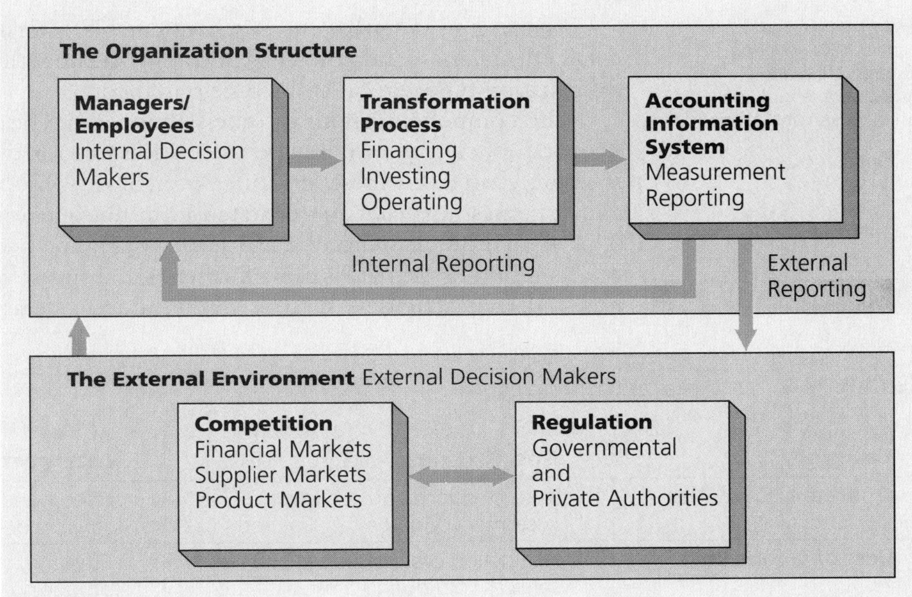

Numerous factors are part of this environment. Understanding interrelationships among these factors is critical to analysis of operating activities. For example, the ability of a company to sell its products depends on the attributes of the products, such as quality and style, and customer demand for products with these attributes. Demand, in turn, is affected by general economic conditions that influence consumer confidence, the availability of money, and the relative prices of domestic and foreign goods. Demand also depends on regulations, such as consumer protection and utilities regulations, that affect the ability of a company to sell its products and that affect the prices of the products. Regulations, such as those protecting workers and the environment, also affect the costs of producing, marketing, and distributing products. The ability of a company to compete in product markets depends on the cost of inputs, such as materials, labor, and equipment. Its ability to acquire these resources may depend on its access to money in financial markets. This chapter examines interrelationships among these factors.

The use of accounting information depends on understanding relationships. The purpose of analysis is to find meaningful patterns and interrelationships in data. Analytical tools can be misused easily. Many tools will lead to the same answers if the user understands the conceptual relationships that make patterns meaningful.

Components of Income

The success of an organization depends on how it responds to its economic environment. Success can be measured in a variety of ways. Most of these measurements relate to two primary attributes, effectiveness and efficiency. An effective organization is one that takes advantage of economic opportunities to provide goods and services demanded by customers. An efficient organization is one that produces goods and services demanded by customers at a low cost relative to their prices.

Objective 2
Explain how an income statement provides information about effectiveness and efficiency.

An income statement reveals considerable information about an organization's effectiveness and efficiency. Exhibit 14-2 identifies the major categories of information reported on an income statement.

The components of an income statement can be used to measure effectiveness and efficiency, to compare these measures for different companies, and to measure changes in these attributes over time. Observe that operating revenues and expenses normally are separated from nonoperating revenues and expenses. This separation facilitates the analysis of operating activities independent of the effects resulting primarily from financing and investing activities. The effects of nonrecurring activities, such as discontinued operations, extraordinary items,

Exhibit 14-2 Income Statement Categories

Category	Description	Interpretation
Operating Revenues	Sales of goods and services to customers during a fiscal period	Effectiveness in providing goods and services demanded by customers
Cost of Goods Sold	Production costs of goods and services sold during a fiscal period	Efficiency in acquiring or producing goods and services
Gross Profit	Excess of operating revenues over production costs for a period	Efficiency in acquiring or producing goods and services
Operating Expenses	Non-production costs expensed during a period	Efficiency in support activities
Operating Income	Excess of operating revenues over expenses of production and operations for a period	Efficiency in production and support activities
Other Revenues and Expenses	Nonoperating revenues and expenses for a period	Effect of financing and investing activities on income
Income Before Taxes	Excess of recurring revenues over recurring expenses before income taxes for a period	Efficiency, considering the effect of financing and investing activities on income
Income Taxes	Expected income taxes on pre-tax income for a period	Effect of income taxes on income
Income Before Special Items	Excess of recurring revenues over recurring expenses after income taxes for a period	Efficiency, considering the effect of financing and investing activities, and taxes on income
Special Items	Nonrecurring revenues and expenses, net of income tax effect for a period	Effect of nonrecurring activities on income
Net Income	Excess of revenues over expenses for a period	Efficiency, considering all income affecting activities

and accounting changes also are separated. The analysis of operating activities normally focuses primarily on operating revenues, cost of goods sold, and operating expenses.

As a basis for illustrating the analysis of income statement components, Exhibit 14-3 provides the income statement for International Paper Company from its 1991 Annual Report.

Exhibit 14-3

International Paper Co.
Consolidated Statement of Earnings

In millions, except per share amounts For the years ended December 31	**1991**	1990	1989
Net Sales	**$12,703**	$12,960	$11,378
Costs and Expenses			
Cost of products sold	**9,341**	9,263	7,918
Depreciation and amortization	**700**	667	559
Distribution expenses	**569**	528	411
Selling and administrative expenses	**945**	934	789
Taxes other than payroll and income taxes	**135**	133	91
Reduction in force charge	**60**		
Business improvement charge		212	
Total Costs and Expenses	**11,750**	11,737	9,768
Earnings Before Interest, Income Taxes and Cumulative Effect of Accounting Change	**953**	1,223	1,610
Interest expense, net	**315**	277	205
Earnings Before Income Taxes and Cumulative Effect of Accounting Change	**638**	946	1,405
Provision for income taxes	**239**	377	541
Earnings Before Cumulative Effect of Accounting Change	**399**	569	864
Cumulative effect of change in accounting for postretirement benefits (less deferred income tax benefit of $135)	**(215)**		
Net Earnings	**184**	569	864
Preferred dividend requirements			19
Earnings Applicable to Common Shares	**$ 184**	$ 569	$ 845
Earnings per Common Share			
Earnings before cumulative effect of accounting change	**$ 3.61**	$ 5.21	$ 7.72
Cumulative effect of change in accounting for postretirement benefits	**(1.95)**		
Earnings per Common Share	**$ 1.66**	$ 5.21	$ 7.72

The income statement reveals an increase in operating revenues (sales) from 1989 to 1990, followed by a decrease from 1990 to 1991. The company's operating and net incomes declined from 1989 to 1990 and from 1990 to 1991. International Paper was less effective in selling its products in 1991 than in 1990. Also, it was less efficient in generating profits from its sales in 1991 than in 1990 and less efficient in 1990 than in 1989.

The following sections analyze International Paper's operating results in greater detail. Also, they illustrate various analytical tools commonly used to evaluate a company's performance.

Percentage Analysis of Income

Objective 3
Analyze the relationships among components of an income statement.

Analysis of income statement components is easier if the amounts are converted to percentages of operating revenues. This presentation is known as a common-sized income statement. Exhibit 14-4 contains these percentages for International Paper. The exhibit also includes percentage changes in each income statement item for 1990 and 1991.

Exhibit 14-4

International Paper Co.
Percentage Analysis of Income Statement

	% of Sales 1991	% of Sales 1990	% of Sales 1989	% Change 1990–1991	% Change 1989–1990
Net Sales	100.0	100.0	100.0	−2.0	13.9
Costs and Expenses					
Cost of products sold	73.5	71.5	69.9	.8	17.0
Gross Profit	26.5	28.5	30.1		
Depreciation and amortization	5.5	5.1	4.9	4.9	19.3
Distribution expenses	4.5	4.1	3.6	7.8	28.5
Selling and administrative expenses	7.4	7.2	6.9	1.2	18.4
Taxes other than payroll and income taxes	1.1	1.0	.8	1.5	46.2
Total Costs and Expenses	92.5	90.6	85.8	0.1	20.2
Operating Income	7.5	9.6	12.7	−22.1	−24.0
Interest expense, net	2.5	2.1	1.8	13.7	35.1
Income Before Taxes	5.0	7.4	11.1	−32.6	−32.7
Provision for income taxes	1.9	2.9	4.8	−36.6	−30.3
Net Earnings	1.4	4.4	7.6	−67.7	−34.1

In the first three columns of numbers, each item is expressed as a percent of net sales for the year. The last two columns contain percentage changes in the item from one year to the next. For example, the percentage change in net sales from 1990 to 1991 was −2.0% [($12,703 − $12,960)/$12,960].

Learning Note

Percentage change from one time to a later time is computed as:

$$\text{Percentage Change} = \frac{\text{Amount at Time 2} - \text{Amount at Time 1}}{\text{Amount at Time 1}}$$

Exhibit 14-4 reveals that International Paper's costs increased as a percentage of sales over the three year period. All expenses, other than income taxes, increased. These expenses, except income taxes, increased more rapidly than sales from 1989 to 1990 and from 1990 to 1991. Increases in distribution expenses, taxes other than payroll and income taxes, and interest expense were especially large from 1989 to 1990 relative to sales. Increases in interest expense normally indicate increases in debt. Higher interest from additional debt financing decreases net income unless the additional financing is used to generate higher revenues. Distribution and interest expenses also increased rapidly from 1990 to 1991. Overall, it is apparent the company's operating results have deteriorated from 1989 to 1991. A general economic recession had a negative effect on most companies in the early 1990s. The adoption of a new accounting standard in 1991 also decreased the company's net income. Detailed analysis is necessary to determine more precisely why changes occurred in International Paper's operating performance.

Operating Revenues

Demand for a company's products is affected by product attributes, general economic conditions, and competition. Product attributes include product type, quality, features, and price. Demand for different types of products changes over time. New or different products may substitute for old products. The demand for horse-drawn carriages declined in the early part of the twentieth century with the increased availability of automobiles. The demand for related products, such as horse collars and buggy whips, also declined. More recently, plastic containers have replaced many glass and paper containers. Aluminum cans have replaced tin and other materials. Factors affecting product demand are considered in the following sections.

Product Demand

Objective 4
Identify factors affecting demand for a company's products.

Products of the same type differ as to quality and features. Automobiles, for example, differ as to reliability and operating costs. Demand for small cars has increased with the need for gas conservation and reduced emissions. Automobiles differ in design, power, comfort, safety, and ease of handling. Prices of automobiles also vary considerably. Different types of automobiles appeal to different customer tastes and income levels.

External economic conditions also affect demand for different products (see Exhibit 14-1). During a period of general prosperity, demand for most products increases relative to demand in recessionary periods. Thus, consumer spending, employment, and industrial production are higher. As the economy slows down, demand decreases. The relative amounts of unemployment, consumer confidence, availability of money and credit, interest rates, and prices of domestic and foreign goods affect demand for different types of goods and services. During the recession of the early 1990s, the demand for many products decreased relative to earlier levels. Many companies found their operating revenues decreased from previous years. Other companies, such as discount stores, experienced increased demand. Many consumers shifted from higher priced goods to lower priced goods because of lower incomes.

Competition in product markets changes over time. New producers or sellers may enter or leave a product market. The early 1990s exhibited a decrease in the number of air lines. The automobile and steel industries experienced sharp increases in international competition in the 1970s and 80s. New markets may become available with changing political conditions. The collapse of communism in eastern Europe provided new markets for many western companies.

Political and social conditions also affect demand and competition. Government regulation may limit competition and may affect prices and costs of products. Utility rates are regulated in most locations. Deregulation of airlines and savings and loan companies contributed to economic problems in these industries. Concern about health and environmental issues has resulted in increased emphasis on pollution control and waste management. Some products, such as cigarettes and alcoholic beverages, are taxed at high levels because they are considered to be health hazards.

Analysis of the demand for a company's products depends on an understanding of its markets. International Paper Company, for example, is a producer of paper and wood products. Its industry segments include: pulp and paper, paperboard and packaging, distribution (primarily of paper), specialty and other products, and timber and wood products. These segments are closely allied because they are all connected with forest products. Within the paper industry, International Paper is a major producer of pulp used in paper production, linerboard used in making corrugated boxes, paperboard for cartons and paper plates, and office papers for stationery, copiers, and printers. Markets are highly competitive for these products because many companies produce similar goods. Profits depend largely on controlling costs. Prices for most of these products change in response to changing economic conditions. Demand for paper products follows closely the general level of industrial production in the economy. Other manufacturers and businesses are the primary consumers of paper products for packaging and office use. As these companies reduced production during early 1990s, their demand for paper products declined. Therefore, paper companies experienced a decline in revenues.

Demand for a company's products has an important effect on a company's operating activities and profitability. High demand usually is associated with increased sales volume and higher prices. A company may increase investment to expand its production capacity. Additional employees are hired to increase productivity. Operating revenues result from two factors, volume and price. If a company can sell its products at favorable prices, normally it will make money. When demand decreases, profitability usually decreases because companies often cut prices and reduce production. Plant assets are underutilized and employees are laid off.

Revenues and resulting profits affect a company's risk and return. Stockholders, in particular, expect to receive higher returns as a company's profits increase. If demand for a product varies considerably over time, sales volume, prices, revenues, and earnings also are likely to vary. Therefore, returns to owners will be more variable than if demand and prices are relatively stable. A company's risk and return are affected by how demand for its products varies in response to changing economic conditions. Indicators of economic activity are useful for evaluating risk and return.

Objective 5
List indicators of economic performance and explain their importance.

Economic Indicators. Economic indicators are indexes of activity for the economy as a whole. They may be expressed as dollar amounts or as quantities of units sold or produced. Dollar amounts may be stated in nominal or real terms. Real dollars are adjusted for inflation and are stated as indexes. These indexes measure the dollar amount of activity relative to dollar amounts in a base year. Exhibit 14-5 illustrates and lists six commonly used indicators for 1981 through 1993. Amounts for 1992 and 1993 are forecasts based on information available in June of 1992.

The indicators are measured on different scales. Gross domestic product and consumer spending are measured in nominal dollars. Industrial production is measured as an index relative to industrial production in 1987. Housing starts and car sales are measured in units, and unemployment is measured as a percent.

Exhibit 14-5 Indicators of Economic Activity

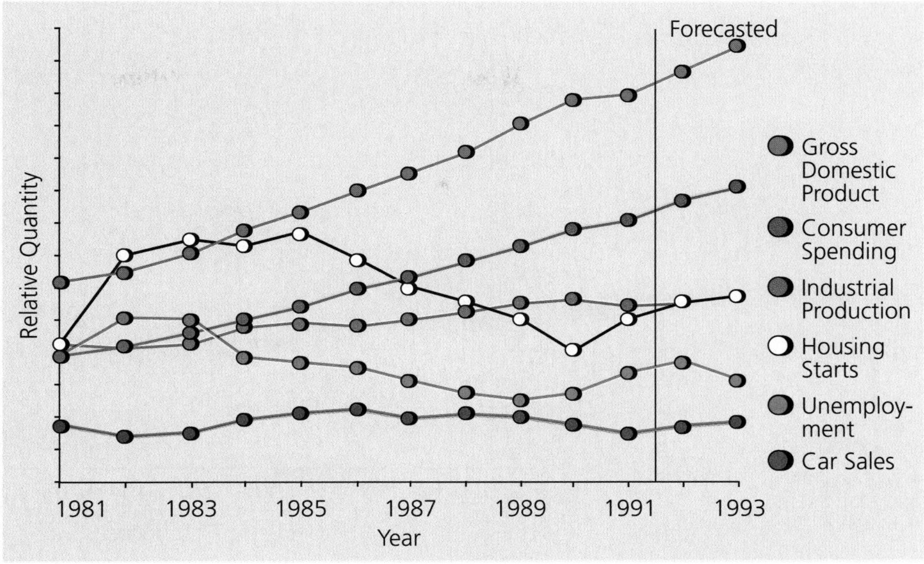

	Gross Domestic Product $ Billion	Consumer Spending $ Billion	Industrial Production Indexed to 1987	Housing Starts Million Units	Car Sales Million Units	Unemployment Percent of Work Force
1981	3031	1926	85.7	1.06	8.5	7.5
1982	3150	2059	81.9	1.7	8.0	9.7
1983	3405	2258	84.9	1.77	8.2	9.6
1984	3777	2460	92.8	1.74	10.4	7.5
1985	4039	2667	94.4	1.81	11.0	7.2
1986	4269	2851	95.3	1.63	11.4	7.0
1987	4540	3052	100.0	1.49	10.2	6.2
1988	4900	3296	105.4	1.38	10.6	5.5
1989	5244	3518	108.1	1.21	9.9	5.3
1990	5514	3743	109.2	1.02	9.3	5.5
1991	5673	3889	107.1	1.26	8.2	6.8
1992f	5956	4115	109.6	1.37	8.6	7.2
1993f	6320	4374	115.0	1.42	9.7	6.6

f = forecasted

Data source: The Value Line Investment Survey, July 24, 1992.

The indexes were scaled in the graph to illustrate their relative movements over time.

A particular indicator may be more useful for one type of product than another. For example, housing starts and car sales are useful for products associated with these industries. Industrial production is a useful indicator for products of many basic manufacturing companies, including paper companies. Exhibit 14-6 illustrates the relationship between industrial production and sales for two companies in the paper industry.

Exhibit 14-6 Effect of Economic Activity on Sales

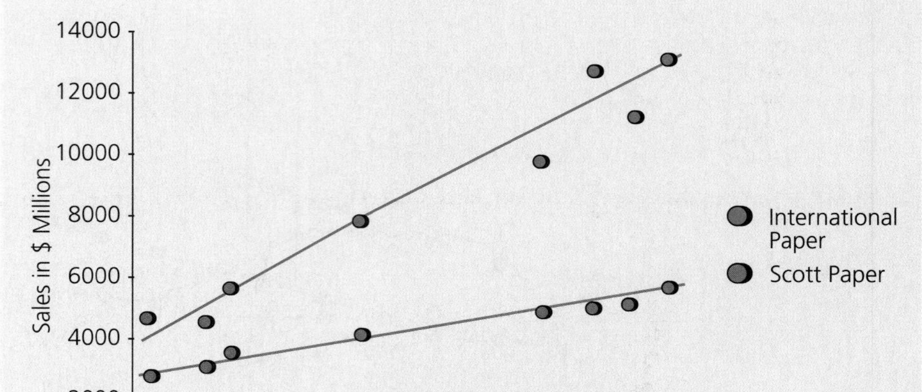

As the level of industrial production increases in the exhibit, the companies' sales increase as well. International Paper's sales are affected more than are those of Scott Paper, as revealed by the steeper slope of the trend line.

Scott Paper's major products differ from those of International Paper. Scott Paper produces primarily consumer paper products, such as tissue and paper towels. Markets for these products are more stable than those for goods produced by International Paper, and prices are not as volatile. For example, pulp prices declined by 19% in 1990 and linerboard prices declined by 11%.[1] These price variations make International Paper's revenues particularly susceptible to changes in demand. The decline in industrial production and the resulting decrease in prices for paper products largely explain International Paper's decline in operating revenues from 1990 to 1991 (see Exhibit 14-3).

International Paper's revenues were less affected by the recession of the early 1990s than those of certain other paper and wood products companies, however. Weyerhaeuser and Georgia-Pacific, for example, were affected by the sharp decline in housing construction (see Exhibit 14-5). These companies are major producers of building materials. As a result, these companies sustained net losses in 1991. The sensitivity of different products to changing economic conditions is a major reason companies often diversify their product lines. By producing a variety of products, a company often is less affected by economic changes than if it produces only one product. Thus, though companies in the paper and wood products industry were affected by the recession, most produced a variety of products. Some products were affected to a greater extent than others.

A comparison of the results of a company's operating activities with an index of economic activity or with other companies in an industry (or industry

[1] This and other industry information comes primarily from Standard and Poor's *Industry Surveys*, February 21, 1991.

averages) provides one means of assessing how well a company is performing. An analyst can determine whether a company's sales are increasing relative to other companies and how demand changes under different economic conditions.

In addition to product demand and pricing, a company's operating results depend on its ability to manage and control costs. Factors affecting this ability are considered next.

Profit Margins

Objective 6
Explain the importance of profit margins.

Profit margin **is the ratio of a company's earnings to its operating revenues.** Several profit margins can be computed. ***Gross profit margin,*** **or** ***gross margin,*** **is the ratio of gross profit to operating revenues:**

$$\text{Gross Profit Margin} = \frac{\text{Gross Profit}}{\text{Net Operating Revenues}}$$

Net operating revenues are sales and other operating revenues net of discounts, returns, and allowances. ***Operating profit margin*** **is the ratio of operating income to operating revenues:**

$$\text{Operating Profit Margin} = \frac{\text{Operating Income}}{\text{Net Operating Revenues}}$$

Net profit margin is the ratio of net income or income before special items to operating revenues:

$$\text{Net Profit Margin} = \frac{\text{Net Income}}{\text{Net Operating Revenues}}$$

The term "profit margin" is defined differently by various users of the term. Even so, the concept is the same. It is a measure of efficiency, of how well a company controls its expenses for the amount of revenue it generates.

Most analysts exclude special (nonrecurring) items, such as discontinued operations, from the analysis of profit margins. Thus, they focus on income from continuing operations and operating income. Including special items can result in misleading performance measures. For example, American Express reported a 76% gain in net income in the first quarter of 1992 though profits on its charge card operations decreased 23%. This decline was due primarily to increased marketing and promotion costs. The increase in net income was due to a change in the method the company used to account for income taxes for financial statement purposes. Because the accounting change was a nonrecurring, nonoperating event, it should not be included in an analysis of operating results.

Exhibit 14-4 contains profit margins for International Paper, as follows:

	% of Sales 1991	**% of Sales 1990**	**% of Sales 1989**
Gross Profit	26.5	28.5	30.1
Operating Income	7.5	9.6	12.7
Net Earnings	1.4	4.4	7.6

Gross margin was 26.5%, operating margin was 7.5%, and net profit margin was 1.4% in 1991. All of the margins decreased from the prior year. As shown in Exhibit 14-3, while the company's operating revenues decreased from 1990 to 1991, its expenses increased, resulting in lower margins. The company was unable to reduce expenses to preserve its margins.

In the short-run, many costs are difficult to control. International Paper has a large investment in plant assets. It has contracts and commitments with suppliers and employees. Many of these costs cannot be reduced substantially, even if production decreases. Recall that operating leverage is the ratio of fixed to variable costs. A company with high operating leverage will experience rapidly increasing profit margins when operating revenues increase, but rapidly decreasing margins when revenues decrease. Thus, operating leverage affects the magnitude and volatility of a company's profits. Also, it affects risk and return for the company's investors.

Exhibit 14-7 illustrates operating revenue and operating expense relationships for five companies.

Exhibit 14-7 Operating Revenues and Expenses

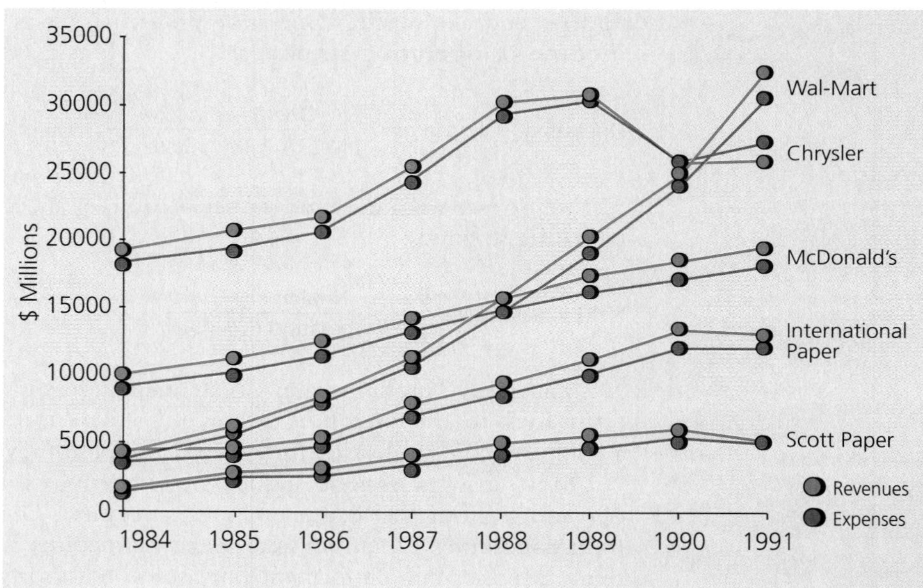

Expenses in this exhibit include cost of goods sold and operating expenses. The difference between the revenue line and the expense line for each company is its operating income. As revenues for most of the companies increased during the 1984 to 1991 period, operating income increased. Overall, except for Chrysler, the companies' expenses increased at a slower rate than their revenues for most of the years shown. Observe that the distance between the revenue and expense lines increases for all companies but Chrysler throughout most years. International Paper and Scott Paper exhibit a decrease in the revenue/expense relationship in 1989 to 1991. The improved performance of most companies was a result of operating leverage and increased efficiency. Many companies can increase sales volume without adding substantially to available plant assets. Operating expenses, such as property taxes, insurance, and amortization of intangibles, also may remain relatively constant with increases in sales and production. As revenues decrease, however, most companies will experience decreasing profits and profit margins. Fixed costs cannot be eliminated and variable operating expenses are difficult to reduce in the short-run.

Scott Paper was operating on a smaller margin than was International Paper throughout the period shown in Exhibit 14-7. The decrease in its revenues in 1991 resulted in the elimination of most of its profits. McDonald's and Wal-Mart were not affected adversely by the recession. McDonald's revenues and profit margin increased throughout the period shown. Wal-Mart's revenues and profits increased dramatically during the early 1990s. The company profited from the recession, as consumers bought larger quantities of discount merchandise.

Chrysler's financial behavior differs from the other companies in the exhibit. Its operating income decreased throughout the period shown, even as its revenues increased. Its operating income was eliminated in 1990 and became negative in 1991 with decreases in revenues. Though Chrysler had high operating leverage, its expenses outpaced its revenues. Therefore, operating leverage does not ensure increased profitability, even in periods of increased sales. Other factors may affect operating expenses. The ability of a company to manage the costs of operations is important. Some companies are able to operate more efficiently by increasing employee productivity, reducing waste, and reducing the time necessary to produce and distribute goods. Demand for a company's products and its ability to control operating costs have important effects on profitability.

SELF-STUDY PROBLEM 14-1

An income statement for Intel Corporation is provided below (earnings per share amounts have been omitted):

Three Years Ended December 28, (In thousands)	**1991**	**1990**	**1989**
Net revenues	**$4,778,616**	**$3,921,274**	**$3,126,833**
Cost of sales	2,315,559	1,930,288	1,720,979
Research and development	618,048	516,747	365,104
Marketing, general and administrative	765,069	615,904	483,436
Operating costs and expenses	3,698,676	3,062,939	2,569,519
Operating income	**1,079,940**	**858,335**	**557,314**
Interest expense	(81,786)	(99,363)	(96,127)
Interest income and other, net	196,475	227,289	121,834
Income before taxes	**1,194,629**	**986,261**	**583,021**
Provision for taxes	376,000	336,000	192,000
Net income	**$ 818,629**	**$ 650,261**	**$ 391,021**

Required

Analyze Intel's operating results for 1989 to 1991. Use a percentage analysis of the company's income statement to evaluate changes in revenues and expenses from 1989 to 1991.

The solution to Self-Study Problem 14-1 appears at the end of the chapter.

COMPARING OPERATING RESULTS AMONG COMPANIES

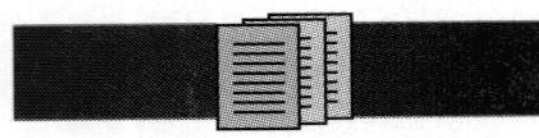

The first part of this chapter examined product demand and cost factors that affect profitability. These factors vary across companies. Therefore, companies use different strategies for creating profits, and decision makers evaluate the results of these strategies. This section describes methods decision makers use to compare the results of strategies used by different companies. Decision makers often use ratios to compare results among companies. As discussed in Chapter 10, return on assets is a commonly used measure of operating results. By dividing earnings by assets, the performances of companies of different sizes can be compared. Return on equity is another commonly used ratio, also discussed in Chapter 10. Return on assets measures the performance of a company relative to its total investment. Return on equity measures performance relative to owners' investments. The analytical methods described below consider the effect of operating, investing, and financing activities on return measures.

Return on Assets

Like other ratios, return on assets is defined in various ways. In its simplest form, it is net income divided by total assets. Interest expense or interest expense net of the tax effect of the interest is often added back to net income in computing the ratio. A frequently used measure of return on assets (ROA) is:

$$\text{ROA} = \frac{\text{Income Before Special Items} + [\text{Interest Expense } (1 - \text{Tax Rate})]}{(\text{Beginning Total Assets} + \text{Ending Total Assets})/2}$$

The numerator excludes nonrecurring items but includes interest expense, net of the tax effect of the expense. Thus, the numerator measures the effect of continuing operating activities as though all financing was provided by equity, and therefore no interest expense was incurred. The effect of capital structure is removed from the equation.

Objective 7
Identify the components of return on assets and explain their importance.

The denominator is the average total assets for the fiscal period. Return on assets can be separated into two components, profit margin and asset turnover:

$$\text{Return on Assets} = \text{Profit Margin} \times \text{Asset Turnover}$$

$$\frac{\text{Net Income} + \text{Interest } (1 - \text{Tax Rate})}{\text{Average Total Assets}} = \frac{\text{Net Income} + \text{Interest } (1 - \text{Tax Rate})}{\text{Operating Revenues}} \times \frac{\text{Operating Revenues}}{\text{Average Total Assets}}$$

Observe that interest expense (net of taxes) is added to net income in this definition of profit margin. ***Asset turnover* is the ratio of operating revenues to average total assets during a fiscal period.** It is a measure of a company's sales volume relative to its (asset) size.

Companies use different strategies for creating profits and return on assets. These strategies depend on the types of products a company provides. These strategies can be examined in terms of profit margin and asset turnover measures, as discussed in the following section.

Strategies for Creating Profits. Two strategies commonly used by companies to create profits are **product differentiation** and **cost leadership.** The strategy a company uses depends on its capital intensity. A company that requires a large investment in plant assets is capital intensive. These companies often rely on high profit margins to generate profits. Low capital intensive companies often rely on high asset turnover:

Capital Intensity	Profit Margin	Asset Turnover	Competitive Strategy
High	High	Low	Product Differentiation
Low	Low	High	Cost Leadership

Profit margin is especially important for companies that are capital intensive. These companies require large investments in plant and other long-term assets. Therefore, their fixed costs and operating leverages are high. Long periods are needed to add production capacity. Example industries include oil, steel, utilities, airlines, automobiles, and telecommunications. Companies in these industries have high levels of average total assets. Consequently, their asset turnover is low. These companies depend on high profit margins to generate profits and return on assets. Because operating leverage is high, profit margins increase rapidly with increases in operating revenues. They also decline rapidly as operating revenues decrease.

To create high profit margins, the companies attempt to differentiate their products from competitors or rely on regulations to control competition. They may develop a specialized product or a niche in the market for their products. Features and quality are important product attributes. Advertising is important to promote the product's special features or quality. High costs of production provide a barrier preventing other companies from entering the industry and reducing competition. Regulations provide control over monopolies, such as utilities. These regulations limit competition in a particular location and provide for a return on assets established by a regulatory board or commission.

At the other extreme are companies whose products are difficult to differentiate from competitors'. Low capital requirements permit many companies to enter an industry. Prices are constrained by intense competition. Therefore, profit margins are low. Profits and return on assets are generated by high asset turnover. Large sales volumes and cost control are keys to success. Many retailers and wholesalers, such as department stores, discount stores, and grocery stores, are in this category. These companies focus on controlling their costs and underpricing their competition.

Companies can be described by positions on a continuum. High asset turnover—low profit margin companies are at one end of the continuum. High profit margin—low asset turnover companies are at the other end. Most companies lie between the two extremes. They can choose to focus on product differentiation or cost leadership. Trading off asset turnover against profit margins may create higher profits and returns.

Exhibit 14-8 summarizes key attributes of cost leadership and product differentiation strategies.[2] The cost leadership strategy depends on competitive pricing and cost control. **Economies of scale** result when production and

2 Adapted from Alfred Rappaport, *Creating Shareholder Value*, The Free Press, 1986, pp. 97-98.

Exhibit 14-8 Strategies for Creating Profits

Cost Leadership Strategy	
Sales	Maintain competitive prices Pursue growth where market share will lead to economies of scale
Operating Margin	Achieve economies of scale and scope Create efficiency through standardization, product design, and scheduling Control costs of purchasing, distribution, and support
Working Capital	Minimize cash balances Increase accounts receivable turnover Minimize inventory
Fixed Capital	Increase utilization Invest in productivity-increasing assets Eliminate unnecessary assets
Product Differentiation Strategy	
Sales	Command a premium price Pursue growth where buyers are willing to pay premium
Operating Margin	Emphasize specialization and quality to meet customer needs
Working Capital	Maintain accounts receivable and inventory levels suitable to customer needs
Fixed Capital	Invest in assets that create product differentiation and quality

sales volumes reach levels sufficient to keep unit costs low. For example, purchasing materials in large quantities normally results in lower per unit costs. Distribution and selling costs can be reduced on a per unit basis when large quantities are shipped, advertised, and sold. Administrative and support costs often remain relatively constant as production and sales volumes increase. Therefore, producing and selling larger quantities results in lower costs for each unit produced. These goods can be sold at lower prices and still yield a profit.

Economies of scope also are becoming increasingly important for many companies. **Economies of scope** result when a company has the ability to produce a variety of products using the same production facilities. By efficient use of inventory, labor, and equipment, a company can produce several products at less cost than if each product were produced in separate facilities. The ability to create new products and introduce new technology quickly also are important. Flexible manufacturing systems permit the company to produce low volumes efficiently and modify products to meet the needs of a variety of customers.

Asset turnover increases when operating revenues increase and when the amount of total assets decrease. Therefore, elimination of unnecessary assets and production costs increases turnover. Large amounts of cash, accounts receivable, and inventory reduce asset turnover. Though some amounts of these assets are necessary, keeping their levels low permits greater investment in productive assets and larger cash flows. Just-in-time inventory systems, for example, permit companies to receive materials and components as they are needed in the production process. Storage and handling costs, as well as the amount invested in inventory, is reduced, permitting higher asset turnover. Discounts and other incentives often are offered to customers to speed payment of receivables.

Production costs can be reduced by standardizing designs to simplify production processes and by reducing the numbers of components. Fewer activities and components often result in a need for less equipment, less time to set up equipment for different product types, and fewer product defects.

The product differentiation strategy also relies on efficiency through cost control. However, this strategy also requires a company to develop products that meet specialized needs of customers. Product design and quality are especially important. Higher investments in assets typically are required in this strategy. More specialized plant assets are needed. Customer service and product promotion often are critical.

To illustrate differences in these strategies, consider the difference between a discount store and a specialty clothing store. Both stores often carry similar clothing items. The discount store emphasizes low prices. Service and quality are secondary. High volumes are used to create profits. The specialty store emphasizes design, quality, and personal service. High profit margins rather than high volumes are used to create profits.

Objective 8
Identify and analyze companies' strategies for success.

Evaluating Strategies. Exhibit 14-9 (at the top of the next page) illustrates the tradeoff between asset turnover and profit margins in creating return on assets.[3] Data are from 1991 annual reports.

Companies successfully using a cost leadership (or high asset turnover) strategy are to the right side of the graph. Companies successfully using a product differentiation (or high profit margin) strategy are to the top of the graph. Companies to the right and top of the graph earned higher return on assets than those to the left and bottom of the graph. Curved lines in the graph indicate amounts of return on assets. A company could move anywhere along one of the lines by trading off profit margin against asset turnover and achieve a return equal to the amount shown for that line.

For example, the points indicated by A and B in the exhibit both would produce a return of 15%. At point A, a 15% return would be generated by a profit margin of 20% and an asset turnover of .75 (.15 = .20 × .75). At point B, a 15% return would be generated by a profit margin of 6% and asset turnover of 2.5 (.15 = .06 × 2.5).

Wal-Mart is an example of a cost leadership company. It was able to create an ROA of approximately 14% through high asset turnover. The Southern Company and Southwestern Bell, both utilities, created an ROA of about 7% through their profit margins. McDonald's ROA of about 10% also resulted primarily from its profit margins. Microsoft was in the enviable position of having both high profit margins and relatively high asset turnover. Its ROA of about 30% resulted from meeting a market need with a differentiated product that required relatively low capital investment.

Most of the companies in this exhibit demonstrate moderate levels of both asset turnover and profit margins. Some were more successful than others, however. General Mills, Toys "R" Us, and Boeing had higher ROA's than other companies using similar strategies. As operating revenues decrease, both profit margin and asset turnover tend to decrease. Exhibit 14-10 provides computations of the amounts illustrated in Exhibit 14-9 for several companies. Revenues, earnings, and assets are expressed in $ millions. Asset turnover is a ratio. The ratio for International Paper, for example, indicates that operating

[3] Adapted from Clyde P. Stickney, *Financial Statement Analysis: A Strategic Perspective*, New York: Harcourt Brace Jovanovich, 1990, p. 167.

Exhibit 14-9 Tradeoffs Between Profit Margin and Asset Turnover

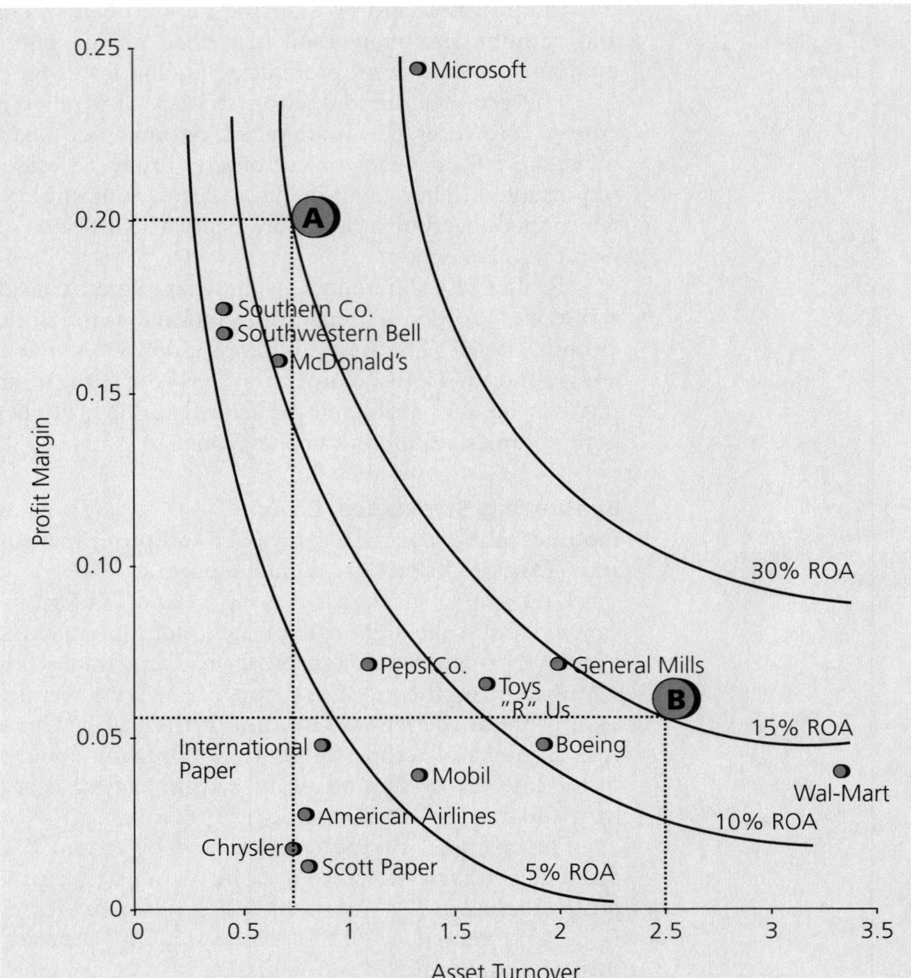

ROA = Return on Assets

revenues were 0.89 times average total assets for 1991. Earnings is defined as income before special items. Tax rates were computed as the ratio of income taxes to income before taxes as reported on the companies' income statements.

Exhibit 14-10 Profit Margin and Asset Turnover Computations

	International Paper	**Scott Paper**	**Wal-Mart**	**McDonald's**	**Chrysler**
Operating revenues	$12,703	$4,977	$32,602	$ 6,695	$29,370
Earnings + interest (after taxes)	596	114	1,398	1,119	703
Average assets	14,305	6,697	9,794	11,008	44,725
Profit margin	4.7%	2.3%	4.3%	16.7%	2.4%
Asset turnover	.89	.74	3.33	.61	.66
Return on assets	4.2%	1.7%	14.3%	10.2%	1.6%

Profit margin and asset turnover can be separated into more detailed components. For example gross profit margins (gross profit ÷ operating revenues) and operating margins (income from operations ÷ operating revenues) for each of the companies in Exhibit 14-10 were:

	International Paper	Scott Paper	Wal-Mart	McDonald's	Chrysler
Gross profit margin	26.5%	31.9%	22.4%	75.7%	20.5%
Operating margin	7.5%	0.8%	6.7%	25.1%	3.6%

Observe that cost of goods sold was a major expense for all of the companies except McDonald's, as shown by gross profit margin. McDonald's earns about $0.75 of gross profit on each $1.00 of merchandise sold. Operating expenses are a major cost for McDonald's, relative to the other companies, as shown by the large decrease from gross margin to operating margin. McDonald's operating expenses include labor and facility costs.

Asset turnover can be separated into accounts receivable, inventory, and fixed (or plant) asset turnover ratios. *Accounts receivable turnover* **is operating revenues divided by average accounts receivable.** It provides a measure of the rate at which cash is being collected from customers. A higher ratio indicates that a greater proportion of sales are being collected in cash during a fiscal period.

Inventory turnover **is cost of goods sold divided by average inventory.** It provides a measure of the amount of inventory a company maintained relative to the amount of inventory sold during a fiscal period. A higher ratio indicates less investment in inventory was needed in proportion to the amount of goods sold. The lower a company's investments in inventory, the greater the amount of cash available for other purposes.

Fixed assets turnover **is operating revenues divided by average fixed assets.** It provides a measure of the amount of plant assets used to generate the amount of sales occuring during a fiscal period. A higher ratio indicates less investment in plant assets was needed for the level of sales generated. As with inventory, the lower a company's investments in plant assets, the greater the amount of cash available for other purposes.

These ratios are shown below for the companies in Exhibit 14-10:

	International Paper	Scott Paper	Wal-Mart	McDonald's	Chrysler
Accounts receivable turnover	6.98	6.64	142.57	29.08	10.25
Inventory turnover	5.47	5.19	4.98	38.07	6.94
Fixed asset turnover	1.68	1.19	10.60	0.72	3.96

Wal-Mart had high accounts receivable and fixed assets turnover. The company sells little merchandise on credit. Therefore, sales are high relative to accounts receivable. The company also invests in relatively small amounts of plant assets. Therefore, fixed asset turnover is high. McDonald's had high accounts receivable and inventory turnover. Like Wal-Mart, McDonald's sells little merchandise on credit. When did you last purchase a hamburger on credit? Also, it maintains relatively small amounts of inventory. Who wants to buy old hamburgers? These ratios provide a measure of the relative amounts of investments in different types of assets necessary for a company's operations. Companies that produce similar products normally will have similar ratios. For example, International Paper and Scott Paper exhibit ratios that are fairly close. Turnover for International Paper was higher than for Scott Paper, indicating lower levels of investment relative to revenues and cost of goods sold.

In addition to use in evaluating a company as a whole, return on assets can be used to evaluate each of a company's major product lines. This analysis provides information about the effect of diversity on a company's risk and return.

Segment Analysis. Many large corporations produce a variety of products and may be involved in several different industries. The strategy employed for one product or industry segment may differ from that employed for another. It may be helpful to examine profit margin and turnover measures for each of a company's segments to analyze their relative performances. The overall profitability of a company depends on the performance of each of its segments.

Following is a description of the performance of each of International Paper's segments for 1991.

	Pulp & Paper	Paper-board	Distribu-tion	Specialty Products	Timber & Wood
Profit margin	7.3%	11.1%	2.0%	9.5%	10.3%
Asset turnover	.75	.99	2.57	.99	.68
Return on assets	5.5%	11.0%	5.3%	9.4%	7.0%

Profit margin was computed from operating profits for each segment. A company's net earnings equals the sum of the operating profits from its segments minus expenses that are common to all of the segments, such as corporate office expenses. Asset turnover was computed from identifiable segment assets, as reported in International Paper's annual report. Therefore, though the ROA numbers are comparable among segments, these numbers are not computed on the same basis as the company's overall ROA. Paperboard and specialty products were the company's most profitable segments. The distribution segment had high asset turnover but a low profit margin.

The analysis of geographical segments also may be useful. Multinational companies may exhibit different performances in different locations. For example, PepsiCo's European operations earned a profit margin of 4.2% in 1991, compared with a profit margin on U.S. operations of 12.1%. Profits earned in some locations may be riskier than those earned in other locations. A company may do well in a new market until competition increases. Economic and political conditions may change quickly in a location, affecting a company's profitability in that location. In 1992, the SEC charged Caterpillar Corporation with failure to inform investors that nearly 25% of its 1989 earnings came from a Brazilian unit. These earnings were unusual and could not be expected to reoccur in future years. Decision makers should be aware of where a company is earning its profits.

Return on assets measures relationships between a company's sales, operating expenses, and assets. Thus, it links operating to investing activities. Return on equity includes the effect of financing activities on operating results, as discussed in the following section.

Return on Equity

Objective 9
Identify and analyze components of return on common equity.

Return on equity (ROE), sometimes referred to as return on common stockholders' equity, is equal to return on assets adjusted for the effects of debt and preferred stock financing:

$$\text{ROE} = \frac{\text{Net Income} - \text{Preferred Dividends}}{\text{Average Common Stockholders' Equity}}$$

Common stockholders' equity is total stockholders' equity minus preferred stock. Net income is included in the numerator. Therefore, the effects of interest expense on operating results are included. Two effects result from financial leverage. One is *earnings leverage,* the effect of interest expense on net income. The other is *capital structure leverage,* the effect of debt financing on total invested capital[4]:

$$\text{ROE} = \text{ROA} \times \text{Earnings Leverage} \times \text{Capital Structure Leverage}$$

$$\text{ROE} = \text{ROA} \times \frac{\text{Net Income} - \text{Preferred Dividends}}{\text{Net Income} + \text{Interest Expense } (1 - \text{Tax Rate})} \times \frac{\text{Average Total Assets}}{\text{Average Common Stockholders' Equity}}$$

Earnings leverage considers the effect of debt and preferred stock financing on income available for common stockholders. Interest expense is computed on an after-tax basis. Higher earnings leverage results in lower net income available for common stockholders. Net income available for common stockholders is reduced by interest and preferred dividends.

Capital structure leverage increases as the percentage of total financing provided by debt and preferred stock increases. Higher capital structure leverage results in higher earnings per share of common stock because fewer common shares are required to provide financing as higher proportions of debt and preferred stock are used.

International Paper's return on common equity for 1991 was:

$$\text{ROE} = \text{ROA} \times \frac{\text{Net Income} - \text{Preferred Dividends}}{\text{Net Income} + \text{Interest Expense } (1 - \text{Tax Rate})} \times \frac{\text{Average Total Assets}}{\text{Average Common Stockholders' Equity}}$$

$$7.1\% = 4.2\% \times \frac{\$399 \text{ million}}{\$399 + \$197 \text{ million}} \times \frac{\$14{,}305 \text{ million}}{\$5{,}686 \text{ million}}$$

$$7.1\% = 4.2\% \times .67 \times 2.52$$

Interest expense after taxes was \$197 million (\$315 million interest expense × 1 − .375 tax rate). International Paper had no preferred stock and paid no preferred stock dividends in 1991. Earnings leverage was 0.67. Thus, net income was 67% of what it would have been if the company had used only equity financing. But, capital structure leverage was 2.52. Consequently, earnings available for common shareholders was 2.52 times what it would have been if only equity financing had been used. Financial leverage was 1.69 (.67 × 2.52). Re-

[4] Adapted from Clyde P. Stickney, *Financial Statement Analysis,* New York: Harcourt Brace Jovanovich, 1990, p. 207.

turn on equity was 1.69 times as much as return on assets because of the effects of financial leverage.

Exhibit 14-11 contains financial leverage and return on equity amounts for several companies.

Exhibit 14-11 Components of Return on Equity

	International Paper	Scott Paper	Wal-Mart	McDonald's	Chrysler
Earnings leverage	.67	−.62	.92	.77	−.77
Capital structure leverage	2.52	3.22	2.10	2.58	6.90
Return on assets	4.2%	1.7%	14.3%	10.2%	1.6%
Return on equity	7.1%	−3.4%	27.6%	20.3%	−8.5%

Observe that financial leverage can have a positive or a negative effect on return on equity. A positive effect results if a company has net income after interest expense. In such situations, as exhibited by International Paper, Wal-Mart, and McDonald's, capital structure leverage results in ROE that is higher than ROA. The difference can be dramatic, as shown for Wal-Mart. A negative effect results if a company has a net loss after interest expense, as exhibited by Scott Paper and Chrysler. Capital structure leverage for these companies makes a poor performance even worse. Return on equity will be lower than return on assets. Like operating leverage, financial leverage is an advantage when a company is doing well and a disadvantage when it is doing poorly.

Financial leverage, asset turnover, and profit margin are important for understanding a company's strategies for earning profits. These measures reveal the potential a company has for earning a favorable return in varying economic conditions. Careful analysis can reveal the potential for risk and return. **Operating, investing, and financing decisions are interrelated.** Therefore, it is important to examine these decisions in relationship to each other. Analysis of interrelationships among income statement, balance sheet, and cash flow statement amounts is useful for this purpose.

SELF-STUDY PROBLEM 14-2

Selected accounting information is presented below for AT&T and Sears. Amounts are for 1991, except as noted.

(In millions)	AT&T	Sears
Operating revenues	$63,089	$ 57,242
Total assets, 1990	48,322	96,253
Total assets, 1991	53,355	106,435
Net income	522	1,279
Interest expense	726	3,252
Income taxes	361	193
Income before taxes	883	1,458
Preferred dividends	0	0
Common equity, 1990	15,883	12,824
Common equity, 1991	16,228	13,863

Required

(a) Compute profit margin, asset turnover, return on assets, earnings leverage, capital structure leverage, and return on equity for each company. (b) Analyze the companies' performances for 1991 using this information.

The solution to Self-Study Problem 14-2 appears at the end of the chapter.

PROBLEMS WITH INTERPRETING EARNINGS

Objective 10
Identify major problems that affect the interpretation of accounting information.

Owners, creditors, suppliers, employees, and other decision makers are concerned with an organization's expected cash flows. They want to know whether a company will be able to pay interest, repay debt, pay for purchases, and pay wages. Owners want to know what amount of return they should expect from their investments. The analysis of earnings is useful for many companies when their earnings are reliable signals of expected cash flows. Care must be used in interpreting earnings, however, because they are not always comparable across companies or time periods and are not always reliable. The analysis of earnings is complicated by the different methods and estimates companies use in computing accrual numbers. Earnings numbers can be managed to look better or worse by using one set of accounting methods or estimates relative to using a different set. The following sections consider these issues.

Choice of Accounting Methods

Prior chapters have described several types of transactions for which choices of accounting methods and estimations are important. Among these are:

Item	Accounting Method Choices and Estimates
Depreciation	Accelerated and straight-line methods and selection of estimated useful lives
Inventory	FIFO, LIFO, and average methods
Accounts receivable	Estimation of doubtful accounts and returns
Employee benefits	Selection of discount and asset earnings rates and amortization periods
Foreign exchange	Choice of functional currency
Leases	Capital or operating
Investments in securities	Lower of cost or market, equity method, or consolidation
Mergers and acquisitions	Purchase or pooling of interests

If management uses the same accounting methods consistently over time, the analysis of a particular company is not likely to be affected to a major extent by these choices. Comparisons among companies may be affected, however.

Analysts often attempt to adjust reported numbers for differences in accounting methods when comparing companies. Some of these adjustments are relatively easy. Companies using LIFO report the effect on earnings of using LIFO rather than FIFO, for example. Thus, an analyst can compute what a company's earnings would have been if it had used FIFO. Then, an analyst can compare a LIFO company with a company using FIFO. Other adjustments are more complex, and information may not be available for adjusting reported numbers. Adjusting employee benefit computations for differences in interest rates and other estimates would be extremely difficult, for example.

Earnings Management

Earnings management results when managers manipulate accounting numbers to make a company's performance for a period appear to be better or worse than it would have without the manipulation. Management compensation agreements, loan and debt covenants, and other contractual arrangements often are based on accrual accounting numbers. Management bonuses, for example, may depend on a company's revenues or profits reaching a specified amount or growth rate. These agreements provide incentives for the managers to manipulate earnings and other accounting numbers. Managers sometimes can increase their compensation by shifting earnings from one fiscal period to another. Many accounting rules are flexible and permit such shifting.

For example, assume a company uses LIFO and has two levels of inventory costs available on October 1, 1994. One level represents units purchased in prior periods at $5 per unit. The other level represents units purchased more recently at a much higher cost of $8 per unit:

Units	Cost per Unit	Total Cost
3,000	$5	$15,000
2,000	$8	$16,000

The company sells 4,000 units during the last quarter of 1994. If it does not purchase additional units during the quarter, it would record cost of goods sold of $26,000 [(2,000 × $8) + (2,000 × $5)] for the quarter. If it purchases 4,000 units during the quarter at the current cost of $10 per unit, it would record cost of goods sold of $40,000 (4,000 × $10). Thus, the management decision of whether to purchase inventory results in an approximately 50% difference in cost of goods sold for the quarter.

When a company and its investors focus on short-run performance indicators, such as current period earnings per share or return on assets, incentives exist for managers to manipulate reported earnings. In addition, managers may wish to reduce the volatility of reported earnings so their operating results will appear to be stable. Volatile earnings may be interpreted by investors as increasing default risk on debt and the uncertainty of returns to stockholders. Investors are concerned with the volatility of expected cash flows. Because these cash flows cannot be observed directly, however, they often rely on earnings to evaluate cash flows. Investors typically prefer a steadily increasing earnings pattern. Therefore, managers may attempt to manipulate earnings to fit this pattern.

The usefulness of accounting information is affected by management choice of accounting methods and by manipulation of accounting numbers. In

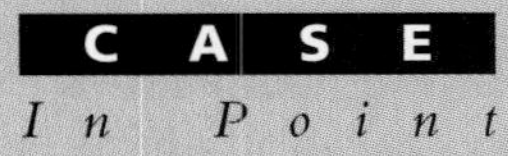

Investors can be misled by management manipulation of earnings. For example, the stock of Chambers Development Co. decreased by more than 50% on one trading day in 1992. The company revised its reported earnings per share from $.83 to $.03. It acknowledged that it had been deferring certain costs and recording them as assets when it should have been expensing them.

addition, companies may record large losses in a fiscal period as part of a corporate restructuring. These losses affect current and future earnings, making operating results more difficult to analyze, as considered below.

Restructuring

Companies experiencing poor performance frequently change their organizational structures in an effort to reduce costs and improve profits. Restructuring occurs when a company writes off inventory or receivables, closes or sells facilities or entire segments, reduces its work force, or makes major changes in its capital structure. A company records the costs associated with restructuring as an expense during the period a restructuring decision is made, often resulting in a major loss for that period. Restructuring is intended to reduce expenses in future years, thereby increasing future profits. If new managers take over a company, they may restructure so future years will appear more profitable than the years prior to their take over. Thus, they can demonstrate improvement in company performance to investors.

Many companies restructured during the late 1980s and early 1990s. For example, in 1990, General Motors recorded expenses of $2.1 billion associated with costs of closing plants and reducing its work force. Some of these closings would not occur for two or three years. Because of these changes, the company expected to reduce annual costs by at least $1 billion. By expensing costs in one year, less cost would need to be expensed in future years, thus increasing future profits. Expensing large costs associated with restructuring is called taking a "big bath." The "bath" cleanses the company of excess labor and plant assets and reduces future costs. A company expects to demonstrate more stable earnings growth after taking a bath.

A big bath is not illegal or dishonest. It does suggest, however, that a company's performance in previous fiscal periods may have been overstated and future period costs may be understated. A company that restructures usually is aware that the book values of some of its assets are greater than their market values. A bath is a way of reducing the book values in a single fiscal period, rather than writing down the assets as the decline in market value occurred in prior years. A company also may reduce the book value of inventory to eliminate items that are obsolete or for which demand and prices have decreased. It may reduce the book value of receivables that it has had difficulty collecting. When all the write-downs are recorded in a single year, the performances of other years appear better than they might actually be.

One reason for restructuring is the use of historical costs in preparing accounting information. The next section examines other problems caused by the use of historical costs.

Historical Costs

The use of historical costs as a basis for reporting the value of many assets also poses problems in interpreting accounting information. Inflation drives the price of resources and products up over time. Inventory, plant assets, and other resources acquired in prior periods are stated at their earlier, uninflated costs. Thus, when these costs are matched against revenues during a later period, profits are inflated over what they would have been if current costs were matched against revenues. During periods of high inflation, a company's profits may appear to be much higher than in previous years. In terms of the current value of the dollar (inflation adjusted) or cash flows, however, the company may not be doing as well as it appears. This was a problem of the late 1970s when inflation was relatively high.

This problem may be especially acute for industries that hold large amounts of physical assets or natural resources. For example, paper companies often own large amounts of timberlands. Relative to the current value of these lands, their purchase prices may be extremely low because they were purchased decades earlier. Expenses associated with these resources are much lower than they would be if a company were purchasing the resources at current market prices. Profits are higher, assets are lower, and thus, return on assets appears to be much higher than it would have if current values were used. Therefore, extreme care is needed in comparing companies in certain industries. Comparing similar companies within an industry is easier than comparing companies in different industries.

CASH FLOW ANALYSIS

Objective 11
Compare a company's cash flow and net income as a basis for identifying potential financial problems.

Along with analysis of earnings and other accrual based numbers, cash flow analysis is important. In some situations, cash flows from operating activities are more important indicators of performance than accrual measures. Companies with large amounts of debt, perhaps from mergers or acquisitions, and interest expense often exhibit low earnings. Solvency rather than profitability may be their major concern. Cash flows from operating activities sometimes are better indicators of operating performance for these companies than earnings. Operating cash flows normally are used to evaluate operating results for some industries, including real estate and oil. Depreciation expenses greatly reduce the profits of real estate companies, even though a company's properties may be appreciating in value. Depletion has a similar effect on earnings of oil companies.

Operating cash flow amounts often are reported by business periodicals as part of their analysis. *Value Line*, for example, reports cash flow per share as a primary factor explaining stock prices. One must be cautious in using these numbers because operating cash flow is defined in various ways. Operating cash flow sometimes is defined as net income plus depreciation and amortization. This is the definition used by *Value Line*. The statement of cash flows adjusts net income for all noncash operating items: depreciation and amortization, changes in current asset and liability accounts, changes in deferred taxes, and other noncash items. Some analysts subtract capital expenditures, and even dividends, from cash flow from operating activities to measure cash available for use by a company. When reviewing an analysis of cash flows, be sure you know how cash flows are being defined.

Comparison of cash flow and accrual measures of operating activities over time can reveal whether accrual measures are good indicators of operating cash flows. Exhibit 14-12 provides a comparison of cash flows from operating activities and net income (before special items) for Vulcan Materials Company. Operating cash flows and earnings follow similar patterns over time. Much of the difference between the two measures is explained by depreciation and amortization. When these non-cash expenses are added to net income, earnings are similar in magnitude to cash flows from operating activities.

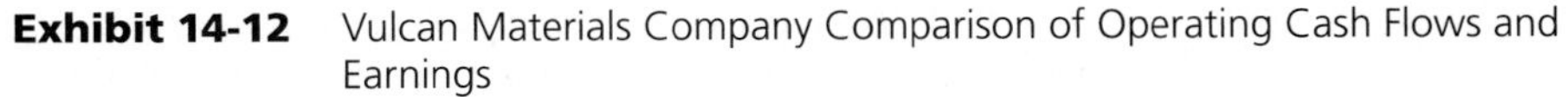

Exhibit 14-12 Vulcan Materials Company Comparison of Operating Cash Flows and Earnings

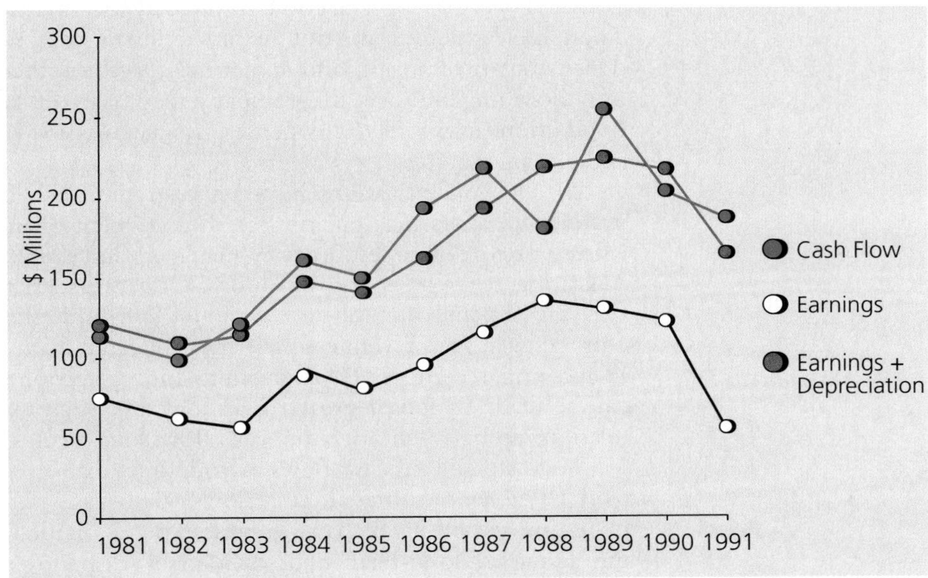

Operating cash flows and earnings do not follow similar patterns for all companies. Exhibit 12-4 illustrated cash flow and accrual measures for Allied Products Company. Cash flow from operating activities and net income varied widely from year to year. Allied's receivables, inventory, and payables also varied widely from year to year as shown below (in $ millions):

	Net Income	Cash—Operating	Change in Receivables	Change in Inventory	Change in Payables
1986	$16.2	−$99.8	$38.3	$15.2	−$66.7
1987	−1.7	−32.1	30.1	4.4	5.7
1988	5.5	−3.6	21.8	17	20.9
1989	−22.4	−8.1	−7.7	24.6	7.6
1990	−5.8	25.7	8.2	−49.9	−25.4
1991	−34	34.5	−44.3	−5.8	−5.6

An increase in receivables results when a company is selling goods and services but is not collecting from customers. Therefore, its cash flow from customers is less than its operating revenues. Inventory increases when a company produces more than its sells. A decrease in payables results when a company pays more cash to its suppliers than it purchases during a period. Therefore, cash outflow will be greater than expenses on the income statement. Observe that in 1986, Allied Products experienced an increase in receivables and inventory and a decrease in payables. It received less cash from customers than the amount of sales revenue recorded for the year. It paid out more for production costs and purchases than it expensed. Consequently, cash flow from operating activities was dramatically less than net income.

Wide variations between earnings and cash flows from operating activities often signal financial problems for a company. In an economic downturn, a company may be able to maintain its earnings by relaxing credit policies and by continuing to produce goods. Accounts receivable increase as credit sales increase. The costs of the goods produced are inventoried until they are sold. Therefore, expenses are not recorded during the period the goods are produced, but inventories, and sometimes payables, increase rapidly. If the economy does not improve, the company may have difficulty collecting receivables. In addition, it will record expenses associated with writing off unsold inventory and closing facilities.

In addition, variations between operating cash flows and net income can indicate earnings manipulation or misstatement of income statement numbers. Misuse of corporate resources by managers and employees often is concealed by misstating receivables and inventories. By overstating receivables and inventories, a company can overstate revenues and understate expenses. For example, consider that sales revenue equals cash collected from customers plus the change in accounts receivable. By overstating ending accounts receivable, sales revenues can be made to appear greater than they are. Such manipulations will affect the relationship between operating cash flows and earnings.

Ratios based on cash flows provide information about the ability of a company to generate sufficient cash flows. Cash basis ratios include cash flow from operating activities per share, interest expense divided by cash flow from operating activities, long-term debt divided by cash flow from operating activities, and common stock price per share divided by operating cash flow per share. A comparison of accrual and cash flow ratios for several companies appears below:

	International Paper	Scott Paper	Wal-Mart	McDonald's	Chrysler
Cash Flow—Operating (millions)	$1,152	$582	$1,296	$1,423	$2,853
Operating Cash Flow per Share	9.81	7.90	1.13	3.89	11.76
Earnings per share	3.61	−0.95	1.14	2.35	−2.22
Price to Earnings	19.60	N/A	26.32	16.17	N/A
Price to Operating Cash Flow	7.21	4.43	26.44	9.77	1.13

N/A = not applicable when earnings are negative

Cash flow from operating activities normally is higher than net income, because it excludes noncash expenses such as depreciation. Therefore, ratios in which operating cash flow is in the numerator often are higher than corresponding earnings-based ratios. Ratios in which operating cash flow is in the denominator normally are lower. These ratios are used in the same manner as earnings-based ratios. Comparing changes in ratios over time can reveal whether a company's performance is improving or deteriorating. Comparisons among companies, particularly if the companies are similar, can reveal relative strengths and weaknesses.

A company creates value for its shareholders by generating cash flows from its operating activities in excess of the amount needed to replace resources consumed by these activities. Therefore, careful attention should be given to operating cash flows in evaluating a company's performance. Both accrual and cash flow measures can be useful for predicting expected future cash flows. Cash flow from operating activities is often a useful indicator of potential business failure, as considered in the next section.

BUSINESS FAILURE

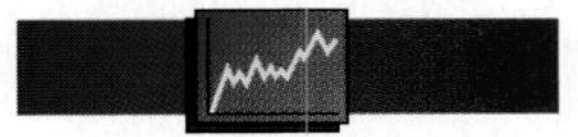

Objective 12
Identify warning signals of impending business failure.

A business failure occurs when a company is forced out of business. Businesses fail when they are unable to generate sufficient cash flows from operating activities to acquire necessary resources and to pay creditors. Sustained losses normally are accompanied by cash flow problems. In some situations, cash flow problems will appear on the statement of cash flows before a loss appears on the income statement. Typically, a business enters bankruptcy when it faces a cash flow crisis. For example, it does not have cash to pay interest or principal on its debt and its major sources of short-term financing refuse to provide additional cash.

Companies may go through several stages of financial decline before they fail. Decreases in net income and cash flow from operating activities often are the first signals of financial problems. Declining sales and narrower profit margins generally lead to these problems. Increases in receivables, inventories, and payables sometimes accompany these trends. Net losses and negative operating cash flows usually are signals of major financial problems. A company that sustains losses will find its equity gradually eliminated as retained earnings decrease. It becomes insolvent when its total liabilities are greater than its total assets.

A company normally declares bankruptcy when it cannot meet cash flow demands, particularly when it cannot pay its creditors. It usually seeks protection under Chapter 11 of the U.S. Bankruptcy Code. This protection provides a period of time during which a company can continue to operate while attempting to seek additional sources of financing, to work out payments with creditors, and to re-establish profitable operations. A bankrupt company also receives favorable tax treatment while it attempts to overcome its financial problems.

A bankrupt company often reorganizes its capital structure as a means of removing itself from bankruptcy. For example, creditors may be willing to lengthen debt terms or accept lower interest rates. They may be willing to accept common or preferred stock in place of notes or bonds. In exchange for accepting these conditions, a company's creditors and board of directors may require changes in management. For example, a reorganization of Greyhound Corporation in 1991 gave creditors 95% of the company's equity. Stock held by the company's previous owners became worthless.

A company that cannot resolve its debt payment problems or is incapable of reestablishing profitable operations normally will liquidate. Liquidation involves the sale of assets and distribution of cash to creditors. Any cash remaining after creditors have been paid is distributed to stockholders, though cash seldom remains. Only at the stage of liquidation does a company cease to exist. Many companies faced with the prospect of bankruptcy or liquidation seek to sell their operations to another company. By merging or being acquired, a company can avoid liquidation and sometimes preserve value for its creditors and stockholders.

Eastern Air Lines provides an example of a recent business failure. Exhibit 14-13 illustrates the financial decline of the company.

Exhibit 14-13 The Failure of Eastern Air Lines

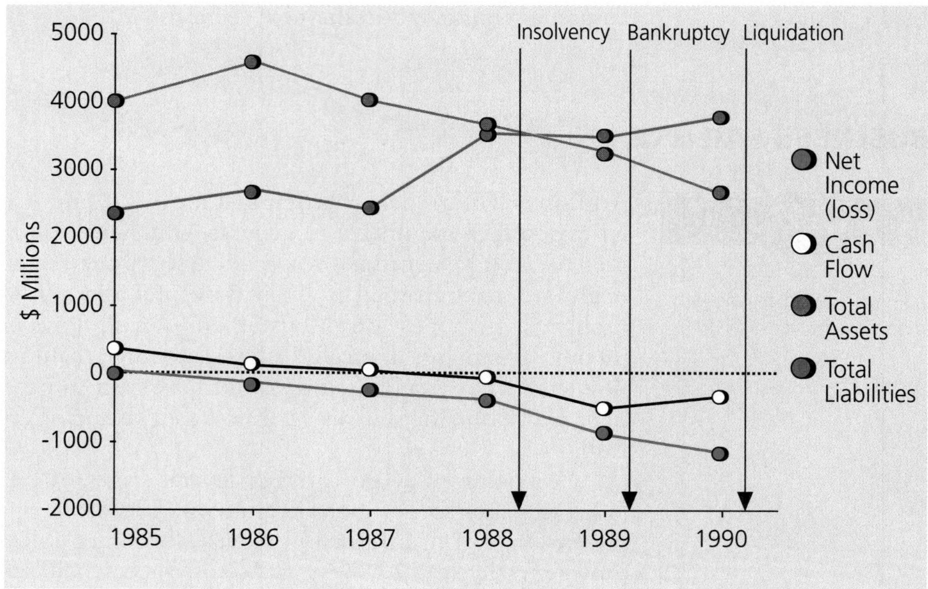

By 1985, the company was sustaining net losses. Its cash flow from operating activities became negative during 1987, and it became insolvent during 1988. A major loss and negative operating cash flow in 1989 led to bankruptcy. Continued losses and negative operating cash flows led to liquidation in 1990. As the company's cash flow from operating activities became negative, it increased debt financing to provide needed cash flows. At the same time, it sold off assets to provide cash and reduce operating costs.

The airlines industry was especially hurt by deregulation, increased fuel and other operating costs, and the general downturn of the economy in the late 1980s and early 1990s. Several major carriers declared bankruptcy (Continental, TWA) and several went out of business (Eastern, Pan Am). These failures, like most, were the result of changing economic conditions and the inability of management to develop successful strategies for dealing with the conditions. Accounting information generally is a useful indicator of these problems.

FORECASTING OPERATING RESULTS

Objective 13
Explain factors that should be considered in forecasting a company's operating results.

Decision makers are interested in what is going to happen to a company in the future. They want to know what amount of return to expect, whether a company will be able to pay its debts and pay dividends. They must decide whether to invest in a company, to lend it money, or to sell it goods and services. They forecast a company's future performance to help with these decisions. Forecasting involves an analysis of past events and expected future conditions. Typically, it requires considerable knowledge of a company and its industry. So many factors are involved in forecasting the future performance of a company that professional financial analysts tend to specialize in particular industries. This section considers some of the factors and approaches used in forecasting. It is intended to provide a general summary.

The following list summarizes important factors considered when forecasting future performance. These are factors that are also important for interpreting a company's past performance.

1. Types of products produced and/or sold and the industries in which the company competes.
2. Management strategies used to generate profits.
3. Expected demand for a company's products.
4. Expected domestic and international economic conditions.
5. Changes in competing products.
6. Population demographics.
7. Foreign exchange rates.
8. Present economic conditions.
9. Political and social factors affecting product demand and pricing or affecting cost and availability of resources.
10. Management abilities.
11. Technology and research and development activities.
12. Access to materials, labor, and other resources.
13. Distribution capabilities.
14. Availability and cost of financing.
15. Employee relations.

These factors provide a basis for estimating future revenues, expenses, and cash flows. Demand factors affect revenues from sales of goods and services. Analysts consider the size of a company's market, how fast it is growing or shrinking, how a company is positioned to compete in the market, how competitive the market is likely to be, who the leading competitors are, what their market shares are, and what competitive factors are important in the market (quality, diversity, pricing, packaging, distribution, advertising, creation of new products, and sales force). They consider the expenses a company is likely to incur for the amount of revenues it is expected to generate. Expenses change over time with improvements in technology, increases in wages and benefits, changes in interest rates, changes in tax rates, changes in environmental regulations, and changes in sources and costs of materials and plant assets.

Products have life cycles. They are born, grow, mature, and die. In the birth or inception stage, costs are high relative to revenues. Major development, design, testing, and marketing efforts are necessary to introduce new products in the market. Therefore, profits and cash flows typically are negative until a product gains acceptance. Cash is paid out for development activities and to purchase new assets. New financing is needed to supply cash needs. During the growth stage, when new markets develop for products, sales increase rapidly and profit margins grow. Cash flow from operating activities increases. Cash is invested to expand production and sales activities. The maturity stage results when sales of a product reach their full potential. New markets become harder to identify and little room for additional growth exists. During this stage, profits and cash flows are relatively stable. Operating activities provide for most cash flow needs. A decline (and eventual death) stage occurs when demand for a product decreases because of newer products or changing customer needs. Profits and cash flow from operating activities decrease. Cash flow is received from the sale of assets no longer needed for producing and selling the product. Cash may be used to repay debt and repurchase stock.

If the life cycle is managed well, a company can remain profitable over a long period. By investing in research and product development, it can plan for new products and replacement of old products to increase profits and cash flows. It may need to shift from one type of product to others as some products mature and die. Management must anticipate these changes to maintain a successful company. If they do not anticipate changes and manage their company accordingly, they are likely to face financial problems. Companies that have been successful in the past fail because they do not adapt to changing conditions. Analysts consider the life cycle of a company's products in forecasting future performance.

To illustrate the importance of these factors, consider the paper industry from the perspective of information available in 1992. Prior sections of this chapter have described some of the goods produced in this industry and the types of strategies companies may use. Though affected adversely by the recession of the early 1990s, prospects for the paper industry appeared favorable in 1992. Industrial production was expected to grow slowly during the mid 1990s. The increase in production was expected to result in higher prices for paper products and, therefore, increased revenues for the industry.

The paper industry in the U.S. is a mature industry. Its future growth is tied to population growth, since each individual can consume a limited amount of paper products each year. Opportunities for growth in international markets are excellent, however. Paper consumption in many developing countries is likely to grow rapidly. U.S. paper companies are the most technologically advanced in the world. Unlike some industries, in which foreign competition has had a technological edge, the U.S. paper industry enjoys a competitive advantage. Careful management has resulted in ample raw material supply. Research has led to improved trees that are straighter and more resistant to diseases than in earlier periods. The industry is not labor intensive. Therefore, competitors in low-wage countries do not have a cost advantage. The dollar's low exchange rate in recent years makes U.S. products more competitive in foreign markets. U.S. companies have begun developing international markets through foreign investments and acquisitions. Therefore, though domestic markets are not likely to expand rapidly, international markets hold considerable promise.

New investment in plant assets should decrease in the U.S. Places to build new mills in the U.S. are limited. Mills require nearby supplies of raw materials and access to water. Most good locations already have been developed. Therefore, expansion is likely to occur in foreign markets. Pollution control and waste reduction also have become major issues in the U.S. Paper companies spend over $750 million a year on pollution control. Sulfur dioxide and other chemical emissions have stimulated tighter federal and state regulations. Concern over the amount of waste created in the U.S. has led to a demand for less packaging, though there has been a movement back to paper and away from plastic.

Increased demand for paper associated with increased industrial production was expected to increase revenues of paper companies in the mid 1990s. *Value Line* forecasted sales of $13,800 million for International Paper in 1992 and sales of $15,250 million in 1993. As the company's sales increase, profit also should increase because of operating leverage. Therefore, *Value Line* anticipated net income for International Paper of $485 million in 1992 and $780 million in 1993.

SELF-STUDY PROBLEM 14-3

Information is provided below for Eli Lilly and Company, a pharmaceutical company:

(In millions)	1990	1989	1988
Net income	$ 1,127.3	$ 939.5	$ 761.0
Operating cash flow	1,474.4	1,032.6	689.6
Investing cash flow	(1,055.9)	(824.8)	(259.1)
Financing cash flow	(393.7)	(537.0)	(672.6)

Required

Analyze the company's performance over the three years presented. In what stage of the life cycle are the company's products? How would you assess the future prospects of the company, given economic conditions during the three years (see Exhibit 14-5)?

The solution to Self-Study Problem 14-3 appears at the end of the chapter.

REVIEW *Summary of Important Concepts*

1. Analysis of revenues and expenses:
   A. An income statement provides information for evaluating the effectiveness and efficiency of a company's operating activities.
   B. Percentage relationships among items on the income statement reveal changes in revenues and expenses that indicate changes in effectiveness and efficiency.
   C. Operating revenues indicate the demand for a company's products. Revenues are affected by the price and quantity of products sold. Demand is affected by product features, economic conditions, competition, and political and social conditions.
   D. Analysis of a company's segments is useful for determining the performance of different product lines and geographic locations.
2. Comparison among companies:
   A. A company's success depends largely on how it responds to internal and external conditions in its economic environment.
   B. Economic indicators measure activity in the economy as a whole. Demand for many products varies in relation to economic indicators. These indicators provide a basis for evaluating how well a company is performing relative to other companies.
   C. Companies use different strategies for creating profits. Some companies use a cost leadership strategy, while others use a product differentiation strategy. Most companies use a combination of these strategies.
3. Interpreting earnings:
   A. Profit margins measure the relationship between earnings and revenues. They are a means of assessing a company's efficiency. Profit margins are affected by operating leverage and the ability of a company to control its costs.
   B. Return on assets results from the ability of a company to sell its product and earn a favorable margin. Asset turnover and profit margin are components of return on assets useful for evaluating this ability.

C. Return on equity depends on the ability of a company to sell its products at favorable margins and on the effect of financial leverage. Earnings leverage and capital structure leverage are components of financial leverage.

4. Analysis of cash flows:
   A. Choice of accounting methods, earnings management, restructuring, and the use of historical costs affect accounting information. Accrual measurements sometimes are distorted by these problems.
   B. Cash flow analysis can be used to evaluate the reliability of accrual measures. Wide variations between earnings and cash flow from operating activities often signal financial problems for a company and may indicate misstatement of income statement numbers.
   C. A company's success depends on its ability to create cash flow from operating activities. Accrual and cash flow measures should be used to evaluate this ability.
5. Business failures:
   A. Businesses go through several stages on the road to failure: net losses, negative cash flows, insolvency, bankruptcy, and eventual liquidation. Failure results from the inability of management to develop effective strategies for dealing with changing economic conditions.
6. Forecasting:
   A. Forecasting future operating results requires considerable insight into a company's economic environment. Numerous factors affect a company's performance. Demand for products can be estimated from expected future economic conditions. Earnings can be estimated from expected profit margins for the forecasted level of sales.

DEFINE *Terms and Concepts Defined in this Chapter*

accounts receivable turnover
asset turnover
fixed assets turnover
gross margin
gross profit margin
inventory turnover
net profit margin
operating profit margin
profit margin

SOLUTIONS

SELF-STUDY PROBLEM 14-1

A percentage analysis of Intel's income statement appears at the top of the next page.

Intel's operating revenues increased during the three year period. A 25% increase in 1990 was followed by a 22% increase in 1991. Cost of sales decreased as a percentage of operating revenues during this period, resulting in higher gross profit margins. Operating expenses also decreased as a percentage of operating revenues, resulting in higher operating profit margins. A dramatic increase in operating profit margin occurred in 1990. Research and development expenses increased markedly in 1990, as well. Interest expense decreased during the three years. Net profit margin increased, especially in 1990. Overall, the company appears to have experienced favorable growth in demand for its products, accompanied by efficient resource use. The result was increased profitability.

	1991	1990	1989	% Change 1990–91	% Change 1989–90
Net revenues	1.00	1.00	1.00	0.22	0.25
Cost of sales	0.48	0.49	0.55	0.20	0.12
Gross profit margin	0.52	0.51	0.45	0.24	0.42
Research and development	0.13	0.13	0.12	0.20	0.42
Marketing, general and administrative	0.16	0.16	0.15	0.24	0.27
Operating costs and expenses	0.77	0.77	0.82	0.22	0.18
Operating profit margin	0.23	0.22	0.18	0.26	0.54
Interest expense	−0.02	−0.03	−0.03	−0.18	0.03
Interest income and other, net	0.04	0.06	0.04	−0.14	0.87
Income before taxes	0.25	0.25	0.19	0.21	0.69
Provision for taxes	0.08	0.09	0.06	0.12	0.75
Net profit margin	0.17	0.17	0.13	0.26	0.66

SELF-STUDY PROBLEM 14-2

(a)

	AT&T	Sears
Income tax rate	361/883 = .409	193/1,458 = .132
Interest after tax effect	726(1 − .409) = 429	3,252(1 − .132) = 2,823
Net income + interest	522 + 429 = 951	1,279 + 2,823 = 4,102
Profit margin	951/63,089 = 1.507%	4,102/57,242 = 7.166%
Average total assets	(48,322 + 53,355)/2 = 50,838.5	(96,253 + 106,435)/2 = 101,344
Asset turnover	63,089/50,838.5 = 1.241	57,242/101,344 = .565
Return on assets	1.507% × 1.241 = 1.87%	7.166% × .565 = 4.05%
Earnings leverage	522/951 = .549	1,279/4,102 = .312
Average common equity	(15,883 + 16,228)/2 = 16,055.5	(12,824 + 13,863)/2 = 13,343.5
Capital structure leverage	50,838.5/16,055.5 = 3.166	101,344/13,343.5 = 7.595
Return on equity	1.87% × .549 × 3.166 = 3.25%	4.05% × .312 × 7.595 = 9.60%

(b) AT&T's profit margin was much lower than Sears', though its asset turnover was higher. Operating revenues were relatively low for AT&T during 1991, depressing profit margins, asset turnover, and return on assets. Sears performed relatively better than AT&T. Sears was able to generate a higher return on equity than AT&T through its greater financial leverage. Thus, its performance for its stockholders was considerably better than that of AT&T in 1991.

SELF-STUDY PROBLEM 14-3

Net income and operating cash flow increased dramatically during the three year period for Eli Lilly. Cash flow from operating activities increased more rapidly than net income. Therefore, the growth in earnings was not the result of earnings management. The company's products appear to be in a growth stage. Cash flow from operating activities increased sharply. The company is reinvesting a large percentage of these cash flows in the business. Operating cash flows are sufficient to meet investment and dividend needs without substantial borrowing. While the economy was suffering a recession in the early 1990s, Eli Lilly was experiencing rapid growth. Therefore, the prospects for continued growth appeared very favorable.

EXERCISES

14-1. Write a short definition for each of the terms listed in the *Terms and Concepts Defined in this Chapter* section.

14-2. What is a company's economic environment? How does this environment affect the company's performance?

14-3. You have accepted a position as local manager of a fast-food franchise, specializing in Tex-Mex cuisine. Identify economic factors that are likely to have an influence on the success of your franchise. Which factors do you consider to be most important?

14-4. Match the income statement category in column 1 with the letter of the appropriate interpretation of the category from column 2. Some items from column 2 may be used more than once.

	1	2
______	1. Operating Revenues	a. Effect of income taxes on income
______	2. Cost of Goods Sold	b. Efficiency, considering the effect of financing and investing activities, and taxes on income
______	3. Gross Profit	c. Efficiency in producing goods and services
______	4. Operating Expenses	d. Effectiveness in providing goods and services demanded by customers
______	5. Operating Income	e. Effect of financing and investing activities on income
______	6. Other Revenues and Expenses	f. Efficiency, considering all income affecting activities
______	7. Income Before Taxes	g. Efficiency in support activities
______	8. Income Taxes	h. Efficiency, considering the effect of financing and investing activities on income
______	9. Income Before Special Items	i. Efficiency in production and support activities
______	10. Special Items	j. Effect of nonrecurring activities on income
______	11. Net Income	

14-5. Information is provided below from the 1991 income statement of Rubbermaid, Incorporated:

		Years ended December 31,	
(Dollars in thousands except per share amounts)	**1991**	**1990**	**1989**
Net sales	$1,667,305	$1,534,013	$1,452,365
Cost of sales	1,102,685	1,014,526	967,563
Selling, general and administrative expenses	307,780	286,647	268,148
Other charges (credits), net:			
Interest expense	8,300	8,627	8,810
Interest income	(5,889)	(5,363)	(5,650)
Miscellaneous, net	(8,158)	(1,693)	8,814
	(5,747)	1,571	11,974
Earnings before income taxes	262,587	231,269	204,680
Income taxes	99,937	87,749	79,696
Net earnings	$ 162,650	$ 143,520	$ 124,984
Net earnings per common share	$ 1.02	$ .90	$ .78

How much did sales grow from 1989 to 1990 and from 1990 to 1991? Restate each item on the income statement (except earnings per share) as a percent of net sales. What important changes occurred in Rubbermaid's relative expenses and income over the three year period? What conclusions can you draw about the company's economic environment? What conclusions can you draw about the company's operating leverage? Are most of its costs fixed or variable?

14-6. Information is provided below from the income statements of the merchandise group of Sears, Roebuck and Company and from Wal-Mart Stores, Incorporated from their 1991 annual reports:

Sears		**Year Ended December 31**	
millions	**1991**	**1990**	**1989**
Revenues	$31,432.9	$31,985.7	$31,599.2
Cost of sales	19,976.6	20,181.4	19,854.7
Selling and administrative	9,668.5	10,167.5	9,288.2
Interest expense	1,022.4	1,238.5	1,324.4
Operating income	$ 765.4	$ 398.3	$ 1,131.9

Wal-Mart		**Year Ended January 31**	
millions	**1991**	**1990**	**1989**
Revenues	$32,863.4	$25,985.3	$20,785.9
Cost of sales	25,499.8	20,070.0	16,056.9
Selling and administrative	5,152.2	4,069.7	3,267.8
Interest expense	168.6	138.0	135.7
Operating income	$ 2,042.8	$ 1,707.5	$ 1,325.5

Compare the effectiveness and efficiency of the two companies for the three years shown.

14-7. Information is provided below about industrial production in the U.S. economy and sales (in millions) for Georgia-Pacific Corporation and Champion International Corporation. Both companies are in the paper and wood products industry:

Year	**Industrial Production**	**Sales—Georgia-Pacific**	**Sales—Champion International**
1982	81.9	5,003	3,737
1983	84.9	6,040	4,264
1984	92.8	6,682	5,121
1985	94.4	6,716	5,770
1986	95.3	7,223	4,388
1987	100.0	8,603	4,615
1988	105.4	9,509	5,129
1989	108.1	10,171	5,163
1990	109.2	12,665	5,090
1991	107.1	11,524	4,786

Draw a graph similar to Exhibit 14-6 to describe the relationship between industrial production and sales for the two companies. What conclusions can you draw from the graph?

14-8. Information from the 1992 income statement of Westinghouse Electric Corporation is provided below:

In millions	1992	1991	1990
Operating revenues	$ 8,447	$ 8,490	$8,646
Cost of sales and services	(6,243)	(6,379)	(6,190)
Income from continuing operations before taxes and minority interest	536	388	1,025
Income from continuing operations	348	265	746
Loss from discontinued operations, net of taxes	(1,301)	(1,351)	(478)
Cumulative effect of change in accounting principles	(338)	—	—
Net income (loss)	(1,291)	(1,086)	268

Calculate the gross profit margin, operating profit margin, and net profit margin for Westinghouse for each of the three years. What information do these amounts provide about the company's operating activities over the three years?

14-9. Selected information from the 1991 income statements of Bristol-Myers Squibb Company and Warner-Lambert Company is provided below:

Bristol-Myers Squibb millions	**Year Ended December 31** 1991	1990	1989
Net sales	$11,159	$10,300	$9,189
Cost of products sold	2,930	2,874	2,656
Operating expenses	5,463	5,037	4,595
Warner-Lambert millions	**1991**	**1990**	**1989**
Net sales	$ 5,059	$ 4,687	$4,196
Cost of goods sold	1,626	1,515	1,383
Operating expenses	2,717	2,509	2,241

Compare the operating margins of the two companies for the three years reported. Use a graph similar to Exhibit 14-7 to illustrate the operating margins of the two companies.

14-10. Selected information from the 1991 annual report of Home Depot, Incorporated is provided below:

In millions	1991	1990
Net sales	$5,137	
Interest expense	12	
Net income	249	
Total assets	2,510	$1,640
Income tax rate	37%	

Calculate Home Depot's profit margin, asset turnover, and return on assets for 1991. Use earnings plus interest adjusted for taxes in your computations. In comparison with the companies shown in Exhibit 14-9, what strategy does Home Depot appear to be using to generate profits?

14-11. Selected information from the 1991 annual reports of American Brands, Incorporated and Philip Morris Companies, Incorporated is provided below. Both companies are in the tobacco and consumer products industry.

In millions	American Brands	Philip Morris
Net sales	$14,064	$56,458
Interest expense	264	1,651
Income before special items	806	3,927
Total assets, 1991	15,116	47,384
Total assets, 1990	13,896	46,569
Income tax rate	35%	44%

Compare the operating strategies of the two companies by calculating profit margin, asset turnover, and return on assets. Which company appears to be doing the better job with its strategy?

14-12. Summarize the primary differences between cost leadership and profit differentiation strategies. How can these strategies be used to improve return on assets and profitability? In particular, how would you expect the choice of strategy to affect the components of return on assets reported by companies using these strategies?

14-13. Information is provided below for three of Monsanto Company's primary segments from its 1991 annual report:

in millions	Net Sales	Operating Income	Average Assets
Agricultural Products	$1,711	$ 400	$1,630
Chemicals	3,740	(154)	3,163
Pharmaceuticals	1,531	170	4,427

Calculate the asset turnover, profit margin, and return on assets of each segment. Evaluate the relative performance of each segment in terms of the strategy the company appeared to be using to generate profits.

14-14. The following information was taken from the 1991 annual report of Champion International Corporation ($ in thousands):

Net income	$ 40,343
Interest expense	210,527
Preferred dividends	27,750
Average total assets	8,503,643
Average common equity	3,675,517
Income tax rate	48.4%

Calculate return on assets, earnings leverage, capital structure leverage, and return on equity. What conclusions can you draw about the effect of financial leverage on return to common stockholders?

14-15. The Home Depot, Incorporated paid a dividend of $.11 per share for the fiscal year ended in February 1992. At the end of the year, the company's stock was selling at $14.66 per share. At the end of the preceding year, the stock was selling at $9.82 per share. Net income for 1992 was $249,150,000. Total common equity at the beginning of the year was $683,402,000, and total common equity at the end of the year was $1,691,212,000. No preferred stock was outstanding. What was the market return on the company's stock for the year ended in February 1992? What was the return on equity? Why did the market and accounting returns differ?

14-16. New Forest Company and Old Forest Company are both in the paper and wood products industry. New Forest began operations in 1990. It purchased 5 million acres of timberland at a cost of $2,000 per acre in 1990. The book value of the timberland at the end of the company's 1994 fiscal year was $9.2 billion, including the effect of depletion for 1994 of $300 million. Old Forest began operations in 1920. It also owns 5 million acres of timberland, but its land was purchased at an average cost of $500 per acre. The book value of the timberland at the end of 1994 was $1.3 billion, including the effect of depletion for 1994 of $80 million. Both companies reported sales of $800 million in 1994. Expenses other than depletion and income taxes were $250 million for each company. Income tax rates for both companies were 34%. Other than timberland, both companies had assets with book values of $3 billion. The estimated market value of the timberland owned by both companies was $10 billion at the end of 1994. Both companies depleted 3% of their estimated timber holdings during 1994. Calculate the ratio of net income to total assets for both companies using GAAP-based accounting rules. Calculate the ratio of net income to total assets for both companies based on market value adjustments to assets and depletion expense. What effect do GAAP-based rules have on the profitability measures of the companies?

14-17. Information is provided below from the 1991 annual report of Rubbermaid, Incorporated:

(in thousands)	**1991**	**1990**	**1989**
Net earnings	$ 162,650	$ 143,520	$124,984
Net cash from operating activities	249,165	157,053	173,672
Net cash from investing activities	(119,980)	(135,919)	(87,532)
Net cash from financing activities	(53,362)	(45,611)	(32,461)

Evaluate Rubbermaid's performance over the three years presented. Would you characterize the company as growing, stable, or declining? Is it surprising that the change in net earnings differs from the change in net cash from operating activities over the period? Which measure of operating activities is more stable? Why?

14-18. The following information was reported by Delta Airlines in its 1991 annual report:

(in thousands)	**1991**	**1990**	**1989**
Net income (loss) available to common	$ (342,972)	$ 284,639	$ 460,918
Net cash from operating activities	$ 323,790	$ 803,766	$1,091,950
Average common shares outstanding	44,370	49,160	49,190
Total assets	$8,410,679	$7,227,002	$6,483,986
Total common stockholders' equity	$2,456,985	$2,595,569	$2,619,707

Evaluate Delta's performance over the three year period. Calculate earnings per share and cash flow per share. Would you expect the company's stock price to have increased or decreased over the three years? Is the company solvent or insolvent? If you were a creditor or owner of Delta would you be concerned about the company declaring bankruptcy in the near future?

14-19. Distinguish between insolvency, bankruptcy, and liquidation. Identify primary reasons for each of these conditions.

14-20. Foreign and Domestic are companies that manufacture and sell the same types of electronic equipment. Both obtain raw materials in the U.S. and maintain their manufacturing facilities in the U.S. Foreign sells most of its products in Europe. Domestic sells most of its products in the U.S. In recent years, the dollar has fluctuated in value against European currencies but generally has declined in value relative to these other currencies. What effect do foreign exchange rates have on the two companies? If the dollar is expected to increase in value relative to European currencies in the near future, what effect would the expectation have on the forecasted earnings of Foreign? What could Foreign do to reduce its foreign exchange risk?

PROBLEMS

PROBLEM 14-1 Percentage Analysis

The income statement of Borden, Incorporated from its 1991 annual report is provided below:

(In millions)	*Year Ended December 31,*	**1991**	**1990**	**1989**
Revenue	Net sales	$7,235.1	$7,632.8	$7,653.3
Costs and Expenses	Cost of goods sold	5,008.1	5,433.5	5,701.1
	Marketing, general and administrative expenses	1,524.7	1,457.5	1,236.0
	Reorganization and restructuring charges	71.6		570.7
	Interest expense	198.4	186.9	160.2
	Equity in income of affiliates	(23.9)	(23.1)	(17.0)
	Other (income) and expense	(4.7)	2.4	(.2)
	Income taxes	166.0	212.0	63.1
		6,940.2	7,269.2	7,713.9
Earnings	Net income (loss)	$ 294.9	$ 363.6	$ (60.6)

Minor modifications have been made to the format.

Required Restate the income statement as a percentage analysis or common-sized statement. Evaluate changes in the company's effectiveness and efficiency over the three years.

PROBLEM 14-2 Product Demand Analysis

You have been hired as a marketing manager for Astro Whiz Appliance Company. The company manufactures major home appliances, such as refrigerators, stoves, and dishwashers. The company has been in existence for only a few years. It has not paid much attention to market demand in the past because it has been able to sell as much as it produced, largely because of special features of its appliances that made them energy efficient. The company is considering the addition of production capacity and has become concerned about demand for its products. Part of your job is to provide top management with demand information. The president of the company, Myrtle Whiz, has asked you to prepare a memo describing the factors you believe the company should consider in its product demand analysis.

Required Write a memo to President Whiz identifying the factors and explaining how they might affect the company's sales revenues.

PROBLEM 14-3 Use of Economic Indicators

The relationship between the sales of Colgate-Palmolive Company and consumer spending in the U.S. in $billions is shown below. Data are for 1985 through 1993. Consumer spending is estimated for 1992 and 1993 at $4,115 billion and $4,375 billion, respectively. As a result, Colgate Palmolive's sales are forecasted at approximately $6,400 million in 1992 and $7,000 million in 1993.

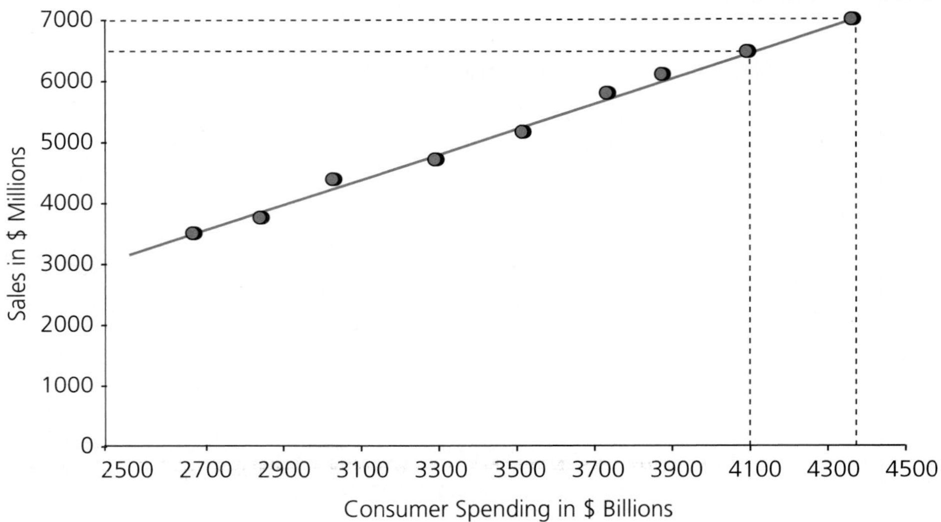

Information from Colgate Palmolive's annual report for 1991 is provided below:

in Millions	**1987**	**1988**	**1989**	**1990**	**1991**
Sales	$4,365.7	$4,734.3	$5,038.8	$5,691.3	$6,060.3
Income from continuing operations (before restructuring charges)	145.7	152.7	280.0	321.0	367.9

Required Assume the relationship between income from continuing operations and sales revenue will continue through 1993. Graph this relationship and forecast the amount of income from continuing operations for Colgate-Palmolive for 1992 and 1993.

PROBLEM 14-4 Comparison of Profit Margins

Information is provided below from the financial statements of Apple Computer, Incorporated and Pacific Gas and Electric Company from their 1991 annual reports:

	1987	1988	1989	1990	1991
Apple Computer					
Operating Revenues	$2,661	$4,071	$5,284	$5,558	$6,308
Operating Income	371	620	634	746	671
Net Income	217	400	454	475	310
Pacific Gas & Electric					
Operating Revenues	7,186	7,646	8,588	9,470	9,778
Operating Income	1,262	1,297	1,623	1,706	1,713
Net Income	689	62	901	987	1,026

Required (a) Calculate the operating and net profit margins for each company for each year. (b) Graph the relationship between operating income and operating revenues for each company for the five years. (c) Which company appears to have the higher operating leverage? What effect does operating leverage have on the risks of the companies?

PROBLEM 14-5 Return Analysis

Information is provided below for five companies in the food and agricultural products industry from their 1991 annual reports.

(in millions)	Archer Daniels Midland	Borden	Coca-Cola	ConAgra	Ralston Purina
Net sales	$8,468.2	$7,235.1	$11,571.6	$19,504.7	$7,375.8
Interest expense	95.8	198.4	192.5	298.0	208.7
Pretax income	718.0	460.9	2,383.3	515.2	647.8
Income taxes	251.2	166.0	765.3	204.0	255.9
Preferred dividends	0	0	0.5	19.5	20.7
Average total assets	5,855.3	5,382.8	9,750.0	7,112.3	4,513.3
Average common equity	3,747.8	1,908.1	4,151.0	1,456.6	684.6

Required (a) Calculate asset turnover, profit margin, return on assets, earnings leverage, capital structure leverage, and return on common equity for each company. (b) Graph the relationship between asset turnover and profit margin using a format similar to Exhibit 14-9. Return on asset curves do not have to be included.

PROBLEM 14-6 Assessing Operating Strategies

Discount Shoes and Elegant Footwear are both retail shoe companies. Both have outlets in major cities throughout the U.S. Discount Shoes uses a cost leadership strategy, and Elegant Footwear uses a product differentiation strategy.

Required Answer each of the following questions:

a. What differences would you expect to observe between the two companies with respect to the location and design of their stores, the types of products they sell, and the types of service they provide?

b. Compare the companies' sales revenues, cost of goods sold, operating expenses, accounts receivable, merchandise inventory, and plant assets based on the strategies they use to generate profits.

PROBLEM 14-7 Asset Turnover and Cash Flow Analysis

Information is provided below for American Home Products Corporation from the 1991 annual report:

$ in millions	1991	1990	1989	1988
Net sales	$7,079	$6,775	$6,747	
Cost of goods sold	2,390	2,453	2,448	
Operating expenses	2,929	2,494	2,885	
Income before taxes	1,760	1,828	1,414	
Income taxes	384	597	312	
Net income	1,375	1,231	1,102	
Accounts receivable, net	1,024	1,021	1,095	$1,037
Inventories	842	796	789	746
Plant assets, net	1,477	1,437	1,373	1,306
Total assets	5,939	5,637	5,681	5,492
Net cash from operating activities	1,898	1,314	1,157	

Required (a) Calculate accounts receivable, inventory, fixed asset, and total asset turnover. (b) Graph the company's operating income and net cash flow from operating activities for the years shown. (c) Describe the relationship between the company's operating income and cash flow from operating activities. How do the asset turnover ratios help explain the relationship?

PROBLEM 14-8 Analysis of Return and Financial Leverage

Information is provided below for H. J. Heinz Company and Sysco Corporation from their 1992 annual reports. Heinz is a manufacturer of food products. Sysco is a marketer and distributor of food products, primarily to hotels, restaurants, and institutions. Neither company had substantial amounts of preferred stock outstanding or paid substantial preferred dividends during 1992.

(In millions)	Heinz	Sysco
Operating revenues	$6,582	$8,893
Total assets, 1991	4,935	2,160
Total assets, 1992	5,932	2,301
Net income	638	172
Interest expense	135	43
Income taxes	346	109
Income before taxes	984	282
Common equity, 1991	2,274	919
Common equity, 1992	2,367	1,057

Required (a) Compute profit margin, asset turnover, return on assets, earnings leverage, capital structure leverage, and return on equity for each company. (b) How did profit margin, asset turnover, and financial leverage affect the companies' returns?

PROBLEM 14-9 Ethics and Choice of Accounting Methods

Horace Stinson is president of My Way Corporation. He built the company from scratch. Starting with a small business, he created a large corporation. His business had shown a steady increase in net income over the past 10 years. Its stock price had quadrupled in the last three years. In late November, 1994, Stinson faced a problem, however. It appeared as though the company's profits would be well below previous levels. A recent projection of the company's income for the fiscal year ended December 31, 1994 revealed:

Net sales	$ 7,400,000
Cost of goods sold	(3,600,000)
Operating expenses	(3,100,000)
Pretax income	700,000
Income tax expense	(210,000)
Net income	$ 490,000

Among the company's assets were long-term investments in marketable securities with costs and market values as follows:

	Cost	Market
Investment in Bridge Company	$4,200,000	$3,800,000
Investment in Tower Company	6,500,000	7,300,000

The company used the LIFO method for its inventories. Its inventories in late November consisted of:

30,000 units at a unit cost of $6	$180,000
12,000 units at a unit cost of $7	84,000

The company projected sales of 40,000 units in December. It follows a normal practice of purchasing from suppliers at the end of each month the number of units it expects to sell during the following month. The expected cost to the company of any inventory purchased at the end of November would be $11 per unit. The revenue and cost of goods sold (at $11 per unit) for the 40,000 units were included in the projected income statement for 1994. An order had not been placed for the units that would be sold in December. The company's income tax rate is 30%.

Required What actions could My Way take to improve its reported earnings in 1994? Calculate the effect these actions would have on the company's income statement. Do you see any ethical problems in these decisions? Explain why or why not.

PROBLEM 14-10 Comparing Accrual and Cash Flow Information

Selected information from the annual report and 10-K of Comptronix Corporation is provided at the top of the next page.

In Thousands	**1987**	**1988**	**1989**	**1990**	**1991**
Sales	$14,251	$29,255	$42,420	$70,229	$102,026
Net Income	311	1,020	1,470	3,028	5,071
Total Assets	11,564	28,306	31,939	59,866	81,204
Net Cash from Operating Activities	−1,831	−3,504	5,717	−5,494	4,936
Net Cash from Investing Activities	−3,141	−3,438	−13,717	−12,360	−19,284
Net Cash from Financing Activities	4,716	8,600	6,379	17,827	15,107

Required (a) Graph the net income and cash flow from operating activities for the company for the years shown. (b) Calculate the total amount of net income and cash flow from operating activities for the five year period. (c) Calculate the ratio of net income to sales and net income to total assets for the company for the five years. (d) Using the data from the table and the information from parts a through c, identify any concerns you might have about Comptronix's financial condition and operating results.

PROBLEM 14-11 Evaluation of Return and Risk

A primary use of accounting information by decision makers is to assess a company's risk and return. The following list identifies information corporations report in their annual reports:

Operating revenues, cost of goods sold and operating expenses, operating income, other revenues and expenses, special items (discontinued operations, extraordinary changes, changes in accounting methods), net income, net income available for common stockholders, accounting policies and methods for depreciation, amortization, inventories, etc., net cash flow from operating activities.

Required (a) Define risk and return and explain why they are important to decision makers. (b) Complete the following table by explaining how each item is useful for explaining a company's risk and return:

RETURN:	
Accrual Basis Measurement:	
Operating Revenues	
Cost of Goods Sold and Operating Expenses	
Other Revenues and Expenses	
Special Items	
Choice of Accounting Methods	
Net Income	
Net Income Available for Common	
Cash Flow Measurement:	
Cash Collected from Customers	
Cash Payments to Suppliers	
Payment for Income Taxes	
RISK:	
Operating Revenues and Cash Inflows	
Operating Expenses, Cash Outflows, and Operating Income	
Interest Expense and Earnings per Common Share	

PROBLEM 14-12 Multiple-Choice Overview of the Chapter

1. The Wool Sweater Company reported sales of $10 million in 1993 and $12 million in 1994. Also, it reported gross profit of $5 million in 1993 and $4.8 million in 1994. From this information, you could conclude:
   a. The company was more effective and efficient in 1993 than in 1994.
   b. The company was more effective and efficient in 1994 than in 1993.
   c. The company was more effective in 1994 than in 1993 but was more efficient in 1993 than in 1994.
   d. The company was more effective in 1993 than in 1994 but was more efficient in 1994 than in 1993.
2. The effect of changing economic conditions on demand for a company's products affects:
   a. the company's risk and return.
   b. the company's risk but not its return.
   c. the company's return but not its risk.
   d. neither the company's risk nor its return.
3. A company's profit margin is the ratio of its earnings to:
   a. total assets
   b. total liabilities
   c. operating income
   d. operating revenues
4. If Alpha Company has higher operating leverage than Beta Company, an equivalent increase in sales for both companies should result in:
   a. a greater increase in operating income for Alpha than for Beta.
   b. a greater increase in operating income for Beta than for Alpha.
   c. the same increase in operating income for Alpha and Beta.
   d. an increase in operating income for Beta but a decrease for Alpha.
5. Chrysanthemum Company reported a profit margin of 2.0% and an asset turnover of 5.0 for its 1994 fiscal year. The company's return on assets for the year was:
   a. 2.0%
   b. 2.5%
   c. 3.0%
   d. 10.0%
6. Green Company reported a profit margin of 2.0 and an asset turnover of 7.0 during 1995. Blue Company reported a profit margin of 4.0 and an asset turnover of 3.0 during the same period. From this information, you would expect that:
   a. Green Company is more capital intensive than Blue Company.
   b. Blue Company is more capital intensive than Green Company.
   c. Blue Company is in a more highly competitive industry than Green Company.
   d. Blue Company earned a higher return on assets than Green Company.
7. The difference between a company's return on assets and its return on equity can be explained by the company's:
   a. operating leverage
   b. variability of sales
   c. financial leverage
   d. profit margin
8. Earnings management:
   a. is prevented by GAAP.
   b. can be used to reduce the volatility of reported earnings.
   c. is not a problem for most companies because of their management compensation agreements.
   d. cannot mislead investors because of information reported in a company's annual report.
9. When comparing a company's net income and cash flow from operating activities, you normally should expect:

a. cash flow to be lower than net income.
b. cash flow to be equal to net income.
c. cash flow to be higher than net income.
d. cash flow to be less volatile than net income.

10. Bankruptcy often results because a company:
    a. cannot earn enough to pay dividends to its stockholders.
    b. has more liabilities than its equity.
    c. earns a low profit margin.
    d. cannot make payments to its creditors.

CASES

CASE 14-1 Analysis of an Investment

You are an investment analyst. Some of your clients have talked with you about an investment they are considering in a new company, Mountain Top Resorts. This company will construct and rent condominiums to tourists on Snowshoe Mountain. The total investment required for the project is $5,000,000. Individual investors are expected to invest not less than $100,000 each. They could borrow up to this amount at 10% annual interest. The development will contain 50 units that will cost $70,000 per unit to construct. Land for the development will cost $250,000. $300,000 will be held in reserve for first year operating costs for the year beginning January 1, 1995. The remaining investment capital will be used for furnishings, streets, parking lots, sidewalks, and landscaping. Buildings will be depreciated over a 20 year period. Other depreciable assets will be depreciated over 5 years. Straight-line depreciation will be used. Based on an analysis of similar developments in the area, units should rent for an average of $1,000 per week. Each unit should rent for a minimum of 25 weeks per year. Each unit is expected to rent for 30 weeks per year. Maintenance and operating costs are expected to average $100 per unit-week for 52 weeks. Management costs will be $250,000 per year. A reserve fund will be established with annual reinvestments of profits of $200,000 for future repair and replacement of property. Remaining profits will be distributed to investors in proportion to their investments. The company is not subject to income tax.

Required (a) Calculate the net income and cash flow to investors from operating activities expected from the project in 1995, assuming average rental of 25 and 30 weeks. Assume cash flows are equivalent to revenues and expenses except for depreciation. Which is more relevant to the investment decision, net income or cash flow? Why? (b) Assume investors could expect to receive net cash flows from their investments for 10 years at the amounts expected for 1995. At the end of 10 years they expect to be able to sell their investments for $2 million. What is the net present value of the cash flows assuming 25 week and 30 week average rentals each year? (c) What effect does the company's operating leverage have on its expected operating results? (d) Would you recommend that your clients invest in Mountain Top Resorts? What factors are important to this decision other than those considered above?

CASE 14-2 Analysis of Operating Activities

Appendix B of this book contains a copy of the 1992 annual report of General Mills, Inc. The company's average assets (in millions) were: 1992, $4,103.4; 1991, $3,595.7; 1990, $3,088.8. Its average stockholders' equity was: 1992, $1,242.2; 1991, $961.6; 1990, $770.8.

Required Review the annual report and answer each of the following questions: (a) Compute profit margin, asset turnover, return on assets, earnings leverage, capital structure leverage, and return on equity for the company for 1990-1992. (b) Evaluate the changes in these amounts over the three year period. (c) What strategy does the company appear to be following to generate profits?

PROJECTS

PROJECT 14-1 Comparing Profit Margins and Asset Turnovers

Obtain the most recent annual reports available for three corporations from your library. Use companies from different industries. Calculate the profit margins, asset turnovers, and return on assets for each company. Write a short report comparing the ratios and summarizing the information they provide about the companies.

PROJECT 14-2 Comparing Operating Leverages

Obtain the most recent annual reports available for three corporations from your library. Prepare a graph illustrating the relationship between operating income and operating revenue for each company using data for the last five years. Use your graph to determine which company appears to have the highest operating leverage and which has the lowest. What can you conclude about the relative risks of the companies? Summarize your findings and conclusions in a short report.

PROJECT 14-3 Comparing Return on Equity

Obtain the most recent annual reports available for three corporations from your library. Find corporations in the same industry. Calculate return on assets, earnings leverage, capital structure leverage, and return on equity for each company. Write a short report comparing the results. What effect does financial leverage have on return on equity for each company? Which companies have the highest and lowest financial leverages? What effect does financial leverage have on the risks of the companies?

PROJECT 14-4 Comparing Net Income and Cash Flow

Use an annual report or other source of accounting information to identify the net income and cash flow from operating activities of a company for a five year period. Graph the relationship between net income and cash flow for the five years. Write a short report comparing the company's net income and cash flow. Explain any concerns raised by your analysis about the company's financial condition or operating results.

PROJECT 14-5 Analyzing Business Failure

Use a business periodicals index or *The Wall Street Journal Index* to identify a recent company that went bankrupt or was liquidated. Use the company's annual report or other sources of accounting information to determine the company's total assets, total liabilities, net income, and cash flow from operating activities for the five years prior to the bankruptcy or liquidation. Graph these amounts for the five year period. Write a short report summarizing any results from your graph that might have been useful for forecasting the company's financial problems.

CHAPTER 15

NONBUSINESS ORGANIZATIONS

CHAPTER *Overview*

Accounting information is important for understanding economic activities of nonbusiness organizations. Nonbusiness organizations include federal, state, and local governments and other nonprofit (or not-for-profit) organizations. Nonbusiness organizations are a major part of the U.S. economy. Citizens have a responsibility to understand the economic activities of these organizations to make informed decisions. Also, the economic activities of nonbusiness organizations, particularly governments, have an important effect on decisions made about business organizations. Therefore, business managers, investors, customers, and other decision makers should understand nonbusiness organization economic activities.

Nonbusiness organizations are similar in many respects to business organizations. They transform cash and other resources into goods and services. Their transformation processes include financing, investing, and operating activities. Accounting systems record transactions, summarize economic activities, and report these summaries to decision makers. Decision makers analyze reported information in much the same way as for business organizations.

Important distinctions exist between nonbusiness and business organizations, however. These organizations function in different economic and legal environments. The processes by which they generate revenues differ. Methods of achieving effectiveness and efficiency vary. Accounting information and systems are different in some important ways. This chapter examines these differences and the effect they have on the reporting and use of accounting information.

Major topics covered in this chapter include:

- Purposes of nonbusiness organizations.
- Control of nonbusiness organizations for effectiveness and efficiency.
- Accounting measurement in nonbusiness organizations.
- Accounting reports of nonbusiness organizations.
- Analysis of nonbusiness accounting information.

CHAPTER *Objectives*

Once you have completed this chapter, you should be able to:

1. Compare the purposes of nonbusiness and business organizations.
2. Identify the types of services provided by governments and revenues that pay for these services.
3. Identify types of services provided by nonprofit organizations and revenues that pay for these services.
4. Compare the transformation processes of nonbusiness and business organizations.
5. Distinguish between democratic and market controls.
6. Explain the purpose of budgets in nonbusiness organizations.
7. Identify the fund types used by governments and nonprofit organizations and explain their purpose.
8. Explain the purpose of encumbrances.
9. Compare the financial resources and capital maintenance measurement focuses.
10. Explain how a government determines its financial reporting entity.
11. Discuss the types of financial statements reported by governments and their contents.
12. Discuss the financial statements reported by nonprofit organizations.
13. Identify sources of accounting standards for nonbusiness organizations.
14. Identify factors that should be considered when analyzing government accounting information.

PURPOSE OF NONBUSINESS ORGANIZATIONS

Objective 1
Compare the purposes of nonbusiness and business organizations.

Businesses sell goods and services to earn revenues. Profits are determined by the difference between revenues and expenses associated with providing goods and services. Nonbusiness organizations provide goods and services, as well. Since many of these services are not sold, revenue is not earned, and associated expenses cannot be matched to determine profits. Thus, profitability, as a measure of effectiveness and efficiency, is not available for many activities of nonbusiness organizations. Other control procedures substitute for the need to earn profits in competitive markets.

This section examines different types of nonprofit organizations. It considers the services they provide and transformation processes in these organizations. A later section examines control procedures for these organizations.

Types of Nonbusiness Organizations

Nonbusiness organizations can be classified into two general groups: governments and nonprofit organizations. Governments provide a variety of services at the federal, state, and local levels. Nonprofit (or not-for-profit) organizations include religious, education, health, and civic organizations.

Governments. Exhibit 15-1 summarizes the primary types of services provided by governments.

Percentage of Total Gross National Product Provided By Governmental and Non-Governmental Organizations

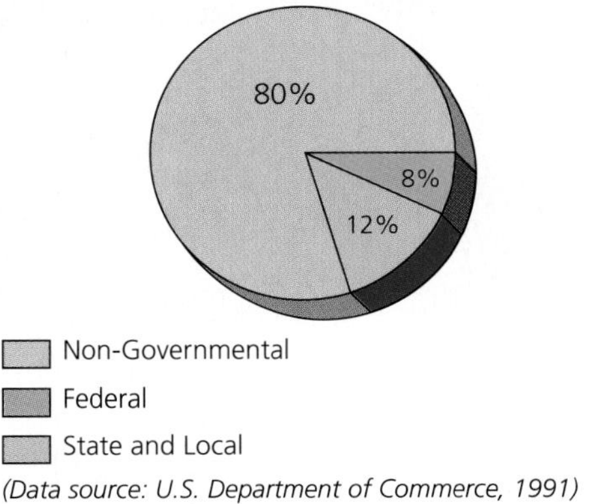

(Data source: U.S. Department of Commerce, 1991)

Exhibit 15-1 Services Provided by Governments

Type of Service	Examples
Education	Public schools, trade schools, community colleges, state colleges and universities
Health Care	State and community hospitals, veterans' hospitals, public health clinics
Public Protection	U.S. military, FBI, state and local police and fire departments
Parks and Recreation	National, state, and city parks, stadiums, golf courses
Cultural Activities	Public libraries and museums
Social Services	Social security, welfare, Medicare, Medicaid, public housing
Streets and Highways	Interstate highways, state, county, and city roads and streets
Transportation	Public transit, airports

Objective 2
Identify the types of services provided by governments and revenues that pay for these services.

Some services are provided without charge to the user. Examples include national defense, police and fire protection, some parks, libraries, and museums, and many public streets and highways. Other services are provided at a charge, but the charge is less, often much less, than the cost of providing the service. Most of the costs of these services are paid from tax revenues.

Income, property, and sales taxes account for the majority of government revenues. Other taxes include excise taxes and those on gasoline, alcoholic beverages and tobacco products, social security, and unemployment. The amount taxpayers contribute to governments depends largely on their income and wealth, not on the public services they consume. Governments sell some goods and services to consumers. Public utilities sell water, electricity, and sanitation services, for example. User charges pay for some highways and bridges. Parking fees pay for many parking facilities. Most government services are not sold at a price to cover the cost of the services, however.

Some services cannot be sold because they are not separable, that is, they cannot be made available to one person without making them available to others. Public protection and streets and highways are examples of nonseparable goods. If the government provides for your protection and defense, it also is providing for the protection and defense of others in society. This type of product is a "public good." People will not purchase public goods in a market because the benefits they receive from the goods cannot be determined from a competitive market price. If you were asked to make a voluntary payment for police and fire protection, how much would you pay? You would have difficulty in determining a fair price because you do not know how much others are paying. A government would have difficulty raising sufficient money to pay for these services if it made requests for voluntary payments. Instead, governments levy taxes to pay for most public goods. Taxpayers share in the cost of these goods to ensure that they are available to the entire society.

Other goods and services are not provided in markets because society desires they be available to everyone. As an example, education and health care services can be provided by business organizations. Privately owned institutions sometimes sell these services to earn a profit. But, our society has decided that these services should be available to all its members. Therefore, public schools provide tuition-free education. Public health care institutions provide low-cost health care services to those who qualify. Governmental organizations levy taxes to pay for these services as they do for public goods.

Objective 3
Identify types of services provided by nonprofit organizations and revenues that pay for these services.

Nonprofit Organizations. Nonprofit organizations cannot levy taxes to pay for services. They depend on charges to users, donations, grants, and membership fees to pay for their services. For example, private, nonprofit educational institutions charge tuition and fees for their services. These charges typically are much higher than those of public institutions. Students pay a higher percentage of the total cost of the services they receive. Like public institutions, nonprofit organizations also depend on contributions and government grants to pay for a portion of their costs. Religious and civic organizations also depend on contributions and membership fees to pay for the costs of their services.

Hospitals and other health care organizations may be governmental, nonprofit, or for-profit institutions. Regardless of how they are organized, they charge for a large portion of the goods and services they provide. These charges often are paid by private insurance companies or by public insurance, such as Medicare or the Veterans' Administration. Government-owned hospitals, in particular, may provide services to those unable to pay for health services. Nevertheless, most costs are charged to patients. Therefore, most hospitals operate much as business organizations. For-profit hospitals attempt to earn a profit by generating revenues in excess of expenses. Governmental and nonprofit hospitals often attempt to generate sufficient revenues to cover the costs of providing services.

The Transformation Process

Objective 4
Compare the transformation processes of nonbusiness and business organizations.

The transformation process is similar for business and nonbusiness organizations. Nonbusiness organizations issue bonds and incur other liabilities. Governments are tax receivers, not tax payers. Most other nonprofit organizations are tax exempt. Therefore, they do not pay income taxes or property taxes and may be exempt from sales and other taxes. Nonbusiness organizations do not have owners. Individuals do not hold title to a nonbusiness organization. Stock is not issued by these organizations. Control resides in elected or appointed oversight groups, such as boards, councils, commissions, trustees, and legislatures. The right to vote in elections is determined by residency, citizenship, or membership requirements.

Oversight groups need information about the operations of the organizations they oversee to assess the efficiency and effectiveness of their operations. They employ administrators to manage the operating activities of these organizations. Most major administrative or executive officers, such as the president, governor, or mayor, are elected in government organizations. Oversight groups are responsible for seeing that managers use resources according to approved plans to provide specific types of services.

Those responsible for overseeing and managing these organizations make investment decisions. Resources are acquired to provide services. Resources include current assets, such as cash, receivables, and inventories. Inventories typically are relatively small portions of assets, often consisting primarily of supplies. Nonbusiness organizations are service organizations, for the most part. Seldom do they manufacture goods or purchase goods for resale. Noncurrent assets include land, buildings, and equipment. Special assets, such as monuments, roads, and waterways, also are part of government fixed assets. Intangible assets are uncommon.

Operating activities are those typical of service organizations. Many services are labor intensive. Teachers, medical doctors, nurses, public protection personnel, and other public or nonprofit employees are responsible for these services. Some government services are purchased from businesses. Governments pay for these purchases from their tax revenues. Road construction and maintenance, sanitation services, jails and prisons are examples of services governments sometimes purchase from the private sector.

EFFICIENCY AND EFFECTIVENESS

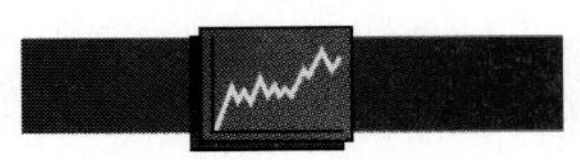

Objective 5
Distinguish between democratic and market controls.

Competitive markets are not available for many services provided by nonbusiness organizations. Profitability cannot be used to impose discipline on these organizations. One cannot judge how well they are performing by examining their net incomes. These organizations can fail financially, but often they cannot be liquidated. For example, a government can default on its debt, but a city or state cannot be sold to pay creditors. The U.S. government had a total deficit of over $4 trillion in 1992. Nevertheless, it continues to function because it is permitted to spend more than it receives in taxes and other revenues. Like businesses, governments can borrow to provide financing in addition to that provided by operating activities. The U.S. government also has the right to print money.

People can choose among various nonprofit organizations for the services they receive. They can choose to join or to contribute to those organizations they perceive to be most effective and efficient. People and businesses can move from one location to another if they perceive a government is not operating efficiently and effectively, but, such moves are costly. Democratic control substitutes for market control in government and nonprofit organizations. Citizens elect representatives who determine public policies and manage the affairs of government. If citizens perceive that their elected representatives are not providing goods and services efficiently and effectively, they can support competing candidates. Governing boards of most nonprofit organizations are selected by members or by major resource providers. Citizens and members sometimes can vote on specific financial issues, as well. For example, citizens may have a right to vote on tax increases or bond issues.

Accounting information is important for nonbusiness as well as for business organizations. The accounting system provides information about the money and other resources available to nonbusiness organizations and how these resources were used to provide goods and services. Managers of nonbusiness organizations use accounting information in planning for the services they provide. This information helps in maintaining effective and efficient operations. Accounting information helps taxpayers and resource providers determine whether their money was spent properly. It informs them of amounts spent for various services.

Because profits and competitive markets are not available as controls, other controls are important in nonbusiness accounting. Accounting controls used by nonbusiness organizations include budgets, fund accounting, and encumbrances.

Budgets

Managers develop plans for future operations and submit these to the oversight group for approval. A budget is a formal plan describing the expected financial resources that will be used to provide services for a particular period. **A *budget* identifies the financial resources that an organization expects to receive, their sources, and how they will be used.** For many nonbusiness organizations, an annual budget provides a basis of comparison for determining whether managers are obtaining and using resources appropriately.

Objective 6
Explain the purpose of budgets in nonbusiness organizations.

Budgets are statements of planned economic activities. They identify the revenues, expenses, and cash flows an organization expects for a fiscal period. Many business organizations use budgets as a means of planning for future activities. Budgets provide goals that can be communicated to the various divisions of an organization. They inform the divisions of the level of production, sales, or costs they are expected to obtain during a period. Budgets provide a benchmark against which actual results can be compared. Managers and employees can evaluate how well they have performed relative to expectations.

Budgets play a special role in governments and many other nonprofit organizations. Budgets constrain the use of resources by some nonbusiness organizations. Government budgets are legal contracts. They specify the amounts various departments are permitted to spend during a fiscal period. Administrators and departmental managers are constrained by the amounts appropriated by the budget. **An *appropriation* is an authorized use of financial resources during a fiscal period.** Budgets can be modified during a fiscal period as available resources and needs change. However, changes in budgets cannot be made without formal approval of the legislative body of the government. Therefore, managers are limited to spending only the amount appropriated in the budget.

Thus, the budget is a critical document. Revenues for a coming fiscal period are forecasted. Expected revenues control the amount of spending planned for the period. Each department of government documents its needs for the coming period; then a legislative body considers these requests and allocates expected resources. Governments, except the federal government, usually cannot spend more than they receive from revenues and other financial resource inflows. Borrowing for operating activities normally is limited to short-term obligations that will be repaid when revenues are received during the current period. Long-term borrowing sometimes is used to finance long-term capital assets, such as the construction of buildings and other facilities. The amounts borrowed are repaid over the lives of the assets. Revenues earned each fiscal year during this period are used to pay interest, to repay principal, and to provide for the costs of current services.

Fund Accounting

Objective 7
Identify the fund types used by governments and nonprofit organizations and explain their purpose.

Most nonbusiness organizations account for their economic activities through funds. Governments use funds and account groups. **A *fund* is a fiscal and accounting entity. A fiscal entity controls financial resources. An accounting entity contains accounts to record and summarize information about economic activities. An *account group* is an accounting entity. It contains accounts but does not control financial resources.** Resources often are restricted for specific purposes. For example, sales taxes may be restricted to providing for education. Gasoline taxes may be restricted for highway use. Donations to a college may be restricted for scholarships or building construction. Funds separate resources according to their intended purposes. Thus, a highway tax fund might be used to account for taxes received and spent for highway maintenance and construction.

Government Funds and Account Groups. State and local governments may use hundreds of funds. They establish separate funds for each type of restricted revenue, for each construction project, and for many other special purposes. There are eight fund types, classified into three categories. The categories include governmental, proprietary, and fiduciary funds. Exhibit 15-2 illustrates the government fund structure. **Governmental funds** account for service activities supported primarily by taxes and fees rather than by sales of goods and services. **Proprietary funds** account for activities involving the sale of goods and services. **Fiduciary funds** account for activities in which a government serves as trustee or agent for resource providers and recipients.

Governmental funds include general, special revenue, debt service, and capital projects funds. A **general fund** accounts for resources used by the general government that are not legally restricted for specific purposes. General fund revenues may be used for a variety of purposes as determined by the government's administrators and oversight group. A government operates only one general fund. Most taxes and services are accounted for through the general

Exhibit 15-2 Government Funds and Account Groups

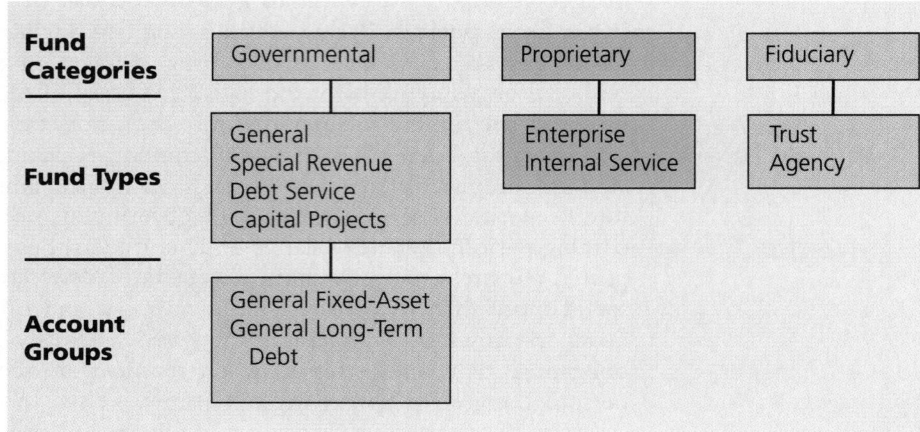

fund. **Special revenue funds** account for resources that are legally restricted to specific purposes, such as gasoline taxes. A government may operate a separate special revenue fund for each activity involving restricted revenues. **Debt service funds** account for resources used to pay interest and principal on general long-term debt. General long-term debt includes obligations that are repaid from general government revenues. A government normally operates only one debt service fund to account for all of its general debt. **Capital projects funds** account for the construction of long-term assets financed by general government revenues. Separate capital projects funds are created for each project. These funds are created when a project is begun and are eliminated when a project is completed.

Proprietary funds include enterprise and internal service funds. **Enterprise funds** account for business activities that involve sales of goods and services to customers external to the government itself. Public utilities, municipal golf courses, and campus bookstores are examples. Separate enterprise funds are maintained for each enterprise activity. **Internal service funds** account for business activities involving sales of goods and services to other divisions of a government. For example, a government might maintain a garage and motor pool to provide vehicles for use by other government departments. These departments pay a fee to the motor pool for using government vehicles. A government maintains separate internal service funds for each type of internal service activity.

Fiduciary funds include trust and agency funds. **Trust funds** manage resources that have been restricted for specific purposes. For example, an employee retirement fund invests financial resources appropriated by government and employee contributions. These investments are used to provide retirement benefits for government employees. A trust fund differs from a special revenue fund because it is responsible for long-term investments, whereas special revenue funds account primarily for current period resources. Most of these resources are consumed during the period in which they are received. **Agency funds** account for resources a government collects or holds for another organization. A county might collect property taxes that are distributed to school districts within the county, and may use an agency fund to account for the collection and distribution of these taxes. A government operates as many trust and agency funds as it requires to account for each of its trust or agency activities.

In addition to these funds, governments use two account groups. The **general fixed asset group** accounts for fixed assets financed by general government revenues. Fixed assets of proprietary and some fiduciary funds are accounted for by those funds rather than in the general fixed asset group. The **general long-term debt group** accounts for long-term obligations that will be paid from general government revenues. Long-term obligations of proprietary and some fiduciary funds are accounted for separately by those funds. Each government normally maintains only one general fixed asset group and one general long-term debt group.

Funds of Other Nonprofit Organizations. Nonprofit organizations such as colleges and hospitals use funds that are separated into two general categories: unrestricted and restricted. An **unrestricted fund** accounts for resources used to provide general services that are not restricted for specific purposes by resource providers. Thus, it is similar to a government's general fund. **Restricted funds** account for resources that are restricted for specific purposes. For example, colleges use loan funds to account for resources used to provide student loans and endowment funds for donations used to fund scholarships, professorships, or other special purposes. An endowment fund is a type of trust fund. A donor's contribution is invested, and earnings from the investment are used to support the particular activity desired by the donor. Nonprofit organizations use plant funds for resources used to finance plant asset acquisition and for the plant assets. Plant funds also account for the long-term debt of most nonprofit organizations, because the debt is used to finance plant assets. Hospitals use plant, endowment, and other special purpose funds. Hospitals separate resources available to provide current services into restricted and unrestricted funds.

Expenditures and Encumbrances

Many funds of governments and other nonprofit organizations account for resources that can be used to provide current services. Most of these are financial resources. An expenditure results when these resources are used to pay the costs of providing services. An important control issue is ensuring that managers do not overspend their resources by expending more than they are permitted to spend.

Objective 8
Explain the purpose of encumbrances.

Governments control financial resources through encumbrances. **An *encumbrance* is a commitment to expend financial resources to acquire goods and services that have been ordered or contracted for but that have not been received.** Encumbrances limit the amount available for additional expenditure from an account. For example, assume a government budget appropriates $100,000 for use by a public library for the purchase of books. The librarian orders books with an expected cost of $80,000. The account used for the books is not reduced by the cost of the books until they are received and a legal obligation for payment arises. Only $20,000 remains in the account for additional purchases, however. Therefore, an adjustment to the account is needed so the librarian will not place additional orders in excess of $20,000. The account is encumbered for $80,000 to limit the amount of any additional expenditure to $20,000. The encumbrance is eliminated once the order is received and an expenditure is recorded. The encumbrance controls the amount available so an account will not be overspent.

SELF-STUDY PROBLEM 15-1

The city of Dry Gulch has experienced a rapid increase in the cost of providing police services. In September 1994, the city council decided to levy a special tax on bars. The tax was to be used for upkeep of the city jail. The levy was 1% of prior year operating revenues. Council members believed the bars were the major source of jail population for the city. The council wants the city manager to account for the taxes so it can determine how much money was received, how the money was spent, and whether the jail overspent its appropriation.

Required

What accounting procedures could the manager use to account for the taxes? Why are these types of procedures needed by a government?

The solution to Self-Study Problem 15-1 appears at the end of the chapter.

ACCOUNTING MEASUREMENT

The types of accounts used by nonbusiness organizations are similar to those of businesses. These accounts are used to measure and report the economic effects of transactions in much the same way as in business organizations. Important differences exist, however, as described in this section. Many important accounting measurement and reporting rules for nonbusiness organizations have been examined and changed in recent years. As a result, accounting reports issued by these organizations are being changed. For example, this section examines certain accounting rules that apply to government financial statements issued after June 15, 1994.

Measurement Focus

Measurement focus refers to what is measured and reported on an entity's financial statements. Governmental funds use a financial resources measurement focus. **The *financial resources measurement focus* reports inflows and outflows of financial resources for a fiscal period.** For purposes of governmental accounting, financial resources include cash, receivables, prepaid items, supplies, and marketable securities. In general, these are the resources businesses would classify as current assets. The financial resources focus is different from the capital maintenance focus used by businesses. The types of accounts used by these funds and the elements of the accounting model depend on which measurement focus a fund uses. Exhibit 15-3 summarizes the two measurement approaches.

Objective 9
Compare the financial resources and capital maintenance measurement focuses.

Instead of investments by owners, nonbusiness organizations are financed by taxes, donations, grants, and fees that are sources of revenues. In addition, they may borrow money from financial institutions and by issuing bonds. Instead of equity, many nonbusiness organization funds use the term "fund balance." ***Fund balance* is the difference between the assets and liabilities reported by a fund.** Funds that account for business-type activities, such as proprietary funds, often use the term "fund equity." Equity for these funds includes earnings from the sale of goods and services, as in business organizations.

Governmental funds account for the flow of financial resources during a fiscal period. The services that a government can provide during a period depend

Exhibit 15-3 Comparison of Measurement Approaches

Financial Resources Measurement Focus
Financial Resources (Assets) = Current Liabilities + Fund Balance
Revenues – Expenditures = Change in Fund Balance

Capital Maintenance Measurement Focus
Assets = Liabilities + Equity
Revenues – Expenses = Net Income and Change in Retained Earnings

on its financial resources to pay for the services. Therefore, the accounting system used by governmental funds measures the financial resources obtained from taxpayers and compares these resource inflows with the use of financial resources to provide services. **An *expenditure* arises when financial resources are consumed or when an obligation is incurred that will require the use of financial resources.** Governmental funds match the inflow of financial resources for a fiscal period with the expenditure of these resources. The change in the fund balance for a period is the excess (or deficiency) of revenues over expenditures.

Governmental revenues and expenditures are measured on an accrual basis. Revenues are recognized in the period in which the event generating revenues occurs and the government has demanded payment. For example, income taxes are recognized when taxable income is earned by taxpayers and when taxes have been demanded as a result of withholdings or from the filing of estimated or actual tax returns. Other revenues, such as fines, fees, and donations, are recognized when an enforceable legal claim to payment arises. Expenditures are recognized when a claim against a government's financial resources arises or when financial resources are consumed.

Proprietary funds account for revenues earned from sales of goods and services and related expenses. An expense arises when resources are consumed or an obligation is incurred that will require the consumption of resources. These resources are not limited to financial resources. Depreciation is an expense arising from the consumption of plant assets, though no payment for the assets is made during the current fiscal period.

Matching revenues with expenses measures whether a fund has maintained its capital during a fiscal period and whether it has earned a profit. Capital maintenance is the measurement focus of proprietary funds and business organizations. Also, it is a focus of certain fiduciary funds that have a responsibility for capital maintenance.

A major observable difference in the transactions recorded by proprietary and governmental funds occurs for long-term resources such as buildings and equipment. Governmental funds record expenditures for these resources when they are purchased because financial resources are consumed by the purchase. Governmental funds do not record depreciation expense because depreciation does not result in a use of financial resources. For example, assume that a business and a government's general fund both purchased equipment on January 1, 1994, and both paid $10,000. Both organizations assume the equipment will have a life of 5 years. The business would depreciate the equipment over the five years at $2,000 per year, assuming straight-line depreciation. It would record $2,000 of depreciation expense each year for five years. The government would report the purchase as a $10,000 expenditure in 1994. This expenditure would be deducted from revenues for the government during 1994 in reporting its operating results. It would record no expenditure or expense associated with the acquisition of the equipment during 1995 or future years.

Some business and nonbusiness organizations, especially small ones, use a cash basis of accounting measurement rather than an accrual basis. The accounting information reported by these organizations does not have the same meaning as that for organizations using the accrual basis. Careful inspection may be needed to determine how economic activities are being measured.

The Financial Reporting Entity

Objective 10
Explain how a government determines its financial reporting entity.

The reporting entity for a business organization includes a parent corporation and its subsidiaries. The entity is determined by the extent of ownership and control by stockholders. Defining a governmental entity is not always easy. Governments do not own other organizations, though they may provide the majority of another organization's revenues. Governments have responsibility for many activities that other organizations or oversight groups administer. For example, some colleges and hospitals are funded largely by state appropriations. These institutions often are administered by boards appointed by the governor or other officials. Management of these organizations may be largely independent of state government, however. Therefore, they may not be included in the state's accounting reports.

A government should include in its accounting reports the activities of the primary government and those organizations for which the primary government is financially accountable. Also, it should include those organizations that would result in misleading reports if they were omitted. Governments may not always agree as to what constitutes the entity about which they are reporting, however. For example, the State of Indiana noted in its 1991 annual report that it included:

> . . . all funds, agencies, boards, commissions and authorities over which the State's executive or legislative branches exercise oversight responsibility. Oversight responsibility is defined to include the following considerations: financial interdependency, selection of governing authority, designation of management, ability to significantly influence operations, and accountability for fiscal matters.

The State did not include colleges and universities as part of its reporting entity. The State of Washington used a similar definition to determine its reporting entity, but included state colleges and universities as part of its reporting entity.

The accounting reports of governments and other nonprofit organizations include those activities management considers to be important parts of their responsibilities. This is a subjective decision.

ACCOUNTING REPORTS

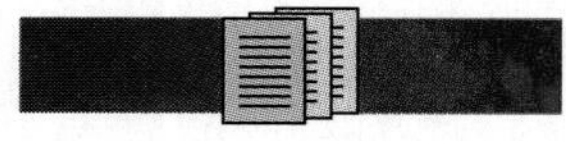

Nonbusiness accounting reports include many of the same components included by businesses. Considerable variation exists among nonbusiness organizations as to the amount of information included in and the format of accounting reports. This section examines some of the primary financial statements of governments and other nonprofit organizations.

Governmental Reporting

Objective 11
Discuss the types of financial statements reported by governments and their contents.

Governmental annual reports, which are often large, contain many schedules and descriptions of governmental activities. Financial statements are presented for the various funds and account groups of the government. Consolidated statements for the government as a whole usually are not presented. The primary financial statements include:

- balance sheets
- statements of revenues, expenditures, and changes in fund balances for governmental and expendable trust funds
- statements of revenues, expenditures, and changes in fund balances—budget and actual
- statements of revenues, expenses, and changes in retained earnings for proprietary, and nonexpendable trust funds
- statements of cash flows for proprietary funds

Combined financial statements report summaries for each fund type. A combined balance sheet presents the total of each asset, liability, and fund balance or equity account according to fund type. In addition, **combining statements** report account balances for all funds of the same type. For example, a combining balance sheet for the special revenue funds presents the asset, liability, and fund balance account balances for each of a government's special revenue funds. Financial statements for each individual fund also may be reported. Exhibit 15-4 illustrates the relationship among the various types of financial statements.

Exhibit 15-4 Relationship Among Combined, Combining, and Individual Fund Balance Sheets

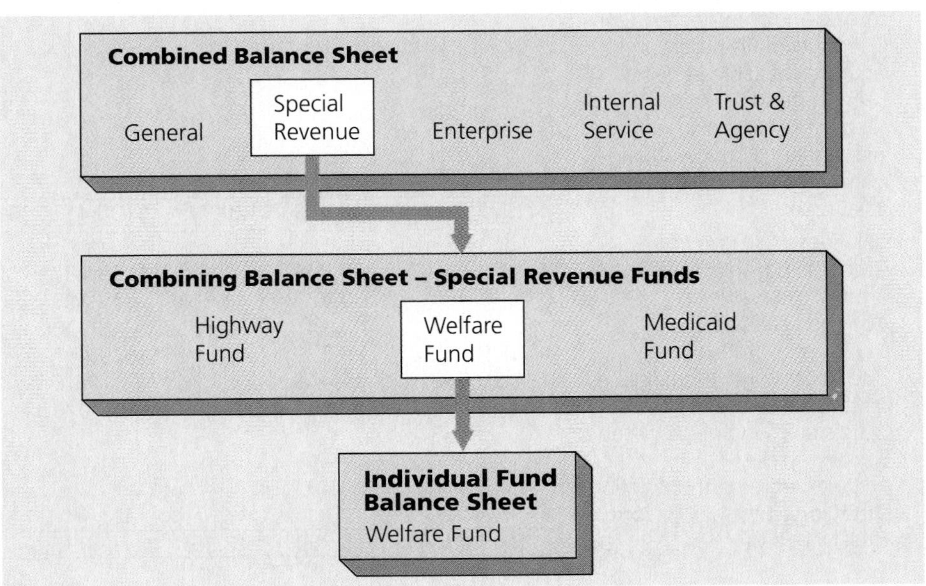

Governmental Funds and Account Groups

This section examines the primary components of financial statements of governmental funds and account groups. Governmental funds report current assets and current liabilities associated with general government activities. Long-term assets and long-term liabilities associated with these activities are reported by the account groups.

Balance Sheet. Exhibit 15-5 provides a combined balance sheet of the governmental funds and account groups for the State of Washington.

Many of the items reported on the balance sheet are similar to those reported by businesses. **Receivables** are reported net of related allowances for doubtful accounts. Interfund receivables (due from other funds) and payables

Exhibit 15-5

STATE OF WASHINGTON: EXCERPT FROM COMBINED BALANCE SHEET
June 30, 1991

(in Thousands)	General	Special Revenue	Debt Service	Capital Projects	General Fixed Assets	General Long-Term Debt
Assets						
Cash and equivalents	$ 986,588	$1,013,273	$101,056	$ 47,673	$	$
Investments	821	6,116		84		
Taxes receivable, net	1,258,329	8,484				
Other receivables, net	95,871	62,540	9,326	169		
Due from other funds	193,560	173,121	10,337	148,486		
Due from other governments	377,911	126,815				
Inventories	12,299	20,140				
Land					526,920	
Buildings					2,189,968	
Other improvements					466,395	
Furnishings and equipment					793,420	
Accumulated depreciation					(1,236,317)	
Construction in progress					267,367	
Amount available in debt service fund						118,561
Amount to be provided for retirement of general long-term obligations						4,585,400
Total Assets	$2,925,379	$1,410,489	$120,719	$196,412	$3,007,753	$4,703,961
Liabilities and Fund Equity						
Accounts payable	$ 385,846	$ 98,549	$	$ 15,287	$	$
Contracts payable	17,467	59,427	1,261	12,708		
Accrued liabilities	90,176	48,146	895	320		
Due to other funds	240,355	82,379	2	29,437		
Due to other governments	25,069	14,443		116		
Deferred revenues	653,059	72,808		228		
Claims and judgments payable	35,458					
Bonds payable						3,721,033
Accrued retirement obligations						791,400
Other long-term obligations						191,528
Total Liabilities	1,447,430	375,752	2,158	58,096		4,703,961

(in Thousands)	General	Special Revenue	Debt Service	Capital Projects	General Fixed Assets	General Long-Term Debt
Fund Equity and Other Credits:						
Investment in general fixed assets					3,007,753	
Fund balances:						
Reserved for:						
Encumbrances	2,702	160,849		106,964		
Inventories	11,273	20,140				
Restricted accounts	477,742					
Working capital	374,750					
Other specific purposes	145,733	14,449		109		
Unreserved:						
Designated for debt service			118,561			
Designated for other specific purposes		87,845		31,243		
Undesignated	465,749	751,454				
Total Fund Equity and Other Credits	1,477,949	1,034,737	118,561	138,316	3,007,753	
Total Liabilities & Fund Equity	$2,925,379	$1,410,489	$120,719	$196,412	$3,007,753	$4,703,961

Minor modifications have been made to the format.

(due to other funds) are included. Unlike corporate statements, which consolidate transactions of companies owned by the parent and eliminate intercompany transactions, governmental financial statements do not eliminate interfund transactions. Total columns are included in many combined financial statements of governments. These columns sum the account balances for the government's funds. The totals can be misleading, however, because interfund transactions have not been eliminated. Therefore, totals should be interpreted cautiously.

Inventories are not a major item for most governmental funds. Therefore, the method used to account for inventories is not especially important for many nonbusiness organizations. FIFO is commonly used. Also, there are no tax implications in the choice of accounting methods as there are for businesses. Thus, the simplest methods are most common.

Governmental funds report only current assets. These assets can be used to provide services during the coming fiscal period. The **general fixed asset account group** reports plant assets for the general government. These assets are recorded at cost. Most governments do not depreciate these assets. Washington is unusual in including accumulated depreciation as part of its balance sheet. **Construction in progress** refers to the cost of construction projects that currently are incomplete. Once completed, these costs are transferred to the buildings or other improvements accounts.

The **general long-term debt (or obligations) account group** reports asset balances to indicate the **amount available in the debt service fund** to pay for interest and principal. Observe that the amount available is approximately equal to the asset balance of the debt service fund. Also, the general long-term debt group reports the **amount to be provided** in the future to pay for long-term obligations. The sum of the amount available and the amount to be provided is equal to the total amount of long-term obligations to be paid from general government revenues. These amounts are bookkeeping entries to offset the amount of liabilities in the account group. They do not represent resources. The only assets currently available to pay for the general long-term obligations are in the debt service fund. Other amounts will be appropriated in future years, as interest and principal on the obligations become due.

Payables reported by governmental funds are similar to those reported by businesses. Governmental funds report only current liabilities. Long-term liabilities that are the responsibility of the general government are included in the general long-term debt group. Amounts currently due are listed as current liabilities of the debt service fund. Thus, though the long-term debt group lists long-term obligations, the debt service fund accounts for payments of the current portions of these obligations.

Fund balance (or equity) includes the excess of assets over liabilities for each fund and account group. The fund balance provides information about claims to the financial resources that are the assets of governmental funds. The unreserved, undesignated portion of the fund balance indicates the portion of resources that are available for use to meet the general operating needs of the government during the coming fiscal period. Reserved fund balance identifies the portion of resources that are not available for future use because they have already been committed for other purposes, such as payment of encumbrances. A portion of the government's financial resources will be used during the coming fiscal period to pay for goods that have been ordered during the previous year. Therefore, these resources are not available for other uses. Designated fund balance refers to management decisions that have been made about how certain resources will be used. Thus, the state's management has decided that $118,561,000 of its available resources (that are available in the debt service fund) will be used in the coming year for debt service needs. Consequently, this portion of the government's resources also is not available to meet general operating needs.

The general long-term debt group does not have a fund balance since its purpose is to list long-term obligations. The equity for the general fixed assets group is a bookkeeping entry to offset the balance reported in the asset section.

Statement of Revenues and Expenditures

Exhibit 15-6 provides a statement of revenues, expenditures, and changes in fund balance for the State of Washington.

Expendable trust funds also are included with the governmental funds on this statement. **Expendable trust funds** are those for which fund resources can be expended to meet the intended purpose of the trust. For example, an unemployment insurance trust fund records employer contributions and invests these until they are needed to pay employee unemployment claims. The amounts contributed, along with earnings on investments of these contributions, can be expended. **Nonexpendable trust funds** are those for which most fund resources cannot be expended. For example, a retirement trust fund records resources from the general government and from government employees. These resources are invested to provide future retirement benefits. The government may be permitted to use only earnings from the fund investments to pay current retirement benefits. The contributions are nonexpendable. The operations of nonexpendable trust funds are reported with proprietary funds because they have a capital maintenance focus.

Exhibit 15-6

STATE OF WASHINGTON
EXCERPT FROM COMBINED STATEMENT OF REVENUES, EXPENDITURES, AND CHANGES IN FUND BALANCE
For the Fiscal Year Ended June 30, 1991

(in Thousands)	General	Special Revenue	Debt Service	Capital Projects	Expendable Trust
Revenues:					
Retail sales taxes	$3,582,346	$ 2,654	$	$	$
Business and occupation taxes	1,154,768				
Property taxes	742,440				
Excise taxes	626,082	101,868			
Motor vehicle and fuel taxes	5,365	581,606			
Other taxes	601,993	145,034			
Licenses, permits, and fees	71,803	310,047			$ 134
Federal grants-in-aid	1,910,843	869,812	164		135,178
Charges for services	220,413	164,003		15,337	12,204
Unemployment compensation contribution					547,203
Miscellaneous revenues	258,324	441,951	14,357	13,838	200,522
Total Revenues	9,174,377	2,616,975	14,521	29,175	895,241
Expenditures:					
Current:					
General government	498,727	243,284		7,046	40,169
Human services	3,687,353	136,557		15,873	557,887
Natural resources and recreation	249,365	261,409		17,324	2,918
Transportation	37,986	572,041		842	127
Education	4,381,444	563,067		27,470	130,583
Capital outlays	165,164	722,745		207,585	73,318
Debt service:					
Principal	3,685	5,950	155,520	219	4
Interest	789	1,702	237,330	10,467	20
Total Expenditures	9,024,513	2,506,755	392,850	286,826	805,026
Excess of Revenues Over (Under) Expenditures	149,864	110,220	(378,329)	(257,651)	90,215
Other Financing Sources (Uses)					
Bond sale proceeds		130,722		377,450	
Operating transfers in	235,621	80,352	415,796	70,604	132,866
Operating transfers out	(544,287)	(215,302)	(28,024)	(39,663)	(25,713)
Capital lease acquisitions	7,770	7,279		280	
Total Other Financing Sources (Uses)	(300,896)	3,051	387,772	408,671	107,153
Excess of Revenues and Other Sources Over (Under) Expenditures and Other Uses	(151,032)	113,271	9,443	151,020	197,368
Fund Balances:					
Fund balances, July 1	1,628,981	920,391	109,118	(13,008)	1,698,563
Residual equity transfers in		1,381		381	1
Residual equity transfers out		(306)		(77)	
Fund Balances, June 30	$1,477,949	$1,034,737	$118,561	$138,316	$1,895,932

Taxes are the primary revenues of governmental funds. Taxes designated for specific purposes, such as motor vehicle and fuel taxes, are reported in the special revenue funds. Grants are another major source of revenues for many governments. States receive grants from the federal government. Local governments receive grants from the federal and state governments. **Charges for services** are a small source of revenues for most governmental funds. Debt service and capital projects funds usually do not levy taxes directly. Most of their resources are transfers from the general or special revenue funds.

Operating statements for governmental funds list **expenditures** by function. Amounts expended for services during the current period are separated from expenditures for long-term assets (capital outlays) and for debt service.

Other financing sources include debt issued to acquire capital assets and transfers among funds. Debt is not revenue, but it is a source of money for current expenditure. Therefore, it is an "other" financing source. Taxes received by one fund, particularly the general fund, are transferred to other funds for expenditure. For example, the debt service fund receives most of its financial resources from tax revenues received by the general fund. These resources are **operating transfers in** to the debt service fund and **operating transfers out** of the general fund.

The **excess of revenues and other sources over (under) expenditures and other uses** indicates whether a government is obtaining sufficient taxes and other revenues to meet its current service needs. Washington incurred a short-fall in its general fund in 1991. The amount was relatively small. The State's beginning general fund balance was sufficient to cover the short-fall. **Residual equity transfers** occur when a new fund is established or eliminated. Equity is created in a fund when resources are transferred in to establish the fund. Equity is eliminated when a fund ceases to exist. The remaining balance in the fund is transferred to other funds.

Comparison of Actual and Budgeted Amounts

Governments report comparisons of actual and budgeted revenues, expenditures, and other financing sources and uses for a fiscal period. Exhibit 15-7 provides an example.

Exhibit 15-7

STATE OF WASHINGTON
EXCERPT FROM STATEMENT OF REVENUES, EXPENDITURES
BUDGET AND ACTUAL
For the Biennium Ended June 30, 1991

(in thousands)	Approved Budget 1989–1991 Biennium	Actual for 1989–1991 Biennium	Variance Favorable (Unfavorable)
Taxes	$13,022,759	$13,024,941	$12,182
Federal grants-in-aid	3,620,925	3,553,712	(67,213)

The exhibit reports information for only two general fund revenue accounts. The complete statement includes all major categories of revenues, expenditures, and other financing sources and uses. The statement contains the amount budgeted, the amount actually recorded, and the difference. This statement is useful for identifying causes of surpluses or deficiencies during a period. Observe that Washington's budget is prepared on a biennium (every two years) basis. Thus, this statement reports comparisons for a two year period.

Proprietary and Fiduciary Funds

Financial statements for proprietary and fiduciary funds are similar to those for governmental funds. These statements also are similar in many respects to those of businesses.

Balance Sheets. Exhibit 15-8 provides an example of a balance sheet for proprietary and fiduciary funds.

Exhibit 15-8

STATE OF WASHINGTON
EXCERPT FROM COMBINED BALANCE SHEET
June 30, 1991

(in Thousands)	Enterprise	Internal Service	Trust and Agency
Assets			
Cash and equivalents	$ 179,619	$105,703	$ 3,700,304
Investments	4,529,842	25,361	15,640,634
Taxes receivable, net	2,569		
Other receivables, net	395,270	3,818	348,947
Due from other funds	87,224	42,118	198,508
Due from other governments	18,043	7,345	112,292
Inventories	44,591	18,779	271
Prepaid expenses	2,724	551	
Other nonfixed assets	253		39
Land	28,886	1,252	
Buildings	739,366	15,092	
Other improvements	137,281	5,743	
Furnishings and equipment	460,532	353,016	
Accumulated depreciation	(353,938)	(205,613)	
Construction in progress	32,693	3,755	
Total Assets	$6,304,955	$376,920	$20,000,995
Liabilities and Fund Equity			
Accounts payable	$ 47,391	$ 23,328	$ 15,601
Contracts payable	39,663	5,974	15,462
Accrued liabilities	110,263	15,075	159,918
Matured bonds payable	11,749		
Due to other funds	61,275	13,780	426,126
Due to other governments	1,421	91	1,678,748
Deferred revenues	13,800	5,961	24,356
Claims and judgments payable	699,000	32,463	
Claims and judgments payable—Long-term	6,876,892	53,982	
bonds payable	388,735		
Other long-term obligations	204,866	6,449	256,909
Total Liabilities	8,455,055	157,103	2,577,120

(in Thousands)	Enterprise	Internal Service	Trust and Agency
Fund Equity and Other Credits:			
Unrealized gain on investments	56,284		
Contributed capital	560,367	34,128	
Retained earnings	(2,766,751)	185,689	
Fund balances:			
Reserved for:			
Inventories			271
Nonexpendable trust corpus			664,964
Unemployment compensation			1,665,027
Retirement systems			14,862,983
Other specific purposes			120,260
Unreserved:			
Designated for other specific purposes			4,919
Undesignated			105,451
Total Fund Equity and Other Credits	(2,150,100)	219,817	17,423,875
Total Liabilities & Fund Equity	$6,304,955	$376,920	$20,000,995

Minor modifications have been made to the format.

Unlike governmental funds, proprietary funds report both current and long-term assets and liabilities. These funds are responsible for maintaining capital, including plant assets. They record depreciation on their plant assets and include accumulated depreciation on their balance sheets. Straight-line depreciation normally is used. They are responsible for meeting their own debt service requirements. Nonexpendable trust funds also have this responsibility. Trust and agency funds are largely investment funds. They seldom require plant assets.

The fund equity of proprietary funds is similar to the equity of corporations. Contributed capital results from equity transfers to establish the funds. Retained earnings result from profits earned by the fund operating activities. A proprietary fund can incur losses as well as profits. Observe that Washington's enterprise funds reported a $2.7 billion deficit in retained earnings in 1991.

Operating Statements. Proprietary and nonexpendable trust funds report income statements and statements of cash flows. Because these statements are very similar to those provided by businesses, an illustration has not been provided. The primary categories included on these statements parallel those of businesses. Income statements list operating revenues, operating expenses, and other revenues and expenses (particularly interest). They may include extraordinary items and the effects of changes in accounting methods. These changes are less common than for businesses. Discontinued operations are extremely rare. Cash flow statements may be prepared using the direct or indirect format. The indirect format adjusts net income for noncash revenues and expenses.

Financial Statements of Other Nonprofit Organizations

Objective 12
Discuss the financial statements reported by nonprofit organizations.

The financial statements of other nonprofit organizations vary considerably. Some organizations, such as hospitals, tend to follow closely the formats of business organizations. They report balance sheets, income statements, and statements of cash flows. In some cases, the statements are divided between unrestricted and various restricted funds.

Colleges and universities, particularly public ones, tend to follow the format of governments. Balance sheets are divided into several funds: current unrestricted (similar to a general fund), current restricted (similar to special revenue funds), loan, endowment, agency, plant, and others. Account groups are not used. Plant funds report most plant assets and long-term liabilities.

Civic, social, and religious organizations may use a variety of funds. Unrestricted, restricted, plant, and endowment funds are common.

The Financial Accounting Standards Board has issued standards requiring nonprofit organizations, other than government controlled organizations, to adopt accounting methods similar to those of businesses. For example, these organizations are required to depreciate fixed assets, a practice uncommon for many of these organizations until recently. Professional accounting organizations also have encouraged a greater similarity in reporting practices among these organizations. Some nonprofit organizations now report financial statements that consolidate fund activities. The statements closely parallel those of businesses.

Considerable diversity in accounting methods and reporting formats continues among nonprofit organizations. Careful inspection of the methods used to prepare the statements and an understanding of their intended purposes are necessary to interpret the statements.

SELF-STUDY PROBLEM 15-2

A combined statement of revenues, expenditures, and changes in fund balances is provided below for Green Acres County.

(in Thousands)	General	Special Revenue	Debt Service	Capital Projects
Revenues:				
Sales taxes	$ 978	$	$	$
Property taxes	524			
Licenses, permits, and fees	95	51		
Grants-in-aid	167	122		
Total Revenues	1,764	173		
Expenditures:				
Current:				
General government	220			8
Human services	494			14
Parks and recreation	112	68		4
Education	743	113		23
Capital outlays	107			144
Debt service:				
Principal			40	
Interest			18	
Total Expenditures	1,676	181	58	193
Excess of Revenues Over (Under) Expenditures	88	(8)	(58)	(193)

(in Thousands)	General	Special Revenue	Debt Service	Capital Projects
Other Financing Sources (Uses)				
Bond sale proceeds				200
Operating transfers in			55	
Operating transfers out	(50)			(5)
Total Other Financing Sources (Uses)	(50)		55	195
Excess of Revenues and Other Sources Over (Under) Expenditures and Other Uses	38	(8)	(3)	2
Fund Balances:				
Fund Balances, July 1	315	109	7	20
Fund Balances, June 30	$ 353	$101	$ 4	$ 22

Required

Answer each of the following questions:

a. What are the county's major sources of revenue?
b. What primary services does the county provide?
c. What were the major revenues of the special revenue funds? What were their primary uses?
d. What is the purpose of each of the funds included in the statement?
e. What is the difference between revenues and other financing sources?

Why are other financing sources included on the statement?

The solution to Self-Study Problem 15-2 appears at the end of the chapter.

ACCOUNTING STANDARDS

Objective 13
Identify sources of accounting standards for nonbusiness organizations.

Until recently, governments and nonprofit organizations established their own accounting standards. Professional organizations, composed of financial managers from a particular type of organization, prepared accounting and reporting guidelines. Therefore, governments, hospitals, colleges, and other nonprofit organizations developed various approaches to accounting and financial reporting. Though similar, these approaches varied considerably. In addition, the American Institute of CPAs (AICPA) developed accounting and auditing guidelines for these organizations. The guidelines were inconsistent and many variations in accounting and reporting existed among these organizations.

Since the early 1980s, a major effort has been made to develop uniform standards of accounting and reporting. The Governmental Accounting Standards Board (GASB) was created in 1984. It is an independent, privately sponsored organization supported by professional organizations and state and local governments. It establishes accounting and financial reporting standards for state and local governments and government sponsored institutions in the U.S. The FASB establishes accounting standards for nonprofit organizations that are not sponsored by governments. Both the GASB and the FASB have been active in improving accounting and reporting practices of nonbusiness organizations. The standards developed by GASB and FASB are not always consistent, however. The philosophy of the FASB has been to increase the consistency between nonprofit and business accounting and reporting. The philosophy of the GASB has been to recognize specific distinctions between governments and businesses. Therefore, public colleges and hospitals may follow accounting standards that differ from those followed by private, nonprofit colleges and hospitals.

Neither the FASB nor the GASB has power to enforce its standards. The SEC enforces FASB standards for publicly-traded corporations. Other organizations adopt standards voluntarily. States may require local governments to adopt standards set by the GASB and many have done so. Much of the variation in accounting and reporting practices among governments and among other nonprofit organizations has been eliminated in recent years. Practices are still much more diverse than among major corporations, however. Knowledge of basic accounting principles, some understanding of the principles of fund accounting, and a careful reading of accounting reports can provide insight into how effectively and efficiently these organizations are performing.

ANALYSIS OF ACCOUNTING INFORMATION

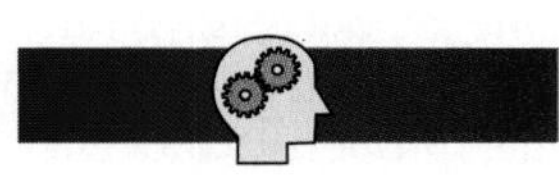

Objective 14
Identify factors that should be considered when analyzing government accounting information.

The keys to success for any organization are how it responds to its economic environment and how effectively and efficiently it provides goods and services demanded by its customers. Like businesses, nonbusiness organizations must generate sufficient cash flows to pay for the cost of services and to make payments on their obligations. Many of the approaches described in earlier chapters for analyzing accounting information of businesses can be used for nonbusiness organizations as well. This section focuses primarily on issues related to the analysis of state and local government accounting information. These organizations differ from businesses more than other nonprofit organizations. Some of this discussion is applicable to both governments and nonprofit organizations. Factors that should be considered in evaluating a government's performance include: its economic environment, effectiveness and efficiency of its operating activities, its operating and financial leverage, and its compliance with legal and other restrictions.

Economic Environment

Governments are regional entities. They derive their revenues and provide services within a specific geographical area. If the State of Alabama is having serious financial problems, it cannot tax incomes of people residing in Florida, for example. The demographic, social, and economic attributes of a particular region affect the financial conditions of governments in the region. Many regions depend heavily on certain companies or industries for jobs. Examples include the automobile industry in Michigan and other midwestern states, the oil industry in Texas, Oklahoma, and Louisiana, and the aerospace industry in California and Washington. Therefore, tax revenues often vary in relation to the profitability of industries that dominate a region. Industrial strength and diversity are important factors affecting the growth and stability of government revenues.

Population demographics also affect government finances. Taxpayers in the 40 to 60 age group generally earn the highest incomes. Therefore, they pay the most taxes. People under 20 and those over 60 generally have low earned incomes. They tend to be more service receivers than taxpayers. Thus, changes in population can have a significant effect on the demand for services and the taxes available to pay for these services. Education and health services are major expenditure items for many governments. Unemployment rates and education levels also affect both taxpaying ability and demand for services. Many large cities have been adversely affected by a migration of high income taxpayers to suburbs. The remaining populations have been dominated by low income families with high birth rates. Thus, service demands have increased while revenues have decreased.

Governments face financial problems when they fail to adjust to changing conditions. California once symbolized prosperity in the U.S. Its booming economic climate and favorable demographics created ample tax revenues to provide for a high level of government services. In recent years the state has faced growing economic problems and major budget reductions, however. The state has depended heavily on defense and aerospace industries. As these industries have declined in the post-cold war era, the state has lost hundreds of thousands of high-paying jobs. Its taxpayer base has decreased, as many in the 40 to 60 age group have left the state. At the same time, the numbers of those requiring government services, students, welfare recipients, and the elderly, have increased. Growing service demands and shrinking revenues are ingredients for financial disaster in any government. The problem is similar to one of decreasing sales and profit margins in the business sector.

Governments derive revenues primarily from income, property, and sales taxes. Property taxes depend on property values. Property values usually change slowly over time. Therefore, property taxes are a relatively stable source of revenues. Income and sales taxes are less stable. In an economic downturn, they decrease as unemployment increases and as commercial activity decreases. Thus, the way a government derives its revenues is important to understanding its ability to respond to economic changes. During the early 1990s many governments faced dwindling tax revenues because of a major and prolonged recession. As business revenues and corporate and individual incomes decreased, government revenues also decreased. Budget cuts and elimination of services resulted.

Effectiveness and Efficiency

Effectiveness is difficult to quantify for governments. Governments are effective if they provide the type, quantity, and quality of services demanded by their citizens. Because citizen tastes differ, determining their demands is not easy. Comparisons among governments can reveal the relative amounts spent for various services. Whether these expenditures are meeting citizen needs cannot be determined directly, however. Recent efforts have been made to develop measures of service efforts and accomplishments. Many of these measures involve quantitative measures of performance, such as numbers of police officers relative to population or response time for fires or other emergencies.

Efficiency also is difficult to quantify. Because most revenues are not earned from the sale of goods or services, a comparison of revenues with the costs of providing services is not a measure of efficiency. Comparisons of expenditures among governments, adjusted for the size of the governments, can reveal which governments are providing services at the lowest cost. Real growth rates (adjusted for inflation) in revenues and expenditures relative to population size can reveal whether the cost of government services is increasing.

The stability and growth of major revenue and expenditure items can be determined by examining changes in these items over time. Real growth can be determined by dividing revenue and expenditure items by an inflation index, such as the consumer price index. Adjustments for population changes can be made by dividing revenues and expenditures by the government's population at different points in time. Resulting amounts are expressed on a per capita basis. For example, Exhibit 15-9 illustrates the real growth per capita in major revenues and expenditures for the State of Washington. The exhibit indicates a higher rate of growth in 1988-1991 than in prior years. A high tax growth rate implies an increasing burden on taxpayers. This burden may be consistent with a demand for greater services. On the other hand, high tax growth may drive out taxpayers and reduce the revenue base of a government.

Exhibit 15-9 State of Washington—Real Growth in Per Capita Revenues and Expenditures

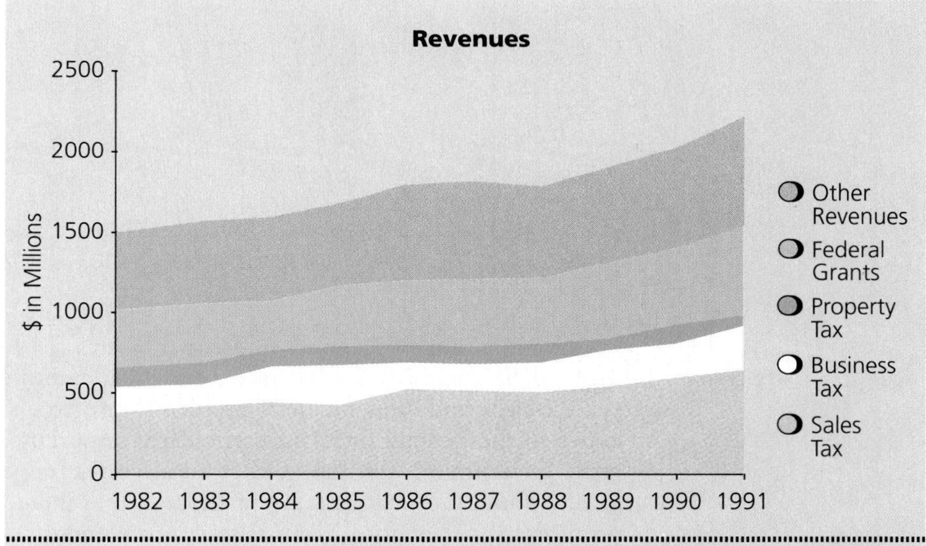

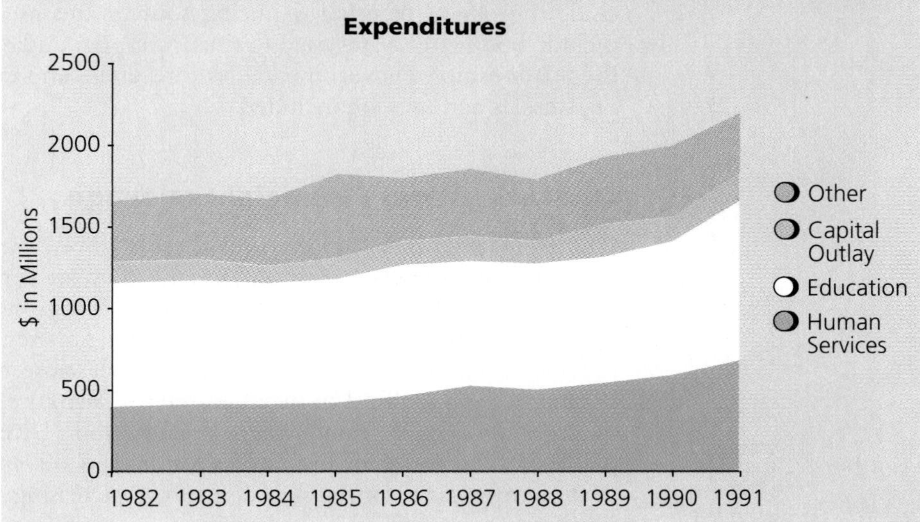

Another factor to consider in assessing growth in a government's revenues and expenditures is change in personal income of taxpayers. If tax revenues are growing at a faster rate than taxpayer income, the tax burden is increasing. Exhibit 15-10 illustrates growth in tax revenues relative to personal income for the State of Washington.

Exhibit 15-10 Tax Revenue Growth Relative to Personal Income—State of Washington

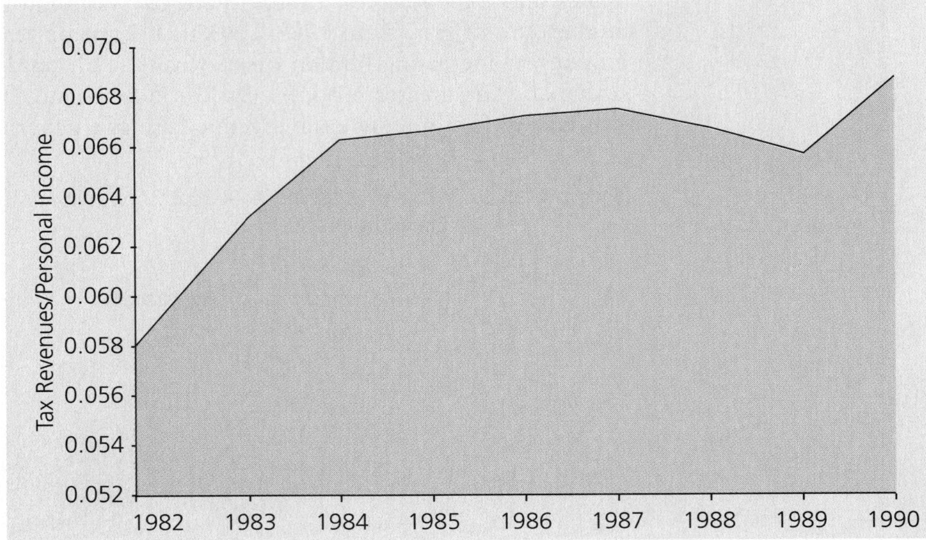

Examination of revenues and expenditures for individual funds reveals any major deficiencies. A significant excess of expenditures over revenues for several years usually indicates financial problems. An excess of expenditures over revenues in the general fund are particularly important because this fund finances most government services. Other funds often depend on transfers from the general fund. Governmental fund expenditures include capital outlays (for long-term assets). Therefore, comparisons of revenues and expenditures should include the effects of other financing sources and uses. Other financing sources include bonds and notes used to finance capital outlays. Exhibit 15-11 illustrates the relationship of governmental fund revenues and expenditures. Other financing sources and uses are included.

Operating and Financial Leverage

Operating and financial leverage affect a government's ability to respond to changing economic conditions. Because they are service providers, most nonbusiness organizations have high fixed costs. They invest in fixed assets, and employees provide most services. Many assets are not readily marketable. They provide specialized functions. A state cannot close or sell its highways simply because it cannot afford to maintain them. Therefore, when faced with decreasing revenues, many nonbusiness organizations have difficulties reducing expenses in the short run. Employees can be laid-off, but the level of services will decline, often at a time when demand is increasing. Unlike a business, a government cannot sell or liquidate itself. It must find ways to increase revenues and/or decrease expenditures when facing economic problems. In the short

Exhibit 15-11 Relationship Between Revenues and Expenditures—State of Washington

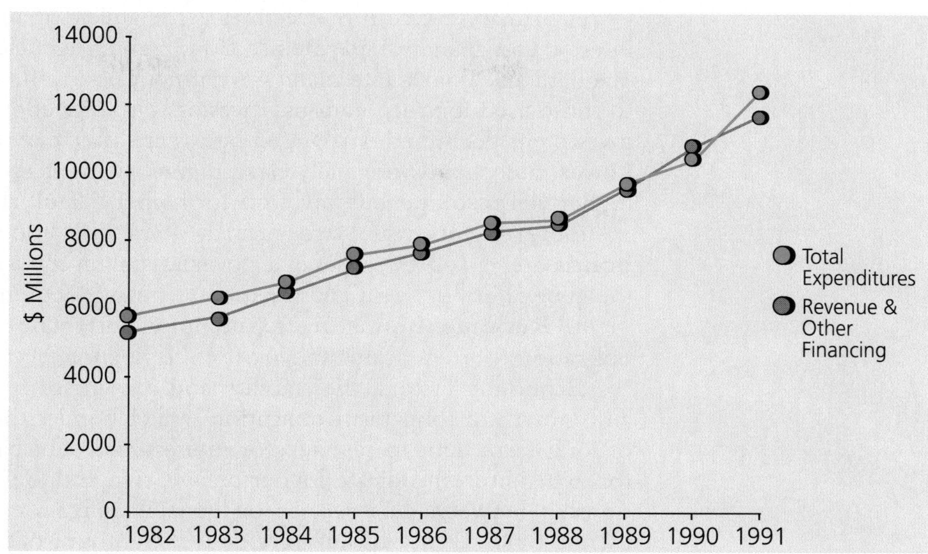

run, governments cut expenditures and reduce services. In the long-run, they attempt to attract investment by new industry and to stimulate business activity. Schools, hospitals, prisons, and other facilities can be closed if the services can be provided by alternate means. Occasionally, a public facility can be sold to private investors. For example, some cities have sold airports to private investors and then have leased the facilities back from the owners.

When revenues increase, because of higher levels of income or sales taxes, for example, governments often expand their operating activities by constructing new facilities and providing new services. These activities are difficult to eliminate when revenues shrink. Therefore, these organizations have difficulties adjusting to decreasing revenues. In the past, a solution often has been to increase taxes or to add additional revenue sources. In many locations, taxpayers have been unwilling to accept additional taxes in recent years. In some cases they have demanded tax reductions. Therefore, many governments have faced increasing financial problems.

The amount of debt a government has outstanding also can affect its ability to respond to changes in its economic environment. High levels of debt require a government to use a high proportion of its revenues to pay interest and repay principal. As revenues decrease, this proportion increases, making it more difficult for a government to meet its other needs. Because a government does not have owners, financial leverage does not increase return on equity as it does for corporations. It does permit a government to provide services it could not otherwise afford. Debt permits a government to acquire long-term assets that would be difficult to finance with current revenues. If debt increases at a higher rate than revenues, however, a government may find it increasingly difficult to meet debt service requirements and other service needs.

Approximately 14% of federal revenues currently are required to meet interest payments. This high debt service requirement makes it more difficult for the federal government to meet its other needs without raising taxes or increasing its deficit. Also, the debt makes it difficult for the federal government to stimulate economic recovery during a recession. This difficulty is one factor contributing to the prolonged recession of the early 1990s.

A primary concern of creditors is the ability of an organization to make its interest and principal payments. Bond rating agencies, such as Moody's and Standard and Poor's, rate many government bonds. Rating categories are similar to those used for corporations. Investors typically consider the rating in making investment decisions. AAA rated bonds are safer than those rated AA or lower. Lower rated bonds normally have higher yields than higher rated bonds. The higher yields compensate investors for higher default risk.

Governments issue two primary types of bonds. **General obligation bonds** are repaid from general government revenues. They are obligations of the general government and are used to finance activities of the general government. **Revenue bonds** are repaid from enterprise fund revenues. They are obligations of these funds and are used to finance their activities.

Economic factors, the stability and growth of revenues and expenditures, and growth in long-term obligations affect bond ratings. Increases in the ratio of long-term debt to revenues or interest and debt payments to total revenues (or expenditures) indicate higher default risk. Exhibit 15-12 illustrates the relationship between debt service on general obligation bonds and total governmental fund revenues. Debt service is the amount of interest and principal paid each year.

Exhibit 15-12 Relationship Between Debt Service and Total Revenues—State of Washington

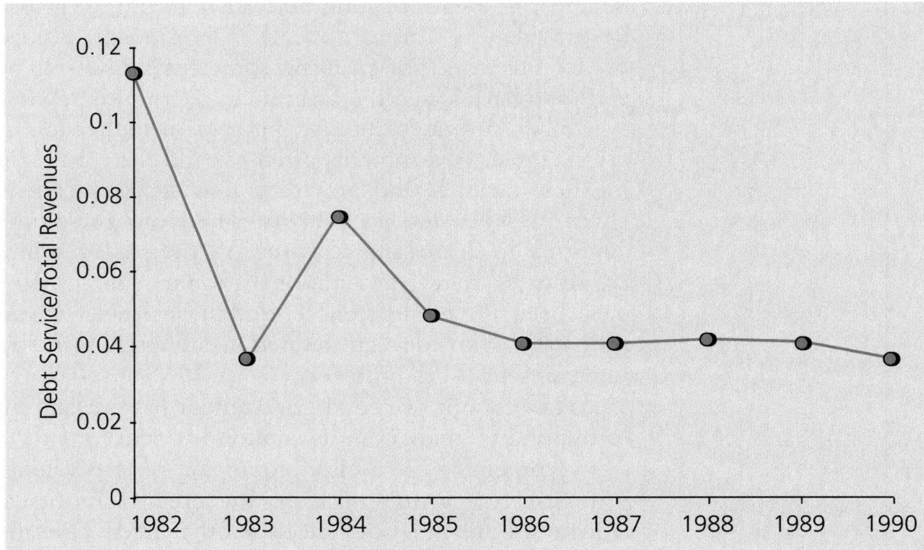

Governments that have defaulted on their debt, such as New York City in the 1970s, generally have experienced a long-run trend in debt growth relative to revenues. A financial crisis occurs when creditors are unwilling to continue to lend to the government. Cash flows from revenues are inadequate to provide required services and make interest and debt payments. Washington's debt service requirements have decreased relative to its revenues since 1982 and have remained relatively stable since 1986.

Default is more common for revenue than general obligation bonds. Revenue bonds finance specific projects, such as utilities. Earnings from the projects are used to repay the debt. Unprofitable projects may be unable to repay interest and principal. The ratio of interest and principal payments to enterprise fund earnings is a commonly used measure of debt paying ability. Some revenue bonds are backed by the general government. If an enterprise fund is unable to make payments, the general government is obligated to make them. Not all revenue bonds are backed in this way. Therefore, investors should be cautious about these arrangements.

Compliance

Compliance is an important issue for governments and some nonprofit organizations. Legal restrictions constrain the use of many resources. They limit the amount of spending for different services and require some resources be used only for specific purposes. Federal and state governments often identify the purpose for which a particular grant can be used. Governments and other grant recipients must demonstrate that they have complied with these requirements. Otherwise, they may be required to repay the grants.

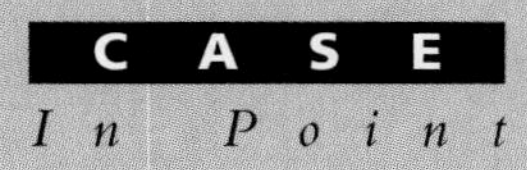

In 1991 and 1992 the federal government required several universities to repay millions of dollars in federal grants. The charging by the universities of certain costs to the grants was considered by the federal government to be improper.

Governments and other grant recipients are audited for compliance with laws and grant restrictions. In addition, most nonbusiness financial statements are audited for conformance with Generally Accepted Accounting Principles (GAAP). Audit reports and other disclosures in annual reports describe the audit findings. Major compliance problems are uncommon. Departure from GAAP is much more common, however, among nonbusiness organizations than it is among major corporations. A review of notes to the financial statements usually will reveal how a government accounts for restricted resources and grants.

SELF-STUDY PROBLEM 15-3

A combined statement of revenues, expenditures, and changes in fund balances is provided below for Green Acres County for the year ended June 30, 1995.

(in Thousands)	General	Special Revenue	Debt Service	Capital Projects
Revenues:				
Sales taxes	$ 978	$	$	$
Property taxes	524			
Licenses, permits, and fees	95	51		
Grants-in-aid	167	122		
Total Revenues	1,764	173		

(in Thousands)	General	Special Revenue	Debt Service	Capital Projects
Expenditures:				
Current:				
General government	220			8
Human services	494			14
Parks and recreation	112	68		4
Education	743	113		23
Capital outlays	107			144
Debt service:				
Principal			40	
Interest			18	
Total Expenditures	1,676	181	58	193
Excess of Revenues Over (Under) Expenditures	88	(8)	(58)	(193)
Other Financing Sources (Uses)				
Bond sale proceeds				200
Operating transfers in			55	
Operating transfers out	(50)			(5)
Total Other Financing Sources (Uses)	(50)		55	195
Excess of Revenues and Other Sources Over (Under) Expenditures and Other Uses	38	(8)	(3)	2
Fund Balances:				
Fund balances, July 1	315	109	7	20
Fund Balances, June 30	$ 353	$101	$ 4	$ 22

Required

Answer each of the following questions:

a. What economic factors are likely to affect each of the county's revenue sources?
b. What economic factors are likely to affect each of its expenditures?
c. Should citizens be concerned about the excess of expenditures over revenues for the special revenue, debt service, and capital projects funds?
d. Does the county appear to be able to meet its service requirements, including debt service?
e. Does the amount of debt issued by the county appear to be reasonable?

The solution to Self-Study Problem 15-3 appears at the end of the chapter.

REVIEW *Summary of Important Concepts*

1. Purposes of nonbusiness organizations:
   A. Nonbusiness organizations can be classified into two general groups: governments and nonprofit organizations. Governments provide a variety of services at the federal, state, and local levels. Nonprofit (or not-for-profit) organizations include religious, education, health, and civic organizations.

   B. Most government services are not sold at a price to cover the cost of the service. Some cannot be sold because they are not separable. Other services are not provided in markets because society desires these be available to everyone.
2. Control:
   A. Individuals do not hold title to a nonbusiness organization. Stock is not issued by these organizations. Control resides in elected or appointed oversight groups, such as boards, councils, commissions, trustees, and legislatures.
   B. Democratic control substitutes for market control in government and nonprofit organizations. Citizens elect representatives who set public policies and manage the affairs of government.
   C. Because profits and competitive markets are not available as controls, other controls are important in nonbusiness accounting. Accounting controls used by nonbusiness organizations include budgets, fund accounting, and encumbrances.
3. Accounting measurement:
   A. A budget identifies the financial resources that an organization expects to receive, their source, and how they will be used. For many nonbusiness organizations, an annual budget provides a basis of comparison for determining whether managers are obtaining and using resources appropriately.
   B. Governmental funds account for service activities supported primarily by taxes and fees rather than by sales of goods and services. Proprietary funds account for activities involving the sale of goods and services. Fiduciary funds account for activities in which a government serves as trustee or agent for resource providers and recipients.
   C. In addition to funds, governments use two account groups. The general fixed asset group accounts for fixed assets financed by general government revenues. Fixed assets of proprietary and some fiduciary funds are accounted for by these funds. The general long-term debt group accounts for long-term obligations that will be paid from general government revenues. Long-term obligations of proprietary and some fiduciary funds are accounted for by these funds.
   D. Nonprofit organizations such as colleges and hospitals use funds that are separated into two general categories: unrestricted and restricted.
   E. Some funds of nonbusiness organizations use a financial resources measurement focus. This focus is different from the capital maintenance focus used by businesses. The types of accounts used by these funds and the elements of the accounting model depend on which measurement focus a fund uses.
4. Accounting reports:
   A. Combined financial statements report summaries for each fund type. Combining statements report account balances for all funds of the same type.
   B. The GASB establishes accounting and financial reporting standards for state and local governments and government sponsored institutions in the U.S. The FASB establishes accounting standards for other nonprofit organizations.
5. Analysis:
   A. Factors that should be considered in evaluating a government's performance include: its economic environment, effectiveness and efficiency of its operating activities, its operating and financial leverage, and its compliance with legal and other restrictions.

DEFINE *Terms and Concepts Defined in this Chapter*

account group
appropriation
budget
encumbrance
expenditure
financial resources measurement focus
fund
fund balance

SOLUTIONS

SELF-STUDY PROBLEM 15-1

A budget could be established to indicate the amount of revenues expected from the tax levy. The amount of the levy determines how much will be appropriated for use by the jail. A comparison of actual and budgeted amounts will demonstrate whether the taxes levied were received and whether the appropriation was overspent. A separate special revenue fund could be established to account for the taxes and their expenditure. Revenues received by the fund would be restricted for use by the jail. Financial statements for the fund would compare revenues and expenditures for the fiscal period. Encumbrance accounting could be used to prevent overspending. As supplies, equipment, and other items are ordered, the expected cost of these items could be encumbered. The encumbrance would reduce the spendable balance in the jail's account, so it could not spend more than was appropriated.

A competitive market does not exist for most government services. Governments must levy taxes to provide resources to pay the cost of services. Without a competitive market, incentives do not exist to control costs and use resources effectively. Accounting controls limit the use of resources and constrain spending to predetermined levels.

SELF-STUDY PROBLEM 15-2

a. Major sources of revenue include sales taxes, property taxes, licenses, fees, permits, and grants.
b. Primary services are human services, such as health care and welfare, education, and parks and recreation.
c. The special revenue funds receive revenues from licenses, fees, and permits and from grants. Fees are probably for use of parks and from recreational activities. They probably are used to support these services. Grants are probably used primarily for education.
d. The general fund accounts for resources used to provide general government services that are not restricted to specific purposes. Special revenue funds account for resources restricted for specific purposes, such as grants restricted for education. The debt service fund accounts for general revenues appropriated to pay interest and repay principal on general government debt. Capital projects funds account for appropriations and other financing sources, such as bonds, used to construct fixed assets.
e. Government revenues are inflows resulting in net increases in government resources. Other financing sources include inflows associated with transfers from one fund to another or with the issuance of debt. Transfers are not a net increase in government resources. They shift resources from one fund to another. Bonds and other obligations must be repaid. Therefore, they are not net increases in government resources, either. Governmental funds use a financial resources measurement focus. They account for inflows and outflows of financial resources during a period. These inflows are recognized if they are available to provide services during a period. Outflows are recognized if they are used to provide services during a period. Thus, the operating statement measures the net change in financial resources associated with services provided for a fiscal period. Both capital outlays, outflows for fixed assets, and inflows from issuing debt are included as part of the total change in financial resources for a period.

SELF-STUDY PROBLEM 15-3

a. Sales taxes are affected by the amount of sales generated by businesses in the county during the year. Tax rates also affect the amount of revenues. Higher sales or higher rates will increase revenues. Property taxes are affected by property values and the assessment of the values, as well as the property tax rate. Licenses, fees, and permits depend on the amount of these items issued during the year. Grants depend on the abilities of grantors to provide grants and on the ability of the county to demonstrate a need for the grants and that grant requirements have been met. Except for grants, these revenues depend on economic and demographic factors, such as the numbers and incomes of tax payers. If personal income is higher, taxpayers will spend more and generate higher sales taxes. An increase in population will increase sales and probably increase property values.

b. The numbers, ages, and incomes of county residents have a major effect on service demands. Expenditures for education increase as the number of children increase. Lower income residents usually require higher levels of human services, such as health care and welfare. Increases in the number of elderly residents also tend to increase human service needs.

c. Debt service and capital projects funds usually do not receive much revenue. These funds receive transfers from the general fund to meet their expenditure requirements. Capital projects funds often issue bonds or other long-term debt to pay for construction. Therefore, excesses of expenditures over revenues in these funds is normal. The excess of expenditures over revenues in the special revenue fund is relatively small. The fund has a sufficient balance to cover the excess. Therefore, it is not likely to be a problem. A problem arises if the general or special revenue funds incur large excesses of expenditures over revenues, after adjusting for other financing sources and uses, over several years.

d. The county's total revenues and other financing sources are larger than its expenditures and other financing uses. The county does not appear to be facing any financial problems at present.

e. Capital outlays of the capital projects funds were $144,000 for the year. Bond proceeds of $200,000 were received. Part of the bond proceeds may be used to fund completion of capital projects funds that were begun in the current year. No indication exists of a problem with the amount of bonds issued and their use. A problem might exist if bonds were issued to meet current operating needs because of a deficit in the general fund.

EXERCISES

15-1. Write a short definition for each of the terms listed in the *Terms and Concepts Defined in this Chapter* section.

15-2. Recipients of government services often do not pay directly for these services or they pay less than the cost of providing the services. Why are the costs of these services not charged directly to users? What effect does the lack of direct payment have on accounting for governments?

15-3. What are the primary differences between governments and other nonprofit organizations? How do the major revenue sources differ between governments and nonprofit organizations?

15-4. Compare the transformation processes of nonbusiness organizations with those of businesses. Who owns nonbusiness organizations?

15-5. How do democratic controls differ from market controls? What are the disadvantages of democratic controls?

15-6. Identify three types of accounting controls often used by nonbusiness organizations and describe the purpose of each.

15-7. The City Council of the City of Lost Valley appropriated $50,000 for office supplies to be used by the general government for the fiscal year beginning October 1, 1994. On October 15, the City's purchasing agent ordered $15,000 of office supplies. The supplies were received on November 8 along with a bill. A check was mailed to the supplier on December 3. Identify the accounting controls that the City should use to ensure proper accounting for the appropriation and purchase of supplies.

15-8. Identify the types of funds and account groups that might appear in each of the following government fund categories: governmental funds, proprietary funds, and fiduciary funds. What is the purpose of each fund category? How do funds differ from account groups?

15-9. The following transactions occurred for the of City of Spruce Gap during a recent fiscal year:

a. Collected property taxes to support public schools.
b. Collected sales taxes to support general government services.
c. Collected gasoline taxes to support street construction and maintenance.
d. Charged users for water.
e. Made investments to provide retirement benefits for employees.
f. Paid principal and interest on general debt.
g. Recorded long-term debt issued by the general government.
h. Paid for the construction of a new fire station.
i. Charged governmental departments for use of services provided by the government's computer center.
j. Recorded general government assets acquired.

Identify the fund type or account group that would be used to account for each transaction.

15-10. The City of Blue Springs purchased a garbage truck on January 1, 1994 at a cost of $40,000. Garbage services are paid out of general government revenues. The truck had an expected useful life of 10 years. The truck was paid for by issuing a long-term note to a local bank. The Garbage Express, a private sanitation company, purchased an identical truck on January 1, 1994. It also issued a long-term note. It depreciated the truck using straight-line depreciation. On December 31, 1998, the City of Blue Springs and The Garbage Express both sold their trucks for $17,000. How would the purchase of the trucks and related transactions affect the financial statements of the city and the company for the fiscal year ended December 31, 1994? How would the sale of the trucks on December 31, 1998 affect the financial statements of the city and the company?

15-11. The County of Dry Gulch adopted an annual budget for its 1995 fiscal year that included an appropriation of $2,300,000 for highway construction and maintenance. Ten months into the 1995 fiscal year, the highway department had spent $2,280,000. What is the purpose of the budget appropriation? What action could the highway department take when it had expended its appropriation?

15-12. Tri-County Community College uses the following funds to account for its financial activities: current unrestricted fund, current restricted fund, loan fund, endowment fund, and plant fund. Explain the purpose of each fund and why the college uses separate funds to control its financial activities.

15-13. The City of Frosty Mountain fire department received an appropriation of $300,000 for equipment for the fiscal year that began on October 1, 1994. By August 1, 1995, the fire department had recorded expenditures of $250,000 for equipment. On August 15, 1995, the fire department ordered additional equipment that it expected to cost $48,000. How would the event of August 15 affect the city's accounting records for the fire department? Why?

15-14. What are the primary distinctions between the financial resources measurement focus used by governments and the capital maintenance focus used by businesses?

15-15. What is meant by a "financial reporting entity?" What criteria should a government consider in determining the organizations to include in its accounting reports? How do these criteria differ from those used by businesses?

15-16. Governmental organizations may include combined and combining individual fund statements in their annual accounting reports. How do these statements differ? Why are these types of financial statements provided?

15-17. During its 1994 fiscal year, the general fund of the City of Stone Ridge reported interfund transfers of $40,000 to the debt service fund and $75,000 to the capital projects fund. What are interfund transfers and how do they affect a government's financial statements?

15-18. The County of Golden Flats reported the following information in its combined fund balance sheet for 1995:

Fund balance:	
Reserved for:	
Encumbrances	$ 6,500
Restricted accounts	28,000
Unreserved:	
Designated for debt service	50,000
Undesignated	260,000
Total fund balance	$344,500

Why does the county separate its fund balance into reserved, unreserved, designated, and undesignated amounts?

15-19. The City of Red Bluff issued $1 million of bonds during its 1995 fiscal year to construct a new city building. Also, it reported a payment of $200,000 during the year to repay principle on debt issued in a prior year that was used to acquire plant assets. How would these transactions affect the statement of revenues, expenditures, and changes in fund balance of the city in 1995? How would similar transactions of a business organization affect its financial statements?

15-20. The City of Rolling Hills received a grant from the federal government to assist in construction of a new elementary school. The city is required to use the grant only for this purpose, or the federal government will require the grant to be repaid. How can the city's accounting system help it ensure compliance with the grant restrictions?

PROBLEMS

PROBLEM 15-1 Fund Accounts

The table provided below lists account titles that might appear in the balance sheets of various governmental funds and account groups.

	General	Debt Service	Capital Projects	General Fixed Assets	General Long-Term Debt
Cash					
Taxes receivable					
Land					
Buildings					
Construction in process					
Amount available for debt service					

	General	Debt Service	Capital Projects	General Fixed Assets	General Long-Term Debt
Amount to be provided for debt retirement					
Accounts payable					
Bonds payable					
Investment in general fixed assets					
Fund balance					

Required Place an X in the appropriate boxes to indicate the funds in which each account might appear. Some accounts might appear in several funds or account groups.

PROBLEM 15-2 Comparing Governmental and Proprietary Balance Sheets

Examine the balance sheets of the governmental (Exhibit 15-5) and proprietary (Exhibit 15-8) funds for the State of Washington provided in this chapter.

Required Identify similarities and differences in the reporting of the following types of accounts on these balance sheets for the general fund and enterprise funds: cash, receivables, due from or due to other funds, plant assets, accounts payable, bonds payable, contributed capital, retained earnings, fund balance. Explain why the similarities or differences occur.

PROBLEM 15-3 Evaluating Fund Statements

A combined statement of revenues, expenditures, and changes in fund balances is provided below for the City of Flint Creek.

(in Thousands)	General	Special Revenue	Debt Service	Capital Projects
Revenues:				
Sales taxes	$1,956	$	$	$
Property taxes	1,048			
Licenses, permits, and fees	190	102		
Grants-in-aid	334	244		
Total Revenues	3,528	346		
Expenditures:				
Current:				
General government	440			16
Human services	988			28
Parks and recreation	224	136		8
Education	1,486	226		46
Capital outlays	214			288
Debt service:				
Principal			80	
Interest			36	
Total Expenditures	3,352	362	116	386

(in Thousands)	General	Special Revenue	Debt Service	Capital Projects
Excess of Revenues Over (Under) Expenditures	176	(16)	(116)	(386)
Other Financing Sources (Uses)				
Bond sale proceeds				400
Operating transfers in			110	
Operating transfers out	(100)			(10)
Total Other Financing Sources (Uses)	(100)		110	390
Excess of Revenues and Other Sources Over (Under) Expenditures and Other Uses	76	(16)	(6)	4
Fund Balances:				
Fund Balances, July 1	730	218	14	40
Fund Balances, June 30	$ 806	$202	$ 8	$ 44

Required Answer each of the following questions:

a. What are the city's major sources of revenue?
b. What primary services does the city provide?
c. What were the major revenues of the special revenue funds? What were their primary uses?
d. Why are bond sale proceeds listed among other financing sources of the capital projects fund?
e. As a taxpayer of the city, would you be concerned that some of the funds reported an excess of expenditures and other uses over revenues and other sources? Evaluate the financial performance of Flint Creek for the current fiscal year.

PROBLEM 15-4 Evaluating Revenues and Expenditures

Information is provided below from the general funds of two counties, Endover and Flagship.

	1990	1991	1992	1993	1994
Endover					
Revenues	$2,645	$2,759	$2,768	$2,755	$2,620
Expenditures	2,497	2,752	2,774	2,786	2,803
Flagship					
Revenues	$ 505	$ 512	$ 524	$ 553	$ 590
Expenditures	500	509	520	557	586

Required Graph the relationship between revenues and expenditures for each city. Evaluate their relative performances and describe any problems you believe the cities are experiencing.

PROBLEM 15-5 Analyzing Fund Statements

Information is provided below from the 1991 statement of revenues, expenditures, and changes in fund balances of the State of Indiana:

(in Thousands)	General	Special Revenue	Expendable Trust
Revenues:			
Taxes	$4,752,819	$1,778,285	
Licenses, Permits and Franchises	15,591	187,669	
Current Service Charges	195,628	289,204	$ 7,464
Sales	17,284	8,089	
Grants	51,493	2,510,923	395,301
Other	9,257	313,574	9,515
Total Revenues	5,042,072	5,087,744	412,280
Expenditures:			
Current:			
General Government	545,459	1,052,422	1,669
Public Safety	216,474	277,964	
Health	327,733	161,407	
Welfare	627,155	2,301,722	
Conservation, Culture and Development	112,657	496,531	377,515
Education	2,576,070	388,765	
Transportation	1,693	858,460	
Miscellaneous	44	67,293	
Capital Outlay	0	0	
Total Expenditures	4,407,285	5,604,564	379,184
Excess of Revenue Over (Under) Expenditures	634,787	(516,820)	33,096
Other Financing Sources (Uses):			
Operating Transfers In	478,652	1,728,110	16,338
Operating Transfers Out	(1,276,371)	(1,160,386)	(11,296)
Total Other Financing Sources (Uses)	(797,719)	567,724	5,042
Excess of Revenues and Other Sources Over (Under) Expenditures and Other Uses	(162,932)	50,904	38,138
Fund Balance, July 1,1990	1,583,020	1,177,722	216,395
Fund Balance, June 30, 1991	1,420,088	1,228,626	254,533

Required Answer each of the following questions:

(a) Did Indiana generate sufficient general government revenues to meet its operating needs during 1991? Explain.

(b) What purposes were served by the special revenue fund? Why were these services not accounted for by the general fund?

(c) What purposes were served by the expendable trust fund? Why were these services not accounted for by the general fund or the special revenue fund?

PROBLEM 15-6 Comparing General Obligation and Revenue Bonds

The City of Silver Falls issued general obligation bonds during its 1996 fiscal year to construct a new city hall. In addition, it issued revenue bonds for construction of a parking garage.

Required (a) Distinguish between general obligation and revenue bonds with respect to purpose, source of funding for repayment of the debt, and risk. (b) Identify how the two bond issues would be reported in the city's 1996 annual report.

PROBLEM 15-7 Evaluating Financial and Operating Leverage

Financial and operating leverage of businesses affect the variability in profitability and return from operating activities of the businesses as operating revenues change. Thus, they affect business risk. Governmental and nonprofit organizations use long-term debt as a source of financing and often employ large proportions of fixed costs.

Required In what ways are financial and operating leverage relevant for analyzing the financial activities of nonbusiness organizations?

PROBLEM 15-8 Evaluating the Purpose of Governmental Accounting Reports

A major concept underlying governmental accounting is the principle of intergenerational equity. This principle maintains that those who are entitled to receive services from a governmental organization during a particular period should be responsible for paying for the services a government provides during that period. Therefore, except for the federal government, most governments are prohibited from using long-term debt to finance operating costs associated with current services. Long-term borrowing for operating purposes permits a government to shift the burden of paying for current services from current taxpayers to future taxpayers.

Required Explain how the accounting measurement and reporting rules used by state and local governments help oversight groups, managers, and citizens evaluate intergenerational equity.

PROBLEM 15-9 Evaluating Tax Burden

Information is provided below from the 1991 annual reports of the State of New Jersey and the State of Ohio. The table provides information about total state tax revenues and about total personal income of residents of each state.

in millions	New Jersey		Ohio	
	Taxes	**Income**	**Taxes**	**Income**
1986	7,783	141,919	8,258	148,972
1987	8,945	156,145	8,855	157,250
1988	9,325	170,914	9,509	168,756
1989	9,870	182,882	10,356	180,197
1990	9,766	192,893	10,875	190,720

Required Calculate the ratio of tax revenues to personal income for each year for each state. Compare these ratios and evaluate the relative tax burdens of citizens in the two states.

PROBLEM 15-10 Multiple Choice Overview

1. A difference between business and nonbusiness organizations is:
   a. nonbusiness organizations do not engage in financing activities.
   b. nonbusiness organizations do not engage in investing activities.

c. nonbusiness organizations do not engage in operating activities.
d. nonbusiness organizations do not receive investments from owners.

2. A plan that identifies how a government expects to obtain financial resources and how it expects to use those resources is:
   a. an appropriation
   b. a fund
   c. a budget
   d. an encumbrance
3. Which of the following attributes describe account groups:

	They are fiscal entities	**They are accounting entities**
a.	Yes	Yes
b.	Yes	No
c.	No	Yes
d.	No	No

4. A government accounts for activities involving the sale of goods and services primarily in its:
   a. governmental funds
   b. proprietary funds
   c. fiduciary funds
   d. account groups
5. Financial resources that will be used to pay interest and principal on long-term debt of a general government are accounted for by a government's:
   a. debt service fund
   b. capital projects fund
   c. fiduciary fund
   d. long-term debt account group
6. When a government orders supplies, it often limits the amount of additional payments that can be made from its supplies account by recording:
   a. an appropriation
   b. an encumbrance
   c. an expenditure
   d. a revenue
7. A financial statement that reports account balances for all capital projects funds would be:
   a. an individual fund statement
   b. a combining statement
   c. a combined statement
   d. a consolidated statement
8. Bonds issued by a general government to pay for the construction of a new building would be reported by the government as:
   a. a liability on the general fund balance sheet but would not be included on the operating statement.
   b. a liability on the general fund balance sheet and as a revenue on the operating statement.
   c. a liability listed on the general long-term debt group balance sheet and as an other revenue source on the operating statement.
   d. would not be reported on the balance sheet but would be listed as an other revenue source on the operating statement.
9. The purchase of equipment by an enterprise fund is:
   a. recorded as an expenditure in the period that it is purchased.
   b. recorded as an asset in the general fixed asset account group.
   c. recorded as an asset of the enterprise fund and depreciated over its useful life.
   d. recorded as an asset of the enterprise fund and is expensed when it is sold or retired from service.
10. The ability to adapt to changing financial conditions is an important attribute of:

	Business Organizations	Nonbusiness Organizations
a.	Yes	Yes
b.	Yes	No
c.	No	Yes
d.	No	No

PROJECTS

PROJECT 15-1 Comparing Financial Statements

Obtain a recent annual report of a nonprofit organization. Compare the organization's financial statements with those of a business organization. Write a short report describing the primary differences you observe.

PROJECT 15-2 Evaluating Governmental Performance

Use a periodical index to identify a recent magazine or newspaper article that describes a bond rating change for a state or local government. Review the article and summarize the primary factors discussed that explain why the rating was changed. Identify any accounting information referenced in the article that was used by the bond rating agency in its decision.

PROJECT 15-3 Evaluating Governmental Revenues

Obtain a recent financial statement for a local government. Examine the revenues reported in the government's statement of revenues, expenditures, and changes in fund balance. Write a short report summarizing the primary sources of revenue for the government. Are revenues derived from a variety of sources, or does the government depend on one or two primary sources? How important are intergovernmental grants to the governments overall revenues? Is the government generating sufficient revenues to meet its current service needs?

PROJECT 15-4 Evaluating Governmental Debt

Use the annual report of a local government to evaluate changes in the government's general long-term debt. How has the amount of long-term debt changed over the last five years? How has the amount of debt changed relative to the government's general revenues? Does the government's ability to meet its debt service requirements appear to be increasing or decreasing?

PROJECT 15-5 Comparing Revenues and Expenditures

Use annual reports or other sources of accounting information to identify the general government revenues and expenditures for three major cities in three different geographic regions. Prepare a table comparing the revenues and expenditures of each city for the past five years. Summarize your findings by describing the relative strengths and weaknesses of each city as revealed by your analysis.

PROJECT 15-6 Organizations Subject to Democratic Control

Identify two organizations in your community that are not subject to market control but are subject to democratic control. For each of those two organizations, find out how democratic control is implemented. Write a brief report discussing your findings. Your report should include, along with other information, the name of the office, group, or governing board making decisions, how many persons serve on the oversight group, how they are selected, and the length of their terms of office.

APPENDICES

APPENDIX A

Sources of Information About Companies and Industries

Many college and public libraries contain publications that provide information about companies and industries. The following listing describes some of the publications you may find useful. The listing is not comprehensive. Check with your librarian for other publications that may be available in your library.

Industry Classification

- The *Standard Industrial Classification Manual* categorizes companies by standard industrial classification (SIC) code. Companies with the same classification codes produce similar products. Other reference materials often use SIC codes to identify companies and industries.

Indexes to Journal and Newspaper Articles

- *Predicasts F&S Index* identifies and summarizes articles from more than 750 publications about products, industries, and companies.
- The *Business Periodicals Index* identifies articles in major business journals by topic.
- *The Accounting and Tax Index* identifies articles in accounting and business journals associated with accounting topics.
- *The Wall Street Journal Index* identifies articles from *The Wall Street Journal* by company and topic.
- The *New York Times Index* identifies articles from the *New York Times* by company and topic.

Business Periodicals

- *Forbes* provides descriptive articles on many companies and industries. Special issues provide summary information for large companies.

- *Fortune* provides descriptive articles on many companies and industries. Special issues provide summary accounting information for large U.S. and foreign companies.
- *Business Week* provides general coverage of a wide variety of business issues, including selected industries and companies.
- *The Wall Street Journal* provides daily coverage of major events related to specific companies and industries.
- *Barron's* provides various economic and financial indicators.

Financial Services

- *Standard & Poor's Corporation Records* provides information on over 6,000 companies.
- Standard & Poor's *Industry Surveys* provides detailed analysis of over 50 industries.
- Standard & Poor's *Stock Reports* provides concise descriptions of major corporations.
- *Moody's Industrial Manual, Moody's Bank and Financial Manual, Moody's Public Utilities Manual, Moody's Transportation Manual,* and *Moody's Municipal & Government Manual* provide detailed information about major organizations of each type. These manuals are published annually.
- *Value Line Investment Survey* provides analysis and commentary on major industries and companies.

Computer Services

- *Dow Jones Information Services* provide on-line computer access to news, financial, and economic indicators.
- *National Automated Accounting Research System (NAARS)* provides computer access to news, financial statement, and other accounting information for major corporations.
- *Compact Disclosure* provides accounting and other information on over 13,000 corporations.

Government Economic and Industry Publications

- A variety of economic indicators are provided in government publications such as *Survey of Current Business, Economic Indicators,* and the *Federal Reserve Bulletin.*
- The Department of Commerce publishes economic censuses of various types of industries, such as retail, wholesale, service, and manufacturing. It also publishes *U.S. Industrial Outlook,* providing an analysis of prospects for major industries.

Industry Ratios

- Industry averages for a variety of ratios and other accounting measures are available in *Standard & Poor's Analysts Handbook,* Robert Morris Associate's *Annual Statement Studies,* Dunn & Bradstreet's *Industry Norms & Key Business Ratios,* and the Department of Commerce's *Statistical Abstract of the United States.*

APPENDIX B

General Mills, Inc. Financial Report

MANAGEMENT DISCUSSION OF RESULTS OF OPERATIONS AND FINANCIAL CONDITION

General Mills' financial goal is to achieve performance that places us in the top 10 percent of major American companies, ranked by the combination of growth in earnings per share and return on capital over a five-year period.

Our major financial targets for top-decile performance include:

- Averaging 13 to 14 percent earnings per share growth over a five-year period. We have exceeded this goal since 1988, delivering average annual growth in earnings per share of 17 percent.
- Improving after-tax return on sales to a minimum of 7.0 percent by 1995. Our previous goal of reaching a 6.5 percent after-tax ROS by 1994 was achieved in 1992.
- Meeting or exceeding a 20 percent after-tax return on invested capital and 38 percent return on equity. Our return on invested capital has averaged 21 percent and our ROE has averaged 44 percent during the past five years.
- Maintaining a solid balance sheet with a strong "A" bond rating. Financial ratios, including a fixed charge coverage of 8.6 times and a debt-to-total-capital ratio of 53 percent, continued strong in 1992. Cash flow from operations also remained strong.
- Increasing dividends in line with long-term growth in earnings per share and paying out up to 50 percent of earnings. The $1.48 per share dividend in 1992 represents 49 percent of earnings per share. The indicated annual dividend of $1.68 per share for 1993 is a 14 percent increase.

The combined earnings per share growth and return on invested capital achieved in 1992 again placed General Mills in the top 10 percent of major corporations. Meeting our financial objectives will help ensure our ability to provide superior returns to shareholders in the years ahead.

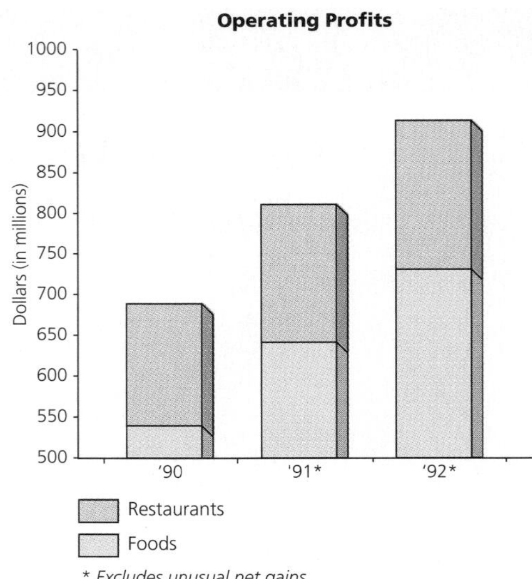

Results of Operations

Earnings per share from continuing operations were $3.05 compared to $2.82 in 1991. After-tax earnings were $505.6 million compared to $464.2 million a year ago. The figures for 1991 include an unusual net after-tax gain of $26.5 million, or 16 cents per share, from the sales of the O-Cel-O sponge and Lancia Bravo pasta operations and restructuring charges for Yoplait yogurt and hot cereals. Excluding these unusual items, earnings and earnings per share for 1992 increased 16 percent and 15 percent, respectively. Sales rose 9 percent to $7.78 billion; excluding revenues from operations disposed of since 1991, sales grew 11 percent.

Segment operating results are summarized in note seventeen to the Consolidated Financial Statements.

Consumer Foods 1992 sales grew 6 percent to $5.23 billion and operating profits increased 8 percent to $744.3 million. Unusual items in 1992 of $17.5 million included a gain on the sale of PYCASA, our Spanish frozen food subsidiary, partially offset by charges for restructuring Betty Crocker packaged mixes production, European food operations and our Consumer Foods national sales organization. Fiscal 1991 operating profits included a net gain of $48.2 million for unusual items. Excluding these items from both years, the increase in 1992 operating profits was 13 percent.

Total domestic retail packaged foods unit volume grew 7 percent, led by gains in Betty Crocker Products, Big G cereals and Yoplait yogurt. In addition, Foodservice and General Mills Canada reported strong volume gains led by ready-to-eat cereals. Only the flour milling businesses reported results substantially below the prior-year level resulting from lower margin levels. In 1991, sales and operating profits grew 9 percent and 20 percent (excluding unusual items), respectively, with market share maintained or increased in all major product categories except Gorton's frozen seafood and Yoplait yogurt, which had declines in volume and market share.

CPW, our international cereal strategic alliance with Nestlé, achieved strong volume and share gains in France, Spain and Portugal, and initiated operations in Italy during 1992. Including operations in the U.K., CPW's sales reached $237 million. Total Consumer Foods 1992 operating profits include a loss of $25.8 million for General Mills' share of CPW's losses. The joint venture is in the heavy investment stage with positive earnings from initial markets expected in the mid-1990s.

Restaurants 1992 sales and operating profits grew 15 percent and 11 percent of $2.54 billion and $190.8 million, respectively. Results reflect increased operational efficiencies at Red Lobster USA and strong gains by The Olive Garden throughout the year, as well as the addition of 120 units in North America. Performance by the Canadian restaurants was well below the prior year's results reflecting depressed consumer spending in a weak economic environment. Restaurants sales and operating profits in 1991 increased 15 percent and 12 percent, respectively, reflecting volume gains by existing restaurants and the addition of 111 units.

Interest expense in 1992 was $75.9 million, down $8.2 million from 1991 due to lower rates and short-term borrowings, increased capitalized interest and reduced interest related to prior year's income taxes. Interest income was $17.7 million, $5.3 million less than 1991 primarily reflecting lower rates. The 1991 interest expense of $84.1 million was $22.8 million greater than 1990. This was attributable to increased long-term borrowings and higher foreign short-term debt levels. Interest income of $23.0 million was $5.9 million less than 1990 as time deposits matured. Based on the purchase in June 1992 of $128.4 million of common stock for treasury and planned investments, interest expense is expected to increase in fiscal 1993.

It is management's view that changes in the rate of inflation have not significantly affected profitability from continuing operations over the three most recent fiscal years. Management attempts to minimize the effects of inflation through appropriate planning and operating practices.

The Financial Accounting Standards Board issued Statement of Financial Accounting Standards No. 109, "Accounting for Income Taxes," in February 1992. This statement requires the use of the liability method of accounting for deferred income taxes and the company is required to adopt the standard by fiscal 1994. At the current corporate income tax rate, the net deferred income tax balance would be reduced upon adoption but the amount of the reduction has not yet been determined.

Financial Condition

General Mills' balance sheet and overall financial condition remain strong. The company intends to manage its businesses and financial ratios so as to maintain a strong "A" bond rating, which will allow access to financing at reasonable costs. Currently, General Mills' publicly issued long-term debt carries "A+" (Moody's Investors Services, Inc.) and "A1" (Standard & Poor's Corporation) ratings. Our commercial paper has ratings of "P-1" (Moody's) and "A-1+" (Standard & Poor's) in the U.S. and "R-1 (middle)" in Canada from Dominion Bond Rating Service.

While there may be fluctuations in financial returns and ratios due to various factors including purchases of common stock for treasury and planned investments, the returns and ratios are expected to be maintained at levels that will sustain our strong "A" bond rating over the long term.

The debt-to-total-capital ratio is based on management's definition of capital structure, as shown in the table at the top of the next page.

Commercial paper has historically been our primary source of short-term financing. Bank credit lines are maintained to ensure availability of short-term funds as needed.

Capital Structure

In Millions	**May 31, 1992**	**May 26, 1991**
Notes payable	**$ 169.3**	$ 23.4
Current portion of long-term debt	**32.6**	129.0
Long-term debt	**920.5**	879.0
Deferred income taxes-tax leases	**203.0**	215.8
Total debt	**1,325.4**	1,247.2
Debt adjustments:		
Leases-debt equivalent	**376.3**	314.4
Domestic cash equivalents	**(.3)**	(20.6)
Marketable investments	**(170.4)**	(167.9)
Adjusted debt	**1,531.0**	1,373.1
Stockholders' equity	**1,370.9**	1,113.5
Total capital	**$2,901.9**	$2,486.6

Our registration statement permits the issuance of up to $307.1 million net proceeds in unsecured debt securities. The registration authorizes a medium-term note program that provides additional flexibility in accessing the debt markets.

Sources and uses of cash in the past three fiscal years are shown in the table below.

Cash Sources (Uses)

In Millions	**1992**	**1991**	**1990**
From operations	**$771.6**	$544.4	$627.8
Fixed assets and other investments—net	**(725.7)**	(670.3)	(562.8)
From dispositions of businesses	**77.7**	114.6	32.6
Increase in outstanding debt—net	**91.0**	160.2	57.2
(Increase) decrease in marketable investments and time deposits	**—**	67.7	(.6)
From tax leases	**(7.9)**	(8.4)	(2.3)
Common stock issued	**39.3**	41.5	168.9
Treasury stock purchases	**(40.1)**	—	(149.9)
Dividends paid	**(245.2)**	(210.6)	(180.8)
Increase (decrease) in cash and cash equivalents	**$ (39.3)**	$ 39.1	$ (9.9)

Operations generated $227.2 million more cash in 1992 than in the previous year. This increase resulted from:

In Millions	
Increased earnings from continuing operations	$125.1
Decreased working capital	116.7
Increased use of cash by discontinued operations	(14.6)
Increase in cash from operations	$227.2

Net cash used for fixed assets and other investments increased $55.4 million over 1991. Fixed asset investments included additional cereal capacity, a new plant for European snacks, and new Red Lobster and The Olive Garden units.

Proceeds from dispositions in 1992 were from the sale of PYCASA.

Our planned fixed asset investments for the years 1993 to 1995 total $1.9 billion. In fiscal 1993, capital expenditures are estimated to be approximately $700 million. The company is anticipating a net cash outflow and will borrow either short or long term depending on market conditions.

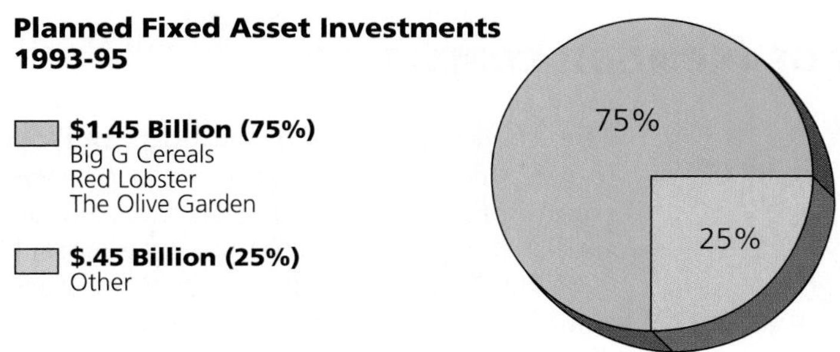

In May 1992, the company announced it entered into a joint venture agreement in principle with PepsiCo Foods International to merge six existing Continental European snack operations into one company to develop, manufacture and market snack foods. General Mills will own 40 percent of the company. The European Commission initiated its review of the joint venture in July.

REPORT OF MANAGEMENT RESPONSIBILITIES

The management of General Mills, Inc. includes corporate executives, operating managers, controllers and other personnel working full time on company business. These managers are responsible for the fairness and accuracy of our financial statements. The Audit Committee of the Board of Directors meets regularly to determine that management, internal auditors and independent auditors are properly discharging their duties regarding internal control and financial reporting.

The financial statements have been prepared in accordance with generally accepted accounting principles, using management's best estimates and judgments where appropriate. The financial information throughout this report is consistent with our financial statements.

Management has established a system of internal controls that provides reasonable assurance that, in all material respects, assets are maintained and accounted for in accordance with management's authorization, and transactions are recorded accurately on our books. Our internal controls provide for appropriate separation of duties and responsibilities, and there are documented policies regarding utilization of company assets and proper financial reporting. These formally stated and regularly communicated policies demand high ethical conduct from all employees.

We maintain a strong audit program that independently evaluates the adequacy and effectiveness of internal controls. The independent auditors, internal auditors and controllers have full and free access to the Audit Committee at any time.

KPMG Peat Marwick, independent certified public accountants, are retained to audit the consolidated financial statements. Their report follows.

H. B. Atwater, Jr.
Chairman of the Board and Chief Executive Officer

J. R. Lee
Vice Chairman and Chief Financial Officer

REPORT OF THE AUDIT COMMITTEE

The Audit Committee of the Board of Directors is composed on six outside directors. Its primary function is to oversee the Company's system of internal controls, financial reporting practices and audits to ensure their quality, integrity and objectivity are sufficient to protect stockholder assets.

The Audit Committee met twice during fiscal 1992 to review the overall audit scope, plans and results of the internal auditor and independent auditor, the Company's internal controls, emerging accounting issues, officer and director expenses, audit fees, goodwill and other intangible values, and the audits of the pension plans. The Committee also met separately without management present and with the independent auditors to discuss the audit. Acting with the other Board members, the Committee reviewed the Company's annual financial statements and approved them before issuance. Audit Committee meeting results were reported to the full Board of Directors. The Audit Committee recommended to the Board that KPMG Peat Marwick be reappointed for fiscal 1993, subject to the approval of stockholders at the annual meeting.

The Audit Committee is satisfied that the internal control system is adequate and that the stockholders of General Mills are protected by appropriate accounting and auditing procedures.

M. D. Rose
Chairman, Audit Committee

INDEPENDENT AUDITORS' REPORT

The Stockholders and the Board of Directors of General Mills, Inc.:

We have audited the accompanying consolidated balance sheets of General Mills, Inc. and subsidiaries as of May 31, 1992 and May 26, 1991, and the related consolidated statements of earnings and cash flows for each of the fiscal years in the three-year period ended May 31, 1992. These consolidated financial statements are the responsibility of the Company's management. Our responsibility is to express an opinion on these consolidated financial statements based on our audits.

We conducted our audits in accordance with generally accepted auditing standards. Those standards require that we plan and perform the audit to obtain reasonable assurance about whether the financial statements are free of material misstatement. An audit includes examining, on a test basis, evidence supporting the amounts and disclosures in the financial statements. An audit also includes assessing the accounting principles used and significant estimates made by management, as well as evaluating the overall financial statement presentation. We believe that our audits provide a reasonable basis for our opinion.

In our opinion, the consolidated financial statements referred to above present fairly, in all material respects, the financial position of General Mills, Inc. and subsidiaries as of May 31, 1992 and May 26, 1991, and the results of their operations and their cash flows for each of the fiscal years in the three-year period ended May 31, 1992 in conformity with generally accepted accounting principles.

KPMG Peat Marwick
Minneapolis, Minnesota
July 1, 1992

Consolidated Statements of Earnings

	Fiscal Year Ended		
Amounts in Millions, Except per Share Data	**May 31, 1992**	**May 26, 1991**	**May 27, 1990**
Continuing Operations:			
Sales	**$7,777.8**	$7,153.2	$6,448.3
Costs and Expenses:			
Cost of sales	**4,123.2**	3,722.1	3,485.1
Selling, general and administrative	**2,504.5**	2,386.0	2,138.0
Depreciation and amortization	**247.4**	218.4	180.1
Interest, net	**58.2**	61.1	32.4
Total Costs and Expenses	**6,933.3**	6,387.6	5,835.6
Earnings from Continuing Operations before Taxes	**844.5**	765.6	612.7
Income Taxes	**338.9**	301.4	239.0
Earnings from Continuing Operations	**505.6**	464.2	373.7
Discontinued Operations after Taxes	**(10.0)**	8.5	7.7
Net Earnings	**$ 495.6**	$ 472.7	$ 381.4
Earnings per Share:			
Continuing operations	**$ 3.05**	$ 2.82	$ 2.27
Discontinued operations	**(.06)**	.05	.05
Net Earnings per Share	**$ 2.99**	$ 2.87	$ 2.32
Average Number of Common Shares	**165.7**	164.5	164.4

See accompanying notes to consolidated financial statements.

Consolidated Balance Sheets

In Millions	**May 31, 1992**	**May 26, 1991**
Assets		
Current Assets:		
Cash and cash equivalents	**$ .5**	$ 39.8
Receivables, less allowance for doubtful accounts of $6.4 in 1992 and $6.0 in 1991	**291.9**	306.3
Inventories	**487.2**	493.6
Prepaid expenses and other current assets	**106.3**	98.5
Deferred income taxes	**148.7**	144.1
Total Current Assets	**1,034.6**	1,082.3
Land, Buildings and Equipment, at cost	**2,648.6**	2,241.3
Other Assets	**621.8**	578.2
Total Assets	**$4,305.0**	$3,901.8

In Millions	**May 31, 1992**	**May 26, 1991**
Liabilities and Stockholders' Equity		
Current Liabilities:		
Accounts payable	**$ 632.5**	$ 578.7
Current portion of long-term debt	**32.6**	129.0
Notes payable	**169.3**	23.4
Accrued taxes	**127.9**	159.2
Accrued payroll	**165.0**	154.7
Other current liabilities	**244.4**	227.4
Total Current Liabilities	**1,371.7**	1,272.4
Long-term Debt	**920.5**	879.0
Deferred Income Taxes	**231.5**	239.4
Deferred Incomes Taxes—Tax Leases	**203.0**	215.8
Accrued Postretirement Benefits	**103.6**	109.5
Other Liabilities	**103.8**	72.2
Total Liabilities	**2,934.1**	2,788.3
Stockholders' Equity:		
Cumulative preference stock, none issued	**—**	—
Common stock, 204.2 shares issued	**343.6**	320.2
Retained earnings	**2,049.0**	1,795.5
Less common stock in treasury, at cost, shares of 38.7 in 1992 and 39.1 in 1991	**(802.9)**	(777.4)
Unearned ESOP and restricted stock compensation	**(172.3)**	(177.6)
Cumulative foreign currency adjustment	**(46.5)**	(47.2)
Total Stockholders' Equity	**1,370.9**	1,113.5
Total Liabilities and Stockholders' Equity	**$4,305.0**	$3,901.8

See accompanying notes to consolidated financial statements.

Consolidated Statements of Cash Flows

	Fiscal Year Ended		
In Millions	**May 31, 1992**	**May 26, 1991**	**May 27, 1990**
Cash Flows—Operating Activities:			
Earnings from continuing operations	**$505.6**	$464.2	$373.7
Adjustments to reconcile earnings to cash flow:			
Depreciation and amortization	**247.4**	218.4	180.1
Deferred income taxes	**13.5**	.9	12.5
Change in current assets and liabilities*	**20.0**	(96.7)	113.3
Other, net	**3.9**	(38.2)	(22.5)
Cash provided by continuing operations	**790.4**	548.6	657.1
Cash provided by discontinued operations	**(18.8)**	(4.2)	(29.3)
Net Cash Provided by Operating Activities	**771.6**	544.4	627.8
Cash Flows—Investment Activities:			
Purchases of land, buildings and equipment	**(695.3)**	(554.6)	(540.0)
Investments in businesses, intangibles and affiliates	**(30.6)**	(91.6)	(.5)
Cash from disposal of land, buildings and equipment	**8.1**	9.8	12.1
Proceeds from dispositions	**77.7**	114.6	32.6
Other, net	**(7.9)**	(33.9)	(34.4)
Net Cash Used by Investment Activities	**(648.0)**	(555.7)	(530.2)

In Millions	Fiscal Year Ended May 31, 1992	May 26, 1991	May 27, 1990
Cash Flows—Financing Activities:			
Increase (decrease) in notes payable	**150.3**	(80.0)	(24.5)
Issuance of long-term debt	**188.7**	373.0	142.4
Payment of long-term debt	**(248.0)**	(132.8)	(60.7)
(Increase) decrease in marketable investments and time deposits	**—**	67.7	(.6)
Cash flows from tax leases	**(7.9)**	(8.4)	(2.3)
Common stock issued	**39.3**	41.5	168.9
Purchases of common stock for treasury	**(40.1)**	—	(149.9)
Dividends paid	**(245.2)**	(210.6)	(180.8)
Net Cash Provided (Used) by Financing Activities	**(162.9)**	50.4	(107.5)
Increase (Decrease) in Cash and Cash Equivalents	**$ (39.3)**	$ 39.1	$ (9.9)
*Cash Flow from Changes in Current Assets and Liabilities:			
Receivables	**$ 2.1**	$(47.4)	$ (1.5)
Inventories	**.6**	(109.8)	(22.4)
Prepaid expenses and other current assets	**(8.9)**	(19.0)	(6.6)
Accounts payable	**54.5**	63.1	79.1
Other current liabilities	**(28.3)**	16.4	64.7
Change in Current Assets and Liabilities	**$ 20.0**	$ (96.7)	$113.3

See accompanying notes to consolidated financial statements.

NOTES TO CONSOLIDATED FINANCIAL STATEMENTS

Note One: Summary of Significant Accounting Policies

A. Principles of Consolidation The consolidated financial statements include the following domestic and foreign operations: parent company and 100% owned subsidiaries, and General Mills' investment in and share of net earnings or losses of 20–50% owned companies.

Our fiscal year ends on the last Sunday in May. Fiscal year 1992 consisted of 53 weeks, and fiscal years 1991 and 1990 each consisted of 52 weeks.

B. Land, Buildings, Equipment and Depreciation Buildings and equipment are depreciated over estimated useful lives ranging from three to 50 years, primarily using the straight-line method. Accelerated depreciation methods are generally used for income tax purposes.

When an item is sold or retired, the accounts are relieved of cost and the related accumulated depreciation; the resulting gains and losses, if any, are recognized.

C. Inventories Inventories are valued at the lower of cost or market. Certain domestic inventories are valued using the LIFO method, while other inventories are generally valued using the FIFO method.

D. Intangible Assets Goodwill represents the difference between purchase prices of acquired companies and the related fair values of net assets acquired and accounted for by the purchase method of accounting. Goodwill acquired after October 1970 is amortized on a straight-line basis over 40 years or less.

Intangible assets include an amount that offsets a minimum liability recorded for a pension plan with assets less than accumulated benefits as required by Financial Accounting Standard No. 87.

The costs of patents, copyrights and other intangible assets are amortized evenly over their estimated useful lives. Most of these costs were incurred through purchases of businesses.

The Audit Committee of the Board of Directors annually reviews goodwill and other intangibles. At its meeting on April 27, 1992, the Board of Directors affirmed that the remaining amounts of these assets have continuing value.

E. Research and Development All expenditures for research and development are charged against earnings in the year incurred. The charges for fiscal 1992, 1991 and 1990 were $62.1 million, $57.0 million and $48.2 million, respectively.

F. Income Taxes Income taxes include deferred income taxes that result from timing differences between earnings for financial reporting and tax purposes.

G. Earnings per Share Earnings per share has been determined by dividing the appropriate earnings by the weighted average number of common shares outstanding during the year. Common share equivalents were not material.

H. Foreign Currency Translation For most foreign operations, local currencies are considered the functional currency. Assets and liabilities are translated using the exchange rates in effect at the balance sheet date. Results of operations are translated using the average exchange rates prevailing throughout the period. Translation effects are accumulated in the foreign currency adjustment in stockholders' equity.

Gains and losses from foreign currency transactions are generally included in net earnings for the period.

We selectively utilize foreign exchange contracts to hedge foreign currency exposure related to operating activities and net investments in foreign operations. Realized and unrealized gains and losses on contracts that hedge operating activities are recognized currently in net earnings. Realized and unrealized gains and losses on contracts that hedge net investments are recognized in the foreign currency adjustment in stockholders' equity. At May 31, 1992, we had forward contracts maturing in fiscal 1993 to sell $297.8 million and purchase $15.5 million of foreign currencies.

I. Statements of Cash Flows For purposes of the statement of cash flows, we consider all investments purchased with a maturity of three months or less to be cash equivalents.

Note Two: Discontinued Operations

No operations were discontinued in fiscal 1992. However, we recorded a net after-tax charge related to previously discontinued operations of $10.0 million ($.06 per share). This charge primarily relates to a lease adjustment with the R. H. Macy Company which is operating under bankruptcy law protection.

In fiscal 1990, we sold Vroman Foods, our frozen novelties operation, for proceeds of $24.5 million and adjusted our estimated disposition loss recorded in fiscal 1989, recording after-tax income of $9.6 million ($.06 per share).

Other minor adjustments were made during fiscal year 1992, 1991 and 1990 for previously discontinued operations.

Sales for the discontinued operations were $9.5 million in fiscal 1990.

Note Three: Unusual Items

In fiscal 1992, we recognized a gain on the sale of the stock of our Spanish frozen food subsidiary, Preparados y Congelados Alimenticios, S.A. (PYCASA) and also recorded charges primarily related to restructuring our Betty Crocker packaged mixes production, European food operations, Consumer Foods national sales organization and the call of our 9⅜% sinking fund debentures. These transactions resulted in no net effect on earnings.

In fiscal 1991, we recognized gains on the sale of the net assets of our O-Cel-O Division, a cellulose sponge operation, and Lancia Bravo, our Canadian pasta operation. We also recorded charges primarily related to restructuring our Yoplait yogurt and hot oatmeal cereal operations. These transactions resulted in an increase in net earnings of $26.5 million ($.16 per share).

Note Four: Investments in Affiliates and Intangibles

During fiscal 1992, we made additional capital contributions and advances of $24.3 million to Cereal Partners Worldwide (CPW), our joint venture with Nestlé S.A.

During fiscal 1991, we invested $88.2 million in CPW. This investment consisted primarily of capital contributions and advances of $70.1 million, and our purchase of intangible assets related to RHM Breakfast Cereals (RHM) for $18.1 million. CPW purchased the RHM business in the United Kingdom.

Note Five: Inventories

The components of inventories are as follows:

In Millions	**May 31, 1992**	**May 26, 1991**
Raw materials, work in process and supplies	**$202.0**	$227.4
Finished goods	**290.3**	274.6
Grain	**61.9**	67.5
Reserve for LIFO valuation method	**(67.0)**	(75.9)
Total inventories	**$487.2**	$493.6

At May 31, 1992 and May 26, 1991, respectively, inventories of $266.3 million and $241.4 million were valued at LIFO. If the FIFO method of inventory accounting had been used in place of LIFO, reported earnings per share would have been lower by $.03 in fiscal 1992 and higher by $.02 in fiscal 1991 and 1990.

Note Six: Balance Sheet Information

The components of certain balance sheet items are as follows:

In Millions	**May 31, 1992**	**May 26, 1991**
Land, Buildings and Equipment:		
Land	**$ 253.9**	$ 215.2
Buildings	**1,302.2**	1,116.6
Equipment	**1,903.2**	1,701.6
Construction in progress	**450.0**	303.7
Total land, buildings and equipment	**3,909.3**	3,337.1
Less accumulated depreciation	**(1,260.7)**	(1,095.8)
Net land, buildings and equipment	**$2,648.6**	$2,241.3
Other Assets:		
Prepaid pension	**$ 217.4**	$ 173.5
Marketable investments, at cost	**170.4**	167.9
Intangible assets	**81.0**	79.2
Investments in and advances to affiliates	**70.2**	70.2
Miscellaneous	**82.8**	87.4
Total other assets	**$ 621.8**	$ 578.2

Note Seven: Notes Payable

The components of notes payable are as follows:

In Millions	**May 31, 1992**	**May 26, 1991**
U.S. commercial paper	**$ 58.0**	$ 70.0
Canadian commercial paper	**103.1**	83.7
Financial institutions	**158.2**	19.7
Amount reclassified to long-term debt	**(150.0)**	(150.0)
Total notes payable	**$169.3**	$ 23.4

To ensure availability of funds, we maintain bank credit lines sufficient to cover our outstanding commercial paper. As of May 31, 1992, we had $225.0 million fee-paid lines and $295.8 million uncommitted, no-fee lines available in the U.S. and Canada. In addition, other foreign subsidiaries had unused credit lines of $79.8 million.

We have a revolving credit agreement expiring in fiscal 1994 that provides for the fee-paid credit lines. This agreement provides us with the ability to refinance short-term borrowings on a long-term basis, and therefore we have reclassified a portion of our notes payable to long-term.

We have U.S. and Canadian interest rate swap agreements with commercial banks that convert variable interest rates to fixed interest rates, as illustrated at the top of the next page.

We have an interest rate swap agreement that converts the fixed interest rate to a variable interest rate on $13.0 million of nine-month commercial paper notes (3.68% at May 31, 1992).

We have a forward agreement to enter into a 10-year interest rate swap to pay 40.5 basis points over 10-year U.S. Treasury securities on a notional amount of $50.0 million with an expiration date of May 1993.

In Millions			Notional Amount	
Expiration Date	**Fixed Rate**	**Type**	**May 31, 1992**	**May 26, 1991**
June 1994	8.83%	Swap	**$ 25.0**	$ 25.0
November 1993	9.53	Swap	**74.0**	74.0
November 1993	7.00	Option	**50.0**	—
May 1992	9.38	Swap	—	25.0
April 1992	9.79	Swap	—	50.0
January 1992	11.04	Swap	—	26.1
August 1991	12.28	Swap	—	21.8
Total notional amount			**$149.0**	$221.9

Any interest rate differential on interest rate swaps is recognized as an adjustment of interest expense over the term of the agreement. We are exposed to credit loss in the event of nonperformance by the other parties to these agreements. However, we do not anticipate any losses.

Note Eight: Long-Term Debt

In Millions	**May 31, 1992**	**May 26, 1991**
Zero coupon notes, yield 11.14%, $481.6 due August 15, 2013	**$ 49.2**	$ 48.4
9⅜% sinking fund debentures due March 1, 2009	—	109.9
ESOP loan guaranty, variable rate (3.2% at May 31, 1992), due December 31, 2007	**50.0**	50.0
8.31% ESOP loan guaranty, due through June 30, 2007	**85.5**	89.8
Zero coupon notes, yield 11.73%, $67.8 due August 15, 2004	**17.0**	15.1
6.24% to 9.14% medium-term notes, due 1993 to 2007	**571.6**	391.3
Currency purchase obligation, yield 9.29%, due through November 15, 1993	**12.5**	19.9
12% notes due December 19, 1991	—	63.7
Zero coupon notes, yield 14⅝%, $49.3 due June 30, 1991	—	48.7
Notes payable, reclassified	**150.0**	150.0
Other, no individual item greater than $3.1	**17.3**	21.2
	953.1	1,008.0
Less amounts due within one year	**(32.6)**	(129.0)
Total long-term debt	**$920.5**	$ 879.0

Our shelf registration statement permits the issuance of up to $307.1 million net proceeds in unsecured debt securities to reduce short-term debt and for other general corporate purposes. This registration authorizes a medium-term note program that allows us to issue debt quickly for various amounts and at various rates and maturities.

In fiscal 1992, we issued $181.3 million of debt under our medium-term note program with maturities from three to 15 years and interest rates from 6.24% to 8.13%. In fiscal 1991, $310.6 million of debt was issued under this program with maturities from three to 15 years and interest rates from 8.46% to 9.14%.

We have an interest rate swap agreement that coverts the fixed interest rate to a variable interest rate on $100.0 million of medium-term notes (3.88% at May 31, 1992).

In fiscal 1992, we called our 9⅜% sinking fund debentures due March 1, 2009 (see note three). This transaction resulted in a decrease in net earnings of $3.5 million ($.02 per share).

The Company has guaranteed the debt of the Employee Stock Ownership Plans; therefore, the loans are reflected on our consolidated balance sheets in long-term debt with a related offset in stockholders' equity, "Unearned ESOP and restricted stock compensation."

The currency purchase obligation had a variable rate at May 31, 1992 of 3.86%. The obligation is secured by $13.0 million of corporate commercial paper, which is held under a trust agreement.

The sinking fund and principal payments due on long-term debt are (in millions) $32.6, $49.3, $37.2, $72.8 and $94.1 in fiscal years ending 1993, 1994, 1995, 1996 and 1997, respectively. The notes payable that are reclassified under our revolving credit agreement are not included in these principal payments.

Our marketable investments consist of corporate commercial paper and zero coupon U.S. Treasury securities. These investments are intended to provide the funds for the payment of principal and interest for the zero coupon notes due August 15, 2013 and 2004, and the currency purchase obligation.

Certain debt issues have been removed from our consolidated balance sheets through the creation of irrevocable trusts. The principal and interest of the securities deposited with the trustee will be sufficient to fund the scheduled principal and interest payments of these debt issues. At May 31, 1992, there was $58.6 million of this debt outstanding.

Note Nine: Stock Options

The following table contains information on stock options:

		Shares	Average Option Price per Share
Granted			
	1992	**2,574,008**	**$58.29**
	1991	2,931,372	42.50
	1990	2,777,196	34.71
Exercised			
	1992	**1,026,760**	**$19.64**
	1991	1,578,774	16.32
	1990	1,101,120	15.58
Expired			
	1992	**175,804**	**$39.12**
	1991	272,910	27.33
	1990	193,458	23.76

	Shares	Average Option Price per Share
Outstanding at year-end		
1992	**13,030,720**	**$35.88**
1991	11,659,276	29.55
1990	10,579,588	23.93
Exercisable at year-end		
1992	**8,938,384**	**$28.71**
1991	7,202,248	24.19
1990	6,139,424	19.15

A total of 9,372,246 shares are available for grants of options or restricted stock to officers and key employees under our 1988 and 1990 stock plans through September 30, 1995. The options may be granted at a price not less than 100% of fair market value on the date the option is granted. Options now outstanding include some granted under the 1980 and 1984 option plans, under which no further options or other rights may be granted. All options expire within 10 years plus one month after the date of grant. The plans provide for full vesting of the option in the event there is a change of control.

The 1988 plan permits awards of restricted stock to key employees subject to a restricted period and a purchase price, if any, to be paid by the employee as determined by the Compensation Committee of the Board of Directors. In fiscal 1992, grants of 79,918 shares of restricted stock were made and on May 31, 1992, there were 256,415 of such shares outstanding.

The 1988 plan also permits the granting of performance units corresponding to stock options granted. The value of performance units will be determined by return on equity and growth in earnings per share measured against preset goals over three-year performance periods. For seven years after a performance period, holders may elect to receive the value of performance units (with interest) as an alternative to exercising corresponding stock options. On May 31, 1992, there were 4,315,214 outstanding options with corresponding performance units or performance unit accounts.

The 1988 plan provides for the granting of incentive stock options as well as non-qualified options. No incentive stock options have been granted.

A total of 62,400 shares are available for grants of options and restricted stock to non-employee directors until September 30, 1995 under a separate 1990 stock plan. An option to purchase 2,500 shares is granted upon becoming a member of the Board of Directors at fair market value on the date of grant. Options expire 10 years after the date of grant. Each year 400 shares of restricted stock will be awarded to each non-employee director, restricted until the later of the expiration of one year of completion of service on the Board of Directors.

Note Ten: Stockholders' Equity

Cumulative preference stock of 5.0 million shares, without par value, is authorized but unissued.

We have a shareholder rights plan that entitles each outstanding share of common stock to one-fourth of a right. Each right entitles the holder to purchase one one-hundredth of a share of cumulative preference stock (or, in cer-

In Millions, Except per Share Data	$.10 Par Value Common Stock (One Billion Shares Authorized)				Retained Earnings	Unearned ESOP and Restricted Stock Compensation	Cumulative Foreign Currency Adjustment	Total
	Issued		Treasury					
	Shares	Amount	Shares	Amount				
Balance at May 28, 1989	204.2	$222.3	(43.0)	$(781.9)	$1,327.8	$ —	$(36.3)	$ 731.9
Net earnings					381.4			381.4
Cash dividends declared ($1.10 per share), net of income taxes of $2.2					(178.6)			(178.6)
Stock option, profit sharing and ESOP plans		74.8	6.5	119.1				193.9
Shares purchased on open market			(4.5)	(149.9)				(149.9)
Unearned compensation related to:								
Guaranties of ESOP's debt						(142.4)		(142.4)
Note receivable from ESOP						(25.0)		(25.0)
Earned compensation						2.7		2.7
Translation adjustments, net of income taxes of $7.2							(4.3)	(4.3)
Balance at May 27, 1990	204.2	297.1	(41.0)	(812.7)	1,530.6	(164.7)	(40.6)	809.7
Net earnings					472.7			472.7
Cash dividends declared ($1.28 per share), net of income taxes of $2.8					(207.8)			(207.8)
Stock option, profit sharing and ESOP plans		23.1	1.9	35.3				58.4
Unearned compensation related to:								
Note receivable from ESOP						(10.0)		(10.0)
Restricted stock awards						(8.2)		(8.2)
Earned compensation						5.3		5.3
Translation adjustments, net of income taxes of $1.4							(6.6)	(6.6)
Balance at May 26, 1991	204.2	320.2	(39.1)	(777.4)	1,795.5	(177.6)	(47.2)	1,113.5
Net earnings					495.6			495.6
Cash dividends declared ($1.48 per share), net of income taxes of $3.1					(242.1)			(242.1)
Stock option, profit sharing and ESOP plans		23.4	1.1	21.5				44.9
Shares purchased on open market			(.7)	(47.0)				(47.0)
Unearned compensation related to restricted stock awards						(4.3)		(4.3)
Earned compensation						9.6		9.6
Translation adjustments, net of income taxes of $.7							(6.7)	(6.7)
Amount charged to gain on sale of foreign operation							7.4	7.4
Balance at May 31, 1992	**204.2**	**$343.6**	**(38.7)**	**$(802.9)**	**$2,049.0**	**$(172.3)**	**$(46.5)**	**$1,370.9**

tain circumstances, common stock or other securities), exercisable upon the occurrence of certain events. The rights are not transferable apart from the common stock until a person or group has acquired 20% or more, or makes a tender offer for 20% or more, of the common stock. If the Company is then acquired in a merger or other business combination transaction, each right will entitle the holder (other than the acquiring company) to receive, upon exercise, common stock of either the Company or the acquiring company having a value equal to two times the exercise price of the right. The rights are redeemable by the Board in certain circumstances and expire on March 7, 1996. At May 31, 1992, there were 41.4 million rights issued and outstanding.

The Board of Directors has authorized the repurchase, from time to time, of common stock for our treasury, provided that the number of shares in the treasury shall not exceed 50.0 million.

Note Eleven: Interest Expense

The components of net interest expense are as follows:

In Millions		Fiscal Year	
	1992	**1991**	**1990**
Interest expense	**$89.5**	$94.0	$75.5
Capitalized interest	**(13.6)**	(9.9)	(14.2)
Interest income	**(17.7)**	(23.0)	(28.9)
Interest expense, net	**$58.2**	$61.1	$32.4

During fiscal 1992, 1991 and 1990, we actually paid interest (net of amount capitalized) of $70.7 million, $64.7 million and $54.6 million, respectively.

Note Twelve: Retirement Plans

We have defined benefit plans covering most employees. Benefits for salaried employees are based on length of service and final average compensation. The hourly plans include various monthly amounts for each year of credited service. Our funding policy is consistent with the funding requirements of federal law and regulations. Our principal plan covering salaried employees has a provision that any excess pension assets would be vested in plan participants if the plan is terminated within five years of a change in control. Plan assets consist principally of listed equity securities and corporate obligations, and U.S. government securities.

Components of the net pension credit are as follows:

In Millions		Fiscal Year	
	1992	**1991**	**1990**
Service cost—benefits earned	**$ 14.2**	$ 12.8	$ 13.0
Interest cost on projected benefit obligation	**51.2**	49.4	46.1
Actual return on plan assets	**(75.0)**	(70.6)	(84.8)
Net amortization and deferral	**(26.1)**	(26.1)	(8.8)
Net pension credit	**$(35.7)**	$(34.5)	$(34.5)

The weighted-average discount rate and rate of interest in future compensation levels used in determining the actuarial present value of the benefit obligations were 9.5% and 6% in fiscal 1992, and 9.73% and 6% in fiscal 1991, respectively. The expected long-term rate of return on assets was 11.35%.

The funded status of the plans and the amounts recognized on the consolidated balance sheets (as determined as of May 31, 1992 and 1991) are as follows:

In Millions	May 31, 1992 Assets Exceed Accumulated Benefits	May 31, 1992 Accumulated Benefits Exceed Assets	May 26, 1991 Assets Exceed Accumulated Benefits	May 26, 1991 Accumulated Benefits Exceed Assets
Actuarial present value of benefit obligations:				
Vested benefits	**$453.6**	**$ 11.3**	$425.4	$ 7.7
Nonvested benefits	**41.7**	**2.2**	37.4	3.3
Accumulated benefit obligation	**495.3**	**13.5**	462.8	11.0
Projected benefit obligation	**568.3**	**19.3**	526.1	17.5
Plan assets at fair value	**824.8**	**—**	786.7	—
Plan assets in excess of (less than) the projected benefit obligation	**256.5**	**(19.3)**	260.6	(17.5)
Unrecognized prior service cost	**28.3**	**.4**	26.9	.5
Unrecognized net loss	**97.9**	**7.1**	67.6	4.9
Recognition of minimum liability	**—**	**(11.4)**	—	(9.6)
Unrecognized transition (asset) liability	**(165.3)**	**9.7**	(181.6)	10.7
Prepaid (accrued) pension cost	**$217.4**	**$(13.5)**	$173.5	$(11.0)

We have defined contribution plans covering salaried and non-union employees. Contributions are determined by matching a percentage of employee contributions. Such plans had net assets of $658.2 million at May 31, 1992. Expense recognized in fiscal 1992, 1991 and 1990 was $12.7 million, $16.1 million and $18.8 million, respectively.

Within our defined contribution plans we have Employee Stock Ownership Plans (ESOP). These ESOPs borrowed funds guaranteed by the Company with terms described in the long-term debt footnote, and borrowed $35.0 million from the Company at a variable interest rate (4.07% at May 31, 1992) with $10.0 million due June 15, 2015 and $25.0 million due December 15, 2014. Compensation expense is recognized as contributions are accrued. Our contributions to the plans, plus the dividends accumulated on the common stock held by the ESOPs, are used to pay principal, interest and expenses of the plans. As loan payments are made, common stock is allocated to ESOP participants. In fiscal 1992, 1991 and 1990, the ESOPs incurred interest expense of $11.3 million, $13.4 million and $12.1 million, respectively, and used dividends received of $7.8 million, $6.4 million and $5.4 million and contributions received from the Company of $7.1 million, $12.1 million and $11.7 million, respectively, to pay principal and interest on their debt.

Note Thirteen: Other Postretirement Benefits

We sponsor several plans that provide health care benefits to the majority of our retirees. The salaried plan is contributory with retiree contributions based on years of service.

We fund a plan for certain employees and retirees on an annual basis. In fiscal 1992, 1991 and 1990 we contributed $4.2 million, $4.0 million and $19.8 million, respectively, to a trust with plan assets consisting principally of listed equity securities and U.S. government securities.

Components of the postretirement health care expense are as follows:

	Fiscal Year		
In Millions	**1992**	**1991**	**1990**
Service cost—benefits earned	**$3.5**	$ 3.8	$ 3.4
Interest cost on accumulated benefit obligation	**9.7**	10.5	9.7
Actual return on plan assets	**(3.0)**	(2.3)	—
Net amortization and deferral	**(1.2)**	(.9)	(.9)
Net postretirement expense	**$9.0**	$11.1	$12.2

We initially adopted accrual accounting for the expense of these plans in fiscal 1989 by setting up a liability of $115.7 million. The amount accrued on the consolidated balance sheets as of May 31, 1992 is $103.6 million. The table below indicates this liability and the funded status of the plans.

In Millions	**May 31, 1992**	**May 26, 1991**
Accumulated benefit obligation:		
Retirees	**$ 56.3**	$ 57.6
Fully eligible active employees	**16.2**	15.5
Other active employees	**46.4**	40.4
Accumulated benefit obligation	**118.9**	113.5
Plan assets at fair value	**28.5**	23.8
Accumulated benefit obligation in excess of plan assets	**90.4**	89.7
Unrecognized prior service cost	**16.4**	18.4
Unrecognized net gain (loss)	**(3.2)**	1.4
Accrued postretirement benefits	**$103.6**	$109.5

There are assumptions used in determining the accumulated postretirement benefit obligation and related expense. The discount rate used in determining the benefit obligation was 9.5% and 8.75% in fiscal 1992 and 1991, respectively. The expected long-term rate of return on assets was 9.6%.

The health care cost trend rate increase in the per capita charges for benefits ranged from 9.4% to 15.4% for fiscal 1993 depending on the medical service category. The rates gradually decrease to 4.5% to 5.8% for fiscal 2017 and remain at that level thereafter. If the health care cost trend rate were increased by one percentage point in each future year, the aggregate of the service and interest cost components of postretirement expense would increase for fiscal 1992 by

$2.3 million and the accumulated postretirement benefit obligation as of May 31, 1992 would increase by $15.3 million.

Note Fourteen: Profit-Sharing Plans

We have profit-sharing plans to provide incentives to key individuals who have the greatest potential to contribute to current earnings and successful future operations. These plans were approved by the Board of Directors upon recommendation of the Compensation Committee. The awards under these plans depend on profit performance in relation to pre-established goals. The plans are administered by the Compensation Committee, which consists solely of outside directors. Profit-sharing expense, including performance unit accruals, was $8.8 million, $11.0 million and $11.2 million in fiscal 1992, 1991 and 1990, respectively.

Note Fifteen: Income Taxes

The components of earnings before income taxes and the income taxes thereon are as follows:

	Fiscal Year		
In Millions	**1992**	**1991**	**1990**
Earnings before income taxes:			
U.S.	**$818.3**	$710.4	$584.9
Foreign	**26.2**	55.2	27.8
Total earnings before income taxes	**$844.5**	$765.6	$612.7
Income taxes:			
Current:			
Federal	$254.0	$238.3	$183.8
State and local	55.1	49.9	37.6
Foreign	16.3	12.3	5.1
Total current	325.4	300.5	226.5
Deferred (principally U.S.)	13.5	.9	12.5
Total income taxes	$338.9	$301.4	$239.0

During fiscal 1992, 1991 and 1990, we paid income taxes of $326.4 million, $257.7 million and $231.3 million, respectively.

In prior years we purchased certain income tax items from other companies through tax lease transactions. Total current income taxes charged to earnings in fiscal 1992, 1991 and 1990 reflect the amounts attributable to operations and have not been materially affected by these tax leases. Actual current taxes payable on fiscal 1992, 1991 and 1990 operations were increased by approximately $10 million, $9 million and $4 million, respectively, due to the effect of tax leases. These tax payments do not affect taxes for statement of earnings purposes since they repay tax benefits realized in prior years. The repayment liability is classified as "Deferred Income Taxes—Tax Leases."

Deferred income taxes result from timing differences in the recognition of revenue and expense for tax and financial statement purposes. The tax effects of these differences follow:

In Millions	Fiscal Year 1992	1991	1990
Depreciation	**$ 6.5**	$10.8	$13.8
Prepaid pension asset	**16.8**	16.1	14.8
Accrued expenses	**(1.1)**	(28.0)	(30.6)
Other	**(8.7)**	2.0	14.5
Total deferred income taxes	**$13.5**	$ .9	$12.5

The following table reconciles the U.S. statutory income tax rate with the effective income tax rate:

	Fiscal Year 1992	1991	1990
U.S. statutory rate	**34.0%**	34.0%	34.0%
State and local income taxes, net of federal tax benefits	**4.9**	4.3	4.2
Other, net	**1.2**	1.1	.8
Effective income tax rate	**40.1%**	39.4%	39.0%

Provision has been made for foreign and U.S. taxes that would be payable on foreign operations' earnings that are not considered permanently reinvested. Additional income taxes have not been provided on unremitted earnings of foreign operations amounting to $106.4 million that are expected by management to be permanently reinvested. If a portion were to be remitted, income tax credits would substantially offset any resulting tax liability.

Note Sixteen: Leases

An analysis of rent expense by property leased follows:

In Millions	Fiscal Year 1992	1991	1990
Restaurant space	**$33.9**	$27.8	$22.9
Warehouse space	**12.6**	11.8	9.7
Equipment	**8.3**	5.9	5.5
Other	**5.4**	4.8	5.2
Total rent expense	**$60.2**	$50.3	$43.3

Some leases require payment of property taxes, insurance and maintenance costs in addition to the rent payments. Contingent and escalation rent in excess of minimum rent payments and sublease income netted in rent expense were insignificant.

Noncancelable future lease commitments are (in millions) $57.0 in 1993, $52.0 in 1994, $50.1 in 1995, $46.5 in 1996, $42.9 in 1997 and $263.9 after 1997, with a cumulative total of $512.4.

Note Seventeen: Segment Information

In Millions	**Consumer Foods**	**Restau-rants**	**Unallocated Corporate Items (a)**	**Consoli-dated Total**
Sales				
1992	**$5,233.8**	**$2,544.0**		**$7,777.8**
1991	4,939.7	2,213.5		7,153.2
1990	4,520.3	1,928.0		6,448.3
Operating Profits				
1992	**744.3(b)**	**190.8**	**$ (90.6)**	**844.5**
1991	689.5(c)	172.2	(96.1)	765.6
1990	533.9	154.2	(75.4)	612.7
Identifiable Assets (d)				
1992	**2,481.2**	**1,419.3**	**404.5**	**4,305.0**
1991	2,189.2	1,256.4	456.2	3,901.8
1990	1,834.2	1,038.2	417.1	3,289.5
Capital Expenditures				
1992	**397.1**	**297.0**	**1.2**	**695.3**
1991	277.6	273.0	4.0	554.6
1990	298.2	239.1	2.7	540.0
Depreciation Expense				
1992	**140.3**	**99.4**	**2.3**	**242.0**
1991	131.7	79.7	2.0	213.4
1990	110.2	64.2	1.7	176.1

In Millions	**U.S.A.**	**Foreign**	**Unallocated Corporate Items (a)**	**Consoli-dated Total**
Sales				
1992	**$7,039.6**	**$738.2**		**$7,777.8**
1991	6,376.8	776.4		7,153.2
1990	5,796.1	652.2		6,448.3
Operating Profits				
1992	**896.3(b)**	**38.8(b)**	**$ (90.6)**	**844.5**
1991	805.8(c)	55.9(c)	(96.1)	765.6
1990	655.9	32.2	(75.4)	612.7
Identifiable Assets (d)				
1992	**3,452.2**	**448.3**	**404.5**	**4,305.0**
1991	3,001.5	444.1	456.2	3,901.8
1990	2,543.3	329.1	417.1	3,289.5

(a) Corporate expenses reported here include net interest expense and general corporate expenses.

(b) Consumer Foods operating profits include a net gain of $17.5 million (U.S.A. $20.5 million loss; Foreign $38.0 million gain) for unusual items described in note three.

(c) Consumer Foods operating profits include a net gain of $48.2 million (U.S.A. $20.9 million; Foreign $27.3 million) for unusual items described in note three.

(d) Identifiable assets for our segments consist mainly of receivables, inventories, prepaid expenses, net land, buildings and equipment, and other assets. Corporate identifiable assets consist mainly of cash, cash equivalents, deferred income taxes and marketable investments.

Note Eighteen: Quarterly Data (unaudited)

Summarized quarterly data for fiscal 1992 and 1991 follow:

In Millions, Except per Share and Market Price Amounts	**First Quarter**		**Second Quarter**	
	1992	**1991**	**1992**	**1991**
Sales	**$1,916.5**	$1,739.5	**$1,992.5**	$1,836.8
Gross profit (a)	**914.6**	828.5	**946.9**	874.1
Earnings after taxes—				
Continuing operations	**142.1**	123.8	**128.3**	118.2(b)
Earnings per share—				
Continuing operations	**.86**	.75	**.77**	.72
Discontinued operations after taxes	—	5.7	—	—
Net earnings	**142.1**	129.5	**128.3**	118.2
Net earnings per share	**.86**	.79	**.77**	.72
Dividends per share	**.37**	.32	**.37**	.32
Market price of common stock:				
High	**64**	47½	**68⅝**	45⅜
Low	**54¼**	37⅞	**58⅝**	39½

In Millions, Except per Share and Market Price Amounts	**Third Quarter**		**Fourth Quarter**		**Total Year**	
	1992	**1991**	**1992**	**1991**	**1992**	**1991**
Sales	**$1,868.3**	$1,747.6	**$2,000.5**	$1,829.3	**$7,777.8**	$7,153.2
Gross profit (a)	**884.9**	870.5	**908.2**	858.0	**3,654.6**	3,431.1
Earnings after taxes—						
Continuing operations	**132.1**	131.3(c)	**103.1**	90.9	**505.6**	464.2
Earnings per share—						
Continuing operations	**.80**	.80	**.62**	.55	**3.05**	2.82
Discontinued operations after taxes	—	2.8	**(10.0)**	—	**(10.0)**	8.5
Net earnings	**132.1**	134.1	**93.1**	90.9	**495.6**	472.7
Net earnings per share	**.80**	.81	**.56**	.55	**2.99**	2.87
Dividends per share	**.37**	.32	**.37**	.32	**1.48**	1.28
Market price of common stock:						
High	**75⅞**	54¾	**70⅛**	60⅞	**75⅞**	60⅞
Low	**64⅛**	43½	**58¾**	52⅛	**54¼**	37⅞

(a) Before charges for depreciation.
(b) Includes a net after-tax gain of $9.2 million ($.096 per share) from the sale of our Lancia Bravo pasta operation and a restructuring charge for Yoplait yogurt operations.
(c) Includes a net after-tax gain of $17.3 million ($.10 per share) from the sale of our O-Cel-O sponge operation and restructuring charges primarily for hot cereal operations.

APPENDIX C

General Mills, Inc. 10-K Report

SECURITIES AND EXCHANGE COMMISSION
Washington, D. C. 20549

FORM 10-K

ANNUAL REPORT PURSUANT TO SECTION 13 OR 15(d) OF
THE SECURITIES EXCHANGE ACT OF 1934

For the fiscal year ended May 31, 1992 Commission File Number 1-1185

GENERAL MILLS, INC.

State of Incorporation: **Delaware**

I.R.S. Employer Identification No: **41-0274440**

Principal Executive Offices:
Number One General Mills Boulevard (Mail: P.O. Box 1113; Zip: 55440)
Minneapolis, Minnesota 55426
Telephone Number: (612) 540-2311

Securities registered pursuant to Section 12(b) of the Act:

Title of each class	Name of each exchange on which registered
Common Stock, $.10 par value	New York Stock Exchange Midwest Stock Exchange
8% Sinking Fund Debentures due February 15, 1999	New York Stock Exchange

Indicate by check mark whether the Registrant (1) has filed all reports required to be filed by Section 13 or 15(d) of the Securities Exchange Act of 1934 during the preceding 12 months, and (2) has been subject to such filing requirements for the past 90 days. Yes _X_ No ___

Indicate by check mark if disclosure of delinquent filers pursuant to Item 405 of Regulation S-K is not contained herein, and will not be contained, to the best of registrant's knowledge, in definitive proxy or information statements incorporated by reference in Part III of this Form 10-K or any amendment to this Form 10-K. [ ]

Aggregate market value of Common Stock held by non-affiliates of the Registrant, based on the closing price of $66.875 per share as reported on the New York Stock Exchange on July 24, 1992: $10,945.6 billion.

Number of shares of Common Stock outstanding as of July 24, 1992: 163,673,130 (excluding 40,480,202 shares held in the treasury)

DOCUMENTS INCORPORATED BY REFERENCE

Portions of Registrant's Proxy Statement dated August 17, 1992 are incorporated by reference into Part III, and portions of Registrant's 1992 Annual Report to Stockholders are incorporated by reference into Parts I, II and IV.

PART I

Item 1. Business.

General Mills, Inc. was incorporated in Delaware in 1928. The Company currently markets consumer goods and services in two principal business areas: Consumer Foods and Restaurants. The terms "General Mills," "Company" and "Registrant" mean General Mills, Inc. and its subsidiaries unless the context indicates otherwise.

During fiscal 1992, the Company sold all of the stock of Preparados y Congelados Alimenticios, S.A., its frozen foods business in Spain. See Note Three to Consolidated Financial Statements as contained in the Company's 1992 Annual Report to Stockholders, incorporated herein by reference. The Company has an agreement to merge its snack food businesses in Holland, France and Belgium with the snack food businesses of PepsiCo, Inc. in Spain, Portugal and Greece forming one company to be owned 59.5% by PepsiCo, Inc. and 40.5% by General Mills. The merged company will develop, manufacture and market snack foods in Continental Europe.

Cereal Partners Worldwide, the Company's joint venture with Nestlé, S.A., initiated marketing activity in Italy during fiscal 1992 and continued to market breakfast cereals in France, Spain, Portugal and the United Kingdom. See Note Four to Consolidated Financial Statements as contained in the Company's 1992 Annual Report to Stockholders, incorporated herein by reference.

Consumer Foods

The Company is a leading producer of packaged consumer foods, including those in the categories set forth below.

Breakfast Products. General Mills produces and sells a number of ready-to-eat cereals, including such brands as: *Cheerios, Honey Nut Cheerios, Apple Cinnamon Cheerios, Wheaties, Lucky Charms, Corn Total, Wheat Total, Trix, Golden Grahams, Kix, Fiber One, Cocoa Puffs, Crispy Wheats 'N Raisins, Cinnamon Toast Crunch, Clusters, Raisin Nut Bran, Total Raisin Bran, Oatmeal Crisp, Oatmeal Raisin Crisp, Triples* and *Basic 4.* In fiscal 1992, the Company introduced three new ready-to-eat cereals, *Wheaties Honey Gold, Multi Grain Cheerios* and *Berry Berry Kix.*

Mixes & Convenience Foods. General Mills makes and sells prepared brownie, muffin, cake, frosting and other dessert mixes under the *Betty Crocker* trademark, including *SuperMoist* layer cakes and *Creamy Deluxe* ready-to-spread frostings. The Company also has reduced-fat versions of its muffin, cake and frosting mixes sold under the *Betty Crocker Light* name and a line of *Supreme Dessert* bar mixes introduced in fiscal 1992 under the *Betty Crocker* trademark. Also under the *Betty Crocker* trademark, the Company sells *Potato Buds* instant mashed potatoes and other potato and pasta specialty mixes, such as *Suddenly Salad* and *Betty Crocker AuGratin* and *Scalloped Potatoes.* The Company markets a variety baking mix under the *Bisquick* trademark and lines of dry packaged dinner mixes under the *Hamburger Helper, Tuna Helper* and *Skillet Chicken Helper* names. The Company also sells pouch mixes under the names *Robin Hood* and *Gold Medal* and sells *Bac★Os* garnish and salad topping. In fiscal 1992 the Company introduced a line of prepared dinner sauces in jars under the *Betty Crocker Recipe Sauce* trademark.

Family Flour, Bakery Flour and Ingredients. General Mills produces family flour under the *Gold Medal* brand, introduced in 1880, and regional brands such as *La Piña, Robin Hood* and *Red Band.* The Company also engages in grain merchandising, produces its own ingredient flour requirements and sells flour to bakeries.

Snack Products and Beverages. General Mills markets *Pop Secret* microwave popcorn, a line of *Nature Valley* granola bars, *Bugles* snacks, a line of real fruit snack including *Fruit Roll-Ups, Garfield, Gushers* and *Fruit By The Foot* and shaped fruit snacks including *Thunder Jets, Shark Bites, The Berry Bears, Sodalicious* and *Surf's Up!* The Company also produces and sells regionally a line of single-serving 10% fruit juice drinks marketed under the *Squeezit* trademark.

Other. The Gorton division sells a variety of seafood entrees and other products, mostly in frozen form, under the *Gorton's* brand name. The Gorton division also markets institutional seafood and supplies frozen fish portions, breadings and coatings to the food service trade. Yoplait USA markets *Yoplait Original* yogurt, *Custard Style* yogurt and *Breakfast* yogurt. New additions to the *Yoplait* line include *Fat-free Fruit on the Bottom, Parfait Style* and *Trix,* a layered yogurt for children. The Foodservice division markets General Mills branded baking mixes and cereals to the commercial and non-commercial sector.

International Food Operations. General Mills Canada, Inc. makes and sells food products in Canada, including ready-to-eat cereals, *Betty Crocker* baking and packaged dinner mixes and snacks. The Company also has interests in companies engaged primarily in flour milling operations in Latin America, licenses food products for manufacture in Europe, Japan and Korea, and exports flour and packaged products throughout the world. The Company has an agreement to merge its snack food businesses in Holland, France and Belgium with the snack food businesses of PepsiCo, Inc. in Spain, Portugal and Greece into one company to be owned 59.5% by PepsiCo, Inc. and 40.5% by General Mills. Cereal Partners Worldwide, the Company's joint venture with Nestlé S.A., continues to market breakfast cereals in the United Kingdom, France, Spain and Portugal and initiated marketing activity in Italy. New products introduced into selected markets in fiscal 1992 include *Trio, Clusters, Nesquik* and *Lucky Charms.*

General Mills markets its packaged food products through its own sales organizations, supported by advertising and other promotional activities. Such products are primarily distributed directly to retail food chains, co-operatives and wholesale outlets. Certain food products, such as seafood and some food service products, are sold through distributors and brokers.

The Company's Consumer Foods business segment is highly competitive, with numerous competitors of varying sizes. In most of its consumer foods lines, General Mills competes not only with other widely advertised branded products, but also with generic products and private label products, which are generally distributed at lower prices.

Restaurants

The Company operates *Red Lobster* full-service specialty seafood restaurants in the United States and Canada and is engaged in a partnership in Japan operating *Red Lobster* restaurants. The Company also operates *The Olive Garden* full-service Italian restaurants in the United States and Canada.

The Company's Restaurant businesses operate in highly competitive segments, with numerous competitors of varying sizes. The restaurant markets rely on the varied tastes, discretionary decisions and available disposable income of individual consumers.

New Ventures

The Company is test marketing *China Coast,* a Chinese restaurant, in Orlando, Florida and has discontinued the testing of *Bringer's,* a home delivery concept.

Executive Officers of the Registrant

The executive officers of the Company, together with their ages and business experience, are set forth below.

H. B. Atwater, Jr., age 61, is Chairman of the Board and Chief Executive Officer, and has been a director since 1971. Mr. Atwater joined the Company in 1958 and was elected an Executive Vice President in 1970, Chief Operating Officer in 1976, President in 1977, Chief Executive Officer in 1981 and Chairman of the Board effective January 1, 1982.

Dean Belbas, age 60, is Vice President and Director of Corporate Communications. Mr. Belbas joined General Mills in 1956, was elected a Vice President in 1977 and was appointed Director of Corporate Communications in 1979.

Edward K. Bixby, age 56, is Senior Vice President; President, Consumer Foods Sales, with additional responsibility for Foodservice and Information Systems. Mr. Bixby joined the Company in 1958 and was named Vice President, General Manager of the Package Foods Operations Division in 1975. He has also served as Vice President, General Manager of the Golden Valley Division and of the Betty Crocker Division after it was combined with the Golden Valley Division in March 1986. Mr. Bixby was elected Senior Vice President, General Manager, Grocery Products Sales Division in 1987, and was named to his present position in 1989.

Walter W. Faster, age 58, is Vice President and Director of Corporate Growth and Development. Mr. Faster joined the Company in 1963 and was elected Vice President and Director of Corporate Growth and Development in 1982.

Charles W. Gaillard, age 51, is Executive Vice President of General Mills; President and Chief Executive Officer of CPW, S.A., a joint venture of General Mills and Nestlé S.A. Mr. Gaillard joined the Company in 1966, became General Manager of the Golden Valley Division and was appointed a Vice President in 1977. He was appointed General Manager of the Big G Division in 1979, was elected a Senior Vice President in 1985 and became Executive Vice President in 1989.

Stephen J. Garthwaite, age 48, is Senior Vice President, Technology and Operations. Mr. Garthwaite joined the Company in 1982 as Vice President, Director of Corporate Research and was named Vice President, Research and Development for the Betty Crocker Division in 1986. He assumed the position of Vice President, Research and Development for Consumer Foods in 1987, was elected Senior Vice President, Research and Development in 1989 and was named Senior Vice President, Technology and Operations in 1990.

David E. Kelby, age 55, is Senior Vice President, Treasurer. Mr. Kelby joined the Company in 1966 as a member of the Law Department. Mr. Kelby left General Mills to join Graco, Inc. as its General Counsel in 1970, and he returned to General Mills in 1972 as Manager of Acquisitions, becoming Vice President, Director of Corporate Growth in 1977. He became Vice President, Control and Administration for Consumer Foods in 1979, was elected Senior Vice President, Treasury, Growth and Planning in 1985 and was elected Senior Vice President, Treasurer in 1986.

Joe R. Lee, age 51, is Vice Chairman and Chief Financial Officer. Mr. Lee was elected a director in 1985. Mr. Lee joined Red Lobster in 1967 as a member of its founding team, and was named its President in 1975. He was elected a Vice President of General Mills in 1976, a Group Vice President in 1979, an Executive Vice President in 1981, named Executive Vice President, Finance and International Restaurants in 1991 and elected to his present position in April 1992.

Ronald N. Magruder, age 44, is Senior Vice President; President, The Olive Garden. Mr. Magruder joined Red Lobster in 1972 and has served as both Vice President of Operations and Vice President of International Growth and Development for Red Lobster. He was named President of Casa Gallardo in 1982, President of York Steak House Systems in 1983, President of The Olive Garden in 1987 and was elected Senior Vice President in 1989.

D. D. Murphy, age 40, is Senior Vice President; President, Big G Division. Mr. Murphy joined the Company in 1976, was appointed Vice President of Marketing Services in 1986 and subsequently Vice President, General Manager of the Minnetonka Division in 1988. He assumed overall responsibility for Betty Crocker Products in 1989, when the Minnetonka and Betty Crocker Divisions were merged. He was elected a Senior Vice President in 1991 and was named President of the Big G Division in 1992.

Sandy J. Navin, age 56, is Vice President and Director of Taxes. Mr. Navin joined General Mills as Tax Counsel in 1969, was named Assistant Director of Taxes in 1974 and was elected Vice President and Director of Taxes in 1988.

Thomas P. Nelson, age 62, is Senior Vice President, Controller. Mr. Nelson joined the Company in 1955 and was named Vice President, Control and Administration for Consumer Foods in 1969. He was elected Vice President, Controller of General Mills in 1979 and was elected Senior Vice President in 1981.

Jeffrey J. O'Hara, age 44, is Senior Vice President; President, Red Lobster. Mr. O'Hara joined the Company in 1970 and was named Vice President of Marketing and Menu Planning for Red Lobster in 1978. He was named President of The Good Earth in 1981, Executive Vice President of Marketing and Development for General Mills Restaurant Group in 1984, President of Red Lobster in 1986 and was elected Senior Vice President in 1989.

Michael A. Peel, age 42, is Senior Vice President, Personnel. Previously, Mr. Peel served as Division Employee Relations Manager, Pepsi-Cola Bottling Group (1977–1980), Director-Personnel Administration, Pepsi-Cola Company (1980–1983), Vice President, Employee Relations, Pepsi-Cola Bottling Group (1984–1987) and Senior Vice President-Personnel, Pepsico Foods International (1987–1991). Mr. Peel joined the Company and was elected to his present position in September 1991.

Stephen W. Sanger, age 46, is Executive Vice President with responsibility for Big G, Yoplait and International Foods. Mr. Sanger joined the Company in 1974 and was named Vice President, General Manager of the Northstar Division in 1983. He was appointed Vice President, General Manager of New Business Development in 1986, President of Yoplait USA in 1986, President of the Big G Division in 1988, elected Senior Vice President in 1989 and Executive Vice President in 1991.

Arthur R. Schulze, age 61, is Vice Chairman with responsibility for Consumer Foods Sales, Marketing Services, Technology and Operations, Foodservice, Information Systems, Health and Human Services, Corporate Public Relations and Corporate Personnel. Mr. Schulze joined the Company in 1962, was appointed Vice President in 1970, elected Group Vice President in 1973 and elected Executive Vice President, Consumer Foods in 1981. He was named Executive Vice President; President, Grocery Products Food Group in 1985, was elected a director in 1986 and was elected Vice Chairman in 1989.

Stephen H. Warhover, age 48, is Senior Vice President; President, The Gorton Division. Mr. Warhover joined the Company in 1968 and was appointed Vice President, General Manager of the Betty Crocker Division in 1980. He was named Vice President, General Manager of the Minnetonka Division in 1983, President of The Gorton Division in 1986 and was elected Senior Vice President in 1989.

Clifford L. Whitehill, age 61, is Senior Vice President, General Counsel and Secretary. Mr. Whitehill joined the Company in 1962 as an attorney in the Law Department. He was appointed Assistant General Counsel in 1968, elected Vice President in 1971, named General Counsel in 1975, elected Senior Vice President in 1981 and elected Secretary in 1983.

Mark H. Willes, age 51, is Vice Chairman with responsibility for Red Lobster, The Olive Garden, China Coast, International Restaurants, Betty Crocker Products, Sperry and Cereal Partners Worldwide. Mr. Willes joined the Company as Executive Vice President and Chief Financial Officer in 1980. He was elected President and became a member of the Board of Directors in 1985 and was elected to his present position in 1992. Previously, Mr. Willes served as Vice President, Director of Research and Senior Economist of the Philadelphia Federal Reserve Bank (1969–1971), First Vice President of the Federal Reserve Bank of Philadelphia (1971–1977) and President of the Federal Reserve Bank of Minneapolis (1977–1980).

General

Trademarks. Trademarks and service marks are vital to the Company's business. Some of the important trademarks and service marks of the Company are contained in the business segment discussions above.

Raw Materials and Supplies. The principal raw materials used by General Mills are cereal grains, sugar, fruits, other agricultural products, vegetable oils, fish for food products, and plastic and paper for packaging materials. Although General Mills has some long-term contracts, the bulk of such raw materials are purchased on the open market. Although prices of most raw materials will probably increase over the long term, General Mills believes that it will be able to obtain an adequate supply of such raw materials. Occasionally and where possible, General Mills makes advance purchases of commodities significant to its business in order to ensure continuity of operations. In many cases, the Company also seeks to protect itself from basic market price fluctuations of commodities through hedging transactions.

Capital Expenditures. During the three fiscal years ended May 31, 1992, General Mills expended approximately $1,790 million for capital expenditures, not including the cost of acquired companies. The Company expects to spend approximately $700 million for such purposes in fiscal 1993.

Research and Development. The main research and development facilities are located at the James Ford Bell Technical Center in Golden Valley (suburban Minneapolis), Minnesota. With a staff of approximately 710, the Center is responsible for most of the food research for the Company. Approximately one-half of the staff hold degrees in various biological and engineering sciences. Research and development expenditures (all Company-sponsored) amounted to approximately $62.1 million in fiscal 1992, $57.0 million in fiscal 1991 and $48.2 million in fiscal 1990. General Mills' research and development resources are focused on new product development, product improvement, process design and improvement, packaging and exploratory research in new business areas.

Employees. At May 31, 1992, General Mills had approximately 111,500 employees, approximately 110,000 of whom were located in the United States and Canada.

Environmental Matters. As of June 30, 1992, the Company has been advised that it is a "potentially responsible party" in 14 environmental matters, five of which are state instituted and the remainder are federal Environmental Protection Agency proceedings; however, based on current facts and circumstances. General Mills believes that neither the results of these proceedings nor its compliance in general with environmental laws or regulations will have a material effect upon the capital expenditures, earnings or competitive position of the Company.

Segment Information. For financial information relating to industry segments of General Mills and foreign and domestic operations and sales, see Note Seventeen to Consolidated Financial Statements appearing on page 35 (see Appendix B of this text) of the Company's 1992 Annual Report to Stockholders, incorporated herein by reference. See Note Two to Consolidated Financial Statements appearing on page 28 (see Appendix B of this text) of the Company's 1992 Annual Report to Stockholders, incorporated herein by reference, with respect to the effect of discontinued operations on such financial information.

Item 2. Properties.

The Company's principal executive offices and main research laboratory are Company-owned and located in the Minneapolis, Minnesota metropolitan area. General Mills operates numerous manufacturing facilities and maintains many sales and administrative offices and warehouses mainly in the United States. Other facilities are also operated in Canada and Europe.

General Mills operates eleven major consumer foods plants for the production of cereal products, prepared mixes, convenience foods and other food products. These facilities have a combined annual production capacity of approximately 1,849,000,000 pounds and are located at Buffalo, New York; Carlisle, Pennsylvania; Ceda Rapids, Iowa; Chicago, Illinois (2); Covington, Georgia; Lodi, California (2); St. Charles, Illinois; Toledo, Ohio; and Etobicoke, Canada. A new consumer foods plant for the production of cereal products in Albuquerque, New Mexico is expected to be fully operational in the fall of 1992. The Company owns seven flour mills, located at Avon, Iowa; Buffalo, New York; Great Falls, Montana; Johnson City, Tennessee; Kansas City, Missouri; Vallejo, California; and Vernon, California. The Company operates seven terminal grain elevators and has country grain elevators in 32 localities, primarily in Idaho and Montana.

General Mills has other facilities for the manufacture of various products with total floor space of approximately 414,000 square feet, including 68,000 square feet of leased space. Such manufacturing facilities consist of seven seafood processing facilities and five other food production facilities.

General Mills also owns or leases warehouse space aggregating approximately 6,059,000 square feet, of which approximately 3,509,000 square feet are leased. A number of sales and administrative offices are maintained worldwide, totaling 1,459,000 square feet.

The Company operates 961 restaurants, including 619 *Red Lobster* and 341 *The Olive Garden* restaurants and one *China Coast* restaurant, in the following locations:

Alabama (16)	Iowa (7)	Nevada (6)	South Carolina (14)
Arizona (16)	Kansas (8)	New Hampshire (1)	South Dakota (2)
Arkansas (7)	Kentucky (9)	New Jersey (20)	Tennessee (20)
California (84)	Louisiana (4)	New Mexico (6)	Texas (91)
Colorado (16)	Maine (3)	New York (29)	Utah (5)
Connecticut (3)	Maryland (8)	North Carolina (21)	Vermont (1)
Delaware (3)	Massachusetts (2)	North Dakota (3)	Virginia (25)
Florida (112)	Michigan (38)	Ohio (53)	Washington (12)
Georgia (34)	Minnesota (15)	Oklahoma (12)	West Virginia (3)
Idaho (2)	Mississippi (2)	Oregon (7)	Wisconsin (14)
Illinois (45)	Missouri (25)	Pennsylvania (30)	
Indiana (29)	Nebraska (4)	Rhode Island (3)	Canada (91)

The Company is also engaged in a partnership which operates 50 *Red Lobster* restaurants in Japan.

Item 3: Legal Proceedings.
In management's opinion, there were no claims or litigation pending at May 31, 1992, the outcome of which could have a significant effect on the consolidated financial position of General Mills, Inc. and its subsidiaries.

Item 4. Submission of Matters to a Vote of Security Holders.
Not applicable.

PART II

Item 5. Market for Registrant's Common Equity and Related Stockholder Matters.
The information relating to the market prices and dividends of the Company's common stock contained in Note Eighteen to Consolidated Financial Statements appearing on page 35 (see Appendix B of this text) of Registrant's 1992 Annual Report to Stockholders, is incorporated herein by reference. As of July 24, 1992, the number of record holders of common stock was 40,639. The Company's common stock ($.10 par value) is listed on the New York and Midwest Stock Exchanges.

Item 6. Selected Financial Data.
The information for fiscal years 1988 through 1992 contained in the Eleven Year Financial Summary As Reported and the Financial Data for Continuing Operations on page 36* of Registrant's 1992 Annual Report to Stockholders, is incorporated herein by reference.

Item 7. Management's Discussion and Analysis of Financial Condition and Results of Operation.
The information set forth in the section entitled "Management Discussion of Results of Operations and Financial Condition" on pages 19 through 21 (see Appendix B of this text) of Registrant's 1992 Annual Report to Stockholders, is incorporated herein by reference.

* Not included in this text.

Item 8. Financial Statements and Supplementary Data.

The information on pages 22 through 35 (see Appendix B of this text) of Registrant's 1992 Annual Report to Stockholders, is incorporated herein by reference.

Item 9. Disagreements on Accounting and Financial Disclosure.

Not applicable.

PART III

Item 10. Directors and Executive Officers of the Registrant.

The sections entitled "Compliance with Section 16(a) of the Securities Exchange Act of 1934" and "Information Concerning Nominees" contained in Registrant's definitive proxy materials dated August 17, 1992 are incorporated herein by reference.

Item 11. Executive Compensation.

Pages 16 through 21, 23 and 24, and 26 through 29 (see Appendix B of this text) of Registrant's definitive proxy materials dated August 17, 1992 are incorporated herein by reference.

Item 12. Security Ownership of Certain Beneficial Owners and Management.

The section entitled "Share Ownership of Directors and Officers" contained in Registrant's definitive proxy materials dated August 17, 1992 is incorporated herein by reference.

Item 13. Certain Relationships and Related Transactions.

Not applicable.

The Company's Annual Report on Form 10-K for the fiscal year ended May 31, 1992, at the time of its filing with the Securities and Exchange Commission, shall modify and supersede all prior documents filed pursuant to Sections 13, 14 and 15(d) of the 1934 Act for purposes of any offers or sales of any securities after the date of such filing pursuant to any Registration Statement or Prospectus filed pursuant to the Securities Act of 1933 which incorporates by reference such Annual Report on Form 10-K.

Auditors' Report

The Stockholders and the Board of Directors
General Mills, Inc.:

Under date of July 1, 1992, we reported on the consolidated balance sheets of General Mills, Inc. and subsidiaries as of May 31, 1992 and May 26, 1991 and the related consolidated statements of earnings and cash flows for each of the fiscal years in the three-year period ended May 31, 1992, as contained in the 1992 annual report to stockholders. These consolidated financial statements and our report thereon are incorporated by reference in the annual report on Form 10-K for the fiscal year ended May 31, 1992. In connection with our audits of the aforementioned consolidated financial statements, we have also audited the related financial statement schedules as listed in the accompanying index. These financial statement schedules are the responsibility of the Company's management. Our responsibility is to express an opinion on these financial statement schedules based on our audits.

In our opinion, such financial statement schedules, when considered in relation to the basic consolidated financial statements taken as a whole, present fairly, in all material respects, the information set forth therein.

KPMG Peat Marwick

Minneapolis, Minnesota
July 1, 1992

Auditors' Consent

The Board of Directors
General Mills, Inc.:

We consent to incorporation by reference in the Registration Statements (Nos. 2-49637, 2-91893, 33-15323, 33-37474 and 33-39927) on Form S-3 and Registration Statements (Nos. 2-13460, 2-50327, 2-53523, 2-66320, 2-91987, 2-95574, 33-24504, 33-27628, 33-32059, 33-36892 and 33-36893) as well as Registration Statement, dated August 19, 1992, covering the issuance of common stock of General Mills, Inc. and plan interests under the Profit Sharing and Savings Plan of General Mills Restaurants Inc. on Form S-8 of General Mills, Inc. of our reports dated July 1, 1992, relating to the consolidated balance sheets of General Mills, Inc. and subsidiaries as of May 31, 1992 and May 26, 1991 and the related consolidated statements of earnings, cash flows and related financial statement schedules for each of the fiscal years in the three-year period ended May 31, 1992, which reports are included or incorporated by reference in the May 31, 1992 annual report on Form 10-K of General Mills, Inc.

KPMG Peat Marwick

Minneapolis, Minnesota
August 25, 1992

PART IV

Item 14. Exhibits, Financial Statement Schedules and Reports on Form 8-K.

(a) 1. Financial Statements:

Consolidated Statements of Earnings for the Fiscal Years Ended May 31, 1992, May 26, 1991 and May 27, 1990 (incorporated herein by reference to page 24 (see Appendix B of this text) of the Registrant's 1992 Annual Report to Stockholders).

Consolidated Balance Sheets at May 31, 1992 and May 26, 1991 (incorporated herein by reference to page 25 (see Appendix B of this text) of the Registrant's 1992 Annual Report to stockholders).

Consolidated Statements of Cash Flows for the Fiscal Years Ended May 31, 1992, May 26, 1991 and May 27, 1990 (incorporated herein by reference to page 26 (see Appendix B of this text) of the Registrant's 1992 Annual Report to Stockholders).

Notes to Consolidated Financial Statements (incorporated herein by reference to pages 27 through 35—see Appendix B of this text—of the Registrant's 1992 Annual Report to Stockholders).

2. Financial Statement Schedules:

For the Fiscal Years Ended May 31, 1992, May 26, 1991 and May 27, 1990:

V—Property, Plant and Equipment
VI—Accumulated Depreciation, Depletion and Amortization of Property, Plant and Equipment
VII—Valuation and Qualifying Accounts
IX—Short-Term Borrowings
X—Supplementary Income Statement Information
XIII—Other Investments

3. Exhibits:

3.1 —Copy of Registrant's Restated Certificate of Incorporation, as amended to date.
3.2 —Copy of Registrant's By-Laws, as amended to date.
4 —Copy of Indenture between Registrant and Continental Illinois National Bank and Trust Company of Chicago, as amended to date by Supplemental Indentures Nos. 1 through 7.
10.1 —Copy of Stock Option and Long-Term Incentive Plan of 1988, as amended to date.
10.2 —Copy of Stock Option and Long-Term Incentive Plan of 1984, as amended to date.
10.3 —Copy of Stock Option and Long-Term Incentive Plan of 1980, as amended to date.
10.4 —Copy of Executive Incentive Plan, as amended to date.
10.5 —Copy of Management Continuity Agreement, as amended to date (incorporated herein by reference to Exhibit 10.6 to Registrant's Annual Report on Form 10-K for the fiscal year ended May 28, 1989).
10.6 —Copy of Supplemental Retirement Plan, as amended to date (incorporated herein by reference to Exhibit 10.7 to Registrant's Annual report on Form 10-K for the fiscal year ended May 28, 1989).
10.7 —Copy of Executive Survivor Income Plan, as amended to date (incorporated herein by reference to Exhibit 10.8 to Registrant's Annual Report on Form 10-K for the fiscal year ended May 26, 1991).
10.8 —Copy of Executive Health Plan, as amended to date (incorporated herein by reference to Exhibit 10.9 to Registrant's Annual Report on Form 10-K for the fiscal year ended May 26, 1991).
10.9 —Copy of Supplemental Savings Plan, as amended to date (incorporated herein by reference to Exhibit 10.10 to Registrant's Annual Report on Form 10-K for the fiscal year ended May 28, 1989).
10.10—Copy of Compensation Plan for Non-Employee Directors, as amended to date.
10.11—Copy of Retirement Plan for Non-Employee Directors, as amended to date (incorporated herein by reference to Exhibit 10.11 to Registrant's Annual Report on Form 10-K for the fiscal year ended May 31, 1987).
10.12—Copy of Deferred Compensation Plan, as amended to date (incorporated herein by reference to Exhibit 10.13 to Registrant's Annual Report on Form 10-K for the fiscal year ended May 26, 1991).

10.13—Copy of Supplemental Benefits Trust Agreement dated February 9, 1987, as amended and restated as of September 26, 1988 (incorporated herein by reference to Exhibit 10.14 to Registrant's Annual Report on Form 10-K for the fiscal year ended May 28, 1989).

10.14—Copy of Supplemental Benefits Trust Agreement dated September 26, 1988 (incorporated herein by reference to Exhibit 10.14 to Registrant's Annual Report on Form 10-K for the fiscal year ended May 28, 1989).

10.15—Agreements dated November 29, 1989 by and between General Mills, Inc. and Nestlé S.A. (incorporated herein by reference to Exhibit 10.16 to Registrant's Annual Report on Form 10-K for the fiscal year ended May 27, 1990).

10.16—Copy of Protocol and Addendum No. 1 to Protocol of Cereal Partners Worldwide (incorporated herein by reference to Exhibit 10.17 to Registrant's Annual Report on Form 10-K for the fiscal year ended May 26, 1991).

10.17—Copy of Stock Plan for Non-Employee Directors, as amended to date.

10.18—Copy of 1990 Salary Replacement Stock Option Plan, as amended to date.

11 —Statement of Determination of Common Shares and Common Share Equivalents (at the end of this Appendix).

12 —Statement of Ratio of Earnings to Fixed Charges (at the end of this Appendix).

13 —1992 Annual Report to Stockholders (only those portions expressly incorporated by reference herein shall be deemed filed with the Commission).

22 —List of Subsidiaries of General Mills, Inc.

24 —Consent of KPMG Peat Marwick (contained on page 7* of this Report).

(b) Reports on Form 8-K—Not applicable.

Not included in this text.

SIGNATURES

Pursuant to the requirements of Section 13 or 15(d) of the Securities Exchange Act of 1934, the Registrant has duly caused this report to be signed on its behalf by the undersigned, thereunto duly authorized.

GENERAL MILLS, INC.

Dated: August 25, 1992

By: /s/C. L. WHITEHILL

C. L. Whitehill

Senior Vice President,

General Counsel and Secretary

Pursuant to the requirements of the Securities Exchange Act of 1934, this report has been signed below by the following persons on behalf of the Registrant and in the capacities and on the dates indicated.

Signature	Title	Date
/s/ H. B. ATWATER, JR. (H. B. Atwater, Jr.)	Chairman of the Board and Chief Executive Officer	August 18, 1992
/s/ R. M. BRESSLER (Richard M. Bressler)	Director	August 19, 1992
/s/ L. D. DE SIMONE (Livio D. DeSimone)	Director	August 19, 1992
/s/ W. T. ESREY (William T. Esrey)	Director	August 20, 1992
/s/ JUDITH RICHARDS HOPE (Judith R. Hope)	Director	August 19, 1992
/s/ JOE R. LEE (Joe R. Lee)	Director, Vice Chairman and Chief Financial Officer	August 19, 1992
/s/ KENNETH A. MACKE (Kenneth A. Macke)	Director	August 18, 1992
/s/ GWENDOLYN A. NEWKIRK (Gwendolyn A. Newkirk)	Director	August 19, 1992
/s/ GEORGE PUTNAM (George Putnam)	Director	August 19, 1992
/s/ M. D. ROSE (Michael D. Rose)	Director	August 20, 1992
/s/ ARTHUR R. SCHULZE (Arthur R. Schulze)	Director, Vice Chairman	August 19, 1992
/s/ A. MICHAEL SPENCE (A. Michael Spence)	Director	August 24, 1992
/s/ M. H. WILLES (Mark H. Willes)	Director, Vice Chairman	August 18, 1992
/s/ C. ANGUS WURTELE (C. Angus Wurtele)	Director	August 18, 1992
/s/ T. P. NELSON (Thomas P. Nelson)	Senior Vice President, Controller	August 18, 1992

General Mills, Inc. and Subsidiaries
Schedule V—Property, Plant and Equipment
(in millions)

Column A	Column B	Column C	Column D	Column E	Column F
Description	Balance at beginning of period	Additions at cost	Retirements (a)	Other changes add (deduct) (b)	Balance at end of period
Year ended May 31, 1992:					
Land	$ 215.2	$ 41.2	$ 1.6	$ (.9)	$ 253.9
Buildings	1,116.6	198.0	10.2	(2.2)	1,302.2
Equipment	1,701.6	307.8	107.3	1.1	1,903.2
Construction in progress	303.7	148.3	2.0	—	450.0
Total	$3,337.1	$695.3	$121.1	$ (2.0)	$3,909.3
Year ended May 26, 1991:					
Land	$ 172.5	$ 42.6	$ .4	$ .5	$ 215.2
Buildings	938.8	197.0	20.6	1.4	1,116.6
Equipment	1,397.0	385.3	80.2	(.5)	1,701.6
Construction in progress	374.9	(70.3)	1.1	.2	303.7
Total	$2,883.2	$554.6	$102.3	$ 1.6	$3,337.1
Year ended May 27, 1990:					
Land	$ 141.9	$ 31.5	$ 1.3	$ .4	$ 172.5
Buildings	801.7	141.7	8.7	4.1	938.8
Equipment	1,214.6	238.3	64.9	9.0	1,397.0
Construction in progress	245.8	128.5	—	.6	374.9
Total	$2,404.0	$540.0	$ 74.9	$14.1	$2,883.2

Notes:
(a) Gross book value of land, buildings and equipment retired or sold.
(b) Changes in dollar value of foreign assets due to changes in foreign currency translation.

General Mills, Inc. and Subsidiaries
Schedule VI—Accumulated Depreciation, Depletion and Amortization of Property, Plant and Equipment
(in millions)

Column A	Column B	Column C	Column D	Column E	Column F
Description	Balance at beginning of period	Additions charged to costs and expenses (a)	Retirements or sales	Other changes add (deduct) (b)	Balance at end of period
Year ended May 31, 1992:					
Buildings	$ 289.1	$ 54.4	$ 7.0	$ .3	$ 336.8
Equipment	806.7	187.6	72.0	1.6	923.9
Total	$1,095.8	$242.0	$79.0	$ 1.9	$1,260.7

Column A	Column B	Column C	Column D	Column E	Column F
Description	Balance at beginning of period	Additions charged to costs and expenses (a)	Retirements or sales	Other changes add (deduct) (b)	Balance at end of period
Year ended May 26, 1991:					
Buildings	$ 249.8	$ 47.9	$ 8.4	$ (.2)	$ 289.1
Equipment	698.9	165.5	56.7	(1.0)	806.7
Total	$ 948.7	$213.4	$65.1	$(1.2)	$1,095.8
Year ended May 27, 1990:					
Buildings	$ 214.1	$ 38.2	$ 4.6	$ 2.1	$ 249.8
Equipment	601.8	137.9	46.8	6.0	698.9
Total	$ 815.9	$176.1	$51.4	$ 8.1	$ 948.7

Notes:
(a) See Note One (B) of Notes to Consolidated Financial Statements contained in the Registrant's 1992 Annual Report to Stockholders.
(b) Changes in dollar value of foreign assets due to changes in foreign currency translation.

General Mills, Inc. and Subsidiaries
Schedule VIII—Valuation and Qualifying Accounts
(in millions)

Column A	Column B	Column C	Column D	Column E
Description	Balance at beginning of period	Additions charged to costs and expenses	Deductions from reserves	Balance at end of period
Allowance for possible losses on accounts receivable:				
Year ended May 31, 1992	$6.0	$1.9	$1.6 (a) (.1)(b)	$6.4
Total	$6.0	$1.9	$1.5	$6.4
Year ended May 26, 1991	$6.0	$2.2	$2.0 (a) .2 (b)	$6.0
Total	$6.0	$2.2	$2.2	$6.0
Year ended May 27, 1990	$6.0	$2.6	$2.8 (a) (.2)(b)	$6.0
Total	$6.0	$2.6	$2.6	$6.0

Notes:
(a) Bad debt write-offs.
(b) Other adjustments and reclassifications.

General Mills, Inc. and Subsidiaries
Schedule IX—Short-Term Borrowings
(in millions)

Column A	Column B	Column C	Column D	Column E	Column F
Category of short-term borrowings	Balance at end of period	Weighted average interest rate	Maximum amount outstanding (at any month-end)	Average amount outstanding*	Weighted daily average interest rate
Year ended May 31, 1992:					
Banks**	$ 66.2	9.2%	$154.3	$106.6	6.1%
U. S. commercial paper**	—	—	—	68.9	4.9
Canadian commerical paper	103.1	6.9	112.9	67.6	8.0
Year ended May 26, 1991:					
Banks**	$ 15.7	9.7%	$131.3	$ 81.0	8.0%
U. S. commercial paper**	—	—	141.1	91.6	7.6
Canadian commercial paper	7.7	9.7	116.2	67.9	12.3
Year ended May 27, 1990:					
Banks**	$ 40.3	8.7%	$ 84.9	$ 83.8	10.9%
U. S. commercial paper**	—	—	92.6	129.9	8.8
Canadian commercial paper	63.0	14.0	63.0	1.6	14.0

**Determined by dividing total of daily balances outstanding by 371 days for fiscal 1992, and 364 days for fiscal 1991 and 1990, excluding any reclassifications.*

***Short-term borrowings of $150.0 million, $150.0 million and $100.0 million wre reclassified to long-term at May 31, 1992, May 26, 1991 and May 27, 1990, respectively, as the Company's revolving credit agreement (See Note Seven of Notes to Consolidated Financial Statements contained in the Registrant's 1992 Annual Report to Stockholders) provides the Company with the ability to refinance short-term borrowings. If the reclassifications had not been made, the maximum amount of bank debt outstanding would have been $194.4 million, $162.1 million and $133.5 million during the years ended May 31, 1992, May 26, 1991 and May 27, 1990, respectively, and the maximum amount of U.S. commercial paper outstanding would have been $131.5 million, $241.1 million and $212.6 million during the years ended May 31, 1992, May 26, 1991 and May 27, 1990, respectively.*

General Mills, Inc. and Subsidiaries
Schedule X—Supplementary Income Statement Information
(in millions)

	For the Fiscal Years Ended		
	May 31, 1992	May 26, 1991	May 27, 1990
Maintenance and repairs	$209.0	$178.5	$163.9
Depreciation and amortization of intangible assets, preoperating costs and similar deferrals	*	*	*
Taxes, other than payroll and income taxes	*	*	*
Royalties	*	*	*
Advertising media expenditures	426.8	419.6	394.9

**Less than 1% of total sales.*

General Mills, Inc. and Subsidiaries
Schedule XIII—Other Investments
(in millions)

Column A	Column B	Column C	Column D	Column E
Name of issuer and title of each issue	Number of shares or units—principal amounts of bonds and notes	Cost of each issue	Market value of each issue at balance sheet date	Amount at which each issue is carried on the balance sheet
As of May 31, 1992:				
Commercial Paper—U.S. Issuers	$108.4	$108.4	$108.4	$108.4
Zero Coupon U. S. Treasury Securities	350.9	62.0	97.0	62.0
Total		$170.4	$205.4	$170.4
As of May 26, 1991:				
Commercial Paper—U.S. Issuers	$108.7	$108.7	$108.7	$108.7
Zero Coupon U. S. Treasury Securities	378.5	59.2	89.7	59.2
Total		$167.9	$198.4	$167.9

Exhibit 11

General Mills, Inc.
Statement of Determination of Common Shares and Common Share Equivalents

	Weighted average number of common shares and common share equivalents assumed outstanding		
	For the Fiscal Years Ended		
	May 31, 1992	May 26, 1991	May 27, 1990
Weighted average number of common shares outstanding, excluding common stock held in treasury (a)	165,679,432	164,504,874	164,369,106
Common share equivalents resulting from the assumed exercise of certain stock options (b)	3,341,623*	2,561,743*	2,026,540*
Shares potentially issuable under compensation plans	28,288*	37,449*	34,598*
Total common shares and common share equivalents	169,049,343	167,104,066	166,430,244

Notes:

(a) Beginning balance of common stock is adjusted for changes in the number of shares outstanding, weighted monthly by the elapsed portion of the period during which the shares were outstanding.

(b) Common share equivalents are computed by the "treasury stock" method. Share amounts represent the dilutive effect of outstanding stock options which have an option price below the average market price for the period concerned.

**Common share equivalents are not material. As a result, earnings per share have been computed using the weighted average of common shares outstanding of 165,679,432, 164,504,874 and 164,369,106 for fiscal 1992, 1991 and 1990, respectively.*

Exhibit 12

General Mills, Inc.
Ratio of Earnings to Fixed Charges

	Fiscal Year Ended				
	May 31, 1992	**May 26, 1991**	**May 27, 1990**	**May 28, 1989**	**May 29, 1988**
Ratio of Earnings to Fixed Charges	8.58	7.82	7.66	7.73	8.47

For purpose of computing the ratio of earnings to fixed charges, earnings represent pretax income from continuing operations plus fixed charges (net of capitalized interest). Fixed charges represent interest (whether expensed or capitalized) and one-third (the proportion deemed representative of the interest factor) of rents of continuing operation.

APPENDIX D

General Mills, Inc. Proxy Statement

General Mills, Inc.

P. O. Box 1113
Minneapolis, MN 55440

August 17, 1992

To Our Stockholders:

You are cordially invited to attend the 1992 Annual Meeting of Stockholders which will be held in the auditorium of the Children's Theatre Company, 2400 Third Avenue South, Minneapolis, Minnesota, on Monday, September 21, 1992, at 11:00 a.m. Central Daylight Savings Time. All holders of the Company's outstanding common stock as of July 24, 1992 are entitled to vote at the Annual Meeting.

Time will be set aside for discussion of each item of business described in the accompanying Notice of Annual Meeting and Proxy Statement. A current report on the business operations of the Company will be presented at the meeting and stockholders will have an opportunity to ask questions. We plan to adjourn the meeting at approximately 12:15 p.m., but members of senior management will remain to answer any additional questions you may have. Also, a report of the Annual Meeting will be mailed to all stockholders in October.

We hope you will be able to attend the Annual Meeting. Whether or not you expect to attend, you are urged to complete, sign, date and return the proxy card in the enclosed envelope in order to make certain that your shares will be represented at the Annual Meeting.

Sincerely,

H. B. Atwater, Jr.
Chairman of the Board and
Chief Executive Officer

GENERAL MILLS, INC.

NOTICE OF ANNUAL MEETING OF STOCKHOLDERS— SEPTEMBER 21, 1992

NOTICE IS HEREBY GIVEN that the Annual Meeting of Stockholders of General Mills, Inc. will be held on Monday, September 21, 1992, at 11:00 a.m., Central Daylight Savings Time, in the auditorium of the Children's Theatre Company, 2400 Third Avenue South, Minneapolis, Minnesota, for the following purposes:

1. To elect fourteen directors;
2. To approve the selection of KPMG Peat Marwick to audit the consolidated financial statements of General Mills, Inc. for the fiscal year beginning June 1, 1992;
3. If presented at the meeting, to consider and act upon one stockholder proposal as described in the proxy materials; and
4. To act upon any other business which may properly be brought before the meeting.

The close of business on July 24, 1992 has been fixed as the record date for determining the stockholders entitled to notice of and to vote at the Annual Meeting.

By Order of the Board of Directors,
CLIFFORD L. WHITEHILL
Secretary

August 17, 1992

GENERAL MILLS, INC.
PROXY STATEMENT
FOR
ANNUAL MEETING OF STOCKHOLDERS
MONDAY, SEPTEMBER 21, 1992

Voting Procedures

This Proxy Statement is being sent beginning on August 17, 1992, to all holders of the common stock ($.10 par value) (the "Common Stock") of General Mills, Inc., P. O. Box 1113, Minneapolis, MN 55440 (the "Company") entitled to vote at the Annual Meeting of Stockholders on September 21, 1992 in order to furnish information relating to the business to be transacted. Stockholders of record at the close of business on July 24, 1992 are entitled to vote at the meeting. As of that date, there were 163,673,130 shares of Common Stock outstanding. Each share of Common Stock entitles the holder to one vote. The 40,480,202 shares of Common Stock held in the Company's treasury will not be voted.

A proxy card is enclosed for your use. **YOU ARE SOLICITED ON BEHALF OF THE BOARD OF DIRECTORS TO SIGN, DATE, AND RETURN THE PROXY CARD IN THE ACCOMPANYING ENVELOPE,** which is postage-paid if mailed in the United States or Canada.

You have three choices on each matter to be voted upon at the Annual Meeting. As to the election of directors, by checking the appropriate box on your proxy card you may: (i) vote for all of the director nominees as a group;

(ii) withhold authority to vote for all director nominees as a group; or (iii) vote for all director nominees as a group except those nominees you identify in the appropriate area. See "General Information" under Item No. 1. Concerning the other items, by checking the appropriate box you may: (i) vote "FOR" the item; (ii) vote "AGAINST" the item; or (iii) "ABSTAIN" from voting on the item.

You may revoke your proxy at any time before it is actually voted at the Annual Meeting by delivering written notice of revocation to the Secretary of the Company, by submitting a subsequently dated proxy, or by attending the meeting and withdrawing the proxy. You may also be represented by another person present at the meeting through executing a form of proxy designating such person to act on your behalf. Each unrevoked proxy card properly executed and received prior to the close of the meeting will be voted as indicated. Where specific instructions are not indicated, the proxy will be voted FOR the election of all directors as nominated, FOR the approval of the selection of KPMG Peat Marwick as independent auditors and AGAINST the stockholder proposal. A majority of the shares represented at the meeting and entitled to vote is required for approval of the stockholder proposal.

The Company has adopted a policy that all shareholder meeting proxies, ballots and vote tabulations that identify the particular vote of a shareholder are to be secret, and no such document shall be available for examination, nor shall the identity and vote of any shareholder be disclosed to any third party except (i) as necessary to meet applicable legal requirements; (ii) to allow the independent election inspectors to certify the results of the vote; or (iii) in the event of a proxy solicitation in opposition to the Board of Directors based on an opposition proxy statement filed with the Securities and Exchange Commission.

The expense of preparing, printing and mailing this Proxy Statement will be paid by the Company. The Company has engaged Georgeson & Company Inc. to assist in the solicitation of proxies from stockholders at a fee of $9,000 plus reimbursement of its out-of-pocket expenses. In addition to the use of the mail, proxies may be solicited personally or by telephone by regular employees of the Company without additional compensation, as well as by employees of Georgeson & Company Inc. The Company will reimburse banks, brokers and other custodians, nominees and fiduciaries for their costs in sending the proxy materials to the beneficial owners of the Common Stock.

A copy of the 1992 Annual Report to Stockholders, which includes the consolidated financial statements of the Company for the fiscal year ended May 31, 1992, was mailed on or about August 10, 1992 to all stockholders entitled to vote at the Annual Meeting. If upon receipt of your proxy material you have not received the Annual Report, please call 1-800-245-5703 and a copy will be forwarded to you.

Shares of Common Stock credited to the accounts of participants in the Automatic Dividend Reinvestment Plan have been added to such persons' other holdings on their proxy cards. If a stockholder is a participant in a savings plan of the Company or a subsidiary and Common Stock has been allocated to such person's account in a plan, the proxy serves as voting instructions to the plan trustee. The trustee also votes allocated shares of Common Stock as to which it has not received direction, as well as unallocated shares held by the trustee in the same proportion as directed shares are voted.

Certain Owners of Common Stock

State Street Bank and Trust Company, Boston, Massachusetts, has advised the Company that as of June 30, 1992, they held 11,292,613 shares of Common

Stock (6.8% of the then outstanding Common Stock) and that (i) 8,019,369 shares were held in its capacity as trustee of the Company's savings plans and 3,273,244 shares were held in its capacity as trustee for various personal trust accounts, other employee benefit plans and index accounts; and (ii) they had sole power to vote 1,952,676 of such shares, shared voting power on 8,235,759 shares, no voting power on 1,104,178 shares, sole dispositive power on 1,875,484 shares, shared dispositive power on 8,350,237 shares and no dispositive power on 1,066,892 shares. The Company knows of no other holder with more than five percent of the outstanding Common Stock.

ITEM NO. 1: ELECTION OF DIRECTORS

General Information

Directors will hold office until the next Annual Meeting and until their successors are duly chosen and qualify, or until their earlier resignation or removal. The Board of Directors has inquired of each nominee and has ascertained that each will serve if elected. In the event that any of these nominees should become unavailable for election, the Board of Directors may designate substitute nominees, in which event the shares represented by the proxy cards returned will be voted for such substitute nominees unless an instruction to the contrary is indicated on the proxy card.

The Board of Directors has adopted a policy regarding tenure which provides that non-employee directors serve on the Board for no more than 12 consecutive years after election.

Board Compensation and Benefits

Employee directors do not receive additional compensation for serving on the Board of Directors. Non-employee directors received an annual retainer for the 1992 fiscal year of $25,000 plus $1,000 for each Board meeting attended and $700 for each committee meeting attended. The directors' remuneration is paid quarterly. Each year the directors may elect to receive all or a portion of their remuneration: (i) in cash payments; (ii) in cash payments deferred until the director retires, with such amounts earning interest; or (iii) in Common Stock having a market value equal to the remuneration due. In 1992 the following directors elected to receive all of their remuneration in Common Stock: Livio D. DeSimone, William T. Esrey, Kenneth A. Macke, Michael D. Rose and C. Angus Wurtele. Gwendolyn A. Newkirk elected to receive 25% in Common Stock and deferred in cash 75%. All other non-employee directors elected to receive full cash payments. Under the Stock Plan for Non-Employee Directors, each such director receives 400 shares of restricted stock annually upon election or re-election, which restrictions lapse at the later of the next year's annual meeting date or the director's termination of service on the Board. Each non-employee director also receives a one-time stock option grant for 2,500 shares upon election to the Board. A retirement plan for non-employee directors provides for an annual retirement benefit for directors who have served at least five years in an amount equal to the retainer fee in effect at the date of the director's retirement, payable for the lesser of (i) the number of years of the director's service; or (ii) the lifetime of the director. The Company also pays the premiums on directors' and officers' liability and travel accident insurance policies covering the directors.

As part of its overall program to promote charitable giving, the Company has established a directors' planned gift program funded by life insurance policies on directors. Upon the death of an individual director, the Company will donate $1 million to one or more qualifying charitable organizations recommended by the individual director and subsequently be reimbursed by life insurance proceeds. Individual directors derive no financial benefit from this program since all charitable deductions accrue solely to the Company. The program does not result in any material cost to the Company.

Committees of the Board

During the fiscal year ended May 31, 1992, the Board of Directors met six times and various committees of the Board met a total of twelve times. Attendance at Board meetings averaged 95% and attendance at committee meetings averaged 95%. Each incumbent director attended more than 75% of the Board meetings and the meetings of Board committees on which the director served, except Richard M. Bressler, who missed one Board meeting and three committee meetings held the same day, which lowered his attendance to 73%.

Audit Committee. The Audit Committee consists of six non-employee directors: Michael D. Rose (Chair), Richard M. Bressler, Livio D. DeSimone, Judith Richards Hope, Kenneth A. Macke and A. Michael Spence (effective 6/22/92). The Committee met twice during fiscal 1992. It also meets separately with representatives of the Company's independent auditors and with the representatives of senior management and the internal auditors. The Committee reviews: (i) the general scope of audit coverages; (ii) the fees charged by the independent auditors; (iii) matters relating to the internal control systems; (iv) the value of goodwill and other intangibles; and (v) the expenses of senior executives.

Compensation Committee. The Compensation Committee consists of five non-employee directors: Richard M. Bressler (Chair), William T. Esrey, George Putnam, Michael D. Rose and C. Angus Wurtele. The Compensation Committee met five times during fiscal 1992. The Committee administers the stock option and long-term incentive plans and the Executive Incentive Plan, and in this capacity it makes or recommends all option grants or awards to Company officers and executives under these plans. In addition, the Committee makes recommendations to the Board with respect to the compensation of the Chairman of the Board and approves the compensation paid to other senior executives. The Committee also recommends the establishment of policies dealing with various compensation, pension and profit-sharing plans for the Company and its subsidiaries. See pages 16-17 (page D-12 in this text) and 19-21 (page D-13 in this text) for their reports on fiscal 1992 compensation and stock ownership programs.

Executive Committee. The Executive Committee consists of seven directors: H. Brewster Atwater, Jr. (Chair), Richard M. Bressler, Livio D. DeSimone, William T. Esrey, Joe R. Lee, George Putnam and Mark H. Willes. The Executive Committee did not meet in fiscal 1992. Pursuant to the By-Laws, the Committee has the authority to take all actions that could be taken by the full Board of Directors. It may meet between regularly scheduled meetings to take such action as is necessary for the efficient operation of the Company.

Finance Committee. The Finance Committee consists of six non-employee directors: George Putnam (Chair), Livio D. DeSimone, Kenneth A. Macke, Gwendolyn A. Newkirk, Michael D. Rose and A. Michael Spence (effective 6/22/92). The Finance Committee met twice during fiscal 1992. It reviews and makes recommendations relating to public offerings of debt and equity securities, major borrowing commitments and other significant financial transactions, including the dividend policy of the Company.

Nominating Committee. The Nominating Committee consists of five non-employee directors: William T. Esrey (Chair), Richard M. Bressler, Judith Richards Hope, George Putnam and C. Angus Wurtele. The Nominating Committee held two meetings during fiscal 1992. The Committee's duties include proposing a slate of directors for election by the stockholders at each annual meeting and proposing candidates to fill vacancies on the Board. It conducts research to identify suitable candidates for Board membership, and seeks individuals who will make a substantial contribution to the Company. It will consider candidates proposed by stockholders. Generally, candidates must be highly qualified and be both willing and affirmatively desirous of serving on the Board. They should represent the interests of all stockholders and not those of a special interest group. A stockholder wishing to nominate a candidate should forward the candidate's name and a detailed background of the candidate's qualifications to the Secretary of the Company.

Public Responsibility Committee. The Public Responsibility Committee consists of five non-employee directors: C. Angus Wurtele (Chair), Livio D. DeSimone, Judith Richards Hope, Kenneth A. Macke and Gwendolyn A. Newkirk. The Public Responsibility Committee met once in fiscal 1992. The duties of the Committee are to review and make recommendations regarding the Company's policies, programs and practices in relation to public issues of significance to the Company. In addition, it reviews and makes recommendations regarding trends in the political and social environment that may affect the operations of the Company.

Share Ownership of Directors and Officers

Set forth in the following table is the beneficial ownership of Common Stock as of August 1, 1992 for all directors as of the date of this Proxy Statement, all nominees to the Board of Directors and all directors and officers as a group. Shares listed as beneficially owned include shares allocated to participant accounts under the Company's savings plans as of July 31, 1992, according to the plans' administrator. No director or officer owns more than 0.86% of the total outstanding shares (including exercisable options). All directors and officers as a group own 3.8% of the total outstanding shares (including exercisable options).

Name	Shares (a)	Name	Shares (a)
H. B. Atwater, Jr.	358,172	G. A. Newkirk	4,375
R. M. Bressler	5,644	G. Putnam	80,800
L. D. DeSimone	2,419	M. D. Rose	16,511(c)
W. T. Esrey	1,200	A. R. Schulze	63,787
J. R. Hope	3,008	A. M. Spence	100
J. R. Lee	75,334(b)	M. H. Willes	104,551(d)
K. A. Macke	900	C. A. Wurtele	9,249
All directors and officers as a group			1,203,513

(a) The amounts shown do not include the following shares that may be acquired within 60 days pursuant to outstanding option grants: H. B. Atwater, Jr., 1,045,068 shares; J. R. Lee, 364,024 shares; A. R. Schulze, 414,084 shares; M. H. Willes, 619,582 shares; all other listed persons except A. M. Spence, 2,500 shares each; and all directors and officers as a group, 5,024,084 shares. (b) Included in the shares for Mr. Lee are 800 shares owned by members of his family, in which he disclaims any beneficial interest. (c) Included in the shares for Mr. Rose are 13,779 shares owned by or held in trust for members of his family, in which he disclaims any beneficial interest. (d) Included in the shares for Mr. Willes are 615 shares owned by members of his family, in which he disclaims any beneficial interest.

Compliance with Section 16(a) of the Securities Exchange Act of 1934

Section 16(a) of the Securities Exchange Act of 1934 requires the Company's executive officers and directors to file initial reports of ownership and reports of changes in ownership with the Securities and Exchange Commission and the New York Stock Exchange. Executive officers and directors are required by SEC regulations to furnish the Company with copies of all Section 16(a) forms they file. Based solely on a review of the copies of such forms furnished to the Company and written representations from the Company's executive officers and directors, the Company notes that one officer, Stephen R. Garthwaite, did not timely report a transaction in Common Stock that occurred in January 1992, although he filed a corrected report shortly thereafter, and that certain family trusts for which a director, Michael D. Rose, or his spouse, acts as trustee, did not timely report transactions in Common Stock that occurred in June 1991. However, all of the holdings and transactions relating to Mr. Rose were included in individual reports which were timely filed by Mr. Rose in his capacity as a director of the Company.

Information Concerning Nominees

H. BREWSTER ATWATER, JR. — Director since 1971

H. Brewster Atwater, Jr., age 61, has been Chief Executive Officer of General Mills, Inc. since 1981. Mr. Atwater joined General Mills in 1958 and served in a variety of sales and marketing positions. He was elected Executive Vice President in 1970, President in 1977 and Chairman of the Board in 1982. Mr. Atwater is a director of General Electric Company and Merck & Co., Inc.; a member of the Policy Committee of the Business Roundtable and The Business Council. He is a member of the International Council of J. P. Morgan & Co. Incorporated and a director of American Public Radio.

RICHARD M. BRESSLER — Director since 1984

Richard M. Bressler, age 61, is Chairman of the Board of Plum Creek Timber Company and El Paso Natural Gas Company. He joined Burlington Northern, Inc. as President and Chief Executive Officer in 1980 and retired from that position in 1990. He previously served as a General Mills director in 1978-79. Mr. Bressler is also a director of El Paso Natural Gas Co., H. F. Ahmanson & Company, Baker Hughes Incorporated and Rockwell International Corporation.

LIVIO D. DeSIMONE — Director since 1989

Livio D. DeSimone, age 56, is Chairman of the Board and Chief Executive Officer, Minnesota Mining and Manufacturing Company (3M). Mr. DeSimone joined 3M in 1957 and has served in various U. S., international and subsidiary capacities. Mr. DeSimone was elected Executive Vice President, Life Sciences Sector in 1981; Executive Vice President, Industrial and Consumer Sector in 1984; and Executive Vice President, Information and Imaging Technologies Sector and Corporate Services, in 1989. He is a director of 3M, Cray Research, Inc., Dayton Hudson Corporation and Vulcan Materials Company, and a trustee of the University of Minnesota Foundation.

WILLIAM T. ESREY — Director since 1989

William T. Esrey, age 52, is Chairman and Chief Executive Officer of Sprint Corporation. He has been Chief Executive Officer of the company since 1985. Prior to joining the company in 1980 as Executive Vice President-Corporate

Planning, he was with Dillon, Read & Co. Inc., where he served from 1970-79 as a managing director. Mr. Esrey is a director of Sprint, The Equitable Life Assurance Society of the United States and Panhandle Eastern Corporation, and an individual general partner of Boettcher Venture Capital Partners, L.P.

JUDITH RICHARDS HOPE **Director since 1989**

Judith Richards Hope, age 51, is a senior partner of the law firm of Paul, Hastings, Janofsky & Walker, Los Angeles, California and Washington, DC. She has been a partner with the firm since 1981. Ms. Hope is a director of The Budd Company, IBM Corporation and Union Pacific Corporation, a member of the Harvard Corporation (The President and Fellows of Harvard College), a director of Cities in Schools and a trustee of Ford's Theatre and of the National Housing Partnership Foundation.

JOE R. LEE **Director since 1985**

Joe R. Lee, age 51, is Vice Chairman, Chief Financial Officer of General Mills, Inc. Mr. Lee joined Red Lobster in 1967 and was a member of its founding team. He was named its President in 1975, a Vice President of General Mills in 1976, a Group Vice President in 1979 and Executive Vice President, Restaurants in 1981. He was named to his current position in April 1992, having served since April 1991 as Executive Vice President, Finance. Mr. Lee is past president of the National Restaurant Association, a member of the Minnesota Advisory Board of the United Negro College Fund, a director of the Minnesota Orchestral Association, a director of the University of Central Florida Foundation, and a Presidential appointee to the Board of Trustees for the Orlando Museum of Art.

KENNETH A. MACKE **Director since 1991**

Kenneth A. Macke, age 53, is Chairman of the Board, Chief Executive Officer and Chairman of the Executive Committee of Dayton Hudson Corporation (DHC). He joined Dayton's as a merchandise trainee and advanced through various management positions at Dayton's and Target. In 1977, he was elected Chairman and Chief Executive Officer of Target and Senior Vice President of DHC. He served as President of DHC from 1981 to 1984. He was elected Chief Operating Officer of DHC in 1982, Chief Executive Officer in 1983, Chairman of the Board in 1984 and Chairman of the Executive Committee in 1985. He is a director of DHC, First Bank System, Inc. and Unisys Corporation.

GWENDOLYN A. NEWKIRK **Director since 1990**

Dr. Gwendolyn A. Newkirk, age 66, is the retired Chairman of the Department of Consumer Science and Education at the University of Nebraska, having joined the University in 1971. She is the author of a number of articles on home economics, consumerism and the black family. Dr. Newkirk previously served as a General Mills director from 1975 to 1989. She received an honorary doctorate degree from Huston-Tillotson College in 1990 and the American Home Economics Education Association Foundation Distinguished Service Award in June 1991. She is a member of the board of directors of Tabitha, Inc. (health care services), Lincoln, Nebraska.

GEORGE PUTNAM **Director since 1981**

George Putman, age 65, is Chairman of The Putnam Management Company, Inc. He is also Chairman and President of each of The Putnam Group of Mutual

Funds. Mr. Putnam joined The Putnam Management Company in 1951 as a security analyst. He became a director in 1960, Executive Vice President in 1961 and President and Chief Executive Officer later that year. He has served as Chairman since 1970. Mr. Putnam is a director of The Boston Company, Inc., Boston Safe Deposit & Trust Co., Inc., Freeport-McMoran Inc., Houghton-Mifflin Co., Marsh & McLennan Companies and Rockefeller Group, Inc. He is on the boards of McLean Hospital, Massachusetts General Hospital, The Colonial Williamsburg Foundation, Museum of Fine Arts (Boston) and The WGBH Foundation.

MICHAEL D. ROSE **Director since 1985**

Michael D. Rose, age 50, is Chairman of the Board and Chief Executive Officer of The Promus Companies Incorporated. Promus, the public parent company of Harrah's Casino/Hotels and Embassy Suites, Hampton Inn and Homewood Suites hotels, was spun-off from Holiday Corporation in early 1990. Mr. Rose joined Holiday in 1974. He was elected President in 1979 and held that position until 1984, was elected Chief Executive Officer in 1981 and Chairman of the Board in 1984. In 1988 he resumed the position as President. Mr. Rose is a director of Ashland Oil, Inc., First Tennessee National Corp. and the Memphis Arts Council, a member of The Business Roundtable and the President's Executive Council at the University of Cincinnati.

ARTHUR R. SCHULZE **Director since 1986**

Arthur R. Schulze, age 61, is a Vice Chairman of General Mills, Inc. Mr. Schulze joined General Mills in 1962 and held various assignments in the Grocery Products Division and the Consumer Foods Group. He was named a Vice President of General Mills in 1970, Group Vice President in 1973, Executive Vice President in 1981, President of the Grocery Products Food Group in 1985 and Vice Chairman in 1989. Mr. Schulze is a director of Tennant Co., Inc. and Inter-Regional Financial Group, a trustee of Carleton College and the Minneapolis Institute of Arts, and a director of Methodist HealthCare.

A. MICHAEL SPENCE **Director elected April 1992**

Dr. A. Michael Spence, age 48, has been Dean of the Graduate School of Business at Stanford University since July 1990. His election to the Board of Directors became effective in June 1992. Dean Spence served on the faculty at Harvard University in both the Business School and the Faculty of Arts and Sciences as professor of economics and business administration from 1975 to 1990. From 1984 to 1990 he served as the Dean of the Faculty of Arts and Sciences at Harvard. Dean Spence is a director of BankAmerica Corporation, Polaroid Corporation and Sun Microsystems, Inc. He also serves on the Board of Trustees of the Joint Council on Economic Education and is a Fellow of the Econometric Society.

MARK H. WILLES **Director since 1985**

Mark H. Willes, age 51, is a Vice Chairman of General Mills, Inc., a position to which he was elected in April 1992. He was Executive Vice President, Chief Financial Officer of General Mills, Inc. from 1980 to 1985, and served as President from 1985 to April 1992. Mr. Willes served as President of the Federal Reserve Bank of Minneapolis from 1977 to 1980, First Vice President of the Federal Reserve Bank of Philadelphia from 1971 to 1977, and as Vice President, Director of Research and Senior Economist at the Philadelphia Federal Reserve Bank. He is a director of The Black & Decker Corporation.

C. ANGUS WURTELE **Director since 1985**

C. Angus Wurtele, age 57, is Chairman of the Board and Chief Executive Officer of The Valspar Corporation. Mr. Wurtele joined Minnesota Paints, Inc. (which later merged into Valspar) as a Vice President in 1962. He was elected as Executive Vice President of Minnesota Paints in 1965 and as President and Chief Executive Officer later that year. In 1970, Mr. Wurtele became President and Chief Executive Officer of Valspar, and he was elected to his current position in 1973. Mr. Wurtele is a director of Donaldson Company, Inc. and The NWNL Companies, Inc. He is also a director of the National Paint and Coatings Association, the Walker Art Center and The Bush Foundation. He is a member of the American Business Conference, the Minnesota Business Partnership and the Advisory Council of the Graduate School of Business, Stanford University.

These fourteen (14) persons will be placed in nomination for election to the Board of Directors. The shares represented by the proxy cards returned will be voted FOR the election of these nominees unless you specify otherwise.

ITEM NO. 2: APPROVAL OF THE APPOINTMENT OF INDEPENDENT AUDITORS

The stockholders are asked to consider and approve the appointment by the Board of Directors of KPMG Peat Marwick ("KPMG"), an independent certified public accounting firm, to audit the consolidated financial statements of the Company for the fiscal year beginning June 1, 1992. KPMG has audited the books of the Company since 1928. During fiscal 1992, KPMG provided General Mills with audit and other services, with fees totalling approximately $2,060,000. Representatives of the firm will attend the Annual Meeting and have the opportunity to make a statement if they desire, and will also be available to answer questions.

The Board of Directors recommends you vote FOR the appointment of KPMG Peat Marwick as the independent auditors and your proxy will be so voted unless you specify otherwise.

ITEM NO. 3: STOCKHOLDER RESOLUTION ON CUMULATIVE VOTING

Lewis D. Gilbert and John J. Gilbert, owner of 616 shares, both of 1165 Park Avenue, New York, New York 10028, who state that they are co-trustees under the will of Minnie D. Gilbert for 800 shares of Common Stock and represent an additional family interest of 2,208 shares, have notified the corporation in writing that they intend to present the following resolution at the Annual Meeting:

> "RESOLVED: That the stockholders of General Mills, Inc., assembled in annual meeting in person and by proxy, hereby request the Board of Directors to take the steps necessary to provide for cumulative voting in the election of directors, which means each stockholder shall be entitled to as many votes as shall equal the number of shares he or she owns multiplied by the number of directors to be elected, and he or she may cast all of such votes for a single candidate, or any two or more of them as he or she may see fit."

The statement of the shareholders in support of the resolution is as follows:

"Continued strong support along the lines we suggest were shown at the last annual meeting when 15.2%, 2,758 owners of 19,367,598 shares were cast in favor of this proposal. The vote against included 9,553 unmarked proxies.

"The Proxy Monitor, Inc., which reviews both management and shareholder proposals on a monthly basis, comments on one of our cumulative voting proposals in its January 1990 Part One issue thus:

'Specifically at issue in the cumulative voting debate are questions as old as the idea representative democracy itself: Can an opposition be loyal? Should minorities be represented? TPM analysts answer yes on both counts. Consequently, we support adoption of the instant initiative.'

"Majority rule is important but potential minority rights of shareholders should not be denied if and when desired. This is the purpose of cumulative voting, in our opinion, it protects everyone.

If you agree, please mark your proxy for this resolution; otherwise it is automatically cast against it, unless you have marked to abstain."

The Board of Directors favors a vote AGAINST the adoption of the shareholder resolution on cumulative voting for the following reasons:

The Board of Directors continues to believe that in order to be effective, each member must feel a responsibility to represent all stockholders. Cumulative voting is undesirable because it is directed toward the election of one or more directors by a special group of stockholders. Directors so elected might be principally concerned with representing and acting in the interest of the special group that elected them rather than in the interest of the stockholders as a whole.

Cumulative voting introduces the possibility of partnership among Board members which could destroy the ability of the Board to work together. These factors could operate to the disadvantage of the Corporation and its stockholders.

The present method of electing directors, where each director is elected by majority vote of the stockholders as a whole, permits the directors to administer the affairs of the Corporation for the benefit of all the stockholders. We believe that each director should serve on the Board only if the majority of the stockholders elect the director to hold that position.

An examination of the past performance and the achievements of the management team selected by the Board of Directors supports the present method of electing the Board, and the Board of Directors is confident that this method will continue to work as successfully in the future as it has in the past, for the benefit of all stockholders.

The Board of Directors recommends you vote AGAINST this stockholder proposal and your proxy will be so voted unless you specify otherwise.

OTHER BUSINESS

The Company is not aware of any business to be acted upon at the annual meeting other than that which is explained in this Proxy Statement. In the event than any other business calling for a vote of the stockholders is properly presented at the meeting, the holders of the proxies will vote your shares in accordance with their best judgment.

REPORT OF COMPENSATION COMMITTEE ON ANNUAL COMPENSATION

The Compensation Committee of the Board of Directors (the "Committee") is composed entirely of independent outside directors (see page 5—page D-5 in this text). The Committee is responsible for setting and administering the policies which govern both annual compensation and stock ownership programs.

The Committee annually evaluates General Mills' corporate performance, actual compensation and share ownership compared with both our own industry and a broader group of companies such as the S&P 500.

The annual compensation programs of the Company are highly leveraged on the basis of performance. General Mills' annual compensation mix generally has lower base salaries than comparable companies, coupled with a highly leveraged incentive system which will pay more with good performance and less with below par performance.

Executive Incentive Plan Description

The Executive Incentive Plan ("EIP") is based on the following factors: corporate performance, business unit performance and personal performance. The corporate performance rating is based on the Company's percentage growth in earnings per share over the prior year and its return on equity. The Committee believes that these two factors are the primary determinants of share price over time. Business unit ratings are based primarily on profit performance (market share performance, new product development, workplace diversity and other factors are considered). Personal ratings can include such qualitative factors as quality of the strategic plan, organizational and management development progress and industry, public affairs, and civic involvement.

Corporate and business unit ratings can range from .5 to 1.8 with top quartile performance represented by a 1.5 or higher rating. Personal ratings can range from 0.0 to 1.5. These ratings are then combined with the participant's target incentive participation rate (a percentage of base salary which increases for higher positions within the Company). Both business unit and personal ratings are heavily dependent on achievement of financial objectives. The weights for executive officers are 50% corporate and 50% personal, while business unit officers are generally 38% unit, 12% corporate and 50% personal.

Under the EIP, incentive awards are made annually to key management employees selected by the Committee. Receipt of cash incentive awards may be deferred to a subsequent date or to retirement. Under the stock matching provisions of the EIP, each participant may deposit shares of Common Stock with a value equal to 25% of the participant's cash incentive award with the Company. Participants age 55 or over may elect not to participate fully in the stock matching provisions of the EIP. If such election is made, those participants receive an additional cash award (which may also be deferred). A participant under age 55 who elects not to deposit shares does not receive an additional cash award. The Company issues one share of "restricted" Common Stock for each share that the participant originally deposits. The shares vest 50% at three years and 50% at six years, provided the participant's deposit shares remain with the Company. A participant may elect to receive directly the dividends paid on all stock held in the participant's account, or reinvest such dividends in Common

Stock. The EIP provides for the full vesting of restricted shares in the event there is a change of control of the Company. The cost of the Common Stock to the Company bears no necessary relation to its market value at the time of ultimate distribution to the participants. Stock matching shares granted in respect of fiscal 1985 and fiscal 1988 were distributed in fiscal 1992 as follows: H. B. Atwater, Jr., 4,679 shares; F. C. Blodgett, 1,384 shares; J. R. Lee, 2,547 shares; A. R. Schulze, 1,049 shares; M. H. Willes, 2,492 shares; and to all executive officers, 24,285 shares. Stock matching shares are included in the table on page 24 (page D-17 in this text) under the "Restricted Stock" heading.

Performance Evaluation

The Committee meets without the Chief Executive Officer's presence to evaluate his performance and reports on that evaluation to the independent directors of the Board.

The Committee's evaluation of corporate performance in fiscal 1992 was 1.72 compared with 1.8 in fiscal 1991. This was based on 1992 earnings per share growth (before unusual items) of 14.7% in fiscal 1992 and 17.2% in fiscal 1991. Return on equity was 40.7% in fiscal 1992 and 45.5% in fiscal 1991. See the tables on page 25 (pages D-17 and D-18 in this text) showing corporate performance over the last five fiscal years. Personal incentive ratings for each participant listed in the table on page 18 (at the top of the next page) were at or near the top of the scale in both fiscal 1992 and 1991. Specific salary and cash incentive payments are disclosed in the same table. None of the executive officers indicated in this table received a merit salary increase in fiscal 1992 as all of the executive officers elected to receive stock option grants in lieu of a merit salary increase.

REPORT OF THE COMPENSATION COMMITTEE ON STOCK OWNERSHIP PROGRAMS

The General Mills Board of Directors, Compensation Committee and management believe that significant stock ownership is a major incentive in building shareholders' wealth and aligning the interests of employees and shareholders. The Committee believes that broad and deep stock ownership is highly motivating and has set an objective that 10% of the Common Stock of General Mills be owned by employees by 1995 and that over 90% of employees with more than three years experience own Common Stock.

Stock Options. The shareholders approved the Stock Option and Long-Term Incentive Plan in 1988 and a Salary Replacement Stock Option Plan in 1990 with favorable votes of 82.4% and 94.4% respectively. The table on page 22 (page D-16 in this text) gives a summary of shares granted under these plans to all employees and to the executive officers.

Included in the totals are options granted under three different programs: regular stock options, deposit stock options and options in lieu of salary. Regular stock options are granted to employees based on their potential impact on corporate results and on their performance. 1,638 employees were granted options on 1,692,600 shares under that program in fiscal 1992. Stock options with performance units as an alternative form of exercise were granted to 29 officers as part of the regular grants outlined above (see page 20—the bottom of page D-14 in this text).

To encourage retention of stock, the deposit stock option program requires the deposit of one share of owned Common Stock for every two options shares

		Annual Compensation			
Name and Principal Position	**Fiscal Year**	**Salary(a)**	**Bonus(b)**	**Other Compensation(c)**	**Total**
H. B. Atwater, Jr.					
Chairman of the Board and Chief	1992	$ 620,591(d)	$ 786,900	$ 20,141	$ 1,427,632
Executive Officer	1991	607,882	823,500	37,197	1,468,579
F. C. Blodgett					
Vice Chairman, Chief Financial					
and Administrative Officer	1992	401,633(e)	620,875	146,283	1,168,791
(retired 5/1/92)	1991	428,507	640,895	17,868	1,087,270
J. R. Lee					
Vice Chairman and Chief					
Financial Officer	1992	396,771(d)	442,700	30,100	869,571
(effective 5/1/92)	1991	357,229	372,400	22,683	752,312
A. R. Schulze	1992	362,181(d)	464,725	12,155	839,061
Vice Chairman	1991	354,764	467,935	6,995	829,694
M. H. Willes	1992	442,553(d)	538,700	13,643	994,896
Vice Chairman	1991	433,490	563,800	14,488	1,011,778
All Executive Officers as a	1992	5,235,564(d)	5,685,525	661,341	11,582,430
Group (20) (f)	1991	4,829,702	5,112,610	420,999	10,363,311

(a) Includes all before-tax contributions to the Voluntary Investment Plan described at page 26 (page D-17 in this text).

(b) These amounts are the cash awards under the Executive Incentive Plan described at pages 16–17 (pages D-12 and D-13 in this text).

(c) Other compensation for Messrs. Atwater, Blodgett, Lee, Schulze and Willes includes personal benefits consisting primarily of personal use of Company automobiles, financial counseling and moving expenses, and the Executive Health Plan, described at page 28 (page D-20 in this text). The total value of the personal benefits in 1992 for all executive officers as a group was $323,584. Mr. Blodgett also received $115,768 for unused vacation at his retirement, and in 1991 Mr. Lee received $9,000 for unused vacation under the Restaurant operations' policy. In addition to the personal benefits described above, certain executive officers received in cash the value of unusued vacation, one executive officer received a housing allowance, another executive officer received foreign service allowances and a third executive officer received a signing bonus.

(d) 53 week fiscal year.

(e) Partial year due to 5/1/92 retirement.

(f) Compensation for all officers as a group covers only the period during which such persons were executive officers of the Company.

granted. The maximum number of shares permitted for deposit is based on the number of shares equivalent to 50% of the executive's prior year incentive payment.

The option in lieu of salary program was available to 72 employees in fiscal 1992. All executive officers received stock option grants in lieu of merit salary increases in 1992.

Stock options are granted to officers by the Board of Directors upon recommendation of the Committee, and are granted at an option price not less than the fair market value of the Common Stock on the grant date. The Stock Option and Long-Term Incentive Plan of 1988 (the "1988 Plan") permits the granting of "incentive stock options" under Section 422 of the Internal Revenue Code (none granted to date) and stock options which are not incentive stock options ("non-qualified options"). Stock options are outstanding under the 1980, 1984, 1988 and 1990 Plans, although options may be granted only under the 1988 and 1990 Plans. No option may be exercised after ten years and one month from the date of grant. These Plans provide for full vesting of options in the event that is a change of control of the Company.

Performance Unit Exercise Alternative. Performance units may be granted as an exercise alternative with the grant of regular non-qualified stock options under the 1988 Plan. Some performance units are outstanding which were granted under the 1980 and 1984 Plans. Performance units are payable in cash and an optionee may exercise them as an alternative to the exercise of regular stock options.

As of August 1, 1992, no performance unit had a value in excess of the value of the stock option available for exercise as an alternative to the performance unit.

The value of performance units is measured over three fiscal years by a formula that compares the Company's compound growth in earnings per share for the three-year period and the after-tax return on average stockholders' equity for the third year of the three-year period, with predetermined goals established by the Committee at the time of grant. The Committee may modify such goals and/or exclude the effect of unusual items from earnings and returns. At the end of the three-year period, the value (if any) of the performance units is credited to a participant's account and thereafter credited quarterly with an amount equal to interest at a rate determined by the Committee. Upon withdrawal of performance units granted before fiscal 1987, the corresponding stock options are forfeited as to a number of shares of which the "appreciated value" (the difference between the market price of stock on the date of withdrawal and the stock price on the grant date) is equal to the amount withdrawn. Comparably, upon the exercise of a corresponding stock option, the participant's account is decreased by the "appreciated value" existing on the date of exercise. For performance unit grants after fiscal 1987, a withdrawal from a performance unit account or the exercise of a stock option cancels the other on a one for one basis. During fiscal 1992, withdrawals from performance units accounts were as follows: F. C. Blodgett, $531,009; M. H. Willes, $116,000; no withdrawals were made by H. B. Atwater, Jr., J. R. Lee or A. R. Schulze; and all executive officers as a group, $796,717.

Performance units awarded in fiscal 1992 will complete the three-year period at the end of fiscal 1994. If the compound growth in earnings per share is between 4% and 16%, a value of between $2 and $13 will be calculated for each unit, and if the after-tax return on average stockholders' equity for fiscal 1994 is between 13% and 25%, a value of between $2 and $13 will be calculated for each unit. The total value of the performance unit will be the sum of the calculations under the two formulas with the maximum value not to exceed $15 per unit. These performance units will have no value if the Company's compound growth rate in earnings per share for the three-year period is less than 4% and the after-tax return on average stockholders' equity for fiscal 1994 is less than 13%. The number of performance units awarded with and as an alternative to stock options granted during fiscal 1992 are as follows: H. B. Atwater, Jr., 80,000; F. C. Blodgett, 44,000; J. R. Lee, 40,000; A. R. Schulze, 40,000; M. H. Willes, 60,000; and all executive officers as a group, 537,000.

Restricted Stock. The 1988 Plan authorizes the Committee to make awards of restricted stock or restricted stock units (for employees of foreign operations) to selected employees, and in that connection, to determine the number of shares to be awarded, the length of the restricted period, the purchase price, if any, to be paid by the participant and whether any other restrictions will be imposed in respect of such awards. Restricted stock or restricted stock units may vest in the participant prior to the completion of the restricted period in the event of permanent disability, retirement, death, change of control or certain terminations of employment as described in the 1988 Plan. One restricted stock grant of 21,618 shares was made under the 1988 Plan to one executive officer in the group and vests in four approximately equal annual installments. Most grants of restricted stock have been made with the requirement that the recipient deposit with the Company one share of Common Stock owned by the recipient for each share of restricted stock awarded, and that such "deposit" shares remain with the Company until the expiration of the restricted period, which is generally three years. This requirement is in keeping

Stock Option Summary Report

Total Number of Common Shares Outstanding at May 31, 1992	165,494,098
Total Number of Common Shares Authorized To Be Granted as Options	18,100,000*
Percentage of Total Common Shares Outstanding Authorized	10.9%
Total Number of Options Granted To Date Under Current Authorizations	8,627,841
Percentage of Total Authorizations	47.7%
Total Number of Options Granted in Fiscal 1992	2,574,008
Total Number of Options Granted to Named Executives in Fiscal 1992	436,496
Percentage of Total Number of Options Granted to Named Executive Officers	17.0%
Total Number of Options Granted to CEO in Fiscal 1992	146,280
Percentage of Total Number of Options Granted to CEO in Fiscal 1992	5.7%
Total Number of Options Granted to Executive Group in Fiscal 1992	932,226
Percentage of Total Options Granted to Executive Group in Fiscal 1992	36.2%

All shares authorized to be granted are issued under plans approved by the shareholders. The 1988 Plan was approved by an 82.4% vote, the 1990 Salary Replacement Stock Option Plan (6,000,000 shares) by a 94.4% vote and the Stock Plan for Non-Employee Directors (100,000 shares) by an 89.6% vote.

Stock Option Table

Name/Group	Number of Options Granted Fiscal 1992(a)	Average Per Share Option Price	Dollar Gains based on Assumed Rates of Stock Price Appreciation(b), (c) 0%	50%	100%	200%
All Shareholders	N/A	N/A	$0	$5,254,437,612	$10,508,875,223	$21,017,750,446
H. B. Atwater, Jr.	146,280	$58.46	$0	$ 4,275,764	$ 8,551,529	$ 17,103,058
CEO gain as % of All Shareholders' gain	N/A	N/A	N/A	0.08%	0.08%	0.08%
F. C. Blodgett	56,240	$57.93	$0	$ 1,628,992	$ 3,257,983	$ 6,515,966
J. R. Lee	65,372	$58.16	$0	$ 1,901,018	$ 3,802,036	$ 7,604,071
A. R. Schulze	75,770	$58.51	$0	$ 2,216,651	$ 4,433,303	$ 8,866,605
M. H. Willes	92,834	$58.05	$0	$ 2,694,507	$ 5,389,014	$ 10,778,027
All Executive Officers as a Group	932,226	$58.44	$0	$ 27,239,664	$ 54,479,287	$ 108,958,575
All Optionees	2,574,008	$58.29	$0	$ 75,019,463	$ 150,038,926	$ 300,077,853

(a) Options generally are exercisable one year from the grant date, although one set of option grants made in fiscal 1992 will not be exercisable for three years.

(b) For the named officers and the groups, other than "All Shareholders," the gain is calculated from the average per share price of fiscal 1992 granted options. For "All Shareholders," the gain is calculated from $63.50, the closing price of the Common Stock on May 29, 1992, based on the outstanding shares of Common Stock on that date.

(c) Pre-tax gains listed for the named officers and the groups other than "All Shareholders" are net of the average option exercise price; the pre-tax gain for "All Shareholders" is net of the Common Stock closing price on May 29, 1992. These amounts represent certain assumed rates of appreciation only. Actual gains, if any, on stock option exercises and Common Stock holdings are dependent on the future performance of the Common Stock and overall stock market conditions. There can be no assurance that the amounts reflected in this table will be achieved.

Total Common Stock Holdings, Option Holdings and Fiscal Year Gains As of May 31, 1992

Name	Unrestricted Stock Beneficially Owned, Excluding Options(a)	Restricted Stock (b)	Option Shares (c)	Fiscal 1992 Number of Options Exercised	Fiscal 1992 Net Value of Option Shares Exercised
H. B. Atwater, Jr.	275,903	92,501	1,097,170	53,544	$ 3,139,997
F. C. Blodgett	68,877	0	569,576	71,033	$ 3,815,402
J. R. Lee	63,041(d)	10,596	385,948	24,068	$ 1,162,032
A. R. Schulze	60,856	1,688	438,380	18,500	$ 1,006,401
M. H. Willes	89,706(e)	12,644	655,256	0	N/A
All Executive Officers	942,517	199,255	5,935,487	310,055	$15,870,229

(a) Includes shares allocated under the Company's savings plans as of May 31, 1992.
(b) Includes shares issued under the stock matching provisions of the EIP. See pages 16–17 (pages D-12 and D-13 in this text).
(c) Includes all exercisable and non-exercisable option shares as of May 31, 1992.
(d) Included in the shares for Mr. Lee are 800 shares owned by members of his family, in which he disclaims any beneficial interest.
(e) Included in the shares for Mr. Willes are 615 shares owned by members of his family, in which he disclaims any beneficial interest.

with the Company's philosophy of encouraging Common Stock ownership by employees.

Savings Plans

Under the Voluntary Investment Plan ("VIP"), participants may elect to contribute up to 15% of their compensation on either an after-tax or before-tax basis. In 1992, total pre-tax savings may not exceed $8,728 annually. Contributions of up to 5% of compensation are supplemented by a base matching contribution from the Company at the rate of fifty cents per dollar contributed. Through an employee stock ownership plan ("ESOP"), all matching contributions are made in shares of Common Stock with a market value equal to the re-

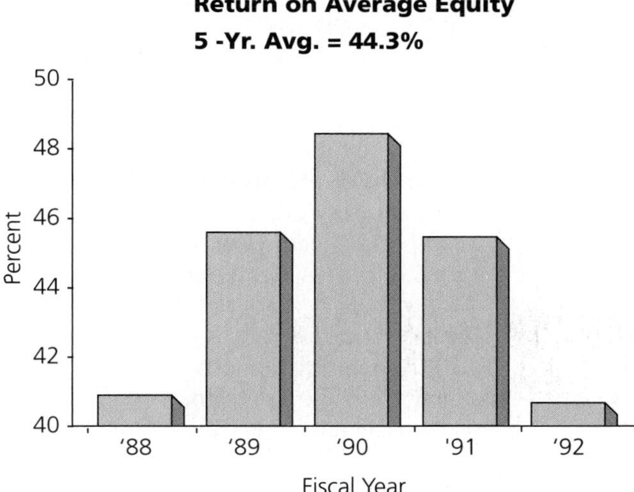

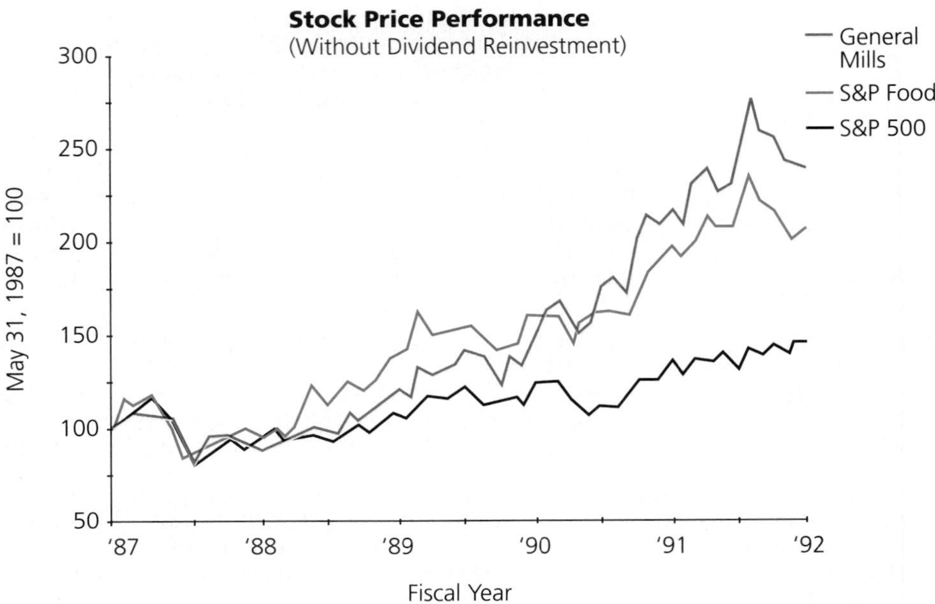

quired amount. At the end of each fiscal year, the Company may make an additional variable match of up to 50% of eligible contributions, determined by the Company's fiscal year performance. Company contributions are vested 25% at two years of service, 50% at three years, 75% at four years and 100% at five years of service. The General Mills Restaurants savings plan (the "PSSP") matches participant contributions of up to 6% of compensation through an ESOP. The matching contributions vary in value from 25 cents up to one dollar for each dollar contributed by the participant, as determined by the related restaurant division. The Company also has a non-qualified Supplemental Savings Plan, which credits amounts to accounts of executive officers who participate in the Company's savings plans but who are affected by the maximum benefit limitations under qualified plans imposed by the Employee Retirement Income Security Act of 1974, as amended ("ERISA"). The Company's contributions or allocations to these plans for the persons named in the compensation table were as follows: H. B. Atwater, Jr., $46,895 in fiscal 1992 and $48,759 in fiscal 1991; F. C. Blodgett, $51,321 in fiscal 1992 and $59,344 in fiscal 1991; J. R. Lee, $42,616 in fiscal 1992 and $21,066 in fiscal 1991; A. R. Schulze, $40,827 in fiscal 1992 and $43,801 in fiscal 1991; M. H. Willes, $53,483 in fiscal 1992 and $50,257 in fiscal 1991; and all executive officers as a group in fiscal 1992, $483,406.

Defined Benefit Retirement Plans

The Company's Retirement Income Plan ("RIP") will provide pension benefits to all persons named in the compensation table. Although J. R. Lee will receive a portion of his retirement benefits from a pension plan sponsored by a Company subsidiary, the total benefits from both plans will approximate the benefits payable from the RIP as if his service had been solely under the RIP. Under the RIP, retirement benefits for salaried non-union employees consist of a fixed benefit providing a normal retirement income equal to the sum of the "Past Service Benefit" and the "Current Service Benefit," subject to a maximum benefit of 50% of "Final Average Earnings." Past Service Benefit is equal to an employee's accrued benefit under the RIP, as of December 31, 1988, adjusted by any increases in Final Average Earnings. The basic formula for such benefits is 50% of Final Average Earnings, less 50% of the employee's projected Social Security benefit, times years of service divided by 30. Current Service Benefit is equal to the sum of 1.1% of Final Average Earnings, plus .65% of the excess of Final Average Earnings over "Covered Compensation," for each year of service after 1988. Final Average Earnings is defined as the average of the five highest consecutive years' remuneration. Such remuneration is generally equal to the salary and bonus reported in the compensation table plus the value of shares of Common Stock granted pursuant to the stock matching provisions of the EIP. Covered Compensation is the average of the Social Security taxable wage bases for the 35-year period ending with the year in which the employee reaches normal retirement age for Social Security purposes.

The following table shows the estimated annual aggregate benefits payable at normal retirement for various classifications of earnings and years of benefit service. This table is based on the maximum benefit under the RIP of 50% of Final Average Earnings for a participant with 30 years of service. The effects of integration with Social Security benefits have been excluded from the table, because the amount of the reduction in benefits due to integration varies depending on the participant's age at the time of retirement and changes in the Social Security laws. The table does not reflect any limitations on benefits imposed by ERISA or federal tax law. The Company's Supplemental Retirement Plan provides for the payment of additional amounts to certain executive officers (including those named in the table) so that they will receive in the aggregate, the benefits they would have been entitled to receive had neither ERISA nor fedral law imposed maximum limitations. The total retirement benefits of executive officers whose sum of age and services as of June 1, 1992 equaled or exceeded 65 will be determined as if the Past Benefit Service formula under the RIP had continued in effect for service after 1988. During fiscal 1992, lump-sum prepayments were made to certain participants, including F. C. Blodgett, and one other executive officer in the group, of the vested accrued retirement benefits they were entitled to under the Supplemental Plan. Accordingly, at the time of retirement or termination, the total benefit paid to these participants will be reduced by the value of the prepayment (plus interest).

Final Average Earnings (as defined)	10 years of service	15 years of service	20 years of service	25 years of service	30 or more years of service
$ 100,000	$ 16,666	$ 25,000	$ 33,333	$ 41,666	$ 50,000
300,000	50,000	75,000	100,000	125,000	150,000
500,000	83,333	125,000	166,666	208,333	250,000
700,000	116,666	175,000	233,333	291,666	350,000
900,000	150,000	225,000	300,000	375,000	450,000
1,100,000	183,333	275,000	366,666	458,333	550,000
1,300,000	216,666	325,000	433,333	451,666	650,000
1,500,000	250,000	375,000	500,000	625,000	750,000
1,700,000	283,333	425,000	566,666	708,333	850,000
1,900,000	316,666	475,000	633,333	791,666	950,000

The persons named in the compensation table have the following full years of benefit service as defined in the RIP: H. B. Atwater, Jr., 34 years; F. C.

Blodgett, 30 years; J. R. Lee, 23 years; A. R. Schulze, 29 years; and M. H. Willes, 12 years.

Other Benefits

The Executive Health Plan is an insured hospital, medical and dental plan covering corporate officers at and above the senior vice president level and their dependents. The plan (paid for in full by the Company) provides coverage for 100% of such expenses, subject to an individual lifetime maximum benefit of $2,000,000. The aggregate cost of these benefits in excess of health benefits provided generally to salaried employees is included in the compensation table on page 18 (page D-14 in this text). The Company also reimburses executive officers for financial counseling expenses, subject to differing maximum payments at various levels, not to exceed $7,500 for any individual. These amounts are also included in the table on page 18 (page D-14 in this text) under "Other Compensation."

The Company maintains management continuity agreements with most of its executive officers (including the current officers specifically named in the compensation table) providing for guaranteed severance payments equal to three times the annual compensation of the officer (salary plus EIP cash award) and continuation of health and similar benefits for a three-year period if there is a change of control of the Company and the officer is terminated within two years thereafter. These agreements also provide for a cash payment of the amount necessary to insure that the foregoing payments are not subject to reduction due to the imposition of excise taxes payable under Section 4999 of the Internal Revenue Code or any similar tax.

The Company has entered into two trust agreements to provide for payment of amounts under its non-qualified deferred compensation plans, including the directors' compensation plans, the EIP, the management continuity agreements and the Supplemental Savings and Retirement Plans. Full funding is required in the event of a change of control. To date, only a nominal amount has been paid into each trust.

The Company maintains at its sole expense a supplemental pre-retirement survivor income plan covering key executives of the Company. In the event of death, the surviving spouse is provided with a lifetime benefit of 25% of the Final Average Earnings of the officer. If there is no surviving spouse, surviving dependent children will be provided a benefit of 12½% of Final Average Earnings so long as dependency requirements are met. Benefits are payable on a monthly basis. All benefits unders this plan are reduced on a dollar for dollar basis for any survivor benefits payable from the qualified pension plans maintained by the Company.

Stockholder Proposals for the 1993 Annual Meeting

Any stockholder proposal intended to be presented for consideration at the 1993 Annual Meeting and to be included in the Company's proxy statement must be received at the principal executive offices of the Company by the close of business on April 19, 1993. Proposals should be sent to the attention of the Secretary.

YOUR VOTE IS IMPORTANT!

Please sign and promptly return your proxy in the enclosed envelope.

APPENDIX E

Compaq Computer Corporation Consolidated Statement of Cash Flows

Compaq Computer Corporation
CONSOLIDATED STATEMENT OF CASH FLOWS

	Year ended December 31,		
	1991	**1990**	**1989**
		(in thousands)	
Cash flows from operating activities:			
Cash received from customers	**$3,325,465**	$3,536,984	$2,771,724
Cash paid to produce inventories	**(2,014,919)**	(2,005,673)	(1,911,970)
Cash paid to other suppliers and employees	**(807,729)**	(715,397)	(521,863)
Interest received	**32,301**	26,889	22,269
Interest paid	**(36,907)**	(46,728)	(38,898)
Income taxes paid	**(104,001)**	(140,294)	(134,619)
Net cash provided by operating activities	**394,210**	655,781	186,643
Cash flows from investing activities:			
Purchases of property, plant and equipment, net	**(188,746)**	(324,859)	(367,151)
Investment in Silicon Graphics, Inc.	**(135,000)**		
Purchases of other assets, net	**(16,636)**	(1,747)	(3,886)
Proceeds from sale of stock of affiliated company			10,815
Net cash used in investing activities	**(340,382)**	(326,606)	(360,222)
Cash flows from financing activities:			
Proceeds from issuance of notes payable			30,000
Purchases of treasury shares	**(82,275)**		
Proceeds from sale of equity securities	**22,637**	22,645	14,820
Repayment of borrowings	**(540)**	(30,561)	(444)
Net cash provided by (used in) financing activities	**(60,178)**	(7,916)	44,376

	Year ended December 31,		
	1991	**1990**	**1989**
		(in thousands)	
Effect of exchange rate changes on cash	**23,824**	(47,872)	9,337
Net increase (decrease) in cash	**17,474**	273,387	(119,866)
Cash and short-term investments at beginning of year	**434,700**	161,313	281,179
Cash and short-term investments at end of year	**$ 452,174**	$ 434,700	$ 161,313
Reconciliation of net income to net cash provided by operating activities:			
Net income	**$ 130,869**	$ 454,910	$ 333,300
Depreciation and amortization	**165,824**	135,305	84,575
Provision for bad debts	**8,542**	3,878	1,014
Equity in net income of affiliated company	**(19,765)**	(29,682)	(13,771)
Unrealized gain on investment in affiliated company		(34,532)	(13,691)
Realized gain on investment in affiliated company			(7,621)
Deferred income taxes	**(9,639)**	40,443	29,315
Loss on disposal of assets	**4,200**	4,887	1,235
Exchange rate effect	**(4,136)**	21,422	5,727
Other changes in net current assets	**118,315**	59,150	(233,440)
Net cash provided by operating activities	**$ 394,210**	$ 655,781	$ 186,643

The accompanying notes are an integral part of these financial statements.

GLOSSARY

A

accelerated depreciation an accounting method that allocates a larger portion of plant asset cost to expense early in the asset's life than does the straight-line method.

account a record of increases and decreases in the dollar amount associated with a specific resource or activity.

accounting an information system for the measurement and reporting of the transformation of resources into goods and services and the sale or transfer of these goods and services to consumers.

accounting changes the effects on income of changes in accounting principles from one fiscal period to another.

accounting cycle the recording, summarizing, and reporting of accounting information.

accounting information system the specific part of the management information system responsible for tracking financial resources, their transformation, and their costs, and for describing the results in financial reports.

accounting standard an official pronouncement establishing acceptable accounting procedures or financial report content.

accounts payable amounts owed by an organization to its suppliers.

accounts receivable amounts of cash to be received in the future from credit sales to customers.

accounts receivable turnover operating revenues divided by average accounts receivable.

accrual basis an accounting system in which revenues are recognized (recorded) when earned and expenses are recognized (recorded) when incurred.

accrued expenses expenses recognized prior to the time cash is paid for resources consumed.

accrued revenues revenues recognized prior to the time cash is received for goods and services sold.

accumulated depreciation the sum of all depreciation expense recorded on plant assets since their acquisition.

acquisition an economic event in which one company acquires a controlling interest in another company, which continues to exist as a separate legal entity.

allowance for doubtful accounts an account that identifies the amount of accounts receivable a company's management expects is likely to become uncollectible.

amortization the process of systematically allocating a cost to expense over a period of time.
annuity a series of equal payments over a specified number of equal time periods.
appropriation of retained earnings a transfer of a portion of retained earnings to a separate account to restrict its use.
articulation the relationship among financial statements in which the numbers on one statement explain numbers on other statements.
asset turnover the ratio of operating revenues to average total assets during a fiscal period.
assets resources controlled by an organization and available for its use in the future.
attestation affirmation by an auditor as to whether financial statements are presented fairly in conformity with generally accepted accounting principles and are reliable representations of an organization's economic activities.
audit a detailed examination of an organization's financial reports and supporting documents; also, a verification process to ensure that information provided by an accounting system is reliable.
audit committee members of a corporation's board of directors who discuss the audit and its findings with the independent auditors.
audit opinion see audit report.
audit report a statement of the auditor's belief about the fairness and reliability of accompanying financial information.
authorized shares the maximum number of shares a corporation can issue without receiving approval from stockholders and the state to amend its charter.

B

balance sheet the financial report commonly used to report the amounts of assets, liabilities, and owners' equity.
bond a certificate of credit that represents an amount owed to a creditor.
book value the net dollar amount reported for an account on an organization's financial statement.
business combination see merger.
business organizations organizations that sell goods and/or services with the intention of earning profits.
business risk uncertainty associated with a company's financing, investing, and operating activities that affects the amount and timing of its cash flows.

C

capital resources invested by owners in a business; sometimes used to refer to resources provided by owners and to resources provided by creditors.
capital expenditures amounts paid for the purchase, lease, and construction of plant assets.
capital lease a contract that permits one organization to use property owned by another organization as though the property had been purchased. Capital leases transfer most of the risks and rights of ownership to the company leasing the assets.
capital maintenance principle returns to owners are to be paid out of profits and not out of owners' contributions to an organization; profits result only when a company earns revenues in excess of costs of resources consumed during a period.
capital stock the ownership rights of investors in a corporation.
capital structure the way a company chooses to finance its assets and operating activities.
cash basis an accounting system in which revenues are recognized when the related cash is received and expenses are recognized when the related cash is paid.
cash equivalent a short-term investment that can be converted to cash quickly and easily.
cash flow the amount of cash received by an organization (cash inflow) or the amount of cash paid out by an organization (cash outflow) during a certain period of time.
certified public accountant (CPA) an accountant who has passed a rigorous exam and has been granted a license to practice by a state or territory of the U.S.
chart of accounts a list of account titles used by an organization in its accounting system.
charter the legal right granted by a state permitting a corporation to exist.
commitment a promise to engage in some future activity that will have an economic effect.
compensation arrangements any wage or salary contract between a company and employees; often refers to incentive plans offered to execu-

tives that will reward them for meeting specified goals.

compilation financial statements prepared by an independent accountant for a client from the client's accounting records.

completed contracts method for long-term contracts an accounting method that recognizes revenue when a long-term contract is completed.

conceptual framework a set of objectives, principles, and definitions to guide the development of new accounting standards.

consolidated financial statements a report of the combined economic activities of two or more corporations owned by the same stockholders.

contingency an existing condition that may result in an economic effect if a future event occurs.

contra-account an account that offsets another account; sometimes referred to as a valuation account.

contracts legally binding agreements for the exchange of resources and rights.

contributed capital the amount of direct investment by owners in a corporation.

control the evaluation of organizational activities and modification of these activities to achieve organization goals.

convertible bonds bonds that can be converted into shares of the issuer's stock.

corporation a legal entity separate and distinct from its owners.

cost accounting those functions necessary to accumulate and report a company's costs.

cost management strategies and methods to reduce costs and increase competitiveness.

cost of goods sold the cost incurred by an organization to acquire or produce the inventory that was sold during a specific period.

coupon rate of return see nominal rate of return.

creditor a person or organization to whom obligations are owed.

credits bookkeeping entries that decrease asset or expense accounts and increase liability, owners' equity, or revenue accounts.

current assets cash or other resources management expects to convert to cash or consume during the next fiscal year, or operating cycle (if longer than a year).

current liabilities obligations management expects to pay during the next fiscal year or operating cycle (if longer than a year).

current ratio see working capital ratio.

D

data base an orderly storage device that allows data to be retrieved and manipulated systematically.

date of declaration the date a corporation's board of directors announces that a dividend will be paid.

date of payment the date dividends are mailed to recipients.

date of record the date used to determine the recipients of a dividend.

debentures bonds that are unsecured by specific assets.

debits bookkeeping entries that increase asset or expense accounts and decrease liability, owners' equity, or revenue accounts.

debt covenants see loan agreements.

debt financing results when a company obtains financial resources from creditors.

debtors those with obligations to an organization.

declining balance depreciation an accounting method that allocates a multiple of the straight-line rate times the book value of an asset to depreciation expense.

deferred charges assets resulting when a company prepays expenses that will result in long-term benefits.

deferred expenses expenses that have not yet been incurred but for which cash has been paid.

deferred income tax the accumulated difference between the amount of income tax expense and income tax liability over the life of a company.

deferred revenues revenues that have not yet been earned but for which cash has been collected.

depletion the systematic allocation of the cost of natural resources to the periods that benefit from their use.

depreciation the process of allocating the cost of plant assets to expense over the accounting periods that benefit from the asset's use.

direct labor wages and benefits of employees who work directly in the manufacturing process that are added to the cost of production.

discontinued operations major lines of business or segments from which a company will no longer derive income.

discount on bonds payable a contra-liability account resulting from the sale of bonds at a price less than their maturity value.

discussion memorandum a document that identifies accounting issues and alternative approaches to resolving the issues that may lead to an accounting standard.

dividend a distribution of assets, usually cash, to stockholders from a corporation's profits.

dividend payout ratio the total cash dividend for a fiscal period divided by net income for the period.

dividend yield the ratio of the dividend paid on each share of stock to the price of the stock.

double-entry bookkeeping a systematic method for recording the effects of transactions in an accounting data base where each transaction is recorded in two or more accounts.

E

earnings per share a measure of earnings performance computed by dividing net income by the average number of shares of common stock outstanding during a fiscal period.

effective business an organization that meets customer needs by producing or providing goods and services that customers demand at a price they are willing to pay.

effective rate of return the actual return earned on an investment or incurred on a liability.

efficient business an organization that produces or provides goods and services at reasonable cost relative to the selling prices of its products.

equity financing the issuance of stock as a means of raising capital for a corporation.

equity method for investments an accounting method that requires an investor company to recognize revenue from an investee company's net income in proportion to the investors' ownership.

expenses the consumption of resources or incurrence of obligations as a result of selling goods or providing services to customers.

exposure draft a document that describes a proposed accounting standard.

extraordinary items gains and losses that are both unusual and infrequent.

F

financial accounting the development and reporting of accounting information for use by interested parties external to an organization.

financial leverage the ratio of debt to equity in a company's capital structure.

financial revenues and expenses another name for revenues and expenses not directly related to primary operating activities.

financial risk the risk that a company may be unable to make promised payments to investors.

financing activities those activities by which an organization raises and maintains capital to be used in the business.

finished goods inventory products awaiting sale.

first-in first-out (FIFO) inventory method an accounting method for estimating inventory cost that assumes those units of inventory acquired first are sold first.

fiscal period any period of time for which operating results are collected and reported; could be a day, week, month, quarter, year, etc.

fixed assets see property, plant, and equipment.

fixed assets turnover operating revenues divided by average fixed assets.

fixed costs costs that do not vary in proportion to sales activity.

foreign currency translation the process of converting the financial results of operations that occur in a foreign currency into U.S. dollars for financial reporting purposes.

form 10-K reports annual registration statements filed by corporations with the SEC.

fully diluted earnings per share earnings per share attributable to common stock after considering all effects of exercising options and warrants and converting debt and preferred stock that would reduce earnings per share.

functional currency the currency a company or division uses in conducting its operating activities.

future value the amount a liability or investment is worth at some time in the future.

G

generally accepted accounting principles (GAAP) the practices and procedures commonly used by accountants in preparing financial reports for external parties.

generally accepted auditing standards (GAAS) procedures used in conducting an audit to help auditors form an opinion about the fairness and reliability of the audited statements.

going concern an organization that can be expected to continue to operate into the foreseeable future.

goodwill the excess of cost over the market value of identifiable net assets resulting from the purchase of one company by another.

governmental and nonprofit organization one whose purpose is to provide goods and services without the intention of earning a profit.

gross margin see gross profit margin.

gross profit the difference between the cost and selling price of goods or services sold to customers during a period.

gross profit margin the ratio of gross profit to operating revenues.

H

historical cost the purchase or exchange price of an asset or liability at the time it is acquired or incurred.

I

income from operations the excess of gross profit over operating expenses.

income statement a commonly used financial statement that reports the profit (net income) earned by a business over a certain period of time.

indirect labor the cost of wages and benefits paid to maintenance and supervisory employees who are associated with the production process.

intangible assets long-term legal rights resulting from the ownership of patents, copyrights, trademarks, and similar items.

interest the cost of borrowed money.

interest expense the cost associated with borrowing money during a fiscal period.

interest payable an amount owed to creditors for the use of the creditors' money during a fiscal period.

interest rate risk uncertainty about future interest rates.

internal control an organization's plan and the procedures it uses to safeguard its assets, ensure reliable information, promote efficiency, and encourage adherence to policies.

inventory turnover cost of goods sold divided by average inventory.

investing activities acquisition or disposal of long-term resources.

investment risk the probability that an investment will be partially or completely lost or that returns on an investment will differ from expectations.

investors owners and creditors who provide money to an organization with the expectation of earning a return.

issued shares the number of shares that have been sold by a corporation to investors.

J

journal an accounting book used for the original recording of transactions in chronological order.

L

last-in first-out (LIFO) inventory method an accounting method for estimating inventory cost that assumes the last units of inventory acquired are sold first.

ledger an accounting data base in which financial information is classified and stored by account.

liabilities obligations owed by an organization to its creditors.

limited liability characteristic of a corporation in which shareholders are not personally liable for the debts of a corporation.

liquid assets resources that can be converted to cash in a relatively short period.

liquidity the extent to which an organization has sufficient cash and other liquid assets to pay current obligations.

loan agreements restrictions placed on a company's economic activities by its creditors.

long-term investments investments in securities that will not mature during the coming fiscal year and that management does not plan to convert to cash during the coming year.

long-term liabilities obligations not classified as current liabilities.

lower of cost or market method for investments an accounting method that requires investments to be reported at their aggregate cost or market value, whichever is lower.

M

managerial accounting the development and reporting of accounting information for use by an organization's managers and employees.

manufacturing companies organizations that build or produce the goods they sell to other organizations or to consumers.

market any location or process that facilitates the exchange of resources.

marketable security a financial instrument (usually a stock or bond) that can be readily sold in an organized market.

master file a computer file that contains relatively permanent information that occurs once for each entity or item (e.g., a customer, vendor, or inventory item).

materiality criteria for establishing the importance of a transaction or of a potential misstatement in financial statements.

merchandising companies organizations that sell tangible products to other organizations or to consumers.

merger an economic event that occurs when companies combine their resources and operations so only one legal entity continues to exist.

minority interest the percentage of a subsidiary not owned by the parent.

minority interest in income of consolidated subsidiaries the portion of subsidiary net income attributable to minority interest.

moral hazard the condition that exists when agents (e.g., managers) have access to information that is not available to principals (e.g., stockholders) and are in a position to use the information to make decisions that are in the best interest of the agents, but not in the best interest of the principals.

multinational corporations companies that operate in foreign and domestic markets.

mutual agency a legal right that permits a partner to enter into contracts and agreements that are binding on all members of a partnership.

N

net cash flow the difference between cash inflows and cash outflows during a specific period of time.

net income the difference between revenues and expenses.

net loss the result when expenses are greater than revenues for a period.

net present value of an investment the excess of the present value of future cash inflows expected from an investment over its cost.

net profit margin the ratio of net income (or income before special items) to operating revenues.

net value the total price of all goods and services provided by the transformation process minus the total cost of all goods and services consumed therein.

nominal rate of return the rate of interest paid on an investment or liability.

nonbusiness organizations governmental or nonprofit organizations, including civic, social, and religious organizations.

notes payable contracts with creditors that affirm the borrower will repay the amount borrowed plus interest at specific dates.

O

operating activities those activities related to the transformation of resources into goods and services.

operating expenses costs of resources consumed as part of operating activities during a fiscal period that are not directly associated with specific goods or services. Operating expenses are period costs because they are recognized in the fiscal period in which they occur.

operating income gross profit minus operating expenses.

operating lease a contract that permits one organization to use property owned by another organization for a limited period of time. The costs of operating leases are expensed in the period in which leased assets are used.

operating leverage the relationship between fixed and variable costs.

operating profit margin the ratio of operating income to operating revenues.

organization a group of people who work together to develop, produce, and/or distribute goods or services.

other assets a general category of assets that sometimes includes long-term investments in other companies, noncurrent receivables, fixed assets held for sale, and long-term legal rights such as patents, trademarks, and copyrights.

other revenues and expenses revenues and expenses that are not directly related to a company's primary operating activities.

outstanding shares the number of a corporation's shares currently held by investors.

overhead production costs other than direct materials and direct labor.

owners' equity the amount of the owners' investment in an organization; legally, the amount of assets remaining after all creditor claims have been satisfied.

P

paid-in capital in excess of par value the excess of the sales price of stock sold by a corporation over its par value.

par value the value assigned to each share of stock by a corporation in its corporate charter.

parent a corporation that controls another corporation, normally by owning more than 50% of the other corporation's common stock.

partnership a business owned by two or more persons, with no legal identity distinct from that of their owners.

percentage of completion method for long-term contracts an accounting method that recognizes revenues and expenses for long-term contracts in proportion to the amount of the contract completed each fiscal period.

period costs all costs except those incurred to manufacture or acquire a product and prepare it for sale. These costs are reported as expenses in the period in which they occur.

periodic measurement estimated results of financing, investing, and operating activities recorded during a particular period.

planning the development of organizational goals and the development of strategies and policies to achieve these goals.

plant assets see property, plant, and equipment.

preemptive right the right of stockholders to maintain the same percentage of ownership when new shares are issued.

preferred stock stock that has a higher claim on dividends and assets than common stock.

premium on bonds payable an amount received by a bond issuer when bonds are sold at more than their maturity value.

present value the amount an investment or liability is worth at the beginning of a time period.

price-earnings (PE) ratio the ratio of price per share to earnings per share.

primary earnings per share earnings per share attributable to common stock outstanding and to common stock equivalents.

primary market the market in which new (or original) issues of stocks and bonds are sold.

principal the amount of a loan that must be repaid.

product costs costs incurred to manufacture or acquire a product and distribute it to customers.

profit the difference between the price received for goods or services sold and the total cost to the seller of all goods and services consumed by the seller in acquiring or producing those goods or services; another name for net income or net earnings.

profit margin the ratio of a company's earnings to its operating revenues.

property, plant, and equipment long-term, tangible assets that are used in a company's operations.

proprietorship a business owned by one person, with no legal identity distinct from that of the owner.

proxy a document that authorizes management to cast votes for its stockholders at a stockholders' meeting.

proxy statement information distributed to stockholders about matters that will be considered at a corporation's annual stockholders' meeting.

public goods nonseparable goods; ones that cannot be made available to one person without making them available to all persons.

R

raw materials inventory the physical ingredients of a product that are used in the manufacturing process.

retail companies organizations that sell tangible products to consumers.

retained earnings the portion of cumulative net income that has been reinvested in an organization.

return of investment an amount received by investors that is paid from the amounts the investors originally invested.

return on assets the ratio of net income plus interest expense adjusted for taxes to average total assets.

return on equity the ratio of net income minus preferred dividends to average common stockholders' equity.

return on investment an amount that could be paid to investors from profits earned by an organization, also see return on assets.

revenue increase in resources or reduction in obligations from selling goods or providing services to customers.

review an examination by an independent accountant of a client's financial statements to provide assurance they appear to be in good order.

risk see investment risk.

S

secondary market a market in which investors sell to each other.

service companies those that sell services instead of tangible goods.

shareholders' equity see stockholders' equity.

short-term security a financial instrument (usually a stock or bond) that can be readily and easily sold in an organized market and is likely to be sold.

sinking fund a long-term investment to which a company makes payments for a period of time to accumulate financial resources to repurchase stock or pay debt.

source documents the original records of transactions, such as invoices, receipts, and shipping documents.

statement of cash flows a financial statement that reports events that resulted in cash inflows and outflows for a fiscal period.

statement of stockholders' equity a financial statement that provides information about changes in owners' equity accounts for a corporation during a fiscal period.

stock certificates of ownership in a corporation.

stock dividends shares of stock distributed by a company to its current stockholders without charge to the stockholders.

stock market an organization established to facilitate the trading of shares of corporate securities; examples include the New York Stock Exchange, the American Stock Exchange, or the Tokyo Stock Exchange.

stock options legal rights that permit the holder, usually an employee of the grantor, to purchase a specified number of shares of a company's stock at a predetermined price.

stock split the issuance by a corporation of a multiple of the number of shares of stock outstanding prior to the split.

stock warrants legal rights that permit the holder to purchase additional shares of the issuer's stock at a future date at a prescribed price.

stockholders owners of a corporation.

stockholders' equity claims by owners of stock to the resources of a corporation.

straight-line depreciation an accounting method that allocates an equal amount of the cost of a plant asset to expense during each fiscal period of the asset's expected useful life.

subsequent events major economic activities occurring after the close of a company's fiscal year but prior to the time its annual report is printed.

subsidiaries corporations controlled by other corporations, normally by ownership of more than 50% of the subsidiaries' common stock.

subsidiary ledger a collection of a related group of accounts such as all accounts receivable or all accounts payable.

sum-of-the-years'-digits depreciation an accounting method that allocates depreciation according to a fraction, n/N, in which n is remaining life of the asset at the beginning of the period and N is the sum of the years of the expected useful life of the asset.

system a group of resources that work together to achieve a goal.

T

transaction an economic event that results in a change in the amount of an asset, liability, equity, revenue, or expense.

transaction analysis the process of evaluating a transaction to determine its effect on specific accounts.

transaction file a computer file that contains transactions during a specific period for the entities contained in a master file.

transformation process a cycle that begins with the acquisition of money from investors and creditors. This money is invested in facilities and equipment used to transform resources into goods and services. Organizations use these resources in producing, distributing, and selling goods and services. Selling goods and services results in the inflow of additional money so that the cycle can continue. An organization's success in the transformation process determines its profitability.

translation adjustment gains or losses resulting from translating the operations of a company's foreign subsidiaries into U.S. dollars for purposes of reporting consolidated financial statements.

treasury stock stock a corporation sold to its investors and then repurchased from them that can be reissued.

trial balance a list of all an organization's accounts and their balances at a specific point in time.

U

unearned revenue an obligation to provide goods or services in the future, usually because cash has been received for the goods or services.

units-of-production depreciation an accounting method that produces a level amount of depreciation expense per unit of output, rather than per fiscal period.

V

variable costs costs that vary in proportion to sales activity.

W

warranty a promise by a seller to repair or replace defective products or to service products over a period of time.

weighted average inventory method an accounting method for estimating inventory cost that assumes an average cost of units available during a period as the cost of units sold.

withdrawals distribution of assets, usually cash, to a proprietor or partner.

work in process inventory goods currently in the process of being manufactured.

working capital the amount of current assets minus the amount of current liabilities.

working capital ratio the amount of current assets divided by the amount of current liabilities.

Y

yield to maturity see effective rate of return.

INDEX

A

Account(s), 4, 63, 142
  chart of, 140
  created as needed, 106
  government funds and, 674
Account balances, 4, 28, 135-137, 139, 144, 182-210
Account groups, 667-669
Accounting, 2, 28-30
  development of, 304-308
  organization environment and, 47
Accounting cycle, 148, 151
Accounting equation, 93, 136, 138-140, 144
Accounting information, see Information
Accounting measurement, 89-111, 565, 576
  cash flows and, 96-98
  nonbusiness organizations and, 670-681
  reports and, 234-263
  rules, 61, 234-263, 354, 471
  time and, 96-105
  transformation process and, 91-96, 105-108
  See also Accrual basis of accounting measurement; Cash basis of accounting measurement
Accounting methods, 297
  earnings and, 633-634
  equity and, 474
  taxes and, 300-301
Accounting periods, 9. See also Fiscal periods
Accounting process, 2-5, 28, 147
Accounting profession, 287-315
Accounting records, 2-3, 162
Accounting reports, see Financial statements; Report(s)
Accounting standards, 54-55, 308-315, 353, 588, 682
Accounting system, 4, 67, 91
  computerized, 149-160
  management and, 163-164
  manual, 135-148
Accounts payable, 64, 143, 248
  cash flows and, 257-258
  computers and, 150, 156
  decision makers and, 164
  decreases in, 637-638
  recording, 406
  significant increases in, 260
Accounts receivable, 63, 141, 569
  accrual accounting and, 99, 246
  asset turnover and, 626, 629
  cash flow associated with, 256
  computers and, 150, 154
  decision makers and, 164
  increase in, 260, 637-638
  uncollectible, 185, 571-572
Accounts receivable ledger, 142
Accounts receivable turnover, 629
Accrual basis of accounting measurement, 98-105, 108-110, 184, 185
  cash measurement and, 103-105, 234-263, 390
  governments and, 671-672
  income statement and, 187, 200, 590
  interest and principal, 393-394
  operating cash flows and, 637
  timing differences and, 245-249
  trial balance and, 147
Accrued expenses, 245, 247-249
Accrued revenues, 245-246
Acid-test ratio, 442
Acquisitions, 301, 394, 477-479, 527-531, 639

Adjustments, 147, 235-244, 290, 346, 349
Advertising, 102, 580
Affiliated companies, 474-475, B11
Allocations, 204, 296
American Institute of Certified Public Accountants (AICPA), 293, 296, 306, 308, 682
Amortization, 196, 259
- bonds, 388, 481-482
- depreciation and, 204
- General Mills, Inc., C15-C16
- intangible assets, 493-494
- leased assets and, 491, 492
- notes receivable and, 480
- statement of cash flows and, 593

Analysis of financing activities, 421-452
- dividend payments and, 439-440
- long-term debt and, 440-444
- nonbusiness organizations and, 683-689
- price-earnings ratio and, 430
- risk and return, 423-438
- security prices and, 424-430
- short-term debt and, 440-444

Analysis of investing activities, 515-546
- acquisitions and, 527
- asset value, 516-524
- cash flows and, 543-545
- comparison over time and, 537
- fair market values and, 531-534
- operating leverage and, 540-543
- ratios and, 535-537
- risk and return and, 524-534

Analysis of operating activities, 611-644
- business failure, 639-640
- cash flow, 636-639
- comparing among companies, 624-632
- earnings management and, 634-635
- expenses, 613-623
- forecasting, 640
- historical costs and, 636
- percentages and, 616-617
- profit margins, 621-623
- restructuring and, 635
- return on assets, 624-631
- return on equity, 631-632
- revenues, 613-623

Annuities, 382-383, 391, 481
Asset(s), 107, 136, 139, 532
- accrual accounting and, 108
- bonds secured by, 385
- book value, 354
- capital improvements, 493
- cash, 468
- construction and, 492
- consumed over time, 248-249
- control of, 496-497
- current, see Current assets
- deferrals and, 250, 494, 584
- depreciation of, see Depreciation
- estimated lives of, 204-205
- fixed, see Fixed assets
- growth rate of, 538-539
- historical cost of, 205, 532
- intangible, see Intangible assets
- investing activities and, 385, 467-468
- leased, 405, 490-492
- liquid, 193-194, 197
- liquidation of, 523, 639
- long-term, see Long-term assets
- mergers and, 477, 529
- nonbusiness organizations and, 670, 675, 676, 680
- plant, see Plant assets
- prepaid taxes, 494
- return on, 432, 521-523, 624-631
- safeguarding, 291
- sale of, 488, 495-496
- securities, 468
- statement of cash flows and, 591
- value of, 354, 516-524, 531-534

Asset accounts, 63, 65, 139, 144, 184, 193
Asset composition, 537, 540-543
Asset turnover, 624, 625, 626
Audit(s), 19, 55, 160, 162
- accounting standards and, 311
- of cash and securities, 497
- external services, 293-299
- federal funding and, 309
- General Mills, Inc., B6-B23, C10-C11
- independent services, 292, 293-299, 311, B6
- internal, 291
- limitations of, 299
- negligence and, 312
- nonbusiness organizations, 302
- standards and, 296, 308
- stockholders and, 307-308

Audit committees, 295, 299, B6
Audit opinion, 294
Authorized shares, 335

B

Balance, 4
Balance sheet, 65, 106, 136, 193-198
- accounts receivable, 572
- adjustments for internal transactions and, 243-244
- assets and, 193-196, 490, 494, 532
- bond investments and, 482
- cash and, 107, 468
- classified, 193, 194
- combined, 673
- comparative, 193, 194
- consolidated, 475
- equity transactions and, 332, 471
- fiduciary funds, 679-680
- foreign currency and, 348
- General Mills, Inc., B7-B8, B11-B12
- governments and, 673, 674-676
- income statement and, 202
- intangible assets and, 494
- inventories on, 573
- investing activities and, 385, 471, 495
- leased assets and, 490
- liabilities and, 196-197, 377-408
- owners' equity section of, 333
- preferred stock and, 351
- proprietary funds, 679-680
- redeemable preferred stock, 353
- securities investment and, 469
- statement of cash flows and, 202
- stockholders' equity and, 192, 197-198
- working capital and, 197

Balance sheet equation, 136, 193
Bankruptcy:
- creditors and, 442, 639
- 1990s and, 437
- resource liquidation and, 50
- subordinated debt and, 386
- suppliers and, 53

Banks, 19, 291
Bank statement, 3-4, 162
Big Six, 293
Billing statements, 141, 144, 150, 155
Board of directors, 16, D4-D10
Bond(s):
- amortization schedule, 388-390
- call provisions, 437

conversion of, 343, 351, 386, 589
government, 688
interest rates and, 386, 436-437
investment in, 481-483
junk, 426
market return on, 386
nonbusiness organizations and, 665, 670
present value and, 387
prices, 387, 424, 426-428
ratings of, 426
repurchase of, 393-394, 468
risk and, 386, 426-428
serial, 393
unsecured, 385
yields and, 427
Bonds payable, 64, 385-391
Book value, 205, 354, 484, 489
Borrowing, see Debt
British corporations, 594-595
Budgets, nonbusiness organizations and, 666-667, 678-679
Buildings, 100-101. See also Depreciation
Business Week, A2
Business failures, 543
Business ownership, 15-19
Business periodicals, A1-A2

C

Capital, 18, 21, 28, 64
average cost of, 518
contributed, 333, 335, 337
participation, 356-357
share, 356
Capital expenditures, 538, 539
Capital improvements, 493, 668
Capital intensity, 543, 624-625
Capitalized interest, 393
Capital leases, 405, 490
Capital maintenance focus, 670
Capital stock, 64, 334
Capital structure, 423-424, 518-519, 631
bankruptcy and, 639
decisions about, 439-449
interest rates and, 437
long-term obligations and, 444
optimal, 436
use of debt in, 434-436
Cash, 3, 440
analysis of, 543-545
asset turnover and, 626
balance sheet and, 107, 468
collection of, 155, 565
control of, 161, 162, 497, 543
financing activities and, 332
investing activities and, 440, 468-470
received before revenue is earned, 249-250
Cash basis of accounting measurement, 185, 200
accrual basis and, 103-105, 234-263, 390
nonbusiness organizations and, 672
Cash dividends, 339-340
Cash flow(s), 96-98, 103
accounts payable and, 257-258
accounts receivable and, 256
accrual basis and, 104, 246
analysis of, 636-639
from bonds, 424, 428
bonds payable and, 390
business failure and, 543, 639
to current maturities of long-term debt ratio, 442
debt principal and, 393
decision-making and, 163, 185
dividends and, 352, 429, 439-440
estimate of, 185
expected, 246-249, 633
financing activities and, 544
future, 246-249, 425
intangible assets and, 259
interest payable and, 258
interpretation of, 260-262
inventory and, 256-257
investing activities and, 495, 519-523, 535, 544
net income and, 253-260
nonbusiness organizations and, 666-667
notes and, 392
paid in future periods, 383
per share, 636
preferred dividends and, 429
present value of, 383, 525
product life cycle and, 641-642
profits and, 443-444
short-term, 440-444
statement of, see Statement of cash flows
stock and, 340, 358
Cash flows from operating activities, 253-260, 519, 592
accrual measures and, 637
analysis of, 636-639
to average total assets ratio, 521-522
business failures and, 543
performance measures and, 97-98
stock value and, 532
to total assets ratio, 537
Cash sales, 137-141
Certified Internal Auditor (CIA) Examination, 292
Certified Management Accountant, 289-290
Certified public accountants (CPAs), 55, 292-293
Chartered Account (CA), 293
Chart of accounts, 140
Chief executive officer, 16
Classified balance sheet, 193, 194
Closing entries, 147-148, 290
Commercial paper, 430-431
Common equity, return on, 631-632
Common stock, 64, 333, 334
net income and, 590
owned by another company, 472-476
prices and, 429-430
repurchase of, 261
Common stockholders'equity, return on, 518
Compaq Computer Corp., E1-E2
Compensation, 51-52, 341, 397-402, 634, D11-D16
Competition, 8, 12, 291, 617
financial resources and, 14, 29
intense, 625
operating activities and, 23
political, 14
regulations and, 625
for resources, 29
risk and return and, 49
in supplier markets, 21
Compilation, 299-300
Computerized accounting systems, 59, 149-160
Computer services, A2
Consolidated financial statements, 203, B6-B23
Construction, 492, 567, 675
Consumers, 24, 25, 618
Continuing education, 292, 293
Continuous lives, 18
Contra account, 101, 570
Contra-asset accounts, 471, 484, 494
Contract(s), 47-48, 69
accounting standards and, 310

bonds as, 385-391
capital structure and, 424
debt and, 378, 379, 391, 442
employees and, 53, 379
exchanges and, 69
extended over time, 99, 235, 445
external transactions and, 235
foreign exchange, 404
government budgets as, 666
investors and, 49, 310
liabilities and, 378, 379
long-term, 567-568
pension plans as, 397
risk and return and, 94
sales and, 99
suppliers and, 379
unearned revenues, 396
Contra-owners' equity account, 192
Contributed capital, 191-192, 333, 335, 337
Control, 142
of assets, 496-497
audits and, 55
computer systems and, 162-163
of costs, 56-57
diversification and, 527
internal, 291-292, 496
inventory and, 574, 579
manual systems and, 161-162
nonbusiness organizations and, 665, 666-670
securities and, 469, 472
Controller, 17
Convertible bonds, 344, 591
Convertible preferred stock, 351, 352, 591
Copyrights, 493
Corporate owners' equity, see Stockholders' equity
Corporations, 15-19
cash payments to owners, 66
charter, 334
contracts and, 47
financial decisions and, 20, 183
functions of, 16-17
income statements and, 183, 190
investing activities, 21-22
management of, 16-18
parent, 203-204
size of, 19
taxes and, 300, 584
Cost accounting, 291
Cost leadership, 624-630
Cost of goods sold, 68, 143
accrual accounting and, 99, 101-102, 248, 257
income statement and, 187-188, 570-579
reporting, 573-576
Cost of services sold, 188
Costs, 56-57, 206
allocation of, 196
capitalized, 492
fixed, 540-543
historical, 205, 354, 532, 636
period, 102
product, 101-102, 580
variable, 540-543
Coupon rate, 386, 388
Creditors, 19-20, 21, 49-50
accounting information and, 442
balance sheet and, 183
bankruptcy and, 442, 639
legal reserves and, 356, 357
obligations to, 395-396
risk and, 20
suppliers as, 53
See also Debt
Credits, 139-141, 161
Credit sales, 141-143, 570
Cumulative stock, 352
Current assets, 440-444, 468
balance sheet and, 193-194
current liabilities and, 197
governmental funds and, 675
operating activities and, 200
timing adjustments and, 251, 254, 259
variable costs and, 540
Current liabilities, 196
ability to pay, 185, 443
compensation and benefits, 397
current assets and, 197
operating activities and, 200
timing adjustments and, 251, 254, 259
Current operating activities, financing, 440
Current ratio, 197, 440-441
Customers:
decision-making and, 53-54
master file, 154
obligations to, 396-397

D

Data base, 59, 61, 63-69, 106, 135, 136, 152
Data entry, 152, 162
Data processing, 59, 163
Debentures, 344, 385
Debits, 139-141, 161
Debt, 49, 377-408, 424
bankruptcy and, 639
bonds payable, 385-391
control of, 406-407
earnings per share and, 435
foreign corporations and, 406
future value and, 380-383
government and, 665-666, 668, 669, 675-676, 687-689
lines of credit, 404
long-term, 384
mergers and, 528-529
nonprofit organizations and, 669
notes payable, 391-393
obligations and, 384-394
present value and, 380-383
price/earnings ratio and, 434, 436
proportion of, 435-436
refinancing, 437
repayment of, 523, 544
repurchase of, 393-394
retired, 261
return on equity and, 433, 631
short-term, 384
statement of cash flows and, 200
subordinated, 386
subsidiary and, 394
types of, 379-380
Debt covenants, 442
Debt ratio, 436, 443
Debt securities, 468, 480-483
Debt service funds, 668
Debt to equity ratio, 435-436, 445, 537
Debt to total assets ratio, 436
Debt to total capitalization ratio, 436
Decisions/decision-making, 5, 14-26, 55
capital structure and, 424, 439-449
cash flows and, 185
company policies and, 292
control and, 56-57
debt-equity mix and, 435
employees and, 53
evaluating exchanges and, 49-54
external, 28-29, 55
financing activities and, 14-21, 49
information for, 47-62
internal, 56

internal auditors and, 291
investing activities and, 21-22, 49-51, 521-524, 535-537
management and, 51, 55, 163
net income and, 565
operating activities and, 22-26
risk and return and, 48-49
strategic, 291
structuring, 28
timely information and, 206
transformation process and, 47
Default risk, 426, 428
Deferrals, 249-251, 494
compensation, 343, 397-401
expenses, 245, 250-251
income, 396
revenues, 245, 249-250
taxes, 403, 584-585, 593
Defined benefit retirement plans, 397, 399-400, B17, D18-D20
Defined contribution retirement plan, 397
Demand for goods and services, 22, 617-621
Depletion, 488-489, C15-C16
Depreciation, 100-101, 144
accelerated, 484-485
accumulated, 101, 238-239, 259
amortization and, 204-205
comparison of methods, 486-487
construction and, 492
declining balance, 485
deferred taxes and, 585-586
fixed assets and, 195
General Mills, Inc., B9, C15-C16
governmental accounting and, 675
income statement and, 188
net income and, 259
period costs and, 102
plant assets and, 483-487
selling activities and, 583
statement of cash flows and, 593
straight-line, 484
sum-of-the-years'-digits, 485
units-of-production, 485
Dilutive securities, 592
Direct format, statement of cash flows, 198-202
Disclaimer, audit reports and, 296
Discontinued operations, 587-588, 591, B10
Discount(s), 626
accounts payable and, 395-396
bonds and, 388, 389, 390
note issued at, 392
sales, 567-568
Discount rate, 424-425, 436
Distribution accounting, 25
Diversification, 525-527
Dividend payout ratio, 346, 439
Dividends, 66, 183, 192, 344-346
accounting for receipt of, 470
cash, 190
decision-making and, 183, 439
declared, 340
preferred stock and, 351-353, 429, 445
right to, 334
statement of cash flows and, 200
Dividends payable, 406
Dividends per share, 439
Double-entry bookkeeping, 135-148, 161, 305

E

Earnings, 10, 183, 437
accounting methods and, 633-634
economic downturn and, 638
future, 206
manipulation of, 638
minority interest in, 475
operating cash flows and, 637
problems with interpreting, 633-636
segment information and, 526
shifting fiscal periods and, 634
Earnings per share, 190
cash flow and, 430
debt and, 435
discontinued operations and, 591
dividends per share and, 439
financing decisions and, 434-435
General Mills, Inc., B10
leverage and, 434-435, 631
price/earnings ratio and, 430
reporting, 589-592
Economic conditions, 436, 617, 638
Economic environment, nonbusiness organizations and, 683-684
Economic indicators, 618-621
Economic policies, 311-312
Economic recovery, government debt and, 688
Economies of scale, 625-626
Economies of scope, 626
Education, 293, 302, 303, 664
Effective organization, 12, 614, 665-670, 684-686
Efficient organization, 12, 56, 614, 665-670, 684-686
Employees, 17-18, 291
accounting information and, 444
computer records and, 151, 157, 162
contracts and, 379
evaluation and, 56
integrity and ability of, 161
obligations to, 206, 397-402, 444
performance of, 53
stock options and, 358
Employee Stock Ownership Plans, 342, B18
Equipment, 100-101, 188, 484
purchases of, 144
secured, 497
See also Depreciation
Equity:
balance sheet and, 332
business failure and, 639
legal reserve, 356, 357
return on, 432, 445, 631
shareholders', see Stockholders' equity
Equity financing, 49, 433, 468, 470-479
Equity income, 583-584, 593
Equity method of accounting, 474
Estimates, 95, 589, 641
audits and, 296
depreciation, 101
inventory, 577-581
long-term contracts and, 567-568
Ethical behavior, 52, 290, 292, 293, 303
Exchange rates, 200, 348, 593
Exchanges, 49-54, 69
Expenditures, nonbusiness organizations and, 669, 671, 676-678
Expense(s), 10, 65-67, 139, 147
accounting equation and, 93, 136
accrual accounting and, 98-102, 109, 187, 245, 247-249
allocated to fiscal periods, 206
analysis of, 613-623
deferred, 245, 250-251
depreciation, 100-101, 238, 483-487
doubtful accounts, 571
estimates, 205
future, 398, 444
income statement and, 184
income tax, 402-403, 582
insurance, 239

nonbusiness organizations and, 666-667
noncash, 259, 260
operating, 188, 614, 622, 580
prepaid, 250, 255, 494
repurchase of debt and, 394
restructuring and, 635
revenue relationship, 621-623
special items, 587-589
timing differences in recognition of, 235, 238
wages, 397
External audit, 293-299
External environment, 28-29, 48
External users, 55, 183, 190, 193, 202, 332

F

Face value, bonds and, 388, 390
Fair business practices, 311-312
Fair market value, 477-478, 533
Federal government:
debt of, 687-688
regulation by, 306-309
See also Government(s)
Federal Reserve Board, 436
Fiduciary funds, 667, 671, 679-680
Financial Accounting Foundation, 309
Financial Accounting Standards Board (FASB), 309, 313-314, 472, 397, 400, 682
Financial condition, 184, 202-203, B3-B5
Financial decision analysis, 445-448
Financial institutions, 470, 534
Financial markets, 10, 15
Financial reports, see Report(s)
Financial resources, 3, 17-19, 28, 135
competition for, 29
investing, 465-499
measurement focus, 670
need for, 51
Financial services, A2
Financial statements, 105-106, 141, 147, 182-210
audited, 295
compilation services and, 299
computers and, 151, 160
consolidated, 203, 475, 477, B6-B23
content and presentation, 186-202
fiduciary funds, 679-680
General Mills, Inc., B1-B23
governments and, 673-681
interrelationships among, 202
limitations of, 204-206
management responsibilities, 298
nonprofit organizations and, 680-681
notes accompanying, 340-341
pro-forma, 433
proprietary funds, 679-680
purpose of, 183-185
timeliness of information, 206
transformation process and, 207-208, 262-263
use of, 202-207
value and, 354, 531-534
See also Balance sheet; Income statement; Statement of cash flows; Statement of stockholders' equity
Financing activities, 14-21, 91
accounts for, 64
analysis of, see Analysis of financing activities
attributes affecting, 436
balance sheet and, 184
cash flows and, 332, 544
commercial paper, 430-431
debt, see Debt
decisions about, 20, 49, 56
equity, 49, 433, 468, 470-479
nonbusiness organizations and, 670
risk and return, 423-438
statement of cash flows and, 200, 593
See also Bond(s); Stock
First-in first-out method (FIFO), 577
Fiscal periods, 9, 208
cash flows and, 252
expense measurement and, 66, 109
inventory measurement and, 578
net income and, 66
revenue recognition and, 65, 66, 96, 567-569
shifting earnings and, 634
Fiscal year, 148, 195
Fixed assets, 100, 144, 195, 669
Fixed assets turnover, 629
Fixed costs, 540-543, 625
Forecasting, 158, 640-642
Foreign corporations:
audit reports for, 298
liabilities and, 406
statement of cash flows, 595-596
wages and, 53
Foreign currency, 346-349, 353, 404, 591, B10
Foreign language, 304
Form 8-K report, 307
Form 10-K reports, 307, C1-C13
Forms, controls and, 162
Fortune, A2
Fraud, 299
Functional currency, 347-348
Fund accounting, 667-669
Fund balance, 670, 676
Future activities, 22, 379, 405
Future cash flows, 383, 445
bonds and, 387
pension plans and, 400
security prices and, 424-425
Future value, 380-383, 398-399

G

Gains, 394, 495
bond investments and, 482
discontinued operations and, 587-588
equity investments and, 470, 471, 475
foreign currency and, 348
statement of cash flows and, 593
General fixed asset group, 669, 675
General fund, 667-668
General journal, 136
General ledger, 136, 151, 160
General long-term debt group, 669, 675
Generally Accepted Accounting Principles (GAAP), 54, 61, 183, 290
American Institute of Certified Public Accountants and, 308
asset measurement and, 354
audits and, 296, 311
balance sheet and, 193
depreciation and, 487
equity securities and, 468
extraordinary items, 588
Financial Accounting Standards Board and, 309
financial statements notes and, 340
going concern and, 96
income statement and, 188-189, 190
intangible assets and, 493
inventory and, 580-581

leased assets and, 492
litigation and, 312
long-term securities and, 472
major departures from, 297
natural resources and, 489
net income, 585
nonbusiness organizations and, 689
pension plans and, 399-400
process of setting, 313
research and development activities, 102, 495
securities investment and, 469-470, 472
statement of cash flows and, 198
stockholders' equity and, 337, 353
subsequent events, 594
taxes and, 403
Generally Accepted Auditing Standards (GAAS), 296
General Mills, Inc.:
annual stockholders' meeting, D1-D20
financial reports, B1-B23
Form 10-K, C1-C13
Global market, 25, 29
Going concern, 95-96, 109
Goods, 6, 566
Goodwill, 529, B9
Government(s), 7, 29, 427
account groups and, 667-669
actual versus budgeted, 678-679
assets and, 675, 676, 680
balance sheet and, 673, 674-676
bonds, 393, 688
debt and, 665-666, 668, 669, 687-689
efficiency and, 684-686
expenditures and, 666, 676-678
financial leverage and, 686-689
funds, 667-670
interest rates, 425
liabilities and, 676
obligations to, 402-403
operating leverage and, 686-689
reporting by, 673-681
reports for, 54, 62
revenues, 302, 664, 668, 669, 671, 676, 677-678, 683-684
services provided by, 663-664
Governmental Accounting Standards Board (GASB), 309, 682-683
Government economic planning, 291
Government publications, A2
Gross profit, 187, 565-572, 621
Growth potential, 439, 440

H

Health care services, 400, 664-665
Historical cost, 205, 354, 532, 533, 636
Human resource activities, 24

I

Income, 189, 614-615
deferred, 396
equity, 583-584
minority interest in, 589-590
operating, 582-583
percentage analysis of, 616-617
pretax, 584
See also Net income; Revenue(s)
Income statement, 10, 19, 565-592
accounting changes, 588
adjustments for internal transactions and, 242
common-sized, 616
components of, 106, 565, 614-615
consolidated, 475
continuing operations, 587
cost of goods sold, 572-581
discontinued operations, 587
equity income, 583-584
extraordinary items, 588
fiduciary funds and, 680
foreign currency and, 348, 353
gross profit, 565-572
income taxes and, 584-586
interest expense, 583-584
investment revenue and, 474
manipulation of, 638
multiple-step, 186-187
net income per share, 590-592
operating activities and, 200
operating income, 582-583
other income, 583-584
proprietary funds and, 680
purpose of, 565
revenue recognition and, 566-569
sale of securities and, 470
single-step, 190
statement of cash flows and, 200
stockholders and, 192, 590
subsidiaries, 589-590
Income taxes, 189-190, 306
adjustment for, 241
deferred, 403
General Mills, Inc., B10, B20-B21
income statement and, 584-586
investments and, 517-518
pension plans and, 398
reporting, 402-403, 591
Independent accountants, 292, 293-299, 311
Industry publications, A2
Inflation, 205, 312, 618
bond prices and, 388
growth rates and, 538-539
interest rates and, 425
multinationals and, 348
profits and, 636
Information, 5, 17, 45-70, 96
audited, 55
capital structure and, 424
contracts and, 47, 69-70
creditors and, 442
customers and, 53-54
default risk and, 428
delay in providing, 206
employees and, 53, 444
false or misleading, 312
investment decisions, 49-51, 521-524
managers and, 51-53, 55-57
mergers and, 527-531
organization size and, 91
processing, 63-69
pro-forma, 433
relationships and, 613
reliability of, 54, 310, 312
reporting, 182-210
risk and return and, 48-49
suppliers and, 53
transformation process and, 207-208
Information over time, 537-540
Information system, 7, 28, 58-62
audits and, 55
development of, 290, 301
investors and, 12-13
measurement rules, 89-111
processing phase, 133-165
See also Decisions; Report(s)
Institute of Internal Auditors, 292
Institute of Management Accountants, 289-290
Insurance, 102, 188
control of assets and, 497
health care and, 664
prepaid, 239, 250, 255
Intangible assets, 196, 259, 493-494, 537, B9-B10

Interest, 11, 407, 381, 393
Interest expense, 189, 240, 541
  accrual accounting and, 100, 102
  bonds and, 389-390
  cash flows and, 258
  construction and, 492-493
  future value and, 381-382
  General Mills, Inc., B17
  income statement and, 583
  notes, 392
  present value and, 387
  return on assets and, 432, 624
  return on equity and, 631
Interest rates, 427
  bonds and, 386, 436-437
  discount rate and, 425
  Federal Reserve and, 436
  notes and, 391
  stock prices and, 436
Interest revenue, 49, 380, 481
Internal control, 161-163, 291, 406, 496
Internal Revenue Service, 302, 306
International Accounting Standards Committee, 309-310
International reporting:
  of operating activities, 594-595
  of stockholders' equity, 355-357
Inventories, 161-164, 572-581
  asset turnover and, 626, 629
  cash flow associated with, 256-257
  computers and, 154, 155-156
  consumed over time, 248-249
  first-in first-out method, 577
  General Mills, Inc., B9
  governmental funds and, 675
  last-in first-out method, 577-579
  lower of cost or market, 580
  manufacturing and, 574-575
  measurement, 576-581
  merchandising companies, 573
  transactions, 137-142
  weighted average method, 580
Investing activities/investment, 21, 28, 91, 365-399
  acquisitions, 477-479
  asset types and, 467-468
  bonds, 426, 481-483
  capital improvement, 493
  cash and, 468-470, 519-523, 535-537, 543-545
  cash flows and, 200, 495-496, 522-523, 544, 593
  construction, 492-493
  debt securities, 480-483
  decisions and, 22, 56, 521, 535
  deferred charges, 494
  diversified, 525-527
  equity securities, 470-479
  fair market values and, 531
  growth rate of, 540
  income tax effects and, 517-518
  intangible assets, 493-494
  long-term, 481-483
  mergers and, 477-479, 527-531
  natural resources and, 488-489
  plant assets, 483-488, 490-493
  research and development, 494-495
  return of, 11
  risk and, 12, 48-49, 52
  securities and, 468-470
  sinking funds, 385
  value and, 380, 517
  See also Analysis of investing activities; Return on investment
Investors, 135
  corporations and, 15
  market for, 12-13
  risk versus return and, 49-50

J

Journal, 136, 138, 140, 149
Journal articles, A1
Junk bonds, 426
Just-in-time manufacturing, 581

L

Labor, 53, 164, 291, 575
Land, 101
Last-in first-out method (LIFO), 577-579
Leases, 405, 445, 490-492, B21
Ledgers, 136, 140, 142-143, 147, 149, 161
Legal rights, 63, 135, 196
Lenders, see Debt
Leverage, 434-438, 540-543
  government and, 686-689
  interest rates and, 436-437
  return on equity and, 631
Leveraged buy-out, 50
Leverage ratios, 443
Liabilities, 64, 65, 136, 139
  accrual accounting and, 108-109
  acquisitions and, 394, 477-478
  balance sheet and, 184, 193, 196-197
  bonds payable, 385-391
  changes in composition of, 532
  contingencies and, 404-406
  control of, 406-407
  current, 440-444
  customers and, 395
  deferred revenues, 249-250
  deferred taxes and, 586
  employees and, 241, 397-402
  foreign corporations and, 406
  governments and, 402, 676
  income taxes, 241, 584
  lease commitments, 445
  mergers and, 529
  nonbusiness organizations and, 665, 670, 676
  notes payable, 391-393
  statement of cash flows and, 593
  types of, 379-380
  unearned revenues, 396
  unfunded, 397
  value and, 205, 380, 531
Lines of credit, 404, 543-544
Liquidation, 50, 352, 639
Liquidity, 193-194, 197, 443
Litigation, 312, 404, 588
Loans, 5, 19, 28, 381, 404, 442
Long-term assets, 195, 200, 468
  financing, 440
  proportion of, 540
  ratios for, 535-537
  receivables, 481
  sale of, 495-496
Long-term contracts, 567-568
Long-term investments, 195, 472-476, 668
Long-term liabilities, 196, 384
  ability to meet, 443
  capital structure and, 444
  current maturities of, 442
  General Mills, Inc., B13-B14
  government and, 676
  notes payable, 242
Losses, 10, 18, 394, 635
  bond investments and, 482
  business failure and, 639
  debt and, 50
  discontinued operations and, 587-588
  equity investments, 470
  foreign currency and, 348
  litigation and, 405, 588
  long-term investments and, 475
  restructuring and, 635

sale of assets and, 495-496
short-term securities and, 471-472
uncollectible accounts, 571-572
Lower of cost or market method, 471, 472-475

M

Management, 12, 15-18, 22, 298
accounting system and, 163-164
bankruptcy and, 639
compensation and, 51-52, 102, 583, 634
contracts and, 310
decision-making and, 21, 51, 59
moral hazard and, 19, 54
nonbusiness organizations and, 665
unscrupulous, 312
Managerial (or management) accounting, 55-57, 58, 62, 289-292
Manual accounting systems, 135-148
Manufacturing companies, 6, 24-25, 543
inventory and, 574-575, 581
investing activities, 21
operating transactions, 565
revenue recognition and, 566
Market(s), 8
demand and, 618
financial, 10, 14
for investors, 12-13
primary, 427
Marketable securities, 468-469, 471
Marketing, 25, 188, 582-583
Market value, 354, 489, 580
Master files, 152-157, 160
Maturity values, 381, 386, 388
Measurement, see Accounting measurement
Merchandising (or retail) companies, 6, 25, 565-566
capital intensive, 543
cost of goods sold and, 187-188
inventory and, 573, 581
Mergers, 301, 477, 527, 537, 639
Minority interest, 349, 445, 475, 589-590
Money, 3, 205, 666
Moody's, 426-427, A2
Moral hazard, 19, 29, 54
Multinational corporations, 19, 29, 152, 304, 346

N

Natural resources, 488, 636
Net income, 10, 12, 65
accumulation of, 337
asset proportion and, 521
business failure and, 639
cash flows and, 104, 107, 187, 253, 353, 429, 638
decision makers and, 565
depreciation and, 259
dividend payments and, 190, 345, 353, 429, 439-440
earnings per share and, 190
economic conditions and, 205
expected, 525-526
gains and losses and, 394
growth rate of, 539
inventory and, 143
leverage and, 541
prepaid expense and, 255
reinvested, 184, 192
return on assets and, 432
return on equity and, 432, 631
sale of plant assets and, 496
statement of cash flows and, 593
stock and, 339, 430, 590
timing differences and, 256-259
transfer to balance sheet, 136
See also Profit(s)
Net loss, 10-11
Net present value, 517
Net profit margin, 621
Net value, 484
New York Stock Exchange, 306
Nominal rate, 386, 387-388
Nonbusiness organizations, 7, 13, 302, 661-691
accounting measurement and, 670-681
accounting standards and, 682-683
analysis and, 683-689
budgets, 666-667, 678-679
efficiency and, 665-670, 684-686
expenditures and, 669, 671, 676-678
fund accounting and, 667-669
purpose of, 663-665
reports and, 672-681
Nonprofit organizations, 7, 302, 664-665, 669, 680
No-par stock, 335
Notes:
investment in, 480-481
promissory, 430-431
Notes payable, 64, 260, 391-393
adjustment for, 241-242
General Mills, Inc., B11-B13
Notes to financial statements, 384, B9-B23

O

Obligations, 379-381
to employees, 397-402
to governments, 402-403
to lenders, 384-394
short-term, 440
to suppliers and creditors, 395-397
Operating activities, 22-26, 91, 563-597
for accounting period, 65
accrual basis and, 98-105, 108-110, 592
cash flows from, see Cash flows from operating activities
current assets and, 468
demand and, 618
information about, 52-53
international reporting of, 594-595
liabilities associated with, 64
nonbusiness organizations and, 665
organizational environment and, 613
reporting, 184, 199-200, 565-596
Operating cycle, 195, 468n.1
Operating expenses, 187-189, 582, 614, 622
Operating income, 188, 582
Operating leases, 405, 490
Operating leverage, 542, 625, 686
Operating results, 624, 640
Operating revenues, 564-567, 614, 617, 622, 626
Organization(s), 5, 11-13
decisions in, 14-26
indefinite life, 95
information in, 45-70
nonbusiness, see Nonbusiness organizations
purpose of, 6-14
size of, 91
structure of, 17, 28, 56
types of, 6-7
Organizational environment, 28-29, 47, 613
Owner(s), 11, 15-19, 21, 49

Owner investment accounts, 64
Owner's capital account, 148
Owners' equity, 64-65, 136, 139
accrual accounting and, 108
balance sheet and, 184, 193, 333
net income and, 190

P

Paid-in capital, 333, 334-335, 340
Par, bonds selling at, 388, 390
Par value, 334
Participation capital, 356-357
Partnerships, 15, 18
cash payments to owners, 66
capital and, 64
contracts and, 47
income taxes and, 189
Payroll, 144, 151, 157, 164
Pension plans, 397-400, 444, 495
Performance, 310, 432
forecasting, 640-642
net income and, 565
over time, 537-540
Period, 9, 65. See also Fiscal periods
Period costs, 102, 188
Physical assets, 497, 636. See also Equipment; Plant assets
Physical controls, 496-497
Plant assets, 100, 490-493, 543
depreciation of, 195, 483-487
disposal of, 487-488, 494
financing, 437
ratios for, 535-537
Plant expansion, 261
Plant funds, 669
Pooling of interests method, 477
Preferred stock, 631
convertible, 351, 591
cumulative, 352
dividends and, 351-353, 429, 445
lower of cost or market and, 472
participating, 353
prices of, 428-429
redeemable, 352, 353, 437
Premium, bonds selling at, 388, 390
Prepaid expenses, 92, 250, 255, 494
Present value, 472, 525
bonds and, 387, 424, 481
lease payments and, 491
net, 517
notes, 391-392
pension benefits, 398, 399, 400
Price, 8-9
bonds and, 386-388
decisions about, 163
See also Stock prices
Price-earnings (PE) ratio, 430, 434, 436, 448, 542
Principal, 49, 392-394
Processing accounting information, 133-165
accounting cycle and, 134, 148
computers and, 149-160
controls and, 161-163
manual systems and, 135-148
management and, 163-164
Product(s), 10, 24
demand for, 617-621
differentiation, 624-630
life cycles, 641-642
pricing records, 150
revenues, 582
Product costs, 101, 157, 188, 582
Production, 24, 156, 164, 574, 625
Product line, 17, 527
Profit(s), 9-10, 65, 621-630
cash flows and, 260
compensation linked to, 52
creation of, 25
decisions and, 21
demand and, 618
dividends and, 352
expected, 261, 525-526
gross, 187-188, 565-572
inflation and, 636
inventory measurement and, 579
inventory reports and, 156
reinvested, 11, 66-67, 93, 106, 107, 439, 440
restructuring and, 635
risk and return and, 52
withdrawn, 11
Profit and loss statement, 184
Profit-sharing plans, B20
Property, plant, and equipment, 195. See also Equipment; Plant assets
Proprietary funds, 667, 671, 679-680
Proprietorships, 15
capital and, 64
cash payments to owners, 66
contracts and, 47
income taxes and, 189
liability and, 18
Proxy statement, 307, D2-D4
Public accounting, 292-301
Publications, A1-A2
Public utilities, 312, 664
Purchase order, 143, 150, 156, 157

Q

Quick ratio, 442

R

Rate of return, 19, 518-521
Ratios, 443-444, 535-537
accounts receivable turnover, 629
acid-test, 442
asset composition, 537
asset turnover, 629
cash flow from operating activities to average total assets, 521-522
cash flow from operating activities to total assets, 537
cash flow to current maturities of long-term debt, 442
cash used in investing activities to long-term assets, 535
comparing among companies, 624-632
current, 440-441
debt, 436, 443
debt to equity, 435-436, 537
debt to total assets, 436
debt to total capitalization, 436
depreciation and amortization expense to long-term assets, 535
dividend payout, 439
fixed assets turnover, 629
gross profit margin, 621
industry, A2
inventory turnover, 629
leverage, 443
liquidity, 443
net plant assets to cost of plant assets, 535
price-earnings, 430, 448, 542
profit margin, 621
quick, 442
return on assets, 432, 521-523
return on equity, 432, 631
times interest earned, 442
Receivables, see Accounts receivable
Recession, 437, 590
Reconciliation, 104, 253-260
Recording transactions, 4, 135-148
Regulation, 18-19, 29, 49
audits and, 302

business practices and, 311-312
competition and, 625
federal, 306-308
reports and, 290-291
taxes and, 300
Report(s), 4, 19, 60, 67, 182-210
accounts payable, 156
accounts receivable and, 155
assets, 107
audit, 294-298
cost of goods sold, 573-576
data base and, 135
deferred compensation, 397
depreciation and, 486
employees, 158, 399-401
erroneous, 161
financial accounting, 57-58
general ledger module and, 160
General Mills, Inc., B1-B23
government and, 54, 307, 673-681
internal, 306, 592
inventory, 156, 573-576
limitations of, 204, 353-354
measurement rules and, 234-263
nonbusiness organizations and, 672-681
operating results, 565-596
regulation and, 290-291
securities investments and, 469-470
segment information and, 526-527
special items, 587-589
stockholders and, 55, 307-308, 332
subsequent events, 592
taxes and, 54, 160, 291, 402-403, 585-586
See also Financial statements
Reporting period, 66, 96, 195
Research and development, 24, 102, 188, 206, 494, 583, 642
Resources, 4, 7-9, 22, 28-29, 139
audits and, 295
balance sheet and, 106, 184
control over, 161-162, 292
corporations and, 15
financial, 14-21
human, 206
income statement and, 106
long-term, physical, 100
net, 9, 11
operating activities, 22-26
portfolio of, 52
recording acquisition of, 135
rented, 92
sources of data about, 60
value of, 52, 516-524, 532
See also Asset(s); Financial resources
Retail companies, see Merchandising companies
Retained earnings, 107, 183, 192, 336-337
appropriated, 349, 355
business failure and, 639
deficit in, 354
dividends and, 340, 344, 352
statement of, 193
Retained earnings account, 64, 148
Retirement benefits, 18, 397-401, 676, B17-B20, D18-D20
Return of investment, 11, 94, 440
Return on assets, 521, 526, 636
Return on equity, 432, 445, 631
Return on investment, 11, 48, 52-54, 93, 423-438
bonds, 386, 387
creditors and, 19
effect of investing activities on, 524-534
expectations about, 202
securities and, 351, 424
uncertainty about, 12
Revenue(s), 10, 12, 65, 139, 147
accounting equation and, 93, 136
accounts receivable and, 256, 569-572
accrual basis, 98, 109, 187, 245
allocated to fiscal periods, 206
analysis of, 613-623
deferred, 245, 249-250
estimates, 205
expenses and, 621-623
government, 302, 664, 668, 669, 671, 676, 677-678, 683-684
income statement and, 183, 184, 186-191
interest, 481
investment, 474
nonbusiness organizations and, 666-667, 670
operating, 570, 614, 617, 622
product, 582
recognition, 235, 242, 566-569
repurchase of debt and, 394
sale of securities and, 470
special items, 587
unearned, 109, 250, 396
Risk, 48-49, 94, 423-438, 517
benefit plans and, 444
bonds and, 386, 426-428
credit, 20, 572
customers and, 54
debt and, 426, 428, 433-436
diversification and, 527
employees and, 53, 398
expectations about, 202
interest rate, 425
investments and, 52, 524-535
return and, 12, 519
security prices and, 424, 428
suppliers and, 53

S

Sale(s), 9, 25, 137-142, 163
accrual basis and, 99
computers and, 149, 154, 158
contract as, 99
costs, 188
intercompany, 203-204
of long-term assets, 495-496
of plant assets, 487-488
reporting of, 155-156
revenue, 141, 154, 256
Sales discounts, 569-570
Sales receipt, 137, 497
Savings and loans failures, 426
Securities, 424-430, 468-470
control and, 469, 497
dilutive, 592
value of, 471, 472-475, 532-534
Securities and Exchange Commission (SEC), 55, 291, 307, 534
Segment information, 526, 630, B22
Service organizations, 7, 24, 135
income statement and, 188
nonbusiness organizations, 663
operating transactions, 565
revenue recognition and, 566
Share, dividends per, 439
Shareholders, see Stockholders
Shipping goods, 566-567
Sinking funds, 352, 385
Statement of cash flows, 106, 183, 332, 592
analysis and, 544, 636
cash needs and, 441
General Mills, Inc., B8-B9, B10
direct format, 198-202, 252
fiduciary funds and, 680
foreign corporations, 595-596
income statement and, 200
indirect format, 198, 253-260

investing activities and, 495-496
proprietary funds and, 680
stock-related items, 358
Statement of financial condition, 65, 184
Stock, 183, 340-343
acquisitions and, 335, 343, 477
authorized shares, 335
bond conversion, 343, 386
capital, 334
classes of, 351-353
common, 334, 429
cumulative, 352
dividends, 344
inside information and, 311
noncash resources for, 337
no-par, 335
outstanding shares, 335
par value of, 334
preferred, 351-353, 428
registration and, 307
repurchase, 336, 352, 358, 468, 544
splits, 344-345
statement of cash flows and, 200
statement of stockholders' equity and, 191-193
treasury, 336, 342
Stockholders, 15, 19, 50, 306
annual meeting, 307, D1
audit report and, 295
contracts and, 310
limited liability of, 18
preemptive right of, 341
reports for, 55
voting and, D10-D11
Stockholders' (or shareholders') equity, 64, 331-359, 472
accounting standards and, 337
appropriation and, 349
balance sheet and, 197-198
contributed capital, 334-335
foreign currency and, 346
General Mills, Inc., B15-B17
international reporting, 355
minority interest and, 349
net income and, 190
statement of, 191-193, 332, 338-349
treasury stock and, 336
Stock markets, 15, 306-308
Stock option, 51, 341, 358, 591, B14, D11-D16
Stock prices, 425, 428-430
cash flows and, 636
contributed capital and, 191-192
debt financing and, 436
expected earnings and, 448
interest rates and, 436
Stock warrants, 591
Straight-line depreciation, 484
Subsidiaries, 203, 394, 445, 475
Sum-of-the-years'-digits depreciation, 485
Suppliers, 10, 21, 53, 143, 379, 395-396
Supplies expense, 24, 188, 239
Support activities, 16, 17, 24

T

Taxes, 64, 157, 188, 585
accounting methods and, 300-301
corporate, 18
deferred, 444, 494, 584, 593
depreciation methods and, 486
government accounting and, 302, 677-678
income statement and, 189-190
inventory measurement and, 579
population demographics and, 683-684
reporting, 54, 147, 160, 291
sales, 138
types of, 664
10-Q's, 307
Time:
accounting measurement and, 96-105, 109-110
comparing companies over, 537-540
Times interest earned ratio, 442
Timing differences, 235, 238-242, 245-251, 254-259
Total capitalization, ratio of debt to, 436
Transaction files, 152-158, 160
Transaction(s), 4, 28, 146
accounts and, 136, 144
contracts and, 69-70
data base storage of, 61
debt, 377-408
equity investments, 470
external, 235-237, 245
internal, 235, 238-242, 245
omitted on financial statements, 206
processing, 135
recording, 61, 96-105
reporting using financial statements, 182-210
source documents and, 137
summary of, 140, 141
Transformation process, 7-8, 21, 52, 135
accounting measurement and, 91-95, 105-108
continuous, 95
information and, 47, 60, 207
nonbusiness organizations and, 665
reporting, 67-69, 207, 262
stockholders' equity and, 338
value created by, 23, 28
Treasury stock, 336, 342
Trial balance, 147, 161
Trust funds, 668, 676

U

Unearned revenues, 109, 249, 396

V

Value, 52, 516-524
book, 354, 484
creation of, 8-11, 23, 28, 65
dividends and, 345-346
fair market, 477-478, 531-534
future, 380-383
lower of cost or market, 580
natural resources and, 489
net present, 517
present, 380-383
residual, 484
salvage, 484
See also Present value
Value Line, 636, A2
Variable costs, 540-543

W

Wages, 99, 241, 397, 583
foreign countries and, 53
manufacturing and, 575
Wages payable, 64, 100
Wall Street Journal, A1, A2
Warranty, 25, 396, 406
Weighted average cost of capital, 518-519
Working capital, 197, 200, 254, 260

The author gratefully acknowledges the talents of the following photographers and studios who furnished the section and chapter opener photographs.

Section 1	© Bruce Ayers/Tony Stone Images
Section 2	© Howard Grey/Tony Stone Images
Appendices Section	© Bruce Ayers/Tony Stone Images
Chapter 1	© Jose L. Pelaez/Stock Market
Chapter 2	© Tim Brown/Tony Stone Images
Chapter 3	© Tim Brown/Tony Stone Images
Chapter 4	© Tim Brown/Tony Stone Images
Chapter 5	© Ian O'Leary/Tony Stone Images
Chapter 6	© Bruce Ayres/Tony Stone Images
Chapter 7	© Stewart Cohen/Tony Stone Images
Chapter 8	© Tim Brown/Tony Stone Images
Chapter 9	© Tim Brown/Tony Stone Images
Chapter 10	© Tim Brown/Tony Stone Images
Chapter 11	© Lonnie Duka/Tony Stone Images
Chapter 12	© Comstock 1991
Chapter 13	© Comstock 1993
Chapter 14	© Tom Tracy/Stock Market
Chapter 15	© Charles Gupton/Tony Stone Images